GENOCIDE

Genocide: A Comprehensive Introduction is the most wide-ranging textbook on genocide yet published. The book is designed as a text for upper-undergraduate and graduate students, as well as a primer for non-specialists and general readers interested in learning about one of humanity's enduring blights.

Fully updated to reflect the latest thinking in this rapidly developing field, this unique book:

- Provides an introduction to genocide as both a historical phenomenon and an analytical-legal concept, including the concept of genocidal intent, and the dynamism and contingency of genocidal processes.
- Discusses the role of state-building, imperialism, war, and social revolution in fueling genocide.
- Supplies a wide range of full-length case studies of genocides worldwide, each with a supplementary study.
- Explores perspectives on genocide from the social sciences, including psychology, sociology, anthropology, political science/international relations, and gender studies.
- Considers "The Future of Genocide," with attention to historical memory and genocide denial; initiatives for truth, justice, and redress; and strategies of intervention and prevention.

Highlights of the new edition include:

- Box-texts on "Physical, Biological, and Cultural Genocide" and "Whatever Happened to Political Groups?" (Chapter 1)
- Nigeria/Biafra as a "contested case" of genocide (Chapter 1)
- Genocide, empire, and modernity in Europe: the "Bloodlands" and "Rimlands" literature (Chapter 2)
- Extensive new material on the Kurds, Islamic State/ISIS, and the civil wars/genocide in Iraq and Syria (Chapter 4)
- "Stalin: Return from the Crypt"—Stalinist dictatorship in Russian popular
- Memory, including a visit to the despot's hometown (Chapter 5)
- Indonesia in 1965—66 as a case of genocide (Chapter 7)

- A reworked and expanded Chapter 9, "Genocide in Africa's Great Lakes Region," with extensive new material on DR Congo and Burundi
- Conflict and atrocities in the world's newest state, South Sudan (Chapter 9)
- Canada's indigenous people and the Truth and Reconciliation process (Chapter 15)
- Nuremberg prosecutor Benjamin Ferencz and the tribunal's legacy, including an encounter with Ferencz in the very courtroom where Nazi mass killers were tried (Chapter 15)
- The role, activities, and constraints of the United Nations Office of Genocide Prevention (Chapter 16)
- "Is Humanity Becoming More Peaceful?"—the implications for genocide studies of Steven Pinker's *The Better Angels of Our Nature* (Chapter 16)
- Many new testimonies from genocide victims, survivors, witnesses—and perpetrators
- Dozens of new images, including a special photographic essay, as well as maps, memorials, engravings, and artworks—the richest collection of genocide-related imagery in a single book.

Genocide: A Comprehensive Introduction remains the indispensable text for new generations of genocide study and scholarship. An accompanying website (www.genocidetext.net) features a broad selection of supplementary materials, teaching aids, and Internet resources.

Adam Jones, Ph.D., is Professor of Political Science at the University of British Columbia Okanagan in Kelowna, Canada. His recent books include *The Scourge of Genocide: Essays and Reflections* (Routledge, 2012) and *Gender Inclusive: Essays on Violence, Men, and Feminist International Relations* (Routledge, 2009). He is also editor of the Genocide and Crimes against Humanity book series for Routledge.

PRAISE FOR THE NEW EDITION

This volume is the most detailed and comprehensive textbook in the field of genocide studies. Anyone who wants to learn about key cases and issues, past and present, needs to read it.

Alexander Hinton, Center for the Study of Genocide and Human Rights, Newark College of Arts & Sciences, USA

PRAISE FOR PREVIOUS EDITIONS

Adam Jones is among today's leading – and most prolific – scholars of genocide. *Genocide: A Comprehensive Introduction* is truly comprehensive, ranging from antiquity to numerous episodes that straddle the porous borders between "genocide" and "mere" crimes against humanity. The book also ventures to offer strong passages on the psychology of perpetrators; genocide denial; international law, and artistic representations. It is perfectly suited for classroom purposes, while challenging scholars with its numerous striking insights regarding gender and other issues.

John Cox, Centre for Holocaust, Genocide and Human Rights Studies, University of North Carolina, USA

With its interdisciplinary approach and bevy of case studies, *Genocide: A Comprehensive Introduction* will surely become the seminal text for students of genocide. Written in an engaging and conversational style, the book not only explores existing frameworks, but expands the boundaries of genocide studies with attention to issues such as gender and the future of genocide. Perhaps best of all, Jones educates and inspires the reader to become an active and responsible global citizen.

Nicholas A. Robins, Duke University, USA

This is the best introductory text available to students of genocide studies. Written in clear, elegant prose and supported by a wealth of authoritative sources, *Genocide: A Comprehensive Introduction* is likely to become the gold standard by which all subsequent introductions to this enormously important subject will be measured.

Kenneth J. Campbell, Professor of Political Science, University of Delaware, USA

Compassionate, searching, up-to-the minute and sometimes even electrifying in its prose, this is *the* book I will be particularly recommending to my university students of genocide.

Mark Levene, University of Southampton, UK

Based on immense scholarship, *Genocide: A Comprehensive Introduction* is much more than an indispensable text for students of this seemingly intractable phenomenon. With its global and interdisciplinary perspectives, it consistently advances our understanding of genocidal events on many fronts.

A. Dirk Moses, University of Sydney and the European University Institute, Florence

This wide-ranging inquest into the dynamics of genocidal violence stands as a major contribution to the dismal science of 'massacrology.' More than a collection of case studies, it offers a depth of critical insight and a richness of data seldom matched in comparative studies of genocide. Informed by a formidable erudition, and a deep personal sensitivity to the horrors that he describes, Adam Jones's splendid book is a milestone in the literature on mass crimes and genocide.

Rene Lemarchand, Department of Political Science, University of Florida, USA

The subtitle says it all: unique in the literature, this book provides a thorough, comprehensive introduction to the subject of genocide. Jones delivers a very readable, intellectually stimulating text. The overall perspective is interdisciplinary. Relevant research and insights from psychology, sociology, and anthropology are included; maps and illustrations complement many of the examples and case studies. . . . Readers are encouraged as responsible citizens to consider their reactions to genocide. Summing Up: Essential. All readership levels.

P.G. Conway, SUNY College at Oneonta, writing in *Choice—Reviews Online*

GENOCIDE

A Comprehensive Introduction

3rd Edition

Adam Jones

Routledge
Taylor & Francis Group

LONDON AND NEW YORK

Third edition published 2017
by Routledge
2 Park Square, Milton Park, Abingdon, Oxon, OX14 4RN

and by Routledge
711 Third Avenue, New York, NY 10017

Routledge is an imprint of the Taylor & Francis Group, an informa business

First edition published by Routledge 2006

British Library Cataloguing in Publication Data
A catalogue record for this book is available from the British Library

Library of Congress Cataloging-in-Publication Data

Names: Jones, Adam, 1963– author.
Title: Genocide : a comprehensive introduction / by Adam Jones.
Description: Third edition. | Abingdon, Oxon ; New York, NY : Routledge, 2016. | Includes bibliographical reference and index.
Identifiers: LCCN 2016025350| ISBN 9781138780439 (hardback) | ISBN 9781138823846 (pbk.) | ISBN 9781315725390 (ebook)
Subjects: LCSH: Genocide. | Genocide—Case studies.
Classification: LCC HV6322.7 .J64 2016 | DDC 304.6/63—dc23
LC record available at https://lccn.loc.gov/2016025350

ISBN: 978-1-138-78043-9 (hbk)
ISBN: 978-1-138-82384-6 (pbk)
ISBN: 978-1-315-72539-0 (ebk)

Typeset in Bembo
by Apex CoVantage, LLC

For my parents, David (1932–2015) and Jo, givers of life.
And for Dr. Griselda Ramírez Reyes, saver of lives.

It is the writer's duty to tell the terrible truth, and it is a reader's civic duty to learn this truth. To turn away, to close one's eyes and walk past is to insult the memory of those who have perished.

Vasily Grossman, "The Hell of Treblinka" (1944)

Vasily Grossman during the battle of Berlin in April 1945—Nazism's final gasp.

Source: Courtesy *Jewish Currents*/www.jewishcurrents.org.

Vasily Grossman was a Soviet-Jewish journalist and novelist who achieved national fame as a correspondent for the *Red Star* newspaper during the "Great Patriotic War" of 1941–1945 (see Chapters 2, 6). Like all other Soviet writers, he was subject to highly restrictive Stalinist censorship (see Chapter 5). The vigilance was only heightened in wartime. He nonetheless produced masterpieces of reporting, as well as poetry and one epic work of fiction deeply informed by his journalism. Many consider *Life and Fate* (trans. Robert Chandler, London: Vintage, 2006) to be "the greatest Second World War novel ever written."[*]

Grossman submitted his semi-autobiographical narrative, with its stinging indictment of Stalinism, during the Khrushchev "thaw" in 1960—only to be told that it

---

[*] Sam Sacks, "Vasily Grossman: Loser, Saint," *The New Yorker*, June 25, 2013, www.newyorker.com/books/page-turner/vasily-grossman-loser-saint—an excellent profile.

was too incendiary to be published for at least two hundred years. Grossman died of cancer in 1964; the novel finally appeared during the Mikhail Gorbachev/*glasnost* era of the 1980s.

Grossman's mother was one of more than a million Jews murdered in the Nazis' "Holocaust by Bullets" in 1941–1942. His essay "The Hell of Treblinka" was written and published in 1944, as the Soviet armies, rolling back the Nazi enemy across Central Europe, were laying bare the death-camp system that still symbolizes, for most people, the Holocaust of European Jews and others (Chapter 6). Grossman's harrowing report appeared in the pages of *Red Star*, and is reprinted in English in the collection *A Writer at War: Vasily Grossman with the Red Army, 1941–1945*, ed. and trans. by Antony Beevor and Luba Vinogradova (London: Pimlico, 2006). Despite minor inaccuracies brought to light by subsequent documentation and discoveries, it remains a seminal account of the death camp, a must-read for any student of the Holocaust and the Nazi-Soviet conflict, and a classic of twentieth-century long-form journalism. The epigraph here is taken from the text as translated by Robert Chandler and published in Chil Rajchman, *Treblinka: A Survivor's Memory, 1942–1943* (London: Maclehose Press, 2011), p. 165.

CONTENTS

ILLUSTRATIONS

FIGURES

Photo Essay

■ FIGURES, CONT.

▮ Maps

▮ Boxes

ABOUT THE AUTHOR

Adam Jones, Ph.D., was born in Singapore in 1963, and grew up in England and Canada. He is currently Professor of Political Science at the University of British Columbia Okanagan in Kelowna, BC. Jones was selected as one of *Fifty Key Thinkers on the Holocaust and Genocide* for the book of that title, edited by Paul Bartrop and Steven Jacobs (Routledge, 2010). He has published various sole-authored and edited works on genocide and related themes, including *The Scourge of Genocide: Essays and Reflections* (2013), *New Directions in Genocide Research* (2012), and *Gender Inclusive: Essays on Violence, Men, and Feminist International Relations* (2009), all with Routledge; *Gendercide and Genocide* (Vanderbilt University Press, 2004); and *Genocide, War Crimes and the West: History and Complicity* (Zed Books, 2004). He has also published books about mass media and political transition, based on his doctoral fieldwork in Russia, Nicaragua, South Africa, and Jordan. Jones has lived and/or traveled in over one hundred countries on every populated continent. His "Global Photo Archive" of more than 17,000 Creative Commons images has been used online by *The New York Times*, *The Washington Post*, the BBC, *The Guardian*, and *The Atlantic*, among many others (see www.flickr.com/adam_jones/sets/). In recent years, Jones has served as review editor of the *Journal of Genocide Research*, and as an expert consultant for the United Nations Office of the Special Adviser on the Prevention of Genocide, based in New York City. Email: adam.jones@ubc.ca

(Photo by Griselda Ramírez—Mrauk U, Myanmar, 2014)

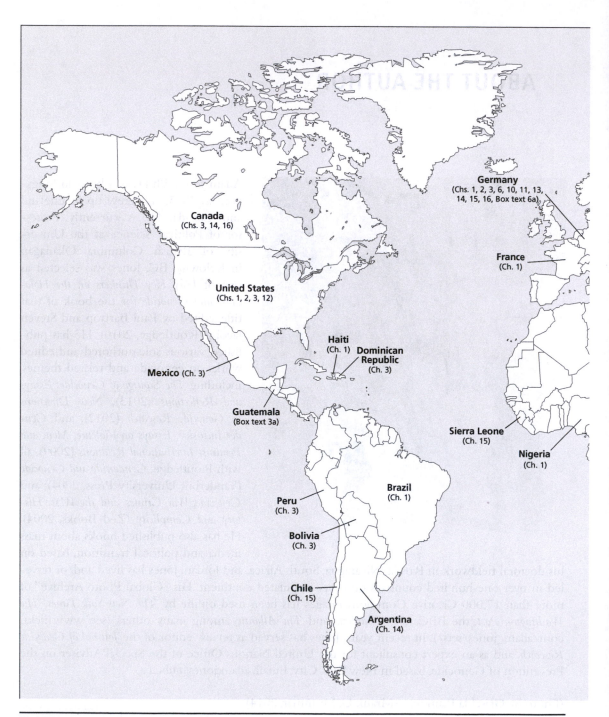

Canada
(Chs. 3, 14, 16)

Germany
(Chs. 1, 2, 3, 6, 10, 11, 13,
14, 15, 16, Box text 6a)

France
(Ch. 1)

United States
(Chs. 1, 2, 3, 12)

Haiti
(Ch. 1)

Dominican
Republic
(Ch. 3)

Mexico (Ch. 3)

Guatemala
(Box text 3a)

Sierra Leone
(Ch. 15)

Nigeria
(Ch. 1)

Brazil
(Ch. 1)

Peru
(Ch. 3)

Bolivia
(Ch. 3)

Chile
(Ch. 15)

Argentina
(Ch. 14)

World Map Cases of genocide and mass conflict referenced in this book

Source: Chartwell Illustrators

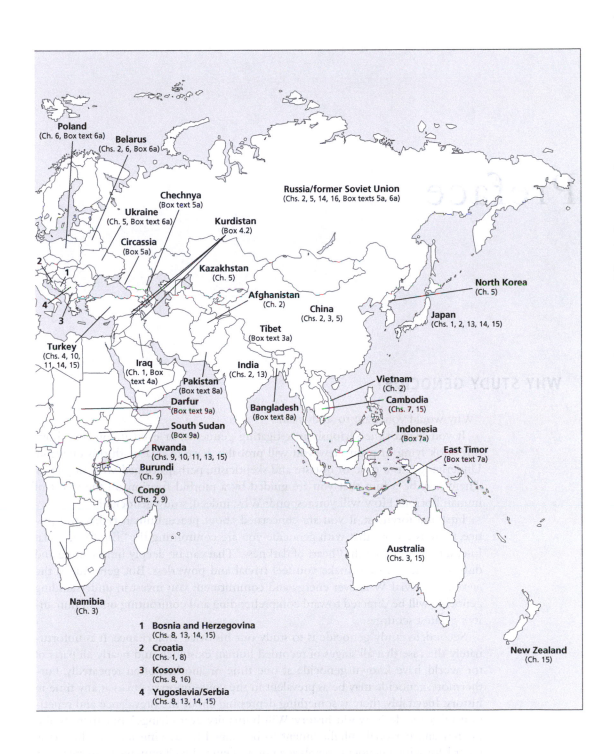

Poland
(Ch. 6, Box text 6a)

Belarus
(Chs. 2, 6, Box 6a)

Chechnya
(Box text 5a)

Ukraine
(Ch. 5, Box text 6a)

Kurdistan
(Box 4.2)

Russia/former Soviet Union
(Chs. 2, 5, 14, 16, Box texts 5a, 6a)

Circassia
(Box 5a)

Kazakhstan
(Ch. 5)

North Korea
(Ch. 5)

2

1

Afghanistan
(Ch. 2)

China
(Chs. 2, 3, 5)

Japan
(Chs. 1, 2, 13, 14, 15)

4

Tibet
(Box text 3a)

3

Turkey
(Chs. 4, 10,
11, 14, 15)

Iraq
(Ch. 1, Box
text 4a)

India
(Chs. 2, 13)

Vietnam
(Ch. 2)

Pakistan
(Box text 8a)

Cambodia
(Chs. 7, 15)

Darfur
(Box text 9a)

Bangladesh
(Box text 8a)

Indonesia
(Box 7a)

South Sudan
(Box 9a)

East Timor
(Box text 7a)

Rwanda
(Chs. 9, 10, 11, 13, 15)

Burundi
(Ch. 9)

Congo
(Chs. 2, 9)

Australia
(Chs. 3, 15)

Namibia
(Ch. 3)

New Zealand
(Ch. 15)

1   Bosnia and Herzegovina
(Chs. 8, 13, 14, 15)

2   Croatia
(Chs. 1, 8)

3   Kosovo
(Chs. 8, 16)

4   Yugoslavia/Serbia
(Chs. 8, 13, 14, 15)

Preface

WHY STUDY GENOCIDE?

"Why would you want to study *that?*"

If you spend time seriously investigating genocide, or even if you only leave this book lying in plain view, you will probably have to deal with this question. Underlying it is a tone of distaste and skepticism, perhaps tinged with suspicion. There may be a hint that you are guided by a morbid fixation on the worst of human horrors. How will you respond? Why, indeed, study genocide?

First and foremost, if you are concerned about peace, human rights, and justice, there is a sense that with genocide you are confronting the "Big One," what Joseph Conrad called the "heart of darkness." That can be deeply intimidating and disturbing. It can even make you feel trivial and powerless. But genocide is the *opposite* of trivial. Whatever energy and commitment you invest in understanding genocide will be directed toward comprehending and confronting one of humanity's greatest scourges.

Second, to study genocide is to study our historical inheritance. It is unfortunately the case that all stages of recorded human existence, and nearly all parts of the world, have known genocide at one time or another, often repeatedly. Furthermore, genocide may be as prevalent in the contemporary era as at any time in history. Inevitably, there is something depressing about the prevalence and repetition of genocide in world history: Will humanity ever change? But there is also interest and personal enlightenment to be gained by delving into the historical record, for which genocide serves as a point of entry. I well remember the period, a decade-and-a-half ago, that I devoted to voracious reading of the genocide studies literature, and exploring the diverse themes this opened up to me. The accounts were grim—sometimes relentlessly so. Yet they were also spellbinding, and they gave me a better grounding not only in world history, but also in sociology, psychology, anthropology, and a handful of other disciplines.

This points to a third reason to study genocide: it brings you into contact with some of the most interesting and exciting debates in the social sciences and humanities. To what extent should genocide be understood as reflecting epic social transformations such as modernity, the rise of the state, and globalization? How has warfare been transformed in recent times, and how are the wars of the present age linked to genocide? How does gender shape genocidal experiences and genocidal strategies? How is history "produced," and what role do memories or denial of genocide play in that production? These are only a few of the themes to be examined in this book. I hope they will lead readers, as they have led me, toward an engagement with debates that have a wider, though not necessarily deeper, significance.

In writing this book, I stand on the shoulders of giants: the scholars without whose trail-blazing efforts my own work would be inconceivable. You may find their approach and humanity inspiring, as I do. One of my principal concerns is to provide an overview of the core genocide studies literature; thus each chapter and box text is accompanied by recommendations for further study.

Modern academic writing, particularly in the social sciences and humanities, is often riddled with jargon and pomposity. It would be pleasant to report that genocide studies is free of such baggage. It isn't; but it is less burdened by it than most other fields. It seems this has to do with the experience of looking into the abyss, and finding that the abyss looks back. One is forced to ponder one's own human frailty and vulnerability; one is even pressed to confront one's own capacity for hating others, for marginalizing them, for supporting their oppression and annihilation. These realizations aren't pretty, but they are arguably necessary. And they can lead to humility—a rare quality in academia. I once described to a friend why the Danish philosopher Søren Kierkegaard (1813–1855) moved me so deeply: "It's like he's grabbing you by the arm and saying, 'Look. We don't have much time. There are important things we need to talk about.'" You sense the same in the genocide-studies literature: that the issues are too vital, and time too limited, to beat around the bush. George Orwell famously described political speech—he could have been referring to some academic writing—as "a mass of words [that] falls upon the facts like soft snow, blurring the outlines and covering up all the details."[1] By contrast, the majority of genocide scholars inhabit the literary equivalent of the tropics. I try to keep a residence there too.

Finally, some good news for the reader interested in understanding and confronting genocide: your studies and actions may make a difference. To study genocide is to study processes by which *hundreds of millions* of people met brutal ends. Yet there are many, many people throughout history who have bravely resisted the blind rush to hatred. They are the courageous and decent souls who gave refuge to hunted Jews or desperate Tutsis. They are the religious believers of many faiths who struggled against the tide of evil, and spread instead a message of love, tolerance, and commonality. They are the nongovernmental organizations that warned against incipient genocides and carefully documented those they were unable to prevent. They are the leaders and common soldiers—American, British, Soviet, Vietnamese, Indian, Tanzanian, Rwandan, and others—who vanquished genocidal regimes in modern times.[2] And yes, they are the scholars and intellectuals who have honed our understanding of genocide, while at the same time working outside the ivory tower to alleviate it. You will meet some of these individuals in this book. I hope their stories and actions will inspire you to believe that a future free of genocide and other crimes against humanity is possible.

But ...

Studying genocide, and trying to prevent it, is not to be entered into lightly: as the French political scientist Jacques Sémelin asks, "Who is ever really prepared for the shock of tales of cruelty in all their naked horror?"[3] The psychological and emotional impact that genocide studies can have on the investigator has yet to be systematically studied. How many genocide students, scholars, and activists suffer, as do their counterparts in the human rights and social work fields?[4] How many experience depression, insomnia, and nightmares as a result of having immersed themselves in the most atrocious human conduct?

The trauma is especially intense for those who have actually witnessed genocide, or its direct consequences. During the Turkish genocide against Armenians (Chapter 4), the US Ambassador to Constantinople, Henry Morgenthau, received a stream of American missionaries who had managed to escape the killing zone. "For hours they would sit in my office with tears streaming down their faces," Morgenthau recalled; many had been "broken in health" by what they had witnessed.[5] In 1948, the Jewish jurist Raphael Lemkin, who learned when World War Two ended that dozens of his family members had perished in the Holocaust (Chapter 6), wrote: "Genocide has taken the lives of my dear ones; the fight against genocide takes my health."[6] My friend Christian Scherrer, who works at the Hiroshima Peace Institute, arrived in Rwanda in November 1994 as part of a United Nations investigation team, only a few months after the slaughter of perhaps a million people had ended (see Chapter 9). Rotting bodies were still strewn across the landscape. "For weeks," Scherrer writes:

> Following directions given by witnesses, I carefully made my way, step by step, over farmland and grassland. Under my feet, often only half covered with earth, lay the remains of hundreds, indeed thousands . . . Many of those who came from outside shared the experience of hundreds of thousands of Rwandans of continuing, for months on end, or even longer, to grieve, to weep internally, and, night after night, to be unable to sleep longer than an hour or two.

Scherrer described the experience as "one of the most painful processes I have ever been through," and the writing of his book, *Genocide and Crisis*, as "part of a personal process of grieving." "Investigation into genocide," he added, "is something that remains with one for life."[7]

I encourage you—especially if you are just beginning your exploration of genocide—to be attentive to signs of personal stress. Talk about it with fellow students, colleagues, family, or friends. Dwell on the positive examples of bravery, rescue, and love for others that the study of genocide regularly brings to light (see especially Chapter 10). If necessary, seek counseling through the resources available on your campus or in your community.

It is also worth recalling that genocide scholars are far from alone as members of a profession that must confront suffering and mortality. Indeed, we are often privileged to maintain an arm's-length distance from those realities, unlike many other (often underappreciated and poorly recompensed) workers. The point was made to me by Meaghen Gallagher, an undergraduate student in Edmonton, Canada, after she first encountered the field of comparative genocide studies. She wrote:

> Really, you chose a very interesting field of study, in my opinion. It might be dark, but it is something that people are so afraid to talk about, when it really needs to be brought into light . . . I guess it is just like anything. Nurses, police, emergency technicians, philanthropists, they all have to deal with some pretty tough things, but someone has to do it, right?[8]

WHAT THIS BOOK TRIES TO DO, AND WHY

I see genocide as among history's defining features, overlapping a range of central historical processes: war, imperialism, state-building, and class struggle, from antiquity to the present. It is intimately linked to key institutions, in which state or broadly-political authorities are often but not always principal actors, such as forced labor, military conscription, incarceration, and female infanticide.

I adopt a comparative approach that resists elevating particular genocides over others, except to the extent that scale and intensity warrant special attention. I argue that virtually all definable human groups—the ethnic, national, racial, and religious ones that anchor the legal definition of genocide, and others besides—have been victims of genocide, and are vulnerable in specific contexts today. Equally, most human collectivities—even vulnerable and oppressed ones—have proven capable of inflicting genocide. This can be painful for genocide scholars to acknowledge. But it will be confronted head-on in this volume. Taboos and tender sensibilities take a back seat to *getting to grips with genocide*—to reduce the chances that mystification and wishful thinking will cloud recognition, and thereby blunt effective opposition.

The first part of *Genocide: A Comprehensive Introduction* seeks to ground readers in the basic historical and conceptual contexts of genocide. It explores the process by which Raphael Lemkin first named and defined the phenomenon, then mobilized a nascent United Nations to outlaw it. His story constitutes a vivid and inspiring portrait of an individual who had a significant, largely-unsung impact on modern history. Examination of legal and scholarly definitions and debates may help readers to clarify their own thinking, and situate themselves in the discussion.

The case study section of the book (Part 2) is divided between longer case studies of genocide and capsule studies that complement the detailed treatments. I hope this structure will catalyze discussion and comparative analysis.

Part 3 explores social-scientific contributions to the study of genocide—from psychology, sociology, anthropology, political science/international relations, and gender studies. Throughout these chapters, my ambition is modest. I am a political scientist by profession, and consider myself a somewhat trained historian, sociologist, and gender scholar. In roaming these fields and beyond, I seek only to introduce readers to some relevant scholarly framings, and to convey something of the extraordinary, still burgeoning *interdisciplinarity* of genocide studies.

Part 4, "The Future of Genocide," seeks to familiarize readers with contemporary debates over historical memory and genocide denial, as well as mechanisms of justice and redress. The final chapter, "Strategies of Intervention and Prevention," invites readers to evaluate options for suppressing the scourge.

"How does one handle this subject?" wrote Terrence Des Pres in the Preface to *The Survivor*, his study of life in the Nazi concentration camps. His answer: "One doesn't; not well, not finally. No degree of scope or care can equal the enormity of such events or suffice for the sorrow they encompass. Not to betray it is as much as I can hope for."[9] His words resonate. In my heart, I know this book is an audacious enterprise, but I have tried to expand the limits of my empathy and, through wide reading, my interdisciplinary understanding. I have also benefited from the insights and corrections of other scholars and general readers, whose names appear in the acknowledgments.

While I must depict particular genocides (and the contributions of entire academic disciplines) in very broad strokes, I have tried throughout to make space for individuals, whether as victims, survivors, rescuers, bystanders—and perpetrators. I hope this serves to counter some of the abstraction and depersonalization that is inevitable in a general survey. A list of relevant internet sources, along with links, teaching resources, and a "Filmography of Genocide and Crimes against Humanity," can be found on the Web page for this book at www.genocidetext.net.[10]

NOTE TO THE THIRD EDITION

Following the principle "If it ain't broke, don't fix it," I have left the core structure of *Genocide: A Comprehensive Introduction* intact from previous editions. Instructors who kindly used the second edition in their classes will find that many sections are reproduced with relatively few alterations. However, arguments, sources, and political developments have been updated throughout.

I offer here a quick summary of major changes for this third edition, aimed especially at educators. The most significant of these changes is the reframing of Chapter 9, formerly titled "Holocaust in Rwanda," as "Genocide in Africa's Great Lakes Region." It has become clearer to me, as to other scholars, that the Rwandan genocide of 1994 must be analyzed alongside parallel, reciprocal, and highly-consequential events in the Democratic Republic of the Congo and Burundi, especially. Adopting a broader framing allows me to incorporate Congo (previously addressed in a box text) in the main narrative; to examine the genocidal outbreaks in Burundi in 1972 and 1993, as well as the severe crisis in that country at the time of writing; and to devote space in the supplementary case study (Box 9a) to the conflict in the world's newest state, South Sudan, together with the previously-featured Sudan and Darfur.

Other sections of the text have also been extensively revised. The early portrait and discussion of Raphael Lemkin in Chapter 1 reflects the recent "return to Lemkin" in genocide studies, gaining steam with the publication of his unfinished history of genocide (*Lemkin on Genocide* [2012], edited by Steven Leonard Jacobs) and his autobiography (*Totally Unofficial: The Autobiography of Raphael Lemkin* [2013], edited by Donna-Lee Frieze). I have also included Nigeria/Biafra as a "contested case" of genocide in Chapter 1. A lengthy box text in Chapter 2 (Box 2.2) explores the case of the Circassians, uprooted and genocided by tsarist Russia in the nineteenth century, and their contemporary efforts to secure recognition, repatriation, and restitution. Chapter 4 now features sustained attention to the Kurds of Turkey, Iraq, and Syria (Box 4.2), as well as to the genocidal Islamic State (IS) movement (Box 4a). The case study of East Timor (Box 7a) now incorporates the earlier genocide in Indonesia (1965–1966)—the subject of advocacy and memorialization campaigns in Indonesia, an Oscar-nominated documentary film (*The Act of Killing*), and some notable recent scholarship, including an extended treatment in Christian Gerlach's *Extremely Violent Societies* (2010).

Several box texts, for example on Buffy Sainte-Marie (Chapter 3) and the gendered politics of lynching in the US South (Chapter 13), have been substituted for this third edition. They are, however, archived in PDF format on www.genocidetext.net (see "Text Excerpts"), and are copyright-cleared for reprinting/reposting or for use as class handouts. Among the other new box texts for this edition are those on physical, biological, and cultural genocide (Box 1.7); "Whatever Happened to Political Groups?" (Box 1.3); Sinéad O'Connor on the Irish famine (Box 2.1); the "Bloodlands" and "Rimlands" of twentieth-century Europe (Box 2.3); "The American West and the Nazi East" (Box 3.1); "Stalin: Return from the Crypt" (Box 5.2); Hermann Gräbe's witnessing of the "Holocaust by Bullets" (Box 6.1); the "Hitler-Mufti" controversy sparked by Israeli prime minister Benjamin Netanyahu (Box 6.4); the "Blood Telegram" sent by US consular officials during the Bangladeshi genocide of 1971 (Box 8a.1); the criminology of genocide (Box 11.1); the gendercidal targeting of gay and trans people worldwide (Box 13.1, adapted and updated from materials in the last edition); the *Stolpersteine* ("stumbling stones") memorialization project in Germany (Box 14.1); the "history wars" over the Canadian Museum for Human Rights (Box 14.2) and Canada's Truth and Reconciliation process for Canadian aboriginals and the residential-school atrocities (Box 15.3); Benjamin Ferencz and the Nuremberg *Einsatzgruppen* trials (Box 15.1); the United Nations Office of Genocide Prevention (OSAPG, Box 16.1); recent studies of state "resilience" to genocide (Box 16.2); and whether humanity is becoming more peaceful (Box 16.6).

For each edition of this book, I replace two or three of the individual "stories" in the case-study chapters, based on my reading in the interim. Fresh stories accompany the case studies of Stalinism (Boris Izvekov, Box 5.1), the Jewish Holocaust (Frieda Wulfovna, Box 6.2), and Cambodia under the Khmer Rouge (Denise Affonço, Box 7.1).

The visual aspect of the book has undergone extensive changes, including the addition of a photo essay/insert between Chapters 9 and 10, though plenty of familiar images remain. Since the last edition, photography and visual representations in general have grown more important to my own scholarship, teaching, and advocacy efforts. Many of this book's images are my own, including the cover photo. Many are gleaned from Wikimedia Commons, Flickr, the US government, and other sources of copyright-free illustrations. I am deeply grateful to the photographers who share their work in this way, as I do. Kudos also to those who scan, catalogue, and supply archival imagery at the US Holocaust Memorial Museum, Yad Vashem in Jerusalem, the Hoover Institution, and elsewhere. The publisher and I must renew our thanks to www.WorldAtlas.com for granting access to the excellent, reader-friendly maps used in the case-study chapters. Where licensing fees were unavoidable, Routledge provided very helpful financial assistance. Thanks to those at the Reuters, Associated Press, Magnum, and UN Photo agencies, who worked efficiently and courteously to make the necessary arrangements. But only a dozen or so of the 250 images in this book required licensing payments, at which point my budget was exhausted. That you hold, nonetheless, perhaps the richest and most diverse collection of genocide-related imagery ever compiled is an indication of what can be accomplished in the Creative Commons and online-institutional realms these days.

In a book of this attempted scope and detail, there are bound to be errors that have survived my fact-checking and various outside proofreadings. For these stumbles, I accept full responsibility. But I also ask you to get in touch when you notice them. The publisher and I can make minor corrections to the digital edition quite rapidly, and to any new printings thereafter. Indeed, I welcome readers' feedback of all kinds (well, most kinds). Write to me at adam.jones@ubc.ca. Now—let's dive in.

NOTES

1 George Orwell, "Politics and the English Language" (1946), in *Inside the Whale and Other Essays* (Harmondsworth: Penguin, 1974). Available online at www.resort.com/~prime8/Orwell/patee.html.

2 The Second World War Allies against the Nazis and Japanese; Tanzanians against Idi Amin's Uganda; Vietnamese in Cambodia in 1979; Indians in Bangladesh in 1971; soldiers of the Rwandan Patriotic Front in 1994. See also Chapter 16.

3 Jacques Sémelin, *Purify and Destroy: The Political Uses of Massacre and Genocide* (New York: Columbia University Press, 2007), p. 6.

4 Writing the first in-depth study of the Soviet "terror-famine" in Ukraine in 1932–1933 (see Chapter 5), Robert Conquest confronted only indirectly the "inhuman, unimaginable misery" of the famine; but he still found the task "so distressing that [I] sometimes hardly felt able to proceed." Conquest, *The Harvest of Sorrow: Soviet Collectivization and the Terror-Famine* (New York: Oxford University Press, 1986), p. 10. Donald Miller and Lorna Touryan Miller, who interviewed a hundred survivors of the Armenian genocide, wrote: "During this project our emotions have ranged from melancholy to anger, from feeling guilty about our own privileged status to being overwhelmed by the continuing suffering in our world." They described experiencing "a permanent loss of innocence about the human capacity for evil," as well as "a recognition of the need to combat such evil." Miller and Miller, *Survivors: An Oral History of the Armenian Genocide* (Berkeley, CA: University of California Press, 1999), p. 4. After an immersion in the archive of S-21 (Tuol Sleng), the Khmer Rouge killing center in Cambodia, David

Chandler found that "the terror lurking inside it has pushed me around, blunted my skills, and eroded my self-assurance. The experience at times has been akin to drowning." Chandler, *Voices from S-21: Terror and History in Pol Pot's Secret Prison* (Berkeley, CA: University of California Press, 1999), p. 145. Brandon Hamber notes that "many of the staff" working with the Truth and Reconciliation Commission in South Africa have experienced "nightmares, paranoia, emotional bluntness, physical problems (e.g., headaches, ulcers, exhaustion, etc.), high levels of anxiety, irritability and aggression, relationship difficulties, and substance abuse related problems." Hamber, "The Burdens of Truth," in David E. Lorey and William H. Beezley, eds., *Genocide, Collective Violence, and Popular Memory: The Politics of Remembrance in the Twentieth Century* (Wilmington, DL: Scholarly Resources, Inc., 2002), p. 96.

5 Peter Balakian, *The Burning Tigris: The Armenian Genocide and America's Response* (New York: HarperCollins, 2003), p. 278.

6 Lemkin quoted in John Cooper, *Raphael Lemkin and the Struggle for the Genocide Convention* (London: Palgrave Macmillan, 2008), p. 169.

7 Christian P. Scherrer, *Genocide and Crisis in Central Africa: Conflict Roots, Mass Violence, and Regional War* (Westport, CT: Praeger, 2002), pp. 1, 7.

8 Meaghen Gallagher, personal communication, October 11, 2009.

9 Terrence Des Pres, *The Survivor: An Anatomy of Life in the Death Camps* (Oxford: Oxford University Press, 1976), pp. v–vi.

10 Readers who are interested in the background to my engagement with genocide studies can consult the short essay, "Genocide: A Personal Journey," at www.genocidetext.net/personal_journey.htm; and my chapter, "Seized of Sorrow," in Samuel Totten, ed., *Advancing Genocide Studies: Personal Accounts and Insights from Scholars in the Field* (New Brunswick, NJ: Transaction Publishers, 2015), pp. 57–77.

Acknowledgments

Routledge Publishers has been the home of most of my recent book publications, both sole-authored and edited. I am deeply grateful to Craig Fowlie, who proposed what became the first edition of *Genocide: A Comprehensive Introduction*, over dinner in Durban, South Africa in 2003. He has continued his unfailing support through to the present. Thanks also to Nicola Parkin, Lydia de Cruz, and Emily Ross on the editorial side, and Luke Allen, who worked closely with me on the visual design and presentation of the volume. Emma Simmons and Jamie Vidich at Bookbright Media provided sterling copy-editing.

This book has its audience because educators around the world have adopted it for their courses on genocide studies. I have benefited from their supportive words and feedback, and it gives me no deeper pleasure in my intellectual life than to know that my work is contributing to the project of educating a new generation of students to an understanding of genocide and the international "epistemic community" that seeks to prevent future outbreaks of the scourge.

Allow me to express gratitude to some cherished colleagues on this path. Elisa von Joeden-Forgey has been one of my most reliable sources of information and inspiration on the gender-and-genocide front, and humanitarian issues more generally. She is unquestionably the best person alive when it comes to staying up late in Yerevan, Armenia, to knock back bottles of white wine and survey the progress of our field, our species, and much else besides. Benjamin Madley at UCLA, so helpful in shaping and polishing previous editions, continued to assist me this time around, as with his updated map of Native Indian massacres in North America (see Map 3.1, pp. 158–159). A core group of younger Canadian genocide scholars has coalesced in recent years. I'm grateful to Christopher Powell, Andrew Woolford (president of the International Association of Genocide Scholars, 2015–2017), Andrew Basso, and Geneviève Parent for nourishing interactions. My graduate students in genocide-related thesis programs at the University of British Columbia have been constant sources of inspiration and insight. Thanks to Jill Mitchell (who also provided diligent research assistance for a couple of the box texts in this book), Jeffrey Stonehouse, Amin Mansouri, and Cathay Gibson. Many undergraduate students, especially in my Poli 382 and 383 (Genocide and Crimes against Humanity) courses, have supplied trenchant insights and the pedagogical pleasure of witnessing and guiding students' first systematic encounters with this subject. Thanks also to my colleagues in UBCO's PoliSci program—Carl Hodge, James Rochlin, David Ding, Carey Doberstein, and Andrew Irvine—as well as unit assistants Shelby Wolfe and Tiffany Clarke.

Over the past few years, I have worked with various institutions devoted to the study and prevention of genocide. At the United Nations Office of the Special Adviser for the Prevention of Genocide (OSAPG) in New York, I thank Mario Buil-Merce and Norul Rashid, who is now with UN Women. My dear friend David Simon of Yale University was my usual confederate and co-presenter in these UN-sponsored settings, and graciously provided feedback on my reworked Chapter 9. At the Holocaust Museum Houston, Mary Lee Webeck, Kelly Webeck, Emily Sample, Matthew Remington, Bruce Kirsch—and the apparently immortal Holocaust survivor and humanitarian, Naomi Warren—have been colleagues and true sweethearts. At the Liberation War Museum in Dhaka, Bangladesh, I thank Mofidul Hoque and Umme Wara. Professor John Cox at the University of North Carolina—Charlotte is a *compadre* of the first order, and the source of memorable speaking invitations to Charlotte, most recently on "ISIS, Religion, and Genocide." Ben Kiernan at Yale University, who provided me with my "break" in the field via a postdoctoral fellowship to Yale's Genocide Studies Program (2005–2007), continues to offer support, friendship, and guidance. Thanks also to Debórah Dwork and Thomas Kühne at the Strassler Center for Holocaust and Genocide Studies, Clark University; Daniel Feierstein at the Universidad Nacional de Tres de Febrero/Universidad de Buenos Aires; Victoria Fontan at the Center for Peace and Human Security, The American University of Kurdistan, Duhok; Ernesto Verdeja at the Kroc Institute for International Peace Studies, University of Notre Dame; Marc Greenside at Columbia Grammar Prep School, New York City; and Graeme Stacey at Kelowna Senior Secondary School.

For the better part of a decade, during the preparation of the current and previous editions of this book, I was privileged to serve as book review editor of the *Journal of Genocide Research*, the oldest and arguably the preeminent journal in the field of comparative genocide studies. This allowed me a perch from which to stay on top of the proliferating literature in the field, and related historical, sociological, and anthropological monographs on the cases addressed here. I thank A. Dirk Moses, one of the most impressive of the new generation of genocide scholars and historians, for collaborating to make the *JGR* review section one of the liveliest in the social sciences, or so I humbly submit. My deep gratitude also to the team of *JGR* book reviewers, including many of the preeminent names in the profession.

Genuine friendships, including with Mark Levene and Martin Shaw, grew out of my review editor role.

Miscellaneous shout-outs to the following friends and colleagues, several of whom provided feedback on this new edition: R. Charli Carpenter, Ferrel Christensen, Wendy Lower, Stephen McLoughlin, the late and much-missed Eric Markusen and Stephen Feinsten, Andrea and Steve Gunner, Rick Feingold, David Buchanan, Luz María Johnson and her son Louis, Diana Henson, Henry Huttenbach, David Liebe, Fabiola Martínez, Miriam Tratt, Paul Cottingham and Sandi Love, Susan Minushkin, Paula Drumond, Lauren Marshall, Hamish Telford, and Laura Shepherd. Marcelle Torres kindly double-checked all URL links in the book to ensure they were "live" as of June 2016. My cherished Facebook friends—my social life, as I sometimes refer to them—have followed my progress on this edition for many months. They have offered unstinting "thumbs up" and moral support, along with much useful feedback. For example, I Facebook-tested close to a dozen designs for this book cover. What you hold was the favorite of an absolute majority of respondents. And my own. And my mother's.

Speaking of whom, this book could not have been written without the nurture and guidance provided by my parents and my brother, Craig. My beloved father, David Jones, died during the preparation of this third edition, at the age of 82.* I miss him immensely, but I know his shaping influence will be with me for the rest of my days. Together with my mother Jo, he proofread and commented on previous editions of this book, so he lives on in these pages. I can still count on Jo's eagle eye for this new edition—thanks as always, Mom.

Dr. Griselda Ramírez Reyes shares the dedication of this work. Griselda is a pediatric neurosurgeon at the Siglo XXI medical center in Mexico City. I have stood literally at her elbow as she opened the head of a three-week-old girl, and extracted a cancerous tumor seemingly half the size of the infant's brain. I hope to open a few minds myself with this work, but I would not pretend the task compares. Throughout the preparation of new editions, Griselda has joined me on journeys to sites of genocide and war that resonated deeply with us—most memorably in Cambodia, Vietnam, Russia, Poland, Romania, Rwanda, Armenia, and indeed Mexico. It is a great salve and pleasure to have her company and solidarity as I try to absorb these horrors and make some sense of them.

Adam Jones
Kelowna, BC, June 2016
adam.jones@ubc.ca

* See "David Gilbert Jones, 1932–2015," *Maclean's*, July 14, 2015, www.macleans.ca/society/david-gilbert-jones-1932-2015/, and the self-authored "Who is David G. Jones?," http://adamjones.freeservers.com/jojones.htm#David.

PART 1 OVERVIEW

CHAPTER 1

The Origins of Genocide

This chapter analyzes the origins of genocide as a global-historical phenomenon, providing a sense of genocide's frequency through history. It then examines the origin and evolution of the concept, unravels some central theoretical debates, and explores "contested cases" that test the boundaries of the genocide framework. No other chapter in the book tries to cover so much ground, and the discussion may at points seem complicated and confusing, so please fasten your seatbelts.*

GENOCIDE IN PREHISTORY, ANTIQUITY, AND EARLY MODERNITY

"The word is new, the concept is ancient," wrote sociologist Leo Kuper in his seminal 1981 text of genocide studies.[1] He echoed the father of genocide studies, Raphael Lemkin, whose unfinished history of genocide—only recently published—declared at its outset: "Genocide is a new word, but the evil it describes is old."[2] The roots of genocide are lost in distant millennia, and will remain so unless an "archaeology of genocide" can be developed.[3] The difficulty, as Frank Chalk and Kurt Jonassohn pointed out in their study *The History and Sociology of Genocide*, is that such historical

---

* Throughout this book, to reduce footnoting, I gather sequential quotations and citations from the same source into an omnibus note at the end of the passage. Epigraphs for chapters and sections are not footnoted. All Web links cited in the notes were "live" as of mid-2016. If you find one broken, search the title of the source in quotation marks; often it will be archived elsewhere. I have included link addresses for media and other reports when they are reasonably concise. Where I consider them too ungainly to print, a Web search by author and title will generally bring up the source.

records as exist are ambiguous and undependable. While history today is generally written with some fealty to "objective" facts, many past accounts aimed to praise the writer's patron (normally a powerful leader) and to emphasize the superiority of one's own religious beliefs. They may also have been intended as good stories— so that when Homer quotes King Agamemnon's quintessential pronouncement of root-and-branch genocide, one cannot know what basis it might have in fact:

> We are not going to leave a single one of them alive, down to the babies in their mothers' wombs—not even they must live. The whole people must be wiped out of existence, and none be left to think of them and shed a tear.[4]

The founder of genocide studies, Raphael Lemkin, quoted the declaration of the Assyrian King Ashur-natsir-pal, boasting about one of his military triumphs:

> I crossed the mountain of Kashiari and toward Kinabu, the fortress of Hulai I advanced. With the multitude of my troops by a charge, tempestuous as the tempest, I fell upon the town. I took it. I put to the sword 600 of their warriors. I delivered 3,000 prisoners over to the flames and I left not a single one of them alive to serve as a hostage. . . . Their carcasses I piled in heaps, their young men and their maidens I delivered to the flames. Hulai, their governor, I flayed; I stretched his skin along the wall of Dadaamusa. The city I destroyed, I ravaged it, I gave it to the flames.[5]

What are we to make of Agamemnon's command and Ashur-natsir-pal's proclamation? Are they factually reliable? Regardless, they encapsulate a fantasy and often an ambition of kings and commoners alike: know thine enemies, and annihilate them.

BOX 1.1 NEANDERTHALS: THE FIRST VICTIMS OF GENOCIDE?

The Neanderthals, humanity's closest cousins, disappeared from their lands in Europe some 26,000 to 32,000 years ago. For many decades, a consensus prevailed that climate change had driven them to extinction. According to more recent research, however, it appears that not only were Neanderthal populations highly resistant to climatic fluctuations, but conditions were quite mild in southwestern Europe, during the period when the Neanderthals "made their last stand" as a species. According to *The Washington Post*'s Rick Weiss, reviewing a 2007 study by Chronis Tzedakis and his colleagues: "That pretty much leaves one suspect: the butler—or more precisely the predecessors to all butlers and to modern humans, generally, who were making their initial sweep across Europe at the time." As Konrad Hughen of the Woods Hole Oceanographic Institution noted: "They [Neanderthals] survived 20,000 years of very unstable climate. Then when you add humans to the mix, they are gone within 10,000 years. You tell me what the most parsimonious explanation is."[6]

In 2013, Spanish anthropologists went further, speculating that "our closest extinct relative was exterminated in the same way as 178 other large mammals, so called

Figure 1.1 Growing evidence points to a human–driven extermination of Europe's Neanderthal population, rather than a slow decline linked to climate change.

Source: © Procyab/Dreamtime.com.

megafauna, which are suspected of going at least partially by the hand of hungry human hunters." That is, the Neanderthals may have been hunted to extinction as food, as well as competitors for land and nutritional resources, as other megafauna were.[7] Or perhaps it was dogs that did most of the eating. Pat Shipman argued in her book *The Invaders* that human beings first partnered with canines to bring about the Neanderthals' extermination.[8]

Regardless of the Neanderthals' fate, archaeological discoveries announced in early 2016 emphasized how deeply-rooted in the human species was the institution of savage intercommunal massacre. For the first time, persuasive evidence was found of such massacres—which bear the hallmarks of "root-and-branch" genocide—occurring some 10,000 years ago, prior to the rise of agriculture and durable human settlements. James Gorman of *The New York Times* reported findings in the journal *Nature* that of "12 relatively complete skeletons" found by Lake Turkana in Kenya, "10 showed unmistakable signs of violent death . . . Partial remains of at least 15 other people were found at the site and are thought to have died in the same attack." The remains of these early hunter-gatherers, Gorman reported, "tell a tale of ferocity. One man was hit twice in the head by arrows or small spears and in the knee by a club. A woman, pregnant with a 6- to 9-month-old fetus, was killed by a blow to the head, the fetal skeleton preserved in her abdomen. The position of her hands and feet suggest that she may have been tied up before she was killed."

Pottery at the site suggested that the targeted population may have harbored food resources that drew the notice of forager-predators. "Or the attackers may have been after captives," Gorman wrote. "Bones from one young teenager were found at the site, and remains of adults and children under 6, but no remains of older children, who might have been taken by the attackers."[9]

Humanity has always nurtured conceptions of social difference that generate a sense of in-group versus out-group, as well as hierarchies of good and evil, superior and inferior, desirable and undesirable. As Chalk and Jonassohn observed:

> Historically and anthropologically peoples have always had a name for themselves. In a great many cases, that name meant "the people" to set the owners of that name off against all other people who were considered of lesser quality in some way. If the differences between the people and some other society were particularly large in terms of religion, language, manners, customs, and so on, then such others were seen as less than fully human: pagans, savages, or even animals.[10]

The fewer the shared values and standards, the more likely members of the out-group were (and are) to find themselves beyond the "universe of obligation," in sociologist Helen Fein's evocative phrase. Hence the advent of "religious traditions of contempt and collective defamation, stereotypes, and derogatory metaphor indicating the victim is inferior, sub-human (animals, insects, germs, viruses) or super-human (Satanic, omnipotent)." If certain classes of people are "pre-defined as alien . . . subhuman or dehumanized, or the enemy," it follows that they must "be eliminated in order that we may live (Them or Us)."[11]

An example of this mindset is the text that underpins the Christian, Jewish, and Muslim cultural traditions: the Old Testament (particularly its first five books, the Pentateuch). In general, these texts depict God as "a despotic and capricious sadist,"[12] and his followers as eager *génocidaires* (genocidal killers). The trend begins in the Book of Genesis (6:17–19), where God decides "to destroy all flesh in which is the breath of life from under heaven," with the exception of Noah and a nucleus of human and animal life.[13] In "the most unequivocally extirpatory of [the] Old Testament texts,"[14] 1 Samuel 15:2–3, "the Lord of hosts" declares: "I will punish the Amalekites for what they did in opposing the Israelites when they came up out of Egypt.

Now go and attack Amalek, and utterly destroy all that they have; do not spare them, but kill both man and woman, child and infant, ox and sheep, camel and donkey."[15]

The Midianites in Numbers 31: 7–18 fare little better, but even the minimal selectivity at the outset vexes Moses:

> They warred against Midian, as the Lord commanded Moses, and slew every male. . . . And the people of Israel took captive the women of Midian and their little ones; and they took as booty all their cattle, their flocks, and all their goods. All their cities . . . they burned with fire. . . . And Moses was angry with the officers of the army. . . . [He] said to them, "Have you let all the women live? Behold, these caused the people of Israel, by the counsel of Balaam, to act treacherously against the Lord . . . and so the plague came to the congregations of the Lord. Now, therefore, kill every male among the little ones, and kill every woman who has known man by lying with him [sexually]. But all the young girls who have not known man by lying with him, keep alive for yourselves.[16]

As this passage suggests, genocides in prehistory and antiquity were often designed not just to eradicate enemy ethnicities, but to incorporate and exploit *some* of their members. Generally, it was children (particularly girls) and women (particularly virgins, or those in the associated age group) who were spared murder. They were simultaneously seen as the group least able to offer resistance, and as sources of off-spring for the dominant group, descent in patrilineal society being traced through the male bloodline.[17] By contrast, "every male" was often killed, "even the little ones." We see here the roots of *gendercide* against men and boys, including male infants, discussed further in Chapter 13.

A combination of gender-selective mass killing and root-and-branch genocide pervades accounts of ancient wars. Chalk and Jonassohn provide a wide-ranging selection of historical events such as the Assyrian Empire's root-and-branch depredations in the first half of the first millennium BCE,* and the destruction of Melos by Athens during the Peloponnesian War (fifth century BCE), a gendercidal rampage described by Thucydides in his "Melian Dialogue."[18]

The Roman siege and eventual razing of Carthage at the close of the Third Punic War (149–46 BCE) has been labeled "The First Genocide" by historian Ben Kiernan.[19] The "first" designation is debatable; the label of genocide seems apt. Fueled by the documented ideological zealotry of the senator Cato, Rome sought to suppress the supposed threat posed by (disarmed, mercantile) Carthage. "Of a population of 2–400,000, at least 150,000 Carthaginians perished," writes Kiernan. The "Carthaginian solution" found many echoes in the warfare of subsequent centuries.[20] Among Rome's other victims during its imperial ascendancy were the followers of Jesus Christ. After his death at Roman hands in 33 CE, Christ's followers were subjected to persecutions and mass murder. The scenes of torture and public spectacle were duplicated by Christians themselves during

---

* "BCE" means "Before the Common Era," and replaces the more familiar but ethnocentric "BC" (Before Christ). "CE" replaces "AD" (Anno Domini, Latin for "year of the Lord"). For discussion, see ReligiousTolerance.org, "The Use of 'CE' and 'BCE' to Identify Dates," www.religioustolerance.org/ce.htm.

Europe's medieval era (approximately the ninth to fourteenth centuries CE). This period produced onslaughts such as the Crusades: religiously sanctified campaigns against "unbelievers," whether in France (the Albigensian crusade against Cathar heretics),[21] Germany (against Jews), or the Holy Land of the Middle East.[22]

BOX 1.2 HUMANITY'S TWENTY DEADLIEST "MULTICIDES"

Matthew White—"self-described atrocitologist, necrometrician, and quantifier of hemoclysms"—presents in his book *Atrocitology* an account of "Humanity's 100 Deadliest Achievements."[23] The death tolls of the twenty leading "multicides"— mass killings—by his calculations are:

1. Second World War (1939–1945)	66,000,000
2. Chinggis [Genghis] Khan (1206–1227)	40,000,000
3. Mao Zedong (1949–1976)	40,000,000
4. Famines in British India (18th–20th centuries)	27,000,000
5. Fall of the Ming Dynasty [China] (1635–1662)	25,000,000
6. Taiping Rebellion (1850–1864)	20,000,000
7. Joseph Stalin (1928–1953)	20,000,000
8. Mideast Slave Trade (7th–19th centuries)	18,500,000
9. Timur (1370–1405)	17,000,000
10. Atlantic Slave Trade (1452–1807)	16,000,000
11. Conquest of the Americas (after 1492)	15,000,000
12. First World War (1914–1918)	15,000,000
13. An Lushan Rebellion [China] (755–763)	13,000,000
14. Xin Dynasty (9–24)	10,000,000
15. Congo Free State (1895–1908)	10,000,000
16. Russian Civil War (1918–1920)	9,000,000
17. Thirty Years War (1618–1648)	7,500,000
18. Fall of the Yuan Dynasty [China] (ca. 1340–1370)	7,500,000
19. Fall of the Western Roman Empire (395–455)	7,000,000
20. Chinese Civil War (1927–1937, 1945–1949)	7,000,000

Of these, the First and Second World Wars, the Russian Civil War, and the Stalin multicide figure in "the Hemoclysm" (Greek: "blood flood") of human history: the destruction of approximately 150 million human lives during the first half of the twentieth century. This epoch and its component genocides are anchors of this book. The depredations of Genghis Khan, famines in British India, the Atlantic Slave Trade, the conquest of the Americas, and the Congo Free State are all referenced here, and have received extended or passing attention from other genocide scholars. The other multicides, with the possible exceptions of Timur (Tamerlane), the Taiping Rebellion, and certain events in the Thirty Years War, have rarely if ever entered the genocide-studies literature.

Génocidaires also arose on the other side of the world. In the thirteenth century, a million or so Mongol horsemen under their leader, Genghis Khan, surged out of the grasslands of East Asia to lay waste to vast territories, extending to the gates of Western Europe; "entire nations were exterminated, leaving behind nothing but rubble, fallow fields, and bones."[24] "If genocide did not take place," wrote Raphael Lemkin, then for the Mongols, "conquest seemed incomplete . . ."[25] Yet Genghis Khan became a towering figure of history, as well as a villain etched deep in the collective memory of the populations ravaged by him and his descendants. One of the small handful of individuals to match or surpass his destructive efforts, Adolf Hitler, praised the Mongol emperor's "annihilative spirit": Genghis Khan "set millions of women and children into death knowingly and cheerfully . . . Yet history sees in him only the great founder of states."[26]

A hunger for wealth, power, and "death-defying" glory seems to have motivated these acts of mass violence (see Chapter 10), along with religious and cultural factors (Chapter 16). These elements combined to catalyze the genocides of the early modern era, dating from approximately 1492, the year of Caribbean Indians' fateful encounter with Christopher Columbus. The consequences of contact between expansionist Europeans and indigenous peoples are detailed in Chapter 3. I now briefly present two cases from the early modern era: one from western Europe, presaging the genocidal civil wars of the twentieth century; and one from southern Africa, reminding us that genocide knows no geographical or cultural boundaries.

The Vendée uprising

In 1789, French rebels, inspired by the American revolutionaries, overthrew King Louis XVI and established a new order based on the "Rights of Man." The French revolution provoked immediate opposition at home and abroad. European armies massed on French borders, and in March 1793—following the execution of King Louis and the imposition of mass military conscription—revolt erupted in the Vendée. The population of this isolated and conservative region of western France declared itself opposed to conscription, and to the replacement of their priests by pro-revolutionary designates. Well trained and led by royalist officers, Vendeans rose up against the rapidly radicalizing central government: the "terror" of the Jacobin faction was instituted in the same month as the rebellion in St.-Florent-le-Vieil. The result was a civil war that, according to French author Reynald Secher, constituted a genocide against the Vendeans—and for historian Mark Levene, a turning point in the evolution of genocide.[27]

Early Vendean victories were achieved through the involvement of all demographic sectors of the Vendée, and humiliated the Republican government. Fueled by the ideological fervor of the Terror, and by foreign and domestic counter-revolution, the Republicans in Paris implemented a campaign of root-and-branch genocide. Under Generals Jean-Baptiste Carrier and Louis Marie Turreau, the Republicans launched a scorched-earth drive by the *colonnes infernales* ("hellish columns"). On December 11, 1793, Carrier wrote to the Committee of Public Safety in Paris, pledging to purge the Vendean peasantry "absolutely and totally."[28] Similar edicts by General Turreau in early 1794 were approved by the Committee, which declared that the "race of brigands" in the Vendée was to be "exterminated to the last." Targeted victims included even children, who were "just as dangerous [as adults], because they were or were in the process of becoming brigands." Extermination was "both sound and pure," the Committee wrote, and should "show great results."[29]

The slaughter targeted all Vendeans, including Republicans (these victims were seen as "collateral damage"). Specifically, none of the traditional gender-selective exemptions was granted to adult females, who stood accused of fomenting the rebellion through their defense of conservative religion, and their "goad[ing] . . . into martyrdom" of Vendean men.[30] In the account of a Vendean *abbé*, perhaps self-interested but buttressed by other, similar testimony:

> There were poor girls, completely naked, hanging from tree branches, hands tied behind their backs, after having been raped. It was fortunate that, with the Blues [Republicans] gone, some charitable passersby delivered them from this shameful torment. Elsewhere . . . pregnant women were stretched out and crushed beneath wine presses. . . . Bloody limbs and nursing infants were carried in triumph on the points of bayonets.[31]

When the last remnants of Vendean resistance were hunted down and slaughtered at the end of 1793, General François-Joseph Westermann was exultant. His "justly notorious" report to the authorities in Paris included one of the most decisive genocidal proclamations on the historical record:

> There is no more Vendée citizens. It has died under our free sword, with its women and children. I have just buried it in the marshes and woods of Savenay. Following the orders you gave me, I have crushed children under the hooves of horses, and massacred women who, these at least, will give birth to no more brigands. I do not have a single prisoner with which to reproach myself. I have exterminated everyone.[32]

Perhaps 150,000 Vendeans died in the carnage, though not all were civilians. The character of the killings was conveyed by post-genocide census figures, which displayed not the usual war-related disparity of male versus female victims, but a rough—and unusual—parity. Only after this "ferocious . . . expression of ideologically charged avenging terror,"[33] and with the collapse of the Committee of Public Safety in Paris, did the genocide wane, though scattered clashes with rebels continued through 1796.

In a comparative context, the Vendée uprising stands as an example of a mass-killing campaign that has only recently been conceptualized as "genocide." This designation is not universally shared, but it seems apt in light of the large-scale murder of a designated group (the Vendean civilian population).[34] In *The First Total War*, his influential study of warfare in the French revolutionary and Napoleonic eras, David A. Bell presents the Vendée slaughter as a vanguard of modernity, a harbinger of the gargantuan slaughters of the twentieth century (see Chapter 2):

> The Vendée was the face of total war, which followed its own dynamic of radicalization. It was the place where the modern version of the phenomenon was first revealed to its full, gruesome extent. As in most modern cases, its "totality" did not derive primarily from the battlefield clashes between organized armies

(World War I is a distracting exception in this case). What made it total was rather its erasure of any line between combatants and noncombatants and the wanton slaughter of both—and at the behest of politics more than military necessity.[35]

Zulu genocide

Between 1810 and 1828, the Zulu kingdom under its dictatorial leader, Shaka Zulu, waged an ambitious campaign of expansion and annihilation. Huge swathes of present-day South Africa and Zimbabwe were laid waste by Zulu armies. The European invasion of these regions, which began shortly after, was greatly assisted by the upheaval and depopulation caused by the Zulu assault.

Oral histories help document the scale of the destruction:[36] "To this day, peoples in Zimbabwe, Malawi, Zambia, Tanzania, Kenya, and Uganda can trace their descent back to the refugees who fled from Shaka's warriors."[37] At times, Shaka apparently implemented a gender-selective extermination strategy that may be unique in the historical record. In conquering the Butelezi clan, Shaka "conceived the then [and still] quite novel idea of utterly demolishing them as a separate tribal entity by incorporating all their manhood into his own clan or following," thereby bolstering his own military; but he "usually destroyed women, infants, and old people," who were deemed useless for his expansionist purposes.[38]

However, root-and-branch strategies reminiscent of the French rampage in the Vendée seem also to have been common. According to historian Michael Mahoney, Zulu armies often aimed not only at defeating enemies but at "their total destruction. Those exterminated included not only whole armies, but also prisoners of war, women, children, and even dogs."[39] In exterminating the followers of Beje, a minor Kumalo chief, Shaka determined "not to leave alive even a child, but [to] exterminate the whole tribe," according to a foreign witness. When the foreigners protested against the slaughter of women and children, claiming they "could do no injury," Shaka responded in language that would have been familiar to the French revolutionaries: "Yes they could," he declared. "They can propagate and bring [bear] children, who may become my enemies . . . therefore I command you to kill all."[40]

Mahoney has characterized these policies as genocidal. "If genocide is defined as a state-mandated effort to annihilate whole peoples, then Shaka's actions in this regard must certainly qualify." He points out that the term adopted by the Zulus to denote their campaign of expansion and conquest, *izwekufa*, derives "from Zulu *izwe* (nation, people, polity), and *ukufa* (death, dying, to die). The term is thus identical to 'genocide' in both meaning and etymology."[41]

NAMING GENOCIDE: RAPHAEL LEMKIN

Genocide is an absolute word—a howl of a word . . .

Lance Morrow

Until the Second World War, genocide was a "crime without a name," in the words of British Prime Minister Winston Churchill.[42] The man who named the crime, placed it in a global-historical context, and demanded intervention and remedial action was a Polish-Jewish jurist, a refugee from Nazi-occupied Europe, named Raphael Lemkin (1900–1959). His story is one of the most remarkable of the twentieth century.

Lemkin is an exceptional example of a "norm entrepreneur" (see Chapter 12). In the space of four years, he coined a term—genocide—that concisely defined an age-old phenomenon. He supported it with a wealth of documentation. He published a lengthy book *(Axis Rule in Occupied Europe)* that applied the concept to campaigns of genocide underway in Lemkin's native Poland and elsewhere in the Nazi-occupied territories. He then waged a successful campaign to persuade the new United Nations to draft a convention against genocide; another successful campaign to obtain the required number of signatures; and yet another to secure the necessary national ratifications. Yet Lemkin lived in penury—in surely his wittiest recorded comment, he described himself as "pleading a holy cause at the UN while wearing holey clothes"[43]—and he died in obscurity in 1959; his funeral drew just seven people. Only in recent years has the promise of his concept, and the UN convention that incorporated it, begun to be realized.

Growing up in a Jewish family in Wolkowysk, a town in eastern Poland, Lemkin developed a passion for reading. But his tastes were strange for a young boy. He recalled in his autobiography, only recently published, that:

> I started to devour books on the persecution of religious, racial, or other minority groups. I was startled by the description of the destruction of the Christians by Nero. They were thrown to the lions while the emperor sat laughing on the Roman arena. The Polish writer Henryk Sienkiewicz's book on this subject, *Quo Vadis*, made a strong impression on me, and I read it several times and talked about it often. I realized, vividly, that if a Christian could have called a policeman to help he would not have received any protection. Here was a group of people collectively sentenced to death for no reason except that they believed in Christ. And nobody could help them. . . . I was fascinated by the frequency of such cases, by the great suffering inflicted on the victims and the hopelessness of their fate, and by the impossibility of repairing the damage to life and culture.[44]

Lemkin's interest in languages (he would end up mastering a dozen or more) drew him to the study of linguistics. But his passionate curiosity about the cultures that nurtured those languages, his instinctive empathy for those destroyed for no other reason than they belonged to the wrong group, and his activist energy—"I always wanted to shorten the distance between the heart and the deed"[45]—combined to produce one of the great legal advocates and moral figures of the twentieth century.

As John Cooper notes, "growing up in a contested borderland over which different armies clashed . . . made Lemkin acutely sensitive to the concerns of the diverse nationalities living there and their anxieties about self-preservation." As a Jew, Lemkin was also conscious of the ever-present danger of *pogroms*, local or regional anti-semitic campaigns. This region, enshrined in recent literature as the "Bloodlands" and "Rimlands" of Europe (see Box 2.3), was the heartland of European anti-Jewish violence. Word reached the young Lemkin of a pogrom in

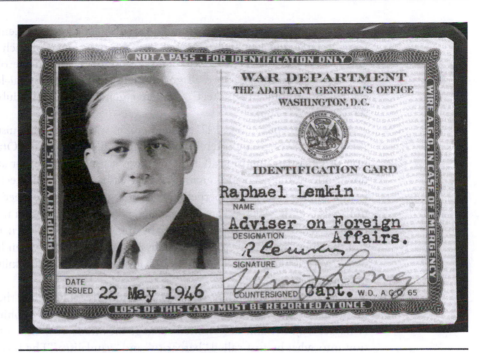

Figure 1.2 Raphael Lemkin first deployed the term "genocide" in his 1944 book *Axis Rule in Occupied Europe*. His study of Nazi occupation legislation was completed under the auspices of the US War Department. He was issued this identity card two years later, as the Nuremberg trials were getting underway in Germany (see Chapter 15). "Lemkin's word" made its first appearance in international jurisprudence at Nuremberg, and underpinned the United Nations Genocide Convention, adopted in 1948.

Source: American Jewish Historical Society (www.ajhs.org).

Bialystok. He perceived "a line, red with blood … from the Roman arena … to the pogrom of Bialystok. I could not define history with my childish mind, but I saw it with my eyes vividly and strongly as a huge torture place of the innocent …"[46]

Despite the chilling proximity of the violence he was studying, at no point in Lemkin's life—from childhood to death—did he particularly emphasize his own Jewishness or the historical suffering of the Jews. Indeed, he might even be accused of downplaying the Jewish experience of persecution and genocide, beyond what might have seemed advisable given the widespread anti-semitism of the pre-World War Two (and postwar) periods. It is striking, for example, that in the substantial portions of his unfinished history of genocide that first reached public view in 2012—four hundred pages of text, in Steven Leonard Jacobs's scrupulous edit—Lemkin mentions Hebrews/Jews only in passing, *and never as victims of violence*. He writes much more about Christian *and Muslim* populations (nearly thirty pages, for example, on "Moors and Moriscos," the Spanish Muslims expelled along with Jews in 1492, and a similarly in-depth treatment of "The Persecution of the Catholics in Japan in the Sixteenth and Seventeenth Centuries").[47] He was never a notable advocate for the state of Israel, which came into being in the same year (1948) that the Genocide Convention was adopted by the General Assembly of the United Nations. For whatever combination of reasons, the vulnerabilities of "his people," and the violence historically directed against them, did not seem *particularly* to interest the eclectic-minded Lemkin. What was most notable and lamentable, he felt, was the prevalence of such vulnerabilities and violence in the *collective* experience of minorities—and the obliviousness of the world community, above all governments and international-legal bodies, to their "responsibility to protect" (as a later generation would dub it; see Chapter 16, pp. 764–765).[48]

A key moment came in 1921, while Lemkin was studying linguistics at the University of Lvov. Soghomon Tehlirian, an Armenian avenger of the Ottoman destruction of Christian minorities (Chapter 4), was arrested for murder after he gunned down one of the genocide's architects, Talat Pasha, in a Berlin street.[49] In the same year, leading planners and perpetrators of the genocide were freed by the British from custody in Malta, as part of the Allies' postwar courting of a resurgent Turkey. Lemkin wrote that he was "shocked" by the juxtaposition: "A nation was killed and the guilty persons were set free. Why is a man punished when he kills another man? Why is the killing of a million a lesser crime than the killing of a single individual?"[50]

Why should this be? Why shouldn't it cease to be? These are the foundational questions of the "norm entrepreneur" seeking to build a "prohibition regime" (Chapter 12). Lemkin determined to stage an intellectual and activist intervention into what he first called "barbarity" and "vandalism." The former referred to "the premeditated destruction of national, racial, religious and social collectivities," while the latter denoted the "destruction of works of art and culture, being the expression of the particular genius of these collectivities."[51] At a conference of European legal scholars in Madrid in 1933, Lemkin's framing was first presented in public (though not by its author; the Polish government denied him a travel visa). Despite the post-First World War prosecutions of Turks for "crimes against humanity" (Chapters 4, 15), governments and public opinion leaders were still wedded to the notion that state sovereignty trumped atrocities against a state's own citizens. It was this legal impunity that rankled and galvanized Lemkin more than anything else. Yet the Madrid delegates did not share his concern. They refused to adopt a resolution against the crimes Lemkin set before them; the matter was tabled.

Undeterred, Lemkin continued his campaign. He presented his arguments in legal forums throughout Europe in the 1930s, and as far afield as Cairo, Egypt. The outbreak of the Second World War found him at the heart of the inferno—in Poland, with Nazi forces invading from the West, and Soviets from the East. As Polish resistance crumbled, Lemkin paid a final visit to his parents. Remembering relatively civilized treatment of Jews by German occupation forces during the First World War, they refused to leave their home. Lemkin had no such illusions about the Nazis. " . . . I felt I would never see them again," he wrote in his autobiography. "It was like going to their funeral while they were still alive."[52]

He took flight, first in eastern Poland, enduring "many months of half-savage existence," then to Vilnius, Lithuania. From that Baltic city he succeeded, through connections, in securing refuge in Sweden.

After teaching in Stockholm, the United States beckoned. Lemkin believed the US would be both receptive to his framework, and in a position to actualize it in a way that Europe under the Nazi yoke could not. An epic 14,000-mile journey took him across the Soviet Union by train to Vladivostok, by boat to Japan, and across the Pacific. At the Seattle customs post, a towering official "gave my valises a superficial examination. Then his big hand landed on my shoulder and squeezed it warmly, and his deep voice boomed out, 'Okay, boy—you're in!'"

Lemkin moonlighted at Yale University's Law School before moving to Durham, North Carolina, where he became a professor at Duke University. He struggled throughout with the concepts and vocabulary that might best evoke the atrocities that galvanized him. "Vandalism" and "barbarity" had failed to strike a chord with his legal audiences. Inspired by, of all things, the Kodak camera,[53] Lemkin trawled through his impressive linguistic resources for a term that was concise and memorable. He settled on a neologism with both Greek and Latin roots: the Greek "genos," meaning race or tribe, and the Latin "cide," or killing. "Genocide" was the intentional destruction of national groups on the basis of their collective identity. In what is perhaps the most eloquent passage in the genocide-studies literature, he presented his concept for the first time in *Axis Rule in Occupied Europe* (1944):

> By "genocide" we mean the destruction of a nation or an ethnic group. . . . Generally speaking, genocide does not necessarily mean the immediate destruction of a nation, except when accomplished by mass killings of all members of a nation. It is intended rather to signify a coordinated plan of different actions aiming at the destruction of essential foundations of the life of national groups, with the aim of annihilating the groups themselves. The objectives of such a plan would be disintegration of the political and social institutions of culture, language, national feelings, religion, and the economic existence of national groups, and the destruction of the personal security, liberty, health, dignity, and even the lives of the individuals belonging to such groups. Genocide is directed against the national group as an entity, and the actions involved are directed against individuals, not in their individual capacity, but as members of the national group. . . . Genocide has two phases: one, destruction of the national pattern of the oppressed group; the other the imposition of the national pattern of the oppressor. This imposition, in turn, may be made upon the oppressed population which is allowed to remain, or upon the territory alone, after removal of the population and the colonization of the area by the oppressor's own nationals.[54]

The critical question, for Lemkin, was whether the multipronged campaign proceeded under the rubric of policy. To the extent that it did, it could be considered genocidal, even if it did not result in the physical destruction of all (or any) members of the group.[55] The issue of whether mass killing is definitional to genocide has been debated ever since, by myriad scholars and commentators, and will be considered further below. Equally vexing for subsequent generations was the emphasis on ethnic and national groups. These predominated as victims in the

Figure 1.3 Samantha Power's book *"A Problem from Hell": America and the Age of Genocide* (2002) won both the Pulitzer Prize and the National Book Critics Circle Award, and contributed to the resurgence of public interest in genocide. Power's work also offered the most detailed and vivid account to that date of Raphael Lemkin's life and his struggle for the UN Genocide Convention. She is shown here speaking in Geneva, Switzerland in June 2010. Under the Barack Obama administration, in 2013, Power was appointed US ambassador to the United Nations.

Source: Photo by Eric Bridiers/United States Mission Geneva/Wikimedia Commons.

decades in which Lemkin developed his framework (and in the historical examples he studied). Yet by the end of the 1940s, it was clear that political groups were often targeted for annihilation.[56] Moreover, the appellations applied to "communists," or by communists to "kulaks" or "class enemies"—when imposed by a totalitarian state—seemed every bit as difficult to shake as ethnic identifications, if the Nazi and Stalinist onslaughts were anything to go by. This does not even take into account the important but ambiguous areas of crossover among ethnic, political, and social categories (see "Multiple and Overlapping Identities," below).

Lemkin, though, would hear little of this. His single-minded, classically romantic focus was on minority nationality and ethnicity (including the religious component of ethnicity), for their culture-carrying capacities as he perceived them.[57] His attachment to these core concerns was almost atavistic, and legal scholar Stephen Holmes, for one, has faulted him for it:

> Lemkin himself seems to have believed that killing a hundred thousand people of a single ethnicity was very different from killing a hundred thousand people of mixed ethnicities. Like Oswald Spengler, he thought that each cultural group had its own "genius" that should be preserved. To destroy, or attempt to destroy, a culture is a special kind of crime because culture is the unit of collective memory, whereby the legacies of the dead can be kept alive. To kill a culture is to cast its individual members into individual oblivion, their memories buried with their mortal remains. The idea that killing a culture is "irreversible" in a way that killing an individual is not reveals the strangeness of Lemkin's conception from a liberal–individualist point of view.
>
> This archaic-sounding conception has other illiberal implications as well. For one thing, it means that the murder of a poet is morally worse than the murder

of a janitor, because the poet is the 'brain' without which the 'body' cannot function. This revival of medieval organic imagery is central to Lemkin's idea of genocide as a special crime.[58]

It is probably true, then, that Lemkin's formulation had its archaic elements.[59] It is certainly the case that subsequent scholarly interpretations of "Lemkin's word" have tended to be more capacious in their framing. What *can* be defended is Lemkin's emphasis on the collective as a target. One can philosophize about the relative weight ascribed to collectives over the individual, as Holmes does; but the reality of modern times is that the vast majority of those murdered *were killed on the basis of a collective identity—even if only one imputed by the killers.* The link between collective and mass, then between mass and large-scale extermination, was the defining dynamic of the twentieth century's unprecedented violence. In his historical studies, Lemkin appears to have read this correctly. Many or most of the examples he cites would be uncontroversial among a majority of genocide scholars today.[60] He saw the Nazis' assaults on Jews, Poles, and Polish Jews for what they were, and labeled the broader genre for the ages.

Still, for Lemkin's word to resonate today, and into the future, two further developments were required. The UN Convention on the Prevention and Punishment of the Crime of Genocide (1948), adopted in remarkably short order after Lemkin's indefatigable lobbying, entrenched genocide in international and domestic law. And beginning in the 1970s, a coterie of "comparative genocide scholars," drawing upon a generation's work on the Jewish Holocaust,* began to discuss, debate, and refine Lemkin's concept—a trend that shows no sign of abating.

DEFINING GENOCIDE: THE UN CONVENTION

Lemkin's extraordinary "norm entrepreneurship" around genocide is described in Chapter 12. Suffice it to say for now that "rarely has a neologism had such rapid success" (legal scholar William Schabas). Barely a year after Lemkin coined the term, it was included in the Nuremberg indictments of Nazi war criminals (Chapter 15). To Lemkin's chagrin, genocide did not figure in the Nuremberg judgments. However, "by the time the General Assembly completed its standard sitting, with the 1948 adoption of the Convention on the Prevention and Punishment of the Crime of Genocide, 'genocide' had a detailed and quite technical definition as a crime against the law of nations."[61]

---

* I use the word "holocaust" generically in this book to refer to especially destructive genocides, such as those against indigenous peoples in the Americas and elsewhere, Christian minorities in the Ottoman Empire during the First World War, Jews and Roma (Gypsies) under the Nazis, extermination campaigns by communist regimes, and Tutsis in Rwanda in 1994. Most scholars and commentators capitalize the "h" when referring to the Nazi genocide against the Jews, and I follow this usage when citing "the Jewish Holocaust" (see also Chapter 6, n. 1).

The "detailed and quite technical definition" is as follows:

Article I. The Contracting Parties confirm that genocide, whether committed in time of peace or in time of war, is a crime under international law which they undertake to prevent and to punish.

Article II. In the present Convention, genocide means any of the following acts committed with intent to destroy, in whole or in part, a national, ethnical, racial or religious group, as such:

(a) Killing members of the group;
(b) Causing serious bodily or mental harm to members of the group;
(c) Deliberately inflicting on the group conditions of life calculated to bring about its physical destruction in whole or in part;
(d) Imposing measures intended to prevent births within the group;
(e) Forcibly transferring children of the group to another group.

Article III. The following acts shall be punishable:

(a) Genocide;
(b) Conspiracy to commit genocide;
(c) Direct and public incitement to commit genocide;
(d) Attempt to commit genocide;
(e) Complicity in genocide.[62]

Thematically, Lemkin's conviction that genocide needed to be confronted, whatever the context, was resoundingly endorsed with the Convention's declaration that genocide is a crime "whether committed in time of peace or in time of war." This removed the road-block thrown up by the Nuremberg trials, which had only considered Nazi crimes committed after the invasion of Poland on September 1, 1939.

The basic thrust of Lemkin's emphasis on ethnic and national groups (at the expense of political groups and social classes) also survived the lobbying and drafting process. Genocide scholars have lamented the absence of political groups, and this omission has become only more glaring as we have grown to appreciate how "political" are the constructions of the Convention's protected groups, as Daniel Feierstein has pointed out. He stresses, for example, "the ideological nature of religious belief," so evident in the case of the Argentine military *junta* of 1976–1983, with its "explicit aim of establishing a 'Western and Christian' order." He argues that "race is really a metaphor for otherness—an otherness constructed as dangerous, deep-seated, and inassimilable. In this sense, race is clearly a political concept, used for political ends." Moreover, Feierstein wonders, how can any decision to target a group "in part—as opposed to in whole . . . be anything but political"?[63]

In the diverse genocidal strategies cited, we see reflected Lemkin's conception of genocide as a "coordinated plan of different actions aiming at the destruction

▌BOX 1.3 WHATEVER HAPPENED TO POLITICAL GROUPS?

It is instructive to trace the appearance and disappearance of political groups among those protected by the United Nations' emerging Convention on the Prevention and Punishment of the Crime of Genocide, eventually signed on December 9, 1948. As late as April 1948, the Ad Hoc Committee on Genocide was defining genocide as the destruction of "a national, racial, religious *or political* group as such." Ominously, however, the chairman "remarked that the words 'or political' had for the time being been put in brackets, because the Committee had not yet taken a decision regarding [their] inclusion . . . "[64] Later in April, the Convention framers again tackled the subject. It noted that while there was unanimous agreement on "protecting *national, racial and religious groups* . . . the inclusion of *political groups* was accepted by four votes to three. The minority pointed out that political groups lack the stability of the other groups mentioned. They have not the same homogeneity and are less well defined."[65]

Joseph Stalin's USSR (Chapter 5) was among the most vocal opponents of extending Convention protection to political groups. Its representative, Platon Mozorov, asserted in May 1948 that

Crimes committed for political motives are crimes of a special kind and have nothing in common with crimes of genocide. The very word "genocide" derived from the word "genus" – race, people – shows that it concerns the destruction of nations or races as such, for reasons of racial or national persecution and not for the particular political opinions of such human groups. Crimes committed for political motives are not connected to propaganda of racial and national hatred and cannot therefore be included in the category of crimes covered by the notion of genocide.[66]

With the Soviet Union fresh from imposing political control over the eastern European "Bloodlands" it had ravaged, together with the Nazis (Box 2.3), it is easy to suspect that its policymakers were anxious to avoid untoward attention to their own domestic atrocities. (For a similar reason, colonial powers tended to downplay the sociocultural destruction and forced assimilation of indigenous peoples—see further below.) But it was not solely the Soviet Union and its satellites that had qualms. Venezuela's representative, V.M. Pérez Perozo, argued that the Convention's "protected groups" should be limited to those

based on permanent and easily recognizable criteria: that of blood for racial groups and that of the Mother Church for religious groups. Political groups lacked permanence: their inclusion in the Convention would be tantamount to the protection of conspiracies and plots and thus place certain governments under the constant threat of being accused of criminal acts. Moreover, the fear of impairing their power to take defensive action against domestic disorders might prevent many States from signing the Convention.

Venezuela "recognized the necessity of protecting political groups," said Pérez Perozo, "but thought that protection should be ensured by other means, in particular by absolute respect for guarantees of individual rights . . . "[67]

Such reasoning did not pass unchallenged, however. Bolivian representative Gustavo Medeiros scoffed at the notion that "genocide meant the physical destruction of a group which was held together by a common origin or a common ideology." "No valid reason" existed, said Medeiros, "for restricting the concept of genocide by excluding political groups. Moreover, no convincing arguments had been produced in favour of that exclusion." He added, a little cheekily, that "the definition might even be broadened still further to include economic groups." Castel Demesmin of Haiti pithily reflected the modern history of his country in his view "that all the crimes [of genocide] envisaged were in reality committed for political reasons, whatever motive might be alleged."[68]

The proponents carried the day: references to both "political groups" and "political opinion" still made the cut in Article II of the Draft Convention dated May 24, 1948. But the struggle for clear consensus, and a desire to move on to other pressing issues, led to "protected groups" being whittled down to their present form—national, "ethnical," racial, and religious alone. (David Nersessian stresses that "this was expressly described as a 'conciliatory' measure to ensure ratificastion, rather than a legalistiac concession that political groups somehow were analytically incongruent.")[69] Under international law, political groups sheltered, or languished, under the catch-all of "crimes against humanity" (see Chapter 15). No fewer than eleven countries "recognize political groups in their domestic legislation on genocide" ("Bangladesh, Cambodia, Col[o]mbia, Costa Rica, Côte d'Ivoire, Ecuador, Ethiopia, Lithuania, Panama, Poland, and Slovenia"), while nine others "recognize a 'broad form' conception of genocide (groups based on 'any arbitrary criterion')" ("Belarus, Burkina Faso, Canada, Congo (DR), Estonia, Finland, France, Latvia, and Romania"). In the most detailed engagement with the subject in the genocide studies literature, Nersessian issues a spirited call for reformulating the Genocide Convention to protect political groups, on four principal grounds:

1. Political rights are important rights that have a similar (albeit not identical) level of international acceptance and recognition;
2. on a theoretical level, political rights correspond closely to the rights underlying the groups included in the Convention in terms of how such rights are implemented and protected, particularly in respect of religion;
3. because national, racial, ethnic and religious characteristics are so often used as a proxy for political identity, in practice political groups often overlap significantly with the enumerated group categories [see below, "Multiple and Overlapping Identities"]; and
4. there have been many historic examples of political genocide.[70]

of essential foundations of the life of national groups, with the aim of annihilating the groups themselves." However, at no point did the Convention's drafters actually define "national, ethnical, racial or religious" groups, and these terms have been subject to considerable subsequent interpretation. The position of the International Criminal Tribunal for Rwanda (ICTR), that "any stable and permanent group" is in fact to be accorded protection under the Convention, is likely to become the norm in future judgments.

With regard to genocidal strategies, the Convention places "stronger emphasis than Lemkin on *physical and biological destruction,* and less on broader *social destruction,*" as sociologist Martin Shaw points out.[71] But note how diverse are the actions considered genocidal in Article II—in marked contrast to the normal understanding of "genocide." One does not need to exterminate or seek to exterminate every last member of a designated group. In fact, *one does not need to kill anyone at all to commit genocide!* Inflicting "serious bodily or mental harm" qualifies, as does preventing births or transferring children between groups. It is fair to say, however, that from a legal perspective, genocide unaccompanied by mass killing is rarely prosecuted.[72] (I return to this subject below.)

Controversial and ambiguous phrases in the document include the reference to "serious bodily or mental harm" constituting a form of genocide. In practice, this has been interpreted along the lines of the Israeli trial court decision against Adolf Eichmann in 1961, convicting him of the "enslavement, starvation, deportation and persecution of . . . Jews . . . their detention in ghettos, transit camps and concentration camps in conditions which were designed to cause their degradation, deprivation of their rights as human beings, and to . . . cause them inhumane suffering and torture." The ICTR adds an interpretation that this includes "bodily or mental torture, inhuman treatment, and persecution," as well as "acts of rape and mutilation." In addition, "several sources correctly take the view that mass deportations under inhumane conditions may constitute genocide if accompanied by the requisite intent."[73] "Measures to prevent births" may be held to include forced sterilization and separation of the sexes. Sexual trauma and impregnation through gang rape have received increasing attention. The destruction of groups "as such" brought complex questions of motive into play. Some drafters saw it as a means of paying lip-service to the element of motive, while others perceived it as a way to sidestep the issue altogether.

Historically, it is intriguing to note how many issues of genocide definition and interpretation have their roots in contingent and improvised aspects of the drafting process. The initial draft by the UN Secretariat defined genocide's targets as "a group of human beings," adoption of which could have rendered redundant the subsequent debate over *which* groups qualified.

Responsibility for the exclusion of political groups was long laid at the door of the Soviet Union and its allies, supposedly nervous about application of the Convention to Soviet crimes (see Box 1.3). Schabas challenges this notion, arguing that "rigorous examination of the *travaux* [working papers] fails to confirm a popular impression in the literature that the opposition . . . was some Soviet machination." Political collectivities "were actually included within the enumeration [of designated groups] until an eleventh-hour compromise eliminated the reference."[74] In the estimation of many genocide scholars, this is the Convention's greatest oversight.[75] As for the provision outlawing the transfer of children between groups to undermine an out group, it "was added to the Convention almost as an afterthought, with little substantive debate or consideration."[76] It was influenced by the Nazi practice of seizing ideal "Aryan" children from occupied countries for induction into the "master race." It has resonated most in subsequent decades in advocacy around indigenous peoples' genocides (Chapter 3). Settler-state authorities have standardly coerced aboriginal parents into surrendering their children to residential schools, some of them exterminatory. Seizures of aboriginal children, by social workers on humanitarian grounds, are rife and controversial today.

In its opening sentence, the Convention declares that the Contracting Parties "undertake to prevent and to punish" the crime of genocide. A subsequent article (VIII) states that "any Contracting Party may call upon the competent organs of the United Nations to take such action under the Charter of the United Nations as they consider appropriate for the prevention and suppression of acts of genocide or any of the other acts enumerated in Article III." Yet this leaves actual policy obligations vague.

BOUNDING GENOCIDE: COMPARATIVE GENOCIDE STUDIES

Between the 1950s and the 1980s, the term "genocide" languished almost unused by scholars. A handful of legal commentaries appeared for a specialized audience.[77] In 1975, Vahakn Dadrian's article "A Typology of Genocide" sparked renewed interest in a comparative framing. It was bolstered by Irving Louis Horowitz's *Genocide: State Power and Mass Murder* (1976), and foundationally by Leo Kuper's *Genocide: Its Political Use in the Twentieth Century* (1981). Kuper's work, including a subsequent volume on *The Prevention of Genocide* (1985), was the most significant on genocide since Lemkin's in the 1940s and '50s. It was followed by edited volumes and solo publications from Helen Fein, R.J. Rummel, Frank Chalk and Kurt Jonassohn, and Robert Melson, among others.

This early literature drew upon more than a decade of intensive research on the Holocaust, and most of the scholars were Jewish. "Holocaust Studies" remains central to the field. Still, rereading these pioneering works, one is struck by how inclusive and comparative their framing is. It tends to be global in scope, and interdisciplinary at many points. The classic volumes by Chalk and Jonassohn *(The History and Sociology of Genocide)* and Totten *et al. (Century of Genocide)* appeared in the early 1990s, and seemed to sum up this drive for catholicity. So too, despite its heavy focus on the Holocaust, did Israel Charny's *Encyclopedia of Genocide* (1999). A rich body of case-study literature also developed, with genocides such as those against the Armenians, Cambodians, and East Timorese—as well as indigenous peoples worldwide—receiving serious and sustained attention.

The explosion of public interest in genocide in the 1990s, and the concomitant growth of genocide studies as an academic field, have spawned a profusion of humanistic and social-scientific studies, joined by memoirs and oral histories. (The wider culture has also produced a steady stream of films on genocide and its reverberations, including *The Killing Fields, Schindler's List*, and *Hotel Rwanda*.)[78]

To capture the richness and diversity of the genocide-studies literature in this short section is impossible. What I hope to do is, first, to use that literature constructively throughout this book; and, second, to provide suggestions for further study, encouraging readers to explore for themselves.

With this caveat in place, let me make a few generalizations, touching on debates that will reappear regularly in this book. Genocide scholars are concerned with two basic tasks. First, they attempt to *define* genocide and *bound* it conceptually. Second, they seek to *prevent* genocide. This implies understanding its comparative dynamics, and generating prophylactic strategies that may be applied in emergencies.

Scholarly definitions of genocide reflect the ambiguities of the Genocide Convention and its constituent debates. They can be confusing in their numerous and often opposed variants. However, surveying most of the definitions on offer—I count twenty-five, so you don't have to—and combining them with the Lemkian and UN Convention framings, we can isolate some key features and variables.

BOX 1.4 GENOCIDE: SCHOLARLY DEFINITIONS (in chronological order)

Peter Drost (1959)

"Genocide is the deliberate destruction of physical life of individual human beings by reason of their membership of any human collectivity as such."

Nehemiah Robinson (1960, interpreting the UN Convention)

"Genocide has been committed when acts of homicide are joined with a connecting purpose, i.e., directed against persons with specific characteristics (with intent to destroy the group or a segment thereof)."

Vahakn Dadrian (1975)

"Genocide is the successful attempt by a dominant group, vested with formal authority and/or with preponderant access to the overall resources of power, to reduce by coercion or lethal violence the number of a minority group whose ultimate extermination is held desirable and useful and whose respective vulnerability is a major factor contributing to the decision for genocide."

Irving Louis Horowitz (1976)

"[Genocide is] a structural and systematic destruction of innocent people by a state bureaucratic apparatus . . . Genocide represents a systematic effort over time to

liquidate a national population, usually a minority . . . [and] functions as a fundamental political policy to assure conformity and participation of the citizenry."

Leo Kuper (1981)

"I shall follow the definition of genocide given in the [UN] Convention. This is not
to say that I agree with the definition. On the contrary, I believe a major omission
to be in the exclusion of political groups from the list of groups protected. In the
contemporary world, political differences are at the very least as significant a basis
for massacre and annihilation as racial, national, ethnic or religious differences.
Then too, the genocides against racial, national, ethnic or religious groups are
generally a consequence of, or intimately related to, political conflict. However,
I do not think it helpful to create new definitions of genocide, when there is an
internationally recognized definition and a Genocide Convention which might
become the basis for some effective action, however limited the underlying conception. But since it would vitiate the analysis to exclude political groups, I shall
refer freely . . . to liquidating or exterminatory actions against them."

Jack Nusan Porter (1982)

"Genocide is the deliberate destruction, in whole or in part, by a government or
its agents, of a racial, sexual, religious, tribal or political minority. It can involve not
only mass murder, but also starvation, forced deportation, and political, economic
and biological subjugation. Genocide involves three major components: ideology,
technology, and bureaucracy/organization."

Yehuda Bauer (1984)

[n.b. Bauer distinguishes between "genocide" and "holocaust"]:

"[Genocide is] the planned destruction, since the mid-nineteenth century, of a
racial, national, or ethnic group as such, by the following means: (a) selective
mass murder of elites or parts of the population; (b) elimination of national
(racial, ethnic) culture and religious life with the intent of 'denationalization';
(c) enslavement, with the same intent; (d) destruction of national (racial, ethnic) economic life, with the same intent; (e) biological decimation through the
kidnapping of children, or the prevention of normal family life, with the same
intent . . . [Holocaust is] the planned physical annihilation, for ideological or
pseudo-religious reasons, of all the members of a national, ethnic, or racial
group."

John L. Thompson and Gail A. Quets (1987)

"Genocide is the extent of destruction of a social collectivity by whatever agents, with whatever intentions, by purposive actions which fall outside the recognized conventions of legitimate warfare."

Isidor Wallimann and Michael N. Dobkowski (1987)

"Genocide is the deliberate, organized destruction, in whole or in large part, of racial or ethnic groups by a government or its agents. It can involve not only mass murder, but also forced deportation (ethnic cleansing), systematic rape, and economic and biological subjugation."

Helen Fein (1988)

"Genocide is any act that puts the very existence of a group in jeopardy."

Barbara Harff and Ted Gurr (1988)

"By our definition, genocides and politicides are the promotion and execution of policies by a state or its agents which results in the deaths of a substantial portion of a group. . . . In genocides the victimized groups are defined primarily in terms of their communal characteristics, i.e., ethnicity, religion, or nationality. In politicides the victim groups are defined primarily in terms of their hierarchical position or political opposition to the regime and dominant groups."

Henry Huttenbach (1988)

"Genocide is a series of purposeful actions by a perpetrator(s) to destroy a collectivity through mass or selective murders of group members and suppressing the biological and social reproduction of the collectivity. This can be accomplished through the imposed proscription or restriction of reproduction of group members, increasing infant mortality, and breaking the linkage between reproduction and socialization of children in the family or group of origin. The perpetrator may represent the state of the victim, another state, or another collectivity."

Frank Chalk and Kurt Jonassohn (1990)

"Genocide is a form of one-sided mass killing in which a state or other authority intends to destroy a group, as that group and membership in it are defined by the perpetrator."

Helen Fein (1993)

"Genocide is sustained purposeful action by a perpetrator to physically destroy a collectivity directly or indirectly, through interdiction of the biological and social reproduction of group members, sustained regardless of the surrender or lack of threat offered by the victim."

Steven T. Katz (1994)

"[Genocide is] the actualization of the intent, however successfully carried out, to murder in its totality any national, ethnic, racial, religious, political, social, gender or economic group, as these groups are defined by the perpetrator, by whatever means." (n.b. Modified by Adam Jones in 2010 to read, "murder in whole or in part. . . . ")

Israel Charny (1994)

"Genocide in the generic sense means the mass killing of substantial numbers of human beings, when not in the course of military action against the military forces of an avowed enemy, under conditions of the essential defencelessness of the victim."

Irving Louis Horowitz (1996)

"Genocide is herein defined as *a structural and systematic destruction of innocent people by a state bureaucratic apparatus* [emphasis in original]. . . . Genocide means the physical dismemberment and liquidation of people on large scales, an attempt by those who rule to achieve the total elimination of a subject people." (n.b. Horowitz supports "carefully distinguishing the [Jewish] Holocaust from genocide"; he also refers to "the phenomenon of mass murder, for which genocide is a synonym".)

Manus I. Midlarsky (2005)

"Genocide is understood to be the state-sponsored systematic mass murder of innocent and helpless men, women, and children denoted by a particular ethno-religious identity, having the purpose of eradicating this group from a particular territory."

Mark Levene (2005)

"Genocide occurs when a state, perceiving the integrity of its agenda to be threatened by an aggregate population—defined by the state as an organic collectivity, or series of collectivities—seeks to remedy the situation by the systematic, *en masse* physical elimination of that aggregate, *in toto*, or until it is no longer perceived to represent a threat."

(Elsewhere: genocide is "the state-organised total or partial extermination of perceived or actual communal groups.")

Jacques Sémelin (2005)

"I will define genocide as that particular process of civilian destruction that is directed at the total eradication of a group, the criteria by which it is identified being determined by the perpetrator."

Daniel Chirot and Clark McCauley (2006)

"A genocidal mass murder is politically motivated violence that directly or indirectly kills a substantial proportion of a targeted population, combatants and noncombatants alike, regardless of their age or gender."

Martin Shaw (2007)

"[Genocide is] a form of violent social conflict, or war, between armed power organizations that aim to destroy civilian social groups and those groups and other actors who resist this destruction."("Genocidal action" is defined as "action in which armed power organizations treat civilian social groups as enemies and aim to destroy their real or putative social power, by means of killing, violence and coercion against individuals whom they regard as members of the groups.")

Daniel Feierstein (2007)

" . . . Genocide should be defined in broad and general terms as the execution of a large-scale and systematic plan with the intention of destroying a human group as such in whole or in part." (English translation, 2014)

Donald Bloxham (2009)

"[Genocide is] the physical destruction of a large portion of a group in a limited or unlimited territory with the intention of destroying that group's collective existence."

Christopher Powell and Julia Peristerakis (2014)

"We define genocide as the violent erasure of a collective identity and understand genocide as a multidimensional process that works through the destruction of the social institutions that maintain collective identity as well as through the physical destruction of human individuals."

Discussion

The elements of definition may be divided into "harder" and "softer" positions, paralleling the international-legal distinction between hard and soft law. According to Christopher Rudolph,

> those who favor hard law in international legal regimes argue that it enhances deterrence and enforcement by signaling credible commitments, constraining self-serving auto-interpretation of rules, and maximizing 'compliance pull' through increased legitimacy. Those who favor soft law argue that it facilitates compromise, reduces contracting costs, and allows for learning and change in the process of institutional development.[79]

In genocide scholarship, harder positions are guided by concerns that "genocide" will be rendered banal or meaningless by careless use. Some argue that such slack usage will divert attention from the proclaimed uniqueness of the Holocaust. Softer positions reflect concerns that excessively rigid framings (for example, a focus on the total physical extermination of a group) rule out too many actions that, logically and morally, demand to be included. Their proponents may also wish to see a dynamic and evolving genocide framework, rather than a static and inflexible one.

It should be noted that these basic positions do not map perfectly onto individual authors and authorities. A given definition may even alternate between harder and softer positions—as with the UN Convention, which features a decidedly "soft" framing of genocidal strategies (including non-fatal ones), but a "hard" approach when it comes to the victim groups whose destruction qualifies as genocidal. Steven Katz's 1994 definition, by contrast, features a highly inclusive framing of victimhood, but a tightly restrictive view of genocidal outcomes: these are limited to the total physical destruction of a group. The alteration of just a few words turns it into a softer definition that happens to be my preferred one (see below).

Exploring further, the definitions address genocide's *agents, victims, goals, scale, strategies*, and *intent*.

Among **agents,** there is a clear emphasis on state and official authorities—Dadrian's "dominant group, vested with formal authority"; Horowitz's "state bureaucratic apparatus"; Porter's "government or its agents"—to cite three of the first five definitions proposed (note also Harff and Gurr [1988], and Levene's exclusively state-focused 2005 definition). However, some scholars abjure the state-centric approach (e.g., Chalk and Jonassohn's "state or other authority"; Fein's [1993] "perpetrator"; Thompson and Quets's "whatever agents"; Shaw's "armed power organizations"; Feierstein's emphasis on the "execution" regardless of the executioner). The UN Convention, too, cites "constitutionally responsible rulers, public officials or private individuals" among possible agents (Article IV).[80] In practice, most genocide scholars continue to emphasize the role of the state, while accepting that in some cases—as with settler colonialism

(Chapter 3)—non-state actors may play a prominent and at times dominant role.[81] The proliferation of detailed historical and social-scientific studies, based on local archives or fieldwork, has also heightened awareness of the *local* dimension of genocides, and the way they are often used as an opportunity for personal gain, or to settle personal scores. Fresh research on the European "Rimlands" and "Bloodlands" (see Box 2.3), as well as many important works on the Rwandan Tutsi genocide, are examples of this trend. It has dovetailed with political scientists' new focus on local dynamics in civil conflicts, sparked by Stathis Kalyvas's book *The Logic of Violence in Civil War.*[82]

As noted earlier, there is a significant "return" to Raphael Lemkin's original, more sociological/cultural framing of genocide as a multifaceted and structural assault on the viability of groups. In this understanding, agency is pervasive, diffused, and institutionalized. Often, adherents to this position simply reference Lemkin's definition; Powell and Peristerakis are an exception.

Victims are routinely identified as *collectivities* and *social minorities.* There is a widespread assumption that victims must be civilians or non-combatants: Charny references their "essential defencelessness," while others emphasize "one-sided mass killing" and the destruction of "innocent and helpless" victims (Midlarsky; see also Dadrian, Horowitz, Chalk and Jonassohn, and Fein [1993]). Interestingly, however, only Sémelin's 2005 definition, and Shaw's 2007 one, actually use the word "civilian." The groups may be internally constituted and self-identified (that is, more closely approximating groups "as such," as required by the Genocide Convention). From other perspectives, however, target groups may and must be defined by the perpetrators (e.g., Chalk and Jonassohn, Katz, Levene).[83] The debate over political target groups is reflected in Leo Kuper's comments. Kuper grudgingly accepts the UN Convention definition, but strongly regrets the exclusion of political groups.

The *goals* of genocide are held to be the destruction/eradication of the victim group, whether this is defined in physical terms or to include "cultural genocide" (see below). But beyond this, the element of motive is little stressed. Lemkin squarely designated genocidal "objectives" as the "disintegration of the political and social institutions of culture, language, national feelings, religion, and the economic existence of national groups." Bauer likewise emphasizes "denationalization"; Martin Shaw, the desire to destroy a collective's (generally a minority's) social power. Dadrian and Horowitz specify that genocide targets groups "whose ultimate extermination is held to be desirable and useful," while Horowitz stresses the state's desire "to assure [sic] conformity and participation of the citizenry."

As for *scale*, this ranges from Steven Katz's targeting of a victim group "in its totality" and Sémelin's "total eradication," to phrasing such as "a substantial portion" (Harff and Gurr) to "in whole or in large part" (Wallimann and Dobkowski). Irving Louis Horowitz emphasizes the absolute dimension of "mass" murder "for which genocide is a synonym."[84] Some scholars maintain a respectful silence on the issue, though the element of mass or "substantial" casualties seems implicit in the cases they select and the analyses they develop.

BOX 1.5 A LEXICON OF GENOCIDES AND RELATED MASS CRIMES

Groups targeted for genocide and related crimes sometimes develop terms in their local languages to denote and memorialize their experiences. The following is a sample of this nomenclature.

Churban—the "Great Catastrophe"—the Yiddish term for the Holocaust/Shoah (see below) of Jews at Nazi hands.

Gukurahundi—"the mass murder of over 20,000 Matabele citizens of Zimbabwe in 1983 and 1984." It "meets the definition of genocide because it was carried out by the North-Korean trained, exclusively [ethnic] Shona Fifth Brigade under President Mugabe and it targeted ethnic Matabele people."[85]

Holocaust—Derived from the Greek word meaning a sacrificial offering completely consumed by fire. In modern usage, "holocaust" denotes great human destruction, especially by fire. It was deployed in contemporary media coverage of the Ottoman genocides of Christian minorities from 1915–1922 (see Chapter 4). Today, "the Holocaust" (note: uppercase "H") is used for the Nazis' attempted destruction of Jews during World War Two (Chapter 6; but see also *Shoah*, below). The phrase "Nazi H/holocaust" is also sometimes used to encompass both Jewish and non-Jewish victims of the Nazis (Box 6a). Use may be made of "holocaust" (with a lowercase "h") to describe "especially destructive genocides" throughout history, as in my own framing (see note, p. 17).

Holodomor—the Ukrainian "famine-extermination" of 1932–1933 at the hands of Stalin's Soviet regime (Chapter 5); "a compound word combining the root *holod* 'hunger' with the verbal root *mor* 'extinguish, exterminate' " (Lubomyr Hajda, Harvard University).

Itsembabwoko—used by Rwandans to describe the genocide of 1994 (see Chapter 9)—Kinyarwanda, "from the verb 'gutsemba'—to exterminate, to massacre, and 'ubwoko' (ethnic group, clan)" (PreventGenocide.org; see their very useful resource page, "The Word 'Genocide' Translated or Defined in 80 Languages," www.preventgenocide.org/genocide/languages-printerfriendly.htm). Rwandans also use *Jenosid*, an adaption of the English/French "genocide/*génocide*."

Lokeli—the "Overwhelming"—term used in the Longo language to describe the ravages of the Congo "rubber terror" at the turn of the twentieth century (Chapter 2).

Medz Yeghern (or Mec Ejer'n)—the "Great Calamity" in Armenian—the Armenian genocide of 1915–1917 (Chapter 4).

Naqba—in Arabic, the "Catastrophe" of the Palestinian people uprooted and dis-possessed in 1947–1948 by the forces of the nascent Israeli state (see Chapter 6).

Porrajmos—the "Devouring"—Romani term for the holocaust of the Roma/Sinti ("Gypsy") population of Europe under Nazi rule from 1941 to 1945 (see Box 6a).

Sayfo—"Year of the Sword"—term used by Assyrian populations to refer to the Ottoman genocide of Christian minorities during World War One (Chapter 4).

Shoah—from the Hebrew for "Catastrophe"—an alternative term for the Jewish Holocaust (Chapter 6), preferred by those who reject the religious-sacrificial con-notations of "holocaust."

Sokumu—the "Unweaving"—Turkish term for the atrocity-laden expulsions of Muslims from lands liberated from the Ottoman Empire, from the 1870s to the end of the Balkan wars in 1913 (see Chapter 4).

Many people feel that lumping together a limited killing campaign, such as in Kosovo in 1999, with an overwhelmingly exterminatory one, such as the Nazis' attempted destruction of European Jews, diminishes the concept of "genocide." However, it is worth noting how another core concept of social science and pub-lic discourse is deployed: *war.* We readily use "war" to designate conflicts that kill "only" a few hundred or a few thousand people (e.g., the Soccer War of 1969 between El Salvador and Honduras; the Falklands/Malvinas War of 1982), as well as epochal descents into barbarity that kill millions or tens of millions. The gulf between minimum and maximum toll here is comparable to that between Kosovo and the Jewish Holocaust, but the use of "war" is uncontroversial. There seems to be no reason why we should not distinguish between larger and smaller, more or less exterminatory genocides in the same way.

Diverse genocidal *strategies* are depicted in the definitions. Lemkin referred to a "coordinated plan of different actions," and the UN Convention listed a range of such acts. For the scholars cited in our set, genocidal strategies may be direct or indirect (Fein [1993]), including "economic and biological subjugation" (Wallimann and Dobkowski). They may include killing of elites (i.e., "eliticide"); "elimination of national (racial, ethnic) culture and religious life with the intent of 'denationalization'"; and "prevention of normal family life, with the same intent" (Bauer). Helen Fein's earlier definition emphasizes "breaking the linkage between reproduction and socialization of children in the family or group of origin," which carries a step further the Convention's injunction against "preventing births within the group.""The New Lemkians," such as Powell and Peristerakis, stress the target-ing of institutions and identities alongside physical destruction.

Regardless of the strategy chosen, a consensus exists that genocide is "com-mitted with intent to destroy" (UN Convention), is "structural and systematic" (Horowitz), "deliberate [and] organized" (Wallimann and Dobkowski), and "a series of purposeful actions" (Fein; see also Thompson and Quets). Porter and Horowitz stress the additional role of the state bureaucracy.

There is something of a consensus that group "destruction" must involve physical liquidation, generally in the form of mass killing (see, e.g., Robinson, Fein [1993], Charny, Horowitz, Katz/Jones, Bloxham). The first UN declaration on the subject, Resolution 96/I of December 1946, stated that "Genocide is a denial of the right of existence to entire human groups, *as homicide is the denial of the right to life of individual human beings.*"[86] In Peter Drost's 1959 view, genocide was "collective homicide and not official vandalism or violation of civil liberties. . . . It is directed against the life of man and not against his material or mental goods."[87] In their 1988 framing of genocide and politicide, Harff and Gurr were emphatic in their emphasis on the UN Convention provisions of "killing members of a group" and "deliberately inflicting on the group conditions of life" that caused physical destruction. They rejected the "innumerable instances of groups which have lost their cohesion and identity, but not necessarily their lives, as a result of processes of socioeconomic change."[88]

This distinction is also central to my own framing of genocide. My definition, cited above, alters only slightly that of Steven Katz as published in his 1994 volume, *The Holocaust in Historical Context, Vol. 1.*[89] Katz stresses physical (and mass) killing as the core element of genocide, as do I. Like him, I prefer to incorporate a much wider range of targeted *groups* under the genocide rubric, as well as an acceptance of diverse genocidal *agents* and *strategies*. Unlike Katz, I adopt a broader rather than narrower construction of genocidal *intent* (see further below). I also question Katz's requirement of the actual or attempted *total* extermination of a group, substituting a phrasing of "in whole or in part," following in this respect the UN Convention's definition.

In my original (2000) reworking of Katz's definition, reproduced in this book's first edition, my alteration read "in whole or in *substantial* part." This was an attempt to emphasize that large numbers (either in absolute numbers or as a proportion of the targeted group) needed to be attacked in order for the powerful term "genocide" to take precedence over, for example, "homicide" or "mass killing." However, on reconsideration, this was to view genocide from the perspective of its elite planners and directors. What of those who kill at the grassroots, and perhaps murder "only" one or several individuals? From this perspective, there is something to commend former UN Secretary-General Kofi Annan's evocative declaration, in his Nobel Peace Prize acceptance speech in 2001, that "a genocide begins with the killing of one man—not for what he has done, but because of who he is. . . . What begins with the failure to uphold the dignity of one life, all too often ends with a calamity for entire nations."[90] Moreover, legal scholars including William Schabas and Chile Eboe-Osuji have cautioned against unnecessarily restricting the application of a genocide framework to "substantial" killing. In Eboe-Osuji's eloquent analysis of the UN definition:

> . . . The theory of *reading in* the word "substantial" to the phrase "in part" is clearly hazardous to the preventive purpose of the Genocide Convention, while arguably not enhancing its punitive purpose. It does not enhance the punitive purpose since it will be harder to convict any single accused of the crime of genocide. Not only will it be more difficult to show that the accused intended to destroy a substantial part of the group, but it arguably needs to be shown that the accused was in a position to destroy the substantial part of a

protected group. . . . The "substantial" part theory is, worse still, hazardous to the preventive purpose. For in the throes of an unfolding apparent genocide, it will, in most cases, be difficult to ascertain the state of mind of the perpetrators and planners in order to establish whether or not they harbour joint or several intent to destroy a "substantial" part of the group. The longer the delay in establishing whether or not the perpetrators and planners harboured that intent, the longer it will take for the international community to react and intervene with the level of urgency and action required.[91]

Eboe-Osuji's framing allows us to bring into the ambit of "genocide" such cases as exterminations of indigenous people which, in their dimension of direct killing, are often composed of a large number of relatively small massacres, not necessarily centrally directed, and generally separated from each other spatially and temporally. A final example of its utility is the case of the lynching of African Americans, noted later in this chapter and in Chapter 13. If there is a case to be made that such murders were and are genocidal, then we must reckon with a campaign in which usually "only" one or two people were killed at a time.

In the cases of both colonial exterminations and lynching, however, what *does* appear to lift the phenomena into the realm of genocide, apart from genocidal intent (see below), is the fact that the local-level killing occurred as part of a "widespread or systematic" campaign against the groups in question—to borrow an important phrase from the legal language of crimes against humanity (see pp. 709–712). What united the killers was a racial-cultural animus and sense of superiority, in which individual actors were almost certainly and always aware that their actions were taken to bolster and "defend" the wider perpetrator group. Demonstrating such a consciousness is not a requirement for a legal finding of genocide, as it appears to be for the findings of crimes against humanity. Nonetheless, in practice, it seems that acts of murder are unlikely to be defined as genocidal—whether in law or in the wider scholarship on the subject—unless they are empirically part of a "widespread or systematic" campaign, and target a substantial or significant portion of the group.[92] The reader should be aware that this requirement, unspoken hereafter, guides the analysis of genocide offered in this book, and the range of cases presented to illustrate it.

The reader should keep in mind throughout, however, that there is just one international-legal definition of genocide. For some scholars and advocates, like Helen Fein, this is sufficient to grant the UN Genocide Convention pride of place in any analysis. "I employ the UNGC definition," Fein wrote, "because I believe that it is useful to maintain a common universe of discourse among genocide scholars, international lawyers and human rights monitors; to discriminate between victims of genocide and the violations of life integrity; and to recognize related violations in international law, such as war crimes and crimes against humanity."[93]

For my part, when I touch on legal aspects of genocide, I highlight the UN Convention definition; but I deploy it and other legal framings instrumentally, not dogmatically. I seek to convey an understanding of genocide in which international law is a vital but not a dominant consideration. In part, this is because at the level of international law, genocide is perhaps being displaced by the framing of "crimes against humanity," which is easier to prosecute and imposes much the same punishments as for genocide convictions. The result may be that "genocide," in the coming years and decades, will prove more significant as *an intellectual and scholarly framework* (a heuristic device, for the jargon-inclined), and as *a tool of advocacy and mobilization.* I return to this argument in Chapter 16.

A final caution: the debate over genocide definitions should not blind us to the core problem to be addressed. As the Zen adage has it, let us not mistake the finger pointing at the moon for the moon itself. Israel Charny has noted the sterility of such "definitionalism," which he described as "a form of maddening resistance to acknowledging a known genocide that is common for academics who enter definitional battles over whether or not a given event really fits the pure form of definition of genocide. So much energy goes into the definitional struggle, and so much emphasis is put on words that minimize the extent of the event, that first the significance of the event and its enormous human tragedy are written out of existence, and then the event itself becomes as if something else."[94]

BOX 1.6 THE OTHER "-CIDES" OF GENOCIDE

The literature on genocide and mass violence has given rise to a host of terms derived from Raphael Lemkin's original "genocide." A sampling follows.

Classicide. Term coined by Michael Mann to refer to "the intended mass killing of entire social classes." Examples: The destruction of the "kulaks" in Stalin's USSR (Chapter 5); Cambodia under the Khmer Rouge (Chapter 7). Source: Michael Mann, *The Dark Side of Democracy* (Cambridge University Press, 2004).

Democide. Term invented by R.J. Rummel to encompass "the murder of any person or people by a government, including genocide, politicide, and mass murder." Examples: Rummel particularly emphasizes the "megamurders" of twentieth-century totalitarian regimes. Source: R.J. Rummel, *Death by Government* (Transaction Publishers, 1997).

Ecocide. The willful destruction of the natural environment and ecosystems, through (a) pollution and other forms of environmental degradation, and (b) military efforts to undermine a population's sustainability and means of subsistence. Examples: Deforestation in the Amazon and elsewhere; US use of Agent Orange and other defoliants in the Vietnam War (see Figure 1.4); Saddam Hussein's campaign against the Marsh Arabs in Iraq.[95] Source: David Zierler, *The Invention of Ecocide: Agent Orange, Vietnam, and the Scientists Who Changed the Way We Think About the Environment* (University of Georgia Press, 2011).

Eliticide. The destruction of members of the socioeconomic elite of a targeted group—political leaders, military officers, businesspeople, religious leaders, and cultural/intellectual figures. (n.b. Sometimes spelled "elitocide.") Examples: Poland under Nazi rule (1939–1945); Burundi (1972); Bosnia-Herzegovina in the 1990s.

Figure 1.4 US aerial spraying with Agent Orange—a 50–50 mixture of the herbicides 2,4-d and 2,4,5-t—over vast areas of South Vietnam in the 1960s and 1970s exemplified and popularized the concept of "ecocide."

Source: US Air Force/Wikimedia Commons.

Source: "Eliticide," in Samuel Totten, Paul R. Bartrop, and Steven L. Jacobs, *Dictionary of Genocide, Vol. 1* (Greenwood Press, 2007), pp. 129–130.

Ethnocide. Term originally coined by Raphael Lemkin as a synonym for genocide; subsequently employed (notably by the French ethnologist Robert Jaulin) to describe patterns of cultural genocide, i.e., the destruction of a group's cultural, linguistic, and existential underpinnings, without necessarily killing members of the group. Examples: The term has been used mostly with reference to indigenous peoples (Chapter 3, Box 5a.1), to emphasize that their "destruction" as a group involves more than simply the murder of group members. Source: Robert Jaulin, *La paix blanche: Introduction a l'ethnocide* ("White Peace: Introduction to Ethnocide") (Seuil, 1970).

Femicide/Feminicide. The systematic murder of females for being female. Examples: female infanticide; killings in Ciudad Juarez, Mexico, in the 1990s and 2000s; the École Polytechnique massacre in Montreal (1989). (See also Gendercide.) Source: Diana E.H. Russell and Roberta A. Harmes, eds., *Femicide in Global Perspective* (Teachers College Press, 2001).

Fratricide. Term coined by Michael Mann to describe the killing of factional enemies within political (notably communist) movements. Examples: Stalin's USSR

(Chapter 5); Mao's China (Chapter 5); the Khmer Rouge (Chapter 7). Source: Michael Mann, *The Dark Side of Democracy* (Cambridge University Press, 2004).

Gendercide. The selective destruction of the male or female component of a group, or of dissident sexual minorities (e.g., homosexuals, transsexuals). Term originally coined by Mary Anne Warren in 1985. Examples: Female infanticide; gender-selective massacres of males (e.g., Srebrenica, Bosnia in 1995) (see Chapter 13). Source: Adam Jones, ed., *Gendercide and Genocide* (Vanderbilt University Press, 2004).

Indigenocide. " . . . Another term used to refer to the particular experiences of Indigenous peoples under colonialism"; coined by Bill Thorpe "to communicate 'an interdependent, three-way onslaught upon lives, land, and culture.' "[96]

Judeocide. The Nazi extermination of European Jews. Term coined by Arno Mayer to avoid the sacrificial connotations of "Holocaust" (see also Shoah). Example: The Jewish Holocaust (1941–1945). Source: Arno J. Mayer, "Memory and History: On the Poverty of Remembering and Forgetting the Judeocide," *Radical History Review*, 56 (1993).

Libricide. "The violent destruction of books and libraries" (Knuth) as a strategy and subset of Ethnocide (see above; see also Linguicide and Memoricide). Examples: Nazi Germany; Cultural Revolution in China (1966–1969). Source: Rebecca Knuth, *Libricide: The Regime-Sponsored Destruction of Books and Libraries in the Twentieth Century* (Praeger Publishers, 2003).

Linguicide. The destruction and displacement of languages. Examples: The forcible supplanting of indigenous tongues as part of a wider ethnocidal campaign (see "Ethnocide," above); Turkish bans on the Kurdish language in education and the media (repealed in 2009, but again under threat). Source: Steven L. Jacobs, "Language Death and Revival after Cultural Destruction: Reflections on a Little Discussed Aspect of Genocide," *Journal of Genocide Research*, 7: 3 (2005).

Memoricide. The destruction "not only . . . of those deemed undesirable on the territory to be 'purified,' but . . . [of] any trace that might recall their erstwhile presence (schools, religious buildings and so on)" (Jacques Sémelin). Term coined by Croatian doctor and scholar Mirko D. Grmek during the siege of Sarajevo. Examples: Israel in Palestine;[97] Bosnia-Herzegovina in the 1990s. Source: Edgardo Civallero, " 'When Memory Turns into Ashes' . . . Memoricide During the XX Century," *Information for Social Change*, 25 (Summer 2007).

Omnicide. "The death of all": the blanket destruction of humanity and other life forms by weapons of mass destruction, especially nuclear weapons. Term coined by John Somerville. Examples: None as yet, fortunately. Source: John Somerville, "Nuclear 'War' is Omnicide," *Peace Research*, April 1982.

Politicide. Barbara Harff and Ted Gurr's term for mass killing according to "hierarchical position or political opposition to the regime and dominant groups," as this identification is imputed by the state (see Box 1.4). Examples: Harff and Gurr consider "revolutionary one-party states" to be the most common perpetrators of genocide. The term may also be applied to the mass killings of alleged "communists" and "subversives" in, e.g., Latin America during the 1970s and 1980s. Source: Barbara Harff, "No Lessons Learned from the Holocaust? Assessing Risks of Genocide and Political Mass Murder since 1955," *American Political Science Review*, 97: 1 (2003). (A blog, "The Liberal Ironist," offers an interesting alternative definition of politicide: "the mass killing by the state of the members of a voluntary association such as a political party, professional group or class of property-holders.")[98]

Poorcide. Coined by S.P. Udayakumar in 1995 to describe "the genocide of the poor" through structural poverty. Example: North–South economic relations. Source: S.P. Udayakumar, "The Futures of the Poor," *Futures*, 27: 3 (1995).

Urbicide. The obliteration of urban living-space as a means of destroying the viability of an urban civilization and eroding its collective values.

Throughout world history, human civilization has meant urbanization (the Latin *civitas* is the etymological root of both "city" and "civilization"). "Cities," wrote Daniel Jonah Goldhagen, "are the principal sites of modernity, of economic productivity, of technological productivity."[99] They are also, as political scientist Allan Cooper noted in *The Geography of Genocide*, sites of "hybridity" and cultural mixing. Cooper considered genocide a "fundamentally anti-city" phenomenon, pointing to the regularity with which genocidal perpetrators focus their assaults on urban environments, seeking to destroy them as symbols of group identity and social modernity.[100] Such campaigns are often accompanied by depictions of cities as cesspools of corruption and of foreign-affiliated cliques, requiring "cleansing" and "purifying" by genocidal agents.

Figure 1.5 The ruins of the Warsaw Ghetto, razed by Nazi forces after the Jewish uprising of April–May 1943. The photo was taken in 1945, after Warsaw's liberation. By that point, the remainder of the city, which rose in rebellion in August 1944, had suffered an only slightly less systematic urbicide at Nazi hands. The communists' meticulous postwar reconstruction of Warsaw's historic center was a notably rare architectural and aesthetic triumph of state socialism.

Source: Photo by Zbyszko Siemaszko/Central Photographic Agency (CAF), Warsaw/Wikimedia Commons.

These "deliberate attempts at the annihilation of cities as mixed physical, social, and cultural spaces"[101] constitute *urbicide*. The term was originally popularized in the Serbo-Croatian language, by Bosnian architects, to describe the Serb assault on Sarajevo and the Croat attack on Mostar during the Balkan wars of the 1990s (see Chapter 8). There are numerous historical precedents; as a strategy and symbol of the wider conquest of enemy populations, the obliteration of urban areas was celebrated with special relish. Raphael Lemkin quoted the Assyrian King Sennacherib's declaration following his conquest of the kingdom of Elam: "The city and houses, from their foundation to their upper chambers, I destroyed, dug up, in the fire I burn." Lemkin says Sennacherib "had canals dug through the city 'in order that, in the course of time, no one may find the place of this city and of its temples. I covered it with water.'"[102]

Another classical example of urbicide, perhaps the most iconic one, is the Roman siege and obliteration of Carthage (c. 149 BCE). Significantly, this was preceded by an ultimatum that the Carthaginians abandon their city for the countryside. When the ultimatum failed to produce the desired results, the Romans made plain their rejection of Carthage as a city. They razed it to rubble, and consigned the surviving population to slavery around the known world; they also inspired a term for indiscriminate destruction (and the "Carthaginian peace" it may impose). The wars of conquest, obliteration, and extermination waged by Genghis Khan and his successors across Central and West Asia represent perhaps the most sustained, geographically far-flung campaign of urbicide on the historical record.

In the modern period, examples of urbicide include the Ottoman destruction of the old city of Van in 1915, depicted and discussed in the photo essay (photo 7). During the Second World War, the Nazis inflicted some of the most ruthless urbicidal assaults on the historical record. The cases of Leningrad and Stalingrad are well known; less so the destruction of Warsaw, massively bombed in 1939, its Jewish ghetto razed Carthage-style after the uprising of 1943, and the rest of the city systematically eviscerated after much of the remaining population rebelled in 1944. The Nazis, wrote Keith Lowe, seemed almost to be working from a prewar Baedeker cultural guide as they set about destroying first every landmark in Warsaw, then entire urban neighborhoods:

> German troops blew up the medieval Royal Castle. They undermined the fourteenth-century cathedral and blew that up too. Then they destroyed the Jesuit Church. The Saxon Palace was systematically blown up over the course of three days just after Christmas 1944, as was the entire complex of baroque and rococo palaces. The European Hotel, recommended by Baedeker, was first burned down in October and then, just to make sure, blown up in January 1945. German troops went from house to house, street to street, systematically destroying the entire city: 93 per cent of Warsaw's dwellings were destroyed or damaged beyond repair. To complete the destruction they burned down the National Archive, the

Archives of Ancient Documents, the Financial Archives, the Municipal Archives, the Archives of New Documents and the Public Library.[103]

More recent iconic instances of urbicide include the Khmer Rouge's forced expulsions from Phnom Penh and other Cambodian cities in 1975 (see Chapter 7); Hafez al-Assad's 1982 assault on the rebellious Syrian city of Hama in 1982 ("The Hama Solution"),[104] and the merciless bombardment of rebel cities and neighborhoods by his son, Bashir, in today's ongoing civil war; the Armenian sacking and leveling of the Azerbaijani city of Agdam in 1992;[105] the siege of Sarajevo, Bosnia, 1992–1996 (see Chapter 8); the Russian pulverizing of Grozny, Chechnya in 1994–1995 (see Box 5a); and repeated Israeli air and artillery assaults on densely-populated urban areas of the Gaza Strip.

WHAT IS DESTROYED IN GENOCIDE?

Many framers of genocide have emphasized physical killing as primary in the equation—perhaps essential. For others, however—including Raphael Lemkin, and to an extent the drafters of the UN Genocide Convention—physical and mass killing is just one of a range of genocidal strategies. These observers stress the destruction of the group *as a sociocultural unit*, not necessarily or primarily the physical annihilation of its members.[106] This question—what, precisely, is destroyed in genocide?—has sparked one of genocide studies' most fertile lines of inquiry. It is closely connected with sociologist Martin Shaw, who in his book *What Is Genocide?* called for a greater emphasis on the social destruction of groups. For Shaw,

> *Because groups are social constructions, they can be neither constituted nor destroyed simply through the bodies of their individual members.* Destroying groups must involve a lot more than simply killing, although killing and other physical harm are rightly considered important to it. The discussion of group "destruction" is obliged, then, to take seriously Lemkin's "large view of this concept," discarded in genocide's reduction to body counts, which centred on social destruction. . . . The aim of "destroying" social groups is not reduced to killing their individual members, but is understood as destroying groups' social power in economic, political and cultural senses. . . . [Genocide] *involves mass killing but . . . is much more than mass killing.*[107]

Daniel Feierstein, and the emerging Argentine "school" of genocide studies, have likewise stressed the destruction of social power and existential *identity* as the essence of genocide. For Feierstein, modern "genocidal social practice" can be conceptualized as a "technology of power—a way of managing people as a group—that aims (1) to destroy social relationships based on autonomy and cooperation by annihilating a significant part of the popular (significant in terms of either numbers or practices), and (2) to use the terror of annihilation to establish new models of identity and social relationships among the survivors."[108]

The question of whether forms of destruction short of, or other than, physical killing can *in themselves* constitute genocide touches directly on one of the oldest debates in genocide studies and law: over ***cultural genocide.*** We have noted that Lemkin placed great emphasis on human groups as culture carriers, and on the destruction of cultural symbols as genocidal in and of itself: *"the destruction of cultural symbols is genocide,* because it implies the destruction of their function and thus menaces the existence of the social group which exists by virtue of its common culture."[109] However, Lemkin felt that cultural genocide had to involve "acts of violence which are qualified as criminal by most of the criminal codes":[110] he was always concerned that patterns of gradual cultural assimilation, for example, should not be depicted as genocidal, or even necessarily malign.

One can argue, in fact, that Lemkin went further. Genocide scholars usually cite him nowadays to justify de-emphasizing the role of physical killing/extermination in genocide, and highlighting cultural/social destruction. But we might note, first, that Lemkin with great deliberation chose a suffix, *-cide,* that is commonly associated with physical killing and extermination (e.g., homicide, suicide, insecticide). Moreover, as Dirk Moses has pointed out, Lemkin at the outset of *Axis Rule in Occupied Europe* "seems to restrict genocide to [physical] extermination, thereby distinguishing it from other techniques" (such as cultural assimilation, already referenced). He wrote in his 1944 volume: "The practice of extermination of nations and ethnic groups as carried out by the invaders is called by the author 'genocide' . . . by way of analogy, see homocide [*sic*], fratricide)."[111] In his unfinished history of genocide, Lemkin declared "actual physical destruction" to be "the last and most effective phase of a genocide. . . . in all genocide cases, there is a gradual descent toward the violence which seeks utter extermination."[112]

Nonetheless, as we have seen, Lemkin was deeply attached to the concept of cultural genocide, and it was his most personally wounding experience, during the drafting of the UN Convention, to see this concept jettisoned. "On this issue the wind was not blowing in my direction," he acknowledged ruefully in his autobiography.[113] The UN Secretariat draft of 1947, prepared with Lemkin's direct input as well as that of legal experts Vespasian Pella and Henri Donnedieu de Vabres, "divided genocide into three categories, physical, biological and cultural genocide"[114] (see Box 1.7). But many expressed discomfort with the "cultural genocide" formula. The Danish delegation, for example, argued that it demonstrated "a lack of logic and of a sense of proportion to include in the same convention both mass murder in gas chambers and the closing of libraries."[115] The Sixth Committee of 1948 eliminated cultural genocide, and the Convention as subsequently passed privileged physical killing first and foremost—even more so in its practical application.

Nonetheless, the Sixth Committee did grant that one aspect of the cultural genocide framework be reinserted in the Convention. It is enshrined as Article 2(e), which outlaws "forcibly transferring children of the group to another group," and the consequent elimination of those children as culture-bearers for the victimized group. Article 2(e) has not, by itself, sustained a conviction for genocide in international law. But it *has* figured in an important quasi-legal process, the Australian governmental commission that issued a report on the forcible transfer of aboriginal children to white families and institutions, *Bringing Them Home*

BOX 1.7 "PHYSICAL," "BIOLOGICAL," AND "CULTURAL" GENOCIDE

Until late in the drafting process of the 1948 Genocide Convention, a category of genocidal strategies (Article III) was reserved for cultural forms of genocide, alongside physical and biological ones. Though cultural genocide was jettisoned for the final Convention,[116] as late as the report of the Ad Hoc Committee on Genocide on May 24, 1948, this categorization was preserved, as shown in the "Draft Convention on the Prevention and Punishment of the Crime of Genocide" attached as an annex to the report. Note that "political groups" are still included as a protected category of victims, though they too would be absent from the final Convention.

THE HIGH CONTRACTING PARTIES . . . HEREBY AGREE TO PREVENT AND PUNISH THE CRIME AS HEREINAFTER PROVIDED:

Substantive Articles

ARTICLE I

(Genocide: a crime under international law)

Genocide is a crime under international law whether committed in time of peace or in time of war.

ARTICLE II

("Physical" and "biological" genocide)

In this Convention genocide means any of the following deliberate acts committed with the intent to destroy a national, racial, religious or political group, on grounds of the national or racial origin, religious belief, or political opinion of its members.

(1) killing members of the group;
(2) impairing the physical integrity of members of the group;
(3) inflicting on members of the group measures or conditions of life aimed at causing their deaths;
(4) imposing measures intended to prevent births within the group.

ARTICLE III

("Cultural" genocide)

In this Convention genocide also means any deliberate act committed with the intent to destroy the language, religion, or culture of a national, racial or religious group on grounds of the national or racial origin or religious belief of its members such as:

(1) prohibiting the use of the language of the group in daily intercourse or in schools, or the printing and circulation of publications in the language of the group;

(2) destroying or preventing the use of libraries, museums, schools, historical monuments, places of worship or other cultural institutions and objects of the group.[117]

(1997). We will see in Chapter 3 that this report controversially used the language of "genocide" on the basis of Article 2(e).

Unsurprisingly, it is aboriginal and indigenous peoples, and their supporters in activist circles and academia, who have placed the greatest emphasis on cultural genocide in issuing appeals for recognition and restitution. Indigenous peoples who experienced settler colonialism, as sociologist Robert van Krieken has argued, have in common "a heartfelt and persistent sense of inflicted violence, pain and suffering at the heart of the settler-colonial project." As a result, they have evinced a "particularly strong . . . support for an understanding [of genocide] which goes beyond outright killing."[118]

Also unsurprisingly, it was the settler-colonial regimes who were most "anxious to exclude cultural genocide" from the Genocide Convention, as Raphael Lemkin's biographer John Cooper points out. South Africa, settler-conquered and racially-ruled, of course voted to delete the clause. So too did "many members of the Commonwealth with indigenous populations," including Canada and New Zealand.[119]

Nonetheless, despite this early and enduring relegation of cultural genocide from legal framings of genocide, the concept has resurged in this setting in the 1990s—*not as genocidal in itself, but as "a marker of intent to commit genocide."*[120] Specifically, as John Quigley notes, "the destruction of cultural objects may provide evidence that such acts were done with intent to destroy the group."[121] This was most prominent in the proceedings of the International Criminal Tribunal for the Former Yugoslavia (ICTY), established in 1993 as war and genocide in the Balkans were still raging. Serbian obliteration of Bosnian Muslim cultural symbols, especially mosques (see Figure 1.4) and the main library complex in Sarajevo, was entered into evidence to demonstrate Serbian intent to destroy Bosnian Muslims as a group, though individual convictions for genocide were based on the perpetrators' physical killing of group members, or the infliction of "serious bodily . . . harm" upon them.

Since the first edition of this book appeared, explorations of genocide as including the destruction of "social power" and group culture have been among the most fertile lines of investigation in genocide studies. Martin Shaw's interpretation of genocidal destruction resonates in the mind long after one has read it, and seems to me one of the most incisive conceptualizations of the subject.

Notions of cultural destruction as suggestive (or legally indicative) of genocidal intent strike me as persuasive and highly meaningful. The full-scale and semi-official destruction of cultural symbols seems powerfully relevant to the study of genocide (notably with regard to indigenous peoples), and to legal prosecutions

Figure 1.6 UN peacekeepers walk by a destroyed mosque in Ahmiçi, Bosnia–Herzegovina, in April 1993. *Génocidaires* often attempt to obliterate a group's cultural, religious, and intellectual symbols as part of their broader campaign of destruction. For Raphael Lemkin, these constituted cultural forms of genocide, and were essential to his understanding of the phenomenon. International law, and most scholarship, has generally made mass killing definitional to the crime of genocide; but such attacks on a group's cultural integrity are considered indicative of a wider genocidal strategy, for legal purposes. Thus, the image shown here was tagged for submission as evidence to the International Criminal Tribunal for the Former Yugoslavia (ICTY) in The Hague, Netherlands (see Chapter 15).

Source: Courtesy International Criminal Tribunal for the Former Yugoslavia (ICTY), www.icty.org.

of genocide in the contemporary period. Lower-level acts of vandalism, defacing, hate speech and graffiti, and book-burning are also significant in developing strategies of prevention and intervention (Chapter 16). They occupy a position on the "genocidal continuum" described by the anthropologist Nancy Scheper-Hughes (see Chapter 11, pp. 590–591). As such, they not only point to everyday patterns of anathematization and exclusion that may otherwise be overlooked, but *may* serve as harbingers of serious acts of violence against targeted groups—up to and including genocidal outbreaks. As such, they should prompt serious concern in the national communities in question, and the international community as well.

The question remains, however, whether strategies of social and cultural "destruction" should be considered genocidal *in the absence of systematic killing, or at least widespread physical attack*. I believe they should not be. I will cite two examples, situated at very different points on the "genocidal continuum," to make my point.

One of the principal cultural divides in Canada is between descendants of Anglo-Saxon and Gallic civilizations in Western Europe. Quebec's "Quiet Revolution" in the 1960s radically destabilized the longstanding hegemony of the Anglos in the province. Francophone nationalism spilled over, at the end of the 1960s, into small-scale acts of terrorism and political assassination, but also gave rise to a mass political movement that brought the separatist Parti Québecois (PQ) to power in 1976. In ensuing years, the PQ pursued a broad nationalist campaign that included seeking political separation through referenda, institutionalizing French-language requirements in all schools and public signage (Bill 101), and requiring bilingualism in workplaces with over fifty employees. Graffiti began to appear around Montreal reading *"101 ou 401"*—accept the nationalist legislation of Bill 101, or take Highway 401 from Montreal to the Anglo bastion of Toronto in next-door Ontario.

The Anglo community in Montreal and elsewhere in Quebec organized to resist these measures, and a regular feature of their discourse was the language of mass atrocity to describe the Anglophone plight in Quebec. PQ cabinet minister Camille Laurin, depicted as "the father of Bill 101," was accused of inflicting "linguistic genocide" on the English minority.[122] "Words like 'cultural re-engineering' and 'akin to ethnic cleansing' were printed" at the time,[123] and they remain popular even in relatively recent times.[124]

I think most readers will agree that such rhetoric was and is overheated. Yet the result of more than four decades of francophone ascendancy in Quebec has indeed been the real displacement of the Anglo community. Hundreds of thousands of Anglos chose Highway 401 over Bill 101. The native English-speaking population of Quebec declined precipitously, from 13.8 percent in 1951 to 8.2 percent in 2006.[125] French is now a requirement of most middle-and upper-level positions in society, politics, and the economy. Proposed measures to ban even the apostrophe in the name of the department store "Eaton's" were overturned in court battles; in 1993, the UN's Human Rights Committee, ruling on a case brought by representatives of Quebec's English minority, found the province's sign laws in contravention of international rights treaties. "A State may choose one or more official languages," declared the UNHCR, "but it may not exclude outside the spheres of public life, the freedom to express oneself in a certain language."[126] Even in the wake of those decisions, French text must be at least twice as large as English on all commercial signage, and street signs are French-only outside spheres of federal jurisdiction.[127]

So has Anglo power been "destroyed" in Quebec, in whole or in substantial part? Arguably, yes. But as with similar affirmative-action measures in countries like Malaysia and (for a while) Lebanon, Bill 101 seems to have achieved a reconfiguration of power relations that is largely acceptable to the Anglos that remain.[128] Again, the genocide framing seems unhelpful and overblown, because whatever measures of positive discrimination/affirmative action have been instituted to benefit the francophone majority, and redress longstanding disadvantages vis-à-vis the Anglos, they have not spilled over into systematic violence, severe persecution, and murderous rampages against the targeted minority.

Consider a second case. In August 1972, the Ugandan dictator Idi Amin—an iconic figure of evil in the 1970s—issued a stunning order. All Ugandan citizens of Asian (overwhelmingly Indian) descent were to be stripped of their property and forced either to leave the country within ninety days, or to accept "banishment to remote and arid areas, where they could occupy themselves as farmers"—a familiar motif in mass atrocity campaigns, forcing a commercially-identified sub-group to engage in "productive" agricultural labor. Despite international protest, as Leo Kuper noted in his seminal 1981 volume, "the expulsions took their uninhibited course. The victims were brutally treated, a few were killed, and they were systematically stripped of their possessions, which were distributed to, or seized as booty by, soldiers and other supporters of the regime."[129]

Here we have an instance of persecution, dispossession, forcible uprooting, and mass expulsion. The result was the *total* destruction of the Indian-descended community of Uganda as a social entity, and the internal displacement or forced exile of the vast majority of its members (about 75,000 people). This would surely meet Shaw's requirement that the essence of the genocidal enterprise be sought in its attempted destruction of a group's social power. Indeed, in his subsequent work *Genocide and International Relations*, Shaw stressed that "expulsions can be considered genocidal because their aims were to wholly or partially destroy unwanted populations *as presences in their homelands*."[130] Yet Shaw does not mention Uganda's Indians in either book. As for Kuper's early analysis, it is not clear that he considers the targeting of the Indians to be genocidal as such—he certainly places more emphasis on "the slaughter . . . [of] almost every conceivable category of victim" in Amin's wider political and ethnic liquidations, nearly all of which occurred *after* the Indian expulsions.[131] Since Kuper's work appeared, I have not seen the Ugandan Indians explored as a case of genocide in the comparative literature—nor do I feel the need to correct a perceived oversight in this regard. The reason for the widespread silence seems to be that Ugandan Indians were largely preserved from the largescale slaughter that Amin meted out to other political and ethnic opponents. The substantial undermining or even outright destruction of a group's social, economic, political, and cultural power and presence does not seem to warrant the "genocide" label if it is not accompanied by mass killing.

To reiterate, though, where such systematic forms of cultural targeting and persecution can be isolated, their significance is considerable for the interpretation, prosecution, and prevention of genocide. And to students of the subject, I stress it is reasonable to cultivate a personal/individual understanding of genocide (or to adopt someone else's, as I have mostly done with Steven Katz's). Many readers will favor a more cultural and sociological interpretation of the subject. As long as genocide remains an essentially contested concept[132]—and it always will—we should continue the discussion and debate, and turn the conceptual ferment to our advantage.

MULTIPLE AND OVERLAPPING IDENTITIES

> . . . Identity markers and their functions are often highly fluid.
>
> Martin Shaw

Vigorous controversy has attended the Genocide Convention's exclusion of all but four human categories—national, ethnic, racial, and religious groups—from the convention's list of protected groups. We are also, as noted, increasingly conscious that the alleged stability and integrity of these groups is very much open to question—not least because group identity is often imposed (even imagined) by perpetrators rather than claimed by targets.

Less recognized is the fact that these identities, along with the "big three" missing from the Genocide Convention (political, social, and gender groups), *never* exist in isolation. Genocidal targeting is *always* the result of a blurring and blending of identities. As psychologist David Moshman has written, "All genocides involve multiple motives, complex interactions of causal factors, *and groups that can be divided and defined in multiple ways*. . . . A purist definition of genocide requiring unmixed motives, singular causes, and discrete groups would render the concept irrelevant to the actual social worlds of human beings."[133]

This is why victims may be simultaneously viewed as (for example) representatives of a dangerous ethnicity, an insurgent or rapacious social class, a threatening political entity, and a malevolent gender group—in fact, with that particular recipe, we have just sketched the outline of a great many modern genocides. It is also why the "other -cides" of genocide studies, rather than being frivolous, are vital to identifying the interwoven threads of identity, whether claimed or imputed. Hence, "a given campaign of mass killing can easily be labeled as genocidal, democidal, politicidal, eliticidal, and gendercidal all at once—with each of these designations representing an analytical cut that exposes one aspect of the campaign and serves to buttress comparative studies of a particular 'cide.'"[134]

The "hard" test for these assertions is the genocide that many still see as having been impelled by perhaps the fiercest racial-ethnic-biological animus imaginable: the Jewish Holocaust (Chapter 6). In his detailed exploration of Nazi anti-semitic propaganda, *The Jewish Enemy*, historian Jeffrey Herf delivered a surprising verdict: "that the radical anti-Semitic ideology that justified and accompanied the mass murder of European Jewry was first and foremost *a paranoid political, rather than biological, conviction and narrative*." What was vital was not "the way Jews were said to look" but what "Hitler and his associates . . . believed 'international Jewry' *did* . . . "[135] This was the foundation of the *mixed* political-ethnic construction of "the threatening Jewish-Bolshevik danger," in the language of a 1943 press report.[136] "Judeo-Bolshevism" was the international communist conspiracy allegedly headed by Jews in order to advance their project of political/economic/ethnic-racial/religious/sexual conquest and domination.[137] A Nazi propaganda pamphlet from 1941 described "Bolshevism"—"this system of chaos, extermination and terror"—as "conceived and led by Jews":

> Through subversion and propaganda, world Jewry attempts to gather the uprooted and racially inferior elements of all peoples together in order to lead an extermination battle [*Vernichtungskampf*] against everything positive, against native customs and the nation, against religion and culture, against order and morals. The goal is the introduction of chaos through world revolution and the establishment of a Jewish state under Jewish leadership.[138]

In a single sentence ("Through subversion . . . "), the Judeo-Bolshevik is depicted as a "racial," "nation[al]," "religi[ous]" and "cultur[al]" enemy, seeking to

Figure 1.7 "Nazi antisemitic propaganda frequently linked Jews to the fears of their German and foreign audiences. This [1943] poster, displayed in the German-occupied Soviet Union to foment both anti-Soviet and antisemitic fervor, uses the stereotype of the bloodthirsty 'Jewish Bolshevik commissar' to associate 'the Jew' with the murder of more than 9,000 Soviet citizens in Vinnytsia, Ukraine, an atrocity committed by Stalin's secret police in 1937–38. German forces uncovered the massacre in May 1943." The identities that *génocidaires* impute to their victims—here, a mix of (Jewish) race/ethnicity, (Bolshevik/communist) political belief, (godless) religion, (masculine) gender, and (lower/lumpen) social class—overlap and intersect in complex ways to produce genocidal outcomes. (The Cyrillic caption reads "Vinnytsia." See also Figure 13.9, p. 648.)

Source: Library of Congress, Prints and Photographs Division, Washington, DC.

erode German "customs," social "order," and "morals" for good measure. Add the identification of the Jew as a *military* enemy—as the Nazi wartime adage had it, "Wherever there is [a] partisan, there is a Jew, and wherever there is a Jew, there is a partisan"[139]—and one has the essential ingredients of the ideological pastiche and *mortal terror* that fueled the architects and perpetrators of the Holocaust.[140] In Martin Shaw's trenchant words:

> SS *Einsatzgruppen* reports in the wake of the invasion of the Soviet Union identified no fewer than forty-four overlapping "target groups" . . . When an *Einsatzgruppen* killer pulled his trigger, could victims always tell—or care—whether they were killed as Slavs, as communists or as Jews, even if the perpetrators later produced grisly reports claiming to itemize the numbers of victims in different categories? Can we, historians and sociologists many decades later, make these distinctions with certainty?[141]

DYNAMISM AND CONTINGENCY

In Chapter 6, we will explore how the historiography of the Holocaust evolved from an "intentionalist" position—depicting the attempted extermination of European Jews as a policy intended from the very outset of the Nazi movement—to a more "functionalist" perspective, emphasizing contingency and situational context, and finally to a synthesis of the two perspectives. Broadly speaking, the Nazi agenda underwent a *cumulative radicalization*. An exterminatory agenda evolved, shaped (though in no way mechanistically determined) by forces beyond the control of the principal perpetrators. Discriminatory legislation gave way to outright persecution, forced migration, ghettoization, enslavement, massacre, and finally industrialized mass killing. In the phrase coined by Karl A. Schleunes, it was a "twisted road to Auschwitz"—and Schleunes can take credit for first supplying an "interpretation of the Final Solution as a product of unplanned evolution rather than premeditated 'grand design,'" in historian Christopher Browning's words.[142]

At each stage, objective factors—notably the bureaucratic challenges of realizing and administering the master-race fantasy—influenced outcomes chosen by at least *somewhat* rational perpetrators. Nonetheless, hateful ideologies and persecutory programs were evident from the outset, and throughout, so that a clear line of connection *can* be drawn from the earliest Nazi activity after World War One and the exterminatory outburst against Jews and others that we know as the Holocaust.

Genocide studies has followed a similar intellectual trajectory. In tandem with an increased recognition of multiple and overlapping identities, monocausal models of carefully-planned and long-nurtured mass slaughters have given way to a recognition that genocide, in Mark Levene's words, "is not necessarily preordained but will come out of a concatenation or matrix of ingredients and contingencies . . . *only* crystallising in specific and usually quite extraordinary circumstances of acute state and societal crisis." In the colonial collision with indigenous peoples worldwide, for example, Levene isolated "a dynamic in which perpetrator-state violence leads to tenacious *people* resistance, provoking in turn a ratcheting up of the perpetrator's response" and a genocidal consequence.[143] Dirk Moses, another leading scholar of colonial and imperial genocides, agrees: "Resistance leads to reprisals and counterinsurgency that can be genocidal when they are designed to ensure that never again would such resistance occur."[144] Nor is the pattern limited to colonial cases. Examining the Rwandan genocide in his 2006 book *The Order of Genocide*, political scientist Scott Straus argued that far from a "meticulously planned" extermination,

> a dynamic of escalation was critical to the hardliners' choice of genocide. The more the hardliners felt that they were losing power and the more they felt that their armed enemy was not playing by the rules, the more the hardliners radicalized. After the president [Juvenal Habyarimana] was assassinated [on April 6, 1994] and the [RPF] rebels began advancing, the hardliners let loose. They chose genocide as an extreme, vengeful, and desperate strategy to win a war that they were losing. Events and contingency mattered.[145]

Levene has theorized this pattern as follows:

> Perhaps, in this way, a set of state plans directed against a communal group might not start out as consciously exterminatory but begins to radically evolve in this direction because, in conditions of usually self-inflicted crisis, other paths are blocked. A default plan, at this point, perhaps has to be improvised and where this in turn proves inadequate to the needs of the original agenda, a process of cumulative radicalization may set in.

If "mass killing can arise out of unforeseen or entirely contingent circumstances," then for Levene, "a more functional analysis" of genocidal intent is required.[146] It is to this vexed subject that we turn next.

THE QUESTION OF GENOCIDAL INTENT

Most scholars and legal theorists agree that intent defines genocide.[147] But what defines intent?

We can begin by distinguishing *intent* from *motive*. According to Gellately and Kiernan, in criminal law, including international criminal law, the specific motive is irrelevant. Prosecutors need only to prove that the criminal act was intentional, not accidental.[148] As legal scholar John Quigley notes,

> In prosecutions for genocide, tribunals have not required proof of a motive....The personal motive of the perpetrator of the crime of genocide may be, for example, to obtain personal economic benefits, or political advantage or some form of power. The existence of a personal motive does not preclude the perpetrator from also having the specific intent to commit genocide.[149]

The notion of *specific* intent (*dolus specialis*) "demands that the perpetrator clearly seeks to produce the act charged" (in the words of the International Criminal Tribunal for Rwanda, ICTR), which "in relation to genocide ... means the perpetrator commits an act while clearly seeking to destroy the particular group, in whole or in part." For many scholars and legal specialists, as Katherine Goldsmith noted, such specificity is "the only appropriate intent level for the crime of genocide, as allowing any lower form of intent would risk situations that result in the destruction of a group, with no intent of this destruction taking place, being wrongly seen as genocide."[150]

As Goldsmith also stressed, however, the central difficulty of a specific-intent requirement for legal purposes lies "in obtaining actual proof, beyond a reasonable doubt, that the perpetrator's intention was to destroy the group ... " But "proving a perpetrator's state of mind is a massive problem. Perpetrators are fully aware that admitting what they are doing could interfere with achieving their objective. They are therefore unlikely to admit what their intentions are and thus risking possible action against them, especially if the objective of destroying the target group is still taking place."[151] She contends, moreover, that this highly-restrictive understanding of intent was neither favored by Raphael Lemkin nor emphasized by the drafters of the Genocide Convention in their *Travaux préparatoires* (see Further Study).[152]

In light of this conundrum, Goldsmith identifies an emerging trend in genocide trials to incorporate a *knowledge-based* understanding of intent. The Rome Statute of the International Criminal Court (1998), for instance, declares that "a person has intent where ... in relation to conduct, that person means to cause that consequence *or is aware that it will occur in the ordinary course of events*."[153] Likewise, the International Criminal Tribunal for Rwanda stated in its historic *Akayesu* judgment (1998) that "the offender is culpable because he knew *or should have known* that the act committed would destroy, in whole or in part, a group."[154] This moves applications of the Genocide Convention closer to the framing of "crimes against humanity" as codified in the Rome Statute. The Statute establishes that an accused may be convicted of a specific crime against humanity (e.g., murder, "extermination," enslavement, rape) if it can be shown (a) that the act was part of a "widespread or systematic attack" against civilians, and (b) *that the perpetrator had "knowledge of the attack,"* that is, an awareness that his or her action was not isolated but part of a broader strategy. In the words of the ICTR's Akayesu judgment, "it is possible to deduce the genocidal intent inherent in a particular act ... from the general context of the perpetration of other culpable acts systematically directed against that same group, whether these acts were committed by the same offender or by others." As Goldsmith summarizes, "the tribunal was working under the assumption that if the perpetrator knows of the intent of others to kill a particular group, and knows his/her actions would contribute to this intent, but continues to participate, then in a sense the perpetrator does want the destruction of the group and is, therefore, guilty of genocide."[155]

The shift away from a strict *dolus specialis* requirement hardly resolves all the evidentiary quandaries of genocide prosecutions, however—notably the requirement to show that a particular "national, ethnical, racial, or religious" group is targeted for attack and destruction. For this reason, in the international-legal sphere, charges of crimes against humanity are increasingly preferred to genocide—especially as the legal sentences upon conviction are broadly comparable. Genocide and crimes against humanity, and genocide *as* a crime against humanity, are discussed further in Chapter 15.

CONTESTED CASES OF GENOCIDE

With the varied academic definitions of genocide, and the ambiguities surrounding both the Genocide Convention and historical interpretation, it is not surprising that nearly every posited case of genocide will be discounted by someone else. Even the "classic" genocides of the twentieth century have found their systematic minimizers and deniers (see Chapter 14). With this in mind, let us consider a few controversial events and human institutions. What can the debate over the applicability of a genocide framework in these cases tell us about definitions of genocide, the ideas and interests that underlie those definitions, and the evolution in thinking about genocide? I will offer my own views in each case. Readers are also encouraged to consult the discussion of "famine crimes" in Chapters 2 and 5, and of genocide against political groups in Chapter 5 on Stalin's USSR.

Atlantic slavery—and after

Slavery is pervasive in human societies throughout history. Arguably in no context, however, did it result in such massive mortality as with Atlantic slavery between the sixteenth and nineteenth centuries.[156]

A reasonable estimate of the deaths caused by this institution is fifteen to twenty million people—by any standard, a major human cataclysm.[157] However, Atlantic slavery is rarely included in analyses or anthologies of genocide. A notable exception—Seymour Drescher's chapter in *Is the Holocaust Unique?*—avoids the "genocide" label, and stresses the differences between slavery and the Holocaust.[158] (Admittedly, these are not few.) More recently, the human rights scholar Michael Ignatieff has cited slavery-as-genocide arguments as a leading example of the tendency to "banalize" the genocide framework:

> Thus slavery is called genocide, when—whatever else it was—it was a system to exploit the living rather than to exterminate them. . . . Genocide has no meaning unless the crime can be connected to a clear intention to exterminate a human group in whole or in part. Something more than rhetorical exaggeration for effect is at stake here. Calling every abuse or crime a genocide makes it steadily more difficult to rouse people to action when a genuine genocide is taking place.[159]

Figure 1.8 Perhaps half of the many millions of African victims of the Atlantic slave trade died before they reached the human markets and plantations of the western hemisphere. Countless numbers died on forced marches to the sea, where European colonialists and slave-traders established fortified outposts like Cape Coast Castle in Ghana, today a UNESCO World Heritage Site. The photo shows the cells where slaves were held in dark, stifling, and fetid captivity (note the open sewer), sometimes for months, awaiting the moment when they would be led in chains through the "Door of No Return" for the "Middle Passage" across the Atlantic. The death toll inflicted in the sea journeys alone likely accounted for over a million victims. On the plantations of North and South America and the Caribbean, slaves toiled in a culture of terror and violence, aimed at keeping them quiescent, hyper-exploited, and in a state of "social death."[160]

Source: Author's photo, June 2010.

Ignatieff's argument—that it was in slaveowners' interest to keep slaves alive, not exterminate them—is probably the most common argument against slavery-as-genocide. Others point to the ubiquity of slavery through time; the large-scale collaboration of African chiefs and entrepreneurs in corralling Africans for slavery; and the supposedly cheery results of slavery for slaves' descendants, at least in North America. Even some African-American commentators have celebrated their "deliverance" from strife-torn Africa to lands of opportunity in America.[161]

My own view is that these arguments are mostly sophistry, serving to deflect responsibility for one of history's greatest crimes. To call Atlantic slavery genocide is not to claim that "every abuse or crime" is genocide, as Ignatieff asserts; nor is it even to designate all slavery as genocidal. Rather, it seems to me an appropriate response to a *particular* slavery institution, or network of institutions, that inflicted "incalculable demographic and social losses" on West African societies,[162] utilizing every genocidal strategy listed in the UN Genocide Convention's definition (Articles 2a–e).[163] The killing and destruction were clearly intentional, whatever the counter-incentives to preserve survivors of the Atlantic passage for labor exploitation. To revisit the issue of intent already touched on: If an institution is deliberately maintained and expanded by discernible agents, though all are aware of the hecatombs of casualties it is inflicting on a definable human group, then why should this not qualify as genocide?

The aftermath of Atlantic slavery—reverberating through African-American societies to the present—also produced one of the very first petitions ever presented to the United Nations on the subject of genocide. In December 1951, "only 11 months after the Genocide Convention went into effect," a petition titled *We Charge Genocide* was submitted by African-American activists, headed by the lawyer and communist activist William L. Patterson, and the great actor, scholar, and singer Paul Robeson. Nearly sixty years later, the document must be regarded as one of the central, and earliest, documents of the US civil rights era. It is also nuanced in its reading of the Genocide Convention, claiming to have "scrupulously kept within the purview" of the new law. It specifies Article II(c) ("deliberately inflicting on the group conditions of life . . . "), that is indirect/structural genocide, as a foundational aspect of the claim. It also "pray[s] for the most careful reading of this material by those who have always regarded genocide as a term to be used only where the acts of terror evinced an intent to destroy a whole nation," arguing instead for a recognition that the Convention prohibits the selective/partial destruction of a group, as well as its wholesale extermination.[164]

Among the atrocities, abuses, and discrimination detailed in *We Charge Genocide* (see Box 1.8) was the murder of "10,000 Negroes . . . on the basis of 'race,'"[166] many of them the widespread "vigilante" lynchings of the post-slavery period. These atrocities were inflicted with the tacit and often enthusiastic approval of local communities and authorities. Nevertheless, the United Nations General Assembly, still dominated by the US at that early stage of the UN's evolution, refused to accept the petition.[167]

Area bombing and nuclear warfare

Controversy has swirled around the morality both of the area bombing of German cities by British and US air forces (see also "Germans as Victims," Chapter 6a), and the US firebombing of the Japanese mainland, culminating in the atomic bombings of Hiroshima and Nagasaki in August 1945. The key issue in both cases is at what point legitimate military action becomes genocide. The line is difficult to draw, in part due to the intimate relationship between war and genocide, discussed in detail in Chapter 2. In the case of "area" bombing (in which cities were blanketed with high explosives), the debate centers on the military utility and morality of the policy. In Germany, "the effects [themselves] are clear and undisputed," according to Markusen and Kopf: "By the end of the war in 1945, every large and medium-sized German city, as well as many smaller ones had been destroyed or badly damaged by the Allied strategic-bombing offensive. . . . Estimates of deaths

BOX 1.8 *WE CHARGE GENOCIDE*

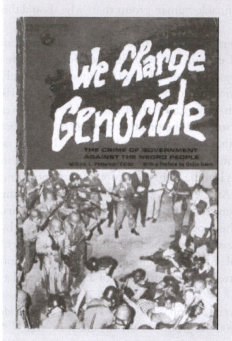

Figure 1.9 *We Charge Genocide*, the text of one of the first genocide declarations ever issued—in 1951, against the US government for its policies toward "the Negro people." This is the cover of the 1970 International Publishers edition.

Source: Courtesy of International Publishers, www.intpubnyc.com.

To the General Assembly of the United Nations:

The responsibility of being the first in history to charge the government of the United States of America with the crime of genocide is not one your petitioners take lightly. . . . But if the responsibility of your petitioners is great, it is dwarfed by the responsibility of those guilty of the crime we charge. Seldom in human annals has so iniquitous a conspiracy been so gilded with the trappings of respectability. Seldom has mass murder on the score of "race" been so sanctified by law, so justified by those who demand free elections abroad even as they kill their fellow citizens who demand free elections at home. Never have so many individuals been so ruthlessly destroyed amid so many tributes to the sacredness of the individual. The distinctive trait of this genocide is a cant that mouths aphorisms of Anglo-Saxon jurisprudence even as it kills. . . .

Our evidence concerns the thousands of Negroes who over the years have been beaten to death on chain gangs and in the back rooms of sheriff's offices, in the cells of county jails, in precinct police stations and on city streets, who have been framed and murdered by sham legal forms and by a legal bureaucracy. It concerns those Negroes who have been killed, allegedly for failure to say "sir" or tip their hats or move aside quickly enough, or, more often, on trumped up charges of "rape," but in reality for trying to vote or otherwise demanding the legal and inalienable rights and privileges of United States citizenship formally guaranteed them by the Constitution of the United States, rights denied them on the basis of "race," in violation of the Constitution of the United States, the United Nations Charter and the Genocide Convention.

We shall offer proof of economic genocide, or in the words of the Convention, proof of "deliberately inflicting on the group conditions of life calculated to bring about its destruction in whole or in part." We shall prove that such conditions so swell the infant and maternal death rate and the death rate from disease, that the American Negro is deprived, when compared with the remainder of the population of the United States, of eight years of life on the average. . . .

We have proved "killing members of the group" [Article II(a) of the UN Genocide Convention]—but the case after case after case cited does nothing to assuage the helplessness of the innocent Negro trapped at this instant by police in a cell which will be the scene of his death. We have shown "mental and bodily harm" in violation of Article II[(b) of the Genocide Convention but this proof can barely indicate the life-long terror of thousands on thousands of Negroes forced to live under the menace of official violence, mob law and the Ku Klux Klan.[165] We have tried to reveal something of the deliberate infliction "on the group of conditions which bring about its physical destruction in whole or in part" [Article II(c)]—but this cannot convey the hopeless despair of those forced by law to live in conditions of disease and poverty because of race, of birth, of color. We have shown incitements to commit genocide, shown that a conspiracy exists to commit it, and now we can only add that an entire people, not only unprotected by their government but the object of government-inspired violence, reach forth their hands to the General Assembly in appeal. Three hundred years is a long time to wait. And now we ask that world opinion, that the conscience of mankind as symbolized by the General Assembly of the United Nations, turn not a deaf ear to our entreaty.

From *We Charge Genocide: The Historic Petition to the United Nations for Relief from a Crime of the United States Government against the Negro People* (New York: International Publishers, 1970 [originally issued in December 1951]), pp. 4–5, 195–196.

range from about 300,000 to 600,000. . . . Most of the civilian victims were women, infants, and elderly people."[168]

Similar destruction was inflicted on Japan, where some 900,000 civilians died in all. A single night's fire-bombing of Tokyo (March 9–10, 1945) killed 90,000 to 100,000 people —"We scorched and boiled and baked to death more people in Tokyo on that night . . . than went up in vapor at Hiroshima and Nagasaki," the attack's architect, US General Curtis LeMay, proudly declared.[169]

Was this militarily necessary, or at least defensible? Did it shorten the war, and thereby save the lives of large numbers of Allied soldiers? Should daylight bombing have been pursued, even though it was of dubious efficacy and led to the deaths

Figure 1.10 The almost unimaginable devastation inflicted on German and Japanese cities in the Allied area bombing campaigns of 1943–1945 led some observers to allege that a "just war" spilled over into genocide. An aerial view of the German city of Wesel is shown after it was pulverized by Allied bombing and street fighting in February 1945.

Source: USAAF/National Archives and Records Administration/Wikimedia Commons.

Figure 1.11 A destroyed temple amidst the ruins of Nagasaki, Japan, following the atomic bombing of August 9, 1945, three days after Hiroshima. An estimated 70,000 people were killed at Nagasaki, either in the explosion or from burns and radiation sickness afterward. The "conventional" Allied bombing of Tokyo on March 9–10, 1945 killed even more—over 100,000 Japanese, overwhelmingly civilians.

Source: Deutsche Fotothek/Wikimedia Commons.

of more Allied pilots? Or was the bombing *in*defensible, killing more civilians than military requirements could justify?

From a genocide-studies perspective, at issue is whether civilian populations were targeted (1) outside the boundaries of "legitimate" warfare, and (2) on the basis of their ethnic or national identity. Answers have differed, with Leo Kuper arguing that area and atomic bombing *were* genocidal.[170] After a nuanced weighing of the issue, Eric Markusen and David Kopf agreed.[171] Others rejected the genocide framework. The Nuremberg prosecutor Telford Taylor argued that the area bombings "were certainly not 'genocides' within the meaning of the Convention . . . Berlin, London and Tokyo were not bombed because their inhabitants were German, English or Japanese, but because they were *enemy* strongholds. Accordingly, the killing ceased when the war ended and there was no longer any enemy."[172]

The genocide framing is perhaps more persuasively applied in the Japanese case, given the racist propaganda that pervaded the Pacific War, including a common depiction of Japanese as apes and vermin (see Chapter 2). As well, the bombing reached a crescendo when Japan was arguably prostrate before Allied air power—though this would also apply to the destruction of Dresden in Germany, when total Allied victory was already assured. At times in both the German and Japanese cases, but particularly in the latter, the destruction caused by the "thousand-bomber" raids and similar assaults appears to have been inflicted as much to test what was technically and logistically possible as to pursue a coherent military objective. After the Japanese surrendered, General LeMay would muse: "I suppose if I had lost the war, I would have been tried as a war criminal. Fortunately, we were on the winning side."[173]

Fewer ambiguities attach to the atomic bombings of Japan at war's end. Both of the Supreme Allied Commanders, General Dwight D. Eisenhower and General Douglas MacArthur, considered them to be "completely unnecessary."[174] Other options were also available to the US planners—including a softening of the demand for unconditional surrender, and demonstration bombings away from major population centers. The destruction of Nagasaki, in particular, seemed highly gratuitous, since the power of atomic weaponry was already evident, and the Japanese government was in crisis talks on surrender.[175]

The Biafra war

When Nigeria won its independence in 1960, many considered the country one of the likeliest to succeed in all of Africa. Only six years later, however, "Nigeria was a cesspool of corruption and misrule."[176] Members of the relatively prosperous Igbo minority who had migrated to the north found themselves the target of attacks by "educationally disadvantaged Northerners."[177] In 1966, a coup attempt by mostly Igbo army officers produced a counter-coup, and a murderous pogrom was launched against northern Igbo, killing several thousand people. This violence marked the first deployment of a "genocide" discourse by Igbo advocates, "and

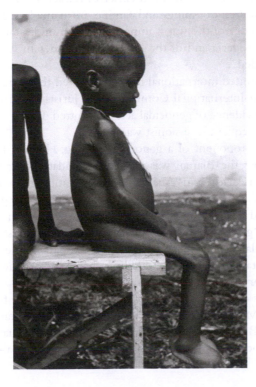

Figure 1.12 The Biafra conflict first established the image of the African child, stomach swollen with starvation, as a humanitarian icon.

Source: Photo by Dr. Lyle Conrad, Public Health Image Library (PHIL)/Wikimedia Commons.

the idea of secession as a protective mechanism for the survival of the Igbo people took hold."[178] In May 1967, an independent state of Biafra was declared in the Igbo-majority southeast. The Nigerian authorities responded by imposing a land blockade as they slowly whittled away at the territory controlled by the Biafran government. By 1968, starvation was rampant, leading US presidential candidate Richard Nixon to declare on the campaign trail:

> Until now efforts to relieve the Biafran people have been thwarted by the desire of the central government of Nigeria to pursue total and unconditional victory and by the fear of the Ibo [sic] people that surrender means wholesale atrocities and genocide. But genocide is what is taking place right now—and starvation is the grim reaper.[179]

The Biafran regime welcomed foreign journalists throughout the war, and imagery of starving Biafrans—above all, children—flooded western mass media. "Even today," wrote Michael Gould, "when asking people in Britain about the war, a common response is: 'Oh! That was the war with the starving, pot-bellied black children?'"[180] The death toll remains a subject of fierce dispute, with estimates ranging from hundreds of thousands to 3.1 million Biafrans killed[181]—in massacres and bombing raids, but mostly from starvation and related causes.

In a groundbreaking special issue of the *Journal of Genocide Research* on the Biafran conflict, Lasse Heerten and A. Dirk Moses noted that "usually, genocide scholars do not even list Biafra among the cases excluded from their definition of genocide."[182] But the authors did not themselves render a verdict, writing only: "Whether the massacres, bombings and famine are named as genocide or not, dealing with the history of the war is important for an understanding of the fabric of postcolonial Nigeria and of the international order in which the conflict emerged and unfolded."[183]

A Nigerian-appointed international mission rejected the genocide charge, but a 1968 report by an International Commission of Jurists (at Biafra's request) *did* point to *prima facie* evidence of genocidal acts committed during both the pogrom of 1966 and the subsequent secessionist war.[184]

The most vocal proponent of a genocide framing, Herbert Ekwe-Ekwe, has argued not only that the Biafran war was "the foundational genocide of post-(European) conquest Africa" and "Africa's most devastating genocide of the twentieth century," but that Nigerian policy toward the Igbo *remains* genocidal.[185] But in the most detailed English-language history of the war, Michael Gould scathingly rejected the "genocide" designation as "completely unjustified"—nothing more than "a popular promotional thought" on the part of the Biafran regime, "which, alongside starvation, death, and killings, helped foster the idea that Biafra should be helped for humanitarian reasons."[186]

Were the actions of the Nigerian state such that a *prima facie* finding of genocide is warranted? My own sense, based on the limited documentation available, is that they were. But I accept Gould's argument that the Biafran authorities exploited the genocide for propaganda purposes, and must also bear a share of responsibility—especially by refusing to accept food aid delivered through Nigerian channels.[187]

UN sanctions against Iraq

Following Saddam Hussein's invasion and occupation of Kuwait in August 1990, the United Nations, spearheaded by the US and Great Britain, imposed sweeping economic sanctions on Iraq. These lasted beyond the 1991 Gulf War and, with modifications, were maintained through to the invasion and occupation of Iraq in 2003. Even under exemptions to the regime, endless and increasing "holds" were placed on humanitarian supplies, allegedly on "security" grounds that must be judged largely specious." . . . The consistent goal" beyond military ones, wrote Joy Gordon, "to reduce Iraq's society and economy to the most primitive conditions possible and keep it in that state indefinitely."[188]

It soon became evident that the sanctions were exacting an enormous human toll on Iraqis, particularly children and nursing mothers. "By 1991, 18 percent of children under five years of age were malnourished; by 1996 that figure had increased to 31 percent; and by 1997, one million children under five were malnourished. As of 1998, 70 percent of Iraqi women were anemic."[189] Asked in May 1996 about statistics indicating 500,000 child deaths from sanctions, US Secretary of State Madeleine Albright notoriously responded: "I think this is a very hard choice. But the price—we think the price is worth it."[190] Is this "infanticide masquerading as policy," as US Congressman David Bonior alleged?[191]

According to a "criminal complaint" filed by former US Attorney General Ramsey Clark before a people's tribunal in Madrid, the policies were indeed nothing short of genocidal:

> The United States and its officials[,] aided and abetted by others[,] engaged in a continuing pattern of conduct . . . to impose, maintain and enforce extreme economic sanctions and a strict military blockade on the people of Iraq for the purpose of injuring the entire population, killing its weakest members, infants, children, the elderly and the chronically ill, by depriving them of medicines, drinking water, food, and other essentials.[192]

The ensuing debate sparked controversy and some rancor among genocide scholars. A majority rejected the idea that genocide can be inflicted by "indirect" means such as sanctions, or assigns the bulk of responsibility for Iraqi suffering to the corrupt and dictatorial regime of Saddam Hussein. Such arguments also emphasized the modifications to the sanctions regime in the 1990s, notably the introduction of an "Oil-for-Food" arrangement by which limited food and humanitarian purchases could be made with Iraqi oil revenues under UN oversight.[193]

Perhaps the most rigorous and recent study of the sanctions regime and its humanitarian effects, Joy Gordon's *Invisible War* (2010), rejected a finding of "genocide or crimes against humanity, as they are defined in international law."[194] But her concluding passages made it clear that she regretted this failure of law to encompass intentional mass atrocities in which "the explicit desire to destroy" cannot be proven. She accused US and British officials, nonetheless, of

> systematically ensur[ing] the conditions that would make Iraq unable to provide decent conditions for human life . . . It is only the type of intent that prevents the Security Council measures, as shaped by the United States, from properly being labeled genocide or extermination. It is not the absence of intent, in the sense of mistake or ignorance. Certainly the U.S. policies were knowing, deliberate, systematic, planned; and the fact that this is not quite sufficient to show culpability tells us more about the limitations of international law than about the good will or good faith of the actors.[195]

In my books and teaching, I have presented the Iraq sanctions regime as a case of genocide. For me, the reluctance to acknowledge sanctions' devastating impact reflects the difficulty that many Western observers have in acknowledging Western-inflicted genocides. In 1998 the UN Humanitarian Coordinator for Iraq, Denis Halliday—who witnessed the impact of sanctions at first hand—resigned in protest over their allegedly genocidal character. "I was made to feel by some that I had crossed an invisible line of impropriety," he stated in the following year. "Since then I have observed that the term 'genocide' offends many in our Western media and establishment circles when it is used to describe the killing of others for which we are responsible, such as in Iraq."[196]

9/11: Terrorism as genocide?

The attacks launched on New York City and Washington, D.C. on the morning of September 11, 2001 constituted the worst terrorist attack in history.[197] Perhaps never outside wartime and natural disasters have so many people been killed virtually at once. But were the attacks, apparently carried out by agents of Osama bin Laden's Al-Qa'eda movement, more than terroristic? Did they in fact constitute genocidal massacres, by Leo Kuper's definition?[198]

In the aftermath of September 11, this question was debated on the H-Genocide academic list. Citing the UN Convention, Peter Ronayne wrote: "[It] seems at least on the surface that the argument could be made that Osama bin Laden and his ilk are intent on destroying, in whole or in part, a national group, and they're more than willing to kill members of the group." Robert Cribb, an Indonesia specialist, differed. "Surely the attacks were terrorist, rather than genocidal. At least 20% of the victims were not American, and it seems pretty likely that the destruction of human life was not for its own sake . . . but to cause terror and anguish amongst a much broader population, which it has done very effectively."[199]

Expanding on Ronayne's reasoning, if we limit ourselves to the UN Convention framing, the 9/11 attacks resulted in "killing members of the group," intentionally and (in most cases) "as such." Also, the "destruction[,] . . . terror and anguish" they inflicted caused serious "bodily [and] mental harm to members"

Figure 1.13 Sunlight streams through the still-smoldering ruins of the World Trade Center in lower Manhattan on September 15, 2001, four days after Al-Qa'eda terrorist attacks on New York and Washington in which nearly 3,000 people were killed, overwhelmingly civilians. Was it an act of genocide?

Source: Kurt Sonnenfeld/FEMA Photo Library/Wikimedia Commons.

of the group. Moreover, it seems likely that the ferocity of the attack was limited only by the means available to the attackers (passenger jets used as missiles). Were nuclear bombs at hand, one suspects that they would be used against civilian populations in the US, and perhaps elsewhere. This brings us close to the Convention requirement that genocidal acts be "committed with intent to destroy, in whole or in part, a national . . . group" (i.e., US Americans).

There was thus, at least, a palpable genocidal impetus and intent in 9/11— one that could yet result in fully-fledged genocide. Only the coming decades will enable us to place the attacks in proper perspective: to decide whether they stand as isolated and discrete events and campaigns, or as opening salvos in a systematic campaign of genocide. Daniel Jonah Goldhagen goes too far in describing "Political Islam" as "currently the one expressly, publicly, and unabashedly genocidal major political movement." It is not a unified movement, nor are its adherents uniformly violent in their programs and actions, as Al-Qa'eda is. But certain strands of political Islam do evince "eliminationist civilizations' hallmark features: tyrannical regimes, eliminationist-oriented leaders, transformative eschatological visions, populaces brimming with eliminationist beliefs and passions, a sense of impunity, and eliminationism at the center of its normal political repertoire and existing practice."[200] At the time of writing, there is no need to look further than the murderous militants of Islamic State (IS) in Iraq, Syria, and Libya to observe this genocidal ideology in proudly-proclaimed practice. See Box 4a for further discussion.[201]

Structural and institutional violence

In the 1960s, peace researchers such as Johan Galtung began exploring the phenomenon of "structural violence": destructive relations embedded in social and economic systems. Some commentators argue that certain forms of structural and institutional violence are genocidal, "deliberately inflicting on [a designated] group conditions of life calculated to bring about its physical destruction in whole or in part," in the language of the UN Convention. For example, the Indian scholar and activist Vandana Shiva has described "the globalization of food and agriculture systems" under neoliberal trade regimes as "equivalent to the ethnic cleansing of the poor, the peasantry, and small farmers of the Third World. . . . Globalization of trade in agriculture implies genocide."[202] Jean Ziegler, the UN Special Rapporteur on the Right to Food, stated in October 2005: "Every child who dies of hunger in today's world is the victim of assassination," and referred to the *daily* death by starvation of 100,000 people as a "massacre of human beings through malnutrition."[203] My own work on gender and genocide

Figure 1.14 Genocide is usually represented as an *event*, and even recent scholarship on genocide as a "process" tends to focus on the structured evolution of a given "case" (the popular case-study format, not avoided in this book, is also biased in this respect). But can genocide take the form of *structural violence*, and vice-versa? Can we speak, for example, of "poorcide" (p. 37) against the world's most underprivileged people, like this child in a Coptic Christian neighborhood of Cairo, Egypt? How are relationships of structural violence evident in the daily practices and exclusions of more privileged societies, as suggested by Nancy Scheper-Hughes's concept of a "genocidal continuum"? (See Chapter 11, pp. 590–591)

Source: Author's photo, 1989.

(see Chapter 13) explores "gendercidal institutions" such as female infanticide and even maternal mortality, suggesting that they are forms of gender-selective mass killing, hence genocidal.

Much of structural violence is diffuse, part of the "background" of human relations. It is accordingly difficult to ascribe clear agency to phenomena such as racism, sexism, and other forms of discrimination. International relations scholar Kal Holsti rejects global-systemic visions of structural violence, like Galtung's, as "just too fuzzy," and evincing a tendency to "place all blame for the ills of the Third World on the first one." In Holsti's view, this overlooks the essential role of many Third World leaders and elites in the suffering and violence experienced by their populations. "It also fails to account for many former Third World countries that today have standards of living and welfare higher than those found in many 'industrial' countries."[204]

These points are well taken. Nonetheless, in my opinion, genocide studies should move to incorporate an understanding of structural and institutional violence as genocidal mechanisms. If our overriding concern is to prevent avoidable death and suffering, how can we shut our eyes to "the Holocaust of Neglect" that malnutrition, ill-health, and structural discrimination impose upon huge swathes of humanity?[205] Are we not in danger of "catching the small fry and letting the big fish loose," as Galtung put it?[206]

Moreover, when it comes to human institutions, it is not necessarily the case that responsibility and agency are impossible to establish. Consider the neoliberal economic policies and institutions that shape the destinies of much of the world's poor. Economist Jeffrey Sachs played a key role in designing the "structural adjustment" measures imposed by the World Bank and International Monetary Fund (IMF) around the Third World and former Soviet bloc. He later turned against such prescriptions, commenting in 2002 that they had "squeezed [targeted] countries to the point where their health systems are absolutely unable to function. Education systems are broken down, and *there's a lot of death associated with the collapse of public health and the lack of access to medicine.*"[207] In such cases, as Holsti has pointed out, "distinct agents with distinct policies and identifiable consequences" may be discerned, and moral and legal responsibility may likewise be imputed.[208]

In a recent essay on the structural genocide question, I argue that a claim of genocide related to structural and institutional forms of violations was *most* sustainable where evidence of debility and death as a result of the event or phenomenon in question is strong; where the causal chain is direct rather than indirect, and agency centralized and individualized rather than decentralized or diffuse; where actors' awareness of the impact of their policies is high; and where a meaningful measure of voluntary agency[209] among victims is lacking. I argue in the same essay that a discourse of genocide and structural/institution violence "deserves to be taken seriously, and moved closer to the mainstream of genocide studies."[210] Among other things, as historian Norbert Finzsch has suggested, it could serve as a useful corrective to the fact that "genocides in modern history tend to be perceived as chronologically limited occurrences that punctuate time, rather than as repetitive and enduring processes.[211]

■ IS GENOCIDE EVER JUSTIFIED?

This question may provoke a collective intake of breath.[212] Examining ourselves honestly, though, most people have probably experienced at least a twinge of sympathy with those who commit acts that some people consider genocidal. Others have gone much further, to outright *celebration* of genocide (see, e.g., Chapter 3). Is any of this justifiable, morally or legally?

In one sense, genocide clearly *is* justified—that is, people often seek to justify it. Perhaps the most common strategy of exculpation and celebration is a utilitarian one, applied most frequently in the case of indigenous peoples (Chapter 3). These populations have been depicted stereotypically as "an inertial drag on future agendas,"[213] failing to properly exploit the lands they inhabit and the rich resources underfoot.[214] A latent economic potential, viewed through the lens of the Protestant work ethic and a capitalist hunger for profit, is held to warrant confiscation of territories, and marginalization or annihilation of their populations.

Those subaltern populations sometimes rose up in rebellion against colonial authority, and those rebellions frequently evoke sympathy—though occasionally they have taken a genocidal form. To the cases of Upper Peru (Bolivia) in the late eighteenth century, and the Caste War of Yucatán in the nineteenth, we might add the revolution in the French colony of Saint-Domingue that, in 1804, created Haiti as the world's first free black republic. This was a revolt not of indigenous people, but of slaves. It succeeded in expelling the whites, albeit at a devastating cost from which Haiti never fully recovered. As in Bolivia and Yucatán, rebellion and counter-rebellion assumed the form of unbridled race war.[215] Yet this particular variant finds many sympathizers. The great scholar of the Haitian revolution, C.L.R. James, described in the 1930s "the complete massacre" of Saint-Domingue's whites: "The population, stirred to fear at the nearness of the counter-revolution, killed all [whites] with every possible brutality." But James's appraisal of the events excused the race war on the grounds of past atrocities and exploitation by whites. Acknowledging that the victims were defenseless, James lamented only the damage done to the souls of the killers, and their future political culture:

> The massacre of the whites was a tragedy; *not for the whites.* For these old slaveowners, those who burnt a little powder in the arse of a Negro, who buried him alive for insects to eat . . . and who, as soon as they got the chance, began their old cruelties again; for these there is no need to waste one tear or one drop of ink. *The tragedy was for the blacks and the Mulattoes* [who did the killing]. It was not policy but revenge, and revenge has no place in politics. *The whites were no longer to be feared*, and such purposeless massacres degrade and brutalise a [perpetrator] population, especially one which was just beginning as a nation and had had so bitter a past. . . . Haiti suffered terribly from the resulting isolation. Whites were banished from Haiti for generations, and the unfortunate country, ruined economically, its population lacking in social culture, had its inevitable difficulties doubled by this massacre.[216]

Figure 1.15 "Burning of the Plaine du Cap—Massacre of Whites by the Blacks," August 1791. This 1832 French depiction of slaves slaughtering Europeans during the uprising in Saint-Domingue/ Haiti (1791–1804) is predictably slanted. For long stretches of the revolutionary period, all sides waged no-holds-barred race war. But the stylized image is not inaccurate in itself. It indicates what elites might expect when underclasses violently rebel—here, against genocidal hyperexploitation on the plantations of the "Plaine du Cap." Our sympathies will likely lie with the oppressed. But we should recognize that out of desperation and a desire for vengeance, subaltern populations frequently employ genocidal strategies mirroring those of their oppressors.

Source: France Militaire/Wikimedia Commons.

Bolivia, Mexico, and Haiti are examples of what Nicholas Robins and I call *subaltern genocide*, or "genocides by the oppressed."[217] In general, genocidal assaults that contain a morally plausible element of revenge, retribution, or revolutionary usurpation are less likely to be condemned, and are often welcomed. Allied fire-bombing and nuclear-bombing of German and Japanese cities, which Leo Kuper and other scholars considered genocidal, are often justified on the grounds that "they started it" (that is, the German and Japanese governments launched mass bombings of civilians before the Allies did). The fate of ethnic-German civilians in Czechoslovakia, Poland, and other Central European countries at the end of the Second World War, and in its aftermath, likewise attracted little empathy until recent times—again because, when it came to mass expulsions of populations and attendant atrocities, the Germans too had "started it." The quarter of a million Serbs expelled from the Krajina and Eastern Slavonia regions of Croatia in 1995 (Chapter 8) now constitute the largest refugee population in Europe; but their plight evokes no great outrage, because of an assignation of collective guilt to Serbs for the Bosnian genocide. (The trend was evident again after the 1999 Kosovo war, when Serb civilians in the province were targeted for murder by ethnic Albanian extremists.)[218]

Even the September 11, 2001 terrorist attacks on the World Trade Center and Pentagon, which could be considered genocidal massacres (see pp. 60–61), secured the equivocal or enthusiastic support of hundreds of millions of people worldwide. Americans were deemed to have gotten what was coming to them after decades of US imperial intervention. A similar vocabulary of justification and celebration may be found among many Arabs, and other Palestinian supporters, after massacres of Jewish civilians in Israel.

Apart from cases of subaltern genocide, the defenders and deniers of some of history's worst genocides often justify the killings on the grounds of *legitimate defensive or retributory action against traitors and subversives.* The Turkish refusal to acknowledge the Armenian genocide (Chapter 4) depicts atrocities or "excesses" as the inevitable results of an Armenian rebellion aimed at undermining the Ottoman state. Apologists for Hutu Power in Rwanda claim the genocide of 1994 was nothing more than the continuation of "civil war" or "tribal conflict"; or that Hutus were seeking to preempt the kind of genocide at Tutsi hands that Hutus had suffered in neighboring Burundi (Chapter 9). Sympathizers of the Nazi regime in Germany sometimes present the invasion of the USSR as a preemptive, defensive war against the Bolshevik threat to Western civilization (Box 6a). Even the Nazis' demonology of a Jewish "cancer" and "conspiracy" resonated deeply with millions of highly educated Germans at the time, and fuels Holocaust denial to the present, though as a fringe phenomenon.

All these cases of denial need to be rejected and confronted (see Chapter 14). *But are there instances when genocide may occur in self-defense?* The Rome Statute of the International Criminal Court abjures criminal proceedings against "the person [who] acts reasonably to defend himself or herself or another person or . . . against an imminent and unlawful use of force, in a manner proportionate to the degree of danger to the person or the other person or property protected." Citing this, William Schabas has noted that "reprisal and military necessity are not formally prohibited by international humanitarian law." However, "reprisal as a defense must be proportional, and on this basis its application to genocide would seem inconceivable."[219] But Schabas has a tendency, in defending his "hard" and predictably legalistic interpretation of the UN Convention, to use terms such as "inconceivable," "obviously incompatible," "totally unnecessary," "definitely inappropriate." Sometimes these may close off worthwhile discussions, such as: What is the acceptable range of responses to genocide? Can genocidal counter-assault be "proportional" in any meaningful sense?

A large part of the problem is that the plausibility we attach to reprisals and retribution frequently reflects our political identifications. We have a harder time condemning those with whom we sympathize, even when their actions are atrocious. Consciously or unconsciously, we distinguish "worthy" from "unworthy" victims.[220] And we may be less ready to label as genocidal the atrocities that our chosen "worthies" commit.

On a personal note, I find myself wrestling with this issue most vexedly in the case of the Islamic State (IS) movement, which burst onto the geopolitical and genocidal map in summer 2014 (see Chapter 4a). I am mistrustful of language like US Secretary of State John Kerry's, in the wake of the Paris mass shootings of November 2015, referring to ISIS militants as "psychopathic monsters."[221] But if the shoe fits ... Many of us across the political spectrum have likely harbored secret fantasies, as I have, of pressing a button and vaporizing all black-flag-waving ISIS *génocidaires* and *génocidaires*-in-training between Tunisia and Afghanistan. Would this be a tragic loss to humanity and civilization, of the kind that Raphael Lemkin feared? Or might the extermination of the members of this criminal conspiracy be a decided gain, and a protection for those minority peoples who would otherwise disappear into the ISIS meat-grinder? But surely any such annihilatory enterprise would meet the requirements of the Genocide Convention for the "crime of crimes," as do the cases I cited of subaltern genocide. ISIS is certainly a distinct religious sect as well as a political movement—the distinction is anyway meaningless, as the term "theocracy" implies. How far are my sentiments, then, from the kind of crusading, militantly anti-Islamic rants that I criticize elsewhere (pp. 121–122)? Far enough to preserve such meaningful distinctions as combatant and civilian, I hope. But this far from resolves the issue, or the moral quandary.

FURTHER STUDY

Hirad Abtahi and Philippa Webb, eds., *The Genocide Convention: The Travaux Préparatoires* (2 vols.). Leiden: Martinus Nijhoff Publishers, 2008. An exhaustive compendium (2,200 pages in total) of the 1946–1948 drafting sessions and negotiations for the UN Genocide Convention. Includes reams of dry procedural material, but also the fascinating debates of the Ad Hoc Committee on Genocide over core issues such as the role of the state in genocide, physical/biological versus cultural forms of genocide, and the inclusion (finally exclusion) of political groups.

Alex Alvarez, *Governments, Citizens, and Genocide: A Comparative and Interdisciplinary Approach*. Bloomington, IN: Indiana University Press, 2001. A tautly-written analysis from a sociological and criminological perspective. See also *Genocidal Crimes*.

Paul Bartrop and Steven L. Jacobs, *Fifty Key Thinkers on the Holocaust and Genocide*. London: Routledge, 2010. Informative short essays on leading figures in Holocaust research and comparative genocide studies.

Donald W. Beachler, *The Genocide Debate: Politicians, Academics, and Victims*. New York: Palgrave MacMillan, 2011. A commendably balanced and fair-minded introduction to some controversial themes in genocide studies.

Donald Bloxham and A. Dirk Moses, eds., *The Oxford Handbook of Genocide Studies*. Oxford: Oxford University Press, 2010. Indispensable, erudite essays, with richly-detailed attention to the pre-modern and early-modern periods, as well as twentieth-century cases. Probably the best book to accompany or replace this one in graduate-level courses.

Frank Chalk and Kurt Jonassohn, *The History and Sociology of Genocide*. New Haven, CT: Yale University Press, 1990. Early and eclectic treatment, still widely read and cited.

John Cooper, *Raphael Lemkin and the Struggle for the Genocide Convention*. London: Palgrave Macmillan, 2008. The first full-length biography of Lemkin and his extraordinary campaign, competently handled.

John Cox, *To Kill a People: Genocide in the Twentieth Century*. Oxford: Oxford University Press, 2016. The best short introduction to the subject: wide-ranging, well-informed, and fluently written, with an excellent bibliographic essay.

Lawrence Davidson, *Cultural Genocide*. New Brunswick, NJ: Rutgers University Press, 2012. Groundbreaking short survey of "the purposeful weakening and ultimate destruction of cultural values and practices of feared out-groups." Includes chapter-length treatments of American Indians, Jews in Russia, Israel—Palestine, and Tibet.

Robert Gellately and Ben Kiernan, eds., *The Specter of Genocide: Mass Murder in Historical Perspective*. Cambridge: Cambridge University Press, 2003. One of the richest edited volumes on genocide; diverse in scope and consistent in quality.

Daniel Jonah Goldhagen, *Worse Than War: Genocide, Eliminationism, and the Ongoing Assault on Humanity*. New York: Basic Books, 2009. Usefully situates genocide within a broader framework of "eliminationist" ideologies and strategies.

Alexander Laban Hinton, Thomas La Pointe, and Douglas Irvin-Erickson, eds., *Hidden Genocides: Power, Knowledge, Memory*. New Brunswick, NJ: Rutgers University Press, 2014. A short but provocative study of genocides usually marginalized in the "canon." Includes my chapter, "The [African] Great Lakes Genocides: Hidden Histories, Hidden Precedents."

Adam Jones, ed., *New Directions in Genocide Research*. London: Routledge, 2012. Highlights contributions from the new generation of genocide scholars.

Ben Kiernan, *Blood and Soil: A World History of Genocide and Extermination from Sparta to Darfur*. New Haven, CT: Yale University Press, 2007. The magnum opus of the director of Yale University's Genocide Studies Program.

Leo Kuper, *Genocide: Its Political Use in the Twentieth Century*. Harmondsworth: Penguin, 1981. The foundational text of comparative genocide studies, still in print.

Raphael Lemkin, *Lemkin on Genocide*, ed. Steven Leonard Jacobs. Lanham, MD: Lexington Books, 2012. At last, Lemkin's unfinished but epoch-spanning history of genocide, ably edited and introduced by Steven Jacobs.

Raphael Lemkin, *Totally Unofficial: The Autobiography of Raphael Lemkin*, ed. Donna-Lee Frieze. New Haven, CT: Yale University Press, 2013. With the publication of Lemkin's autobiography, previously available only in excerpts and archives, the core of Lemkin's corpus on genocide is now complete (see *Lemkin on Genocide*, above).

Mark Levene, *Genocide in the Age of the Nation State, Vol. 1: The Meaning of Genocide* and *Vol. 2: The Rise of the West and the Coming of Genocide* (London: I.B. Tauris, 2005); *The Crisis of Genocide, Vol. 1: Devastation: The European Rimlands 1912–1938* and *Vol. 2: Annihilation: The European Rimlands 1939–1953* (Oxford: Oxford University Press, 2013). Levene's four-volume masterwork is the most nourishing and mind-expanding work of genocide studies. The first two volumes trace the rise of modern genocide and link it conceptually and historically to European state-building and processes of imperialism/colonialism. The concluding installments make a seminal contribution to the literature on the European "Rimlands" in an age of toxic nationalisms and world wars (see Box 2.3). Frustratingly, both volumes were unavailable in paperback nearly three years after publication.

Jens Meierhenrich, ed., *Genocide: A Reader*. Oxford: Oxford University Press, 2014. Appealingly diverse, bite-sized selections from the literature; another volume worth considering to accompany this one in the classroom (see also Totten and Parsons, eds., below).

David L. Nersessian, *Genocide and Political Groups*. Oxford: Oxford University Press, 2010. The first in-depth study of the controversial exclusion of political groups from the Genocide Convention, with proposals for reform.

Samantha Power, *"A Problem from Hell": America and the Age of Genocide*. New York: Basic Books, 2002. Power's multiple award-winning work focuses on the US response to various genocides.

John Quigley, *The Genocide Convention: An International Law Analysis*. London: Ashgate, 2006. Stimulating analysis of the Convention, especially provocative on framings of genocidal intent.

Nehemiah Robinson, *The Genocide Convention: A Commentary*. New York: Institute of Jewish Affairs, 1960. If you can find this book it will be on a dusty shelf, but Robinson's short early work provides an incisive legal commentary on the 1948 UN Convention and the debates that attended its drafting.

Richard L. Rubenstein, *The Age of Triage: Fear and Hope in an Overcrowded World*. Boston, MA: Beacon Press, 1983. Groundbreaking study of the elimination of unwanted populations.

Martin Shaw, *What is Genocide?*, 2nd edn. Cambridge: Polity Press, 2015. Thoughtful examination of what, exactly, genocide "destroys," revised and updated to deepen the conceptual discussion.

Dinah Shelton, ed., *Encyclopedia of Genocide and Crimes Against Humanity* (3 vols). Detroit, MI: Macmillan Reference, 2005. Massive and admirably inclusive; so far the leading work of this type.

Dan Stone, ed., *The Historiography of Genocide*. London: Palgrave Macmillan, 2008. Wide-ranging compilation examining core themes of the genocide studies literature.

Samuel Totten and William S. Parsons, eds., *Centuries of Genocide: Essays and Eyewitness Accounts* (4th edn). New York: Routledge, 2013. Unparalleled collection of analyses and testimonies, richer than ever in this edition. From an instructor's perspective, perhaps the best companion to the book you're reading.

Samuel Totten and Paul R. Bartrop, eds., *The Genocide Studies Reader*. London: Routledge, 2009. A comprehensive selection of essays from the literature. As Totten/Parsons (above) is ideal for undergraduate courses, this is a highly useful volume for graduate students.

Hannibal Travis, *Genocide in the Middle East: The Ottoman Empire, Iraq, and Sudan*. Durham, NC: Carolina Academic Press, 2010. Broader in scope than its title suggests: one of the most meticulously documented of the major histories of genocide, with a solid focus on the contemporary period.

Benjamin Whitaker, *Revised and Updated Report on the Question of the Prevention and Punishment of the Crime of Genocide* (The Whitaker Report). ECOSOC (United Nations), July 2, 1985, available in full at www.preventgenocide.org/prevent/UNdocs/whitaker. A significant attempt to rethink and revise the UN Genocide Convention.[222]

Matthew White, *Atrocitology: Humanity's 100 Deadliest Achievements*. Edinburgh: Canongate, 2011. Not entirely reliable, but certainly the most encyclopedic compendium of mass atrocities throughout history, and amusing (!) to boot.

NOTES

1 Leo Kuper, *Genocide: Its Political Use in the Twentieth Century* (Harmondsworth: Penguin, 1981), p. 9.

2 Raphael Lemkin, *Lemkin on Genocide*, ed. Steven Leonard Jacobs (Lanham, MD: Lexington Books, 2012), p. 20.

3 Frank Chalk and Kurt Jonassohn, *The History and Sociology of Genocide: Analyses and Case Studies* (New Haven, CT: Yale University Press, 1990), p. 64.

4 Quoted in Chalk and Jonassohn, *The History and Sociology of Genocide*, p. 58. Notably, when Troy did finally fall, women and girl children were spared extermination, and instead abducted as slaves (Israel Charny, ed., *The Encyclopedia of Genocide* [Santa Barbara, CA: ABC-CLIO, 1999], p. 273). See the discussion of gender and genocide in Chapter 13.

5 Quoted in Lemkin, *Lemkin on Genocide*, p. 90 (citing L. Delaporte, *Mesopotamia: The Babylonian and Assyrian Civilization*, 1925).

6 Rick Weiss, "Climate Link to Neanderthal Demise Abates, *Washington Post*, September 13, 2007, www.washingtonpost.com/wp-dyn/content/article/2007/09/12/AR2007091202323.html.

7 Larry O'Hanlon, "Shocking New Theory: Humans Hunted, Ate Neanderthals," *NBCNews.com*, May 21, 2013, www.nbcnews.com/science/shocking-new-theory-humans-hunted-ate-neanderthals-6C10012944.

8 Pat Shipman, *The Invaders: How Humans and Their Dogs Drove Neanderthals to Extinction*, 3rd edn. (Cambridge, MA: The Belknap Press, 2015).

9 James Gorman, "Prehistoric Massacre Hints at War Among Hunter-Gatherers," *The New York Times*, January 20, 2016, www.nytimes.com/2016/01/21/science/prehistoric-massacre-ancient-humans-lake-turkana-kenya.html.

10 Chalk and Jonassohn, *The History and Sociology of Genocide*, p. 28.

11 Helen Fein, *Genocide: A Sociological Perspective* (London: Sage, 1993), p. 26.

12 Karen Armstrong, *A History of God;* quoted in Roy F. Baumeister, *Evil: Inside Human Violence and Cruelty* (New York: W.H. Freeman, 1999), p. 171. For other examples of Old Testament genocide, see Chalk and Jonassohn, *The History and Sociology of Genocide*, pp. 62–63; Eric D. Weitz, *A Century of Genocide: Utopias of Race and Nation* (Princeton, NJ: Princeton University Press, 2003), p. 18, citing Joshua's "destruction by the edge of the sword [of] all in the city [of Jericho], both men and women, young and old, oxen, sheep, and donkeys."

13 "Genocide, God, and the Bible," http://stripe.colorado.edu/~morristo/genocide.html.

14 Mark Levene, *Genocide in the Age of the Nation State, Vol. 1: The Meaning of Genocide* (London: I.B. Tauris, 2005), p. 151.

15 Cited in Louis W. Cable, "The Bloody Bible," *Freethought Today*, June/July 1997. http://ffrf.org/legacy/fttoday/1997/june_july97/cable.html. See also the numerous examples of "God-ordered genocide" cited in Bill Moyers, "9/11 and the Sport of God," *CommonDreams.org*, September 9, 2005, www.commondreams.org/views/2005/09/09/911-and-sport-god.

16 Numbers 31, Revised Standard Edition, quoted in Daniel Chirot and Clark McCauley, *Why Not Kill Them All? The Logic and Prevention of Mass Political Murder* (Princeton, NJ: Princeton University Press, 2006), pp. 29–30. For discussion and debates over biblical genocide, see J. Harold Ellens, ed., *The Destructive Power of Religion: Violence in Judaism, Christianity, and Islam* (Westport, CT: Praeger, 2007); Paul Copan and Matthew Flannagan, *Did God Really Command Genocide? Coming to Terms with the Justice of God* (Grand Rapids, MI: Baker Books, 2014); C.S. Cowles *et al.*, *Show Them No Mercy: Four Views on God and Canaanite Genocide* (Grand Rapids, MI: Zondervan, 2003); from an openly Christian-apologist perspective, Douglas S. Earl, *The Joshua Delusion? Rethinking Genocide in the Bible* (Eugene, OR: Wipf & Stock, 2011); Paul Copan, *Is God a Moral Monster? Making Sense of the Old Testament God* (Ada, MI: Baker Publishing Group, 2012). On religiously-inspired terrorism and genocide in general, see Omer Bartov and Phyllis Mack, eds., *In God's Name: Genocide and Religion in the Twentieth Century* (New York: Berghahn Books, 2001); Steven Leonard Jacobs, ed., *Confronting Genocide: Judaism, Christianity, Islam* (Lanham, MD: Lexington Books, 2009); James W. Jones, *Blood That Cries Out From the Earth: The Psychology of Religious Terrorism* (Oxford: Oxford University Press, 2012).

17 Hans van Wees wrote that "if a distinction by gender and age was made, it was because communities were conceived of as consisting essentially of adult men. Women, children, and the aged were mere dependants. The death of the men amounted to the annihilation of the community; killing the others was not necessary," and often they could be usefully employed as slaves. Van Wees, "Genocide in the Ancient World," in Donald Bloxham and A. Dirk Moses, eds., *The Oxford Handbook of Genocide Studies* (Oxford: Oxford University Press, 2013), p. 245.

18 For a nuanced exploration of classical strategies of genocide (and non-genocide), see van Wees, ibid., pp. 239–258.

19 Ben Kiernan, "The First Genocide: Carthage, 146 BC," *Diogenes*, 203 (2004), pp. 27–39.

20 Ibid., p. 202.

21 See "The Albigensians," in Lemkin, *Lemkin on Genocide*, pp. 59–81; Sean Martin, *The Cathars: The Rise and Fall of the Great Heresy* (Harpenden: Pocket Essentials, 2014), especially chs. 3–4.

22 Andrew Bell-Fialkoff writes that the First Crusade (1096–1099) left "a trail of blood and destruction, throughout the Rhine and the Moselle valleys, as well as in Prague and Hungary. Entire communities, perhaps tens of thousands of people in all, were wiped out. The Crusade culminated in a wholesale massacre of all non-Christians in Jerusalem." Bell-Fialkoff, *Ethnic Cleansing* (New York: St. Martin's Griffin, 1999), p. 13.

23 Matthew White, *Atrocitology: Humanity's 100 Deadliest Achievements* (Edinburgh: Canongate, 2011). The full list of 100 multicides is at pp. 529–531. The "self-described atrocitologist" quote is from Steven Pinker's foreword.

24 Eric S. Margolis, *War at the Top of the World: The Struggle for Afghanistan, Kashmir, and Tibet* (New York: Routledge, 2001), p. 155. In Hannibal Travis's summary: "After 1200 CE, Genghis Khan led a campaign through Asia that destroyed millions of lives and many ancient cities. In Beijing in 1219, the Mongols slaughtered thousands of people and set the city ablaze, causing it to burn for a month. . . . In present-day Konye-Urgench in Turkmenistan, then called Gurganj, a contingent from Genghis Khan's army, with 100,000 Mongols in all, killed over a million people, in house-to-house fighting that burned large sections of the city. . . . " Matthew White recorded that when Genghis Khan "finally beat the Tatars, he is said to have lined up all of the men and boys alongside a wagon and ordered his followers to kill every Tatar male who stood taller than the lynch pin of the wagon wheel." According to Travis, Genghis Khan's grandson, Hulagu Khan, "reached Baghdad in the 1250s and massacred 100,000 to two million people there, seizing enormous amounts of gold and treasure, destroying libraries, and soiling and ruining mosques. Mesopotamia's irrigation system was severely damaged, leaving a legacy of dependency on imported food that would have catastrophic consequences during U.N. sanctions in the 1990s." Travis, *Genocide in the Middle East:*

The Ottoman Empire, Iraq, and Sudan (Durham, NC: Carolina Academic Press, 2010), pp. 167–168; White, *Atrocitology*, p. 117.

25 Lemkin, *Lemkin on Genocide*, p. 115.

26 Hitler quoted in Cathie Carmichael, *Genocide before the Holocaust* (New Haven, CT: Yale University Press, 2009), p. 102.

27 See Reynald Secher, *A French Genocide: The Vendée*, trans. George Holoch (Notre Dame, IN: University of Notre Dame Press, 2003); Mark Levene, "The Vendée—A Paradigm Shift?," in Levene, *Genocide in the Age of the Nation State, Vol. 2: The Rise of the West and the Coming of Genocide* (London: I.B. Tauris, 2005), pp. 103–161. This section also draws on Adam Jones, "Why Gendercide? Why Root-and-Branch? A Comparison of the Vendée Uprising of 1793–94 and the Bosnian War of the 1990s," *Journal of Genocide Research*, 8: 1 (2006), pp. 9–25. For an interesting reportage of travel in the Vendée region, including sites connected with the genocide, see Anthony Peregrine, "France: Vengeance on the Vendée," *The Telegraph*, August 18, 2009, www. telegraph.co.uk/travel/destinations/europe/france/6048204/France-Vengeance-on-the-Vendee.html. The war and atrocities are depicted in Victor Hugo's renowned final novel, *Ninety-Three* (1874), available online at https://en.wikisource.org/wiki/Ninety-three.

28 Cited in Alain Gérard, *"Par principe d'humanité . . ." La Terreur et la Vendée* (Paris: Librairie Artheme Fayard, 1999), p. 295.

29 Cited in Arno J. Mayer, *The Furies: Violence and Terror in the French and Russian Revolutions* (Princeton, NJ: Princeton University Press, 2000), p. 353.

30 In the estimation of France's greatest historian, Jules Michelet; quoted in Mayer, *The Furies*, p. 325.

31 Quoted in Secher, *A French Genocide*, p. 132.

32 Westermann quoted in David A. Bell, *The First Total War: Napoleon's Europe and the Birth of Warfare As We Know It* (Boston, MA: Houghton Mifflin Company, 2007), p. 173.

33 Mayer, *The Furies*, p. 340.

34 For a perceptive analysis of the French Revolutionary and Napoleonic Wars as a "watershed" in the transition between "the uncoordinated, retributive massacres of the *ancien régime*, and the bureaucratized, purposeful massacres of the latter nineteenth and twentieth centuries," see Philip G. Dwyer, "Violence and the Revolutionary and Napoleonic Wars: Massacre, Conquest and the Imperial Enterprise," *Journal of Genocide Research*, 15: 2 (2013), pp. 117–131 (quote p. 127).

35 Bell, *The First Total War*, p. 184, emphasis added. Bell is skeptical of the "genocide" label for the Vendée (p. 158), but on grounds that are more restrictive (emphasizing ethnicity) than the definition and framing deployed in this book.

36 Michael R. Mahoney, "The Zulu Kingdom as a Genocidal and Post-genocidal Society, c. 1810 to the Present," *Journal of Genocide Research*, 5: 2 (2003), p. 263.

37 Chalk and Jonassohn, *The History and Sociology of Genocide*, p. 223.

38 Ibid., pp. 224–225, citing Eugene Victor Walter, *Terror and Resistance: A Study of Political Violence*.

39 Mahoney, "The Zulu Kingdom," p. 254.

40 Chalk and Jonassohn, *The History and Sociology of Genocide*, pp. 224–225.

41 Mahoney, "The Zulu Kingdom," p. 255.

42 See *PreventGenocide.org*, "A Crime without a Name," www.preventgenocide.org/genocide/crimewithoutaname.htm.

43 John Cooper, *Raphael Lemkin and the Struggle for the Genocide Convention* (London: Palgrave Macmillan, 2008), p. 213.

44 Raphael Lemkin, *Totally Unofficial: The Autobiography of Raphael Lemkin* (New Haven, CT: Yale University Press, 2013), pp. 1–2.

45 Ibid., p. 2.

46 Ibid., p. 17.

47 Lemkin, *Lemkin on Genocide*, pp. 157–185, 343–370.

48 Michael Ignatieff puts it well: "[Lemkin's] self-identification as a Jew was always relatively weak, and his objective was never to save the Jewish people from genocide but mankind as a whole. This is why, when other Jews who survived the Holocaust became Zionists and put their faith in a defensible state of their own, Lemkin put his faith instead in international law and a convention that would proscribe the crime forever for every victim group." Ignatieff adds: "This does not mean he was not shaped, through and through, by Jewish fate, in his case, by the glory and the burden of being born a Jew in what the historian Timothy Snyder has taught us to call the Bloodlands [see Box 2.3], the killing fields of Byelorussia, Lithuania and eastern Poland." Ignatieff, "Raphael Lemkin and Genocide," 2013, www.michaelignatieff.ca/assets/pdfs/LemkinandGeno cide2013.pdf, pp. 13–14.

49 Tehlirian's testimony at his trial—that he personally witnessed the murder of his family members on a death march—was a cover story. He did indeed lose loved ones to the Turkish genocide, but this occurred while he was fighting against the Turks, as an Armenian revolutionary attached to Russian forces. He subsequently joined a hit squad organized by the Dashnak Party that worked to track down and assassinate perpetrators of the genocide, especially those convicted *in absentia* by the postwar Constantinople tribunal (see Chapters 4, 15). For a full account of the assassination campaign and Tehlirian's role, see Eric Bogosian, *Operation Nemesis: The Assassination Plot That Avenged the Armenian Genocide* (New York: Little, Brown and Company, 2015).

50 Lemkin quoted in Travis, *Genocide in the Middle East*, p. 28.

51 Lemkin quoted in Power, *"A Problem from Hell,"* p. 21.

52 Ibid., p. 58.

53 "Of particular interest to Lemkin were the reflections of George Eastman, who said he had settled upon 'Kodak' as the name for his new camera because: 'First. It is short. Second. It is not capable of mispronunciation. Third. It does not resemble anything in the art and cannot be associated with anything in the art except the Kodak.'" Power, *"A Problem from Hell,"* pp. 42–43. It had, Eastman said, a "rigorous and distinctive personality" (quoted in Lemkin, *Lemkin on Genocide*, p. 24).

54 Lemkin, *Axis Rule in Occupied Europe*, p. 79. Michael Ignatieff called Axis Rule "one of the very rare examples of scholarship as heroism: patient, dogged empirical research by a legal scholar, whose purpose is to discern the infernal logic of despotism." Ignatieff, "The Legacy of Raphael Lemkin," address to the United States Holocaust Memorial Museum, December 13, 2000, www.ushmm.org/confront-genocide/ speakers-and-events/all-speakers-and-events/the-legacy-of-raphael-lemkin.

55 On this point, see Thomas M. Butcher, "A 'Synchronized Attack': On Raphael Lemkin's Holistic Conception of Genocide," *Journal of Genocide Research*, 15: 3 (2013), pp. 253–271.

56 David Nersessian, citing research by Barbara Harff and Ted Gurr (see Chapter 12), estimates that "in the four decades following World War II, the destruction of opposition groups on political grounds outnumbered destruction on xenophobic or hegemonical grounds by four to one." Nersessian, *Genocide and Political Groups* (Oxford: Oxford University Press, 2010), p. 189.

57 See Douglas Irvin-Erickson, "Genocide, the 'Family of Mind' and the Romantic Signature of Raphael Lemkin," *Journal of Genocide Research*, 15: 3 (2013), pp. 273–296.

58 Stephen Holmes, "Looking Away," *London Review of Books*, November 14, 2002 (review of Power, *"A Problem from Hell"*).

59 See also Mark Levene's interesting observations: "Like [Johann] Herder a century and a half earlier, Lemkin's starting point was to both accept and celebrate the existence of primordial national groups as an ostensible fact of humanity's natural history. Like Herder, too, what mattered about this 'reality' was enabling the sum of the nations' diverse parts to operate within an ecumenical discourse, the consequence of which would be the creation of a truly cosmopolitan, international civilization. Lemkin's idea

of the nation thus derived from a firm Enlightenment optimism." Levene, *The Crisis of Genocide, Vol. 1: Devastation: The European Rimlands 1912–1938* (Oxford: Oxford University Press, 2013), p. 242.

60 According to Helen Fein, Lemkin's "examples of genocide or genocidal situations include: Albigensians, American Indians, Assyrians in Iraq, Belgian Congo, Christians in Japan, French in Sicily (c. 1282), Hereros, Huguenots, Incas, Mongols, the Soviet Union/Ukraine, [and] Tasmania." Fein, *Genocide: A Sociological Perspective*, p. 11. Lemkin's study of Tasmania was edited by Ann Curthoys and published in *Patterns of Prejudice*, 39: 2 (2005), pp. 170–196 (and Curthoys's introduction, pp. 162–169).

61 William A. Schabas, *Genocide in International Law* (Cambridge: Cambridge University Press, 2000), p. 14.

62 As supplied in W. Michael Reisman and Chris T. Antoniou, eds., *The Laws of War: A Comprehensive Collection of Primary Documents on International Laws Governing Armed Conflict* (New York: Vintage Books, 1994), pp. 84–85.

63 Daniel Feierstein, *Genocide as Social Practice: Reorganizing Society under the Nazis and Argentina's Military Juntas* (New Brunswick, NJ: Rutgers University Press, 2014), p. 20.

64 Ad Hoc Committee on Genocide, "Summary Record of the Twelfth Meeting," April 19, 1948. In Abtahi and Webb, eds., *The Travaux Préparatoires*, Vol. 1, p. 861.

65 Ad Hoc Committee on Genocide, "Commentary on Articles Adopted by the Committee," April 26, 1948. In Abtahi and Webb, eds., *The Travaux Préparatoires*, Vol. 1, p. 980 (emphasis in original).

66 Ad Hoc Committee on Genocide, "Report of the Committee and Draft Convention Drawn Up by the Committee," May 24, 1948, in Abtahi and Webb, eds., *The Travaux Préparatoires*, Vol. 1, p. 1125.

67 "Two Hundred and Eighteenth Meeting," in Abtahi and Webb, eds., *The Travaux Préparatoires*, Vol. 1, p. 1222.

68 Economic and Social Council, "Seventy-Fourth Meeting," October 14, 1948. In Abtahi and Webb, eds., *The Travaux Préparatoires*, Vol. 2, pp. 1391, 1396.

69 Nersessian, *Genocide and Political Groups*, p. 70.

70 Nersessian, *Genocide and Political Groups*, p. 76.

71 Martin Shaw, *What is Genocide?* (Cambridge: Polity, 2007), p. 22.

72 L.J. van den Herik concurs that "it is not likely that genocidal acts other than killing—sub (b) to (e)—will be perceived as genocide when they are committed outside a context of mass killing." Van den Herik, *The Contribution of the Rwanda Tribunal to the Development of International Law* (Leiden: Martinus Nijhoff Publishers, 2005), p. 146.

73 Cited in Steven R. Ratner and Jason S. Abrams, *Accountability for Human Rights Atrocities in International Law: Beyond the Nuremberg Legacy* (2nd edn) (Oxford: Oxford University Press, 2001), pp. 30, 32.

74 Schabas, *Genocide in International Law*, p. 140.

75 See Beth Van Schaack, "The Crime of Political Genocide: Repairing the Genocide Convention's Blind Spot," *Yale Law Journal*, 106 (1997), pp. 2259–2291.

76 Schabas, *Genocide in International Law*, pp. 175, 178.

77 For a survey of the early legal literature, see David Kader, "Law and Genocide: A Critical Annotated Bibliography," *Hastings International and Comparative Law Review*, 11 (1988).

78 See my "Filmography of Genocide and Crimes Against Humanity" at www.genocide text.net/gaci_filmography.htm.

79 Christopher Rudolph, "Constructing an Atrocities Regime: The Politics of War Crimes Tribunals," *International Organization*, 55: 3 (Summer 2001), p. 659. Rudolph cites Kenneth Abbott and Duncan Snidal, who "define 'hard' legalization as legally binding obligations characterized by high degrees of obligation, precision, and delegation, and define 'soft' legalization as a more flexible manifestation characterized by varying degrees along one or most of these same dimensions."

80 See also the "Comments on Article IV" in the early (June 1947) Secretariat Draft E/447 of the UN Convention: "The heaviest responsibility [for genocide] is that of statesmen or rulers in the broad sense of the word, that is to say, heads of state,

ministers and members of legislative assemblies . . . Officials who commit genocide at government orders—the most frequent case—or do so on their own initiative, also bear a heavy responsibility. Finally, private persons, that is to say, persons who are neither rulers nor officials, can also commit acts of genocide . . . either by collective action (through a political group, league, or clandestine or other association), or by individual action." In Abtahi and Webb, eds., *The Travaux Préparatoires*, Vol. 1, p. 241.

81 In this context, it is worth noting the verdict of the ICTR that the law of genocide "did not include a requirement that the perpetrator be a State official. Hence, individuals connected to non-State actors, such as the *Interahamwe* [genocidal militia] and RTLM [extremist radio station], and other persons not affiliated with the government, such as businessmen, who had all played a major role in the preparation, organization and execution of the genocide, could also be held responsible for genocide" (see Chapter 9). Van den Herik, *The Contribution of the Rwanda Tribunal*, p. 269.

82 Stathis Kalyvas, *The Logic of Violence in Civil War* (Cambridge: Cambridge University Press, 2006), focusing on the Greek civil war of the 1940s.

83 This element of *imputed/assigned identity* is essential to understanding the nature of genocidal targeting, as international law (most notably the International Criminal Tribunal for Rwanda) have acknowledged. It was hardly necessary for women and men in early-modern Europe to be self-identified witches in order for them to be targeted as such. Indeed, it is a reasonable proposition that "witches" as imagined by the perpetrators were precisely that—imaginary. Likewise, there were few card-carrying "enemies of the people" in the populations genocided as class enemies in Lenin's and Stalin's USSR and Maoist China (Chapter 5), or in Cambodia under the Khmer Rouge (Chapter 7). As Christopher Powell eloquently argued: "Once individuals are assigned to the victim group, they belong to it for all practical purposes—or at least, for the practical purposes that matter most in such a situation. Such groups are, in effect, *constituted through genocide*." Powell, *Barbaric Civilization: A Critical Sociology of Genocide* (Montreal & Kingston: McGill-Queen's University Press, 2011), p. 82. Patrick Wolfe likewise contends that a property like "race cannot be taken as given. It is made in the targeting." Wolfe, "Structure and Event: Settler Colonialism, Time, and the Question of Genocide," in A. Dirk Moses, ed., *Empire, Colony, Genocide: Conquest, Occupation, and Subaltern Resistance in World History* (New York: Berghahn Books, 2008), p. 111. Scott Straus writes that "Genocide is not carried out against a group bounded by essential internal properties. Rather, genocide is carried out against a group that the perpetrator *believes* has essential properties . . . however fictive such a belief may be." Straus quoted in Levene, *Genocide in the Age of the Nation State, Vol. 1*, p. 87.

84 Irving Louis Horowitz, *Taking Lives: Genocide and State Power* (4th edn) (New Brunswick, NJ: Transaction Publishers, 1996), p. 265. Benjamin Whitaker, in his mid-1980s reevaluation of the Genocide Convention for the UN, likewise contended that "in part" should mean a "reasonably significant number, relative to the total of the group as a whole, or else a significant section of a group such as its leadership." Quoted in John Quigley, *The Genocide Convention: An International Law Analysis* (London: Ashgate, 2006), p. 141.

85 "Genocide Watch Calls for Prosecution of Zimbabwe's Robert Mugabe for Genocide," press release, September 16, 2010.

86 The December 11, 1946 General Assembly declaration, "The Crime of Genocide," is available online at https://documents-dds-ny.un.org/doc/RESOLUTION/GEN/NR0/033/47/IMG/NR003347.pdf?OpenElement.

87 Drost quoted in Curthoys and Docker, "Defining Genocide," p. 22.

88 Barbara Harff and Ted Robert Gurr, "Toward Empirical Theory of Genocides and Politicides: Identification and Measurement of Cases Since 1945," *International Studies Quarterly*, 32: 3 (1988), p. 360.

89 Steven Katz, *The Holocaust in Historical Context, Vol. 1: The Holocaust and Mass Death before the Modern Age* (New York: Oxford University Press, 1994), p. 131.

90 "Annan's Nobel Speech in Oslo," *The New York Times*, December 11, 2001. Also eloquent were French representative Charles Chaumont's comments at an October 1948 meeting of the UN Economic and Social Council, shortly before the General Assembly voted to adopt the Genocide Convention. Chaumont "held that the crime of genocide existed as soon as an individual became the victim of acts of genocide. If a motive for the crime existed, genocide existed even if only a single individual were the victim. The French delegation had therefore proposed to replace the words 'acts committed with the intent to destroy a . . . group' by the words 'an attack on life directed against a human group, or against an individual as a member of a human group . . .' The group was an abstract concept; it was an aggregate of individuals; it had no independent life of its own; it was harmed when the individuals composing it were harmed." In Abtahi and Webb, eds., *The Travaux Préparatoires*, Vol. 2 (Leiden: Martinus Nijhoff Publishers, 2008), p. 1380.

91 Chile Eboe-Osuji, "Rape as Genocide: Some Questions Arising," *Journal of Genocide Research*, 9: 2 (2007), pp. 262–263. Eboe-Osuji adds: "This mischief was especially evident during the Rwandan genocide, when the US government refused to acknowledge that a genocide was in progress, for fear of being impelled to do something about it, while semantically acknowledging that 'acts of genocide' (rather than genocide) were occurring."

92 UN-appointed commissioner Benjamin Whitaker (see note 220) wrote that the phrase "in part" denotes "a reasonably significant number, relative to the total of the group as a whole, or else a significant section of a group such as its leadership." Quoted in William A. Schabas, "The Law and Genocide," in Donald Bloxham and A. Dirk Moses, eds., *The Oxford Handbook of Genocide Studies* (Oxford: Oxford University Press, 2013), pp. 136–137.

93 Fein quoted in René Lemarchand, "Introduction," in Lemarchand, ed., *Forgotten Genocides: Oblivion, Denial, and Memory* (Philadelphia, PA: University of Pennsylvania Press, 2011), p. 9. I must say that between the last edition and this, the most cogent framing of genocide I have come across is a very old one: Nehemiah Robinson's, in his 1960 work *The Genocide Convention: A Commentary* (New York: Institute of Jewish Affairs; see p. 23).

94 Charny quoted in Edina Becirevic, *Genocide on the Drina River* (New Haven, CT: Yale University Press, 2014), p. 173.

95 On the Marsh Arabs, see Joseph W. Dellapenna, "The Iraqi Campaign against the Marsh Arabs: Ecocide as Genocide," *Jurist*, January 31, 2003. www.jurist.org/forum/forumnew92.php.

96 Andrew Woolford, *This Benevolent Experiment: Indigenous Boarding Schools, Genocide, and Redress in Canada and the United States* (Winnipeg, MB: University of Manitoba Press, 2015), p. 27.

97 See Ilan Pappé, "The Memoricide of the Nakba," in Pappé, *The Ethnic Cleansing of Palestine* (Oxford: Oneworld, 2006), pp. 225–234; Jonathan Cook, "Memoricide in the West Bank," *Counterpunch.org*, March 10, 2009, www.counterpunch.org/2009/03/10/memoricide-in-the-west-bank/.

98 The Liberal Ironist, "Harff's Genocide Typology, Along with Some Explanation," January 25, 2011, https://liberalironist.wordpress.com/2011/01/25/harffs-genocide-typology-along-with-some-explanation/.

99 Daniel Jonah Goldhagen, *Worse Than War: Genocide, Eliminationism, and the Ongoing Assault on Humanity* (New York: Basic Books, 2009) p. 122.

100 Allan D. Cooper, *The Geography of Genocide* (Lanham, MD: University Press of America, 2009), p. 67. Provocatively, Cooper asserts a gender dimension to urbicide: for genocidal perpetrators, who generally adhere to a traditional patriarchal model of gender relations, "the city, in particular, becomes a female terrain marked by chaos and uncontrolled sexual license where patriarchal social controls are surrendered. And by

female I really mean that which is not heterosexually male" (p. 73). See the discussion of gender and genocide in Chapter 13.

101 The quoted passage is drawn from a posted announcement of "an international and interdisciplinary academic workshop" entitled "Urbicide: The Killing of Cities," at the University of Durham, November 24–25, 2005.

102 Lemkin, *Lemkin on Genocide*, p. 95.

103 Keith Lowe, *Savage Continent: Europe in the Aftermath of World War II* (New York: St. Martin's Press, 2012), pp. 25–26 (e-book). Urbicides may have numbered in the *thousands* across Nazi-occupied Europe, especially eastern Europe. "About 80 per cent of the city of Minsk in Belarus was destroyed: only 19 of 332 major factories in the city survived, and only then because mines set by the retreating Germans were defused by Red Army sappers just in time. Approximately 1,700 towns and cities were devastated in the USSR, 714 of them in Ukraine alone" (Lowe, p. 28, e-book).

104 On the urbicide of Hama in 1982 by the forces of Hafez al-Assad, father of the current Syrian dictator, see Scott Peterson, "How Syria's Brutal Past Colors Its Future," *The Christian Science Monitor*, June 20, 2000, www.csmonitor.com/2000/0620/p1s3. html—strikingly prescient in retrospect.

105 On the urbicide of the city of Agdam by victorious Armenian forces in the Nagorno-Karabakh war, including some powerful images, see "Agdam, Azerbaijan: Ghost Town of War," http://sometimes-interesting.com/2011/08/04/agdam-azerbaijan-ghost-town-of-war/. I toured the ruins of Agdam with my companion Griselda Ramírez in July 2015, but we were prohibited from taking photos by our rather nervous taxi driver. The former city is today inhabited only by Armenian soldiers, police, and a few traders and squatters. There are no utilities or public services, and indeed no highway signs for what was once a thriving urban center of 50,000 people, overwhelmingly ethnic Azeris who were comprehensively "cleansed" after the Armenian conquest. For more on Nagorno-Karabakh, see pp. 232–233.

106 Of Lemkin, Thomas M. Butcher wrote that he "conceived of genocide in a fundamentally cultural manner, because the ultimate purpose of genocide (under his definition of the term) is to destroy a cultural unit." See Butcher, "A 'Synchronized Attack': On Raphael Lemkin's Holistic Conception of Genocide," *Journal of Genocide Research*, 15: 3 (2013), p. 254.

107 Shaw, *What is Genocide?*, pp. 34, 106, 156. Emphasis in original.

108 Feierstein, *Genocide as Social Practice*, p. 14. For a concise summation, see Daniel Feierstein, "The Concept of 'Genocidal Social Practices,'" in Adam Jones, ed., *New Directions in Genocide Research* (London: Routledge, 2012), pp. 18–35; also Feierstein, "Beyond the Binary Model: National Security Doctrine in Argentina as a Way of Rethinking Genocide as a Social Practice," in Alexander Laban Hinton, Thomas La Pointe, and Douglas Irvin-Erickson, eds., *Hidden Genocides: Power, Knowledge, Memory* (New Brunswick, NJ: Rutgers University Press), pp. 68–80.

109 Lemkin quoted in Cooper, *Raphael Lemkin*, p. 241.

110 A. Dirk Moses, "Empire, Colony, Genocide: Keywords and the Philosophy of History," in Moses, ed., *Empire, Colony, Genocide*, pp. 12, 15.

111 Lemkin quoted (my emphasis) in Dirk Moses, "Raphael Lemkin, Culture, and the Concept of Genocide," in Donald Bloxham and A. Dirk Moses, eds., *The Oxford Handbook of Genocide Studies* (Oxford: Oxford University Press, 2013), p. 33.

112 Lemkin, *Lemkin on Genocide*, pp. 35, 72.

113 Lemkin, *Totally Unofficial*, p. 172.

114 William A. Schabas, "Convention on the Prevention and Punishment of the Crime of Genocide," United Nations Treaty Collection, http://legal.un.org/avl/ha/cppcg/cppcg.html.

115 Danish delegation quoted in A. Dirk Moses, "The Holocaust and Genocide," in Dan Stone, ed., *The Historiography of the Holocaust* (London: Palgrave Macmillan, 2004), p. 541.

116 See Elisa Novic, "Physical-Biological or Socio-Cultural 'Destruction' in Genocide? Unravelling the Legal Underpinnings of Conflicting Interpretations," *Journal of Genocide Research*, 17: 1 (2015), pp. 63–82.

117 Text as supplied in Abtahi and Webb, eds., *The Travaux Préparatoires*, Vol. 1, pp. 1155–1156.

118 Robert van Krieken, "Cultural Genocide in Australia," in Stone, ed., *The Historiography of Genocide* (London: Palgrave Macmillan, 2008), p. 131. For a nuanced exploration of the applicability of the genocide framework to indigenous peoples' experiences, see Andrew Woolford, "Ontological Destruction: Genocide and Canadian Aboriginal Peoples," *Genocide Studies and Prevention*, 4: 1 (2009), pp. 81–97.

119 Cooper, *Raphael Lemkin*, p. 158. The statements of the Canadian government representative during the drafting of the Genocide Convention seem self-interested in retrospect. The Canadian government "was opposed to inclusion under the term 'genocide,' and within the framework of the Convention, of a form of cultural destruction which appeared to it to be wholly and essentially a matter of minority rights and would, as such, best be dealt with in the Covenant on Human Rights. It was a far cry from the unspeakable crimes which had been perpetrated at the Nazi crematoria, and which had so fundamentally shocked mankind, to the prohibition of the use of a museum cherished by some particular cultural group or other acts of cultural repression, deplorable and revolting though they might be." He added: "The Convention would enjoy the overwhelming popular support of decent people throughout the world, if they understood that it was intended to prevent and punish the slaughter of whole racial, national, religious *or political* [n.b.] groups. . . . But if the term were broadened to include the suppression of a minority-language newspaper or the closing of a school, confusion would inevitably ensue." "Two Hundred and Eighteenth Meeting," in Abtahi and Webb, eds., *The Travaux Préparatoires*, Vol. 1, p. 1219, emphasis added.

120 Lawrence Davidson, *Cultural Genocide* (New Brunswick, NJ: Rutgers University Press, 2012), p. 128.

121 John Quigley, *The Genocide Convention: An International Law Analysis* (London: Ashgate, 2006), p. 105.

122 CBC Digital Archives, "Fighting Words: Bill 101," www.cbc.ca/archives/topic/fighting-words-bill-101.

123 Benoit Aubin, "Bill 101: 30 Years On," *The Canadian Encyclopedia*, August 13, 2007.

124 "The UN says ethnic cleansing is by genocide or forced migration. In black and white I guess Bill 101 fits pretty well" (blog post by Wheresmyneighbours, February 28, 2009, http://blog.fagstein.com/2009/02/24/journal-lockout-1-month). A March 31, 2009 post by blogger Steve Karmazenuk, apparently a disenchanted member of the provincial Liberal Party, assailed "Quebec's War on Anglos," alleging an "underreported and ongoing campaign of ethnic cleansing by attrition [which] has continued to be ignored" by the Liberals (http://kspaceuniverse.blogspot.com/2009/03/message-to-anglo-community.html). Interestingly, the language of genocide has recently been revived on the other side of the language fence—reflecting francophone concerns over creeping Anglicization and bilingualism. In a TV interview in 2008, the writer Victor-Levy Beaulieu declared that "If all Quebec becomes bilingual, what awaits us is a slow genocide." Graeme Hamilton, "Lost in Translation: 30 Years On, Quebecers Are Still Hot about Bill 101," *National Post*, February 16, 2008.

125 Government of Canada Privy Council Office figures cited and supplemented in "English-Speaking Quebecker," *Wikipedia*, http://en.wikipedia.org/wiki/English-speaking_Quebecker. See also Garth Stevenson, *Community Besieged: The Anglophone Minority and the Politics of Quebec* (Montreal, PQ: McGill-Queen's University Press, 1999).

126 *CBC News Online*, "Language Laws in Quebec," March 30, 2005.

127 *CBC Digital Archives*, "Fighting Words."

128 "A generation later, the language charter is widely accepted as an intrinsic part of Quebec's social fabric. Both anglos and francophones of moderate persuasion say the law has engendered an unprecedented era of social peace and easing of language

tensions and fostered a cross-cultural communication between English and French Quebecers that has served as an important bridge between the storied 'two solitudes' of the bad old days." Hubert Bauch, "Bill 101 Paved Way for Peace," *The Gazette* (Montreal), August 25, 2007.

129 Kuper, *Genocide*, p. 166.

130 Martin Shaw, *Genocide and International Relations: Changing Patterns in the Transitions of the Late Modern World* (Cambridge: Cambridge University Press, 2013), p.79. Emphasis added.

131 Kuper, *Genocide*, p. 166.

132 See the discussion of genocide as an essentially contested concept in Powell, *Barbaric Civilization*, pp. 66–70.

133 David Moshman, "Conceptions of Genocide and Perceptions of History," in Dan Stone, ed., *The Historiography of Genocide* (London: Palgrave Macmillan, 2008), p. 86.

134 Adam Jones, "Problems of Gendercide," in Jones, ed., *Gendercide and Genocide* (Nashville, TN: Vanderbilt University Press, 2004), p. 260.

135 Jeffrey Herf, *The Jewish Enemy: Nazi Propaganda during World War II and the Holocaust* (Cambridge, MA: The Belknap Press of Harvard University Press, 2006), pp. 150–151. For another important study of the "Judeo-Bolshevik" motif, see Lorna Waddington, *Hitler's Crusade: Bolshevism and the Myth of the International Jewish Conspiracy* (London: Tauris Academic Studies, 2007). Like Herf, Waddington contends that in Hitler's mind, "the scourge of Bolshevism had always been inextricably linked to the wider danger presented to Germany and the world by the machinations of international Jewry. That fact alone is indicative of the profound significance of anti-Bolshevism as a determinant of his political actions" (p. 210), and as a determinant of how the Jew was depicted in the Nazi *Weltanschauung* (world-view).

136 Nazi press report quoted in Herf, *The Jewish Enemy*, p. 189. Daniel Feierstein likewise emphasizes that "Nazi ideology made a clear link between the ethnic and the political. To claim, as many have done, that the victims [of the Holocaust] 'were killed simply because they were Jews' erases the political nature of extermination and treats ethnicity as if it were singular and set in stone." Feierstein, *Genocide as Social Practice*, p. 172.

137 Mark Levene writes that for Hitler and the Nazis, "the international Jewish conspiracy" "operat[ed] through manifold, multi-layered forces of subversion and pollution, including Bolshevism, capitalism, cultural modernism, sexual contamination, racial emasculation and disease . . ." Levene, *Genocide in the Age of the Nation State, Vol. 1*, p. 69.

138 Nazi pamphlet quoted in Herf, *The Jewish Enemy*, p. 101. In fact, as Herf shows (p. 96), while at one point Jews constituted over a quarter of Bolshevik Central Committee members (around 1917), by 1939 (when World War Two erupted, supposedly at Jewish behest) it was roughly 10 percent. At no time did Jewish members of the Communist Party exceed around 5 percent of the total.

139 Peter Fritzsche, *Life and Death in the Third Reich* (Cambridge, MA: The Belknap Press of Harvard University Press, 2008), p. 196.

140 Saul Friedländer similarly notes that "on occupied Soviet territory . . . the extermination was first aimed at Jews as carriers of the Soviet system, then as Jews as potential partisans and finally as hostile elements living in territories ultimately destined for German colonization: The three categories merged of course into one." Friedländer, *The Years of Extermination: Nazi Germany and the Jews, 1939–1945* (New York: Harper-Collins, 2007), p. 237.

141 Shaw, *What is Genocide?*, p. 117.

142 Karl A. Schleunes, *The Twisted Road to Auschwitz: Nazi Policy toward German Jews, 1933–1939* (Urbana, IL: University of Illinois Press, 1990); Browning's comment is in his back-cover endorsement.

143 Levene, *Genocide in the Age of the Nation State, Vol. 1*, p. 61.

144 A. Dirk Moses, "Empire, Colony, Genocide: Keywords and the Philosophy of History," in Moses, ed., *Empire, Colony, Genocide*, p. 29.

145 Scott Straus, *The Order of Genocide: Race, Power, and War in Rwanda* (Ithaca, NY: Cornell University Press, 2006), p. 12.

146 Mark Levene, "The Tragedy of the Rimlands, Nation-State Formation and the Destruction of Imperial Peoples, 1912–48," in Panikos Panayi and Pippa Virdee, eds., *Refugees and the End of Empire: Imperial Collapse and Forced Migration in the Twentieth Century* (New York: Palgrave Macmillan, 2011), pp. 55–56. From a similar historical-political-sociological perspective, Martin Shaw asserts: "Genocidal policies often represent more pragmatic situational responses to threats, difficulties and the actions of others, including the target groups as well as third parties. We must take seriously the idea that genocide often constitutes *policy* and like all policy develops situationally, rather than as some sort of unbending implementation of an original idea." Shaw, *Genocide in International Relations: Changing Patterns in the Transitions of the Late Modern World* (Cambridge: Cambridge University Press, 2013), p. 40.

147 As the International Law Commission, "which drafts treaties for the UN General Assembly," analyzed the question of genocidal intent: "The prohibited acts enumerated in subparagraphs (a) to (e) [of the Genocide Convention] are *by their very nature conscious, intentional or volitional acts* which an individual could not usually commit without knowing that certain consequences were likely to result." Quoted in Quigley, *The Genocide Convention*, p. 91. Emphasis added.

148 Robert Gellately and Ben Kiernan contend that under the prevailing international-legal understanding, "genocidal intent also applies to acts of destruction that are not the specific goal but are predictable outcomes or by-products of a policy, which could have been avoided by a change in that policy." Gellately and Kiernan, "The Study of Mass Murder and Genocide," in Gellately and Kiernan, eds., *The Specter of Genocide: Mass Murder in Historical Perspective* (Cambridge: Cambridge University Press, 2003), p. 15. Helen Fein has argued along similar lines: "Intent or purposeful action—or inaction—is not the same in law or everyday language as either motive or function. An actor performs an act, we say, with intent if there are foreseeable ends or consequences: for what purpose is different from why or for what motive is the act designed." Quoted in Martin Shaw, "Sociology and Genocide," in Bloxham and Moses, eds., *The Oxford Handbook*, p. 149.

149 Quigley, *The Genocide Convention*, pp. 121–122.

150 Katherine Goldsmith, "The Issue of Intent in the Genocide Convention and Its Effect on the Prevention and Punishment of the Crime of Genocide: Toward a Knowledge-Based Approach," *Genocide Studies and Prevention*, 5: 3 (2010), p. 241.

151 Ibid., p. 242.

152 In his "Proposed Convention on Prevention and Punishment of the Crime of Genocide," Churchill maps "gradations of culpability" for genocide onto domestic law's concept of "degrees" of homicide. He distinguishes among "(a) *Genocide in the First Degree*, which consists of instances in which evidence of premeditated intent to commit genocide is present. (b) *Genocide in the Second Degree*, which consists of instances in which evidence of premeditation is absent, but in which it can be reasonably argued that the perpetrator(s) acted with reckless disregard for the probability that genocide would result from their actions. (c) *Genocide in the Third Degree*, which consists of instances in which genocide derives, however unintentionally, from other violations of international law engaged in by the perpetrator(s). (d) *Genocide in the Fourth Degree*, which consists of instances in which neither evidence of premeditation nor other criminal behavior is present, but in which the perpetrator(s) acted with depraved indifference to the possibility that genocide would result from their actions and therefore [failed] to effect adequate safeguards to prevent it." Ward Churchill, *A Little Matter of Genocide: Holocaust and Denial in the Americas, 1492 to the Present* (San Francisco, CA: City Lights Books, 1997), pp. 434–435.

153 Alexander K.A. Greenawalt, "Rethinking Genocidal Intent: The Case for a Knowledge-based Interpretation," *Columbia Law Review*, 99: 8 (1999), p. 2269. Emphasis added.

154 *Akayesu* judgment quoted in Schabas, *Genocide in International Law*, p. 212. Emphasis added. Schabas considers this approach "definitely inappropriate in the case of genocide."

155 Goldsmith, "The Issue of Intent," p. 246.

156 For a superbly accessible introduction to the institution of Atlantic slavery, see Robert Harms, *The Diligent: A Voyage Through the Worlds of the Slave Trade* (New York: Basic Books, 2002).

157 After conducting a useful review of available sources, Matthew White concludes: "If we assume the absolute worst, a death toll as high as 60 million is at the very edge of possibility; however, the likeliest number of deaths would fall somewhere from 15 to 20 million." White, "Twentieth Century Atlas—Historical Body Count," http:// users.erols.com/mwhite28/warstatv.htm. To arrive at such a total, one can begin with the figure of eleven to fifteen million slaves "shipped between the fifteenth and the nineteenth century," cited in Hugh Thomas, *The Slave Trade: The Story of the Atlantic Slave Trade: 1440–1870* (New York: Touchstone, 1997), p. 862. (Thomas himself argues for an "approximate figure . . . [of] something like eleven million slaves, give or take 500,000.") A widely held view is that approximately 50 percent of those captured as slaves died before they were shipped from West African ports. To these eleven to fifteen million victims, one adds approximately two million more who died on the "middle passage" between Africa and the Americas, and an unknown but certainly very large number who perished after arrival, either during the brutal "seasoning" process or on the plantations.

158 Seymour Drescher, "The Atlantic Slave Trade and the Holocaust: A Comparative Analysis," in Alan S. Rosenbaum, ed., *Is the Holocaust Unique? Perspectives on Comparative Genocide* (Boulder, CO: Westview Press, 2001), pp. 97–117. See also Jeffrey Herf, "Comparative Perspectives on Anti-Semitism, Radical Anti-Semitism in the Holocaust and American White Racism," *Journal of Genocide Research*, 9: 4 (2007), pp. 575–600; and A. Dirk Moses, "The Fate of Blacks and Jews: A Response to Jeffrey Herf," *Journal of Genocide Research*, 10: 2 (2008), pp. 269–287.

159 Michael Ignatieff, "Lemkin's Word," *The New Republic*, February 26, 2001.

160 The "social death" concept, explored by Orlando Patterson in his magisterial *Slavery and Social Death: A Comparative Study* (Cambridge, MA: Harvard University Press, 1982), has also been deployed in the genocide studies literature, notably by Claudia Card. See her article "Genocide and Social Death," *Hypatia*, 18: 1 (2003), pp. 63–79: "Social death, central to the evil of genocide (whether the genocide is homicidal or primarily cultural), distinguishes genocide from other mass murders. Loss of social vitality is loss of identity and thereby of meaning for one's existence. Seeing social death at the center of genocide takes our focus off body counts and loss of individual talents, directing us instead to mourn losses of relationships that create community and give meaning to the development of talents" (from the article's abstract). The usage thus ties in with discussions of cultural genocide (Chapter 1)—and also with discussions of gender and genocide, notably the mental suffering inflicted by genocidal rape (Chapter 13). Raped women and men in a traditional society, for instance, are exposed to much the same kind of shame, stigmatization, and anathematization as the slave. In a genocidal and post-genocidal situation, the intent is often (and the consequences more often still) to undermine the "relationships that create community" and erode the cohesion of the targeted ethnic or national group.

161 See, e.g., the African-American journalist Keith Richburg's controversial article, "American in Africa," in *Washington Post Magazine*, March 26, 1995, available online at www. washingtonpost.com/wp-srv/inatl/longterm/richburg/richbrg1.htm.

162 Orlando Patterson, *Slavery and Social Death: A Comparative Study* (Cambridge, MA: Harvard University Press, 1982), p. 164.

163 The fact that slavery in the United States was far less destructive of slaves' lives, compared to the Caribbean or Portuguese America (Brazil), is an important factor in weighing the applicability of the genocide framework to different slavery institutions

in the Americas. Life for slaves in the US was a calvary; in French-controlled Haiti it was a holocaust. Recall, however, that millions of slaves died *en route* to West African ports and New World plantations. These rates do not seem to have been lower for slaves shipped to US destinations.

164 *We Charge Genocide: The Historic Petition to the United Nations for Relief from a Crime of the United States Government against the Negro People* (New York: International Publishers, 1970), p. xv.

165 The Ku Klux Klan was, and in a somewhat transformed guise still is, a white-supremacist organization based in the US South. It began as an armed militia in the post-Civil War era, and was responsible for many acts of terrorism and violent vigilantism against blacks. See Allen W. Trelease, *White Terror: The Ku Klux Klan Conspiracy and Southern Reconstruction* (Baton Rouge, LA: Louisiana State University Press, 1995); Stephen Budiansky, *The Bloody Shirt: Terror after the Civil War* (New York: Plume, 2008).

166 *We Charge Genocide*, p. 6.

167 Raphael Lemkin's response to the controversy was illuminating, and not in a way that reflects well on the founder of genocide studies. According to Ann Curthoys and John Docker, Lemkin "argued vehemently that the provisions of the Genocide Convention bore no relation to the US Government or its position vis-à-vis Black citizens." He was anxious that the charges not derail American ratification of his cherished Genocide Convention. Moreover, Lemkin was ardently wooing the Slavic and Baltic populations that had fallen under Soviet rule (and receiving significant funding from their usually self-appointed representatives). Thus we have his frankly craven comments to *The New York Times* on December 18, 1951, accusing Patterson and Robeson of being "un-American," and declaring that *We Charge Genocide* was a communist ploy to "divert attention from the crimes of genocide committed against Estonians, Latvians, Lithuanians, Poles and other Soviet-subjugated peoples." For Curthoys and Docker, his response raises "disturbing questions . . . concerning Lemkin and his attitudes to African American history and people: perhaps there was a fundamental lack of sympathy." Ann Curthoys and John Docker, "Defining Genocide," in Stone, ed., *The Historiography of Genocide*, pp. 19–20. In this respect, the authors contend, Lemkin was "conforming to a long tradition of European superiority and contempt towards Africa" (p. 21).

168 Eric Langenbacher, "The Allies in World War II: The Anglo-American Bombardment of German Cities," in Jones, ed., *Genocide, War Crimes and the West*, pp. 117–119. See also Howard Zinn, "Hiroshima and Royan," in William L. Hewitt, ed., *Defining the Horrific: Readings on Genocide and Holocaust in the Twentieth Century* (Upper Saddle River, NJ: Pearson, 2004), pp. 187–199. Zinn, a renowned dissident historian, was also a US veteran of the area-bombing campaign against Germany; the chapter relates some of his personal experiences.

169 LeMay quoted in Paul Ham, *Hiroshima Nagasaki: The Real Story of the Atomic Bombings and Their Aftermath* (New York: Thomas Dunne Books, 2011), pp. 482–483. See the description of the Tokyo raid in Eric Markusen and David Kopf, *The Holocaust and Strategic Bombing: Genocide and Total War in the Twentieth Century* (Boulder, CO: Westview Press, 1995), pp. 175–180.

170 "I cannot accept the view that . . . the bombing, in time of war, of such civilian enemy populations as those of Hiroshima, Nagasaki, Hamburg, and Dresden does not constitute genocide within the terms of the [UN] convention." Kuper, *Genocide*, cited in Chalk and Jonassohn, *The History and Sociology of Genocide*, p. 24. Mary Kaldor also argues that "the indiscriminate bombing of civilians . . . creat[ed] a scale of devastation of genocidal proportions." Mary Kaldor, *New and Old Wars: Organized Violence in a Global Era* (Stanford, CA: Stanford University Press, 2001), p. 25.

171 "Was strategic bombing genocidal? Put bluntly, our answer is yes." Markusen and Kopf, *The Holocaust and Strategic Bombing*, p. 255; see the extended discussion at pp. 244–258. For a judgment of the area bombings of German and Japanese cities as "moral crimes," see A.C. Grayling, *Among the Dead Cities: The History and Moral Legacy of the WWII*

Bombing of Civilians in Germany and Japan (New York: Walker & Company, 2006). On Germany, see also W.G. Sebald, *On the Natural History of Destruction* (New York: Modern Library, 2004); Richard Overy, *The Bombers and the Bombed: Allied Air War over Europe, 1940–1945* (New York: Viking, 2013); and Keith Lowe, *Inferno: The Fiery Destruction of Hamburg 1943* (New York: Scribner, 2007). On the atomic bombings of Hiroshima and Nagasaki, see Daniel Jonah Goldhagen, *Worse Than War: Genocide, Eliminationism, and the Ongoing Assault on Humanity* (New York: Basic Books, 2009), pp. 3–8, arguing that "the willful slaughter of more than a quarter of a million people, in full view of the world, should be universally recognized for what it was, causing the label 'mass *murderer*' to be affixed to [President Harry] Truman's name ... putting Truman and his deeds into the same broad categories of Hitler and the Holocaust, Stalin and the gulag, Pol Pot, Mao, Saddam Hussein, and Slobodan Milosevic and their victims," though "without judging them morally as being equivalent" (pp. 6, 8).

172 Taylor quoted in Chalk and Jonassohn, *The History and Sociology of Genocide*, p. 25.

173 LeMay quoted in Donald L. Miller, *D-Days in the Pacific* (New York: Simon & Schuster, 2005), p. 252.

174 Ronald Takaki, *Hiroshima: Why America Dropped the Atomic Bomb* (Boston, MA: Little, Brown, 1995), pp. 30, 153 (n. 3).

175 Paul Ham's detailed recent investigation concludes: "While the bombs obviously contributed to Japan's general sense of defeat, not a shred of evidence supports the contention that the Japanese leadership surrendered *in direct response* to the atomic bombs. On the contrary, Tokyo's hardline militarists shrugged as the two irradiated cities were added to the tally of 66 already destroyed [by 'conventional' bombing], and overrode the protests of the moderates.... In the eyes of the Imperial forces ... the decisive factor in the surrender was the Soviet invasion [of Manchuria on August 8, 1945].... The most that may be said in defence of the bombing of Hiroshima—in strictly military and political terms—is that it bounced the Russians into the war a week or so earlier than Moscow planned. Whether that justified the destruction of a city is a different question. There appears to be no justification—in military or political terms—for Nagasaki.... The truth is, the bombs were militarily unnecessary, as the plain facts show and the leading American commanders confirmed after the war ... The atomic attacks were the culmination of [a] process of deliberate civilian annihilation." Ham, *Hiroshima Nagasaki*, pp. 404, 473, 485, 509–510. Some 20,000 of those killed in the Hiroshima attack were Korean slave-laborers; hundreds of enslaved Chinese also died (Ham, p. 408).

176 Chinua Achebe, *There Was a Country: A Personal History of Biafra* (New York: The Penguin Press, 2012), p. 51.

177 Michael Gould, *The Biafran War: The Struggle for Modern Nigeria* (London: I.B. Tauris, 2013), p. 34.

178 Ibid., p. 34.

179 Nixon quoted in Achebe, *There Was a Country*, p. 231.

180 Gould, *The Biafran War*, p. 131.

181 Herbert Ekwe-Ekwe, "The Nigerian State, Igbo Genocide and the Africom," *Tensões Mundiais/World Tensions*, 7: 13 (July/December 2011), p. 157.

182 Lasse Heerten and A. Dirk Moses, "The Nigeria-Biafra War: Postcolonial Conflict and the Question of Genocide," *Journal of Genocide Research*, 16: 2–3 (2014), p. 184.

183 Ibid., p. 185.

184 The major English-language reportage on Biafra at the time of the conflict, by Frederick Forsyth, also found "a reasonable suspicion of genocide," but stated "it would be presumptuous for a writer to arrogate to himself the functions either of an inquiry or of a court." Forsyth, *The Biafra Story* (Barnsley: Pen & Sword Books, 2007 [reprint edition]), p. 229.

185 Ekwe-Ekwe, "The Nigerian State," p. 157. See also Ekwe-Ekwe, "Longest Genocide—Since 29 May 1966," paper presented to the conference of the International Association of Genocide Scholars (IAGS), Winnipeg, Manitoba, July 19, 2014.

186 Gould, *The Biafran War*, pp. 146–147.

187 See, e.g., "Revealed: 'How Ojukwu Rejected Food Aid for Starving Biafrans,'" *The Nation*, October 20, 2012, http://thenationonlineng.net/revealed-how-ojukwu-rejected-food-aid-for-starving-biafrans/.

188 Joy Gordon, *Invisible War: The United States and the Iraq Sanctions* (Cambridge, MA: Harvard University Press, 2010), p. 190.

189 Ibid., p. 33.

190 Albright on *60 Minutes*, May 12, 1996. She later disowned the comment.

191 Bonior quoted in "US Congressmen Criticise Iraqi Sanctions," BBC Online, February 17, 2000, http://news.bbc.co.uk/1/hi/world/middle_east/646783.stm.

192 See Ramsey Clark, "Criminal Complaint against the United States and Others for Crimes against the People of Iraq (1996) and Letter to the Security Council (2001)," in Jones, ed., *Genocide, War Crimes and the West*, p. 271. The forum in question was the International Court on Crimes Against Humanity Committed by the UN Security Council on [*sic*] Iraq, held on November 16–17, 1996. For more on citizens' tribunals, see Chapter 15. Clark's phrase "for the purpose of" is not clearly supported by the evidence; an accusation of genocide founded on willful and malignant negligence is, for me, more persuasive.

193 For an argument along these lines, see John G. Heidenrich, *How to Prevent Genocide: A Guide for Policymakers, Scholars, and the Concerned Citizen* (Westport, CT: Praeger, 2001), pp. 101–103.

194 Gordon, *Invisible War*, p. 221. She provides a detailed evaluation of the legal provisions for genocide and crimes against humanity at pp. 221–230.

195 Ibid., p. 244.

196 Denis J. Halliday, "US Policy and Iraq: A Case of Genocide?," in Jones, ed., *Genocide, War Crimes and the West*, p. 264 (based on a November 1999 speech in Spain).

197 A useful definition of terrorism is offered by the US Congress: "any [criminal] activity that . . . appears to be intended (i) to intimidate or coerce a civilian population; (ii) to influence the policy of a government by intimidation or coercion; or (iii) to affect the conduct of a government by assassination or kidnapping." Quoted in Noam Chomsky, *9–11* (New York: Seven Stories Press, 2001), p. 16 (note).

198 For Kuper, genocidal massacres are "expressed characteristically in the annihilation of a section of a group—men, women and children, as for example in the wiping out of whole villages." Kuper, *Genocide*, p. 10.

199 See the H-Genocide discussion logs for September 2001, searchable at www.h-net.org/logsearch/. The posts cited here can be found in the archives for September 16, 2001 (Ronayne) and September 20 (Cribb).

200 Goldhagen, *Worse Than War*, pp. 490–491. Goldhagen defines "Political Islam" as a "phenomenon includ[ing] only Islamic-grounded *political* regimes, organizations, and initiatives that share . . . a common ideological foundation about Islam's *political* primacy or its need to systematically and politically roll back the West—a conviction that the fundamentally corrupt modern world must be refashioned, including by annihilating others" (p. 492). In addition to the terrorists of Al-Qa'eda, he cites established regimes such as Iran's (see p. 521) and Omar al-Bashir's in Sudan (Box 9a).

201 The Islamists of the Boko Haram movement and proto-state, centered in northeastern Nigeria and now formally allied with Islamic State/ISIS, are comparably genocidal and millenarian in their ideology and praxis. See, e.g., Emmanuel Ogebe, "Time to Recognize Boko Haram's Genocide," *LinkedIn*, February 2, 2016, www.linkedin.com/pulse/time-recognize-boko-harams-genocide-emmanuel-ogebe. On the parallel al-Shabaab movement in Somalia, see Stig Jarle Hansen, *Al-Shabaab in Somalia: The History and Ideology of a Militant Islamist Group, 2005–2012* (Oxford: Oxford University Press, 2012).

202 Vandana Shiva, "War against Nature and the Peoples of the South," in Sarah Anderson, ed., *Views from the South* (San Francisco, CA: Food First Books, 2000), pp. 93, 113. See also Paul Farmer, "On Suffering and Structural Violence: A View from Below," in

Nancy Scheper-Hughes and Philippe Bourgois, eds., *Violence in War and Peace* (London: Blackwell, 2004), pp. 281–289.

203 Ziegler quoted in "UN Expert Decries 'Assassination' By Hunger of Millions of Children," UN News Center, October 28, 2005. An assistant to Ziegler confirmed that the comments were "directly translated from the French," and added that in the past Ziegler had described the "world order" as "murderous" (Sally-Anne Way, personal communication, November 3, 2005). In a similar vein, Stephen Lewis, the UN Special Envoy for HIV/AIDS in Africa, stated of the global AIDS crisis: "This pandemic cannot be allowed to continue, and those who watch it unfold with a kind of pathological equanimity must be held to account. There may yet come a day when we have peacetime tribunals to deal with this particular version of crimes against humanity." Lewis quoted in Michael Mann, *Incoherent Empire* (London: Verso, 2005), p. 61.

204 Kal Holsti, personal communication, June 29, 2005.

205 See Henry Shue, *Basic Rights: Subsistence, Affluence, and U.S. Foreign Policy* (2nd edn) (Princeton, NJ: Princeton University Press, 1996), p. 207 (n. 17). I am citing Shue somewhat out of context: his phrase refers to specific historical events during the Second World War, when "over 6 million Asians were . . . allowed to starve" under colonial (British and French) dominion. See also the discussion of imperial famines in Chapter 2. In his study of Belgian genocide in the Congo (see Chapter 2), Martin Ewans also refers to "genocide by neglect" in post-independence Africa, "with a massive, on-going loss of life . . . being treated in Europe [and elsewhere] with near total indifference." Ewans, *European Atrocity, African Catastrophe: Leopold II, the Congo Free State and its Aftermath* (London: RoutledgeCurzon, 2002), p. 252.

206 Galtung quoted in Joseph Nevins, *A Not-So-Distant Horror: Mass Violence in East Timor* (London: RoutledgeCurzon, 2002), p. 252.

207 Sachs quoted in J. Tyrangiel, "Bono," *Time* (Latin American edition), March 4, 2002. Princeton professor Stephen F. Cohen has argued that the death toll exacted by the "nihilistic zealotry" of proponents of "savage capitalism" was *tens of millions in Russia alone* following the collapse of the Soviet Union: to US supporters of radical free-market policies there, "the lost lives of perhaps 100 million Russians seem not to matter, only American investments, loans, and reputations." See Cohen, *Failed Crusade: America and the Tragedy of Post-Communist Russia* (New York: W.W. Norton, 2000), pp. 38, 50.

208 Holsti, personal communication, June 29, 2005.

209 The issue of "voluntarism" is pertinent, for example, in the case of tobacco sale and consumption. It kills millions of people each year around the world, and is strongly "pushed" by corporate actors; but it is also to a significant extent "pulled" by the voluntary (though also dependent) agency of the tobacco consumer.

210 Adam Jones, "Genocide and Structural Violence: Challenges of Definition, Prevention, and Intervention," in Jones, ed., *New Directions in Genocide Research* (London: Routledge, 2012), pp. 132–151.

211 Norbert Finzsch, "'The Aborigines . . . Were Never Annihilated, and Still They are Becoming Extinct': Settler Imperialism and Genocide in Nineteenth-Century America and Australia," in Moses, ed., *Empire, Colony, Genocide*, p. 253.

212 Ervin Staub does ask "Is mass killing ever justified?," but quickly answers in the negative, and even rejects the notion that "genocides and mass killings [are] ever 'rational' expressions of self-interest." Staub, *The Roots of Evil: The Origins of Genocide and Other Group Violence* (Cambridge: Cambridge University Press, 1989), pp. 11–12.

213 Levene, *Genocide in the Age of the Nation State, Vol. 2*, p. 8.

214 For example, this comment by "a British observer" of the genocide against Herero and Nama in German South-West Africa (Chapter 3): "There can be no doubt, I think, that the war has been of an almost unmixed benefit to the German colony. Two warlike races have been exterminated, wells have been sunk, new water-holes discovered, the country mapped and covered with telegraph lines, and an enormous amount of

capital has been laid out." Quoted in Mark Levene, "Why Is the Twentieth Century the Century of Genocide?" *Journal of World History*, 11: 2 (2000), pp. 315–316.

215 For a study of French genocidal violence during the revolution, see Philippe R. Girard, "French Atrocities during the Haitian War of Independence," *Journal of Genocide Research*, 15: 2 (2013), pp. 133–149; Philip G. Dwyer, "Memories of Massacres and Atrocities during the Revolutionary and Napoleonic Wars," in Philip G. Dwyer and Lyndall Ryan, eds., *Theatres of Violence: Massacre, Mass Killing and Atrocity throughout History* (New York: Berghahn Books, 2012), pp. 157–169.

216 C.L.R. James, *The Black Jacobins: Toussaint L'Ouverture and the San Domingo Revolution*, 2nd rev. edn (New York: Vintage Books, 1989), pp. 373–374. Emphasis added.

217 "Subaltern genocide" and "genocides by the oppressed" are terms that Nicholas Robins and I coined in 2004, and deployed in our edited volume, *Genocides by the Oppressed: Subaltern Genocide in Theory and Practice* (Bloomington, IN: Indiana University Press, 2009). Robins elsewhere explores the wider implications for genocide studies: "Such cases of subaltern genocides [by indigenous peoples in Latin America] call into question widely held views of genocide. For example, such uprisings were the means to establishing an Indian state, not an expression of state policy. Furthermore, genocidal movements are not bound to any specific time period, and subaltern genocides demonstrate that genocides are not always from above or about the strong over the weak. . . . Unlike genocides from above, subaltern perpetrators of genocide often were defeated by their enemies. Subaltern genocide also challenges prevailing concepts of leadership," with some movements characterized by "highly fragmented, confederational, and far from bureaucratic" leadership structures. "In some cases . . . the objectives of the formal leadership were considerably more limited in scope and generally more conservative than that of those who operated in their name." Robins, "Colonial Latin America," in Bloxham and Moses, eds., *The Oxford Handbook*, p. 319. The only legal-political articulation of this dynamic that I know of is that of Lin Mousheng, the Chinese representative to the Ad Hoc Committee on Genocide that framed the UN Genocide Convention. At a committee meeting in April 1948, in countering Soviet assertions that "the crime of genocide is organically bound up with Fascism–Nazism and other similar race 'theories'," Lin "added the following considerations": "so-called racial theories were not necessarily bound up with genocide, *and so-called 'inferior' races were capable of acts of genocide against so-called 'superior' races.*" In Abtahi and Webb, eds., *The Travaux Préparatoires, Vol. 1*, p. 964, emphasis added.

The Soviet Union's consistent pressing of a "Fascism–Nazism" phrasing sparked some exasperation during UN deliberations. This was reflected in the comments of UK representative Gerald Fitzmaurice at an October 1948 meeting: he "was sorry to have to note that the USSR representatives were unable to discuss a draft or advance arguments without attributing base motives to their colleagues. He must repeat once again that the United Kingdom delegation did not concede to the Soviet Union any moral authority over other delegations. The USSR representatives had no monopoly of wisdom; and the other representatives were not children." It reads like a "War Room" speech by US president Merkin Muffley (Peter Sellers) in Stanley Kubrick's *Dr. Strangelove* (1964). Quoted in ibid., p. 1419.

218 Martin Shaw writes: "Groups are always to some extent actors, participants in conflict, as well as victims of it. . . . Liberal humanitarianism often finds it easiest to represent victim groups as pure victims—innocent civilian populations attacked by state or paramilitary power. Thus the West sees Iraqi Kurds and Kosova Albanians only as helpless civilians, not as groups that have supported political movements or guerrilla struggle. . . . Armed groups may even carry out mutually genocidal war, against each others' populations. In these situations, we need to recognize the complex patterns that make groups—and often individuals—both participants and victims, at different times." Shaw, *War and Genocide: Organized Killing in Modern Society* (Cambridge: Polity Press, 2003), p. 187.

219 Schabas, *Genocide in International Law*, p. 341.

220 The terms "worthy" and "unworthy" victims are deployed by Edward S. Herman and Noam Chomsky in *Manufacturing Consent: The Political Economy of the Mass Media* (New York: Pantheon, 1988).

221 "John Kerry Calls ISIS 'Psychopathic Monsters' After Paris Attacks," *Time*, November 17, 2015, http://time.com/4115823/paris-attacks-john-kerry-isis-terrorism/.

222 In 1982, the Englishman Benjamin Whitaker was appointed Special Rapporteur by the UN's Economic and Social Council (ECOSOC) to revise a previously commissioned study on reform to the Genocide Convention. Whitaker's report was submitted in 1985 and "made a number of innovative and controversial conclusions . . . Whitaker wanted to amend the Convention in order to include political groups and groups based on sexual orientation, to exclude the plea of superior orders, to extend the punish-able acts to those of 'advertent omission' and to pursue consideration of cultural genocide, 'ethnocide' and 'ecocide.'" Schabas, *Genocide in International Law*, p. 467. Whitaker's proposals so divided his sponsors that his report was tabled and never acted upon—in my view, an opportunity missed to substantially advance legal and scholarly understandings of genocide.

CHAPTER 2

State and Empire;
War and Revolution

No study of genocide can proceed without attention to the four horsemen of the genocidal apocalypse, enumerated in this chapter's title. Tracing the connections between state-formation and empire-building; incorporating an understanding of war and revolution; and linking all these to genocidal outbreaks, is arguably genocide studies' single most fertile line of recent inquiry.

At the heart of these phenomena is the nation-state, contests over it, and resistance to it. Mark Levene's two-volume work, *Genocide in the Age of the Nation State*, gives the game away in the title.[1] For Levene, and for many other scholars, the emergence of the modern nation-state represents a qualitative irruption in history, and the advent of a new form of genocide—perhaps even of "genocide" as such. Whether or not ancient leaders can be branded as *génocidaires* remains a matter of dispute. I did not hesitate to do so in Chapter 1. Yet however one chooses to classify the state violence inflicted over millennia, it is clear that it was common in the pre-modern age. Exterminatory mass violence, in short, is inseparable from the human record. And generally, it has been the agents of states and quasi-states— military and police formations, colonists, bureaucratic administrators—that have been the most prominent and *essential* perpetrators. Their systematic behavior in various locations over time is what helps to distinguish genocide—legally, practically, and historically—from other patterned and collective violence, like the "riots and pogroms" of Paul Brass's classic study (see Chapter 12).

The central emphasis on state and empire in recent key works of genocide studies pivots on the concepts of social ordering and "legibility," ethnonational collectivity, and racial hierarchy and "purity" that emerged from the Enlightenment and its multiple philosophical and scientific revolutions. The modern state developed into a bureaucratically complex and administratively capacious entity. As it did, it tried to impose a "legible" order upon social formations that were often patchwork and fragmented, from the state's Olympian perspective. Political scientist James C. Scott's *Seeing Like a State* shows how this produced not only ugly, hyperrational architectural schemes (viz. Brasilia), but also a hubris that fueled, in turn, some of modernity's greatest catastrophes, such as Stalin's collectivization campaigns and Mao's "Great Leap Forward" (Chapter 5).[2]

Classical and modern states alike have coalesced and expanded through acts of imperialism and colonization. The growing emphasis on these processes in genocide studies, led by the European/Australasian school gathered in Dirk Moses's *Empire, Colony, Genocide* collection, has supplemented the previous focus on the atrocities of fascism and communism. The new agenda, for the first time, directs systematic attention to a third major genocidal "-ism"—colonialism—and to the imperial holocausts that Western and other countries unleashed on indigenous populations during the great waves of Western colonization (sixteenth to twentieth centuries). Most of this colonial expansion was capitalist or proto-capitalist in nature, certainly with regard to the most destructive institutions imposed on native peoples. Indeed, it was the gold and silver of the Spanish American mines, sustained by genocidal slave labor and circulated throughout Europe by indebted Spanish rulers, that helped to kick-start modern capitalism. These tendencies remain prominent today, in a post-colonial period in which capitalism reigns supreme as a system of economic organization and exploitation. The fact that the most powerful "neo-colonial" players continue to be self-proclaimed democratic exemplars, as they were in the eighteenth and nineteenth centuries, may undermine the "democratic peace" hypothesis that figured in some early formulations of genocide and genocide prevention (see further discussion in Chapter 12).

Incorporating a global-comparative perspective on the genocides of the last half-millennium has enabled important advances in the understanding of events central to the genocide studies field—such as the process of Ottoman imperial dissolution, *reciprocal* genocidal killing (during the "Unweaving" in the Balkans), and complex international jockeying that factored into the massive anti-Christian slaughters in Anatolia in 1915 and thereafter (Chapter 4). Perhaps surprisingly, it is the most iconic genocide of all, the Jewish Holocaust, that has benefited most from these new framings. Analysts from Raul Hilberg to Zygmunt Bauman and Götz Aly had emphasized the statist-bureaucratic dimension of the Holocaust. Daniel Feierstein has now expanded on this to suggest that the Nazi state's very self-conception, its "reading" of the German population, led it to fundamentally distrust and anathematize "cosmopolitan" and "stateless" elements—Jews and Roma/Gypsies above all. These were depicted as standing in opposition, not only to the *German* state, but to the very *idea* and *project* of a state. Moreover, thanks to the work of historians like Benjamin Madley, Jürgen Zimmerer, and Jan-Bart Gewald, we better perceive the link between the Nazis and earlier German imperialists—notably those who orchestrated the systematic mass murder of the Herero and Nama peoples of present-day Namibia in 1904–1907 (see Chapter 3). In the wake of seminal studies by (among others) historians Karel Berkhoff, Wendy Lower, and Mark Mazower, we also have for the first time a clear sense of the imperial contours and character of Nazi policies, in the occupied east above all (Poland, Belorussia, Ukraine, Russia).[3] We see how this empire was imagined, "sold" to Germans, and administered along traditional Western colonial lines—in part as a claiming or reclaiming of Germany's "place in the sun," following the failed imperial projects of previous decades.

If Germany's annihilation war in the east was fundamentally one of imperial conquest, then this points to war's role in enabling and justifying genocides throughout history. And as a vision of radical social revolution through titanic social engineering, it attests to the connection between genocide and the world-changing hubris that often underpins it—whether from a leftist-communist or rightist-capitalist direction. Such grand projects of social revolution, state-building, and political-imperial expansion inevitably generate resistance—and so, much of the war-making of revolutionary and irredentist states becomes *counterinsurgent* violence. This dynamic is no less central to an understanding of war, revolution, and genocide for its involving, to some extent, a *reactive* stance and *retributive* policy on the state's part.

The present chapter addresses these "four horsemen" of genocide—state-building, imperialism/colonialism, war, and social revolution—and explores their interactions and interpenetrations. This paves the way for the exploration of genocide case-studies presented in Part 2 of the book.

THE STATE, IMPERIALISM, AND GENOCIDE

Imperialism is "a policy undertaken by a state to directly control foreign economic, physical, and cultural resources."[4] Colonialism is "a specific form of imperialism involving the establishment and maintenance, for an extended period of time, of rule over an alien people that is separate from and subordinate to the ruling power."[5]

Imperialism and colonialism are mapped into the DNA of the state, both in its classical and modern guise. The units that we know as states or nation-states were generally created by processes of imperial expansion followed by *internal* colonialism.[6] The designated or desirable boundaries of the state were first imposed on coveted lands through imperialism, then actualized, rationalized, made "legible" and exploitable by the imposition of members of the dominant group or its surrogates upon adjacent or nearby territories and populations. The internal expansion of the state's capacities continued apace throughout the early modern period. Processes of turning *Peasants into Frenchmen*, to cite Eugen Weber—and into Germans, Britons, Americans, Soviets—could be evolutionary and benign, in Raphael Lemkin's view. But often, as in the Vendée case described in Chapter 1, the state's centralizing project was perceived as a mortal threat by other populations and power centers. The crushing of resistance to the statist-expansionist enterprise inevitably assumed a genocidal scale and character, and continues to do so.

The greatest relevance of the internal-colonialism concept is for indigenous populations worldwide. Native people occupy marginal positions both territorially and socially; their traditional homelands are often coveted by expanding state settlement from the center. Profits flow from periphery to core; the environment is ravaged. The result is the undermining and dissolution, often the destruction, of indigenous societies, accomplished by massacres, selective killings, expulsions, coerced labor, disease, and substance abuse. Other examples of internal colonialism in this book include the Chinese in Tibet (Chapter 5); Stalin's USSR vis-à-vis both the Soviet countryside and minority ethnicities (Chapter 5);[7] and Indonesia in East Timor (Chapter 7a).

Genocide is further interwoven with colonialism in the phenomenon of *settler colonialism*. Here, the metropolitan power encourages or dispatches colonists to "settle" the territory. (In the British Empire, this marks the difference between settler colonies such as Canada, Australia, and New Zealand; and the Indian subcontinent, where just 25,000 Britons administered a vast realm.) Settler colonialism implies occupation of the land, and is often linked to genocide against indigenous peoples (and genocidally-tinged rebellions against colonialism) (see Chapter 3). Settler colonies may also be born of expansionist and internal-colonialist projects close to the metropolitan core. The genocidal or near-genocidal campaigns against Ireland's and Scotland's native inhabitants from the sixteenth to nineteenth centuries,[8] for example, prompted the migration under massive duress of millions of Irish and Scottish to the British settler colonies and the United States. Likewise, the drive against "asocial" elements and political dissidents resulted in the transportation of tens of thousands of prisoners to the Australian penal colonies.[9] Ironically, it was sometimes representatives of these invaded and criminalized populations, thrust to the "sharp end" of colonial invasions, who proved energetic exponents and practitioners of genocide against indigenous populations.

Finally, we should expand upon the dimension of *neo-colonialism*. The concept is ambiguous and contested, but also useful. Under neo-colonialism, formal political rule is abandoned, while colonial structures of economic, political, and cultural control remain. The resulting exploitation may have genocidal consequences. Individual interventions with arguably genocidal consequences may be linked to prior colonial or quasi-colonial relationships (e.g., France in Rwanda before and during the 1994 genocide; Britain and the US in Iraq in 1991 and 2003). Many commentators also consider *structural violence*—that is, the destructive power residing in social and economic structures—to reflect neo-colonialism: the former colonial powers have maintained their hegemony over the formerly colonized ("Third") world, and immense disparities of wealth and well-being remain, producing "poorcide" in S.P. Udayakumar's framing (see p. 37).

The brief examination of genocide in classical and early modern times (Chapter 1) showed how frequently genocide accompanied imperial expansion and colonialism. In the modern era, the destruction of indigenous peoples has been a pervasive feature of these institutions, and is analyzed as a global phenomenon in

Chapter 3. The communist tyrannies studied in Chapters 5 and 7 had a brazenly statist and imperial dimension, to be considered in its place. It remains here to provide an overview of some other key cases of genocide under colonial and imperial regimes in the past two centuries.

Imperial famines

"Famine crimes" or "genocidal famines" have increasingly drawn genocide scholars' attention.[10] The most extensively studied cases are Stalin's USSR (Chapter 5), Mao's China, and Ethiopia under the Dergue regime. Recently the North Korean case, in which up to two million people may have starved to death while the government remained inert, has sparked outrage (also explored in Chapter 5). The literature has focused strongly on cases of famine under dictatorial and authoritarian regimes. Influenced by Nobel Prize-winning economist Amartya Sen, who demonstrated that "there has never been a famine in a functioning multiparty democracy,"[11] this has produced groundbreaking case studies such as Robert Conquest's *The Harvest of Sorrow* (USSR) and Frank Dikötter's *Mao's Great Famine* (China). The millions of dead in these catastrophes, from starvation and disease, form a substantial part of the indictment of communist regimes in the compendium, *The Black Book of Communism*.[12] However, historian Mike Davis's *Late Victorian Holocausts* reminds us that liberal regimes have also been complicit in such crimes—extending far beyond the notorious example of the Great Hunger in 1840s Ireland (see Box 2.1). Davis's subject is the epic famines of the later nineteenth and early twentieth centuries, linked both to nature (the El Niño phenomenon) and state policy, which devastated peasant societies from China to Brazil. He shares Sen's conviction that famines are not blows of blind fate, but "social crises that represent the failures of particular economic and political systems." Specifically, he asserts that "imperial policies towards starving 'subjects' were often the exact moral equivalents of bombs dropped from 18,000 feet."[13]

India was largely free of famine under the Mogul emperors, but British administrators refused to follow the Mogul example of laying in sufficient emergency grain stocks. When famine struck, they imposed free-market policies that were nothing more than a "mask for colonial genocide," according to Davis. They continued ruinous collections of tax arrears, evincing greater concern for India's balance of payments than for "the holocaust in lives." When the British did set up relief camps, they were work camps, which "provided less sustenance for hard labor than the infamous Buchenwald concentration camp and less than half of the modern caloric standard recommended for adult males by the Indian government." The death toll in the famine of 1897–1898 alone, including associated disease epidemics, may have exceeded eleven million, while grain exports continued apace.[14] "Twelve to 16 million was the death toll commonly reported in the world press, which promptly nominated this the 'famine of the century.' This dismal title, however, was almost immediately usurped by the even greater drought and deadlier famine of 1899–1902." In 1901, the leading British medical journal the *Lancet* suggested that "a conservative estimate of excess mortality in India in the previous decade . . . was 19 million," a total that "a number of historians . . . have

BOX 2.1 SINÉAD O'CONNOR ON THE IRISH FAMINE

Figure 2.1 Sinéad O'Connor in concert at the Festival interceltique de Lorient in France, August 2013.

Source: Photo by Pymouss/Creative Commons/Flickr.

The 1994 song "Famine," by the Irish singer Sinéad O'Connor, is a remarkably clear-eyed and empathetic evocation of the colonial impact and its enduring legacy. Those who favor a more cultural/sociological interpretation of genocidal "destruction" (see "What Is Destroyed in Genocide?," Chapter 1) will find support in the kinds of structural violence and psychological traumas that O'Connor describes, particularly as they afflict indigenous peoples worldwide (Chapter 3). Allowing for poetic license, O'Connor's depiction of the Irish famine of 1846–1848 squares with most scholarly interpretations (see note 8). Her "famine" anyway is as much metaphorical and existential as historical.

> Okay, I want to talk about Ireland
> Specifically I want to talk about the "famine"
> About the fact that there never really was one
> There was no "famine"
> See Irish people were only allowed to eat potatoes
> All of the other food
> Meat fish vegetables
> Were shipped out of the country under armed guard
> To England while the Irish people starved

And then in the middle of all this
They gave us money not to teach our children Irish
And so we lost our history
And this is what I think is still hurting we

See we're like a child that's been battered
Has to drive itself out of its head because it's frightened
Still feels all the painful feelings
But they lose contact with the memory

And this leads to massive self-destruction
Alcoholism, drug addiction
All desperate attempts at running
And in its worst form
Becomes actual killing

And if there ever is gonna be healing
There has to be remembering
And then grieving
So that there then can be forgiving
There has to be knowledge and understanding [. . .]

An American army regulation
Says you mustn't kill more than ten percent of a nation
'Cos to do so causes permanent "psychological damage"
It's not permanent but they didn't know that
Anyway, during the supposed "famine"
We lost a lot more than ten percent of our nation
Through deaths on land or on ships of emigration
But what finally broke us was not starvation
But its use in the controlling of our education
Schools go on about "Black '47"
On and on about "the terrible famine"
But what they don't say is in truth
There really never was one [. . .]

So let's take a look, shall we
The highest statistics of child abuse in the EEC [EU]
And we say we're a Christian country
But we've lost contact with our history
See we used to worship God as a mother
We're suffering from post-traumatic stress disorder
Look at all our old men in the pubs
Look at all our young people on drugs

We used to worship God as a mother
Now look at what we're doing to each other

We've even made killers of ourselves
The most child-like trusting people in the universe
And this is what's wrong with us
Our history books, the parent figures, lied to us

I see the Irish as a race like a child
That got itself bashed in the face
And if there ever is gonna be healing
There has to be remembering
And then grieving
So that there then can be forgiving
There has to be knowledge and understanding [. . .]

Excerpts from "Famine," lyrics © by Sinéad O'Connor, Tim Simenon, John Reynolds, John Lennon, Paul McCartney, and David Clayton. Used by permission of Hal Leonard Corporation, Warner/Chappell Music, and Nettwerk One Publishing.[15]

accepted . . . as an order–of–magnitude approximation for the combined mortality of the 1896–1902 crisis."[16]

Overall, Davis argued that market mechanisms imposed in colonial (e.g., India) and neo–colonial contexts (e.g., China and Brazil) inflicted massive excess mortality. "There is persuasive evidence that peasants and farm laborers became dramatically more pregnable to natural disaster after 1850 as their local economies were violently incorporated into the world market. . . . Commercialization went hand in hand with pauperization."[17] He explicitly linked colonial and neo–colonial relations to the economic structures and policies that devastated once–thriving economies, and produced the "Third World" of the post–colonial era.

In 1940s Bengal, liberal economics was supplanted by "security" considerations. The British empire had been humiliated and pushed to its extremity by the Japanese, who had occupied Burma, and were now massing at the borders of India, together with their allies of the Indian National Army, a guerrilla force under the command of Subhas Chandra Bose. Among the little-known aspects of this little-known "theater" of the Pacific War, a massive cyclone triggered crop failure across Bengal. Emergency relief was desperately required. "With the empire at risk from a military invasion, and discord rife even as Bengal's people began to starve, Churchill was called upon to make a choice that would tilt the balance between life and death for millions: whether or not to expend valuable wheat and shipping space on providing famine relief to Bengalis."

But the Bengali masses were never likely to loom large in Churchill's considerations. "I hate Indians," he proclaimed frankly. "They are a beastly people with a beastly religion [Hinduism]." (At the war's end he would describe Hindus as "a

Figure 2.2 "The Famine in India—Natives Waiting for Relief in Bangalore." Engraving in *The Illustrated London News*, 1877. In subjugated India and Ireland in the nineteenth century, British imperialists pioneered the "faminogenic" catastrophes of the modern period, with famine relief sacrificed to the laws of the market or, in the Stalinist and Maoist cases, the drive for communist utopia (see Chapter 5). In all these cases, the ruling regimes exported foodstuffs on a large scale throughout the famines.

Source: Scanned from the original October 20, 1877 issue of *The Illustrated London News*, in the author's collection.

foul race" kept alive only by out-of-control breeding. Air Chief Marshall Arthur Harris, who had lately bombed German cities to rubble, should "send some of his surplus bombers to destroy them.") Churchill ascribed the burgeoning famine of 1943 "to the improvidence of the various [colonial] Governments in the East concerned, and the failure of their crops." With shipping resources desperately scarce, he wrote to his minister of transport: "I hope you will be as stiff as you can. There is no reason why all parts of the British Empire should not feel the pinch in the same way as the Mother Country has done." (In fact, noted Madhusree Mukerjee, "the sole sacrifice that ordinary Britons were asked to make in response to the shipping crisis of 1943 was to eat multigrain bread.")

The decisions of Churchill and his commanders in the field would exact a death toll comparable to the Indian famines just mentioned, though not on the same territorial scale. "In a replay" of earlier policies, domestic rice production was devoted to the armed forces. *And once again food was exported*—not for profit, and not on so massive a scale as in the past, but Mukerjee estimates that the rice and wheat could have kept 390,000 to 2 million Bengalis alive for a full year. The Churchill government repeatedly stonewalled on offers by Australia and Canada to send wheat to Bengal. Strategic considerations were cited—the grain was needed for the population of the soon-to-be-occupied Balkans. But the obstinate refusal to utilize available resources to provide available relief is a key feature in determining the presence, or degree, of genocidal intent in a "faminogenic" situation like Bengal's. And Churchill's racist malice bordered on the pathological, marking him as a genuine *génocidaire* in this case. (His views would mellow somewhat in later years, as he interacted more with the Indian leader Jawaharlal Nehru, among others.) His subordinates regularly pressed him to do more for the Bengalis, but as the Secretary of State for India, Leopold Amery, noted caustically in his diary: "Winston so dislikes India and all to do with it that he can see nothing but the mere waste of shipping space involved" in rescuing it.

The chief consequence of these policies and prejudices was the extermination by starvation and disease of at least one million Bengalis. Estimates range far higher. The Nobel Prize-winning economist Amartya Sen "took the registered deaths for West Bengal, extended them to East Pakistan (nowadays Bangladesh), and applied corrections to get around 3 million for the famine toll."[18] Sen's Nobel Prize derived above all from his work on famines, buttressed by the Bengali case and others. He proposed, in a thesis that has become a virtual law of political economy, that *famines do not occur in democracies*, because democracy provides counterweights—in the form of popular mobilizations and media exposure, for example—that are not available under dictatorial rule. This holds whether the dictatorial authority is colonially imposed or homegrown. The two most destructive famines of the twentieth century—in Soviet Ukraine and Kazakhstan in 1932–1933, and in Maoist China during the "Great Leap Forward" of 1958–1961—further validate Sen's argument, which is also relevant to the discussion of democracy and genocide in Chapter 12.

The Congo "rubber terror"

Thanks to novelist Joseph Conrad's *Heart of Darkness*, published early in the twentieth century, the murderous exploitation of the Congo by Belgium's King Leopold has attained almost mythic status. However, not until the publication of Adam Hochschild's *King Leopold's Ghost*, at the end of the last century, did contemporary audiences come to appreciate the scale of the destruction inflicted on the Congo, as well as the public outcry at the time that produced one of the first truly international campaigns for human rights.[19]

Conrad's novella was based on a river voyage into the interior of the Congo, during which he witnessed what he called "the vilest scramble for loot that ever disfigured the history of human conscience and geographical exploration."[20] The territory that became the so-called Congo Free State was, and remains, immense. In 1874, King Leopold commissioned British explorer Henry Stanley to secure for the monarch a place in the imperial sun. By 1885, Leopold had established the Congo as his personal fief, free of oversight from the Belgian parliament. Ivory was the prize he first hungered for, then rubber as the pneumatic tire revolutionized road travel. To muster the forced labor *(corvée)* needed to supply these goods, Leopold's agents imposed a reign of terror on African populations.

The result was one of the most destructive and all-encompassing *corvée* institutions the world has known. It led to "a death toll of Holocaust dimensions," in Hochschild's estimation,[21] such that "Leopold's African regime became a byword for exploitation and genocide."[22] Male rubber tappers and porters were mercilessly exploited and driven to death. A Belgian politician, Edmond Picard, encountered a caravan of conscripts:

> Incessantly, we met these porters ... black, miserable, their only clothing a horrible dirty loincloth ... most of them sickly, their strength sapped by exhaustion and inadequate food, which consisted of a handful of rice and stinking dried fish, pitiable walking caryatids ... organised in a system of human transport, requisitioned by the State with its irresistible *force publique* [militia], delivered by chiefs whose slaves they are and who purloin their pay ... dying on the road or, their journey ended, dying from the overwork in their villages.[23]

The precipitous population decline during Leopold's rule remains astonishing. Hochschild accepted the conclusions of a Belgian government commission that "the population of the territory had 'been reduced by half.'" "In 1924," he added, "the population was reckoned at ten million, a figure confirmed by later counts. This would mean, according to the estimates, that during the Leopold period and its immediate aftermath the population of the territory dropped by approximately ten million people."[24] During this time, the region was also swept by an epidemic of sleeping sickness, "one of the most disastrous plagues recorded in human history."[25] However, as with indigenous peoples elsewhere, the impact of disease was exacerbated by slavery and privation, and vice versa: "The responsibility for

Figure 2.3 "A child victim of Belgian atrocities in Congo stands with a missionary (probably Mr. Wall-baum), Congo, ca. 1890–1910." The atrocious practice, during King Leopold's reign and "Rubber Terror," of severing the hands of Congolese males who failed to meet their slave labor quotas aroused international revulsion, and produced some of the earliest iconic images of humanitarian photography. They were shown to public audiences in the form of lantern slides like this one, especially by Christian missionaries and advocates in Europe, North America, and beyond.[29] Religious and other opponents of Belgian depredations utilized existing networks and discourses of anti-slavery, pro-emancipation movements decades earlier, in a classic instance of "norm grafting" (see Chapter 12).

Source: University of Southern California Digital Library/Wikimedia Commons.

this disaster is no less Leopold's because it was a compound one."[26] And the demographic data presented by Hochschild demonstrated a shocking under-representation of adult males in the Congolese population, indicating that genocide claimed millions of lives.[27] "Sifting such figures today is like sifting the ruins of an Auschwitz crematorium," wrote Hochschild. "They do not tell you precise death tolls, but they reek of mass murder."[28]

The only bright side to this, "one of the most appalling slaughters known to have been brought about by human agency,"[30] was an international protest movement, the Congo Reform Association, led by Joseph Conrad, Sir Arthur Conan Doyle—author of the Sherlock Holmes stories—and the Irishman Roger Casement. The Association spread across Europe and North America, and sponsored investigative exposes of Leopold's Congo.[31] All of this increased pressure on King Leopold to subject his territory to outside oversight. Finally, in 1908, Leopold agreed to sell his enormous fief to the Belgian government. Subsequent parliamentary monitoring appears to have substantially reduced mortality, though the "rubber terror" only truly lapsed after the First World War.

Belgium remained the colonial power in the territory until 1960, when it handed over the Congo to the pro-Western dictator, Mobutu Sese Seko. Early in the twenty-first century, the Congo was again torn apart by genocide, amidst the most destructive military conflict since the Second World War—a grim echo of the killing that rent the region under Leopold's rule (see Chapter 9).

The Japanese in East and Southeast Asia

Japanese imperialism, founded on invasions of Korea and Taiwan in the late nineteenth century, grew by leaps and bounds under the military regime established during the 1930s. Domestic persecution of communists and other political opponents merged with aggressive expansion. In 1931, the Japanese invaded the mineral-rich Chinese region of Manchuria, setting up the puppet state of Manchukuo the following year.

In 1937, Japan effectively launched the Second World War, invading China's eastern seaboard and key interior points. The campaign featured air attacks that killed tens of thousands of civilians and even more intensive atrocities by troops on the ground. The occupation of the Chinese capital, Nanjing, in December 1937 became a global byword for war crimes. Japanese forces slaughtered as many as 200,000 Chinese men of "battle age," and raped tens of thousands of women and children—often murdering and mutilating their victims thereafter (see Chapter 13). "There are executions everywhere," wrote John Rabe, a German businessman who witnessed the atrocities of the "Rape of Nanjing," and worked indefatigably to save civilian lives (see p. 632). "You hear of nothing but rape. . . . The devastation the Japanese have wreaked here is almost beyond description."[32] Over the course of the Japanese occupation (1937–1945), "nearly 2,600,000 unarmed Chinese civilians" were killed, together with half a million to one million prisoners-of-war.[33]

In December 1941, Japan coordinated its surprise attack on the US Pacific Fleet at Pearl Harbor with a lightning invasion of Southeast Asia. This brought the Philippines, Malaya (peninsular Malaysia), Singapore, and Indonesia under its direct rule. (Satellite control was established in Indochina, in collusion with the Vichy French regime.) Large-scale summary killings of civilians, death marches of Asian and European populations, and atrocities against Allied prisoners-of-war all figured in the postwar war-crimes trials (Chapter 15). The Japanese also imposed a *corvée* labor system, one of the worst in modern history,

Figure 2.4 Furious at popular resistance, Japanese forces used captured Chinese prisoners-of-war as targets for bayonet practice, while others stood and enjoyed the spectacle.

Source: www.nanking-massacre.com.

Figure 2.5 Allied prisoners-of-war and their native auxiliaries were also killed *en masse* by Japanese troops—on death marches, in prison camps, and in executions like this one, of Australian commando Sgt. Leonard G. Siffleet at Aitape, New Guinea, in October 1943.

Source: Collection Database of the Australian War Memorial/Wikimedia Commons.

throughout the occupied territories. Not only did the notorious Burma–Thailand railroad kill 16,000 of the 46–50,000 Allied prisoners forced to work on it, but "as many as 100,000 of the 120,000 to 150,000 Asian forced laborers may have died. . . . "[34] The trafficking of Asian women for prostitution (the so-called "comfort women") formed an integral part of this forced-labor system. Region-wide, the death toll of *corvée* laborers probably approached, or even exceeded, one million. Both the "comfort women" and male forced laborers have in recent years petitioned the Japanese government for acknowledgment and material compensation, with some success but also much stonewalling (see Chapter 14).[35]

Like their Nazi counterparts, the Japanese believed themselves to be superior beings. Subject races were not considered "subhuman" in the Nazi fashion, but they were clearly regarded as inferior, and were usually assigned a helot status in the "Greater Asian Co-Prosperity Sphere." Japanese fantasies of racial supremacy also led to a Nazi-style preoccupation with genocidal technologies, reflected most notably in the biological warfare program and gruesome medical experiments. Unit 731 in Manchuria produced chemical and biological weapons that were tested on prisoners-of-war and civilians, and deployed throughout the war theater. In China, according to Japanese historian Yuki Tanaka,

> In Zhejiang province, biological weapons were used six times between September 18 and October 7, 1940. . . . Around the same time 270 kilograms of typhoid, paratyphoid, cholera, and plague bacteria were sent to Nanjing and central China for use by Japanese battalions on the battlefield. . . . After the outbreak of World War II, the Japanese continued to use biological weapons against the Chinese. They sprayed cholera, typhoid, plague, and dysentery pathogens in the Jinhua area of Zhejiang province in June and July 1942. . . . It is [also] well known that Unit 731 used large numbers of Chinese people for experiments. Many Chinese who rebelled against the Japanese occupation were arrested and sent to Pingfan where they became guinea pigs for Unit 731. . . . When they were being experimented on, the [subjects] were transferred from the main prison to individual cells where they were infected with particular pathogens by such means as injections or being given contaminated food or water. . . . After succumbing to the disease, the prisoners were usually dissected, and their bodies were then cremated within the compound.[36]

In an ironic outcome from which Nazi scientists also benefited, after the Second World War the participants in Unit 731 atrocities were granted immunity from prosecution—so long as they shared their knowledge of chemical and biological warfare, and the results of their atrocious experiments, with US authorities (see Chapter 15).[37]

The US in Indochina

With the possible exception of the French war to retain Algeria (1958–1962), no imperial intervention in the twentieth century provoked as much dissent and political upheaval in the colonial power as the US's long war in Vietnam. And in the post–World War Two period, none was so destructive.

A French attempt in 1945–1954 to reconquer Vietnam was defeated by a nationalist guerrilla movement under Ho Chi Minh and his military commander, Vo Nguyen Giap. The country was divided between a Chinese client regime in the North and a US client regime in the South. Under the Geneva agreements of 1954, this was supposed to be temporary. But recognizing that Ho would likely win nationwide elections scheduled for 1956, Ngo Dinh Diem's regime refused to hold them. After 1961, the US stepped up direct military intervention. In 1965, hundreds of thousands of US troops occupied the country to combat the South Vietnamese guerrillas (Viet Cong or VC), as well as regular North Vietnamese forces infiltrating down the "Ho Chi Minh Trail" through southern Laos and eastern Cambodia.

About seven million tons of bombs and other munitions were dropped on North and (especially) South Vietnam during the course of the war. *This was more than was dropped by all countries in all theaters of the Second World War.* The bombing was combined with the creation of a network of "model villages" in the South Vietnamese countryside, kept under close US and South Vietnamese military observation.

Beyond these villages, essentially concentration camps, large swathes of the countryside were liable to be designated as "free-fire zones," in which anyone living was assumed to be an enemy. In a highly racialized war in which Vietnamese were reviled as "dinks" and "gooks" and "slopes" (i.e., slant-eyed), a war of mass and localized atrocity was waged, well-captured by the title of Nick Turse's important investigation, *Kill Anything That Moves.* For American soldiers, especially those delivering death and ruin from the air, the atmosphere resembled that of the US Plains Indians wars and massacres of the nineteenth century. A reporter in the Mekong Delta, the rice bowl of South Vietnam, described US helicopter pilots who "seemed to fire whimsically and in passing even though they were not being shot at from the ground nor could they identify the people as NLF [guerrillas]. They did it impulsively for fun, using farmers for targets as if in a hunting mood."[38] The pervasive "body count" system, in which murdered civilians were generally counted as dead combatants, spawned "a real incentivizing of death . . . [that] just fucked with our value system," as one US infantry medic recalled.[39] A 1st Cavalry battle song captured the ambience of cheerful slaughter:

> We shoot the sick, the young, the lame,
> We do our best to kill and maim,
> Because the kills count all the same,
> Napalm sticks to kids.
> Ox cart rolling down the road,
> Peasants with a heavy load,
> They're all VC when the bombs explode,
> Napalm sticks to kids.[40]

Populations who resisted evacuation risked annihilation from the air and massacre by US and South Vietnamese ground forces. The most infamous such event was the My Lai massacre—a four-hour-long rampage by US troops on March 16, 1968, in the village of Son My and its constituent hamlets of My Lai, My Khe, and Co Luy in Quang Ngai province. Infuriated by guerrilla attacks, US troops of Charlie Company, 1st Battalion, slaughtered, raped, and wreaked material destruction.[41] The My Lai memorial plaque today lists 504 victims. A handful of troops resisted orders to kill, and genuine rescuers emerged—most heroically Lt.-Col. Hugh Thompson, Jr., who witnessed the killing from his helicopter, landed, and interposed himself between fleeing villagers and their would-be murderers, ordering his men to fire on the US forces if they advanced (see pp. 553–556). An extensive official cover-up of the massacre was mounted, until investigative reporter Seymour Hersh blew the lid off the case in articles for the *St. Louis Post-Dispatch* in November 1969.[42] An investigation was launched, but only one perpetrator—Lt. William Calley—was convicted. After sentence reductions and a couple of years of house arrest, he was paroled in 1974 by the Secretary of the Army, "after having served one-third of his twice-reduced sentence."[43] Calley lived on in obscurity, until he emerged in 2009 to publicly apologize for his crimes.[44] Research by investigative reporters from the *Toledo Blade* and other publications has established that My Lai was no isolated incident. Rather, massacres were common for US forces fighting to "pacify" the south, after the Viet Cong/North Vietnamese "Tet Offensive" of 1968 rocked US popular support of the war to its foundations.[45]

In 1970, Nixon widened the war, stepping up the "secret" bombing of neighboring Cambodia on a scale that is only now being recognized (and fueling the rise of the genocidal Khmer Rouge; see Chapter 7). Extensive areas of Laos, notably the Plain of Jars and the Bolaven Plateau, were subjected to saturation bombing that killed their inhabitants or terrorized them into flight. The bombing continued until 1973, when a peace agreement was signed and most US soldiers withdrew from South Vietnam. Two years later, North Vietnamese forces invaded and conquered South Vietnam.

The human cost of the war to the US was some 58,000 soldiers killed. In Indochina, the toll was catastrophic. The Vietnamese government in 1995 estimated over three million war dead, including two million civilians; a 2008 report co-sponsored by the Harvard Medical School found that 3.8 million Vietnamese may have died violently during the war, and "there are good reasons to believe that even this staggering figure may be an underestimate."[46] Millions more were wounded, mutilated, disfigured, or poisoned by "the massive application of chemical warfare," aimed primarily at defoliating the countryside of forest cover in

Figure 2.6 The My Lai massacre of March 16, 1968, was the largest, but far from the only, genocidal massacre inflicted during the US imperial "pacification" of South Vietnam in 1968–1969. Ronald K. Haeberle, an army photographer, captured this image of Vietnamese children and women rounded up in My Lai hamlet, seconds before they were gunned down by US troops. According to an army publicist accompanying the photographer (*LIFE*, December 5, 1969), "Haeberle jumped in to take a picture of the group of women. The picture shows the thirteen-year-old girl hiding behind her mother, trying to button the top of her pyjamas. When they noticed Ron, they left off and turned away as if everything was normal. Then a soldier asked, 'Well, what'll we do with 'em?' 'Kill 'em,' another answered. I heard an M60 go off, a light machine-gun, and when we turned all of them and the kids with them were dead."

Source: Ronald K. Haeberle/US Army/Wikimedia Commons.

Figure 2.7 A visitor views another of Haeberle's images at the My Lai memorial museum.
Source: Author's photo, July 2009.

which guerrilla forces could hide, poisoned the soil and food chain.[47] "The lingering effects of chemical warfare poisoning continue to plague the health of adult Vietnamese (and ex-GIs) while causing increased birth defects. Samples of soil, water, food and body fat of Vietnamese continue to the present day to reveal dangerously elevated levels of dioxin." An estimated "3.5 million landmines and 300,000 tons of unexploded ordnance [UXO]" still litter the countryside, killing "several thousand" Vietnamese every year—at least 40,000 since the war ended in 1975.[48] Laos, too, is laced with UXO; hundreds of rural residents are killed and maimed annually, particularly younger children.[49]

The international revulsion that the Indochina war evoked led to the creation, in 1966, of an informal International War Crimes Tribunal under the aegis of the British philosopher Bertrand Russell. The Russell Tribunal panelists were "unanimous in finding the US guilty for using illegal weapons, maltreating prisoners-of-war and civilians, and aggressing against Laos." Most controversially, "there was a unanimous vote of guilty on the genocide charge."[50] A leading figure in this "citizens' tribunal" (see Chapter 15) was the French philosopher Jean-Paul Sartre, who wrote "On Genocide," an essay that made "a striking case for regarding the American war in Vietnam as genocide legally and conceptually."[51] Those fighting the war, Sartre argued, were *"living out* the only possible relationship between an overindustrialized country and an underdeveloped country, that is to say, a genocidal relationship implemented through racism."[52] Genocide scholar Leo Kuper likewise called the war's conduct "suggestive of genocide."[53]

The Soviets in Afghanistan

Soviet intervention in Afghanistan was a continuation of the historic Russian drive for influence and control along the imperial periphery. Severely mauled by the Nazi invasion during the Second World War, the Soviets thereafter established authoritarian police states in Eastern Europe, with forays beyond, notably in Asia and Africa.

Within the Soviet empire, governance strategies varied, but they were frequently murderous, particularly in the decade or so following the Second World War and the lowering of a communist "Iron Curtain" over Central and Eastern Europe.[54] Hundreds of thousands of German and other prisoners-of-war and civilian men were shipped off to distant corners of the Gulag prison-camp and slave-labor system. Most did not survive to see freedom. In 1956, when Hungary rose in revolt against its Soviet satraps, the USSR invaded and crushed the uprising, killing some 25,000 Hungarians and sending hundreds of thousands more fleeing into exile.[55]

The worst barbarism of the Soviet empire, however, occurred in Afghanistan, which shared a border with the USSR's Central Asian territories. Years of growing Soviet influence there culminated in the establishment of a Soviet client government in Kabul in April 1978. In 1979, a reign of terror inflicted by President Hafizullah Amin further destabilized Afghan society. Finally, in December 1979, 25,000 Soviet troops invaded to "restore stability." Amin, who had outlived his usefulness, was killed at the outset of the invasion, and replaced by a more compliant Soviet proxy, Babrak Karmal. Occupying forces rapidly swelled to around 85,000.

The occupation spawned an initially ragtag but, with US assistance, increasingly coherent Islamist-nationalist resistance, the *mujahedin*. Osama bin Laden began his trajectory as a foreign volunteer with the *mujahedin*, as did others who would later wage war on the West. The Soviets responded with collective atrocity. In "a ferocious scorched-earth campaign that combined the merciless destructiveness of Genghis Khan's Mongols with the calculated terrorism of Stalin,"[56] the Soviets inflicted massive civilian destruction, recalling the worst US actions in Indochina. According to Afghanistan specialist Rosanne Klass,

> From January 1980 on . . . the Soviets made genocide a coherent, systematic policy. . . . Soviet and local communist forces targeted the rural civilian population, not the armed resistance. . . . Operational patterns (particularly air attacks) indicated a systematic effort to depopulate selected areas on an ethnic basis. . . . Overall Soviet strategy focused on emptying out the predominantly Pashtun areas, thereby altering the ethnic makeup of Afghanistan. . . . Thousands of very young children were (often forcibly) sent to the USSR and Eastern Europe for ten years for preparatory indoctrination; few if any have returned.

Figure 2.8 Soviet troops round up young Afghan men in a counterinsurgency sweep in 1985. The fate of the men is unknown, but such sweeps were typically accompanied by harsh interrogation or torture, and widespread summary execution. Such measures are the norm when imperial powers seek, sometimes by genocidal means, to cow and subjugate a restive population (see Chapter 13). The Soviets repeated them in the campaign against the population of Chechnya in the 1990s and 2000s (Box 5a). In central respects, Russia's wars in Chechnya were racist acts of vengeance against Muslim populations, fueled by the humiliating defeat in Afghanistan. As many as two million people were killed during the decade-long Soviet occupation of the country (1979–1989).

Source: Wikimedia Commons.

Air attacks through the southern and eastern provinces methodically killed hundreds of thousands and resulted in the mass exodus of millions, creating a depopulated no-man's-land in large areas along the Afghanistan-Pakistan border. In addition to the bombings, which reached their peak in 1986, the Soviets used terror—chemical weapons, weapons targeting children, gruesome localized atrocities, and the destruction of crops, orchards, animals, food supplies, and water sources—to empty out whole districts.[57]

Aerial bombing never assumed the saturation levels of Indochina. But once the Soviets realized that a genuinely popular insurgency had taken root, aerial attacks became collective and indiscriminate in their targeting. A former Soviet fighter pilot, Alexander Rutskoi, related during a conversation on the war in Chechnya in the 1990s (Box 5a) his view "that Russia should use the same approach he had employed in Afghanistan: 'A *kishlak* [village] fires at us and kills someone. I send a couple of planes and there is nothing left of the *kishlak*. After I've burned a couple of *kishlaks* they stop shooting.'"[58] As US atrocities in Vietnam mirrored the "Indian wars" of the past,[59] there are clear echoes in the Afghanistan campaign of Russia's ruthless wars of imperial expansion against minority populations in the nineteenth century, most notably the Circassians (see Box 2.2).

BOX 2.2 THE CIRCASSIANS

Figure 2.9 A t-shirt produced by the No Sochi 2014 campaign. Writes the photographer, a Jordanian Circassian: "On 22 October 2010 I wore this T shirt while running in the Amman Marathon. I did it for my brave ancestors who fought fiercely for 101 years!"

Source: Photo by pshegubj/Flickr/Creative Commons.

YOU'LL BE SKIING ON MASS GRAVES. The protest signs at the 2010 Winter Olympics in Vancouver, Canada were probably the first that most visitors to the games had ever heard of Circassia. But in a chilling harbinger of the type of imperial violence that Soviet and post-Soviet governments would inflict on Afghans, Chechens (Box 5a), and others, this ancient nation was obliterated in the final stages of a Russian imperial conquest that took nearly a century. The climactic battle, in May 1864, took place at Krasnaya Polyana, "the location of [the Circassians'] first and only parliament," which in the Russian invasion became "a site of suffering and death." A century-and-a-half later, Krasnaya Polyana—developed in Soviet times as a ski resort—was the principal site chosen for the 2014 Sochi Olympics. "The notion of medals symbolizing peaceful competition between nations being awarded on the very ground where military decorations were handed out for the annihilation of the Circassian nation exactly 150 years earlier filled many with indignation."[60]

The Circassians, who adopted Islam in the eighteenth century, were a tribal people whose "identity was defined by a series of overlapping kinship groups, stretching outwards from the individual's closest kin to the Circassian nation (or proto-nation if one prefers) as a whole."[61] In the mid-eighteenth century, some two million Circassians inhabited a long stretch of the northwestern Caucasus mountains straddling the Black Sea coast.[62] For the Russian imperial regime, the Circassians were nothing more than "primitive warlike barbarians and savage bandits,"[63] and an obstacle to imperial expansion and colonization of the Caucasus.[64]

The final stage of the conquest, in 1862–1864, was guided by the conviction of the Russian commander-in-chief, Alexander Baryatinsky, that "we must assume that we will need to exterminate the mountaineers before they will agree to our demands."[65] The climactic expeditions were commanded by Count Nikolai Evdokimov. His soldiers burned villages, massacred inhabitants, forcibly resettled Circassian survivors who pledged allegiance to the tsar, and expelled nearly all the remaining population under horrific conditions to the coast (see Figure 2.10).[66] There, they festered and tens of thousands died of exposure, malnutrition, and disease in "one of the worst winters in recent history [to] hit the Black Sea."[67] Evdomikov was kept fully apprised of the humanitarian crisis, but he cared not a jot, expressing frustration at one Count Sumarokov who "keeps reminding me in every report concerning the frozen bodies which cover the roads." By the autumn of 1864, "there were so many corpses on the shore . . . that Staff Captain Sme-kalov frankly stated, "I have no data because it's impossible to gather up [the dead] . . . "[68] Those who did not perish on the shore were transported on "barges

Figure 2.10 The mass expulsion of the Circassians from their mountainous homeland was depicted by Pyotr Nikolayevich Gruzinsky in this painting, "The Mountaineers Leave the Aul [Village]," from 1872. In the collection of the State Russian Museum, St. Petersburg.

Source: Wikimedia Commons.

and small Turkish and Greek ships, loaded with several times as many passengers as they could carry. Many of these sank and their passengers drowned in the open sea."[69] The ships that arrived deposited the Circassians in an Ottoman empire that had agreed to receive them, but was "completely unprepared to deal with the half million or more sick and starving people who arrived." Uncounted numbers perished. Walter Richmond, who has written the first scholarly monograph on the Circassian genocide, contends that "even with the most conservative mortality estimates, at least 625,000 Circassians died during Evdokimov's operations."[70] Shenfield wrote that the toll "could hardly . . . have been fewer than one million, and may well have been closer to one-and-a-half million."[71] Ninety-five to 97 percent of the entire Circassian population had been killed or deported in what contemporary Russian field reports referred to as an *ochischenie* ("cleansing").[72]

The Circassian diaspora today encompasses several million descendants in Turkey, as well as substantial communities in Russia (the Karachai-Cherkess Autonomous Province, where mountain populations who submitted to tsarist rule were resettled), Jordan, Syria, and the Balkans. Advocates have pressed Russia to allow largescale immigration of Circassians to their ancestral home, and circulated petitions calling on "the United Nations, the US Congress, and the European Union to recognize the Circassian genocide."[73] In 2011, Georgia became the first country to extend such recognition. The "No Sochi 2014" mobilization produced no boycotts of the Winter Olympics, but notably succeeded in raising awareness of this "forgotten" imperial genocide. Richmond's powerfully-written monograph has accomplished something similar in the field of genocide studies.[74]

Ground-level counterinsurgency campaigns in Vietnam produced genocidal massacres at My Lai and elsewhere. Much the same occurred in the Soviets' Afghan war, in which the imperial strategy, according to Jeri Laber and Barnett Rubin, was "to spread terror in the countryside so that villagers will either be afraid to assist the resistance fighters who depend on them for food and shelter or be forced to leave." Benjamin Valentino described the mass-murderous consequences:

Executions often were carried out with extreme savagery and in full public view, presumably to further intimidate the population. Since the Soviets generally lacked the information necessary to identify guerrilla supporters on an individual basis, they often slaughtered entire villages, including women and children. Two defectors from the Soviet army claimed that these atrocities were not merely the actions of out-of-control troops. In a typical operation, rather, "an officer decides to have a village searched to see if there are any rebels in it. . . . What usually happens is we found a cartridge or a bullet. The officers said: 'This is a bandit village; it must be destroyed.' . . . The men and young men are usually shot right where they are. And the women, what they do is try to kill them with grenades."[75]

"Conservative estimates put Afghan deaths at 1.25 million, or 9 percent of the population, with another three-quarters of a million wounded."[76] Some five million Afghans fled to Pakistan and Iran—one of the largest refugee flows in history.[77]

The Afghanistan-Vietnam comparison explored in these passages has often been advanced, but sometimes with attention to alleged differences between the two. In a well-known article for the *Denver Journal of International Law and Policy*, sociologist Helen Fein undertook to examine whether either or both cases constituted genocide. Her verdict on Vietnam was that while "repeated and substantive charges of war crimes . . . appear well-founded," the charge of "genocide . . . simply [is] not supported by the acts cited." In the Soviet case, however, Fein catalogued "repeated and substantive charges of 'depopulation,' massacre, deliberate injury, forced transfer of the children of Afghanis, and occasional charges of genocide." Combined, they "sustain[ed] a prima facie charge of genocide as well as charges of war crimes."[78]

One may disagree with Fein's gentler judgment about US conduct in Indochina (which featured bombing on a scale and of an intensity never matched in Afghanistan, for example). But it is hard to dispute the validity of the genocide framework for this instance of Soviet imperialism.

IMPERIAL ASCENT AND DISSOLUTION

Chaos is deadlier than tyranny.

Matthew White

Empires are most destructive in their waxing and waning phases. The onset of empire is often marked by vigorous imperial violence, much of which derives from—and is sometimes a desperate response to—the resistance of indigenous populations which may remain unvanquished, even against all technological and epidemiological odds.

BOX 2.3 THE "RIMLANDS," "BLOODLANDS," AND "SHATTERZONES" OF EMPIRE

Some of the most stimulating historical research—and one of the most vigorous intellectual debates—of recent years has deployed concepts of "rimlands," "bloodlands," and "shatterzones" to convey the macro-dynamics of imperial and ethnonational collisions, with their frequently genocidal consequences. The trend, including its offshoot in genocide studies crowned by the work of Mark Levene—reflects diverse historical and social-scientific influences. They include Immanuel Wallerstein's "world systems" theory of international relations; the school of subaltern studies rooted in the Global South;[79] seminal Marxist studies by Eric Hobsbawm, Perry Anderson, and Negri/Hardt;[80] multinational "integrated" histories of the Jewish *Shoah*, notably by Saul Friedlander (see Further Study, Chapter 6); and growing attention to local-level, grassroots dynamics and actors in research on mass violence and genocide, anchored by the writings of Charles Tilly and Paul Brass (Chapter 11) and more recently spurred by Stathis Kalyvas's classic 2006 study, *The Logic of Civil War*.[81]

The term "shatterzones," wrote Mark Levene, "stress[es] points, fault lines and tectonic plates" in imperial-political-economic systems, usually regional in scope.[82] As succinctly summarized by the editors of *Colonial Genocide in Indigenous North America*, the concept "implies the violence and destructiveness that results when multiple forces, such as slaving, global capital, and imperialism, come together and ignite patterns of destruction, loss, coalescence, and regeneration."[83] Omer Bartov and Eric Weitz,[84] as well as Donald Bloxham, Benjamin Lieberman, and Jacques Sémelin (see Further Study, this chapter, and Chapter 1), have drawn attention to these "fragile, if not uncontrollable . . . buffer zones between two worlds, [and] between two or more empires."[85]

Mark Levene's epic four-volume work (Further Study, Chapter 1) meticulously charts the rise and fall of imperial and national formations in the age of modern empires and late-imperial nationalist struggles. His focus is the "Rimlands" of eastern and southeastern Europe: "those frontier and (by extension) contested regions of the Ottoman, Russian and Austrian empires, where the 'Western formula' [of sovereign state-building and capitalist economics] most keenly collided with time-honoured notions of sacralized political authority, legitimacy and governance." These were largely agrarian societies with nodes of capitalist investment and state-sponsored industry, and growing cities that were the sites of both cosmopolitanism and ethnic-political collisions. For these were territories of great "ethnographic heterogeneity" and "social, linguistic and cultural diversity,"[86] in which most of the population self-identified "by way of religion, family, extended family, possibly the fact that they were not Muslim, or rich, or part of a ruling elite," not as a member of an ethnic group or the citizen of a nation-state.[87]

But the spirit of the age—even the professedly-liberal spirit—dictated that these "backward" peoples must toe the new nationalist line. If they found themselves on the wrong side of the demographic majority, they were prone to be forcibly assimilated, violently expelled, or exterminated. The result was forced population transfers and genocidal eruptions on a scale probably unprecedented in history. The main arc of holocaust scythed across the "Lands Between": from the Baltic and Belarus to "right-bank Ukraine in the east, modern-day Poland as far as Silesia in the west, and through the Carpathians and sub-Carpathian ranges towards an intersection with the Danube at its deltaic point of entry into the Black Sea" (see Map 2.1, zone 2).[88] Their epicenter lay in the "Bloodlands" analyzed in Timothy Snyder's 2010 volume.

Amplified by an extraordinary and unexpected historical conjuncture—the near-simultaneous collapse of all three Rimland empires (Ottoman, Austro-Hungarian, and Russian) in 1917–1918—genocidal violence spilled beyond Christian and Muslim Europeans to shape the destinies of eastern Europe under the Nazi and Stalinist empires, along with contemporary shatterzones such as the Middle East and Caucasus regions (see Box 4a, Chapter 5, Box 5a).

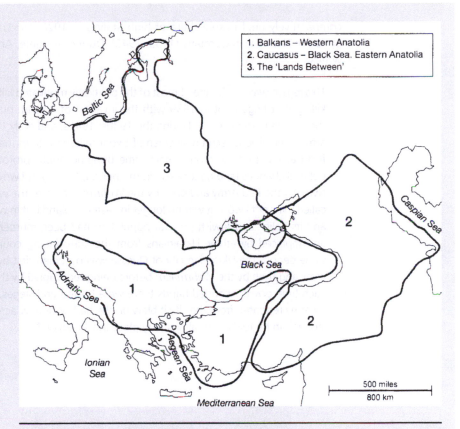

Map 2.1 The European Rimlands.

Source: Scanned from Mark Levene, *The Crisis of Genocide, Vol. 1* (Oxford University Press).

The "Bloodlands" debate

Perhaps no book in the past decade has aroused such interest, readership, and controversy in European and genocide studies as Timothy Snyder's *Bloodlands: Europe between Hitler and Stalin* (2010). Instead of strictly dividing the Nazi and Stalinist dictatorships and treating them in isolation or in sequence, Snyder produced a synoptic and highly readable treatise on the most sanguinary of the "rimland" zones—the same "Lands Between" (today's Lithuania, Poland, Belarus, Ukraine, and western Russia). Usually addressed marginally and derivatively in the European and genocide studies literatures, these regions are now receiving sustained study, their polyglot populations are increasingly studied as actors with their own agendas, rivalries, and entrenched ethnic-political-religious conflicts. Snyder's work, more than any other, has also driven home the unprecedented, almost incomprehensible scale and severity of the human destruction during the comparatively brief historical era of high Stalinism (1928–1953) subsuming the period of Nazi rule in Germany (1933–1945). During this time, Anne Applebaum writes:

> This region was . . . the site of most of the politically motivated killing in Europe— killing that began not in 1939 with the invasion of Poland, but in 1933, with the famine in Ukraine. . . . During the 1930s, 1940s, and early 1950s, the lethal armies and vicious secret policemen of two totalitarian states marched back and forth across these territories, each time bringing about profound ethnic and political changes [and genocides]. In this period, the city of Lwów was occupied twice by the Red Army and once by the *Wehrmacht*. After the war ended it was called L'viv, not Lwów, it was no longer in eastern Poland but in western Ukraine, and its Polish and Jewish pre-war population had been murdered or deported and replaced by ethnic Ukrainians from the surrounding countryside. In this same period, the Ukrainian city of Odessa was occupied first by the Romanian army and then by the *Wehrmacht* before being reoccupied by the Soviet Union. Each time power changed hands there were battles and sieges, and each time an army retreated from the city it blew up the harbor or massacred Jews. Similar stories can be told about almost any place in the region.[89]

Figure 2.11 Yale University historian Timothy Snyder's 2010 work *Bloodlands: Europe between Hitler and Stalin* drew attention to the historical and genocidal experiences of eastern European states, where the full violence of the Nazi and Soviet holocausts was concentrated. Snyder's dual framing, and his argument that Stalin's genocidal policies (Chapter 5) preceded and shaped the Nazi version (Chapter 6, Box 6a), has generated substantial discussion and some controversy. He is pictured at the Frankfurt book fair (*Buchmesse*) in October 2015.

Source: Wikimedia Commons.

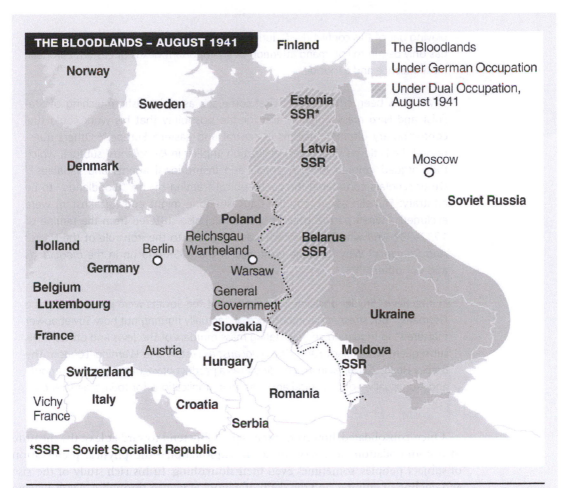

Map 2.2 The "Bloodlands" of present-day Lithuania, Poland, Belarus, Ukraine, and western Russia in August 1941, shortly after the German invasion of Soviet Russia and the onset of the "Holocaust by Bullets" against eastern European Jews (see Chapter 6, pp. 325–332).

Source: Courtesy of *Ha'aretz*, Israel.

It was the claimed linkage and mutually reactive/constitutive character of the "Bloodlands" genocides that provoked the most discussion and scholarly push-back. Reading in all the relevant languages—a rarity in itself—Snyder sought, in Anne Applebaum's summary, "to show that the two systems committed the same kinds of crimes at the same times and in the same places, that they aided and abetted one another, and above all that their interaction with one another led to more mass killing than either might have carried out alone."[90] He is among a handful of recent scholars to highlight the "truly genocidal Polish—Ukrainian confrontation," building on prewar repression of the ethnic-Ukrainian majority in the eastern territories of the newly reconstituted Polish state, but with the ethnic-Polish minority in the region highly vulnerable to victimization in acts of "subaltern" violence.[91] The playing out of this conflict dyad, during World War Two and for several years after, has only begun to command attention as an important nexus of eastern European mass violence and genocide.

Snyder has been criticized for what some see as a simplistic mulching of Stalinist and Nazi mass violence; and for the possibility that his work could fuel contemporary ultranationalisms in central and eastern Europe.[92] Others questioned the Hitler-vs.-Stalin personalization implicit in *Bloodlands'* subtitle, which they argued ignored local, regional, and institutional agents and variables.[93] Other scholars considered the geographical framing of the "Bloodlands" to be arbitrary: Sémelin asked why the Caucasus (one might add Kazakhstan) were excluded, "when part of [their] population[s] also suffered from the famine of 1932–33? And why Serbia, which was subjected to the iron rule of the Nazis? And Romania? Why do some territories in the USSR end up in the *bloodlands* and not others?"[94]

In interviews, Snyder disclaimed the view "that the Soviets were just as bad as the Germans," but stressed the importance of "actually figuring out how Soviet power mattered" in triggering and facilitating mass murders of the Jews and others.[95] His subsequent work, *Black Earth: The Holocaust as History and Warning* (London: The Bodley Head, 2015), examines the *Shoah* as a product of vacuums of state authority and—unusually—of ecological anxieties, with implications for today's generations.

Once consolidated, however, empires probably tend toward at least the measure of accommodation necessary for stable exploitation—the physical preservation of subject peoples, sometimes even their flourishing. In his rich study of the rise and decline of empires, and the skein of genocide woven through it, Mark Levene argued that "colonial genocides made no obvious sense," because empires have "inbuilt, usually self-interested and self-regulatory mechanisms for the avoidance of exterminatory conflict with subject peoples ... "These include "political policies and administrative practices" that "at least allow[ed] their diverse peoples to co-exist with one another, often even where this involved widely divergent cultures, not to mention social and economic habits."[96]

When that order breaks down, and especially when multiethnic empires begin to dissolve in intercommunal strife, genocide rears anew. Now it is fueled and exacerbated by fear, even terror, at the encirclement, besieging, and looming collapse of the imperial order, and a sudden pervasive insecurity at the grassroots. When the heart of the empire is under threat of conquest, partition, and extinction, as with Constantinople and Vienna during the waning days of the Ottoman and Austro-Hungarian empires, the imperial backlash may be especially violent. When those empires experienced "relatively stable conditions" and "did not feel threatened," "ethnographic diversity ... remained tenable." But "take away this stability and the most immediate and likely effect was a much more pronouncedly aggressive state ethnic policy with particularly dire consequences ... "[97]

An essential element here is the perception of *diminution, humiliation,* and *dispossession.* From a psychopathological perspective, no context is more toxic, no fuel more combustible. We consider fear and humiliation more closely—along with the subaltern desires for vengeance that they engender—in Chapter 10's discussion of psychological perspectives on genocide.

These tendencies also shape the aftermath of empire—sometimes for centuries. Memories of past dispossessions become inextricably bound up with a sense of victimization, and the contemporary need for violent redress of perceived wrongs. For Levene, this is one of the features that may partly explain a specifically German *Sonderweg* (special path) to the Holocaust:

> The German example may help identify a particular type of state with the potentiality for genocide not so much on the basis of whether it is labeled as authoritarian, revolutionary, ethnically stratified or whatever . . . so much as one which suffers from what one might call a chronic 'strong' state—'weak' state syndrome. . . . Such states seem to have what one might only describe as a collective inferiority complex: that is, of a conviction shared by policy makers, opinion formers and possibly significant sections of their general population that the position which they believe *ought* to be theirs in terms of international status is forever being denied or blocked off to them.[98]

This mentality pervaded not only Nazi actions, but the Ottoman empire's destruction of its Christian minorities (Chapter 5), the Khmer Rouge genocide in Cambodia in the 1970s (Chapter 7), and the Serb victimization narrative that fueled the Bosnian genocide of the 1990s (Chapter 8).[99] A final example displaying this trajectory of genocidal ascent and genocidal decline is the Russian/Soviet/Chechen/Circassian experiences (see Box 2.2, Chapter 5, Chapter 5a). The frequently exterminatory violence of tsarist Russia's conquest of the Caucasus, from the late 1820s to the 1860s, was followed by a measure of stability in the final decades of the tsarist empire, and sporadic stability—to the extent that any population enjoyed it—under Soviet and early Stalinist rule. But when the Stalinist regime felt itself mortally threatened in 1941–1942, particularly in the peripheral areas conquered by its tsarist forebears, the uprooting was again epic in scale and the violence again mass-murderous, for Chechens and for other minority peoples besides. And the tendency can be traced to the contemporary period, with the wars-unto-genocide launched by the Yeltsin and Putin regimes against rebellious Chechnya (Box 5a). The pathological excesses of the violence reflect a post-Soviet Russia reduced and vulnerable, stripped of its quasi-colonies in eastern Europe and central Asia, and obsessed with holding onto minority-dominated territories on the fringes of the shrunken empire.

GENOCIDE AND WAR

> Such a radical, dehumanizing approach only had a chance of being put into practice in wartime, in a more generally brutalizing atmosphere in which the existence of the individual was already to an extent devalued.
>
> Peter Longerich, *Holocaust*

If state formation, imperialism, war, and social revolution are genocide's "four horsemen," then war and genocide might be described as its conjoined twins. The intimate bond between the two is evident from the twentieth-century record alone. All three of the century's "classic" genocides—against Armenians in Turkey, Jews in Nazi-occupied Europe, and Tutsis in Rwanda—occurred in a context of civil and/or international war. The wartime context is only a necessary, not a sufficient, explanation; but as historian Christopher Fettweis asked of the Jewish Holocaust, "Should one be surprised that the most destructive war in history was accompanied by one of the most dramatic instances of violence against civilians?"[100] A sagacious scholar of the relationship, Martin Shaw, considered genocide to be an offshoot of "degenerate" warfare, with its large-scale targeting of civilian populations.[101]

The line between "legitimate" war and genocide is hard to draw. Still, most genocide scholars acknowledge intimate connections between the two, and many rank war as genocide's greatest single enabling factor. "Thank God that now, during wartime, we have a whole series of opportunities that would be closed off to us in peacetime," Nazi leader Joseph Goebbels exulted in his diary in March 1942, as the machinery of full-scale Holocaust geared up around him.[102]

What are these points of connection between war and genocide?

- ***War accustoms a society to violence and dehumanization.*** Large portions of the male population may be drawn into institutions, the prime purpose of which is to inflict violence. " . . . Clad in a stiff uniform, a heart does not beat as it wants to," wrote German soldier Kresten Andresen in the early weeks of World War One. "We aren't ourselves. We're hardly human any longer, at most we are well-drilled automatons who perform every action without any great reflection."[103] Much of the non-combatant population is cast in various war-related productive and reproductive roles. Nearly all adults are therefore complicit in the war machine. The boundaries between legality and criminality erode. Psychological and social inhibitions diminish, often to be replaced by blood-lust.

- ***War increases the quotient of fear and hatred in a society.*** "War creates a type of mass psychosis to which societies at peace cannot relate."[104] Both soldiers and civilians live in dread of death. Propaganda emphasizes the "traitor within": "Know that the person whose throat you do not cut now will be the one who will cut yours," warned Hutu intellectual Ferdinand Nahimana before the outbreak of the Rwandan genocide against Tutsis and moderate Hutus in 1994.[105] Fear fuels hatred of the one allegedly responsible for the fear, and dependence on the authority that pledges deliverance from the threat. The ideology of militarism inculcates "a condition of slavish docility" and "stolid passivity" throughout the militarized society.[106] Societies grow more receptive to state vigilance and violence, as well as to suspensions of legal and constitutional safeguards.[107] Dissidence threatens unity and stability, and provokes widespread loathing and repression.

- ***War eases genocidal logistics.*** With the unified command of society and economy, it is easier to mobilize resources for genocide. State power is increasingly devoted to inflicting mass violence. (Indeed, the state itself, "evolving as it did within the crucible of endless rounds of combat, served initially as a more efficient apparatus to fight wars.")[108] For example, the wartime marshalling of rail and freight infrastructure was essential to the "efficient" extermination of millions of Jews, and others, in the Nazi death camps. Much of that infrastructure was built and/or maintained by forced laborers captured as spoils, another regular phenomenon in wartime.

- *War provides a smokescreen for genocide.*[109] "That's war" becomes the excuse for extermination. Traditional sources of information, communication, and denunciation are foreclosed or rigidly controlled. "Journalism is highly restricted, and military censorship prevents the investigation of reported atrocities. The minds of nations and of the international community are on other issues in time of war."[110]

- *War fuels intracommunal solidarity and intercommunal enmity.* Many who experienced the wars of the twentieth century recalled them with mingled pain and pleasure. Few had ever before considered themselves citizens swept up in a common cause. Most soldiers experienced "a new kind of community held together by common danger and a common goal,"[111] which forged the most enduring friendships of their lives. In general, war "exaggerates nationalistic impulses as populations come together under outside threats. . . . During conflict group identities are strengthened as the gap between 'us' and 'them' is magnified, and individuals increasingly emphasize their solidarity with the threatened group."[112] As psychologist David Barash put it succinctly:

Figure 2.12 Wartime propaganda often dehumanizes the enemy, magnifying sentiments of fear, hatred, and superiority (see Chapter 10). With rare exceptions, and according to patriarchal-military logic, the racial/civilizational threat is gendered male/masculine (see Chapter 13). A US recruiting poster from World War One (adapting an image previously used in Britain) depicts Germany as a slavering ape arriving on American shores, wielding a club ironically labeled "Kultur" (culture), with the virtuous national maiden crooked in his simian arm.

Source: H.R. Hopps (artist)/Wikimedia Commons.

Figure 2.13 Propaganda also stresses the need for conformity, obedience to state authority, and the obligation to "play one's part." Military and civilian men, depicted marching lemming-like in this 1915 poster of the UK Parliamentary Recruiting Committee, are the principal targets. But women, too, are lured and conscripted into the great national struggle (see Chapter 13). Dissenters are now "traitors" and "defeatists," to be harassed, jailed, or worse. The population can thus be primed to accept, indeed celebrate, the genocidal destruction of designated enemies, both foreign and internal.

Source: Lithograph by David Allen & Sons Ld., Harrow, Middlesex. Artist Posters Collection, US Library of Congress/Flickr.

"In enmity, there is unity."[113] "What is France if not as defined against England or Germany? What is Serbia if not as defined against Germany or Croatia?"[114] Solidarity may coalesce around a dominant ethnicity within the society, prompting the anathematizing of Other-identified minorities.

- *War magnifies humanitarian crisis.* Refugee flows—whether of internally or internationally displaced peoples—may destabilize the society at war, and others around it. War complicates or prevents the provision of humanitarian assistance. Millions may starve to death beyond the reach of aid agencies, as in Congo's messy and multifaceted wars (Chapter 9). "New wars" (see Chapter 12) may come to feed on war-related humanitarian assistance, which can also buttress genocidally-inclined state authorities, as in Rwanda in the early 1990s.[115]
- *War stokes grievances and a desire for revenge.* Large numbers of Serbs were spurred to support Slobodan Milosevic's ultranationalist option by the collective memory of genocide committed against Serbs during World War Two. Fewer Germans would have supported Hitler or the Nazis (Chapter 6) without an abiding sense of grievance generated by the 1919 Versailles Treaty. Cambodia's Khmer Rouge (Chapter 7) would have enjoyed less popular support if years of American bombing had not terrorized, enraged, and displaced much of the country's peasant population.

It would be comforting to think that democratic societies are immune to these responses. Yet when liberal societies are under stress, as during the present "war on terror," they can slide toward genocidal mindsets, motifs, and sometimes policies. In the first edition of this book, I cited comments on a rightwing blog (The Anti-Idiotarian Rottweiler) posted in the wake of the May 2004 execution, by slow decapitation, of an American journalist in Iraq. I suggested that the statements, of the exterminate-all-the-brutes variety, "exposed a brazenly genocidal discourse."[116] In November 2009, the UK *Guardian* reported that after the shooting rampage at Fort Hood, Texas, by an American Muslim army officer who shouted "Allahu Akhbar!" ("God is great!" in Arabic) as he fired, websites "filled with hate mail questioning [US Muslims'] loyalty."[117] I suspected that the Anti-Idiotarian Rottweiler might have something to say on the matter, and indeed it did. Its contributors were also vocal about a news item that followed immediately after Major Nadil Malik Hasan's atrocity at Fort Hood: the announcement that accused Al-Qa'eda mastermind Khaled Sheik Muhammed would be tried for the 9/11 attack (see pp.) in New York City, the main attack site. A quite representative sample of the posted comments follows (there were also a few tentatively liberal responses):

Define "win" [in the "war on terror"]? Okay, how's this: Make the enemy . . . fear you at a genetic level and never ever want to go anywhere near you for a thousand years or more. You use Genghis Khan level brutality. Men, women, children, young, old, sick or well, you erase them. You scrape the Earth and salt it. They want to go to Allah, you help them in every way possible. They behead a journalist, we destroy a city. And by destroy I mean down to the cockroaches in their sewers. . . . Absolute total decimation. That is the only thing these barbarians truly understand.

(DJ Allyn, November 16, 2009)

Extermination, root and branch, to the third generation. Plow and salt the ground followed by the blood of swine. . . . They [Muslims] are a festering pustule everywhere they go. They will *not* "assimilate," not ever. They are instructed by the unHoly Quran to convert, or destroy, the whole world. There is no such thing as a permanent peace treaty with them . . .

(LC Jon Imperial Hunter, November 11 and 12, 2009)

I honestly do not see any other option to deal with these mutant freaks save overwhelming, make-them-shit-the-diapers-on-both-ends violence. Coddling them does not work. They are using our own morality against us. . . . Sometimes, the only MORAL and RIGHT thing to do is to unleash the beast. . . . It is time to stand up to them and kick their ass, like it was done to the filthy Nazis.

(Princess Natasha, November 16, 2009)

As for the shitstain in question [Major Hasan]. He again proves my point that American Muslims are Muslims first, and Americans a distant second. They should all be deported back to whatever goat-molesting shithole they came from.

(LC Beaker, November 6, 2009)[118]

Such rhetoric reminds us of the genocidal potential lurking in *all* societies. The comments are representative and generic; there is nothing uniquely American about them. They are not even especially sadistic, compared to other examples that could be cited from the same "discussion" on the same website. Some posts have a timeless air, reminiscent of the proclamations of Assyrian kings or Mongol emperors as they prepared to embark on genocidal war and empire-building. (Note the references to classical precedents—Genghis Khan; the ancient sowing of destroyed cities with salt.)

But if something in war's extremism is timeless, something is also distinctively modern, and this merits exploration.

The First World War and the dawn of industrial death

In July 1916, my grandfather, Alfred George Jones (1885–1949), a British volunteer soldier, arrived on the Somme farmlands of the western front in France. This terrain had just witnessed the most massive and disastrous Allied offensive of the First World War. On July 1, commemorated as the "Black Day" of the British Army, an offensive by 100,000 troops produced 60,000 Allied casualties *in a single day*, including 20,000 killed. The image of British troops walking at a parade-ground pace, bayonets fixed, across the gently rolling landscapes of the Somme, and directly into German machine-gun fire, is iconic: "the Somme marked the end of an age of vital optimism in British life that has never been recovered"[119] (see Figures 2.14 and 2.15).

Figure 2.14 Alfred George Jones (1885–1949), the author's grandfather, a British First World War veteran. The photo appears to have been taken shortly after he volunteered for service, in time to be drawn into the maelstrom of the Battle of the Somme in July 1916.

Source: Author's collection.

Figure 2.15 An iconic image of the twentieth century: soldiers go "over the top" at the Battle of the Somme on July 1, 1916—the "Black Day" of the British Army." The soldier at right has already been shot and fallen into the barbed wire of the Allied trenchline. Nearly a century later, the Somme still symbolizes the futility of modern war, and the impersonal, industrialized mass killing that would reach its apogee with the Nazi Holocaust (see Chapter 6 and Box 6a).

Source: Imperial War Museum, London.

My grandfather was thrown into the meat-grinder that followed, which claimed 630,000 Allied casualties and a similar number of Germans over four-and-a-half months. A sapper in the Royal Engineers, he was blown up and buried for three days by an artillery shell in "no man's land" (a term that has since become a metaphor of the social and cultural dislocation wrought by the First World War). He was discovered by chance. Shell-shocked, he was shipped to England to convalesce. The experience triggered epileptic attacks that haunted him to the end of his days; but he survived to father my father. Thus, for better or worse, you hold this book in your hands because someone stumbled across my grandfather in no man's land nearly a century ago, during the definitive war of modern times.[120]

The crisis caused by the "Great War" derived from its combination of industrial technology and physical immobility. As millions of tons of munitions were unleashed, soldiers cowered in trenches that trembled or collapsed from the bombardments, and that between assaults were a wasteland of mud, rats, and corpses. Ten million soldiers died on all sides—a previously unimaginable figure, and one that left a gaping and traumatic hole where a generation of young men should have been. For sociologist Martin Shaw,

> The slaughter of the trenches was in many ways the definitive experience of modern mass killing, seminal to virtually all the mass killing activities of the twentieth century. The massacre of conscripts was a starting-point for the development of each of the other strands. As the soldier-victims were mown down in their hundreds of thousands in the Somme and elsewhere, they provided a spectacle of mass death that set the tone for a century. . . . All the main paradigms of twentieth-century death were already visible in this first great phase of total war.[121]

Adolf Hitler spent four years in the trenches of the western front. He had been swept up in nationalist euphoria at the war's outbreak—there is a photograph of a Munich crowd celebrating the declaration of war, in which Hitler's face may be seen, rapt with enthusiasm. As a soldier, he fought bravely, receiving the Iron Cross Second Class. He was nearly killed in an Allied gas attack that left him blind and hospitalized—the prone, powerless position in which he first heard of the "humiliating" armistice Germany had accepted. (For more on genocide and humiliation, see Chapter 10.) In the war's aftermath, Hitler joined millions of demobilized soldiers struggling to find a place in postwar society. His war-fueled alienation, his newly pungent anti-semitism (based on the conviction that "the Jews" had delivered a "stab in the back" to bring about German defeat),[122] and his nostalgic longing for the solidarity and comradeship of the trenches—all marked Hitler for life.[123] And the aftershocks of the war continued to fuel his rise in nationalist politics, as his biographer Ian Kershaw has noted:

> The First World War made Hitler possible. Without the experience of war, the humiliation of defeat, and the upheaval of revolution the failed artist and social drop-out would not have discovered what to do with his life by entering politics and finding his métier as a propagandist and beerhall demagogue. And

without the trauma of war, defeat and revolution, without the political radicalization of German society that this trauma brought about, the demagogue would have been without an audience for his raucous, hate-filled message. The legacy of the lost war provided the conditions in which the paths of Hitler and the German people began to cross.[124]

The Bolshevik Revolution in Russia, which spawned large-scale killing under Vladimir Lenin and epic slaughter under Joseph Stalin (Chapter 5), is scarcely conceivable without the trauma of the war. The conflict also directly sparked genocide against the Christian minorities of the Ottoman realm (see Chapter 4). The genocide was carried out on the grounds of military "self-defense" against minority groups accused of seeking to subvert the Ottoman state, in alliance with a historic adversary (Russia). Genocidal logistics, particularly transport, were greatly facilitated by the requisites of wartime emergency.

The Second World War and the "barbarization of warfare"

The European theater of the Second World War consisted of two quite different conflicts. In the west, Nazi occupation authorities were more disciplined and less brutal, though not where Jews or partisans were concerned. In the east, and in the Balkans to the south, crimes against humanity were the norm. Genocide featured prominently among them.

The heart of the eastern war was primarily the struggle between Nazi-led forces and the Soviet people in arms.[125] Soviet formations were dealt a massive blow by the German *Blitzkrieg* (lightning-war) of June to December 1941, an invasion—dubbed Operation Barbarossa—that "dwarfs everything else in the history of warfare"[126] and pushed all the way to the suburbs of Moscow.

There ensued a titanic struggle between two totalitarian systems—the largest and most destructive military conflict in history. For Hitler, according to historian Omer Bartov, it was from the start "an ideological war of extermination and enslavement":

> Its goal was to wipe out the Soviet state, to enslave the Russian people after debilitating them by famine and all other forms of deprivation, systematically to murder all "biological" and political enemies of Nazism, such as the Jews, the Gypsies [Roma], members of the Communist Party, intellectuals, and so forth, and finally to turn the Soviet Union west of the Ural mountains into a German paradise of "Aryan" colonizers, served by hordes of Slav helots.[127]

Wendy Lower calls it "the most radical colonization campaign in the history of European conquest and empire building."[128] It might be the most extreme in the history of the world, with due acknowledgment to the Mongols. Reflecting this racial animus and political extremism, the restraints that generally governed German troops in the west—the preservation of prisoners-of-war, a degree of respect for civilian lives and property—were abandoned from the outset. "This struggle

Figure 2.16 The Nazi–Soviet war of 1941–1945 was the most titanic armed conflict in human history, and arguably the most consequential. In Operation Barbarossa, launched on June 22, 1941, German armies and their Romanian, Italian, and Finnish allies invaded along a 2,900-kilometer front with *4.5 million* troops. They drove Soviet forces to the gates of Moscow before a successful counteroffensive was launched. Until the cauldron of the battle of Kursk in July–August 1943— accurately depicted in this vivid Russian mural and diorama—the war seesawed militarily. This was the main period of Nazi holocaust against subject Jewish and Slavic populations in the eastern occupied territories, including millions of Soviet prisoners-of-war (see Chapter 6, Box 6a). After Kursk, in which the Soviets battled huge German tank formations to a stalemate, the Nazis never again mounted a major offensive in the east. By the time Allied armies landed at Normandy, France, on "D-Day" (June 6, 1944), Soviet armies of staggering size, growing skill, and unvanquishable morale had pushed the Nazis back as far as Warsaw, Poland. They were poised to deliver the crushing blow to German Army Group Center in Operation Bagration. This offensive matched Barbarossa in scale, and brought Soviet armies onto German soil, where they committed widespread atrocities, including the notorious mass rape of German women. Soviet armies conquered the German capital, Berlin, and went on to impose the tyrannical Stalinist system on the newly conquered populations of eastern (now central) Europe, though this moderated in the decades leading to the successful anti-Soviet revolutions of 1989. A Nazi-ruled order would have been inconceivably worse, with the programmed mass extermination of tens of millions of "useless eaters," and the enslavement of remaining populations. Today, the memory of the "Great Patriotic War," in which *between twenty-five and forty million* Soviet citizens died, is carefully nurtured by Russian president Vladimir Putin to legitimize both his authoritarian regime and a new era of Russian expansionism. See note 125, this chapter, for a detailed literature review of the Nazi–Soviet war and its many genocidal components.

Source: Russian museum diorama and mural, artist unknown/Reddit.com.

must have as its aim the demolition of present Russia and must therefore be conducted with unprecedented severity," declared Panzer Group Colonel-General Hoepner before the invasion. "Both the planning and the execution of every battle must be dictated by an iron will to bring about a merciless, total annihilation of the enemy. Particularly no mercy should be shown toward the carriers of the present Russian-Bolshevik system."[129]

The result was a "demodernization" of the eastern front from 1941 to 1945, and a concomitant "barbarization of warfare," to cite historian Omer Bartov's term. Amidst physical travails, primitive conditions, and endless harassment by partisans, German troops turned readily to atrocity. They were granted a "license to murder disarmed soldiers and defenseless civilians," and often carried out the task with an indiscriminate enthusiasm that transported them beyond the limited controls established by the army.

The Soviet stance toward the German invader could also be blood-curdling. The poet Ilya Ehrenburg penned a leaflet for circulation among Soviet frontline troops titled simply, "Kill": "The Germans are not human beings. From now on the word 'German' is for us the worst imaginable curse.... We shall kill. If you have not killed at least one German a day, you have wasted that day."[130]

Thus conditioned, when Soviet troops reached German soil in East Prussia they unleashed a campaign of mass rape, murder, and terror against German civilians, who were overwhelmingly children and women. The campaign of gang rape, which Stalin notoriously dismissed as the Soviet soldier "having fun with a woman," is seared into the German collective memory.[131] As many as two million German women were sexually assaulted: "it was not untypical for Soviet troops to rape every female over the age of twelve or thirteen in a village, killing many in the process."[132] One Soviet officer described an encounter with a unit that had captured a group of German refugees. "Women, mothers and their children lie to the right and left along the route, and in front of each of them stands a raucous armada of men with their trousers down. The women who are bleeding or losing consciousness get shoved to one side, and our men shoot the ones who try to save their children." "Grinning" officers stood by, ensuring "that every soldier without exception would take part."[133]

Whatever else may be said, however, Soviet ideology lacked a strong racist component. Perhaps as a result, after months of rape and killing, the regime finally imposed on the Soviet client-state of East Germany was much less malevolent a "new order" than Slavs experienced under Nazi rule.

Barbarization was also evident in the war in the Pacific, which pitted the US, UK, China, and their allies against Japanese occupation forces. In his *War Without Mercy*, historian John Dower examined the processes of mutual demonization and bestialization by the US and Japanese polities. These processes both conditioned and reflected the broader popular hostility in wartime. The American public's view of the Japanese enemy was conveyed in a poll taken in December 1944, in which, according to Gary Bass, "33 percent of Americans wanted to destroy Japan as a country after the war, 28 percent wanted to supervise and control Japan—and fully 13 percent wanted to kill *all* Japanese people."[134] Among soldiers consulted in both the Pacific and European theatres in 1943–1944, between 42 percent (Pacific) and 67 percent (Europe) considered "wiping out the whole Japanese nation" as the most desirable option.[135]

GENOCIDE AND SOCIAL REVOLUTION

It is on a blank page that the most beautiful poems are written.

Mao Zedong, Chinese revolutionary leader

Revolutions are sudden, far-reaching, and generally violent transformations of a political order. Social revolutions, which go beyond a change of political regime to encompass transformations of the underlying class structure, are particularly wrenching.

Beginning with the English Civil War of 1648, the American Revolution of 1776, and the French Revolution of 1789, the modern era has witnessed an escalating series of such transformations. Revolution has been closely linked to struggles for national independence, as well as to attempts to engineer fundamental changes in the social order. The uprisings against the crumbling Ottoman Empire in the early twentieth century provided the template for the century's national liberation struggles. These coalesced as a comprehensive movement for decolonization following the Second World War.

The Soviet Revolution of 1917, which grew out of the chaos and privation of the First World War, epitomized the Marxist-Leninist variant of social-revolutionary strategy. This strategy viewed "all history [as] the history of class struggle" (to cite Marx and Engels's *Communist Manifesto*).[136] Under the influence of Vladimir Lenin, it stressed the role of a vanguard party in dragging the workers and peasants to liberation, kicking and screaming if necessary (as it indeed proved to be). Social-revolutionary struggle in the early part of the twentieth century also took a fascist form, as in Mussolini's Italy and Hitler's Germany.[137] Fascism found its shock troops among workers and the *lumpenproletariat* (lower social orders and riffraff). Its peasant following was also considerable. Nevertheless, its base resided in the lower-middle class, and featured an alliance—or marriage of convenience—with traditional, conservative sectors.

Both communist and fascist variants of revolution are highly militarized. This reflects the clandestine organizing and cell-based struggle of revolutionary strategy, as well as the need to crush counter-revolutionary opposition before, during, and after the revolution. It also attests to the conviction of some revolutionaries that the world should share in their victory, or be subjugated by it. As Martin Shaw noted,

> *revolution itself . . . increasingly took the form of war*, particularly guerrilla war . . . Revolutionaries pursued armed struggle not as a conclusion to political struggle, but as a central means of that struggle from the outset. Likewise, established power has used force not merely to defeat open insurrection, but to stamp out revolutionary forces and terrorize their actual or potential social supporters. As revolution became armed struggle, counter-revolution became counter-insurgency. In this sense there has been a radical change in the character of many revolutionary processes.[138]

Research into the Turkish and Nazi revolutions produced a key work of comparative genocide studies, political scientist Robert Melson's *Revolution and Genocide* (1996), which summarized the linkages as follows:

1. Revolutions created the conditions for genocidal movements to come to power.

2. Revolutions made possible the imposition of radical ideologies and new orders that legitimated genocide.

3. The social mobilization of low status or despised groups [e.g., in struggles for national liberation] helped to make them targets of genocide.

4. Revolutions leading to wars facilitated the implementation of genocide as a policy of the state.[139]

While revolution, especially social revolution, may take a genocidal form, so too may counter-revolution. This book contains numerous instances of revolutions that spawned genocides (Turkey's against Christian minorities, Lenin's and Stalin's terrors, the Nazis, the Khmer Rouge in Cambodia, "Hutu Power" in Rwanda). Yet it includes even more cases in which colonial and contemporary state authorities sought to stamp out "revolutionary" threats through genocide. The Germans in Southwest Africa (Chapter 3), the Chinese in Tibet (Chapter 5), West Pakistan in East Pakistan/ Bangladesh (Box 8a), Serbia in Kosovo, Russia in Chechnya (Box 5a), and Sudan in Darfur (Box 9a)—all fit the pattern, as does the Guatemalan army's rampage against Mayan Indians in the 1970s and 1980s (Box 3a). In all cases, once war is unleashed, the radicalization and extremism of organized mass violence, described previously, come to dominate the equation.

THE NUCLEAR REVOLUTION AND "OMNICIDE"

Total war is no longer only between all members of one national community and all those of another: it is also total because it will very likely set the whole world up in flames.

Jean-Paul Sartre, *On Genocide*

As revolutions in the social and political sphere represent dramatic irruptions of new actors and social forces, so technological revolutions transform the world and human history. This was the case prior to the First World War, when scientific knowledge, wedded to an industrial base, facilitated the mass slaughter of 1914–1918. An even more portentous transformation was the nuclear revolution—the discovery that the splitting (and later the fusion) of atoms could unleash unprecedented energy, and could be directed toward military destruction as well as peaceful ends. Atomic bombs had the power to render conventional weapons obsolete, while "the destructive power of the hydrogen bomb was as revolutionary in comparison with the atomic bomb as was the latter to conventional weaponry."[140]

The invention of nuclear weapons, first (and fortunately last) used in war at Hiroshima and Nagasaki in August 1945, transformed civilization to its very roots. "In a real way we all lead something of a 'double life,'" wrote psychologists Robert Jay Lifton and Eric Markusen. "We are aware at some level that in a moment we and everyone and everything we have ever touched or loved could be annihilated, and yet we go about our ordinary routines as though no such threat exists."[141] In his classic cry for peace, social critic Jonathan Schell described *The Fate of the Earth* as being "poised on a hair trigger, waiting for the 'button' to be 'pushed' by some misguided or deranged human being or for some faulty computer chip to send out the instruction to fire. That so much should be balanced on so fine a point . . . is a fact against which belief rebels."[142]

Lifton and Markusen compared the mindset of Nazi leaders and technocrats with those managing nuclear armories today. Both cultures reflected deep, sometimes hysterical preoccupations with "national security," which could be employed to depict one's own acts of aggression as preemptive. Both involved professionals whose specialization and distancing from the actuality of destruction helped them to inflict or prepare to inflict holocaust. A dry, euphemistic language rendered atrocity banal. Both mindsets accepted megadeath as necessary:

> With [nuclear] deterrence, there is the assumption that we must be prepared to kill hundreds of millions of people in order to prevent large-scale killing, to cure the world of genocide. With the Nazis, the assumption was that killing all Jews was a way of curing not only the Aryan race but all humankind. Involvement in a therapeutic mission helps block out feelings of the deaths one is or may be inflicting.[143]

Whatever the parallels, the immensity of modern nuclear weapons' destructive power was beyond Hitler's wildest fantasies. Scholars coined the term "omnicide"—total killing—to describe the extinction that nuclear arms could impose: not only on humans, but on the global ecosystem and all complex life forms, with the possible exception of the cockroach. Nuclear weapons are the one threat that can make past and present genocides seem small.

Younger readers of this book may find such comments melodramatic. They will lack direct memories of the "balance of terror" and the (il)logic of "mutually assured destruction" that pervaded the Cold War. These spawned a degree of fear and mass psychosis that marked for life many of those who lived under it, including myself. Antinuclear sentiment sparked moves toward a prohibition regime (see Chapter 12), built around arms control treaties between the superpowers and monitoring the peaceful use of nuclear energy. This left the situation still extremely volatile, as populations across the Western world recognized in the 1980s: they staged the largest protest demonstrations in postwar European and North American history.

Since that time, immediate tensions have subsided. Few today feel themselves under the perpetual shadow of the mushroom cloud; but, arguably, this reflects no diminution of the threat. Thousands of missiles remain in the armories of the major nuclear powers—enough to destroy the world many times over. While a number of nuclear or proto-nuclear powers have abandoned their programs (South Africa, several former Soviet republics, Brazil, Argentina), other states have joined the nuclear club, including India, Pakistan, and North Korea. At least one "conflict dyad" seems capable of sparking a nuclear holocaust on short notice: that of India and Pakistan. These countries have fought four wars since 1947, and seemed poised for a fifth as recently as 2001.

In another way, too, the nuclear threat has multiplied. The Soviet collapse left thousands of missiles in varying states of decay, and often poorly guarded.[144] They made attractive targets for *mafiosi* and impoverished military officers seeking the

Figure 2.17 Hiromichi Matsuda took this photo of the second atomic attack in history, by the US against the population of Nagasaki, Japan, on August 9, 1945. The image was captured about thirty minutes after the blast that killed some 80,000 people, instantly and over time, including from flash burns and long-term radiation poisoning. The bombings of Hiroshima (August 6) and Nagasaki (see also Figure 1.11) inaugurated the "nuclear age" in world politics, and in the evolution of genocidal and "omnicidal" technologies.

Source: Hiromichi Matsuda/Nagasaki Atomic Bomb Museum (http://nagasakipeace.jp)/Wikimedia Commons.

ultimate black-market payoff. The client might be a rogue state or terrorist movement that would have little compunction about using its prize against enemies or "infidels." The next chapter of the nuclear saga thus remains to be written. It is possible that it will be a genocidal, even omnicidal one.

FURTHER STUDY

Omer Bartov, *Hitler's Army: Soldiers, Nazis, and War in the Third Reich*. New York: Oxford University Press, 1992. Short and seminal study; see also *The Eastern Front, 1941–45*.

David A. Bell, *The First Total War: Napoleon's Europe and the Birth of Warfare as We Know It*. Boston, MA: Houghton Mifflin Company, 2007. Examines the wars of 1792–1815 as harbingers of the exterminatory warfare of the twentieth century.

Iris Chang, *The Rape of Nanking*. New York: Penguin, 1998. Examines Japan's genocidal massacres and mass rape in China in 1937–1938.

Mike Davis, *Late Victorian Holocausts: El Niño Famines and the Making of the Third World*. New York: Verso, 2001. Influential exploration of how early capitalist economics in the colonial world combined with environmental stresses to inflict mass death.

John Dower, *War Without Mercy: Race and Power in the Pacific War*. New York: Pantheon, 1986. Analyzes the racism of both the US and Japanese war efforts, and its transformation into peaceful cooperation after 1945.

Barbara Ehrenreich, *Blood Rites: Origins and History of the Passions of War*. New York: Metropolitan Books, 1997. Intriguing interpretation of warfare as a vestige of human beings' prehistoric struggle against predators.

Marcia Esparza, Henry R. Huttenbach, and Daniel Feierstein, eds., *State Violence and Genocide in Latin America: The Cold War Years*. London: Routledge, 2010. The first volume to systematically explore genocide in a modern Latin American context; focuses on the "dirty wars" and genocides of the 1970s and 1980s, along with the US imperial role.

J. Glenn Gray, *The Warriors: Reflections on Men in Battle*. Omaha, NE: University of Nebraska Press, 1998. Evocation of the soldier's soul, first published in 1959.

Paul Ham, *Hiroshima Nagasaki: The Real Story of the Atomic Bombings and Their Aftermath*. New York: St. Martin's Press, 2011. "A provocative reassessment . . . Ham writes with anger and a journalist's eye" (*The Daily Telegraph*).

Thomas Keneally, *Three Famines: Starvation and Politics*. New York: PublicAffairs, 2011. Readable and well-informed study of famine crimes in colonial India and Ireland, as well as Ethiopia under the Dergue regime.

Alan Kramer, *Dynamic of Destruction: Culture and Mass Killing in the First World War*. Oxford: Oxford University Press, 2007. How the First World War served as a precursor and prototype for the mass slaughters of the twentieth century.

René Lemarchand, ed., *Forgotten Genocides: Oblivion, Denial, and Memory*. Philadelphia, PA: University of Pennsylvania Press, 2011. Short, trenchant volume examining genocides that are usually excluded from the "canon," and why they are excluded. The focus is on colonial/imperial genocides, including cases of "internal colonialism" (Tibet, Iraqi Kurdistan).

Benjamin Lieberman, *Terrible Fate: Ethnic Cleansing in the Making of Modern Europe*. Chicago, IL: Ivan R. Dee, 2006. Moving, highly readable account of state formation and imperial collapse in Europe, and the human destruction it wrought.

Robert Jay Lifton and Eric Markusen, *The Genocidal Mentality: Nazi Holocaust and Nuclear Threat*. New York: Basic Books, 1990. Compares the mindset of Nazi leaders and functionaries with that of their counterparts in the nuclear age.

Eric Markusen and David Kopf, *The Holocaust and Strategic Bombing: Genocide and Total War in the Twentieth Century*. Boulder, CO: Westview Press, 1995. Excellent analysis of points of sociological and psychological crossover.

Arno J. Mayer, *The Furies: Violence and Terror in the French and Russian Revolutions*. Princeton, NJ: Princeton University Press, 2000. Epic study of two epochal revolutions.

Robert Melson, *Revolution and Genocide: On the Origins of the Armenian Genocide and the Holocaust*. Chicago, IL: University of Chicago Press, 1996. The interweaving of war, revolution, and genocide.

Jean-Paul Sartre and Arlette El Kai'm-Sartre, *On Genocide*. Boston, MA: Beacon Press, 1968. Sartre's controversial essay, set alongside evidence of US crimes in Vietnam.

Jonathan Schell, *The Fate of the Earth and the Abolition*. Stanford, CA: Stanford University Press, 2000. Two key works on nuclearism, now in a combined edition; see also *The Seventh Decade: The New Shape of Nuclear Danger*.

Martin Shaw, *War and Genocide: Organized Killing in Modern Society*. Cambridge: Polity Press, 2003. The best introduction to the subject.

Yukiko Tanaka, *Hidden Horrors: Japanese War Crimes in World War II*. Boulder, CO: Westview Press, 1997. Examines biological experiments, sexual enslavement, and atrocities against prisoners-of-war.

Nick Turse, *Kill Anything That Moves: The Real American War in Vietnam*. New York: Metropolitan Books, 2013. An encompassing treatment of US crimes in Vietnam.

NOTES

1 Mark Levene, *Genocide in the Age of the Nation State, Vol. 1: The Meaning of Genocide* and *Vol. 2: The Rise of the West and the Coming of Genocide* (London: I.B. Tauris, 2005).

2 James C. Scott, *Seeing Like A State: How Certain Schemes to Improve the Human Condition Have Failed* (New Haven, CT: Yale University Press, 1998).

3 Karel C. Berkhoff, *Harvest of Despair: Life and Death in Ukraine under Nazi Rule* (Cambridge, MA: Harvard University Press, 2004); Wendy Lower, *Nazi Empire-Building and the Holocaust in Ukraine* (Chapel Hill, NC: The University of North Carolina Press, 2004); Mark Mazower, *Hitler's Empire: How the Nazis Ruled Europe* (New York: Penguin, 2008).

4 Leonard Seabrooke, "Imperialism," in Martin Griffiths, ed., *Encyclopedia of International Relations and Global Politics* (London: Routledge, 2005), p. 398.

5 Ripon College, "Important Concepts in Global Studies" (link now defunct).

6 The term "internal colonialism" was first deployed by leading Marxist theoreticians such as Lenin and Gramsci. The most prominent treatment of the theme is that of Michael Hechter, who built his analysis around the English conquest of the "Celtic Fringe" (Scotland, Wales, and Ireland). See Hechter, *Internal Colonialism: The Celtic Fringe in British National Development, 1536–1966* (Berkeley, CA: University of California Press, 1975).

7 This is the interpretation advanced by Lynne Viola in *The Unknown Gulag*. "The peasantry would serve as an internal colony for Soviet economic development. . . . The countryside became a foreign country to be invaded, occupied, and conquered." She cites a fascinating speech by the Soviet dictator, Joseph Stalin (see Chapter 5), to the Communist Party Central Committee in July 1928, which is worth reproducing at length for the insights it offers into state-building, internal colonialism, and class-driven genocidal processes:

> In capitalist countries industrialization was usually based not only on internal accumulation but also on the plundering of other countries, the plundering of colonies

or vanquished countries, or on substantial loans from abroad. . . . Our country differs from the capitalist countries . . . in that it cannot and must not engage in the plundering of colonies or in the plundering of other countries in general. Therefore this path is closed to us. But our country doesn't have loans from abroad either. Consequently, this path is closed to us as well. In that case what is left for us? One choice is left: to develop industry, to industrialize the country on the basis of internal accumulation [n.b. effectively, internal colonialism]. . . . But where are the sources of this accumulation? . . . There are two such sources: first, the working class, which creates valuable output and moves industry forward; and second, the peasantry.

The situation in our country with regard to the peasantry in this case is the following: it pays the state not only ordinary taxes, direct and indirect, but it also pays relatively high prices for goods from industry—that is first of all—and it doesn't receive the full value of the prices of agricultural products—that is second of all. This is an additional tax on the peasantry in the interests of developing industry, which serves the whole country, including the peasantry. This is something like a 'tribute,' something like a surtax, which we are forced to take temporarily in order to sustain and further develop the current rate of industrial growth. . . . This situation, needless to say, is unpleasant. But we would not be Bolsheviks if we papered over this fact and closed our eyes to the fact that, unfortunately, our industry and our country cannot manage without this additional tax on the peasantry. (Quoted in Viola, *The Unknown Gulag: The Lost World of Stalin's Special Settlements* [Oxford: Oxford University Press, 2007], pp. 15, 32.)

Compare this with Frank Dikötter's description of Mao Zedong's communist regime in China during the "Great Leap Forward" of the late 1950s and early 1960s (Chapter 5): " . . . The party had evolved a set of political priorities which ignored the needs of the countryside. The leadership decided to increase grain exports to honour its foreign contracts and maintain its international reputation, to such an extent that a policy of 'export above all else' was adopted in 1960. . . . Priority was also given to the growing populations of Beijing, Tianjin, Shanghai and the province of Liaoning—the heartland of heavy industry—followed by the requirements of city people in general. The consequence of these political decisions was not only an increase in the proportion of procurements, but also an increase in the overall amount of grain handed over to the state out of these procurements. . . . The net effect of these policy priorities was that the lives of many villagers were destroyed." Dikötter, *Mao's Great Famine: The History of China's Most Devastating Catastrophe, 1958–62* (London: Bloomsbury, 2010), pp. 133–134.

8 On the Irish famine of the 1840s, see John Kelly, *The Graves Are Walking: The Great Famine and the Saga of the Irish People* (New York: Henry Holt and Company, 2012); Tim Pat Coogan, *The Famine Plot: England's Role in Ireland's Greatest Tragedy* (London: Palgrave Macmillan, 2012); Christine Kinealy, *A Death-Dealing Famine: The Great Hunger in Ireland* (London: Pluto Press, 1997); Robbie McVeigh, "'The Balance of Cruelty': Ireland, Britain and the Logic of Genocide," *Journal of Genocide Research*, 10: 4 (December 2008), pp. 541–561. According to Hannibal Travis, after the famine, "An Irish official accused the British prime minister of having 'smitten and offered up as a holocaust' a total of a 'million and a half Irish people.' The lord lieutenant of Ireland in 1849 condemned Parliament for pursuing a cold, calculating 'policy of extermination.'" Hannibal Travis, *Genocide in the Middle East: The Ottoman Empire, Iraq, and Sudan* (Durham, NC: Carolina Academic Press, 2010), p. 142. The usage in this early context of the modern-seeming language of "holocaust" and "extermination" is notable (see more on "extermination" in Chapter 15).

9 A readable popular account is Robert Hughes, *The Fatal Shore: The Epic of Australia's Founding* (New York: Vintage, 1988).

10 For an overview of the literature and law surrounding "famine crimes," see David Marcus, "Famine Crimes in International Law," *The American Journal of International Law*, 97 (2003), pp. 245–281. See also Rhoda E. Howard-Hassmann, "Genocide and State-Induced Famine: Global Ethics and Western Responsibility for Mass Atrocities in Africa," *Perspectives on Global Development and Technology*, 4: 3–4 (2005), pp. 487–516.

11 Amartya Sen, *Development as Freedom* (New York: Anchor, 1999), p. 168. Sen's 1977 study of the 1943–1945 famine in colonial Bengal, in which some three million Indians died, prompted Henry Shue to coin his famous phrase, "the Holocaust of Neglect." Sen, "Starvation and Exchange Entitlements: A General Approach and Its Application to the Great Bengal Famine," *Cambridge Journal of Economics*, 1:1 (1977), pp. 33–59; Shue, *Basic Rights: Subsistence, Affluence, and U.S. Foreign Policy* (2nd edn) (Princeton, NJ: Princeton University Press, 1996), p. 207 (n. 17).

12 Stéphane Courtois *et al.*, *The Black Book of Communism: Crimes, Terror, Repression* (Cambridge, MA: Harvard University Press, 1999).

13 Mike Davis, *Late Victorian Holocausts: El Niño Famines and the Making of the Third World* (London: Verso, 2001), pp. 158, 174.

14 "Three-fourths of a million bushels of grain was exported from Berar province in the north even as 143,000 people starved to death there. When Kansas Populists in the United States shipped 200,000 bags of grain to ease the famine 'in solidarity with India's farmers,' British officials taxed the shipment. The standing order among officials was that 'the revenue must at all costs be gathered in.'" Matthew White, *Atrocitology: Humanity's 100 Deadliest Achievements* (Edinburgh: Canongate, 2011), pp. 314–315.

15 The lyrics of "Famine" include a sample from Lennon and McCartney's "Eleanor Rigby" ("All the lonely people . . . "), as well as a concluding excerpt from a 1970 speech by Irish Taoiseach (prime minister) Jack Lynch. Neither is included here. The studio recording of the hip-hop-driven song, from Sinéad O'Connor's 1994 album *Universal Mother*, can be heard at www.youtube.com/watch?v=Z0K2kaG3VhM. There is a live performance from *Later . . . with Jools Holland* at www.youtube.com/watch?v=Ts8QyK6nm34.

16 Davis, *Late Victorian Holocausts*, pp. 15, 22, 37–38, 152, 287–288, 290. Eric Hobsbawm has also pointed out that colonial policy during the Indian famines occurred against a backdrop of Britain's "virtual destruction . . . of what had been a flourishing domestic and village industry which supplemented the rural incomes" across India, but which competed with British products. This "deindustrialization made the peasant village itself more dependent on the single, fluctuating fortune of the harvest," and correspondingly more vulnerable when famine struck. Hobsbawm, *The Age of Revolution, 1789–1848* (London: Abacus, 1994), p. 201.

17 The influence of Conrad's novella continues to the present, entrenching a notion of Congo, in Daniel Magnowski's words, "as being beyond anyone's help. . . . The idea of a dark, savage place resonates deeply in the Western psyche, to the point at which violence has become the expected national trait of Congo, and the country a canvas upon which the worst excesses of depravity have been painted." Magnowski, "'Cursed' Congo Still Shocks and Fascinates," Reuters dispatch, November 21, 2008.

18 Madhusree Mukerjee, *Churchill's Secret War: The British Empire and the Ravaging of India during World War II* (New York: Basic Books, 2010), pp. xxxi, 78, 117, 121, 130, 207, 269.

19 Adam Hochschild, *King Leopold's Ghost* (Boston, MA: Houghton Mifflin, 1998), p. 4. A potent two-hour television documentary, *Congo: White King, Red Rubber, Black Death* (dir. Peter Bate, 2003), was streaming on Google Videos (http://video.google.com/) at the time of writing.

20 Martin Ewans, *European Atrocity, African Catastrophe: Leopold II, the Congo Free State and its Aftermath* (London: RoutledgeCurzon, 2002), p. 3.

21 Hochschild, *King Leopold's Ghost*, p. 233.

22 Neal Ascherson, *The King Incorporated: Leopold the Second and the Congo* (London: Granta, 1999), p. 251.

23 Quoted in Ewans, *European Atrocity, African Catastrophe*, pp. 112–113. Caryatids are (female) figures in the columns of Greek architecture, "used as pillar[s]" to support friezes and other stonework *(The Concise Oxford Dictionary).*

24 Hochschild, *King Leopold's Ghost*, p. 233.

25 Neal Ascherson, *The King Incorporated: Leopold the Second and the Congo* (London: Granta, 1999), p. 251.

26 Ascherson, *The King Incorporated*, p. 9.

27 For more on the gendering of the catastrophe, see Adam Jones/Gendercide Watch, "Case Study: *Corvée* (Forced) Labour," www.gendercide.org/case_corvee.html.

28 Hochschild, *King Leopold's Ghost*, p. 232. Nor were the Belgians the only imperial power to inflict genocidal atrocities in Congo: according to Hochschild (p. 280), French rule in "their" part of the Congo resulted in population losses also approaching 50 percent in the most afflicted regions. See also Raphael Lemkin's historical study of roughly contemporaneous imperial atrocities, "The Germans in Africa," with special attention to Cameroon, in Raphael Lemkin, *Lemkin on Genocide*, ed. Steven Leonard Jacobs (Lanham, MD: Lexington Books, 2012), pp. 189–222.

29 See Christina Twoney, "Severed Hands: Authenticating Atrocity in the Congo, 1904–1913," in Geoffrey Batchen *et al.*, eds., *Picturing Atrocity: Photography in Crisis* (London: Reaktion Books, 2014), pp. 39–50.

30 Ascherson, *The King Incorporated*, p. 9.

31 See also E.D. Morel's influential contribution, *Red Rubber: The Story of the Rubber Slave Trade Which Flourished on the Congo for Twenty Years, 1890–1910* (Manchester: The National Labour Press, 1920). A digital facsimile is available online at http://catalog.hathitrust.org/Record/008416679.

32 John Rabe, *The Good Man of Nanking: The Diaries of John Rabe*, trans. John E. Woods (New York: Alfred A. Knopf, 1998), pp. 76–77, 134. Notoriously, the *Japan Advertiser* of December 7, 1937 related the "friendly contest" held between two Japanese sub-lieutenants "to see which of them will first fell 100 Chinese in individual sword combat" (i.e., the execution of Chinese male non-combatants).

> [Toshiaki] Mukai has a score of 106 and his rival [Takeshi Noda] has dispatched 105 men, but the two contestants have found it impossible to determine which passed the 100 mark first. Instead of settling it with a discussion, they are going to extend the goal by 50. . . . Mukai's blade was slightly damaged in the competition. He explained that this was the result of cutting a Chinese in half, helmet and all. The contest was 'fun,' he declared, and thought it a good thing that both men had gone over the 100 mark without knowing that the other had done so. (Quoted in Rabe, *The Good Man of Nanking*, p. 283.)

33 R.J. Rummel, *Death by Government* (New Brunswick, NJ: Transaction Publishers, 1997), pp. 146, 151.

34 Ibid., p. 150.

35 For in-depth treatments of Japanese forced prostitution in the occupied territories, see Yuki Tanaka, *Japan's Comfort Women: The Military and Involuntary Prostitution During War and Occupation* (London: Routledge, 2002); George L. Hicks, *The Comfort Women: Japan's Brutal Regime of Enforced Prostitution in the Second World War* (New York: W.W. Norton, 1997). See further discussion in the context of memory issues and redress claims in Chapter 14.

36 Yukiko Tanaka, *Hidden Horrors: Japanese War Crimes in World War II* (Boulder, CO: Westview Press, 1997), pp. 137–138. A good, brief introduction to Japanese crimes is

Laurence Rees, *Horror in the East: Japan and the Atrocities of World War II* (Cambridge, MA: Da Capo Press, 2002).

37 See Sheldon H. Harris, *Factories of Death: Japanese Biological Warfare, 1932–45 and the American Cover-Up* (rev. edn) (London: Routledge, 2001).

38 Katsuichi Honda, quoted in Nick Turse, *Kill Anything That Moves: The Real American War in Vietnam* (New York: Metropolitan Books, 2013), p. 212. See also Deborah Nelson, *The War Behind Me: Vietnam Veterans Confront the Truth about U.S. War Crimes* (New York: Basic Books, 2008).

39 Quoted in Turse, *Kill Anything that Moves*, p. 45.

40 Quoted in ibid., pp. 48–49.

41 The most detailed account of the massacre is Michael Bilton and Kevin Sim, *Four Hours in My Lai* (New York: Penguin, 1992). The wrenching TV documentary of the same name can be searched on YouTube, and makes clear also the resulting trauma (in one case, to the point of self-destruction) for many of the guilt-ridden soldier-perpetrators.

42 Hersh's original dispatches on the My Lai massacre are compiled at www.pierretristam.com/Bobst/library/wf-200.htm.

43 Trent Angers, *The Forgotten Hero of My Lai: The Hugh Thompson Story* (Lafayette, LA: Acadian House Publishing, 1999), p. 184.

44 In August 2009, in a speech to his local Kiwanis Club in Columbus, Georgia, Calley made his first public comment on the massacre: "There is not a day that goes by that I do not feel remorse for what happened that day in My Lai. I feel remorse for the Vietnamese who were killed, for their families, for the American soldiers involved and their families. I am very sorry." See "Calley Apologizes for Role in My Lai Massacre," Associated Press dispatch on MSNBC.com, August 21, 2009, www.msnbc.msn.com/id/32514139/ns/us_news-military.

45 See the account by *Toledo Blade* journalists Michael Sallah and Mitch Weiss, based on their Pulitzer Prize-winning reportage: *Tiger Force: A True Story of Men and War* (New York: Back Bay Books, 2006); and Deborah Nelson, *The War Behind Me: Vietnam Veterans Confront the Truth about US War Crimes* (New York: Basic Books, 2008).

In 2001, the former US Senator and Navy Seal, Bob Kerrey, confessed his involvement in one such massacre of civilians. See Douglas Valentine, "Bob Kerrey, CIA War Crimes, and the Need for a War Crimes Trial," *Counterpunch.org*, May 17, 2001, available at www.whale.to/b/val1.html. Valentine's earlier book, *The Phoenix Program* (Authors Guild, 2000), analyzes the post-Tet "pacification" atrocities, and is also essential. For a discussion of remarkably similar acts by US forces during the Korean War, only recently unearthed, see Charles J. Hanley, Sang-Hun Choe, and Martha Mendoza, *The Bridge at No Gun Ri: A Hidden Nightmare from the Korean War* (New York: Henry Holt & Company, 2001). For an argument that "the No Gun Ri incident . . . may be the tip of the iceberg in regards [sic] to the matter of mass killings committed by US and South Korean troops during the Korean War," citing "more than sixty cases of mass killing committed by US troops, by shooting, bombing, strafing or other means," see Dong Choon Kim, "Forgotten War, Forgotten Massacres: The Korean War (1950–1953) as Licensed Mass Killings," *Journal of Genocide Research*, 6: 4 (2004), pp. 523–544. As Kim notes (p. 531), "In every aspect of the war—America's use of napalm, indiscriminate bombing, and the shooting of 'voiceless' civilians of the Third World, the Korean War preceded the Indochina War in many tragic ways."

46 Turse, *Kill Anything That Moves*, p. 13.

47 Martha Ann Overland, "Agent Orange Poisons New Generations in Vietnam," *Time*, December 19, 2009, www.time.com/time/world/article/0,8599,1948084,00.html.

48 S. Brian Willson, "Bob Kerrey's Atrocity, the Crime of Vietnam and the Historic Pattern of US Imperialism," in Adam Jones, ed., *Genocide, War Crimes and the West: History and Complicity* (London: Zed Books, 2004), pp. 167–169.

49 As I learned on a visit to the Plain of Jars in summer 2009, one treads gingerly on narrow paths cleared by the dedicated workers of the Mines Advisory Group (MAG), even in areas at the heart of Laos's attempt to revive a tourist economy. To ramble away from the path is to risk death or disfigurement—nearly four decades after the bombing assault climaxed. See the website of the Mines Advisory Group (MAG), www.maginternational.org, and that of the organization devoted to crafting prosthetic limbs for UXO victims in Laos, the Cooperative Orthotic and Prosthetic Enterprise (COPE), www.copelaos.org.

50 Arthur Jay Klinghoffer, "International Citizens' Tribunals on Human Rights," in Adam Jones, ed., *Genocide, War Crimes and the West: History and Complicity* (London: Zed Books, 2004), p. 355.

51 Ann Curthoys and John Docker, "Defining Genocide," in Dan Stone, ed., *The Historiography of Genocide* (London: Palgrave Macmillan, 2008), p. 25.

52 Jean-Paul Sartre, "On Genocide," in Jean-Paul Sartre and Arlette El Ka'im-Sartre, *On Genocide* (Boston, MA: Beacon Press, 1968), p. 82.

53 Kuper, *Genocide*, p. 35.

54 See Anne Applebaum, *Iron Curtain: The Crushing of Eastern Europe, 1944–1956* (New York: Anchor, 2013).

55 See Victor Sebestyen, *Twelve Days: The Story of the 1956 Hungarian Revolution* (New York: Vintage, 2007) and Michael Korda, *Journey to a Revolution* (New York: Harper-Collins, 2006).

56 Eric Margolis, *War at the Top of the World: The Struggle for Afghanistan, Kashmir, and Tibet* (New York: Routledge, 2001), p. 18.

57 Rosanne Klass, "Afghanistan," in Israel W. Charny et al., eds., *The Encyclopedia of Genocide, Vol. 2* (Santa Barbara, CA: ABC-CLIO, 2000), pp. 48–49. Benjamin Valentino's summary of Soviet scorched-earth strategies is succinct: "In regions of high guerrilla activity, Soviet forces systematically burned crops and dwellings, reducing vast swaths of territory to wasteland. Soviet aircraft employed incendiary weapons, including napalm and phosphorus cluster munitions, to burn crops from the air. Entire herds of livestock were slaughtered or confiscated. Irrigation systems were intentionally destroyed, rendering agriculture in Afghanistan's arid climate all but impossible. Some reports suggest that Soviet forces deliberately poisoned village grain stores and water supplies. Houses and agricultural fields were heavily mined. By 1984 these tactics and the ensuing exodus of the rural population resulted in a 75 to 80 percent decline in agricultural production compared to pre-1979 levels." Valentino, *Final Solutions: Mass Killing and Genocide in the 20th Century* (Ithaca, NY: Cornell University Press, 2004), p. 224. As with the US "free-fire zones" in Vietnam, or the Mayan highlands of Guatemala during the military's campaign of "scorched communists" (Box 3a), this is precisely the kind of coordinated campaign to deliberately inflict "conditions of life calculated to bring about [the] physical destruction" of a group that is referenced in Article 2(c) of the UN Genocide Convention.

58 Ibid., p. 222.

59 As explored by Richard Drinnon in *Facing West: The Metaphysics of Indian Hating and Empire Building* (New York: Schocken Books, 1990).

60 Walter Richmond, *The Circassian Genocide* (New Brunswick, NJ: Rutgers University Press, 2013), pp. 161, 162.

61 Stephen D. Shenfield, "The Circassians: A Forgotten Genocide?," in Mark Levene and Penny Roberts, eds., *The Massacre in History* (New York: Berghahn Books, 1999), p. 150.

62 See the 1840 map of Circassia by James Stanislaus Bell at https://en.wikipedia.org/wiki/Russo-Circassian_War#/media/File:CIRCASSIA1840.jpg.

63 Shenfield, "The Circassians," p. 156.

64 The flavor of the Russian conquest of the Caucasus is conveyed by the proclamation of General Alexei Yermolov, Russian viceroy in the region between 1816 and 1827: "I desire that the terror of my name should guard our frontiers more potently than

chains of fortresses, that my word should be for the natives a law more inevitable than death." Quoted in Oliver Bullough, *Let Our Fame Be Great: Journeys Among the Defiant People of the Caucasus* (New York: Basic Books, 2010), p. 60. Bullough writes that Yermolov "became a byword for massacre and horror, especially in the eastern Caucasus."

65 Baryatinsky quoted in Richmond, *The Circassian Genocide*, p. 71.
66 A "clearly appalled" Russian observer in Circassia, the geographer Mikhail Venyukov, wrote: "The war was conducted with implacable, merciless severity. We went forward step by step, irrevocably cleansing the mountaineers to the last man from any land the soldiers set foot on. The mountaineers' auls [settlements] were burned by the hundreds . . . We trampled and destroyed their crops with our horses. If we were able to capture the villagers by surprise we immediately sent them via convoy to the shore of the Black Sea, and farther, to Turkey. . . . Sometimes—to the credit of our troops, rarely—there were atrocities bordering on barbarity"—which were in fact far from "rare." Quoted in Richmond, *The Circassian Genocide*, p. 80; see also p. 65.
67 Richmond, *The Circassian Genocide*, p. 85.
68 Ibid., pp. 85, 91.
69 Shenfield, "The Circassians," p. 153.
70 Richmond, *The Circassian Genocide*, pp. 92, 101.
71 Shenfield, "The Circassians," p. 154.
72 Richmond, *The Circassian Genocide*, p. 132.
73 Ibid., p. 159.
74 For a concise treatment of the Circassian case, see Walter Richmond's chapter, "Circassia: A Small Nation Lost to the Great Game," in Alexander Laban Hinton, Thomas La Pointe, and Douglas Irvin-Erickson, eds., *Hidden Genocides: Power, Knowledge, Memory* (New Brunswick, NJ: Rutgers University Press, 2013), pp. 109–125.
75 Valentino, and Laber and Rubin quoted in Valentino, *Final Solutions*, pp. 221–222.
76 Gregory Feifer, *The Great Gamble: The Soviet War in Afghanistan* (New York: HarperPerennial, 2009), p. 4.
77 Boulouque, "Communism in Afghanistan," p. 717.
78 Helen Fein, "Discriminating Genocide from War Crimes: Vietnam and Afghanistan Reexamined," *Denver Journal of International Law and Policy*, 22: 1 (1993), p. 61. Hannibal Travis also refers to "the genocidal war between Soviet and Afghan communist forces and the fundamentalist insurgents backed by the Western and wider Islamic worlds." Travis, *Genocide in the Middle East*, p. 385.
79 See, e.g., Ranajit Guha, *A Subaltern Studies Reader, 1986–1995* (Minneapolis, MN: University of Minnesota Press, 1997).
80 See Eric Hobsbawm's *Age* series, especially *The Age of Empire, 1875–1914* (New York: Vintage, 1989) and *The Age of Extremes: A History of the World, 1914–1991* (New York: Vintage, 1996); Perry Anderson, *Lineages of the Absolutist State* (London: NLB, 1977), a masterpiece of vast scope and erudition that is too rarely read in genocide studies; and Antonio Negri and Michael Hardt, *Empire* (Cambridge, MA: Harvard University Press, 2001).
81 Stathis Kalyvas, *The Logic of Violence in Civil War* (Cambridge: Cambridge University Press, 2006). For a groundbreaking Europe-wide survey of civil strife and mass violence between the end of the Second World War and the mid-1950s, see Keith Lowe, *Savage Continent: Europe in the Aftermath of World War II* (New York: St. Martin's Press, 2013), including attention to many of the cases analyzed by Kalyvas, Levene, and Snyder, among others.
82 Levene, "The Tragedy of the Rimlands," p. 54.
83 Jeff Benvenuto, Andrew Woolford, and Alexander Laban Hinton, "Introduction: Colonial Genocide in Indigenous North America," in Woolford, Benvenuto, and Hinton, eds., *Colonial Genocide in Indigenous North America* (Durham, NC: Duke University Press, 2014), p. 14. The specific "shatter zone" referenced is the early-eighteenth-century Mississippian one—a reminder that the concept has informed historical interpretations well beyond the European continent. The Caucasus, Northwest Asia (Afghanistan,

Pakistan, India, China) and the modern Middle East seem apt examples. Perhaps also the Great Lakes region of Africa (Chapter 9)?

84 Omer Bartov and Eric Weitz, eds., *Shatterzone of Empires: Coexistence and Violence in the German, Habsburg, Russian, and Ottoman Borderlands* (Bloomington, IN: Indiana University Press, 2013).

85 Sémelin, *Purify and Destroy: The Political Uses of Massacre and Genocide* (New York: Columbia University Press, 2007), p. 118.

86 Mark Levene, "The Tragedy of the Rimlands, Nation-State Formation and the Destruction of Imperial Peoples, 1912–48," in Panikos Panayi and Pippa Verdee, eds., *Refugees and the End of Empire* (London: Palgrave Macmillan, 2011), pp. 51, 63. See the exchange on Levene's *Crisis of Genocide* volumes in *Journal of Genocide Research*, 17: 2 (2013), pp. 221–254.

87 Levene, "The Tragedy of the Rimlands," pp. 72–73 (quoting Duncan M. Perry). Elsewhere, Levene has cited British observer Arthur Ransome's account from eastern Galicia during the First World War: "The peasants working on the land were very unwilling to identify themselves as belonging to *any* of the warring nations. Again and again, on asking a peasant to what nationality he belonged: [Muscovite] Russian, Little [southern] Russian, or Polish, I heard the reply 'Orthodox,' and when the men were pressed to say what actual race he belonged to [*sic*] I heard him answer safely: 'We are local.'" Quoted in Levene, *The Crisis of Genocide, Vol. 1*, p. 9.

88 Ibid., p. 63.

89 Anne Applebaum, "The Worst of the Madness," *The New York Review of Books*, November 11, 2010, www.nybooks.com/articles/2010/11/11/worst-madness/.

90 Ibid.

91 Mark Levene and Jan Gross are among the scholars who have highlighted the Polish-Ukrainian genocidal dyad. It was largely subsumed, of course, by Nazi empire-building between 1939 and 1945, and by Soviet imperialism from 1939 until the early 1950s. See, e.g., Levene, *The Crisis of Genocide, Vol. 2: Annihilation: The European Rimlands 1939–1953* (Oxford: Oxford University Press, 2013), pp. 290–300, concluding his excellent chapter on the "wars of all against all" during this period of Rimlands history. See also "The Ethnic Cleansing of Ukraine and Poland," in Keith Lowe, *Savage Continent: Europe in the Aftermath of World War II* (London: Picador, 2013), pp. 212–270 (e-book); Wendy Lower, "Pogroms, Mob Violence and Genocide in Western Ukraine, Summer 1941: Varied Histories, Explanations and Comparisons," *Journal of Genocide Research*, 13: 3 (2011), pp. 217–246.

92 On Snyder's deployment of a "Great Man" model of history, and the reported use of his book as an ultranationalist and Holocaust-denier "bible," see Thomas Kühne, "Great Men and Large Numbers: Undertheorizing a History of Mass Killing," *Contemporary European History*, 21: 2 (2012), p. 135–137. See also Daniel Lazare's polemic, "Timothy Snyder's Lies," *Jacobin*, September 2014, www.jacobinmag.com/2014/09/timothy-snyders-lies/.

93 For Thomas Kühne, "a regional history of the 'bloodlands' would be one that catches on local views, local traditions and local agency. It would explore how local traditions, local people and local choices clashed with the changing terrorist regimes; it would compare how different localities struggled with different regimes in different ways and possibly with different results. None of these themes are subject[s] of *Bloodlands*, which is even more surprising as Snyder is the author of a brilliant book on them"— that is, *The Reconstruction of Nations: Poland, Ukraine, Lithuania, Belarus, 1569–1999* (New Haven, CT: Yale University Press, 2004). Kühne, "Great Men," p. 139.

94 Sémelin, "Timothy Snyder and His Critics." See also the forum on *Bloodlands* with John Connelly, Mark Roseman, Andriy Portnov, Michael David-Fox, and a response by Snyder: *Journal of Genocide Research*, 13: 3 (2011), pp. 313–352.

95 Ibid.

96 Levene, *Genocide in the Age of the Nation State, Vol. 2*, pp. 217, 232, 274.

97 Ibid., pp. 223–224.

98 Levene, *Genocide in the Age of the Nation State, Vol. 1*, pp. 186–187.

99 On the Serb case, see David B. MacDonald, "From Jasenovac to Srebrenica: Subaltern Genocide and the Serbs," in Nicholas A. Robins and Adam Jones, eds., *Genocides by the Oppressed: Subaltern Genocide in Theory and Practice* (Bloomington, IN: Indiana University Press, 2009), pp. 103–121.

100 Christopher J. Fettweis, "War as Catalyst: Moving World War II to the Center of Holocaust Scholarship," *Journal of Genocide Research*, 5:2 (2003), p. 225.

101 "Genocide can be regarded as a particular form of modern warfare, and an extension of the more common form of *degenerate* war," which "involves the deliberate and systematic extension of war against an organized armed enemy to war against a largely unarmed civilian population. . . . Therefore, the best way of making sense of genocide is to see it as *a distinctive form of war.*" Martin Shaw, *War and Genocide: Organized Killing in Modern Society* (Cambridge: Polity Press, 2003), p. 5. Mark Levene proposes the term "degenerative warfare" as a "more adjectivally dynamic term" to capture "the unfolding, worsening, and by degree more 'totalist' pursuit of war by belligerents over time [which] might bring in its wake a greater readiness to dispense with normative rules . . . a consequence of which could well be genocidal outcomes." Levene, *The Crisis of Genocide, Vol. 2: Annihilation* (Oxford: Oxford University Press, 2013), p. 235.

102 Goebbels quoted in Jeffrey Herf, *The Jewish Enemy: Nazi Propaganda during World War II and the Holocaust* (Cambridge, MA: The Belknap Press of Harvard University Press, 2006), p. 149.

103 Andresen quoted in Max Hastings, *Catastrophe 1914: Europe Goes to War* (New York: Borzoi Books, 2014), p. 353.

104 Fettweis, "War as Catalyst," p. 228.

105 Sémelin, *Purify and Destroy*, p. 172.

106 Barbara Ehrenreich, *Blood Rites: Origins and History of the Passions of War* (New York: Metropolitan Books, 1997), pp. 180–181.

107 Mark Levene notes the "instrumental opportunities" that war provides "for governments to increase surveillance and censorship of their own populations under the guise of fighting espionage and flagging morale." Levene, *The Crisis of Genocide, Vol. 1*, pp. 73–74.

108 Alex Alvarez, *Governments, Citizens, and Genocide: A Comparative and Interdisciplinary Approach* (Bloomington, IN: Indiana University Press, 2001), p. 68.

109 I am grateful to Benjamin Madley for this insight.

110 Norman M. Naimark, *Fires of Hatred: Ethnic Cleansing in Twentieth-Century Europe* (Cambridge, MA: Harvard University Press, 2001), p. 187.

111 George L. Mosse, quoted in Ehrenreich, *Blood Rites*, p. 183.

112 Alvarez, *Governments, Citizens, and Genocide*, p. 68.

113 Barash quoted in Michael Shermer and Alex Grobman, *Denying History: Who Says the Holocaust Never Happened and Why Do They Say It?* (Berkeley, CA: University of California Press, 2002), p. 93.

114 Ehrenreich, *Blood Rites*, p. 196.

115 Peter Uvin, *Aiding Violence: The Development Enterprise in Rwanda* (West Hartford, CT: Kumarian Press, 1998).

116 Quoted in Adam Jones, *Genocide: A Comprehensive Introduction* (1st edn) (London: Routledge, 2006), pp. 50–51.

117 Ewen MacAskill, "Fort Hood Backlash Feared," *The Guardian Weekly*, November 13, 2009.

118 Quoted passages from The Anti-Idiotarian Rottweiler (http://nicedoggie.net/), November 2009 archives, http://nicedoggie.net/2009/index.php/archives/date/2009/11. All typography as in the original.

119 John Keegan, *The First World War* (New York: Vintage, 1998), p. 299.

120 In 1989, I walked the Somme battlefields; the experience is described, with accompanying photos, in "No Man's Land," *The Gazette* (Montreal), December 11, 1989, http://adamjones.freeservers.com/nomans.htm.

121 Shaw, *War and Genocide*, p. 172. According to Lance Morrow, "Trench warfare prefigured the fatal industrialism of the Nazi death camps: there cling[s] to the gray, corpse-littered wastelands of World War I something of the same atmosphere: individual life stripped of meaning, dignity, all life and all death rendered purposeless, and reduced to absolute metaphysical insignificance." Morrow, *Evil: An Investigation* (New York: Basic Books, 2003), p. 47.

122 Jeremy Noakes, citing the research of Brigitte Hamann, disputes the "claim that Hitler was already a strong anti-Semite" during his time as a struggling artist in Vienna prior to World War One; indeed, "Hitler had a number of Jewish acquaintances and used them to sell his paintings, though not very successfully." See Noakes, "Hitler and the Third Reich," in Dan Stone, ed., *The Historiography of the Holocaust* (London: Palgrave Macmillan, 2004), p. 25.

123 "'No Hitler, no Holocaust' is the well-rehearsed maxim. But without the First World War, no Hitler either. At least, not in any conceivable position of power." Mark Levene, *The Crisis of Genocide, Vol. 1: Devastation: The European Rimlands 1912–1938* (Oxford: Oxford University Press, 2013), p. 2.

124 Ian Kershaw, *Hitler 1889–1936: Hubris* (London: Penguin, 2000), p. 74.

125 *The Nazi-Soviet war*. For solid social histories of the Soviet side of this titanic conflict, the most destructive in human history, see Richard Overy, *Russia's War* (London: Penguin, 1997), and Catherine Merridale, *Ivan's War: Life and Death in the Red Army, 1939–1945* (New York: Picador, 2007). See also Robert W. Thurston and Bernd Bonwetsch, eds., *The People's War: Responses to World War II in the Soviet Union* (Champaign, IL: University of Chicago Press, 2000).

Nearly all military historians of the Nazi-Soviet war acknowledge the seminal two-volume study by the late John Erickson, *The Road to Stalingrad* and *The Road to Berlin* (New Haven, CT: Yale University Press, 1999 [1975, 1983]). Erickson, however, lacked the current generation's access to the Soviet archives. Chris Bellamy, *Absolute War: Soviet Russia in the Second World War* (New York: Vintage, 2008) is the best single-volume military history, reflecting the archival revolution. But it is 800 pages long. Even longer, but compulsively readable, is British diplomat Alexander Werth's towering memoir, *Russia at War, 1941–1945* (New York: Carroll & Graf, 2000). See also two indelible portraits of besieged Russian cities: Antony Beevor, *Stalingrad: The Fateful Siege, 1942–1943* (London: Penguin, 1999) and Brian Moynahan, *Leningrad: Siege and Symphony* (New York: Atlantic Monthly Press, 2014). Both are Tolstoyan in their sweep and humanity.

Over the past couple of decades, a series of fascinating revisionist assessments of the Nazi-Soviet war have appeared, mostly in the military history field. A notable few incorporate the Holocaust of the Jews as a central element of Operation Barbarossa and subsequent occupation policies (see also Box 2.3 on recent study of the "Bloodlands" and "Rimlands" of Central and Eastern Europe). Emblematic and readable, though based on no fresh archival research, are Geoffrey P. Megargee, *War of Annihilation: Combat and Genocide on the Eastern Front, 1941* (Lanham, MD: Rowman & Littlefield, 2007), and Stephen G. Fritz, *Ostkrieg: Hitler's War of Extermination in the East* (Lexington, KY: University of Kentucky Press, 2011). Also highly recommended are Alex J. Kay, Jeff Rutherford, and David Stahel, eds., *Nazi Policy on the Eastern Front, 1941: Total War, Genocide, and Radicalization* (see Further Study, Chapter 6), and the superb 2014 monograph by Waitman Wade Beorn, *Marching Into Darkness: The Wehrmacht and the Holocaust in Belarus* (see Further Study, Chapter 6). On the role of the "partisan war," which often served as a cover for Nazi extermination policies, see Ben Shepherd, *War in the Wild East: The German Army and Soviet Partisans* (Cambridge, MA: Harvard University Press, 2004), and Alexander Hill, *The War Behind the Eastern Front: The Soviet Partisan Movement in North-West Russia 1941–1944* (London: Frank Cass, 2005).

Meanwhile, new research on the first several months of the Nazi-Soviet war, centered on the meticulous archival work of David M. Glantz and David Stahel, has fundamentally shifted understandings of the "turning point" of the conflict from the iconic battle of Stalingrad (November 1942–February 1943) to earlier moments: not only the gargantuan battle of Moscow (November 1941–January 1942), but the clashes along the Nazis' route to Moscow between July and September 1941, especially at Smolensk and Kiev. "Beginning at Smolensk," writes Stephen Fritz, "the Ostheer found itself drawn increasingly into a series of operations that ended in victories but that taxed its already strained logistics system to the limit, eroded irreplaceable combat strength, and gave the Soviets time both to call up new levies of manpower and to organize their remaining economic potential" (*Ostkrieg*, p. 121). Despite losing millions of men in encirclements, most of whom would be genocided as prisoners-of-war (see Box 6a and Figure 6a.2), desperate resistance by Soviet forces at first slowed, then stalled the Nazi juggernaut. It was at this stage that Franz Halder, chief of the German general staff, famously diagnosed the *Wehrmacht's* military quandary, writing in his diary:

> The whole situation makes it increasingly plain that we have underestimated the Russian colossus, who consistently prepared for war with that utterly ruthless determination so characteristic of totalitarian states. . . . At the outset of the war we reckoned with about 200 enemy divisions. Now we have already counted 360. These divisions indeed are not armed and equipped according to our standards, and their tactical leadership is often poor. *But they are there,* and if we smash a dozen of them, the Russians simply put up another dozen. The time factor favors them, as they are near their own resources, while we are moving farther and farther away from ours. And so our troops, sprawled over an immense front line, without any depth, are subjected to the incessant attacks of the enemy. (Quoted in Fritz, *Ostkrieg*, p. 130, emphasis added.)

The autumn 1941 weather, which turned the few main roads glutinous, is often mentioned as a contributing factor. But what made Halder's diagnosis a terminal one was the ability of the Red Army to bend but not break—or break but not collapse. With the Germans at the outer suburbs of Moscow, fresh Soviet formations arrived from Siberia, and Hitler's forces were thrown back in the first strategic defeat they had suffered in all the war. In hindsight, despite some grim moments for the Soviets in 1942, Hitler's dream of *Lebensraum* and empire in the east never recovered. Its fate was sealed by the entry of the mighty United States to the war in December 1941— gleefully provoked by Hitler, who declared war on America at a moment when he considered European hegemony within his grasp. The most accessible overview of the 1941 battles is David M. Glantz, *Operation Barbarossa: Hitler's Invasion of Russia 1941* (Stroud: The History Press, 2011); the best detailed study is David Stahel, *Operation Barbarossa and Germany's Defeat in the East* (Cambridge: Cambridge University Press, 2009). See also David M. Glantz and Jonathan House, *When Titans Clashed: How the Red Army Stopped Hitler* (Edinburgh: Birlinn Limited, 2000); David M. Glantz, *Barbarossa Derailed: The Battle for Smolensk, 10 July–10 September 1941*, 3 vols. (Solihull: Helion and Company, 2010); David Stahel, *Kiev 1941: Hitler's Battle for Supremacy in the East* (Cambridge: Cambridge University Press, 2012); David Stahel, *Operation Typhoon: Hitler's March on Moscow, October 1941* (Cambridge: Cambridge University Press, 2013); and Rodric Braithwaite, *Moscow 1941: A City and Its People at War* (New York: Vintage Books, 2006). The protracted battle of Moscow is still the largest in world history, with *seven million* soldiers fighting on both sides.

The renewed but ultimately failed German offensives of 1942, aimed at Stalingrad on the Volga river and the oil fields of the Caucasus, are surveyed in Robert M. Citino, *Death of the Wehrmacht: The German Campaigns of 1942* (Lawrence, KS: University of Kansas Press, 2007). The pivotal battle of Kursk (July–August 1943—see Figure 2.16), after which Nazi armies never again mounted an offensive in the east, is vividly rendered by Dennis E. Showalter in *Armor and Blood: The Battle of Kursk: The Turning Point of World War II* (New York: Random House, 2013), and analyzed at an almost forensic level by David M. Glantz and Jonathan M. House in *The Battle of Kursk* (Lawrence, KS: University of Kansas Press, 1999). Some might be interested in my impressions and photographs of the Kursk battlefields, "Pilgrimage to Prokhorovka," at http://adamjones.freeservers.com/prokhorovka.htm. Operation Bagration, the Soviets' summer 1944 pulverizing of Army Group Center in Belorussia/Belarus, awaits its great chronicler. In the meantime, there is Paul Adair, *Hitler's Greatest Defeat: The Collapse of Army Group Centre, June 1944* (London: Brockhampton Press, 1998), and Walter S. Dunn, Jr., *Soviet Blitzkrieg: The Battle for White Russia, 1944* (Mechanicsburg, PA: Stackpole Books, 2000).

126 Andrew Roberts, *The Storm of War: A New History of the Second World War* (London: Penguin, 2009), p. 160.

127 Omer Bartov, *Germany's War and the Holocaust: Disputed Histories* (Ithaca, NY: Cornell University Press, 2003), p. 7.

128 Wendy Lower, "'On Him Rests the Weight of the Administration': Nazi Civilian Rulers and the Holocaust in Zhytomyr," in Ray Brandon and Wendy Lower, eds., *The Shoah in Ukraine: History, Testimony, Memorialization* (Bloomington, IN: Indiana University Press, 2010), p. 225.

129 Omer Bartov, *Hitler's Army: Soldiers, Nazis, and War in the Third Reich* (New York: Oxford University Press, 1992), p. 129.

130 Ehrenburg quoted in Alfred-Maurice de Zayas, *A Terrible Revenge: The Ethnic Cleansing of the East European Germans, 1944–1950* (New York: St. Martin's Press, 1994), p. 34.

131 Stalin quoted in Milovan Djilas, *Wartime* (New York: Harvest, 1980), p. 435.

132 Norman M. Naimark, *The Russians in Germany: A History of the Soviet Zone of Occupation, 1945–1949* (Cambridge, MA: The Belknap Press, 1995), pp. 72, 133; see also pp. 235–250 on the postwar uranium mining that killed thousands of German workers.

133 Quoted in Richard J. Evans, *The Third Reich at War: How the Nazis Led Germany from Conquest to Disaster* (London: Penguin, 2009), p. 710.

134 Gary Paul Bass, *Stay the Hand of Vengeance: The Politics of War Crimes Tribunals* (Princeton, NJ: Princeton University Press, 2000), p. 198.

135 Daniel Chirot and Clark McCauley, *Why Not Kill Them All? The Logic and Prevention of Mass Political Murder* (Princeton, NJ: Princeton University Press, 2006), p. 216.

136 Karl Marx and Friedrich Engels, *The Communist Manifesto* (London: Penguin, various editions); available online at www.gutenberg.org/ebooks/61.

137 Fascism "is closely associated with imperialism, militarism and nationalism. The logic of belief in racial superiority leads to policies of conquest, domination and even elimination of lesser races." Graham Evans and Richard Newnham, *The Penguin Dictionary of International Relations* (London: Penguin, 1999), p. 168. For a penetrating psychological study, see Israel Charny, *Fascism and Democracy in the Human Mind* (Lincoln, NB: University of Nebraska Press, 2006).

138 Shaw, *War and Genocide*, p. 29.

139 Robert Melson, *Revolution and Genocide: On the Origins of Armenian Genocide and the Holocaust* (Chicago, IL: University of Chicago Press, 1996), p. 18.

140 Eric Markusen and Matthias Bjørnlund, "*Hiroshima: Culmination of Strategic Bombing, Beginning of the Threat of Nuclear Omnicide*," paper prepared for the symposium "Terror in the Sky: Indiscriminate Bombing from Hiroshima to Today," Hiroshima Peace Institute, August 2, 2003.

141 Robert Jay Lifton and Eric Markusen, *The Genocidal Mentality: Nazi Holocaust and Nuclear Threat* (New York: Basic Books, 1990), p. 38.

142 Jonathan Schell, *The Fate of the Earth and the Abolition* (Stanford, CA: Stanford University Press, 2000), p. 182.

143 Lifton and Markusen, *The Genocidal Mentality*, p. 226.

144 See Terrence Henry, "Russia's Loose Nukes," *The Atlantic Monthly*, December 2004, pp. 74–75.

PART 2 CASES

Genocides of Indigenous Peoples

INTRODUCTION

This chapter considers the impact of European invasion upon diverse indigenous peoples. Vast geographic, temporal, and cultural differences exist among these cases, but there are important common features in the strategies and outcomes of genocide.[1] To grasp this phenomenon, we must first define "indigenous peoples." The task is not easy. Indeed, both in discourse and in international law, the challenge of definition remains a "complex [and] delicate" one, in anthropologist Ronald Niezen's appraisal.[2] Nevertheless, there are "some areas of general consensus among formal attempts at definition," well captured in a 1987 report by the UN Special Rapporteur on indigenous issues, José Martínez Cobo:

> Indigenous communities, peoples and nations are those which, having a historical continuity with pre-invasion and pre-colonial societies that developed on their territories, consider themselves distinct from other sectors of the society now prevailing in those territories, or parts of them. They form at present nondominant sectors of society and are determined to preserve, develop and transmit to future generations their ancestral territories and their ethnic identity, as the basis of their continued existence as peoples, in accordance with their own cultural patterns, social institutions and legal systems.[3]

By this definition, "indigenous" peoples are inseparable from processes of colonialism and imperialism that consigned the previously dominant population of a colonized territory to a marginal status.[4] A nexus of indigenous identity and structural subordination is generally held to persist today.

The political and activist components of the indigenist project are also clear from Martínez Cobo's definition. Indigenous peoples proclaim the validity and worth of their cultures, languages, laws, religious beliefs, and political institutions; they demand respect and political space. Increasingly, they have mobilized to denounce the genocides visited upon them in the past and demand their rights in the present. In large part thanks to the growth of international governmental and nongovernmental organizations, notably the United Nations system, these mobilizations have assumed a global character. This is analyzed further in the section on "Indigenous revival," below.

COLONIALISM AND THE DISCOURSE OF EXTINCTION

The histories of indigenous peoples cannot be understood without reference to imperialism and colonialism, examined in the previous chapter. In general, though not overlooking the counterexample of African slavery, the destruction of indigenous peoples was less catastrophic in cases of "empire lite," where foreign settlement was mostly limited to coastal settlements, and networks of trade and exploitation were predominantly in the hands of native satraps. Correspondingly, policies of extermination and/or exploitation unto death were most pronounced in areas where Europeans sought to conquer indigenous territories and both displace and supplant their native populations. The focus here is on this latter variant, known as "settler colonialism."

Three ideological tenets stand out as justifying and facilitating European[5] conquest, "pacification," and "settlement." The first, most prominent in the British realm (especially the United States, Canada, and Australasia), was a *legal-utilitarian* justification, according to which native peoples had no right to territories they inhabited, owing to their "failure" to exploit them adequately. As Benjamin Madley has pointed out, this translated in Australasia to the fiction of *terra nullius*, i.e., that the territories in question had no original inhabitants in a legal sense; and, in America, to the similar concept of *vacuum domicilium*, or "empty dwelling." The second tenet, most prominent in Latin America, was a religious ideology that justified invasion and conquest as a means of saving native souls from the fires of hell. The third, more diffuse, underpinning was a *racial-eliminationist* ideology. Under the influence of the most modern scientific thinking of the age, world history was viewed as revolving around the inevitable, sometimes lamentable supplanting of primitive peoples by more advanced and "civilized" ones. This would be engineered through military confrontations between indigenous peoples and better-armed Europeans, and "naturally," through a gradual dying-off of the native populations. "Genocide began to be regarded as the inevitable byproduct of progress," as literary scholar Sven Lindqvist observed—even if its perpetrators and supporters grew misty-eyed in the process.[6]

A sophisticated study of this pervasive ideology of inevitable extinction is Patrick Brantlinger's *Dark Vanishings*. Brantlinger pointed to the remarkable "uniformity . . . of extinction discourse," which pervaded the speech and writings of "humanitarians, missionaries, scientists, government officials, explorers, colonists, soldiers, journalists, novelists, and poets." Extinction discourse often celebrated the destruction of native peoples, as when the otherwise humane author Mark Twain wrote that the North American Indian was "nothing but a poor, filthy, naked scurvy vagabond, whom to exterminate were a charity to the Creator's worthier insects and reptiles."[7] Often, though, the discourse was more complex and ambivalent, including nostalgia and lament for vanishing peoples. English naturalist Alfred Russel Wallace, who shared credit with Charles Darwin for the theory of natural selection, wrote:

> The red Indian in North America and in Brazil; the Tasmanian, Australian, and New Zealander in the southern hemisphere, die out, not from any one special cause, but from the inevitable effects of an unequal mental and physical struggle. The intellectual and moral, as well as the physical qualities of the European are superior; the same powers and capacities which have made him rise in a few centuries from the condition of the wandering savage . . . to his present state of culture and advancement . . . enable him when in contact with the savage man, to conquer in the struggle for existence, and to increase at the expense of the less adapted varieties in the animal and vegetable kingdoms,—just as the weeds of Europe overrun North America and Australia, extinguishing native productions by the inherent vigor of their organization, and by their greater capacity for existence and multiplication.[8]

Several features of extinction discourse are apparent here, including the parallels drawn with natural biological selection, and the claims of racial superiority imputed to northern peoples. Yet it is interesting that Wallace depicted the European conquerors as analogous to "weeds . . . overrun[ning] North America and Australia," rather than as representatives of a noble race. Wallace was in fact an "anti-imperialist and anti-capitalist";[9] hence his critical edge. But like some contemporary observers (several of whom are cited in the section on "Denying genocide, celebrating genocide," below), Wallace found little difficulty in reconciling the extermination of native peoples with his progressive political views.

There is a close link between extinction discourse and the more virulent and systematically hateful ideologies that fueled the Nazi Holocaust in Europe (Box 6a). The Nazis, wrote Lindqvist, "have been made sole scapegoats for ideas of extermination that are actually a common European heritage."[10] We should also note the interaction of extinction discourse with ideologies of modernization and capitalist development, which created "surplus or redundant population[s]," in genocide scholar Richard Rubenstein's phrase. As Rubenstein explained in his *Age of Triage*, these ideologies produced destructive or genocidal outcomes in European societies as well, as with the colonial famines of the nineteenth century, or the Holocaust.[11] Ironically, this modernizing ideology also resulted in the migration—as convicts or refugees from want, political persecution, and famine—of millions of "surplus" Europeans to the New World. In Australia and the United States, among other locations, these settlers would become key, often semi-autonomous instruments of genocide against indigenous peoples. Brendan Lindsay described the dynamic of "California's Native American Genocide" in a way that echoes many others worldwide: "rather than a government orchestrating a population to bring about the genocide of a group, the population orchestrated a government to destroy a group."[12]

THE CONQUEST OF THE AMERICAS

The reader may ask himself if this is not cruelty and injustice of a kind so terrible that it beggars the imagination, and whether these poor people would not fare far better if they were entrusted to the devils in Hell than they do at the hands of the devils of the New World who masquerade as Christians.

Bartolomé de las Casas, Spanish friar, 1542

I have been looking far,
Sending my spirit north, south, east and west.
Trying to escape death,
But could find nothing,
No way of escape.

Song of the Luiseno Indians of California

The European holocaust of indigenous peoples in the Americas may have been the most extensive and destructive genocide ever. Ethnic studies scholar Ward Churchill has called it "unparalleled in human history, both in terms of its sheer magnitude and its duration."[13] Over nearly five centuries, and perhaps continuing to the present, wide-ranging genocidal measures have been imposed.[14] These include:

- genocidal massacres;
- biological warfare, using pathogens (especially smallpox and plague) to which the indigenous peoples had no resistance;
- spreading of disease via the "reduction" of Indians to densely crowded and unhygienic settlements;
- slavery and forced/indentured labor, especially though not exclusively in Latin America,[15] in conditions often rivaling those of Nazi concentration camps;
- mass population removals to barren "reservations," sometimes involving death marches *en route*, and generally leading to widespread mortality and population collapse upon arrival;
- deliberate starvation and famine, exacerbated by destruction and occupation of the native land base and food resources;
- forced education of indigenous children in white-run schools, where mortality rates sometimes reached genocidal levels.

Spanish America

The Spanish invasion, occupation, and exploitation of "Latin" America began in the late fifteenth century, and resulted, according to American studies scholar David Stannard, in "the worst series of human disease disasters, combined with the most extensive and most violent program of human eradication, that this world has ever seen."[16] The tone was set with the first territory conquered, the densely-populated Caribbean island of Hispaniola (today the Dominican Republic and Haiti). Tens of thousands of Indians were exterminated: the Spanish "forced their way into native settlements," wrote eyewitness Bartolomé de las Casas, "slaughter-ing everyone they found there, including small children, old men, [and] pregnant women."[17] Those men not killed at the outset were worked to death in gold mines; women survivors were consigned to harsh agricultural labor and sexual servitude. Massacred, sickened, and enslaved, Hispaniola's native population collapsed, "as would any nation subjected to such appalling treatment"[18]—declining from as many as eight million people at the time of the invasion to a scant *20,000* less than three decades later.[19] African slaves then replaced native workers, and toiled under similarly genocidal conditions.

Rumors of great civilizations, limitless wealth, and populations to convert to Christianity in the Aztec and Inca empires lured the Spanish on to Mexico and Central America. Soon thereafter, assaults were launched against the Inca empire in present-day Peru, Bolivia, and Ecuador. The Incas constituted the largest empire in the world, but with their leader Atahualpa captured and killed, the empire was decapitated, and quickly fell. "It is extremely difficult now to grasp the beliefs and motives of the Conquistadores [conquerors] as they cheated, tortured, burnt, maimed, murdered and massacred their way through South and Meso-America, causing such ferocious destruction that their compatriot Pedro de Cieza de León complained that 'wherever Christians have passed, conquering and discovering, it seems as though a fire has gone, consuming.'"[20] A holocaust it indeed proved for the Indians enslaved on plantations and in silver mines. Conditions in the mines—notably those in Mexico and at Potosí (see Figure 3.2) and Huancavelica in Upper

Figure 3.1 After invading Hispaniola, the Spanish enslaved the population and inflicted systematic atrocities, like the severing of limbs depicted here, upon natives who failed to deliver sufficient gold to the Spaniards. In two or three decades, the indigenous population of Hispaniola was exterminated. The carnage sparked outrage in Europe, resulting in some stylized but basically accurate contemporary representations, like this (sixteenth-century?) rendering.

Source: Wikimedia Commons.

Figure 3.2 The Cerro Rico overlooking Potosí, Bolivia. Following the discovery of silver in the mid-sixteenth century, this mountain largely paid for the profligacy and foreign wars of the Spanish Crown for some two hundred years. Millions of Indians and some African slaves were forced to work in horrific conditions, making the Cerro possibly the world's single biggest graveyard: anywhere from one million to eight million forced laborers perished in the mines, or from silicosis and other diseases soon after. By some estimates, the mines killed seven out of every ten who worked there. Time for a Potosí holocaust museum, perhaps?

Source: Author's photo, May 2005.

Peru (Bolivia)—resulted in death rates matching or exceeding those of Hispaniola. According to Stannard, Indians in the Bolivian mines had a life expectancy of three to four months, "about the same as that of someone working at slave labor in the synthetic rubber manufacturing plant at Auschwitz in the 1940s."[21] In his unfinished history of genocide, Raphael Lemkin noted that the compulsory-labor system, or *mita*, practiced in Inca society as a "humane . . . system of state-sponsored work," was transformed by the Spanish overlords into a system "*of the most brutal and genocidal slavery.*"[22]

Only in the mid-sixteenth century did the exterminatory impact of Spanish rule begin to wane. A *modus vivendi* was established between colonizers and colonized, featuring continued exploitation of surviving Indian populations, but also a degree of autonomy for native peoples. It survived until the mid-nineteenth century, when the now-independent governments of Spanish America sought to implement the economic prescriptions then popular in Europe. This resulted in another assault on "uneconomic" Indian landholdings, the further erosion of the Indian land base and impoverishment of its population, and the "opening up" of both land and labor resources to capitalist transformation. Meanwhile, in both South America and North America, expansionist governments launched "Indian wars" against native nations that were seen as impediments to economic development and progress. The campaigns against Araucana Indians in Chile and the Querandí in Argentina form part of national lore in these countries. Only relatively recently have South American scholars and others begun to examine such exterminations under the rubric of genocide.[23]

The United States and Canada

...It must be admitted that the actual treatment [the Indians] have received has been unjust and iniquitous beyond the power of words to express. Taught by the government that they had rights entitled to respect; when those rights have been assailed by the rapacity of the white man, the arm which should have been raised to protect them has been ever ready to sustain the aggressor.

> Report of the Peace Commission including Nathaniel Taylor
> (Commissioner for Indian Affairs) and General William
> Tecumseh Sherman, 1867

The first sustained contact between Europeans and the indigenous peoples of North America developed around the whaling industry that, in the sixteenth century, began to cross the Atlantic in search of new bounty. Whaling crews put ashore to process the catch, and were often welcomed by the coastal peoples. Similarly, when the Pilgrims arrived at Plymouth Rock, Massachusetts, in 1608, their survival through the first harsh winters was due solely to the generosity of Indians who fed them and trained them in regional agriculture. The settlers, though, responded to this amity with contempt for the "heathen" Indians. In addition, as more colonists flooded into the northeastern seaboard of the future United States, they brought diseases that wreaked havoc on Indian communities, leading to depopulation that paved the way for settler expansion into the devastated Indian heartlands.

■ BOX 3.1 "THE AMERICAN WEST AND THE NAZI EAST"

One of the most significant historiographical advances in analyses of the Nazi race-war against the peoples of Eastern Europe and the USSR (Chapter 6) is the recognition that, in central respects, it mirrored strategies of European colonialism during the previous centuries. The difference, it is often argued, was that the Nazis sought their settler-colonial *Lebensraum* ("living space") *in Europe*, specifically its "rimlands" and "borderlands" in the east and southeast. European countries had generally projected their expansionism outwards and overseas, in large part to preserve a peace among themselves. Hitler's challenge to the continental system was all-consuming, but it was not unprecedented in the German *Sonderweg* (historical path). We will explore the exterminatory policy adopted to the Herero and Nama peoples of Namibia, then German South-West Africa, below; the direct and indirect linkages to Nazi *Lebensraum* policies are well established.[24] Additional research has shown how the Nazi enterprise drew upon an almost unknown and unstudied German colonial experience, in precisely the same eastern European borderlands that the Nazis would seek to conquer in the 1940s. As V.G. Liulevicius and Mark Levene have memorably explored, Germany in the late stages of the First World War—with imperial Russia's armies and state structures collapsing—gained military and administrative control over *a territory that was initially even larger than that conquered and occupied by German forces in World War II*. The "Ober Ost" included almost all of present-day Belarus, and most centrally Ukraine. The fixing of Ukraine in the German imperial mind during this period, as the Reich's resource-base and breadbasket, is reflected also in Hitler's early postwar declarations and writings, including *Mein Kampf*. Even after the German defeat and armistice in the West, in November 1918, the Allies found it useful to continue German occupation in the rimlands, as long as it could serve as a bulwark against Bolshevik/Soviet expansion. Much of the defeated imperial force and administration was not repatriated until 1920. For Liulevicius, this early experience of eastern European "cleansing," "ordering," and *racializing* of territories and populations "had enormous consequences" for the Nazis' substantially similar enterprise.[25]

There is another fascinating aspect to the Nazi colonial vision: the way in which it both paralleled and drew specific inspiration from the American "conquest of the West." The expropriation, and often extermination, of indigenous populations in the western hemisphere prompted Hitler to declare: "Here in the East a similar process will repeat itself as in the conquest of America." "There is only one duty: to Germanize [the East] by the immigration of Germans, and to look upon the natives as Redskins," the derogatory term applied to Native Americans during the period of US continental invasion and expansion in the eighteenth and nineteenth centuries. In his provocatively-titled *The American West and the Nazi East*, Carroll Kakel cites numerous such examples, and uses them as a springboard to a rigorous and eye-opening comparison of the two imperial and settler-colonial systems.[26]

While acknowledging important differences of "scale, intensity, and duration"—most significantly, there is no US parallel for the Nazis' " 'conveyor belt' industrial killing of Jews"[27]—Kakel stressed that "far from being an inexplicable anomaly," "much Nazi genocidal violence and many of the events we have come to call the Holocaust were a radicalized blend of several forms of mass political violence whose patterns, logics, and pathologies can be located in the Early American project, a project which provides a unique window onto the colonial origins, context, and content of Nazi genocide . . ."[28] The "Early American and Nazi-German national

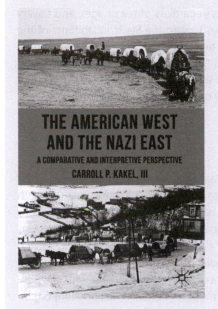

Figure 3.3 Cover of Carroll P. Kakel's *The American West and the Nazi East*.

Source: Courtesy of Palgrave Macmillan.

projects . . . can (and should) be read and understood as remarkably similar national projects of 'space' and 'race', with genocidal consequences for allegedly 'inferior' peoples in metropolitan and colonized 'living space', projects whose distinct (but linked) histories bear an unsettling and disturbing resemblance to each other."[29]

Kakel devotes considerable space to exploring the "imperialist and expansionist vision" of American "founding fathers" such as George Washington, Thomas Jefferson, and James Madison.[30] He shows that the American Revolution was driven more by frustration at British restrictions on American continental conquest than by ideals of liberty and equality for all. Jefferson even envisaged white American settlers coming, through "rapid multiplication," to "cover the whole northern, if not the southern continent," that is, the entire western hemisphere.[31] The indigenous populations that still dominated west of the Appalachians were depicted as "merciless Indian savages," to cite the language of the US Declaration of Independence, in much the way that Slavs and Jews would be demonized in the Nazi realm. The untold story of the Revolutionary War of 1776–1783, for Kakel, is the "brutal genocidal war without mercy on the 'frontier' fringes of the 13 rebellious colonies," targeting Indian populations whether allied with the British or not.[32] The "radicalization of racial 'othering' within Early American and Nazi-German popular and political cultures produced similarly strong notions of the inevitable 'disappearance' of targeted 'out-groups', thus making 'ordinary' citizens more likely to support (or at least be indifferent to) even more radical policies designed to 'hasten' the 'disappearance' of those identified as racial and ethnic 'enemies' of the nation-state."[33] In the US case, this meant "the subjugation and dispossession of 'the natives' by force, their segregation and removal from 'white' settlement zones, brutal attacks on warrior combatants and non-combatants (regardless of sex or age), and slavery for the Indian survivors."[34] The Nazis' policies toward the Slavic inhabitants of the German "East" were more concentrated in time and systematic in their execution, but fundamentally differed little from the US "Indian wars" that partly inspired and justified Nazi empire-building strategies. An agrarian cult of the conquering white "settler-farmer" underpinned the worldview of successive American leaders no less than their Nazi counterparts.

Kakel summarizes his findings as follows:

> In both the 'American West' and the 'Nazi East', genocide became intrinsically linked to the 'acquisition' of new 'living space' for agricultural settlement. In both cases, a comparable genocidal dynamic shared strikingly similar preconditions (political elite obsessions with territorial expansion, racial and ethnic prejudice, settler colonization, and agrarian idealism), causalities (settler-colonial policies and practices aimed at the 'elimination' of indigenes from the settler 'living space'), and triggers or immediate catalysts (settler-colonial wars for *Lebensraum* . . .). Both cases, moreover, featured similar colonial modalities of violence (including organized killing, a declared policy of 'depopulation' of the indigenes and 'repopulation' by settler colonists, 'slow death' by attrition, and forced assimilation of 'selected' indigene children by 'Americanization' or 'Germanization'). In both cases, genocide reflected common schema of motive (an identical perceived settler-state need for more 'living space' for agricultural settlement), intent (the intention to 'eliminate' the indigenes from the settler *Lebensraum*), genocidal agency ('ordinary Americans' and 'ordinary Germans' acting in a dual capacity of agents of empire and instruments of extreme political violence), and legitimation (justification of extreme political violence against largely unarmed civilian indigene populations as necessary measures of self-defence or pre-emption in the wars for settler 'living space'). In the 'American West' and the 'Nazi East', both state and non-state actors carried out exterminationist assaults, in the form of mobile killing operations, against the indigenous inhabitants of the newly acquired settler *Lebensraum*. And in both cases, 'concentration' centres—whether called 'reservations' or 'ghettos'—facilitated the removal of 'inferior', 'unwanted' populations away from the 'living space' of the 'superior', dominant societies (to await 'their fate').[35]

According to demographer Russell Thornton, disease was "without doubt . . . the single most important factor in American Indian population decline,"[36] which in five centuries reduced the Indian population of the present-day United States from between seven and ten million (though anthropologist Henry Dobyns has estimated as many as eighteen million) to *237,000* by the end of the nineteenth century.[37] Smallpox was the biggest killer: uncounted numbers of Indians died as did O–wapa–shaw, "the greatest man of the Sioux, with half his band . . . their bodies swollen, and covered with pustules, their eyes blinded, hideously howling their death song in utter despair."[38] At least one epidemic was deliberately spread, by British commander Lord Jeffery Amherst in 1763. Amherst ordered a commanding officer in 1763: "You will Do well to try to Inoculate the Indians [with smallpox] by means of Blanketts, as well as to try Every other method that can serve to extirpate this Execrable Race."[39] It is likely that other attempts were made to infect Indian populations with the pox, according to Norbert Finzsch, though their "success" is harder to determine.[40] Cholera, measles, plague, typhoid, and alcoholism also took an enormous toll. Other, often interlocking factors included "the often deliberate destructions of flora and fauna that American Indians used for food and other purposes,"[41] whether as a military strategy or simply as part of the exploitation of the continent's resources. An example of both was the extermination of the bison, which was hunted into near extinction. Perhaps sixty million buffalo roamed the Great Plains before contact. "... By 1895 there were fewer than *1,000* animals left," and the ecocidal campaign (see pp. 34–35) "had not only driven [the Indians] to starvation and defeat but had destroyed the core of their spiritual and ceremonial world."[42]

Genocidal massacres were also prominent.[43] According to Thornton, though direct slaughter was a subsidiary cause of demographic decline, it was decisive in the trajectories of some Indian nations "brought to extinction or the brink of extinction by . . . genocide in the name of war."[44] Perhaps the first such instance in North America was the Pequot War (1636–1637) in present-day Connecticut, when Puritan settlers reacted to an Indian raid by launching an extermination campaign.[45] This "created a precedent for later genocidal wars,"[46] including that targeting Apaches in the 1870s. "As there has been a great deal said about my killing women and children," the civilian scout leader King Woolsey wrote to military authorities, "I will state to you that we killed in this Scout 22 Bucks [males] 5 women & 3 children. We would have killed more women but [did not] owing to having attacked in the day time when the women were at work gathering Mescal. It sir is next to impossible to prevent killing squaws in jumping a rancheria [settlement] even were we disposed to save them. For my part I am frank to say that I fight on the broad platform of extermination."[47]

Perhaps most infamous was Colonel John Chivington's command to his volunteer soldiers, in November 1864 at Sand Creek, Colorado, to "kill and scalp all, little and big." Children could not be exempted, Chivington declared, because "Nits make lice."[48] The ensuing massacre prompted a government inquiry, at which Lieutenant James Connor testified:

> I did not see a body of man, woman or child but was scalped, and in many instances their bodies were mutilated in the most horrible manner—men, women and children's privates cut out, &c; I heard one man say that he cut out a woman's private parts and had them for exhibition on a stock . . . I also heard of numerous instances in which men had cut out the private parts of females and stretched them over their saddle-bows and wore them over their hats . . . [49]

Recalling this rampage, US President Theodore Roosevelt would call it "as righteous and beneficial a deed as ever took place on the frontier."[50]

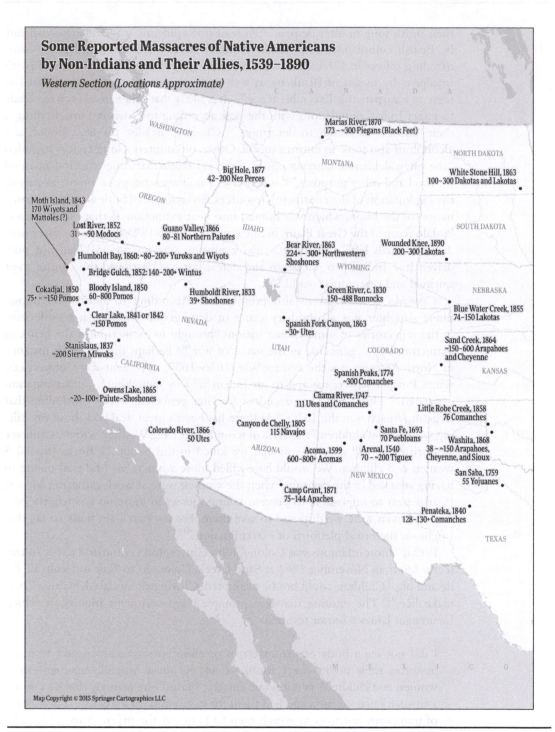

Some Reported Massacres of Native Americans by Non-Indians and Their Allies, 1539–1890

Western Section (Locations Approximate)

CANADA

WASHINGTON

Marias River, 1870
173 – ~300 Piegans (Black Feet)

MONTANA

NORTH DAKOTA

White Stone Hill, 1863
100–300 Dakotas and Lakotas

Big Hole, 1877
42–200 Nez Perces

OREGON

Moth Island, 1843
170 Wiyots and
Mattoles (?)

Lost River, 1852
31 – ~90 Modocs

Guano Valley, 1866
80–81 Northern Paiutes

IDAHO

SOUTH DAKOTA

Bear River, 1863
224+ – 300+ Northwestern
Shoshones

Wounded Knee, 1890
200–300 Lakotas

Humboldt Bay, 1860: ~80–200+ Yuroks and Wiyots

WYOMING

Bridge Gulch, 1852: 140–200+ Wintus

Cokadjal, 1850
75+ – ~150 Pomos

Bloody Island, 1850
60–800 Pomos

Humboldt River, 1833
39+ Shoshones

Green River, c. 1830
150–488 Bannocks

NEBRASKA

Blue Water Creek, 1855
74–150 Lakotas

Clear Lake, 1841 or 1842
~150 Pomos

NEVADA

Spanish Fork Canyon, 1863
~30+ Utes

Stanislaus, 1837
~200 Sierra Miwoks

CALIFORNIA

UTAH

COLORADO

Sand Creek, 1864
~150–600 Arapahoes
and Cheyenne

KANSAS

Spanish Peaks, 1774
~300 Comanches

Owens Lake, 1865
~20–100+ Paiute-Shoshones

Chama River, 1747
111 Utes and Comanches

Little Robe Creek, 1858
76 Comanches

Colorado River, 1866
50 Utes

Canyon de Chelly, 1805
115 Navajos

Santa Fe, 1693
70 Puebloans

ARIZONA

Acoma, 1599
600–800+ Acomas

Arenal, 1540
70 – ~200 Tiguex

Washita, 1868
38 – ~150 Arapahoes,
Cheyenne, and Sioux

NEW MEXICO

San Saba, 1759
55 Yojuanes

Camp Grant, 1871
75–144 Apaches

Penateka, 1840
128–130+ Comanches

TEXAS

MEXICO

Map Copyright © 2015 Springer Cartographics LLC

Map 3.1 Historian Benjamin Madley of the University of California—Los Angeles has published prizewinning investigations of systematic violence, including genocidal massacres, against Native Americans. This map, his latest (2015), shows the locations of colonial and postcolonial massacres at dozens of different sites across the present-day territory of the United States.

Source: Map provided by Benjamin Madley.

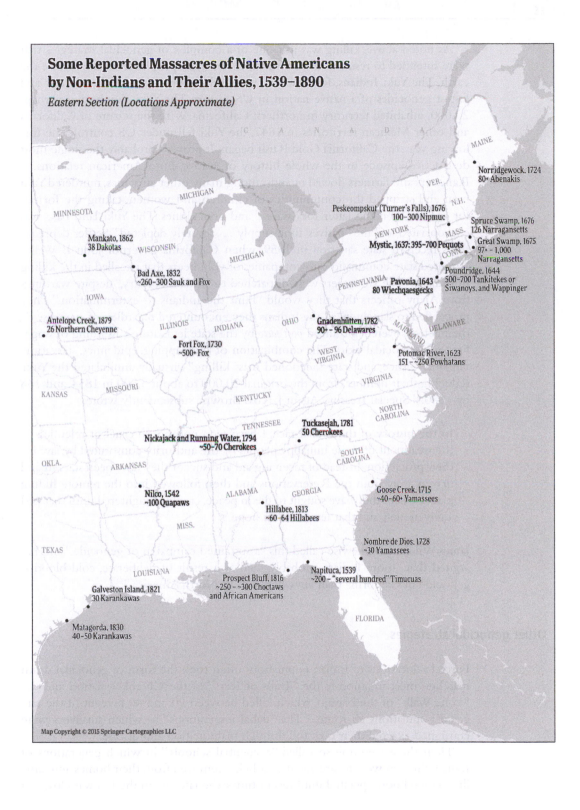

Some Reported Massacres of Native Americans by Non-Indians and Their Allies, 1539–1890

Eastern Section (Locations Approximate)

Norridgewock, 1724
80+ Abenakis

Peskeompskut (Turner's Falls), 1676
100–300 Nipmuc

Spruce Swamp, 1676
126 Narragansetts

Mankato, 1862
38 Dakotas

Mystic, 1637: 395–700 Pequots

Great Swamp, 1675
97+ – 1,000
Narragansetts

Poundridge, 1644
500–700 Tankitekes or
Siwanoys, and Wappinger

Pavonia, 1643
80 Wiechqaesgecks

Bad Axe, 1832
~260–300 Sauk and Fox

Antelope Creek, 1879
26 Northern Cheyenne

Gnadenhütten, 1782
90+ – 96 Delawares

Fort Fox, 1730
~500+ Fox

Potomac River, 1623
151 – ~250 Powhatans

Tuckasejah, 1781
50 Cherokees

Nickajack and Running Water, 1794
~50–70 Cherokees

Goose Creek, 1715
~40–60+ Yamassees

Nilco, 1542
~100 Quapaws

Hillabee, 1813
~60–64 Hillabees

Nombre de Dios, 1728
~30 Yamassees

Napituca, 1539
~200 – "several hundred" Timucuas

Prospect Bluff, 1816
~250 – ~300 Choctaws
and African Americans

Galveston Island, 1821
30 Karankawas

Matagorda, 1830
40–50 Karankawas

As noted above, killing was just one of a complex of genocidal strategies that were intended to result in the elimination of Indian peoples from the face of the earth. The Yuki Indians, for example, were subjected to one of the clearest and fastest genocides of a native nation in US history. The Yuki, numbering perhaps 20,000, inhabited territory in northern California. With the seizure of California and other Mexican territories in 1847, the Yuki fell under US control. The following year, the California Gold Rush began. It proved "probably the single most destructive episode in the whole history of Native/Euro-American relations."[51] Ranchers and farmers flowed in and, among many other atrocities, murdered Yuki men and stripped the communities of children and women, taking the former for servants and the latter for "wives" and concubines. The Yuki land base was expropriated and the "natives' food supply ... severely depleted." Settler depredations received state sanction in 1859, when California governor John B. Weller "granted state commissions to companies of volunteers that excelled in the killing of Indians." The volunteers were dispatched to "Indian country," despite warnings from Army officers that they would "hunt the Indians to extermination." They proceeded to slaughter "all the Indians they encountered regardless of age or sex"; their actions were legitimized *post facto* by the state legislature's awarding of wages for their genocidal work. The combination of "kidnapping, epidemics, starvation, vigilante justice, and state-sanctioned mass killing" virtually annihilated the Yuki, reducing their numbers from the original 20,000 to about 3,500 in 1854, and *168* by 1880.[52] Special Treasury Agent J. Ross Browne subsequently wrote:

> In the history of the Indian race, I have seen nothing so cruel or relentless as the treatment of those unhappy people by the authority constituted by law for their protection. Instead of receiving aid and succor they have been starved and driven away from the Reservations and then followed into the remote hiding places where they have sought to die in peace, cruelly slaughtered until that [sic] a few are left and that few without hope.[53]

James Wilson has likewise called this "a sustained campaign of genocide," and has argued that "more Indians probably died as a result of deliberate, cold-blooded genocide in California than anywhere else in North America."[54]

Other genocidal strategies

Forced relocations of Indian populations often took the form of genocidal death marches, most infamously the "Trails of Tears" of the Cherokee nation and the "Long Walk" of the Navajo, which killed between 20 and 40 percent of the targeted populations en route.[55] The "tribal reservations" to which survivors were consigned exacted their own toll through malnutrition and disease.

Then there were the so-called "residential schools," in which generations of Indian children were incarcerated after being removed from their homes and families. The schools operated until recent times; the last one in the US was closed in

Figure 3.4 US soldiers load the corpses of Indian victims of the Wounded Knee massacre for burial in mass graves, December 1890.

Source: Smithsonian Institution National Archives.

1972. In an account of the residential-school experience, titled "Genocide by Any Other Name," Ward Churchill describes the program as

> the linchpin of assimilationist aspirations . . . in which it was ideally intended that every single aboriginal child would be removed from his or her home, family, community, and culture at the earliest possible age and held for years in state-sponsored "educational" facilities, systematically deculturated, and simultaneously indoctrinated to see her/his own heritage—and him/herself as well—in terms deemed appropriate by a society that despised both to the point of seeking as a matter of policy their utter eradication.[56]

As Churchill has pointed out, the injunction in the UN Genocide Convention against "forcibly transferring children of the [targeted] group to another group" qualifies this policy as genocidal—and in Australia, where a similar policy was implemented, a government commission found that it met the Convention's definition of genocide (see further below). In addition, there was much that was genocidal in the operation of the North American residential schools apart from the "forcible transfer" of the captive native children. Crucially, "mortality rates in the schools were appalling from the outset," resulting in death rates—from starvation, disease, systematic torture, sexual predation,[57] and shattering psychological dislocation—*that matched or exceeded the death rates in Nazi concentration camps.* In Canada, for example, the 1907 "Bryce Report," submitted by the Indian Department's chief medical officer,

> revealed that of the 1,537 children who had attended the sample group of facilities since they'd opened—a period of ten years, on average—42 per cent had died of "consumption or tuberculosis," either at the schools or shortly after being discharged. Extrapolating, Bryce's data indicated that of the 3,755 native children then under the "care" of Canada's residential schools, 1,614 could be expected to have died a miserable death by the end of 1910. In a follow-up survey conducted in 1909, Bryce collected additional information, all of it corroborating his initial report. At the Qu'Appelle School, the principal, a Father Hugonard, informed Bryce that his facility's record was "something to be proud of" since "only" 153 of the 795 youngsters who'd attended it between 1884 and 1905 had died in school or within two years of leaving it.[58]

The experience of the residential schools reverberated through generations of native life in Canada and the US. Alcoholism and substance abuse are now increasingly understood to reflect the "worlds of pain" inflicted by residential schooling, and the traumas that Indians in turn inflicted on their own children. Churchill wrote of a "Residential School Syndrome" (RSS) studied in Canada, which

> includes acutely conflicted self-concept and lowered self-esteem, emotional numbing (often described as "inability to trust or form lasting bonds"), somatic

disorder, chronic depression and anxiety (often phobic), insomnia and night-mares, dislocation, paranoia, sexual dysfunction, heightened irritability and tendency to fly into rages, strong tendencies towards alcoholism and drug addiction, and suicidal behavior.[59]

AUSTRALIA'S ABORIGINES AND THE NAMIBIAN HEREROS

The cases of the aboriginal populations of British-colonized Australia and German-colonized Namibia further illuminate the fate of indigenous peoples worldwide. In both instances, decades of denial gave way, at the twentieth century's close, to a greater readiness to acknowledge the genocidal character of some colonial actions.

Genocide in Australia

In 1788, the "First Fleet" of British convicts was dumped on Australian soil. Over the ensuing century-and-a-half, the aboriginal population—estimated at about 750,000 when the colonists arrived—was reduced to just 31,000 by 1911. As in North America, the colonists did not arrive in Australia with the explicit intention of exterminating the Aborigines. The destruction inflicted on Australian Aborigines instead reflected a concatenation of ideologies, pressures, and circumstances. Arriving whites were aghast at the state of the Aborigines, and quickly determined that they were (1) barely, if at all, human,[60] and (2) largely useless. Aboriginal lands, however, were coveted, particularly as convicts began to be freed (but not allowed to return to England) and as new waves of free settlers arrived. As the Australian colonial economy came to center on vast landholdings for sheep-raising and cattle-grazing, expansion into the interior brought colonists into ever-wider and more conflictive contact with the Aborigines. Through measures including direct massacre—"at least 20,000 aborigines, perhaps many more, were killed by the settlers in sporadic frontier skirmishes throughout the nineteenth century and lasting into the late 1920s"[61]—Aborigines were driven away from areas of white colonization and from their own sources of sustenance. When they responded with raids on the settlers' cattle stocks, colonists "retaliated" by "surround[ing] an aborigine camp at night, attack[ing] at dawn, and massacr[ing] men, women, and children alike."[62]

Formal colonial policy did not generally favor genocidal measures. Indeed, the original instructions to colonial Governor Arthur Phillip were that he "endeavour by every means in his power to open an intercourse with the natives and to con-ciliate their goodwill, requiring all persons under his Government to live in amity and kindness with them." But these "benign utterances of far-away governments" contrasted markedly with "the hard clashes of interest on the spot."[63] Colonial officials often turned a blind eye to atrocities against the Aborigines, and failed to intervene effectively to suppress them. The most murderous extremes were reached in Queensland, where a state militia—effectively a death squad—was "given carte blanche to go out and pursue 'niggers' far into the bush and indiscriminately shoot them down—often quite regardless of whether a particular tribal group had been responsible for an alleged wrongdoing or not—with the rape of cornered women inevitably being one unofficially sanctioned perk of these operations."[64] Historian Henry Reynolds estimated between 8,000 and 10,000 Aborigines murdered in Queensland from 1824 to 1908.[65]

Legal discrimination, and the imposition of broader "social death" measures, buttressed these frequent genocidal massacres. Until the late nineteenth century, no Aborigine was allowed to give testimony in a white man's court, rendering effective legal redress for dispossession and atrocity a practical impossibility. Moreover, extinction discourse took full flight, with the British novelist Anthony Trollope, for example, writing in the 1870s that the Aborigines' "doom is to be exterminated; and the sooner that their doom is accomplished,—so that there can be no cruelty [!],—the better will it be for civilization."[66]

The combination of clashes between colonists and natives, disease, and extermination campaigns was strikingly similar to the North American experience. The destruction of the aboriginal population of the island of Tasmania is often cited as a paradigmatic colonial genocide. The 3,000–15,000 native inhabitants were broken down by the usual traumas of contact, and survivors were dispatched (in a supposedly humanitarian gesture) to barren Flinders Island.[67] There "they died, if not directly from observable neglect, bad conditions and European illness, then from alcohol-assisted anomie, homesickness and the pointlessness of it all. Tellingly, there were few and ultimately no births on the island to make up for deaths."[68]

The destruction was so extensive that many observers contended that the island's aboriginals had been completely annihilated. This appears to have been true for full-blooded aboriginals, one of the last of whom, a woman named Truganini (Figure 3.5), died in 1876. It ignored, however, aboriginals of mixed blood, thousands of whom live on today.[69]

Figure 3.5 Truganini (also known as Trugernanner) (1812–1876) was often described as the last of the full-blooded aboriginal population of Tasmania, though in fact several may have outlived her. "Before she was eighteen, her mother had been killed by whalers, her first fiancé died while saving her from abduction, and in 1828, her two sisters, Lowhenunhue and Maggerleede, were abducted and taken to Kangaroo Island, off South Australia and sold as slaves." ("Trugernanner," http://en.wikipedia.org/wiki/Trugernanner.) Truganini was one of the approximately two hundred Aborigines removed to Flinders Island off the Tasmanian coast, where most died from disease between 1833 and 1847. After her death in 1876, Truganini's skeleton was displayed by the Royal Society of Tasmania. Only in 1976 were her remains removed and cremated; fragments of her skin and hair housed in the Royal College of Surgeons, UK, were returned for burial in Tasmania in 2002. The date of the photo is uncertain.

Source: Anton Brothers/Wikimedia Commons.

Figure 3.6 Children at a school in Perth, Australia, join forces to spell out "Sorry," shortly before the country's prime minister issued a formal apology to the "Stolen Generations" of aboriginal children. A national "Sorry Day," expressing remorse for Australia's treatment of its indigenous population, has become a national institution since it was first launched in 1998.[70]

Source: Courtesy Mark Binns/Flickr, February 2008.

As was true for indigenous peoples elsewhere, the twentieth century witnessed not only a demographic revival of the Australian Aborigines but—in the latter half of the century—the emergence of a powerful movement for land rights and restitution. Subsequently, this movement's members worked to publicize the trauma caused by the kidnapping of aboriginal children and their placement in white-run institutional "homes." These were strikingly similar, in their underlying (assimilationist) ideology, rampant brutality, and sexual predation, to the "residential schools" imposed upon North American Indians. In response to growing protest about these "stolen generations" of aboriginal children (the title of a landmark 1982 book by Peter Read),[71] a national commission of inquiry was struck in 1995. Two years later it issued *Bringing Them Home*, which stated that Australia's policy of transferring aboriginal children constituted genocide according to the UN Convention definition. This claim provoked still-unresolved controversy (and the report's co-author later abjured the term).[72] The Australian Prime Minister at the time, John Howard, denounced the "black armband" view of his country's history (that is, a focus on negative elements of the Australian and aboriginal experience). However, although many voices were raised in public fora and Australian media generally supported Howard's rejectionist stance, the report ensured that "the dreaded 'g' word is firmly with us," as Colin Tatz wrote. "Genocide is now in the vocabulary of Australian politics, albeit grudgingly, or even hostilely."[73]

In February 2008, incoming Labour prime minister Kevin Rudd declared as his government's first act of parliament: "We apologise for the laws and policies of successive parliaments and governments that have inflicted profound grief, suffering and loss on these our fellow Australians. . . . For the pain, suffering and hurt of these stolen generations, their descendants and for their families left behind, we say sorry."[74]

The Herero genocide

It is now widely acknowledged that the first genocide of the twentieth century was committed by German colonial forces in their near-extermination of the

Herero nation in present-day Namibia, which took place during the century's first decade.[75] The pattern of colonial invasion and occupation that provoked the Herero uprising was a familiar one. Drawn by the opportunities for cattle ranching, some 5,000 Germans had flooded into the territory by 1903. Colonists' deception, suasion, and violent coercion pushed the Hereros into an ever-narrower portion of their traditional landholdings. In 1904, the Hereros rose up against the Germans. Declaring, "Let us die fighting rather than die as a result of maltreatment, imprisonment, or some other calamity,"[76] Herero paramount chief Samuel Maharero led his fighters against military outposts and colonists, killing about 120 Germans. This infuriated the German leader Kaiser Wilhelm II, who responded by dispatching the hardline Lt.-Gen. Lothar von Trotha. Von Trotha arrived with a reputation for brutality that was already well-established. He reviled the Hereros as *Untermenschen* (subhumans), the same term the Nazis would deploy to designate racial enemies for extermination.[77] Africans were "all alike," Von Trotha proclaimed. "They only respond to force. It was and is my policy to use force with terrorism and even brutality. I shall annihilate the revolting [rebellious] tribes with rivers of blood and rivers of gold. Only after a complete uprooting will something emerge."[78]

After five months of sporadic conflict, about 1,600 German soldiers armed with machine guns and cannons decisively defeated the Hereros at the Battle of Waterberg.[79] After vanquishing the Hereros, the German Army launched a "mass orgy of killing":

> Not only were there repeated machine gunnings and cannonades, but Herero men were slowly strangled by fencing wire and then hung up in rows like crows, while young women and girls were regularly raped before being bayoneted to death. The old, the sick, the wounded were all slaughtered or burnt to death. Nor were children spared, one account describing how men, women and children were corralled into a high thorn and log enclosure before being "doused with lamp oil and burnt to a cinder."[80]

Survivors fled into the Omahake desert. Von Trotha then issued his notorious "annihilation order" *(Vernichtungsbefehl)*. In it, he pledged that "within the German borders every Herero, with or without a gun, with or without cattle, will be shot. I will no longer accept women and children [as prisoners], I will drive them back to their people or I will let them be shot at."[81] The order remained in place for several months, until a domestic outcry led the German Chancellor to rescind it. A contemporary account described Hereros emerging from the desert "starved to skeletons with hollow eyes, powerless and hopeless."[82] The German Official History of the Battle of Waterburg was triumphalist in its genocidal zeal:

> The hasty exit of the Herero to the southeast, into the waterless Omaheke, would seal his fate; the environment of his own country was to bring about his extermination in a way that no Germany weapon, even in a most bloody or deadly battle, ever could . . . [their] death rattle and furious cry of insanity echoed in the exalted silence of eternity.[83]

In October 1904, another tribal nation, the Namas (sometimes called the Namaquas), also rose up in revolt against German rule and was crushed, with approximately half the population killed. Many scholars thus refer to the genocide of the Hereros and Namas. Survivors of the slaughters and the desert wastes were then moved to concentration camps, most notoriously Shark Island (today a camping site), where conditions often rivaled Nazi slave-labor camps (Chapter 6). Historian Benjamin Madley cited "official German figures [that] of 15,000 Hereros and 2,200 Namas incarcerated in camps, some 7,700 or 45 percent perished."[84] Olusoga and Erichsen wrote that the Nama on Shark Island "were not simply left to die . . . They were systematically worked to death." While the indigenous population was also exploited as slave laborers,

> the equanimity with which this resource was squandered strongly suggests that forced labour was a secondary function of the Shark Island camp. The camp's main focus from September 1906 onwards was the extermination of Nama prisoners. Nama deaths were the "product" of the Shark Island camps; forced labour was merely one of the means by which those deaths were brought about. Shark Island was a death camp, perhaps the world's first.[85]

Conditions were equally wanton in their murderousness for the Hereros incarcerated at the Swakopmund camp. A German missionary, Heinrich Vedder, described Hereros "placed behind a double row of barbed wire . . . and housed in pathetic structures constructed out of simple sacking and planks . . ." They worked from morning to night "under the clubs of the raw overseers until they broke down." Starvation further ground down bodies "already weakened . . . from the cold and restless exertion of all their powers in the prison conditions in Swakopmund." Hundreds of them "were driven to death" like "cattle."[86]

A comparative and global-historical approach to genocide allows us to perceive important connections between campaigns of mass killing and group destruction that are widely separated in time and space. Scholarship on the genocide against the Hereros provides an excellent example. It is increasingly acknowledged that it paved the way, in important respects, for the prototypical mass slaughter of that century—Nazi mass murder (Chapter 6 and Box 6a). As summarized by Olusogo and Ericksen,

> So much of what took place in German South-West Africa at the beginning of the twentieth century horribly prefigures the events of the 1940s: concentration camps, the bureaucratization of killing, meticulous record-keeping of death tolls and death rates, the use of work as a means of extermination, civilians transported in cattle trucks then worked to death, their remains experimented upon by race scientists, and the identification of ethnic groups who had a future as slaves and those who had no future of any sort. All were features of the German South-West African genocides that were replicated in different forms and on a much vaster scale in Europe in the 1940s.[87]

Figure 3.7 Famished Hereros after emerging from the Omahake desert in Namibia, c. 1907.
Source: Ullstein Bilderdienst, Berlin/Wikimedia Commons.

Following the independence of Namibia in 1990 (from South Africa, which had conquered the territory during the First World War), survivors' descendants called on Germany to apologize for the Herero genocide, and provide reparations. In August 2004—the centenary of the Herero uprising—the German development-aid minister, Heidemarie Wieczorek-Zeul, attended a ceremony at Okakarara in the region of Otjozondjupa, where the conflict had formally ended in 1906. The minister eloquently stated that:

> A century ago, the oppressors—blinded by colonialist fervour—became agents of violence, discrimination, racism and annihilation in Germany's name. The atrocities committed at that time would today be termed genocide—and nowadays a General von Trotha would be prosecuted and convicted. We Germans accept our historical and moral responsibility and the guilt incurred by Germans at that time. And so, in the words of the Lord's Prayer that we share, I ask you to forgive us.[88]

Of Wieczorek-Zeul's declaration, Jurgen Zimmerer wrote: "To my knowledge it is the first and only apology by a high-ranking member of the government of a former colonial power referring to genocide for colonial crimes."[89] Moves were afoot early in 2010 to offer millions of euros in reparations in the form of German development aid aimed at traditionally Herero regions of Namibia.

DENYING GENOCIDE, CELEBRATING GENOCIDE

> I celebrated Thanksgiving in an old-fashioned way. I invited everyone in my neigh-
> borhood to my house, we had an enormous feast, and then I killed them and took
> their land.
>
> Jon Stewart, US comedian

Denial is regularly condemned as the final stage of genocide (see Chapter 14). How, then, are we to class the mocking or *celebrating* of genocide? These are sadly not uncommon responses, and they are nowhere more prominent than with regard to genocides of indigenous peoples.

Among most sectors of informed opinion in the Americas—from Alaska to Tierra del Fuego—the notion that indigenous peoples experienced genocide at the hands of their white conquerors is dismissed and derided.[90] In a September 2001 post to the H-Genocide academic mailing list, Professor Alexander Bielakowski of the University of Findlay engaged in what seemed outright genocidal denial, writing that "if [it] was the plan" to "wipe out the American Indians ... the US did a damn poor job following through with it."[91] This is a curious way to describe the annihilation of up to 98 percent of the indigenous population of the United States over three centuries. The fine British historian Michael Burleigh took a similarly flippant jab in his book *Ethics and Extermination*, scoffing at notions of "the 'disappearance' of the [Australian] Aboriginals or Native Americans, some of whose descendants mysteriously seem to be running multi-million dollar casinos."[92] How can a tiny Indian elite be considered representative of the poorest, shortest-lived ethnic minority in the US and Canada?

Celebrations of indigenous genocide also have no clear parallel in mainstream discourse. Thus one finds prominent essayist Christopher Hitchens describing protests over the Columbus quincentenary (1992) as "an ignorant celebration of stasis and backwardness, with an unpleasant tinge of self-hatred." For Hitchens, the destruction of Native American civilization was simply "the way that history is made, and to complain about it is as empty as complaint about climatic, geological or tectonic shift." He justified the conquest on classic utilitarian grounds:

> It is sometimes unambiguously the case that a certain coincidence of ideas, technologies, population movements and politico-military victories leaves humanity on a slightly higher plane than it knew before. The transformation of part of the northern part of this continent into "America" inaugurated a nearly boundless epoch of opportunity and innovation, and thus *deserves to be celebrated with great vim and gusto*, with or without the participation of those who wish they had never been born.[93]

The arrogance and contempt in these comments are echoed in the pervasive appropriation of Indian culture and nomenclature by North American white culture. Note, for example, the practice of adopting ersatz Indian names and motifs for professional sports teams. James Wilson has argued that calling a Washington, DC football franchise the "Redskins" is "roughly the equivalent of calling a team 'the Buck Niggers' or 'the Jewboys.'"[94] Other acts of appropriation include naming gas-guzzling vehicles (the Winnebago, the Jeep Cherokee) after Indian nations, so that peoples famous for their respectful custodianship of the environment are instead associated with technologies that damage it. This is carried to extremes with the grafting of Indian names onto weaponry, as with the Apache attack helicopter and the Tomahawk cruise missile. In Madley's opinion, such nomenclature "casts Indians as threatening and dangerous," subtly providing "a post-facto justification for the violence committed against them."[95]

COMPLEXITIES AND CAVEATS

Several of the complicating factors in evaluating the genocide of indigenous peoples have been noted. Prime among them is the question of intent.

Genocidal intent (see pp. 49–51) is easy enough to adduce in the consistent tendency toward massacre and physical extermination, evident from the earliest days of European conquest of the Americas, Africa, Australasia, and other parts of the world. Yet in most or perhaps all cases, this accounted for a minority of deaths among the colonized peoples.

The forced-labor institutions of Spanish America also demonstrated a high degree of specific intent. When slaves are dying in large numbers, after only a few months in the mines or on the plantations, and your response is not to improve conditions but to feed more human lives into the inferno, this is direct, "first-degree" genocide (in Ward Churchill's conceptualizing; see note 152, p. 80). The mechanisms of death were not appreciably different from those of many Nazi slave-labor camps.

Disease was the greatest killer. Here, specific intent arguably prevailed only in the direct acts of biological warfare against Indian nations. More significant was a general genocidal intent, with disease tolls greatly exacerbated by malnutrition, overwork, and outright enslavement.[96] In some cases, though, entire Indian nations were virtually wiped out by pathogens before they had ever set eyes on a European. In addition, many of the connections between lack of hygiene, overcrowding, and the spread of disease were poorly understood for much of the period of the attack on indigenous peoples. Concepts of second- and third-degree genocide might apply here, if one supports Churchill's framing.

Further complexity arises in the agents of the killing. Genocide studies emphasizes the role of the state as the central agent of genocide, and one does find a great deal of state-planned, state-sponsored, and state-directed killing of indigenous peoples. In many and perhaps most cases, however, the direct perpetrators of genocide were colonial *settlers* rather than authorities. Indeed, colonists often protested the alleged lack of state support and assistance in confronting "savages." To the extent that policies were proposed to halt the destruction of native peoples, it was often those in authority who proposed them, though effective measures were rarely implemented. Measures were taken, as at Flinders Island, to "protect" and "preserve" aboriginal groups, but these often *contributed* to the genocidal process. As Colin Tatz has pointed out, "nowhere does the [Genocide] Convention implicitly or explicitly rule out intent with *bona fides*, good faith, 'for their own good' or 'in their best interests.'"[97]

Helpful here might be historian Patrick Wolfe's notion of a "logic of elimination,"[98] and Tony Barta's influential concept of the "genocidal *society*—as distinct

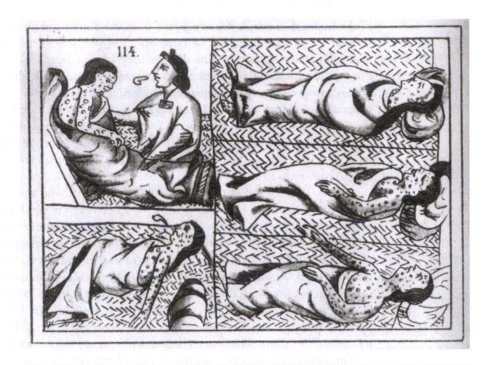

Figure 3.8 Nahua victims of a sixteenth-century smallpox epidemic in Mexico, with the distinctive vomiting and spotted appearance of the infected.

Source: Nahua artist in the *Florentine Codex* compiled by Fray Bernardino de Sahagun in the sixteenth century/Wikimedia Commons.

from a genocidal state." This is defined as a society "in which the whole bureau-cratic apparatus might officially be directed to protect innocent people but in which a whole race is nevertheless subject to remorseless pressures of destruction inherent in the very nature of the society."[99] The nature of settler colonialism, in other words, made conflict with native peoples, and their eventual large-scale destruction, almost inevitable. As Mark Levene has phrased it, while benevolent intentions sometimes existed, "the problem was that these good intentions were at odds with the very colonial project itself." Whenever push came to shove, "the 'Anglo' state always ultimately sided with the interests of capital, property and development, whatever the murderous ramifications."[100] State authorities, though they might occasionally have decried acts of violence against natives, were above all concerned with ensuring that the colonial or post-colonial endeavor succeeded. As one British House of Commons committee reported in the 1830s, "Whatever may have been the injustice of this encroachment [on indigenous lands], there is no reason to suppose that either justice or humanity would now be consulted by receding from it."[101] If the near-annihilation of the indigenous population none-theless resulted, this was sometimes lamented (perhaps with romantic and nostalgic overtones, as described in Brantlinger's *Dark Vanishings*), but it was never remotely sufficient to warrant the cancellation or serious revision of the enterprise.[102]

A few other ambiguous features of genocides against indigenous peoples may be cited. First, the prevailing elite view of history has tended to underestimate the role of the millions of people who migrated from the colonial metropole to the "New World." These settlers and/or administrators were critical to the unfolding of the genocides, not only through the diseases they carried, but (notably in Australasia) through the massacres they authorized and implemented.[103] It should not be forgotten, however, that many of them were fleeing religious persecution or desperate material want. Think of the millions of Irish who abandoned their homeland during the Great Hunger of 1846–1848, or the English convicts shipped off for minor crimes to penal colonies in the Antipodes. Settlers and administrators often suffered dreadful mortality rates. As with the indigenous population, death usually resulted from exposure to pathogens to which they had no resistance. To cite an extreme example, "it is said that 6,040 died out of the total of 7,289 immigrants who had come to Virginia by February, 1625, or around 83 percent."[104] Elsewhere, "tropical maladies turn[ed] assignments to military stations, missions, or government posts into death watches."[105]

Finally, we should be careful not to romanticize indigenous peoples and their pre-contact societies. To limit the discussion to the Americas: it was broadly true that genocide, and war unto genocide, featured only rarely. War among North American Indian communities (excluding present-day Mexico) was generally "farre lesse bloudy and devouring than the cruell Warres of Europe," as one European observer put it.[106] But there were notable exceptions. According to genocide scholars Daniel Chirot and Clark McCauley, "Before widespread contact with the Europeans, warfare among the stateless societies of [the North American northwest], ranging from Puget Sound through the coasts of British Columbia and into the Alaskan panhandle, was frequent and bloody, with exterminations of whole tribes, except for those taken as slaves, not uncommon."[107] Aboriginal slavery institutions could also be genocidal; of the Indians of the same northwest coastal region, sociologist Orlando Patterson has written that "*nothing in the annals of slavery*" can match them "for the number of excuses a master had for killing his slaves and the sheer sadism with which he destroyed them."[108] Post-contact warfare also assumed a virulent form, as with the Iroquois territorial expansion of the sixteenth and seventeenth centuries, which anthropologist Jeffrey Blick has studied as a case of genocide.[109]

Mass violence seems to have been more pervasive among the native populations of Central America and Mexico, at least during certain periods. In the classic era of Mayan civilization (600–900 CE), war seems to have been waged with frequency and sometimes incessantly; many scholars now link endemic conflict to the collapse of the great Mayan cities, and the classical civilization along with it. The Aztecs of Mexico, meanwhile, warred to capture prisoners for religious sacrifice, sometimes thousands at a time, at their great temple in Tenochtitlan. The Aztecs so ravaged and alienated surrounding nations that these subjects enthusiastically joined with invading Spanish forces to destroy them.

Collaboration with the colonizing force, often arising from and exacerbating the tensions of indigenous international relations, was quite common throughout the hemisphere.[110] Soon Indians, too, became participants in genocidal wars against other Indian nations—and sometimes against members of the colonizing society as well. In Mexico, for example, the myth of a few hundred *conquistadores* overthrowing the Aztec Empire has been decisively debunked. It was their tens of thousands of Indian allies, rebelling against the Aztec imperial yoke, who provided the critical military forces and know-how. "The conquest was a war of Indians against Indians," argued historian Andrea Martínez. "The Spaniards were far too small a force to do it by themselves."[111]

Reference has also been made (Chapter 1) to *subaltern genocide* (see pp. 64–66), in which oppressed peoples adopt genocidal strategies against their oppressors. Latin America offers several examples, studied in detail by historian Nicholas Robins in *Native Insurgencies and the Genocidal Impulse in the Americas*.[112] The millenarian "Great Rebellion" in Upper Peru (Bolivia) in the 1780s explicitly aimed to slaughter or expel all white people from the former Inca realm. In Mexico's Yucatán peninsula in the mid-nineteenth century, Mayan Indians rose to extirpate the territory's whites or drive them into the sea.[113] In both cases, the genocidal project advanced some distance before the whites launched a successful (and genocidal) counter-attack. I believe we can sympathize with the enormous and often mortal pressure placed upon indigenous peoples, while still recognizing that a genocidal counter-strategy sometimes resulted.

INDIGENOUS REVIVAL

As the Guatemala case study (Box 3a) demonstrates, assaults on indigenous peoples—including genocide—are by no means confined to distant epochs. According to Ken Coates, "the era from the start of World War II through to the 1960s . . . [was] an era of unprecedented aggression in the occupation of indigenous lands and, backed by the equally unprecedented wealth and power of the industrial world, the systematic dislocation of thousands of indigenous peoples around the world."[114] In many regions, invasions and occupations by colonists and corporations, seeking to exploit indigenous lands and resources, continues. And in the "developed world"—Canada, the US, Australasia—the situation of indigenous peoples "is as deplorable as in the very poorest [parts] of the third world."[115]

Figure 3.9 As a symbol of the need to redress past injustices, US indigenous people have focused advocacy efforts around Columbus Day, a national holiday created in the 1930s to cater to Italian-American political constituencies. Their push to replace the homage to Columbus—responsible for slavery and mass murder in Hispaniola (see p. 151)—with "Indigenous People's Day" has gained considerable traction. In 1992, the quincentenary of Columbus's invasion of the Americas, the city council of Berkeley, California declared the first Indigenous People's Day. In 2014, Seattle and Minneapolis likewise voted "to shift the holiday's focus . . . to the people [Columbus] encountered in the New World and their modern-day descendants." The Minneapolis council stated that the new designation would encourage reflection "upon the ongoing struggles of indigenous people on this land" and celebration of "the thriving culture and value that Dakota, Ojibwa and other indigenous nations add to our city."[117]

Source: Courtesy of American Indian Movement Colorado.

Figure 3.10 For half a century, Cree-Canadian singer Buffy Sainte-Marie has been perhaps the most prominent Native North American artist, and a vigorous advocate for indigenous cultures and causes. Her early song, "My Country 'Tis of Thy People You're Dying" (1966), is both one of the most poetic evocations of Native peoples' experiences in North America, and possibly the first popular song to deploy the word "genocide." Sainte-Marie's album, *Power in the Blood*, won Canadian Album of the Year at the 2015 Polaris Music Prize awards. She is pictured at a June 2015 concert to commemorate the work of the Canadian Truth and Reconciliation Commission (TRC) (see Box 15.3, pp. 726–730).

Source: Photo by Dr. Peter Stockdale/Wikimedia Commons.

Measured in life expectancy, malnutrition, vulnerability to infectious disease, and many other basic indices, indigenous peoples in most of the countries they inhabit are the most marginalized and deprived of all.[116]

No less than in past periods, however, invasion, deprivation, and attempted domination have fueled indigenous resistance. In recent decades, this has taken the form of a *global* indigenous mobilization. The "indigenous revival" is powerfully linked to decolonization. It also reflects the development of human-rights philosophies and legislation—particularly in the period following the Second World War, when numerous rights instruments were developed (including the UN Genocide Convention). Decolonization brought to fruition the pledges of self-determination that had featured in the charter of the League of Nations, but had withered in the face of opposition from colonial powers. But this was liberation from domination only by external colonial forces. As Niezen has pointed out, the horrors of the Nazi era in Europe "contributed to a greater receptiveness at the international level to measures for the protection of minorities," given the increasing recognition "that states could not always be relied upon to protect their own citizens, that states could even pass laws to promote domestic policies of genocide."[118] At the same time as this realization was gaining ground, so was an acceptance among the diverse colonized peoples that they were members of a global indigenous class. The United Nations, which in 1960 declared self-determination to be a human right, became a powerful forum for the expression of indigenous aspirations, particularly with the creation in 1982 of a Working Group on Indigenous Populations in the UN Economic and Social Council (ECOSOC). Attending a session of the working group, Australian aboriginal representative Mick Dodson described his dawning recognition that, "We were all part of a world community of Indigenous peoples spanning the planet; experiencing the same problems and struggling against the same alienation, marginalisation and sense of powerlessness."[119]

An event of great significance in the Western hemisphere was the first Continental Indigenous International Convention, held in Quito, Ecuador in July 1990, and "attended by four hundred representatives from 120 indigenous nations and organizations."[120] Simultaneously, the number of nongovernmental organizations (NGOs) grew exponentially, so that by 2000 the UN High Commissioner for Human Rights could cite some 441 organizations of indigenous peoples worldwide. And indigenous peoples in many parts of the world strove to use the "master's tools"—the educational and legal systems of the dominant society—to reclaim the lands, political rights, and cultural autonomy stripped from them by their colonial conquerors.

At the national level, the impact of these movements is increasingly far-reaching. In the United States, an ever-greater number of individuals are choosing to self-identify as Native Americans,[121] and more and more native nations are petitioning for federal recognition; an "Indigenous Peoples' Day" has supplanted Columbus Day in some US cities. In Latin America, the impact has been more dramatic still. Indigenous peoples in Ecuador and Bolivia have "converged in mass mobilizations, breathtaking in their scale and determination," that overthrew governments and ushered in "a new revolutionary moment in which indigenous actors have acquired the leading role," led by current president Evo Morales.[122] In Mexico on January 1, 1994, indigenous peoples in the poverty-stricken southern state of Chiapas rose up in revolt against central authorities—the so-called Zapatista rebellion—protesting the disastrous impact on the native economy of cheap, subsidized corn exports from the US under the recently signed North American Free Trade Agreement (NAFTA). The Zapatistas have since established substantial local autonomy in their zone of control.

On September 13, 2007, nearly nine in ten member states of the United Nations General Assembly voted in favor of the UN Declaration on the Rights of Indigenous Peoples. The document expressed its concern "that indigenous peoples have suffered from historic injustices as a result of, *inter alia* [among other things], their colonization and dispossession of their lands, territories and resources, thus preventing them from exercising, in particular, their right to development in accordance with their own needs and interests . . ." In refutation of these imperial strategies, the declaration emphasized that,

> Indigenous peoples have the right to the full enjoyment, as a collective or as individuals, of all human rights and fundamental freedoms as recognized in the Charter of the United Nations, the Universal Declaration of Human

Rights and international human rights law. . . . Indigenous peoples and individuals are free and equal to all other peoples and individuals and have the right to be free from any kind of discrimination, in the exercise of their rights, in particular that based on their indigenous origin or identity. . . . Indigenous peoples have the right to self-determination. By virtue of that right they freely determine their political status and freely pursue their economic, social and cultural development. . . . Indigenous peoples, in exercising their right to self-determination, have the right to autonomy or self-government in matters relating to their internal and local affairs, as well as ways and means for financing their autonomous functions. . . . Indigenous peoples have the right to maintain and strengthen their distinct political, legal, economic, social and cultural institutions, while retaining their right to participate fully, if they so choose, in the political, economic, social and cultural life of the State.[123]

Despite the historic nature of the declaration, there were some notable holdouts among UN member states. Not surprisingly, the most prominent opponents—the only ones voting against the declaration—were delegates of countries responsible for some of the most brazen acts of colonial invasion and dispossession: the United States, Canada, New Zealand, and Australia.[124]

FURTHER STUDY

Alex Alvarez, *Native America and the Question of Genocide*. Lanham, MD: Rowman and Littlefield, 2014. A brief but comprehensive overview of the history and contemporary debates.

Richard Arens, ed., *Genocide in Paraguay*. Philadelphia, PA: Temple University Press, 1976. The first indigenous (Aché Indian) focused volume in the genocide literature, and one of the earliest books on genocide. With a widely-cited epilogue by the Holocaust survivor and (subsequently) Nobel Prize laureate, Elie Wiesel.

Patrick Brantlinger, *Dark Vanishings: Discourse on the Extinction of Primitive Races, 1800–1930*. Ithaca, NY: Cornell University Press, 2003. Examines European attitudes toward "primitive" races and their extinction.

Dee Brown, *Bury My Heart at Wounded Knee: An Indian History of the American West*. New York: Owl Books, 2001. First published in 1971, and still a classic introduction to the native North American experience.

Bartolomé de las Casas, *A Short Account of the Destruction of the Indies*. London: Penguin, 1992. First published in 1552: a Spanish friar's unrelenting description of colonial depredations in the Americas.

Alfred A. Cave, *The Pequot War*. Amherst, MA: University of Massachusetts Press, 1996. Definitive work on the Pequot genocide.

Ward Churchill, *A Little Matter of Genocide: Holocaust and Denial in the Americas, 1492 to the Present*. San Francisco, CA: City Lights Books, 1997. A forceful and well-documented polemic, with notable insights on genocide as a legal and academic concept.

Ken S. Coates, *A Global History of Indigenous Peoples: Struggle and Survival*. Basingstoke: Palgrave Macmillan, 2004. A solid introduction, especially good on the Second World War and postwar period.

Mark Cocker, *Rivers of Blood, Rivers of Gold: Europe's Conquest of Indigenous Peoples*. New York: Grove Press, 2001. Comprehensive survey, ranging from the Americas to Africa and Australasia.

Richard Drinnon, *Facing West: The Metaphysics of Indian Hating and Empire Building*. New York: Schocken Books, 1990. The racist ideology underlying US wars against American Indians, Filipinos, and Indochinese.

Theodore Fontaine, *Broken Circle: The Dark Legacy of Indian Residential Schools: A Memoir*. Toronto: Heritage House, 2010. Moving first-person account of life and suffering at the Fort Alexander Indian Residential school near Winnipeg, Manitoba.

Francis Jennings, *The Invasion of America: Indians, Colonialism, and the Cant of Conquest*. New York: W.W. Norton, 1975. Early, widely-cited account of the formative period of white–Indian interaction in North America.

Carroll P. Kakel, III, *The American West and the Nazi East: A Comparative and Interpretive Perspective*. New York: Palgrave MacMillan, 2013. Fascinating exploration of the parallels and discontinuities between the Nazi and US policies of imperial expansion and conquest (see Box 3.1).

Sven Lindqvist, *"Exterminate All the Brutes": One Man's Odyssey into the Heart of Darkness and the Origins of European Genocide*. New York: The New Press, 1996. Epigrammatic meditation on the links between colonialism and Nazi genocide.

Brendan C. Lindsay, *Murder State: California's Native American Genocide, 1846–1873*. Lincoln, NE: University of Nebraska Press, 2012. Winner of the 2014 Presidents' Award of the Western Social Science Association; an important contribution to the literature on Native American massacre.

Alan Moorehead, *The Fatal Impact: The Invasion of the South Pacific, 1767–1840*. New York: HarperCollins, 1990. First published in 1966, this remains a moving introduction to the destruction of Pacific indigenous peoples.

A. Dirk Moses, ed., *Genocide and Settler Society: Frontier Violence and Stolen Indigenous Children in Australian History*. New York: Berghahn Books, 2004. Seminal collection of essays.

Ronald Niezen, *The Origins of Indigenism: Human Rights and the Politics of Identity*. Berkeley, CA: University of California Press, 2003. The growth of contemporary indigenous identities and movements.

David Olusoga and Casper W. Ericksen, *The Kaiser's Holocaust: Germany's Forgotten Genocide and the Colonial Roots of Nazism*. London: Faber and Faber, 2010. Exemplary, fast-paced study of the Namibian genocide, including the Nazi connections and present-day struggles for recognition and restitution.

Daniel K. Richter, *Facing East from Indian Country: A Native History of Early America*. Cambridge, MA: Harvard University Press, 2001. "May be as close as any scholar has come to synthesizing an 'Indian perspective' on early American history" (Philip J. Deloria).

Nicholas Robins, *Native Insurgencies and the Genocidal Impulse in the Americas*. Bloomington, IN: Indiana University Press, 2005. Groundbreaking study of

Indian millenarian movements that adopted genocidal strategies against the European invader.

David E. Stannard, *American Holocaust: The Conquest of the New World*. New York: Oxford University Press, 1992. Perhaps the most enduring of the works published for the Columbus quincentenary.

Russell Thornton, *American Indian Holocaust and Survival: A Population History since 1492*. Norman, OK: University of Oklahoma Press, 1990. Foundational text on the demographic impact of European conquest and colonization.

James Wilson, *The Earth Shall Weep: A History of Native America*. New York: Atlantic Monthly Press, 1998. Fine overview of the native experience in North America.

Ronald Wright, *Stolen Continents: The "New World" Through Indian Eyes*. Boston, MA: Houghton Mifflin, 1993. Like Richter (above), examines the conquest from the perspective of its victims, but across the western hemisphere.

Andrew Woolford, *This Benevolent Experiment: Indigenous Boarding Schools, Genocide, and Redress in Canada and the United States*. Winnipeg, MB: University of Manitoba Press, 2015. A rigorous and penetrating study; by far the most systematic comparison of the US and Canadian residential-school experiences and the physical and cultural devastation they wreaked.

Andrew Woolford, Jeff Benvenuto, and Alexander Laban Hinton, eds., *Colonial Genocide in Indigenous North America*. Durham, NC: Duke University Press, 2014. A wide-ranging and inclusive collection.

Geoffrey York, *The Dispossessed: Life and Death in Native Canada*. London: Vintage UK, 1990. Harrowing journalistic account of poverty and cultural dislocation among Canada's native peoples.

NOTES

1 For concise overviews, see Robert K. Hitchcock and Tara M. Twedt, "Physical and Cultural Genocide of Various Indigenous Peoples," in Samuel Totten *et al.*, eds., *Century of Genocide: Eyewitness Accounts and Critical Views* (New York: Garland Publishing, 1997), pp. 372–407; and Elazar Barkan, "Genocides of Indigenous Peoples: Rhetoric of Human Rights," in Robert Gellately and Ben Kiernan, eds., *The Specter of Genocide: Mass Murder in Historical Perspective* (Cambridge: Cambridge University Press, 2003), pp. 117–140.

2 Ronald Niezen, *The Origins of Indigenism: Human Rights and the Politics of Identity* (Berkeley, CA: University of California Press, 2003), p. 18.

3 Quoted in ibid., p. 20.

4 However, some have criticized definitions that emphasize colonialism as being too Eurocentric, denying agency to indigenous peoples, and overlooking imperial conquests by non-Western societies. See, e.g., Ken S. Coates, *A Global History of Indigenous Peoples: Struggle and Survival* (Basingstoke: Palgrave Macmillan, 2004), pp. 8–9.

5 See Benjamin Madley, "Patterns of Frontier Genocide, 1803–1910: The Aboriginal Tasmanians, the Yuki of California, and the Herero of Namibia," *Journal of Genocide Research*, 4: 2 (2004), p. 168.

6 Sven Lindqvist, *"Exterminate All the Brutes": One Man's Odyssey into the Heart of Darkness and the Origins of European Genocide* (New York: The New Press, 1996), p. 123.

7 Twain quoted in Patrick Brantlinger, *Dark Vanishings: Discourse on the Extinction of Primitive Races, 1800–1930* (Ithaca, NY: Cornell University Press, 2001), p. 10. Twain's

complete essay on "The Noble Red Man," originally published in *The Galaxy* in 1870, is available on the Web at www.twainquotes.com/Galaxy/187009c.html.

8 Wallace quoted in Brantlinger, *Dark Vanishings*, pp. 185–186. President Andrew Jackson, one of the great tormentors of indigenous populations in US history, noted that "humanity has often wept over the fate of the aborigines of this country," and indeed, "to follow to the tomb the last of [this] race and to tread on the graves of extinct nations excite melancholy reflections. But," Jackson declared, "true philanthropy reconciles the mind to these vicissitudes as it does the extinction of one generation to make room for another." Jackson quoted in A. Dirk Moses, "Empire, Colony, Genocide: Keywords and the Philosophy of History," in Moses, ed., *Empire, Colony, Genocide: Conquest, Occupation, and Subaltern Resistance in World History* (New York: Berghahn Books, 2008), p. 19.

9 Brantlinger, *Dark Vanishings*, p. 186.

10 Lindqvist, *"Exterminate All the Brutes,"* p. 9.

11 Richard L. Rubenstein, *The Age of Triage: Fear and Hope in an Overcrowded World* (Boston, MA: Beacon Press, 1983), p. 1.

12 Brendan C. Lindsay, *Murder State: California's Native American Genocide, 1846–1873* (Lincoln, NE: University of Nebraska Press, 2012), p. 22.

13 Ward Churchill, *A Little Matter of Genocide: Holocaust and Denial in the Americas, 1492 to the Present* (San Francisco, CA: City Lights Books, 1997), p. 97.

14 Russel Lawrence Barsh points to the concentration of Indians on "reservations" (a system that "undoubtedly brought chronic malnutrition to a great proportion of North America's indigenous population"), destruction of forests, and denial of access to clean water as additional factors promoting high Indian mortality (his analysis concentrates on the later nineteenth century). See Barsh, "Ecocide, Nutrition, and the 'Vanishing Indian,'" in Pierre L. van den Berghe, ed., *State Violence and Ethnicity* (Niwot, CO: University Press of Colorado, 1990), pp. 224, 231, 239.

15 See Elizabeth A. Fenn, "Biological Warfare in Eighteenth-century North America: Beyond Jeffery Amherst," *The Journal of American History*, 86: 4 (March 2000), pp. 1552–1580.

16 David E. Stannard, *American Holocaust: The Conquest of the New World* (New York: Oxford University Press, 1992), p. 54.

17 Bartolomé de las Casas, *A Short Account of the Destruction of the Indies* (London: Penguin, 1992), p. 15. Raphael Lemkin praised las Casas for efforts that "went much beyond the ordinary ecclesiastic opposition to genocide in the Indies; he preached a doctrine of humanitarianism which was actually beyond the values of his own time. . . . [His] name has lived on through the centuries as one of the most admirable and courageous crusaders for humanity the world has ever known." Quoted in John Docker, "Are Settler-Colonies Inherently Genocidal?," in Moses, ed., *Empire, Colony, Genocide*, p. 92; and A. Dirk Moses, "Raphael Lemkin, Culture, and the Concept of Genocide," in Donald Bloxham and A. Dirk Moses, eds., *The Oxford Handbook of Genocide Studies* (Oxford: Oxford University Press, 2013), p. 26; Moses states straightforwardly that "Las Casas was [Lemkin's] hero." However, whether las Casas was truly "beyond the values" of his era is questionable, since others advanced similar values—sometimes in a more rigorous way. While las Casas did accept the basic right of Spain to occupy territories in the Americas and incorporate their populations, his contemporary Francesco de Vitoria (1485–1546) rejected this utterly: "it is clear . . . that the Spaniards, when they first sailed to the land of the barbarians [*sic*], carried with them no right at all to occupy their countries." The contributions of Hugo Grotius (1583–1645) and Samuel von Pufendorf (1632–1694) are also vital in demonstrating that far from being a universally held norm, a sophisticated contemporary critique of Western imperialism existed. For a cogent discussion, see Andrew Fitzmaurice, "Anticolonialism in Western Political Thought: The Colonial Origins of the Concept of Genocide," in Moses, ed., *Empire, Colony, Genocide*, pp. 55–80 (Vitoria quoted p. 58).

18 De las Casas, *A Short Account*, p. 24.

19 James Wilson, *The Earth Shall Weep: A History of Native America* (New York: Atlantic Monthly Press, 1998), p. 34.

20 Ibid., p. 35.

21 Stannard, *American Holocaust*, p. 89.

22 Lemkin, *Lemkin on Genocide*, p. 384, emphasis added.

23 See, e.g., Alvaro Kaempfer, "Lastarria, Bello y Sarmiento en 1844: Genocidio, historiografía y proyecto nacional," *Revista de Crítica Literaria Latinoamericana*, 32: 63–64 (2006), pp. 9–24; Florencia Roulet, "Genocidio en las Pampas. Crónica de una polémica abortada," Argentina Indymedia, February 11, 2005, http://argentina.indymedia.org/news/2005/02/264061.php.

24 See the sources on Namibia/German South-West Africa in Further Study, this chapter, especially David Olusoga and Casper W. Erichsen, *The Kaiser's Holocaust: Germany's Forgotten Genocide and the Colonial Roots of Nazism* (London: Faber and Faber, 2010). Elisa von Joeden-Forgey broadens the German-colonial framing in "Hidden in Plain Sight: Atrocity Concealment in German Political Culture before the First World War," in Alexander Laban Hinton, Thomas La Pointe, and Douglas Irvin-Erickson, eds., *Hidden Genocides: Power, Knowledge, Memory*, (New Brunswick, NJ: Rutgers University Press, 2014), pp. 52–67.

25 Vejas Gabriel Liulevicius, *War Land on the Eastern Front: Culture, National Identity, and German Occupation in World War I* (Cambridge: Cambridge University Press, 2000), p. 9 and *passim*. See also Elisa von Joeden-Forgey, "Hidden in Plain Sight: Atrocity Concealment in German Political Culture before the First World War," in Alexander Laban Hinton, Thomas La Pointe, and Douglas Irvin-Erickson, eds., *Hidden Genocides: Power, Knowledge, Memory* (New Brunswick, NJ: Rutgers University Press, 2014), pp. 52–67; Jürgen Zimmerer, "The Birth of the *Ostland* out of the Spirit of Colonialism: A Postcolonial Perspective on the Nazi Policy of Conquest and Extermination," *Patterns of Prejudice*, 39: 2 (2005), pp. 197–219; and the opening section on "The Great War: Site of Genocide or Signpost to its Future Enactment?" in Mark Levene, *The Crisis of Genocide, Vol. 1: Devastation: The European Rimlands 1912–1938* (Oxford: Oxford University Press, 2013), pp. 35–94. Scholars have also cited and explored the important precedent of the German conquest and occupation of Belgium at the outset of World War One. The policies of mass retribution, particularly the largescale killing of civilian hostages and the destruction of libraries and cultural monuments, served as a template for the Nazi invasion and occupation of Poland in 1939–1940, and the "war of annihilation" against the Soviet Union beginning in June 1941. Much of the literature cited in the lengthy endnote 125, pp. 141–143, points to this precedent. On the Belgian atrocities and occupation, Matthew White wrote: "The Germans moved quickly into Belgium. To ensure speed, they ruthlessly suppressed every hint of resistance they spotted in the Belgian populace. A single potshot from a sniper was often punished with the execution of all of the men in town. They shot 211 Belgian civilians at Andenne, 384 more at Tamines, and 612 at Dinant. . . . In all, the passing Germans killed some 5,500 Belgian civilians to quiet the population." White, *Atrocitology: Humanity's 100 Deadliest Achievements* (Edinburgh: Canongate, 2011), p. 347. For detailed histories, see Jeff Horne and Alan Kramer, *German Atrocities, 1914: A History of Denial* (New Haven, CT: Yale University Press, 2001), and the vast study by Jeff Lipkes, *Rehearsals: The German Army in Belgium, August 1914* (Leuven: Leuven University Press, 2007). The German destruction of Leuven/Louvain and its great library has become an iconic example of both urbicide and libricide/bibliocide— see the itemization at pp. 36, 37–39, and Bruno Waterfield, "The City That Turned Germans into 'Huns' Marks 100 Years Since It Was Set Ablaze," *The Telegraph*, August 25, 2014, www.telegraph.co.uk/news/worldnews/europe/belgium/11053962/The-city-that-turned-Germans-into-Huns-marks-100-years-since-it-was-set-ablaze.html.

26 Carroll P. Kakel, III, *The American West and the Nazi East: A Comparative and Interpretive Perspective* (New York: Palgrave Macmillan, 2011). Hitler also considered British rule in India a "model for domination and exploitation. . . . To Hitler, the raj represented

not just an example of how a small country could control a large area, but power and prosperity, the means by which Great Britain had become a world power." Stephen G. Fritz, *Ostkrieg: Hitler's War of Extermination in the East* (Lexington, KY: The University Press of Kentucky, 2011), p. 91. Hitler referred to "the Russian space" as "our India": "Like the English, we shall rule this empire with a handful of men." See the interesting quotes compiled by Andy Lee Chaisiri, "What Did Hitler Think of India and Indian People?," Quora.com, www.quora.com/What-did-Hitler-think-of-India-and-Indian-people. According to Madhusree Mukerjee, Hitler's "favourite movie" was "the 1935 Hollywood production *Lives of a Bengal Lancer*," with its depiction of heroic English officers on the Indian "frontier." Mukerjee, *Churchill's Secret War: The British Empire and the Ravaging of India during World War II* (New York: Basic Books, 2010), p. 34.

27 Kakel, *The American West*, pp. 202, 210. The motherlode of such critiques is Hannah Arendt, *The Origins of Totalitarianism* (New York: Harvest, 1976 [1951]). For an overview of other recent theorizing along these lines, see Thomas Kühne, "Colonialism and the Holocaust: Continuities, Causations, and Complexities," *Journal of Genocide Research*, 15: 3 (2013), pp. 339–362. For a counterargument addressing Kakel's work among others', see Jens-Uwe Guettel, "The US Frontier as Rationale for the Nazi East? Settler Colonialism and Genocide in Nazi-Occupied Eastern Europe and the American West," *Journal of Genocide Research*, 15: 4 (2013), pp. 401–419.

28 Ibid., p. 3.

29 Ibid., p. 214.

30 Ibid., p. 27.

31 Jefferson writing in 1786, quoted in ibid., p. 28.

32 Ibid., p. 53. "On General George Washington's orders, Continental Army and militia units attacked Indian towns and villages along the New York, Pennsylvania, and Ohio 'frontiers', with the goal of destroying 'native' food sources, livestock, homes, fields, and orchards. In the Revolutionary era, these so-called 'burnt earth' tactics (sometimes called 'feedfight') aimed at the intentional destruction of the Indian subsistence economy and the deliberate production of mass starvation, leaving the Indian survivors without shelter or food. . . . General Washington . . . ordered the 'total destruction and devastation of [Indian] settlements" (p. 197).

33 Ibid., p. 65.

34 Ibid., p. 86.

35 Ibid., pp. 209–210.

36 Russell Thornton, *American Indian Holocaust and Survival: A Population History since 1492* (Norman, OK: University of Oklahoma Press, 1987), p. 44.

37 Churchill, *A Little Matter of Genocide*, p. 97.

38 Testimony cited in Thornton, *American Indian Holocaust and Survival*, p. 95.

39 Amherst quoted in Ben Kiernan, *Blood and Soil: A World History of Genocide and Extermination from Sparta to Darfur* (New Haven, CT: Yale University Press, 2007), p. 245.

40 See Norbert Finzsch, "' [. . .] Extirpate or Remove That Vermine': Genocide, Biological Warfare, and Settler Imperialism in the Eighteenth and Early Nineteenth Century," *Journal of Genocide Research*, 10: 2 (2008), pp. 215–232.

41 Thornton, *American Indian Holocaust and Survival*, p. 51.

42 Wilson, *The Earth Shall Weep*, p. 283. See also Tasha Hubbard's chapter, "Buffalo Genocide in Nineteenth-Century North America: 'Kill, Skin, and Sell'," in Andrew Woolford, Jeff Benvenuto, and Alexander Laban Hinton, eds., *Colonial Genocide in Indigenous North America* (Durham, NC: Duke University Press, 2014), pp. 292–305. Hubbard's essay is additionally relevant to the study of "ecocide"—see pp. 34–35.

43 Genocidal massacres of Native Americans are the principal subject of Benjamin Madley's article, "Reexamining the American Genocide Debate: Meaning, Historiography, and New Methods," *American Historical Review*, 120: 1 (February 2015), pp. 98–139.

44 Thornton, *American Indian Holocaust and Survival*, p. 95.

45 On the Pequot War and its genocidal character, see Alfred A. Cave, *The Pequot War* (Amherst, MA: University of Massachusetts Press, 1996); Michael Freeman, "Puritans

and Pequots: The Question of Genocide," *New England Quarterly*, 68 (1995), pp. 278–293; "'We Must Burn Them,'" in Francis Jennings, *The Invasion of America: Indians, Colonialism, and the Cant of Conquest* (New York: W.W. Norton, 1975), pp. 202–227.

46 Wilson, *The Earth Shall Weep*, p. 94.

47 Karl Jacoby, *Shadows at Dawn*, quoted in Tim Morrison, "A Massacre Explained," *Time*, Monday, November 24, 2008, www.time.com/time/arts/article/0,8599, 1861448,00.html. Emphasis in original.

48 Chivington quoted in Michael Mann, *The Dark Side of Democracy: Explaining Ethnic Cleansing* (Cambridge: Cambridge University Press, 2005), p. 98. Chivington also stated: "Damn any man who sympathizes with Indians! I have come to kill Indians, and believe it is right and honorable to use any means under God's heaven to kill Indians." Quoted in David M. Crowe, *War Crimes, Genocide, and Justice: A Global History* (New York: Palgrave Macmillan, 2014), p. 48.

49 Connor quoted in Wilson, *The Earth Shall Weep*, p. 274. See also the description in Mark Levene, *Genocide in the Age of the Nation State, Vol. 2: The Rise of the West and the Coming of Genocide* (London: I.B. Tauris, 2005), pp. 93–94.

50 Roosevelt quoted in Paul R. Bartrop, "Punitive Expeditions and Massacres: Gippsland, Colorado, and the Question of Genocide," in A. Dirk Moses, ed., *Genocide and Settler Society: Frontier Violence and Stolen Indigenous Children in Australian History* (New York: Berghahn Books, 2004), p. 209.

51 Wilson, *The Earth Shall Weep*, p. 228.

52 The figures were provided by Benjamin Madley. See his essays exploring the fates of not only the Yuki but also the Yana and Tolowa peoples of California and Oregon: "California's Yuki Indians: Defining Genocide in Native American History," *Western Historical Quarterly*, 39: 3 (2008), pp. 303–332; "The Genocide of California's Yana Indians," in Samuel Totten and William S. Parsons, eds., *Centuries of Genocide: Essays and Eyewitness Accounts*, 4th edn (London: Routledge, 2013), pp. 17–53; and "When 'The World Was Turned Upside Down': California and Oregon's Tolowa Indian Genocide, 1851–1856," in Adam Jones, ed., *New Directions in Genocide Research* (London: Routledge, 2012), pp. 170–196.

53 Frank Chalk and Kurt Jonassohn, *The History and Sociology of Genocide* (New Haven, CT: Yale University Press, 1990), pp. 197–199.

54 Wilson, *The Earth Shall Weep*, pp. 228, 231.

55 "The Trail Where They Cried," translated from Cherokee (Coates, *A Global History*, p. 185). For a detailed account, see John Ehle, *Trail of Tears: The Rise and Fall of the Cherokee Nation* (New York: Doubleday, 1988).

56 Ward Churchill, "Genocide by Any Other Name: North American Indian Residential Schools in Context," in Adam Jones, ed., *Genocide, War Crimes and the West: History and Complicity* (London: Zed Books, 2004), p. 87.

57 Canada's Ministry of National Health and Welfare cited evidence in 1993 that "100% of the children at some [residential] schools were sexually abused between 1950 and 1980" *(The Globe and Mail);* in the United States a "wall of silence" still surrounds this subject. Churchill, "Genocide by Any Other Name," pp. 104–105.

58 Ibid., p. 97. See also Debora Mackenzie, "Canada Probes TB 'Genocide' in Church-Run Schools," *New Scientist*, May 5, 2007. Andrew Woolford's judgment is notable: "Tuberculosis was rampant through many residential schools until the 1940s, and reports suggest that the staff at these schools did little to help the infected children. Susceptibility to this and other diseases was increased by the poor nutrition and inadequate clothing provided to students. In addition, there are reports of students' being required to bunk with others who were infected. With death tolls from tuberculosis reaching as high as 50% in some schools, any claim that this was simply 'natural' is exposed as disingenuous at best." Woolford, "Ontological Destruction: Genocide and Canadian Aboriginal Peoples," *Genocide Studies and Prevention*, 4: 1 (April 2009), pp. 90–91.

59 Churchill, "Genocide by Any Other Name," pp. 105–106.

60 "Whites spoke of Aborigines as 'horribly disgusting,' lacking 'any traces of civilization,' 'constituting in a measure the link between the man and the monkey tribe,' or 'undoubtedly in the lowest possible scale of human nature, both in form and intellect.'" Madley, "Patterns of Frontier Genocide," p. 169.

61 Mann, *The Dark Side of Democracy*, p. 80.

62 Ibid., p. 81.

63 Colin Tatz, "Genocide in Australia," *AIATSIS Research Discussion Papers No. 8*, 1999, www.kooriweb.org/gst/genocide/tatz.html.

64 Levene, *Genocide in the Age of the Nation State, Vol. 2*, p. 75.

65 Reynolds cited in Ben Kiernan, *Blood and Soil: A World History of Genocide and Extermination from Sparta to Darfur* (New Haven, CT: Yale University Press, 2007), p. 308.

66 Trollope quoted in Mark Cocker, *Rivers of Blood, Rivers of Gold: Europe's Conquest of Indigenous Peoples* (New York: Grove Press, 2001), p. 178.

67 Benjamin Madley, "From Terror to Genocide: Britain's Tasmanian Penal Colony and Australia's History Wars," *Journal of British Studies*, 47 (2008), p. 78 (fn. 7).

68 Levene, *Genocide in the Age of the Nation State, Vol. 2*, p. 42. The exterminatory character of the Flinders system was acknowledged in 1999 by the Tasmanian Premier, Jim Bacon, who referred to the Wybalenna concentration camp as "a site of genocide." Quoted in Madley, "Patterns of Frontier Genocide," p. 175. Madley added (p. 176): "From the outset, British authorities knew that conditions on Flinders Island were lethal. Inaction despite clear warnings and high mortality rates suggests that population decline was government policy, or was considered preferable to returning the survivors to their homes. . . . In 1836 the commander of Launceston visited Flinders Island and warned that if conditions were not improved, 'the race of Tasmania . . . will . . . be extinct in a quarter of a century.' . . . Still, the government did not address the issues contributing to mortalities. In fact, they operated Flinders Island with virtually no policy amendments for over a decade, until closing the reserve in 1847. The colonial government may not have planned to kill large numbers of Aborigines on Flinders Island, but they did little to stop mass death when they were clearly responsible for it."

69 Madley, "From Terror to Genocide," p. 104.

70 See Jennifer Latson, "This Is Why Australia Has 'National Sorry Day'," *Time*, May 25, 2015, http://time.com/3890518/national-sorry-day/.

71 Peter Read, *The Stolen Generations: The Removal of Aboriginal Children in NSW, 1883–1969* (Sydney: Government Printer, 1982); revised edition available on the Web at http://dmsweb.daa.asn.au/files/Recognition_of_Overseas/Reading%207_Stolen-Generations.pdf.

72 "With hindsight, I think it was a mistake to use the word genocide . . . once you latch onto the term 'genocide,' you're arguing about the intent and we should never have used it." Sir Ronald Wilson, quoted in Robert van Krieken, "Cultural Genocide in Australia," in Dan Stone, ed., *The Historiography of Genocide* (London: Palgrave Macmillan, 2008), p. 130. For more on the international law surrounding forcible child transfer, see Kurt Mundorff, "Other Peoples' Children: A Textual and Contextual Interpretation of Article 2(e) of the Genocide Convention," *Harvard International Law Journal*, 50: 1 (2009), pp. 61–127.

73 Colin Tatz, *With Intent to Destroy: Reflecting on Genocide* (London: Verso, 2003), p. xvi.

74 For text and video of Rudd's apology, see www.australia.gov.au/about-australia/our-country/our-people/apology-to-australias-indigenous-peoples.

75 For a solid overview, see Dominik J. Schaller, "The Genocide of the Herero and Nama in German South-West Africa," in Totten and Parsons, eds., *Centuries of Genocide*, pp. 89–116.

76 Maharero quoted in Mark Levene, *Genocide in the Age of the Nation State, Vol. 2: The Rise of the West and the Coming of Genocide* (London: I.B. Tauris, 2005), p. 248.

77 Von Trotha quoted in David Olusoga and Casper W. Erichsen, *The Kaiser's Holocaust: Germany's Forgotten Genocide and the Colonial Roots of Nazism* (London: Faber and Faber, 2010), p. 140.

78 Von Trotha quoted in Jon Bridgman, *The Revolt of the Hereros* (New York: Berkeley, 1981), pp. 111–112.

79 Benjamin Madley, "From Africa to Auschwitz: How German South West Africa Incubated Ideas and Methods Adopted and Developed by the Nazis in Eastern Europe," *European Historical Quarterly*, 35: 3 (2005), p. 430.

80 Levene, *Genocide in the Age of the Nation State, Vol. 2*, p. 234.

81 Von Trotha quoted in Jan-Bart Gewald, "Imperial Germany and the Herero of Southern Africa: Genocide and the Quest for Recompense," in Jones, ed., *Genocide, War Crimes and the West*, p. 61.

82 Quoted in Gewald, "Imperial Germany and the Herero," p. 62.

83 German Official History quoted in Olusoga and Erichsen, *The Kaiser's Holocaust*, p. 148.

84 Madley, "Patterns of Frontier Genocide," p. 188; Madley, "From Africa to Auschwitz," p. 181.

85 Olusoga and Erichsen, *The Kaiser's Holocaust*, p. 220, emphasis added.

86 Vedder quoted in ibid., pp. 163–164.

87 Olusoga and Erichsen, *The Kaiser's Holocaust*, p. 361.

88 Wieczorek-Zeul quoted in Jurgen Zimmerer, "Colonial Genocide: The Herero and Nama War (1904–08) in German South West Africa and Its Significance," in Stone, ed., *The Historiography of Genocide*, p. 323. See also Andrew Meldrum, "German Minister Says Sorry for Genocide in Namibia," *The Guardian*, August 16, 2004, www.theguardian.com/world/2004/aug/16/germany.andrewmeldrum. An excellent BBC documentary on the genocide of the Hereros and Namas, *Genocide and the Second Reich*, can be viewed on YouTube at www.youtube.com/watch?v=fhhOOPVdRQk.

89 Zimmerer, "Colonial Genocide," p. 323. Olusoga and Erichsen note, however, that "although a brave and admirable step . . . for which Wieczorek-Zeul was roundly condemned by parts of the German press," the official apology was in some ways lacking: it "made no mention of the concentration camps, and seemed to place blame for the genocides on von Trotha and the *Schutztruppe* [colonial expeditionary force]." *The Kaiser's Holocaust*, p. 359.

90 In academia, the denialist position is associated with scholars such as Steven Katz, Guenter Lewy, William Rubinstein, and (in Australia) Keith Windschuttle.

91 Alexander Bielakowski, post to H-Genocide, September 26, 2001; see my response of the same date in the H-Genocide archives, http://h-net.msu.edu/cgi-bin/logbrowse.pl?trx=lmandlist=H-Genocide.

92 Michael Burleigh, *Ethics and Extermination: Reflections on Nazi Genocide* (Cambridge: Cambridge University Press, 1997), p. 181.

93 Christopher Hitchens, "Minority Report," *The Nation*, October 19, 1992, emphasis added. Hitchens's "vulgar social Darwinism, with its quasi-Hitlerian view of the proper role of power in history" is effectively pilloried in David E. Stannard's essay, "Uniqueness as Denial: The Politics of Genocide Scholarship," in Alan S. Rosenbaum, ed., *Is the Holocaust Unique? Perspectives on Comparative Genocide* (2nd edn) (Boulder, CO: Westview Press, 2001), pp. 245–290 (on Hitchens, p. 248).

94 Wilson, *The Earth Shall Weep*, p. xx.

95 Benjamin Madley, personal conversation, August 16, 2005.

96 See Tzvetan Todorov, *The Conquest of America: The Question of the Other* (New York: Harper Perennial, 1992), pp. 135–138. Ben Kiernan argues that "Whether genocide accounted for more or fewer deaths than other causes is irrelevant . . . Nor should larger, unplanned tragedies like epidemics obscure lesser crimes, even if unconnected, that lead to the extinction of a population also ravaged by disease. In other words, it is possible neither to convict microbes of genocide nor to present their great destruction as a defense exhibit for perpetrators." Kiernan, *Blood and Soil: A World History of Genocide and Extermination from Sparta to Darfur* (New Haven, CT: Yale University Press, 2007), p. 35.

97 Tatz, *With Intent to Destroy*, p. 99.

98 Patrick Wolfe, "Structure and Event: Settler Colonialism, Time, and the Question of Genocide," in Moses, ed., *Empire, Colony, Genocide*, p. 102.

99 Tony Barta, "Relations of Genocide: Land and Lives in the Colonization of Australia," in Isidor Wallimann and Michael N. Dobkowski, eds., *Genocide and the Modern Age: Etiology and Case Studies of Mass Death* (Westport, CT: Syracuse University Press, 2000), p. 240.

100 Levene, *Genocide in the Age of the Nation State, Vol. 2*, p. 44. He adds (p. 78) in the Australian context: "What had begun as a seemingly benign, implicitly anti-genocidal native policy thus became not just a *failed* policy but actually took on its reverse nightmare image; the very logic of non-negotiable, not to say accelerated, land seizure and conquest in the face of aboriginal resistance inevitably forcing Crown colonial good intentions into a cul-de-sac from which they could only be extricated through explosions of extreme, exterminatory violence."

101 Quoted in Ann Curthoys, "Genocide in Tasmania," in Moses, ed., *Empire, Colony, Genocide*, p. 233.

102 Another sophisticated analysis of the issues of agency and intent is A. Dirk Moses, "An Antipodean Genocide? The Origins of the Genocidal Moment in the Colonization of Australia," *Journal of Genocide Research*, 2:1 (2000), pp. 89–106.

103 For example—to cite a case where colonial administrators have often been credited with seeking to prevent or impede genocide against indigenous peoples—the Lieutenant Governor of Tasmania, Sir George Arthur, imposed martial law in the territory in 1828. He called for "the most energetic measures on the part of the settlers themselves," though adding that "the use of arms is in no case to be resorted to until other measures for driving them off have failed." As Benjamin Madley notes, "Martial law made killing Aborigines legal until they had all been 'driven off,' resulting, within a year of the issuing of the decree, in the slaughter of over two-thirds of Tasmania's Aboriginal population." Madley, "Patterns of Frontier Genocide," p. 174.

104 Thornton, *American Indian Holocaust and Survival*, p. 69.

105 Coates, *A Global History*, p. 132.

106 Roger Williams, quoted in Wilson, *The Earth Shall Weep*, p. 55. Writes G.B. Nash: "The nature of pre-contact Indian war was far different than the wars known in Europe, both in duration and in scale of operations. Unlike the Europeans, Native Americans could not conceive of total war that was fought for months or even years, that did not spare non-combatants, and that involved the systematic destruction of towns and food supplies. Wars among Indians were conducted more in the manner of short forays, with small numbers of warriors engaging the enemy and one or the other side withdrawing after a few casualties had been inflicted." Quoted in Jeffrey P. Blick, "Genocidal Warfare in Tribal Societies as a Result of European-induced Culture Conflict," *Man*, New Series, 23:4 (1988), p. 658. See also "Savage War," in Jennings, *The Invasion of America*, pp. 146–170, pointing (among other things) to the extent to which Europeans themselves imported methods of warfare that were subsequently depicted as "savage" customs.

107 Daniel Chirot and Clark McCauley, *Why Not Kill Them All? The Logic and Prevention of Mass Political Murder* (Princeton, NJ: Princeton University Press, 2006), pp. 113–114.

108 Orlando Patterson, *Slavery and Social Death: A Comparative Study* (Cambridge, MA: Harvard University Press, 1982), p. 191.

109 Jeffrey P. Blick, "The Iroquois Practice of Genocidal Warfare (1534–1787)," *Journal of Genocide Research*, 3: 3 (2001), pp. 405–429.

110 See, e.g., Laura E. Matthew and Michel R. Oudijk, eds., *Indian Conquistadors: Indigenous Allies in the Conquest of Mesoamerica* (Norman, OK: University of Oklahoma Press, 2007).

111 "On the Trail of Hernán Cortés," *The Economist*, December 20, 2014, www.economist.com/news/christmas-specials/21636686-journey-past-most-mexicans-would-rather-forget-trail-hern-n.

112 Nicholas Robins, *Native Insurgencies and the Genocidal Impulse in the Americas* (Bloomington, IN: Indiana University Press, 2005).

113 See Nelson Reed, *The Caste War of Yucatan* (Stanford, CA: Stanford University Press, 1964); Don E. Dumond, *The Machete and the Cross: Campesino Rebellion in Yucatan* (Lincoln, NE: University of Nebraska Press, 1997).

114 Coates, *A Global History*, pp. 226–227. See also Richard Arens's edited volume on the Aché Indians, *Genocide in Paraguay* (Further Study, this chapter).

115 Levene, *Genocide in the Age of the Nation State, Vol. 2*, p. 99.

116 For example, Ward Churchill notes that US Indians in the contemporary era "incur by far the lowest annual and lifetime incomes of any group ... and the highest rates of infant mortality, death by malnutrition, exposure, and plague disease. Such conditions produce the sort of endemic despair that generates chronic alcoholism and other forms of substance abuse among more than half the native population—factors contributing not only to further erosion in physical health but to very high accident rates—as well as rates of teen suicide up to 14.5 times the national average. ... 'Genocidal' is the only reasonable manner in which to describe the imposition, as a matter of policy, of such physiocultural effects upon any target group." Churchill, *A Little Matter of Genocide*, pp. 247–248. Conditions among Australian aboriginals are strikingly similar: this group "ended the twentieth century at the very top, or bottom, of every social indicator available." See the statistics cited in Tatz, *With Intent to Destroy*, pp. 104–105. In Australia, "the standard of health of Aborigines lags almost 100 years behind that of other Australians, with some indigenous people still suffering from leprosy, rheumatic heart disease and tuberculosis, according to a report for the World Health Organisation. The report said that Aborigines and Torres Strait Islanders, which make up about 2.5% of Australia's population, have an average life expectancy 17 years below their fellow countrymen. The average age of death for Aboriginal men in some parts of New South Wales is 33." Barbara McMahon, "Aboriginal Health '100 Years Behind' Other Australians," *The Guardian*, May 1, 2007, www.theguardian.com/world/2007/may/01/australia.barbaramcmahon.

117 Emanuella Grinberg, "Instead of Columbus Day, Some U.S. Cities Celebrate Indigenous People's Day," *CNN.com*, October 13, 2014, www.cnn.com/2014/10/12/living/columbus-day-indigenous-people-day/. See also "Indigenous Peoples Day Celebrated alongside Columbus Day in US," Associated Press dispatch in *The Guardian*, October 11, 2015, www.theguardian.com/us-news/2015/oct/11/indigenous-peoples-day-columbus-day-native-americans. (Diverse spellings have been adopted: "People's," "Peoples," "Peoples'.")

118 Niezen, *The Origins of Indigenism*, p. 40.

119 Quoted in ibid., p. 47.

120 Elazar Barkan, *The Guilt of Nations: Restitution and Negotiating Historical Injustices* (New York: W.W. Norton, 2000), p. 161.

121 For a survey of the trend, see Jack Hitt, "The Newest Indians," *New York Times Magazine*, August 21, 2005.

122 "Bolivia Fights Back: An Introduction," and Forrest Hylton and Sinclair Thomson, "Insurgent Bolivia," both in *NACLA Report on the Americas*, November to December 2004, pp. 14–15.

123 "United Nations Declaration on the Rights of Indigenous Peoples," adopted by *General Assembly Resolution 61/295*, September 13, 2007, www.un.org/esa/socdev/unpfii/documents/DRIPS_en.pdf.

124 Haider Rizvi, "UN Adopts Historic Statement on Native Rights," *CommonDreams.org*, September 14, 2007, www.commondreams.org/archive/2007/09/14/3831. However, the Rudd government in Australia endorsed the declaration in 2009, and in November 2015, the Liberal government in Canada announced it would do likewise. See Joanna Smith, "Canada Will Implement UN Declaration on Rights of Indigenous Peoples, Carolyn Bennett Says," *TheStar.ca*, November 12, 2015, www.thestar.com/news/canada/2015/11/12/canada-will-implement-un-declaration-on-rights-of-indigenous-peoples-carolyn-bennett-says.html.

BOX 3A THE GENOCIDE OF GUATEMALA'S MAYANS

Map 3a.1 Guatemala. The mountainous sierra zone is the heartland of Mayan culture and settlement, and was devastated in the genocide of 1981–1983.

Source: Map provided by WorldAtlas.com.

Guatemala's Mayans are the inheritors of one of the world's great civilizations, which erected the temple complexes of Tikal, Copán, Palenque, and Chichen Itzá (the last three lying just outside Guatemala's present-day boundaries, in Honduras and Yucatán, Mexico). The causes of the collapse of these civilizations, and the reversion of their monuments to the jungle, remain something of an enigma. But what is known suggests that two hugely destructive institutions in the west—war and environmental despoliation—were far from unknown to indigenous civilizations in the Americas. While (and in part because) growing populations placed great strain on available land and resources, patterns of Mayan warfare seem to have grown increasingly uncompromising—perhaps exterminatory and genocidal, as for the Aztecs of the valley of Mexico several centuries later (see pp. 172–173).

After the collapse of classical Mayan culture, descendent populations gravitated toward the Guatemalan sierra and other mountainous regions, such as Chiapas in southern Mexico.[1] The Mayan region experienced one of the most savage of all sixteenth-century conquistador campaigns, when Pedro de Alvarado arrived to lay the territories waste and claim them for the Spanish crown. In his *Brief Account of the Destruction of the Indies*, the Spanish friar and Indian advocate, Bartolomé de las Casas, wrote of Alvarado's rampage through Guatemala that his forces had:

> plundered and ravaged an area of more than a hundred leagues by a hundred leagues that was among the most fertile and most heavily peopled on earth, killing all the leaders among the native population and, with all men of military age dead, reducing the survivors to the Hell of slavery. . . . As this very butcher himself was quite accurately to record in writing, there were more people in this region than in the whole of the kingdom of Mexico. Yet, in this same area, he and his brothers, together with their comrades-in-arms, were responsible for the deaths of more than four or five million souls over the fifteen or sixteen years, from 1524 to 1540. Nor is the butchery and destruction over, for those natives who

have survived so far will soon perish in the same ways as have all the others in the region.[2]

Mark Levene aptly notes that what these conquistadors "did in mass murder was quite equal to the accomplishment of *Einsatzgruppen* [killing] units operating in the Russian borderlands of 1941–42" (see the discussion of the "Holocaust by Bullets" on pp. 325–332).[3] Unlike the Arawaks of Hispaniola or the Beothuks of Newfoundland,[4] the Mayans were not hounded to complete extinction. But along with the other Indians of Mesoamerica, they experienced the most calamitous demographic collapse in recorded history. Las Casas's casualty estimate is far from untenable, given the densely-woven populations that inhabited much of the isthmus at the time of the conquest. And his prediction that the "same ways" of extermination and enslavement would be employed against Mayan populations in the future was prescient.

One important legacy of Spanish colonialism in Mesoamerica was the advent of a *ladino* (Hispanic) culture which, since *ladino* was a cultural rather than racial identification, gradually eroded and supplanted the native culture. Another crucial legacy, which afflicts neighboring El Salvador as well, was the glaringly unequal division of land and wealth resulting from the parceling up of conquered territories into vast *latifundias* (plantations), worked by armies of dragooned Indians. Mayan populations were squeezed to the point of bare subsistence and beyond, occupying tiny plots in inaccessible areas, so they would be forced to enter the cash economy in planting and harvest seasons, toiling in abominable conditions. During the great coffee boom of the nineteenth century, highland Indians were both pressed into forced labor and coerced into debt peonage—with the debts often passed down for generations.[5] In the twentieth century, they were transported in cattle trucks to the lowland *fincas* (plantations) that grew crops, especially cotton, for export.[6] It was in such conditions that the global symbol of the Guatemalan Mayans, Rigoberta Menchú, labored alongside her family as a child, and lost two of her brothers to the *fincas*—one to malnutrition, the other to pesticide poisoning. Menchú would go on to be awarded the Nobel Peace Prize in 1992, the quincentenary of Columbus's invasion of the Americas.[7]

In 1944, Guatemala was ruled by Jorge Ubico, the latest in a long line of dictators. But an impetus for change was building, inspired both by the decolonization movements of the era and by US president Franklin Roosevelt's proclamation of "Four Freedoms" to guide the postwar era (freedom of speech and religion; freedom from want and fear). That same year, 1944, the first democratic wave crested with the deposing of Ubico and the election of a reformist government under Juan José Arevalo. He was succeeded in 1950 by an even more energetic reformer, Jacobo Arbenz, who introduced measures aimed at dissolving Guatemala's institutions of privilege and inequality, and sparking a *capitalist* modernization of the country. Fatefully,

Figure 3a.1 The awarding of the Nobel Peace Prize in 1992 to Rigoberta Menchú, a Quiche Indian from the highlands of Guatemala, symbolized the increased recognition of indigenous people's experiences worldwide. Menchú lost several family members to the state-sponsored genocide that swept Guatemala in the late 1970s and early 1980s; her autobiography, *I, Rigoberta Menchú* (see Further Study), is a classic of modern Latin American literature and indigenous advocacy. Menchú is shown speaking at a ceremony for the Odebrecht Award for Sustainable Development in Quito, Ecuador, in November 2014.

Source: Photo by Carlos Rodriguez/ANDES/Wikimedia Commons.

among Arbenz's decrees was the nationalization of the United Fruit Company—which enjoyed intimate access to the upper level of the Eisenhower administration in the US. The company was compensated, but based on the declared tax-value of its immense and unproductive holdings. This was of course the lowest possible amount. Confronted by such a flagrant refusal of a formerly client regime to play its assigned role in US hemispheric designs, the Eisenhower administration declared Arbenz a dangerous communist— pointing to the "evidence" of four communist representatives out of fifty-one in Congress, along with a handful of sub-cabinet appointees.

The years 1944–1954 are known as the "Ten Years of Spring" in Guatemala. They marked the only time in the country's postcolonial history where genuine attention was paid to the needs of the vast majority of the population. But they were about to be foreclosed, and followed by a genocidal winter.

On June 18, 1954, a force scarcely 150 strong—led by Castillo Armas, a military officer on the CIA payroll—"invaded" Guatemala from Honduras. There they paused, while the CIA organized a campaign of propaganda aimed at spreading terror of an impending foreign assault. The plan worked. Arbenz's nerve broke, and he was carted off to exile in his underclothes.[8] Armas and his military cronies took over and, with extensive US assistance, launched a counterinsurgency campaign against Arbenz's supporters and other opposition. Eventually, young officers rebelled against the dictatorial new order, forming the nucleus of a guerrilla group that fled the cities for the guerrilla redoubt of the highlands. The army's extermination campaign against them, this time conducted in close coordination with the US military, killed thousands of mostly Mayan civilians, at the same time as it routed the guerrilla insurgency.

Yet nothing had changed politically. By the end of the 1970s, populations were boiling over in Guatemala, as in nearby El Salvador and Nicaragua.[9] Trade-union mobilization swept the cities, while in the Mayan sierra, a *ladino-led* but mostly Indian force, the Guerrilla Army of the Poor (EGP), launched a fresh insurrection. The response of the Guatemalan army and security forces between 1978 and 1983—with critical political, economic, and military support from the United States and Israel[10]—was probably the worst holocaust unleashed in the Americas in the twentieth century.

"Though their official targets were left-wing guerrillas," writes Patrick Brantlinger, "the army and the death squads tortured, raped, and killed indiscriminately, massacring entire Mayan villages in a patently genocidal campaign . . ."[11] In just six years, peaking under the regime of General Efraín Ríos Montt (see Figure 3a.3) in 1982–1983, some 440 Indian villages were obliterated. The author, visiting the ravaged highlands of El Quiché department in 1987, found scorched earth dotting the roadsides where peasant dwellings had once stood. Much of the remaining Mayan population—there were few men to be seen—was corralled in concentration camps behind barbed wire and army watchtowers. Russell Schimmer's research for Yale University's Genocide Studies Program, which uses remote sensing technologies to detect changes to vegetation and land use caused by genocidal outbreaks, found signs of extensive destruction and despoliation in Quiché's "Ixil Triangle," where the most merciless scorched-earth measures were imposed. ("We have no scorched-earth policy," Ríos Montt notoriously declared after a meeting with President Reagan in Honduras. "We have a policy of scorched communists.")[12]

At least 200,000 and as many as 250,000 people—mostly Mayans, about 75 percent males[13]—were massacred, often after torture. The barbarism was fully comparable to the early phase of Spanish colonization under Pedro de Alvarado half a millennium earlier: indeed, Virginia Garrard-Burnett described the counterinsurgency campaign of the early 1980s as "the worst calamity to befall Mayan life and culture in Guatemala since the sixteenth–century Spanish conquest."[14] It involved acts of "extreme cruelty . . . such as the killing of defenseless children, often by beating them against walls or throwing them alive into pits where the corpses of adults were later thrown; the amputation of limbs; the impaling of victims; the killings of persons by covering them in petrol and burning them alive," all part of "military operations directed towards the physical annihilation" of opposition forces.

Such was the verdict of the Historical Clarification Commission (CEH), established after the United Nations brokered a peace agreement between the Guatemalan government and guerrilla forces in 1996.[15] The Commission's final report on the atrocities of the 1970s and 1980s, released in February 1999, ascribed responsibility for fully 93 percent of them to the government and its paramilitary allies. Most of the atrocities, it found, "occurred with the knowledge or by the order of the highest authorities of the State." Finally, and crucially, the Commission declared, on the basis of its survey of four regions of the Mayan zone, that

> the acts committed with the intent to destroy, in whole or in part, numerous groups of Mayans were not isolated acts or excesses committed by soldiers who were out of control, nor were they the result of possible improvisation by mid-level Army command. With great consternation, the CEH concludes that many massacres and other human rights violations committed against these groups obeyed a higher, strategically planned policy, manifested in actions which had a logical and coherent sequence. . . . In consequence, the CEH concludes that agents of the State of Guatemala, within the framework of counterinsurgency operations carried out between 1981 and 1983, committed acts of genocide against groups of Mayan people which lived in the four regions analysed. This conclusion is based on the evidence that, in light of Article II of the Convention on the Prevention and Punishment of the Crime of Genocide, the killing of members of Mayan groups occurred (Article II.a), serious bodily or mental harm was inflicted (Article II.b) and the group was deliberately subjected to living conditions calculated to bring about its physical destruction in whole or in part (Article II.c). The conclusion is also based on the evidence that all these acts were committed "with intent to destroy, in whole or in part," groups identified by their common ethnicity, by reason thereof, whatever the cause, motive or final objective of these acts may have been (Article II, first paragraph).[16]

Since the ceasefire, the return of the tens of thousands of refugees who had fled to southern Mexico and elsewhere,[17] and the release of the Clarification Commission's report, measures have been instituted to bolster Mayan rights.[18]

Figure 3a.2 "Queqchí people carrying their loved ones' remains after an exhumation in Cambayal in Alta Verapaz department, Guatemala," February 2012. The exhumation was carried out by the Centre of Forensic Anthropology and Applied Sciences (CAFCA), which "since 1997 . . . has been helping to heal the deep wounds caused by Guatemala's internal conflict. The impact of CAFCA's forensic work is twofold: It helps families to find their loved ones and come to terms with their loss and it gathers the evidence needed to bring their murderers to justice." For more on the forensics of genocide, see Chapter 11, pp. 592–594.

Source: CAFCA archive/Wikimedia Commons.

In 1996, for example, twenty-one Mayan tongues were formally recognized by the state as official languages. Education in these languages is more widely available than previously. Exhumations and reburials, of the kind depicted in Victoria Sanford's book *Buried Secrets*,[19] have brought a measure of closure to thousands of indigenous families. And in December 2009, Col. Marco Antonio Sanchez was found guilty of the forcible disappearance of eight people during the war and genocide, and sentenced to fifty-three years in prison. It was the first such conviction ever rendered by a Guatemalan court, and human rights organizers expressed their hope that the trial would serve as a "test case" for future prosecutions.[20]

As for the profound disparities of wealth and land ownership that spawned rebellion in the first place, they seem only to have deepened, and are now some of the worst in the world.[21] According to Inter-American Development Bank statistics, cited by *NotiCen Report* in 2007, "Guatemala has surpassed Brazil as the most unequal country in Latin America. . . . Most of these impoverished people are indigenous and campesinos [peasants]. . . . Two-thirds of Guatemala's children, 2,700,000 of them, live in poverty, a poverty that will follow them all their lives in the form of decreased life expectancy and health outlook."[22]

Figure 3a.3 General Efraín Ríos Montt testifying at his first trial in Guatemala, September 2013.
Source: Photo by Elena Hermosa/Wikimedia Commons.

Also generating deep concern is the skyrocketing male violence—principally against other males, but increasingly against women[23]—that pervades "postwar" Guatemala. In this respect, the traumatized land stands as emblematic of many post-genocide societies[24]—awash with arms, drugs, and gangs; with military and security forces still rampaging as off-duty death squads, though now against "socially deviant" elements (street children, drug dealers and gang members, homosexuals and transvestites); pervaded by extreme *machismo* that fuels an epidemic of rape-murders of young women.

The quest for justice for the Guatemalan genocide for years centered on Efraín Ríos Montt—the former genocidal general and putative president of Guatemala during the worst of the genocide. Reelected to the national Congress in 2007, Ríos Montt took full advantage of the immunity from prosecution that this afforded him. But his pursuers proved surprisingly tenacious, especially given the co-opted status of most of the judiciary and political spectrum. In November 2011, Ríos Montt was charged with genocide *and convicted of the crime in 2013*—though the verdict was subsequently overturned. As 2016 began, the trial was due to resume, though without Ríos Montt present: the former dictator was in failing health.[25]

Another, even more substantive and taboo-shattering process was launched at the outset of 2016. Eighteen officers of the 1980s military regime—including Gen. Manuel Benedicto Lucas García, brother of the *génocidaire* who preceded Ríos Montt in power, and a former chief of military intelligence—were arrested for their alleged involvement in massacres and forcible disappearances. "These are the big fish," said Victoria Sanford, author of *Buried Secrets* and other anthropological works on Guatemala (see Further Study, ch. 12). According to *The New York Times*, "Most of the arrests stem from a three-year investigation on a military base in Cobán in the central region of Alta Verapaz, where investigators have found the remains of 558 people, including 90 children ... DNA testing confirmed the identities of 97 people at the site who disappeared from 1981 to 1986, when the accused officers were commanding the base or in the chain of command."[26] A further milestone was reached in February 2016 with the conviction of a pair of military officers, Heriberto Valdez Asij and Esteelmer Reyes Girón, for sexually enslaving fifteen Mayan women, an "emblematic case" that "made visible the kind of violence visited upon women's bodies during the armed conflict and sends a very powerful message that the justice system can hold these perpetrators to account," in the estimation of US political scientist Jo-Marie Burt.[27] As with many other cases explored in this book, however, the key foreign enablers, suppliers, and co-conspirators in the Guatemalan genocide—notably political and military figures in the United States and Israel—have yet to be meaningfully exposed and pursued, let alone prosecuted.

FURTHER STUDY

Virginia Garrard-Burnett, *Terror in the Land of the Holy Spirit: Guatemala under General Efraín Ríos Montt, 1982–1983*. Oxford: Oxford University Press, 2010. Powerfully written account of the worst period of genocide against Mayan Indians and others during Guatemala's civil war.

Guatemala: Memory of Silence: Report of the Commission for Historical Clarification, February 1999. Available online at www.aaas.org/sites/default/files/migrate/uploads/mos_en.pdf.

Ételle Higonnet, ed., *Quiet Genocide: Guatemala 1981–1983*, trans. Marcie Mersky. New Brunswick, NJ: Transaction Publishers, 2009. Analyzes modern Guatemala through a lens of genocide and crimes against humanity.

Carlota McAllister and Diane M. Nelson, eds., *War by Other Means: Aftermath in Post-Genocide Guatemala*. Durham, NC: Duke University Press, 2013. Diverse and insightful collection exploring the social and structural violence that continues to afflict Guatemala.

Rigoberta Menchú with Elisabeth Burgos-Debray, *I, Rigoberta Menchú: An Indian Woman in Guatemala*. New York: Verso, 1987. Memoir, by the Nobel Peace Prize-winner, of her family's experience in the genocide against Mayan Indians.

Victoria Sanford, *Buried Secrets: Truth and Human Rights in Guatemala*. New York: Palgrave Macmillan US, 2003. Moving study of post-genocide Guatemala, centered on the forensic exhumations of victims.

Daniel Wilkinson, *Silence on the Mountain: Stories of Terror, Betrayal, and Forgetting in Guatemala*. Boston, MA: Houghton Mifflin Company, 2002. The historical roots and human consequences of the Guatemalan genocide.

NOTES

1   It was in Chiapas, as noted, that the Spanish friar Bartolomé de las Casas centered his efforts to preserve the Indian population; the city of San Cristobal de las Casas bears his name. It was also in Chiapas that modern oppression and marginalization of Mexico's Mayan Indian population erupted in the Zapatista uprising of January 1, 1994—the same date that the North American Free Trade Agreement was scheduled to come into effect, which many Indian communities saw as a mortal threat to their subsistence-agricultural economy.

2   Bartolomé de las Casas, *A Short Account of the Destruction of the Indies*, trans. Nigel Griffin (London: Penguin, 1991), pp. 61–62.

3   Mark Levene, *Genocide in the Age of the Nation State, Vol. 2: The Rise of the West and the Coming of Genocide* (London: I.B. Tauris, 2005), p. 12.

4   On the extermination of the Indians of Hispaniola, see las Casas, *A Short Account*, pp. 18–25; David Stannard, *American Holocaust: The Conquest of the New World* (New York: Oxford University Press, 1992), pp. 62–75. On the Beothuks, see Frederick W. Rowe, *Extinction: The Beothuks of Newfoundland* (Toronto, ON: McGraw-Hill Ryerson, 1977); Arthur Grenke, *God, Greed, and Genocide: The Holocaust through the Centuries* (New Academic Publishing, 2005), pp. 170–173.

5   See Jim Handy, *Gift of the Devil: A History of Guatemala* (Toronto, ON: Between the Lines, 1984); Julio C. Cambranes, *Coffee and Peasants in Guatemala* (South Woodstock, VT: CIRMA/Plumsock Mesoamerican Studies, 1985); Adam Jones, *Guatemala Insurgent: Roots of Rebellion from the Rise of the Coffee Economy to the Present Day* (unpublished manuscript, University of British Columbia, 1989; available as a PDF file from the author).

6   A fine and succinct summary of Guatemalan historical, social, and economic development is Greg Grandin, "Five Hundred Years," in Carlota McAllister and Diane M. Nelson, eds., *War by Other Means: Aftermath in Post-Genocide Guatemala* (Durham, NC: Duke University Press, 2013), pp. 49–70.

7   Rigoberta Menchú with Elisabeth Burgos-Debray, *I, Rigoberta Menchú: An Indian Woman in Guatemala* (New York: Verso, 1987), chs. 4, 7. Menchú's autobiography is a classic of indigenous literature, though controversy has attended some of the personal history that Menchú recounts—a notable case of the struggle over history and memory examined in Chapter 14. For an overview, see Arturo Arias, ed., *The Rigoberta Menchú Controversy* (Bloomington, MN: Minnesota University Press, 2001).

8   The coup, and its prelude and aftermath, have been well studied as a paradigmatic case of US intervention. The fullest account is Stephen C. Schlesinger and Stephen Kinzer, *Bitter Fruit: The Story of the American Coup in Guatemala*, expanded edn (Cambridge, MA: Harvard University Press, 1999). See also Richard H. Immerman, *The CIA in Guatemala: The Foreign Policy of Intervention* (Austin, TX: University of Texas Press, 1982), and, on the aftermath, Stephen M. Streeter, *Managing the Counterrevolution: The United States and Guatemala, 1954–1961* (Athens, OH: Ohio University Press, 2000).

9   Nicaragua would experience a seizure of power by leftist revolutionaries, the Sandinistas, in 1979, prompting another Reagan administration-sponsored

terrorist campaign, spearheaded by the so-called *Contras* (counter-revolutionaries). An estimated 20,000–30,000 Nicaraguan civilians were killed before the war wound down later in the 1980s, and the Sandinistas were voted out of power in 1990. As for El Salvador in the late 1970s and 1980s, it has not yet been studied as a case of genocide, and should be, if political groups (real or imagined) are included in the framing. See Americas Watch, *El Salvador's Decade of Terror: Human Rights since the Assassination of Archbishop Romero* (New Haven, CT: Yale University Press, 1991), and *New York Times* correspondent Raymond Bonner's devastating exposé, *Weakness and Deceit: US Policy and El Salvador* (New York: Times Books, 1984). The emblematic genocidal massacre of the war, inflicted by the US-trained Atlacátl battalion at the village of El Mozote in December 1981—and followed by a US-engineered cover-up—is memorably described by Mark Danner in *The Massacre at El Mozote: A Parable of the Cold War* (New York: Vintage, 1994).

10 On the US role during the peak years of the genocide, see Michael McClintock, *The American Connection, Vol. 2: State Terror and Popular Resistance in Guatemala* (London: Zed Books, 1985). Of President Ronald Reagan, who directly sponsored the "anti-communist" campaigns of state terror and extermination in Central America, Robert Parry wrote that he "found virtually every anti-communist action justified, no matter how brutal. From his eight years in the White House, there is no historical indication that he was troubled by the bloodbath and even genocide that occurred in Central America during his presidency, while he was shipping hundreds of millions of dollars in military aid to the implicated forces." Parry, "Reagan and Guatemala's Death Files," in William L. Hewitt, ed., *Defining the Horrific: Readings on Genocide and Holocaust in the Twentieth Century* (Upper Saddle River, NJ: Pearson Education, 2004), p. 247; available online at www.consortiumnews.com/1999/052699a1.html. Reagan also infamously described the Guatemalan commander at the peak of the genocide, Efraín Ríos Montt, as a "man of great personal integrity and commitment"; accusations that Ríos Montt was inflicting mass atrocities were a "bum rap." Quoted in Garrard-Burnett, *Terror in the Land of the Holy Spirit*, p. 158. On the basis of the US orchestration of genocide in El Salvador and Nicaragua (c. 100,000 killed), and also considering the "fundamental political support" (McClintock, p. 199) that his government extended to Guatemala and other atrocious regimes throughout Latin America, there are grounds to regard Reagan as the single worst purveyor of mass atrocity in the western hemisphere during the twentieth century. Very little of this surfaced in the nauseating encomiums in the US media following the president's death in 2004. See my chapter, "Genocide in Central America," in Adam Jones and John Cox, eds., *The Routledge Handbook of Genocide Studies*, forthcoming.

A crucial element of US support to Guatemala and El Salvador, under both Reagan and his predecessor Jimmy Carter, was the drafting of key clients—Israel and South Korea—to fill gaps in military and "security" assistance, especially when the US Congress restricted direct aid. Of Israel's quite remarkable level of involvement in Guatemala, *The Washington Post* reported that not only had Israel trained Guatemalan *génocidaires*, but "Israeli advisers—some official, others private—helped Guatemalan internal security agents hunt underground rebel groups." Quoted in Benjamin Beit-Hallahmi, *The Israeli Connection: Who Israel Arms and Why* (New York: Pantheon Books, 1987), pp. 79, 81. See also McClintock, *The American Connection, Vol. 2*, pp. 192–196. "During the height of the Guatemalan civil war," reports Stephen Kinzer, "Israeli companies supplied nearly all of the army's weaponry—$20 million worth in 1984 alone. The Uzi submachine gun is the preferred weapon of the liquidation units operating in the early hours against dissidents, Indians and non-Indians, or against campesinos, the poor farmers, whenever they take the initiative to organize agricultural cooperatives or attempt to find out the fate of disappeared relatives,' the Israeli newspaper *Ha'aretz* reported in 1985." Kinzer, *Reset: Iran, Turkey, and America's Future* (New York: St. Martin's Press, 2010), p. 162. Israel was likewise instrumental in arming the military and security forces who perpetrated genocide, by this book's anchoring definition (pp. 32–33), in next-door El Salvador in the 1970s and early 1980s. "During the 1970s, 80 percent of arms imports to El Salvador came from Israel, but after the United States resumed sales in 1980, Israel became only its second largest supplier" (Beit-Hallahmi, *The Israeli Connection,* p. 85).

According to Kinzer, "Central American armies were not the only ones that turned to Israel for help. Dictators around the world, from Bolivia, Chile, and the Dominican Republic to Burma, the Philippines, and Indonesia, equipped their soldiers with Galil assault rifles and Uzi submachine guns. Israel also became the principal arms supplier for the apartheid regime in South Africa, which President Reagan fervently supported but could not arm because of congressional restrictions. Israelis trained South Africa's elite police and military units, sold tanks and aviation technology to its army, licensed the production of Galil rifles at a factory in South Africa, and even advised the regime on developing nuclear weapons." Israel also "trained more than a dozen guerrilla and paramilitary forces blessed by Washington. They established private security forces in Colombia that ranchers and drug traffickers used to protect themselves and dispatch their enemies, and did the same in the Philippines during the Ferdinand Marcos dictatorship" (*Reset*, pp. 164–165). Israel also assisted the apartheid regime of South Africa in developing nuclear, biological, and chemical weapons that clearly envisaged the mass extermination of African populations if white rule was pushed to the wall. "Although [the regime's] nuclear weapons were never used, this created one of history's most extraordinary and bitter ironies. The Jewish state, born of European racism and forged by Nazi genocide, armed the world's last ideologically Nazi state of the twentieth century with chemical, nuclear and biological weapons, the weapons of genocide." Richard Dowden, *Africa: Altered States, Ordinary Miracles* (New York: PublicAffairs, 2009), pp. 401–402. Is there a Ph.D. student in genocide studies or a related field seeking a dissertation subject?

11 Patrick Brantlinger, reviewing recent books on Guatemala in *Journal of Genocide Research*, 11: 4 (2009), p. 531. The genocide was labeled as such at the time (May 1982) in a statement by Guatemalan bishops: "never in our national history have we arrived at such a grave extreme. These assassinations now belong in the category of genocide." Quoted in Garrard-Burnett, *Terror in the Land of the Holy Spirit*, p. 114. Two important chapter-length treatments of the genocide are Victoria Sanford, *"¡Si Hubo Genocidio en Guatemala!* Yes! There Was Genocide in Guatemala," in Dan Stone, ed., *The Historiography of Genocide* (London: Palgrave Macmillan, 2008), pp. 543–576; and Marc Drouin, "Understanding the 1982 Guatemalan Genocide," in Marcia Esparza, Henry R. Huttenbach, and Daniel Feierstein, eds., *State Violence and Genocide in Latin America* (London: Routledge, 2010), pp. 81–104.

12 Ríos Montt quoted in Daniel Wilkinson, *Silence on the Mountain: Stories of Terror, Betrayal, and Forgetting in Guatemala* (Durham, NC: Duke University Press, 2004), p. 327. Ríos Montt's press secretary, Francisco Bianchi, also notoriously stated: "The Indians were subversives, right? And how do you fight subversion? Clearly

you had to kill the Indians because they were collaborating with subversion. And then they would say, 'You're massacring innocent people.' But they weren't innocent. They had sold out to subversion." Quoted in McClintock, *The American Connection, Vol. 2*, p. 258.

13 "One of the most striking effects of the scorched-earth campaign is that it left much of the countryside largely devoid of men. . . . Approximately 75 percent of the people killed over the course of Guatemala's long conflict were men, a cold statistic that, in isolation, fails to convey the loss of wage-earners, family providers, and beloved husbands, sons, and fathers—the heads of households and communities. . . . While the killing of both men and women peaked in 1982, women and children, not surprisingly, were much more likely to die in massacres than in selective killings or assassinations. Men, however, were highly vulnerable in either scenario. . . . During (and after) the Ríos Montt period, some villages, having lost their men to violence, flight, migration to the south coast, conscription by the army (or the guerrillas), or obligations with the civil patrols [conscripted Mayan paramilitaries] became virtual 'cities of women'—villages in which adult males were, for all intents and purposes, almost entirely absent. The absence of men, in turn, helped to contribute to an overall collapse of traditional community and family hierarchies." Virginia Garrard-Burnett, *Terror in the Land of the Holy Spirit: Guatemala under General Efraín Ríos Montt, 1982–1983* (Oxford: Oxford University Press, 2010), p. 105.

14 *Ibid.*, p. 7.

15 For an overview of the Historical Clarification Commission's work, and the truth and reconciliation process in Guatemala more generally, see Anita Isaacs, "Truth and the Challenge of Reconciliation in Guatemala," in Joanna R. Quinn, ed., *Reconciliation(s): Transitional Justice in Postconflict Societies* (Montreal, QC: McGill-Queen's University Press, 2009), pp. 116–146. Genocide was also the verdict of an important human rights report on Guatemala issued while the slaughter was still underway: Craig W. Nelson and Kenneth I. Taylor, *Witness to Genocide: The Present Situation of Indians in Guatemala* (London: Survival International, 1983).

16 All quotes from *Guatemala: Memory of Silence: Report of the Commission for Historical Clarification*, February 1999. Available online at www.aaas.org/sites/default/files/migrate/uploads/mos_en.pdf.

17 On the plight of the refugees, see Beatriz Manz, *Refugees of a Hidden War: The Aftermath of Counterinsurgency in Guatemala* (Albany, NY: State University of New York Press, 1988).

18 For an overview of decades of Mayan activism on this front, see Edward F. Fischer and R. McKenna Brown, *Maya Cultural Activism in Guatemala* (Austin, TX: University of Texas Press, 1996).

19 Victoria Sanford, *Buried Secrets: Truth and Human Rights in Guatemala* (New York: Palgrave Macmillan, 2003).

20 Stephen Gibbs, "Guatemala Colonel Given 53 Years for Civil War Crime," *BBC Online*, December 5, 2009, http://news.bbc.co.uk/2/hi/americas/8396691.stm.

21 In the 2015 *Human Development Report*, Guatemala ranked 128th out of 188 countries (see http://hdr.undp.org/en/countries/profiles/GTM).

22 "Hardly a Dent in Guatemalan Poverty, as Wealth Distribution Becomes World's Worst," *NotiCen: Central American & Caribbean Affairs*, October 4, 2007. See also "Malnutrition in Guatemala: A National Shame," *The Economist*, August 27, 2009, noting that "in parts of rural Guatemala, where the population is overwhelmingly of Mayan descent, the incidence of child malnutrition reaches 80%."

23 On the *feminicidio* (femicide/feminicide) in Guatemala, see Victoria Sanford, *Guatemala: Del Genocidio al Feminicidio* (Guatemala City: F&G Editores, 2008); the stark documentary, *Guatemala: Killer's Paradise* (National Film Board of Canada, 2006), available on YouTube; and Sanford's essay on this film, "Images of Impunity," in Adam Jones, ed., *Evoking Genocide: Scholars and Activists Describe the Works That Shaped Their Lives* (Toronto, ON: The Key Publishing House Inc., 2009), pp. 210–214. See also the broader discussion of gender and genocide in Chapter 13.

24 See Alessandro Preti, "Guatemala: Violence in Peacetime—A Critical Analysis of the Armed Conflict and the Peace Process," *Disasters*, 26: 2 (2002), pp. 99–119.

25 Elisabeth Malkin, "Genocide Retrial Is Set for Guatemalan Former Dictator," *The New York Times*, August 25, 2015, www.nytimes.com/2015/08/26/world/americas/genocide-retrial-is-set-for-guatemalan-former-dictator.html.

26 Elisabeth Malkin, "Guatemala Arrests Former Military Officers in Connection with Massacres," *The New York Times*, January 6, 2016, www.nytimes.com/2016/01/07/world/americas/guatemala-arrests-former-military-officers-in-connection-with-massacres.html. The account added that "the arrests pose a direct challenge to the president-elect, Jimmy Morales, a political neophyte who ran as the candidate of a party dominated by former officers."

27 Nina Lakhani, "Justice at Last for Guatemalan Women as Military Officers Jailed for Sexual Slavery," *The Guardian*, March 1, 2016, www.theguardian.com/world/2016/mar/01/guatemala-sexual-slavery-sepur-zarco-military-officers-jailed. The article notes that "the women will be awarded compensation for the long-term physical, psychological and economic harm suffered as a consequence of being systematically raped and forced into bondage for up to six years."

CHAPTER 4

The Ottoman Destruction of Christian Minorities

They hate the Christians.

Charlotte Kechejian, survivor of the Armenian genocide

INTRODUCTION

The murder of over a million Armenians in Turkey between 1915 and 1923 presaged Adolf Hitler's even more gargantuan assault on European Jews in the 1940s. However, for decades, the events were almost forgotten. War crimes trials—the first in history—were held after the Allied occupation of Turkey, but were abandoned in the face of Turkish opposition. In August 1939, as he prepared to invade western Poland, Hitler mused to his generals that Mongol leader "Genghis Khan had millions of women and men killed by his own will and with a gay heart. History sees in him only a great state builder." And in noting his instructions to the Death's Head killing units "to kill without mercy men, women and children of Polish race or language," Hitler reportedly uttered some of the most resonant words in the history of genocide: "*Who, after all, talks nowadays of the annihilation of the Armenians?*"[1]

Fortunately, Hitler's rhetorical question cannot sensibly be asked today—except in Turkey. Over the past four decades, a growing movement for apology and restitution has established the Armenian catastrophe as one of the three canonical genocides of the twentieth century, alongside the Holocaust and Rwanda. The widespread commemorations of the centenary of the genocide's outbreak, in 2015, further entrenched this status.[2]

However, a variant of Hitler's question *could* still obtain: who, today, talks of the genocides of the *other* Christian minorities of the Ottoman realm, notably the Assyrians (including Chaldeans, Nestorians, and Syrian/Syriac Christians)[3] and the Anatolian and Pontian Greeks?*

Historian Hannibal Travis, who has done more than any other scholar to bring the Assyrian catastrophe into mainstream genocide studies, notes that at the time of the anti-Christian genocides, "newspapers in London, Paris, New York, and Los Angeles regularly reported on the massacres of Assyrians living under Ottoman occupation." According to Travis, the attention the Assyrians received was such, and so intertwined with the Armenian atrocities, that when Raphael Lemkin pondered early versions of what would become his "genocide" framework, he had two main instances in mind: the Armenian holocaust, and a renewed round of anti-Assyrian persecutions, this time in post-Ottoman Iraq in 1933.[4]

As for the Anatolian, Thracean, and Pontian Greeks, they had been vulnerable ever since their linguistic brethren in the Greek mainland had become the first to successfully fling off Ottoman dominion—with numerous atrocities committed on both sides. This marked the beginning of the "Great Unweaving" that dismantled the Ottoman empire, and sent terrorized and humiliated Muslim refugees fleeing toward the Constantinople and the Anatolian heartland. By the beginning of the First World War, a majority of the region's ethnic Greeks still lived in present-day Turkey, mostly in Thrace (the only remaining Ottoman territory in Europe, abutting the Greek border), and along the Aegean and Black Sea coasts. They would be targeted both prior to and alongside the Armenians of Anatolia and the Assyrians of Anatolia and Mesopotamia.

For these reasons, while the events of the 1914–1922 period have long been depicted in terms of the Armenian genocide and its aftermath, one is justified in portraying it instead as a unified campaign against all the empire's Christian minorities. This does greater justice to minority populations that have generally been marginalized in the narrative. The approach mirrors the discourse and strategizing of the time. Sultan Abdul Hamid II lamented "the endless persecutions and hostilities of the *Christian* world" as a whole.[5] Historian Donald Bloxham refers to "a general anti-Christian chauvinism" in which Christians "were cast as collective targets."[6] The German ambassador to the Ottoman empire, Baron Hans Freiherr von Wangenheim, described the regime's "internal enemies" as "local Christians."[7]

A "Christian genocide" framing acknowledges the historic claims of the Assyrian and Greek peoples, and the movements now stirring for recognition and restitution among Greek and Assyrian diasporas. It also brings to light the quite staggering cumulative death toll among the various Christian groups targeted. In Thea Halo's estimation, "Armenian deaths were estimated at 1.5 million.

---

* Anatolia is the "Asian" region of Turkey, extending east from the Bosphorus Strait, which bisects the city of Istanbul. The major populations of "Anatolian Greeks" include those along the Aegean coast and in Cappadocia (central Anatolia), but not the Greeks of the Thrace region west of the Bosphorus. In a geographical sense, Anatolia technically includes the Pontus region along the Black Sea coast, but the Pontian Greeks are culturally and historically such a distinct community that I designate them separately.

According to figures compiled by the Greek government in collaboration with the Patriarchate, of the 1.5 million Greeks of Asia Minor—Ionians, Pontians, and Cappadocians—approximately 750,000 were massacred and 750,000 exiled. Pontian deaths alone totaled 353,000."[8] As for the Assyrian victims, the Assyrian delegation to the Paris Peace Conference cited a figure of 250,000 killed, a figure which has been accepted by Hannibal Travis and David Gaunt, arguably the two leading scholars of the Assyrian genocide.[9]

A broader framing also encourages attention to vulnerable Christian populations in the region today—most notably in Iraq, home to the descendants of the Assyrian populations targeted in earlier rounds of persecution and genocide. I return to the movements for recognition at the end of this chapter.

ORIGINS OF THE GENOCIDE

Three factors combined to produce the genocide of Christian minorities: (1) the decline of the Ottoman Empire, which provoked desperation and humiliation among Turkey's would-be revolutionary modernizers, and eventually violent reaction;* (2) Christians' vulnerable position in the Ottoman realm; and (3) the First World War, which confronted Turkey with attack from the west (at Gallipoli) and invasion by the Russians in the northeast. Significant as well was the Turkish variant of racial hygiene theory, echoing many motifs familiar from the subsequent Nazi period in Europe. According to Vahakn Dadrian, "measures for the better 'health' of the national body, [and for] 'eugenic improvements' of the race" were actively promoted.[10] Young Turk racial theory, according to Ben Kiernan, connected the Turks with the heroic Mongols, and contrasted them with inferior and untrustworthy Greeks, Armenians, and Jews.[11]

In Chapter 10, I argue that *humiliation* is one of the greatest psychological spurs to violence, including mass violence and genocide. Theories of Turkish racial superiority certainly provided a salve for the psychic wounds inflicted by the almost unbroken string of humiliations that constituted Ottoman history in its final decades. Indeed, the empire had been in decline ever since its armies were repulsed from the gates of Western Europe, at Vienna in 1688. "As well as the loss of Greece and effectively Egypt, in the first twenty-nine years of the nineteenth century alone the empire had lost control of Bessarabia, Serbia, Abaza, and Mingrelia." In 1878, the empire "cede[d] ownership of or genuine sovereignty over . . . Bosnia, Herzegovina, Bulgaria, Kars, Ardahan, and Cyprus," with "the losses of that year alone comprising one-third of Ottoman territory and 20 per cent of the empire's inhabitants."[12]

The human toll of this "Great Unweaving," from Greece's independence war in the early nineteenth century to the 1912–1913 Balkan wars, was enormous. Hundreds of thousands of Ottoman Muslims were massacred in the secessionist drive. The victims of these atrocities were hardly Muslims exclusively, or overwhelmingly.

---

* Throughout this chapter, I refer to "Turkey" and "the Ottoman Empire" interchangeably.

When Paul Mojzes rightly states that "the first European genocide of the twentieth century took place during the Balkan wars of 1912–1913," and that "it is a heretofore unrecognized genocide," he is thinking in the singular about a roiling zone of genocide in which dozens of ethnic and political entities and forces, both major and minor, were swept up in violence that was exceptionally vicious, intercommunal, and mutual[13]—"not quite a war of all against all but of most against most," as Timothy Snyder has described the "Bloodlands" of eastern Europe and the western USSR during the 1940s (see Box 2.3).[14] Other ready parallels are the catastrophe attending Indian Partition in 1947–1948, and the reciprocal genocides in Iraq from 2005, discussed in Box 4a.

Nonetheless, Bloxham argued that "in the years up to the First World War, Muslims were the primary victims of violence in the region by state and sub-state Christian actors working in the name of nationalist liberation and self-determination for their ethno-religious group."[15] Hundreds of thousands more were expelled as refugees from the former imperial periphery to the heartland. There, many of these so-called *muhajirs* festered in humiliating poverty, and many yearned for revenge.[16] According to Taner Akçam, "it was precisely those people who, having only recently been saved from massacre themselves, would now take a central and direct role in cleansing Anatolia of 'non-Turkish' elements."[17] In this, they were joined by "bullyboys" drawn from the "most recalcitrant elements" of Circassians in Turkey—the survivors or descendants of those expelled in 1864 from Russia's new empire in the Caucasus *to* the Ottoman empire (see Box 2.2). After what Mark Levene has called "the most dramatic—and genocidal" forced deportations of the entire Unweaving, the arrival of half a million to a million destitute and starving Circassians, mostly along the Black Sea coast, "had profound knock-on effects on an already vastly destabilized empire."[18] This traumatized population regrettably, but predictably, produced many eager recruits for the Young Turks' atrocities against Bulgarian Christians in the 1870s. And their paramilitary formations would be deployed as death squads against the Christian population of Anatolia in 1915–1916.

The situation within the shrinking empire was ripe for nativist backlash, and when it occurred, Ottoman Armenians were predictable targets. They are an ancient people who, by the late nineteenth century, constituted the largest non-Muslim population in eastern Anatolia.[19] In the 1870s and 1880s, Armenian nationalist societies began to form—part of a broader "'Armenian Renaissance' *(Zartonk)* that gained momentum from the middle of the nineteenth century on."[20] Like the small number of Armenian political parties that mobilized later, they demanded full equality within the empire, and occasionally appealed to outside powers for protection and support. These actions aroused the hostility of Muslim nationalists, and eventually prompted a violent backlash.[21] Suspicions were heightened by the advent, in the 1870s and 1880s, of a small number of Armenian revolutionary societies that would later carry out robberies and acts of terrorism against the Ottoman state.

With the Ottomans' hold over their empire faltering, foreign intervention increasing, and Armenian nationalists insurgent, vengeful massacres swept across Armenian-populated territories. Between 1894 and 1896, "the map of Armenia in Turkey went up in flames. From Constantinople to Trebizond to Van to Diyar-bekir, and across the whole central and eastern plain of Anatolia, where historic Armenia was lodged, the killing and plunder unfolded."[22] Vahakn Dadrian, the leading historian of the Armenian genocide, considered the 1894–1896 massacres "a test case for the political feasibility, if not acceptability by the rest of the world, of the enactment by central authorities of the organized mass murder of a discordant nationality."[23] The killings were, however, more selective than in the 1915–1917 conflagration, and central state direction more difficult to discern. According to Bloxham, the main role was played by "Muslim religious leaders, students, and brotherhoods," though many ordinary Muslims, especially Kurds, also participated.[24] Between 80,000 and 200,000 Armenians were killed.[25]

In the first few years of the twentieth century, outright collapse loomed for the Ottoman Empire. In 1908, Bulgaria declared full independence, Crete's parliament proclaimed a union with Greece, and the Austro-Hungarian Empire annexed Bosnia and Herzegovina. Italy seized Libya in 1912. The following year, Albania and Macedonia seceded. Summarizing these disasters, Robert Melson noted that "out of a total area of approximately 1,153,000 square miles and from a population of about 24 million, by 1911 the Turks had lost about 424,000 square miles and 5 million people";[26] and by 1913, only a narrow strip of European territory remained in their grasp.

In 1908, the tottering Ottoman sultanate was overthrown in the Young Turk revolution, led by a group of modernization-minded military officers. Christian minorities joined with other Ottoman peoples in welcoming the transformations. In the first blush of post-revolutionary enthusiasm, "a wave of fraternal effusions between Ottoman Christians and Muslims swept the empire."[27] It seemed there was a place for all, now that despotism had been overturned. Indeed, Christians (together with Jews and other religious minorities) were now granted full constitutional rights.[28]

Unfortunately, as with many revolutionary movements, the new Ottoman rulers (grouped under the Committee of Union and Progress, CUP) were split into liberal-democratic and authoritarian factions. The latter was guided by a "burgeoning ethnic nationalism (still informed by Islam) blended with a late-imperial paranoid chauvinism";[29] its leading ideologist was Ziya Gokalp, whose "pan-Turkism was bound up in grandiose romantic nationalism and a 'mystical vision of blood and race.'"[30] "Turks," declared Gokalp, "are the 'supermen' imagined by the German philosopher Nietzsche . . . New life will be born from Turkishness."[31] Within the CUP, amidst "economic and structural collapse, the vision of a renewed empire was born—an empire that would unite all Turkic peoples and stretch from Constantinople to central Asia. This vision, however, excluded non-Muslim minorities."[32]

In January 1913, in the wake of the shattering Balkan defeats of the previous year, the extremist CUP launched a coup against the moderates and took power. The new ruling triumvirate—Minister of Internal Affairs Talat Pasha; Minister of War Enver Pasha; and Minister of the Navy Jemal Pasha—quickly established a *de facto* dictatorship. Under the so-called Special Organization of the CUP that they directed, this trio would plan and oversee the genocides of the Christian minorities, with the Special Organization's affiliates in the Anatolia region serving as ground-level organizers.[33]

WAR, DEPORTATION, AND MASSACRE

The Ottoman genocide of Christians has long been depicted as starting in April 1915, when with Allied invaders on the doorstep in the Dardanelles, the Ottoman authorities rounded up Armenian notables, and the CUP's "final solution" to the Armenian "problem" was implemented. If we speak of systematic, generalized destruction of a Christian population, either through direct murder or through protracted death marches, this may be true. Armenians, moreover, had been targeted for a premonitory wave of killings in 1909. The so-called "Adana events" extended well beyond this heavily Armenian city in Cilicia (southeastern Turkey), killing some 21,000 Armenians. Though the immediate perpetrators were drawn from the ranks of regional CUP members and their conservative and Kurdish allies, Raymond Kévorkian has argued persuasively that the central Young Turk authorities at the very least approved of the massacres if they did not actually order them.[34]

But the multipronged holocaust that swept the Ottoman realm during World War One was presaged by atrocities not only against Armenians, but against Greeks as well. It erupted in 1913–1914, before the outbreak of the war, with massive "group persecution" directed by the CUP against the "Ottoman Greeks living along the Aegean littoral," in Matthias Bjørnlund's account.[35] Historian Arnold Toynbee described a campaign of "general" attacks in which

> entire Greek communities were driven from their homes by terrorism, their houses and land and often their moveable property were seized, and individuals were killed in the process. . . . The terror attacked one district after another, and was carried on by "chette" bands, enrolled from the Rumeli refugees [i.e., Muslim populations "cleansed" from the Balkans by Christian terror] as well as from the local population and nominally attached as reinforcements to the regular Ottoman gendarmerie.[36]

This was almost precisely the pattern—Taner Akçam calls it a "trial run"[37]—that would be followed in the 1915 extermination campaign against all Christian minorities, though with a starker emphasis on direct killing.[38] US ambassador Henry Morgenthau cited testimony from his Turkish informants that they "had expelled the Greeks so successfully that they had decided to apply the same method toward all the other races in the empire."[39] Again the looting and destruction would be voracious; again the "Rumeli refugees," the most humiliated and dispossessed of the population, would be encouraged to avenge themselves on Christians; again the *chettes* would be mobilized for genocidal service under gendarmerie control.

When those "other races" were targeted in the full-scale genocide of 1915, the Aegean Greeks would again be among those exposed to the same process of concentration, deportation, and systematic slaughter as the Armenians and Assyrians. Of this second and more far-reaching wave of anti–Christian policies, Morgenthau wrote that the Ottoman authorities

> began by incorporating the Greeks into the Ottoman army and then transforming them into labor battalions using them to build roads in the Caucasus and other scenes of action. These Greek soldiers, just like the Armenians, died by thousands from cold, hunger, and other privations ... The Turks attempted to force the Greek subjects to become Mohammadans; Greek girls ... were stolen and taken to Turkish harems and Greek boys were kidnapped and placed in Muslim households ... Everywhere, the Greeks were gathered in groups and, under the so-called protection of Turkish gendarmes, they were transported, the larger part on foot, into the interior.[40]

Alfred Van der Zee, Danish consul in the port city of Smyrna, reported in June 1916:

> A reign of terror was instituted and the panic stricken Greeks fled as fast as they could to the neighbouring island of Mitylene. Soon the movement spread to Kemer, Kilissekeuy, Kinick, Pergamos and Soma. Armed *bashibozuks* [Turkish irregular troops] attacked the people residing therein, lifted the cattle, drove them from their farms and took forcible possession thereof. The details of what took place [are] harrowing, women were seduced, girls were ravished, some of them dying from the ill-treatment received, children at the breast were shot or cut down with their mothers.[41]

That same year, 1916, Ottoman deputy Emanuel Emanuelidi Efendi announced that some "550,000 [Greeks] ... were killed."[42] By this point, the slaughter had spread to the Armenian population; to the Assyrians of southeast Anatolia and Mesopotamia (present-day Iraq); and to the Pontian Greek population of the Black Sea coast. We will consider the experiences of these groups in turn.

THE ARMENIAN GENOCIDE

> It appears that a campaign of race extermination is in progress under a pretext of reprisal against rebellion.
>
> Ambassador Morgenthau to the US Secretary of State, July 16, 1915

As with the other Christian minorities, war catalyzed the onset of mass murder against the Armenians of the Ottoman empire. As early as December 1914 or January 1915, a special conference of the CUP issued a "strictly confidential" document ordering its agents to "close all Armenian Societies, and arrest all who worked against the Government at any time among them and send them into the provinces such as Bagdad or Mosul [i.e., in the distant eastern corner of the empire], *and wipe them out either on the road or there.*" Measures were to be implemented "to exterminate all males under 50, priests and teachers, leav[ing] girls and children to be Islamized," while also "kill[ing] off" all Armenians in the army.[43] This was essentially a blueprint for the genocide that followed.

In April 1915, just as the Allies were about to mount their invasion of the Dardanelles, the Turkish army launched an assault on Armenians in the city of Van, who were depicted as traitorous supporters of the Russian enemy. In scenes that have become central to Armenian national identity, the Armenians of Van organized a desperate resistance that succeeded in fending off the Turks for weeks. Eventually, the resistance was crushed, but it provided the "excuse" for genocide, with the stated justification of removing a population sympathetic to the Russian army. As one Young Turk, Behaeddin Shakir, wrote to a party delegate early in April: "It is the duty of all of us to effect on the broadest lines the realization of the noble project of wiping out of existence the Armenians who have for centuries been constituting a barrier to the Empire's progress in civilization."[44]

On April 24, in an act of "eliticide" in Constantinople and other major cities, hundreds of Armenian notables were rounded up and imprisoned. The great majority were subsequently murdered, or tortured and worked to death in isolated locales. (To the present, April 24 is commemorated by Armenians around the world as Genocide Memorial Day.) This was followed by a coordinated assault

Figure 4.1 The genocide of the Christian populations of present-day Turkey produced "the first international human rights movement in American history," according to poet and genocide scholar Peter Balakian. The campaign spearheaded by the American Committee for Relief in the Near East, symbolized by this contemporary poster, raised an astounding $116 million between 1915 and 1930—equivalent to over a billion dollars today. Nearly two million refugees benefited from the assistance.

Source: Wikimedia Commons.

on Armenians throughout most of the Armenian-populated zone; a few coastal populations were spared, but would be targeted later.

The opening phase of the assault consisted of a gendercide against Armenian males. Like the opening eliticide, this was aimed at stripping the Armenian community of those who might mobilize to defend it. Throughout the Armenian territories, males of "battle age" not already in the Ottoman Army were conscripted. In Ambassador Morgenthau's account, Armenians "were stripped of all their arms and transformed into workmen," then worked to death. In other cases, it "became almost the general practice to shoot them in cold blood."[45] By July 1915, some 200,000 Armenian men had been murdered,[46] reducing the remaining community "to a condition of near-total helplessness, thus an easy prey for destruction."[47]

The CUP authorities turned next to destroying the surviving Armenians. A "Temporary Law of Deportation" and "Temporary Law of Confiscation and Expropriation" were passed by the executive.[48] Armenians were told that they were to be transferred to safe havens. However, as Morgenthau wrote, "The real purpose of the deportation was robbery and destruction; it really represented a new method of massacre. When the Turkish authorities gave the orders for these deportations, they were merely giving the death warrant to a whole race; they understood this well, and, in their conversations with me, they made no particular attempt to conceal the fact."[49] Modern bureaucratic structures and communications technologies, especially the railroad and telegraph, were critical to the enterprise. In his most recent work, Taner Akçam (see Figure 4.16) has shown that the genocidal deportations—and renewed rounds of them in 1916–1917—were coordinated according to a sophisticated demographic strategy, aimed not necessarily at the extermination of the Armenians and other minorities *in toto*, but at scattering and fragmenting those not slaughtered so that they constituted no more than five or ten percent of the remaining population, which could then be considered "Turkified."[50]

The pattern of deportation was consistent throughout the realm, attesting to its central coordination.[51] Armenian populations were called by town criers to assemble in a central location, where they were informed that they would shortly be deported—a day to a week being the time allotted to frantically gather belongings for the journey, and to sell at bargain-basement prices whatever they could. The Italian consul general at Trebizond supplied a haunting account of the deportations from his city. Writing shortly after the events, Commissioner Giacomo Gorrini described

the lamentations, the tears, the abandonments, the imprecations, the many suicides, the instantaneous deaths from sheer terror, the sudden unhingeing of men's reason, the conflagrations, the shooting of victims in the city, the ruthless searches through the houses and in the countryside; the hundreds of corpses found every day along the exile road; the young women converted by force to Islam or exiled like the rest; the children torn away from their families or from the Christian schools, and handed over by force to Moslem families, or else placed by hundreds on board ship in nothing but their shirts, and then capsized and drowned in the Black Sea and the River Deyirmen Deré—these are my last ineffaceable memories of Trebizond, memories which still, at a month's distance, torment my soul and almost drive me frantic.[52]

Figure 4.2 A Danish missionary, Maria Jacobsen, took this photo of Armenian men in the city of Harput being led away for mass murder on the outskirts of town, May 1915.

Source: Maria Jacobsen/Courtesy Karekin Dickran's Danish-Armenian archive collection.

In scenes that prefigured the Nazi deportation of Jews, local populations eagerly exploited Armenians' dispossession. "The scene reminded me of vultures swooping down on their prey," wrote US Consul Leslie Davis. "It was a veritable Turkish holiday and all the Turks went out in their gala attire to feast and to make merry over the misfortunes of others. . . . [It was] the opportunity of a lifetime to get-rich-quick."[53] "Armenian women," wrote Faiz el-Ghusein in *Martyred Armenia*, "were sold like pieces of old furniture, at low prices, varying from one to ten liras, or from one to five sheep."[54]

Looting, pillage, and rapine were accompanied by a concerted campaign to destroy the Armenian cultural heritage. "Armenian monuments and churches were dynamited, graveyards were plowed under and turned into fields of corn and wheat, and the Armenian quarters of cities were torn down and used for firewood and scrap, or occupied and renamed."[55] The Armenian population was led away on foot—or in some cases dispatched by train—to the wastelands of the Deir el-Zor desert in distant Syria, in conditions calculated to kill tens of thousands en route.

Kurdish tribespeople swooped down to pillage and kill, but the main strike force mobilized for mass killing was the *chettes*, bands of violent convicts who had been active since the 1914 "cleansings" of the Aegean Greeks, released from prison to exterminate Armenians and other Christians. The genocide's organizers believed that using such forces "would enable the government to deflect responsibility. For as the death tolls rose, they could always say that 'things got out of control,' and it was the result of 'groups of brigands.'"[56]

Figure 4.3 "An Armenian woman kneeling beside a dead child in field 'within sight of help and safety at Aleppo,' an Ottoman city." Armenian children and women suffered systematic atrocities during the deportations; the minority that reached refuge were often on the verge of death from starvation, wounds, and exhaustion.

Source: American Committee for Relief in the Near East/Wikimedia Commons.

Figure 4.4 The US Ambassador to Constantinople, Henry Morgenthau, Sr., who fielded reports and firsthand accounts of the genocide from across Anatolia, and wrote a classic memoir of the period.

Source: Photographer unknown/from the original edition of *Ambassador Morgenthau's Story* (1918).

Attacks on the surviving children, women, and elderly of the deportation cara-vans gave rise to hellish scenes. "The whole course of the journey became a per-petual struggle with the Moslem inhabitants," wrote Morgenthau:

> Such as escaped . . . attacks in the open would find new terrors awaiting them in the Moslem villages. Here the Turkish roughs would fall upon the women, leaving them sometimes dead from their experiences or sometimes ravingly insane. . . . Frequently any one who dropped on the road was bayoneted on the spot. The Armenians began to die by hundreds from hunger and thirst. Even when they came to rivers, the gendarmes [guards], merely to torment them, would sometimes not let them drink.[57]

"In a few days," according to Morgenthau,

> what had been a procession of normal human beings became a stumbling horde of dust-covered skeletons, ravenously looking for scraps of food, eating any offal that came their way, crazed by the hideous sights that filled every hour of their existence, sick with all the diseases that accompany such hardships and privations, but still prodded on and on by the whips and clubs and bayonets of their executioners.[58]

In thousands of cases, children and women were kidnapped and seized by villagers; the women were kept as servants and sex-slaves, the children converted to Islam and raised as "Turks." One young male survivor described his group being gathered together in a field while word went out to the local population: "Whoever wants a woman or child, come and get them." "Albert said that people came and took whomever they wanted, comparing the scene to sheep being sold at an auction."[59]

BOX 4.1 ONE WOMAN'S STORY: ESTER AHRONIAN

Ester Ahronian remembered her childhood in the Anatolian town of Amasia as idyl-lic. "In the center of our courtyard we had a large mulberry tree with the sweetest mulberries I ever tasted. I would lie under the thick branches and reach up for hand-fuls of soft berries. Sometimes they fell off the branches onto my face and eyes. The cool, sweet juice ran down my cheeks into my ears. . . . I believed with all my heart that my world would never change. Nothing bad could ever happen to me."

But in May 1915, dark rumors began reaching Amasia—rumors of persecution of the Ottoman empire's Armenian population. One day, returning from school, Ahro-nian witnessed a young Armenian man being dragged to the town's central square and hanged. By the end of the month, "the streets were crowded with soldiers carrying rifles with fixed bayonets," and a Turkish leader of the town announced that all able-bodied Armenian males were to present themselves to the authorities. "I watched from my window as groups of men gathered daily in the street. Then, bunches of twenty or thirty were marched out of the city by the soldiers." "As soon as they are outside the city limits they will kill them and come back for more," a neighbor declared.

Shortly after, Ester observed a group of Turkish soldiers approaching an Armenian church. She "watched as a soldier threw a lit torch into an open window. The other soldiers laughed and shouted, 'Let's see your Christian God save you now. You will roast like pigs.' Then the screaming began . . ." Her father was taken away to detention by Turkish forces—never to be seen again. In the face of the mounting persecution, some Armenian girls agreed to be married to Muslim men, "promis[ing] never to speak the Armenian language or practice Christianity again." But Ester refused, and instead joined one of the caravans leaving Amasia as the town was emptied of its Christian population. "Aksor—the deportation word everyone in town was whispering. What did it mean? What would it be like?"

She soon learned. "We were only a half hour out of town when a group of Kurds charged down from the mountains and attacked the first group at the front of the caravan." The soldiers allegedly guarding them joined, instead, in the slaughter and pillage. "Then the soldiers came for the girls. The prettiest ones were taken first." Ester's grandmother clad her in baggy garb and smeared her with mud and raw garlic, and she was momentarily spared.

Her caravan "passed a deep pit by the side of the road filled with the naked bodies of young and old men." Another attack by soldiers: "Wagons were overturned. The sound of bullets filled the air. . . . Around us lay the dead and near-dead." Pausing by a river, she watched bodies and parts of bodies floating by. Almost comatose with trauma and exhaustion, she was seized by Kurds who thought she had expired; they stripped her and threw her "into a wagon filled with naked dead bodies. I lay there, not moving under the pile of rotting flesh." She was dumped with the bodies over a cliff. An elderly Armenian woman, disguising her ethnicity in order to work for Kurds, rescued her, and offered her a life-saving proposition: to toil as a domestic with a Muslim notable, Yousouf Bey, and his family. "Yes, if they'll have me, I'll work for them," Ester agreed.[60]

In Yousouf Bey's home, she overheard Turks boasting of their massacre of Armenians. She was told that when she had recovered from her ordeal, she would be married off to a Muslim. She entreated Yousouf Bay to release her. He agreed to send her to an orphanage in the city of Malatya—but before doing so, he drugged her and raped her, brutally taking her virginity. "It was his parting gift to me."

At the orphanage, "once a week, Turks came and took their pick of the girls. They chose as many as they wanted for cooks, field workers, housekeepers, or wives. Like slaves, no one asked any questions. No one had any choice." She was claimed by Shamil, a teenage Muslim boy, and forced to marry him. In Shamil's poor household, "three times a day we faced Mecca and chanted Muslim prayers." When she was discovered in possession of a cherished crucifix, Shamil whipped her until blood flowed.

Finally seizing her opportunity, Ester fled and took refuge with the Bagradians, one of the few Armenian families allowed to survive—they were blacksmiths, deemed essential laborers by the Turks. Finally, she was able to make her way back to her hometown of Amasia. "A heavy silence hung over the streets like a dark cloud. . . . I was returning to the scene of a violent crime." Approaching her house, she found it occupied by a Turkish woman. "You have no rights," the woman told her. "I'm leaving, so you can have your house back but I'm taking everything in it with me. If you make a fuss, I'll have you arrested." Hunkering down there, she discovered that "those Armenian families that remained in the city spoke only Turkish. All the Armenian churches were boarded up and stood as empty shadows against the clear sky."

She was befriended by Frau Gretel, the wife of a distant relative. Eventually, the war ended; but in 1920 a new wave of killings of Armenians descended. "Escape with us to America," Gretel implored her, and she consented. "The only thing I brought with me to America was my memory—the thing I most wanted to leave behind." Ester forged a new life on the east coast of the US, living to the ripe age of 98. Resident in an old-age home, she finally opened up to her daughter, Margaret, about her experiences during the genocide of Anatolia's Christian population. She disclaimed any feeling of hatred for her Turkish persecutors: "Hatred is like acid, it burns through the container. You must let go of bad memories." Margaret published her mother's recollections several years after Ester's death, in 2007.[61]

For those not abducted, the death marches usually meant extermination. Morgenthau cited one convoy that began with 18,000 people and arrived at its destination with 150. The state of most survivors was such that they often died within days of reaching refuge. J.B. Jackson, the US consul in Aleppo, Syria, recounted eyewitness descriptions of

over 300 women [who] arrived at Ras-el-Ain, at that time the most easterly station to which the German—Baghdad railway was completed, entirely naked, their hair flowing in the air like wild beasts, and after travelling six days afoot in the burning sun. Most of these persons arrived in Aleppo a few days afterwards, and some of them personally came to the Consulate and exhibited their bodies to me, burned to the color of a green olive, the skin peeling off in great

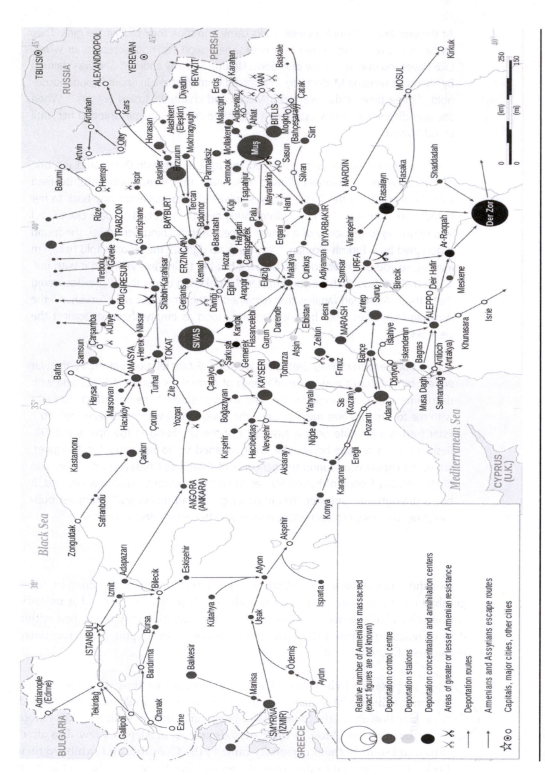

Map 4.1 The geography of the Armenian genocide.

Source: Map by Sémhur/Wikimedia Commons.

blotches, and many of them carrying gashes on the head and wounds on the body as a result of the terrible beatings inflicted by the Kurds.[62]

By 1917, between half and two-thirds of Ottoman Armenians had been exterminated. Large-scale massacres continued. In the final months of the First World War, Turkey crossed the Russian frontier and occupied sizable parts of Russian Armenia. There, according to Dadrian, "the genocidal engine of destruction unleashed by the Young Turk Ittihadists was once more activated to decimate and destroy the other half of the Armenian population living beyond the established frontiers of Turkey. . . . According to Soviet and Armenian sources, in five months of Turkish conquest and occupation about 200,000 Armenians of the region perished."[63] Meanwhile, "Armenians attacked civilian populations in Turkish towns and villages, massacring civilians and doing as much damage as they could. Having survived genocide, some of the Armenian irregulars were attempting to avenge the atrocities of 1915."[64]

THE ASSYRIAN GENOCIDE

In his careful research, beginning with a groundbreaking article in *Genocide Studies and Prevention* and continuing through his meticulous 2010 study of *Genocide in the Middle East*, Hannibal Travis has shown that the targeting of the Assyrians was fully comparable to that of the Armenians, in scale, strategy, and severity—and was recognized as such at the time it was inflicted. "The Assyrian genocide," he wrote, is "indistinguishable in principle from the Armenian genocide, despite being smaller in size":

> Starting in 1914 and with particular ferocity in 1915 and 1918, Ottoman soldiers and Kurdish and Persian militia subjected hundreds of thousands of Assyrians to a deliberate campaign of massacre, torture, abduction, deportation, impoverishment, and cultural and ethnic destruction. Established principles of international law outlawed this campaign of extermination before it was embarked upon, and ample evidence of genocidal intent has surfaced in the form of admissions by Ottoman officials. Nevertheless, the international community has been hesitant to recognize the Assyrian experience as a form of genocide.[65]

The foundation for the campaign against the Assyrians was an October 1914 edict from the Interior Ministry that the Assyrian population of the Van region should "depart." In June 1915, it was the same region that served as a flashpoint for both the Armenian and Assyrian mass killings, and the suffering of the Assyrian Christians was, as Travis says, "indistinguishable" from that of the Armenians. As David Gaunt describes the slaughter,

> The degree of extermination and the brutality of the massacres indicate extreme pent-up hatred on the popular level. Christians, the so-called *gawur*

215

infidels, were being killed in almost all sorts of situations. They were collected at the local town hall, walking in the streets, fleeing on the roads, at harvest, in the villages, in the caves and tunnels, in the caravanserais [travelers' inns], in the prisons, under torture, on the river rafts, on road repair gangs, on the way to be put on trial. There was no specific and technological way of carrying out the murders like the Nazis' extermination camps. A common feature was that those killed were unarmed, tied up, or otherwise defenseless. All possible means of killing were used: shooting, stabbing, stoning, crushing, throat cutting, throwing off of roofs, drowning, decapitation. Witnesses talk of seeing collections of ears and noses and of brigands boasting of their collections of female body parts.[66]

Joseph Naayem, an Assyro-Chaldean priest, received firsthand reports from the town of Sa'irt (also known as Seert) in Bitlis province. Assyro-Chaldean deaths in Sa'irt were later estimated as numbering 7,000 to 8,000—with massacres of Chaldeans substantially adding to the toll.[67] Naayem cited testimony that the *chettes* (Ottoman paramilitaries, usually criminals conscripted straight from jail) had gathered Sa'irt's men, marched them to the valley of Zeryabe, and massacred them. Women and girls were then set upon.[68] An Ottoman officer, Raphael de Nogales, described the aftermath:

> The ghastly slope was crowned by thousands of half-nude and still bleeding corpses, lying in heaps, or interlaced in death's final embrace. . . . Overcome by the hideous spectacle, and jumping our horses over the mountains of cadavers, which obstructed our passage, I entered Siirt with my men. There we found the police and the populace engaged in sacking the homes of the Christians. . . . I met various sub-Governors of the province . . . who had directed the massacre in person. From their talk I realized at once that the thing had been arranged the day before . . . Meanwhile I had taken up my lodging in a handsome house belonging to Nestorians, which had been sacked like all the rest. There was nothing left in the way of furniture except a few broken chairs. Walls and floors were stained with blood.[69]

Ambassador Morgenthau's account of the destruction of the Christian minorities asserted that the "same methods" of attack were inflicted on the Assyrians ("Nestorians" and "Syrians," as he called them) as on Armenians and Greeks. "The greatest crime of all ages," as he called it in a missive to the White House, was "the horrible massacre of helpless Armenians *and Syrians*."[70]

A British officer based in Persia, Sir Percy Sykes, later suggested that if the Assyrians had not fled in terror to northern Persia, they would have experienced "extermination at the hands of Turks and Kurds."[71] But as many as 65,000 died from exhaustion, malnourishment, and disease en route to refuge in Persia, or after their arrival.[72] The suffering of Assyrians in Mesopotamia (Iraq) was no less.[73] All told, "about half of the Assyrian nation died of murder, disease, or exposure as refugees during the war," according to Anglican Church representatives on the ground. "Famine and want were the fate of the survivors, whose homes, villages, churches and schools were wiped out."[74] The remnants of the Assyrian population of southeastern Anatolia crossed into Mesopotamia, then under British control, and settled in refugee camps there. The British brought no resolution to their plight, though a civil commissioner of the time acknowledged it was "largely of our own creation and a solution has been made more difficult by our own action, or rather inaction."[75] It is in that zone of present-day Iraq that their descendants have been exposed to new rounds of persecution, "ethnic cleansing," and genocidal killing, as described in Box 4a.

BOX 4.2 THE KURDS: TRAGEDY AND HOPE

I have always had a soft spot for the underdog,[76] hence for the Kurds. By most reckonings, they are the world's largest nation without a state to call their own—some thirty-two million people spread across southeastern Turkey, northern Iraq and Syria, and northwestern Iran. I have had the pleasure of traveling in all the major Kurdish regions except the Syrian one, and there is no denying that everywhere the Kurds leave an indelible impression: with their hospitality and gregariousness, their vigorous culture and colorful dress, their relatively emancipated women, their sense of collective destiny despite sometimes byzantine factional divisions.

The story of the Kurds in the twentieth century is one of genocide, betrayal, and resurrection. Unfortunately, the Kurds' initial experience with genocide was as its perpetrators. During the early twentieth century, and continuing through the full-scale holocaust of 1915–1917, Turkish tribespeople were instrumental in the Ottoman genocide against Armenians and Assyrians. With their hallowed tradition of raiding, looting, and vendetta, they were ideal agents of murder and rapine for the Ottoman authorities—who could thereby further divide the populations of the fractious southeast against each other.[77] As explored later in the chapter (see p. 237), numerous Kurdish spokespeople, organizations, and political parties have recently issued apologies for Kurdish complicity in the genocide of Ottoman Christians.

In Turkey in the late stages of the First World War and during its aftermath, the Kurds shifted from being agents of state violence to becoming its targets. This was evident as early as 1916–1917, when "hundreds of thousands were deported from their homelands," with "tens of thousands perish[ing] from privation."[78] In the Treaty of Sèvres (1920), the victorious allies promised the Kurds a homeland of their own in Anatolia. However, they backed away from the pledge in an attempt to court the new Turkish regime of Kemal Ataturk, and fearful of destabilizing the British and French mandates in Iraq and Syria. Instead, the Kurds were left marooned in three Arab-dominated countries, along with Persian Iran.[79] In Turkey, they rapidly fell afoul of the nationalizing, modernizing agenda of the Kemalist state.[80] Since Turkey was now to be for Turks alone, the existence of millions of Kurds was denied by a linguistic trope: they were merely "mountain Turks," and viewed with racist contempt. "For Ankara, the whole of Kurdish-dominated eastern Anatolia was an embarrassment, a throwback to the sort of backward, feud-ridden tribal society, to which Turkification was the state's unyielding riposte." Repeated clashes with rebellious Kurdish tribes, challenging the state's attempts to consolidate control over eastern Anatolia, led in 1937–1938 to one of the most ferocious (and least known) genocidal campaigns of that decade—against the Kurds of the Dersim region. Mark Levene described a "picture . . . of unadulterated and unforgiving atrocity," bearing all the hallmarks of a "colonial-style military massacre":

> of *aghas* [tribal leaders] and their retainers tortured and then brutally killed; of women and children burnt in haylofts—on specific occasions doused in kerosene and set alight; and of other instances, where they were bricked up in caves and these then set alight. There appear to have been instances where surrendering communities who had survived the artillery fire and aerial bombing of their towns or villages were then lined up and machine-gunned to death. And then, there were specific instances where the women and girls of the Kureyshan and Bakhtiyar tribes threw themselves from the high cliffs of the Munzur and Parchik ravines to avoid what they certainly would have perceived as a worse fate from the Turkish soldiery.[81]

Levene lamented that the Dersim genocide "is passed over in nearly all standard Western texts, either in silence or in the briefest and most opaque of commentaries." But this served "to reinforce the Kemalist point of the exercise. Until 1981 there was no further politico-military challenge to Ankara's authority from eastern Anatolia."[82] The *carte blanche* that the western powers (and the Soviet Union) gave Turkey to resolve its Kurdish "problem" also attests to the broad political indulgence of the Kemalist state, and (after World War Two) the various Turkish regimes incorporated into NATO and the western defense structure. This had important negative consequences not only for Kurdish nationalism, but for Armenian attempts to win recognition of the Turkish genocide against them, discussed at the chapter's close.

In the 1980s and 1990s, southeastern Turkey descended into civil war as *Peshmerga* of the Kurdistan Workers' Party (PKK) led a fierce resistance struggle, including targeted killings of Turkish soldiers, police, and civilians. The response of the Turkish state, then under the control of a military dictatorship, at times recalled the scorched-earth policies of the Dersim genocide—and the atrocities inflicted upon fellow Kurds in Saddam Hussein's Iraq during the same period (see below). Death squads linked to the Turkish "deep state" (the military/security apparatus) ran amok, killing and "disappearing" several thousand Kurds. Tens of thousands of Kurdish men were detained, interrogated, often tortured, and regularly

Figure 4.5 "Lost Girls of Dersim": Kurdish refugee women and their children in December 1937.
Source: Turkish Army image courtesy of Dünya Bülteni/Wikimedia Commons.

extrajudicially executed, in classic and gendercidal "filtration" strategies. In the cities, Kurdish politicians, journalists, and activists were hunted down. In the countryside and mountains, genocidal policies combined mass killing with much more massive displacement, à la Bangladesh in 1971 (see Box 8a) and the Balkan wars of the 1990s (Chapter 8). The Turkish government and military "sought to drain the swamp of support for the PKK" by inflicting sufficient indiscriminate violence to massively uproot the Kurdish civilian population. Tens of thousands of Kurds were killed in counterinsurgency sweeps, aerial and artillery bombardments, and through mass "disappearances" of alleged PKK activists. Fully 3 to 3.5 million Kurds fled the ravaged rural areas for shantytowns in the cities, or for refuge abroad[83]—one of the largest forced migrations anywhere in the world during the last half-century, comparable in scale to the dislocations and dispossessions of the current Syrian and Iraqi conflicts (see Box 4a).

Despite early peace feelers under the regime of Reccep Tayip Erdogan, these core patterns of violence, repression, and mass resistance have continued to the time of writing. In fact, they surged dramatically in 2015–2016, reflecting the prominent showing of the Kurdish-dominated Peoples' Democratic Party (HDP) in national elections, as well as the reverberations and cross-pollinations of war and insurgency in neighboring Iraq and Syria. At the end of 2015, *The New York Times* reported that renewed Turkish military assaults had "turned dozens of urban districts into bloody battlefields, displacing hundreds of thousands of civilians and shattering hopes of reviving peace as an old war reaches its deadliest level in two decades." Residents described "chaos and destruction" with "black smoke rising above shelled buildings and neighborhoods." "People are dying in their own homes," a teacher, Nurettin Kurtay, told the *Times*. "Our schools and our infrastructure has been destroyed. There is no difference between what is going on here and next door in Iraq and Syria." President Erdogan ratcheted up the rhetoric in a way that could only set alarm bells ringing among scholars of genocide and counterinsurgency. "You will be annihilated in those houses, those buildings, those ditches which you have dug." Erdogan pledged to "continue this fight until it"—the Kurdish region?—"has been completely cleansed and a peaceful atmosphere established." A Kurd who fled to Istanbul, Engin Gur, said: "The east of the country is burning . . . What people here in the west [of Turkey] do not realize is that we are one step away from a civil war."[84]

Like the Kurds of Turkey—one is tempted to say Kurds everywhere—those of Iraq had long chafed against centralized role. After peace feelers with the new Ba'thist regime proved abortive, the Kurdish Democratic Party (KDP) led Iraqi Kurds in full-scale

Figure 4.6 Demonstration against renewed Turkish military attacks on the country's Kurds, London, September 2015.
Source: Photo by Ron Fassbinder/The Weekly Bull/Flickr.

rebellion against the Ba'thist regime. As civil war ensued, 130,000 refugees fled to Iran. But in 1980, Iraq launched an opportunistic war against the new regime of the Ayatollahs in Iran.[85] It turned into one of the most protracted and arguably gendercidal meat-grinders of recent decades, with hundreds of thousands of soldiers, including young boys, killed in World War One-style trench warfare and massed assaults. In this climate of national emergency and total war, the Kurds were viewed as dangerous subversives, and the full force of state terror was unleashed against them. A particularly restive Kurdish clan, the Barzanis, was destroyed by gendercide and deportation in 1980. Eight thousand of its menfolk were rounded up, transported to southern Iraq, and murdered—a death toll on the order of the Srebrenica massacre in Bosnia in 1995 (see Chapter 8). The Barzanis had "betrayed the country," Hussein proclaimed, "and we meted out a stern punishment to them, and they went to hell."[86]

Yet Kurdish resistance persisted. In 1987, Saddam Hussein's cousin, Ali Hassan al-Majid, was assigned the task of imposing a "final solution" on the rebellious Kurdish population. In February–March 1988, the first of eight distinct "Anfal" operations was launched (the Arabic word means "the Spoils," and references a verse of the Koran). Though it was not strictly part of Anfal, the March 16, 1988 chemical attack on the Kurdish town of Halabja, which killed upward of 5,000 civilians, entered the record of twentieth-century infamy when photographers were able to reach the site from the Iranian side of the frontier (see Figures 4.7 and 4.8). It was "the world's first chemical assault against noncombatants."[87] It earned al-Majid the sobriquet "Chemical Ali," and in January 2010, execution at the hands of the post-Ba'thist regime for crimes against humanity.[88] Hussein himself had been hanged in 2006. But the atrocities that earned their architects the death penalty were not enough to arouse sustained international opposition at the time they were committed. Governments, both western and non-western, were too committed to supporting Iraq as a bulwark against Iran, too covetous of the country's oil, and too anxious to sell the Ba'thists their weapons and chemicals, to care much about the fate of a dispossessed minority.[89]

Throughout the Anfal genocide, the standard Iraqi strategy was to attack Kurdish settlements with artillery and airstrikes, conduct mass killings on the spot, and cart off the remainder of the population for "processing" further south. Hundreds of thousands of Kurds were trucked to concentration camps, most notoriously the Topzawa camp near the northern Iraqi city of Kirkuk. There the standard gendercidal selection procedure was implemented, with adult and teenage males separated for execution. The operations of the killers were "uncannily reminiscent of . . . the activities of the *Einsatzkommandos*, or mobile killing units, in the Nazi-occupied lands of Eastern Europe" (see Chapter 6), with prisoners "lined up, shot from the front, and dragged into predug mass graves . . . Bulldozers then pushed earth or sand loosely over the heaps of corpses."[90] Children, women, and the elderly were also swept up in the mass executions, killed in bombardments and gassings, or selectively targeted after the "battle-age" males had been destroyed.

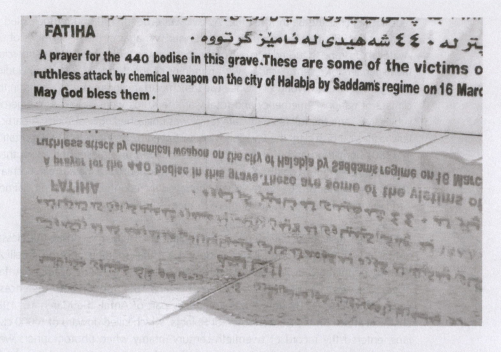

Figures 4.7 and 4.8 Remembering the Anfal genocide: a memorial in the city of Halabja, Iraq, commemorating the chemical attack of March 1988; a photograph from an exhibition in Rizgary, southern Kurdistan, depicts a woman survivor holding a letter from a "disappeared" relative.

Sources: Author's photos, April 2011.

Others perished from starvation or disease in the concentration camps. Some three thousand villages were destroyed,[91] and at least 100,000 Kurds—Kurdish estimates range up to 180,000—perished in Anfal, "systematically put to death in large numbers by order of the central Iraqi government."[92]

At the end of the 1991 Gulf War, Kurdish aspirations for autonomy were finally realized. When Kurds rose up in renewed rebellion, Hussein—a ceasefire with Allied forces freshly signed—turned his army against them. Hundreds of thousands fled to Iran and Turkey, prompting the Allies to create a safe area and no-fly zone. This provided the Kurds with a territorial autonomy that was further entrenched after the 2003 fall of the Ba'thist regime, and has lasted until the present.[93]

The proto-state that Iraqi Kurds have established in northern Iraq is one of the most intriguing actors in international relations. As an oil-rich territory with ambitions to control even more oil-rich territory, it has positioned itself as a viable and prosperous entity with a capital, Erbil, that resembles the Gulf states in its peripatetic construction and booming economic activity. It has allied itself with the "war on terror"—providing the most reliable foot-soldiers in the battle against Islamic State (see Box 4a); welcoming tens of thousands of refugees from elsewhere in Iraq, including thousands of Christians, and providing protection to minorities outside Kurdistan proper;[94] offering the use of its prisons to the US military for the detention (sometimes indefinite) of accused rebels and militants;[95] and demonstrating a degree of internal security that the remainder of Iraq could only dream of. (In this, Kurdish authorities have benefited "from the most decisive factor in counterinsurgency: a civilian population completely aligned with the government against suicidal car bombers and mass murderers."[96]) At a time when Turkey has renewed its assaults on Kurds across the border, Iraqi Kurdistan has worked nimbly to sidestep the conflict, dependent as it is on the Turks for the bulk of the statelet's imports (including, ironically, gasoline—Kurdistan is rich in petroleum but not in refineries). This has included allowing Turkish bombing raids on PKK bases inside Iraqi Kurdish territory.[97]

Within the Iraqi federation, the Kurdistan Regional Government (KRG)—its official name, though a Kurdish national flag flies everywhere—poses as a "team player." Despite numerous tensions with the central authority, and internally as well, the KRG has officially supported Iraqi federalism, and presented itself as a model of pluralism, democracy, and development for the rest of the country to follow. But the effective collapse of Iraqi central-state authority in northern Iraq has allowed the Kurds, no less than the extremists of Islamic State, to exploit the vacuum of power and expand their political and military control. Kurds have long nurtured aspirations of seizing the oil-rich region around Kirkuk—a historically Kurdish center, but also a patchwork of ethnicities, including Turkmens, indigenous Arabs, and tens of thousands of southern Sunnis imported by the Ba'thists to erode the Kurds' demographic preponderance. The crisis of 2014–2016, with IS's declaration of a

Mosul-based "caliphate" (Box 4a), brought Kirkuk firmly in the grasp of Kurdish Peshmerga forces, which were also able to extend their control of the disputed Nineveh plains abutting Mosul. They benefited from the "pragmatic considerations" of the "vulnerable religious minorities," including Yazidis and Shia Shabaks, that have demonstrated "unprecedented support for the Peshmerga."[98] But there have also been widespread reports of Peshmerga-inflicted atrocities against communities accused of harboring or otherwise supporting Islamic State. In February 2015, for example, Human Rights Watch accused Iraqi Kurdish forces of "confin[ing] thousands of Arabs in 'security zones' in areas of northern Iraq." The Peshmerga had "barred Arabs displaced by fighting from returning to their homes in portions of Ninewa and Erbil provinces, while permitting Kurds to return to those areas and even to move into homes of Arabs who fled." KRG soldiers were likewise alleged to have detained Arab males for long periods and "destroyed dozens of Arab homes in the areas, which the KRG appears to be seeking to incorporate into Kurdish autonomous territory." Human Rights Watch detected a consistent pattern of "apparently discriminatory acts," which KRG authorities defended on the grounds that the communities in question had collaborated with IS and might do so again.[99] Amnesty International followed in January 2016 with a condemnation and satellite imagery of the systematic destruction of Arab homes and properties in Pershmerga-controlled zones.[100]

In Syria, comment and controversy have swirled around the People's Protection Units (YPG) in the strip of Kurdish-controlled territory dubbed Rojava (from the Kurdish word for "sun") along the Turkish border. For Turkey, the resilience of the YPG, the military wing of the Democratic Union Party (PYD), and its successes in 2015 in seizing territory from Islamic State, raised anxieties about "a strong new Kurdish entity emerging in Syria."[101] Erdogan's government reacted to the rise of Rojava with hardline policies aimed at strangling the quasi-state in its infancy. For many on the global left, this bolstered the image of the PYD/YPG as a brave underdog threatened by two powerful states (Turkey and Syria) and a reactionary/theocratic non-state actor (IS). Meanwhile, the social order established in Rojava evoked the kind of enthusiasm among progressives that was once directed toward the Sandinista revolutionaries in Nicaragua, the FMLN guerrillas in El Salvador, and the EPLF rebels battling for Eritrean secession from Ethiopia. In all these cases, nationalist/anti-imperialist struggles were combined with far-reaching social transformations, especially with regard to popular democracy, cultural revival, and women's new rights and roles. For many, the iconic image of the People's Defense Units is their women's battalions (the YPJ), fighting both Islamic State and the "patriarchal norms of their own culture"[102] (see Figure 4.9; I hope that is enough acronyms for one paragraph).

As with the Iraqi Kurds, however, the lionizing of the YPG obscured a darker and more destructive component. As the Kurds rolled back the militants of Islamic State in northern Syria, symbolized by the recapture of the key city of Kobani, Amnesty

Figure 4.9 Fighters of the Women's Protection Units (YPJ) guarding the Kurdish quasi-state in northern Syria, March 2014.

Source: Kurdishstruggle/Creative Commons/Flickr.

International accused them of inflicting "a wave of forced displacement and home demolitions amounting to war crimes," principally against Arab and Turkmen populations. Amnesty posted images of the village of Husseiniya before and after its occupation by the YPG, showing "225 buildings standing in June 2014 but only 14 remaining in June 2015—a shocking reduction of 93.8%." Residents told the investigators of threats intended to coerce them into flight, including retribution from the coalition fighting IS: "They told us we had to leave or they would tell the US coalition that we were terrorists and their planes would hit us and our families." While the YPG justified the widespread displacement as "necessary for the civilians' own protection or militarily necessary," Amnesty called its actions "a violation of international humanitarian law."[103] Clearly, there was much that was admirable in these Kurdish social experiments—and attractive to some minority populations that saw Kurdish forces as the most viable shield against IS. But the temptation to consolidate political control through ethnic "cleansing" and reconfiguring remained a potent one for the increasingly powerful and influential Kurds, no less than for other actors in the Iraqi and Syrian imbroglios.

THE PONTIAN GREEK GENOCIDE

Approximately 350,000 Pontian Greeks are believed to be among the Christian minorities slaughtered between 1914 and 1922. The Turks began targeting the millennia-old community along the Black Sea coast as early as 1916. Their extermination therefore long predated the renewed killings and persecutions of the post–World War One period, accompanying the Greek invasion of Anatolia. Missionary testimony cited by George Horton in his account of the late-Ottoman genocides, *The Blight of Asia*, dated the onset of "the Greek deportations from the Black Sea" to January 1916:

> These Greeks came through the city of Marsovan by thousands [reported a missionary], walking for the most part the three days' journey through the snow and mud and slush of the winter weather. Thousands fell by the wayside from exhaustion and others came into the city of Marsovan in groups of fifty, one hundred and five hundred, always under escort of Turkish gendarmes. Next morning these poor refugees were started on the road and destruction by this treatment was even more radical than a straight massacre such as the Armenians suffered before.[104]

BOX 4.3 ONE WOMAN'S STORY: SANO HALO

Figure 4.10 Sano Halo (seated at left), aged 100, takes her oath of honorary Greek citizenship at the Greek consulate in New York City, June 11, 2009. Sano was accompanied by her daughter Thea Halo, who told Sano's story of surviving the Pontian Greek genocide in her book *Not Even My Name*. Sano died in 2014, just shy of her 105th birthday.

Source: Photo by Costas Euthalitsidis/Courtesy of Thea Halo.

Once Sano was Themia: like so many survivors of genocide, she was stripped of her name along with the life she was born into, in the Pontian Greek-dominated region along the Black Sea coast, in 1909.

"We never thought that one day we would be forced to leave our paradise," Sano related in her daughter Thea's memoir, *Not Even My Name*. "Our history went back too far to believe that, and we had survived invasion after invasion for 3,000 years. By the time of Alexander the Great's short rule between 336 and 323 BC, Greeks had already been living in Asia Minor, or Ionia as they called it, for over

800 years. . . . Pontus flourished as a great commercial and educational center. After decades of war, the Romans finally conquered the kingdom of Pontus in 63 BC. But the Greek culture continued to have great influence. The conquered gave culture to the conqueror."

During the First World War, Halo's mountain village was not attacked, but her father was one of the many Greek men swept up by the notorious labor battalions, or *Amele Tabourou*. He managed to escape, and conveyed a chilling report to his family: "The camps are cold and full of vermin. We're worked day and night without enough food to eat or a decent place to sleep or wash. In some camps the Greeks are just left to die with nothing at all. Even when the war was still being fought, the Turks left the Greeks behind to be killed without arms to defend themselves or food to eat. I think that's what they want, for all of us to die."

When Themia and her family were finally swept up in the carnage, in 1921–1922, the campaign bore the same genocidal hallmarks of massacre and death march that had been deployed against diverse Christian populations during the war period. Themia and her family were launched on a march that lasted "for seven to eight months from the frigid mountainous regions of the north through the desert-like plains of the south without concern for food, water, or shelter." The landscape changed from green to "jagged cliffs and parched, coarse earth . . . The sun beat down on us all day . . ." After four months, Themia's "shoes wore out completely. Walking through this barren land with bare feet was like walking on pitted glass. The food we had brought was also gone. Each day brought another death, another body left to decompose on the side of the road. Some simply fell dead in their tracks. Their crumpled bodies littered the road like pieces of trash flung from a passing cart, left for buzzards and wolves."[105]

To save her from starvation, Themia's mother left her with an Assyrian family in the south of Turkey, where she received the Kurdish name Sano. After she ran away, an Armenian family took Themia in and brought her to Aleppo, Syria. There she was presented to Abraham, an Assyrian Christian who had emigrated to America twenty years before. She agreed to marry him, beginning a new life across the oceans and surviving to the present day. In 2000, her daughter Thea published Sano's story, based in part on a journey that mother and daughter made to the Pontian village of Sano's youth. In 2009, on her centennial birthday, Sano was granted honorary Greek citizenship (see Figure 4.10). Sano Halo "died peacefully at home in her sleep on April 28, 2014, just two weeks shy of her 105th birthday."[106]

As the Paris Peace Negotiations ground on in 1919, the victorious Allies invited Greece, which had joined their side in 1917, to occupy the city of Smyrna on Turkey's Aegean coast. A large Greek community still resided there, even after the 1914–1915 "cleansings," and by the end of the war, the Christian population

Figure 4.11 "Weeding Out the Men: All men of military age were torn away from their wives and children and led away in groups for deportation to the interior" (original caption). Image from the Pontian Greek genocide—the date is given as 1915; the precise location is uncertain.

Source: George Horton, *The Blight of Asia* (1926)/Pontian.info.[107]

of the city had been swelled by Armenian and Assyrian refugees. The 1920 Treaty of Sèvres, though never implemented, formally recognized Greece's intervention.

The problems associated with the decision to dispatch Turkey's historic enemy to occupy a major city and stretch of Turkish coastline were compounded by the further failure to specify how far the Greek zone of occupation extended. The result was a violent occupation of Smyrna in 1919, with the Greeks and fellow Christians inflicting atrocities while "pacifying" the city and expanding into surrounding areas. This was followed by an opportunistic invasion of the Anatolian heartland.[108] Ill-judged, abjured by the Allies, increasingly unpopular with the Greek population and its soldiers, this invasion was also accompanied by atrocities and destruction, in proclaimed vengeance for the wartime genocides of Greeks and other Christians. The atrocities and the strategic nature of the invasion appeared to "put the very survival of any Turkish state in question," wrote historian Benjamin Lieberman. ". . . With the Greek invasion there was no obvious end in sight, no boundary to fall back on, and no security for a new Turkey. Many Turks saw their nation threatened by nothing less than extermination."[109]

Turkish fury and vengefulness ignited a further genocidal explosion against Anatolian Greeks, including Pontians, before the Greek army was finally driven from Turkish soil at Smyrna in 1922. The resultant Turkish-directed destruction of Smyrna by fire has become a poignant symbol of the catastrophe of Ottoman Greeks.[110]

An estimate of the Pontian Greek death toll at all stages of the anti-Christian genocide is about 350,000; for all the Greeks of the Ottoman realm taken together, the toll surely exceeded half a million, and may approach the 900,000 killed that a team of US researchers found in the early postwar period. Most surviving Greeks were expelled to Greece as part of the tumultuous "population exchanges" that set the seal on a heavily "Turkified" state. Apart from an anti-Greek pogrom in Istanbul in 1955 (the culmination of a series that reduced the Greek population from 297,788 in 1924 to fewer than 3,000 today),[111] only the restive Kurdish minority remained to challenge ethnic-Turkish hegemony within the new state boundaries. The Kurds, accordingly, were mercilessly repressed from the 1930s to the 1980s, a story that lies beyond the bounds of this account.[112]

AFTERMATH: ATTEMPTS AT JUSTICE

Turkey's defeat in the First World War, and the subsequent collapse and occupation of the Ottoman Empire, offered surviving Armenians an opportunity for national self-determination. In 1918, an independent Republic of Armenia was declared in the southwestern portion of Transcaucasia, a historically Armenian territory that had been under Russian sovereignty since the early nineteenth century. US President Woodrow Wilson was granted the right to delimit a new Armenian nation,

Figure 4.12 Armenian orphan boys at Anatolia College in Merzifon in 1918, as the world war and Ottoman genocide abated.
Source: Tsolag Dildilian/Wikimedia Commons.

formalized at the Treaty of Sèvres in 1920. Later that year, Wilson supervised the drawing of boundaries for independent Armenia that included parts of historic Ottoman Armenia in eastern Turkey.

Turkey, however, staged a rapid political recovery following its abject military defeat. The new leader, Mustafa Kemal (known as Ataturk, "father of the Turks"), repelled the Greek invasion through the bloody and indiscriminate countermeasures as described above; renounced the Sèvres Treaty; and in a secret gathering, declared it "indispensable that Armenia be annihilated politically and physically."[113] The Kemalist forces invaded, and reconquered six of the former Ottoman provinces that had been granted to independent Armenia under Sèvres. What remained of Armenia was swallowed up by the new Soviet Union. Following a brief period of cooperation with Armenian nationalists, the Soviets took complete control in 1921, and Armenia was incorporated into the Transcaucasian Soviet Federated Socialist Republic (TSFSR) in 1922. A separate Armenian Soviet Socialist Republic was created in 1936. Greeks had nearly all been killed or expelled, and surviving Assyrian populations were clustered outside Anatolia, under British mandatory control in Mesopotamia. The stage was set for the rebirth of Turkish nationalism and the resuscitation of Turkish statehood.

In the interim (1918–1920) between the Ottoman collapse and the ascendancy of the Ataturk regime, and at the insistence of the Allies (who, as early as 1915, with an eye on the postwar dismemberment of the Turkish heartland, had accused the Young Turk rulers of "crimes against humanity"), the Turkish government—at British insistence, and in the hope of winning more favorable terms from the Allies

Figure 4.13 A statue in Istanbul's Taksim Square of Mustafa Kemal, known as Ataturk—"father of the Turks"—in the early 1920s. After the crushing defeat of the First World War, Ataturk used his common touch and charisma to rally the Turks to expel foreign occupiers and restore Anatolia as the heartland of a post-Ottoman state. He modernized and secularized Turkish society, and established the country as an influential and strategic player in international politics. But the Turkish ethnonationalism that he both mobilized and catalyzed has proved to be a volatile quantity. It led to further massacres of Christians in the early Kemalist period, and the marginalization and persecution of the country's large Kurdish minority thereafter. And it impeded Turks' honest engagement with their country's past, including the genocides of the First World War period. Turks are, of course, hardly alone in such nationalistic/patriotic hubris and selective readings of history. See Chapters 2, 10, 14, and 16 for examples and further discussion.

Source: Author's photo, May 2011.

at the Paris Peace Conference—held a remarkable series of trials of those accused of directing and implementing the Armenian genocide.

In April 1919, the Court pronounced that "the disaster visiting the Armenians was not a local or isolated event. It was the result of a premeditated decision taken by a central body . . . and the immolations and excesses which took place were based on oral and written orders issued by that central body."[114] Over a hundred former government officials were indicted, and a number were convicted, with Talat, Enver, and a pair of other leadership figures sentenced to death in absentia. After three relatively minor figures were executed, nationalist sentiment in Turkey exploded, greatly strengthening Ataturk's revolution. The British Foreign Office reported that "not one Turk in a thousand can conceive that there might be a Turk who deserves to be hanged for the killing of Christians"[115]—and in the face of that opposition and Allied pandering, the impetus for justice began to waver. "Correspondingly the sentences grew weaker, as the court refrained from handing down death sentences, finding most of the defendants only 'guilty of robbery, plunder, and self-enrichment at the expense of the victims.'"[116]

Eventually, in a tactic duplicated by Serbs in Bosnia-Herzegovina decades later (Chapter 8), Ataturk took dozens of British hostages from among the occupying forces. For Britain, which had decided some time earlier that the best policy was "cutting its losses," this was the final straw.[117] Anxious to secure the hostages' release, and to placate the new Turkish regime, the British freed many of the Turks in its custody. In July 1923, the Allies signed the Treaty of Lausanne with the Turks, which made no mention of the independent Armenia pledged at Sevres. It was an "abject, cowardly and infamous surrender," in the estimation of British politician Lloyd George.[118]

Denied formal justice, Armenian militants settled on a vigilante version. All three of the main organizers of the genocide were assassinated: Talat Pasha in Berlin in 1921, at the hands of Soghomon Tehlirian, who had lost most members of his family in the genocide; Enver Pasha while leading an anti-Bolshevik revolt in Turkestan in 1922 (in an ambush "led by an Armenian Bolshevik officer");[119] and Jemal Pasha, by Armenians in Tiflis in 1922.

TURKEY: DENIAL . . . AND GROWING RECOGNITION

"The evidence [of the Armenian genocide] is so overwhelming that its denial clearly stems from a collective neurosis."[120] Nonetheless, for decades such denial has been force-fed to the international community by a sustained Turkish government campaign. As Bloxham summarized, Turkey has "written the Armenians out of its history books, and systematically destroyed Armenian architecture and monuments to erase any physical traces of an Armenian presence." Moreover, "Armenian genocide denial is backed by the full force of a Turkish state machinery that has pumped substantial funding into public-relations firms and American university endowments to provide a slick and superficially plausible defence of its position."[121] In these efforts (analyzed in comparative context in Chapter 14), Turkey has been greatly assisted by its alliance with the US.[122] For the US, Turkey was critically important in the "containment" of the Soviet Union during the Cold War. Today, it is seen as a secular bulwark against Muslim-fundamentalist ferment in the Middle East. Accordingly, US military leaders, as well as "security"-minded politicians, have played a key role in denial of the genocide.[123] The close US–Turkish relationship means that Turkish studies in the United States is well-funded, not only through Turkish government sources, but thanks to the large number of contractors (mainly arms manufacturers) who do business with Turkey.

In recent years, however, the denial efforts of the Turkish government and its supporters have met with decreasing success. According to the tally of the Armenian National Institute in early 2016, twenty-six countries and the Vatican city-state had passed resolutions recognizing the genocide.[124] To this can be added the International Center for Transitional Justice, with perhaps the most nuanced legal reading of the Armenians' *Mets Yeghern* (Great Catastrophe).[125] A 1998 resolution by the French National Assembly consisted of a single sentence reading, "France recognizes the Armenian genocide of 1915."[126] This was passed over strong Turkish objections and threats of economic reprisals against French companies doing business with Turkey. In April 2004, the Canadian House of Commons recognized "the death of 1.5 million Armenians between 1915 and 1923 as a genocide . . . and condemn this act as a crime against humanity."[127] Most recently, in June 2016, the German Parliament voted "nearly unanimous[ly]" for recognition, prompting another angry riposte from the Turkish government.[128]

The United States still held out. President-to-be Barack Obama expressed his support on the campaign trail for formal recognition of the Armenian genocide, including the proposed congressional resolution, while campaigning in 2008: "As a US Senator, I have stood with the Armenian American community in calling for Turkey's acknowledgement of the Armenian Genocide." But as president, he has refrained from issuing a presidential declaration on the subject—as he pledged to do—and he carefully avoided using the word "genocide" during his April 2009 visit to Turkey.[129] He continued to do so throughout the remainder of his presidency, though he did employ the Armenian term, *Meds Yeghern*, on several occasions.[130] In 2015, an unnamed US official again rejected use of the "genocide" label: "We know and respect that there are some who are hoping to hear different language this year. We understand their perspective . . . [but] the approach we have taken in previous years remains the right one, both for acknowledging the past, and for our ability to work with regional partners to save lives in the present." According to Noah Bierman of *The Los Angeles Times*, this was "a reference to U.S. hope for cooperation from Turkey, particularly in the civil war in Syria."[131]

One reason cited for Obama's demurral was the sensitive question of Turkish–Armenian relations, which had been frozen since the outbreak of war between Armenia and Azerbaijan over the disputed Armenian-majority territory of Nagorno-Karabakh (hereafter, Karabakh). Turkish prime minister Reccep Tayip Erdogan took power as the leader of the moderate-Islamist Justice and Development Party (AKP) in the transformative 2002 general election. Turkey supported a multitrack peace process between Armenia and Azerbaijan that nearly culminated in an agreement to reestablish diplomatic and economic relations in 2009, until Erdogan bowed to intense appeals for Muslim and "Turkic" solidarity by the Azerbaijani government, and declared their border would remain closed until the Karabakh issue was resolved.

Before Turkey backed away, however, the negotiators had agreed to set aside the genocide recognition issue, establishing only a joint "impartial historical commission" to examine the matter. This drove a notable wedge into a little-explored element of the political equation: relations between the government and population of independent Armenia, on one hand, and the far-flung diaspora of Armenians, concentrated especially in Lebanon and the United States. Many diaspora Armenians, for whom the genocide of 1915 was "a core part of their identity,"[132] argued that establishing a fact-finding commission implied that the historical veracity of the genocide remained to be determined. In Armenia itself, however, the unifying cause was the struggle first to conquer, then to hold onto Karabakh. (The diaspora backed the project also, including supplying the $10 million required to build a modern highway connecting Armenia and Armenian-conquered Karabakh, via the "Lachin corridor" through a further swath of occupied Azerbaijani territory.) According to Thomas de Waal, the word "genocide" was more likely to be deployed in Armenia against the Azerbaijani "Turks" in the context of the Karabakh conflict, rather than with regard to the holocaust a century distant.[133] They were prepared to be flexible on the question of Turkish recognition of the Ottoman genocide: more flexible, certainly, than on the territory of Karabakh, from which the last two presidents of Armenia have hailed. Gerard Libaridian, a historian who served as a foreign policy advisor to the first post-independence government in Armenia, put it bluntly: "Do we want Turkey to recognize the Genocide? Of course. But is that a pre-condition [for negotiations]? Of course not. Why not? Because that doesn't resolve any particular issue that the country is facing, that our people are facing."[134]

Within Turkey, policy remained marked by "advances, ambiguities, and reversals."[135] But the advances were notable, even dramatic, at the level of both government and civil society. After 2002, the new administration of Recep Tayyip Erdogan (then prime minister, now president; see Figure 4.14) reined in anti-Armenian

Figure 4.14 Turkish president Recep Tayyip Erdogan. Leading the originally moderate-Islamist Justice and Development party (AKP), and arguably steering contemporary Turkey in an increasingly Islamist direction, Erdogan has also confronted the continuing "history wars" over Ottoman-era genocides. He has shifted the official Turkish position very little: considerations of national "honor" and *Realpolitik* still underpin widespread reticence and denialism at the state level. But transformations in Turkish civil society have spawned increased ties between ethnic Turks and Armenians (see Figure 4.17), acknowledgments of the Armenian genocide, and several prominent apologies for it. Erdogan is shown speaking in the Polish Senate in November 2013. In the past several years, the spillover of the Syrian civil war— and Erdogan's meddling in it—have prompted renewed largescale assaults on Turkey's Kurdish population in the southeast, as well as against Kurdish-led forces in Syria and Iraq (see Box 4.2).

Source: Photo by Michal Jozefaciuk, Senat Rzeczypospolitej Polskiej/Wikimedia Commons.

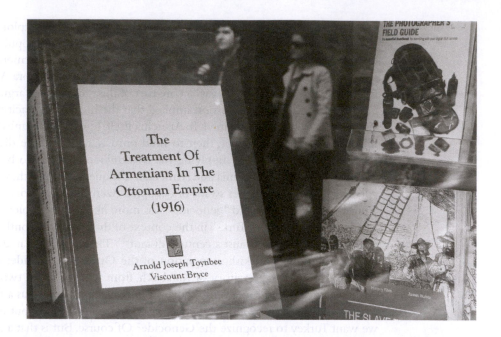

Figure 4.15 The 1916 British government publication, *The Treatment of Armenians in the Ottoman Empire*—the so-called "Blue Book"—was long dismissed by Turkey and its supporters as an enemy concoction at the height of the world war. It is in fact a reliable compilation of testimonies and documentation pertaining to the Ottoman genocides of Christian populations. To see it prominently displayed in a bookstore window in Turkey's showcase metropolis, Istanbul, was eye-catching indeed. The fact that the window remained unsmashed also attested to a new tolerance in Turkish society for reminders of the "shameful act" against the Armenians and other Christians.

Source: Author's photo, May 2011.

propaganda, and made halting moves toward recognition and reconciliation.[136] In 2011, Erdogan formally apologized to the country's Kurdish population for the mass killing of tens of thousands of Kurds in 1938–1939 in the Dersim genocide (see Box 4.2).[137] As the Kurds were Muslim coreligionists, this was an easier stance for Erdogan to take than acknowledging mass atrocities against Ottoman Christians would have been. He still reserved the word "genocide" for crimes against Muslims worldwide—the term was inapplicable to Turkey, Erdogan claimed, because "a Muslim could not commit genocide, by definition."[138] Erdogan became the country's first elected president in August 2014; in the run-up to the vote, with Armenians around the world preparing for the April 24 commemoration, he offered an unprecedented but still heavily-hedged statement of sympathy: "We wish that the Armenians who lost their lives in the context of the early twentieth century rest in peace, and we convey our condolences to their grandchildren."[139] His equivocal stance, and the broader process of democratization that the AKP symbolized, opened space for others to take the lead: on a 2015 visit to Istanbul, for example, I was surprised to see a copy of the British-authored "Blue Book" on Ottoman atrocities against their Christian subjects prominently displayed in a bookstore window (see Figure 4.15). In 2012, one of Turkey's best-known journalists, Hasan

Cemal, published a work titled simply *1915: The Armenian Genocide*, "a shockingly straightforward account of this historic event" which "became a bestseller, piled high in bookstore windows and fuelling intellectual debate."[140]

Arguably more significant were the transformations underway in Turkish society and intellectual culture. In September 2005, a groundbreaking academic conference was held at Bilgi University on the "Ottoman Armenians during the Decline of the Empire." In a tense atmosphere characterized by threats, legal challenges, and demonstrations, some two hundred academics participated, including Turkish intellectuals who asserted that they used the term "Armenian genocide" in their work. The brave scholarship of Taner Akçam, notably his key works *A Shameful Act* and *The Young Turks' Crime Against Humanity* (see Further Study), deepened understanding of the genocide. Akçam visited his homeland, was granted access to key Turkish archives to pursue his investigations, and found Turkish publishers for his books.[141] But he also chose to base himself outside Turkey—at Clark University in Massachusetts, where he holds the Chair in Armenian Genocide Studies. Even in the United States, his speaking appearances remain controversial; when I saw Akçam speak at the Holocaust Museum Houston in July 2015 (see Figure 4.16), police were on hand for his and the audience's protection. Other prominent figures who have spoken about the genocide, including the Nobel Prize-winning author Orhan Pamuk, have likewise been hounded, threatened, and charged with the serious (but also rather comical) "crime" of "insulting Turkishness."[142]

A critical figure in promoting dialogue and reconciliation was the Turkish-Armenian activist and newspaper editor, Hrant Dink—a "born communicator,"

Figure 4.16 Taner Akçam, who now teaches at Clark University in Massachusetts, is the leading Turkish exponent of Armenian genocide recognition. His diligent research in Ottoman/Turkish archives has added immeasurably to our understanding of the genocides against the Armenians and other Christian minorities. He is shown here speaking at the Holocaust Museum Houston in August 2015.

Source: Photo by Kelly Webeck/Courtesy Holocaust Museum Houston.

Figure 4.17 In summer 2015, the centenary of the Armenian genocide, I encountered these two young Turkish citizens at the genocide memorial and museum in Yerevan, capital of the Armenian republic. They were members of the Hrant Dink Society, which commemorates the life and martyrdom of Turkey's most prominent advocate for the Armenian cause. With the Turkish-Armenian frontier still closed, they had journeyed via neighboring Georgia to reach Yerevan and the memorial. I photographed them in front of a display dedicated to Dink, including his massive funeral procession in Istanbul. See the main text for further discussion.

Source: Author's photo, June 2015.

according to the Turkish academic Cengiz Aktar, who "was capable of convincing the worst denialist in 20 minutes—and this is probably why he was assassinated."[143] Indeed, on January 19, 2007, Dink was shot to death in an Istanbul street by a Turkish youth from the heavily-nationalist city of Trabzon. The assassin and one of his co-conspirators were sentenced to lengthy prison terms, though many in Turkey believed the origins of the plot lay in the Turkish "deep state," dominated by diehard militarists and nationalists who viewed Dink as a subversive and a traitor. Dink's funeral produced extraordinary scenes, as some two hundred thousand Turkish mourners marched in his procession: "cries of *Hepimiz Ermeniz* ('We are all Armenians!') [sounded] in the throats of tens of thousands of Turks."[144] The following year, a quartet of Turkish intellectuals—Ahmet Insel, Baskin Oran, Ali Bayramoglu, and Cengiz Aktar—risked the wrath of the state and nationalist vigilantes by issuing a "public apology" for the Armenian genocide, in which the signatories declared:

> My conscience does not accept the insensitivity showed to and the denial of
> the Great Catastrophe that the Ottoman Armenians were subjected to in 1915.
> I reject this injustice and for my share, I empathise with the feelings and pain of
> my Armenian brothers. I apologise to them.[145]

Ayşe Günaysu of the Turkish Human Rights Association likewise recognized the
genocide unconditionally. "Recognition is a prerequisite, without which nothing
else is possible. It's a moral and ethical position, and nothing must be expected in
return. We must humbly make amends because it was our ancestors who carried
out the genocide."[146] An especially vocal figure has been Osman Baydemir, the
mayor of the predominantly Kurdish, perennially restive city of Diyarbekir in the
southeast. Baydemir was one of a number of prominent Kurds who issued public
apologies to Armenians for the participation of Kurdish tribespeople in the massacres and expropriations of the Christian population.[147] In 2012, he proclaimed:
"We refuse the legacy of the grandparents who participated in this massacre; we
refuse to be a part of that history; and we honour those of our grandparents who
opposed the massacre and the cruelty. To deny the crimes . . . would be to perpetu-
ate them in some way. We must first acknowledge the suffering of the people so we
can start to heal the wounds." (The strategy had obvious political payoffs for the
Kurdish national cause as well—see Box 4.2. Its proponents "have a clear interest
in goading the Turkish state about its past," and the Armenian genocide "could
remind people of more recent atrocities [e.g., against Kurds] and further shake the
country's foundations.)[148]

A remarkable additional component of the new reckoning with the "Armenian ghost" is the growing number of Turkish citizens willing to acknowledge—or only now learning of—their Armenian ancestry and heritage. These
are the "crypto-Armenians" who survived in the Turkish Republic by avoiding
the Armenian language, Christian religious practice, and so on. Then there are
the "leftovers of the sword," as they are called in Turkish.[149] We saw that the massacres and deportations of Armenians and other Christians were accompanied
by the widespread kidnapping of children and adolescent girls. Sometimes, too,
Christian children were surrendered to be raised as Muslims by parents desperate to save their lives. One Turkish journalist, Bekir Coskun, published an essay,
"My Armenian Question," in the leading newspaper *Hurriyet*. He described being
raised by his grandmother, who

> wasn't like our aunts and the other women in the household. She was tall
> and thin with blond hair and grey-blue eyes. . . . The whole family loved
> her and treated her with respect. . . . Time passed, and we grew older. And
> we learned that she wasn't our real grandmother, that she had entered our
> home after our real grandmother had died. She was an Armenian. . . . What
> I want to know is who took my grandmother away from her home, from
> her safe place, when she was just a young girl. I want to know who is
> responsible for the pain she tried to keep from us, for the homesickness she
> tried to hide, for the tears she must have shed on her pillow every night,
> behind closed doors. I don't know anything about one million Armenians

[killed]. Just this one woman. This terribly sad woman I loved so much. My Armenian.[150]

Recognition of the genocides of the other Christian populations of the Ottoman realm has also proceeded incrementally. In an announcement which ran counter to a tendency toward an "exclusivity of suffering,"[151] the Armenian National Committee of America (ANCA) "join[ed] with Pontian Greeks—and all Hellenes around the world—in commemorating ... the genocide initiated by the Ottoman Empire and continued by Kemalist Turkey against the historic Greek population of Pontus along the southeastern coast of the Black Sea." "We join with the Hellenic American community in solemn remembrance of the Pontian Genocide, and in reaffirming our determination to work together with all the victims of Turkey's atrocities to secure full recognition and justice for these crimes," said ANCA's director, Aram Hamparian. A number of US states, including Florida, New York, New Jersey, Massachusetts, and Pennsylvania, have also passed formal acts of recognition.

Another initiative was spearheaded in the International Association of Genocide Scholars (IAGS). A resolution was placed before the IAGS membership to recognize the Greek and Assyrian/Chaldean components of the Ottoman genocide against Christians, alongside the Armenian strand of the genocide (which the IAGS had already formally acknowledged). The result, passed emphatically in December 2007 despite not inconsiderable opposition, was a resolution which I co-drafted, reading as follows:

WHEREAS the denial of genocide is widely recognized as the final stage of genocide, enshrining impunity for the perpetrators of genocide, and demonstrably paving the way for future genocides;

WHEREAS the Ottoman genocide against minority populations during and following the First World War is usually depicted as a genocide against Armenians alone, with little recognition of the qualitatively similar genocides against other Christian minorities of the Ottoman Empire;

BE IT RESOLVED that it is the conviction of the International Association of Genocide Scholars that the Ottoman campaign against Christian minorities of the Empire between 1914 and 1923 constituted a genocide against Armenians, Assyrians, and Pontian and Anatolian Greeks.

BE IT FURTHER RESOLVED that the Association calls upon the government of Turkey to acknowledge the genocides against these populations, to issue a formal apology, and to take prompt and meaningful steps toward restitution.[152]

In my view, the initiative typified one of the more positive aspects of genocide studies: the opportunity to help in resuscitating long-forgotten or marginalized events for a contemporary audience; in acknowledging the victims and survivors of the genocide; and in exposing accepted framings and discourses to critical reexamination. Such processes themselves represent a kind of "humanitarian intervention"—primarily in the realms of history and memory, but also in contemporary crises, by highlighting the plight of vulnerable descendant populations today.

FURTHER STUDY

Taner Akçam, *A Shameful Act: The Armenian Genocide and the Question of Turkish Responsibility*. New York: Metropolitan Books, 2006. Explores the planning, perpetration, and aftermath of the Armenian holocaust, drawing on extensive research in Turkish archives. See also *The Young Turks' Crime Against Humanity*.

Peter Balakian, *The Burning Tigris: The Armenian Genocide and America's Response*. New York: HarperCollins, 2003. The best overview of the genocide and the US humanitarian response; see also *Black Dog of Fate* (memoir).

Donald Bloxham, *The Great Game of Genocide: Imperialism, Nationalism, and the Destruction of the Ottoman Armenians*. Cambridge: Cambridge University Press, 2005. Excellent on the international machinations surrounding the "Armenian question." See also *Genocide, the World Wars and the Unweaving of Europe*.

Sébastien de Courtois, *The Forgotten Genocide: Eastern Christians, The Last Arameans*, trans. Vincent Aurora. Piscataway, NJ: Gorgias Press, 2004. One of the very few studies of the destruction of Assyrian/Syriac communities under the Ottomans. Other exemplary accounts are found in Hannibal Travis, *Genocide in the Middle East* (see Further Study, ch. 1) and Mark Levene, *The Crisis of Genocide, Vol. I: Devastation* (see Further Study, ch. 1).

Thomas de Waal, *Great Catastrophe: Armenians and Turks in the Shadow of Genocide*. Oxford: Oxford University Press, 2015. Incisive study of the international politics surrounding the Armenian genocide. Especially good on the Armenian diaspora in the United States, its internal divisions, and its sometimes tense relationship with post-Soviet Armenia.

Marjorie Housepian Dobkin, *Smyrna 1922: The Destruction of a City*. New York: Newmark Press, 1998 (reprint). A useful though partisan account of one of the last spasms of war and "cleansing" in the Ottoman period.

David Gaunt, *Massacres, Resistance, Protectors: Muslim-Christian Relations in Eastern Anatolia during World War I*. Piscataway, NJ: Gorgias Press, 2006. Exhaustive survey of the mass violence in this little-studied corner of the empire.

Thea Halo, *Not Even My Name*. New York: Picador, 2001. Moving account of a survivor of the Pontian Greek genocide—the author's mother, Sano Halo, who died in 2014, aged 104.

Tessa Hofmann, Matthias Bjørnlund, and Vasileios Meichanetsidis, *The Genocide of the Ottoman Greeks: Studies on the State-Sponsored Campaign of Extermination of the Christians of Asia Minor (1912–1922) and Its Aftermath: History, Law, Memory*. New York: Aristide D. Caratzas, 2011. By far the most complete engagement with the genocide of Ottoman Greeks available in English.

Raymond Kévorkian, *The Armenian Genocide: A Complete History*. London: I.B. Tauris, 2011. Daunting in its length—a thousand pages—and in its regional detail. But beautifully written, and essential for any serious student of the genocide.

Laure Marchand and Guillaume Perrier, *Turkey and the Armenian Ghost: On the Trail of the Genocide*, trans. Debbie Blythe. Montreal: McGill-Queen's University Press, 2015. The physical and human legacy of the Armenian genocide.

Donald E. Miller and Lorna Touryan Miller, *Survivors: An Oral History of the Armenian Genocide*. Berkeley, CA: University of California Press, 1999. Focuses on the experiences of Armenian children.

Henry Morgenthau, *Ambassador Morgenthau's Story*. http://net.lib.byu.edu/estu/wwi/comment/morgenthau/MorgenTC.htm. Memoirs of the US Ambassador to Constantinople.

Merrill D. Peterson, *"Starving Armenians": America and the Armenian Genocide, 1915–1930 and After*. Charlottesville, VA: University of Virginia Press, 2004. As the title suggests, a study of Americans' roles in publicizing the Armenian genocide and rescuing some of its survivors; includes a study of the activities of the Near East Relief committee.

Ronald Grigor Suny, *"They Can Live in the Desert but Nowhere Else": A History of the Armenian Genocide* (Princeton, NJ: Princeton University Press, 2015). The most notable of the books published for the 2015 centenary, and probably the best general history of the genocide (but see Balakian and Kévorkian, above).

The Treatment of Armenians in the Ottoman Empire, 1915–16. http://net.lib.byu.edu/~rdh7/wwi/1915/bryce/. Text of the British "Blue Book," published in 1916, on atrocities against the Armenians (see Figure 4.15).

NOTES

1 In German, *"Wer redet heute noch von der Vernichtung der Armenier?"* Hitler quoted in Ronnie S. Landau, *The Nazi Holocaust* (Chicago, IL: Ivan R. Dee, 1994), p. 15. On the documentary evidence for Hitler's statement, see Vahakn N. Dadrian, *The History of the Armenian Genocide: Ethnic Conflict from the Balkans to Anatolia to the Caucasus* (6th rev. edn) (New York: Berghahn Books, 2003), pp. 403–409.

2 For a fine brief survey of recent historiographical contributions and debates, see Uğur Ümit Üngör, "Fresh Understandings of the Armenian Genocide: Mapping New Terrain with Old Questions," in Adam Jones, ed., *New Directions in Genocide Research* (London: Routledge, 2012), pp. 198–213.

3 I follow Travis in referring "to the Assyrians, Nestorians, Chaldeans, and Syrian/Syriac Christians collectively as Assyrians. All of them are descended from the indigenous inhabitants of Mesopotamia, southeastern Anatolia, and northwestern Persia; Persian, Greek, and Arab rulers, as well as Chaldean Patriarchs, Syrian/Syriac priests and monks, and their Armenian neighbors, have referred to all three groups together as 'Assyrians.'" Travis, *Genocide in the Middle East: The Ottoman Empire, Iraq, and Sudan* (Durham, NC: Carolina Academic Press, 2010), p. 237 (n. 2).

4 Travis, *Genocide in the Middle East*, p. 299. As Travis points out, the original title of the famous "Blue Book," the Allied compilation of documents on Turkish atrocities, was *Papers and Documents on the Treatment of Armenians and Assyrian Christians by the Turks, 1915–1916, in the Ottoman Empire and North-West Persia*. The phrase "and Assyrian Christians" was deleted prior to the book's publication in Britain, and all references to anti-Assyrian atrocities were removed from the French version presented at the postwar Paris Peace Conference *(Genocide in the Middle East*, p. 253).

5 Taner Akçam, *A Shameful Act: The Armenian Genocide and the Question of Turkish Responsibility* (New York: Metropolitan Books, 2006), p. 43.

6 Donald Bloxham, *The Great Game of Genocide: Imperialism, Nationalism, and the Destruction of the Ottoman Armenians* (Cambridge: Cambridge University Press, 2005), p. 71.

7 Wangenheim quoted in Akçam, *A Shameful Act*, p. 121.

8 Thea Halo, *Not Even My Name* (New York: Picador USA, 2001), p. 131. For a fine survey with some ethnonationalist blind spots, see Vasileios Th. Meichanetsidis, "The Genocide of the Greeks of the Ottoman Empire, 1913–1923: A Comprehensive Overview," *Genocide Studies International*, 9: 1 (2015), pp. 104–173.

9 Hannibal Travis, personal communication, January 25, 2010 (he notes that the estimate squares with that of David Gaunt, and also the figures submitted to the Paris Peace Conference shortly after the events). On the wider politics of genocide recognition in the former Ottoman realm, see Travis, "Constructing the 'Armenian Genocide': How Scholars Unremembered the Assyrian and Greek Genocides in the Ottoman Empire," ch. 9 in Alexander Laban Hinton, Thomas La Pointe, and Douglas Irvin-Erickson, eds., *Hidden Genocides: Power, Knowledge, Memory* (New Brunswick, NJ: Rutgers University Press, 2014, pp. 170–192.

10 Vahakn Dadrian, "Documentation of the Armenian Genocide in Turkish Sources," in Israel Charny, ed., *Genocide: A Critical Bibliographic Review, Vol. 2* (New Brunswick, NJ: Transaction Publishers, 1991); Dadrian, "The Role of Turkish Physicians in the World War I Genocide of Ottoman Armenians," *Holocaust and Genocide Studies*, 1 (1986), pp. 172–175, 184.

11 Ben Kiernan, *Blood and Soil: A World History of Genocide and Extermination from Sparta to Darfur* (New Haven, CT: Yale University Press, 2009), p. 402.

12 Bloxham, *The Great Game of Genocide*, pp. 30–31.

13 Paul Mojzes, *Balkan Genocides: Holocaust and Ethnic Cleansing in the Twentieth Century* (Lanham, MD: Rowman & Littlefield, 2011), p. 25. He describes the Balkan wars as "a case of mutual genocide by the participant nations."

14 Snyder quoted in Levene, *The Crisis of Genocide, Vol. 1*, p. 431 (n. 35).

15 Donald Bloxham, *Genocide, the World Wars and the Unweaving of Europe* (London: Vallentine Mitchell, 2008), p. 1. However, Hannibal Travis contests Bloxham's claim of a clear primacy of Muslim victims: it "seems to ignore the massacres of 200,000 to 450,000 Ottoman Christians, including 30,000 Armenians in the 1900s, 100,000 to 300,000 mostly Armenians in the 1890s, about 15,000 Armenians and Slavs in the 1870s, about 12,000 Maronites in Lebanon around 1860, and about 70,000 Greeks in the 1820s." Travis, personal communication, January 24, 2010. Justin McCarthy's revisionist study, *Death and Exile: The Ethnic Cleansing of Ottoman Muslims, 1821–1922* (Princeton, NJ: The Darwin Press, 1995), claims that during the period under consideration, "Five and one-half million Muslims died, some of them killed in wars, others perishing as refugees from starvation and disease" (p. 1). McCarthy has been justifiably criticized for his efforts to downplay the genocide of Ottoman Armenians, sometimes radically. But his work is an important counter to mainstream narratives "in that it debunks the myth of the eternally innocent Christians forever pillaged by the demonic Turk that is present, explicitly or implicitly, in so much of the literature on the Armenian genocide." Donald Beachler, *The Genocide Debate: Politicians, Academics, and Victims* (New York: Palgrave Macmillan, 2011), p. 102.

16 The sense of humiliation was profound at elite levels as well, as Mark Levene notes: "the Ottoman fantasy was so out of kilter with reality as to produce nothing less than absolute trauma, absolute bitterness, hurt, and, above all, humiliation when the actual result [of the Balkan wars] sank in. The very nadir of imperial fortunes, to add insult to injury, had not even come at the hands of a *great* nation, but in Ottoman minds, at those of the most miserable and inferior of former subject peoples [principally Serbs]. Worse still, it actually brought those for whom the empire *really* mattered face to face with the possibility of its complete extinction." Levene, *The Crisis of Genocide, Vol. 1*, p. 112.

17 Akçam, *A Shameful Act*, p. 87. Eric Bogosian notes that the Central Committee of the CUP, likewise, was disproportionately composed of "men . . . from Balkan Ottoman

territories. They were very familiar with the massacres of Muslims during the Balkan wars and . . . held little sympathy for the Armenians once the decision was made to wipe them out." Bogosian, *Operation Nemesis: The Assassination Plot that Avenged the Armenian Genocide* (New York: Little, Brown and Company, 2015), p. 250.

18 Mark Levene, "The Tragedy of the Rimlands, Nation-State Formation and the Destruction of Imperial Peoples, 1912–48," in Panikos Panayi and Pippa Virdee, eds, *Refugees and the End of Empire: Imperial Collapse and Forced Migration in the Twentieth Century* (London: Palgrave Macmillan UK, 2011), pp. 60–61.

19 The shrinking of the empire meant that the Ottoman realm became more homogeneous, and the minority Christians of the realm (the Armenians, Assyrians, and Pontian Greeks) stood out more prominently. Whereas the Ottoman Empire had once been unusually diverse, cosmopolitan, and tolerant, its dissolution spurred those who yearned for an ethnically "pure" Turkish homeland. I am indebted to Benjamin Madley for this point.

20 Stephan Astourian, "The Armenian Genocide: An Interpretation," *The History Teacher*, 23: 2 (February 1990), p. 123.

21 Levene supplies a scathing verdict: "By seeking to encourage revolt, sabotage, or even plain dissent among ethnic communities who were the subjects of enemy powers," European countries "were not simply implicating such communities in their own devious stratagems but encouraging them, whether through passive non-action or even active betrayal, to behave treasonably. Rather, in an already highly charged situation, it was as if they were offering on a plate to enemy state and dominant demos just cause to vent their wrath against these communities." Levene, *The Crisis of Genocide, Vol. 1*, p. 49.

22 Balakian, *The Burning Tigris*, p. 59.

23 Dadrian, *The History of the Armenian Genocide*, p. 151. Daniel Jonah Goldhagen points out that "the Turks' massive assault upon the Armenians from 1894 to 1896 would rightly be called the Armenian Genocide—had an even more massive mass murder and elimination not followed twenty years later." Daniel Jonah Goldhagen, *Worse Than War: Genocide, Eliminationism, and the Ongoing Assault on Humanity* (New York: Basic Books, 2009), p. 302.

24 Bloxham, *The Great Game of Genocide*, p. 55.

25 For analysis of the death toll, see Dadrian, *The History of the Armenian Genocide*, pp. 153–157.

26 Melson quoted in Donald E. Miller and Lorna Touryan Miller, *Survivors: An Oral History of the Armenian Genocide* (Berkeley, CA: University of California Press, 1999), p. 47.

27 Astourian, "The Armenian Genocide," p. 129.

28 For a detailed account of Ottoman-Armenian relations and negotiations during this period, see Raymond Kévorkian, *The Armenian Genocide: A Complete History* (London: I.B. Tauris, 2011), Part II.

29 Donald Bloxham, personal communication, August 31, 2005.

30 Balakian, *The Burning Tigris*, p. 164.

31 Gökalp quoted in Akçam, *A Shameful Act*, p. 88.

32 Miller and Miller, *Survivors*, p. 39.

33 For example, Bahaeddin Sakir, who headed the Special Organization in the eastern Ottoman provinces, wrote in February 1915 of the CUP's decision that "the Armenians living in Turkey will be destroyed to the last. The government has been given ample authority. As to the organization of the mass murder, the government will provide the necessary explanations to the governors, and to the army commanders. The delegates of [the CUP] in their own regions will be in charge of this task." Cited in Astourian, "The Armenian Genocide," p. 139.

34 See Kévorkian, *The Armenian Genocide, Part II*, chs. 2–3. See also Bedross Der Matossian, "From Bloodless Revolution to Bloody Counterrevolution: The Adana Massacres of 1909," *Genocide Studies and Prevention*, 6: 2 (2011), pp. 152–173. While dozens of Muslims were eventually tried and executed for their crimes, so too were Armenians who

had killed in self-defense, and the leading organizers and supervisors of the slaughter retained impunity.

35 Matthias Bjørnlund, "The 1914 Cleansing of Aegean Greeks as a Case of Violent Turkification," *Journal of Genocide Research*, 10: 1 (2008), p. 42. See also the expanded and revised version of the argument in Bjørnlund, "The Persecution of Greeks and Armenians in Smyrna, 1914–1916: A Special Case in the Course of the Late Ottoman Genocides," in George N. Shirinian, ed., *The Asia Minor Catastrophe and the Ottoman Greek Genocide* (Bloomingdale, IL: The Asia Minor and Pontos Hellenic Research Center, Inc., 2012), pp. 89–133.

36 Toynbee quoted in Akçam, *A Shameful Act*, p. 105.

37 See Taner Akçam, "The Greek Deportations and Massacres of 1913–1914: A Trial Run for the Armenian Genocide," in Shirinian, ed., *The Asia Minor Catastrophe*, pp. 69–88. This is probably the best short account of the ideological and programmatic overlaps in the Greek/Armenian experiences. "Even if we currently possess no direct proof as to whether or not these two separate cleansing operations were the result of a single, overall plan," writes Akçam (p. 85), "we can at the very least confidently point to a clear continuity between these two actions, both in regard to their general lines of organization and the personalities involved."

38 Taner Akçam described the "characteristic" but "unofficial policy" of this campaign against the Greeks as "implemented through: (1) Attacks on Greek villages and villagers by Special Organization (SO) units, with the central government claiming and acting as if it were not involved in the matter; (2) terror and killings to force individuals and communities from their homes; (3) the emptying of entire villages and conscription into labor brigades of all military-age male inhabitants; and (4) the seizure and redistribution of Greek-owned businesses to Muslims." Akçam, *The Young Turks' Crime Against Humanity: The Armenian Genocide and Ethnic Cleansing in the Ottoman Empire* (Princeton, NJ: Princeton University Press, 2012), p. 69. See also Ambassador Morgenthau's comments, quoted on p. 96, that in the deportations of 1913–1914, "the Turks adopted almost identically the same procedure against the Greeks as that which they had adopted against the Armenians. They began by incorporating the Greeks into the Ottoman army and then transferring them into labour battalions, using them to build roads in the Caucasus and other scenes of [military] action. These Greek soldiers, just like the Armenians, died by the thousands from cold, hunger, and other privations. . . . Everywhere the Greeks were gathered in groups and, under the so-called protection of the Turkish gendarmes, they were transported, the larger part on foot, into the interior." For an interpretation running somewhat counter to the one offered here, see Bloxham, *The Great Game of Genocide*, pp. 64, 164. He described the policy adopted toward Ottoman Greeks from 1913 to 1916 as "a combination of population engineering and economic appropriation, using boycotts, murders, terrorization, and then deportation" (*The Great Game of Genocide*, p. 64). However, he argues that generalized killing of Greeks did not occur until 1921–1922, following the Greek invasion and occupation of large parts of Turkey; and then it took place in the context of a "war of extermination" featuring comparably widespread atrocities against civilians by both Greek and Turkish forces.

39 Morgenthau quoted in Akçam, *A Shameful Act*, p. 111.

40 Morgenthau quoted in ibid., pp. 105–106.

41 Van der Zee quoted in Bjørnlund, "The 1914 Cleansing," p. 46.

42 Emanuelidi Efendi quoted in Akçam, *A Shameful Act*, p. 107.

43 CUP document cited in Kiernan, *Blood and Soil*, p. 408.

44 Shakir quoted in Ronald Grigor Suny, *Looking Toward Ararat: Armenia in Modern History* (Bloomington, IN: Indiana University Press, 1993), p. 112.

45 Henry J. Morgenthau, *Murder of a Nation*, http://net.lib.byu.edu/estu/wwi/comment/morgenthau/Morgen24.htm.

46 Michael Mann, *The Dark Side of Democracy: Explaining Ethnic Cleansing* (Cambridge: Cambridge University Press, 2005), p. 148.
47 Dadrian, *The History of the Armenian Genocide*, p. 226.
48 Ibid., pp. 221–222.
49 Morgenthau, *Murder of a Nation*.
50 See Akçam, *The Young Turks' Crime Against Humanity*, especially ch. 8, "Demographic Policy and the Annihilation of the Armenians," pp. 227–285. He quotes a telegram from Abdullahad Nuri, an official in the resettlement office in Aleppo in present-day Syria, sent to central authorities on January 10, 1916: "Enquiries having been made, it is understood that hardly 10 percent of the Armenians subjected to the general deportations have reached the places destined for them; the rest have died from natural causes, such as hunger and sickness. *We inform you that we are working to bring about the same result with regard to those who are still alive, by using severe measures*" (quoted p. xviii, emphasis added). This "second wave of massacres" in 1916, according to Akçam, was "motivated primarily by demographic anxieties, along with security concerns" related to Russian military advances (p. xix).
51 "Some regional variations notwithstanding," wrote Taner Akçam, "the expulsions and massacres proceeded in the same way everywhere and are well documented in American, British and German archival materials, missionary reports, and survivors' accounts. The very persistence of the pattern indicates central planning." Akçam, *A Shameful Act*, p. 174.
52 Gorrini quoted in Bogosian, *Operation Nemesis*, p. 61.
53 Davis quoted in Balakian, *The Burning Tigris*, p. 234.
54 El-Ghusein quoted in Akçam, *The Young Turks' Crime Against Humanity*, p. 315.
55 Norman M. Naimark, *Fires of Hatred: Ethnic Cleansing in Twentieth-century Europe* (Cambridge, MA: Harvard University Press, 2001), p. 41.
56 Balakian, *The Burning Tigris*, pp. 182–183.
57 Morgenthau, *Murder of a Nation*.
58 Ibid.
59 Miller and Miller, *Survivors*, p. 110.
60 For an overview of this practice, see Ara Sarafian, "The Absorption of Armenian Women and Children into Muslim Households as a Structural Component of the Armenian Genocide," in Omer Bartov and Phyllis Mack, *In God's Name: Genocide and Religion in the Twentieth Century* (New York: Berghahn Books, 2001), pp. 209–221.
61 Margaret Ajemian Ahnert, *The Knock at the Door: A Journey through the Darkness of the Armenian Genocide* (New York: Beaufort Books, 2007). The quoted passages are drawn from pp. 10, 15, 88–89, 91, 117, 121, 138, 168, 176.
62 Miller and Miller, *Survivors*, p. 119.
63 Vahakn N. Dadrian, "The Comparative Aspects of the Armenian and Jewish Cases of Genocide: A Sociohistorical Perspective," in Alan S. Rosenbaum, ed., *Is the Holocaust Unique? Perspectives on Comparative Genocide* (Boulder, CO: Westview Press, 1998), pp. 127–128.
64 Balakian, *The Burning Tigris*, p. 320.
65 Ibid., p. 245. David Gaunt likewise contends that the CUP viewed "the Syriac groups in the Ottoman Empire . . . with the same degree of suspicion as they did the Armenians." Gaunt, *Massacres, Resistance, Protectors: Muslim–Christian Relations in Eastern Anatolia during World War I* (Piscataway, NJ: Gorgias Press, 2006), p. 122.
66 Gaunt, *Massacres, Resistance, Protectors*, p. 304.
67 Ibid., p. 252 (citing Arthur Beylerian, *Les Grandes Puissances: L'Empire Ottoman, et les Arméniens dans les archives françaises (1914–1918)* [New York: Holmes & Meier Publishers, 1983]), pp. 478–479; Viscount James Bryce and Arnold Joseph Toynbee, *The Treatment of Armenians in the Ottoman Empire, 1915–1916: Documents Presented to Viscount Grey of Fallodon*, ed. Ara Sarafian (Reading: Taderon Press, 2000), p. 120.

68 Joseph Naayem, *Shall This Nation Die?* (New York: Chaldean Rescue, 1921), pp. 145–162.

69 Nogales quoted in Travis, *Genocide in the Middle East*, p. 248.

70 Morgenthau quoted in ibid., p. 257. Emphasis added.

71 Sykes quoted in Lt. Col. Ronald S. Stafford, "Iraq and the Problem of the Assyrians," *International Affairs*, March 1934, p. 182.

72 Christoph Baumer, *The Church of the East: An Illustrated History of Assyrian Christianity* (London: I.B. Tauris, 2006), p. 263. I am grateful to Hannibal Travis for bringing this source and the preceding one to my attention.

73 Stafford, *Iraq and the Problem of the Assyrians*, p. 177.

74 Travis, *Genocide in the Middle East*, p. 256.

75 Quoted in ibid., p. 207.

76 See my autobiographical essay, "Seized of Sorrow," in Samuel Totten, ed., *Advancing Genocide Studies: Personal Accounts and Insights from Scholars in the Field* (New Brunswick, NJ: Transaction Publishers, 2015), pp. 57–77.

77 According to Mark Levene, "without strong Kurdish involvement in the genocide, the CUP would not have been able to fully implement it." Levene, *The Crisis of Genocide, Vol. 1: Devastation* (Oxford: Oxford University Press, 2013), p. 158.

78 Donald Bloxham, *Genocide, the World Wars and the Unweaving of Europe* (London: Vallentine Mitchell, 2008), p. 199.

79 For a lucid and lively study of the Kurds in the twentieth century, see Jonathan C. Randal, *After Such Knowledge, What Forgiveness? My Encounters with Kurdistan* (Boulder, CO: Westview Press, 1999). Also recommended is John Bulloch, *No Friends but the Mountains: The Tragic History of the Kurds* (Oxford: Oxford University Press, 1993).

80 The standard biography is Andrew Mango, *Atatürk: The Biography of the Founder of Modern Turkey* (Woodstock, NY: The Overlook Press, 2000). See also M. Şükrü Hanioğlu, *Atatürk: An Intellectual Biography* (Princeton, NJ: Princeton University Press, 2011).

81 Mark Levene, *The Crisis of Genocide, Vol. 2: Annihilation* (Oxford: Oxford University Press, 2013), pp. 13–14.

82 Ibid., p. 18.

83 David L. Philips, *The Kurdish Spring: A New Map of the Middle East* (New Brunswick, NJ: Transaction Publishers, 2015), p. 57.

84 Ceylan Yeginsu, "Turkey's Campaign Against Kurdish Militants Takes Toll on Civilians," *The New York Times*, December 30, 2015, www.nytimes.com/2015/12/31/world/europe/turkey-kurds-pkk.html.

85 See Dilip Hiro, *The Longest War: The Iran-Iraq Military Conflict* (London: Paladin, 1990); Pierre Razoux, *The Iran-Iraq War* (Cambridge, MA: The Belknap Press of Harvard University Press, 2015).

86 See Martin van Bruinessen, "Genocide in Kurdistan?," in George J. Andreopoulos, ed., *Genocide: Conceptual and Historical Dimensions* (Pittsburgh, PA: University of Pennsylvania Press, 1994), pp. 156–157.

87 Lawrence, *Invisible Nation*, p. 34.

88 See "'Chemical Ali' Executed in Iraq," *AlJazeera.com*, January 25, 2010, www.aljazeera.com/news/middleeast/2010/01/201012514645847464.html.

89 See Joost R. Hilterman, *A Poisonous Affair: America, Iraq, and the Gassing of Halabja* (Cambridge: Cambridge University Press, 2007).

90 Human Rights Watch-Middle East, *Iraq's Crime of Genocide: The Anfal Campaign Against the Kurds* (New Haven, CT: Human Rights Watch/Yale University Press, 1995), p. 12. For a good short account, see Choman Hardi, "The Anfal Campaign Against the Kurds: Chemical Weapons in the Service of Mass Murder," in René Lemarchand, ed., *Forgotten Genocides: Oblivion, Denial, and Memory* (Philadelphia, PA: University of Pennsylvania Press, 2011), pp. 106–122.

91 Quil Lawrence, *Invisible Nation: How the Kurds' Quest for Statehood is Shaping Iraq and the Middle East* (New York: Walker & Company, 2008), p. 40.

92 Ibid., p. x.

93 For a good overview of Iraqi Kurdish autonomy, see "Self-Rule in Iraq," in Phillips, *The Kurdish Spring*, pp. 97–123.

94 See Mohammed A. Salih, "Iraq's Christians Seek Refuge with Kurds," *AlJazeera.com*, June 26, 2014, www.aljazeera.com/news/middleeast/2014/06/iraq-christians-seek-refuge-with-kurds-2014624867119947.html. The article describes the situation in Iraq, a "serene and tranquil"-seeming town just 50km from IS-administered Mosul. Under the protection of Kurdish Peshmerga forces, "we feel safe," said Yusef, one of the majority of Mosul's Christians who fled IS rule. Father Jebrail Gorgis Toma stated: "We are fed up with the conditions in other parts of the country. But Kurdistan has proven itself in terms of stability, economic development and democratic measures." Mayor Ali Mohammed Fathi, the Shabak mayor of Bartalla, declared: "We are a threatened people. Without Peshmerga forces, our future as Shabaks and Christians here will be genocide."

95 Lawrence, *Invisible Nation*, p. 266.

96 Ibid., p. 309.

97 See "Turkish Jets Strike PKK in Iraq as Conflict Escalates," *France24.com*, September 11, 2015, www.france24.com/en/20150911-many-killed-turkey-cizre-pkk-hdp-mps-march-blocked-kurds-curfew.

98 Salih, "Iraq's Christians."

99 "Iraqi Kurdistan: Arabs Displaced, Cordoned Off, Detained," *Human Rights Watch* bulletin, February 25, 2015, www.hrw.org/news/2015/02/25/iraqi-kurdistan-arabs-displaced-cordoned-detained. See also Sara Elizabeth Williams, "Destroying Homes for Kurdistan," *ForeignPolicy.com*, July 23, 2015, http://foreignpolicy.com/2015/07/23/peshmerga-war-crimes-ethnic-cleansing-islamic-state-iraq/.

100 See the Amnesty International report, *Banished and Dispossessed: Forced Displacement and Deliberate Destruction in North Iraq*, January 20, 2016, www.amnesty.org/down load/Documents/MDE1432292016ENGLISH.PDF.

101 Jonathan Steele, "The Syrian Kurds Are Winning!," *The New York Review of Books*, December 3, 2015, www.nybooks.com/articles/2015/12/03/syrian-kurds-are-winning/. The best scholarly analysis of this sociopolitical experiment, and its conflicts and frictions, is Michael M. Gunter, *Out of Nowhere: The Kurds of Syria in Peace and War* (Oxford: Oxford University Press, 2014).

102 See Amy Austin Holmes, "What Are the Kurdish Women's Units Fighting For in Syria?," *The Washington Post*, December 23, 2015, www.washingtonpost.com/news/monkey-cage/wp/2015/12/23/what-are-the-kurdish-womens-units-fighting-for-in-syria/.

103 "Syria: US Ally's Razing of Villages Amounts to War Crimes," *Amnesty International* press release, October 13, 2015, www.amnesty.org/en/press-releases/2015/10/syria-us-allys-razing-of-villages-amounts-to-war-crimes/.

104 Horton cited in Travis, *Genocide in the Middle East*, p. 287.

105 Halo, *Not Even My Name*, pp. 98, 131, 135–136.

106 "Obituary: Sano Themia Halo (1909–2014)," *Armenian Weekly*, May 4, 2014, http://armenianweekly.com/2014/05/04/obituary-sano-themia-halo-1909–2014/.

107 The image with its original caption appears online at www.hri.org/docs/Horton/pictures.html.

108 A British commission investigating the occupation of Smyrna and environs delivered a "verdict on Greek behavior during the offensive of 1921 [that] was damning in the extreme. The commissioners wrote of the 'burning and looting of Turkish villages' and the explosion of violence of Greeks and Armenians against the Turks . . .: 'There is a systematic plan of destruction and extinction of the Moslem population. This plan is being carried out by Greek and Armenian hands, which appear to operate under Greek instruction and sometimes even with the assistance of detachments of regular

troops.'" Norman M. Naimark, *Fires of Hatred: Ethnic Cleansing in Twentieth-Century Europe* (Cambridge, MA: Harvard University Press, 2001), p. 45.

109 Benjamin Lieberman, *Terrible Fate: Ethnic Cleansing in the Making of Modern Europe* (Chicago, IL: Ivan R. Dee, 2006), p. 123.

110 See Matthew Stewart, "The Immediate Context of the Smyrna Catastrophe," in Tessa Hofmann, Matthias Bjørnlund, and Vasileios Meichanetsidis, eds., *The Genocide of the Ottoman Greeks: Studies on the State-Sponsored Campaign of Extermination of the Christians of Asia Minor (1912–1922) and Its Aftermath: History, Law, Memory* (New York: Aristide D. Caratzas, 2011), pp. 245–263.

111 See Speros Vryonis, Jr., *The Mechanism of Catastrophe: The Turkish Pogrom of September 6–7, 1955, and the Destruction of the Greek Community of Istanbul* (New York: Greekworks, 2007), pp. 16, 565.

112 See Jonathan C. Randal, *After Such Knowledge, What Forgiveness? My Encounters with Kurdistan* (Boulder, CO: Westview Press, 1999).

113 Cited in Balakian, *The Burning Tigris*, p. 328. In a precursor to subsequent Turkish campaigns of genocide denial, Ataturk claimed that the Armenians killed were "victims of foreign intrigues" and guilty of abusing "the privileges granted them."

114 Quoted in Gary Jonathan Bass, *Stay the Hand of Vengeance: The Politics of War Crimes Tribunals* (Princeton, NJ: Princeton University Press, 2000), p. 127.

115 British Foreign Office dispatch quoted in Akçam, *A Shameful Act*, p. 294.

116 Balakian, *The Burning Tigris*, p. 341. For more on the trials, see Akçam, *A Shameful Act*, part 3; Vahakn Dadrian, "The Turkish Military Tribunal's Prosecution of the Authors of the Armenian Genocide," *Holocaust and Genocide Studies*, 11: 1 (1997), pp. 28–59.

117 Bass, *Stay the Hand of Vengeance*, p. 136.

118 Lloyd George quoted in Bass, *Stay the Hand of Vengeance*, p. 144.

119 Balakian, *The Burning Tigris*, p. 345.

120 Laure Marchand and Guillaume Perrier, *Turkey and the Armenian Ghost: On the Trail of the Genocide* (Montreal, PQ: McGill-Queen's University Press, 2015), p. 6.

121 Bloxham, *The Great Game of Genocide*, pp. 211, 228. See also Amy Magaro Rubin, "Critics Accuse Turkish Government of Manipulating Scholarship," *Chronicle of Higher Education*, October 27, 1995. See also Marc A. Mamigonian, "Academic Denial of the Armenian Genocide in American Scholarship: Denialism as Manufactured Controversy," *Genocide Studies International*, 9: 1 (Spring 2015), pp. 61–82.

122 On the Turkish-Israeli relationship, see Yair Auron, *The Banality of Denial: Israel and the Armenian Genocide* (New Brunswick, NJ: Transaction Publishers, 2003). See also Robert Melson, "Responses to the Armenian Genocide: America, the Yishuv, Israel" (review article), *Holocaust and Genocide Studies*, 20: 1 (2006), pp. 103–111. It should be stressed that some Israeli scholars have persistently pressed the Israeli government to recognize the genocide. Israel Charny and Yehuda Bauer deserve special mention in this respect.

123 The trend began early on. Colby Chester, a retired US admiral, wrote in 1922 in the *New York Times Current History*: "The Armenians were moved from the inhospitable regions where they were not welcome and could not actually prosper but to the most delightful and fertile parts of Syria . . . where the climate is as benign as in Florida and California whither New York millionaires journey each year for health and recreation. . . . And all this was done at great expense of money and effort." Quoted in Balakian, *The Burning Tigris*, p. 376.

124 Aside from the Vatican, the countries that have recognized the Armenian genocide are, in alphabetical order: Argentina, Austria, Belgium, Bolivia, Brazil, Bulgaria, Canada, Chile, Cyprus, France, Germany, Greece, Italy, Lebanon, Lithuania, Luxembourg, Netherlands, Paraguay, Poland, Russia, Slovakia, Sweden, Switzerland, United States (apparently on the basis of the 43 US states that have passed resolutions), Uruguay, and Venezuela. See www.armenian-genocide.org/recognition_countries.html.

125 The Turkish-Armenian Reconciliation Committee, a US-based nongovernmental organization, "commissioned a report on the legal status of the 1915 killings from the International Center for Transitional Justice (ICTJ), a non-profit organization that helps societies address legacies of large-scale human rights violations. ICTJ's report, delegated to an independent expert, came out in February 2003. It reviewed the coining of the word 'genocide' and the adoption of the 1948 UN convention. It concluded that the killing of the Ottoman Armenians in 1915 did constitute genocide under the Convention, as 'the overwhelming majority of the accounts conclude that the Events occurred with some level of intent to effect the destruction of the Armenian communities in the eastern provinces of the Ottoman Empire, with many claiming that this was the specific intent of the most senior government officials.'" But the ICTJ also found that the Genocide Convention could not be applied retroactively, because "negotiators understood that they were accepting prospective, not retrospective, obligations ... including the 'prevention of future crimes.'" Thomas de Waal calls the decision "a draw": "The Armenians were vindicated by a legal opinion that the crime against their ancestors was genocide. The Turkish side could be reassured that the verdict had no retroactive legal validity." De Waal, *Great Catastrophe: Armenians and Turks in the Shadow of Genocide* (Oxford: Oxford University Press, 2015), pp. 212–213.

126 "French Parliament Recognises 1915 Armenian Genocide," Reuters dispatch, May 29, 1998. However, "the wording of the resolution was deliberately designed to remove any suggestion of the responsibility of the modern Turkish state for the genocide; indeed no perpetrator agency of any sort was recalled in the brief statement of recognition." Bloxham, *The Great Game of Genocide*, p. 224.

127 "Turkey Denounces Armenian Genocide Vote in Commons," CBC News, April 22, 2004.

128 Alison Smale, "German Parliament Recognizes Armenian Genocide, Angering Turkey," *The New York Times*, June 2, 2016, www.nytimes.com/2016/06/03/world/europe/armenian-genocide-germany-turkey.html.

129 See Pierre Tristam, "Obama, Turkey and the Armenian Genocide," Pierre's Middle East Issues Blog, March 18, 2009; "Barack Obama Sidesteps Armenian Genocide Row on Trip to Turkey," *The Times*, April 6, 2009, www.thetimes.co.uk/tto/news/world/europe/article2599624.ece.

130 See, e.g., "Obama Avoids Using 'Genocide,' Opting for 'Meds Yeghern' in April 24 Commemoration," *Hurriyet Daily News*, April 24, 2014.

131 Noah Bierman, "Armenian Hopes Crushed as Obama Decides Not to Use the Word 'Genocide'," *The Los Angeles Times*, April 21, 2015, www.latimes.com/nation/la-na-obama-armenian-genocide-20150421-story.html.

132 Gwynne Dyer, "Ending the Debate on an Armenian Genocide," *Straight.com*, October 15, 2009, www.straight.com/article-264662/gwynne-dyer-ending-debate-armenian-genocide.

133 The Azerbaijanis, the decisive losers in the conflict, ended up surrendering not just the near-entirety of administrative Karabakh, but "wholly or partly, seven regions around it" (de Waal, *Great Catastrophe*, p. 198), accompanied by the systematic "cleansing" of ethnic Azeris from both Armenia and Karabakh, so that both territories today are among the most ethnically homogeneous anywhere in Europe. This state of affairs holds at the time of writing, though tentatively renewed talks between the two sides were underway, with the largely independent authority of Karabakh also to consider. (Even Armenia does not recognize the self-declared state of Artsakh in Karabakh, but it supports it in every conceivable way, including by joining it to Armenia proper in state-produced maps.) The humiliation at Armenian and Karabakhti hands, along with the recognition of the political and moral capital that Armenia gleans from the genocide legacy, has produced an intriguing Azerbaijani counter-propaganda, as

I discovered on an extended visit to the country in summer 2015. The Armenian massacre of hundreds of fleeing Azerbaijanis, mostly civilians, at Khojaly in February 1992, has been enshrined as "the Khojaly genocide," while an earlier round of tit-for-tat communal killings in the capital, Baku, in 1918 is also memorialized exclusively as an Armenian genocide against Azeris. An impressive "genocide memorial" to this version of events, including an excavated mass grave of alleged victims of "Dashnak" (Armenian-nationalist) *génocidaires*, has been erected in the city of Quba. The standard work on the Nagorno-Karabakh conflict is again by Thomas de Waal: see *Black Garden: Armenia and Azerbaijan through Peace and War*, revised and updated edn (New York: New York University Press, 2013). See also Adam Jones, "Nagorno-Karabakh and the Armenian-Azerbaijani Conflict: A Genocide Studies Perspective," forthcoming.

134 Libaridian quoted in de Waal, *Great Catastrophe*, p. 202.
135 Marchand and Perrier, *Turkey and the Armenian Ghost*, p. 69.
136 According to Turkish historian Halil Berktay, speaking in 2013: "What has happened is over the past few years the official production and reproduction of Turkish denialism has stopped. The factory is no longer operating. . . . Few people have noticed it but the Turkish government has fallen silent on this question. It is an unnoticed silence, a reverberating silence—a loud silence." Quoted in de Waal, *Great Catastrophe*, p. 181.
137 On the Dersim genocide and related atrocities, see Mark Levene, *The Crisis of Genocide, Vol. 2: Annihilation: The European Rimlands 1939–1953* (Oxford: Oxford University Press, 2013), pp. 12–18.
138 De Waal, *Great Catastrophe*, p. 210.
139 Erdogan quoted in de Waal, *Great Catastrophe*, p. 253.
140 Marchand and Perrier, *Turkey and the Armenian Ghost*, p. 168. The authors point out that ironically, Cemal's grandfather "is none other than Djemal Pasha, one of the Three Pashas . . . that ruled the Ottoman Empire during World War I," and supervised the destruction of Ottoman Christian minorities.
141 See de Waal, *Great Catastrophe*, p. 182.
142 Alison Flood, "Pamuk 'Insult to Turkishness' Claims Return to Court," *The Guardian*, May 15, 2009, www.guardian.co.uk/books/2009/may/15/pamut-insult-turkishness-court (*n.b.* "pamut" as given).
143 Aktar quoted in de Waal, *Great Catastrophe*, p. 187. De Waal supplies an extended profile of Hrant Dink and the scenes surrounding his funeral at pp. 185–195.
144 Hratch Tchilingirian, "Hrant Dink and Armenians in Turkey," *OpenDemocracy.net*, February 23, 2007, www.opendemocracy.net/democracy-turkey/dink_armenian_4378.jsp.
145 Robert Tait, "Writers Risk Backlash with Apology for Armenian Genocide," *The Guardian*, December 8, 2008.
146 Günaysu quoted in Marchand and Perrier, *Turkey and the Armenian Ghost*, p. 165.
147 See Uzay Bulut, "Armenian Genocide: Kurdish Leaders Set Moral Example to Turkey by Facing Their Crimes," *International Business Times*, April 23, 2015, www.ibtimes.co.uk/armenian-genocide-kurdish-leaders-set-moral-example-turkey-by-facing-their-crimes-1498053.
148 Marchand and Perrier, *Turkey and the Armenian Ghost*, pp. 181–182.
149 Ibid., p. 38.
150 Quoted in ibid., pp. 45–46.
151 Thea Halo, "The Exclusivity of Suffering: When Tribal Concerns Take Precedence over Historical Accuracy," unpublished research paper, 2004.
152 A facsimile of the resolution as passed is available at www.greek-genocide.org/iags_resolution.html. For a discussion and critique of the resolution process, see Israel W. Charny, "The Integrity and Courage to Recognize All the Victims of a Genocide," in Hofmann *et al.*, eds., *The Genocide of the Ottoman Greeks*, pp. 33–38.

BOX 4A IRAQ, SYRIA, AND THE RISE OF ISLAMIC STATE (IS)

The crackup of the Ottoman Empire has yet to settle down into anything stable.

Michael J. Totten

In spring and summer 2014, as though out of nowhere, the gleeful *génocidaires* of the Islamic State (IS, also widely known as ISIS) roared out of their bases in the Sunni heartland of Iraq, and the city of Raqqa across the border in Syria, to assert hegemony over a territory the size of Great Britain. On June 28, 2014, their leader, Abu-Bakr al-Baghdadi, appeared at the Great Mosque of newly-conquered Mosul, Iraq's second-largest city, to proclaim a new "Caliphate" that would reestablish the glories of Islamic civilizations past, and pave the way for an apocalyptic showdown with the *kuffar* (unbelievers).

Unlike previous terrorist manifestations of Saudi Arabian–derived Salafist religious extremism, such as Al-Qa'eda (see pp. 60–61), this theocratic project would not limit itself to confronting the forces of the West and Israel, together with their decadent so-called minions in the Arab Gulf states. It was to target with even greater ferocity the "apostates" of the Muslim world—the Shia Muslims who had split from the dominant Sunni tendency early in the life of the Islamic faith. Al-Qa'eda's Osama Bin Laden had held back

Figure 4a.1 Islamic State leader Abu Bakr al-Baghdadi has declared a new "Caliphate" to rally Sunni Muslims in Iraq, Syria, and beyond to his extremist and "eliminationist" cause.

Source: Artwork by Thierry Ehrmann/Creative Commons/Flickr.

from such sectarian assaults, not least because his own mother was of the Alawite sect, a Shia offshoot that *de facto* ruled Bashar al-Assad's Syria. But under Abu Musab al-Zarqawi, who formally declared himself the leader of "Al-Qa'eda in Iraq" and struck a formal alliance with Bin Laden before his death under US bombs in 2006,[1] "made no secret of his pathological hatred of Iraq's demographic majority"—close to two-thirds of the population, versus the Sunnis' one-fifth. His savagery, including beheadings of Iraqis and foreigners filmed and posted to the Internet, earned him the sobriquet of "The Sheikh of the Slaughterers" among his admiring followers. Like him, they saw the Shia as "grave-worshippers, idolaters, and polytheists," a stain on Islam to be cleansed.[2] As for ancient ethnic groups like the Yazidis and Mandeans, with their partly pre-Islamic, neo-pagan beliefs,[3] or the Kurds—their males were to be exterminated, and their females enslaved.[4] (Curiously, Christians and Jews, as "people of the book," were nominally to be protected under the Islamic State—though many were massacred anyway, places of worship were closed or destroyed, and few surviving believers stayed to discover the practical extent of the regime's tolerance.)

Yet in crucial respects, the only surprising thing about IS was the speed with which, in summer 2014, it was able to conquer a huge swath of territory in a matter of weeks (including Mosul, Iraq's second-largest city), sending Iraqi forces that on paper were ten or twenty times their size fleeing in disarray. From the early months following the US invasion of Iraq in February 2003 to overthrow the brutal Ba'thist regime of Saddam Hussein, a potent alliance had emerged between tribes of the Iraqi Sunni minority, feeling excluded and humiliated in a Shia-dominated "new order"; commanders and foot-soldiers of the former regime, now fired from their jobs under the "de-Ba'thization" program—instituted by the Bush government in a nod to postwar denazification in Germany, but far more sweeping and indiscriminate; and crucially, leftover radical-Sunni-Islamist elements from the war against the Soviet occupation of Afghanistan (see pp. 106–107, 110–111), calling for the creation of a murderous and ultra-puritanical new order reminiscent of the Khmer Rouge's millenarian fanaticism (Chapter 7).[5] An abiding antipathy toward Shia, both politically- and religiously-inspired, united these elements, which have coexisted (not without friction) throughout the contemporary operations of Islamic State.

At both main stages of their ascent—2004–2006 and 2014–2015—the Sunni-Islamist new order drew its strength from power vacuums. The United States invaded Iraq with almost no clue as to what would follow the destruction of the Ba'thist state. Security collapsed, looting was widespread—including of priceless historical artifacts—electricity supplies were worse than under the sanctions-crippled Hussein dictatorship,[6] and sewage and garbage piled up in the streets. Whatever claim to legitimacy the American occupiers possessed at the outset vanished with the revelations of US forces' torture and abuse of detained (almost exclusively Sunni) men at the

Abu Ghraib prison. Apart from its vulnerability to US raids on households and the mass seizure of menfolk for detention and interrogation, Sunni-dominated Anbar Province, west of the capital Baghdad, was left to fester. It was in that context that the Sunni militants—many of them foreigners, like the notorious former gangster al-Zarqawi, a Jordanian—could present themselves as allies and protectors of the Sunni tribes, their shield against the Shia threat.

It was the Islamists who introduced to postwar Iraq the terrifying new phenomenon of the suicide bomber, especially one armed with a "vehicle-borne improvised explosive device" (VBIED)—a car or truck bomb, often targeting civilians *en masse*.[7] Soon after the destruction of the Ba'thist regime, al-Zarqawi's terrorists launched devastating suicide attacks in Baghdad against the Jordanian embassy in Baghdad, symbol of al-Zarqawi's homeland where the *Mukhabarat* (secret police) had hounded him mercilessly; a hotel occupied by UN Special Representative Sérgio Vieira de Mello and his team (Vieira de Mello was killed along with twenty-one others in the explosion);[8] and Shia markets and religious sites in the south of the capital. A senior CIA counterterrorism expert, Bruce Riedel, described it as a "brilliant strategy." "By attacking the UN, he drove out all the nongovernmental organizations and discouraged anyone from opening an embassy." The slaughter of Shia "apostates" irrevocably divided communities that had generally coexisted and cohabited for centuries. "So first he isolated us [the American occupiers] in Iraq, then he put us in the midst of a civil war."[9]

In February 2006, the al-Zarqawi-organized destruction of the al-Askari mosque in Samarra, a sacred Shia shrine, launched the genocidal paroxysm that engulfed Iraq from 2005 to 2007. Such a provocation could only bring a massive repressive response from the now Shia-dominated Iraqi government (installed in dubiously democratic elections in January 2005) and its burgeoning security apparatus. As Sunni terrorists—al-Zarqawi's forces, but also many experienced former Ba'thist officers and soldiers—blew up mosque after market, killing hundreds of defenseless Shia, the regime promptly organized a network of death squads,[10] composed mostly of police officers (often in uniform), Interior Ministry paramilitaries, and forces led by the Shia "Mahdi army" of hardline cleric Moqtada al-Sadr. In 2005, they were unleashed, and by November of that year *The Los Angeles Times* was reporting "hundreds of bodies ... discovered in rivers, garbage dumps, sewage treatment facilities and alongside roads and in desert ravines."[11] The UK *Independent* wrote that "bodies appear every week of men, and sometimes women, executed with their hands tied behind their backs. Some have been grotesquely mutilated with knives and electric drills before their deaths."[12] In October 2006, Peter Beaumont of the UK *Guardian* reported that "there are so many bodies that their disposal has become a problem of waste management."[13] No refuge was safe: by December, *The Sunday Times* was noting "mounting evidence that Shi'ite death squads are being encouraged to roam hospitals in search of fresh Sunni victims," including Sunni doctors found in the wards.[14]

On both sides, the overwhelming majority of those murdered were male, making Iraq unquestionably the worst political-military "gendercide" of the early twenty-first century (see chs. 1, 13).[15] The trend continued in the IS period, with Shia and Yazidi men the primary targets. "When the [Iraqi] government's Badush prison, near Mosul, was captured by ISIS [in 2014], its fighters slaughtered 670 Shia prisoners. At Camp Speicher, outside Tikrit, 800 Shia cadets were lined up in front of trenches and machine-gunned. Pictures of the scene resemble those of atrocities carried out by the German army in Russia in 1941."[16] IS merrily circulated videos of Egyptian Coptic and Ethiopian Christians being marched to their executions along the Mediterranean shoreline of Libya—yet another power vacuum that the extremists sought to fill. In August 2014, IS seized control of Yazidi villages abutting Mount Sinjar in Iraq's far north:

> Survivors say that men and women were separated within the first hour of their capture. Adolescent boys were told to lift up their shirts, and if they had armpit hair, they were directed to join their older brothers and fathers. In village after village, the men and older boys were driven or marched to nearby fields, where they were forced to lie down in the dirt and sprayed with automatic fire.[17]

The atrocities inflicted on the Yazidi women and girls who were spared execution attracted worldwide attention. After distributing a *fatwa* (religious ruling) that captive women could be sexually enslaved, female Yazidis were consigned to a modern-day slave market built around "a network of warehouses where the victims are held, viewing rooms where they are inspected and marketed, and a dedicated fleet of buses used to transport them" to their new "owners." ". . . The practice has become an established recruiting tool to lure men from deeply conservative Muslim societies, where casual sex is taboo and dating is forbidden." "I kept telling him it hurts—please stop," one Yazidi survivor—a 12-year-old girl "whose body is so small an adult could circle her waist with two hands"—testified to the *The New York Times*. "He told me that according to Islam he is allowed to rape an unbeliever. He said that by raping me, he is drawing closer to God."[18] Another survivor described prospective slave-owners circulating among captive women, pinching and groping and jeering at them. "I want a Yazidi with blue eyes and pale skin," one declared. "Those are the best apparently. I am willing to pay the price."[19]

At the time of writing, an international coalition had mustered to confront IS militarily in Iraq and Syria, with successes such as the recapture of the cities of Ramadi and Fallujah in the "Sunni Triangle" west of Baghdad. However, regardless of the fate of the IS caliphate and its administrative hold over urban areas, a long-term resolution seemed unlikely without concerted

Figure 4a.2 "Displaced people from the minority Yazidi sect hold banners as they take part in a demonstration at the Iraqi—Syrian border crossing," near Dohuk, Iraqi Kurdistan, August 2014.

Source: Photo by Youssef Boudlal/Reuters.

attempts to address the "sectarian-existential" conflict between Sunni and Shia Muslim populations.[20] The legacy of the reciprocal Iraqi genocides of the mid-2000s was that many Sunnis in that shattered country considered IS, for all its barbarities, to be preferable to conquest and massacre "cleansing" by Shia militias. The Sunni majority in Syria likewise appeared to fear a reimposition of Assad's dictatorial order, buttressed by the Shia-offshoot Alawite community, more than the pro-Sunni extremists of IS. Meanwhile, what Patrick Cockburn called "the most powerful and effective jihadi group in the world"[21] was extending its reach, launching largescale terrorist attacks in the European heartland—most notably the mass slaughter in cafés and a concert hall in Paris in November 2015—while establishing branches and bases from Egypt's Sinai peninsula to the failing state of Afghanistan, and beyond.[22]

FURTHER STUDY

See sources in the footnotes for Box 4a.

NOTES

1 In an "unprecedented" move in February 2014, Al-Qa'eda formally renounced Islamic State—the former Al-Qa'eda in Iraq—citing IS's "intractability" and lack of "consultation." See Liz Sly, "Al-Qaeda Disavows Any Ties with Radical Islamist ISIS Group in Syria, Iraq," *The Washington Post*, February 3, 2014.

2 Michael Weiss and Hassan Hassan, *ISIS: Inside the Army of Terror* (New York: Regan Arts, 2015), p. 43 (e-book). See also Loretta Napoleoni, *Insurgent Iraq: Al Zarqawi and the New Generation* (London: Constable & Robinson Ltd., 2005).

3 ". . . Large pockets of neo-pagans practicing the remnants of ancient Assyrian beliefs survived in Iraq until the present day. These neo-pagans, known as Mandaeans and Yezidis, retain references in their holy scriptures to the ancient Assyrian deities such as Shamash, Sin, Bel, Ishtar, and Tammuz." Hannibal Travis, "The Assyrian Genocide: A Tale of Oblivion and Denial," in René Lemarchand, ed., *Forgotten Genocides: Oblivion, Denial, and Memory* (Philadelphia, PA: University of Pennsylvania Press, 2011), pp. 124–125.

4 According to Middle East specialist Rex Brynen, "ISIS is ideologically committed to the forced conversion or elimination of all non-Sunni Muslims (with minor exceptions) world-wide, making it genocidal in intent on a scale equivalent to the Nazis. It currently follows a policy of executing almost 100% of all non-Sunni POWs and military aged males, and has explicitly authorized and provided legal guidance for the sexual slavery of 100% of non-Sunni females that come under its areas of control. . . . And they're less self-consciously defensive about it than the Nazis. They revel in videoing and glorifying mass executions and torture (and use it for recruitment), whereas we have remarkably few grainy films of Nazi executions in WWII because many of the participants had a sense that it should somehow remain hidden—a necessary evil as it were." Brynen, Facebook post, March 7, 2015; reproduced by permission.

5 An excellent analysis of Islamic State's ideology is Graeme Wood, "What ISIS Really Wants," *The Atlantic*, March 2015, www.theatlantic.com/magazine/archive/2015/03/what-isis-really-wants/384980/. For a chilling up-close portrait of life inside IS-controlled Raqqa, Syria, see the VICE News documentary, "The Islamic State," August 2014, www.youtube.com/watch?v=AUjHb4C7b94. For an examination of IS's propaganda and media strategies, which are anything but archaic, see Jessica Stern and J.M. Berger, *ISIS: The State of Terror* (New York: Ecco Press, 2015).

6 See, at pp. 59–60, the discussion of the arguably genocidal impact of UN-sponsored sanctions against Iraq during the 1990s.

7 See Mike Davis, *Buda's Wagon: A Brief History of the Car Bomb* (London: Verso, 2008).

8 Vieira de Mello had previously headed the United Nations' exemplary reconstruction effort and peacebuilding effort in East Timor following the referendum and related mass violence in the Indonesian-occupied territory (Chapter 7a). The follow-up work of Samantha Power to her groundbreaking *"A Problem from Hell": America in the Age of Genocide* (see Further Study, Chapter 1) was a lengthy biography of this much-missed figure, likely a future UN Secretary-General had al-Zarqawi and his truck-bomber not dictated otherwise. See Power, *Chasing the Flame: One Man's Fight to Save the World* (New York: Penguin Books, 2008).

9 Riedel quoted in Joby Warrick, *Black Flags: The Rise of ISIS* (New York: Doubleday, 2015), pp. 141–142 (e-book).

10 Solomon Moore, "Killings Linked to Shiite Squads in Iraqi Police Force," *The Los Angeles Times*, November 29, 2005. "The Death Squads," an up-close and stomach-churning documentary produced by *Britain's Channel 4*, can be searched on Google Videos (http://videos.google.com).

11 Kim Sengupta, "Raid on Torture Dungeon Exposes Iraq's Secret War," *The Independent*, November 16, 2005. See also Kim Sengupta, "The Dirty War: Torture and Mutilation Used on Iraqi 'Insurgents,'" *The Independent*, November 20, 2005; Dexter Filkins, "Sunnis Accuse Iraqi Military of Kidnappings and Slayings," *The New York Times*, November 29, 2005; Moore, "Killings Linked to Shiite Squads."

12 Patrick Cockburn, "Death Squads on the Prowl in a Nation Paralysed by Fear," *The Independent*, March 20, 2006, www.independent.co.uk/news/world/middle-east/death-squads-on-the-prowl-in-a-nation-paralysed-by-fear-470650.html.

13 Peter Beaumont, "Aura of Fear and Death Stalks Iraq," *The Guardian*, October 12, 2006, http://www.guardian.co.uk/world/2006/oct/12/iraq.peterbeaumont.

14 Hala Jaber, "Death Squads Roam Baghdad's Hospitals," *The Sunday Times*, December 3, 2006, www.thesundaytimes.co.uk/sto/news/world_news/article175108.ece. See also Christian Berthelsen, "Iraqis Turn to Tattoos as Indelible IDs," *The Los Angeles Times*, April 20, 2007. A Baghdad morgue worker related a macabre detail: that "the fear of leaving the bereaved without a corpse to bury is so strong that some Iraqi men now tattoo their names, phone numbers and other identifying information on their upper thighs, despite Islam's strict disapproval against such practices." "Baghdad's Morgues Working Overtime," Associated Press dispatch on *MSNBC.com*, November 12, 2006, www.msnbc.msn.com/id/15690725. See also Hala Jaber, "The Accursed: Widows of Iraq's Torn-Apart Society," *The Sunday Times*, April 29, 2007, www.thesundaytimes.co.uk/sto/news/world_news/article63848.ece. Gendercidal killings of women for alleged transgressions of Islamic morality were also reported, particularly in the southern city of Basra at the hands of "Propagation of Virtue and Prevention of Vice" squads set up by the Shia authorities controlling the city. See Yifat Susskind, "Who Is Killing the Women of Basra?," *CommonDreams.org*, January 10, 2008, www.commondreams.org/archive/2008/01/10/6287. "City officials reported on December 31 [2007] that 133 women were killed and mutilated last year, their bodies dumped in trash bins with notes warning others against 'violating Islamic teachings . . .' But ambulance drivers who are hired to troll the city streets in the early mornings to collect the bodies confirm what most residents believe: the actual numbers are much higher. The killers' leaflets are not very original. They usually accuse the women of being prostitutes or adulterers. But . . . most of the women who have been murdered 'are PhD holders, professionals, activists, and office workers.' Their crime is not 'promiscuity,' but rather opposition to the transformation of Iraq into an Islamist state. That bloody transition has been the main political trend under US occupation." Gay and trans Iraqis were additionally targeted in genocidal/gendercidal fashion: see the discussion in Chapter 13, pp. 637–639.

15 How many Iraqis were murdered and otherwise died violently between the 2003 invasion and the climax of the initial wave of genocide in 2007 remains a subject of intense and sometimes vituperative dispute. But a civilian toll in the many hundreds of thousands seems in keeping with the most systematic and consistent data. Indeed, according to those data, by 2007 when the most devastating wave of killing had subsided (at least temporarily), *over a million* Iraqis had died violently. As Joshua Holland noted at the time, it may well be that "the

human toll exceeds the 800,000 to 900,000 believed killed in the Rwandan genocide in 1994, and is approaching the number (1.7 million) who died in Cambodia's infamous 'Killing Fields' during the Khmer Rouge era of the 1970s" (see Chapters 7 and 9). Holland, "Iraq Death Toll Rivals Rwanda Genocide, Cambodian Killing Fields," *AlterNet.org*, September 17, 2007, www.alternet.org/ waroniraq/62728. The calculations and sources were described in greater detail in the second (2011) edition of this book, at pp. 183–184.

16 Patrick Cockburn, "Life under Isis," *The Independent*, March 18, 2015, www. independent.co.uk/news/world/middle-east/life-under-isis-the-everyday-reality-of-living-in-the-islamic-caliphate-with-its-7th-century-laws-10109655. html.

17 Rukmini Callimachi, "ISIS Enshrines a Theology of Rape," *The New York Times*, August 13, 2015, www.nytimes.com/2015/08/14/world/middleeast/ isis-enshrines-a-theology-of-rape.html. In November 2015, the US Holocaust Memorial Museum stated that a "preponderance of the evidence" indicated that the Yazidis were suffering genocide at the hands of IS. According to USHMM researcher Naomi Kikoler, "IS specifically notes that its treatment of the Yazidis differs from its treatment of *ahl al kitab*, the 'people of the book,' Christians and Jews, who had the option of paying the *jizya* (tax) to avoid conversion or death. By refusing Yezidis [*sic*; an alternate spelling] any option to avoid death or forced conversion, IS demonstrates that its actions were calculated with the intent of destroying the community and thereby different from its attacks against other minorities, which were part of a campaign of ethnic cleansing." See Adam Taylor, "Yes, the Islamic State's Attacks on the Yazidis Constitute Genocide, New Report Says," *The Washington Post*, November 12, 2015, www.washingtonpost. com/news/worldviews/wp/2015/11/12/yes-the-islamic-states-attacks-on-the-yazidis-are-a-genocide-new-report-says/. As this edition was going into production, in June 2016, the United Nations' Human Rights Council also found that genocide of the Yazidis was "ongoing." See Matt Brown, "Islamic State Militants Committing Genocide against Yazidis in Syria, Iraq: UN Investigation," *ABC.net*, June 16, 2016, www.abc.net.au/news/2016–06–17/islamic-state-committing-genocide-against-yazidis-un/7518978; the full text of the UN report is available at www.ohchr.org/Documents/HRBodies/HRCouncil/ CoISyria/A_HRC_32_CRP.2_en.pdf.

18 Callimachi, "ISIS."

19 Michel Moutot, "'I Want a Blue-Eyed Yazidi': Teen Describes ISIS Slave Market," AFP Paris dispatch in *The Times of India*, September 2, 2014, http://timesofindia. indiatimes.com/world/europe/I-want-a-blue-eyed-Yazidi-Teen-describes-IS-slave-market/articleshow/48770814.cms.

20 Weiss and Hassan, *ISIS*, p. 44 (e-book).

21 Patrick Cockburn, *The Rise of Islamic State: ISIS and the New Sunni Revolution* (London: Verso, 2015), p. 13 (e-book).

22 Lynne O'Donnell and Humayoon Babur, "ISIS is Expanding Its 'Caliphate' to Afghanistan," Associated Press dispatch in *Business Insider*, December 19, 2015, www. businessinsider.com/isis-is-expanding-its-caliphate-to-afghanistan-2015–12.

CHAPTER 5

Stalin and Mao

Enemies are not people. We're allowed to do what we like with them. People indeed!

Soviet secret police interrogator to Eugenia Ginzburg,
in *Journey into the Whirlwind*

"No other state in history," wrote genocide scholar Richard Rubenstein, "has ever initiated policies designed to eliminate so many of its own citizens as has the Soviet Union."[1] His contention can be challenged. In absolute numbers, the death toll inflicted on the Chinese people by Mao Zedong's communists was significantly greater than the Soviet one. And per capita, Cambodia's Khmer Rouge government (see Chapter 7) devised policies that destroyed fully one-quarter of the country's population in less than four years. A striking feature of these cases is the links among them. Mao's communists were in many ways Stalin's protégés; the Sino-Soviet split of the late 1950s, which irretrievably sundered the world communist movement, reflected Mao's conviction that the Soviets had betrayed Stalin's great legacy. The Khmer Rouge, in turn, took its inspiration from both Stalinism and Maoism, but particularly from the latter's ultra-collectivism and utopianism.

The version of communism instituted in these three regimes was in central respects a perversion of the original doctrine, developed by Karl Marx and others in the nineteenth century. "Marxism" defines society and historical evolution in terms of social classes, inevitably unequal and opposed, and therefore destined for "class struggle." It posits that when the proletariat—the urban working classes created by modern capitalism—finally takes control of the commanding heights of the economy and political structure, the state will wither away, and a world without hierarchy will come into being, in which humans work according to their ability, and receive according to their need.

Marxism and socialism were crucial in spurring modern conceptions and movements of human rights, women's rights, workers' rights, anti-colonialism, and anti-racism. As Cathie Carmichael rightly asserted, during the nineteenth and early twentieth centuries, "there was an elective affinity between the left and humanism."[2] Today, many of the most prosperous societies in the world are those built on broadly democratic-socialist foundations, as in Scandinavia.

Yet the focus of a book on genocide must be on those twentieth-century rulers who proclaimed themselves "socialist" while imposing states that were more or less despotic, and sometimes mega-murderous on a scale that rarely if ever has been matched in history. Proclaimed socialist-humanist values were trumped and trampled by messianic narcissism and power-hunger, by nationalist and racist hubris, by security fears, and by flat-out paranoia. In Stalin's Soviet Union, communist China, and Cambodia under the Khmer Rouge, all those outside the party faithful (and eventually many of the faithful too) were labeled "enemies," denounced, humiliated, and destroyed. Moreover, notions of incremental advance toward communism were replaced by a conviction that paradise was just around the corner—if only the population could be induced to haul the state and economy toward it. Given that all three countries were predominantly agricultural, massive "collectivization" of the rural population was used to yoke them to their revolutionary task, and to support the headlong drive for urbanization and industrialization that figured so prominently in the Soviet and Chinese models.

The consequence of this ideological extremism was human destruction on a scale that beggars belief. Much of it took the form of outright murder. But most victims were killed *indirectly*, through incarceration and forced labor, or manipulated famines. The famines were not planned as such, but they were the predictable result of regime policies, exacerbated by leaders' conscious refusal to intervene and ameliorate them. In that sense, genocidal intent may be discerned in both the direct and indirect forms of killing. And while in all three cases the majority of victims were drawn from the same ethnonational group as the perpetrators, a more "orthodox" genocidal targeting of ethnic minorities also featured. This chapter explores the Stalinist and Maoist cases with, as noted, the Khmer Rouge genocide examined separately in Chapter 7.

THE SOVIET UNION AND STALINISM

1917: The Bolsheviks seize power

The Bolshevik Revolution took place after centuries of dictatorship and underdevelopment in Russia, as well as the most destructive war to that point in European history (see Chapter 2). By 1917, Russian armies facing German and Austro-Hungarian forces had been pushed to the brink of collapse, and the Russian population confronted famine. Bread riots broke out in the capital, Petrograd (St. Petersburg). In the face of growing popular and elite opposition, Tsar Nicholas II abdicated, turning over power to a liberal-dominated provisional government under Alexander Kerensky. Fatefully, Kerensky's regime chose to continue the war. Russian forces crumbled in a poorly conceived military offensive. Hundreds of thousands of soldiers deserted. Across Russia's fertile regions, spontaneous seizures of land added to the chaos.

Poised to exploit the turmoil was Lenin's Bolshevik party. Lenin was a Russian of noble birth who had discovered Marxist socialism and agitated from exile for the overthrow of the tsarist regime. Spirited back to Russia on a sealed train by the German government, which saw Lenin (presciently) as a means of removing Russia from the war, Lenin and the Bolsheviks found themselves in a minority position *vis-à-vis* the leading socialist faction, the Mensheviks. Lenin improved Bolshevik fortunes by promising "Bread, Peace, Land." But the party was still a marginal force, almost non-existent outside the major cities, when Lenin launched a coup against the weak Kerensky regime.

After storming Petrograd's Winter Palace and seizing key infrastructure, the Bolsheviks found themselves in power—but with many predicting that their regime would last only weeks or months. To bolster their position and popular base, they quickly sued for peace with Germany and, in the Treaty of Brest-Litovsk (March 1918), gave up some of Russia's most fertile, resource-rich territories.

"There can be no revolution without counterrevolution," wrote historian Arno Mayer.[3] A potent counter-revolution now confronted the new "Soviet Union" (the "soviets" were workers' councils taken over by the Bolsheviks as a means of controlling Russia's working classes). "Whites"—anti-Bolshevist Russians—sought to overthrow the Bolshevik "Reds." Russia's former allies, notably Britain and the United States, were furious at Lenin's retreat from the First World War, and terrified at the prospect of socialist revolution spreading across Europe. With funding, arms, and tens of thousands of troops on the ground, they backed the Whites in a three-year struggle with the Bolshevik regime.

This civil war, one of the most destructive of the twentieth century, lasted until 1921 and claimed an estimated nine million lives on all sides. According to historian Alec Nove, "[its] influence . . . on the whole course of subsequent history, and on Stalinism, cannot possibly be overestimated. It was during the civil war that Stalin and men like Stalin emerged as leaders, while others became accustomed to harshness, cruelty, terror."[4] Red forces imposed "War Communism," an economic policy that repealed peasants' land seizures, forcibly stripped the countryside of grain to feed city dwellers, and suppressed private commerce. All who opposed these policies were "enemies of the people." "This is the hour of truth," Lenin wrote in mid-1918. "It is of supreme importance that we encourage and make use of the energy of mass terror directed against the counterrevolutionaries."[5] The Cheka, the first incarnation of the Soviet secret police (later the NKVD and finally the KGB), responded with gusto. Lenin and other Bolshevik leaders may have viewed mass terror as a short-term measure,[6] but its widespread use belies claims that it was Stalin's invention.[7]

The civil war left the Reds victorious but the Soviet Union shattered. Famine had struck large areas of the country, and millions in rural areas were kept alive only through foreign, especially US, generosity.[8] Acknowledging reality—a capacity not yet extinguished among Bolsheviks—Lenin repealed the War Communism measures. He allowed peasants to return to the land, and instituted the so-called New Economic Policy (NEP). Under the NEP, market mechanisms were revived, and the economy was regenerated.

Weakened by an assassination attempt and a series of strokes, Lenin died in 1924, leaving the field open for an up-and-coming Bolshevik leader to launch his drive for absolute power.

Joseph Stalin was born Joseph Dzhugashvili in Gori, Georgia, in 1879. His Caucasian background, his abusive upbringing, and the years he spent in Russian Orthodox seminaries have all been linked to his personality and subsequent policies: "There has been too much cod-psychology about Stalin's childhood," cautioned Simon Sebag Montefiore in his Stalin biography, "but this much is certain: raised in a poor priest-ridden household, he was damaged by violence, insecurity and suspicion but inspired by the local traditions of religious dogmatism, blood-feuding and romantic brigandry."[9] In the pre-revolutionary period, the brigand led a series of bank robberies that brought him to the attention of high officials. It was at this time that Dzhugashvili adopted his party moniker, Stalin, meaning "Man of Steel." Captured by tsarist authorities, he endured two spells of exile in Siberia.

After the Bolsheviks seized power, Stalin was appointed General Secretary of the Communist Party in 1922. In itself, the post was an administrative one. But it was ideally suited to one who "did not dazzle in theoretical discussions, but . . . knew how to assemble a coalition."[10] Stalin used the secretariat to build a power base and establish control over the party bureaucracy, while also earning a reputation as "a dynamic leader who had a hand in nearly all the principal discussions on politics, military strategy, economics, security and international relations."[11] When Lenin died in 1924, a struggle for supremacy pitted Stalin against his nemesis, Leon Trotsky, and a host of lesser figures. Stalin's victory was slow and hard-won, but by 1927 he and his allies had succeeded in expelling Trotsky from the party and, in 1929, from the country.[12]

By 1928, Stalin was entrenched as supreme Soviet leader. With world revolution a distant prospect, Stalin chose the course of "socialism in one country," which for him meant "a new programme of extremely—almost hysterically—rapid industrialization."[13] In this decision lay the seeds of two principal genocidal policies: the massive expansion of the Gulag, or prison, system, and the campaign against the peasantry, whose grain was needed to feed cities swelled by Stalin's crash industrialization program.

The two strategies intersected. By waging class warfare in the countryside, Stalin could expropriate the holdings of the wealthier (or less poor) peasants; conscript millions of them into forced labor on industrial projects; and also use the new bounty of prisoners to extract natural resources (especially gold and timber) that could be sold abroad for the hard currency needed to purchase industrial machinery and pay foreign advisors. The policies were driven both by desperation and by an abiding contempt for the "backward" peasantry and its allegedly coun-ter-revolutionary inclinations. Mark Levene draws an important connection when he notes that Soviet peasants

> were to the party what colonial natives were to settlers and imperial adminis-trators: they could only be redeemed from their uncouth drunken sloth, stu-pidity, and slovenliness through assimilation into the Soviet model. Their ability to act of [their] own volition, or for goals which were anything but reactionary, was nil.

And just as the "colonialist counter-response" to native resistance was "invariably one of massive, retributive, exterminatory overkill," Levene writes, "so it was with the Bolsheviks."[14]

Collectivization and famine

Whatever their rhetorical claims to represent working people, the Soviet attitude toward peasants was one of thinly disguised contempt. "On the one hand they were the People incarnate, the soul of the country, suffering, patient, the hope of the future," wrote Robert Conquest, a leading historian of the Stalinist era. "On the other, they appeared as the 'dark people,' backward, mulish, deaf to argument, an oafish impediment to all progress."[15]

Of this group, it was the so-called "kulaks" who aroused the greatest Bolshe-vik hatred. The definition of "kulak" (the word means "fist," as in "tight-fisted") was subject to terrifyingly random variations, and remained "abstract, unclear, and contested" throughout the life of the Stalinist regime.[16] In general, at least at the outset of the campaign, the kulaks were better-off peasants, perhaps only slightly better-off. Owning a cow or hiring a helper could be enough to earn the des-ignation, with consequences that were often fatal, even in the earliest phase of Bolshevik rule. Lenin, for example, referred to kulaks as "avaricious, bloated, and bestial," "spiders," "leeches," "vampires," and "the most brutal, callous, and savage exploiters."[17] "Merciless mass terror against the kulaks. . . . Death to them!" Lenin pronounced, before death took him as well.[18]

As was his habit, Stalin carried things to extremes. The definition of "kulak" grew ever more expansive: "As the state entered into what would be a protracted war with the peasantry," wrote historian Lynne Viola, "the kulak came to serve as a political metaphor and pejorative for the entire peasantry."[19] In January 1930, Stalin formally "approved the liquidation of kulaks as a class."[20] Bolshevik leader Mendel Khataevich then instructed Communist Party functionaries to "throw your bourgeois humanitarianism out the window" and "beat down the kulak agent wherever he raises his head. It's war—it's them or us. The last decayed rem-nant of capitalist farming must be wiped out at any cost."[21] Party militants duti-fully mouthed slogans like: "We will exile the kulak by the thousands and when necessary—shoot the kulak breed"; "We will make soap of kulaks"; "Our class enemy must be wiped off the face of the earth."[22]

In a taste of the quota-fueled terror that would prevail later in the decade, Orlando Figes noted that "in some villages the peasants chose the 'kulaks' from their own number. They simply held a village meeting and decided who should go as a 'kulak' (isolated farmers, widows and old people were particularly vulnerable)."[23] "At least 10 million 'kulaks' were expelled from their homes and villages between 1929 and 1932." About 1.4 million were dispatched to the Gulag concentration-camp system (see next section) or attached forced-labor camps. The conditions under which they were transported frequently killed them before they arrived, including months spent "in primitive detention camps, where children and the elderly died like flies in the appalling conditions."[24] As for the "special settlements" themselves, they were generally established in remote and inhospitable northern regions—part of the regime's designs to open up the mineral-and timber-rich north, to which free laborers could not readily be lured. Virtually no preparations were made for their arrival, leading to mortality rates (15 percent in the Northern Territory of Siberia in 1930 alone)[25] that can be considered as genocide implemented through intentional negligence and willful disregard for subsistence needs. Mark Levene eloquently describes the process:

> Brought to collection points by carts or forced march, from February [1930] onwards, with the minimum of possessions—though supposedly with enough food to sustain them for an initial two-month period—deportees found themselves rail-freighted in cattle wagons for days and weeks, in utterly cramped, freezing, entirely inhumane and degrading conditions. For survivors, however—that is, for those not "abandoned in deportation"—the journey was only the first part of a living hell. Arriving in distant destinations, very often in the middle of nowhere and without any shelter or food to rest and sustain them, they were put to work, usually scores, if not hundreds, of kilometres from their yet-to-be[-]built settlements: mostly in felling and hewing timber, mining, and other extractive projects organized under [police-militia] commandants. . . . It was Russian-style hyper-exploitation pure and simple: shambolically implemented, viciously brutal, vastly under-resourced. Starvation for the ablebodied—this, remember, before the famine sequence of 1932–3—rapidly kicked in, as either insufficient food to hand or operating regimes in which deportees were only fed if they fulfilled their production quota inevitably created a vicious circle. The more exhausted and ill they became from overwork, the more they failed to deliver, the less gruel they received. . . . Herded together thus, in these insanitary conditions and with few medical carers to tend to their misery let alone drugs available to check the rampant spread of measles, diphtheria, pneumonia, and whooping cough, public health collapse did much of the work which direct genocidal shooting or gassing might otherwise have done.[26]

After the "kulaks" were destroyed or banished, the regime's agents scoured the newly collectivized countryside for grain to feed the cities. Often the tax imposed on peasants exceeded the amount that could be harvested. The result was widespread famine, not only in Ukraine, but in the Volga region, Kazakhstan, and other territories afflicted by the twin evils of forced collectivization and grain seizures.

Figure 5.1 "Enemies of the Five Year Plan." The plan imposed collectivization on the Soviet countryside, with genocidal consequences. "This poster from 1929 attacks eight groups that were frequently scapegoated [in the USSR] (clockwise from top left): landlords, kulaks, journalists, capitalists, White Russians [supporters of the former tsarist regime], Mensheviks [factional opponents of the Bolsheviks], priests, and drunkards. . . . The poem at the bottom of the poster was written by Demyan Bedny, one of Stalin's favorite poets. The poem harshly ridicules these members of the 'old order,' describing them as 'hounds that have not yet been caged.' The group is condemned for 'declaring war' on the Five-Year Plan because 'they understand that it will bring about their final destruction.'"

Source: Gareth Jones collection (www.garethjones.org); artwork by Viktor Deni; caption text from *Hoover Digest*, 1998: 3 (www.hoover.org/research/documents-terror).

Stalin and his associates cared little. In their minds, famine was the price of progress and national security; the Soviet Union would "develop," and buttress itself against a hostile world. Moreover, just as the British architects of nineteenth-century Irish and Indian famines had stockpiled and exported food throughout the crises (see Chapter 2), so did Stalin's Soviet Union. ". . . It is imperative to export without fail immediately," Stalin declared in June 1932.[27] Thus, "while millions of peasants were dying of hunger,""the Soviet government was exporting 1,800,000 tons of cereals to honour its debts to Germany and to buy foreign machinery intended to make possible the accelerated industrialization plans. In that year of 1933, the state's strategic reserves, held in case of war, exceeded three million tons—a quantity more than sufficient to save millions of the starving populations."[28] And just as in its Maoist protégé, Stalin refused "to accept any help from the outside world," as the death rate rose to 10,000 a day.[29]

Figure 5.2 Slave labor on Stalinist megaprojects like the White Sea Canal, pictured here in 1932, killed hundreds of thousands of "kulaks" and "enemies of the people."

Source: Government of the Russian Federation/Wikimedia Commons.

Then, as the crisis escalated, it appears that Stalin and his henchmen seized the opportunity to wreak havoc on Ukrainian nationalism, embedded as it was in peasant culture and society. Most scholars now reject Robert Conquest's initial argument that Stalin *planned* the famine to this end.[30] But pre-planning is hardly necessary for a finding of genocide, and the results of intentional actions that aggravated the famine—the seizure of crops, seed grain, and livestock—were no less devastating than if they had been meticulously plotted in advance.[31] As collectivization spread, "a veritable crescendo of terror by hunger" descended on Ukraine and Kazakhstan.[32] "A former activist" in Ukraine described the consequences, particularly for the most vulnerable:

The most terrifying sights were the little children with skeleton limbs dangling from balloon-like abdomens. Starvation had wiped every trace of youth from their faces, turning them into tortured gargoyles; only in their eyes still lingered the reminder of childhood. Everywhere we found men and women lying prone, their faces and bellies bloated, their eyes utterly expressionless.[33]

The massive mortality was covered up by, among other measures, systematically expunging data from village records. In April 1934, for instance, secret instructions were issued to the Odessa region in Ukraine "to withdraw death registration books from village councils: for 1933 from all village councils without exception and for 1932 according to the list provided . . . To transfer the withdrawn village council registration books to the raion [district] executive committees for safe-keeping as classified material."[34] For decades, it was possible to refer to the famine only with euphemisms like "food difficulties."

A credible estimate of excess deaths in the famine, across all regions of the USSR from 1930 to 1933, is 5.7 million[35]—approximately the number of European Jews killed by the Nazis, including those murdered indirectly by starvation and disease. Perhaps 3.9 million perished from unnatural causes in Ukraine between 1926 and 1937, mostly during what succeeding generations of Ukrainians have come to know as the *Holodomor*, or "hunger-extermination."[36] The overwhelmingly majority were ethnic Ukrainians, and for those who allow for notions of cultural genocide, the gutting of Ukrainian society's integrity and identity in

Figure 5.3 "Passers-by no longer pay attention to the corpses of starved peasants on a street" in Kharkov, Ukraine, during Stalin's "terror-famine" of 1932–1933.

Source: Famine in the Soviet Ukraine 1932–1933: A Memorial Exhibition, Widener Library, Harvard University/Wikimedia Commons.

the decades following the Holodomor could serve as a prime example. (Raphael Lemkin considered the Ukrainian holocaust "the classic example of Soviet geno-cide.")[37] The lives of perhaps 1,450,000 Kazakhs were extinguished during the same period—almost unnoticed, then or since. Proportional to their population, this marks the Kazakhs as the national group that "suffered the most consequences of the 'revolution from above' in the rural sector."[38]

The Gulag

As noted, hundreds of thousands of the "kulaks" deported during the collectiviza-tion drive were deposited in the Gulag prison system ("GULag" was an acronym for administrative use). They joined other class enemies in a vast slave-labor net-work that had swelled to 2.4 million inmates by 1936[39] (see Map 5.1). Much of their labor was diverted to hare-brained schemes such as the White Sea Canal, which claimed tens of thousands of lives but fell into near-disuse after its comple-tion.[40] In general, they were concentrated in climatically extreme environments, virtually devoid of infrastructure, which free workers shunned. Typical was the fate of "scores of thousands of prisoners, almost entirely peasants . . . thrown ashore at Magadan [in Siberia] in an ill-considered crash programme to exploit the newly discovered gold seams in the area." Conquest wrote that "whole camps perished to a man, even including guards and guard dogs"; "not more than one in fifty of the prisoners, if that, survived" their first year of incarceration in the remote region.[41]

Of the "476 camp complexes" in the Gulag, "to which some eighteen million people would be sentenced, of whom between a million and a half and three mil-lion would die during their periods of incarceration,"[42] it was the Siberian camps, devoted to gold-mining or timber harvesting, that inflicted the greatest toll. Such camps "can only be described as extermination centres," according to Leo Kuper.[43] The camp network that came to symbolize the horrors of the Gulag was centered on the Kolyma gold-fields, where "outside work for prisoners was compulsory until the temperature reached −50C and the death rate among miners in the goldfields was estimated at about 30 per cent per annum."[44] Apart from death by starvation, disease, accidents, and overwork, NKVD execution squads pronounced death sentences on a whim. In just one camp, Serpantinka, "more prisoners were executed . . . in the one year 1938, than the total executions throughout the Russian Empire for the whole of the last century of Tsarist rule."[45] The number of victims claimed by the Kolyma camps was between a quarter of a million and over a million; in the today lightly populated region, "skeletons in frozen, shallow mass graves far outnumber the liv-ing."[46] Other names engraved on Russians' historical memory include Norilsk, "the centre of a group of camps more deadly than Kolyma"; and Vorkuta, with a regime characterized by "extravagant cold," "exhaustion," and a "starvation diet."[47]

Were the imprisoned multitudes in the Soviet Union *meant* to die? Can we speak of genocidal intent in that sense? The answer may vary according to location and historical-political context. The deaths in the northern camps of the Arctic Circle appear to have exhibited a high degree of genocidal intent, both specific and general. The predominantly peasant and political prisoners were regularly depicted

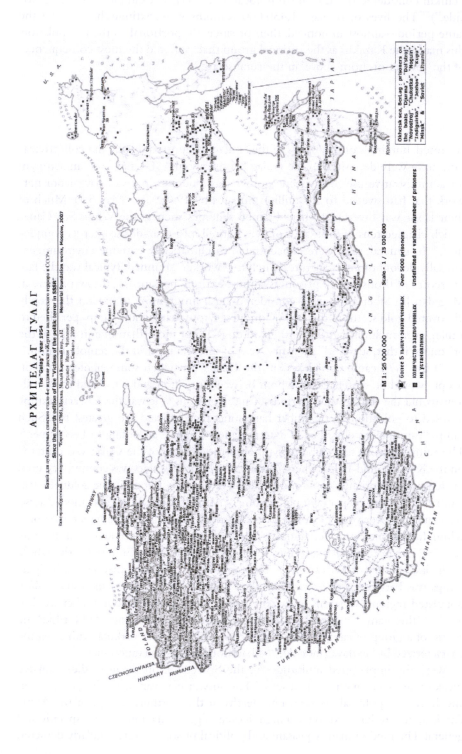

Map 5.1 A Russian map of the Gulag labor–camp system prepared by Memorial, a citizens' organization that works to document the crimes of the former USSR (see also pp. 278–279). The map shows the reach of the Gulag "across the length and breadth of the Soviet Union, from the islands of the White Sea to the shores of the Black Sea, from the Arctic Circle to the plains of central Asia, from Murmansk to Vorkuta to Kazakhstan, from central Moscow to the Leningrad [St. Petersburg] suburbs." The major network in the far northeast includes the Kolyma gold fields in Siberia, where some of the most murderous camps were located.

Source: Memorial/www.memo.ru.

Figure 5.4 "The fence and guard tower at the Soviet forced labor camp Perm–36 100 km northeast of the city of Perm in Russia, part of the prison camp system operated by the Soviet Union in the Stalin era known as the GULag. The last remaining example of a GULag labor camp, the site has been preserved as a museum and is open to the public as 'The Museum of the History of Political Repression Perm–36.'" In 2016, however, *The New York Times* reported that the complex "was recently taken over by the [Putin] government, which changed the site's focus to its contribution to the victory in World War II."[48]

Source: July 2011 photo by Gerald Praschl/Wikimedia Commons.

as subhuman or (in the case of "politicals") the most dangerous of enemies. At best, they were viewed as fodder for the mines and quarries and frozen forests: "A main goal of the Soviet labor-camp system," Ian Frazier wrote, "was to take those citizens the Soviet Union did not need, for political or social or unfathomable reasons, and convert their lives to gold and timber that could be traded abroad."[49] Since the most dangerous conditions imaginable were inflicted, tolerated, and perpetuated; since life expectancy in the camps was often measured in weeks and months; and since almost no measures were proposed or successfully introduced to keep prisoners alive, their fate seems no less genocidal than that of the American Indians worked and starved to death in the Spanish silver mines (Chapter 3).

However, unlike the Spanish mines or the Nazi death camps, conditions varied significantly across the vast Gulag system (apart from the worst of the war years, when privation reigned all across the USSR). Outside the Arctic camps, work regimes were less harsh and death rates far lower. Here, indeed—and even in Siberia after 1938–1939—high mortality rates could be viewed as undermining socialist production. While work regimes in the Nazi death camps were specifically designed to inflict mass murder, the intended function of the Soviet camps was primarily political and economic (though the Gulag never turned a profit). Camp commanders who impeded these functions by imposing an overly destructive regime could be sanctioned, even dismissed. Finally, at no point did the Soviets institute a "selection" process analogous to the Nazi ritual of dispatching older or weaker prisoners (along with children and pregnant women) for immediate slaughter. In fact, Soviet practice differed sharply.[50]

The Great Purge of 1937–1938

It is the purge of the Communist Party that many view as the nadir of Stalinist terror. However, as the Gulag's chronicler, Anne Applebaum, pointed out, this is misleading. Millions had already died—in famines, while undergoing deportation, in exile, and in camps—before Stalin turned against the "Old Bolsheviks" and their alleged legions of co-conspirators. The apex of the Gulag system actually came much later, after the Second World War. Moreover, as historians Orlando Figes, Lynne Viola, and Timothy Snyder have all noted, the largest category of victims in 1937–1938 was not the communist elite, but "kulaks" in the "second dekulakization campaign" known as "mass operation 00447." Hundreds of thousands had fled the "special settlements," and Stalin regarded them with fear as a potential fifth column. The remaining "kulaks" were, Stalin declared in July 1937, "the primary ringleaders of all sorts of anti-Soviet and diversionary crimes both in the collective farms and the state farms and in transport and other branches of industry." By this time, according to Viola, "the appellation of kulak had lost any residual socioeconomic meaning . . . retaining only a political content that could be molded according to regime needs."[51] Ethnic groups deemed subversive, in this period of war scares, were also emasculated[52]—particularly Poles in western Ukraine, tens of thousands of whom were swept up in the Terror. "Very good!" declared Stalin in response to a round of mass arrests of Poles. "Keep on digging up and cleaning out this Polish filth. Eliminate it in the interests of the Soviet Union." According to Timothy Snyder, "the kulak operations and the national operations were the essence of the Great Terror. Of the 681,692 executions carried out for political crimes in 1937 and 1938, the kulak and national [campaigns] accounted for 625,483."[53]

In its way, though, the purge of the Communist Party displays better than any other event Stalin's ruthless megalomania and intense paranoia. The campaign began with moves against the "Right opposition," led by Nikolai Bukharin, which had questioned the crash-collectivization and crash-industrialization campaigns, and was now calling for a return to the New Economic Policy and reconciliation with the shattered peasantry. Three separate "show trials" targeted the opposition between 1936 and 1938, in which Bukharin and others were accused of conspiring with Trotskyite and foreign elements to sabotage communism in the Soviet Union. The evidence presented was almost non-existent, with convictions based on absurd confessions extracted through torture, threats against family members, and (bizarrely) appeals to revolutionary solidarity.[54]

The old guard was convicted almost *en bloc*, and usually sentenced to execution. "Of the 139 Central Committee members elected at the Seventeenth Party Congress in 1934, 102 were arrested and shot, and five more killed themselves in 1937–38."[55] The military, too, was ravaged: "of the 767 members of the high command . . . 412 were executed, 29 died in prison, 3 committed suicide, and 59 remained in jail."[56] This would have catastrophic consequences in the early stages of the Nazi-Soviet war of 1941–1945, when the USSR's poorly-trained armies were vanquished and nearly annihilated by the German army.

Everyone who confessed named names (and more names, and still more names). Investigations and arrests snowballed; detention centers and execution lists were filled by quota.[57] Meanwhile, the prevailing paranoia meant that sabotage lurked around every corner, in every seemingly innocuous situation. A "choking medieval nightmare of plague-dread, xenophobia, and persecution" prevailed.[58] According to the Soviet dissident Alexander Solzhenitsyn, "any adult inhabitant of this country, from a collective farmer up to a member of the Politburo, always knew that it would take only one careless word or gesture and he would fly off irrevocably into the abyss."[59] "In the years of the terror," wrote Nadezhda Mandelstam (herself eventually consigned to the Gulag), "there was not a home in the country where people did not sit trembling at night, their ears straining to catch the murmur of passing cars or the sound of the elevator."[60]

Terror became routine. "People say 'He was shot' as if they were saying 'He went to the theatre,'" marveled the Leningrad theatre director Lyubov Shaporina in a secret diary.[61] Routinized, too, was the assembly-line character of the killing. The façade of legalism, meanwhile, was derisory at best, as the Leningrad case also exemplifies:

> The numbers came down from the center, but the corpses were made locally. The troikas [tribunals] . . . were responsible for sentencing the prisoners, with no need for any confirmation from Moscow, and no possibility for appeal. The three members of a troika would meet at night with investigating officers. For each case they would hear a very brief report, along with a recommendation for sentencing: death or the Gulag. (Only a very few of those arrested were not sentenced at all.) The troikas would almost always accept these recommendations. They handled hundreds of cases at a time, at a pace of sixty per hour or more; the life or death of an individual human was decided in a minute or less. In a single night the Leningrad troika for example, sentenced to death 658 prisoners of the concentration camp at Solovki.[62]

Like careerists and *génocidaires* everywhere, NKVD officials and others in "the exterminating profession" were anxious to match, and if possible exceed, their commanders' expectations. If "enemies of the people" could not be found in sufficient numbers, individuals—overwhelmingly adult men—were rounded up, shot, or convicted under Article 58 and shipped off to the Gulag.

The Great Purge ended only when it became clear that "at the rate arrests were going, practically all the urban population would have been implicated within a few months."[63] As usual, Stalin's underlings took the fall. The NKVD was purged, and its leader, Nikolai Yezhov—whom Norman Naimark calls "as vile a perpetrator as one will find in the history of modern genocide"—was arrested and executed.[64] Stalin went on to preside over the eighteenth Party Congress in March 1939, proclaiming the accomplishments of the purge. Only 35 of the nearly 2,000 delegates who had attended the previous Party Congress were still around to celebrate with him.[65]

The war years

The 1939 Soviet invasion of Poland, following the signing of a non-aggression pact with Nazi Germany, brought with it atrocities that are still relatively little known. The exception is the mass murder, on Stalin's orders, of some 22,000 Polish officers and other prisoners—the "wet work" (*mokraya rabota*), as the NKVD assassins called it.[66] The victims were then buried in sites including the Katyn forest.[67] This was only a small part of a wider Soviet campaign against the Polish nation. Apart from military officers, the campaign concentrated on destroying political leaders, professionals, intellectuals, and businesspeople.[68] The war against the Ukrainian people was thus paralleled in Poland, and subsequently in the Baltic states, which the Soviets invaded and occupied in 1940.

The "eliticidal" character of the Soviets' Baltic campaign is conveyed by a list of those officially designated for arrest and deportation from Lithuania. According to Applebaum, the targets included members of "political parties; former members of the police or the prison service; important capitalists and bourgeoisie; former officers of the national armies; family members of all of the above; anyone repatriated from Germany; refugees from 'former Poland'; as well as thieves and prostitutes." However, this was not sufficient for one Soviet commissar, who added (in his words): "Esperantists [those speaking the 'universal language' of Esperanto]; philatelists; those working with the Red Cross; refugees; smugglers; those expelled from the Communist Party; priests and active members of religious congregations; the nobility, landowners, wealthy merchants, bankers, industrialists, hotel and restaurant owners."[69]

BOX 5.1 ONE MAN'S STORY: BORIS IZVEKOV

"Someone must have been telling lies about Joseph K.," writes Franz Kafka in one of the most famous opening lines in literature, "for without having done anything wrong he was arrested one fine morning."[70] The experiences of Joseph K., intended to symbolize the existential conundrum of the human condition (see Chapter 10), were tragically mirrored in the arrest, detention, and interrogation of millions of Soviet citizens by Stalin's feared secret police, the NKVD, who consigned nearly all their detainees either to the Gulag or the execution cellar.

One of those who fell into their clutches was Boris Izvekov, a renowned scholar of physics and meteorology at Leningrad Technical University. Brian Moynahan describes him as "a strikingly handsome and intelligent man in his early fifties."[71] He had a wife, Olga Alexandrovna, and a young daughter, Tatiana. It was February 1942, and Leningrad was under one of the most destructive sieges ever imposed, with Nazi and allied Finnish forces ringing the city. Starvation was killing thousands daily, but Izvekov, as a member of the intellectual elite, enjoyed access to both spacious housing and special food rations, even amidst intense wartime privations. His daughter Anufriyevka remembered him as a man who loved poetry, history, and the theater. On summer weekends at their dacha (country home), "We went swimming and sailing, we picked mushrooms and berries. . . . Before I fell asleep, he'd come to my room and ask . . . 'are you cosy in your little nest'? And we prayed every night."

Izvekov's "Kafkaesque" nightmare began as it did for so many Soviet citizens, high and low: with a late-night knock on the door from NKVD functionaries. They instructed him to gather a few personal items and accompany them.

Again in common with millions of his fellow citizens, Izvekov had been denounced by a colleague swept up in the dragnet of Soviet purges and persecutions. Izvekov, who had traveled regularly to Europe and met with foreign academicians during the pre-Bolshevik period and after, was denounced as an "active participant" in a German-run spy group—one of the most severe accusations possible. A background check determined that he was the son of a priest. This highly unfavorable finding marked him out as a likely "class enemy."

In an interrogation cell at the notorious "Bolshoi Dom" (Big House), the NKVD's headquarters in Leningrad (today St. Petersburg), his interrogator, Lieutenant Kruzhkov, embarked on the prisoner's slow destruction. "Tell us about your counter-revolutionary activities," Kruzhkov demanded. "I am not engaged in counter-revolutionary activities," Izvekov replied. "Moreover, I have no information about any such activity or of people engaged in it."

After hours of relentless questioning, he was returned to a cell filled with cannibals and fellow political prisoners, and fed starvation rations. Daily interrogations continued. "You are lying," his interrogators shouted, accusing him of "hid[ing] the truth from the Soviet government." "I never fought the Soviet government," Izvekov protested wearily.

It was no use. He held out longer than most, but everyone was broken in the end. Moreover, his tormentors had discovered a new and terrible vulnerability: his wife Olga had been first exiled, then incarcerated in the Gulag. She, too, had been swept up in the new dragnet. It is uncertain if Izvekov knew this, but he knew her background doomed him further.

The fantastic confessions at last came spilling out. Izvekov named six of his colleagues as traitors and spies. The interrogators wanted more denunciations, and they got them from their exhausted and humiliated prisoner. Professor Roze, Izvekov now claimed, was the leader of an intricate conspiracy at the Technical University. Together with German agents, he had recruited Izvekov "because he knew my anti-Soviet views. . . . Roze explained that there was a counter-revolutionary group among the professors who were waiting for the arrival [invasion] of the Germans. . . . We had to prepare a political-scientific declaration in the name of professors and express our wish to cooperate with the Germans and fight against the Soviet Union. After explaining this, Roze asked me to join the group."

The dénouement came on March 6, 1942. Lieutenant Kruzhkov extracted four final names from Izvekov. The prisoner was sent back to his cell to await judgment. It was delivered on April 25. Izvekov and eleven co-defendants were found guilty of crimes including "sabotage, spreading false rumours and ideas, preparing to meet German troops, establishing communications with the German army command, and identifying and recruiting 'anti-Soviet determined individuals.'" All were sentenced under the notorious Article 58 "to the highest criminal sentence, SHOOTING, and their personal belongings to be confiscated." The verdict was "final and not liable to appeal."

Professor Roze, the supposed arch-conspirator, had already perished under brutal interrogation. Izvekov survived the prison cannibals and slave rations long enough to be hauled out, like hundreds of thousands of others, and shot in an NKVD execution chamber. The date of his state-decreed murder is not recorded. He was "rehabilitated" in the post-Stalinist period, when a measure of honor was restored to many of the millions accused, killed, and enslaved in Stalin's genocides.

Tens of thousands of people were executed, and hundreds of thousands more consigned to the Gulag, which now expanded to include camps in occupied territories.[58] When the Nazi-Soviet Pact collapsed and Germany invaded Soviet-occupied Poland in June 1941, fresh catastrophe descended. Forced into retreat, NKVD killing squads massacred many of those whom they had imprisoned on Polish territory. Legions of others were deported on foot, in scenes "hauntingly similar to the marches undertaken by the prisoners of the Nazi concentration camps four years later"[72] (see Chapter 6).

The tide turned in 1943, with the Soviet victories in the battles of Stalingrad and Kursk. By 1944, in the juggernaut of Operation Bagration, the Soviets were reinvading Poland and pushing into German territory in East Prussia. (The destruction wreaked upon German civilians by vengeful Soviet soldiers is discussed in Box 6a on "The Nazis' Other Victims"; see also the literature review in note 125, pp. 141–143.) Notable here is the Gulag's expansion into Germany and other invaded lands (Romania, Bulgaria). In Germany, the so-called *spetslagerya* were sometimes established in former Nazi concentration camps. Again, Soviet policy aimed to undermine any national resistance to Soviet occupation. Inmates were predominantly "judges, lawyers, entrepreneurs, businessmen, doctors and journalists." Of the 240,000 incarcerated, over one-third—95,000 people—perished in the *spetslagerya*, while camps in Romania were more deadly still.[73] In addition, as many as 760,000 Japanese prisoners were captured during the few days that the two countries were at war in August 1945, and dispatched to the Gulag, where tens of thousands died, predominantly during the 1945–1946 winter.[74] The camp system in fact reached its apogee in 1950, well after the Second World War had ended.

Figure 5.5 Soviet dictator Joseph Stalin with his foreign minister, Vyacheslav Molotov. They are pictured during the Allied negotiations in Yalta, Crimea in February 1945 that gave the western imprimatur to postwar Soviet control over eastern Europe.[75] Molotov had earlier leant his name to the infamous non-aggression pact with Nazi Germany (August 1939) that provided for the brutal invasion, occupation, and dismemberment of Poland by the Nazi and Soviet regimes.

Source: US National Archives and Records Administration/Wikimedia Commons.

Finally, in one of modern history's most tragic ironies, repatriated Soviet prisoners-of-war (Box 6a) were arrested *en masse* in the USSR on suspicion of collaboration with the Germans. Most were sentenced to long terms in the Gulag, with hundreds of thousands consigned to mine uranium for the Soviet atomic bomb. "Few survived the experience."[76] As Solzhenitsyn noted: "In Russian captivity, as in German captivity, the worst lot of all was reserved for the Russians."[77]

The destruction of national minorities

As already mentioned, Soviet belligerence toward any ethnic nationalism but the Russian produced a genocidal famine in Ukraine, whose people were the most powerful and resource-rich of those inclined toward autonomy or independence.[78] Both before and during the Second World War, suspicion of national minorities as potential "fifth columnists" led to their deportation from regions deemed vulnerable to foreign attack and occupation. Though the wartime deportations are reasonably widely known, historian Alexander Statiev has shown that the trend actually began several years before the outbreak of the conflict. The first to suffer were tens of thousands of Germans, Poles, Finns, and Iranians, among others. Subsequent measures included "the resettlement of all 171,781 Koreans . . . from the Far East to Central Asia in October 1937," which "initiated the deportations of entire ethnic groups."[79] They joined the kulaks in the catastrophic conditions of the "special settlements." The onset of the Second World War in 1939–1940, and the Soviet occupation of the Baltic states and eastern Poland, "triggered another series of deportations," of national elements deemed hostile and subversive. "About 400,000 Poles were exiled in 1940–41 . . . while 133,138 Germans were repatriated from Moldavia alone. In addition, in May and June 1941, the government banished 85,716 'socially dangerous elements,' mostly members of the titular majorities of the western republics."[80]

The shocking mortality rates among many of the prewar deportees means, according to Statiev, that when the Soviets initiated new rounds of deportations during the war, they "must have understood that in wartime their capacity to . . . [provide for] the accommodation and supply of exiles would be even more limited, which would result in far greater privations for the blacklisted minorities." Implicit here is a case for genocidal intent—constructive or general intent, rather than a specific and explicit exterminatory desire—in what followed, and indeed in much that had preceded it.[81]

After the German invasion of the Soviet Union in June 1941, Soviets of ethnic German origin in the Volga region, numbering well over a million, were a predictable target. Again depicted as potential saboteurs and subversives, some 1.2 million people were rounded up and deported from territories they had inhabited for centuries.[82] The Nazi offensive in the Caucasus and Crimea in 1942 spelled doom for a host of minorities there and in Soviet Central Asia. Accused of collaborating with the German invader, polyglot groups were rounded up by the NKVD and expelled from their homelands—generally under terrible conditions—and to desolate territories where agriculture was difficult and infrastructure non-existent. "The seven peoples deported during the war were: Balkars, Chechens, Crimean Tatars,[83] Ingushi, Karachai, Kalmyks, and Meskhetians."[84]

With the translocation went a systematic assault on the foundations of these minorities' cultures:

> For the first time, Stalin had decided to eliminate not just members of particular, suspect nationalities, or categories of political "enemies," but entire nations—men, women, children, grandparents. . . . After they had gone, the names of all of the deported peoples were eliminated from official documents—even from the *Great Soviet Encyclopedia*. The authorities wiped their homelands off the map, abolishing the Chechen-Ingush Autonomous Republic, the Volga-German Autonomous Republic, the Kabardino-Balkar Autonomous Republic, and the Karachai Autonomous Province. The Crimean Autonomous Republic was also liquidated, and Crimea simply became another Soviet province.[85]

The devastation of the Chechen nation was only one of many such atrocities, but it had especially fateful consequences. The Chechen genocide—Applebaum estimates that 78,000 Chechens died on transport trains alone[86]—resonates to the present day. The fierce Chechen struggle for independence in the 1990s and 2000s reflects memories of the genocide during the Second World War. The response of the post-Soviet Russian government was a new round of genocide, with tens of thousands of Chechens killed and hundreds of thousands more displaced as refugees (Box 5a).[87] In the final months of his life, Stalin directed his paranoid zeal against a minority that so far had largely escaped targeting as such: Soviet Jews. Those arrested in the so–called "Doctors' Plot" in January 1953 were mostly Jewish, and it seemed the arrests might presage a repeat of the Great Purge. But in March, the dictator died. Rapidly, a "thaw" spread through Soviet life. Over the following decade, the vast majority of Gulag prisoners were released, the "camp-industrial complex" was shut down, and many of the dead and still living were officially rehabilitated. Limited criticism was permitted of Stalin and the cult of personality, "the most grandiose in history,"[88] that surrounded him.

BOX 5.2 STALIN: RETURN FROM THE CRYPT

It is one of striking features of Russia and some of the other post-Soviet nations that Stalin's dictatorship has experienced something of a nostalgic revival. Perhaps the "Man of Steel's" core constituency remains the aging diehards selectively recalling a time when the Soviet Union was a political, military, and technological superpower, and the man they credit with bringing it about. They contrast this with the crumbling post-Soviet polity, in which the imposition of brutal neoliberal measures spawned a catastrophic collapse in living and health standards, as well as an unprecedented demographic decline particularly affecting Russian males, whose life expectancy fell *by* a decade *in* a decade. Equally pervasive were feelings of psychological dislocation and humiliation. Russia seemed to be returning to its historical role as a poor and backward source of raw materials for prosperous Western states.

Through glasses tinted by these sudden and varied traumas, the "stability" and "unity" of the Stalinist period can seem highly attractive—certainly preferable to the chaos and corruption of the post-Soviet period. In January 2016, *Guardian* journalist Daniil Turovsky reported from the town of Penza, where a culture center devoted to Stalin was being inaugurated by local Communist Party rank-and-file. "Penza's communists declared 2016 to be the Year of Stalin throughout the region, and promised to hold Stalinist events every month—literary evenings, round table discussions and tours of the Stalinist architecture of Penza." Long-time Communist Party leader Gennady Zyuganov recalled the advent of the Stalinist period as "a Stalinist spring," declaring that "those times demanded him . . . All government figures who wish Russia well should imbibe the genius of Stalin."

Georgy Kamnev, who organized the "space for studying the Stalinist experience" in Penza, likewise argued that "the historical conditions have to be taken into account. Some things which were then morally permissible are now impermissible." What of the Gulag? asked Turovsky. "The state had the right to do [that], and to suppress its people. . . . But that's not all he did. There were a lot of good things. . . . Today, everything has become worse." A woman listening nearby chimed in: "What was the Gulag? Such things will always happen in Russia. Back then, at least the pensions were good."[89]

Under the *glasnost* (openness) regime of Mikhail Gorbachev during the terminal phase of the USSR, the Memorial society formed to expose the crimes of Stalin's purges and slave-labor camps (see Map 5.1). Long-suppressed literary critiques of Stalinism saw the light of day, such as Vasily Grossman's *Life and Fate* (see the opening epigraph for this book) and *Children of the Arbat* by Anatoly Rybakov. Alexander Solzhenitsyn's epochal three-volume work, *The Gulag Archipelago*, long read in the West, was freely available (see Figure 5.6). New media voices emerged across the political spectrum.[90] In a move of huge historical importance, archives were opened to Soviet/Russian and western scholars alike, fueling a boom in Soviet and Stalinist studies just as the USSR was collapsing and reconstituting as the Commonwealth of Independent States (CIS). In the post-Soviet period, physical memorials to Stalin's victims began to sprout, the result of nongovernmental initiatives, such as the "Solovetsky Stones" in St. Petersburg and Moscow. These Memorial-sponsored sites incorporated granite boulders from the Solovetsky Islands, where one of the most feared slave-labor camps of the Soviet Gulag was located. The inscription includes a haunting line from the poem "Requiem" by

Figure 5.6 The Russian Gulag survivor and Nobel Prize laureate, Alexander Solzhenitsyn, documented the daily reality of Stalin's Gulag in his early novella, *One Day in the Life of Ivan Denisovich*, published in the magazine *Novy Mir* in 1962 during the post-Stalinist "thaw." But it was his three-volume masterwork, *The Gulag Archipelago*, that most extensively and indelibly chronicled the great prison network and its millions of captives (see Further Study). Written between 1958 and 1967, it was smuggled out of the Soviet Union and published in various translations. Solzhenitsyn was expelled from his homeland in 1974, the year this photo was taken—he was too famous to jail or consign to a psychiatric hospital, the fate of many other dissidents. The author and his wife, Natalia, settled in the United States until 1994, when they returned permanently to Russia. He lived in western Moscow until his death in 2008, aged 89; Natalia survives and remains active and outspoken.[91]

Source: Dutch National Archives, The Hague/Wikimedia Commons.

Figure 5.7 Anne Applebaum, currently Director of Global Transitions at London's Legatum Institute, authored the definitive account of Soviet mass incarceration, *Gulag: A History* (2003). Her subsequent work, *Iron Curtain: The Crushing of Eastern Europe, 1944–1956*, detailed Stalinist oppression in the "eastern bloc" of neocolonies established at the end of World War Two (see Further Study). Applebaum is pictured in September 2013.

Source: Wikimedia Commons.

Anna Akhmatova, perhaps the iconic literary voice of the Stalinist Terror: "I'd like to name you all by name, but . . ."

When the corrupt but comparatively liberal regime of Boris Yeltsin gave way to the autocracy of Vladimir Putin—a former official in the KGB intelligence services—dissident media and civil-society voices like Memorial's were gradually crowded out. Russian authorities raided Memorial's offices in December 2008, confiscating computer drives and disks containing databases of Gulag victims.[92] Russian president Vladimir Putin (or is he again prime minister as you read this?) has both nurtured the Stalin cult and distanced himself from it. On one hand, Putin has sought to establish post-Soviet Russia as a "responsible partner" in a western-dominated international system. Stalin-style mass violence is considered déclassé, unless directed against rebellious Chechens (see the supplementary case study at the end of this chapter). Putin and his protégé, Dmitry Medvedev, have paid public tribute to Stalin's victims. Laying a memorial wreath in 2007, Putin declared that "hundreds of thousands, millions of people were killed and sent to camps, shot and tortured." Such atrocities "happen when ostensibly attractive but empty ideas are put above fundamental values, values of human life, of rights and freedom."[93] Even more notably and recently, Putin reached out to near-neighbor Poland, to jointly memorialize the Stalin-directed execution of thousands of Polish officers at Katyn and other massacre sites in 1940 (p. 272).[94] But his overall stance—and that of the state educational system—toward Stalin's crimes can best be described as ambivalent. Putin has, after all, sought to recapture the "Great Russian" sentiment that Stalin tapped so effectively during the "Great Patriotic War" of the 1940s. The war experience is memorialized to the point of fetishism, and used to build support for rearmament and military expansionism, as in Crimea and eastern Ukraine in summer 2014.

The Stalin cult extends beyond the Great Russian heartland—certainly to Belarus, whose dictator Alexander Lukashenko strikes a vaguely similar pose, and lionizes the period of the "Great Patriotic War" with its Stalin-era connotations.[95] (There are grounds for this: Belarus was at the heart of the "Bloodlands," the most intensive killing zone of World War Two—see Box 2.3). But nowhere does the cult thrive as in Gori, the dictator's hometown in the now-independent country of Georgia. When I visited in summer 2015, I found my hotel was on Stalin Avenue, across from Stalin Park, with its imposing Stalin Museum. The pleasant park, in which USAID was operating a bright kiosk, was created when the neighborhood surrounding Stalin's boyhood home was bulldozed—all except the very modest dwelling, of course. It holds pride of place in the museum's courtyard, alongside a huge statue of the "Man of Steel." The museum exhibits did some justice to Stalin's pathological violence, as well as his imputed accomplishments. But any critical tenor was offset by the bounty of Stalin memorabilia available in the gift shop: Stalin watches, badges, lighters, liquor flasks, and the like (see Figure 5.8).

It seemed a time warp, and it was—the city that "destalinization" forgot. But Stalin's mainstream popularity, in Russia and the wider region, was real—and growing. A poll by the Levada Centre in March 2015 found that "the proportion of respondents ready to excuse the Soviet leader's brutality had almost doubled in less than two and a half years." Seven percent of those surveyed "agreed fully with the statement, 'The price paid by the Soviet people in the Stalin epoch was justified by great aims and results achieved in a short time', while 38 per cent said they agreed 'to a certain extent.' That compared to four per cent and 21 per cent in a poll taken in November 2012." Arseny Roginsky—head of the Memorial society, which still functioned despite years of harassment—considered the survey "a very worrying sign." But he also stressed that the lingering cult was a proxy for contemporary anxieties and frustrations. It "testifies less to attitudes towards Stalin than to mutual relations between the individual and the state. Stalin is perceived as the symbol of a strong and powerful state[,] and the fact that Stalin and all his politics were inhuman is a secondary concern for people."[96]

Figure 5.8 Memorabilia for sale in the gift shop of the Stalin Museum in Gori, Georgia, the city where Josef Dzhughashvili—the future "Man of Steel"—was born and raised.

Source: Author's photo, June 2015.

The thaw after Stalin's death peaked with his eventual successor, Nikita Khrushchev. A Ukrainian who had helped to consign millions of his fellow Ukrainians to death or the Gulag, Khrushchev nonetheless allowed something of the truth of life in the camps to be published for the first time, with Alexander Solzhenitsyn's 1961 novella *One Day in the Life of Ivan Denisovich*. But in 1964, Khrushchev was ousted for his failed brinkmanship during the Cuban Missile Crisis, and his disastrous agricultural policies. A new chill descended. When Solzhenitsyn completed his three-volume study of *The Gulag Archipelago*, he could publish it only abroad; and though the work won its author the Nobel Prize for literature, it led to his house arrest and forced exile (see Figure 5.6). Only with a new and deeper thaw under Mikhail Gorbachev did a genuine reckoning with the Stalinist and Gulag legacies begin—although post-Soviet citizens have proven notably reluctant to revisit this aspect of the national past.

CHINA AND MAOISM

The ravages of Stalinism in the USSR were, if anything, outdone by the twentieth century's other leading Stalinist, Mao Zedong. According to Matthew White, "Mao is almost certainly the deadliest individual in history to have wreaked havoc inside a single country."[97] The carnage occurred, according to political scientist R.J. Rummel,

> for the same reason it occurred in the Soviet Union . . . In each case, Power was nearly absolute, the central tenets of Marxism the bible, high communist officials its priests, the Communist Party its church, and the achievement of the Marxist paradise—communism—the ultimate goal. In each country, the same classes— bourgeoisie, priests, landlords, the rich, and officers and officials of the previous regime—were sinful, enemies of the Good. Capitalists or their offspring were especially evil. The verdict for such class membership was often death.[98]

At the apex of the system stood Mao, basking in the adoration of the masses. "What is wrong with worship?" he demanded of those who questioned the snowballing "cult of personality" that surrounded him. ". . . Each group must worship its leader, it cannot but worship its leader."[99]

Like the Soviet Bolsheviks, the Chinese Communist Party began as a reaction to centuries of despotic rule. Like the Bolsheviks, most of the early Chinese communist leaders were well educated, generally prosperous individuals moved by the plight of the masses. Unlike the Bolsheviks, however, the Chinese communists recognized early on that the heart of China's revolutionary potential lay in the peasantry, the large majority of the population, rather than in the tiny urban proletariat, as Marxist orthodoxy dictated. In stark contrast to the Bolsheviks' seizure of power in St. Petersburg, which was essentially a coup by a marginal political force, in China the communists seized power after decades of patient mobilization and expansion in the countryside. Throughout, they were hounded—at times almost to extinction—by their opponents, notably Chiang Kai-shek's Nationalist Party *(Guomindang,* or KMT). This persecution, for which there is no real parallel in the Soviet case, spawned a mentality of paranoia and vengeful hatred toward all "class enemies."

In 1925, Chiang Kai-shek's forces inflicted a devastating massacre on CCP ranks—a moment that genocide scholar Ben Kiernan describes as a "watershed." Thereafter, as Haifeng regional party secretary Peng Pai declared, "We have to shift from sorrow to power. We are mad for merciless extermination of the enemy: we thirst for the last drop of the enemy's blood as compensation for our martyred comrades. . . . From now on we . . . must exterminate our enemy to the last."[100] When the communists retook Haifeng, they announced a "Workers–Peasants' Dictatorship" whose primary purpose was "the extermination of anti-revolutionaries": "All persons aiding the enemy and all reactionaries, such as corrupt officials, greedy bureaucrats, bully landowners, evil gentry, spies, propagandists, policemen, Peace Preservation corps-men, messengers and tax collectors for the enemy, and all those who work in their offices must be seized and executed."[101]

When Chiang's Nationalists destroyed an abortive communist "commune" in Guangdong in 1927, Mao rose to the forefront of the movement. The killings initiated under his regime were initially selective, mostly targeting landlords whom peasants denounced as particularly brutal and exploitative. Both violence and land seizures were de-emphasized during the 1937–1945 war against the Japanese, when the Communist Party formed a fragile common front with the Nationalists against the invader (see Chapter 3). Following the Japanese defeat, however, the Communists and Nationalists turned to their final confrontation, and extremism increased on both sides. By this time, the communists had established a state-within-a-state in Henan province. There, Mao fine-tuned the pattern of denunciation, public humiliation, and often murder of "spies" and "class enemies" that would become his regime's hallmark after 1949. "Bad landlords," in particular, were exposed to indiscriminate violence—and as with Stalin's targeting of so-called "kulaks," such a designation could be terrifyingly random. It was often filled by quota (10 percent of the population was an accepted norm), and often based on grudges and personal rivalries in the local community. "Those designated as targets were made to stand facing large crowds," which would "shout slogans while brandishing fists and farm tools. Village militants and thugs would then inflict physical abuse, which could range from making the victims kneel on broken tiles on their bare knees, to hanging them up by their wrists or feet, or beating them, sometimes to death, often with farm implements."[102] There was little danger that the functionaries organizing such proceedings would be punished. Indeed, they were encouraged to excel in their infliction of violence. "Without using the greatest force," Mao wrote in an essay titled "The Question of 'Going Too Far,'" "the peasants cannot possibly overthrow the deep-rooted authority of the landlords . . . To put it bluntly, it is necessary to create terror for a while in every rural area, or otherwise it would be impossible to suppress the activities of the counterrevolutionaries in the countryside or overthrow the authority of the gentry."[103]

According to Mao biographers Jung Chang and Jon Halliday, "Hundreds of thousands, possibly as many as a million, were killed or driven to suicide" during this period of communist expansion.[104] Yet it was only a foretaste of the terror that would sweep the countryside when the communists, having crushed Chiang's KMT and sent it into exile on Taiwan, declared a "People's Republic" on August 1, 1949. "China has stood up," Mao declared; now all enemies would be brought low. A radical land reform program was instituted at breakneck speed, and the main targets were again to be the Chinese equivalent of the kulaks—not just landlords, but any peasant accused of owning marginally more than his or her neighbor. As with Soviet collectivization under Stalin in 1929–1930, large-scale resistance resulted as the communists pushed their "reform" program into the Chinese hinterland. According to political scientist Benjamin Valentino,

Figure 5.9 If measured by the mortality he inflicted, Mao Zedong is probably history's worst mass murderer. He took power at the helm of the Chinese communist party in 1949; this photo was taken during the first year of the new People's Republic. In addition to Stalinist-style collectivization, political purges, and campaigns against minorities (especially Tibetans), Mao launched the "Great Leap Forward" (1958–1961) to crash-industrialize the largely agrarian nation. The result was China's worst-ever disaster, humanity's worst famine, and a death toll numbering in the tens of millions. The witch-hunt of the Great Proletarian Cultural Revolution, peaking in 1965–1966, was Mao's encore and swan song. His death in 1976 began the economic and social transformations, under strict single-party control, that have transformed China and the world in recent decades.

Source: Washington Area Spark/Creative Commons/Flickr. ("The photographer is unknown. The image is an auction find.")

In some regions, communist officials were assassinated and large-scale riots and armed rebellions erupted. CCP cadres were dispatched to the villages with orders to identify landlords and other village "exploiters" and confiscate virtually all of their land, animals, and personal possessions. In an effort to incite "class struggle," landlords were dragged in front of village meetings where cadres encouraged poor peasants to "speak bitterness" against them. The meetings often culminated in brutal beatings or executions.[105]

Presaging the Khmer Rouge's genocidal campaigns in Cambodia, this first post-1949 phase of Maoist repression also targeted "urban elites (especially the capitalists, the westernized intellectuals and the Christians), and even more the former Guomindang cadres, civilian as well as military, down to the lowest ranks."[106] Mao himself acknowledged that 800,000 people had been executed between 1949 and 1954,[107] while Valentino estimated that "between one million and four million people were probably killed" during roughly these years.[108] Many of them perished in the *laogai* (labor camps). At least 2.5 million "class enemies" were dispatched to the camps in this first period of national rule, and conditions there were no less murderous than in the Soviet Gulag which had served as their model. "To be sent to *lao-gai* meant being condemned to backbreaking labor in the most hostile wastelands and down the most contaminating mines, while being hectored and harassed incessantly."[109] Throughout Mao's reign, and especially in the 1960s, the camps accounted for a majority of those killed by the regime. Chang and Halliday estimate that "the number of people in detention in any one year under Mao has been calculated at roughly 10 million. It is reasonable to assume that on average 10 percent of these were executed or died of other causes."[110]

BOX 5.3 TIBET: REPRESSION AND GENOCIDE

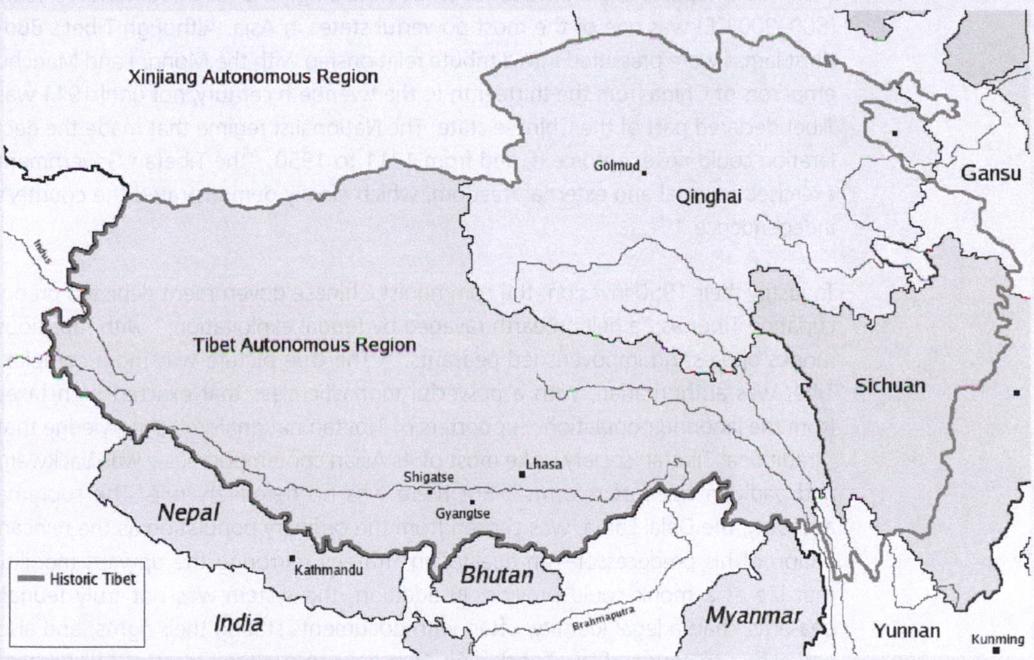

Map 5.2 Chinese Tibet (the Tibet Autonomous Region), showing also the contours of historic Tibet and of significant Tibetan population today (especially in Qinghai). The plateau of Buddhist Tibetans, traditionally herders ruled over by a small religious-political elite, has been penetrated by Chinese roads and railways, and inundated by Han Chinese military and civilian personnel. Allegations of physical genocide against Tibetans center mostly on the period during the late 1950s and early 1960s, when Tibet was arguably the region hardest hit by the disastrous "Great Leap Forward," and when Tibetans were heavily overrepresented in often lethal slave-labor camps. Advocates of a concept of "cultural genocide" cite Tibet as a paradigmatic example.

Source: Wikimedia Commons.

In exploring Chinese policies toward Tibet, we must distinguish between two versions of Tibet that are often confused. Ethnic Tibet—the area in which self-identified Tibetans reside—covers more or less the area of the Tibetan plateau.[111] But it also includes the areas of Amdo and Kham (often referred to as "eastern Tibet"). These were traditionally controlled by warlords more beholden to the Han Chinese center than to the Tibetan authorities in central Tibet—with its capital at Lhasa, home to the supreme religious authority, the Dalai Lama. "Tibet" today is generally held—except by Tibetans—to refer to the Tibet Autonomous Region (TAR) declared by China in 1965. This constitutes barely half the territory of ethnic Tibet, while the more populous territories of "Outer Tibet" (including Amdo and Kham) are mostly divided between the Chinese provinces of Sichuan and Qinghai. Although home to about half of all ethnic Tibetans, these provinces are populated by a Han Chinese majority, and the demographic disparity is increasing.[112]

Historically, Tibet was the product of empire-building, and for three hundred years (600–900 CE) was one of the most powerful states in Asia. Although Tibet's Buddhist lamas were pressured into a tribute relationship with the Mongol and Manchu emperors of China from the thirteenth to the twentieth century, not until 1911 was Tibet declared part of the Chinese state. The Nationalist regime that made the declaration could never enforce it, and from 1911 to 1950, "the Tibetan Government exercised internal and external freedom, which clearly demonstrated the country's independence."[113]

To justify their 1950 invasion, the communist Chinese government depicted preoccupation Tibet as "a hell on earth ravaged by feudal exploitation," with rapacious monks oppressing impoverished peasants.[114] The true picture was more complex. Tibet was authoritarian, with a powerful monastic class that exacted high taxes from the laboring population. Supporters of Tibetan nationalism acknowledge that "traditional Tibetan society—like most of its Asian contemporaries—was backward and badly in need of reforms." But there was no hereditary rule. The supreme authority, the Dalai Lama, was chosen from the ordinary population as the reincarnation of his predecessor—an egalitarian strategy mirroring the upward mobility that life as a monk could provide. In addition, the system was not truly feudal: peasants "had a legal identity, often with documents stating their rights, and also had access to courts of law," including "the right to sue their masters."[115] Peasant holdings appear to have provided adequate subsistence, with crop failures and other agricultural emergencies offset by state reserves.

During the Nationalist era, as noted above, Tibet was claimed but not administered by China. That changed in 1949–1950, after Mao's Communist Party took power in Beijing. With rationales that ranged from bringing civilization to the natives, to the need to counter moves by American "hegemonists," the Chinese invaded and partially occupied Tibet in October 1950. "Tibet's frantic appeals for help to the United Nations, India, Britain, and the United States were ignored, or rebuffed with diplomatic evasions. No nation was about to challenge the new People's Republic of China, which had some ten million men under arms, over the fate of an obscure mountain kingdom lost in the Himalayas."[116] The logistical difficulty of doing so would also have been nightmarish.

In May 1951, China imposed a punitive Seventeen-Point Agreement on Tibet. It guaranteed Tibetan political, religious, and educational rights, but allowed the People's Liberation Army (PLA) to enter the territory, and gave the Chinese control over Tibetan foreign affairs.[117] The Chinese also enjoyed a free hand in the eastern Tibetan territories. They used it to impose communist measures such as collectivization of agriculture. Rebellion against the measures gradually swelled among the Tibetans of the east. The Chinese responded with greater violence, killing thousands of Tibetans and incarcerating tens of thousands under brutal conditions.

When rebellion reached central Tibet, in 1959, it sparked a general uprising that the Chinese rapidly suppressed. The Dalai Lama fled across the border into India, where he still resides in Dharamsala, presiding over a 20,000-strong Tibetan exile community.[118] The Chinese government then extended their regime of "struggle" against supposedly reactionary elements to Tibet. Communist cadres denounced, tortured, and frequently executed "enemies of the people." "These struggle sessions resulted in more than 92,000 deaths" out of a total Tibetan population of about six million people.[119] The killings may be seen as part of a genocidal strategy against Tibetans as a whole, but also as an "eliticide," targeting the better-educated and leadership-oriented elements among the Tibetan population.

After the 1959 uprising, a catastrophic toll was inflicted by the forced-labor camps of Qinghai and Sichuan, which swept up hundreds of thousands of Tibetans.[120] They were set to work extracting Tibet's minerals and building Chinese military infrastructure, especially roads and railways. Toiling at high, frozen altitudes and with minimal food rations, tens of thousands of Tibetans died in the first half of the 1960s, in conditions that rivaled the Soviet Gulag. According to Jean-Louis Margolin,

> it appears that very few people (perhaps as few as 2 percent) ever returned alive from the 166 known camps, most of which were [established] in Tibet or the neighboring provinces. Entire monastic communities were sent to the coal mines. Detention conditions on the whole appear to have been dreadful, with hunger, cold, or extreme heat the daily lot of the prisoners. There are as many tales of execution of prisoners refusing to renounce Tibetan independence as there are tales of cannibalism in prison during the Great Leap Forward. It was as though the entire population of Tibet . . . were suspects.[121]

The second Chinese campaign to devastate Tibet occurred during the "Great Proletarian Cultural Revolution," unleashed in 1966. Tibet was seen as a hotbed of "reaction" and "feudalism," and persecution and cultural destruction occurred there on a vast scale, with thousands killed and further widespread destruction of religious sites and artifacts.

Mao died in 1976, and the extremist phase of the Chinese revolution passed with him. The 1980s were marked by an opening up to the West that launched a remarkable transformation of China's economy and society, which continues today.

This opening has been characterized by something of a softening of China's policies toward Tibetan national and cultural rights.[122] However, with increasing Han Chinese migration, Tibetans have become a minority in their capital of Lhasa—a trend only exacerbated in the 2000s by the opening of a new railway from central China to the Tibetan heartland.[123] Renewed ideological campaigns, such as the "Strike Hard" and "Spiritual Civilization" initiatives, have been aimed at the so-called "Dalai Clique"—notably representatives of the Tibetan religious institutions that have revived since the Cultural Revolution. Hundreds of monks and nuns have been arrested, and thousands more expelled from their institutions. Finally, "in a massive campaign that recalls the socialist engineering of an earlier era, the Chinese

Figure 5.10 The 14th Dalai Lama, Tenzin Gyatso, attending the Hind Swaraj International Centenary Conference in Delhi, November 2009. The Dalai Lama has become the face of Tibetan nationalism and a leading exponent of Buddhism and nonviolence. The Tibetan government-in-exile which he leads has pursued an accommodationist line toward the Chinese government, rejecting violence while seeking autonomy within China, rather than full independence.

Source: Pankaj Mistry/www.pankajfineart.com.

government has relocated some 250,000 Tibetans—nearly one-tenth of the population—from scattered rural hamlets to new 'socialist villages' . . . The broader aim seems to be remaking Tibet—a region with its own culture, language, and religious traditions—in order to have firmer political control over its population."[124]

Tibetan resistance continued beneath the surface, occasionally erupting in open revolt. In March 1989 there occurred "the largest anti-Chinese demonstration in [Lhasa] since 1959."[125] It was met by crackdowns, mass roundups, and torture. Renewed protests in 2008 led to the deaths of dozens of demonstrators (and Tibetan vigilante attacks on Han Chinese). The repression prompted the Dalai Lama to accuse China of imposing a "rule of terror" in the territory, adding: "Whether intentionally or unintentionally, some cultural genocide is taking place. . . . [An] ancient nation with ancient cultural heritage is actually dying."[126] He deployed similar language in March 2010, accusing the Chinese government of seeking to "deliberately annihilate Buddhism."[127]

Overall, perhaps hundreds of thousands of Tibetans likely have died at Chinese hands since 1950, mostly in the decade following the 1959 invasion. The Tibetan government-in-exile estimates 1.2 million deaths, but Margolin calculated a death toll "as high as 800,000—a scale of population loss comparable to that in Cambodia under the Khmer Rouge" (see Chapter 7).[128]

As early as 1960, the International Commission of Jurists declared that there existed "a *prima facie* case that on the part of the Chinese, there has been an attempt to destroy the national, ethnical, racial and religious group of Tibetans by killing members of the group and causing serious bodily harm to members of the group. . . . These acts constitute the crime of genocide under the Genocide Convention of the United Nations of 1948."[129] Since then, supporters of Tibetan self-determination have frequently deployed a genocide discourse. For example, in 1998 Maura Moynihan of Refugees International argued that Tibet suffered "a grimly familiar, twentieth-century, state-sponsored genocide."[130] Such claims are hotly disputed by the Chinese government and its supporters.

Meanwhile, Tibet's government-in-exile has proposed realistic and moderate responses to Chinese occupation. A five-point plan that the Dalai Lama presented in a 1987 speech to the US Congress included the following:

1. Transformation of the whole of Tibet into a zone of peace.
2. Abandonment of China's population transfer policy which threatens the very existence of the Tibetan people.
3. Respect for the Tibetan people's fundamental human rights and democratic freedoms.
4. Restoration and protection of Tibet's natural environment and the abandonment of China's use of Tibet for the production of nuclear weapons and dumping of nuclear waste.

> 5. Commencement of earnest negotiations on the future status of Tibet and of relations between the Tibetan and Chinese people.[131]
>
> The Dalai Lama has made it clear that Tibetans are willing to accept autonomy within China, rather than full independence. Such an arrangement seems remote, however, given China's ambitions for Tibet, and its growing military and colonizing presence.[132]

Gargantuan death tolls left Mao and most of his associates unfazed. Conscious that he was overlord of the most populous country on earth, confronting a super-power (the United States) armed with nuclear weapons, Mao was notorious for blasé statements that anticipated and accepted almost unimaginable hecatombs of dead in pursuit of political goals. "We are prepared to sacrifice 300 million Chinese for the victory of the world revolution," he declared on a visit to Moscow in 1957,[133] and in May 1958 he told the 8th Party Congress: "Don't make a fuss about a world war. At most, people die . . . Half the population wiped out—this happened quite a few times in Chinese history . . . It's best if half the population is left, next best one third."[134]

This world view, blended with Mao's desire to project China as the rightful leader of world communism, led to the greatest disaster of the Maoist period—the "Great Leap Forward" in 1958–1961. The "Great Leap" was supposed to accomplish for China what Stalin had sought in the Soviet Union: to collectivize all agriculture and industrialize a peasant nation in short order. Stalin, at monumental human cost, achieved his goal. The Chinese "Leap," however, was an unmitigated economic and human disaster. "Mao proceeded by simply asserting that there was going to be an enormous increase in the harvest, and got the provincial chiefs to proclaim that their area would produce an astronomical output." When the harvest arrived, the chiefs, fearing for their jobs and their lives, duly "declare[d] that their areas had indeed produced fantastic crops."[135] The "surpluses" were a cruel fiction. But as under Stalin, they served as the basis for grain seizures that provoked mass famine—the worst in China's famine-plagued history, and according to Margolin, "probably the worst in the history of the world."[136] The famine claimed the lives of "an estimated 40 million people" in just three years;[137] Chang and Halliday reported that in 1960 alone, no fewer than "22 million people died of hunger."[138] Yang Jisheng's meticulous study, *Tombstone*, found:

> The number of people who starved to death from 1958 to 1962 was many times greater than the number who died in any previous disaster in China. . . . Tens of millions departed this world in an atmosphere of mute apathy [because of starvation]. Some villages transported corpses by the truckload for burial in common graves. In villages where survivors lacked the strength for proper interment, the limbs of the dead protruded from the ground. In some places, the dead remained along the roadsides where they had dropped in their futile search for food. . . . I estimate that the Great Famine brought about 36 million unnatural deaths, and a shortfall of 40 million births. *China's total population loss during the Great Famine then comes to 76 million.*[139]

Many victims perished in colossal public-works projects, usually white elephants that debilitated the forced laborers and left the countryside worse off than before. "Mass mobilization on water-conservancy schemes," for example, claimed "the lives of hundreds of thousands of exhausted villagers already weakened by hunger. In a chilling precursor of Cambodia under the Khmer Rouge, villagers in Qingshui, Gansu [province], called these projects the 'killing fields.'"[140]

According to Martin Shaw, "the famine clearly demonstrated the genocidal mentality ingrained in Maoism, in which huge numbers of peasants were considered physically dispensable and catastrophic mass death an acceptable price to pay for policy goals."[141] In a macabre touch, as the British had done throughout the Irish and Indian famines of the nineteenth century and as Stalin decreed during the 1930s, food was actually *exported* on a massive scale during the famine:

> Net grain exports, principally to the USSR, rose from 2.7 million tons in 1958 to 4.2 million in 1959, and in 1960 fell only to the 1958 level. In 1961, 5.8 million tons were actually imported, up from 66,000 in 1960, but this was still too little to feed the starving. Aid from the United States was refused for political reasons. The rest of the world, which could have responded easily, remained ignorant of the scale of the catastrophe.[142]

The arrangement apparently struck even the Soviets as perverse. In 1961, they offered "to suspend the repayment of the loans and to furnish emergency food deliveries." Mao, however, rejected the offer.[143] For a long time, he was apparently convinced by his own propaganda that the problem was not famine but surplus. "With so much grain," he assured Chinese as the country hurtled toward crisis, ". . . you should eat more. Even five meals a day is fine!"[144] "Now we've seen the [food] supply increase by hundreds of billions of kilos in just one year," he urged,[145] people should "plant *less*."[146]

Figure 5.11 Beijing-based historian Yang Jisheng's epic 2008 study of "the Great Chinese Famine" was published in English in 2012 as *Tombstone*. The two-volume original was published in Chinese (in Hong Kong), but remains banned elsewhere in China, though it circulates widely in clandestine form. Yang himself maintains an uneasy position as a tolerated but invigilated academic. In 2015 he resigned from the journal, *Yanhuang Chunqiu* (China through the Ages), "a monthly publication known for challenging Party-approved accounts of history—particularly on the Maoist political mania that rocked China in decades past. Because of its limited circulation, specialist content, and the backing it has received by a group of Party elders concerned with reform, the publication has been able to operate for over two decades. But pressure has always been looming. . . . Yang said in one of his letters that from 2010 to 2014, only about a fifth of the articles they submitted to the censors made it into print."[147]

Source: Photo © Kim Rathcke Jensen. Used by permission.

The final paroxysm of Maoist violence was the "Great Proletarian Cultural Revolution" of 1966–1976 (peaking, it seems, in 1968). This equivalent of the Stalinist purges was designed to "cleanse the class ranks" of remaining classical influences and counter-revolutionary elements. It produced some of the notorious images of suspects clad in dunce caps and paraded for public humiliation and violence. Lee Ta-ling, a former Red Guard, remembered seeing

> rows of teachers, about 40 or 50 in all, with black ink poured over their heads and faces so that they were now in reality a "black gang." Hanging on their necks were placards with words such as "reactionary academic authority so-and-so," "corrupt ringleader so-and-so," "class enemy so-and-so," "capitalist roader so-and-so"; all epithets taken from the newspapers. On each placard was a red cross, making the teachers look like condemned prisoners awaiting execution. They all wore dunce caps painted with similar epithets and carried dirty brooms, shoes, and dusters on their backs. Hanging from their necks were pails filled with rocks. . . . All were barefoot, hitting broken gongs or pots as they walked around the field crying out: "I am black gangster so-and-so." Finally, they all knelt down, burned incense, and begged Mao Zedong to "pardon their crimes." . . . Beatings and torture followed. I had never seen such tortures before: eating nightsoil [human waste] and insects, being subjected to electric shocks, being forced to kneel on broken glass, being hanged "like an airplane" by the arms and legs. . . . The heaviest blow to me that day was the killing of my most respected and beloved teacher, Chen Ku-teh.[148]

Tens of thousands apparently chose suicide over further persecution. In Beijing, for example, where "the cleansing of the class ranks resulted in the deaths of 3,731 people between January 1968 and May 1969 . . . more than 94 percent of the deaths [were] registered as suicide."[149]

Figure 5.12 Spectators look on as purge victims are paraded for public humiliation during the Cultural Revolution, the last bout of Maoist extremism before the dictator's 1976 death.

Source: University of Florida.

Chang and Halliday estimated that "in the ten years from when Mao started the Purge until his death in 1976, at least 3 million people died violent deaths, and post-Mao leaders acknowledged that 100 million people, one-ninth of the entire population, suffered in one way or another."[150] Eventually the so-called "Red Guard" factions that Mao had mobilized began running out of targets and fighting among themselves. What had begun as "a massive pogrom against people of exploiting class background" became, in many areas, "a campaign of retribution and murder against factional rivals."[151]

The terror ended with Mao's death in 1976 at the age of 82. The "Gang of Four" (including Mao's wife, Jiang Qing), which had supervised the day-to-day logistics of his later-life derangements, was purged and incarcerated by reformists headed by Deng Xiaoping, who sought the equivalent of a "destalinization" campaign. However, China's revision of Maoism went only so far: to reveal all of Mao's crimes, genocidal and otherwise, would have risked undermining the

BOX 5.4 NORTH KOREA AND "THE CLEANEST RACE"

Figure 5.13 "The Koreas at Night." Nighttime images from space, of South Korea blazing brilliantly while North Korea languishes in darkness, have become emblematic of the sealed and mind-bogglingly despotic state. The single bright light in this photo, taken by a crewmember of NASA's Expedition 38 in January 2014, is the North Korean capital, Pyongyang.

Source: NASA/Wikimedia Commons.

The tyrannical and ultra-isolated nation of North Korea is one inheritor of Stalinist and Maoist patterns of rule. These include a "cult of personality" surrounding the family dictatorship that has run the country (into the ground) since the Second World War, political persecution, and widespread famine.[152] Unlike either of these models, however, North Korea also indulges in "explicit racial theorizing," including a "strident acclamation of Koreans as the world's 'cleanest' or 'purest' race."[153] The concern with purity (see the discussion of this psychological phenomenon in Chapter 10) is reflected in the regime's ultra-isolation from the rest of the world, and its suffocation of modernity in nearly every area save military hardware (see, e.g., Figure 5.13). The ideology, which also includes strong elements of paranoia and dependency, is examined in a groundbreaking 2010 work, *The Cleanest Race*, by B.R. Myers. One of Myers's insights is that to the extent the North Korean ideology is defined by its "race-based worldview," it may make "more sense to posit it on the extreme right than on the far left. Indeed, the similarity to the worldview of fascist Japan is striking."[154]

It was Japan that colonized Korea in the nineteenth century, and divided after the Second World War into northern and southern zones under different occupation regimes, Korea solidified into two opposing states. Conflict between them flared into open war—with Soviet, Chinese, and US backing—from 1950 to 1953. After a truce was agreed, North Korea, under its dictator and "Dear Leader" Kim Il Sung, became "the Hermit kingdom"—the most tightly sealed and secretive dictatorship in the world.

The fall of communism elsewhere changed nothing in North Korea. The Kim dynasty continued with the ascent of Kim Jong Il following his father's 1994 death. Privation and mass suffering increased after the fall of the Soviet Union and Chinese policy transformations dramatically cut foreign aid. The result, in 1994, was one of the worst famines in recent history, killing two to three million North Koreans. As international aid flooded in, the regime conducted a brutal "triage," denying food to those "not seen as critical to the survival of the state." "The corrupt cadres are stealing the food and selling it on the markets for their own profit while we starve," refugees told investigators.[155] As under Stalin, forced requisitions exacerbated the famine: "to feed the army, Kim Jong Il sent soldiers directly to the farms at harvest time to forcibly grab the harvest" and "did everything to prevent the population from finding alternative ways of feeding themselves." So wrote journalist Jasper Becker in his study of the North Korean *Rogue Regime*. While acknowledging that "genocide is normally interpreted to mean the mass killings of another race," Becker contended that "this too"—the death of vast numbers of people through politically-manipulated famine—"is a form of genocide."[156]

In the face of the rampant starvation, North Koreans staged acts of resistance, including "protests, strikes, local uprisings, the sabotage of official buildings, and the murder of officials and their families."[157] Successive Kim regimes, of course, had viewed all such manifestations as "traitorous." Those not subjected to summary execution were dispatched to the North Korean version of the Gulag. Since its founding, North Korea has operated a network of "special control institutions" *(Kwanliso)*, some of them up to twenty miles long and half as wide. If they were not summarily shot, prisoners were forced into mortally dangerous slave labor. According to Young Howard, a South Korean activist working with the US National Endowment for Democracy:

> Prisoners are provided just enough food to be kept perpetually on the verge of starvation. They are compelled by their hunger to eat, if they can get away with it, the food of the labor-camp farm animals, as well as plants, grasses, bark, rats, snakes and anything remotely edible. In committing such desperate acts driven by acute hunger the prisoners simultaneously incur the extreme risk of being detected by an angry security guard and subjected to a brutal, on-the-spot execution. Not surprisingly, the prisoners are quickly reduced to walking skeletons after their arrival. All gulag survivors said they were struck by the shortness, skinniness, premature aging, hunchbacks, and physical deformities of so many of the inmates they saw upon arriving at the gulag. These descriptions parallel those provided by survivors of the Holocaust in infamous camps like Auschwitz.

In its 2007 report, *North Korea: A Case to Answer, A Call to Act*, the nongovernmental organization Christian Solidarity Worldwide (CSW) contended that the conditions inflicted on prisoners had killed hundreds of thousands of inmates over the decades—with estimates ranging from 380,000 to over 1 million. This could qualify as both genocide and the crime against humanity of "extermination" (see pp. 710–711). "The political prison camp policy," wrote CSW, "appears *calculated to cause the death of a large number of persons* who form a part of the population, namely those labelled as 'enemies' who suffer on account of their genuine or alleged political beliefs or other crimes."[158]

In December 2015, the United Nations General Assembly cast fresh light on North Korea's abysmal record. A hundred and nineteen countries united to condemn "long-standing and ongoing systematic, widespread and gross violations of human rights" in the Kim tyranny (with nineteen countries opposed and forty-eight abstaining). The resolution pointed to

> torture, severe violations of the rights of women and rights of children, the "existence of an extensive system of political prison camps," and "all-pervasive and severe restrictions on the freedoms of thought, conscience, religion or belief, opinion and expression, peaceful assembly and association.

The resolution called on the UN Security Council to consider referring (though not actually to refer) North Korea to the International Criminal Court (see Chapter 15). The prospect seemed quite likely at the time of writing, if China withheld its veto.

The General Assembly also pledged to "discuss imposing" (though not actually to impose) "effective targeted sanctions" against key officials. Human Rights Watch focused on the positive, applauding the "strong message [sent] to the government of North Korea that its human rights record has made it a pariah on the global stage." The organization's Asia advocacy director, John Sifton, declared: "Senior North Korean leaders have been put on notice: their crimes against humanity and gross human rights abuses are documented, and they will one day face justice."[159]

government's claim to legitimacy. Deng Xiaoping, who had been suppressed under Mao's regime, provided the official formula: Mao was "seven parts good, three parts bad."[160] His portrait still hangs over the entrance to the imperial city on the edge of Tiananmen Square, and despite his "errors," he is still revered as the father of modern China.[161] One-party rule persists, bolstered by selective violence—notably the Tiananmen Square massacre of 1989, in which several thousand Chinese were slaughtered by government forces.[162] Resurgent nationalist protests on the Chinese periphery, in Tibet and in the Muslim-majority region of Xinjiang, have also been ruthlessly quashed.

STALIN, MAO, AND GENOCIDE

Genocide scholars increasingly accept that the tyrannies of both Joseph Stalin and Mao Zedong produced "canonical" cases of genocide. But this is a relatively recent phenomenon—in large part because both Stalin's and Mao's violence was primarily inflicted upon *political* and *class* "enemies," and these groups lie outside the bounds of the UN Genocide Convention (see Chapter 1). As with the Cambodian case discussed in Chapter 7, however, there is now a greater awareness of the extent to which "traditional" groups were targeted for genocide (notably national minorities like the Chechens and Tibetans), as well as a greater willingness among scholars to incorporate political groups and social classes into a broad genocide framing.

In evaluating the Stalinist period, the application of a genocide framework to the Ukrainian famine (1931–1932) remains a controversial subject of debate. But even some of those once skeptical of the label have shifted toward it. Nicholas Werth declined to register a verdict of genocide in his long chapter on Stalinist crimes for *The Black Book of Communism* in 1999. But by 2008, his position had shifted:

A whole panoply of repressive measures was put in place, ranging from closure of shops to police questioning of any peasants trying to flee from their starving villages. Over and above this range of repressive measures, it is clear that Stalin, *from the end of the summer of 1932*, really had decided to worsen the famine that was beginning, to turn it into a weapon, to *extend it deliberately*. . . . Recent research has shown, without any doubt, that the Ukrainian case is quite specific, at least from the second half of 1932 onwards. On the basis of these new

Figure 5.14 This towering statue of Mao Zedong was erected in late 2015 in Henan province, central China—ironically, one of the provinces most devastated by the "great famine" of the Great Leap Forward period. Mao remains an untouchable Communist Party icon in China, but in the new era of greater freedom of expression, much of his darker side has become known to the general public. The ridicule that greeted news of the statue was such that it was dismantled only a few days after photographs of it went viral.

Source: ChinaFotoPress/Getty Images.[163]

considerations, it seems to me legitimate to classify as genocide the totality of the actions taken by the Stalin regime to punish, by means of famine and terror, the Ukrainian peasantry.[164]

Lynne Viola similarly contended that "the famine was the natural conclusion of the disasters of collectivization, dekulakization, and merciless grain levies; it was minutely observed and publicly ignored by a regime and a dictator that viewed the peasantry as less than human, as raw material to be exploited to the maximum."[165]

Scholars of such calamities who accept the validity of a genocide framework, including this one, generally argue that *culpable negligence may constitute genocidal intent*, as Martin Shaw has suggested with specific reference to the Chinese famine in 1959–1962: "If leaders know that their policies may lead (or are leading) to the social and physical destruction of a group, and fail to take steps to avoid (or halt) it—as Mao Zedong, for example, knew of the effects of the Great Leap Forward but continued his policies—then they come to 'intend' the suffering they cause and may similarly be guilty [of genocide]."[166]

Both Stalin and Mao, as we have seen, also targeted ethnic minorities like the Chechens in the Soviet Union (Box 5a) and Tibetans (Box 5.3 above). But it was in the targeting of "enemy" classes and political tendencies—whether real or imagined—that these regimes truly served as twentieth-century prototypes. By means of direct execution (and, especially in the Chinese case, by deliberately driving numerous victims to suicide), these regimes killed millions of innocent people. Though their image as a "socialist vanguard" for the world's oppressed waned long ago, the Stalinist and Maoist models survive in North Korea, which, ironically, seems to serve both present-day Russia and China as a useful buffer against democratic reform from abroad (see Box 5.4).

FURTHER STUDY

Stalin and Stalinism

Note: The Stalinist period in the USSR has become a classic study of dictatorship and political terror. The following is a small sampling of works in English.

Anne Applebaum, *Gulag: A History.* London: Penguin, 2003. Winner of the Pulitzer Prize; an epic single-volume history of the Soviet forced-labor camps. See also *Iron Curtain: The Crushing of Eastern Europe, 1944–1956.*

Robert Conquest, *The Harvest of Sorrow: Soviet Collectivization and the Terror-Famine.* New York: Oxford University Press, 1986. Conquest retreated from his thesis that Stalin planned the famine of the early 1930s, but his groundbreaking work well conveys the scale and horror of the human destruction wreaked by collectivization. See also *The Great Terror: A Reassessment.*

Stéphane Courtois *et al., The Black Book of Communism: Crimes, Terror, Repression,* trans. Jonathan Murphy and Mark Kramer. Cambridge, MA: Harvard University Press, 1999. Massive indictment of communist regimes; includes Nicolas Werth's penetrating study of the USSR, "A State Against Its People."

R. W. Davies and Stephen G. Wheatcroft, *The Years of Hunger: Soviet Agriculture, 1931–1933.* Basingstoke: Palgrave Macmillan, 2004. Volume in the series "The Industrialisation of Soviet Russia"; usefully consulted alongside Conquest (above).

Miron Dolot, *Execution by Hunger: The Hidden Holocaust.* New York: W. W. Norton, 1985. Memoir of the Ukrainian famine.

Orlando Figes, *The Whisperers: Private Life in Stalin's Russia.* New York: Henry Holt and Company, 2007. Searing vignettes of life under Stalinist terror. See also *Just Send Me Word: A True Story of Love and Survival in the Gulag.*

Sheila Fitzpatrick, *Everyday Stalinism: Ordinary Life in Extraordinary Times: Soviet Russia in the 1930s.* Oxford: Oxford University Press, 1999. Individual perspectives on social transformations; see also *Stalin's Peasants: Resistance and Survival in the Russian Village after Collectivization.*

Eugenia Ginzburg, *Journey into the Whirlwind*. New York: Harvest, 2002. Account of arrest and the Gulag; see also the sequel, *Within the Whirlwind*.

Adam Hochschild, *The Unquiet Ghost: Russians Remember Stalin*. New York: Viking, 1994. Taut work on history and memory.

Halyna Hryn, ed., *Hunger by Design: The Great Ukrainian Famine and Its Soviet Context*. Cambridge, MA: Harvard University Press, 2008. Slender volume capturing the "state of the art" of Holodomor research.

David King, *Ordinary Citizens: The Victims of Stalin*. London: Francis Boutle Publishers, 2003. Haunting portraits of political prisoners from the purge period, mostly destined for execution.

Nadezhda Mandelstam, *Hope Against Hope*, trans. Max Hayward. New York: The Modern Library, 1999. Powerful, poetic recollections of Stalinist terror.

Simon Sebag Montefiore, *Stalin: The Court of the Red Tsar*. London: Phoenix, 2004. Montefiore's description of life in Stalin's "court" is gossipy but galvanizing.

Norman M. Naimark, *Stalin's Genocides*. Princeton, NJ: Princeton University Press, 2010. An extremely concise and punchy examination of Stalin's crimes in comparative-genocide perspective.

Robert Service, *Stalin: A Biography*. Cambridge, MA: The Belknap Press, 2005. A very serviceable biography, though brisk with the human consequences of Stalin's rule.

Varlam Shalamov, *Kolyma Tales*. London: Penguin, 1994. Documentary-style short stories about the Kolyma camps, by a former inmate.

Alexander Solzhenitsyn, *The Gulag Archipelago, 1918–1956*. New York: Harper-Perennial, 2002. Abridged one-volume version of Solzhenitsyn's classic three-volume study of the camp system.

Robert W. Thurston, *Life and Terror in Stalin's Russia, 1934–1941*. New Haven, CT: Yale University Press, 1996. Fine, revisionist social history.

Lynne Viola, *The Unknown Gulag: The Lost Worlds of Stalin's Special Settlements*. Oxford: Oxford University Press, 2007. Moving, intensively-researched study of the "kulak" deportations during the period of Stalinist collectivization and political purges.

Chris Ward, ed., *The Stalinist Dictatorship* (2nd edn). London: Arnold, 1998. Comprehensive survey of the roots and functioning of the Stalinist system.

Mao, Maoism, and Tibet

Jasper Becker, *Hungry Ghosts: Mao's Secret Famine*. New York: Henry Holt, 1998. Describes the catastrophe of Mao's "Great Leap Forward," with particular attention to ethnic Tibetan suffering.

Jung Chang and Jon Halliday, *Mao: The Unknown Story*. New York: Anchor Books, 2005. Borders on caricature in places, but sobering and myth-shattering on many counts.

Mary Craig, *Tears of Blood: A Cry for Tibet*. Washington, DC: Counterpoint Press, 2000. Impassioned overview of Tibet under Chinese rule.

Frank Dikötter, *Mao's Great Famine: The History of China's Most Devastating Catastrophe, 1958–1962*. London: Bloomsbury, 2010. Scathing account of the world's worst famine, inflicted under the auspices of the disastrous "Great Leap Forward" economic plan. See also *The Tragedy of Liberation: A History of the Chinese Revolution, 1945–1957*; a concluding volume in Dikötter's trilogy on Maoist atrocities focuses on the Cultural Revolution (see MacFarquhar and Schoenhals, next).

Roderick MacFarquhar and Michael Schoenhals, *Mao's Last Revolution*. Cambridge, MA: The Belknap Press of Harvard University Press, 2006. The most detailed treatment in English of the Cultural Revolution of 1966–1976.

Jean-Louis Margolin, "China: A Long March into Night," in Courtois *et al.*, *The Black Book of Communism* (see Stalin and Stalinism, above), pp. 463–546. Detailed evaluation of Chinese communism's bloody record.

Tsering Shakya, *The Dragon in the Land of Snows: A History of Modern Tibet Since 1947*. New York: Penguin Compass, 2000. "The first scholarly history of Tibet under Chinese occupation" *(Time);* fair-minded throughout.

Yang Jisheng, *Tombstone: The Great Chinese Famine, 1958–1962*. New York: Farrar, Straus and Giroux, 2012. The English translation of Yang's massive two-volume Mandarin-language study; see Figure 5.11.

▮ NOTES

1 Richard Rubenstein, *The Age of Triage: Fear and Hope in an Overcrowded World* (Boston, MA: Beacon Press, 1983), p. 19.

2 Cathie Carmichael, *Genocide before the Holocaust* (New Haven, CT: Yale University Press, 2009), p. 61. In her study of *The History of Human Rights: From Ancient Times to the Globalization Era* (Berkeley, CA: University of California Press, 2008), Micheline R. Ishay contends: "it would be wrong to overlook Marxism's (or socialism's) nineteenth-century historical contributions because of the human rights abuses later inflicted by communist regimes. If liberalism—rightly celebrated for its contribution to civil rights—is more than its colonial legacy, socialism—which championed the rights of the hardworking and powerless poor—is more than Stalinism and Maoism." She demonstrates how "the socialist movement shifted to the forefront of the struggle for civil, political, and economic rights" during the industrial revolution and European political revolutions of nineteenth century, and this continued into the twentieth century with "the struggle[s] for universal suffrage, social justice, and workers' rights," which "were socialist in origin" and overlapped importantly with anti-colonial movements (pp. 119–120). See, too, her analysis of the rights potential of contemporary liberal- and capitalist-driven globalization (pp. 292–293), which Marx also recognized.

3 Arno J. Mayer, *The Furies: Violence and Terror in the French and Russian Revolutions* (Princeton, NJ: Princeton University Press, 2000), p. 45.

4 Alec Nove, *Stalinism and After* (London: George Allen & Unwin, 1975), p. 23.

5 Lenin quoted in Nicolas Werth, "A State Against Its People: Violence, Repression, and Terror in the Soviet Union," in Stéphane Courtois *et al.*, *The Black Book of Communism: Crimes, Terror, Repression*, trans. Jonathan Murphy and Mark Kramer (Cambridge, MA: Harvard University Press, 1999), p. 70.

6 Werth, no friend of Leninism, argues that "the use of terror as a key instrument in the Leninist political project had been foreseen during the outbreak of the civil war, and was intended to be of limited duration" ("A State Against Its People," p. 265).

7 Indeed, Mark Levene locates the roots of the Soviet police state much further back in Russian history, describing the NKVD during the high-Stalinist period as "an updated version of a sixteenth-century political police force whose only role was to protect a supposedly all-powerful but paranoid tsar and quash whatever disloyalty he imagined." Levene, *The Crisis of Genocide, Vol. 2: Annihilation* (Oxford: Oxford University Press, 2013), p. 61.

8 "At the maximum, the American Relief Administration and its associated organizations were feeding over 10,400,000 mouths, and various other organizations nearly two million more, for a total of more than 12,300,000." Robert Conquest, *The Harvest of Sorrow: Collectivization and the Terror-Famine* (New York: Oxford University Press, 1986), p. 56. This must qualify as one of the most extraordinary and successful "humanitarian interventions" in history, saving millions of lives.

9 Simon Sebag Montefiore, *Stalin: The Court of the Red Tsar* (London: Phoenix, 2004), p. 27. See also Montefiore's portrait of *Young Stalin* (Toronto: McArthur and Company, 2007).

10 Timothy Snyder, *Bloodlands: Europe Between Hitler and Stalin* (New York: Basic Books, 2010), p. 13.

11 Robert Service, *Stalin: A Biography* (Cambridge, MA: The Belknap Press, 2005), p. 174.

12 In exile, Trotsky founded the "Fourth International" of the socialist movement, and became the most outspoken opponent of Stalin's policies. A Stalinist agent tracked him and killed him in Mexico City in 1940.

13 Anne Applebaum, *Gulag: A History* (London: Penguin, 2004), p. 62.

14 Mark Levene, *The Crisis of Genocide, Vol. 1: Devastation: The European Rimlands 1912–1938* (Oxford: Oxford University Press, 2013), p. 209.

15 Conquest, *The Harvest of Sorrow*, p. 19.

16 Lynne Viola, *The Unknown Gulag: The Lost World of Stalin's Special Settlements* (Oxford: Oxford University Press, 2009), p. 5.

17 Lenin quoted in *ibid.*, p. 110.

18 Lenin quoted in Montefiore, *Stalin: The Court of the Red Tsar*, p. 45.

19 Viola, *The Unknown Gulag*, p. 6.

20 Service, *Stalin: A Biography*, p. 267.

21 Khataevich quoted in Applebaum, *Gulag*, p. 515.

22 Norman M. Naimark, *Stalin's Genocides* (Princeton, NJ: Princeton University Press, 2010), p. 57.

23 Figes, *The Whisperers*, p. 87.

24 See Werth, "A State Against Its People," p. 155, with an "estimate that approximately 300,000 deportees died during the process of deportation"; Figes, *The Whisperers*, p. 88.

25 Viola, *The Unknown Gulag*, p. 114.

26 Levene, *The Crisis of Genocide, Vol. 1*, pp. 327–328. Norman M. Naimark cited "the January 1932 report of one frustrated and angry lower-level official" in the Siberian Gulag machinery who protested the treatment of political prisoners. "Comrade Shpek, you don't understand anything about the policies of our government!" he was told. "Do you really think that these elements have been sent here to be re-educated? No, Comrade, we have to see to it that by spring they're all dead, even if we have to be clever about it: dress them in such a way that they'll at least cut down a little wood before they die." Naimark, *Stalin's Genocides*, p. 61.

27 Stalin quoted in Snyder, *Bloodlands*, p. 35.

28 Nicholas Werth, "The Crimes of the Stalin Regime: Outline for an Inventory and Classification" (trans. Mike Routledge), in Dan Stone, ed., *The Historiography of Genocide* (London: Palgrave Macmillan, 2008), p. 408.

29 Snyder, *Bloodlands*, pp. 42, 47.

30 See, for example, the judicious assessment of Andrea Graziosi: "Between the end of 1932 and the summer of 1933 [i.e., at the height of the famine], . . . Stalin and the regime he controlled and coerced . . . consciously executed, as part of a drive directed at

breaking the peasantry, an anti-Ukrainian policy aimed at mass extermination and caus-ing a genocide ... whose physical and psychological scars are still visible today. ...This genocide was the product of *a famine that was not willfully caused with such aim in mind, but was willfully maneuvered towards this end once it came about as the unanticipated result of the regime policies ...*" Graziosi, "The Soviet 1931–1933 Famines and the Ukrainian Holodomor: Is a New Interpretation Possible, and What Would Its Consequences Be?," in Halyna Hryn, ed., *Hunger by Design: The Great Ukrainian Famine and Its Soviet Context* (Cambridge, MA: Harvard University Press, 2008), p. 11; emphasis added. See also the verdict of Nicolas Werth (pp. 296–297).

31 This was Robert Conquest's assertion *(The Harvest of Sorrow*, p. 196), but is contested by R. W. Davies and Stephen G. Wheatcroft in *The Years of Hunger: Soviet Agriculture, 1931–1933* (Basingstoke: Palgrave Macmillan, 2004), pp. 440–441. Conquest himself later abandoned a strongly "intentionalist" position.

32 Conquest, *The Harvest of Sorrow*, p. 224.

33 Testimony quoted in ibid., p. 245. The writer Arthur Koestler (see also note 54) described an experience outside Kharkiv train station, when local women mutely pleaded for help by lifting "to the carriage windows horrible infants with enormous wobbling heads, sticklike limbs, and swollen, pointed bellies." The children of Ukraine he described as resembling "embryos out of alcohol bottles." Quoted in Timothy Sny-der, *Bloodlands: Europe Between Hitler and Stalin* (New York: Basic Books, 2010), p. 23.

34 The document is reproduced and translated in Hryn, ed., *Hunger by Design*, pp. 44–45.

35 Davies and Wheatcroft, *The Years of Hunger*, p. 415. According to Werth, about four mil-lion of the victims were Ukrainian ("A State Against Its People," p. 167).

36 Sergei Maksudov, "Victory over the Peasantry," in Hryn, ed., *Hunger by Design*, pp. 92, 94.

37 Lemkin quoted in Snyder, *Bloodlands*, p. 53.

38 Niccolò Pianciola, "The Collectivization Famine in Kazakhstan, 1931–1933," in Hryn, ed., *Hunger by Design*, p. 103. See also Mukhamet Shayakhmetov, *The Silent Steppe: The Memoir of a Kazakh Nomad Under Stalin*, trans. Jan Butler (New York: Overlook/Rook-ery, 2007).

39 Figes, *The Whisperers*, p. 208.

40 See Applebaum, *Gulag*, ch. 4.

41 Conquest, *The Harvest of Sorrow*, pp. 127–128.

42 Snyder, *Bloodlands*, p. 27.

43 Leo Kuper, *Genocide: Its Political Use in the Twentieth Century* (Harmondsworth: Penguin, 1981), p. 150.

44 Ibid.

45 Robert Conquest, *Kolyma: The Arctic Death Camps* (London: Methuen, 1978), p. 229.

46 Adam Hochschild, *The Unquiet Ghost: Russians Remember Stalin* (New York: Viking, 1994), p. xxv. "I asked four ... researchers, who between them have written or edited more than half a dozen books on the *gulag*, what was the total Kolyma death toll. One estimated it at 250,000, one at 300,000, one at 800,000, and one at 'more than 1,000,000.' ... We will probably never know the answer" (p. 237).

47 Kuper, *Genocide*, p. 150.

48 Alec Luhn, "Stalin, Russia's New Hero," *The New York Times*, March 11, 2016, www.nytimes.com/2016/03/13/opinion/sunday/stalinist-nostalgia-in-vladimir-putins-russia.html.

49 Ian Frazier, *Travels in Siberia* (New York: Picador, 2011), p. 424.

50 In Timothy Snyder's dictum: "Only an unabashed acceptance of the similarities between the Nazi and Soviet systems permits an understanding of their differences." In his view, a notable difference is that while "Stalin, no less than Hitler, spoke of liquida-tions, and cleansings," these "could never be anything more than a successful defense of socialism, or an element in a story of progress toward socialism; it was never the politi-cal victory itself" *(Bloodlands*, pp. 389, 391). Norman Naimark's distilled and insightful

analysis of *Stalin's Genocides* (Princeton, NJ: Princeton University Press, 2010) argues persuasively that both Nazi and Stalinist systems "were genocidal by their very character, meaning that their distinct combinations of charismatic leaders . . . dictatorial powers, ideological motivations, and Promethean transformative aspirations, led them to use the mass killing of groups of their own citizens (and others) as a way to achieve the impossible future that defined their very essence" (p. 129). He points, however, to the fact that "minors were usually not executed by the Soviet regime. . . . This is different from the fearsome Nazi elimination of Jewish children in the death camps and at thousands of sites of mass murder across Eastern Europe and Russia," although "children of the 'repressed' population were highly susceptible to disease, hunger, exposure, and various forms of exploitation while in transport, in 'special settlements,' in orphanages, and in work camps" (p. 127). Note also the root-and-branch targeting of Jews in the Holocaust, contrasted with the essentially gendercidal slaughter in the Gulag and the purges. In her voluminous study *Gulag*, Anne Applebaum further noted the absence of Soviet "'selections' of the sort that took place in German death camps. That is, I have not read of regular selections which ended in weak prisoners being taken aside and shot. . . . Weak prisoners were not murdered upon arrival in some of the further-flung camps, but rather given a period of 'quarantine,' both to ensure that any illnesses they were carrying would not spread, and to allow them to 'fatten up,' to recover their health after long months in prison and terrible journeys" (Applebaum, *Gulag*, p. 175). Mark Levene argued along similar lines that "there was no equivalent of Treblinka in Kazakhstan" (Levene, *The Crisis of Genocide, Vol. 1*, p. 20). He has also pointed to the "time-consuming" process of arresting and interrogating "each and every suspect," which "speaks of a modus operandi not well suited to rapid mass slaughter" (p. 355). For a unique memoir of survival in the prison systems of both Soviet and Nazi regimes, see Margarete Buber-Neumann, *Under Two Dictators: Prisoner of Stalin and Hitler* (New York: Random House, 2013). Matthew White offered a deliberately flippant insight: "the West generally considers Hitler worse than Stalin because Hitler's evil disgusts more successfully on a gut level. The human face of the Holocaust is Anne Frank, an innocent little girl hunted down and exterminated because of dangerous racist pseudoscience. The human face of the Gulag is Aleksandr Solzhenitsyn [author of *The Gulag Archipelago*, see Figure 5.6], a cranky old guy in a wild beard who survived." White, *Atrocitology: Humanity's 100 Deadliest Achievements* (Edinburgh: Canongate, 2011), p. 394.

51 Viola, *The Unknown Gulag*, pp. 163, 165. Figes wrote that "By far the biggest of [the] mass campaigns was the 'kulak operation' instituted by the infamous Directive 00447: it accounted for half of all arrests (669,929) and more than half the executions (376,202) in 1937–38. Nearly all the victims were former 'kulaks' and their families who had recently returned from 'special settlements' and Gulag labour camps . . ." "As a result of the 'national operation' against the Poles, launched by Directive 00485 in August 1937, almost 140,000 people were shot or sent to labour camps by November 1938" *(The Whisperers*, p. 241). Overall, the "kulak" death toll during the 1930s was "roughly half a million" (Viola, *The Unknown Gulag*, p. 183).

52 "Those arrested were almost always men," Snyder notes. For a survivor of the Stalinist terror against ethnic Poles, Hanna Sobolewska, the overriding memory was: "children cry, women remain." Snyder, *Bloodlands*, p. 103.

53 Ibid., pp. 96, 107. Snyder calculates that "as of the end of 1938, the USSR had killed about a thousand times more people on ethnic grounds than had Nazi Germany" (p. 111).

54 The strength of appeals to solidarity and party unity in extracting confessions from the "Old Bolsheviks" was memorably captured in Arthur Koestler's 1940 novel, *Darkness at Noon* (New York: Bantam, 1984). A parallel phenomenon among survivors is examined in Nanci Adler, *Keeping Faith with the Party: Communist Believers Return from the Gulag* (Bloomington, IN: Indiana University Press, 2012).

55 Figes, *The Whisperers*, p. 238.

56 Ibid., pp. 238–239.
57 The infamous Order 00447, also known as the "Kulak Eradication Program," established "for every region . . . initial quotas for those to be executed and for those to be imprisoned for 8–10 years. The quota for the Moscow region was 5,000 people to be shot and 30,000 incarcerated; for Leningrad, 4,000 and 10,000 respectively. Ukraine's quota was set at 8,000 to be shot and 20,800 incarcerated." Ben Kiernan, *Blood and Soil: A World History of Genocide and Extermination from Sparta to Darfur* (New Haven, CT: Yale University Press, 2007), p. 508.
58 Christopher Hitchens, *Arguably: Essays* (Toronto: Signal, 2011), p. 589.
59 Alexander Solzhenitsyn, *The Gulag Archipelago Two* (New York: Harper & Row, 1975), p. 633.
60 Nadezhda Mandelstam, *Hope Against Hope* (New York: Modern Library, 1999), pp. 322–323, 352.
61 Shaporina quoted in Moynahan, *Leningrad: Siege and Symphony* (London: Quercus Editions, 2013), p. 42.
62 Snyder, *Bloodlands*, p. 82. In many cases, Snyder records (pp. 100–101), "NKVD task forces appeared suddenly, with instructions to arrest and execute a certain number of people. They would begin from the assumption that an entire village, factory, or collective farm was guilty, surround the place by night, and then torture the men until they got the results they needed. Then they would carry out the executions and move on."
63 Conquest, *The Great Terror: A Reassessment*, p. 433.
64 Naimark, *Stalin's Genocides*, p. 107. In part to shift blame from Stalin, the purge became known subsequently as the *Yezhovshchina*, or "The Reign of Yezhov," in Werth's translation ("A State Against Its People," p. 184).
65 Conquest, *The Great Terror: A Reassessment*, p. 438.
66 David M. Crowe, *War Crimes, Genocide, and Justice: A Global History* (New York: Palgrave Macmillan, 2014), p. 149.
67 See Allen Paul, *Katyń: Stalin's Massacre and the Triumph of Truth* (DeKalb, IL: Northern Illinois University Press, 2010). The Nazis uncovered some 4,000 of the corpses during Operation Barbarossa in 1941. The Soviet regime accused them of spreading libels, and blamed the Nazis for the crime at the Nuremberg tribunal; the other Allies acquiesced in the charade.
68 The standard and excellent history of the Soviet occupation of Poland (1939–1941) is Jan T. Gross, *Revolution from Abroad: The Soviet Conquest of Poland's Western Ukraine and Western Belorussia*, expanded edition (Princeton, NJ: Princeton University Press, 2002). See also Roger Moorhouse, *The Devils' Alliance: Hitler's Pact with Stalin, 1939–1941* (New York: Basic Books, 2014). For a concise overview, see Levene, *The Crisis of Genocide, Vol. 2*, pp. 35–45.
69 Applebaum, *Gulag*, pp. 382–383.
70 Franz Kafka, *The Trial* (New York: Schocken Books, 1968), p. 1.
71 Brian Moynahan, *Leningrad: Siege and Symphony* (London: Quercus Editions, 2013). The quoted passages and biographical details are drawn from the narrative of Izvekov's arrest, trial, and execution at pp. 302–305, 322–330, 351–354, 359–361, and 364–365.
72 Applebaum, *Gulag*, pp. 378–379.
73 Ibid., p. 410.
74 See the various prisoner totals and casualty estimates cited in "Japanese Prisoners of War in the Soviet Union," Wikipedia.org, http://en.wikipedia.org/wiki/Japanese_prisoners_of_war_in_the_Soviet_Union.
75 A sweeping survey of the period that produced the "Iron Curtain" examined in Anne Applebaum's work (see Figure 5.7) is Michael Dobbs, *Six Months in 1945: FDR, Stalin, Churchill and Truman— From World War to Cold War* (New York: Alfred A. Knopf, 2012).
76 Applebaum, *Gulag*, p. 410.
77 Alexander Solzhenitsyn, *The Gulag Archipelago One* (New York: Harper & Row, 1974), p. 240.

78 An earlier precedent, important for understanding Leninist–Stalinist continuity, is the genocide against the Don and Kuban Cossacks during the civil war of 1919 to 1920. According to Eric Weitz, "'Cossack' came to mean anti-Soviet, a synonym for 'enemy' that carried an implicit racialization of a group defined not even by ethnicity but by its special service relationship to the czarist state." The death toll was 300,000 to 500,000 out of a population of three million. Eric D. Weitz, *A Century of Genocide: Utopias of Race and Nation* (Princeton, NJ: Princeton University Press, 2003), p. 69; see also Werth, "A State Against Its People," pp. 98–102.

79 Alexander Statiev, "Soviet Ethnic Deportations: Intent versus Outcome," *Journal of Genocide Research*, 11: 2–3 (2009), pp. 243–244.

80 Ibid., p. 244.

81 Ibid., p. 246. Statiev, however, bound by a highly restrictive definition of (specific) "intent," contends that the fact that the deportations did not constitute planned exterminations means that they do not constitute "a clear-cut case of genocide and any further discussion on whether the government committed genocide would be not only ideologically loaded but also sterile" (p. 260). I believe this gives short shrift to more flexible and encompassing understandings of genocidal intent. It also overlooks the legal definition of "extermination" as a crime against humanity, and its overlap with Article 2(c) of the Genocide Convention: that is, the infliction of conditions of life which it is known, or should be known, will cause the destruction of the designated groups in whole or in part. See further discussion on pp. 710–711.

82 Finnish speakers in the Karelia region of northwest Russia also suffered after the Finns, seeking to regain territories lost to Stalin in the winter war of 1939–1940, joined the Nazi thrust into the Soviet Union.

83 On the Crimean Tatars, see Brian Glyn Williams, "Hidden Ethnocide in the Soviet Muslim Borderlands: The Ethnic Cleansing of the Crimean Tatars," *Journal of Genocide Research*, 4: 3 (2002), pp. 357–373; Stephen Blank, "A Double Dispossession: The Crimean Tatars After Russia's Ukrainian War," *Genocide Studies and Prevention*, 9: 1 (2015), http://scholarcommons.usf.edu/cgi/viewcontent.cgi?article=1271&context=gsp. In May 2016, Ukraine won the Eurovision song contest with "1944," about the mass deportations of the Tatars. Singer/songwriter Jamala (Susana Jamaladinova) "is herself a Crimean Tatar and has spoken of the importance of the people knowing about the deportations. 'The main message is to remember and to know this story,' she said. 'When we know, we prevent.' Her song opens with the uncompromising lyrics: 'When strangers are coming. They come to your house, they kill you all and say: 'We're not guilty . . . not guilty.' Jamala's great-grandmother was deported along with her four sons and one daughter. 'This song really is about my family,' Jamala said. 'I had to write it. It is a memorial song and it is difficult for me to sing it.'" Mark Brown, "Ukraine's Eurovision Entry Takes Aim at Russian Oppression," *The Guardian*, February 22, 2016, www.theguardian.com/world/2016/feb/22/ukraines-eurovision-entry-takes-aim-at-russian-oppression. The article notes that "the song also feeds into contemporary geopolitical tensions, with Russia's seizure of Crimea in 2014 still fresh in people's memories." See also Ivan Nechepurenkomay, "Ukraine's Eurovision Win Rouses a Chorus of Anger and Suspicion in Russia," *The New York Times*, May 16, 2016, www.nytimes.com/2016/05/17/world/europe/ukraines-eurovision-win-rouses-a-chorus-of-anger-and-suspicion-in-russia.html.

84 See Lyman H. Legters, "Soviet Deportation of Whole Nations: A Genocidal Process," in Samuel Totten *et al., Century of Genocide: Eyewitness Accounts and Critical Views* (New York: Garland Publishing, 1997), pp. 112–135. See also Robert Conquest, *The Nation Killers: The Soviet Deportation of Nationalities* (London: Macmillan, 1970); Aleksander M. Nekrich, *The Punished Peoples: The Deportation and Tragic Fate of Soviet Minorities at the End of the Second World War*, trans. George Saunders (New York: Norton, 1978); and J. Otto Pohl, "Stalin's Genocide against the 'Repressed Peoples,'" *Journal of Genocide Research*, 2: 2 (June 2000), pp. 267–293.

85 Applebaum, *Gulag*, p. 388.

86 Ibid. According to Nicolas Werth, "Of the 608,749 people deported from the Caucasus, 146,892, or nearly 1 in 4, had died by 1 October 1948. . . . Of the 228,392 people deported from the Crimea, 44,887 had died after four years." Werth, "A State Against Its People," p. 223.

87 After Stalin's death, the remnants of some deported nationalities were allowed to return to their former territories, but the extinguished political units were not always revived.

88 Service, *Stalin: A Biography*, p. 592.

89 Daniil Turovsky, "Russian City Opens Cultural Centre Celebrating Stalin," *The Guardian*, January 11, 2016, www.theguardian.com/world/2016/jan/11/stalin-russia-penza-cultural-centre-meduza.

90 I studied the post-Soviet media scene intensively, including through fieldwork in Moscow, for my Ph.D. thesis, *The Press in Transition: A Comparative Study of Nicaragua, South Africa, Jordan, and Russia*, subsequently published by the Deutsche Übersee-Institut in Hamburg (2002). See also Adam Jones, "The Russian Press in the Post-Soviet Era: A Case Study of *Izvestia*," *Journalism Studies*, 3: 3 (2002), pp. 359–375.

91 See, e.g., "Alexander Solzhenitsyn's Widow on What Went Wrong [in Ukraine]," *The Economist*, November 26, 2015, www.economist.com/blogs/prospero/2015/11/russia-and-west.

92 Orlando Figes, "The Raid on Memorial," *The New York Review of Books*, 56: 1 (January 15, 2009), www.nybooks.com/articles/22248.

93 "Putin Honors Stalin Victims 70 Years after Terror," Reuters dispatch, October 30, 2007, www.reuters.com/article/idUSL3072723020071030. For his part, Medvedev stated in October 2009 that "even now we can hear voices saying that these numerous deaths were justified by some supreme goals of the state. Nothing can be valued above human life, and there is no excuse for repressions. . . . It is . . . important to prevent the justification, under the pretext of putting historical records straight, of those who killed their own people." Ellen Barry, "Don't Gloss Over Stalin's Crimes, Medvedev Says," *The New York Times*, October 30, 2009, www.nytimes.com/2009/10/31/world/europe/31russia.html.

94 This model rapprochement was marred by catastrophe on April 10, 2010, when Polish president Lech Kaczynski, his wife, and much of the country's senior political and military leadership were killed in the crash of their Russian Tupolev jet on approach to a fogbound Russian airstrip near Smolensk. The dignitaries were arriving to commemorate, jointly with Putin and other Russian leaders, the 1940 massacre of Polish officers by Stalinist NKVD security forces at Katyn and elsewhere (see p. 272). As an additionally tragic component, the toll of ninety-six crash victims included relatives of several of those killed at Katyn.

95 "Belarusian ruler Alexander Lukashenka frequently refers to the Second World War in his quarrels with the West. Lukashenka added to the Soviet Victory Day celebrated on 9 May another official holiday, 3 July, the day when the Red Army took Minsk in 1944. In 2003 the government introduced the History of the Great Patriotic War as an obligatory and separate subject not only in schools but also at all universities. The authorities are also building a new grand museum devoted to the war." Siarhei Bohdan, "Why Belarus is Missing in World War II History," *Belarus Digest*, May 8, 2012, http://belarusdigest.com/print/9168.

96 Tom Parfitt, "Proportion of Russians Who Respect Stalin is Growing, Poll Suggests," *The Telegraph*, March 31, 2015, www.telegraph.co.uk/news/worldnews/europe/russia/11506970/Proportion-of-Russians-who-respect-Stalin-is-growing-poll-suggests.html. See also Luhn, "Stalin, Russia's New Hero."

97 Matthew White, *Atrocitology: Humanity's 100 Deadliest Achievements* (Edinburgh: Canongate, 2011), p. 429.

98 R.J. Rummel, *Death by Government* (New Brunswick, NJ: Transaction Publishers, 1994), p. 101.

99 Mao quoted in Frank Dikötter, *Mao's Great Famine: The History of China's Most Devastating Catastrophe, 1958–1962* (London: Bloomsbury, 2010), p. 19.

100 Peng Pai quoted in Kiernan, *Blood and Soil*, p. 519.

101 Kiernan, *Blood and Soil*, p. 521.

102 Jung Chang and Jon Halliday, *Mao: The Unknown Story* (New York: Anchor Books, 2006), p. 309.

103 Mao quoted in Sudeep Chakravarti, *Red Sun: Travels in Naxalite Country* (New Delhi: Viking, 2008), p. 169.

104 Chang and Halliday, *Mao*, p. 311.

105 Benjamin Valentino, *Final Solutions: Mass Killing and Genocide in the 20th Century* (Ithaca, NY: Cornell University Press, 2004), p. 121.

106 Jean-Louis Margolin, "Mao's China: The Worst Non-Genocidal Regime?," in Dan Stone, ed., *The Historiography of Genocide* (London: Palgrave Macmillan, 2008), p. 453.

107 Kiernan, *Blood and Soil*, p. 529.

108 Margolin, "Mao's China," p. 453. The slaughter was carefully monitored and regulated, according to Frank Dikötter. "Mao handed down a killing quote as a rough guide for action. The norm, he felt, was one per thousand, a ratio he was willing to adjust to the particular circumstances of each region. His subordinates kept track of local killing rates like bean counters, occasionally negotiating for a higher quota. . . . Villages, counties and provinces emulated each other, preferring to kill too many rather than too few—and risk being purged . . . Thousands were silently executed in order to fulfill and surpass the quota." Dikötter, *The Tragedy of Liberation: A History of the Chinese Revolution, 1945–1957* (London: Bloomsbury, 2013), p. 88.

109 Chang and Halliday, *Mao*, p. 319.

110 Ibid.

111 Central Tibetan Administration (hereafter, CTA), *Tibet under Communist China—Fifty Years* (2001), http://tibet.net/2001/01/tibet-under-communist-china-50-years-2001/, p. 54.

112 The distinction between "Outer Tibet" and "Inner Tibet" was first made in the 1913–1914 Simla Conference and Convention, in which Tibet, China, and Britain participated. "Chinese suzerainty over the whole of Tibet was recognized but China engaged not to convert Tibet into a Chinese province. The autonomy of Outer Tibet was recognised and China agreed to abstain from interference in its internal administration which was to rest with Tibetans themselves. In Inner Tibet the central Tibetan Government at Lhasa was to retain its existing rights." George N. Patterson, "China and Tibet: Background to the Revolt," *The China Quarterly*, 1 (January–March 1960), p. 90.

113 Tsering Shakya, *The Dragon in the Land of Snows: A History of Modern Tibet since 1947* (New York: Penguin Compass, 2000), p. xxx.

114 Ibid., p. xxviii.

115 CTA, *Tibet under Communist China*, p. 130.

116 Eric S. Margolis, *War at the Top of the World: The Struggle for Afghanistan, Kashmir, and Tibet* (New York: Routledge, 2001), p. 195.

117 See the full text of the "Agreement of the Central People's Government and the Local Government of Tibet on Measures for the Peaceful Liberation of Tibet" at www.china-un.org/eng/gyzg/xizang/t424244.htm.

118 See Frank Morales, *The Revolt in Tibet* (New York: Macmillan, 1960).

119 CTA, *Tibet under Communist China*, p. 9.

120 Shakya refers to "areas where all able young men had been arrested and imprisoned, leaving the villages inhabited only by old people and women." *The Dragon in the Land of Snows*, p. 271.

121 Jean-Louis Margolin, "China: A Long March into Night," in Courtois *et al.*, eds., *The Black Book of Communism*, p. 545.

122 For an overview of this period, see Solomon M. Karmel, "Ethnic Tension and the Struggle for Order: China's Policies in Tibet," *Pacific Affairs*, 68 (Winter 1995–1996), pp. 485–505.

123 See Anita Chang, "Group [the International Campaign for Tibet] Says Railway Threatens Tibet," Associated Press dispatch on *Yahoo! News*, February 27, 2008.

124 Tim Johnson, "China Orders Resettlement of Thousands of Tibetans," *Realcities.com*, May 6, 2007.

125 Shakya, *The Dragon in the Land of Snows*, p. 430.

126 Tristan Stewart-Robertson, "80 People Dead in 'Cultural Genocide,'" *The Scotsman*, 17 March 2008. See also Isabel Hilton, "The World Is No Longer Looking—But Tibet's Plight Isn't Over," *The Independent*, March 10, 2009.

127 "China 'Annihilating Tibetan Buddhism,'" Associated Press dispatch in *The Sydney Morning Herald*, March 11, 2010, www.smh.com.au/world/china-annihilating-tibetan-buddhism-20100311-pzj2.html.

128 Margolin, "China," p. 546.

129 Quoted in Shakya, *The Dragon in the Land of Snows*, p. 223; see the "ICJ Report on Tibet 1960."

130 Maura Moynihan, "Genocide in Tibet," *The Washington Post*, January 25, 1998. Tibetan nationalists have often alleged that China is guilty of another strategy of genocide under the terms of the UN Convention: preventing Tibetan births through forcible sterilization of Tibetan women. However, the evidence does not support this. See Melvyn C. Goldstein and Cynthia M. Beall, "China's Birth Control Policy in the Tibet Autonomous Region: Myths and Realities," *Asian Survey*, 31: 3 (March 1991), pp. 285–303.

131 See "The Five Point Peace Plan for Tibet, by His Holiness the Dalai Lama, Washington, DC, 21 September 1987," http://tibet.net/important-issues/sino-tibetan-dialogue/important-statements-of-his-holiness-the-dalai-lama/five-point-peace-plan-for-tibet/. The proposals were "further clarified" but "also developed . . . further" in the Dalai Lama's speech to European Parliament representatives in June 1988; for details, see Shakya, *The Dragon in the Land of Snows*, p. 423.

132 For an account of strategic rethinking now underway in the Tibetan exile community, see "Tibetans Meet to Rethink Autonomy," *AlJazeera.net*, November 17, 2008.

133 Chang and Halliday, *Mao*, p. 431.

134 Margolin, "Mao's China," p. 446.

135 Chang and Halliday, *Mao*, pp. 418–419. "People lied to survive," wrote Frank Dikötter, "and as a consequence information was distorted all the way up to the Chairman." Dikötter, *Mao's Great Famine: The History of China's Most Devastating Catastrophe, 1958–1962* (London: Bloomsbury, 2010), p. xiv.

136 Margolin, "China," p. 495.

137 Shakya, *The Dragon in the Land of Snows*, p. 262.

138 Chang and Halliday, *Mao*, p. 443.

139 Yang Jisheng, *Tombstone: The Great Chinese Famine, 1958–1962* (New York: Farrar, Straus and Giroux, 2012), pp. 13, 430. Emphasis added. Frank Dikötter supplies an estimate of "at least 45 million people [who] died unnecessarily between 1958 and 1962." *Mao's Great Famine*, p. x; see the discussion at pp. 324–325.

140 Dikötter, *Mao's Great Famine*, p. 33.

141 Martin Shaw, *Genocide and International Relations: Changing Patterns in the Transitions of the Late Modern World* (Cambridge: Cambridge University Press, 2013), p. 104.

142 Ibid. In 1958–1959, according to Chang and Halliday, "Grain exports alone, almost exactly 7 million tons, would have provided the equivalent of over 840 calories per day for 38 million people—the difference between life and death. And this was only grain; it does not include the meat, cooking oil, eggs and other foodstuffs that were exported in very large quantities. Had this food not been exported (and instead distributed according to humane criteria), very probably not a single person in China would have had to die of hunger" (*Mao*, p. 430).

143 Margolin, "Mao's China," p. 459. See also Dikötter, *Mao's Great Famine*, p. 106.

144 Frank Fang and Larry Ong, "Esteemed Chinese Editor Quits Amid Political Pressure, But It's Unclear Who's Behind the Pressure," *The Epoch Times*, July 20, 2015, www.theepochtimes.com/n3/1467823-chinese-editor-quits-amid-political-pressure-but-its-unclear-whos-behind-the-pressure/.

145 Mao quoted in Dikötter, *Mao's Great Famine*, p. 41.

146 Mao quoted in Yang, *Tombstone*, p. 330.

147 Mao quoted in Dikötter, *Mao's Great Famine*, p. 136. Emphasis added.

148 Lee quoted in Margolin, "China," p. 495.

149 Roderick MacFarquhar and Michael Schoenhals, *Mao's Last Revolution* (Cambridge, MA: The Belknap Press of Harvard University Press, 2006), p. 258.

150 Chang and Halliday, *Mao*, p. 536.

151 Walder quoted in MacFarquhar and Schoenhals, *Mao's Last Revolution*, p. 256.

152 This box text includes and adapts passages from Adam Jones, *Crimes Against Humanity: A Beginner's Guide* (Oxford: Oneworld, 2008), pp. 81–84.

153 B.R. Myers, *The Cleanest Race: How North Koreans See Themselves—and Why It Matters* (Brooklyn, NY: Melville House, 2010).

154 Ibid., p. 15.

155 Andrew Natsios, "The Politics of Famine in North Korea," United States Institute of Peace report, August 2, 1999, www.usip.org/files/resources/sr990802.pdf.

156 Jasper Becker, *Rogue Regime: Kim Jong Il and the Looming Threat of North Korea* (New York: Oxford University Press, 2006), pp. 32–33, 266. Rhoda Howard-Hassmann cites a careful South Korean estimate of "between 580,000 and 1.1 million people [who] lost their lives during the famine of 1994–2000, or 3–5% of the population." Howard-Hassmann, "State-Induced Famine and Penal Starvation in North Korea," *Genocide Studies and Prevention*, 7: 2–3 (2012), p. 150.

157 Becker, *Rogue Regime*, p. 36.

158 Christian Solidarity Worldwide, *North Korea: A Case to Answer, a Call to Act* (New Malden: Christian Solidarity Worldwide, 2007), p. 43. Emphasis added. The report can be downloaded in PDF format at www.csw.org.uk/2007/06/20/report/35/article.htm. See also Blaine Harden, "Escapee Tells of Horrors in North Korean Prison Camp," *The Washington Post*, December 11, 2008.

159 "North Korea: UN Condemns Systemic Rights Abuses," Human Rights Watch press release, December 17, 2015, www.hrw.org/news/2015/12/17/north-korea-un-condemns-systemic-rights-abuses. See also the text of a February 2016 European Parliament resolution at www.europarl.europa.eu/sides/getDoc.do?type=MOTION&reference=B8–2016–0089&language=EN.

160 Jonathan Watts, "China Must Confront Dark Past, Says Mao Confidant," *The Guardian*, June 2, 2005, www.guardian.co.uk/world/2005/jun/02/china.jonathanwatts. See also Andrew Jacobs, "China Is Wordless on Traumas of Communists' Rise," *The New York Times*, October 1, 2009 (60th anniversary of the victory of the communist revolution), www.nytimes.com/2009/10/02/world/asia/02anniversary.html.

161 See, e.g., Jonathan Watts, "Mao Casts Long Shadow Over China," *The Guardian*, May 15, 2006, www.guardian.co.uk/world/2006/may/16/china.jonathanwatts.

162 Robin Munro, "Remembering Tiananmen Square," *The Nation*, June 2, 2009, www.thenation.com/article/remembering-tiananmen-square/.

163 See "'Mega Mao' No More as Ridiculed Golden Statue Destroyed," *The Guardian*, January 8, 2016, www.theguardian.com/world/2016/jan/08/giant-golden-chairman-mao-statue-destroyed-henan-province.

164 Werth, "The Crimes of the Stalin Regime," p. 415. Emphasis in original.

165 Viola, *The Unknown Gulag*, p. 133.

166 Martin Shaw, *What is Genocide?* (Cambridge: Polity, 2007), p. 85.

BOX 5A CHECHNYA

As discussed in Chapter 5, the people of Chechnya were among a number of nationalities accused of complicity with the Nazis during the Second World War, rounded up, and deported under murderous conditions to distant and barren lands. At least 390,000 Chechens—perhaps many more—were uprooted in this way. Fully a quarter of them died *en route* to their exile, and survivors faced a constant struggle against the elements and poor soils.[1] After Stalin's death, most of these populations were returned to their homelands. Yet bitter memories lingered, and they explain something of the extraordinary persistence of Chechen rebel forces in their war for independence.[2]

One must dig deeper for the roots of Chechen nationalism and its conflict with "Greater Russia." Chechens were at the forefront of efforts to resist Russian expansion during the mid-nineteenth century. For three decades after 1829, the expansionist tsarist state waged "almost unremitting warfare" in the Caucasus, with "hundreds upon hundreds of villages . . . razed, accompanied by terrorist reprisal and atrocity directed against their inhabitants."[3] When the North Caucasus was finally overwhelmed and incorporated into the empire, some 600,000

Map 5a.1 Chechnya.

Source: Map courtesy of WorldAtlas.com

Caucasians—100,000 of them Chechens—"were sent to the Ottoman Empire, where tens of thousands perished from starvation and disease."[4]

The Chechens rallied after the Bolshevik Revolution of 1917, but their aspirations for independence were doomed by renewed Russian (now Soviet) expansionism. The Bolsheviks occupied Chechnya, and in 1924 established the Chechen-Ingush Autonomous Region, which Stalin would cancel in the 1940s.

The liberalizing wave that struck the Soviet Union and Eastern Europe in the late 1980s resulted in the breakup of the Soviet empire; but Chechnya was a federal unit of Russia, not a Soviet Union republic. When Russian president Boris Yeltsin took over from Soviet president Mikhail Gorbachev, he decided that no secession from Russia itself would be permitted. In the Chechen case, there were material considerations: a major oil pipeline ran through Chechnya, which was home to substantial petroleum resources of its own. Whoever controlled them was guaranteed a strategic presence in the region as a whole.

Russian policy reflected an ingrained racism toward Chechens. Chechnya had long been an "obsession" for the Russians, wrote journalist David Remnick: "an image of Islamic defiance, an embodiment of the primitive, the devious, the elusive." Chechens were seen as bumpkins and "black asses." "Yeltsin knew well that for many Russians the Chechens were nothing more than a tribe of 'thieving niggers.'"[5] The conflict can also be viewed in light of the Russian humiliation in the war against Afghanistan (1979–1990; see Chapter 2). As Gregory Feifer noted in his 2009 history of that war, "the Kremlin calls the [Chechen] rebels 'bandits' and 'terrorists'—echoing the same words the Soviet Union used to describe the Afghan mujahideen [Islamic warriors]—and claims the conflict in Chechnya was part of the global war against terrorism."[6]

In 1991, the mercurial Chechen leader, Dzhokar Dudayev—previously a general in the Soviet air force—rebelled against Moscow and declared Chechnya independent. Under his rule, "Chechnya became an epicenter of financial scams and illegal trade in oil and contraband, and a safe haven for criminals from all over Russia," while violence against ethnic Russians in the territory rose alarmingly.[7]

The bombastic, alcoholic Yeltsin countered by seeking to undermine the Chechen regime from within.[8] When a Russian-led assault on Grozny, using Chechen forces opposed to Dudayev, ended in a shambles, the Russians reacted with fury. In December 1994, 40,000 Russian troops—mostly ill-trained conscripts—were sent into Chechnya. Yeltsin apparently believed the declaration of his defense minister, Pavel Grachev, that the territory could be conquered "in two hours by a single paratrooper regiment."[9] Two years later, Russian forces were still there.

The first assault on Grozny was disastrous. Russian tank columns and troop formations were torn apart by hit-and-run rebel attacks. The Russians responded with "the heaviest artillery bombardment that anyone had seen since the Second World War."[10] "Indiscriminate strikes became the preferred mode of warfare against a ground war the Russian armed forces were unfit to win."[11] Numerous towns and villages were pulverized. Tens of thousands of Chechen residents were killed, overwhelmingly civilians. In a grim irony, many of the victims were ethnic Russians who lacked the contacts in the countryside that allowed many Chechen Muslims to find refuge. When the Russians finally claimed control of Grozny in March, visiting journalists marveled at "the sheer scale of the destruction," with the city "not only in ruins but . . . destroyed [to] its very foundations." Even years later, the heart of the city remained "a desert scene of rubble and burnt-out buildings."[12]

To the extent that Russians discriminated in their killing, the strategy was predominantly gendercidal (see Chapter 13). "I killed a lot," a Russian soldier returned from Chechnya told Maura Reynolds of the *Los Angeles Times:*

I wouldn't touch women or children, as long as they didn't fire at me. But I would kill all the men I met during mopping-up operations. I didn't

Figure 5a.1 A Chechen man prays during the first battle of Grozny, December 1994.

Source: Photo by Mikahil Evstafiev/Wikimedia Commons.

feel sorry for them one bit. They deserved it. I wouldn't even listen to the pleas or see the tears of their women when they asked me to spare their men. I simply took them aside and killed them.[13]

In keeping with such strategies, mass round-ups and detentions of Chechen men were staged, with detainees passed through "filtration camps" run by the Russian military and FSB (formerly the KGB). Torture was frequent in the camps, and "disappearances" rampant.[14]

All of this occurred in Europe; yet few Europeans, or others, raised their voices in protest. Russia, even in its post-Soviet incarnation, is a great power, and a nuclear one. European governments have been more interested in courting it and exploiting its immense resources than in criticizing "internal" practices, even genocidal ones. The response of the Clinton and Bush administrations was likewise "woefully late and pitifully restrained."[15]

Destructive as the war was, it was just the first round. In 1996, remarkably, rebel forces reoccupied Grozny, holding it for weeks against an indiscriminate Russian counter-attack that consolidated Grozny's status as "the most destroyed city on earth," in the UN's later verdict.[16] For the Russian public, this was the final straw. Public opposition to the slaughter (albeit mainly to the deaths of Russian conscripts) drove Yeltsin's approval ratings to dismally low levels. The Russian media enjoyed their most brilliant moment since 1917, with press reports and TV investigations carefully documenting the Chechen chaos. Finally, Russian forces pulled out in defeat, leaving the territory still nominally part of Russia, but effectively in the hands of Chechen rebels and warlords.

With the economy and infrastructure virtually destroyed, Chechnya again lapsed into lawlessness. In September 1999, Yeltsin, now a lame duck, sent the troops back in. His policy was energetically continued and expanded by Vladimir Putin, who pungently pledged to "corner the bandits in the shithouse and wipe them out."[17] Putin calculated that a hard line on Chechnya would help him consolidate his power and appeal to voters in future elections.[18]

Under Putin, the Russian tactics of the previous conflict were revived, from indiscriminate bombardment to filtration camps. Again adult men were special targets. Human Rights Watch stated that "every adult Chechen male" was treated "as if he were a rebel fighter."[19] Chechen women were also assaulted and raped on an increasing scale.[20]

Once again, Russian forces became mired in an intractable guerrilla war with rebels whose behavior in turn grew more atrocious, indiscriminate, and terroristic. In 2004, hundreds of schoolchildren died in the town of Beslan in neighboring Ingushetia, when Russian forces stormed a school seized by rebels. Two civilian passenger planes downed by female Chechen rebels—the so-called "Black Widows"[21]—added to the casualty count. The toll among Chechen civilians, though, was much greater, probably reaching 100,000 people. Since the mid-2000s, killings have continued on a selective rather than mass scale. Evaluating Russia's overall record during the Chechen wars, Matthew Evangelista considered it "plausible" that Russia had "violated the Genocide Convention for 'acts committed with intent to destroy, in whole or in part, a national, ethnical, racial, or religious group'"[22]

Putin, recognizing the growing quagmire, sought to indigenize the war. "Chechenization" became the new buzzword, and achieved success from the Russian perspective. Chechnya was placed under the ruthlessly authoritarian grip of a "Chief Mufti," Akhmad Kadyrov, a former rebel. When Kadyrov's erstwhile comrades blew him up during a May 2004 parade, his son, Ramzan, promptly flew to Moscow to pledge his loyalty and receive Putin's blessing. He has since largely suppressed rebel activity, by coopting some fighters and hunting down others. He has also forged a cult of personality in Chechnya for both himself and his patron. "... Chechnya is the only place in Russia where Putin is so openly and publicly worshipped," reported Simon Shuster; the "central drag" in Grozny was renamed V.V. Putin Avenue.[23]

Apart from infusing his warriors with a carefully-crafted Islamist-jihadist ideology, Kadyrov's tactics varied little from those of his Russian sponsors. Targeted detentions and killings of young men, a long-established aspect of the "Chechen style," still featured.[24] Freedom House in 2009 selected Kadyrov's regime as one of the most repressive in the world—one of only two sub-state territories, along with Tibet, to be so designated.[25] The organization has not addressed Chechnya separately from Russia since. But the verdict seemed little less fitting in 2016.[26]

Figure 5a.2 Ramzan Kadyrov, Chechen strongman and Vladimir Putin's enforcer, pictured in December 2014.

Source: Kremlin.ru/Wikimedia Commons.

"We declare to the whole world that we are the foot soldiers of Vladimir Putin," Kadyrov told Chechen troops in mid-2015. "We will carry out any order he gives us in any part of the world." Indeed, thousands of Kadyrov's militiamen fought in eastern Ukraine (the president himself pledged to send 74,000), consolidating Putin's grip over the breakaway region. According to "one of Putin's most experienced advisers": "They're very useful to have around. . . . [We can say,] 'You don't want to talk to us? Fine, then deal with these 10,000 thugs we have standing by. They'll go over there and bust some heads. And maybe then we'll talk.'"[27] The Ukraine involvement prompted both the United States and the European Union to impose sanctions against the upper tier of the Chechen regime. This included Kadyrov, who responded by announcing that President Obama and senior EU officials would likewise be banned from Chechnya.

Was Putin playing with fire by granting such a free hand to his surrogate? The leader of a Chechen battalion, Zaur Dadaev, was accused in 2015 of the Moscow murder of a leading opposition politician, Boris Nemtsov—"the highest-profile killing of a dissident during Putin's tenure." (Chechen assassins had been implicated in other such cases, such as the murder of journalist Anna Politkovskaya [see Further Study], an outspoken critic of the Chechen wars.) Putin's remaining opponents feared similar Chechen-mounted "hits," and even Kremlin insiders began to wonder whether Putin had "created a monster he cannot fully control." But former Kremlin adviser Gleb Pavlovsky claimed in 2015 that "Putin cannot remove Kadyrov now. It would require a military campaign, and a major one."[28] In any case, the notion of Putin deposing one of his most valuable clients seemed improbable as this book went to press.

FURTHER STUDY

Arkady Babchenko, *One Soldier's War.* New York: Grove Press, 2008. Grim memoir by a Russian soldier who fought in both Chechen wars.

Matthew Evangelista, *The Chechen Wars: Will Russia Go the Way of the Soviet Union?* Washington, DC: Brookings Institution Press, 2002. Astute political analysis, with a chapter on "War Crimes and Russia's International Standing."

Carlotta Gall and Thomas de Waal, *Chechnya: Calamity in the Caucasus.* New York: New York University Press, 1998. Journalistic account of the first Chechen war.

Emma Gilligan, *Terror in Chechnya: Russia and the Tragedy of Civilians in War.* Princeton, NJ: Princeton University Press, 2010. The best study of the human rights dimension of the second Chechen war and its aftermath.

Human Rights Watch, *Swept Under: Torture, Forced Disappearances, and Extrajudicial Killings during Sweep Operations in Chechnya.* February 2002. Report on atrocities in the renewed war against Chechens, available online at www.hrw.org/en/reports/2002/02/02/swept-under.

Anna Politkovskaya, *A Small Corner of Hell: Dispatches from Chechnya*. Chicago, IL: University of Chicago Press, 2003. Account by the renowned Russian investigative journalist, assassinated in 2006. See also *A Dirty War: A Russian Reporter in Chechnya*.

NOTES

1 On the struggle to survive after deportation, see Michela Pohl, "'It Cannot Be That Our Graves Will Be Here': The Survival of Chechen and Ingush Deportees in Kazakhstan, 1944–1957," *Journal of Genocide Research*, 4: 3 (2002), pp. 401–430.

2 See Birgit Brauer, "Chechens and the Survival of Their Cultural Identity in Exile," *Journal of Genocide Research*, 4: 3 (2002), pp. 387–400.

3 Mark Levene, *Genocide in the Age of the Nation State, Vol. 2: The Rise of the West and the Coming of Genocide* (London: I.B. Tauris, 2005), p. 299.

4 Tony Wood, "The Case for Chechnya," *New Left Review*, 30 (November–December 2004), p. 10.

5 David Remnick, *Resurrection: The Struggle for a New Russia* (New York: Vintage, 1998), pp. 266, 271. Likewise, during the second Chechen war, "Chechens were dehumanized with racially bigoted language that depicted the enemy as 'blacks' *(chernye)*, 'bandits' *(banditi)*, 'terrorists' *(terroristi)*, 'cockroaches' *(tarakany)*, and 'bedbugs' *(klopi)*"—all terms familiar to the student of genocidal propaganda. Emma Gilligan, *Terror in Chechnya: Russia and the Tragedy of Civilians in War* (Princeton, NJ: Princeton University Press, 2010), p. 6.

6 Gregory Feifer, *The Great Gamble: The Soviet War in Afghanistan* (New York: HarperPerennial, 2009), p. 276.

7 Nabi Abdullaev, "Chechnya Ten Years Later," *Current History* (October 2004), p. 332.

8 President Dudayev was assassinated by a Russian missile in April 1996; his successor, Aslan Maskhadov, was killed in March 2005.

9 Grachev quoted in Remnick, *Resurrection*, p. 278.

10 Carlotta Gall and Thomas de Waal, *Chechnya: Calamity in the Caucasus* (New York: New York University Press, 1998), p. 219.

11 Gilligan, *Terror in Chechnya*, p. 26.

12 Ibid., p. 227.

13 Maura Reynolds, "War Has No Rules for Russian Forces Battling Chechen Rebels," *The Los Angeles Times*, September 17, 2000.

14 See Human Rights Watch, *"Who Will Tell Me What Happened to My Son?,"* report, September 2009, www.hrw.org/report/2009/09/27/who-will-tell-me-what-happened-my-son/russias-implementation-european-court-human.

15 Gilligan, *Terror in Chechnya*, p. 26.

16 2003 UN report, quoted in Simon Shuster, "Putin's Secret Army," *Time*, June 29, 2015, http://time.com/3926053/putins-secret-army/.

17 Remnick, *Resurrection*, p. 284.

18 See the trenchant analysis of Putin's policies, and their underlying motivations, in Wood, "The Case for Chechnya," pp. 27–31.

19 Human Rights Watch cited in Geoffrey York, "Russians Accused of Executing Chechens," *The Globe and Mail*, February 14, 2000.

20 See "Serious Violations of Women's Human Rights in Chechnya," *Human Rights Watch* backgrounder, January 2002, www.hrw.org/en/news/2002/01/09/russian-federation-serious-violations-womens-human-rights-chechnya.

21 See Chris Stephen, "The Black Widows of Chechnya," *The Scotsman*, September 17, 2004, http://news.scotsman.com/chechnya/The-Black-Widows-of-Chechnya.

22 Matthew Evangelista, *The Chechen Wars: Will Russia Go the Way of the Soviet Union?* (Washington, DC: Brookings Institution Press, 2002), p. 142; see also p. 177. Emma Gilligan echoes the judgment, writing: "If we look at the conflict in Chechnya from the vantage point of the 1948 UN Convention on the Prevention and Punishment of the Crime of Genocide, the acts committed by the Russian armed forces might well be framed under article 2 of the convention." Gilligan, *Terror in Chechnya*, p. 9.

23 Shuster, "Putin's Secret Army." See also Joshua Yaffa, "Putin's Dragon," *The New Yorker*, February 8–15, 2016, www.newyorker.com/magazine/2016/02/08/putins-dragon.

24 A defector, Umar Israilov—subsequently murdered—"described many brutal acts by Mr. Kadyrov and his subordinates, including executions of illegally detained men" and the sodomizing "by a prominent police officer" of "another prisoner," who was then "at Mr. Kadyrov's order put to death." See C.J. Chivers, "Slain Exile Detailed Chechen Ruler's Systematic Cruelty," *The New York Times*, January 31, 2009, www.nytimes.com/2009/02/01/world/europe/01torture.html.

25 Freedom House, "Freedom in the World 2009: Freedom Retreats for Third Year" (press release), January 12, 2009.

26 A notably detailed recent evaluation is the International Crisis Group's "Chechnya: The Inner Abroad," *Europe Report no. 236*, June 30, 2015, www.crisisgroup.org/~/media/Files/europe/caucasus/236-chechnya-the-inner-abroad.pdf.

27 Shuster, "Putin's Secret Army."

28 Ibid.

CHAPTER 6

The Jewish Holocaust

INTRODUCTION

The genocide of European Jews—which many scholars and others call simply "the Holocaust"[1]—"is perhaps the one genocide of which every educated person has heard."[2] Between 1941 and 1945, five to six million Jews were systematically murdered by the Nazi regime, its allies, and its surrogates in the Nazi-occupied territories.[3] Yet despite the extraordinary scale and intensity of the genocide, its prominence in recent decades was far from preordained. The Second World War killed upwards of fifty million people in all, and attitudes following the Nazi defeat tended to mirror those during the war, when Western leaders and publics generally refused to ascribe special urgency to the Jewish catastrophe. Only with the Israeli capture of Adolf Eichmann, the epitome of the "banality of evil" in Hannah Arendt's famous phrase, and his trial in Jerusalem in 1961, did the Jewish *Shoah* (catastrophe) begin to entrench itself as the paradigmatic genocide of human history. Even today, in the evaluation of genocide scholar Yehuda Bauer, "the impact of the Holocaust is growing, not diminishing."[4]

This impact is expressed in the diverse debates about the Holocaust. Among the questions asked are: How could the systematic murder of millions of helpless individuals have sprung from one of the most developed and "civilized" of Western states? What are the links to European anti-semitism? How central a figure was Adolf Hitler in the genesis and unfolding of the slaughter? What part did "ordinary men" and "ordinary Germans" play in the extermination campaign?

How extensive was Jewish resistance? What was the role of the Allies (notably Britain, France, the USSR, and the United States), both before and during the Second World War, in abandoning Jews to destruction at Nazi hands? And what is the relationship between the Jewish Holocaust and the postwar state of Israel? This chapter addresses these issues in its later sections, while also alighting on the debate over the alleged "uniqueness" of the *Shoah*.

ORIGINS

Until the later nineteenth century, Jews were uniquely stigmatized within the European social hierarchy, often through stereotypical motifs that endure, in places, to the present.[5] Medieval Christianity "held the Jews to violate the moral order of the world. By rejecting Jesus, by allegedly having killed him, the Jews stood in defiant opposition to the otherwise universally accepted conception of God and Man, denigrating and defiling, by their very existence, all that is sacred. As such, Jews came to represent symbolically and discursively much of the evil in the world."[6] Jews—especially male Jews—were reviled as "uprooted, troublesome, malevolent, shiftless." The Catholic Church, and later the Protestant offshoot founded by the virulently anti-semitic Martin Luther, assailed Jews as "thirsty bloodhounds and murderers of all Christendom."[7] The most primitive and powerful myth was the so-called "blood libel": the claim that Jews seized and murdered Gentile children in order to use their blood in the baking of ceremonial bread for the Passover celebration.[8] Fueled by this and other fantasies, anti-Jewish *pogroms*—localized campaigns of violence, killing, and repression—scarred European Jewish history. The spread of the Black Death—bubonic plague—throughout Europe in the mid-14th century led to a hysterical scapegoating of Jews, accompanied by massacres "of a quite new extent and thoroughness"; rumors and accusations that the malady was caused by Jews poisoning water supplies "became a pretext for the systematic killing of entire Jewish communities."[9] At various points in late-medieval and early-modern Europe, Jews were liable to be rounded up and expelled, most notoriously from Spain and Portugal in 1492.

The rise of modernity and the nation-state recast traditional anti-semitism in new and contradictory guises. (The term "anti-semitism" is a product of this era, coined by the German Wilhelm Marr in 1879.) On one hand, Jews were viewed as *enemies* of modernity. Cloistered in the cultural isolation of the ghetto (to which previous generations had consigned them), they could never be truly part of the nation-state, which was rapidly emerging as the fulcrum of modern identity.[10] On the other hand, for sectors suspicious of or threatened by change, Jews were seen as dangerous *agents* of modernity: as key players in oppressive economic institutions. They were also reviled as urbanite, cosmopolitan elements who threatened the unity and identity of the *Volk* (people). The Jews' "general readiness to embrace multiple identities" and "their recognition of the multiplicity, complexity, and dynamism of identity formation" challenged "the

Figure 6.1 Jews were scapegoated and persecuted by many Christian regimes and populations in Europe. A woodcut from 1493 depicts a mass burning of Jews, who were often targeted *en masse* for supposedly bringing the plague and other disasters to European populations.

Source: Louis Golding, *The Jewish Problem* (1938)/Wikimedia Commons.

Figure 6.2 The Nazis revived and vigorously inculcated anti-semitic stereotypes. This cartoon from the propaganda newspaper *Der Stürmer* (The Stormtrooper) depicts innocent Aryan womanhood about to be ensnared and drained of her blood by the monstrous Jewish spider. That the monster's face is male is no accident; it is virtually never otherwise in Nazi anti-semitic propaganda. Such masculinized and sexualized images were used to "prime" Nazi henchmen and killing squads—and the German population at large—for first rounding up Jewish men (November 1938), and later mass-murdering them (summer 1941). The gendercidal massacres of the early phase of the "Holocaust by Bullets" was, in turn, the harbinger or "tripwire" for the onset of root-and-branch Holocaust. See "The Turn to Mass Murder," below, and Chapter 13, pp. 325–332.

Source: The David S. Wyman Institute for Holocaust Studies/Wikimedia Commons.

narrow nationalisms prevailing in Europe at the time . . . which sought to sub-ordinate all such identifications to those of the organic *Volk* of a well-defined national territory."[11]

It would be misleading, however, to present European history as one long campaign of discrimination and repression against Jews. For several centuries Jews in Eastern Europe "enjoyed a period of comparative peace, tranquility and the flowering of Jewish religious life."[12] They were even more prominent, and valued, in Muslim Spain. Moreover, ideologies of nationalism sometimes followed the liberal "melting-pot" motif exemplified by the United States. Those Jews who sought integration with their societies could be accepted. The late nineteenth and early twentieth centuries are seen as something of a golden age for Jews in France, Britain, and Germany, even while some two-and-a-half million Jews were fleeing pogroms in tsarist Russia.[13]

Germany was widely viewed as one of the more tolerant European societies; Prussia, the first German state to grant citizenship to its Jews, did so as early as 1812. How, then, could Germany turn first to persecuting, then to slaughtering, nearly two-thirds of the Jews of Europe? Part of the answer lies in the fact that, although German society was in many ways tolerant and progressive, German politics was never liberal or democratic, in the manner of both Britain and France.[14] Moreover, German society was deeply destabilized by defeat in the First World War, and by the imposition of a humiliating peace settlement at Versailles in 1919. Germany was forced to shoulder full blame for the outbreak of the "Great War." It lost its overseas colonies, along with some of its European territories; its armed forces were reduced to a fraction of their former size; and onerous reparations were demanded. "A tidal wave of shame and resentment, experienced even by younger men who had not seen military service, swept the nation," wrote Richard Plant. "Many people tried to digest the bitter defeat by searching furiously for scapegoats."[15] These dark currents ran beneath the political order, the Weimar Republic, established after the war. Democratic but fragile, it presided over economic chaos—first, the hyperinflation of 1923, which saw the German mark slip to 4.2 trillion to the dollar, and then the widespread unemployment of the Great Depression, beginning in 1929.

The result was political extremism. Its prime architect and beneficiary was the NSDAP (the National Socialist or "Nazi" party), founded by Adolf Hitler and sundry alienated colleagues. Hitler, a decorated First World War veteran and failed artist from Vienna, assumed the task of resurrecting Germany and imposing its hegemony on all Europe. This vision would lead to the deaths of tens of millions of people. But it was underpinned in Hitler's mind by an epic hatred of Jews—"these black parasites of the nation," as he called them in *Mein Kampf* (My Struggle), the tirade he penned while in prison following an abortive coup attempt in 1923.[16]

As the failed *putsch* indicated, Hitler's path to power was far from direct. By 1932, he seemed to many to have passed his peak. The Nazis won only a minority of parliamentary seats in that year's elections; more Germans voted for parties of the Left than of the Right. But divisions between the Socialists and Communists

Figure 6.3 Adolf Hitler leaves a Nazi party gathering in December 1931. A little over a year later, the formerly obscure Austrian artist and First World War corporal would be appointed German chancellor, and rapidly consolidate the Nazi dictatorship.

Source: Recuerdos de Pandora/Creative Commons/Flickr.

made the Nazis the largest single party in the Reichstag, and allowed Hitler to become Chancellor in January 1933.

Once installed in power, the Nazis proved unstoppable. Within three months, they had seized "total control of [the] German state, abolishing its federalist structure, dismantling democratic government and outlawing political parties and trade unions." The Enabling Act of March 23, 1933 gave Hitler *"carte blanche* to terrorize and neutralize all effective political opposition."[17] Immediately thereafter, the Nazis' persecutory stance toward Jews became plain. Within a few months, Jews saw their businesses placed under Nazi boycott; their mass dismissal from hospitals, the schools, and the civil service; and public book-burnings of Jewish and other "degenerate" works. The Nuremberg Laws of 1935 stripped Jews of citizenship and gave legal shape to the Nazis' race-based theories: intermarriage or sexual intercourse between non-Jews and Jews was prohibited.

With the Nuremberg edicts, and the threat of worse measures looming, increasing numbers of Jews fled abroad. The abandonment of homes and capital in Germany meant penury abroad—the Nazis would allow only a fraction of one's wealth to be exported. The unwillingness of the outside world to accept Jewish refugees meant that many more Jews longed to leave than actually could. Hundreds of those who remained committed suicide as Nazi rule imposed upon them a "social death."[18]

Figure 6.4 The synagogue in Baden-Baden, Germany, gutted by fire on *Kristallnacht*, November 9–10, 1938. While many Germans strongly supported the Nazis' anti-semitic policies, many also bridled at the violence of the "Night of Broken Glass," and the "un-German" disorder it typified. The Nazis monitored public opinion carefully. Such sentiments prompted them, when the time came to impose a "final solution of the Jewish problem," to "outsource" the mass extermination to the occupied territories in Poland and the USSR.

Source: Yad Vashem, Jerusalem/Wikimedia Commons.

The persecution mounted further with the *Kristallnacht* (Night of Broken Glass) on November 9–10, 1938, "a proto-genocidal assault"[19] that targeted Jewish properties, residences, and persons. Several dozen Jews were killed outright, billions of deutschmarks in damage was inflicted, and some 30,000 male Jews were rounded up and imprisoned in concentration camps.[20] Now attempts to flee increased dramatically, but this occurred just as Hitler was driving Europe toward crisis and world war, and as Western countries all but closed their frontiers to Jewish would-be emigrants.

"ORDINARY GERMANS" AND THE NAZIS

In recent years, a great deal of scholarly energy has been devoted to Hitler's and the Nazis' evolving relationship with the German public. Two broad conclusions may be drawn from the work of Robert Gellately, Eric Johnson, and David Bankier—and also from one of the most revelatory personal documents of the Nazi era, the diaries of Victor Klemperer (1881–1960). (Klemperer was a Jew from the German city of Dresden who survived the Nazi period, albeit under conditions of privation and persecution, thanks to his marriage to an "Aryan" woman, Eva.)

The first insight is that Nazi rule, and the isolation of the Jews for eventual expulsion and extermination, counted on a broad wellspring of popular support. This was based on Hitler's pledge to return Germany to social order, economic stability, and world-power status. The basic thesis of Gellately's book, *Backing Hitler: Consent and Coercion in Nazi Germany*, is that "Hitler was largely successful in getting the backing, one way or another, of the great majority of citizens." Moreover, this was based on the anathematizing of whole classes of citizens: "the Germans generally turned out to be proud and pleased that Hitler and his henchmen were putting away certain kinds of people who did not fit in, or who were regarded as 'outsiders,' 'asocials,' 'useless eaters,' or 'criminals.'"[21]

Victor Klemperer's diaries provide an "extraordinarily acute analysis of the day-to-day workings of German life under Hitler" and "a singular chronicle of German society's progressive Nazification."[22] Klemperer oscillated between a conviction that German society had become thoroughly Nazified, and the ironic conviction (given his expulsion from the body politic) that the Germany he loved would triumph. "I certainly no longer believe that [the Nazi regime] has enemies inside Germany," he wrote in May 1936. "The majority of the people is content, a small group accepts Hitler as the lesser evil, no one really wants to be rid of him. . . . And all are afraid for their livelihood, their life, all are such terrible cowards." Yet as late as March 1940, with the Second World War well underway, "I often ask myself where all the wild anti-Semitism is. For my part I encounter much sympathy, people help me out, but fearfully of course." He noted numerous examples of verbal contempt, but also a surprising number of cases where colleagues and acquaintances went out of their way to greet him warmly, and even police officers who accorded him treatment that was "very courteous, almost comically courteous." "Every Jew has his Aryan angel," one of his fellow inmates in an overcrowded communal house told him in 1941.

Nonetheless, there is a scholarly consensus that the German public was largely indifferent to the plight and persecution of the Jews, evincing discomfort and concern only when it (a) confronted them directly, and offended their sense of civic order, and (b) made them fearful of retribution by "the Jews," an anxiety that reflected the anti-semitic trope of an all-powerful global Jewry.[23] By the time Klemperer and his wife had been consigned to communal housing, he had been stripped of his job, pension, house, and typewriter, with no apparent protest by the German population against these persecutory measures. He would shortly lose his right to indulge even in his cherished cigarettes. In September 1941, Klemperer was forced to put on a yellow Star of David identifying him as a Jew. It left him feeling "shattered": nearly a year later, he would describe the star as "torture—I can resolve a hundred times to pay no attention, it remains torture."[24] Hundreds of miles to the east, the program of mass killing was gearing up, as Klemperer and other Jews—not to mention ordinary Germans—were increasingly aware.

If Jews came to be the prime targets of Nazi demonization and marginalization, they were not the only ones, and for some years they were not necessarily the main ones. Communists (depicted as closely linked to Jewry) and other political opponents, handicapped and senile Germans, homosexuals, Roma (Gypsies), Polish intellectuals, vagrants, and other "asocial" elements all occupied the attention of the Nazi authorities during this period, and were the victims of "notorious achievements in human destruction" exceeding the persecution of the Jews until 1941.[25] Of these groups, political opponents (especially communists) and the handicapped and senile were most at risk of extreme physical violence, torture, and murder. "The political and syndical [trade union] left," wrote Arno Mayer, "remained the principal target of brutal repression well past the time of the definitive consolidation of the new regime in July–August 1934."[26] In the slaughter of the handicapped, meanwhile, the Nazis first "discovered that it was possible to murder multitudes," and that "they could easily recruit men and women to do the killings."[27] Box 6a explores the fate of political oppositionists and the handicapped under Nazi rule in greater detail.

THE TURN TO MASS MURDER

> I also took part in the day before yesterday's huge mass killing [of Jews in Belarus] . . . When the first truckload [of victims] arrived my hand was slightly trembling when shooting, but one gets used to this. When the tenth load arrived I was already aiming more calmly and shot securely at the many women, children and infants. . . . Infants were flying in a wide circle through the air and we shot them still in flight, before they fell into the pit and into the water. Let's get rid of this scum that tossed all of Europe into the war . . .
>
> Walter Mattner, a Viennese clerk recruited for service in the *Einsatzgruppen* during the "Holocaust by Bullets"; letter to his wife (!), October 5, 1941

Between the outbreak of the Second World War in September 1939 and the onset of full-scale extermination in mid-1941, the Nazis were hard at work consolidating and confining the Jews under their control. The core policy in the occupied territories of the East was *ghettoization*: confinement of Jews in overcrowded neighborhoods of major cities. One could argue that with ghettoization came genocidal intent: "The Nazis sought to create inhuman conditions in the ghettos, where a combination of obscene overcrowding, deliberate starvation . . . and outbreaks of typhus and cholera would reduce Jewish numbers through 'natural wastage.'"[28] Certainly, the hundreds of thousands of Jews who died in the ghettos are numbered among the victims of the Holocaust.

In the two years following the German invasion of the Soviet Union on June 22, 1941, some 1.8 million Jews were rounded up and murdered, mostly by point-blank rifle fire, in what the Catholic priest Patrick Desbois has dubbed "the Holocaust by Bullets." The direct genocidal agents included the so-called *Einsatzgruppen*, four death-squad battalions—some 3,000 men in all—who followed behind the regular German army.[29] They were accompanied by SS formations and police units filled out with middle-aged recruits plucked from civilian duty in Germany—such as the "ordinary men" of Reserve Police Battalion 101, studied by both historian Christopher Browning and political scientist Daniel Goldhagen (see Further Study; Figures 6.10–6.11). Most of the killings occurred before the machinery of industrial killing was erected in the death camps of Occupied Poland in spring 1942. They continued mercilessly thereafter, hunting down

Figure 6.5 A German soldier, Heinrich Jöst, captured this grim image of an unnamed woman in the Jewish ghetto established by the Nazis in Warsaw, Poland.[30] Starvation, destitution, and disease killed hundreds of thousands of Jews before, and during, the turn to direct mass murder. The impoverishment, debilitation, and destruction of the Jewish ghetto populations under Nazi occupation is a canonical example of the genocidal strategy—"deliberately inflicting on the group conditions of life calculated to bring about its physical destruction"—enshrined in Article 2(c) of the UN Genocide Convention. Those who survived the ghettos were overwhelmingly destined for extermination in the Nazi death factories located elsewhere in occupied Poland (see Map 6.1).

Source: Photo by Heinrich Jöst/Courtesy melyli.wordpress.com.

the last Jews still in flight or hiding. Bruno Mayrhofer, a German gendarme in Ukraine, reported in chillingly clinical language:

On 7 May 1943, 21.00 hours, following a confidential report [n.b. probably by a Ukrainian collaborator], 8 Jews, that is 3 men, 2 women and 3 children were flushed out of a well-camouflaged hole in the ground in an open field not far from the post here, and all of them were ["]shot while trying to escape["]. This case concerned Jews from Pohrebyshche who had lived in this hole in the ground for almost a year. The Jews did not have anything else in their possession except their tattered clothing. . . . The burial was carried out immediately on the spot.[31]

BOX 6.1 THE "HOLOCAUST BY BULLETS" IN MICROCOSM: DUBNO, UKRAINE, OCTOBER 1942

One of the most dramatic pieces of evidence submitted at the Nuremberg trials of 1946–1947 was the affidavit of Hermann Gräbe, a German engineer who observed the mass slaughter of the Jewish population of Dubno, Ukraine. Gräbe's testimony, which was also cited by the Nuremberg tribunal in passing its verdicts on Nazi génocidaires, provides an extraordinary eyewitness account of an ordinary massacre—one of hundreds of such slaughters that the Nazis perpetrated during the "Holocaust by Bullets" of 1941–1942.[32]

On October 5, 1942, at the time of my visit to the construction offices in Dubno, my foreman, Hubert Moennikes, living at 21 Aussenmühlenweg, Hamburg—Haarburg, told me that some Dubno Jews had been shot near the building in three huge ditches about 30 meters long and 3 meters deep. The number of people killed daily was about 1,500. The 5,000 Jews who had lived in Dubno before the Pogrom were all marked for liquidation. Since the executions took place in the presence of my employee, he was painfully impressed by them.

Accompanied by Moennikes, I then went to the work area. I saw great mounds of earth about 30 meters long and 2 high. Several trucks were parked nearby. Armed Ukrainian militia were making people get out, under the surveillance of SS soldiers. The same militiamen were responsible for guard duty and driving the trucks. The people in the trucks wore the regulation yellow pieces of cloth that identified them as Jews on the front and back of their clothing.

Figure 6.6 Hermann Gräbe, Holocaust witness.
Source: Courtesy Yad Vashem, Jerusalem.

Moennikes and I went straight toward the ditches without being stopped. When we neared the mound, I heard a series of rifle shots close by. The people from the trucks—men, women and children—were forced to undress under the supervision of an SS soldier with a whip in his hand. They were obliged to put their effects in certain spots: shoes, clothing, and underwear separately. I saw a pile of shoes, about 800–1,000 pairs, great heaps of underwear and clothing. Without weeping or crying out, these people undressed and stood together in family groups, embracing each other and saying goodbye while waiting for a sign from the SS soldier, who stood on the edge of the ditch, a whip in his hand, too. During the fifteen minutes I stayed there, I did not hear a single complaint, or plea for mercy. I watched a family of about eight: a man and woman about fifty years old, surrounded by their children of about one, eight, and ten, and two big girls about twenty and twenty-four. An old lady, her hair completely white, held the baby in her arms, rocking it, and singing it a song. The infant was crying aloud with delight. The parents watched the groups with tears in their eyes. The father held the ten-year-old boy by the hand, speaking softly to him: the child struggled to hold back his tears. Then the father pointed a finger to the sky, and, stroking the child's head, seemed to be explaining something. At this moment, the SS near the ditch called

Figure 6.7 Members of an *Einsatzgruppe* death squad execute Jewish children and women from the Mizocz ghetto in Wolyn, Ukraine, on October 14, 1942. Wolyn is only 29 km from Dubno, where Hermann Gräbe witnessed a similar genocidal massacre on October 5.

Source: United States Holocaust Memorial Museum (USHMM).

something to his comrade. The latter counted off some twenty people and ordered them behind the mound. The family of which I have just spoken was in the group.

I still remember the young girl, slender and dark, who, passing near me, pointed at herself, saying, "twenty-three [years old]." I walked around the mound and faced a frightful common grave. Tightly packed corpses were heaped so close together that only the heads showed. Most were wounded in the head and the blood flowed over their shoulders. Some still moved. Others raised their hands and turned their heads to show that they were still alive. The ditch was two-thirds full. I estimate that it held a thousand bodies. I turned my eyes toward the man who had carried out the execution. He was an SS man; he was seated, legs swinging, on the narrow edge of the ditch; an automatic rifle rested on his knees and he was smoking a cigarette. The people, completely naked, climbed down a few steps cut in the clay wall and stopped at the spot indicated by the SS man. Facing the dead and wounded, they spoke softly to them. Then I heard a series of rifle shots. I looked in the ditch and saw their bodies contorting, their heads, already inert, sinking on the corpses beneath. The blood flowed from the nape of their necks. I was astonished not to be ordered away, but I noticed two or three uniformed postmen nearby. A new batch of victims approached the place. They climbed down into the ditch, lined up in front of the previous victims, and were shot.

On the way back, while rounding the mound, I saw another full truck, which had just arrived. This truck contained only the sick and crippled. Women already naked were undressing an old woman with an emaciated body; her legs frightfully thin. She was held up by two people and seemed paralyzed. The naked people led her behind the mound. I left the place with Moennikes and went back to Dubno in a car.

The next morning, returning to the construction, I saw some thirty naked bodies lying thirty to fifty yards from the ditch. Some were still alive; they stared into space with a set look, seeming not to feel the coolness of the morning air; nor to see the workers standing around. A young girl of about twenty spoke to me, asking me to bring her clothes and to help her escape. At that moment we heard the sound of a car approaching at top speed; I saw that it was an SS detachment. I went back to my work. Ten minutes later rifle shots sounded from the ditch. The Jews who were still alive had been ordered to throw the bodies in the ditch; then they had to lie down themselves to receive a bullet in the back of the neck.

Gräbe's witnessing of the Dubno massacre constituted a "transforming encounter" in psychological parlance, described by Eva Fogelman as "an incident of such jolting power that the person who experiences it is forever changed." Thereafter, "while working on assignments for the German railroad, Gräbe deliberately recruited Jewish labor for his projects and, using all the authority of his position as chief construction engineer, fiercely protected them from Nazi murder squads. Thanks to his extraordinary effort, the lives of more than 300 Jews in the Ukraine, Poland, and Germany were protected. . . . The killing of 800 to 1,000 men, women, and children had so revolted him, he wrote, that he vowed to do what he could to prevent further Jewish deaths."[33] *Gräbe's affidavit was also read into the record at the trial of Adolf Eich-mann, a key Holocaust perpetrator, in Jerusalem in 1961 (see Figure 15.6, p. 714).*

"On any given day in the second half of 1941," writes Timothy Snyder, "the Germans shot more Jews than had been killed by pogroms in the entire history of the Russian Empire."[34] The role of the regular German army, or *Wehrmacht*, in this eruption of full-scale genocide was noted at the Nuremberg trials of 1945–1946 (see Chapter 15). However, in part because the Western allies preferred to view the *Wehrmacht* as gentlemanly opponents, and subsequently because the German army was reconstructed as an ally by both superpowers in the Cold War, a myth was cultivated that the *Wehrmacht* had acted "honorably" in the occupied territories. Scholarly inquiry has now demonstrated that this is "a wholly false picture of the historical reality."[35] "The mentality of Germany's military elite . . . hardly varied from that of the Führer," argues Stephen Fritz. "Both saw the world in social Dar-winist terms, accepted the need for *Lebensraum* [imperial "living space"], regarded the Slavs as inferior and fitting subjects for German domination, and viewed com-munism as a malignancy that had to be eliminated. Crucially, both also accepted the need for a war of annihilation, within which the destruction of the Jews played a key role."[36] Accordingly, and with the addition of a heavy dose of Nazi racist and strategic indoctrinations, the *Wehrmacht* proved key to engineering the mass mur-der of 3.3 million Soviets seized as prisoners-of-war (see Box 6a).[37] The *Wehrmacht* was also central to the perpetration of the Jewish Holocaust. "'Suspect' civilians— mostly Jews—were routinely handed over" for inevitable execution, according to Peter Longerich; "the Wehrmacht delivered Jewish prisoners of war and others defined by racist or political criteria, to the SS; *Einsatzkommandos* and police units were requested by offices of the Wehrmacht for 'cleansing' or 'pacification opera-tions', or for 'collective reprisal measures'; intelligence officers, the military police and the Secret Field Police made themselves available for 'operations'."[38] The *Ein-satzgruppen* in particular, only 3,000 strong, "needed and got the close coopera-tion of the Armed Forces," wrote Hannah Arendt, noting that "relations between them were usually 'excellent' and in some instances 'affectionate' (*herzlich*, literally 'heartfelt')."[39] A great many soldiers "felt drawn to the killing operations . . . stand-ing around as spectators, taking photographs, and volunteering to be shooters."[40] As SS Lieutenant-Colonel Karl Kretschmer wrote home in September 1942: "Here in Russia, wherever the German soldier is, no Jew remains."[41]

This was true also of the Romanian soldiers accompanying German troops in occupied Transnistria, in southwestern Ukraine. Their atrocities against Jews aroused protest from no less than *Einsatzgruppe* D—for the killers' deficient means of massacre:

The Romanians act against the Jews without any idea of a plan. No one would object to the numerous executions of Jews if the technical aspect of their prepa-ration as well as the manner in which they are carried out were not wanting.

Figure 6.8 Sites of the "Holocaust by Bullets" (1). A commemorative stone with the Star of David in the Bikernieku forest outside Riga, Latvia, where an estimated 25–40,000 Jews from across Europe were massacred by *Einsatzgruppen* forces in summer–autumn 1941.

Source: Author's photo, June 2011.

Figure 6.9 Sites of the "Holocaust by Bullets" (2). A mass grave of Jews in the nearby Rumbula forest, where some 25,000 Jews were murdered in November–December 1941.

Source: Author's photo, June 2011.

The Romanians leave the executed where they fall, without burial. The Ein-satzkommando [present] urged the Romanian police [soldiers] to proceed with more order from this point of view.[42]

Even such intensive slaughter, however, could not eliminate European Jewry in a "reasonable" time. Moreover, the intensely intimate character of murder by gun-fire, with human tissue and brain matter spattering onto the clothes and faces of the German killers, began to take a psychological toll. The difficulty was especially pronounced in the case of murders of children and women. While it was rela-tively easy for executioners to persuade themselves that adult male victims, even unarmed civilians, were dangerous and deserved their cruel fate, the argument was harder to make for people traditionally viewed as passive, dependent, or helpless.[43] "I simply couldn't [do it]," recalled one captured *Wehrmacht* soldier, in a conversa-tion secretly taped by British intelligence. "I could kill fellows who [I believed] had committed crimes, but women and children—and tiny children! The children scream and everything."[44]

To reduce this stress on the killers, and to increase the logistical efficiency of the killing, the industrialized "death camp" with its gas chambers was moved to the fore. Both were refinements of existing institutions and technologies. The death camps grew out of the concentration-camp system the Nazis had established upon first taking power in 1933, while killings by gas were first employed in 1939 as part of the "euthanasia" campaign that was such a vital forerunner of the genocide of the Jews. (It was wound down, in fact, at the precise point that the campaign against European Jews turned to root-and-branch extermination.) Gas chambers allowed for the desired psychological distance between the killers and their victims: "It was the gas that acted, not the man who pulled the machine-gun trigger."[45]

Principally by this means, nearly one million Jews were killed at Auschwitz—a complex of three camps and numerous satellites, of which Auschwitz II (Birk-enau) operated as the main killing center. Zyklon B (cyanide gas in crystal form; see Figure 11.2) was overwhelmingly the means of murder at Auschwitz. Nearly two million more Jews died by gas, shootings, beatings, and starvation at the other "death camps" in occupied Poland, which were distinguished from the vastly larger Nazi network of concentration camps by their core function of extermi-nation. These death camps were Chelmno (200,000 Jews slaughtered); Sobibor (260,000); Belzec (500,000); Treblinka (800,000, mostly from the Polish capital, Warsaw); and Majdanek (130,000).[46]

It would be misleading to distinguish too sharply between the "death camps," where gas was the normal means of extermination, and the broader network of camps where "destruction through work" (the Nazis' term) was the norm.[47] Kill-ings of Jews reached exterminatory levels in the latter institutions as well. As Daniel Goldhagen has argued, "after the beginning of 1942, the camp system in general was lethal for Jews," and well over a million died outside the death camps, killed by starvation, disease, and slave labor.[48] Perhaps 500,000 more, in Raul Hilberg's estimate, succumbed in the Jewish ghettos, themselves a kind of concentration camp (see Figure 6.5). Finally, tens of thousands died on forced marches, often in the dead of winter, as Allied forces closed in.[49]

Figure 6.10 A gas chamber, one of two extant (there were originally three) at the Majdanek death camp on the outskirts of Lublin, Poland. Thousands of Soviet prisoners-of-war, Poles, Jews, and political enemies were gassed here, though many more were worked, starved, and shot to death (the total death toll at Majdanek reached 360,000, including about 130,000 Jews). At least one gas chamber used the Zyklon B chemical, the only use of this insecticide derivative outside Auschwitz-Birkenau. To my knowledge, in all other camps and mobile gas vans, carbon monoxide was the chosen killing agent. Majdanek's are the only intact gas chambers actually used by the Nazis for mass murder. Others were destroyed before the Nazis retreated, as at Auschwitz (see Figure 6.11).

Source: Author's photo, July 2013.

What did the German public know of this massive extermination campaign? Large numbers of "ordinary Germans" were certainly aware of widespread atrocities among *Einsatzgruppen* and *Wehrmacht* forces on the eastern front, including mass shootings of Jews. Photos and written reports of some of the grisly executions circulated on the home front. But they seem to have been subsumed in a war generally perceived as "total" and necessarily savage. The shift in 1942, from mass shootings of Jews close to their places of residence, to their transport over great distances to isolated, purpose-built death camps with gas chambers, sharply reduced the number of German forces in the field who had direct contact with the Holocaust. The camps were of course in occupied Poland, situating them "out of sight and out of mind" of the German woman or man in the street. Finally, precisely as the Holocaust was reaching its destructive apex, German civilians

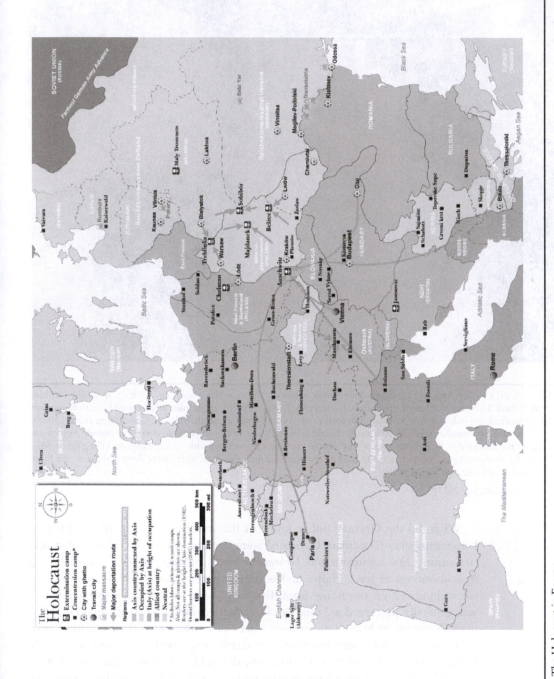

Map 6.1 The Holocaust in Europe.

Source: Map by Dennis Nilsson/Wikimedia Commons.

Figure 6.11 The haunting ruins of the Crematorium III death factory at Auschwitz-Birkenau outside Oswiecim, Poland, dynamited by the Nazis just before the camp was liberated by Soviet soldiers in January 1945. The view is looking down the steps which victims, mostly Jews transported from all over Europe, were forced to tread en route to the undressing room within. They were then murdered in an underground gas chamber (at top left, not clearly visible), and cremated in ovens under the (now collapsed) roof-and-chimney complex at the rear. More than one million children, women, and men—overwhelmingly Jews, but also Roma/Gypsies and Soviet prisoners-of-war—were murdered at Auschwitz-Birkenau. The site has become synonymous with the Jewish Holocaust and modern genocide.

Source: Author's photo, November 2009.

Figures 6.12 and 6.13 Two indelible images of the Jewish Holocaust. *Above:* Near Novgorod, Russia, in 1942, a German soldier takes aim at civilian victims in the killing fields; the rifles of other members of the execution squad are partially visible at left (note also the victim—wounded? killed?—lying prone at the soldier's right foot). *Below:* The notorious "selection" process underway on the railway ramp at Auschwitz-Birkenau. The image is from "The Auschwitz Album," "the only surviving visual evidence of the process leading to the mass murder at Auschwitz-Birkenau. It is a unique document and was donated to Yad Vashem by Lilly Jacob-Zelmanovic Meier. The photos were taken at the end of May or beginning of June 1944, either by Ernst Hofmann or by Bernhard Walter, two SS men whose task was to take ID photos and fingerprints of the inmates (not of the Jews who were sent directly to the gas chambers). The photos show the arrival of Hungarian Jews from Carpatho-Ruthenia. Many of them came from the Berehovo Ghetto, which itself was a collecting point for Jews from several other small towns. Early summer 1944 was the apex of the deportation of Hungarian Jewry."

Sources: Wikimedia Commons (6.12); Yad Vashem, Jerusalem (6.13).

increasingly were suffering under Allied aerial bombardment. This would be intensified through the final extermination spree in the camps (the slaughter of the Hungarian Jews in 1944), and it was supplemented, in 1944–1945 and into the postwar period, by the plight of millions of ethnic Germans uprooted from their ancestral homes in Central Europe and expelled to the war-shattered German heartland. None of this was likely to evoke much empathy for *any* of the Nazis' victims. It was widely known that awful things were happening to the Jews in the east. But at least after the tide of war turned in 1942–1943, this provoked mostly self-centered preoccupations that "Jewish revenge" would now be visited upon Germany (indeed *was* being inflicted, via the devastating bombing of the German heartland; see Box 6a).[50]

Thus, in Ian Kershaw's estimation:

Most ordinary citizens appear to have given no consideration to the actual fate of the Jews or to have pondered much about what might have happened to them. Relatively few people within Germany had first-hand, detailed knowledge of the murderous events that continued to unfold to the east; the 'Final Solution' was, of course, officially still preserved as a closely guarded state secret. But, in any case, overwhelmed by their own anxieties, few Germans were interested in what was happening, far away, to an unloved, where not thoroughly hated, minority.[51]

None of this, of course, prevented Germans from profiting from the persecution, expulsion, and mass murder of their country's Jewish population (see Chapter 10 for more on the role of greed in genocide). The mayor of Berlin, in a report issued in January 1939, called for "a certain order" in distributing the spoils of Jewish dispossession. The "Aryanization" campaign (see Figure 10.4) had left an "overall impression" that was "not pleasant," producing "an extraordinary rush of applications," even from "circles of whom it would not have been expected"—the middle and upper classes, presumably.[52]

BOX 6.2 ONE WOMAN'S STORY: FRIEDA WULFOVNA

Frieda Wulfovna was born in the city of Minsk—then in the Soviet republic of Belorussia, today the capital of the independent state of Belarus—and lived her entire life there before the Nazi invasion of the Soviet Union in June 1941. Her narrative of Holocaust suffering and survival allows a glimpse not only into the Nazis' genocidal assault on European Jews, but of the desperate and sometimes successful means that Jews found to evade the execution squads and gas chambers.

"Before the war, the city was home to a large Jewish community," Frieda related. "You could hear Yiddish spoken all over town. There were many Jewish schools and

Figure 6.14 Frieda Wulfovna is pictured in April 2014 at the Zaslavskaya Jewish Memorial in Minsk, Belarus, where she endured a ghetto existence and survived a series of genocidal Nazi *Aktions* (extermination sweeps).

Source: Photo © Nigel Roberts. Used by permission.

synagogues, only one of which remains from that time. It was never given back to the community and now it's a theatre."

When Nazi occupation forces arrived in Minsk—in the lightning early stages of the *Blitzkrieg* meant to shatter Hitler's main geopolitical and ideological adversary—they implemented a policy that was by then well-established in occupied Poland. Jews were moved into ghettoes—in Frieda's case, "on the very first day it was established" in Minsk. "I came with my mother, my father, and two older brothers aged 15 and 17. I was seven years old."

Conditions in the ghetto were crowded and hopelessly unsanitary—exactly as the Nazis intended, to reduce Jews to the filthy and animal-like portrait they had constructed in their anti-semitic imaginations. A hundred and fifty thousand Jews were crammed into single-story houses. "Every room in every house was filled with as many sofas and beds as could be made to fit, with one family allocated to each. This was all the living space each family had . . ." Without running water or (when the furniture had been burned) fuel, and with permitted caloric consumptions set by the Nazis at below-survival levels, catastrophe descended on the Jews of Minsk and other ghettoized populations well before the first mass executions took place. "Many people starved to death, including children. Every morning, families would take their dead out into the streets for special teams to take the bodies to the pit. For three winters the frosts were very heavy and some people froze to death in their houses."

The Nazis had been exterminating Jews by rifle fire in the "Holocaust by Bullets" since the very first days of the invasion of the USSR. In early 1942, they installed the machinery of the death factories, and over the following two years launched systematic *Aktions* to "reduce" the Jewish ghettoes and deport the inhabitants in waves for extermination—those, anyway, who were not murdered in the *Aktions* themselves. Frieda survived six *Aktions*, "with thousands dying in each. Over time the population of the Ghetto grew smaller and smaller. Many children were orphaned"—and then the Nazis massacred the helpless population of the orphanage itself. "It was a terrible sight. All of the children had been murdered in their beds, even toddlers and babies. There was blood everywhere."

It was Frieda's mother who kept the family alive, "always trying to barter for food, exchanging items of clothing or possessions." Her father, a respected shoemaker, himself an orphan with a seemingly independent and self-reliant mindset, moved to join partisan forces waging a guerrilla war against the German occupiers. "His task was to bring arms into the Ghetto and to save as many lives as he could. I remember sleeping on my mattress with guns and grenades hidden underneath."

Nazi troops soon came looking for her father. The family evaded them and scattered to four different refuges around the ghetto. Frieda was reunited with her mother, and taken by resistance soldiers to a safe house outside the ghetto walls. Later her father and elder brother rejoined them, all confined to a small room. "That was the beginning of my survival. My mother managed to get a job working in government buildings, and we changed our names. I was blond and blue-eyed. I didn't look like a Jew."

The war had turned against the Nazis by the time Frieda escaped the ghetto, and German armies were retreating in the face of gargantuan Soviet offensives and constant partisan attacks. Her father joined her brother with the partisans. When her brother won a medal for heroism in late 1943, he saw that a fellow soldier was eyeing it covetously. He offered a trade—the medal for Frieda and her mother's safety. The two of them were evacuated from Minsk, finally arriving in a "very poor" village where "the people . . . had nothing, but they were so kind to us. They were not Jews, but they hid us and gave us their last piece of bread. We stayed there until the Red Army liberated us." Only much later was she able to discover the fate of her other brother. ". . . He had been murdered in the Ghetto and his body taken to Maly Trostenets extermination camp to be burned."

Nigel Roberts recounts Frieda's experiences in his *Belarus* guidebook for Bradt Publications. "For years," he writes, "she couldn't talk about the things she had seen as a young girl. She didn't think people would believe her. Then one day, whilst visiting the Jewish Centre in Minsk that had been established to record all that happened here between 1941 and 1944, she opened a book written by a fellow survivor and began to read about all the terrible things she had witnessed for herself as a young child. Screams, executions, rivers of blood. From that moment she knew that people would believe her own story, and she began to find the words to articulate her memories."[53] At the time of writing, Frieda Wulfovna was Chairwoman of the Minsk Jewish Ghetto Survivors Association.

DEBATING THE HOLOCAUST

Many of the central themes of the Nazis' attempted destruction of European Jews have served as touchstones for the broader field of comparative genocide studies. No other genocide has generated remotely as much literature as the Holocaust, including thousands of books and essays. It is important, therefore, to explore some major points of debate, not only for the insights they give into the events described in this chapter, but for their relevance to genocide studies as a whole.

Intentionalists vs. functionalists

The core of the debate over the past two decades has revolved around a scholarly tendency generally termed "intentionalist," and a contrasting "functionalist" interpretation. Intentionalists, as the word suggests, place primary emphasis on the *intention* of the Nazis, from the outset, to eliminate European Jews by means that eventually included mass slaughter. Such an approach emphasizes the figure of Adolf Hitler and his monomaniacal zeal to eliminate the Jewish "cancer" from Germany and Europe. ("Once I really am in power," Hitler allegedly told a journalist as early as 1922, "my first and foremost task will be the annihilation of the Jews.")[54] Necessary as well was the anti-semitic dimension of both Nazi ideology and European history. This fueled the Nazis' animus against the Jews, and also ensured there would be no shortage of "willing executioners" to do the dirty work.

The functionalist critique, on the other hand, downplays the significance of Hitler as an individual. It "depicts the fragmentation of decision-making and the blurring of political responsibility," and emphasizes "the disintegration of traditional bureaucracy into a crooked maze of ill-conceived and uncoordinated task forces," in Colin Tatz's summary.[55] Also stressed is the evolutionary and contingent character of the campaign against the Jews: from legal discrimination, to concentration, to mass murder. In this view, "what happened in Nazi Germany [was] an unplanned 'cumulative radicalization' produced by the chaotic decision–making process of a polycratic regime and the 'negative selection' of destructive elements from the Nazis' ideological arsenal as the only ones that could perpetually mobilize the disparate and otherwise incompatible elements of the Nazi coalition."[56]

This sometimes acrimonious debate[57] gave way, in the 1990s, to a recognition that the intentionalist and functionalist strands were not irreconcilable—were perhaps complementary. Peter Longerich reflects the shift toward "intentional functionalism," or "integrationism,"[58] in evaluating the interaction between center and periphery during the Holocaust:

> . . . It would seem pointless to try to debate whether the policies of the centre and the initiatives of the periphery were crucial for the unleashing of the Holocaust. It would be more true to say that they stood in a dialectical relationship to one another, that is, that the centre could only act because it knew that its impulses would fall on fertile ground at the periphery, and the decision makers at the periphery based their own actions on the assumption that they were in harmony with the policy pursued by the centre.[59]

BOX 6.3 POLAND TODAY: "ANTI-SEMITISM WITHOUT JEWS"

The destruction of Polish Jewry was the cornerstone of the Nazis' genocidal enterprise. Fully half of the Jews murdered in the Holocaust—some three million people—were Polish. But Poland's Jews were also afflicted by the long tradition of European anti-semitism. Perhaps nowhere was it more virulent than in the "Rimlands" and "Bloodlands" of eastern Poland, the Baltic states, and the western Soviet Union (including Ukraine), as these territories stood in 1939 (see Box 2.3). Traditionally, whenever restraining authority collapsed, or authorities actively encouraged the violence, Jews were liable to be viciously targeted as "retribution" for imagined crimes and conspiracies.

In July 1941, in Jedwabne and nearby communities, Polish thugs exploited the arrival of Nazi invaders to organize a pogrom against the region's Jews. Several thousand defenseless Jewish villagers were killed, with over a thousand locked in a village barn on the outskirts of Jedwabne and burned to death. Local residents joined in the carnage and, especially, in the free-for-all looting afterward. The massacre, first explored by Jan Gross in his 2001 work Neighbors, *was plumbed far more deeply and resonantly in Anna Bikont's extraordinary book* The Crime and the Silence: Confronting the Massacre of Jews in Wartime Jedwabne, *published in Polish in 2004 and in English in 2015 (see Further Study, this chapter). Bikont's intimate, almost anthropological investigation turned up jaw-dropping examples of the classical anti-semitic tropes that still pervade*

Figure 6.15 Anna Bikont, Polish journalist and author of *The Crime and the Silence: Confronting the Massacre of Jews in Wartime Jedwabne.*

Source: Photo © Anna Wahlgren.

everyday discourse in Poland. The country is not alone in Europe in this respect, but it is unusual in its combination of a pervasive anti-semitism with a near-total absence of Jews—only about 1,100 reside in Poland today, according to Bikont. Perhaps most disturbing is the fury directed at those, in Jedwabne and beyond, who seek to memorialize the massacre. A sampling of Bikont's gathered testimonies attests to the enduring power of "Judeophobia" in European society and politics.

High school teacher, Jedwabne: The only accepted life model here is to put money in the tray on Sunday and then drink all week, beat your wife, and moan about the Jews. You should hear the things that are said in the teachers' lounge. The atmosphere is so tense that arguments don't get through to people. And the kids at school are constantly telling Jewish jokes. They even get up in class and ask why there are so many Jews in Poland [n.b. there are approximately 1,100 in the entire country]. . . . One pupil got up and said, "Why should I study if the Jews are in charge anyway."

Halina Zalewska, retired seamstress, Warsaw: Holy Scripture tells us the Jews are a tribe of vipers, perverts, they're untrustworthy and faithless. They played tricks on the Lord himself, and He had to send down plagues on them. He made them wander in the wilderness for thirty years. It's no accident He punished them the way He did. I've known about that from before the war, from religious studies. I remember everything. I'm seventy-three and . . . I don't eat margarine, only butter, because it's Jewish companies that make margarine.

Kazimierz Laudanski, villager, Jedwabne: "There was a lot of revenge [when the Soviets left in 1941]. But who did they kill? It was the Communists and snitches who were tried by mobs and lynched. They were the ones who got it. The Jewish community is one thing, Communist gangs another. Our guys acted in self-defense, just like in all the other uprisings, which we're not ashamed of. But when you make an omelette you've got to break some eggs. And since there were some uneducated people there, they might have caused the deaths of a lot of innocent people. . . . Traitors get their throats cut.

A Jedwabne man known for giving rides to the massacre memorial: My wife is unemployed, I'm unemployed, but around here they say we get paid well for lighting a candle from time to time, that we're living on Jewish money. People call my aunt to say they're going to burn her. Now, would it be so hard to pour gasoline in the window at night, and who would ever trace the person who did it?

Ewa, married to Leszek, whose father rescued Jews: I have no friends anymore. I lost them all. If my husband weren't a hunter who keeps a gun in the house, I wouldn't get a single night's sleep. I wake up at night and cry. The priest slanders us, saying Leszek isn't a Catholic anymore since he says the things he does [about the massacre of Jedwabne's Jews]. People call us: "Hello, is that Israel?"; "Hello, is that the rabbi?" It's awful to walk down the street and hear "Jewish lackeys." And in shops my neighbors turn away from me as if I were a leper.

Anna Bikont: In the *Gazeta* editorial offices I read letters sent to me after my piece today on Jedwabne: "Woman, what's keeping you in Poland? May you be consumed by hellfire for your perversity and lies. Poland for the Poles"; "Miss Bikont, Jewess possessed by crazy anti-Polonism, we'll be meeting soon. A kamikaze has already been assigned to you"; "You've managed to ignite a Polish-Jewish war in your newspaper. A few more such stories in your pages, and I'll become an anti-Semite, I already associate Jews with lying and swindling."[60]

Figure 6.16 February 2015: a Jewish rabbi stands amidst smashed tombstones in a cemetery in Sarre-Union, eastern France. Approximately 250 graves were desecrated in the anti-semitic attack.

Source: Photo by Patrick Seeger/EPA.

Jewish resistance

The depiction of Jews as having gone meekly to their deaths was first advanced by Raul Hilberg in his 1961 treatise *The Destruction of the European Jews*, and was then enshrined by Hannah Arendt in her controversial account of *Eichmann in Jerusalem*. Both Hilberg and Arendt noted the close prewar coordination between the Jewish Agency (which sought to promote Jewish immigration to Palestine) and the Nazi authorities.[61] They also stressed the role of the Jewish councils (*Judenräte*), bodies of Jews delegated by the Nazis to oversee the ghettos and the round-ups of Jewish civilians. "The whole truth," as Arendt summarized it, was that without Jewish leadership and organization, the Jewish people would have suffered "chaos and plenty of misery" at Nazi hands, "but the total number of victims would hardly have been between four and a half and six million people."[62]

While it may be true that a "salient characteristic of the Jewish community in Europe during 1933–1945 was its step-by-step adjustment to step-by-step destruction,"[63] this is only part of the picture. Scholars have described how, under horrific circumstances, Jews found ways to resist: going into hiding; struggling to preserve Jewish culture and creativity; and even launching armed uprisings. (The Warsaw ghetto uprising which peaked in April–May 1943, and the mass escape from the Sobibor death camp in October 1943, are the most famous of these rebellions against the Nazis.)[64] Large numbers of Jews also joined the armed forces of the Allies, or fought as partisans behind German lines.

On balance, "it is pure myth that the Jews were merely 'passive,'" wrote Alexander Donat in his memoir *The Holocaust Kingdom*:

> The Jews fought back against their enemies to a degree no other community anywhere in the world would have been capable of were it to find itself similarly beleaguered. They fought against hunger and starvation, against disease, against a deadly Nazi economic blockade. They fought against murderers and against traitors within their own ranks, and they were utterly alone in their fight. They were forsaken by God and by man, surrounded by hatred or indifference. Ours was not a romantic war. Although there was much heroism, there was little beauty—much toil and suffering, but no glamour. We fought back on every front where the enemy attacked—the biological front, the economic front, the propaganda front, the cultural front—with every weapon we possessed.[65]

Moreover, to the extent that Jews did *not* mount an effective resistance to their extermination, it is worth noting—as Daniel Goldhagen does—that "millions of Soviet POWs, young military men with organization, and leadership, and initial vigor, died passively in German camps [see Box 6a]. If these men, whose families were not with them, could not muster themselves against the Germans, how could the Jews be expected to have done *more*?"[66]

The Allies and the churches: Could the Jews have been saved?

> By my death, I wish to make my final protest against the passivity with which the world is looking on and permitting the extermination of the Jewish people.
> Smul Zygielbojm, Jewish exile in London; suicide note, May 12, 1943

The genocide against European Jews *could* have been avoided, argues the historian Yehuda Bauer, just as the Second World War itself might never have occurred— "had the Great Powers stopped Nazi Germany when it was still weak." But at this point, "nobody knew that a Holocaust was even possible, because nobody knew what a Holocaust was; the Germans had not decided on anything like it in the 1930s."[67] The Allies, haunted by the carnage of the First World War, sought accommodation ("appeasement") rather than confrontation.

The Evian Conference of July 1938, held in a French town on Lake Geneva, brought together representatives of Western countries to address the Jewish plight. In retrospect, and even at the time, it offered the best chance to alleviate the plight of German Jews, through the simple expedient of opening up Western borders to Jewish refugees. But instead, the West ducked its responsibility. In Germany, Hitler could barely conceal his delight. The rejection of the Jews not only further humiliated Jews themselves, but highlighted the hypocrisy of the West's humanitarian rhetoric.

Turning to the period of full-scale genocide against the Jews, it seems clear that details of the killing operations were known to the Allies early on. For example, radio communications of the Nazi Order Police were intercepted, alluding to mass murder during the "Holocaust by Bullets." But the Allies were observing from a distance, with Germany at the height of its power on the European continent. The sheer speed of the slaughter also militated against meaningful intervention. "From mid-March 1942 to mid-February 1943," that is, in less than a year, "over one-half the victims of the Jewish Holocaust . . . lost their lives at the hands of Nazi killers."[68]

It may be argued that the inclusion of targets such as Auschwitz's gas chambers and crematoria in the Allied bombing campaign, along with key transport points for Jews, could have disrupted the Nazi killing machine. The case is especially cogent for the later stages of the war, as with the genocide of the Hungarian Jews in 1944–1945 (when the USSR might also have been able to intervene). But on prewar evidence, it is hard to believe that, if more effective military measures could have been found, the Allies would have placed saving Jews higher on the list of military priorities—or that doing so would have made much difference.

The role of the Christian churches has also been scrutinized and criticized. Pope Pius XII's placating of the Nazi regime in Germany, and his silence on the persecution of the Jews, are notorious.[69] While "the Holy See [Vatican] addressed numerous protests, demands, and inquiries *via diplomatic channels* both regarding the situation of Catholics in Poland and about the killing of the mentally ill . . . *Not one such diplomatic intervention dealt with the overall fate of the Jews.*" Regarding the fate of "non-Aryans in the territories under German authority," Pius wrote to a German bishop who had protested deportations of Jews: "Unhappily, in the present circumstances, We cannot offer them effective help other than through Our prayers."[70]

Within Germany, the churches did virtually nothing to impede the genocide and indeed strove not to notice it, thereby facilitating it. The Nazis at numerous points demonstrated a keen sensitivity to public opinion, including religious opinion—protests from German churches were partly responsible for driving the "euthanasia" campaign underground after 1941. But such protests were not forthcoming from more than a handful of principled religious voices. When it came to defending co-parishioners whom the Nazis deemed of Jewish origin, "both Church and Church members drove away from their community, from their churches, people with whom they were united in worship, as one drives away mangy dogs from one's door."[71]

The most successful examples of resistance to Hitler's genocidal designs for European Jewry came from a handful of western and northern European countries that were either neutral or under relatively less oppressive occupation regimes.[72] Here, sometimes, extension of the killing campaign could impose political costs that the Nazis were not willing to pay. The most vivid display of public opposition swept up virtually the entire adult population of Denmark, led by the royal family. When the Nazis decreed the imposition of the Jewish yellow star, non-Jewish Danes adopted it in droves as well, as a powerful gesture of solidarity. The regulation was rescinded. Subsequently, Danes arranged for the evacuation of the majority of the country's Jews to neutral Sweden, where they lived through the rest of the war (see Chapter 10). Sweden, meanwhile, saved "about half of Norwegian Jewry and almost all of the Danish Jews," and in 1944

> involved herself more heavily in the heart of Europe, particularly in Budapest, where, along with Switzerland, Portugal, and the Vatican, the Swedish legation issued "protective passports," established safe houses, and generally attempted to restrain the German occupants and their Hungarian puppets from killing more Jews on Hungarian soil in the final hours of the war. Upon the liberation of Jews in concentration camps in the spring of 1945, Sweden accepted thousands of victims for medical treatment and rehabilitation.[73]

Willing executioners?

Just as scholars have demonstrated increased interest in "micro-histories" of public opinion under the Nazis, and the role of ordinary German citizens in accepting and sustaining the regime, so have questions been raised about the role of different sectors of the German population in the genocide. After decades of research by Raul Hilberg and many others, it is a truism that not only German social and economic elites, but all the professions (up to and including the clergy, as we have seen), were corrupted or compromised by the Nazi state. In Michael Burleigh's words, an "understanding of the process of persecution [on racial grounds] now includes greater awareness of the culpable involvement of various sections of the professional intelligentsia, such as anthropologists, doctors, economists, historians, lawyers and psychiatrists, in the formation and implementation of Nazi policies."[74] For such figures, "the advent of the Nazi regime was coterminous with the onset of 'boom' conditions. No one asked or compelled these academics and scientists actively to work on the regime's behalf. Most of them could have said no. In fact, the files of the regime's many agencies bulge with their unsolicited recommendations."[75]

What of the genocidal participation of ordinary Germans? This subject has spawned the most vigorous debate in Holocaust studies over the past decade, though the illumination has not always matched the heat generated.

At the heart of the controversy was the publication, in 1992 and 1996 respectively, of Christopher Browning's *Ordinary Men: Reserve Police Battalion 101 and the Final Solution in Poland*, and Daniel Goldhagen's *Hitler's Willing Executioners: Ordinary Germans and the Holocaust*. Both scholars examined the same archives on Reserve Police Battalion 101, which consisted overwhelmingly of Germans drafted from civilian police units (often too old for regular military service). The records described in detail the battalion's killings of helpless, naked Jewish civilians in occupied Poland during 1941–1942, and the range of reactions among group members.

In interpreting the records, Browning acknowledged the importance of "the incessant proclamation of German superiority and incitement of contempt and hatred for the Jewish enemy." But he also stressed other factors: "conformity to the group," that is, peer pressure; the desire for praise, prestige, and advancement; and the threat of marginalization and anathematization in highly dangerous wartime circumstances. He referred to "the mutually intensifying effects of war and racism. . . . Nothing helped the Nazis to wage a race war so much as the war itself."[76]

Goldhagen, dismissing Browning's work, advanced instead an essentially mono-causal thesis. The Jewish Holocaust was the direct outgrowth of "eliminationist" anti-semitism, which by the twentieth century had become "common sense" for Germans. By 1941, "ordinary Germans easily became genocidal killers . . . [and] did so even though they did not have to." They "kill[ed] Jews willingly and often eagerly,"[77] though Goldhagen did recognize the importance of Nazi leaders in activating and channeling the anti-semitic impulse.

With the controversy now cooled, it is easier to appreciate the significance of "the Goldhagen debate."[78] Goldhagen did counter a trend toward bloodless analysis and abstract theorizing in studies of the Jewish catastrophe. In addition, by achieving mass popularity, Goldhagen's book, like Samantha Power's *"A Problem from Hell"* (2002), broke down the usual wall between scholarship and public debate. However, the core elements of Goldhagen's thesis—that there was something unique about German anti-semitism that spawned the Holocaust; that Germans were only too ready to leap to bloodthirsty murder of Jews—have been decisively countered. Not only was anti-semitism historically stronger in

Figures 6.17 and 6.18 The exchange between Christopher Browning (left), author of *Ordinary Men* (1992), and Daniel Jonah Goldhagen, author of *Hitler's Willing Executioners* (1996), centered on the motivations of "ordinary" German killers of Jews during the Holocaust. Was "eliminationist anti-semitism" the central factor, as Goldhagen argued? Or was it secondary to peer pressure and masculine bonding in wartime, as Browning suggested? The result was a defining—and continuing—debate in Holocaust and genocide studies.

Sources: *The Gazette*, University of North Carolina (Browning); JTN Productions (Goldhagen).

countries other than Germany, but the virulence of its expression during the Second World War in (for example) Lithuania and Romania exceeded that of Germany. The Nazis, as noted above, were reluctant to confront "ordinary Germans" with bloody atrocity, though according to Saul Friedländer, "recent historical research increasingly turns German ignorance of the fate of the Jews into a mythical postwar construct."[79] Nor could they rely on a widespread popular desire to inflict cruelty on Jews as the foundational strategy for implementing their genocide.

Israel, the Palestinians, and the Holocaust

Occasionally an experience of great suffering has been recognized as warranting creation or recognition of a homeland for the targeted group. Such was the case with East Timor (Box 7a), born from Indonesian occupation and genocide. The Kurdish protected zone and *de facto* state in northern Iraq may also qualify (Box 4.2), together with the widespread recognition of Kosovo's declaration of independence from Serbia in 2008 (Chapter 8). But no case is as dramatic as that of Israel in the wake of the Second World War. The dream of the Zionist movement founded in the nineteenth century, to establish a Jewish homeland in Palestine through mobilization and mass immigration, became a reality in the postwar period, as Britain abandoned its territorial mandate over Palestine, and Arabs and Jews fought over the territory. "Anti-Zionism in the Jewish community collapsed, and a consensus that Jewry, abandoned during the war, had to have a home of its own crystallized overnight."[80] Jewish survivors of Nazi genocide provided Palestine with a critical mass of Jewish immigrants and, in the decades following the declaration of the Israeli state on May 15, 1948, Israel received tens of billions of dollars from the Federal Republic of Germany as reparations for the Holocaust of the Jews.

To a significant degree, successive Israeli governments have relied on the Holocaust as a touchstone of Jewish experience and national identity, and have used the threat of another genocide of the Jews to justify military and security policies.[81] Israeli prime minister Benjamin Netanyahu, for example, commemorated the country's Holocaust Remembrance Day on April 21, 2009, by declaring that "Holocaust deniers cannot commit another Holocaust against the Jewish people. This is the state of Israel's supreme obligation."[82]

In October 2015, Netanyahu attracted unexpected attention and near-universal scorn when his comments surfaced accusing Amin al-Husseini, the Palestinian *Mufti* (Muslim religious leader) of Jerusalem, of having played *the* key role in persuading Hitler and the Nazis to pursue a policy of mass extermination against the Jews of Europe, rather than the forced-emigration policy they allegedly still favored. Unmentioned by Netanyahu was that by the time the *Mufti* met Hitler on November 28, 1941, many hundreds of thousands of Jews—perhaps over one million—had already been murdered in the "Holocaust by Bullets" and Nazi-established ghettoes (see Box 6.4).

BOX 6.4: NETANYAHU, THE *MUFTI*, AND THE POLITICS OF HOLOCAUST MEMORY

In a speech to the 37th Zionist Congress on October 20, 2015, Israeli Prime Minister Benjamin Netanyahu digressed to advance an extraordinary interpretation of the Holocaust of the Jews, centered on the figure of Haj Amin al-Husseini, the grand *mufti*—Muslim leader—of Jerusalem "and the Zionist movement's key enemy" during the formative years of its expansion in Palestine. The Mufti, said Netanyahu, "had a central role in fomenting the final solution. He flew to Berlin," where he held a meeting with Adolf Hitler on November 28. "Hitler didn't want to exterminate the Jews at the time, he wanted to expel the Jews," Netanyahu asserted. "And Haj Amin al-Husseini went to Hitler and said, 'If you expel them, they'll all come here.' 'So what should I do with them?' he asked. [Al-Husseini] said, 'Burn them.' "[83]

Christopher Browning, probably the senior scholar of the Holocaust in the English-speaking world (see pp. 347–348), published a devastating rebuttal of Netanyahu's account in the journal *Foreign Policy*, describing the prime minister's claims as "an historical fabrication, or more simply a lie." In no minutes or other account of the November 28 meeting did the exchange quoted by Netanyahu appear. Browning pointed out that by the time Hitler met with the *mufti*, the exterminatory phase of the Nazi persecution of the Jews was already well advanced. Many hundreds of thousands of Jews had been murdered in the "Holocaust by Bullets" beginning in June 1941 (see, e.g., Box 6.1). The early infrastructure of the death factories, purpose-built in Nazi-occupied Poland for the mass murder of Europe's Jewish population, was already in place:

> Hitler had opted for the total and systematic killing of Jews on Soviet territory in mid-July 1941, and German killing units on the eastern front began targeting the entire Jewish population—including women, children, and the elderly—beginning in late July and early August. The two-day massacre of over 33,000 Jews at Babi Yar outside Kiev took place in late September. Hitler approved the extension of the mass murder program to Jews west of Soviet territory in late October, and two death camps using poison gas were under construction at Belzec and Chelmno [in occupied Poland] by early November. When Hitler met with Husseini [on November 28], the fateful shift in Nazi Jewish policy from expulsion and decimation to systematic and total mass murder had already occurred.

Browning extended his critique beyond Netanyahu's historical misreading to the repressive political purpose it was intended to serve:

> There were many thousands of Holocaust perpetrators more historically significant than the grand mufti of Jerusalem, but for Netanyahu they have no useful

Figure 6.19 Adolf Hitler meets with Haj Amin al–Husseini, the Muslim *mufti* (religious leader) of Jerusalem, Berlin, November 28, 1941.

Source: Courtesy WGBH News. Original source unknown.

Figure 6.20 Israeli Prime Minister Benjamin Netanyahu at a March 2011 press conference.

Source: US Department of Defense/Wikimedia Commons.

political significance—which is to say they were not Palestinian. His extraordinary exaggeration of Husseini's complicity, and by implication that of the entire Palestinian people, is a blatant attempt to stigmatize and delegitimize any sympathy or concern for Palestinian rights and statehood. Netanyahu's shameful and indecent speech is a disservice to anyone—Jew and non-Jew—for whom research, teaching, and preservation of the historical truth of the Holocaust has value, meaning, and purpose.[84]

With Israeli public opinion scarcely less withering in its condemnation, Netanyahu was forced to backpedal. A little over a week after his speech, he retracted his allegation: "The decision to move from a policy of deporting Jews to the Final Solution was made by the Nazis and was not dependent on outside influence. The Nazis saw in the Mufti a collaborator, but they did not need him to decide on the systematic destruction of European Jewry, which began in June 1941." He ended on an accusatory and equally political note, however, accusing al-Husseini of inciting violence against Jews by claiming they sought to destroy Jerusalem's al-Aqsa mosque. "Incitement," specifically rumor-mongering over al-Aqsa, was at the heart of Netanyahu's accusations against Palestinian leaders and public figures, as a fresh Palestinian *intifada* (uprising) against Israeli occupation appeared to be looming. Hence, for Netanyahu, the mufti's "lie lives on and continues to exact a price in [Jewish] blood. . . . That the mufti remains an iconic figure among the Palestinian leadership today speaks volumes about that leadership's real attitude towards Israel." The controversy, fleeting though it was,[85] served as a reminder of the continuing centrality of the Holocaust in Israeli and Diaspora politics, and the attractiveness of manipulating this most traumatic incarnation of Jewish suffering for contemporary political and personal advantage.[86]

Palestinians and their supporters, for their part, have tended to adopt the genocide framework as well—but to attract attention to the Palestinian cause. The choice of the term *Naqba* (catastrophe) to describe the Palestinian experience of mass expulsion and dispossession at Israeli hands was clearly meant to echo the Jewish adoption of the Hebrew word *Shoah*, with its parallel meaning, to reference the Jewish Holocaust.[87] Palestinian advocates have sought to draw parallels between Israel's repressive policies and those of the Nazis against Jews. Often such comparisons have seemed hysterical and/or counterproductive;[88] but sometimes they have resonated. Notable was Israeli general (later prime minister) Ariel Sharon's dispatching of Christian Phalangist militia to the Palestinian refugee camps of Sabra and Shatila, during the Israelis' 1982 invasion of Lebanon. This led predictably to the *Einsatzgruppen-style* massacre of thousands of Palestinian civilians, as Israeli troops stood by. Renewed denunciations, employing the language of genocide and crimes against humanity, were issued after Israel imposed a ruinous blockade on the Gaza Strip, still largely in place. The blockade was described as a "genocidal policy" by Israeli historian

Ilan Pappé.[89] It prompted Richard Falk, subsequently the UN Human Rights Council's monitor for Israel-Palestine, to write in 2007 that Israeli strategies toward Gaza were reminiscent of Nazi ghettoization policies toward Jews, displaying "a deliberate intention . . . to subject an entire human community to life-endangering conditions of utmost cruelty."[90] In December 2008, and again in July–August 2014, Israel launched a massive assault on the Gaza Strip, killing many hundreds of Palestinian civilians on each occasion, and laying waste to the already battered territory. In the estimation of UN investigator Judge Richard Goldstone, the 2008 attack was "deliberately disproportionate," ". . . designed to punish, humiliate and terrorize a civilian population, radically diminish its local economic capacity both to work and to provide for itself, and to force upon it an ever-increasing sense of dependency and vulnerability."[91] The same verdict can be rendered on the 2014 assault—the kind of violent and disproportionate atrocity that is carefully calibrated to fall short of indiscriminate massacre and (by my favored definition) genocide.[92]

Is the Jewish Holocaust "uniquely unique"?

Few historical and philosophical issues have generated such intense scholarly debate in genocide studies as the question of Holocaust uniqueness. On one level, it is clearly facile. As Alex Alvarez put it: "All genocides are simultaneously unique and analogous."[93] The question is whether the Jewish Holocaust is *sui generis*—that is, "uniquely unique."[94]

In genocide studies, a well-known exponent of the uniqueness thesis is Steven Katz, who devoted his immense tome *The Holocaust in Historical Context, Vol. 1* to arguing that the Jewish Holocaust was "phenomenologically unique by virtue of the fact that never before has a state set out, as a matter of intentional principle and actualized policy, to annihilate physically every man, woman, and child belonging to a specific people."[95] The Nazi campaign against the Jews was the only true genocide, as Katz defined the term (see p. 26; recall that my own preferred definition of genocide reworks Katz's).

Other scholars have argued against the uniqueness hypothesis. Historian Mark Levene has pointed to an "obvious contradiction": "while, on the one hand, the Holocaust has come to be commonly treated as the yardstick for all that might be described as 'evil' in our world, on the other, it is . . . a subject notably cordoned off and policed against those who might seek to make connections [with other genocides]."[96] Writer and poet Phillip Lopate has likewise argued that claims of uniqueness tend to bestow "a sort of privileged nation status in the moral honor roll."[97] This claim of privilege then carries over to "the Jewish state," Israel, helping to blunt criticism of its treatment of the Palestinians.

My own view should be clearly stated: the Jewish Holocaust was *not* "uniquely unique." On no major analytical dimension—speed, scale, scope, intensity, efficiency, cruelty, ideology—does it stand alone and apart. If it is unique in its mix of these ingredients, so too are most of the other major instances of mass killing in their own way.[98] I also believe that uniqueness proponents, like the rest of us, were severely shaken by the holocaust in Rwanda in 1994 (see Chapter 9). The killing there proceeded much faster than the slaughter of the Jews; destroyed a higher proportion of the designated victim group (some 80 percent of Rwandan Tutsis versus two-thirds of European Jews); was carried out by "a chillingly effective organizational structure that would implement the political plan of genocide more efficiently than was achieved by the industrialized death camps in Nazi Germany";[99] and—unlike the Jewish catastrophe—featured active participation by a substantial portion of the general population. Was Rwanda, then, "uniquely unique"? The claim seems as tenable as in the case of the Jewish Holocaust—but in both cases, a nuanced comparative framework is preferable.[100]

The uniqueness of the Jews *as a target of the Nazis* at first sight seems self-evident. "In the end," for Raul Hilberg, ". . . the Jews retained their special place."[101] Even the leading scholar of Romani/"Gypsy" genocide—the Nazi murder campaign that most closely parallels the Jewish *Shoah*—acknowledges that while both groups were considered racial threats, "Romanies were only ever a 'racial' threat," while "Jews were considered a threat on a number of other grounds as well, political, philosophical and economic . . ."[102] According to Omer Bartov,

> It was *only* in the case of the Jews that there was a determination to seek out every baby hidden in a haystack, every family living in a bunker in the forest, every woman trying to pass herself off as a Gentile. It was only in the case of the Jews that vast factories were constructed and managed with the sole purpose of killing trainload after trainload of people. It was only in the case of the Jews that huge, open-air, public massacres of tens of thousands of people were conducted on a daily basis throughout Eastern Europe.[103]

However, as Christian Gerlach notes, other groups sometimes suffered before, or worse than, Jews under Nazi terror:

> The first to be systematically murdered by gas were disabled people. The first to be made [to] wear a mark in public in Nazi Germany were Polish forced workers. The first to be gassed in Auschwitz, and the first to get their prisoner numbers tattooed there, were (for the most part) Soviet prisoners of war. Other prisoners, including Jews, noticed that these POWs received considerably less food even than themselves, and in vain tried to help them.[104]

The Holocaust certainly holds a unique place in genocide studies. Among all the world's genocides, it alone produced a scholarly literature that spawned, in turn, a comparative discipline. Specialists on the subject played a central role in constituting the field and its institutions, such as the International Association of Genocide Scholars (IAGS) and the *Journal of Genocide Research:* "Genocide studies is really the outgrowth of the study of the Holocaust," as sociologist Thomas Cushman has noted; according to historian Dan Stone, "for good or ill," the Holocaust "has provided many of the theoretical frameworks and research strategies for analyzing other genocides."[105]

Still, there is no denying that the Holocaust has been significantly de-centered from comparative genocide studies since the emergence of the post–Lemkin research agenda in the 1970s and 1980s. In introducing the third edition of his edited collection *Is the Holocaust Unique?* (2009), Alan S. Rosenbaum acknowledged that

> since [my] initial conception of this project some fifteen years ago, the center of gravity for the once-intense debate about the overall arguable claim for the significant uniqueness of the Holocaust may gradually but perceptibly be shifting. . . . It is not that the Holocaust is considered by most responsible or fair-minded scholars as any less paradigmatic, but rather [that] as the Holocaust recedes into history and other genocidal events occur, its scope and dimensions may naturally be better understood in the context of a broader genocide studies investigation.[106]

FURTHER STUDY

Note: No genocide has generated remotely as much scholarly attention as the Nazis' Holocaust against the Jews. The following is a bare sampling of core works in English; others are cited in subsequent chapters.

Irving Abella and Harold Troper, *None is Too Many: Canada and the Jews of Europe, 1933–1948.* Toronto, ON: Key Porter Books, 2002. Canada's shameful treatment of Jewish would-be refugees from Germany and Nazi-occupied Europe; one facet of the West's abandonment of the Jews.

Götz Aly, *"Final Solution": Nazi Population Policy and the Murder of the European Jews.* London: Arnold, 1999. Aly's "functionalist" argument stresses the role of Nazi bureaucrats confronted with problems of population management in the occupied territories. See also *Hitler's Beneficiaries: Plunder, Racial War, and the Nazi Welfare State.*

Yitzhak Arad, *Belzec, Sobibor, Treblinka: The Operation Reinhard Death Camps.* Bloomington, IN: Indiana University Press, 1999. Detailed, readable study of these lesser-known Nazi death factories.

Omer Bartov, *Germany's War and the Holocaust: Disputed Histories.* Ithaca, NY: Cornell University Press, 2003. Essays by the principal scholar of the *Wehrmacht's* war on the eastern front; see also *Hitler's Army.*

Waitman Wade Beorn, *Marching Into Darkness: The Wehrmacht and the Holocaust in Belarus.* Cambridge, MA: Harvard University Press, 2014. Groundbreaking study of war and Holocaust in then–Belorussia. Beorn, a student of Christopher Browning (see below), produces a work every bit the equal of his mentor's.

Anna Bikont, *The Crime and the Silence: Confronting the Massacre of Jews in Wartime Jedwabne,* trans. Alissa Valles. New York: Farrar, Straus and Giroux, 2015. In this indelible book, Bikont explores the same atrocities unearthed by Jan Gross in *Neighbors* (see below). She provides the definitive account of Jedwabne and related massacres of Jews by their fellow Poles, as well as a shocking portrait of anti-semitism in contemporary Poland (see Box 6.3).

Daniel Blatman, *The Death Marches: The Final Phase of Nazi Genocide*, trans. Chaya Galai. Cambridge, MA: The Belknap Press of Harvard University Press, 2011. Encyclopedic account of the murderous forced marches from concentration camps and slave-labor sites in the last months of the war. Shows how diverse was their composition (*contra* Goldhagen, below).

Donald Bloxham, *The Final Solution: A Genocide*. Oxford: Oxford University Press, 2009. A nuanced and fluidly-written comparative treatment, by one of genocide studies' most dynamic younger scholars.

Ray Brandon and Wendy Lower, eds., *The Shoah in Ukraine: History, Testimony, Memorialization*. Bloomington, IN: Indiana University Press, 2010. Superb collection of essays, reflecting the growing focus on the former Soviet Union in Holocaust studies.

Christopher Browning, *Ordinary Men: Reserve Police Battalion 101 and the Final Solution in Poland*. New York: Perennial, 1993. Based on some of the same archival sources as Goldhagen's *Hitler's Willing Executioners* (see below), but emphasizes group dynamics in addition to anti-semitism. See also *The Origins of the Final Solution: The Evolution of Nazi Jewish Policy, September 1939–March 1942*.

Michael Burleigh and Wolfgang Wippermann, *The Racial State: Germany 1933–1945*. Cambridge: Cambridge University Press, 1991. How Nazi racial ideology inspired genocidal policy.

Father Patrick Desbois, *The Holocaust by Bullets: A Priest's Journey to Uncover the Truth behind the Murder of 1.5 Million Jews*. London: Palgrave Macmillan, 2008. The efforts of a French priest to document atrocities against Jews on the eastern front.

Saul Friedländer, *The Years of Extermination: Nazi Germany and the Jews, 1939–1945*. New York: HarperCollins, 2007. Friedländer's work won the Pulitzer Prize, and has been praised for integrating firsthand testimonies with the historical and archival record. See also *Nazi Germany and the Jews, Volume I: The Years of Persecution, 1933–1939*.

Peter Fritzsche, *Life and Death in the Third Reich*. Cambridge, MA: Harvard University Press, 2008. Up-close, galvanizing account of daily life in Germany as the Nazi Holocaust was unleashed on Central and Eastern Europe.

Robert Gellately, *Backing Hitler: Consent and Coercion in Nazi Germany*. Oxford: Oxford University Press, 2001. Argues that ordinary Germans generally supported Nazi policies, often exhibiting enthusiasm beyond the call of duty.

Daniel J. Goldhagen, *Hitler's Willing Executioners: Ordinary Germans and the Holocaust*. New York: Vintage, 1997. Controversial book ascribing a monocausal explanation for the genocide, rooted in Germans' visceral hatred of the Jews.

Gideon Greif, *We Wept Without Tears: Testimonies of the Jewish Sonderkommando from Auschwitz*. New Haven, CT: Yale University Press, 2014. Chilling, intimate portraits of Jews forced to do the filthiest work of the Nazi death camps.

Jan T. Gross, *Fear: Anti-Semitism in Poland after Auschwitz*. New York: Random House, 2007. How murderous pogroms of Jews continued in Poland after the fall of the Third Reich. See also *Neighbors: The Destruction of the Jewish Community in Jedwabne, Poland*; *Golden Harvest: Events at the Periphery of the Holocaust* (with Irena Grudzinska Gross). See also Bikont, above.

Jeffrey Herf, *The Jewish Enemy: Nazi Propaganda during World War II and the Holocaust*. Cambridge, MA: The Belknap Press of Harvard University Press, 2006. Eye-opening study of the Nazi conception of Jews as political threats ("Judeo-bolsheviks") above all else.

Raul Hilberg, *The Destruction of the European Jews* (3rd edn), 3 vols. New Haven, CT: Yale University Press, 2003. Massive, meticulous study of the bureaucracy of death.

Adolf Hitler, *Mein Kampf* (My Struggle), trans. Ralph Mannheim. Boston, MA: Houghton Mifflin, 1943. First published in 1925–1926; lays out Hitler's vision of German destiny, as well as his virulent anti-semitism.

Eric A. Johnson and Karl-Heinz Reuband, *What We Knew: Terror, Mass Murder, and Everyday Life in Nazi Germany: An Oral History*. New York: Basic Books, 2005. Rich study based on interviews with German-Jewish Holocaust survivors.

Alex J. Kay, Jeff Rutherford, and David Stahel, eds., *Nazi Policy on the Eastern Front, 1941: Total War, Genocide, and Radicalization*. Rochester, NY: University of Rochester Press, 2012. First-rate collection providing an overview of recent historiographical advances on the Nazi war of extermination.

Ian Kershaw, *The Nazi Dictatorship: Problems and Perspectives of Interpretation* (4th edn). London: Arnold, 2000. Overview of, and contribution to, scholarly debates about the nature of the Nazi regime. (See also Kershaw's classic two-volume study, *Hitler, 1889–1936: Hubris* and *1936–1945: Nemesis*, now the standard biography of the Nazi dictator. A condensed single-volume edition is available.)

Victor Klemperer, *I Will Bear Witness: A Diary of the Nazi Years*, 2 vols. New York: Modern Library, 1999, 2001. An essential document of the twentieth century: the testimony of a German Jewish professor who survived the entire Nazi era. See also *The Lesser Evil: The Diaries of Victor Klemperer, 1945–59*; and *The Language of the Third Reich: LTI—Lingua Tertii Imperii: A Philologist's Notebook*.

Ronnie S. Landau, *The Nazi Holocaust*. Chicago, IL: Ivan R. Dee, 1994. A good, accessible primer on the origins and course of the Jewish catastrophe.

Primo Levi, *Survival in Auschwitz*. New York: Touchstone, 1996. Haunting account of a year and a half in the Nazi death camp; also *The Drowned and the Saved*, which includes Levi's classic essay, "The Gray Zone" (inspiring Petropoulos and Roth's volume—see below).

Peter Longerich, *Holocaust: The Nazi Persecution and Murder of the Jews*. Oxford: Oxford University Press, 2010. The best single-volume academic study of the Holocaust, superlative in its breadth, depth, and intellectual rigor. The book was extensively revised and updated for its long-overdue English publication.

Wendy Lower, *Nazi Empire-Building and the Holocaust in Ukraine*. Durham, NC: University of North Carolina Press, 2005. How Nazism exposed its imperial and genocidal nature most nakedly in the occupied territories of the east.

David B. MacDonald, *Identity Politics in the Age of Genocide: The Holocaust and Historical Representation*. London: Routledge, 2008. How non-Jews have deployed the language and motifs of the Holocaust to highlight their own and others' victimization.

Jonathan Petropoulos and John K. Roth, eds., *Gray Zones: Ambiguity and Compromise in the Holocaust and its Aftermath*. New York: Berghahn Books, 2005. An essential and deeply rewarding collection, inspired by Levi (see above), on the ambiguities and moral conundrums of Holocaust survival.

Alan S. Rosenbaum, ed., *Is the Holocaust Unique? Perspectives on Comparative Genocide*, 3rd edn. Boulder, CO: Westview Press, 2009. Important and controversial essays, including some significant new ones for this third edition.

Ron Rosenbaum, *Explaining Hitler: The Search for the Origins of His Evil*. New York: Perennial, 1999. Quest for the essence of the malignancy that was Hitler.

Dan Stone, ed., *The Historiography of the Holocaust*. London: Palgrave Macmillan, 2004. Sweeping overview of the Holocaust literature and its core debates.

NOTES

1 In religious usage, a "holocaust" is "a sacrificial offering wholly consumed by fire in exaltation of God" (Arno J. Mayer, *Why Did the Heavens Not Darken? The "Final Solution" in History* [New York: Pantheon, 1988], p. 16). However, in the twentieth century, this was supplanted by a secular usage, in which "holocaust" designates "a wide variety of conflagrations, massacres, wars, and disasters." See Jon Petrie's fascinating etymological study, "The Secular Word HOLOCAUST: Scholarly Myths, History, and 20th Century Meanings," *Journal of Genocide Research*, 2: 1 (2000), pp. 31–64.

2 Donald L. Niewyk, "Holocaust: The Jews," in Samuel L. Totten *et al.*, eds., *Century of Genocide: Eyewitness Accounts and Critical Views* (New York: Garland Publishing, 1997), p. 136. The figure of 5.1 to 5.4 million killed is used by the US Holocaust Museum; see Peter Balakian, *The Burning Tigris: The Armenian Genocide and America's Response* (New York: HarperCollins, 2003), p. 195.

3 Statistics cited in Michael Shermer and Alex Grobman, *Denying History: Who Says the Holocaust Never Happened and Why Do They Say It?* (Berkeley, CA: University of California Press, 2002), p. 174. Saul Friedländer also estimates "between five and six million Jews . . . killed" in the Holocaust: Friedländer, *The Years of Extermination: Nazi Germany and the Jews, 1939–1945* (New York: HarperCollins, 2007), p. 662.

4 Yehuda Bauer, *Rethinking the Holocaust* (New Haven, CT: Yale University Press, 2001), p. xi.

5 See Marvin Perry and Frederick M. Schweitzer, eds., *Antisemitic Myths: A Historical and Contemporary Anthology* (Bloomington, IN: Indiana University Press, 2008).

6 Daniel Jonah Goldhagen, *Hitler's Willing Executioners: Ordinary Germans and the Holocaust* (New York: Vintage, 1997), pp. 37–38. For a detailed study of the progressive demonization of the Jews, see Steven T. Katz, "Medieval Antisemitism: The Process of Mythification," in Katz, *The Holocaust in Historical Context, Vol. 1: The Holocaust and Mass Death before the Modern Age* (Oxford: Oxford University Press, 1994), pp. 225–316. However, as Mark Levene has pointed out to me, there was also a sense in which medieval Christianity *needed* the Jews—"for its own Christological endtime" and teleological myth. It may thus have been constrained from launching a full-scale genocidal assault on them. Levene, personal communication, August 26, 2005.

7 Luther quoted in Raul Hilberg, *The Destruction of the European Jews, Vol. 1* (3rd edn), (New Haven, CT: Yale University Press, 2003), p. 13. For a recent and revealing study of early European anti-semitism, see Sara Lipton, *Dark Mirror: The Medieval Origins of Anti-Jewish Iconography* (New York: Metropolitan Books, 2014).

8 The most infamous anti-semitic tract of modern times is the *Protocols of the Elders of Zion* (1903), a pamphlet that is now generally held to have been devised by the

Tsar's secret police in pre-revolutionary Russia, but which purported to represent the ambitions and deliberations of a global Jewish conspiracy against Christian civilization. For the complete text of the *Protocols*, and a point-by-point refutation, see Steven Leonard Jacobs and Mark Weitzman, *Dismantling the Big Lie: the Protocols of the Elders of Zion* (Jersey City, NJ: Ktav Publishing House, 2003—*n.b.* the centenary of the *Protocols*). For a consideration of its bizarrely enduring influence, see Evan Derkacz, "Again With the 'Jewish Conspiracy,'" *AlterNet.org*, April 11, 2006. www.alternet.org/story/34812.

9 Len Scales, "Central and Late Medieval Europe," in Donald Bloxham and A. Dirk Moses, eds., *The Oxford Handbook of Genocide Studies* (Oxford: Oxford University Press, 2010), p. 300.

10 In addition, for exponents of biological anti-semitism (a nineteenth-century invention), Jews came to be viewed as *innately* at odds with Western-Christian civilization. Religious conversion could no longer expunge their Jewishness—which helps to explain why this option was denied to Jews under Nazi rule. My thanks to Benjamin Madley for this point.

11 Daniel Feierstein, *Genocide as Social Practice: Reorganizing Society under the Nazis and Argentina's Military Juntas* (New Brunswick, NJ: Rutgers University Press, 2014), p. 124.

12 Ronnie S. Landau, *The Nazi Holocaust* (Chicago, IL: Ivan R. Dee, 1994), p. 44.

13 On the pogroms against Russian Jews between 1881 and 1921 (extending throughout the territories of the "Bloodlands" or the "Lands Between," that is, present-day Belarus, western Ukraine, and eastern Poland [see ch. 2]), see John D. Klier and Shlomo Lambroza, eds., *Pogroms: Anti-Jewish Violence in Modern Russian History* (Cambridge: Cambridge University Press, 1992). Recall that these were also the pogroms that reached the ears and influenced the thinking of the young Raphael Lemkin (ch. 1).

14 In the case of France, strong arguments have been made that anti-semitism was far more widespread and virulent, in elite and popular opinion, than was true in Germany. But "in France—unlike Germany—whatever the strength of anti-semitic feeling on the streets, in the bars and in the universities, political power always remained in the hands of the liberal republicans, a government which never endorsed political antisemitism" (Landau, *The Nazi Holocaust*, p. 63). However, when dictatorial government and "eliminationist anti-semitism" (Daniel Goldhagen's term) *were* imposed in France from 1940 to 1944—under direct Nazi occupation and under the Vichy puppet regime—the authorities and a key section of the population cooperated enthusiastically in the transport for mass execution of the Jews.

15 Richard Plant, *The Pink Triangle: The Nazi War against Homosexuals* (New York: Owl Books, 1988), p. 23.

16 Adolf Hitler, *Mein Kampf*, trans. Ralph Mannheim (Boston, MA: Houghton Mifflin, 1943), p. 562.

17 Landau, *The Nazi Holocaust*, pp. 317, 122.

18 See Orlando Patterson, *Slavery and Social Death: A Comparative Study* (Cambridge, MA: Harvard University Press, 1982), and the discussion in Goldhagen, *Hitler's Willing Executioners*, pp. 168–170.

19 Goldhagen, *Hitler's Willing Executioners*, p. 141. Alan E. Steinweis's *Kristallnacht 1938* (Cambridge, MA: The Belknap Press, 2009) is an excellent short treatment. For a still more concise account, see Leonidas E. Hill, "The Pogrom of November 9–10, 1938 in Germany," in Paul R. Brass, ed., *Riots and Pogroms* (Washington Square, NY: New York University Press, 1996), pp. 89–113.

20 For accounts of the fate of the male "November Jews" rounded up in the wake of the countrywide Nazi pogrom, see Alan E. Steinweis, *Kristallnacht 1938* (Cambridge, MA: The Belknap Press, 2009), pp. 91–98; and Kim Wünschmann, *Before Auschwitz: Jewish Prisoners in the Prewar Concentration Camps* (Cambridge, MA: Harvard University Press, 2015), pp. 196–210. The largest group of prisoners was incarcerated at Buchenwald. Wünschmann describes the "constant violent excesses" there, especially during the

"'murder week' of November 10–14, when SS guards, mostly during the night, raided the barracks and beat up the helpless and terrified inmates." Buchenwald also witnessed "the first epidemic in the history of the Nazi concentration camps," a typhoid outbreak in December. Most of the imprisoned Jews were released upon signing promises to emigrate, but an estimated one thousand men were killed in the camps, or "died, after release, from the consequences of their imprisonment" (Wünschmann, pp. 203–204).

21 Robert Gellately, *Backing Hitler: Consent and Coercion in Nazi Germany* (Oxford: Oxford University Press, 2001), p. vii.

22 Omer Bartov, *Germany's War and the Holocaust: Disputed Histories* (Ithaca, NY: Cornell University Press, 2003), p. 197.

23 Ian Kershaw noted that while criticisms of "anti-semitic thuggery" were aired as of 1935, "not much of the criticism was on humanitarian grounds. Economic self-interest played a large part," as when "people ignored exhortations to boycott Jewish shops and stores" in order to continue benefiting from superior goods, prices, and services there. German Christians worried, too, that the thugs and persecutors might turn on them next. "The methods rather than the aims were attacked. There were few principled objections to discrimination against Jews. What concerned people above all were the hooliganism, mob violence, distasteful scenes, and disturbances of order." Kershaw, *Hitler 1889–1936: Hubris* (London: Penguin, 2001), p. 594.

24 Victor Klemperer, *I Will Bear Witness 1933–1941* (New York: The Modern Library, 1999), pp. 165, 329–330, 393, 422, 429; Klemperer, *I Will Bear Witness 1942–1945* (New York: The Modern Library, 2001), pp. 66, 71. Elisabeth Freund, a Jewish Berliner, also described the mixed but frequently sympathetic reaction that German Jews received from "Aryans" when forced to don the yellow star in September 1941: "I am greeted on the street with special politeness by complete strangers, and in the street car ostentatiously a seat is freed for me, although those wearing a star are allowed to sit only if no Aryan is still standing. But sometimes guttersnipes call out abusive words after me. And occasionally Jews are said to have been beaten up. Someone tells me of an experience in the city train. A mother saw that her little girl was sitting beside a Jew: 'Lieschen, sit down on the other bench, you don't need to sit beside a Jew.' At that an Aryan worker stood up, saying: 'And I don't need to sit next to Lieschen.'" Quoted in Friedländer, *The Years of Extermination*, p. 253.

The important study by Eric A. Johnson and Karl-Heinz Reuband, *What We Knew: Terror, Mass Murder, and Everyday Life in Nazi Germany: An Oral History* (New York: Basic Books, 2005), further buttresses Klemperer's impression that anti-semitism was not widespread in Germany before 1933. Most German Jewish Holocaust survivors interviewed for the volume "stated that they and their families had felt well accepted and integrated in German society. Only a few believed that anti-Semitism was especially prevalent in Germany before the Nazi takeover in January 1933." However, and again meshing with Klemperer's documentation of a swiftly darkening situation, "the figures show that after Hitler took power in 1933, the once positive relations between Jews and non-Jews deteriorated. Whereas over two-thirds of the survivors' families before 1933 had friendly relations with non-Jews in their communities, after 1933 nearly two-thirds had relations that the survivors described as clearly worse or even hostile . . . Very few Jewish families in any German communities after 1933 maintained friendly associations with non-Jews . . . Even more disturbing, 22 percent of the survivors . . . suffered physical beatings from German civilians, and this was nearly three times the percentage of those who suffered beatings from Nazi policemen or other officials . . ." (pp. 269, 273, 279). While one-third of survivors "received significant help and support from non-Jewish German civilians during the Third Reich," it was also the case that "about two-thirds could not find a single German willing to help them, and one can only wonder about the Jews who did not survive" (p. 283).

25 Christopher R. Browning, *The Path to Genocide: Essays on Launching the Final Solution* (Cambridge, MA: Cambridge University Press, 1992), p. ix.

26 Mayer, *Why Did the Heavens Not Darken?*, pp. 114, 116–117.

27 Michael Burleigh, "Psychiatry, German Society and the Nazi 'Euthanasia' Programme," in Omer Bartov, ed., *The Holocaust: Origins, Implementation, Aftermath* (London: Routledge, 2000), p. 70.

28 Landau, *The Nazi Holocaust*, pp. 154–155. In his memoir of the Warsaw ghetto, Alexander Donat gives a figure for half a million ghetto internees as "27,000 apartments in an area of 750 acres, with six or seven persons to a room." Donat, *The Holocaust Kingdom* (Washington, DC: Holocaust Library, 1999), p. 24.

29 See Gunther Schwarberg, *In the Ghetto of Warsaw: Photographs by Heinrich Jöst* (Gottingen: Steidl Publishing, 2001).

30 See Richard Rhodes, *Masters of Death: The SS-Einsatzgruppen and the Invention of the Holocaust* (New York: Alfred A. Knopf, 2002).

31 Mayrhofer quoted in Wendy Lower, *Nazi Empire-Building and the Holocaust in Ukraine* (Durham, NC: University of North Carolina Press, 2005), pp. 133–134.

32 Text as supplied on the Yad Vashem website, www.yadvashem.org/yv/en/righteous/stories/related/nuremberg_trials.asp.

33 Eva Fogelman, *Conscience and Courage: Rescuers of Jews during the Holocaust* (New York: Anchor Books, 1994), pp. 11, 52. For a succinct account of Gräbe's dramatic actions, see his "Righteous Among the Nations" entry on the Yad Vashem website, www.yadvashem.org/yv/en/righteous/stories/graebe.asp.

34 Snyder, *Bloodlands*, p. 227.

35 Omer Bartov, *Germany's War and the Holocaust: Disputed Histories* (Ithaca, NY: Cornell University Press, 2003), p. 14. See also the excellent two-part essay by Wolfgang Weber, "The Debate in Germany over the Crimes of Hitler's *Wehrmacht*," *World Socialist Web Site*, September 19–20, 2001, www.wsws.org/articles/2001/sep2001/wehr-s19.shtml and www.wsws.org/articles/2001/sep2001/wehr-s20.shtml.

36 Stephen G. Fritz, *Ostkrieg: Hitler's War of Extermination in the East* (Lexington, KY: The University Press of Kentucky, 2011), p. 70.

37 A key "tipping point" for the *Wehrmacht*'s "indiscriminate, systematic and wholesale resort to carnage" was the Commissar Order issued on June 6, 1941, which called for "Communist Party functionaries . . . to be identified . . . and murdered by the army either on the spot or in rear areas." "Effectively," notes Michael Burleigh, "the army was assuming the functions hitherto performed by the Einsatzgruppen, namely the killing of an entire group of people solely by virtue of their membership of that group and without formal process." Burleigh, *Ethics and Extermination: Reflections on Nazi Genocide* (Cambridge: Cambridge University Press, 1997), p. 67.

38 Longerich, *Holocaust*, p. 243.

39 Hannah Arendt, *Eichmann in Jerusalem: A Report on the Banality of Evil* (New York: The Viking Press, 1965), p. 107. An *Einsatzgruppe* report cited by Ian Kershaw described "the relationship to the Wehrmacht . . . now, as before, [as] wholly untroubled . . . Above all, a constantly growing interest in and understanding for the tasks and business of the work of the security police can be seen in Wehrmacht circles. *This could especially be observed at the executions.*" Quoted in Kershaw, *Hitler, 1936–1945: Nemesis* (London: Penguin, 2001), p. 465.

40 Peter Fritzsche, *Life and Death in the Third Reich* (Cambridge, MA: The Belknap Press of Harvard University Press, 2008), p. 200.

41 Kretschmer quoted in Shermer and Grobman, *Denying History*, p. 185.

42 *Einsatzgruppe* D report (July 31, 1941) quoted in Dennis Deletant, "Transnistria and the Romanian Solution to the 'Jewish Problem,'" in Ray Brandon and Wendy Lower, eds., *The Shoah in Ukraine: History, Testimony, Memorialization* (Bloomington, IN: Indiana University Press, 2010), p. 163.

43 This gendered element of the slaughter is discussed further in Chapter 13.

44 Prisoner Lt. Priebe, quoted in Sönke Neitzel and Harald Welzer, *Soldiers: German POWs on Fighting, Killing, and Dying* (Toronto: Signal, 2013), p. 123. This study of the

intelligence transcripts reveals "that many soldiers were astonishingly well aware of the specific details of the extermination of European Jews. ... The soldiers' conversations make it clear that practically all German soldiers knew or suspected that Jews were being murdered en masse. . . . It was clear to the soldiers that the extermination was happening, and the extermination was integrated into their frame of reference. But it remained quite marginal in terms of what commanded their attention" (pp. 99, 101, 111).

45 Jacques Sémelin, *Purify and Destroy: The Political Uses of Massacre and Genocide* (New York: Columbia University Press, 2007), p. 276.

46 The statistics are drawn from Landau, *The Nazi Holocaust*.

47 Fritzsche, *Life and Death in the Third Reich*, p. 215.

48 "Whether the Germans were killing [Jews] immediately and directly in the gas chambers of an extermination camp or working and starving them to death in camps that they had not constructed for the express purpose of extermination (namely in concentration or 'work' camps), the mortality rates of Jews in camps was at exterminatory, genocidal levels and typically far exceeded the mortality rates of other groups living side by side with them. . . . The monthly death rate for Jews in Mauthausen [camp] was, from the end of 1942 to 1943, 100 percent. Mauthausen was not formally an extermination camp and, indeed, it was not for non-Jews, who at the end of 1943 all had a mortality rate below 2 percent." Goldhagen, *Hitler's Willing Executioners*, p. 173. For more on the Nazi system of forced and slave labor, see Wolf Gruner, *Jewish Forced Labor Under the Nazis: Economic Needs and Racial Aims, 1938–1944*, trans. Kathleen M. Dell'Orto (Cambridge: Cambridge University Press, 2006).

49 See Daniel Blatman, *The Death Marches: The Final Phase of Nazi Genocide*, trans. Chaya Galai (Cambridge, MA: The Belknap Press, 2011).

50 As David Bankier summarizes: "There is no indication that the Nazi policy against Poles, Serbs or Russians ever troubled the ordinary Germans. . . . From 1943 onwards only the murder of Jews (not of Gypsies, Slavs, mentally ill, or other crimes) raises among the public fears of divine or human retribution." Bankier, personal communication, December 17, 2009.

51 Ian Kershaw, *The End: Germany 1944–45* (London: Penguin, 2011), p. 124.

52 Quoted in Longerich, *Holocaust*, p. 119.

53 This account is excerpted from Nigel Roberts, "Life in the Minsk Ghetto—Frieda's Story," http://frsonline.org/community/frs-belarus-project-2/friedas-story/.

54 Hitler quoted in Gerald Fleming, *Hitler and the Final Solution* (Berkeley, CA: University of California Press, 1984), p. 17.

55 Tatz, *With Intent to Destroy*, p. 22.

56 Browning, *The Path to Genocide*, p. 86.

57 For a brief overview, see Richard Bessel, "Functionalists vs. Intentionalists: The Debate Twenty Years On *or* Whatever Happened to Functionalism and Intentionalism?," *German Studies Review*, 26: 1 (February 2003), pp. 15–20.

58 Shermer and Grobman, *Denying History*, p. 213 ("intentional functionalism"); Dan Michman, "Jewish Leadership *in Extremis*," in Dan Stone, ed., *The Historiography of the Holocaust* (London: Palgrave Macmillan, 2004), p. 326 ("integrationists"). Dan Stone likewise contends that "there are now very few historians who would take either an extreme intentionalist or an extreme functionalist position, since most now recognize both that before 1941 or 1942 there was no clearly formulated blueprint for genocide and that a worldview built on mystical race thinking, especially anti-Semitism, lay at the heart of the regime." Stone, "The Holocaust and its Historiography," in Dan Stone, ed., *The Historiography of Genocide* (London: Palgrave Macmillan, 2008), p. 377.

59 Longerich, *Holocaust*, p. 304. "The crucial point," he writes at p. 426, "is that there was from the outset a consensus among the decision makers that the persecution of the Jews should be further and further radicalized in the further course of the war. On the basis of this consensus, general instructions in line with the intuition of the

subordinates were issued in certain situations; in this way wider scope was given to independent initiatives. In the end the entire process was coordinated and standardized at the top. The leadership at the centre and the executive organizations on the periphery radicalized one another through a reciprocal process." Ian Kershaw has captured something of this dynamic in his heuristic of "working towards the Führer," in which he uses a Nazi subordinate's words to describe how peripheral actors sought to harmonize their actions with their understanding of regime policies and Hitler's personal desires and ambitions. See Kershaw, "'Working Towards the Führer': Reflections on the Nature of the Hitler Dictatorship," in Christian Leitz, ed., *The Third Reich: The Essential Readings* (London: Blackwell, 1999), pp. 231–252.

60 The quotes in the box text are from Anna Bikont, *The Crime and the Silence: Confronting the Massacre of Jews in Wartime Jedwabne* (New York: Farrar, Straus and Giroux, 2015), pp. 77, 135, 154, 208, 223, 271, 273 (e-book).

61 Hilberg, *The Destruction of the European Jews*, Vol. 1, pp. 139–140; Arendt, *Eichmann in Jerusalem*, pp. 59–60. For a scholarly study of Eichmann, challenging many of Arendt's framings in particular, see David Cesarani, *Becoming Eichmann: Rethinking the Life, Crimes, and Trial of a "Desk Murderer"* (New York: Da Capo Press, 2007). See also Bettina Stangneth, *Eichmann Before Jerusalem: The Unexamined Life of a Mass Murderer* (New York: Vintage, 2015).

62 Arendt, *Eichmann in Jerusalem*, pp. 117–118, 125. See also the discussion in Hilberg, *The Destruction of the European Jews*, Vol. 1, pp. 218–222. "With the growth of the destructive function of the Judenrate, many Jewish leaders felt an almost irresistible urge to look like their German masters" (p. 219).

63 Raul Hilberg, *Perpetrators, Victims, Bystanders: The Jewish Catastrophe 1933–1945* (New York: Perennial, 1993), p. 170. In *The Destruction of the European Jews* (Vol. 2, p. 901), Hilberg referred to "masses of Jewish deportees, numb, fantasy-ridden, and filled with illusions, [who] reacted with mechanical cooperation to every German command" (the specific reference is to the Hungarian deportations of 1944).

64 See Richard Rashke, *Escape from Sobibor* (Champaign, IL: University of Illinois Press, 1995); Israel Gutman, *Resistance: The Warsaw Ghetto Uprising* (Boston, MA: Houghton Mifflin, 1998). Also notable was the doomed rebellion of the *Sonderkommando* (Jews selected to do the dirty work in the gas chambers and crematoria) at Auschwitz-Birkenau in October 1944, and the Polish Jewish partisan movement led by the three Bielski brothers, depicted in the 2008 film *Defiance* (based on Nechama Tec, *Defiance: The True Story of the Bielski Partisans* [Oxford: Oxford University Press, 1994]).

65 Donat, *The Holocaust Kingdom*, p. 7.

66 Daniel Jonah Goldhagen, *Worse Than War: Genocide, Eliminationism, and the Ongoing Assault on Humanity* (New York: Basic Books, 2009), p. 133.

67 Bauer, *Rethinking the Holocaust*, p. 213.

68 Browning, *The Path to Genocide*, p. ix.

69 See John Cornwell, *Hitler's Pope: The Secret History of Pius XII* (New York: Penguin, 2008); Daniel Jonah Goldhagen, *A Moral Reckoning: The Role of the Catholic Church in the Holocaust and Its Unfulfilled Duty of Repair* (New York: Alfred A. Knopf, 2002).

70 Friedländer, *The Years of Extermination*, pp. 568, 572.

71 Reginald H. Phelps, quoted in Goldhagen, *Hitler's Willing Executioners*, p. 443.

72 In the case of Denmark, Saul Friedländer wrote: "The Germans had allowed a semi-autonomous Danish government to stay in place, and their own presence as occupiers was hardly felt. Hitler had decided on this peculiar course to avoid unnecessary difficulties in a country [that was] strategically important . . . 'racially related' to the community of Nordic peoples, and mainly an essential supplier of agricultural products . . ." Friedländer, *The Years of Extermination*, p. 545.

73 Hilberg, *Perpetrators, Victims, Bystanders*, p. 258.

74 Burleigh, *Ethics and Extermination*, pp. 155, 164.

75 Burleigh and Wippermann, *The Racial State*, p. 51.

76 Christopher Browning, *Ordinary Men: Reserve Police Battalion 101 and the Final Solution in Poland* (New York: HarperPerennial, 1998), pp. 184, 186.

77 Goldhagen, *Hitler's Willing Executioners*, pp. 277, 446.

78 See Robert R. Shandley, ed., *Unwilling Germans? The Goldhagen Debate* (Minneapolis, MN: The University of Minnesota Press, 1998).

79 Friedländer, *The Years of Extermination*, p. 511. See Chapter 14 for further discussion of history and memory in Germany after the Second World War.

80 Hilberg, *Perpetrators, Victims, Bystanders*, p. 191. As Martha Minow comments, "The creation of Israel could be viewed as a kind of international reparation effort." Minow, *Between Vengeance and Forgiveness: Facing History after Genocide and Mass Violence* (Boston, MA: Beacon Press, 1998), p. 133.

81 See Idith Zertal, *Israel's Holocaust and the Politics of Nationhood* (Cambridge: Cambridge University Press, 2005).

82 "Israel Pledges to Protect Itself from 'New Holocaust' Threat Posed by Iran's Nuclear Programme," *Daily Telegraph*, April 21, 2009. Ahmadinejad's comments, made to a "World Without Zionism" conference in Tehran on October 26, 2005, were translated in many media as "Israel must be wiped off the map," suggesting the country and its population should be physically destroyed. However, this is disputed by, among others, Juan Cole, who claims a more accurate translation is: "This regime occupying Jerusalem must vanish from the page of time." In this reading, asserts Cole, "Ahmadinejad was not making a threat, he was quoting a saying of [Ayatollah] Khomeini and urging that pro-Palestinian activists in Iran not give up hope—that the occupation of Jerusalem was no more a continued inevitability than had been the hegemony of the Shah's government," overthrown in Iran in 1979. See Cole, "Informed Comment," May 3, 2006, www.juancole.com/2006/05/hitchens-hacker-and-hitchens.html.

83 See the official transcript of Netanyahu's speech to the 37th Zionist Congress, www.pmo.gov.il/English/MediaCenter/Speeches/Pages/speechcongress201015.aspx.

84 Christopher Browning, "A Lesson for Netanyahu From a Real Holocaust Historian," *Foreign Policy* (online), October 22, 2015, http://foreignpolicy.com/2015/10/22/a-lesson-for-netanyahu-from-a-real-holocaust-historian/. Israeli critics were no less scathing. Roy Isacowitz wrote in *Ha'aretz*: "Himself the son of a crackpot historian, Bibi has adopted a fringe and discredited theory with no historical basis and made it the cornerstone of his understanding of the most traumatic and decisive event in Jewish history. . . . To put anyone on a par with Hitler as regards the Holocaust is a form of Holocaust denial. It perverts the historical truth of the Holocaust and opens the door to all sorts of other lunatic and dangerous theories. It is something that no intelligent and aware person should do, let alone the prime minister of Israel." Roy Isacowitz, "In Mufti Speech, Netanyahu Showed His Obsessive Hatred of the Palestinians," *Ha'aretz*, October 22, 2015, www.haaretz.com/opinion/.premium-1.681790 (requires registration). See also Rabbi Eliyahu Fink's hilarious and cutting reworking of a Hitler rant from the 2004 German film *Downfall* (*Der Untergang*) at www.facebook.com/rabbieliyahufink/videos/788769714567405/.

85 Jodi Rudoren, "Netanyahu Retracts Assertion That Palestinian Inspired Holocaust," *The New York Times*, October 30, 2015, www.nytimes.com/2015/10/31/world/middleeast/netanyahu-retracts-assertion-that-palestinian-inspired-holocaust.html.

86 For explorations and critiques by Jewish authors of the place of the Holocaust in Israeli and Jewish identity politics, see Peter Novick, *The Holocaust in American Life* (Boston, MA: Mariner, 2000); Idith Zertal, *Israel's Holocaust and the Politics of Nationhood* (Cambridge: Cambridge University Press, 2005); Norman Finkelstein, *The Holocaust Industry: Reflections on the Exploitation of Jewish Suffering*, 2nd edn (New York: Verso Books, 2015); Gilad Atzmon, *The Wandering Who? A Study of Jewish Identity Politics* (Winchester: Zero Books, 2011); Judith Butler, *Parting Ways: Jewishness and the Critique of Zionism* (New York: Columbia University Press, 2012); Avraham Burg, *The Holocaust is Over, We Must*

Rise from Its Ashes (London: Palgrave Macmillan, 2008); and Peter Beinart, *The Crisis of Zionism* (New York: Times Books, 2012).

87 For a sensitive deployment of "a theoretical framework for shared and inclusive Jewish and Palestinian deliberation on the memories of the Holocaust and the Nakba," see Bashir Bashir and Amos Goldberg, "Deliberating the Holocaust and the Nakba: Disruptive Empathy and Binationalism in Israel/Palestine," *Journal of Genocide Research*, 16: 1 (2014), pp. 77–99 (quote p. 77).

88 See, e.g., "[Palestinian Authority president Mahmoud] Abbas: IDF [Israel Defense Forces] Action Worse than Holocaust," *The Jerusalem Post*, March 2, 2008; "Iran: Israeli Crimes Outstrip Holocaust," Reuters dispatch on *Aljazeera.net*, February 12, 2006.

89 Ilan Pappé, "Genocide in Gaza," *The Electronic Intifada*, September 2, 2006, http://electronicintifada.net/v2/article5656.shtml.

90 Richard Falk, "Slouching toward a Palestinian Holocaust," The Transnational Foundation for Peace and Future Research, June 29, 2007, www.oldsite.transnational.org/Area_MiddleEast/2007/Falk_PalestineGenocide.html. A Red Cross report leaked in 2008 described a "progressive deterioration in food security for up to 70 per cent of Gaza's population" as a result of the Israeli siege, adding that "Chronic malnutrition is on a steadily rising trend and micronutrient deficiencies are of great concern." Quoted in Donald Macintyre, "Chronic Malnutrition in Gaza Blamed on Israel," *The Independent*, November 15, 2008. Former US president Jimmy Carter stated in 2008 that the Palestinian population of Gaza was being "starved to death," with caloric intakes lower than in the poorest African countries: "It's an atrocity what is being perpetrated as punishment on the people in Gaza. . . . I think it is an abomination that this continues to go on." Jonathan Wright, "Carter Calls Gaza Blockade a Crime and Atrocity," Reuters dispatch on *Yahoo! News*, April 18, 2008.

91 Goldstone report cited in Rory McCarthy, "UN Investigation Finds Evidence of War Crimes in Gaza Campaign," *The Guardian*, October 25, 2009. On the two most recent assaults on Gaza (at the time of writing—another is quite predictable during the life of this edition), see Norman G. Finkelstein, *"This Time We Went Too Far": Truth & Consequences of the Gaza Invasion* (New York: OR Books, 2010), and Max Blumenthal's *The 51 Day War: Ruin and Resistance in Gaza* (New York: Nation Books, 2015). Blumenthal's *Goliath: Life and Loathing in Greater Israel* (New York: Nation Books, 2013) is the most hard-hitting survey of contemporary Israeli atrocity in the occupied Palestinian territories and within Israel proper, including regular outbreaks of genocidal discourse at high levels of the political and religious establishment. In July 2014, for example, Ayelet Shaked of the far-right Jewish Home Party approvingly posted the 2002 comments of an Israeli settler: "Behind every terrorist stand dozens of men and women, without whom he could not engage in terrorism. They are all enemy combatants, and their blood shall be on all their heads. Now this also includes the mothers of the martyrs, who send them to hell with flowers and kisses. They should follow their sons, nothing would be more just. They should go, as should the physical homes in which they raised the snakes. Otherwise, more little snakes will be raised there." Following national elections in March 2015, Shaked was appointed to the Israeli cabinet—as Justice Minister. See Robert Tait, "New Israeli Justice Minister Notorious for Anti-Palestinian Rhetoric Given Bodyguard after 'Nazi' Death Threats," *The Telegraph*, May 12, 2015, www.telegraph.co.uk/news/worldnews/middleeast/israel/11599932/New-Israeli-justice-minister-notorious-for-anti-Palestinian-rhetoric-given-bodyguard-after-Nazi-death-threats.html.

92 See Adam Jones, "Genocide in Gaza? Notes toward an Answer," post to the International Association of Genocide Scholars (IAGS) mailing list, January 26, 2009, www.genocidetext.net/israel_palestine01.htm; Jones, "Israel and Genocide," presentation to the IAGS conference in Winnipeg, Manitoba, July 16, 2014 (notes available from the author). For a critique of the inattention to the Palestinian–Israeli conflict in genocide studies, see Haifa Rashed, Damien Short, and John Docker, "Nakba Memoricide:

Genocide Studies and the Zionist/Israeli Genocide of Palestine," *Holy Land Studies*, 13: 1 (2014), pp. 1–23. For an article around the same time in the genocide studies literature, see Bashir Bashir and Amos Goldberg, "Deliberating the Holocaust and the Nakba: Disruptive Empathy and Binationalism in Israel/Palestine," *Journal of Genocide Research*, 16: 1 (2014), pp. 77–99.

93 Alex Alvarez, *Governments, Citizens, and Genocide: A Comparative and Interdisciplinary Approach* (Bloomington, IN: Indiana University Press, 2001), p. 14.

94 The phrase "uniquely unique" was first used by Alice L. Eckhardt and Roy Eckhardt; see Gunnar Heinsohn, "What Makes the Holocaust a Uniquely Unique Genocide?," *Journal of Genocide Research*, 2: 3 (2000), p. 430 (n. 95). For a trenchant overview of the uniqueness debate and its ideological underpinnings, see Daniel Blatman, "Holocaust Scholarship: Towards a Post-Uniqueness Era," *Journal of Genocide Research*, 17: 1 (2015), pp. 21–43.

95 Katz, *The Holocaust in Historical Context*, p. 28.

96 Mark Levene, *Genocide in the Age of the Nation-State, Vol. 1: The Meaning of Genocide* (London: I.B. Tauris, 2005), p. 2.

97 Lopate, cited in Helen Fein, *Genocide: A Sociological Perspective* (London: Sage Publications, 1993), p. 52.

98 As David Moshman put it: "True, the Holocaust is phenomenologically distinct from every other genocide, but so is every other genocide distinct from every other. Every genocide is unique, and the Holocaust is no exception." Moshman, "Conceptions of Genocide and Perceptions of History," in Stone, ed., *The Historiography of Genocide*, p. 72.

99 Nicholas Wheeler, *Saving Strangers: Humanitarian Intervention in International Society* (Oxford: Oxford University Press, 2000), p. 212.

100 Interestingly, volume 2 of Steven Katz's *The Holocaust in Historical Context*, which was supposed to apply his uniqueness thesis to twentieth-century cases of mass killing, was scheduled for publication many years ago, but has yet to appear. I have often wondered whether Katz hit an insuperable roadblock in applying his uniqueness thesis to the Rwandan genocide, which occurred the same year his first volume was published.

101 Hilberg, *The Destruction of the European Jews, Vol. 3*, p. 1075.

102 Ian Hancock, "Romanies and the Holocaust: A Re-evaluation and Overview," in Dan Stone, ed., *The Historiography of the Holocaust* (London: Palgrave Macmillan, 2004), p. 383.

103 Bartov, *Germany's War and the Holocaust*, p. 106. According to Donald Bloxham, "the Jews had a paramount and peculiar place in Nazi ideology and the relentlessness of the 'final solution' when it was underway was unquestionably greater than in other Nazi programmes." Bloxham, *Genocide, the World Wars and the Unweaving of Europe* (London: Vallentine Mitchell, 2008), p. 113. A recent study of the place of Jews in the Nazi *Weltanschauung* (worldview) is Alon Confino, *A World Without Jews: The Nazi Imagination from Persecution to Genocide* (New Haven, CT: Yale University Press, 2014).

104 Christian Gerlach, *Extremely Violent Societies: Mass Violence in the Twentieth-Century World* (Cambridge: Cambridge University Press, 2010), pp. 236–237. Ian Hancock points out that "the first mass genocidal action of the Holocaust," in January 1940, "took place when 250 Romani ['Gypsy'] children from Brno [Czechoslovakia] were murdered in Buchenwald, where they were used as guinea-pigs to test the efficacy of the Zyklon B cyanide gas crystals that were later used in the gas chambers" (see Figure 11.2). Hancock, "Romanies and the Holocaust," p. 389.

105 Thomas Cushman, "Is Genocide Preventable? Some Theoretical Considerations," *Journal of Genocide Research*, 5: 4 (2003), p. 528; Dan Stone, "Introduction," in Stone, ed., *The Historiography of Genocide*, p. 2. Interestingly, the fate of the Jews was not primary in Raphael Lemkin's framing of genocide in his 1944 book, which first propounded the concept. Martin Shaw has written: "For Lemkin (although himself Jewish and absolutely concerned about the horrors inflicted on the Jews), Nazi genocide

was never exclusively or primarily an anti-Jewish campaign; that was not the standard against which other Nazi persecutions were measured. On the contrary, his book aimed to demonstrate (by placing on record translations of Nazi laws in the occupied countries) how comprehensively, against a range of subject peoples, the Nazis had attempted to destroy the existence of nations, their well-being, institutions and ways of life." Shaw, *What is Genocide?* (Cambridge: Polity, 2007), pp. 20–21.

106 Alan S. Rosenbaum, "Introduction to the Third Edition," in Rosenbaum, ed., *Is the Holocaust Unique? Perspectives on Comparative Genocide* (Boulder, CO: Westview Press, 2009), p. 21. Martin Shaw goes further: "In order to understand other genocides … the imperative is not to compare them with the Holocaust—which as a specific episode was necessarily unique in many respects—but to interpret them in terms of a coherent general conception. We don't need a standard that steers all discussion towards a maximal concept of industrial extermination, a standard that distorts even the Nazi genocide against the Jews. We do need a coherent, generic, sociological concept of genocide that can make sense of a range of historical experiences." Shaw, *What is Genocide?*, p. 45.

While most people associate Nazi genocide with the Jewish Holocaust, a plethora of other victim groups accounted for the majority of those killed by the Nazis. Only in 1942 did the mass murder of Jews come to predominate, as historian Christopher Browning pointed out:

> If the Nazi regime had suddenly ceased to exist in the first half of 1941, its most notorious achievements in human destruction would have been the so-called euthanasia killing of seventy to eighty thousand German mentally ill and the systematic murder of the Polish intelligentsia. If the regime had disappeared in the spring of 1942, its historical infamy would have rested on the "war of destruction" against the Soviet Union. The mass death of some two million prisoners of war in the first nine months of that conflict would have stood out even more prominently than the killing of approximately one-half million Jews in that same period.

"Ever since," wrote Browning, the Jewish Holocaust "has overshadowed National Socialism's other all-too-numerous atrocities."[1] It does so in this book as well. Yet it is important to devote attention, however inadequate, to the Nazis' other victims.

PRE-WAR PERSECUTIONS AND THE "EUTHANASIA" CAMPAIGN

Communists and socialists

The first Nazi concentration camp was located at Dachau, near Munich. Opened in March 1933—two months after the Nazis seized power—its stated purpose was "to concentrate, in one place, not only all Communist officials but also, if necessary, the officials of . . . other Marxist formations who threaten the security of the state."[2] Bolshevism was as central to Hitler's *Weltanschauung* (worldview) as anti-semitism, embodying the decadent modernist tendencies that he loathed. In fact, Hitler's ideology and geopolitical strategy are best seen as motivated by a hatred of "Judeo-Bolshevism," and a conviction that the Nazis' territorial ambitions in Central and Eastern Europe could be realized only through victory over "the Marxist-cum-Bolshevik 'octopus' and the Jewish world conspiracy."[3]

One can distinguish between prewar and wartime phases of the campaign against communists and socialists. In the prewar stage, these sectors dominated the security policies of the Reich. They were the major targets of state violence and incarceration in camps; Jews-as-Jews were not targeted for substantial physical violence or imprisonment until *Kristallnacht* in 1938, by which time the German Left had been crushed. Communists, socialists, and other Left-oppositionists were also purged from public institutions in a manner very similar to Jews.[4] Historian Arnold Sywottek estimates that the Gestapo murdered in excess of 100,000 communists during the twelve years of the Third Reich.[5]

After the occupation of western Poland in September–October 1939, and especially with the invasion of eastern Poland and the Soviet Union in June 1941, the struggle against Bolshevism became bound up with the Nazis' ambition to enslave and exterminate the Slavic "subhuman." "What the Bolsheviks are must be clear to anybody who ever set sight upon the face of a Red Commissar," declared an article in the Nazi military paper, *Mitteilungen für die Truppe* (Information for the Troops), as the invasion of the Soviet Union was launched in June 1941. "Here no theoretical explanations are necessary anymore. To call beastly the traits of these people, a high percentage of whom are Jews, would be an insult to animals. . . . In these Commissars we see the uprising of subhumans against noble blood."[6] As this quotation suggests, the Nazis' ideological struggle against communists and socialists became intertwined with the national and military struggle with the USSR; the threat of ethnic swamping by "barbarians from the East"; and the assault on European Jewry.

"Asocials" and other undesirables

The Nazis' quest for racial purity and social homogeneity meant that "asocial" elements were to be annihilated or, in some cases, reformed. An effective study of this phenomenon is Robert Gellately's book on Nazism and German public opinion, *Backing Hitler*. Considered asocial was "anyone who did not participate as a good citizen and accept their social responsibilities." Among the groups harassed and punished were men seen as "shirking" paid work, or otherwise congenitally prone to unemployment or vagabondage.[7] Gellately describes a "special action" organized by Nazi police chief Heinrich Himmler in March 1937 "to arrest 2,000 people out of work":

> The instruction was to send to concentration camps, those who "*in the opinion of the Criminal Police*" were professional criminals, repeat offenders, or habitual sex offenders. The enthusiasm of the police was such that they arrested not 2,000, but 2,752 people, only 171 of whom had broken their probation. Police used the event as a pretext to get rid of "problem cases." Those arrested were described as break-in specialists (938), thieves (741), sex offenders (495), swindlers (436), robbers (56), and dealers in stolen goods (86). Only 85 of them [3 percent] were women.[8]

According to Gellately, "A recurrent theme in Hitler's thinking was that in the event of war, the home front would not fall prey to saboteurs, that is, anyone vaguely considered to be 'criminals,' 'pimps,' or 'deserters.'" The result was that "asocial" men, along with some women accused of involvement in the sex trade or common crimes, were confined in "camps [that] were presented as educative institutions . . . places for 'race defilers, rapists, sexual degenerates and habitual criminals'" (quoting an article in *Das Schwarze Korps* newspaper). Although "these camps were nothing like the death camps in the eastern occupied territories, the suffering, death, and outright murder in them was staggering."[9] Just as Jews and Bolshevism blurred in the Nazis' ideology, it is important to recognize the overlap among asocials, Jews, and Roma (Gypsies). It was a cornerstone of the Nazi demonization of Jews that they were essentially a parasitic class, incapable of "honest" work and thus driven to usury, lazy cosmopolitanism, and criminality. Likewise, perhaps the *core* of the Nazi racial hatred of Roma lay in their stereotypical depiction as shiftless and inclined to criminal behavior. The genocidal consequences of these stereotypes are examined in the "Other Holocausts" section, below.

Homosexual men

For all the promiscuous hatreds of Adolf Hitler, "homophobia was not one of his major obsessions,"[10] and Hitler does not seem to have been the moving force behind the Nazi campaign against gay men. (Lesbian women were never systematically outlawed or arrested.)[11] Rather, that dubious honor goes to the owlish Heinrich Himmler, supreme commander of the SS paramilitary force, "whose loathing of homosexuals knew no bounds."[12] As early as 1937, in a speech to the SS academy at Bad Tölz, Himmler pledged: "Like stinging nettles we will rip them [homosexuals] out, throw them on a heap, and burn them. Otherwise . . . we'll see the end of Germany, the end of the Germanic world." Later he would proclaim to his Finnish physiotherapist, Dr. Felix Kersten:

> We must exterminate these people root and branch. Just think how many children will never be born because of this, and how a people can be broken in nerve and spirit when such a plague gets hold of it. . . . The homosexual is a traitor to his own people and must be rooted out.[13]

As these comments suggest, the reviling of gays was linked to Nazi beliefs surrounding asocial and "useless" groups, who not only contributed nothing productive to the body politic, but actively subverted it. Gay males—because they chose to have sex with men—"were self-evidently failing in their duty to contribute to the demographic expansion of the 'Aryan-Germanic race,' at a time when millions of young men had perished in the First World

War."[14] Just as Roma and (especially) Jews were deemed parasites on German society and the national economy, so were gays labeled "as useless as hens which don't lay eggs" and "sociosexual propagation misfits."[15] (They did, however, have their uses: among some conquered peoples, homosexuality was to be encouraged, since it "would hasten their degeneracy, and thus their demise.")[16]

Richard Plant's study of the Nazi persecution of gays, *The Pink Triangle*, estimated the number of men convicted for homosexual "crimes" from 1933 to 1944 to be "between 50,000 and 63,000, of which nearly 4,000 were juveniles."[17] In the concentration camps that were the destiny of thousands of them, their "fate . . . can only be described as ghastly."[18] Like the Jews, they were forced to wear a special badge (the pink triangle of Plant's title), were referred to contemptuously as *Mannweiber* ("manwives"), and were segregated from their fellow prisoners, who often joined in the derision and brutalization. An inmate at Dachau reported that "the prisoners with the pink triangle did not live very long; they were quickly and systematically exterminated by the SS."[19] According to Konnilyn Feig, they found themselves "tormented from all sides as they struggle[d] to avoid being assaulted, raped, worked, and beaten to death."[20] Gay men were also among the likeliest candidates for medical experiments. At no point was support and solace likely from relatives or friends, because of the shame and stigma attaching to their "crimes." Plant estimates that the large majority of homosexuals consigned to concentration camps perished there—some 5,000 to 15,000 men.[21]

Jehovah's Witnesses and religious dissidents

If gays were dragged into the Nazi holocaust by their "traitorous" reluctance to contribute to Germany's demographic revival, Jehovah's Witnesses— already anathematized as a religious cult by the dominant Protestant and Catholic religious communities—were condemned for refusing to swear loyalty to the Nazi regime and to serve in the German military. In April 1935 the faith was formally outlawed, and later that year the first four hundred Jehovah's Witnesses were consigned to the Sachsenhausen concentration camp. By 1939 the number incarcerated there and in other prisons and camps had ballooned to 6,000.

When war broke out in September 1939, the Witnesses' rejection of military service aroused still greater malevolence. Only a few days after the German invasion of Poland, a believer who refused to swear loyalty to the regime, August Dickmann, was executed by the Gestapo "in order to set an example."[22] In all, "Over the course of the dictatorship, as many as 10,000 members of the community were arrested, with 2,000 sent to concentration camps, where they were treated dreadfully and as many as 1,200 died or were murdered."[23]

In a curious twist, however, a positive stereotype also arose around the Witnesses. They came to be viewed in the camps as "industrious, neat, and tidy, and uncompromising in [their] religious principles." Accordingly,

> the SS ultimately switched to a policy of trying to exploit [the Witnesses'] devotion to duty and their reliability. . . . They were used as general servants in SS households or put to work in small Kommandos [work teams] when there was a threat that prisoners might escape. In Ravensbruck [women's concentration camp], they were showcased as "exemplary prisoners," while in Niederhagen, the only camp where they constituted the core population, they were put to work on renovations.[24]

As for mainstream religion, in general the Nazis distrusted it, preferring their own brand of mysticism and Volk-worship. Their desire not to provoke unrest among the general population, or (before the war) international opposition, limited their campaign against the main Protestant dominations and the large Catholic minority in Germany. No such restraint obtained in occupied Poland, however, where leading Catholic figures were swept up in the campaign of eliticide against the Polish intelligentsia. At home, as the war turned against Germany, religious dissidents of all stripes came to be hounded, imprisoned, and killed. The best-known case is that of the Protestant pastor Dietrich Bonhoeffer, who declaimed against the Nazi regime from his pulpit, and was hanged in Flossenburg concentration camp shortly before the war ended. His *Letters and Papers from Prison* has become a classic of devotional literature.[25]

The handicapped and infirm

As with every other group the Nazis targeted, the campaign against the handicapped and infirm exploited a popular receptiveness based on long-standing patterns of discrimination and anathematization in European and Western culture. An offshoot of the Western drive for modernity was the development of a science of eugenics, taking both positive and negative forms: "Positive eugenics was the attempt to encourage increased breeding by those who were considered particularly fit; negative eugenics aimed at eliminating the unfit."[26] The foci of this international movement were Germany, Great Britain, and the United States (the US pioneered the use of forced sterilization against those considered "abnormal").[27] In Germany in the 1920s, treatises by noted legal and medical authorities railed against those "unworthy of life" and demanded the "destruction" of disabled persons in institutions. This was not murder but "mercy death."[28] Such views initially received strong public backing, even among many relatives of institutionalized patients.[29]

Once in power, the Nazis intensified the trend. Within a few months, they had promulgated the Law for the Prevention of Hereditarily Diseased Progeny, beginning a policy that by 1945 had led to the forced sterilization of some 300,000 people. The Marriage Health Law followed in 1935, under which Germans seeking to wed were forced to provide medical documentation proving that they did not carry hereditary conditions or afflictions. If they could not so demonstrate, the application was rejected.[30]

In the two years prior to the outbreak of the Second World War, Hitler and other Nazi planners began paving the way for the collective killing of disabled infants and children, then of adults. Hitler used the "fog of war" to cover the implementation of the campaign (the authorization, personally signed by Hitler on September 8, 1939, was symbolically backdated to September 1 to coincide with the invasion of Poland). "An elaborate covert bureaucracy"[31] was established in a confiscated Jewish property at Tiergartenstrasse 4 in Berlin, and "Aktion T-4"—as the extermination program was dubbed—moved into high gear. The program's "task was to organise the registration, selection, transfer and murder of a previously calculated target group of 70,000 people, including chronic schizophrenics, epileptics and long-stay patients."[32] All were deemed *unnütze Esser*, "useless eaters"—surely one of the most macabre phrases in the Nazi vocabulary. In the end, the human destruction exceeded the original ambitions. Among the victims were an estimated 6,000 to 7,000 children, who were starved to death or administered fatal medication. Many adults were dispatched to a prototype gas chamber.[33]

At every point in the chain of death, the complicity of nurses, doctors, and professionals of all stripes was enthusiastic. Yet as the scope of the killing widened, the general population (and Germany's churches) proved more ambivalent, eventually leading to open protest. In August 1941, "Aktion T-4" was closed down in Germany. But a decentralized version continued in operation until the last days of the war, and even beyond (the last victim died on May 29, 1945, under the noses of Allied occupiers). Meanwhile, the heart of the program—its eager supervisors and technicians—was bundled east, to manage the extermination of Jews and others in the death camps of Treblinka, Belzec, and Sobibor in Poland. Thus, "the euthanasia program was the direct precursor of the death factories—ideologically, organizationally, and in terms of personnel."[34]

Predictably, then, mass murder in the eastern occupied territories also targeted the handicapped. "In Poland the Germans killed almost all disabled Poles . . . The same applied in the occupied Soviet Union."[35] With the assistance of the same *Einsatzgruppen* death squads who murdered hundreds of thousands of Jews in the first year of the war, some 100,000 people deemed "unworthy of life" were murdered at a single institution, the Kiev Pathological Institute in Ukraine.[36] In all, perhaps a quarter of a million handicapped and disabled individuals died to further the Nazis' fanatical

Figure 6a.1 A farmer took this clandestine photo of smoke billowing from the crematorium chimney of the Schloss Hartheim killing complex in Austria, as Aktion (Operation) T-4—the mass murder of the handicapped—was underway in 1940–1941. Hartheim was one of six main facilities for the Nazi "euthanasia" campaign, which served as a trial run for the Holocaust, including the use of gas chambers to kill victims.

Source: Wolfgang Schuhmann/ United States Holocaust Memorial Museum.

social-engineering scheme. "With the 'euthanasia' programmes," asserts Peter Longerich, "the National Socialist regime had crossed the threshold to a systematic, racially motivated policy of annihilation a little under two years before the mass murder of the Jews began."[37]

OTHER HOLOCAUSTS

The Slavs

The ethnic designation "Slav" derives from the same root as "slave," and that is the destiny to which Nazi policies sought to consign Poles, Russians, Ukrainians, White Russians (Belorussians), and other Slavic peoples. "The Slavs are a mass of born slaves, who feel the need of a master," Hitler declared, making clear his basically colonialist fantasies for the east: "We'll supply the Ukrainians with scarves, glass beads and everything that colonial peoples like."[38]

But if they were primitive and contemptible, the Slavic "hordes" were also dangerous and expansionist—at least when dominated and directed by Jews (i.e., "Judeo–Bolsheviks"; see Figure 1.7, p. 47). It may be argued that the confrontation with the Slavs was inseparable from, and as central as, the campaign against the Jews. Consider the words of Colonel–General Hoepner, commander of Panzer Group 4 in the invasion of the Soviet Union, on sending his troops into battle:

> The war against the Soviet Union is an essential component of the German people's struggle for existence. It is the old struggle of the Germans against the Slavs, the defense of European culture against the Muscovite-Asiatic flood, the warding off of Jewish Bolshevism. This struggle must have as its aim the demolition of present Russia and must therefore be conducted with unprecedented severity. Both the planning and the execution of every battle must be dictated by an iron will to bring about a merciless, total annihilation of the enemy.[39]

The first victims of the anti–Slav genocide were, however, Polish. Hitler's famous comment, "Who, after all, talks nowadays of the annihilation of the Armenians?" (see Chapter 4), is often mistaken as referring to the impending fate of Jews in Nazi-occupied territories. In fact, Hitler was speaking just before the invasion of Poland on September 1, 1939, referring to commands he had issued to "kill without pity or mercy all men, women, and children of Polish descent or language. Only in this way can we obtain the living space we need."[40] Richard Lukas is left in little doubt of Nazi plans:

> While the Germans intended to eliminate the Jews before the end of the war, most Poles would work as helots until they too shared the fate of the Jews. . . . The conclusion is inescapable that had the war continued, the Poles would have been ultimately obliterated either by outright slaughter in gas chambers, as most Jews had perished, or by a continuation of the policies the Nazis had inaugurated in occupied Poland during the war—genocide by execution, forced labor, starvation, reduction of biological propagation, and Germanization.

Others dispute the claim that non-Jewish Poles were destined for annihilation. Nonetheless, as Lukas notes, "during almost six years of war, Poland lost 6,028,000 of its citizens, or 22 percent of its total population, the highest ratio of losses to population of any country in Europe." Nearly three million of the murdered Poles were Jews, but "over 50 percent . . . were Polish Christians, victims of prison, death camps, raids, executions, epidemics, starvation, excessive work, and ill treatment."[41] The Germans massacred tens of thousands of Polish males from the prewar political elite and professions in one of the classic eliticides, and gendercides, in modern history. ". . . Only a nation whose upper levels are destroyed can be pushed into the ranks of slavery," Hitler declared.[42] The Soviet Union, too, had done its part during the two years that it dismembered and occupied Poland in league with the Nazis: "Together, between September 1939 and June 1941, in their time as allies, the Soviet and German states . . . killed perhaps two hundred thousand Polish citizens, and deported about a million more."[43] The Nazis also dispatched fully six million Poles to Germany as slave laborers. The Soviets' depredations during their relatively brief occupation of eastern Poland (September 1939 to June 1941), and again after 1944, also contributed significantly to the death toll (see Chapter 5).

As for the Slavs of Ukraine, Russia, and other parts of the Soviet Union, their suffering is legendary. A commonly-cited estimate is that *about twenty-seven million* Soviet citizens died. The disproportionate number of militarized male victims would have "catastrophic . . . demographic consequences" for decades after, with women of the relevant age groups outnumbering men by two or even three to one.[44] But two-thirds of the victims—*about eighteen million people*—were civilians.[45] Exploitation of Slavs as slave laborers was merciless and genocidal. According to historian Catherine Merridale, "At least three million [Soviet] men and women (one famous Russian source gives a figure of over five million) were shipped off to the Reich to work as slaves. Many of these—probably more than two million—were worked so hard that they joined Europe's Jews in the death camps, discarded by the Reich for disposal like worn-out nags sent to the abattoir."[46]

Soviet Slavs were the primary intended victims of the Nazis' infamous "hunger policy" (*Hungerpolitik*) codified in a series of dictates in the months prior to the launching of Operation Barbarossa. The strategy of requiring German troops to "live off the land" meant a radical planned reduction in the nutritional resources available to the civilian population of both the occupied and unoccupied Soviet territories. It was anticipated that mass death would result: "The purpose of the Russian campaign is to decimate the Slavic population by thirty millions," announced Heinrich Himmler, Hitler's leading genocidal henchman, at a dinner party shortly before the invasion.[47] With Operation Barbarossa well underway, an *Einsatzgruppe* chief, Franz Alfred Six, declared coolly on a visit to Army Group Center headquarters:

> Hitler intends to extend the eastern border of the Reich as far as the line Baku-Stalingrad-Moscow-Leningrad. Eastward of this line as far as the Urals, a "blazing strip" will emerge in which all life is to be erased. It is intended to decimate [i.e., exterminate] the around thirty million Russians living in this strip through starvation, by removing all foodstuffs from this enormous territory. All those involved in this operation

are to be forbidden on pain of death to give a Russian even a piece of bread. The large cities from Leningrad to Moscow are to be razed to the ground . . . [48]

As historian Alex Kay notes, when German troops crossed the border into the Soviet-occupied regions of eastern Poland in June 1941, "Germany's leading military and political institutions had all contributed to formulating the starvation policy or signaled their explicit endorsement of it. It had become state policy."[49] But with the German setbacks after December 1941, the principal victims of the starvation policy—millions of them—were the Soviet prisoners-of-war captured in the great encirclement campaigns of the invasion's early stages (see following section).

Andrew Roberts pointed out in his history of the Second World War that "in a conflict that claimed the lives of fifty million people . . . the USSR lost more than the whole of the rest of the world put together."[50] Titanic Soviet sacrifices, and crushing military force, proved key to Nazi Germany's defeat, with the other Allies playing important supporting roles. ". . . The Red Army, at the cost of perhaps 12 million dead (or approximately thirty times the number of the Anglo-Americans), broke the back of the Wehrmacht,"[51] most spectacularly in Operation Bagration in mid-1944, an offensive against the Germans' Army Group Center that inflicted a defeat "as decisive as anything seen in the history of warfare," on a scale that "utterly dwarfed the contemporaneous Operation Overlord" in western France.[52] Between the German invasion of the USSR in June 1941 and the D-Day invasion of France in June 1944, some 80 percent of German forces were deployed in the East, and the overwhelming majority of German military casualties occurred there.[53] As Yugoslav partisan leader Arso Jovanovic put it at the time: "Over there on the Eastern front—that's the real war, where whole divisions burn up like matchsticks"—and millions of civilians along with them.[54]

"A genocidal captivity":[55] Soviet prisoners-of-war

"Next to the Jews in Europe," wrote Alexander Werth, "the biggest single German crime was undoubtedly the extermination by hunger, exposure and in other ways of . . . Russian [sic: Soviet] war prisoners."[56] Donald Bloxham noted that the toll of at least 3.3 million murdered POWs "add[s] up to approximately the same number as the combined total of Armenians, Cambodians and Rwandans killed in genocides in the twentieth century."[57] Yet the murder of at least 3.3 million Soviet POWs is one of the least-known of modern genocides; there is still no full-length book on the subject in English.[58] It also stands as one of the most intensive genocides of all time: "a holocaust that devoured millions," as Catherine Merridale acknowledges.[59]

The large majority of POWs, some 2.8 million, were killed in just eight months of 1941–1942, a rate of slaughter matched (to my knowledge) only by the 1994 Rwanda genocide.[60]

The Soviet men were captured in massive encirclement operations in the early months of the German invasion, and in gender-selective round-ups that occurred in the newly-occupied territories. "It was clear to the Wehrmacht on exactly what scale they could expect to capture Soviet troops," wrote Alex Kay, "and yet they neglected to make the requisite preparations for feeding and sheltering the captured soldiers, who were viewed by the economic planners and the military leadership alike as the German troops' direct competitors when it came to food."[61] Nor was military service a strict requirement for this atrocious treatment. All males between the ages of 15 and 65 were deemed to be prisoners-of-war, and liable to be "sent to the rear," a phrase that was merely a euphemism for mass murder.

The POW camps, in Timothy Snyder's estimation, "were designed to end life."[62] According to Alexander Dallin, "Testimony is eloquent and prolific on the abandonment of entire divisions under the open sky":

Epidemics . . . decimated the camps. Beatings and abuse by the guards were commonplace. Millions spent weeks without food or shelter. Carloads of prisoners were dead when they arrived at their destination. Casualty figures varied considerably but almost nowhere amounted to less than 30 percent in the winter of 1941–42, and sometimes went as high as 95 percent.[63]

A Hungarian tank officer who visited one POW enclosure described "tens of thousands of Russian prisoners. Many were on the point of expiring. Few could stand on their feet. Their faces were dried up and their eyes sunk deep into their sockets. Hundreds were dying every day, and those who had any strength left dumped them in a vast pit."[64] German guards took their amusement by "throwing a dead dog into the prisoners' compound," citing an eyewitness account: "Yelling like mad, the Russians would fall on the animal and tear it to pieces with their bare hands. . . . The intestines they'd stuff in their pockets—a sort of iron ration."[65] Cannibalism was rife. Nazi leader Hermann Göring joked that "in the camps for Russian prisoners of war, after having eaten everything possible, including the soles of their boots, they have begun to eat each other, and what is more serious, have also eaten a German sentry."[66]

"On any given day in the autumn of 1941," noted Anne Applebaum, "as many Soviet POWs died as did British and American POWs during the entire war."[67] Hundreds of thousands of Soviet prisoners were sent to Nazi concentration camps, including Auschwitz, which was originally built to house and exploit them. Thousands died in the first tests of the gas chamber complex at Birkenau. Like the handicapped and Roma, then, Soviet POWs

Figure 6a.2 Summer 1942: an emaciated Soviet prisoner-of-war in the Zeithain camp in Saxony, Germany, is selected for slave labor in Nazi-occupied Belgium. Over three million Soviet prisoners died in Nazi captivity, mostly through starvation, exposure, and disease in 1941–1942, before the policy shifted from extermination to enslavement and hyper-exploitation. Had the Nazis' imperial enterprise (see Chapter 2) collapsed around the time this image was captured—with the machinery of the death camps still in its early stages—the mass murder of Soviet POWs would have stood as the regime's greatest atrocity.

Source: Wikimedia Commons.

were guinea-pigs and stepping-stones in the evolution of genocide against the Jews. The overall estimate for POW fatalities—3.3 million—is probably low. An important additional group of victims consists of Soviet soldiers, probably hundreds of thousands, who were killed shortly after surrendering.

In one of the twentieth century's most tragic ironies, the two million or so POWs who survived German incarceration were arrested upon forced repatriation to the USSR, on suspicion of collaboration with the Germans.[68] Most were sentenced to long terms in the Soviet concentration camps, where tens of thousands died in the final years of the Gulag (see Chapter 5).

The Romani genocide (*Porrajmos*)

Perhaps more than any other group, the Nazi genocide against Romani (Gypsy) peoples parallels the attempted extermination of European Jews. Roma were subjected to virulent racism in the centuries prior to the Holocaust—denounced as dirty, alien, and outside the bonds of social obligation.[69] As the legal scholar David Crowe summarizes:

> Though there were only 20,000–26,000 Roma in Germany when Hitler came to power, they were universally despised for what most Germans believed were their lazy, criminal ways. By 1933, there was already a mature body of restrictive anti-Roma laws throughout Germany that placed severe restrictions on their movements under the watchful eye of the police. These laws were such that the Nazis felt all they needed to do was enforce them more rigorously as part of their efforts to deal with what they called the Gypsy plague (*Zigeunerplage*).[70]

The Nazis targeted the Roma as racial enemies alongside the Jew, and more or less simultaneously with the evolution of anti-Jewish policy from persecution and legal restriction to genocidal extermination. The grim phrase "lives undeserving of life," which most people associate with Nazi policy toward Jews and the handicapped, was coined with reference to the Roma in a law passed only a few months after Hitler's seizure of power. Mixed marriages between Germans and Roma, as between "Aryan" Germans and Jews, were outlawed in 1935. The 1935 legislation against "hereditarily diseased progeny," the cornerstone of the campaign against the handicapped, specifically included Roma among its targets.

In July 1936, more than two years prior to the first mass round-up of Jewish men, Romani men were dispatched in their hundreds to the Dachau concentration camp outside Munich. (The measures were popular: Michael Burleigh noted "the obvious glee with which unwilling neighbours and local authorities regarded the removal of Sinti and Roma from their streets and neighbourhoods.")[72] While Hitler decreed a brief moratorium on

Figure 6a.3 Roma interned in the Nazis' Belzec death camp in Poland. Of all demographic groups in Europe, the Roma and Sinti—long known as "Gypsies"*—were probably the only ones destroyed in the Nazi holocaust in about the same proportion as European Jews. Roma and Sinti remain vulnerable across much of Europe, from Ireland in the west (where they are known as "Travellers") to Romania in the east. They are widely depicted as a shiftless and/or criminal element, and are liable to discrimination, harassment, and vigilante violence.[71]

Source: United States Holocaust Memorial Museum.

anti-Jewish measures prior to the 1936 Berlin Olympics, raids were conducted in the vicinity of Berlin to capture and incarcerate Roma.

"On Combating the Gypsy Plague" was the title of a 1937 polemic by Heinrich Himmler, taking a break from his fulminations on homosexuals and Jews. It "marked the definitive transition from a Gypsy policy that was understood as a component of the extirpation of 'aliens to the community' . . . to a persecution *sui generis*."[73] The following year, the first reference to an *endgültige Lösung der Zigeunerfrage*, a "total solution" to the Romani "question," appeared in a Nazi pronouncement.[74] A thousand more Roma were condemned to concentration camps in 1938.

A few months after the outbreak of the Second World War, some 250 Romani children at Buchenwald became test subjects for the Zyklon B cyanide crystals later used to exterminate Jews. In late 1941 and early 1942, about 4,400 Roma were deported from Austria to the death camp at Chelmno, where they were murdered in the mobile gas vans then being deployed against Jews in eastern Poland and the Soviet Union.[75]

* The term "Gypsy" has derogatory connotations for some, and is now often substituted by Roma/Romani, a practice I follow here.

Up to a quarter of a million more Roma perished in German *Einsatzgruppen* and Order Police Battalion executions, "legitimised with the old prejudice that the victims were 'spies.'"[76] These produced micro-level scenes of mass killing every bit as appalling and gut-wrenching as the Jewish murder sites of the "Holocaust by Bullets." An eyewitness, Lidiia Krylova, described to a postwar commission a typical cold-blooded massacre of Roma in April 1942 in the Russian village of Aleksandrovka, home to a large Roma community:

> Each family was led separately to the pit, and if someone did not move to it, they lugged him [or her]. The shooting was carried out by a soldier with a pistol. First the ten- to twelve-year-old children were shot in front of their mothers' eyes, then the babies were torn out of the mothers' arms and thrown alive into the pit. Only after all this was the mother shot. Some of the mothers could not stand the torture and jumped alive after their babies. . . . But not only children were thrown alive into the pit. With my own eyes I saw how they threw [in] the old woman Leonovich, who could not move and was put into a blanket by her daughters and carried by hand.[77]

In December 1942, Himmler decreed that Roma be deported to the most notorious of the death camps, Auschwitz-Birkenau. There they lived in a "family camp" (so named because Romani families, unlike Jewish ones, were not broken up), while the Nazi authorities decided what to do with them. A camp doctor who spoke with psychologist Robert Jay Lifton described conditions in the Romani barracks as "extraordinarily filthy and unhygienic even for Auschwitz, a place of starving babies, children and adults."[78] Those who did not die from privation, disease, or horrific medical experiments were finally consigned to the gas chambers in August 1944. In all, "about 20,000 of the 23,000 German and Austrian Roma and Sinti deported to Auschwitz were killed there."[79]

When the toll of the death factories is combined with that of the mass executions by gunfire, the outcome in terms of Romani mortality rates was not very different from the Jewish Holocaust. From a much smaller population, the Roma lost between 500,000 and 1.5 million of their members in the catastrophe that they call the *Porrajmos* ("Devouring"). While the lower figure is standard, Romani scholar Ian Hancock argues that it is "grossly underestimated," failing to recognize the extent to which Romani victims of (for example) the *Einsatzgruppen* death squads were designated as "partisans" or "asocials," or assigned other labels that tended to obscure ethnic identity.[80] When to the camp victims are added the huge numbers of Roma—perhaps more than perished in the camps—who "were murdered in the fields and forests where they lived,"[81] the death toll may well match that of the Armenian genocide.

Until recent years, however, the *Porrajmos* has been little more than a footnote in histories of Nazi mass violence. In part, this reflects the fact that Roma constituted a much smaller proportion of the German and European population than did Jews—about 0.05 percent. In addition, most Roma before and after the Second World War were illiterate, and thus unable to match the outpouring of victims' testimonies and academic analyses by Jewish survivors and scholars. Finally, and relatedly, while anti-semitism subsided dramatically after the war, Roma continued to be marginalized and stigmatized by European societies, as they remain today.

The result, in historian Sybil Milton's words, was "a tacit conspiracy of silence about the isolation, exclusion, and systematic killing of the Roma, rendering much of current Holocaust scholarship deficient and obsolete."[82] Even in contemporary Europe, Roma are the subject of violence and persecution; in a 2009 essay, Hancock declared that "anti-Gypsyism is at an all-time high."[83] Only since the late 1970s has a civil-rights movement, along with a body of scholarly literature, arisen to confront discrimination and to memorialize Romani suffering during the Nazi era.

Germans as victims

For decades after the end of the Second World War, it was difficult to give voice to German suffering in the war. Sixty years after the war's end, it is easier to accept claims that the Germans, too, should be numbered among the victims of Nazism—and victims of Nazism's victims.

Predictably, the debate is sharpest in Germany itself (see further discussion in Chapter 14). Two books published in 2003 symbolized the new visibility of the issue. A novel by Nobel Prize-winning author Günter Grass, *Im Krebsgang (Crabwalk)*, centers on the twentieth century's worst maritime disaster: the torpedoing of the *Wilhelm Gustloff* by a Soviet submarine, as the converted liner attempted to carry refugees (and some soldiers) from East Prussia to the German heartland, ahead of advancing Soviet armies. Nine thousand people died. In addition, a revisionist historian, Jörg Friedrich, published *Brandstätten (Fire Sites)*, a compendium of grisly, never-before-seen archival photographs of German victims of Allied fire-bombing (see Chapter 14).[84]

Estimates of the death toll in the area bombing of German cities "range from about 300,000 to 600,000, and of injuries from 600,000 to over a million." The most destructive raids were those on Hamburg (July 27–28, 1943) and Dresden, "the German Hiroshima" (February 13, 1945).[85] Both strikes resulted in raging fire-storms that suffocated or incinerated almost all life within their radius. As discussed in Chapter 1, various genocide scholars have described these and other aerial bombardments as genocidal.

Among the estimated four million German soldiers killed on all fronts during the war were those who died as prisoners-of-war in the Soviet Union. Many German POWs were executed; most were sent to concentration camps where, like their Soviet counterparts, they died of exposure, starvation, and additionally overwork. "In all, at least one million German prisoners died out of the 3,150,000 [captured] by the Red Army," and this does not reflect those summarily shot before they could be taken prisoner.[86] "An even greater percentage of German prisoners died in two years of Russian captivity before the end of the war than Russians died in four years of German captivity."[87] In one of the most egregious cases, of 91,000 Sixth Army POWs seized following the German surrender at Stalingrad in 1943, only 6,000 survived to be repatriated to Germany in the 1950s.[88]

Approximately 6.5 million German nationals—soldiers and civilians—were killed in the Second World War, including the hundreds of thousands of

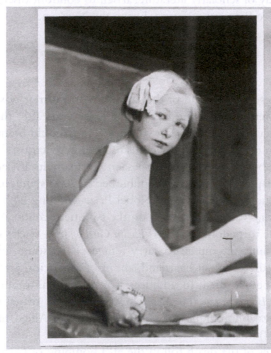

Margot R.
9½ Jahre alt
Gewicht: 21,5 Kg (Norm: 27,8 Kg)
ausgeprägte Hungeroedeme
besonders in den Beinen, im Rücken
und im Gesicht —
hochgradige Magerkeit
erholt sich nur sehr langsam, da
Neigung zu Durchfällen

Margot R.
9½ years of age
weight: 21,5 kilos
(normal standard: 27,8 kilos)
expressive hunger-oedemas
especially at the legs, in the back
and in the face — **high leanness**
recovers very slowly, as inclines
for diarrhoea

see next page, please
Fortsetzung nächste Seite

Figure 6a.4 Margot R., an ethnic-German refugee from Poland. Her medical condition was catalogued as part of the British-supervised "Operation Swallow" of 1946–1947, in which millions of Germans from the former Nazi-occupied territories of central and eastern Europe were evacuated—or "cleansed." Hundreds of thousands of Germans died in this series of mass expulsions by vengeful governments and populations. It may have been the largest such uprooting in history (see also Figure 14.3, p. 669).

Source: Hoover Institution Archives/Christopher Emmet Papers.

German victims of the Nazi regime.[89] A final horror was the reprisal killing and mass expulsion of ethnic Germans from the Soviet Union and Eastern Europe, often from territories their forebears had inhabited for centuries. As early as September 1939, in the opening weeks of the Nazi invasion of Poland, an estimated 60,000 ethnic Germans were allegedly murdered by Poles.[90] With the German army in retreat across the eastern front in 1944–1945, large numbers of Germans fell prey to the vengeful atrocities of Soviet troops (notably in East Prussia) and local populations (especially in Poland and Czechoslovakia). Some twelve to fourteen million ethnic Germans were uprooted in what the historian R.M. Douglas has called "not merely the largest forced migration but probably the largest single movement of population in human history," implemented "largely by state-sponsored violence and terror."[91] Approximately 1.71 million perished or were murdered en route.[92] Much of this occurred after the war had ended, sometimes well after; and it took place under the aegis of Allied occupation authorities, as the philosopher Bertrand Russell noted in an October 1945 protest letter:

> In Eastern Europe now mass deportations are being carried out by our allies on an unprecedented scale, and an apparently deliberate attempt is being made to exterminate millions of Germans, not by gas, but by depriving them of their homes and of food, leaving them to die by slow and agonizing starvation. This is not done as an act of war, but as a part of a deliberate policy of "peace."[93]

Moreover, an agreement reached among the Allies at the Yalta Conference (February 1945) "granted war reparations to the Soviet Union in the form of labor services. According to German Red Cross documents, it is estimated that 874,000 German civilians were abducted to the Soviet Union." They suffered a higher casualty rate even than German prisoners-of-war, with some 45 percent dying in captivity.[94]

FURTHER STUDY

Michael Berenbaum, ed., *A Mosaic of Victims: Non-Jews Persecuted and Murdered by the Nazis.* New York: New York University Press, 1990. A wide-ranging collection.

Michael Burleigh, *Ethics and Extermination: Reflections on Nazi Genocide.* Cambridge: Cambridge University Press, 1997. Essays on themes including "euthanasia," the German-Soviet war, and the racial state.

R.M. Douglas, *Orderly and Humane: The Expulsion of the Germans after the Second World War.* New Haven, CT: Yale University Press, 2012. The most detailed and scholarly investigation of the uprooting of eastern Europe's ethnic-German populations.

Henry Friedlander, *The Origins of Nazi Genocide: From Euthanasia to the Final Solution*. Chapel Hill, NC: University of North Carolina Press, 1995. Traces the evolution of the Nazi killing machine from the initial targeting of disabled and handicapped Germans to the mass slaughter of Jews and Roma.

Robert Gellately and Nathan Stoltzfus, eds., *Social Outsiders in Nazi Germany*. Princeton, NJ: Princeton University Press, 2001. Examines the Nazi campaign against "unwanted populations."

Gerhard Hirschfeld, ed., *The Policies of Genocide: Jews and Soviet Prisoners of War in Nazi Germany*. Boston, MA: Allen & Unwin, 1986. The links between the fate of the Jews and the Soviet prisoners.

Norman M. Naimark, *The Russians in Germany: A History of the Soviet Zone of Occupation, 1945–1949*. Cambridge, MA: The Belknap Press, 1995. Especially strong on atrocities against German women and workers under Soviet occupation.

Richard Plant, *The Pink Triangle: The Nazi War against Homosexuals*. New York: Owl, 1986. The persecution and killing of homosexuals, described by a refugee of the Nazi regime.

Alexander B. Rossino, *Hitler Strikes Poland: Blitzkrieg, Ideology, and Atrocity*. Lawrence, KS: University Press of Kansas, 2003. First-rate survey of the Nazi rampage in Poland, which served as a trial run for the war against the Soviet Union.

Martin K. Sorge, *The Other Price of Hitler's War: German Military and Civilian Losses Resulting from World War II*. Westport, CT: Greenwood Press, 1986. Concise account of German suffering in the war.

Timothy Snyder, *Bloodlands: Europe Between Hitler and Stalin*. New York: Basic Books, 2010. Focuses on the killing fields of Central and Eastern Europe (present-day eastern Poland, Belarus, and western Ukraine) as the heartland of both Nazi and Stalinist genocide. Perhaps the most widely-read book in Holocaust and genocide studies since Goldhagen's *Hitler's Willing Executioners* (see Further Study, Chapter 6). See also Box 2.3.

Frederick Taylor, *Dresden: Tuesday, February 13, 1945*. New York: HarperCollins, 2004. In-depth study of the Allied fire-bombing of the historic German city.

NOTES

1 Christopher R. Browning, *The Path to Genocide: Essays on Launching the Final Solution* (Cambridge: Cambridge University Press, 1992), p. ix.

2 Heinrich Himmler's announcement of Dachau's opening, quoted in Arno J. Mayer, *Why Did the Heavens Not Darken? The Final Solution in History* (New York: Pantheon, 1988), p. 125.

3 Mayer, *Why Did the Heavens Not Darken?*, pp. 107–108.

4 According to Dominique Vidal, approximately 150,000 communists and left-leaning social democrats were incarcerated in concentration camps between

1933 and 1939. Vidal, "From 'Mein Kampf to Auschwitz," *Le Monde diplomatique*, October 1998.

5 Sywottek estimate cited in Adam LeBor and Roger Boyes, *Seduced by Hitler: The Choices of a Nation and the Ethics of Survival* (New York: Barnes & Noble, 2000), p. 69.

6 Quoted in Saul Friedländer, *The Years of Extermination: Nazi Germany and the Jews, 1939–1945* (New York: HarperCollins, 2007), pp. 134–135.

7 "The 'work-shy' were [defined as] males medically fit to work, but who (without good reason) refused jobs on two occasions, or quit after a short time." Robert Gellately, *Backing Hitler: Consent and Coercion in Nazi Germany* (Oxford: Oxford University Press, 2001), p. 98.

8 Ibid., p. 96.

9 Ibid., pp. 60, 63, 68, 70.

10 Geoffrey J. Giles, "The Institutionalization of Homosexual Panic in the Third Reich," in R. Gellately and J. Stoltzfus, eds., *Social Outsiders in Nazi Germany* (Princeton, NJ: Princeton University Press, 2001), p. 233.

11 "Lesbians were not subjected to formal persecution in the Third Reich, despite the fact that some zealous legal experts demanded this. . . . In a state which extolled manly, martial roughness, lesbians were less of a threat to the regime than men who subverted its crude stereotypes of 'normal' male behaviour." Michael Burleigh and Wolfgang Wippermann, *The Racial State: Germany 1933–1945* (Cambridge: Cambridge University Press, 1991), p. 268.

12 Richard Plant, *The Pink Triangle: The Nazi War against Homosexuals* (New York: Owl Books, 1988), p. 62.

13 Himmler quoted in ibid., pp. 89, 99.

14 Michael Burleigh, *Ethics and Extermination: Reflections on Nazi Genocide* (Cambridge: Cambridge University Press, 1997), p. 162.

15 Quoted in Plant, *The Pink Triangle*, p. 102.

16 Ibid., p. 99.

17 Ibid., p. 149.

18 Quoted in ibid., p. 166.

19 Saul Friedländer, *Nazi Germany and the Jews, Volume 1: The Years of Persecution, 1933–1939* (New York: HarperCollins, 1997), p. 206.

20 Konnilyn Feig, "Non-Jewish Victims in the Concentration Camps," in Michael Berenbaum, ed., *A Mosaic of Victims: Non-Jews Persecuted and Murdered by the Nazis* (New York: New York University Press, 1990), p. 163.

21 Plant, *The Pink Triangle*, p. 154.

22 Gellately, *Backing Hitler*, p. 75.

23 Ibid. For Web links and a bibliography on the persecution and killings of Jehovah's Witnesses, see "A Teacher's Guide to the Holocaust: Jehovah's Witnesses," http://fcit.coedu.usf.edu/holocaust/people/VictJeho.htm.

24 Wolfgang Sofsky, *The Order of Terror: The Concentration Camp*, trans. William Templer (Princeton, NJ: Princeton University Press, 1999), pp. 122–123.

25 Dietrich Bonhoeffer, *Letters and Papers from Prison* (New York: Touchstone, 1997). See also the United States Holocaust Memorial Museum page on Bonhoeffer's life and work at www.ushmm.org/information/exhibitions/online-features/special-focus/dietrich-bonhoeffer.

26 Henry Friedlander, "The Exclusion and Murder of the Disabled," in Gellately and Stolzfus, eds., *Social Outsiders in Nazi Germany*, p. 146.

27 "Between 1907 and 1939, more than 30,000 people in twenty-nine [US] states were sterilized, many of them unknowingly or against their will, while they were incarcerated in prisons or institutions for the mentally ill." See "Handicapped:

Victims of the Nazi Era, 1933–1945," *A Teacher's Guide to the Holocaust*, http://fcit.coedu.usf.edu/holocaust/people/USHMMHAN.HTM.

28 Friedlander, "The Exclusion and Murder of the Disabled," p. 147.

29 An opponent of such views, Ewald Meltzer, the director of Katherinenhof juvenile asylum in Saxony, decided in 1925 "to carry out a poll of the views on 'euthanasia' held by the parents of his charges. To his obvious surprise, some 73 per cent of the 162 respondents said that they would approve 'the painless curtailment of the life of [their] child if experts had established that it is suffering from incurable idiocy.' Many of the 'yes' respondents said that they wished to offload the burden repre-sented by an 'idiotic' child, with some of them expressing the wish that this be done surreptitiously, in a manner which anticipated later National Socialist practice." Burleigh, *Ethics and Extermination*, p. 121.

30 Recall that under the UN Convention definition of genocide, preventing births within a group may be considered genocidal.

31 Burleigh, *Ethics and Extermination*, p. 123.

32 Ibid.

33 See "'Wheels Must Roll for Victory!' Children's 'Euthanasia' and 'Aktion T-4,'" in Michael Burleigh, *Death and Deliverance: 'Euthanasia' in Germany c. 1900–1945* (London: Pan Books, 1994), pp. 97–127.

34 Sofsky, *The Order of Terror*, p. 243. Peter Fritzsche also points to the connections between the "euthanasia" campaign and the Holocaust that would erupt shortly after: "Figuring out by trial and error the various stages of the killing process, from the identification of patients to the arrangement of special transports to the murder sites to the killings by gas in special chambers to the disposal of the bodies, and mobilizing medical experts who worked in secret with a variety of misleading euphemisms to conceal their work . . . the Nazis built important bureaucratic bridges that would lead to the extermination of Jews and Gypsies." Fritzsche, *Life and Death in the Third Reich* (Cambridge, MA: The Belknap Press of Harvard University, 2008), p. 118.

35 Friedlander, "The Exclusion and Murder of the Disabled," p. 157.

36 Friedlander, *The Origins of Nazi Genocide*, p. 142.

37 Peter Longerich, *Holocaust: The Nazi Persecution and Murder of the Jews* (Oxford: Oxford University Press, 2010), p. 141.

38 Hitler quoted in Jürgen Zimmerer, "The Birth of the *Ostland* out of the Spirit of Colonialism: A Postcolonial Perspective on the Nazi Policy of Conquest and Extermination," *Patterns of Prejudice*, 39: 2 (2005), p. 202. Raphael Lemkin recognized the colonialist core of the Nazi enterprise: "Hitler's plan covered the Poles, the Serbs, the Russians, the Frenchmen. . . . The main purpose of the Nazis was a commission of a G[enocide] against nations in order to get hold of their territory for colonisation purposes. This was the case of the Poles, and the Russians and the Ukrainians." Quoted in A. Dirk Moses, "Empire, Colony, Genocide: Keywords and the Philosophy of History," in Moses, ed., *Empire, Colony, Genocide: Conquest, Occupation, and Subaltern Resistance in World History* (New York: Berghahn Books, 2008), p. 21.

39 Quoted in Omer Bartov, *Hitler's Army: Soldiers, Nazis, and War in the Third Reich* (New York: Oxford University Press, 1992), p. 129.

40 Heinrich Himmler, tasked with engineering the destruction of the Polish people, parroted Hitler in proclaiming that "all Poles will disappear from the world. . . . It is essential that the great German people should consider it as its major task to destroy all Poles." Hitler and Himmler quoted in Richard C. Lukas, "The Polish Experience during the Holocaust," in Berenbaum, ed., *A Mosaic of Victims*, p. 89.

41 Lukas, "The Polish Experience," p. 90. Timothy Snyder rejects Lukas's calcula-
    tion of the death toll, suggesting that the "six million" figure was "generated
    . . . for the domestic [Polish] political purpose of creating an apparent balance
    between the Polish and Jewish dead" of the Second World War. He argues that
    a total Polish mortality of 4.8 million during the war "is probably closer to the
    truth," of whom "about three million were Jews." Snyder, *Bloodlands*, p. 406. For
    detailed studies of the Nazi occupation of Poland, see Richard C. Lukas, *For-
    gotten Holocaust: The Poles under German Occupation, 1939–1944*, rev. edn (New
    York: Hippocrene Books, 1997), and Alexander B. Rossino, *Hitler Strikes Poland:
    Blitzkrieg, Ideology, and Atrocity* (Lawrence, KS: University Press of Kansas, 2003).
42 Hitler quoted in Snyder, *Bloodlands*, p. 126.
43 Snyder, *Bloodlands*, p. 153.
44 Orlando Figes, *The Whisperers: Private Life in Stalin's Russia* (New York: Metro-
    politan Books, 2007), p. 457.
45 Antony Beevor, *Stalingrad* (New York: Viking Press, 1998), p. 428.
46 Catherine Merridale, *Ivan's War: Life and Death in the Red Army, 1939–1945*
    (New York: Picador, 2006), p. 291.
47 Himmler quoted in Andrew Roberts, *The Storm of War: A New History of the
    Second World War* (London: Penguin, 2009), p. 165. See the massive biography
    by Peter Longerich (trans. Jeremy Noakes and Lesley Sharpe), *Heinrich Himmler*
    (Oxford: Oxford University Press, 2012), which is still on my reading list.
48 Six quoted in Alex J. Kay, "'The Purpose of the Russian Campaign is the Deci-
    mation of the Slavic Population by Thirty Million': The Radicalization of Ger-
    man Food Policy in Early 1941," in Alex J. Kay, Jeff Rutherford, and David
    Stahel, eds., *Nazi Policy on the Eastern Front, 1941: Total War, Genocide, and Radi-
    calization* (Rochester, NY: University of Rochester Press, 2012), p. 113.
49 Ibid., p. 114. See also Alex J. Kay, *Exploitation, Resettlement, Mass Murder: Political
    and Economic Planning for German Occupation Policy in the Soviet Union, 1940–
    1941* (New York: Berghahn Books, 2011).
50 Roberts, *The Storm of War*, p. 557.
51 Stephen G. Fritz, *Ostkrieg: Hitler's War of Extermination in the East* (Lexington,
    KY: The University Press of Kentucky, 2010), pp. xxi–xxii. Fritz adds: "That it
    took the most murderous regime in Europe's history to defeat its most genocidal
    certainly tarnishes Western notions of a good war."
52 Roberts, *The Storm of War*, p. 605.
53 ". . . It cannot be reiterated enough that out of every five Germans killed in
    combat—that is, on the battlefield rather than in aerial bombing or through
    other means—four died on the Eastern Front. It is the central statistic of the
    Second World War." Ibid., p. 603.
54 Quoted in Milovan Djilas, *Wartime* (New York: Harvest, 1980), p. 73. Omer Bar-
    tov has written: "It was in the Soviet Union that the Wehrmacht's back was bro-
    ken long before the Western Allies landed in France, and even after June 1944
    it was in the East that the Germans continued to commit and lose far more
    men. . . . By the end of March 1945 the *Ostheer's* [German eastern front] cas-
    ualties mounted to 6,172,373 men, or double its original manpower on 22
    June 1941, a figure which constituted fully four-fifths of the [Germans'] total
    losses . . . on all fronts since the invasion of the Soviet Union." Bartov, *Hitler's
    Army*, pp. 29, 45. Alec Nove points out that more Russians died in the German
    siege of Leningrad alone (1941–1943) "than the total of British and Americans
    killed from all causes throughout the war." Nove, *Stalinism and After* (London:
    George Allen & Unwin, 1975), p. 93. See further discussion in Chapter 2, pp.
    124–126 and note 125.

55 Roberts, *The Storm of War*, p. 153.
56 Alexander Werth, *Russia at War, 1941–45* (New York: Carroll & Graf, 1999), p. 634.
57 Donald Bloxham, *Genocide, the World Wars and the Unweaving of Europe* (London: Vallentine Mitchell, 2008), p. 241.
58 See also the slim volume edited by Gerhard Hirschfeld: *The Policies of Genocide: Jews and Soviet Prisoners of War in Nazi Germany* (London: Allen & Unwin, 1986).
59 Merridale, *Ivan's War*, p. 149.
60 Anne Applebaum notes that "On any given day in the autumn of 1941, as many Soviet POWs died as did British and American POWs during the entire war." Applebaum, "The Worst of the Madness," *The New York Review of Books*, November 11, 2010, www.nybooks.com/articles/archives/2010/nov/11/worst-madness/.
61 Kay, "'The Purpose of the Russian Campaign,'" pp. 115–116.
62 Snyder, *Bloodlands*, p. 176.
63 Alexander Dallin, *German Rule in Russia, 1941–45: A Study of Occupation Policies* (2nd edn) (London: Macmillan, 1981), pp. 414–415; Omer Bartov, *The Eastern Front, 1941–45: German Troops and the Barbarization of Warfare* (Basingstoke: Macmillan, 1985), p. 110.
64 Quoted in Werth, *Russia at War*, pp. 635–636.
65 Merridale, *Ivan's War*, p. 290.
66 Göring quoted in Dallin, *German Rule in Russia*, p. 415.
67 Anne Applebaum, "The Worst of the Madness," *The New York Review of Books*, November 11, 2010, www.nybooks.com/articles/2010/11/11/worst-madness/.
68 On Allied complicity in these forced repatriations, see Nikolai Tolstoy, *Victims of Yalta: The Secret Betrayal of the Allies, 1944–1947* (London: Pegasus, 2013).
69 For a concise treatment linking historical prejudices against Roma with the widespread discrimination against them in contemporary Europe, see Michael Stewart, "The 'Gypsy Problem': An Invisible Genocide," in René Lemarchand, ed., *Forgotten Genocides: Oblivion, Denial, and Memory* (Philadelphia, PA: University of Pennsylvania Press, 2011), pp. 137–156.
70 Ironically, the Roma "were originally from North India and belonged to the Indo-Germanic speaking, or as Nazi racial anthropologists would have it, 'Aryan' people." Burleigh and Wippermann, *The Racial State*, p. 116.
71 See, e.g., Anna Porter, "Fascism: The Next Generation," *The Globe and Mail*, May 9, 2009; "Bottom of the Heap," *The Economist*, June 21, 2008.
72 Burleigh, *Ethics and Extermination*, p. 167.
73 Michael Zimmermann, "The National Socialist 'Solution of the Gypsy Question,'" in Ulrich Herbert, ed., *National Socialist Extermination Policies: Contemporary German Perspectives and Controversies* (New York: Berghahn Books, 2000), p. 194.
74 Sybil H. Milton, "'Gypsies' as Social Outsiders in Nazi Germany," in Gellately and Stoltzfus, eds, *Social Outsiders in Nazi Germany*, p. 222.
75 Friedländer, *The Years of Extermination*, p. 317.
76 Burleigh and Wippermann, *The Racial State*, p. 125.
77 Krylova quoted in Martin Holler, "Extending the Genocidal Program: Did Otto Ohlendorf Initiate the Systematic Extermination of Soviet 'Gypsies'?," in Alex J. Kay, Jeff Rutherford, and David Stahel, eds., *Nazi Policy on the Eastern Front, 1941: Total War, Genocide, and Radicalization* (Rochester, NY: Rochester University Press, 2012), p. 278. "After the shooting," writes Holler, "the male 'Gypsies' had to fill the mass grave with earth, before they were shot in the second pit.

Returning to the town of Smolensk, the Germans took with them the valuables and some clothes of the murdered victims. The exhumation of the dead bodies revealed that 176 persons were shot on April 24, 1942. One hundred forty-three of them—62 women, 29 men, 52 children—were identified . . . Among the adult victims were kolkhoz [collective farm] workers, educators, and three teachers" (p. 278).

78 Robert Jay Lifton, *The Nazi Doctors: Medical Killing and the Psychology of Genocide* (New York: Basic Books, 1986), p. 161 (the quoted passage is Lifton's paraphrase).

79 Milton, "'Gypsies' as Social Outsiders," p. 226.

80 Ian Hancock, "Responses to the Porrajmos: The Romani Holocaust," in Alan S. Rosenbaum, ed., *Is the Holocaust Unique? Perspectives on Comparative Genocide*, 3rd edn (Boulder, CO: Westview Press, 2009), p. 86.

81 Sybil Milton, "Holocaust: The Gypsies," in Samuel Totten *et al.*, eds., *Century of Genocide* (New York: Garland Publishing, 1997), p. 188.

82 Ibid., p. 92.

83 Hancock, "Responses to the Porrajmos."

84 Günter Grass, *Crabwalk*, trans. Krishna Winston (New York: Harvest, 2004); Jörg Friedrich, *Brandstätten* (Berlin: Propylaen, 2003).

85 Eric Langenbacher, "The Allies in World War II: The Anglo-American Bombardment of German Cities," in Adam Jones, ed., *Genocide, War Crimes and the West: History and Complicity* (London: Zed Books, 2004), p. 118. See also Hermann Knell's study of the lesser-known attack on Würzburg in March 1945, *To Destroy a City: Strategic Bombing and Its Human Consequences in World War II* (Cambridge, MA: Da Capo Press, 2003).

86 S.P. MacKenzie, "The Treatment of Prisoners in World War II," *Journal of Modern History*, 66: 3 (1994), p. 511.

87 Roberts, *The Storm of War*, p. 343.

88 Beevor, *Stalingrad*, p. 430.

89 Richard Bessel, *Germany 1945: From War to Peace* (New York: HarperPerennial, 2010), p. 388.

90 Martin K. Sorge, *The Other Price of Hitler's War: German Military and Civilian Losses Resulting from World War II* (Westport, CT: Greenwood Press, 1996), p. 89.

91 Douglas quoted in Adam Taylor, "The Forgotten Story of When the Germans Were the Refugees," *The Washington Post*, September 3, 2015, www.washington post.com/news/worldviews/wp/2015/09/03/the-forgotten-story-of-when-the-germans-were-the-refugees/. The best scholarly studies in English are Ulrich Merten, *Forgotten Voices: The Expulsion of the Germans from Eastern Europe after World War II* (New Brunswick, NJ: Transaction Publishers, 2012), and R.M. Douglas, *Orderly and Humane: The Expulsion of the Germans after the Second World War* (New Haven, CT: Yale University Press, 2012).

92 Roberts, *The Storm of War*, p. 562.

93 Russell cited in Alfred-Maurice de Zayas, *A Terrible Revenge: The Ethnic Cleansing of the East European Germans, 1944–1950* (New York: St. Martin's Press, 1994), p. 111.

94 De Zayas, *A Terrible Revenge*, p. 116.

CHAPTER 7

Cambodia and the Khmer Rouge

ORIGINS OF THE KHMER ROUGE

A prevalent view of Cambodia prior to the upheavals of the late 1960s and 1970s was of a "gentle land," with peaceful Buddhist authorities presiding over a free and relatively prosperous peasantry. This picture is far from false. Indeed, Cambodia was abundant in rice, and peasant landownership was comparatively common. But the stereotype overlooks a darker side of Cambodian history and culture: absolutism, a politics of vengeance, and a frequent recourse to torture. "Patterns of extreme violence against people defined as enemies, however arbitrarily, have very long roots in Cambodia," acknowledged historian Michael Vickery.[1] Anthropologist Alex Hinton pointed to "a Cambodian model of disproportionate revenge"—"a head for an eye," in the title of his seminal essay on the subject—which was well entrenched by the time the Khmer Rouge communists took power in 1975.[2]

This is not to say that "a tradition of violence" determined that the Khmer Rouge (KR) would rule. In fact, until relatively late in the process, the movement was a marginal presence. Neither, though, was the Khmer Rouge an outright aberration. Certainly, the KR's emphasis on concentrating power and wielding it in tyrannical fashion was in keeping with Cambodian tradition. "Absolutism . . . is a core element of authority and legitimacy in Cambodia," wrote David Roberts.[3] As for the supposedly pacific nature of Buddhism, the religion that overwhelmingly predominated in Cambodia, Vickery denounced it as "arrant nonsense." "That Buddhists may torture and massacre is no more astonishing than that the Inquisition burned people or that practicing Catholics and Protestants joined the Nazi SS."[4]

Another element of Cambodian history and politics is an aggressive nostalgia for past glories. Cambodia under the Angkor Empire, which peaked from the twelfth to the fourteenth centuries, was a powerful nation, incorporating sizable territories that today belong to neighbors. It extended to the South China Sea, and included southern regions of Vietnam as well as parts of present-day Laos, Thailand, and Burma. At the height of its power, forced laborers built the great temples of Angkor Wat, the world's largest religious complex. Ever since, including for the Khmer Rouge, Angkor Wat has served as Cambodia's national symbol.

Cambodian nationalists harked back constantly to these halcyon days, and advanced irredentist claims with varying degrees of seriousness. Most significantly, the rich lands of today's southern Vietnam were designated Kampuchea Krom, "Lower Cambodia" in nationalist discourse—though they have been part of Vietnam since at least 1840. This rivalry with Vietnam, and a messianic desire to reclaim "lost" Cambodian territories, fueled Khmer Rouge fanaticism. The government led by the avowedly anti-imperialist Communist Party of Cambodia (the official name of the KR) proved as xenophobic and expansionist as any regime in modern Asian history.

By the nineteenth century, Cambodia's imperial prowess was long dissipated, and the country easily fell under the sway of the French. On the pretext of creating a buffer between their Vietnamese territories, British-influenced Burma, and independent Siam (Thailand), the French established influence over the Court of King Norodom. The king, grandfather of Prince Norodom Sihanouk who would rule during the KR's early years, accepted protectorate status. He eventually became little more than a French vassal.

As elsewhere in their empire, France provoked nationalist sentiments in Cambodia—through economic exploitation and political subordination, but also through the efforts of French scholars who worked to "'recover' a history for Cambodia." This project bolstered "Khmer pride in their country's heritage," providing "the ideological foundation of the modern drive for an expression of an independent Khmer nation."[5]

Another French contribution to Khmer nationalism was the awarding of academic scholarships to Cambodians for study in Paris. In the 1950s, the French capital was likely the richest environment for revolutionary ferment anywhere in the world. The French Communist Party, which had led the resistance to Nazi occupation, emerged as a powerful presence in postwar politics. In earlier years, Paris had nurtured nationalists from the French colonies, including Vietnam's Ho Chi Minh. The Paris of the 1950s likewise provided a persecution-free environment in which revolutionaries from the Global South could meet and plot. Among the beneficiaries were most of the leaders of the future Khmer Rouge,[6] including:

- Saloth Sar, who subsequently took the name Pol Pot, "Brother Number One" in the party hierarchy, and became Prime Minister of Democratic Kampuchea during the KR's period in power;
- Khieu Samphan, later President of Democratic Kampuchea (DK);
- Son Sen, DK's deputy Prime Minister and Minister of Defense and Security;

- Ieng Sary, deputy Prime Minister in charge of foreign affairs during the DK period;
- his wife, Ieng (Khieu) Thirith, Minister of Social Action for the DK regime.[7]

In retrospect, Khmer Rouge fanaticism was fueled by some of the ideological currents of the time. The French Communist Party was in its high-Stalinist phase, supporting campaigns against "enemies of the people." Intellectuals like Frantz Fanon, another denizen of Paris at the time, espoused the view "that only violence and armed revolt could cleanse the minds of Third World peoples and rid them of their colonial mentalities."[8]

The 1950s and 1960s were a period of nationalist ferment throughout the Global South. The government of Prince Norodom Sihanouk was positioning itself as an anti-colonialist, politically-neutral force in Southeast Asia. Sihanouk was a leader of the Non-Aligned Movement that burst onto the world stage at the Bandung Conference in 1955.

Many returning students flocked to the Indochinese Communist Party, which united communist movements in Vietnam and Cambodia. Tensions soon developed between the two wings, however. Cambodians like Pol Pot felt they "had to

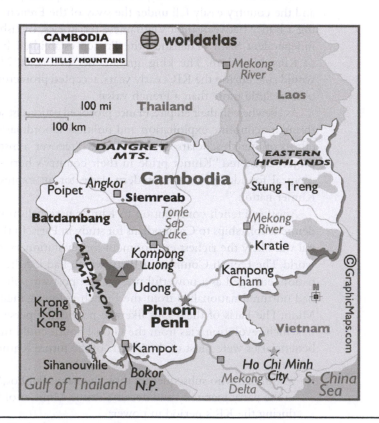

Map 7.1 Cambodia

Source: Map provided by WorldAtlas.com.

carry excrement for the Vietnamese," according to Khieu Thirith.[9] Following the 1954 Vietnamese victory over the French at Dien Bien Phu, and the signing of the Geneva Accords, the Vietnamese withdrew from Cambodia. As they did, they split the Cambodian party membership by transferring some one thousand cadres to Vietnam, leaving another one thousand in Cambodia—including Pol Pot and the future core leadership of the Khmer Rouge. This would have fateful consequences when returning cadres who had spent their formative period in Vietnam were targeted by the KR for extermination, together with all ethnic Vietnamese in Cambodia (or within reach on the other side of the border). In the case of Vietnamese remaining in Cambodia, the destruction was *total*.

In 1966, Sihanouk, whose police had been quietly implementing a campaign of "government murder and repression" against communists in the countryside,[10] launched a crackdown on members of the urban left whom he had not fully co-opted. Khieu Samphan and Hou Youn were forced underground. Not the least of the party's problems was its estrangement from Hanoi. The North Vietnamese regime chose to support the neutralist and anti-imperialist Sihanouk, rather than aid a rebellion by its Cambodian communist "brothers." Hanoi valued Sihanouk as a bulwark against US domination of Southeast Asia, and therefore as an ally in the Vietnamese national struggle. By contrast, Pol Pot's new Cambodian communist leadership considered Sihanouk a US lapdog. It decided to abandon political activity in the city for armed struggle in remote parts of the countryside, where the Khmer Rouge could nurture its revolution beyond Sihanouk's reach.

WAR AND REVOLUTION, 1970–1975

How did Cambodia's communists, politically marginal throughout the 1960s, manage to seize national power in 1975? The explanation, according to Cambodia specialist David Chandler, lies in a combination of "accidents, outside help, and external pressures. . . . Success, which came slowly, was contingent on events in South Vietnam, on Vietnamese communist guidance, on the disastrous policies followed by the United States, and on blunders made by successive Cambodian governments."[11]

After the US invasion of South Vietnam in 1965, conflict spilled into Cambodia. Supplies from the North Vietnamese government, destined for the guerrillas of the National Liberation Front in the south, moved down the "Ho Chi Minh Trail" through Laos and eastern Cambodia. US bombing of the trail, including areas inside Cambodia, pushed Vietnamese forces deeper into Cambodia, until they came to control significant territory in border areas. The Vietnamese, prioritizing their own liberation struggle, urged restraint on their Cambodian communist allies. But in 1970, as war spread across Cambodia, the extension of Vietnamese power provided a powerful boost for the Khmer Rouge, including vital training. In the early 1970s, the Vietnamese forces were inflicting far more damage on Cambodian government forces than was the KR.

The Vietnamese occupation of Cambodian border areas provoked two major responses from the United States, both central to what followed. First, in 1970, came US support for a coup against Prince Sihanouk, whom the US saw as a dangerous socialist and neutralist. He was replaced by Lon Nol, Sihanouk's former right-hand man and head of the armed forces, a religious fanatic who believed that "Buddhist teaching, racial virtues, and modern science made the Khmers invincible."[12] (Clearly, extreme chauvinism in Cambodia was not an invention of Democratic Kampuchea.) Lon Nol duly repaid his benefactors by inviting the US and South Vietnam to launch an invasion of Cambodian territory which lasted for three months.[13]

The significance of this action was outweighed by a second US response: the escalation, from 1970, of the saturation bombing campaign first launched against Vietnamese border sanctuaries in Cambodia in 1969. The campaign climaxed in 1973, a year that saw *a quarter of a million tons* of bombs dropped on Cambodia in just six months. This was one-and-a-half times as much high explosive as the US had unleashed on Japan during the whole of the Second World War—a country with which it was at least formally at war.

The impact was devastating. "We heard a terrifying noise which shook the ground," one villager recalled; "it was as if the earth trembled, rose up and opened beneath our feet. Enormous explosions lit up the sky like huge bolts of light-ning."[14] After bombing raids, "villagers who happened to be away from home returned to find nothing but dust and mud mixed with seared and bloody body parts."[15] Moreover, the assault effectively destroyed the agricultural base of an agrarian nation—more effectively, in fact, than Stalin had with his collectivization drive against the Soviet peasantry (Chapter 5). "The amount of acreage cultivated for rice dropped from six million at the beginning of the war to little more than one million at the end of the bombing campaign," wrote Elizabeth Becker.[16] Mal-nutrition was rampant, and mass starvation was kept at bay only by food aid from US charitable organizations. (This should be borne in mind when the aftermath of the Khmer Rouge victory is considered, below.)[17]

Probably genocidal in itself, the US bombing of a defenseless population was certainly "one of the worst aggressive onslaughts in modern warfare."[18] The best available estimate is that "between 1969 and 1973, more than half a million tons of munitions" had been unleashed on Cambodia.[19] In *The Pol Pot Regime* (1996), Kiernan estimated the death toll inflicted by the bombing at between 50,000 and 150,000. Others have cited much higher figures, including an estimate of 600,000 proposed by Christopher Hitchens in *The Trial of Henry Kissinger* (2001).[20]

The US bombing of the Cambodian rural population was also the most impor-tant factor in bringing the genocidal Khmer Rouge to power. "Civilian casualties in Cambodia drove an enraged populace into the arms of an insurgency that had enjoyed relatively little support until the bombing began, setting in motion ... the rapid rise of the Khmer Rouge, and ultimately the Cambodian genocide," wrote Owen and Kiernan.[21] One KR leader who defected, Chhit Do, eloquently cap-tured the political impact of the bombardment:

> Every time after there had been bombing, [the Khmer Rouge guerrillas] would take the people to see the craters, to see how big and deep the craters were,

to see how the earth had been gouged out and scorched. . . . The ordinary people . . . sometimes literally shit in their pants when the big bombs and shells came. . . . Their minds just froze up and they would wander around mute for three or four days. Terrified and half-crazy, the people were ready to believe what they were told. . . . That was what made it so easy for the Khmer Rouge to win the people over. . . . It was because of their dissatisfaction with the bombing that they kept on cooperating with the Khmer Rouge, joining up with the Khmer Rouge, sending their children off to go with them.[22]

"This is not to say that the Americans are responsible for the genocide in Cambodia," as social critic Michael Ignatieff noted. "It is to say that a society that has been pulverised by war is a society that is very susceptible to genocide."[23]

Under the Paris Peace Accords of 1973, Vietnamese forces left Cambodia, but the focus of military opposition to the Lon Nol regime had already shifted to the Khmer Rouge. Buoyed by Vietnamese arms and training, they were now a hardened force—at least a match for poorly motivated and half-starved government conscripts. The KR moved rapidly to besiege Phnom Penh and other cities. Meanwhile, in the areas of the countryside already under their control, they implemented the first stage of their distinctive—and destructive—revolutionary ideology.

A GENOCIDAL IDEOLOGY

In their jungle camps, the Khmer Rouge developed the philosophy that would guide their genocidal program and turn Cambodia "into our time's arguably most murderous, brutal, inhuman small country."[24] Let us consider the basic elements of this world view, and its consequences from 1975 to 1979:

- *Hatred of "enemies of the people."* Like many communist revolutionaries of the twentieth century—notably those in the USSR and China—the KR exhibited a visceral hatred of the revolution's enemies. As with Lenin–Stalin and Mao Zedong, too, "enemies" were loosely defined. They could be members of socioeconomic classes. The Khmer Rouge targeted the rich/bourgeoisie; professionals (including those who returned from abroad to help the new regime); "imperialist stooges" (collaborators with the US and its client regime in Phnom Penh); and the educated class. In effect, this swept up most urbanites. Enemies could also be designated on ethnic grounds. Just as Stalin waged genocide against the people of Ukraine and the Caucasus, so the Khmer Rouge exterminated ethnic Vietnamese, Chinese, Muslim Chams—in fact, almost every ethnic minority in Cambodia. (Even geographically–defined Khmers were targeted for annihilation, such as those from southern Vietnam or the "traitorous" Eastern Zone in 1978.) The enemy could also be religious believers seen to be out of step with the KR pseudo-religion that now ruled the roost.

Lastly, enemies could be purged on the basis of supposed subversion or betrayal of the revolution from within. Stalin's purges of the Soviet Communist Party (Chapter 5) would be matched and exceeded, relative to population and party membership, by the Khmer Rouge's attacks on internal enemies.

- *Xenophobia and messianic nationalism.* As noted, the KR—in tandem with other Cambodian nationalists—harked back to the Angkor Empire. As is standard with nationalism, territorial claims reflected the zenith of power in the nation's past. Pol Pot and his regime apparently believed in their ability to reclaim the "lost" Cambodian territories of Kampuchea Krom in southern Vietnam. Territorial ambitions were combined with a fear and hatred of ethnic Vietnamese, seen both as Cambodia's historical enemy and the betrayer of Cambodian communism. The desire was imputed to Vietnamese to conquer Cambodia and destroy its revolution—a paranoid vision that harmonized with the Khmer Rouge's narcissistic sense of Cambodia as "the prize other powers covet."[25]

Racism and xenophobia produced an annihilationist ideology that depicted Cambodia's ethnic Vietnamese minority as a deadly internal threat to the survival of the Khmer nation. Khmer Krom from the historically Cambodian territories of southern Vietnam were targeted with similar venom. Finally, the xenophobia led to repeated Cambodian invasions of Vietnamese territory in 1977 and 1978. These eventually sparked the Vietnamese invasion that overthrew the regime.

- *Peasantism, anti-urbanism, primitivism.* Like the Chinese communists, but unlike the Soviets, the Khmer Rouge gleaned most of their support from rural rather than urban elements. Peasants were the guardians of the true and pure Cambodia against alien, cosmopolitan city-dwellers. However, the Khmer Rouge vision of the peasantry was misguided from the first. As Ben Kiernan pointed out, the DK regime attacked the three foundations of peasant life: religion, land, and family. The KR rejected the peasants' attachment to Buddhist religion; imputed to peasants a desire for agricultural collectivization that was alien to Cambodia; revived the hated *corvée* (forced labor); and sought to destabilize and dismantle the family unit.

The primitivist dimension of Khmer Rouge ideology seems to have been influenced by the tribal peoples among whom KR leaders lived in Cambodia's eastern jungles. These people, in particular the Khmer Loeu (highland Khmer), provided indispensable refuge and sustenance for the party in its nascent period. "Pol Pot and Ieng Sary . . . claimed later to have been inspired by the spirit of people who had no private property, no markets, and no money. Their way of life and their means of production corresponded to the primitive communist phase of social evolution in Marxist thinking," and likely influenced the KR decision to abandon the market and the money economy.[26] Soldiers from the highland tribes played an important role in the KR's final campaign to crush the Lon Nol regime, but increasingly fell victim to the genocide against ethnic minorities under DK (see below).[27]

A bizarre aspect of KR primitivism was the conviction that no natural challenge was insuperable, no scientific accomplishment unattainable, if peasant energies and know-how were tapped. "The young are learning their science from the workers and peasants, who are the sources of all knowledge," declared Radio Phnom Penh.[28] "Formerly to be a pilot required a high school education—twelve to fourteen years," declared another classic piece of propaganda. "Nowadays, it's clear that political consciousness is the decisive factor. . . . As for radar, we can learn how to handle it after studying for a couple of months."[29] Not surprisingly, the Khmer Rouge air force never amounted to much.

In Mao Zedong's "Great Leap Forward," an almost identical mentality had produced catastrophic outcomes (see Chapter 5). Undeterred, the DK regime announced that an even more impressive *"Super* Great Leap Forward" would be initiated in Cambodia. Like Mao's experiment, the Super Great Leap would be about self-sufficiency. Foreign help was neither desirable nor required, and even the Chinese model was dismissed. Indeed, the country would be all but sealed off from the outside world.[30]

- *Purity, discipline, militarism.* Like the Nazis, the Khmer Rouge expressed their racism through an emphasis on racial purity. Like the Soviets and Chinese, purity was also defined by class origin, and by an unswerving loyalty to revolutionary principle and practice. Self-discipline was critical. It demonstrated revolutionary ardor and self-sacrifice. In most revolutions of Left and Right, rigorous discipline has spawned an ideology of chaste sexuality— though this was not necessarily realized in practice. There is little question that the Khmer Rouge presided over a regime of "totalitarian puritanism"[31] perhaps without equal in the twentieth century. Among other things, "any sex before marriage was punishable by death in many cooperatives and zones."[32]

Discipline among revolutionaries also buttresses the inevitable military confrontation with the counter-revolution. Ben Kiernan and Chanthou Boua consider militarism to be *the* defining feature of Khmer Rouge rule, reflected in "the forced evacuation of the cities, the coercion of the population into economic programmes organized with military discipline, the heavy reliance on the armed forces rather than civilian cadres for administration, and the almost total absence of political education or attempts to explain administrative decisions in a way that would win the psychological acceptance of the people affected by them."[33]

Some of the ironies and contradictions of Khmer Rouge ideology should be noted. Despite their idealization of the peasants, no senior Khmer Rouge leader was of peasant origin. Virtually all were city-bred intellectuals. Pol Pot came from the countryside, but from a prosperous family with ties to the Royal Court in Phnom Penh. As noted earlier, the core leadership belonged to a small, privileged intellectual class able to study overseas on government scholarships. These racist chauvinists, opposed to any foreign "interference" including aid, were by background among the most "cosmopolitan" Cambodians in history. The genocide they inflicted on intellectuals and urban populations in general, as well as on hundreds of thousands of peasants, was hypocritical as well as indelibly brutal.

A POLICY OF "URBICIDE," 1975

In Chapter 1 (Box 1.6), we explored the phenomenon of "urbicide," the destruction of urban areas and the extermination and/or expulsions of their populations, as a genocidal strategy. There are few more vivid instances than the policy imposed by the Khmer Rouge on Phnom Penh and other cities in March 1975. "For most of the people in Cambodia's towns what happened during those few days literally overturned their lives."[34]

Within hours of arriving in the capital, the Khmer Rouge set about rounding up its two million residents and deporting them to the countryside. Bedraggled caravans of deportees headed back to their old life (in the case of refugees from rural areas) or to a new one of repression and privation (for urbanites). Similar scenes occurred in other population centers nationwide. Without damage to a single building, whole cities were destroyed.

To residents, the Khmer Rouge justified the deportations on the grounds that the Americans were planning bombing attacks on Cambodian cities. (Given recent history, this was not an inconceivable prospect.) To an international audience—on the rare occasions when KR leaders bothered to provide rationales—the urbicide was depicted as a humanitarian act. With the end of the US aid that had fed swollen city populations, albeit inadequately, "the population had to go where the food was," in the words of Ieng Sary.[35] But this excuse faltered in light of the KR's obstinate emphasis on self-sufficiency. Most revealingly, foreign donations of food and other aid went unsolicited, and were rejected when offered. And there is no doubting the murderous destructiveness of the forced marches themselves, in which "the Khmer Rouge intentionally killed and drove to death many tens of thousands of people, perhaps as many as 400,000 people."[36]

After the urbicide, and for the remainder of the DK period, Phnom Penh and other cities remained ghost towns. They were inhabited by only a skeleton crew of KR leaders, cadres, and support staff. The countryside thus served as the backdrop for the Khmer Rouge assault on Cambodia's culture and people.

"BASE PEOPLE" VS. "NEW PEOPLE"

The peasantry, the base of Khmer Rouge support, were depicted as "base" people *(neak moultanh)*. Deported city-folk were "new" people *(neak thmey)*, late arrivals to the revolution. In a sense, though, all of Cambodia was new and revolutionary in the Khmer Rouge conception. The year 1975 was declared "Year Zero"—a term that evokes the nihilistic core of KR policies.

The reception that awaited new people varied significantly, in ways that decisively affected their survival chances. Some reports attested to a reasonably friendly welcome from peasants. In other cases, the peasants—who had suffered through the savage US bombing campaign and the violence and upheaval of civil war—felt the newcomers had received a just comeuppance. This feeling was bolstered by the preferential treatment the base people received from most KR authorities. Srey Pich Chnay, a Cambodian former urbanite, described his experiences to Kiernan and Boua in 1979:

> The Khmer Rouge treated the peasants as a separate group, distributing more food to them than to the city people, and assigning them easier tasks (usually around the village), whereas the city people almost always worked in the fields. Sometimes the peasants, as well as the Khmer Rouge themselves, would say to the newcomers, "You used to be happy and prosperous. Now it's our turn."[37]

The memoir of Loung Ung, who was a young girl in the KR period, conveyed the tension of this confrontation between different worlds, and the experience, unfamiliar to an urbanite, of finding herself despised:

> The new people are considered the lowest in the village structure. They have no freedom of speech, and must obey the other classes. The new people . . . cannot farm like the rural people. They are suspected of having no allegiance to the Angkar [i.e., the KR leadership] and must be kept under an ever-watchful eye for signs of rebellion. They have led corrupt lives and must be trained to be productive workers. To instill a sense of loyalty . . . and break what the Khmer Rouge views as an inadequate urban work ethic, the new people are given the hardest work and the longest hours.[38]

There is the flavor here of *subaltern genocide*, a "genocide by the oppressed" against those seen as oppressors, and indeed the anthropologist and Cambodia specialist Alex Hinton has explored the KR period in these terms.[39] Michael Vickery argued that the DK period was characterized *above all* by the revolutionary terror of the peasantry against urbanites and the intellectual/professional classes: "It is certainly safe to assume that [KR leaders] did not foresee, let alone plan, the unsavory developments of 1975–79. *They were petty-bourgeois radicals overcome by peasant romanticism.*"[40]

However, there are difficulties with this framing. One, as Kiernan has pointed out, is that Vickery's informants were predominantly non-peasants, poorly placed to describe the dynamics of a peasant revolution. Another is that, as we have seen, power was centralized in a leadership that was overwhelmingly urban and intellectual. Even at the regional and local level, where KR cadres with a peasant background were more likely to hold sway, there is little evidence that their policies *responded* to a groundswell of peasant resentment. Rather, they reflected instructions and frameworks supplied by the center, with subaltern animosities channeled into genocidal duties. "By 1977," wrote Kiernan, "the DK system was so tightly organized and controlled that little spontaneous peasant activity was possible,"[41] but there was no shortage of peasant involvement—and eager, virulently hostile involvement too—in the genocide against designated class enemies.

CAMBODIA'S HOLOCAUST, 1975–1979

> Our brothers and sisters of all categories, including workers, peasants, soldiers, and revolutionary cadres have worked around the clock with soaring enthusiasm, paying no attention to the time or to their fatigue; they have worked in a cheerful atmosphere of revolutionary optimism.
>
> Radio Phnom Penh broadcast under the KR

> There were no laws. If they wanted us to walk, we walked; to sit, we sat; to eat, we ate. And still they killed us. It was just that if they wanted to kill us, they would take us off and kill us.
>
> Cham villager interviewed by Ben Kiernan

In Cambodia between 1975 and 1978, the KR's genocidal ideology found full expression. The result was one of the worst genocides, relative to population, in recorded history. In less than four years—mostly in the final two—mass killing swept the Cambodian population. In part it resulted from direct KR murders of anyone perceived as an enemy. Internal purges reached a crescendo in 1977–1978, claiming hundreds of thousands of lives. Even more significant, though, were the indirect killings through privation, disease, and ultimately famine. These swelled the death toll to an estimated 1.7 to 1.9 million, out of a population estimated at just under eight million in April 1975. Between 21 and 24 percent of the entire Cambodian population died in the short period under discussion.[42]

Most scholars accept that "complex regional and temporal variations" were evident under the KR.[43] Temporally, life in many regions appears to have been spartan but tolerable for most of the first two years of KR rule. State terror had yet to descend with full force. Thousands of executions certainly accompanied the forced evacuations of Phnom Penh and other cities, and more took place in the countryside, but there are also accounts of moderate and reasonable Khmer Rouge cadres.

Then things changed. "Most survivors of DK agree that living conditions (that is, rations, working hours, disruptions to family life, and the use of terror) deteriorated sharply in 1977." Chandler pointed to three reasons for the shift: "the regime's insistence on meeting impossible agricultural goals at a breakneck pace"; growing leadership paranoia about "plots"; and, further fueling that paranoia, the mounting conflict with Vietnam.[44] The most exterminatory period was probably the final one: in 1978, prior to Vietnam's successful invasion in December. The repression visited upon the Eastern Zone over the preceding months had turned it into a graveyard, with up to a quarter of a million people killed.[45]

The extent of regional variation in Democratic Kampuchea is one of the most hotly debated aspects of the KR regime. Michael Vickery has argued that "almost no two regions were alike with respect to conditions of life":

> The Southwestern and Eastern Zones, the most important centers of pre-1970 communist activity, were the best organized and most consistently administered, with the East, until its destruction in 1978, also providing the more

favorable conditions of life, in particular for "new" people. In contrast, the West, the Northwest, except for [the region of] Damban 3, and most of the North–Center, were considered "bad" areas, where food was often short, cadres arbitrary and murderous, and policy rationales entirely beyond the ken of the general populace.[46]

Other scholars, however, emphasize the "unchanging character" and "highly centralized control" that marked KR rule.[47] Central direction was certainly evident in the establishment and operation of three key genocidal institutions: the forced-labor system, the mass executions, and the internal purge.

BOX 7.1 ONE WOMAN'S STORY: DENISE AFFONÇO

The world of Denise Affonço's Cambodian childhood was one of comfort and privilege. She was born to a Vietnamese mother and a French father, of Indian-Portuguese descent, who served as the private tutor to King Sihanouk until his untimely death when Denise was twelve. Money soon ran short, but her mother made sure the family never experienced true privation. "I still admire my mother's heroism," Denise wrote in her memoir, *To the End of Hell*.[48] "Maybe it was her example that, twenty years later, gave me the moral strength to fight and survive in the hell of the Cambodian forests."

Denise married an ethnic-Chinese businessman, Phou Teang Seng, who frustrated her by singing the praises of Mao Zedong and the Chinese Communist revolution. "That said, we got on well if we avoided politics." Again living in comparative luxury—"our life was a long tranquil river"—she bore three children, of whom two survived: Jean-Jacques and Jeannie.

In early 1975, Cambodia's civil war ground to its bloody conclusion. The capital, Phnom Penh, was besieged by the Khmer Rouge. The French embassy began arranging evacuation flights for the country's nationals. They would not, however, pay for a ticket for Denise's husband and his family. Unable to afford the cost themselves, Denise decided to stay on, comforting herself with the thought "that life will surely return to normal."

An initial euphoria greeted the arrival of the Khmer Rouge in Phnom Penh on April 17, 1975. But almost immediately, rebel troops began fanning out across the city, commanding residents: "You must evacuate the town . . . just for two or three days . . . as Angkar wants you to be safe from the American air raids." Who or what is Angkar? wondered Denise. She learned when she herself, together with her family, was swept up in the "urbicide" of the capital and the mass expulsions to the countryside: "Three million people thrown onto the streets overnight . . . walking towards the unknown; yes, the complete unknown, and this uncertainty is very difficult to bear."

At the first camp to which Denise and her family were assigned, she was indoctrinated in the Khmer Rouge's new order—above all, the need to serve and worship Angkar, the quasi-divine authority that was to replace all traditional spiritual and family allegiances. She learned the "ten commandments" of the new religion, including:

- Obey Angkar whatever the circumstances.
- It is forbidden to show feelings; joy or sadness.
- It is forbidden to be nostalgic about the past—the spirit must not *vivoat* (stray).
- It is forbidden to beat children, as from now on they are the children of Angkar.

Like all the other urban deportees, Denise was shocked and flummoxed by her new and burdensome work in the fields. "How do you walk barefoot, on ploughed earth, baked and hardened by the sun, when you aren't used to it? . . . The heartless villagers mock me viciously: 'Look how those townies walk!' " They, the Khmer Rouge-designated "Old People" (*neak chak*), received double or more the food rations of the "New People" (*neak thmey*) forced out of the cities. "Within a few weeks both the young and old lose several kilos. The children no longer have any vitality, no inclination to play or to laugh." The food situation only worsened. "At the age of thirty-one, I've suddenly become an old woman. I'm completely dried up."

In July 1975, Denise's husband, whom she had frequently cautioned for "talk[ing] far too much," was taken away by the Khmer Rouge for "reeducation." She never saw him again.

The following month, Denise and other Phnom Penh deportees were moved to a new camp, where she was put to work in the rice paddies. She was tormented by hunger, overwork, and endless leeches. But she managed to devise strategies to keep complete starvation at bay. Threshing rice allowed her to collect the nutrient-rich husks. And there was fishing: "tadpoles, little freshwater crabs, small fish, snails, sometimes little water-snakes and always more leeches. Leaving those aside, the rest can all be eaten; the smallest shrimp is a source of protein." Increasingly, she realized that the brutal conditions were part of the Khmer Rouge plan: "Angkar wants to see us all die: one after the other, of exhaustion, hunger and sickness . . . It is a gentle death sentence which costs nothing."

At her next and final destination, the "village" of Loti-Batran, she found "not even a straw hut." Among all her other worries, Denise noted that her son, Jean-Jacques, was slipping from her grasp. "I no longer have any authority over [him] . . . he has no need of me and I none of him. It isn't me who feeds him, but Angkar . . ." Nonetheless, Jean-Jacques retained enough of a sense of fealty to steal over occasionally from his separate camp with a little extra food for his mother, sister, and in-laws.

"All our emotions must be suppressed deep inside ourselves. We have become robots, the living dead." Then the real dying began: "Death touches every family. In the evening, you can hear the moans and suffering cries of the sick. In the morning, out come one or two corpses from the huts." In August 1976, Denise's sister-in-law, Li, expired from hunger. And then her daughter, Jeannie, died—agonizingly slowly—as Denise could only offer words of comfort. It was an "unbearable torture."

Yet somehow she persevered. "I say over again like a refrain: 'Denise, don't die, stay alive to be a witness to all these atrocities; the world must know what's happening here . . . You must do this for your children and for the loved ones you've lost . . .'" She stole, she begged, she cajoled, as around her the Khmer Rouge's purge mania metastasized, especially against male heads of household: "those few men who have survived previous purges all disappear in their turn." Only now did she learn for certain that her husband had been killed: her overseers told her mockingly that a dyke she and other women were laboring at would be dubbed the "Widows' Dyke." And she had to applaud the announcement—or risk joining the ranks of the murdered.

She hoped against hope for help to arrive "from the outside . . . is there, somewhere in the world, someone who knows what we are going through?" Her deliverance arrived in the form of the Vietnamese invasion of December 1978, which sent the Khmer Rouge fleeing to bases along the Thai border. She was reunited with her last surviving child: "I'm happy, my son is still here with me, skeletal, but a survivor . . . the Good Lord has heard my prayers, He has not abandoned us." Her strength returned under the care of Vietnamese doctors, and with her language skills, she was able to establish herself as a translator for several months. She went on to testify at the genocide trials-in-absentia of key Khmer Rouge figures, held under the Vietnamese proxy government in 1979. "I'm happy to relate the suffering that I've endured for four years, naming all the loved ones I've lost."

Denise's encounters with foreign journalists led to media coverage in France, and the French government agreed to receive them. In November 1979, Denise left Cambodia. After intensive study of shorthand, she secured a low-grade secretarial post in the Ministry of Foreign Affairs. It was a "difficult" life, but "nothing compared to the hell that I have lived through." She watched with pride as Jean-Jacques struggled to make up for his missing years of schooling. "He succeeds, little by little, in catching up . . . Fighting against all the odds, just as he fought in the camps, he has managed today to make himself a little place in the sun."

- *Forced labor* imposed a work regime that was unprecedented in modern Cambodia. Both base people and new people arose before dawn and were allowed to rest only after dark.[49] Food was distributed exclusively in communal kitchens, and after the 1975–1976 interlude there was almost never enough. What could be harvested was mostly confiscated by KR cadres. The population could not buy extra supplies: money and markets were outlawed. They could not supplement rations with produce from their own plots, since private property was banned. They could not engage—legally, at least—in traditional foraging for alternative food sources. Any attempt to do so was seen as "sabotaging" the work effort, and was severely punished. They could not even draw upon networks of family solidarity and sharing. Although the KR never banned the family per se, they invigilated and eroded it by various means.[50]

  Those who fell sick from overwork and malnutrition, or from the malaria that spread across Cambodia when the KR decided to refuse imports of pesticide, had little hope of treatment. Medicine was scarce, and usually reserved for the KR faithful. In addition, former urban residents from the Southwestern Zone, one of six main administrative zones in the DK, were again relocated to the Northwestern Zone. Some 800,000 people were dumped in the northwest with desperately inadequate provisions. Perhaps 200,000 died of starvation, or in the mass killings that descended in 1978 when cadres imported from the Southwestern Zone imposed a new round of purges (described below).

- *Mass executions.* These were conducted against "class enemies," on the one hand, and ethnic minorities on the other. Suspect from the start, "new people" were the most likely Khmer victims of such atrocities. Frequently, entire families would be targeted. "The Khmer Rouge actually had a saying . . . which encouraged such slaughter: 'To dig up grass, one must also dig up the roots' (*chik smav trauv chik teangreus*). . . . This phrase meant that cadres 'were supposed to "dig up" the entire family of an enemy—husband, wife, kids, sometimes from the grandparents down—so that none remained . . . to kill off the entire line at once so that none of them would be left to seek revenge later, in turn.'"[51] A witness, Bunhaeng Ung, described one such execution:

  > Loudspeakers blared revolutionary songs and music at full volume. A young girl was seized and raped. Others were led to the pits where they were slaughtered like animals by striking the backs of their skulls with hoes or lengths of bamboo. Young children and babies were held by the legs, their heads smashed against palm trees and their broken bodies flung beside their dying mothers in the death pits. Some children were thrown in the air and bayoneted while music drowned their screams. . . . At the place of execution nothing was hidden. The bodies lay in open pits, rotting under the sun and monsoon rains.[52]

  These were the "killing fields" made infamous by the 1985 film of the same name (Box 7.2). How many died in such executions is uncertain, but it was doubtless in the hundreds of thousands.

- *Violent internal purges* were a feature of KR insurgent politics well before the revolutionary victory. But after Democratic Kampuchea was established, the leadership's paranoia increased, and the zeal for purges with it. Pol Pot declared before a party audience in 1976 that "a sickness [exists] inside the party": "As our socialist revolution advances . . . seeping more strongly into every corner of the party, the army and among the people, we can locate the ugly microbes."[53] The language was strikingly similar to that employed by Stalin's henchmen against "enemies of the people" in the 1930s.

During the DK period, two major regional purges occurred. Both were carried out by Ta Mok, nicknamed "The Butcher" for his efforts. The first, as noted above, occurred in 1977–1978 in the Northwestern Zone. The second, more of a "conventional military suppression campaign,"[54] was launched in May 1978 against the sensitive Eastern Zone bordering Vietnam. The east, "the heartland of Khmer communism," was the best-administered zone in the country; but the Phnom Penh authorities viewed its residents and cadres as "Khmer bodies with Vietnamese minds."[55] The campaign pushed the Eastern Zone into open rebellion against the center, and finally into the arms of Vietnam. Eastern Zone

Figure 7.1 A cell in the Tuol Sleng S-21 detention and torture center in Phnom Penh, Cambodia. When Vietnamese forces liberated Phnom Penh early in 1979, they discovered days-old corpses still shackled to this and other bedframes in the facility—the last victims of S-21.

Source: Author's photo, May 2009.

Figure 7.2 Victims of Khmer Rouge purges, after incarceration and interrogation at Tuol Sleng and other centers, were executed in the "killing fields," such as this one at Cheung Ek outside Phnom Penh. They are now key memorial sites of the Cambodian genocide.

Source: Author's photo, May 2009.

rebels would give a "Cambodian face" to the Vietnamese invasion at the end of the year, and to the People's Republic of Kampuchea which it established.

Tens of thousands of victims of these and other purges passed through KR centers established for interrogation, torture, and execution. The most notorious was Tuol Sleng in the capital, codenamed "S-21," where an estimated 14,000 prisoners were incarcerated during the KR's reign. Only *ten* are known to have survived.[56] Now a Museum of Genocide in Phnom Penh, Tuol Sleng was one of many such centers across Democratic Kampuchea (see Figures 7.1, 7.5, 7.6, and the photo essay, photos 10 and 16).

As in Mao's China and Stalin's USSR, the purges fed on themselves, and undermined the capacity of the revolution to resist its enemies. Just as Stalin's purges of the Soviet military and bureaucracy increased the country's vulnerability to Nazi invasion, the Khmer Rouge killing sprees paved the way for Vietnam's rapid conquest of Cambodia in 1978.

GENOCIDE AGAINST BUDDHISTS AND ETHNIC MINORITIES

Early commentaries on Khmer Rouge atrocities emphasized the targeting of class and political enemies. Subsequent scholarship, especially by Ben Kiernan, has revealed the extent to which the KR also engaged in genocidal targeting of religious groups and ethnic minorities.

Cambodian Buddhism suffered immensely under the genocide: "the destruction was nearly complete, with more devastating consequences for Cambodia than the Chinese attack on Buddhism had had for Tibet" (Chapter 5).[57] Religious institutions were emptied, often obliterated. Monks were sent to the countryside or executed. "Of the sixty thousand Buddhist monks, only three thousand were found alive after the Khmer Rouge reign; the rest had either been massacred or succumbed to hard labor, disease, or torture."[58]

A patchwork of ethnic minorities, together constituting about 15 percent of the population, was exposed to atrocities and extermination. Local Vietnamese were most virulently targeted. Kiernan offers the stunning estimate that *fully 100 percent of ethnic Vietnamese perished under the Khmer Rouge*.[59] The Muslim Chams were despised for their religion as well as their ethnicity. "Their religion was banned, their schools closed, their leaders massacred, their villages razed and dispersed."[60] Over one-third of the 250,000 Chams alive in April 1975 perished under DK.[61]

As for Cambodia's Chinese population, it was concentrated in the cities, and it is sometimes hard to distinguish repressive action based on racial hatred from repression against the urbanite "new people." Regardless, in DK this group "suffered the worst disaster ever to befall any ethnic Chinese community in Southeast Asia."[62] Only half the Chinese population of 430,000 at the outset of Khmer Rouge rule survived to see its end.

The grim tale of minority suffering under the Khmer Rouge does not end there. "The Thai minority of 20,000 was reportedly reduced to about 8,000. Only 800 families survived of the 1,800 families of the Lao ethnic minority. Of the 2,000 members of the Kola minority, 'no trace . . . has been found.'"[63]

BOX 7.2 CAMBODIA: KILLING FIELDS AND *THE KILLING FIELDS*

Figure 7.3 Dith Pran (left), the journalist whose odyssey under the Khmer Rouge inspired the 1984 film *The Killing Fields*, poses with Haing S. Ngor, himself a survivor of the Cambodian genocide, who won an Oscar for his performance as Dith in the film. The two were photographed on a joint return to Phnom Penh in 1986.

Source: Photo by Steve McCurry/Magnum Photos.

In the early 1980s, Cambodia/Kampuchea struck most Westerners, if it struck them at all, as a somehow undifferentiated humanitarian crisis. *The Killing Fields*, a British film directed by Roland Joffe and released in 1984, changed all that. "In a matter of months," wrote Elizabeth Becker, *"The Killing Fields* catapulted Cambodia from Cold War politics to mass culture. Black-pajamaed Khmer Rouge joined the brown-shirted Nazis as recognizable villains of the twentieth century. The term killing fields became part of the American vocabulary."[64] It remains so today, as a generic descriptor for the mass gravesites that symbolize atrocity zones worldwide.

The Killing Fields is arguably the greatest dramatic film about genocide, though votes for *Schindler's List* and *Son of Saul* will be counted. This is despite the fact that the iconic scenes of suffering at the hands of Khmer Rouge *génocidaires* occupy only half an hour or so of a movie that pushes two-and-a-half hours, straddling conventional war-movie and press-movie genres as well. *The Killing Fields* tells the story of Dith Pran (pictured at left in Figure 7.3), who worked as an assistant and translator for *New York Times* journalist Sydney Schanberg during and after the fall of Phnom Penh to the Khmer Rouge in April 1975. Sending his family to safety in the US, Dith stayed behind. On one occasion shortly after, he risked his life to save Schanberg's and that of two cohorts, including Al Rockoff (see Figure 7.4), threatened with execution by Khmer Rouge cadres. When Schanberg and other foreigners took refuge in the French embassy, Dith was forced to leave, and began a journey to the heart of the "killing fields." (It was Dith, in fact, who coined that iconic term to describe his ordeal.)[65]

The Killing Fields follows Dith as he is drafted as a forced laborer, reduced to a filthy, malnourished state, and forced to witness the depravities of the Khmer Rouge regime up close. Dith's trajectory was depicted by Haing S. Ngor (at right in Figure 7.3)—himself a Cambodian refugee and genocide survivor. Ngor's performance would win him an Academy Award for Best Supporting Actor; he told his personal story of suffering and survival in a memoir, *A Cambodian Odyssey* (1987). Tragically, Ngor, who had endured four years under the Khmer Rouge, was killed in a street hold-up in Los Angeles in February 1996. For his part, after his successful escape from Cambodia and reunion with Schanberg, Dith Pran rejoined the staff of *The New York Times* as a photographer, and became a regular speaker on genocide prevention. He died of pancreatic cancer in March 2008.

In 2009, on my first visit to Phnom Penh, I was introduced to none other than Al Rockoff, the US photojournalist played by John Malkovich in *The Killing Fields*. Over a couple of drinks, Rockoff (see Figure 7.4) derided the movie for portraying him as failing to "fix" a passport image for Dith Pran, thus guaranteeing Dith's

Figure 7.4 Al Rockoff, *Killing Fields* photojournalist (John Malkovich's character), at a Mexican cantina in Phnom Penh, Cambodia.

Source: Author's photo, May 2009.

expulsion from the French embassy. It never happened, Rockoff insisted; he would never be so amateurish. But he allowed that the heart-stopping scene in which he, Schanberg, British journalist Jon Swain, and Dith are detained and nearly gunned down by the Khmer Rouge, as Dith desperately cajoles and pleads with their captors, depicted the events accurately. It was one of several occasions during the Indochina wars when Rockoff nearly died prematurely. He is working on a photo project documenting Cambodian history since 1970, and in 2013 testified before the Extraordinary Chambers in the Courts of Cambodia (the country's genocide tribunal) about the atrocities he had witnessed during the fall of Phnom Penh and its occupation and emptying by the Khmer Rouge.[66]

In his memoir, Haing Ngor wrote that until *The Killing Fields* came out, "relatively few people knew what had happened in Cambodia during the Khmer Rouge years—intellectuals and Asia experts had, maybe, but not the general public. The film put the story of those years in terms that everybody could understand."[67] As such, it remains a classic instance of a cultural product becoming so intertwined with the events it describes that it can be difficult for the layperson to separate them. How many people, one wonders, have mistaken the survivor and original inspiration Dith Pran for Haing Ngor, the survivor who immortalized him on film?

AFTERMATH: POLITICS AND THE QUEST FOR JUSTICE

On December 25, 1978, 150,000 Vietnamese soldiers, accompanied by 15,000 Cambodian rebels and air support, crossed the border of Democratic Kampuchea and seized Phnom Penh in two weeks. The Khmer Rouge leadership fled to sanctuaries in western Cambodia and across the border in Thailand.[68] It used these for the next decade-and-a-half as it fought to return to power at the head of a coalition of forces opposed to Vietnamese occupation. (Prince Sihanouk, who had spent most of the DK years under *de facto* house arrest in Phnom Penh, served as figurehead for the coalition from 1982.) Meanwhile, former KR leaders, the rebels from the Eastern Zone, were appointed as Vietnamese surrogates to run the new People's Republic of Kampuchea (PRK). While Heng Samrin was appointed president, real power eventually fell into the hands of his former subordinate in the Eastern Zone, Hun Sen.

Throughout the 1980s, in one of the twentieth century's "more depressing episodes of diplomacy,"[69] the Western world moved from branding the Khmer Rouge as communist monsters to embracing them as Cambodia's legitimate representatives. At the United Nations, the US led a push to grant Cambodia's General Assembly seat to the anti-Vietnamese coalition dominated by the Khmer Rouge. Why this Orwellian flip-flop? US hostility to Vietnam was still pronounced after the US defeat of 1975. An enemy of Vietnam was America's friend, regardless of its sanguinary past. In the words of US Secretary of State Henry Kissinger, speaking to the Thai Foreign Minister Chatichai Choonhavan a few months after the Khmer Rouge takeover:

> We are aware that the biggest threat to Southeast Asia at the present time is North Vietnam . . . Cambodia [is] a barrier to the Vietnamese. . . . You should . . . tell the Cambodians that we will be friends with them. They are murderous thugs, but we won't let that stand in our way.[70]

Thus one witnessed the anomalous sight, throughout the 1980s, of genocidal communists receiving some of their firmest backing from Washington, DC. China was also an important player—as it had been throughout the Khmer Rouge years in power, despite KR pledges to make Cambodia "self-sufficient."

In October 1991, with the Cold War at an end, the Comprehensive Political Settlement of the Cambodian Conflict was signed in Paris. Vietnamese forces had left the country in 1989. The United Nations stepped in to supervise the peace process. It launched UNTAC, the UN Transitional Authority in Cambodia, "the

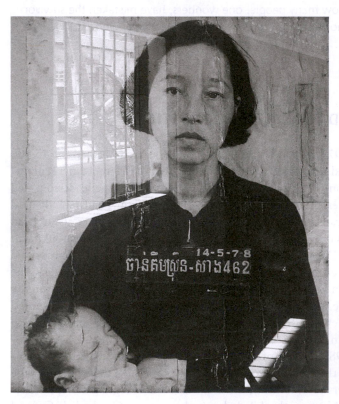

Figures 7.5 and 7.6 Images of victims of the Tuol Sleng torture and execution center in Phnom Penh (Figure 7.1), today a Museum of Genocide. The Khmer Rouge carefully photographed and catalogued their prisoners; today, these images serve as valuable documentation of the Cambodian genocide.

Sources: (woman/infant) Adapter-Plug/Creative Commons/Flickr; (boy) Museo del Comunismo (www.museodelcomunismo.it).

single most ambitious field operation in [UN] history" to that point.[71] However, the path to national elections in 1993 was fraught with difficulties. The Khmer Rouge boycotted the vote, and stepped up military attacks.

Ultimately, in May 1993, elections were held, but they did not produce the results Hun Sen desired. Voters gave a plurality of votes to Prince Ranariddh, son of Norodom Sihanouk. Hun Sen, the "great survivor of Cambodian politics,"[72] then used his control over Cambodia's key institutions to strong-arm Ranariddh into accepting a coalition government. By 1997, Hun Sen had tired of the arrangement. He launched what was in essence a *coup d'état*, re-establishing himself as the supreme authority. The absolutist strain in Cambodian politics was proving difficult to shake, especially against a backdrop of economic and social breakdown.

The campaign to bring surviving Khmer Rouge leaders to justice proceeded, albeit haltingly.[73] The project was marginalized throughout the 1980s by US and communist Chinese opposition. The 1998 death of Pol Pot in his jungle exile, apparently from natural causes, further hampered the process, as did messy wrangling between the United Nations and the Cambodian government over the nature and composition of any tribunal. In June 2003, the two parties finally reached agreement. The Cambodian tribunal would include "international jurists, lawyers and judges [who] will occupy key roles as the co-prosecutor, co-investigating judge and two out of five trial court judges, and must be a party to conviction or exoneration of any accused."[74] This "mixed tribunal" constituted an interesting new legal institution to try genocide cases.

It was this tribunal, based only a short distance from the Cheung Ek "killing fields" site outside Phnom Penh, that was functioning when I visited in May 2009 (see the further discussion of the "mixed tribunals" in Chapter 15). The first of five leadership figures to be tried (though, in this case, for crimes against humanity and war crimes, not genocide) was Kaing Guek Eav, "Comrade Duch" (pronounced "Doik"), former commander of the infamous Tuol Sleng/S-21 killing center. Duch, "a wiry, compact man, expressionless, his silver hair combed tidily to the side,"[75] took occasional notes as his lawyers wrangled over procedure. He showed emotion, according to observers, only when he was taken to the Cheung Ek site where so many of S-21's prisoners were taken for execution. Duch was reportedly "moved to tears" by the experience, "especially . . . when he stood before a tree with a sign describing how executioners disposed of child victims by bashing their heads against its trunk."[76]

In July 2010, Duch was found guilty of crimes against humanity including "enslavement, torture, sexual abuses, and other inhumane acts," and finally sentenced (on the prosecution's appeal) to life imprisonment.[77] The following year the showpiece trial of the ECCC was launched, with four principal Khmer Rouge figures in the dock: Nuon Chea, "Brother Number Two" to the deceased leader Pol Pot; Ieng Sary, the former Khmer Rouge foreign minister, and his wife and former Minister of Social Affairs, Ieng Thirith; and Khieu Samphan, the head of state during the Khmer Rouge period. In November 2011, the charges against Ieng Thirith were dropped after medical specialists diagnosed her with dementia rendering her unfit to stand trial; she died in 2014, aged 87. The remaining trio of defendants faced charges of genocide, crimes against humanity, and war crimes.

Figure 7.7 Nuon Chea at a trial hearing before the Extraordinary Chambers in the Courts of Cambodia, December 5, 2011.

Source: Photo by Nhet Sok Heng/Extraordinary Chambers in the Courts of Cambodia/Wikimedia Commons.

Scheduled to appear next was Khieu Samphan, the 78-year-old former head of state under the Khmer Rouge. Khieu had always denied knowledge of the atrocities committed by the regime, declaring that he became aware of them only after viewing a documentary on S-21 in 2003.[78]

The restriction of the trials to these five figures—at a cost running into hundreds of millions of US dollars—generated discontent in the international community, and among legal specialists. Prime Minister Hun Sen, however, was adamant that no further trials would be countenanced—he claimed because they risked provoking domestic unrest; skeptical observers pointed to the likelihood that additional prosecutions would lead to the summoning of witnesses of senior Cambodian political figures, many of whom (including Hun Sen himself) were tainted by a Khmer Rouge affiliation. "For those benefiting from the status quo," wrote Donald Beachler, "there was nothing to be gained by extensive probing into the past actions of government officials on the part of the ECCC or anyone else,"[79] and in April 2011 the court announced the end of investigations into "Case 3," targeting Sou Met and Meas Mut, the former heads of the Khmer Rouge's Navy and Air Force, accused of overseeing mass purges of supposed traitors in the KR's ranks.

By this point, the tribunal's operations were running more than $100 million over budget. The cost of the proceedings, together with the advanced age of the defendants, allegations of political interference,[80] and the fact that the foreign (especially Chinese and US) role in the genocide was ignored, evoked ambivalence in Cambodia. The majority of Cambodians, after all, were born after the Khmer Rouge were toppled from power—while many current leaders, notably Prime Minister Hun Sen, were themselves Khmer Rouge functionaries until breaking with the movement and joining in its overthrow. For survivors of the genocide, however, the priority was swift justice. "If the process of the trial continues to be too slow, then the aging former Khmer Rouge leaders will die before facing trial," said Yin Kean, a nun in her seventies who joined hundreds of others in a demonstration protesting the numerous delays in the proceedings. "I wish to see these leaders taken to court soon so that they will reveal who is responsible for the deaths of Cambodians under their regime."[81]

FURTHER STUDY

Denise Affonço, *To the End of Hell: One Woman's Struggle to Survive Cambodia's Khmer Rouge*, trans. Margaret Burn and Katie Hogben. London: Reportage Press, 2007. Memoir of forced labor and privation, sampled in this chapter.

Elizabeth Becker, *When the War Was Over: Cambodia and the Khmer Rouge Revolution*. New York: Public Affairs, 1998. The most accessible overview of the Khmer Rouge years.

David P. Chandler, *The Tragedy of Cambodian History: Politics, War and Revolution since 1945*. New Haven, CT: Yale University Press, 1991. A fine short history.

Thierry Cruvellier, *The Master of Confessions: The Making of a Khmer Rouge Torturer*, trans. Alex Gilly. New York: HarperCollins, 2014. A penetrating account of the trial of Kaing Guek Eav ("Comrade Duch"), director of the infamous S-21 detention and torture facility.

Tom Fawthrop and Helen Jarvis, *Getting Away with Genocide? Cambodia's Long Struggle against the Khmer Rouge*. London: Pluto Press, 2004. Justice in post-genocide Cambodia.

Alexander Laban Hinton, *Why Did They Kill? Cambodia in the Shadow of Genocide*. Berkeley, CA: University of California Press, 2005. Insightful anthropological analysis, also drawing on social and existential psychology.

Ben Kiernan, *The Pol Pot Regime: Race, Power and Genocide in Cambodia under the Khmer Rouge*, 3rd edn. New Haven, CT: Yale University Press, 2008. Detailed study of the Khmer Rouge years; a sequel to *How Pol Pot Came to Power*.

Haing Ngor with Roger Warner, *A Cambodian Odyssey*. New York: Macmillan, 1987. Memoir by the Cambodian doctor and genocide survivor who won an Oscar for playing Dith Pran in *The Killing Fields* (see Box 7.2).

William Shawcross, *Sideshow: Kissinger, Nixon and the Destruction of Cambodia* (rev. edn). New York: Cooper Square Press, 2002. The US air war against Cambodia and its role in bringing the Khmer Rouge to power.

Philip Short, *Pol Pot: Anatomy of a Nightmare*. New York: Henry Holt and Company, 2004. The most detailed biography of "Brother Number One" in the Khmer Rouge regime.

Loung Ung, *First They Killed My Father: A Daughter of Cambodia Remembers*. New York: HarperCollins, 2000. Memoir of a Chinese–Cambodian girl who lived through the genocide.

Michael Vickery, *Cambodia 1975–1982*. Boston, MA: South End Press, 1984. Revisionist study, arguing for an emphasis on local/regional dynamics of Khmer Rouge rule.

■ NOTES

1 Michael Vickery, *Cambodia 1975–1982* (Boston, MA: South End Press, 1984), p. 7.

2 Alexander Laban Hinton, "A Head for an Eye: Revenge in the Cambodian Genocide," in Hinton, ed., *Genocide: An Anthropological Reader* (Malden, MA: Blackwell, 2002), pp. 254–285. See also Hinton, *Why Did They Kill? Cambodia in the Shadow of Genocide* (Berkeley, CA: University of California Press, 2005).

3 David W. Roberts, *Political Transition in Cambodia, 1991–1999: Power, Elitism and Democracy* (New York: St. Martin's Press, 2001), p. 205.

4 Vickery, *Cambodia 1975–1982*, p. 9.

5 Elizabeth Becker, *When the War Was Over: Cambodia and the Khmer Rouge Revolution* (New York: Public Affairs, 1998), p. 37.

6 "Khmer Rouge" (Red Khmers) is actually a label applied derisively to the CPK by Cambodian President Norodom Sihanouk.

7 Two other members of the core KR group would hold important regional posts under DK. These were Mok, who would serve as party secretary in the DK's Southwest Zone, and carry out a vicious purge of the Northwest Zone in 1977; and Ke Pauk, a key military leader who directed the Kampuchean army to genocidal ends. A more independent member of the Paris group, Hou Youn, was purged and killed in 1975, at the dawn of the DK era, apparently for his opposition to the forced evacuation of Phnom Penh. Ke Pauk died of natural causes in February 2002. The seminal study of the origins of Cambodian communism is Ben Kiernan, *How Pol Pot Came to Power: Colonialism, Nationalism, and Communism in Cambodia, 1930–1975* (2nd edn) (New Haven, CT: Yale University Press, 2004).

8 Frank Chalk and Kurt Jonassohn, *The History and Sociology of Genocide* (New Haven, CT: Yale University Press, 1990), p. 400.

9 Khieu Thirith quoted in Becker, *When the War Was Over*, p. 75.

10 Becker, *When the War Was Over*, p. 87.

11 David P. Chandler, *The Tragedy of Cambodian History: Politics, War, and Revolution since 1945* (New Haven, CT: Yale University Press, 1991), p. 108.

12 Ibid., p. 205.

13 The coup, invasion, and subsequent bombing campaign are memorably described in William Shawcross, *Sideshow: Kissinger, Nixon, and the Destruction of Cambodia* (rev. edn) (New York: Cooper Square Press, 2002).

14 Quoted in Taylor Owen and Ben Kiernan, "Bombs Over Cambodia," *The Walrus*, October 2006, http://gsp.yale.edu/sites/default/files/walrus_cambodiabombing_oct06.pdf.

15 Samantha Power, *"A Problem from Hell": America and the Age of Genocide* (New York: Basic Books, 2002), p. 94.

16 Becker, *When the War Was Over*, p. 17.

17 In the view of genocide scholar Leo Kuper, "the [Khmer Rouge] government of Kampuchea [Cambodia] had every justification for its indictment of American imperialists. . . . They had left the new rulers with a most desperate food crisis and the overwhelming task of immediately restoring the cultivation of rice in a war-shattered country. They bear a heavy responsibility for many of the subsequent developments under the revolutionary government." Kuper, *Genocide: Its Political Use in the Twentieth Century* (Harmondsworth: Penguin, 1981), p. 159.

18 Vickery, *Cambodia 1975–1982*, p. 15. Kiernan cites "one peasant youth [who] recalled B-52s bombing his village three to six times per day for three months. Over one thousand people were killed, nearly a third of the population. Afterwards, 'there were few people left . . . and it was quiet.'" Kiernan, *The Pol Pot Regime*, p. 23.

19 In the second edition of this book, I cited Kiernan and Owen's dramatic upward revision of the bombing tonnage from roughly 500,000 to 2,756,941. Subsequent data provided to the authors by Australian researchers corrected the "mistaken technical analysis" in the Pentagon database used by Kiernan and Owen, who accepted the

new data and returned to their original estimate. For a discussion and explanation, see Ben Kiernan and Taylor Owen, "Making More Enemies than We Kill? Calculating U.S. Bomb Tonnages Dropped on Laos and Cambodia, and Weighing Their Implications," *The Asia–Pacific Journal*, 13: 3 (April 26, 2015), http://apjjf.org/2015/13/16/Ben-Kiernan/4313.html.

20 Christopher Hitchens, *The Trial of Henry Kissinger* (New York: Verso, 2001), pp. 25–43.

21 Owen and Kiernan, "Bombs Over Cambodia."

22 Chhit Do quoted in Power, *"A Problem from Hell,"* pp. 94–95.

23 Ignatieff quoted in *Crimes against Humanity*, documentary produced by the Imperial War Museum, London, December 2002 (from the official transcript supplied by the IWM).

24 Daniel Jonah Goldhagen, *Worse Than War: Genocide, Eliminationism, and the Ongoing Assault on Humanity* (New York: Basic Books, 2009), p. 123.

25 Becker, *When the War Was Over*, p. 304. According to Pol Pot, speaking in July 1975: "In the whole world, since the advent of the revolutionary war and since the birth of US imperialism, no country, no people, and no army has been able to drive the imperialists out to the last man and score total victory over them [as we have]." This was "a precious model for the world's people." Quoted in Kiernan, *The Pol Pot Regime*, p. 94.

26 Chandler, *The Tragedy of Cambodian History*, p. 175.

27 On the fate of the tribal peoples, see Kiernan, *The Pol Pot Regime*, pp. 302–309.

28 Cited in Chalk and Jonassohn, *The History and Sociology of Genocide*, p. 405.

29 Cited in Eric D. Weitz, *A Century of Genocide: Utopias of Race and Nation* (Princeton, NJ: Princeton University Press, 2003), p. 152.

30 "The borders were closed, foreign embassies and press agencies expelled, newspapers and television stations shut down, radios confiscated, mail and telephone use suppressed, the speaking of foreign languages punished." Kiernan, *The Pol Pot Regime*, p. 9.

31 Tom Fawthrop and Helen Jarvis, *Getting Away with Genocide? Cambodia's Long Struggle against the Khmer Rouge* (London: Pluto Press, 2004), p. 94.

32 Becker, *When the War Was Over*, p. 224.

33 Ben Kiernan and Chanthou Boua, *Peasants and Politics in Kampuchea, 1942–1981* (London: Zed Press, 1982), p. 239.

34 Chandler, *The Tragedy of Cambodian History*, p. 250.

35 Quoted in Chalk and Jonassohn, *The History and Sociology of Genocide*, p. 403.

36 Goldhagen, *Worse Than War*, p. 108.

37 Kiernan and Boua, *Peasants and Politics in Kampuchea*, pp. 345–346. Urban folk, for their part, "often found it impossible to accept that they had become the servants of dark, uneducated people." Chandler, *The Tragedy of Cambodian History*, p. 243.

38 Loung Ung, *First They Killed My Father: A Daughter of Cambodia Remembers* (New York: HarperCollins, 2000), p. 62.

39 Alexander Laban Hinton, "Oppression and Vengeance in the Cambodian Genocide," in Nicholas A. Robins and Adam Jones, eds., *Genocides by the Oppressed: Subaltern Genocide in Theory and Practice* (Bloomington, IN: Indiana University Press, 2009), pp. 84–102.

40 Vickery, *Cambodia 1975–1982*, pp. 66, 286–287, emphasis added. Curiously, Vickery echoes these prejudices, describing Cambodian urbanites as "spoiled, pretentious, contentious, status-conscious at worst, or at best simply soft, intriguing, addicted to city comforts and despising peasant life" (p. 26).

41 Kiernan, *The Pol Pot Regime*, p. 212.

42 The statistics are of course subject to dispute. For calculations, see Ben Kiernan, "The Demography of Genocide in Southeast Asia: The Death Tolls in Cambodia, 1975–79, and East Timor, 1975–80," *Critical Asian Studies*, 35: 4 (2003), pp. 586–587.

43 Chandler, *The Tragedy of Cambodian History*, p. 265.

44 Ibid., pp. 270–271.

45 Hinton, *Why Did They Kill?*, p. 167.

46 Vickery, *Cambodia 1975–1982*, pp. 68–69, 86.

47 Chandler, *The Tragedy of Cambodian History*, p. 265.

48 Denise Affonço, *To the End of Hell: One Woman's Struggle to Survive Cambodia's Khmer Rouge* (London: Reportage Press, 2007). The quoted passages in this box text are from pp. 5, 8, 17, 21, 25, 34–35, 37, 38, 44, 48, 69, 70, 79, 82, 99, 101, 105, 115, 144, 167, 193.

49 "1978 was the year of hardest work, night and day. We planted from 4 a.m. to 10 a.m., then ate a meal. At 1 p.m. we started again, and worked until 5 p.m., and then from 7 to 10 p.m. . . . There was not enough food, and foraging was not allowed." Testimony of Nao Gha, a Cham Muslim woman, in Ben Kiernan, "The Cambodian Genocide—1975–1979," in Samuel Totten and William S. Parsons, eds., *Centuries of Genocide: Essays and Eyewitness Accounts*, 4th edn (New York: Routledge, 2013), p. 341.

50 These included valuing children over parents (the young were the "blank slates" of the revolution); encouraging children to spy on their elders and report "suspicious activities" to KR cadres; and, in later stages, the outright seizure and sequestering of children to be raised and indoctrinated by party representatives.

51 Hinton, "A Head for an Eye," p. 273.

52 Ung quoted in Alexander Laban Hinton, *Why Did They Kill? Cambodia in the Shadow of Genocide* (Berkeley, CA: University of California Press, 2005), p. 168.

53 Pol Pot quoted in Kiernan, *The Pol Pot Regime*, p. 336.

54 Kiernan, "The Cambodian Genocide," pp. 338–339.

55 Ben Kiernan, "Genocidal Targeting: Two Groups of Victims in Pol Pot's Cambodia," in P. Timothy Bushnell *et al.*, eds., *State Organized Terror: The Case of Violent Internal Repression* (Boulder, CO: Westview Press, 1991), pp. 209, 212. In an echo of Nazi Germany's labeling of Jews with the Star of David, inhabitants of the Eastern Zone were outfitted with blue scarves *(kromar)* that allowed them to be easily identified and eliminated once deported from the zone (see pp. 213–218).

56 Statistics cited in Fawthrop and Jarvis, *Getting Away with Genocide?*, p. 245. On Tuol Sleng, see David Chandler, *Voices from S-21: Terror and History in Pol Pot's Secret Prison* (Berkeley, CA: University of California Press, 1999).

57 Becker, *When the War Was Over*, p. 254.

58 Sydney Schanberg, "Cambodia," in Hewitt, ed., *Defining the Horrific*, p. 261. Ironically, as Alexander Hinton notes, "the DK regime's glorification of asceticism, detachment, the elimination of attachment and desire, renunciation (of material goods and personal behaviors, sentiments, and attitudes), and purity paralleled prominent Buddhist themes that were geared toward helping a person attain greater mindfulness." Hinton, *Why Did They Kill?*, p. 197.

59 Kiernan, *The Pol Pot Regime*, p. 458.

60 Kiernan, "Genocidal Targeting," p. 218.

61 Kiernan, *The Pol Pot Regime*, p. 461.

62 Kiernan, "The Cambodian Genocide," p. 341.

63 Ibid., p. 342.

64 Becker, *When the War Was Over*, p. 459.

65 See Jon Swain, "War Reporter Jon Swain Pays Tribute to Dith Pran," *The Sunday Times*, April 6, 2008, www.thesundaytimes.co.uk/sto/news/uk_news/article83985.ece. See also Swain's vivid account of "The Fall of Phnom Penh" in his memoir *River of Time* (New York: Berkley Books, 1995), pp. 119–170.

66 See Doreen Chen, "Fall of Phnom Penh Comes to Life in Photographer's Eyewitness Testimony," *Cambodia Tribunal Monitor*, January 28, 2013, www.cambodiatribunal.org/2013/01/28/fall-of-phnom-penh-comes-to-life-in-photographers-eyewitness-testimony/.

67 Haing Ngor with Roger Warner, *A Cambodian Odyssey* (New York: Macmillan, 1987), p. 455.

68 On the Vietnam–Cambodia relationship during the Khmer Rouge era, and the Vietnamese invasion of 1978–1979, see Nayan Chanda, *Brother Enemy: The War after the War* (New York: Collier, 1986).

69 Eric Hobsbawm, *The Age of Extremes: A History of the World, 1914–1991* (New York: Vintage Books, 1994), p. 451.

70 Kissinger quoted in Ben Kiernan, "Documentation Delayed, Justice Denied: The Historiography of the Cambodian Genocide," in Dan Stone, ed., *The Historiography of Genocide* (London: Palgrave Macmillan, 2008), p. 469.

71 Mats Berdal and Michael Leifer, "Cambodia," in James Mayall, ed., *The New Interventionism, 1991–1994: United Nations Experience in Cambodia, Former Yugoslavia and Somalia* (Cambridge: Cambridge University Press, 1996), p. 36.

72 Nicholas Wheeler, *Saving Strangers: Humanitarian Intervention in International Society* (Oxford: Oxford University Press, 2000), p. 84.

73 For an overview of the twisted course of justice in Cambodia, see "A Case Study: The Atrocities of the Khmer Rouge," Part III in Steven R. Ratner and Jason S. Abrams, *Accountability for Human Rights Atrocities in International Law: Beyond the Nuremberg Legacy*, 2nd edn (Oxford: Oxford University Press, 2001), pp. 267–328.

74 Fawthrop and Jarvis, *Getting Away with Genocide?*, p. 240.

75 Miriama Kamo, "Killing Fields Executioner Faces Justice," *The Independent*, March 13, 2009.

76 "Khmer Rouge Defendant Weeps at Site of Mass Graves," Associated Press dispatch in the *International Herald Tribune*, February 26, 2008, www.iht.com/articles/2008/02/26/asia/cambo.php.

77 Donald W. Beachler, "The Quest for Justice in Cambodia: Power, Politics, and the Khmer Rouge Tribunal," *Genocide Studies and Prevention*, 8: 2 (2014), p. 70.

78 Seth Mydans, "Khmer Rouge Leader Is Arrested," *The New York Times*, November 20, 2007, www.nytimes.com/2007/11/20/world/asia/20cambo.html.

79 Beachler, "The Quest for Justice," p. 72.

80 Seth Mydans, "Efforts to Limit Khmer Rouge Trials Decried," *The New York Times*, January 31, 2009, www.nytimes.com/2009/02/01/world/asia/01cambodia.html.

81 "Cambodians Seek Quick Genocide Trials," Associated Press dispatch on *ABCNews.com*, December 25, 2007.

BOX 7A   INDONESIA AND EAST TIMOR

INDONESIA AND THE "BLACK HOLE" OF 1965–1966

Time magazine trumpeted it as "the West's best news for years in Asia."[1] The ruthless, military-supervised slaughter of at least 500,000 Indonesians accused of communist affiliations—perhaps over a million—was widely viewed as a Cold War victory, crushing the world's second-largest Communist Party (after China's) in a matter of months. At a time when the war in Vietnam was raging (see pp. 102–106), Indonesia was a "domino" that firm action had kept upright. Perhaps because of this Cold War prism; perhaps because little documentation existed at the time to demonstrate the scale of the mass killings; and perhaps because the efforts of the anti-genocide community in the 1980s and 1990s were focused on the occupied territory of East Timor (see below), the Indonesian genocide of 1965–1966 has occupied at best a marginal position in comparative genocide studies.[2] What John Gittings, writing in 1999, called "one of the biggest black holes of modern history" began to receive hesitant examination in Indonesia after the overthrow of Suharto's military dictatorship in 1998. In the West, Joshua Oppenheimer's twin documentaries, *The Act of Killing* (2012) and its sequel *The Look of Killing* (2014), were vital in drawing increased attention to the genocide.

The Indonesian Communist Party (PKI) had risen to national prominence—perhaps dominance—under the rule of President Sukarno, who earned the ire of the West for his role as a leader of the Non-Aligned Movement of Global South states, and for fomenting a confrontation (*Konfrontasi*) over Malaysian control of the territories of Sabah and Sarawak on the otherwise Indonesian-ruled island of Borneo. On September 30, 1965, a coup attempt was launched by mostly junior army and air force officers, supposedly to stave off an incipient CIA-supported coup against Sukarno. Six generals were murdered, but crucially, Major-General Suharto was not targeted. Though communist complicity in the attempted coup has never been demonstrated conclusively, Suharto emerged from hiding to accuse the PKI of being behind it, to sideline President Sukarno (he would die under house arrest in 1970), and to oversee the massacres that would follow.

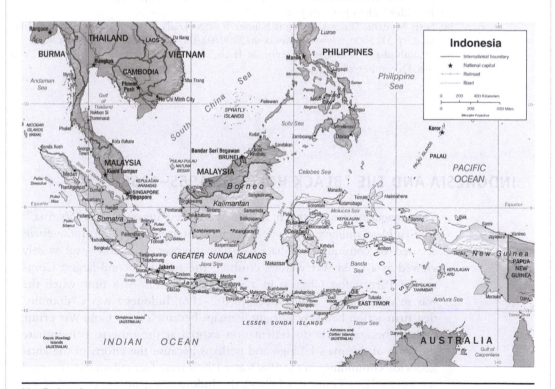

Map 7a.1 Indonesia.

Source: US Central Intelligence Agency (*n.b.* appropriately)/Library of Congress/Wikimedia Commons.

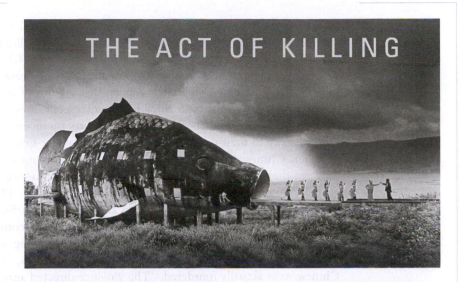

Figure 7a.1 The 2012 documentary *The Act of Killing*, directed by Joshua Oppenheimer, took a unique approach to its subject. Oppenheimer invited declared mass killers of "communists" to explore their retrospective sentiments by acting out scenes in various film genres, such as westerns and gangster films. Since the killers were lionized as heroes in post-genocide Indonesia, they took to their task with gusto, and with extraordinary and chilling cinematic results. The film was nominated for an Academy Award for best documentary, and spawned a sequel, *The Look of Killing*, in 2014.

Source: Courtesy of Final Cut for Real (www.final-cut.dk).

"Within a week," wrote John Gittings, "an elaborate funeral had been held for the generals murdered in the coup, and lurid tales (which appear to have been unfounded) were published alleging that Communist women had first mutilated the [generals'] bodies and even, according to some versions, committed sexual orgies with them. The army had found its martyrs," and the excuse it sought to destroy the PKI.[3] In this project, they were enthusiastically assisted by the US Johnson Administration, which "pushed for the annihilation of the PKI, providing covert assistance and urging the Indonesian army to complete the job."[4] Among the US contributions was providing the military with "lists of PKI members—perhaps with thousands of names" of party members who could then be hunted down by military-backed death squads.[5]

Initially centered on the Indonesian capital, Jakarta, the genocide spread rapidly across Java, and beyond to Sumatra, Bali, and other islands in the vast archipelago. According to genocide scholar Christian Gerlach, "by far most of the murders happened within only three months from mid-October 1965 to mid-January 1966." Of the hundreds of thousands of victims, "it seems that only a minority were shot by the military. Most were beheaded, stabbed, or had their throats slit with knives or swords (sometimes after they had been tied up), others were hacked to death, strangled, slain with clubs or rocks, drowned, or burned or buried alive."[6] "Spectacularized atrocities" and "verificationist mutilation" were prominent in the killing.[7] In an eerie harbinger of some scenes from the Rwandan genocide (Chapter 9), some witness accounts attest to a surreal "passivity [among] those who went to their deaths."[8] Robert Cribb cites "reports that victims in one place in the province of North Sumatra formed long, acquiescent lines at a river's edge while they waited to be decapitated. In Bali, party members are said to have gone placidly to their deaths wearing traditional white funeral clothes."[9]

Ethnic Chinese were significantly targeted throughout the genocide. Not only did they constitute a classic "market-dominant minority" (see Chapter 11), evoking feelings of envy and hostility, but given the PKI's links with the communist Chinese regime of Mao Zedong (Chapter 5), it was easy to depict them as "communists" *tout court*. However, despite contemporaneous claims of hundreds of thousands of ethnic Chinese being murdered, and despite documented massacres on the island of Lombok, "relatively few" Chinese were actually murdered.[10] The violence directed against their communities generally took the form of looting and destruction of property, along with largescale expulsions.

The degree of central control over the mass killing remains a subject of debate. Examining evidence gleaned from field research in Java, Mathias Hammer acknowledged that the Suharto-directed military ordered the genocide, but claimed that "unleashing political violence is not the same as controlling it."[11] At the grassroots, Hammer contended, the military's role was secondary to that of local actors, with their political-religious rivalries and personal disputes. However, the Australian scholar Jess Melvin has cited fresh archival data that "have made it possible to establish beyond reasonable doubt that the Indonesian genocide should be understood as the result of an intentional and centralised military campaign."[12] Indeed, one of the principal henchmen of the genocide, Colonel Sarwo Edhie Wibowo, told a reporter: "we gathered together the youth, the nationalist groups, the religious [Muslim] organizations. We gave them two or three days' training, then sent them out to kill the Communists."[13]

Also atrocious were the prisons in which many survivors of the main phase of the genocide were incarcerated. According to Sri Lestari Wahyuningroem, "the numbers of detainees reached more than one million, and these people were held for up to twenty years, depending on their alleged level of involvement with the PKI. Many detainees were tortured and raped during imprisonment."[14] Gittings described killings occurring "many months or even years after the original period of massacre."[15] Those who were eventually released found that "their lives were blighted by continuing discrimination, they were banned from government jobs, they were not permitted to vote and they faced difficulties in day-to-day dealings with the authorities." Jobs in key sectors, including "education, the media and law . . . were expected to come from a family and social environment untainted by communism. In other words, communism was treated as a permanent, semi–hereditary condition which might afflict even people born after 1965."[16]

The veil of silence over the mass atrocities was lifted, albeit tentatively, during the period of reform (*Reformasi*) inaugurated after the fall of the Suharto regime in 1998. "Nearly 50 years after the events of those years, the National Commission for Human Rights conducted a four–year–long investigation into the case and concluded that crimes against humanity were committed and that the military was responsible."[17] Wahyuningroem stresses that "victims' organisations and groups . . . projected a clear message to the wider public for the need to understand victims' perspectives as well as calling for solidarity." They also launched initiatives "for truth and justice, including the weekly silent Thursday peace demonstrations, or Kamisan, which take place in front of the Presidential Palace." Such projects "have contributed to a wider discourse on the missing stories of what happened after 30 September 1965 by bringing to light victims' stories and working towards community reconciliation." Unfortunately, "the state has responded to these only sporadically and unsustainably."[18]

EAST TIMOR

The Indonesian military regime inaugurated in September 1965 had exterminatory implications for the territory of East Timor, occupying the eastern half of the island of Timor at the eastern tip of the archipelago. East Timor's road to independence began in the same year—1975—that the Khmer Rouge took power in Cambodia. For four years following the Indonesian invasion and occupation of East Timor in December, events in these two Southeast Asian lands moved in grim tandem. Both witnessed genocides as severe, in terms of proportion of population killed, as any since the Jewish Holocaust. The Khmer Rouge regime became a byword for ideological fanaticism and the brutal exercise of power, sparking international condemnation. In contrast, the genocide in East Timor was protested and publicized only by a small group of Timorese exiles, human rights activists, and concerned scholars. In the 1990s, as Indonesian atrocities continued, the Timor solidarity movement grew. The global network it established was a key ingredient in confronting the final blast of Indonesian genocide, in 1999, aiming to overturn a pro–independence referendum result. East Timor thus offers an inspiring example of a genocide ended, in large part, by popular mobilization and protest.

East Timor owes its distinctiveness from the rest of the island of Timor, and the wider Indonesian archipelago, to its colonization by the Portuguese in the mid–seventeenth century. In April 1974, a left–wing military coup against the fascist government in Lisbon established a democratic government, leading Portugal to stage a rapid retreat from its overseas empire (including Angola and Mozambique). Indigenous political parties sprang up in East Timor, the largest of which was Fretilin (the Revolutionary Front of Independent East Timor). In 1975, Fretilin won village-level elections over its main competitor, the Timorese Democratic Union (UDT). Disaffected UDT members, responding to Indonesian machinations, refused to accept the result. Their abortive coup was quickly crushed, with a death toll of several thousand. The UDT leadership fled to Indonesia, and Fretilin issued a declaration of independence on November 28, 1975.

Just over a week later, on December 7—after receiving the green light from visiting US president Gerald Ford and Secretary of State Henry Kissinger[19]—the Indonesians launched an invasion of East Timor by land, sea, and air. In the largest city, Dili, the Indonesian military murdered thousands of Timorese in mass executions. Fretilin forces were driven into the mountainous interior. Over the following years, tens of thousands of Timorese civilians would join them there, preferring isolation in harsh conditions to Indonesian violence and repression.

With Dili and secondary towns under their control, Indonesian forces fanned out across the territory. Massacres occurred almost everywhere they went. Families of suspected Fretilin supporters were killed along with the suspects themselves. In some cases, whole villages were exterminated. This strategy reached its apogee in the Aitana region in July 1981, where "a ghastly

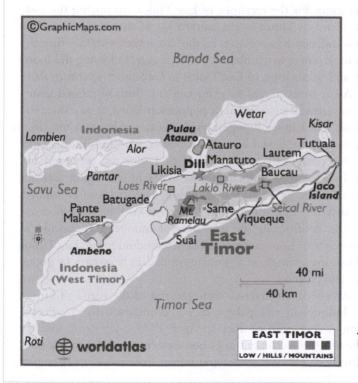

Map 7a.2 East Timor.

Source: Map provided by WorldAtlas.com

massacre . . . murdered everyone, from tiny babies to the elderly, unarmed people who were not involved in the fighting but were there simply because they had stayed with Fretilin and wanted to live freely in the mountains."[20] Perhaps 10,000 Timorese died in this killing spree alone.

The atrocities continued on a smaller scale throughout the 1980s. At Malim Luro in August 1983, for example, "after plundering the population of all their belongings, [Indonesian troops] firmly tied up men, women and children, numbering more than sixty people. They made them lie on the ground and then drove a bulldozer over them, and then used it to place a few centimetres of earth on top of the totally crushed corpses."[21]

Survivors of the rampages were confined to "model villages" invigilated by Indonesian soldiers and local paramilitaries. Disease, starvation, and forced labor caused numerous deaths. The territories not under full Indonesian control also suffered genocide. Indonesian forces launched repeated scorched-earth sorties; rained bombs on civilian populations; and imposed a strict blockade on Fretilin-held areas that led, as designed, to starvation. According to Timor specialist John Taylor, tens of thousands of Timorese died as a result of this war of "encirclements, bombing, uprooting of the population, malnutrition and generalized brutalities."[22] In total, an estimated 170,000 Timorese—"24 to 26 percent of East Timor's 1975 population"— died between 1975 and 1999.[23]

In the 1990s, however, Indonesia's hold over East Timor weakened. On November 12, 1991, some 270 civilians were slaughtered by Indonesian troops in Dili's Santa Cruz cemetery. Witnessed by several foreign observers, who managed to escape with film footage, the Dili massacre provoked the first substantial international outcry against the Indonesian genocide. The territory's profile was raised further in 1996, when the Nobel Peace Prize was awarded to the leader of the East Timor Catholic Church, Carlos Filipe Ximenes Belo, and Fretilin's leader in exile, José Ramos Horta. Meanwhile, the international Timorese solidarity movement—spearheaded by the East Timor Action Network (ETAN)—organized demonstrations and lobbied governments to condemn Indonesian repression.

The overthrow of the Suharto regime in Indonesia catalyzed East Timor's final drive for independence. Suharto's successor, the former vice-president B.J. Habibie, stunned the world by announcing, in January 1999, that Indonesia was willing to "let East Timor go" if its people chose independence in a referendum. The United Nations, with Portugal taking the lead, rapidly organized a vote, scheduled for August 30.

Behind the scenes, the Indonesian military—which had amassed huge economic holdings in East Timor over the previous twenty-five years— prepared to sabotage the independence process. It relied on locally raised paramilitary forces (the so-called *ninjas*), overseen by the elite Kopassus army unit, to terrorize the population into voting to stay with Indonesia. In the prelude to the referendum, hundreds of Timorese, especially activist youth, were murdered by death squads or in local-level massacres.[24] Despite these atrocities, the UN fatefully chose to leave "security" in the hands of the Indonesian army.

The stage was thus set for the violence and destruction unleashed at the end of August 1999. Voting peacefully and in overwhelming numbers, 78.5 percent of Timorese opted for independence. The Indonesian military and its local allies swung immediately into action. As international observers looked on in horror, and the UN hunkered down in its headquarters, militia killed unknown numbers of Timorese. (A regularly cited figure is 1,500, but this may be a substantial undercount.)[25] Indonesian troops and local militias burned swathes of territory and whole city neighborhoods to the ground, in a campaign aimed at "the virtual demolition of the physical basis for survival in the territory."[26]

The UN decided to evacuate staff from its Dili compound, and leave the terrified Timorese gathered there to their fate. This craven action was only avoided by an unprecedented staff rebellion against the edict (see Chapter 16, pp. 767–770). Meanwhile, hundreds of thousands of demonstrators took to the streets in North America, Europe, and Australia, bringing sustained pressure to bear on their governments.[27] "Portugal came to a halt on 8 September, when the prime minister himself took part in a kilometres-long human chain in Lisbon."[28] With memories of Rwanda and Bosnia (see Chapters 8 and 9) doubtless reverberating in his mind, UN Secretary-General Kofi Annan issued a strongly worded warning to Indonesia. The Clinton administration in the US also announced that it was prepared to suspend the military aid on which the Indonesian armed forces depended. The Australian government, for its part, offered to lead a stabilization force to occupy and patrol the territory. Faced with this concerted opposition, the Indonesian government backed down. Australian forces deployed in Dili on September 20; a week later, Indonesia ceded control to the international contingent.

East Timor became an independent nation two years later, in August 2001. The happy ending, however, was undermined by material and human devastation, spiraling unemployment, and social dislocation. Street violence waged by frustrated, demobilized members of the army and police, as well as by gangs and political factions, left the country in a "fragile and precarious" state by 2007, according to then-prime minister José Ramos Horta.[29] Open violence has been relatively rare since, but the country remains one of the world's poorest and least developed.

Attempts to investigate the mass violence of 1999—and the quarter-century preceding it—were confounded by a lack of resources,[30] and by the reluctance of Indonesian and (more surprisingly) East Timorese authorities to pursue justice. The most significant effort to document the atrocities throughout the period of Indonesian rule was launched by the UN-sponsored Commission for Reception, Truth and Reconciliation,

Figure 7a.2 Australian soldiers of the UN-sponsored INTERFET (International Forces East Timor) patrolling the streets of Dili in February 2000, a few months after the paroxysm of violence surrounding the territory's vote for independence from Indonesia.

Source: Photo by Dan Mennuto/USS Blue Ridge/Wikimedia Commons.

established in 2001. The commission reported its findings to the East Timorese government in October 2005—but the government "suppressed [them] for months," fearing destabilization of its relations with its huge neighbor and former occupier.[31] Finally leaked to the media, the report proved explosive. The commission chose to deploy the language of "extermination" as a crime against humanity, rather than "genocide," to describe Indonesian actions—in part to encompass the indirect and structural forms of violence that accounted for a majority of the victims. (See further discussion of "extermination" and crimes against humanity legislation in Chapter 15, pp. 709–712.) But it pulled no punches in detailing the nature and extent of the crimes, finding that "the Indonesian military used starvation as a weapon to exterminate the East Timorese," killing "as many as 180,000 civilians" throughout its dominion over the territory. "Napalm and chemical weapons, which poisoned the food and water supply, were [also] used," and the report documented "a litany of massacres, thousands of summary executions of civilians and the torture of 8500 East Timorese—with horrific details of public beheadings, the mutilation of genitalia, the burying and burning alive of victims, use of cigarettes to burn victims, and ears and genitals being lopped off to display to families."[32]

The commission was also blunt in its assessment of the role played by the United States and Australia in supporting the invasion and turning a blind eye to the ensuing exterminations. US "political and military support [was] fundamental to the Indonesian invasion and occupation," the report's authors declared; the support arose from "a strategically-motivated desire to maintain a good relationship with Indonesia, whose anti-communist regime was seen as an essential bastion against the spread of communism."[33] As for Australia, the report accused the then-government of "contribut[ing] significantly to denying the people of Timor-Leste their right to self-determination before and during the Indonesian occupation," eager to preserve good relations with its powerful neighbor and to secure favorable terms in boundary negotiations over the oil-and gas-rich "Timor Gap."[34] The commissioners insisted that the two countries, along with Britain, France, and others who funded and armed Indonesia's military dictatorship, should pay reparations to the Timorese who died as a consequence. Predictably, the demand fell on deaf ears.

FURTHER STUDY

Peter Carey and G. Carter Bentley, eds., *East Timor at the Crossroads: The Forging of a Nation*. Honolulu, HI: University of Hawaii Press, 1995. Essays on the Timorese independence struggle.

Irena Cristalis, *East Timor: A Nation's Bitter Dawn*, 2nd edn. London: Zed Books, 2009. A highly personal account of the occupation and post-occupation periods, by a journalistic stalwart.

Tim Fischer, *Seven Days in East Timor: Ballots and Bullets*. London: Allen & Unwin, 2000. Eyewitness account of the 1999 independence vote.

Joseph Nevins, *A Not-so-distant Horror: Mass Violence in East Timor*. Ithaca, NY: Cornell University Press, 2005. Good on the post-1999 quest for justice.

Geoffrey Robinson, *"If You Leave Us Here, We Will Die": How Genocide Was Stopped in East Timor*. Princeton, NJ: Princeton University Press, 2010. The inspiring story, by a participant, of how rebellion in UN ranks helped to prompt a humanitarian intervention in 1999.

John G. Taylor, *East Timor: The Price of Freedom*. London: Zed Books, 2000. The best all-around study of the Indonesian occupation, with a useful chronology.

NOTES

1 Quoted in Robert Cribb, "The Indonesian Massacres," in Samuel Totten, William Parsons, and Israel Charny, eds., *Century of Genocide: Eyewitness Accounts and Critical Views* (New York: Garland Publishing, 1997), p. 245. Cribb's chapter appeared through the third edition of *Century of Genocide*, but is curiously absent from the fourth (*Centuries of Genocide*, 2013; see Further Study, Chapter 1).

2 As John Gittings wrote in a 1999 book chapter, the massacres "remain to a large extent a series of events located outside any meaningful context, historical

framework or explanation. Indeed, the very fact that so little is known or under-stood about them has become their most noted characteristic[,] thereby serving, perhaps, as a substitute for more extended analysis." Gittings, "The Indonesian Massacres, 1965–1966: Image and Reality," in Mark Levene and Penny Roberts, eds., *The Massacre in History* (New York: Berghahn Books, 1999), p. 249. This is despite the dedicated efforts of, above all, Robert Cribb to move the Indonesian genocide closer to the mainstream of genocide studies.

3 Gittings, "The Indonesian Massacres," p. 250.

4 Margaret Scott, "The Indonesian Massacre: What Did the US Know?," *The New York Review of Books*, November 2, 2015, www.nybooks.com/daily/2015/11/02/indonesian-massacre-what-did-us-know/. Foreign involvement in the geno-cide, including by the UK, West German, and Dutch governments (Indonesia was the "Dutch East Indies" until independence in 1948), is examined in Alex de Jong, "The Forgotten Massacres," *Jacobin*, June 2, 2014, www.jacobinmag.com/2015/06/indonesian-communist-party-suharto-massacre-purge/. See also Gittings, "The Indonesian Massacres," pp. 258–260; David Easter, "'Keep the Indonesian Pot Boiling': Western Covert Intervention in Indonesia, Octo-ber 1965–March 1966," *Cold War History*, 5: 1 (2005), pp. 55–73; Adam Hughes Henry, "Polluting the Waters: A Brief History of Anti-Communist Propaganda during the Indonesian Massacres," *Genocide Studies International*, 8: 2 (2014), pp. 153–175; and by the director of *The Act of Killing*, Joshua Oppenheimer, contending that "the extent of America's role remains hidden behind a wall of secrecy": "Suharto's Purge, Indonesia's Silence," *The New York Times*, Sep-tember 29, 2015, www.nytimes.com/2015/09/30/opinion/suhartos-purge-indonesias-silence.html.

5 Scott, "The Indonesian Massacre."

6 Christian Gerlach, *Extremely Violent Societies: Mass Violence in the Twentieth-Cen-tury World* (Cambridge: Cambridge University Press, 2010), pp. 21, 34.

7 See Annie Pohlman, "Spectacular Atrocities: Making Enemies during the 1965–1966 Massacres in Indonesia," in Philip G. Dwyer and Lyndall Ryan, eds., *Thea-tres of Violence: Massacre, Mass Killing and Atrocity throughout History* (New York: Berghahn Books, 2012), pp. 199–212.

8 Quoted in Gittings, "The Indonesian Massacres," p. 254.

9 Robert Cribb, "Genocide in Indonesia, 1965–1966," *Journal of Genocide Research*, 3: 2 (2001), pp. 233–234.

10 This is the verdict delivered in Robert Cribb and Charles A. Coppel in "A Gen-ocide That Never Was: Explaining the Myth of Anti-Chinese Massacres in Indo-nesia, 1965–66," *Journal of Genocide Research*, 11: 4 (2009), p. 447. The authors sample Xinhua (Chinese news agency) reports of "a thousand Chinese driven from their homes in Bali and thousands more put to flight in Sumatra, especially in Aceh, wild demonstrations calling for the expulsion of all Chinese, the smash-ing and looting of Chinese shops and houses in more than a dozen cities (2,000 Chinese shops were said to have been destroyed in Makassar), the beating of teachers and students at Chinese schools, attacks on the Chinese embassy and Chinese consulate buildings . . . the rape of Chinese girls and plundering of the possessions of Chinese refugees" (p. 451).

11 Mathias Hammer, "The Organisation of the Killings and the Interaction between State and Society in Central Java, 1965," *Journal of Current Southeast Asian Affairs*, 32: 3 (2013), p. 38.

12 Jess Melvin, "Why Not Genocide? Anti-Chinese Violence in Aceh, 1965–1966," *Journal of Current Southeast Asian Affairs*, 32: 3 (2013), p. 64.

13 Edhie quoted in Gerlach, *Extremely Violent Societies*, p. 33.

14 Sri Lestari Wahyuningroem, "Seducing for Truth and Justice: Civil Society Initiatives for the 1965 Mass Violence in Indonesia," *Journal of Current Southeast Asian Affairs*, 32: 3 (2013), pp. 119–120.

15 Gittings, "The Indonesian Massacres," p. 257.

16 Cribb, "Genocide in Indonesia," pp. 236–237. See also Leslie Dwyer, "Building a Monument: Intimate Politics of 'Reconciliation' in Post-1965 Bali," in Alexander Laban Hinton, ed., *Transitional Justice: Global Mechanisms and Local Realities after Genocide and Mass Violence* (New Brunswick, NJ: Rutgers University Press, 2010), pp. 227–248.

17 Syarina Hasibuan, "Indonesia's Killing Fields," AlJazeera.com, December 21, 2012, www.aljazeera.com/programmes/101east/2012/12/2012121874846805636.html.

18 Wahyuningroem, "Seducing for Truth and Justice," pp. 124, 125, 134. For a study of memorialization efforts as part of the "Intimate Politics of 'Reconciliation' in Post-1965 Bali," see Leslie Dwyer, "Building a Monument," in Alexander Laban Hinton, ed., *Transitional Justice: Global Mechanisms and Local Realities after Genocide and Mass Violence* (New Brunswick, NJ: Rutgers University Press, 2010), pp. 227–248.

19 See the declassified documents posted by the National Security Archive on "Ford, Kissinger and the Indonesian Invasion, 1975–76," December 6, 2001, www.gwu.edu/~nsarchiv/NSAEBB/NSAEBB62/index2.html.

20 Source cited in John G. Taylor, *East Timor: The Price of Freedom* (London: Zed Books, 2000), p. 118. See also Taylor's fine chapter, "'Encirclement and Annihilation': The Indonesian Occupation of East Timor," in Robert Gellately and Ben Kiernan, eds., *The Specter of Genocide: Mass Murder in Historical Perspective* (Cambridge: Cambridge University Press, 2003), pp. 163–185.

21 Source cited in Taylor, *East Timor*, p. 103. Together with indiscriminate, "root-and-branch" massacres of this type, a pattern of gendercidal killings of males was also evident, as it would be after the independence referendum in 1999. For a detailed investigation, see Adam Jones/Gendercide Watch, "Case Study: East Timor, 1975–99," www.gendercide.org/case_timor.html, from which passages in this box text are adapted.

22 Taylor, *East Timor*, p. 151.

23 Ben Kiernan, "The Demography of Genocide in Southeast Asia: The Death Tolls in Cambodia, 1975–79, and East Timor, 1975–80," *Critical Asian Studies*, 35: 4 (2003), p. 594, citing research by Gabriel Defert.

24 Roy quoted in Irena Cristalis, *East Timor: A Nation's Bitter Dawn*, 2nd edn (London: Zed Books, 2009), p. 83.

25 See, e.g., Ellen Nakashima, "For Survivors of E. Timor Massacres, Justice Still Elusive," *The Washington Post*, September 16, 2005. For an examination of the physical, eyewitness, and circumstantial evidence pertaining to the Timorese death toll in 1999, see Jones/Gendercide Watch, "Case Study: East Timor."

26 Noam Chomsky, "East Timor Is Not Yesterday's Story," *ZNet*, October 23, 1999.

27 The fact that the Timor events followed closely on the war in Kosovo (March–June 1999), which *had* prompted Western intervention, added to the pressure on governments—an interesting case of "norm grafting" (see Chapter 12).

28 Cristalis, *East Timor*, p. 225.

29 Lindsay Murdoch, "East Timor Asks for Help as Street Violence Escalates," *The Sydney Morning Herald*, February 14, 2007.

30 Only the most cursory investigation was launched into the atrocities inflicted before and after the independence vote. By contrast with the hundreds of forensic investigators dispatched to Kosovo after the 1999 war there (Chapter 8),

fewer than a dozen were allotted to East Timor, and only for a short period. As a result, no clear picture of the scale of the Indonesian-directed killing has yet emerged, though internationally-sponsored forensic work has been carried out.

31 Sian Powell, "UN Verdict on East Timor," *The Australian*, January 19, 2006. Progress was made, however, by the Serious Crimes Unit within East Timor, established with UN assistance. "This body has indicted some 375 people and secured more than 50 convictions. Most of those convicted are militiamen who say they were acting under the orders of the Indonesian armed forces. About 280 indictees remain at large in Indonesia. They include the Indonesian commander at the time, General Wiranto, for whom the unit has issued an arrest warrant," though the Timorese government (!) refused to forward it to Interpol. It is notable that all of the accusations and legal initiatives relate to the 1999 atrocities; even leading human rights organizations such as Amnesty International have avoided recommending prosecutions for the genocide committed against Timorese over the previous quarter-century (see Joseph Nevins, *A Not-so-distant Horror: Mass Violence in East Timor* (Ithaca, NY: Cornell University Press, 2005), p. 165).

32 Powell, "UN Verdict."

33 Colum Lunch, "Report: US Arms Helped Indonesia Attack East Timor," *The Washington Post*, January 25, 2006.

34 "East Timor Report Scathing of Downer," Australian Associated Press dispatch in *The Sydney Morning Herald*, February 2, 2006.

CHAPTER 8

Bosnia and Kosovo

The dissolution of Yugoslavia in the early 1990s returned genocide to Europe after nearly half a century's absence. During those years, European states and the wider world looked on ineffectually as the multiethnic state of Bosnia-Herzegovina collapsed into genocidal conflict. The most extensive and systematic atrocities were committed by Serbs against Muslims, but clashes between Croats and Serbs, and between Muslims and Croats, claimed thousands of lives. The restive Serb province of Kosovo, with its ethnic-Albanian majority, was another tinder-box, though mass violence did not erupt there until spring 1999.

ORIGINS AND ONSET

> The Yugoslav War was not the result of "ancient ethnic hatreds" but the work of political elites who invoked myths and symbolic politics to mobilize their populations at a time of systemic crisis.
>
> Mark Bondioch

Yugoslavia, the federation of "Southern Slavs," was cobbled together from the disintegrated Ottoman Empire after the First World War. Fragile federations everywhere are prone to violence in times of crisis (see, e.g., Chapter 4, Box 4a, Chapter 5, Box 5a). For Yugoslavia, the crisis came in the Second World War, when the federation was riven by combined Nazi invasion and intercommunal conflict. Yugoslavia in fact became one of the most destructive theaters of history's most destructive war.[1] Under the German occupation regime in Serbia and the fascist Ustashe government installed by the Nazis in Croatia, most of Yugoslavia's Jewish population was exterminated. Hundreds of thousands of Croatian Serbs were rounded up by the Ustashe and slaughtered, most notoriously at the Jasenovac death camp.

Muslims in Bosnia mostly collaborated with the Nazis, earning them the enduring enmity of the Serb population. The Serbs themselves were divided between the Chetniks, who supported the deposed royalist regime, and a partisan movement led by Josip Broz, known as Tito. Chetnik massacres and other atrocities prompted an equally murderous response from Tito's forces. After the partisans seized power in the Yugoslav capital, Belgrade, in the late stages of the war, thousands of Chetniks fled to neighboring countries. The Allies returned the majority of them to Yugoslavia to face summary punishment. Throughout 1945–1946, Tito's forces killed tens of thousands of Chetniks and other political opponents.

One should be cautious about the "buried hatreds" thesis for the former Yugoslavia, the most prominent articulation of which is Robert Kaplan's *Balkan Ghosts*. Those interested in political-psychological factors in genocide, however, have emphasized the importance of "forgotten traumas"—officially forgotten through state neglect and suppression, but constituting part of the fabric of popular/collective memory, and prone to cynical exploitation by the new generation of nationalist leaders in the late 1980s and early 1990s. Edina Becirevic writes in her study of *Genocide on the Drina River*:

> Painful memories of the Nazi invasion during World War II—when Bosnia, like other Yugoslavia territories, was caught up in a parallel civil war—were covered over with politically motivated silence as Tito promoted the ethics of "brotherhood and unity" instead of implementing a proper reconciliation process. Growing up under Tito's regime, many young people in Bosnia, especially in urban areas, were ignorant of how deeply the wounds of World War II were still felt. Thus, when Milosevic's propaganda started in 1987, we could not imagine that it would have such a huge impact on the Serb population ... the demons of the past appeared in prewar propaganda in deviously smart ways; and the results were devastating.[2]

The implications for strategies of genocide prevention (see Chapter 16) should be clear.

The socialist state that Tito instituted was, however, liberal by the standards of Central and Eastern Europe. Yugoslavs enjoyed extensive freedom of movement: millions worked overseas, especially in Germany. The country gained a reputation not only for comparative openness, but for successful ethnic pluralism. Tito, a Croat, worked to ensure that no ethnic group dominated the federation. Political mobilization along ethnic lines was banned (resulting in a wave of detention and imprisonment in the 1970s, when Croatian leaders within the Yugoslav Socialist Party sought greater autonomy for Croatia). State authorities worked hard to defuse ethnic tensions and generate an overarching Yugoslav identity, with some success, notably in the cities.

But Tito died in May 1980, and the multinational federation rapidly unraveled amidst pervasive economic strife. The weak collective leadership faltered when confronted by an emerging generation of ethnonationalist politicians, most prominently Slobodan Milosevic in Serbia and Franjo Tudjman in Croatia.[3] Tudjman, "a small-minded, right-wing autocrat,"[4] led a political movement—the HDZ—that explicitly revived Ustashe symbolism and rhetoric. He also allowed, and probably supervised, a campaign of harassment and violence against the large Serb population of the Krajina region. Serbs were dismissed from their jobs, allegedly to redress preferential treatment granted to them in the past. Worse would follow.

In Milosevic of Serbia, meanwhile, we see one of the most influential European politicians of the second half of the twentieth century—albeit a malign influence. This did not reflect any special talent or charisma. Rather, Milosevic was an *apparatchik* (child of the state-socialist system) who realized sooner than most that rousing nationalist passions was an effective way to exploit the Yugoslav upheavals for personal power.

Milosevic sowed the seeds for genocide in April 1987, on a visit to the restive Albanian-dominated province of Kosovo. (Ironically, it was over Kosovo that the term "genocide" was first deployed in a contemporary Balkans context—by Serbs, to describe the fate that supposedly awaited their people at the hands of a swelling Albanian majority.)[5] Dispatched by Serb president Ivan Stambolic, his mentor, to hold talks with the local Communist Party leadership, Milosevic was greeted by a rowdy outpouring of Serbs* barely kept in check by police. Rocks were thrown, apparently as a provocation. The police reacted with batons. Milosevic was urged to calm the crowd. Instead, he told them: "No one should dare to beat you," "unwittingly coining a modern Serb rallying call."[6]

Transformed by the ecstatic reaction to his speech, Milosevic forged ahead with his nationalist agenda. A few months later, in September 1987, he shunted aside his mentor, Ivan Stambolic, and took over the presidency. In 1989, Serbs initiated a repressive drive in Kosovo that ended the province's autonomy within Serbia, dismissed tens of thousands of Kosovars (ethnic Albanians) from their jobs, and made of Kosovo "one large militia camp . . . a squalid outpost of putrefying colonialism."[7] More than a hundred Kosovars were killed in the repression.[8] In retrospect, this was the key event that unraveled Yugoslavia. After the Kosovo crackdown, no ethnic group could feel safe in a Serb-dominated federation.

In 1991–1992, Yugoslavia exploded into open war. On June 25, 1991, Croatia and Slovenia declared independence. A surreal ten-day war for Slovenia resulted in the withdrawal of the Yugoslav Army (JNA) and the abandonment of Yugoslav claims to the territory. Croatia, though, was a different matter. It included sizable Serb populations in Krajina (the narrow strip of territory running adjacent to the Dalmatian coast and bordering Serb-dominated areas of Bosnia-Herzegovina) and Eastern Slavonia.

Milosevic recognized the inevitability of Croatia's secession, but sought to secure territories in which Serbs were strongly represented for his "Greater Serbia." In December 1991, after several months of fighting, the Krajina Serbs declared independence from Croatia. Meanwhile, the world's attention was captured by the artillery bombardment of the historic port of Dubrovnik; less so by the far more severe JNA assault on Vukovar, which reduced the city to rubble and was followed by the genocidal massacre of some 200 wounded Croatian soldiers in their hospital beds.

The independence declarations by Slovenia and Croatia left multiethnic Bosnia-Herzegovina in an impossible position. As epitomized by its major city, Sarajevo—hitherto a model of ethnic tolerance—Bosnia was divided among

---

* Throughout this chapter and volume, I use "Croatian" and "Croat," "Serbian" and "Serb," to refer to the polity and ethnicity respectively.

Map 8.1 Bosnia and Herzegovina today.

Source: Map provided by WorldAtlas.com.

Muslims, Serbs, and Croats. If it sought to secede, the result would surely be a secession by Bosnian Serbs in turn to integrate "their" zone of Bosnia into Milo-sevic's Greater Serbia, while remaining within the federation meant enduring Serb domination. This was the scenario that played out when, in February 1992, the Muslim-dominated federation declared its independence from Yugoslavia.

In this atmosphere of pervasive fear and uncertainty, populations sought safety in ethnic exclusivity—as leaders, especially Milosevic and Tudjman, presumably anticipated. "Before, we shared the good times and the bad. . . . [Now,] we hardly wish anyone good-day or good-evening any more. Suddenly people have a different look about them, their faces have changed. For me it all happened in one day. It is indescribable."[9] So stated a Bosnian Muslim woman, recalling the breakdown of relations with her Croat neighbors.

Bosnia promptly became the most brutal battlefield of the Balkan wars. Serb gunners launched a siege and artillery bombardment of Sarajevo that evoked global outrage. Apart from killing thousands of civilians, they also staged a systematic campaign of urbicide, targeting the cultural repositories of the Bosnian Muslim and cosmopolitan Sarajevan civilizations:

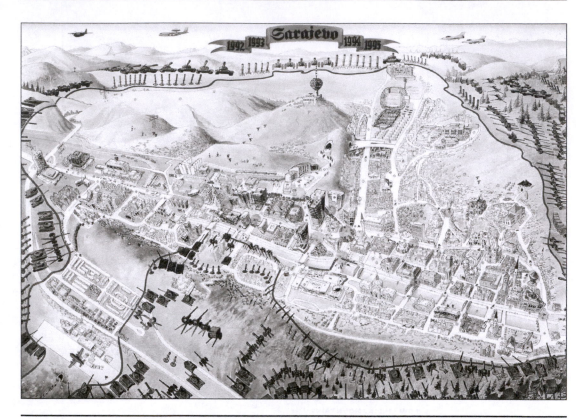

Figure 8.1 The siege of the cosmopolitan city of Sarajevo became the focal point of the Bosnian war for the outside world, though the bulk of the killing occurred elsewhere. The siege and bombardment can also be considered an important contemporary case of *urbicide*, the destruction of an urban living space and its population as part of a broader genocidal strategy (see pp. 37–39). FAMA International produced this map of the siege, showing the ring of Serb gun emplacements around the city, broken only by the UN airport zone at the bottom left. Enterprising Sarajevans dug a tunnel under the airport runway to connect their city with Bosnian government-held territory beyond. Today the tunnel is a tourist attraction.

Source: FAMA International/www.famainternational.com.

Serbs purposely shelled the major cultural institutions . . . as they sought not only to eliminate Bosniaks [Bosnian Muslims] from Bosnia but also to obliterate their communal and cultural existence's foundation. They first destroyed the Oriental Institute, burning the largest collection of Islamic and Jewish manuscripts in southeastern Europe, then the National Museum, and finally the National Library, incinerating more than one million books, more than 100,000 manuscripts and rare books, and centuries of the country's historical records. For the artist Aida Musanovic, and certainly for other Sarajevans, seeing their principal cultural repository engulfed in flames and then having the smoke, ash, and wisps of burnt paper hovering over and raining down on their city, "was the most apocalyptic thing I'd ever seen."[10]

The attack on Sarajevo and its cultural landmarks also distracted international attention from the far greater killing elsewhere in Bosnia, especially in the industrialized east.[11] The Yugoslav army was ordered out, but left most of its weapons in the hands of Bosnian Serbs, who now constituted a formidable 80,000-man army.

Figure 8.2 "Sarajevo siege life, winter of 1992–1993. Cutting branches from Sarajevo's trees—often at risk of being sniped—as fuel for stoves to heat water and provide occasional meagre warmth."

Source: Photo by Christian Maréchal/Wikimedia Commons.

Bosnian Muslims, hampered by their land-locked territory and limited resources, were in most places rolled over by Serb forces. Then—from early 1993—they found themselves fighting their Croatian former allies as well, in a war nearly as vicious as the Serb-Muslim confrontation. Not surprisingly, the Muslims responded by generating "a strident, xenophobic Muslim nationalism" mirroring that of their tormentors.[12] However, neither it nor its Croatian counterpart ever matched Serb nationalism in destructiveness. An in-depth United Nations report subsequently ascribed 90 percent of atrocities in Bosnia-Herzegovina to Serbs, and just 10 percent to Croats and Muslims combined.[13]

In August 1992, Western reporters broke the story of Serb-run concentration camps in Bosnia where Muslim males, and some females, were detained.[14] At Omarska, the grimmest of these camps, "there were routine and constant beatings; in the dormitories, on the way to and from the canteen or the latrines, all the time. The guards used clubs, thick electrical cable, rifle butts, fists, boots, brass knuckle-dusters, iron rods. . . . Every night, after midnight, the guards called out the names of one or more prisoners. These prisoners were taken out and beaten bloody, their bones often broken and their skin punctured."[15] Hundreds, if not thousands, died. Penny Marshall of ITN wrote that survivors were reduced to "various stages of human decay and affliction; the bones of their elbows and wrists protrude like pieces of jagged stone from the pencil thin stalks to which their arms have been reduced."[16] Such images, reminiscent of Nazi concentration camps, sparked an international uproar. Combined with revelations of mass executions and the rape of Bosnian-Muslim women, the camps spawned the first widespread use of the term "genocide" in a Balkans context.[17]

GENDERCIDE AND GENOCIDE IN BOSNIA

The strategy of "ethnic cleansing," as it became known in Western media and public discussion, was intended not only to ensure military victory and the expulsion of target populations, but to establish the boundaries of a post-genocide territorial arrangement.[18] As Laura Silber and Alan Little argue, "the technique . . . was designed to render the territory ethnically pure, and to make certain, by instilling a hatred and fear that would endure, that Muslims and Serbs could never again live together."[19]

Central to this policy was killing civilians, overwhelmingly men of "battle age." The war in Bosnia-Herzegovina offers one of the most vivid modern examples of gendercide, or gender-selective mass killing, discussed in a comparative context in Chapter 13. As with most cases of gendercide, the gender variable interacted with those of *age* and *community prominence* to produce a genocidal outcome in Bosnia (and again in Kosovo in 1999). Journalist Mark Danner described the *modus operandi* of Serb forces as follows:

1. *Concentration.* Surround the area to be cleansed and after warning the resident Serbs—often they are urged to leave or are at least told to mark their houses with white flags—intimidate the target population with artillery fire and arbitrary executions and then bring them out into the streets.
2. *Decapitation.* Execute political leaders and those capable of taking their places: lawyers, judges, public officials, writers, professors.
3. *Separation.* Divide women, children, and old men from men of "fighting age"—sixteen years to sixty years old.
4. *Evacuation.* Transport women, children, and old men to the border, expelling them into a neighboring territory or country.
5. *Liquidation.* Execute "fighting age" men, dispose of bodies.[20]

Throughout the Bosnian war, this strategy was systematically implemented—primarily, but not solely, by Serb military and paramilitary forces. The Srebrenica slaughter of July 1995 was by far the most destructive instance of gendercidal killing in the Balkans (brace yourself, then see the photo essay, photo 5); but there are dozens of more quotidian examples. Some are cited in a short section of the Helsinki Watch report, *War Crimes in Bosnia-Hercegovina*, covering the first and most murderous phase of the war:

> In my village, about 180 men were killed. The army put all men in the center of the village. After the killing, the women took care of the bodies and identified them. The older men buried the bodies. (Trnopolje)

> The army came to the village that day. They took us from our houses. The men were beaten. The army came in on trucks and started shooting at the men and killing them. (Prnovo)

> The army took most of the men and killed them. There were bodies everywhere. (Rizvanovici)

> Our men had to hide. My husband was with us, but hiding. I saw my uncle being beaten on July 25 when there was a kind of massacre. The Serbs were searching for arms. Three hundred men were killed that day. (Carakovo)[21]

The trend culminated in the genocidal slaughter of some 8,000 Bosnian Muslim men and boys, described in Box 8.1. In a tally supplied several years after the war and genocide ended, the International Committee of the Red Cross (ICRC) noted that of the thousands of Bosnians still registered as missing, "92% are men and 8% are women."[22]

As in Armenia in 1915, with community males murdered or incarcerated, Serb soldiers and paramilitaries were better able to inflict atrocities on remaining community members. Women, especially younger ones, were special targets. They were subject to rape, often repeatedly, often by gangs, and often in the presence of a father or husband. Typical was the testimony offered by "E.," just 16 years old:

> Several Chetniks arrived. One, a man around 30, ordered me to follow him into the house. I had to go. He started looking for money, jewelry and other valuables. He wanted to know where the men were. I didn't answer. Then he ordered me to undress. I was terribly afraid. I took off my clothes, feeling that I was falling apart. The feeling seemed under my skin; I was dying, my entire being was murdered. I closed my eyes, I couldn't look at him. He hit me. I fell. Then he lay on me. He did it to me. I cried, twisted my body convulsively, bled. I had been a virgin.
>
> He went out and invited two Chetniks to come in. I cried. The two repeated what the first one had done to me. I felt lost. I didn't even know when they left. I don't know how long I stayed there, lying on the floor alone, in a pool of blood.
>
> My mother found me. I couldn't imagine anything worse. I had been raped, destroyed and terribly hurt. But for my mother this was the greatest sorrow of our lives. We both cried and screamed. She dressed me.
>
> I would like to be a mother some day. But how? In my world, men represent terrible violence and pain. I cannot control that feeling.[23]

It was in the Bosnian context that the term "genocidal rape" was minted, stressing the centrality of sexual assaults of women to the broader campaign of "cleansing." It should be noted that men and adolescent boys were also sexually assaulted and tortured on a large scale in detention facilities such as Omarska and Trnopolje.[24]

THE INTERNATIONAL DIMENSION

If the caliber of the political leadership on all sides of the Balkan wars left much to be desired, the same may be said of international policymaking, beginning with Germany's machinations over Croatian and Slovenian independence. Animated by a vision of expanding economic and political influence, Germany—led by foreign minister Hans-Dietrich Genscher—pressed the rest of the European Union to support Yugoslavia's dissolution. The campaign was fiercely opposed by British representative Lord Carrington, whose plan to safeguard peace in the Balkans depended upon a carrot of recognition being extended only in return for guarantees of minority rights. Bosnian Muslim leader Alija Izetbegovic desperately tried to head off a German/EU declaration of support, while UN Secretary-General Perez de Cuellar warned Genscher that recognizing Croatia would unleash "the most terrible war" in Bosnia-Herzegovina.[25] The efforts were to no avail, and

German/EU recognition was duly granted in May 1992. Many see this as an important spur to the genocide unleashed across Bosnia in ensuing months.

The pivotal role of the United States was characterized by vacillation on the independence issue, guided by a conviction that "we don't have a dog in this fight" (George H.W. Bush's Secretary of State, James Baker, speaking in 1992). The besieging of Srebrenica and other Muslim-majority cities in Bosnia in spring 1993 prompted a US-led response to establish six "safe areas" under UN protection, but these were never effectively defended. When Srebrenica fell to the Serbs, it was "protected" by fewer than four hundred Dutch peacekeepers, mostly lightly armed and under orders not to fire their weapons except in self-defense. Genocidal massacres of Bosnian Muslim men and boys were the predictable result. Suspicion has swirled that, mass atrocities aside, the US and EU were not unhappy to see the "safe areas" fall to the Serbs. (An unnamed US official stated at the time that "While losing the enclaves has been unfortunate for Bosnia, it's been great for us.")[26]

Figure 8.3 Coffins containing the exhumed remains of Srebrenica massacre victims are prepared for reinterment at the annual memorial ceremony in Potocari, Bosnia and Herzegovina, July 2007.

Source: Author's photo.

Figure 8.4 Bosnian Muslim women mourners at the Srebrenica reinterment ceremony depicted in Figure 8.3.

Source: Author's photo, July 2007.

BOX 8.1 ONE MAN'S STORY: NEZAD AVDIC

July 1995. For three years, the city of Srebrenica, with its majority Bosnian-Muslim population, had been one of the major conflict points of the war in Bosnia-Herzegovina. In April 1993, with Srebrenica on the verge of falling to Bosnian Serb forces, the United Nations oversaw the evacuation of children, women, and the elderly, while accepting Serb demands that no males of "battle age" be allowed to leave. It then declared Srebrenica a UN-protected "safe haven." This status held for a little over two years, overseen by first Canadian, then Dutch peacekeepers. The population experienced ever greater hunger and material deprivation. It also fell under the sway of Naser Oric, a Muslim paramilitary leader who organized murderous raids out of the enclave against Serb civilians in surrounding villages.[27]

Finally, on July 6, 1995, the Bosnian Serbs decided to implement their "endgame."[28] Serb General Ratko Mladic promised his men a "feast": "There will be blood up to your knees."[29] The peacekeepers watched without firing a shot as the Serbs overcame light Bosnian-Muslim resistance and rounded up most of the population.

Understanding immediately that they were at mortal risk, thousands of "battle-age" men sought to flee through the surrounding hills to Muslim-controlled territory. Most were killed in the hills, or massacred *en masse* after capture. The men who remained behind, including elderly and adolescent males, were systematically separated from the children and women, who—as in 1993—were allowed to flee in buses to safety. The captured males were trucked off to be slaughtered.

441

Nezad Avdic, a 17-year-old Bosnian Muslim, was among the intended victims. "When the truck stopped, we immediately heard shooting outside," he recalled. "The Chetniks [Serb paramilitaries] told us to get out, five at a time. I was in the middle of the group, and the men in front didn't want to get out. They were terrified, they started pulling back. But we had no choice, and when it was my turn to get out with five others, I saw dead bodies everywhere."

Avdic was lined up in front of a mass grave. "We stood in front of the Chetniks with our backs turned to them. They ordered us to lie down, and as I threw myself on the ground, I heard gunfire. I was hit in my right arm and three bullets went through the right side of my torso. I don't recall whether or not I fell on the ground unconscious. But I remember being frightened, thinking I would soon be dead or another bullet would hit. I thought it would soon be all over."

Lying among wounded men, "hear[ing] others screaming and moaning," Avdic maintained his deathlike pose. "One of the Chetniks ordered the others to check and see what bodies were still warm. 'Put a bullet through all the heads, even if they're cold.' " But his partner replied: "Fuck their mothers! They're all dead."[30]

They weren't. "I heard a truck leave," Avdic said. "I didn't know what to do. . . . I saw someone moving about ten metres away from me and asked, 'Friend, are you alive?' "

With his companion, Avdic managed to flee the scene after Serb forces departed. He was one of a tiny handful of survivors of a connected series of genocidal massacres that claimed more than 7,000 lives. This made Srebrenica the worst slaughter in Europe since the killings of political opponents by Yugoslav partisan forces after the Second World War. Srebrenica was also the crowning genocidal massacre of the Balkan wars of the 1990s—but not, unfortunately, the final one. The Serb assault on Kosovo, with its ethnic-Albanian majority, followed in 1999, with genocidal atrocities reminiscent of Srebrenica, though on a smaller scale.

The Americans and Europeans turned a blind eye to Croatia's rearmament, which violated the arms embargo formally imposed on all sides. The US also forged a "tacit agreement to allow Iran and other Moslem countries to expand covert arms supplies to the Bosnians."[31] A month after Srebrenica fell, the Croatians combined with Muslim forces to launch Operation Storm, a dramatic offensive against the Serb–held Krajina region.[32] Milosevic, once the Bosnian Serbs' ardent champion, now abandoned them, the better to present himself as a Balkans peacemaker, and secure the lifting of economic sanctions.

In a matter of days, the Croatian–Muslim offensive overran Krajina, resulting in "another biblical movement of people" as up to 200,000 Serbs fled to Serb-populated regions of Bosnia.[33] "Greater Serbia is in refugee convoys," commented

Figure 8.5 The Dayton Accords, reached in Dayton, Ohio, in November 1995, brought an end to the war in Bosnia, establishing the unstable multiethnic state of Bosnia and Herzegovina. Shown at the official signing ceremony in Paris on December 14, 1995, are former Yugoslav president Slobodan Milosevic (seated third from left); to Milosevic's left, Bosnian prime minister Alija Izetbegovic; and past the assistant's outstretched arm, Croatian president Franjo Tudjman. All three leaders are now dead. While Izetbegovic bore a measure of responsibility for fueling intercommunal tensions in the prelude to the war, it was Tudjman and, above all, Milosevic who fomented the genocidal outbreak of the 1990s. Milosevic went on to order an assault on the Kosovar Albanian population of Kosovo in 1998–1999. He died of a heart attack on March 11, 2006, while on trial for genocide, crimes against humanity, and war crimes at the International Criminal Tribunal for the Former Yugoslavia (ICTY) in The Hague, Netherlands (see Chapter 15).

Source: Brian Schlumbohm/US Air Force/Wikimedia Commons.

a Belgrade observer.[34] Croatian President Tudjman celebrated the expulsions, declaring that the country's Serbs had "disappeared ignominiously, as if they had never populated this land."[35] The Krajina *fait accompli* left in its wake Europe's largest refugee population, but it was welcomed by the West, especially the US.[36] In the aftermath, the Clinton government invited the warring parties to talks at Wright–Patterson Air Force Base in Dayton, Ohio. These resulted in the signing of a comprehensive peace agreement (the Dayton Accords) in November 1995, and the introduction of 60,000 NATO peacekeepers to oversee it.

An estimated 102,000 people had died in the Bosnian war and genocide, about 50 percent of them Muslim and 30 percent Serbs. "However, while Serb casualties were overwhelmingly among military personnel, Muslim casualties were evenly split between military and civilian, so that the great majority of civilian casualties were Muslims."[37] And there was still a final genocidal act to be inflicted on a Muslim population in pursuit of Greater Serbia—in Kosovo, the Serb province where Milosevic first unveiled his nationalist agenda.

KOSOVO, 1998–1999

To counter the Serb police state imposed in 1989, a parallel political structure arose in Kosovar Albanian communities, built around the non-violent resistance movement led by Ibrahim Rugova. Remarkably, this parallel authority managed to preserve Albanian-language education and a semblance of social services for ethnic Albanians.

Eventually, after nearly a decade of "a system of apartheid that excluded the province's majority Albanian population from virtually every phase of political, economic, social, and cultural life,"[38] an armed guerrilla movement—the Kosovo Liberation Army (KLA)—launched attacks in 1997. Many KLA leaders desired the political union of Kosovo's Albanians with their "compatriots" across the border in Albania proper. Guerrilla war through 1998 and into 1999 resulted in the Serb killing of hundreds of ethnic-Albanian civilians, and the internal displacement of 200,000 more.

Milosevic now began to plot a decisive resolution of the Kosovo quandary. "In a long career, this would be his masterpiece, cleansing the Serb homeland of its Albanian interlopers in a matter of weeks."[39] US General Wesley Clark witnessed a "choleric" outburst by Milosevic against Kosovar Albanians in 1998. "We know how to deal with those murderers and rapists," Milosevic raged. "They are killers, killers of their own kind, but we know how to deal with them and have done it before. In 1946, in Drenica [in post-World War Two reprisals], we killed them all. . . . Well, of course, we didn't [kill them] all at once. It took several years." Clark described it as "like watching a Nuremberg rally."[40]

European countries sought to head off full-scale war, dispatching an observer team (the Kosovo Verification Commission) to monitor a ceasefire between the Serbs and the KLA. Both sides were guilty of violations, but Serb paramilitaries' mass murder of dozens of Kosovar men at the village of Racak (January 16, 1999) sparked the greatest protest. Abortive negotiations under Western auspices at Rambouillet, France, ended in impasse and acrimony. Pro-Serb commentators have accused Western countries, in league with the KLA, of stage-managing a crisis at Rambouillet in order to justify a quick military defeat to bring Milosevic into line.[41]

It did not transpire that way. On March 19, 1999, the Serbs launched "a massive campaign of ethnic cleansing, aimed not only at tipping the demographic balance [of Kosovo] in Belgrade's favor but also—by driving hundreds of thousands of desperate Albanians over the border into the fragile neighboring states of Macedonia and Albania—at threatening the Western allies with the destabilization of the entire Balkan peninsula."[42] The campaign reached its peak after March 24, when NATO began high-altitude bombing of Serb positions in Kosovo and other targets throughout Yugoslavia. This would remain NATO's exclusive, and ineffective, military tactic. The Allies seemed terrified of taking casualties, on the ground or in the air, and jeopardizing popular support for the war. They also assumed that Milosevic would quickly crumble in the face of Allied aerial assault. It proved "a colossal miscalculation," and there are grounds for arguing that the bombing in fact prompted an escalation of the Serb campaign. "NATO leaders, then, stand

Map 8.2 Kosovo.

Source: Map provided by WorldAtlas.com.

accused of exacerbating the very humanitarian disaster that their actions were justified as averting."[43]

The Serb assault on Kosovar Albanians bore many of the hallmarks of earlier Serb campaigns. Army units and paramilitary forces worked in close coordination to empty the territory of ethnic Albanians through selective acts of terror and mass murder. Gendercidal killing again predominated, as in the largest massacre of the war, at the village of Meja:

Shortly before dawn on April 27, according to locals, a large contingent of Yugoslav army troops garrisoned in Junik started moving eastward through the valley, dragging men from their houses and pushing them into trucks. "Go to Albania!" they screamed at the women before driving on to the next town with their prisoners. By the time they got to Meja they had collected as many as 300 men. The regular army took up positions around the town while the militia and paramilitaries went through the houses grabbing the last few villagers and shoving them out into the road. The men were surrounded by fields most of them had worked in their whole lives, and they could look up and see mountains they'd admired since they were children. Around noon the first group was led to the compost heap, gunned down, and burned under piles of cornhusks. A few minutes later a group of about 70 were forced to lie down in three neat rows and were machine-gunned in the back. The rest—about 35 men—were taken to a farmhouse along the Gjakove road, pushed into one of the rooms, and then shot through the windows at point-blank range. The militiamen who did this then stepped inside, finished them off with shots to the head, and burned the house down. They walked away singing.[44]

About 10,000 ethnic Albanians died during the war, along with some Serbs and Roma (Gypsies).[45] The killings were accompanied by the largest mass deportation of a civilian population in decades. Some 800,000 Kosovar Albanians were rounded up and expelled to Albania and Macedonia. Pictures of the exodus bolstered Western resolve, and the Allies began to discuss sending ground forces into the conflict.

In response to growing Allied resolve, Russian pressure, and perhaps the war-crimes indictment issued against him in late May 1999, Milosevic agreed to a ceasefire. The arrangement provided for the withdrawal of Serb forces from Kosovo, and the introduction of 18,000 NATO troops along with 3,500 UN police. These outside forces arrived quickly, but not rapidly—or resolutely—enough to prevent a round of revenge attacks by ethnic Albanians against Serb civilians in northern Kosovo. These prompted 150,000 Serbs to flee to the Serbian heartland, where they joined the 200,000 refugees still stranded by Operation Storm in 1995.

AFTERMATHS

The Dayton Accords brought peace to Bosnia-Herzegovina, and between Croatia and what was left of Yugoslavia. They also froze in place the genocidal "ethnic cleansing" of preceding years. The peace was the peace of the grave: in addition to the more than 100,000 people killed, an astonishing 1,282,000 were registered as internally displaced persons (IDPs).[46] Despite formal declarations that all IDPs should be allowed to return to their homes, in Bosnia the "ground reality . . . in many ways resembles *de facto* nationalist partition rather than a single, sovereign state. . . . The overwhelming majority of Bosnians, well over 90%, now live in areas that are largely homogeneous in the national sense."[47]

The new state of Bosnia-Herzegovina was administered by the Organization for Security and Cooperation in Europe (OSCE). Its High Representative had "far-reaching powers . . . extend[ing] well beyond military matters to cover the most basic aspects of government and state."[48] Over US$5 billion was pledged to "the largest per capita reconstruction plan in history,"[49] and tens of thousands of NATO troops arrived to police the peace. (In December 2004, NATO was replaced by a 7,000-strong European Union force, though most of the troops simply switched insignias.)

An important test of the post-Dayton era was the peace agreement between Croatia and rump Yugoslavia. In 2004, with Croatia pushing for membership in the European Union, the new Prime Minister Ivo Sanader shifted away from the extreme nationalism of Franjo Tudjman, who had died in 2001. After years of "insurmountable impediments" being placed in the way of Serbs attempting to return to their homes (according to Human Rights Watch), Sanader promised a more constructive approach. As the British newspaper *The Guardian* pointed out, however, he ran "little political risk" for doing so, "simply because so few Serbs are returning." While some 70,000 mostly elderly Serbs had accepted the offer, over 200,000 remained as refugees in Bosnia and Herzegovina along with Serbia.[50]

What of those who supervised and committed the atrocities? Many lived comfortably, protected by their ethnic communities and by NATO forces' gossamer commitment to rounding them up. But international justice did register some successes. The International Criminal Tribunal for the Former Yugoslavia (ICTY), established by the UN Security Council in May 1993, began proceedings at The Hague on May 16, 1996. Many greeted the tribunal with derision, viewing it as too little, too late. Nonetheless, by late 2004 the Tribunal had conducted fifty-two prosecutions and sentenced thirty individuals. Its greatest coup came on June 28, 2001, when former Yugoslav president Slobodan Milosevic was transported to The Hague to stand trial. (Milosevic had been toppled by a popular uprising in September 2000, after refusing to recognize unfavorable election results.) The successor government under Vojislav Kostunica saw surrendering Milosevic as the price of rejoining the international community (see further discussion in Chapter 16). Milosevic, charged with genocide for crimes in Bosnia-Herzegovina,[51] waged a spirited defense before the tribunal, but died in March 2006 before a verdict was reached.

Gradually, more of Milosevic's key partners in crime in Bosnia-Herzegovina have been brought to justice. Bosnian Serb commander, General Radislav Krstic, was captured and turned over to The Hague, where he was found guilty in August 2001 of the crime of genocide for his leading role in the carnage at Srebrenica. The biggest coup was the capture of Radovan Karadzic (see Figure 8.6), former prime minister of the Bosnian Serbs, in July 2008. Karadzic's trial by the International Criminal Tribunal for the Former Yugoslavia (ICTY) was one of the setpiece international-legal showdowns of its time. As this edition was going into production, in March 2016, Karadzic was convicted of genocide at Srebrenica, as well as "five counts of crimes against humanity and four of war crimes."[52] He received a 40-year sentence, which many Bosnian survivors considered too lenient[53]—though Karadzic, aged 70 at the time of his conviction, is unlikely to see freedom again.

Croatian, Bosnian Muslim, and Kosovar Albanian suspects have also faced the ICTY—as with the 2001 indictment of Croatian General Ante Gotovina for atrocities committed in Krajina (convicted in 2011, but controversially acquitted on appeal the following year), and Kosovo Prime Minister Ranush Haradinaj, indicted by the tribunal in March 2005 on charges of "murder, rape and deportation of civilians"[54] (acquitted in 2008, acquitted again on appeal in 2012). The ecumenical approach to indictments and prosecutions was commendable, but many critics—and certainly many Serbs in Bosnia and Serbia—considered the acquittals (including that of Naser Oric, see p. 455, n. 27) to be evidence of anti-Serb bias in the tribunal's operations.[55]

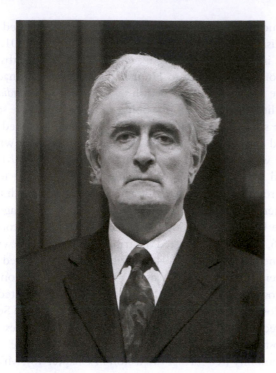

Figure 8.6 Radovan Karadzic, a former psychiatrist, was prime minister of the breakaway Bosnian Serb republic throughout the war and genocide of the 1990s. Karadzic was captured in Serbia in July 2008 following a tipoff, and turned over to the International Criminal Tribunal for the Former Yugoslavia (ICTY). This photo was taken at his first court appearance before the tribunal in The Hague, Netherlands, in November 2009.[56]

Source: Courtesy ICTY.

Another precedent-setting legal case was brought by the government of Bosnia and Herzegovina against Serbia and Montenegro (Montenegro left the federation in 2006) before the venerable International Court of Justice. The suit claimed compensation from Serbia for the genocide inflicted at Srebrenica. In a February 2007 decision that surprised many observers, the Court rejected the genocide charge, ruling that Bosnia and Herzegovina had not proved that the authorities in Belgrade had ordered the massacre, and indeed that "all indications are to the contrary: that the decision to kill the adult male population of the Muslim community of Srebrenica was taken by the VRS [Bosnian Serb Army] Main Staff, but without instructions from or effective control by" Serbia and Montenegro. For this reason, "the [court] . . . found that Serbia had not committed genocide, incited the commission of genocide, conspired to commit genocide, or been complicit in the commission of genocide in Bosnia, but that it had violated the Genocide convention by failing to prevent genocide in Srebrenica and by not arresting general Ratko Mladic."[57]

On the ground in Bosnia and Herzegovina, there were indications in 2008–2009 that an intercommunal truce was solidifying—but also that it was eroding. "Significant riots or civil disturbances are rare," wrote Valery Perry of the OSCE in a 2009 "survey of reconciliation processes." "Having experienced three and a half years of war, people prefer this cold peace. Yet a true peace awaits." Perry pointed to a still-toxic political atmosphere: one "in which all parties have defined politics as a zero-sum game," and in which "compromise is viewed as loss, and long-term possibilities are sacrificed for short-term gains." Moreover, "much of society remains dangerously politicized . . . Civil society is still very weak and has been unable to begin to effectively and consistently shape and determine the political agenda."[58]

As so often, the city of Mostar (see the photo essay, photo 9) provided a litmus test. A triangular conflict there among Muslims, Serbs, and Croats had produced some of the fiercest fighting of the war. In the conflict's wake, a gradual remingling of the population began, as this author witnessed on a visit to Mostar in July 2007. It was acceptable for Croats to visit the Muslim side and vice versa, to shop, to stroll, to eat in restaurants. Along the shattered main strip of the city—still the single most war-damaged urban landscape I have ever seen, though I have not been to Grozny (Box 5a)—a unique experiment was thriving at the Mostar Gymnasium (high school). The Gymnasium was heavily damaged in the war, and after a lengthy spell in which only Croat students occupied a single floor of it, it became the only mixed public school in the city. As Nicole Itano of the *Global Post* noted, however, "even here, the integration only goes so far: there are two separate curricula for Croatian and Muslim students." Nevertheless, "sports, school activities and a few classes, such as technology, are combined," and students mingled relatively freely during recess and in other social contexts. Significant intercommunal flirting was also reported—always a good sign. On the third floor of the refurbished building, the institution that gave me my start in international life—the United World College network (www.uwc.org)—had set up its latest college promoting coexistence and mutual understanding. Graduates, including scholarship students from around the world, received internationally-recognized accreditation through the Swiss-based International Baccalaureate system.[59]

Yet the Gymnasium was an oasis in a city where the reconciliation process still seemed fragile. Informants who stated that either "side" could stroll freely on the other's territory also stressed that it would be unwise for out-group members to purchase property or otherwise establish residence on the "wrong" side of the river. In 2008, a politically significant clash broke out in Mostar over a football (soccer) game. Turkey and Croatia were playing in a tense quarter-final at the Euro 2008 championship. Mostar's Muslim population rooted publicly for the Turks; the city's Croats were predictably otherwise inclined. The result (of a match which Turkey won) was a fierce confrontation between "rival fans, who hurled rocks and bottles at each other," while "gunshots and car alarms could be heard as fans attacked cars and smashed nearby shop windows."[60] Renewed soccer clashes in Mostar in 2011 were accompanied by similar ethnically-based rioting in Sarajevo and Banja Luka.[61]

It was entirely possible that, following a "decent interval," the ethnic cantons of Bosnia and Herzegovina would become independent countries, as other former Yugoslavian territories like Montenegro and Kosovo (see below) had done in the postwar period. This would place something of a seal on the genocidal "cleansings" of the 1990s. At the same time, one could imagine such a patchwork of smaller states being reabsorbed into larger associations, both continental and regional, which are a prominent feature of the European political landscape (see further discussion in Chapter 16). Such fragmentation might not, therefore, impede efforts to reestablish historic linkages across these sundered lands and traumatized populations. Symbolic in this respect was the reopening in 2010 of the Belgrade-Sarajevo train route, abandoned since the federation collapsed in the early 1990s. Younger travelers, in particular, expressed optimism that such linkages could overcome the chasms of the recent past. Twenty-one-year-old passenger Sasa Mehmedagic defined himself as "half-Muslim and half-Serb and . . . proud of it," adding: "I think young people realize that nationalism and racism are wrong because we are all from the same flesh." He and his friends "said they no longer wanted to be defined along ethnic or religious lines but viewed themselves simply as Bosnians. They believed that their people were ready to move beyond the ethnic divisions that led their parents' generation to war, they said, if their leaders stopped agitating for political gain."[62]

As for Kosovo, its trajectory since the first edition of *Genocide: A Comprehensive Introduction* was published in 2006 has been dramatic. With its declaration of independence on February 17, 2008, it became an independent state—at least for the 112 governments that had recognized it by June 2015.[63] While many observers, this one included, welcomed Kosovo's entry to the community of nations, concerns persisted over the fate of the now-stranded Serb minority, concentrated around Mitrovica in the north of the state. In March 2004, an anti-Serb pogrom in Kosovo had killed nineteen people and destroyed hundreds of Serb homes. Human Rights Watch criticized international forces for doing little to prevent or stop the violence: "In many cases, minorities under attack were left entirely unprotected and at the mercy of the rioters. . . . In too many cases, NATO peacekeepers locked the gates to their bases and watched as Serb homes burned."[64]

A visit to Kosovo in 2013 found the northern town of Mitrovica more divided than ever, with Italian troops from NATO's KFOR (Kosovo Force) policing a tense *de facto* ethnic boundary at the bridge across the Ibar river (Figure 8.7). Strolling the Serb neighborhoods on the northern side, with their disproportionately elderly population, my eyes were assailed by banners and graffiti equating the European Union with Nazi imperialism (Figure 8.8) and calling for a "BOJKOT" of Kosovo-wide elections, which Serb nationalists contended would simply seal the fate of the Serb community in Kosovo. Elsewhere in the territory, I came across more KFOR troops guarding the beautiful medieval Serb monasteries at Peje (Pec) and Decani, the only defense against anti-Serb vandalism and violence. In the southern city of Prizren, I walked up footpaths in the surrounding hills, past gutted and burnt-out residences and churches from the 2004 anti-Serb pogrom (Figure 8.9). A United Nations official with long experience in the region told me, with some anger and frustration, that the Albanian-nationalist project of "cleansing" Kosovo of its Serb population was largely completed, and unlikely to be reversed.

IMAGES OF KOSOVO

Figure 8.7 An Italian carabinieri member of KFOR patrols at the bridge across the Ibar river in the ethnically divided town of Mitrovica, Kosovo.

Figure 8.8 Anti-EU graffiti on the northern (Serb) side of Mitrovica.

Figure 8.9 A view over the city of Prizren, with a residence gutted and destroyed during the 2004 anti-Serb pogrom.

Sources: Author's photos, October 2013.

Since the second edition of this book appeared, I have participated as an expert consultant in several UN-cosponsored conflict prevention seminars in the former Yugoslavia (Sarajevo, Skopje, Belgrade, and Budva in Montenegro, with side-travels in Kosovo).[65] It is the youth of the region who most inspire me with their determination to transcend the hatreds and vendettas of the past. As welcome as their core humanism is their skeptical/ironic political stance and their cosmopolitan-bohemian flair. As someone who first viewed the region while it was still an intact Yugoslavia—picnicking on the hills around Sarajevo in 1982, which a decade later would be emplacements for Serb artillery; as one who studied in the same United World College system that gave rise to the only intercommunal educational curriculum in Mostar, Bosnia; and as a European citizen, I join Mark Biondich in believing that:

> The solution for the region's remaining problems lies in its complete integration into multilateral security and political arrangements. While there will be no small measure of irony if the *Pax Ottomanica* [Ottoman empire] is eventually supplanted in the Balkans by the *Pax Europea*, this process would help to transform historically contested frontiers into relatively symbolic borders, and alleviate the severity of, if not resolve, the region's remaining national questions, appreciably diminishing their potential to destabilize while affording minority populations appropriate guarantees of their national and civil rights. . . . There is cause for cautious optimism . . . For the first time in modern Balkan history, a majority of Balkan states have been integrated into a democratic, multilateral security arrangement (NATO), while four are EU member states. There is good reason to believe that the remaining western Balkan states may join the EU over the next decade. These societies are today literate, industrial, and highly urbanized. The institutions of political democracy and civil society have undeniably grown stronger since 1989. A reversion to the violence of the early 1990s thus seems improbable.[66]

FURTHER STUDY

Fred Abrahams, Gilles Peress, and Eric Stover, *A Village Destroyed, May 14, 1999: War Crimes in Kosovo*. Berkeley, CA: University of California Press, 2001. Vivid photographic record and text.

Edina Becirevic, *Genocide on the Drina River*. New Haven, CT: Yale University Press, 2014. Wrenching account of Serb genocide in Bosnia from 1992 to 1995, by a survivor who went on to become a distinguished writer and scholar.

Mark Biondich, *The Balkans: Revolution, War, & Political Violence since 1878*. Oxford: Oxford University Press, 2011. A synoptic treatment usefully read alongside Mojzes (below); a little drier.

Carl T. Dahlman and Gerard Toal, *Bosnia Remade: Ethnic Cleansing and Its Reversal*. Oxford: Oxford University Press, 2011. The most wide-ranging survey of post-Dayton politics and processes of reconciliation.

Misha Glenny, *The Fall of Yugoslavia: The Third Balkan War* (3rd rev. edn). London: Penguin, 1996. Solid journalistic overview, best read alongside Silber and Little (see below).

Helsinki Watch, *War Crimes in Bosnia-Hercegovina, Vol. 2*. New York: Human Rights Watch, 1993. Detailed investigation of atrocities in the first phases of the Bosnian war.

Michael A. Innes, ed., *Bosnian Security after Dayton: New Perspectives*. London: Routledge, 2006. Essays examining the first decade of peacemaking (1995–2005) in Bosnia, including mine on post-genocide media.

Ivana Macek, *Sarajevo under Siege: Anthropology in Wartime*. Philadelphia, PA: University of Pennsylvania Press, 2009. Anthropological study of life during the three-year siege of Bosnia's cosmopolitan capital.

Paul Mojzes, *Balkan Genocides: Holocaust and Ethnic Cleansing in the Twentieth Century*. Lanham, MD: Rowman & Littlefield, 2011. An encompassing overview, with extended attention to "the first European genocide of the twentieth century" (the Balkan wars of 1912–1913) and the "multiple genocides of World War II," along with the 1990s atrocities.

Organization for Security and Cooperation in Europe (OSCE), *Kosovo/Kosova: As Seen, As Told*. Available at www.osce.org/odihr/17772?download=true. Detailed report on atrocities in Kosovo.

David Rohde, *Endgame: The Betrayal and Fall of Srebrenica, Europe's Worst Massacre since World War II*. Boulder, CO: Westview Press, 1998. Heart-stopping account of the only slaughter in the Bosnian conflict so far labeled "genocide" by the Yugoslavia tribunal (ICTY).

Louis Sell, *Slobodan Milosevic and the Destruction of Yugoslavia*. Durham, NC: Duke University Press, 2002. Incisive study of Milosevic's rise and fall.

Laura Silber and Allan Little, *The Death of Yugoslavia* (rev. edn). London: BBC Books, 1996. The best broad overview of the breakup of Yugoslavia.

Chuck Sudetic, *Blood and Vengeance: One Family's Story of the War in Bosnia*. London: Penguin, 1998. Intimate portrait of Bosnia in upheaval.

Ed Vulliamy, *Seasons in Hell: Understanding Bosnia's War*. New York: St. Martin's Press, 1994. Pulitzer Prize–winning reportage from the war zone.

NOTES

1 See Stevan K. Pavlowitch, *Hitler's New Disorder: The Second World War in Yugoslavia* (London: Hurst Publishers Ltd., 2008); Ben H. Shepherd, *Terror in the Balkans: German Armies and Partisan Warfare* (Cambridge, MA: Harvard University Press, 2012).

2 Edina Becirevic, *Genocide on the Drina River* (New Haven, CT: Yale University Press, 2014), p. xi. See also Cathie Carmichael, *Ethnic Cleansing in the Balkans: Nationalism and the Destruction of Tradition* (London: Routledge, 2002).

3 Paul Mojzes pulls few punches in describing Tudjman and Milosevic as the "couple from hell": "they reinforced each other, since the policies of one worked to the advantage of the sinister policies of the other. They helped each other achieve their initial goals; for Tudjman, the international recognition of Croatia's independence regardless of cost, and for Milosevic, battlefield victories in pursuit of expanding Serbia to incorporate all territories inhabited by Serbs. It is very likely that had different men been at

the helm of these two states, war may have been avoided and thousands of lives may have been saved." Mojzes, *Balkan Genocides: Holocaust and Ethnic Cleansing in the Twentieth Century* (Lanham, MD: Rowman & Littlefield, 2011), p. 157.

4 Misha Glenny, *The Fall of Yugoslavia* (3rd rev. edn) (London: Penguin, 1996), p. 86.

5 On the early deployment of the rhetoric of "genocide" in the Balkan wars, see Bette Denich, "Dismembering Yugoslavia: Nationalist Ideologies and the Symbolic Revival of Genocide," *American Ethnologist*, 21 (1994), pp. 367–390. In 1986, a declaration by the Serbian Academy of Sciences and Arts referred to "the physical, political, legal, and cultural genocide of the Serbian population of Kosovo" (quoted in Peter Ronayne, "Genocide in Kosovo," *Human Rights Review*, 5: 4 [July 2004], p. 59). Kosovo was additionally significant to Serbs as the site of "the Serbian Golgotha," a famous 1389 battle with the Ottoman armies that Serbs viewed as a heroic defeat, though most historians regard its outcome as inconclusive. See Michael Sells, "Kosovo Mythology and the Bosnian Genocide," in Omer Bartov and Phyllis Mack, eds., *In God's Name: Genocide and Religion in the Twentieth Century* (New York: Berghahn Books, 2001), pp. 180–205.

6 Laura Silber and Allan Little, *The Death of Yugoslavia* (rev. edn) (London: BBC Books, 1996), p. 37.

7 Glenny, *The Fall of Yugoslavia*, pp. 46, 67.

8 Louis Sell, *Slobodan Milosevic and the Destruction of Yugoslavia (Durham, NC: Duke University Press, 2002)*, p. 83.

9 Quoted in the film by Tone Bringa, *We Are All Neighbours*, cited in Jacques Sémelin, *Purify and Destroy: The Political Uses of Massacre and Genocide* (New York: Columbia University Press, 2007), p. 144.

10 Daniel Jonah Goldhagen, *Worse Than War: Genocide, Eliminationism, and the Ongoing Assault on Humanity* (New York: Basic Books, 2009), p. 142.

11 "Though Sarajevo grabbed the headlines, it was clear from the first day of the war that eastern Bosnia, with its hydroelectric dams, highways, and Muslim-majority population, was the key to the Serb leaders' plans to partition Bosnia." Chuck Sudetic, *Blood and Vengeance: One Family's Story of the War in Bosnia* (London: Penguin, 1998), p. 100. Silber and Little also note that "during the summer months of 1992 . . . the world's media concentrated almost exclusively on the siege and bombardment of [Sarajevo], even though much more decisive battles and campaigns were being waged elsewhere. . . . [This] suited Serb leaders very well." Silber and Little, *The Death of Yugoslavia*, p. 253.

12 Aside from the thousands of human casualties, the Muslim–Croat conflict claimed the famous bridge at Mostar, which mirrored Sarajevo with its Catholic, Greek Orthodox, and Muslim populations. The bridge was completely destroyed by Croatian shelling, rebuilt with international assistance, and reopened in 2004.

13 Cited in James Waller, *Becoming Evil: How Ordinary People Commit Genocide and Mass Killing* (Oxford: Oxford University Press, 2002), p. 262.

14 Among the reporters was Ed Vulliamy, who has given a detailed description of the camps and their discovery in his book *Seasons in Hell* (New York: St. Martin's Press, 1994).

15 David Hirsh, *Law against Genocide: Cosmopolitan Trials* (London: Glasshouse Press, 2003), pp. 66–67.

16 Marshall quoted in Silber and Little, *The Death of Yugoslavia*, p. 250.

17 Mark Biondich describes the culture of the Bosnian Serb-run Trnopolje camp as follows. "The abuse of camp detainees began immediately upon their arrival, and thereafter was constant and widespread. They were beaten as they were led from the buses which brought them to the camps and often had their identity documents and money stolen from them. Many were forced to sing Serb nationalist songs and to sit on the burning asphalt for hours without being allowed to move. All were interrogated and many were repeatedly tortured. Scores of detainees, probably several hundred, were killed. Detainees were held in crowded conditions, with little food or water and with

no real toilets. The sick and wounded received little or no medical treatment. Some women were molested and raped. There was a pervasive climate of violence and fear. The ICTY Trial Chamber concluded, in a case against several former camp personnel, that the crimes [against humanity] of persecution, murder, torture, and cruel treatment were widespread." Bondioch, *The Balkans: Revolution, War, & Political Violence since 1878* (Oxford: Oxford University Press, 2011), p. 220.

18 The UN Commission of Experts appointed for the former Yugoslavia defined "ethnic cleansing" in 1994 as "a purposeful policy designed by one ethnic or religious group to remove by violent and terror-inspiring means the civilian population of another ethnic or religious group from certain geographic areas." Quoted in Benjamin Lieberman, "'Ethnic Cleansing' Versus Genocide?" in Donald Bloxham and A. Dirk Moses, eds., *The Oxford Handbook of Genocide Studies* (Oxford: Oxford University Press, 2013), p. 44.

19 Silber and Little, *The Death of Yugoslavia*, p. 245.

20 Mark Danner, "Endgame in Kosovo," *The New York Review of Books*, May 6, 1999, p. 8.

21 Helsinki Watch, *War Crimes in Bosnia-Hercegovina, Vol. 2* (New York: Human Rights Watch, 1993), pp. 82–83.

22 International Committee of the Red Cross, "The Impact of Armed Conflict on Women," March 6, 2001, available at www.refworld.org/pdfid/46e943750.pdf.

23 Slavenka Draculic, "Rape After Rape After Rape," *The New York Times*, December 13, 1992.

24 For example, the most bestial of the camps, Omarska, held some 2,000 men and 33 to 38 women (Helsinki Watch, *War Crimes in Bosnia-Hercegovina*, p. 87).

25 Perez de Cuellar quoted in Glenny, *The Fall of Yugoslavia*, p. 164.

26 Quoted in Sell, *Slobodan Milosevic*, p. 234.

27 The raids were accompanied by "a horde of Muslim refugees, men and women, young and old, who were driven by hunger and, in many cases, a thirst for revenge. Thousands strong, these people would lurk behind the first wave of attacking soldiers and run amok when the defenses around Serb villages collapsed. Some of the refugees used pistols to do the killing; others used knives, bats, and hatchets. But most of them had nothing but their bare hands and the empty rucksacks and suitcases they strapped onto their backs. They came to be known as *torbari*, the bag people. And they were beyond [Naser] Oric's control" — or under it, in a less generous estimation. Sudetic, *Blood and Vengeance*, p. 157. Oric was indicted and tried by the ICTY tribunal, but was acquitted in 2008 for lack of evidence. However, a renewed legal process led to him being extradited from Switzerland to Bosnia and Herzegovina, to stand trial in a national court for war crimes. The trial began in January 2016: see "War Crimes Trial of Naser Oric Begins in Bosnia," *B92.net*, January 26, 2016.

28 See David Rohde, *Endgame: The Betrayal and Fall of Srebrenica, Europe's Worst Massacre since World War II* (New York: Farrar, Straus and Giroux, 1997).

29 Quoted in Mark Danner, "The Killing Fields of Bosnia," *The New York Review of Books*, September 24, 1998 (citing reporting by Roy Gutman of *Newsday*).

30 Avdic's testimony is recounted in Jan Willem Honig and Norbert Both, *Srebrenica: Record of a War Crime* (London: Penguin, 1996), p. 62.

31 Sell, *Slobodan Milosevic*, p. 215.

32 See Mark Danner, "Operation Storm," *The New York Review of Books*, October 22, 1998.

33 Glenny, *The Fall of Yugoslavia*, p. 284.

34 Quoted in Benjamin Lieberman, *Terrible Fate: Ethnic Cleansing in the Making of Modern Europe* (Chicago, IL: Ivan R. Dee, 2006), p. 322.

35 Tudjman quoted in "Stormy Memories," *The Economist*, July 30, 2005.

36 Stated one European diplomat: "Until now at least the international community has been united in its condemnation of ethnic cleansing. Now it seems one of its members is openly supporting the mass movement of population by the most terrible force." Quoted in Glenny, *The Fall of Yugoslavia*, p. 285. On the present-day situation

of the refugees, and the continuing drain of Serbs from Croatia, see Giulia Bertoluzzi and Tanja Jovetic, "Displaced for Life? Serbs in Croatia Struggle to Regain Housing Rights," September 15 [2014?], www.dispatchesinternational.org/?p=979.

37 Robert M. Hayden, "Mass Killings and Images of Genocide in Bosnia, 1941–5 and 1992–5," in Dan Stone, ed., *The Historiography of Genocide* (London: Palgrave Macmillan, 2008), p. 487.

38 Sell, *Slobodan Milosevic*, p. 93.

39 Danner, "Endgame in Kosovo," p. 11.

40 Sell, *Slobodan Milosevic*, p. 269.

41 This is a common theme of the literature cited in Chapter 16, n. 36.

42 Sell, *Slobodan Milosevic*, p. 304.

43 Nicholas Wheeler, *Saving Strangers: Humanitarian Intervention in International Society* (Oxford: Oxford University Press, 2000), p. 269.

44 Sebastian Junger, "The Forensics of War," in Junger, *Fire* (New York: W.W. Norton, 2001), p. 158. Another reporter estimates that 500 men were killed in the Meja massacre: see Joshua Hammer, "On the Trail of Hard Truth," *Newsweek*, July 9, 2000.

45 The debate over the alleged "exaggeration" of Kosovar Albanian deaths was spirited after the war, and reflects, in Samantha Power's estimation, "the inescapable difficulty of accurately gauging the scale of atrocities while they are being committed." Power, *"A Problem from Hell": America and the Age of Genocide* (New York: Basic Books, 2002), p. 467. Power notes that the ICTY "has received reports that some 11,334 Albanians are buried in 529 sites in Kosovo alone"; moreover, "In 2001 some 427 dead Albanians from Kosovo were exhumed in five mass graves that had been hidden in Serbia proper. An additional three mass grave sites, containing more than 1,000 bodies, were found in a Belgrade suburb and awaited exhumation. Each of the newly discovered sites lies near Yugoslav army or police barracks" (pp. 471–472). For a critique of attempts to downplay genocide in Kosovo, mostly by my colleagues on the left, see Adam Jones, "Kosovo: Orders of Magnitude," *IDEA: A Journal of Social Issues*, 5: 1 (July 2000), available at www.ideajournal.com/articles.php?id=24. A couple of the same culprits figure in denialism around the 1994 genocide of Rwandan Tutsis (see Box 9.2).

46 Figures on dead and displaced from Rory Keane, *Reconstituting Sovereignty: Post-Dayton Bosnia Uncovered* (Burlington, VT: Ashgate, 2002), p. 69.

47 Sumantra Bose, *Bosnia after Dayton: Nationalist Partition and International Intervention* (London: Hurst & Co., 2002), pp. 22, 34.

48 David Chandler, *Bosnia: Faking Democracy after Dayton* (2nd edn) (London: Pluto Press, 1999), p. 43.

49 Bose, *Bosnia after Dayton*, p. 6.

50 Ian Traynor, "Croatia Builds Goodwill in Serb Villages," *The Guardian*, June 19, 2004.

51 Genocide was "curiously absent" from the charge-sheet for Milosevic's actions in Kosovo, "despite the fact that the arc of crime and atrocity in Kosovo seems to fit the Convention's legal definition quite neatly." Ronayne, "Genocide in Kosovo," p. 66.

52 Julian Borger and Owen Bowcott, "Radovan Karadzic Sentenced to 40 Years for Srebrenica Genocide," *The Guardian*, March 24, 2016, www.theguardian.com/world/2016/mar/24/radovan-karadzic-criminally-responsible-for-genocide-at-srebenica.

53 Julian Borger and Owen Boycott, "'Is the Tribunal Not Ashamed?' Karadzic Sentence Angers Victims," *The Guardian*, March 24, 2016, www.theguardian.com/world/2016/mar/24/radovan-karadzic-hague-tribunal-sentence-survivors-victims-reaction.

54 "Ex-Kosovo PM Pleads Not Guilty to War Crimes," Reuters dispatch, March 14, 2005.

55 "Bosnian State Court Rejects Anti-Serb Bias Claims," *Balkan Transitional Justice*, October 22, 2015, www.balkaninsight.com/en/article/bosnian-court-warns-against-irresponsible-criticism-10–21–2015.

56 For a recent biography, see Robert J. Donia, *Radovan Karadžić: Architect of the Bosnian Genocide* (Cambridge: Cambridge University Press, 2015).

57 Hayden, "Mass Killings," p. 506.

58 Valery Perry, "A Survey of Reconciliation Processes in Bosnia and Herzegovina: The Gap between People and Politics," in Joanna R. Quinn, ed., *Reconciliation(s): Transitional Justice in Postconflict Societies* (Montreal, QC: McGill-Queen's University Press, 2009), pp. 226–228.

59 Nicole Itano, "Meet the Students at an Integrated Bosnian High School," *Global Post*, October 15, 2009, www.globalpost.com/dispatch/europe/091014/mostar-bosnia-high-school. I was a scholarship student at the United World College of South-East Asia in Singapore from 1979 to 1981, and credit it with much of the international consciousness I've displayed since. Readers in the relevant age range are encouraged to apply (www.uwc.org).

60 "Bosnian Muslims and Croats Clash after Euro Match," Reuters dispatch, June 21, 2008.

61 Budo Vukobrat, "Ethnic-Related Soccer Clashes in Bosnia Revive Old Fears," *Rferl .org*, October 11, 2011, www.rferl.org/content/ethnic_soccer_clashes_revive_old_bosnia_fears/24356205.html.

62 Nicholas Kulish, "Train Line Across the Balkans Restitches a Region," *The New York Times*, January 10, 2010, www.nytimes.com/2010/01/11/world/europe/11train.html.

63 "International Recognition of Kosovo," *Wikipedia*, https://en.wikipedia.org/wiki/International_recognition_of_Kosovo.

64 "UN and NATO Slammed over Kosovo," *BBC Online*, July 26, 2004, http://news.bbc.co.uk/2/hi/europe/3928153.stm.

65 See Box 16.1 on the United Nations Office of the Special Adviser for the Prevention of Genocide (OSAPG), for which I served as an expert consultant during conflict-prevention seminars in the former Yugoslavia.

66 Biondich, *The Balkans*, p. 266.

BOX 8A GENOCIDE IN BANGLADESH

By some estimates, the mass killings in Bangladesh—at the time, East Pakistan—are on a par with the twentieth century's most destructive genocides. At least one million Bengalis, perhaps as many as three million,[1] were massacred by the security forces of West Pakistan, assisted by local allies. Yet the genocide remains almost unknown in the West. Only recently has its prominence increased slightly, as a result of a handful of educational and memorialization projects.[2] Although it preceded events in the Balkans by two decades, the Bangladeshi genocide is usefully placed alongside the Bosnia and Kosovo case study. Both conflicts had at their core a militarized security threat, a crisis surrounding secession of federal units, and ethnic conflict. On a strategic and tactical level, both genocides featured strong elements of "eliticide" (destruction of the socioeconomic and intellectual elites of a target group—see pp. 34–35), as well as the gendercidal targeting of adult and adolescent males (see Chapter 13).

The federation of East and West Pakistan was forged in the crucible of Indian independence in 1947–1948. Most of India had been under British rule for two centuries. As independence loomed after the Second World War, two distinct political projects arose. One, associated with the century's leading proponent of non-violence, Mohandas (Mahatma) Gandhi, sought to keep India whole and prevent division along religious and ethnic lines. However, strong Hindu and Muslim nationalist movements, along with the departing British, pressed for the creation of two states—one Hindu-dominated (India), the other Muslim-dominated (Pakistan). This project triumphed, but not without cataclysmic violence. The partition of India in 1947 witnessed one of the greatest movements of peoples in modern times, as millions of Muslims fled India for Pakistan, and millions of Hindus moved in the other direction. Hundreds of thousands of people, perhaps over a million, were slaughtered on both sides.[3]

Not the least of Pakistan's post-independence difficulties was its division into two wings, separated by 1,200 miles of Indian territory and an ethno-linguistic gulf. West Pakistan, home to some 55 million people in 1971, was predominantly Urdu-speaking. The Bengali speakers of East Pakistan occupied only one-third of total Pakistani territory, but were the demographic majority—some 75 million people. Most were Muslim, but there was also a large Bengali Hindu minority (the Biharis) that was especially targeted during the genocide. Even Bengali Muslims were viewed as second-class citizens by the inhabitants of wealthier West Pakistan. I originally credited Pakistani Lieutenant-General A.A.K. Niazi with one of the wittiest genocidal quips on the historical record, when he referred to the Ganges river plain—home to most Bengalis and the largest city, Dhaka—as a "low-lying land of low, lying people." (I learned only lately that this was originally a British colonial slur, which is revealing in itself.)[4] The West Pakistani prejudice was often explicitly racial: another senior general, on a December 1970 visit to Dhaka, "reassured his fellow officers, 'Don't worry . . . we will not allow those black bastards to rule over us.'"[5] As for the minority Hindu population of Bengal, they "were as Jews to the Nazis: scum and vermin that [had] best be exterminated."[6]

Reacting to West Pakistan's persistent discrimination and economic exploitation,[7] a strong autonomy movement arose in the east, centered on the Awami League of Sheikh Mujibur Rahman. The spark for the conflagration came in December 1970, with national elections held to pave the way for a transition from military rule. The Awami League won a crushing victory—167 out of East Pakistan's 169 parliamentary seats. This gave the League a majority in the Pakistani parliament as a whole, and the right to form the next government. West Pakistani rulers, led by General Yahya Khan, saw this as a direct threat to their power and interests. After negotiations failed to resolve the impasse, Khan met with four senior generals on February 22, 1971, and issued orders to annihilate the Awami League and its popular base. From the outset, they planned a campaign of genocide. "Kill three million [Bengalis]," said Khan, "and the rest will eat out of our hands."[8]

Map 8a.1 Bangladesh.

Source: Map provided by WorldAtlas.com.

On March 25, the genocide was launched—though the initial blast of violence, I believe, was intended to *preclude* the massive, protracted, nation-wide genocide that rapidly unfolded. In an attempt to decapitate East Pakistan's political and intellectual leadership, Dhaka University—a center of nationalist agitation—was attacked. Hundreds of students were killed in what was dubbed "Operation Searchlight." Working from prepared lists, death squads roamed the streets. Perhaps 7,000 people died in a single night, 30,000 over the course of a week. The terror sparked an epic flight: "it was estimated that in April some thirty million people [!] were wandering help-lessly across East Pakistan to escape the grasp of the military."[9] The ten to twelve million-strong Hindu community of East Pakistan was also targeted *en bloc;* Hindus comprised most of the ten million people who fled to India as refugees. This spurred increasing calls for Indian military intervention, which would have the added advantage—from India's perspective—of dis-membering Pakistan. (The countries had already fought two full-scale wars by 1971; they were, and remain, poised for another one.) The surviving Awami League leadership moved quickly to declare a fully independent Bangladesh, and to organize a guerrilla resistance.

Figure 8a.1 Bengali victims of genocide by Pakistani forces in Dhaka, 1971, most with their hands bound before execution.

Source: Articlebase.com.

With the opening eliticide accomplished, the West Pakistani leadership moved to eradicate the nationalist base. As the election results suggested, this comprised the vast majority of Bengalis. Genocidal killing, however, followed a gendercidal pattern, with all males beyond childhood viewed as actual or potential guerrilla fighters. To produce the desired number of corpses, the West Pakistanis set up "extermination camps"[10] and launched a wave of gender-selective killing:

> The place of execution was the river edge [here, the Buriganga River outside Dhaka], or the shallows near the shore, and the bodies were disposed of by the simple means of permitting them to flow downstream. The killing took place night after night. Usually the prisoners were roped together and made to wade out into the river. They were in batches of six or eight, and in the light of a powerful electric arc lamp, they were easy targets, black against the silvery water. The executioners stood on the pier, shooting down at the compact bunches of prisoners wading in the water. There were screams in the hot night air, and then silence. The prisoners fell on their sides and their bodies lapped against the shore. Then a new bunch of prisoners was brought out, and the process was repeated. In the morning the village boatmen hauled the bodies into midstream and the ropes binding the bodies were cut so that each body drifted separately downstream.[11]

Figure 8a.2 A boy stands by a memorial at one of the killing fields in the 1971 Bangladeshi genocide. Outside Srimangal, Sylhet division, in the country's northern tea-growing region.

Source: Author's photo, March 2014.

The West Pakistani campaign extended to mass rape, aimed at "dishonoring" Bengali women and undermining Bengali society. Between 200,000 and 400,000 women were attacked. "Girls of eight and grandmothers of seventy-five had been sexually assaulted," wrote feminist author Susan Brownmiller in her book, *Against Our Will: Men, Women and Rape*.[12] An unknown number of women were gang-raped to death, or executed after repeated violations.[13]

■ "MUTE AND HORRIFIED WITNESSES": THE BLOOD TELEGRAM

"The Blood Telegram"—a collective statement of outrage by twenty-nine staff at the US consulate in Dhaka, headed by the redoubtable consul-general, Archer Blood—"was probably the most blistering denunciation of US foreign policy ever sent by its own diplomats." So argued Gary J. Bass in his riveting 2013 book, *The Blood Telegram: Nixon, Kissinger, and a Forgotten Genocide* (see Further Study).[14] Furious that the White House under Nixon and Kissinger "was actively and

3.7   POL / PAK-US

Department of State
TELEGRAM

CONFIDENTIAL   084

PAGE 01   DACCA 01138   061008Z

21
ACTION NEA-08

INFO OCT-01 SS-20 AID-12 USIE-00 NSC-10 NSCE-00 CIAE-00

INR-07 SSO-00 RSR-01 RSC-01 /060 W

092431

P 060730Z APR 71
FM AMCONSUL DACCA
TO SECSTATE WASHDC PRIORITY 3124
AMEMBASSY ISLAMABAD
INFO AMCONSUL KARACHI
AMCONSUL LAHORE

C O N F I D E N T I A L DACCA 1138
LIMDIS
SUBJ: DISSENT FROM U.S. POLICY TOWARD EAST PAKISTAN

JOINT STATE/AID/USIS MESSAGE

1. AWARE OF THE TASK FORCE PROPOSALS ON "OPENESS" IN
THE FOREIGN SERVICE, AND WITH THE CONVICTION THAT U.S.
POLICY RELATED TO RECENT DEVELOPMENTS IN EAST PAKISTAN
SERVES NEITHER OUR MORAL INTERESTS BROADLY DEFINED NOR
OUR NATIONAL INTERESTS NARROWLY DEFINED, NUMEROUS OFFICERS
OF AMCONGEN DACCA, USAID DACCA AND USIS DACCA CONSIDER
IT THEIR DUTY TO REGISTER STRONG DISSENT WITH FUNDAMENTAL
ASPECTS OF THIS POLICY. OUR GOVERNMENT HAS FAILED TO
DENOUNCE THE SUPPRESSION OF DEMOCRACY. OUR GOVERNMENT
HAS FAILED TO DENOUNCE ATROCITIES. OUR GOVERNMENT HAS
FAILED TO TAKE FORCEFUL MEASURES TO PROTECT ITS CITIZENS
WHILE AT THE SAME TIME BENDING OVER BACKWARDS TO PLACATE
THE WEST PAK DOMINATED GOVERNMENT AND TO LESSEN LIKELY
AND DESERVEDLY NEGATIVE INTERNATIONAL PUBLIC RELATIONS
IMPACT AGAINST THEM. OUR GOVERNMENT HAS EVIDENCED WHAT
MANY WILL CONSIDER MORAL BANKRUPTCY, IRONICALLY AT A
TIME WHEN THE USSR SENT PRESIDENT YAHYA A MESSAGE DEFEND-
ING DEMOCRACY, CONDEMNING ARREST OF LEADER OF DEMOCRATI-
CALLY ELECTED MAJORITY PARTY (INCIDENTALLY PRO-WEST) AND
CALLING FOR END TO REPRESSIVE MEASURES AND BLOODSHED.
IN OUR MOST RECENT POLICY PAPER FOR PAKISTAN, OUR IN-
TERESTS IN PAKISTAN WERE DEFINED AS PRIMARILY HUMAN.

CONFIDENTIAL

Figure 8a.3 First page of the "Blood Telegram" of April 6, 1971, sent by the US consul-general in Dhaka, Archer Blood, and twenty-eight others, to the Secretary of State (Henry Kissinger) in Washington, DC.

Source: US Government-Department of State/National Security Archives/Wikimedia Commons.

knowingly supporting a murderous regime" committing mass murder all around them, Blood first drafted and sent to Washington a personal cable titled, provocatively, "Selective Genocide" (March 27, 1971). Blood "was not a lawyer," wrote Bass, "but the use of the word 'genocide' was meant to shock, to slice through the anodyne bureaucratic niceties of State Department cables."[15]

The communiqué read, in part:

1. Here in Dacca we are mute and horrified witnesses to a reign of terror by the Pak[istani] military. Evidence continues to mount that the MLA authorities have a list of Awami League supporters whom they are systematically eliminating by seeking them out in their homes and shooting them down.
2. Among those marked for extinction in addition to [the Awami League] hierarchy, are student leaders and university faculty. . . . Also on list are bulk of [Bengali] MNA's [Members of the National Assembly] elect[ed] and number of MPA's [Members of the Parliamentary Assembly].
3. Moreover, with support of Pak[istani] military, non-Bengali Muslims [an apparent reference to the Urdu-speaking "Biharis"—see main text] are systematically attacking poor people's quarters and murdering Bengalis and Hindus. Streets of Dacca are aflood with Hindus and others seeking to get out of Dacca. Many Bengalis have sought refuge in homes of Americans, most of whom are extending shelter. . . .

The cable concluded by cautioning that the "full horror of Pak[istani] military atrocities will come to light. I, therefore, question continued advisability of present USG [US government] posture of pretending to believe GOP [Government of Pakistan] false assertions . . . We should be expressing our shock, at least privately to GOP, at this wave of terror directed against their own countrymen by Pak military." It was signed, simply and appropriately, "Blood."[16]

On April 6, 1971, the "Blood Telegram" "detonated in all directions, to diplomats in Washington, Islamabad, Karachi, and Lahore." Titled "Dissent from US Policy toward East Pakistan," Blood and his co-signatories declared that "numerous officers" of the US Consulate in Dhaka, together with USAID representatives in the country, "consider it their duty to register strong dissent with fundamental aspects" of US policy toward the Bangladesh crisis. It continued (with emphasis added):

Our government has failed to denounce atrocities. Our government has failed to take forceful measures to protect its citizens while at the same time bending over backwards to placate the West Pak[istani] dominated government and to lessen likely and deservedly negative international public relations impact against them. Our government has evidenced what many will consider moral bankruptcy, ironically at a time when the USSR sent [Pakistani] president Yahya a message defending democracy, comdemning [sic] arrest of leader of democratically elected majority party (incidentally pro-West) and calling for end to repressive measures and bloodshed. In our most recent policy paper for Pakistan, our interests in Pakistan were defined as primarily humanitarian, rather than strategic. But we have chosen not to intervene, even morally, on the grounds that the Awami conflict, in which unfortunately the overworked term genocide is applicable, is purely internal matter of a sovereign state. Private Americans have expressed *disgust*. We, as professional public servants[,] express our dissent with current policy and fervently hope that our true and lasting interests here can be defined and our policies redirected in order to salvage our nation's position as a moral leader of the free world.[17]

The "Blood Telegram" provoked fury in the Nixon White House; it is unlikely that it effected any meaningful policy shift. For Blood personally, it was a career-ender. He was stripped of his post as Dhaka consul and forced into early retirement. But he and his confederates seemed never to regret their decision. "Had Blood not done this," said a colleague, "he would have hit rock bottom in a different way. And possibly a worse way. Not for everyone, but for a man like Arch, there are worse things than losing your career. I don't like using words that don't have an accurate meaning, but he was a man of honor. In his own view, he would have lost his honor."

Bass's *Blood Telegram*, a Pulitzer Prize finalist, rendered the diplomats' lonely but eloquent protest iconic. It serves as a reminder of the vital role that diplomats and their ilk have often played in rescues from genocide, from the Armenian and Jewish holocausts to the United Nations compound in Dili, East Timor (see pp. 767–770).[18]

The slaughter and other atrocities were ended by one of the rare instances of successful outside intervention in genocide.[19] Indian troops invaded in December 1971, vanquishing West Pakistani forces in a couple of weeks. The independence of Bangladesh was sealed, though at a staggering human cost.

In the blood-letting following the expulsion of the West Pakistani army, perhaps 150,000 people were murdered by independence forces and local vigilantes. Biharis who had collaborated with West Pakistani authorities were dealt with especially harshly.[20] Themes of the post-genocide era include the continued suffering and social marginalization of hundreds of thousands of Bengali rape victims, and the enduring impunity of the *génocidaires*. They also, in a tragic irony, featured a turn to genocide in independent Bangladesh—grounded in much the same neocolonial mentality of ethnic superiority and wanton exploitation that West Pakistani leaders exhibited toward Bengalis in 1971. The indigenous population of the Chittagong Hill Tracts in the southeast, which had been granted considerable autonomy under British rule, suffered largescale massacres and expropriation throughout the 1970s. The lone treatment of the Hill Tracts from a genocide studies perspective is Mark Levene's.[21]

None of the principal West Pakistani leaders of the 1971 genocide has ever been brought to trial; those not yet deceased remain comfortably ensconced in Pakistan and other countries. However, with the return to power in Bangladesh of the Awami League, led by Sheikh Hasina (the daughter of the murdered Mujibur Sheikh Rahman), a controversial round of domestic trials was launched in 2010, and is ongoing at the time of writing.

The origins of Bangladesh's International Crimes Tribunal (ICT) lay in legislation passed as early as 1973, but the process was first stalled, and then stymied by the military coup of 1975. For decades after, successive military regimes collaborated with the Jamaat-e-Islaami party, which had opposed an independent Bangladesh and stood accused of collaborating with the West Pakistani military throughout the 1971 genocide.[22] After the return to parliamentary democracy in 1990, Jamaat figures were prominent in coalition governments led by the Bangladesh National Party (BNP) under its leader—and Sheikh Hasina's perennial rival and nemesis—Khaleda Zia, widow of the country's first military ruler. Only with the Awami League's victory in 2008 was the process revived, leading to the founding of the ICT tribunal in 2010.

Millions of Bangladeshis perceived the tribunal as an opportunity to secure, at last, a measure of justice for the genocide and crimes against humanity that accompanied the birth of their independent state. The hunger for this long-delayed reckoning was amply evident to me in the public forums that I addressed during an extended visit to Dhaka in April 2014.

International criticism of the process was forceful, however. The punishments available to the ICT's judges included the death penalty, which was the first sentence passed, in December 2013 against Delwar Hossein Sayeedi, a leader of Jamaat-e-Islami. Sayeedi's punishment was reduced to life imprisonment the following year. But when another Jamaat leader, Abdul Quader Mollah, likewise received a life sentence, massive protests erupted in the streets of Dhaka. The government of Sheikh Hasini responded by not only reformulating the ICT's mandate to allow for prosecutorial appeals, but making the measure retroactive so that Quader Mollah could be sentenced to death—and he was executed in December 2013. A second defendant, Muhammad Kamaruzzaman, was executed in April 2015, while two other accused had died in jail.

The Bangladeshi government responded peremptorily to expressed concerns about due process and the death penalty. Foreign media and human-rights advocates who published exposés of collusion between government officials and ICT judges, such as *The Economist* and Human Rights Watch, were charged with contempt of court.[23] Many observers accused Sheikh

Hasini's Awami League administration of using the tribunal as a cudgel against its rival the BNP, and the trial process fueled regular outbreaks of violence, often deadly, between supporters of the two parties.[24] Certainly, in no other setting—not even in post-genocide Bosnia—had tribunal proceedings become such a central and controversial factor in domestic politics.

FURTHER STUDY

Note: The past several years have witnessed a spurt of scholarly and editorial interest in the Bangladesh genocide, connected with growing interest and institutional activity in Bangladesh itself, and a sense that the country is underexplored in genocide studies and other literatures.

Gary J. Bass, *The Blood Telegram: Nixon, Kissinger, and a Forgotten Genocide.* New York: Alfred A. Knopf, 2013. Riveting, highly critical account of the foreign-policy machinations surrounding the genocide; see also Raghavan (below).

Anthony Mascarenhas, *The Rape of Bangla Desh.* Delhi: Vikas Publications, 1971. Early account by a renegade Pakistani journalist whose exposé of the atrocities first generated outrage in the West.

Fazlul Quader Quaderi, ed., *Bangladesh Genocide and World Press.* Dhaka: Songha Prokashan, 2013. Difficult to find outside Bangladesh, but a highly useful resource for any specialist researcher: an encyclopedic compilation of the contemporary global press coverage in English—surprisingly extensive, given the Bangladeshi genocide's subsequent obscurity. Contact the publisher at songhaprokashan@yahoo.com.

Srinath Raghavan, *1971: A Global History of the Creation of Bangladesh.* Cambridge, MA: Harvard University Press, 2013. Groundbreaking analysis of the international dimension of the crisis.

"Special Issue: East Pakistan War, 1971," *Journal of Genocide Research*, 13: 4 (2011). Edited by A. Dirk Moses, a stimulating collection of articles published on the 40th anniversary of Bangladesh's wrenching birth. For contents, see www.tandfonline.com/toc/cjgr20/13/4.

Willem Van Schendel, *A History of Bangladesh.* Cambridge: Cambridge University Press, 2009. Surely the best general history in English; possibly the only one. Pages 121–171 cover the crisis of the Pakistani federation and the course of the independence struggle and genocide.

NOTES

1 There is considerable debate over the scale of the genocide in Bangladesh. At one end of the spectrum, Bangladeshi government sources and NGO initiatives often cite a figure of three million killed, which R.J. Rummel considers within

the bounds of possibility. See Rummel, *Death by Government* (New Brunswick, NJ: Transaction Publishers, 1994), p. 331. A notorious minimizing of the death toll was Sarmila Bose's in her book *Dead Reckoning: Memories of the 1971 Bangladesh War* (London: C. Hurst & Co., 2011), and related articles, including a high-profile one in the genocide-studies literature: see Sarmila Bose, "The Question of Genocide and the Quest for Justice in the 1971 War," *Journal of Genocide Research*, 13: 4 (2011), pp. 393–419. For a penetrating critique of Bose's work, see Naeem Mohaiemen, "Flying Blind: Waiting for a Real Reckoning on 1971," *Economic and Political Weekly*, 46: 36 (September 2011), pp. 3–9. Christian Gerlach considers it "very unlikely that the fatalities in 1971 exceeded one million people." See Gerlach, *Extremely Violent Societies: Mass Violence in the Twentieth-Century World* (Cambridge: Cambridge University Press, 2010), p. 136. My own conviction is that a surplus mortality of three million Bengalis, disproportionately Hindus, is probably outsized, but not out of the question. Much depends on the death rates among internally-displaced and refugee populations, which remain a matter of extrapolation and sometimes speculation. Direct murders of noncombatants by West Pakistani forces and their East Pakistani allies, disproportionately of younger men, almost certainly numbered in the hundreds of thousands. Killings by Bengali rebels, vigilantes, and vengeance-seekers were probably in the several tens of thousands.

2 See in particular the Liberation War Museum Online at www.liberation warmuseum.org/.

3 On Partition, see Nisid Hajari, *Midnight's Furies: The Deadly Legacy of India's Partition* (New York: Houghton Mifflin Harcourt, 2015); Yasmin Khan, *The Great Partition: The Making of India and Pakistan* (New Delhi: Penguin Books India, 2007); Vazira Fazila-Yacoobali Zamindar, *The Long Partition and the Making of Modern South Asia: Refugees, Boundaries, Histories* (New York: Columbia University Press, 2007); Gyanendra Pandey, *Remembering Partition: Violence, Nationalism and History in India* (Cambridge: Cambridge University Press, 2004); Urvashi Butalia, *The Other Side of Silence: Voices from the Partition of India* (Durham, NC: Duke University Press, 2000); and Paul R. Brass, "The Partition of India and Retributive Genocide in the Punjab, 1946–47: Means, Methods, and Purposes," *Journal of Genocide Research*, 5: 1 (March 2003), pp. 71–101. My review article on Partition in *Journal of Genocide Research*, 10: 4 (2008), pp. 625–632, includes discussion of the Khan and Zamindar volumes.

4 Niazi quoted in R.J. Rummel, *Death by Government*, p. 335. On the colonial usage, see Richard Holt, *Sport and the British: A Modern History* (Oxford: Clarendon, 1992), p. 217 ("a low, lying people in a low-lying land").

5 Srinath Raghavan, *1971: A Global History of the Creation of Bangladesh* (Cambridge, MA: Harvard University Press, 2013), p. 35.

6 Rummel, *Death by Government*, p. 335.

7 "The Bangladesh nationalist movement was also fueled by a sense of economic exploitation. Though jute, the major export earning commodity, was produced in East Pakistan, most of the economic investments took place in West Pakistan. A systematic transfer of resources took place from East to West Pakistan, creating a growing economic disparity and a feeling among the Bengalis that they were being treated as a colony by Pakistan." Rounaq Jahan, "Genocide in Bangladesh," in Samuel Totten and William S. Parsons, eds., *Centuries of Genocide: Essays and Eyewitness Accounts*, 4th edn (London: Routledge, 2012), p. 252. Jahan's chapter, which has been in the *Century/Centuries of Genocide* volume from the first edition, remains the best short introduction to the Bangladeshi genocide.

8 Quoted in Robert Payne, *Massacre* (London: Macmillan, 1973), p. 50.

9 Payne, *Massacre*, p. 48.

10 Leo Kuper, *The Prevention of Genocide* (New Haven, CT: Yale University Press, 1985), p. 47.

11 Payne, *Massacre*, p. 55. For more on the gendercidal character of the large majority of killings during the genocide, see Adam Jones/Gendercide Watch, "Case Study: Genocide in Bangladesh, 1971," www.gendercide.org/case_bangladesh. html., from which Box 8a is adapted.

12 Susan Brownmiller, *Against Our Will: Men, Women and Rape* (New York: Bantam, 1975), p. 83.

13 "We are going," a West Pakistani soldier allegedly shouted as he was being evacuated following the army's defeat. "But we are leaving our seed behind." Quoted in Christian Gerlach, *Extremely Violent Societies: Mass Violence in the Twentieth-Century World* (Cambridge: Cambridge University Press, 2010), p. 156.

14 Gary J. Bass, *The Blood Telegram: Nixon, Kissinger, and a Forgotten Genocide* (New York: Alfred A. Knopf, 2013). Irritatingly, the e-book lacks the print pagination, the Kindle version on Amazon's website is not searchable, and the Google Books version also lacks pagination. Search the text on books.google.com to check quotes.

15 The cable also reflected the common misperception that under international law, genocide must target a group *in toto*, rather than "in whole or in part," as the UN Convention provides. The intended partial destruction of the group is not selective genocide, legally speaking, but simply genocide.

16 Transcribed from the digital reproduction of the February 27, 1971 "Selective Genocide" cable, http://nsarchive.gwu.edu/NSAEBB/NSAEBB79/BEBB3. pdf, posted by the National Security Archive in its document collection, "The Tilt: The U.S. and the South Asian Crisis of 1971," http://nsarchive.gwu.edu/ NSAEBB/NSAEBB79/. The original telegrams are of course in all-caps.

17 Transcribed from the digital reproduction of the April 6, 1971 cable, "Dissent from US Policy toward East Pakistan," posted by the National Security Archive at http://nsarchive.gwu.edu/NSAEBB/NSAEBB79/BEBB8.pdf.

18 A later round of whistleblowing led by Peter Galbraith of the US Senate Foreign Relations Committee, denouncing Saddam Hussein's Anfal genocide of Iraqi Kurds (see pp. 222–223), was memorably detailed by Samantha Power in *"A Problem from Hell": America and the Age of Genocide* (New York: Basic Books, 2002), pp. 171–245.

19 For a concise overview of the Indian intervention, see Nicholas J. Wheeler, "India as Rescuer? Order versus Justice in the Bangladesh War of 1971," in Wheeler, *Saving Strangers: Humanitarian Intervention in International Society* (Oxford: Oxford University Press, 2000), pp. 55–77.

20 During the genocide, Urdu-speaking Biharis in East Pakistan "joined the West Pakistanis in killing the Bengalis." This exposed them to retaliation from "Awami League supporters [who] also engaged in killing the West Pakistanis and Biharis in East Pakistan. A White Paper issued by the Pakistani government shows that the Awami League had massacred at least 30,000 Biharis and West Pakistanis," atrocious behavior that nonetheless does not match the systematic slaughter of Bengalis by the West Pakistanis and their Bihari allies. See Wardatul Akman, "Atrocities against Humanity during the Liberation War in Bangladesh: A Case of Genocide," *Journal of Genocide Research*, 4: 4 (2002), p. 549; also "The Right to Self Determination: The Secession of Bangladesh," in Kuper, *The Prevention of Genocide*, pp. 44–61.

21 See Mark Levene, "The Chittagong Hill Tracts: A Case Study in the Political Economy of 'Creeping' Genocide," *Third World Quarterly*, 20: 2 (1999),

pp. 339–369. For a full treatment, see Wolfgang Mey, ed., *They Are Now Burning Village After Village: Genocide in the Chittagong Hill Tracts, Bangladesh* (Copenhagen: International Work Group for Indigenous Affairs, 1984).

22 In Donald W. Beachler's summary, "The military regimes that ran Bangladesh from 1975 to 1990 . . . had little incentive to promote study of the 1971 geno-cide. . . . The military regimes were allied with those who wished to make Islam predominant in Bangladeshi politics. . . . Accordingly, the military regimes courted religious elements that had opposed independence and even collabo-rated in the genocide. . . . The issue of the 1971 atrocities was a weapon in the struggle between Islamists and secularists in Bangladesh for decades after independence. . . . It has often been in the interest of governments and powerful political factions within Bangladesh to ignore or distort the genocide. The fact that local volunteers, or *razakars*, aided in the genocide makes the events of 1971 even more politically complex for any government in Bangladesh." Beachler, "The Politics of Genocide Scholarship: The Case of Bangladesh," *Patterns of Prejudice*, 41: 5 (2007), p. 491.

23 See Surabhi Chopra, "The International Crimes Tribunal in Bangladesh: Silenc-ing Fair Comment," *Journal of Genocide Research*, 17: 2 (2015), pp. 214–216. In November 2015, Human Rights Watch called for the ICT to "immediately suspend the death sentences" of two other convicted perpetrators, Ali Ahsan Mohammed Mujahid of Jamaat-e-Islami and Salahuddin Qader Chowdhury of the BNP, "pending an independent and impartial review of their cases." HRW's Asia director, Brad Adams, declared that "justice and accountability for the terrible crimes committed during Bangladesh's 1971 war of independ-ence are crucial." But "unfair trials can't provide real justice, especially when the death penalty is imposed," as it was against another convicted Jamaat leader, Muhammed Kamaruzzaman, hanged in April 2015 "even though wit-nesses and documents were arbitrarily limited by the courts and inconsistent prior and subsequent statements of prosecution witnesses were not allowed into evidence." See Human Rights Watch, "Bangladesh: Halt Imminent War Crimes Executions," November 20, 2015, www.hrw.org/news/2015/11/20/bangladesh-halt-imminent-war-crimes-executions.

24 See, e.g., "Bangladesh War Crimes Verdict Sparks More Violence," *BBC Online*, March 1, 2013, www.bbc.com/news/world-asia-21626843.

CHAPTER 9

Genocide in Africa's Great Lakes Region

Since the Jewish Holocaust (Chapter 6), no genocide has attracted as much analysis and reflection, and produced such institutional innovation and transformation, as the catastrophe that consumed the tiny Central African country of Rwanda from April to July 1994. This is reflected in the decision of nearly everyone writing or editing a volume on genocide to include detailed attention to the Hutu-extremist genocide of Rwandan Tutsis. The first two editions of this book were no exception. For this new edition, however, I have reworked and reorganized the chapter on the "Apocalypse in Rwanda" much as the chapter on the Armenian genocide in the first edition morphed into "The Ottoman Destruction of Christian Minorities" in subsequent ones. As the Democratic Republic of the Congo (DRC) has received ever greater study and investigation, notably with the 2010 release of the long-delayed, UN-sponsored "Mapping Report" of atrocities; as Burundi, Rwanda's ethnic twin to the south, took center stage in global humanitarian concerns in 2015–2016; and as I, personally, have attained a deeper understanding of political and historical processes in the African Great Lakes region, it has become clearer that a more synoptic and *relational* treatment is necessary. Only with this framing can we understand how the conflicts, ethnic divisions, migrant and refugee flows, and postcolonial policies of each state have reverberated with the others. I have argued elsewhere that the 1994 genocide of Rwandan Tutsis merits an "anchoring" position in the narrative.[1] But it has also served to sideline, discursively and legally, the genocidal atrocities inflicted by the post-genocide RPF regime in Rwanda against Hutu refugees in the DRC (see "The genocide of the camps," below). In Burundi, outbreaks of anti-Hutu genocide by the Tutsi-dominated military in 1972, and of reciprocal genocidal atrocities in 1993 and since, have failed to arouse much notice, in either academic or humanitarian circles. Despite the dedicated efforts of René Lemarchand (see Further Study), there is only the tiniest smattering of monographs, book chapters, and scholarly articles on Burundi and its ongoing conflicts. This left governments and journalists struggling to situate the outbreak of renewed mass violence in 2015–2016, when probably no country outside the Middle East was setting off as many alarms in the humanitarian and genocide-prevention communities.

THE AFRICAN GREAT LAKES COUNTRIES IN REGIONAL CONTEXT

Several significant factors and processes unite the genocidal experiences of the Great Lakes countries of Congo, Burundi, and Rwanda:

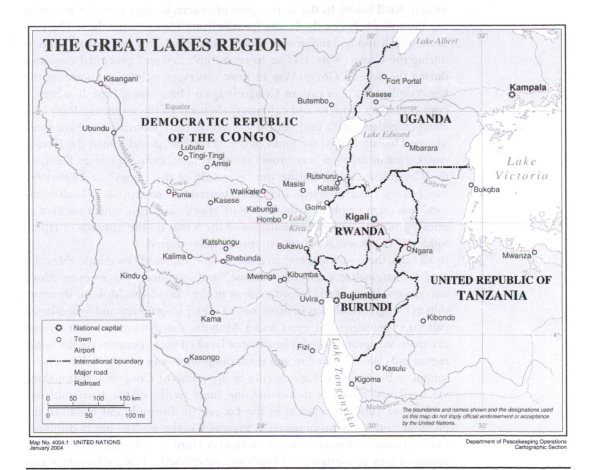

Map 9.1 Geographers and cartographers differ on the boundaries of Africa's Great Lakes region. This is the most common configuration, comprising eastern Democratic Republic of the Congo (DRC), Rwanda, Burundi, Uganda, and Tanzania. Uganda figures only peripherally in this chapter, as the sponsor of the Tutsi-dominated RPF that seized power in Rwanda in 1994, and as its ally, then enemy in the First and Second Congo Wars (1996–2003). Despite its multiethnic and multi-religious makeup, Tanzania has experienced little violence in the postcolonial period, and has played a marginal role in the conflicts and genocides of the region, refugee inflows and the city of Arusha aside.[2] It is analyzed instead as a "success story" of genocide prevention in Chapter 16.

Source: United Nations Department of Peacekeeping Operations, Cartographic Division.

(1) All three countries were administered under Belgian mandates from the post-World War One period through to independence in the early 1960s. (Burundi and Rwanda formed a single colony, Ruanda-Urundi.)

(2) Everywhere, the colonizer played favorites among ethnicities and deepened ethnic cleavages. In Rwanda and Burundi, this meant a privileged role—in the civil service and religio-educational sphere, especially—for the Tutsis. They constituted about 15 percent of the population of the colony (and of each country after independence). They were encouraged to lord it over the masses of Hutu peasants, making up nearly all the remaining population apart from pygmies (the Twa) and Europeans. Under Belgian rule, the previous permeability of Hutu/Tutsi *caste* identities (as peasants and pastoralists, respectively) was transformed into codified *ethnic* identities—as will be shown in greater detail below. In the Ituri region of eastern Congo, a similar hierarchy was instituted between the Lendu (peasants) and Hema (pastoralists). The tensions, which also had indigenous roots,[3] were refueled by Ugandan occupiers during the Congo wars, leading to severe upheaval and genocidal massacres during the Second Congo War. In most observers' estimation, however, the key "conflict dyad" in eastern Congo is again Hutu versus Tutsi. It incorporates expatriate (refugee and colonizer) elements of the respective Rwandan *ethnies*, together with a long-settled Congolese Tutsi population, the Banyamulenge. The latter filled the ranks of the AFDL militia and joined the Rwandan/Ugandan drive to overthrow the tottering Mobutu regime in Kinshasa, the Congolese capital, during the "genocide of the camps" in 1996–1997 (see below). Their presence, and their vulnerability to reprisal as "collaborators," was often invoked by the Tutsi RPF regime in Kigali, which justified its ongoing occupation and exploitation of the Kivus on the grounds of ethnic solidarity and fraternal obligation, among other tropes.

(3) In all cases, the post-independence states were "captured" by ethnic elites and used to marginalize, persecute, "cleanse," and sometimes exterminate ethnic out-groups. The pattern is least evident in the case of the Mobutu dictatorship in Congo, which was in many ways a classic kleptocracy and urban-based patronage machine. But even under Mobutu, the dynamic of capture and exclusion was pronounced. The dictator lavished state resources on his home region and clan of Gdabolite, and at various points—notably toward the end—sought to bolster his collapsing rule by appealing to Congolese nationalism, via legislation aimed at denationalizing huge swaths of the Banyamulenge (Congolese Tutsi) population in the far east. In Burundi and Rwanda, the phenomenon was as pronounced as anywhere in the world—but in diametrically opposite configurations. The Rwandan Hutu Revolution of 1959–1961 uprooted tens of thousands of Tutsis and established a Hutu ethnocracy that lasted through to the genocide and military defeat of 1994, when the state was "captured" in turn by a Tutsi-exile ethnocracy. In Burundi, where the Tutsi were a similarly small minority of the population, the capture of the military and security apparatus in the early post-independence period allowed a Tutsi ethnocracy to hold power, albeit precariously. The situation lasted at least until the mid-2000s, and arguably still obtains today.

(4) The crises, conflicts, and genocides in Burundi, Congo, and Rwanda were mutually constitutive. The first wave of anti-Tutsi pogroms sent tens of thousands of refugees fleeing to Congo, Burundi—and Uganda, where they and their offspring formed the nucleus of the RPF invading force of 1990. Ethnic discrimination and persecution within Congo (against the Banyamulenge above all) destabilized the eastern border regions and strengthened cross-border alliances between Congolese and Rwandan Tutsis, especially during the collapse of the Mobutu regime and its chaotic aftermath. Genocide by the Tutsi-dominated Burundian military against Hutus in 1972, and again in 1993, sent hundreds of thousands of Burundian Hutus fleeing to neighboring Rwanda, where they were often eager conscripts in the genocide against Tutsis in 1994. And of course, the Congo wars of 1996–2003 represented the internationalization of the Rwandan genocide, sparking new rounds of genocidal killing—most notably by the Tutsi RPF against Rwandan Hutu refugees.

If you are confused, I suspect you are not alone. These are some of the most intricate and protean political configurations in the world, exotic to most western readers. But a grasp of the interrelated historical and genocidal processes can lend coherence to the more detailed discussion ahead. We begin with the "anchoring" cataclysm with which most readers will already be somewhat familiar: the Rwandan genocide.

RWANDA, 1994: HORROR AND SHAME

The genocide that consumed the tiny Central African country of Rwanda from April to July 1994 was in some ways without precedent. The international law specialist John Quigley has called it "probably the most concentrated mass killing ever seen,"[4] and this in no way exhausts the holocaust's extraordinary and even unique aspects. In just twelve weeks, approximately one million people—overwhelmingly Tutsis, but also tens of thousands of Hutus opposed to the genocidal government—were murdered, primarily by machetes, clubs, and small arms. About 80 percent of victims died in a "hurricane of death ... between the second week of April and the third week of May," noted Gérard Prunier. "If we consider that probably around 800,000 people were slaughtered during that short period ... the daily killing rate was at least five times that of the Nazi death camps."[5]

While debate has raged over the extent of the complicity of "ordinary Germans" in the genocide against the Jews and others, the German killers were in uniform, and strict measures were taken to ensure that the civilian population did not witness the mass slaughter. In Rwanda, by contrast, the civilian Hutu population—men, women, and even children—was actively conscripted and comprised the bulk of *génocidaires:* "For the first time in modern history, a state succeeded in transforming the mass of its population into murderers."[6]

Despite noble pledges of "Never Again" following the Jewish Holocaust, the international community stood by while a million defenseless victims died. Numerous warnings of impending genocide were transmitted, and an armed

United Nations "assistance mission" (UNAMIR), under the command of Canadian Major-General Roméo Dallaire, had been in place in the capital, Kigali, since October 1993. In what one UNAMIR officer would later refer to as an "act of total cowardice,"[7] well-armed foreign forces were flown in when the genocide broke out—but only to evacuate whites. In a notorious instance captured on video, at the Caraes Psychiatric Hospital in Ndera, Kigali prefecture, a few sobbing whites were evacuated while rapacious militia cruised just outside the gates, and hundreds of terrified Tutsi refugees begged the foreign troops for protection. "Solve your problems yourselves," shouted one soldier to the crowd, and left with his comrades. The Tutsis were massacred within hours of the troops' departure.[8]

For all the lofty rhetoric of universal human rights, it seemed "Rwanda was simply too remote, too far, too poor, too little, and probably too black to be worthwhile," in the scathing assessment of human rights investigator Alison Des Forges.[9] General Dallaire issued a blistering denunciation at the end of his tenure in 1994: "Although Rwanda and UNAMIR have been at the centre of a terrible human tragedy, that is not to say Holocaust, and although many fine words had been pronounced by all, including members of the Security Council, the tangible effort ... has been totally, completely ineffective."[10] In March 2004, UN Secretary-General Kofi Annan offered a qualified apology for member states' unwillingness to confront the Rwandan catastrophe. "The international community failed Rwanda, and that must leave us always with a sense of bitter regret and abiding sorrow." A decade after the slaughter, Annan asked: "Are we confident that, confronted by a new Rwanda today, we can respond effectively, in good time?" His response was sobering: "We can by no means be certain we would."[11]

BACKGROUND TO GENOCIDE

As with the Balkan genocide (Chapter 8), foreign observers tended to view the Rwandan conflict as an expression of "ancient tribal hatreds." Until the twentieth century, however, "Hutus" and "Tutsis" did not constitute separate nations. It is hard even to describe them as distinct ethnicities, since they share the same language, territory, and religion. Rather, the two groups in the pre-colonial period may be viewed as *social castes*, based on material wealth. Broadly speaking, Tutsis were those who owned cattle; Hutus tilled the land and provided labor to the Tutsis. The designations were hardly arbitrary, and they indeed had a basis in physiognomic differences (see below). But they were fluid and permeable, as the Africa specialist Mahmood Mamdani notes: "The rare Hutu who was able to accumulate cattle and rise through the socioeconomic hierarchy could *kwihutura*—shed Hutuness—and achieve the political status of a Tutsi. Conversely, the loss of property could also lead to the loss of status, summed up in the Kinyarwanda word *gucupira.*" These processes were "of little significance statistically," but "their social and political significance cannot be overstated."[12] Thus, "although Rwanda was definitely not a land of peace and bucolic harmony before the arrival of the Europeans, there is no trace in its precolonial history of systematic violence between Tutsi and Hutu as such."[13]

From its beginnings around the seventeenth century, the political organization of Rwandan society featured "centralised forms of political authority and ... a high degree of social control," reflecting "the fact that the land is small, the population density is (and has always been) high and social interactions are constant, intense and value-laden."[14] This authoritarianism reached its apogee under the rule of Mwami Kigeri Rwabugiri (1860–1895), at which point traditional obligations of *corvée* labor came to be imposed on Hutus alone, "thereby polarizing the social difference between Hutu and Tutsi."[15]

In 1894, Germany established indirect suzerainty over Rwanda, co-opting and taking over the pyramidal structure of political rule. The Germans gave way, after their defeat in the First World War, to Belgian colonial administration. The Belgians were the first to rigidly codify Hutu and Tutsi designations. In the divide-and-rule tradition, Tutsis became colonial favorites and proteges.[16] In part, this reflected the Tutsis' minority status—it is often easier for colonizers to secure the allegiance of a minority, which recognizes that its survival may depend on bonds with the imperial authority (see Chapter 11). It also derived from an egregious nineteenth-century contribution by the nascent discipline of anthropology. Early explorers of Central Africa, notably the Englishman John Hanning Speke, propounded the "Hamitic hypothesis." This depicted the Hutus as offspring of Ham, the black son of Noah, cursed by God and destined forever to serve as "hewers of wood and drawers of water"; and, by noble contrast, the Tutsi caste, descended from the Nilotic civilization of classical Egypt. As was typical of imperial racial theorizing, the mark of civilization was grafted on to physiognomic difference, with the generally taller, supposedly more refined Tutsis destined to rule, and shorter, allegedly less refined Hutus to serve.[17]

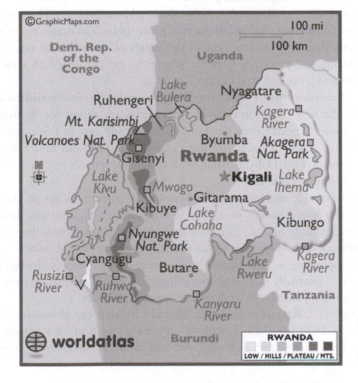

Map 9.2 Rwanda.

Source: Map provided by WorldAtlas.com

Under Belgian rule and afterwards, both Tutsis and Hutus were indoctrinated with this Hamitic hypothesis. It served both to justify Tutsi overlordship under the Belgian colonial power, and resentment and vengefulness among Hutu,[18] which would erupt first in the massacres of 1959–1960 and culminate, in 1994, in full-scale genocide. In 1994, taller Hutus died at roadblocks because they were assumed to be Tutsis, whatever their identity cards said. And the corpses of thousands of Tutsi victims were dumped into the Nyabarongo river, which flowed into Lake Victoria, the source of the Nile—thus symbolically dispatching Tutsis back to their "Nilotic" origins (see Chapter 11 for more on the symbolic dimension of the Rwandan genocide).[19]

It was under the Belgians, too, that a new, racially-segregated state, church, and education system was constructed. Tutsis were assigned a dominant role in each.[20] The symbol of the newly-bureaucratized system was the distribution of identity cards defining every Rwandan as either Hutu, Tutsi, or Twa/pygmy. The institution of these identity cards was perpetuated by the postcolonial government, and in 1994 proved a key genocidal facilitator. At the thousands of roadblocks established across the country, carrying a Tutsi identity card meant a death sentence.

After the Second World War, with anti-colonial national liberation movements in ascendance, Belgian authorities performed a dramatic about-face. Pro-independence movements were springing up throughout the colonized world, and in Rwanda the Tutsis, having benefited from their positions of dominance in education and the state bureaucracy, moved to the forefront of the various anti-colonial initiatives. The Belgians, perceiving the threat—and perhaps also influenced by the democratizing tendency unleashed by the Second World War—switched their favor to the less-educated, less-threatening Hutu majority. This unleashed pent-up Hutu frustrations, and led to the first proto-genocidal massacres of Tutsis, claiming several thousand victims. Tens of thousands of Tutsis fled to neighboring Congo, Tanzania, and especially Uganda, where the exiles formed an armed rebel movement and launched attacks into Rwanda.

Throughout the 1960s, remaining Rwandan Tutsis established a *modus vivendi* with the new Hutu-dominated order. Although almost totally frozen out of formal political power, they were not systematically expelled from other institutional spheres, such as schools and the Catholic Church; and under the rule of Hutu dictator Juvénal Habyarimana, who seized the presidency in a 1973 coup, their conditions improved.

But trouble was brewing just beneath the surface. Although Habyarimana projected a liberal image to attract foreign aid, his regime was dominated by the *akazu*, or "little house": "a tightly knit mafia" of Hutus from the north of Rwanda that coalesced around the figure of Habyarimana's wife, Agathe.[21] It was the *akazu* that, operating as "the 'invisible government' of Rwanda during Habyarimana's reign,"[22] gradually increased ethnic hatred against the Tutsis, encouraging a climate of fear and panic to forestall demands for democracy.

In 1987, Rwandan exiles in Uganda formed the Rwandan Patriotic Front, and in 1990 the RPF launched a military invasion of Rwanda.[23] This offensive had three crucial results. First, it brought immediate outside assistance to prop up the Habyarimana regime—from France, a country that had constructed its postcolonial role in Africa around support for *La Francophonie*, the network of French-speaking countries that Paris viewed as a bulwark against the "Anglo" influence typified by Uganda. French forces succeeded in stalling the RPF invasion, and they remained to train and advise the Hutu military and militias that would implement the 1994 genocide. Second, military conflict exacerbated the economic crisis in Rwanda. "Fragile at the start, the Rwandan economy . . . crumbled under the burden of the costs of war," wrote Alison Des Forges. "Living conditions worsened dramatically as per capita income that stood at US $320 in 1989 (nineteenth poorest in the world) fell to US $200 in 1993."[24] Third, the invasion, with its abuses and atrocities against Hutu civilians, contributed to a growing climate of fear among ordinary Hutus, already deeply anxious after genocidal massacres of Hutus in next-door Burundi by the Tutsi-dominated armed forces there.

Invasion from without; economic crisis; growing domestic and international support for extremists—it is hard to imagine more propitious circumstances for genocide. Between 1990 and 1993, "a series of minipogroms against Tutsi [took place] in different parts of the country," which in retrospect appear to be "rehearsals for the conflagration of 1994."[25] Perhaps 2,000 people were murdered. A UN Special Rapporteur, Bacre Waly Ndiaye, visited Rwanda in April 1993 and "decided that the word genocide was appropriate and that the Convention on the Prevention and Punishment of the Crime of Genocide of 1948 was applicable" to these killings. His superiors in Geneva warned him to avoid the term, but he used it nonetheless in his report, which was quickly buried ("Ndiaye said later that he might just as well have put the report in a bottle and thrown it into the sea").[26]

Exterminationist propaganda against Tutsis became commonplace in Rwanda. As early as December 1990, the infamous "Hutu Ten Commandments" were issued by the Hutu extremist paper *Kangura;* "The Hutu must be firm and vigilant against their common Tutsi enemy," read one of the commandments. In August 1993, the radio station RTLM (Radio-Télévision Libre des Mille Collines) began broadcasting, with funding from the Christian Democratic International.[27] RTLM transformed the staid Rwandan media, and fueled a hysterical fear of the threat posed by RPF forces and their "fifth column" inside Rwanda—the Tutsi minority, designated by RTLM as *inyenzi*, or "cockroaches." "The cruelty of the *inyenzi* is incurable," declared one broadcast; it could only be remedied "by their total extermination."[28]

Propaganda and militia killings reached a peak precisely when the Habyarimana regime was being pressured to respect its 1990 pledge to implement multiparty democracy and seek peace with the RPF. The Arusha Peace Accords of August 1993 guaranteed free elections in less than two years, to include the RPF, which had been allowed to install several hundred troops in Kigali. Some 2,500 foreign peacekeepers arrived to establish the United Nations Assistance Mission for Rwanda (UNAMIR); their task was to monitor the ceasefire and the prelude to elections.

The Arusha Accords and the UNAMIR intervention proved to be the last straw for "Hutu Power" extremists. Genocide against the Tutsi minority would simultaneously eliminate the perceived constituency for the RPF; resolve the economic crisis through distribution of Tutsi land, wealth, and jobs; and bind the Hutu majority in genocidal complicity. The extremists imported hundreds of thousands of machetes in 1993–1994; this weapon would become the symbol of the Rwanda genocide.

GENOCIDAL FRENZY[29]

At 8:30 p.m. on April 6, 1994, the plane carrying President Habyarimana back from talks in Tanzania was shot down as it neared Kigali airport—by either Hutu Power or RPF elements anxious to scuttle the Arusha peace process.[30] By 9:18, the Presidential Guard had begun to erect roadblocks around Kigali.

The following day, working from carefully prepared lists, soldiers and militias began murdering thousands of Tutsis and oppositionist Hutus. Crucially, ten Belgian peacekeepers protecting the moderate Prime Minister, Agathe Uwimiliyana, were seized, tortured, and murdered, along with Uwimiliyana herself. The murders prompted Belgium to withdraw its remaining forces from Rwanda. Over the heated protests of UNAMIR commander Dallaire, other countries followed suit. In the end, Dallaire would be left with "454 [peacekeepers] of all ranks, along with [one] dozen UN civilians" to stop perhaps the most explosive genocide in recorded history.[31] Foreign journalists also departed *en bloc.*

Figure 9.1 Lt.-Gen. Roméo Dallaire. He led UN peacekeeping troops in Rwanda before and during the 1994 genocide. His was indeed a skeleton force, often reduced to counting and collecting corpses, but their efforts in the face of great obstacles saved thousands of lives. Dallaire's emotional breakdown after his return to Canada, and his galvanizing memoir *Shake Hands with the Devil* (see Further Study), established him as a central witness of the Rwandan holocaust, and a leading anti-genocide advocate. He subsequently served in the Canadian Senate. He is pictured at a rally for Darfur (see Box 9a) in November 2007.

Source: Wikimedia Commons.

From the start, the extremist government capitalized on several factors that they appear to have known would limit outside opposition to the genocide. First, they played upon widespread ignorance about Rwanda. "Hutu and Tutsi?" wrote Richard Dowden. "News editors giggled and spoke about Tutus and Whoopsies in news conference. Even when they took it seriously they came up against an extremely complicated history, and they doubted that readers needed to know about it."[32] This meshed neatly with stereotypes of African "tribal conflict," depicting the killings as reciprocal excesses between atavistic and primitive communities. Second, they seem to have realized that killing some foreign troops would scare away the remainder, with memories still fresh of the 1993 Battle of Mogadishu, when two dozen Pakistani troops and eighteen US Rangers died at the hands of Somali militias.[33] Third, the extremists benefited from the "blind commitment" of the French government to its Rwandan counterpart: "the Rwandese leadership kept believing that *no matter what it did*, French support would always be forthcoming. And it had no valid reasons for believing otherwise."[34] Lastly, the "Hutu Power" regime exploited the limited energy and resources of international media and public opinion where Africa was concerned, and the fact that media attention was overwhelmingly directed toward the inaugural free elections in South Africa.

Army and militia forces went street to street, block by block, and house to house, in Kigali and every other major city save Butare in the south (which resisted the genocidal impetus for two weeks before its prefect was deposed and killed, and replaced by a compliant *génocidaire*). Tutsis were dragged out of homes and hiding places and murdered, often after prolonged torture and rape. At the infamous roadblocks, those carrying Tutsi identity cards—along with some Hutus who were deemed to "look" Tutsi—were shot or hacked to death. Often the killers, whether drunk and willing or conscripted and reluctant, severed the Achilles' tendons of their victims to immobilize them. They would be left for hours in agony, until the murderers mustered the energy to return and finish them off. Numerous accounts exist of Tutsis paying to be killed by rifle bullets, rather than slowly and agonizingly with machetes and hoes.

In what can only be called "an incomprehensible scandal,"[35] the killings took place literally before the eyes of UNAMIR and other foreign forces, whose mandate and orders forbade them to intervene beyond saving white lives. As early as April 9, in the church at Gikondo in Kigali, a slaughter occurred that presaged the strategies to be followed in coming weeks—one that was witnessed by Polish nuns, priests, and UN military observers:

A Presidential Guard officer arrived and told the soldiers not to waste their bullets because the Interahamwe [Hutu Power militia] would soon come with machetes. Then the militia came in, one hundred of them, and threatening the [Polish] priests they began to kill people, slashing with their machetes and clubs, hacking arms, legs, genitals and the faces of the terrified people who tried to protect the children under the pews. Some people were dragged outside the church and attacked in the courtyard. The killing continued for two hours as the whole compound was searched. Only two people are believed to have survived the killing at the church. Not even babies were spared. That day in Gikondo there was a street littered with corpses the length of a kilometre. . . . The killing in Gikondo was done in broad daylight with no attempt to disguise the identity of the killers, who were convinced that there would be no punishment for their actions.[36]

The following day, April 10, the UN established contact with military observers in Gisenyi, the heartland of Hutu extremism, where mass killing had erupted three days earlier. The stunned observers described "total chaos" with "massacres everywhere," leaving tens of thousands of Tutsi corpses.[37] With such reports to hand, and the eyewitness testimony of observers in Gikondo, the UN and the international community were fully aware, within a few days of Habyarimana's death on April 6, that killing of a genocidal nature and on a genocidal scale was occurring in Rwanda. They did nothing to stop it, though there were more than enough troops on hand to suppress the killing in Kigali at the very least—and thousands more arrived in the early days of the genocide, albeit to evacuate foreigners (and their pets), not to prevent genocidal killings of Tutsis.[38] Indeed, Security Council members—notably France and the US—would wrap themselves in knots during the ensuing weeks to avoid rendering an unambiguous verdict of genocide. "Be Careful," warned an internal memo following a May 1 meeting at the Pentagon. "Legal [department] at State [Department] was worried about this yesterday— Genocide finding could commit US government to actually do something."[39] Most notorious was the painfully awkward response by State Department spokeswoman Christine Shelly to reporters who sought to pin her down on the genocide question (reproduced from the official State Department transcript, mangled syntax included):

> SHELLY: Based on the evidence we have seen from observations on the ground, we have every reason to believe that acts of genocide have occurred in Rwanda.
>
> REPORTER: What's the difference between "acts of genocide" and "genocide"?
>
> REPORTER: How many acts of genocide does it take to make genocide?
>
> SHELLY: Alan, that's just not a question that I'm in a position to answer.
>
> REPORTER: Well, is it true that you have specific guidance not to use the word "genocide" in isolation but always to preface it with these words "acts of"?
>
> SHELLY: I have guidance which I try to use as best as I can. There are formulations that we are using that we are trying to be consistent of our use of. I don't have an absolute categorical prescription against something, but I have the definitions. I have phraseology which has been carefully examined and arrived at as best as we can apply to exactly the situation and the actions which have taken place. . . . [40]

It seems evident, in retrospect, that the *génocidaires* were not only hoping for such a response, but were awaiting it before launching a full-scale slaughter. Linda Melvern's book *Conspiracy to Murder* conveys the sense of suspended animation in the first week of the genocide, while Hutu Power gauged international reactions to the opening wave of killing. When it became clear there would be no outside impediment, murder spread like a virus across the territories under extremist control. By April 23, Roméo Dallaire, on a journey north from the capital, was "pass[ing] over bridges in swamps that had been lifted by the force of the bodies piling up on the struts. We had inched our way through villages of dead humans. . . . We had created paths amongst the dead and half-dead with our hands. And we had thrown up even when there was nothing in our stomachs."[41]

Parish churches, along with schools and similar facilities, were soon piled thigh-high with the shot, hacked, and savaged corpses of the victims.[42] One such massacre, in fact, may stand as the most concentrated ground-level slaughter of the twentieth

Figure 9.2 David Blumenkrantz, working in neighboring Uganda at the time of the Rwandan genocide, captured this extraordinary image of victims' corpses pulled from Lake Victoria by Ugandan fishermen. Murdered Tutsis were often dumped into tributaries of the lake, which is the source of the Nile River. As explored by the anthropologist Christopher Taylor (see Chapter 11, p. 589), this was a means of symbolically expunging the Tutsis from Rwanda, and returning them to their supposedly foreign, "Nilotic" origins.

Source: Courtesy of David Blumenkrantz.

century (by which I mean a mass killing inflicted in hours or days rather than months or years, and by means other than aerial bombing). On April 20, at the parish of Karama in Butare prefecture, "between thirty-five and forty-three thousand people died *in less than six hours.*"[43] This was more than were killed in the Nazis' two-day slaughters of Jews outside Odessa and Kiev (at Babi Yar) in 1941, or in the largest single-day extermination spree in the gas chambers of Auschwitz-Birkenau.[44]

Tens of thousands of Tutsis sought sanctuary in schools, stadiums, and especially places of worship. But there was no sanctuary to be had. In fact, those encouraging them to seek it were usually *génocidaires* working to concentrate their victims for mass killing. Astonishingly, church figures across Rwanda played a leading role in legitimizing and even inflicting genocidal killing (although "many priests, pastors and nuns" also displayed "courage and compassion," hiding and protecting potential victims).[45]

Figure 9.3 Tutsis were murdered *en masse* in Rwanda in part because they flocked to places of worship for refuge—such sanctuaries had been respected in past outbreaks of violence. In fact, both the Catholic and Anglican churches in Rwanda were deeply complicit in the genocide; Hutu priests, nuns, and lay workers often cooperated with the authorities and with *interahamwe* killers to target Tutsi members of their congregations. The Nyamata Memorial Site, shown here, is centered on a church and surrounding area where some 2,500 Tutsis were butchered in April 1994. "Government soldiers surrounded it and threw in grenades. After that, militiamen, many from the surrounding villages, entered the church with machetes, axes, even screwdrivers and hacked at the survivors."[46] The bodies were removed for burial; bullet holes are still visible in the roof. Many such massacre sites across Rwanda are now carefully maintained memorials to the holocaust that swept the country in 1994.

Source: Fanny Schertzer/Wikimedia Commons.

BOX 9.1 ONE WOMAN'S STORY: GLORIOSE MUKAKANIMBA

A Tutsi woman and mother of three, Gloriose Mukakanimba lived in the Rwandan capital of Kigali, where she ran a tailoring shop. On April 7, 1994, she witnessed the outbreak of the most intensive mass-killing spree in human history. Hutu militias— the so-called *interahamwe* ("those who fight together")—went door-to-door. They first targeted "prominent and rich people," Gloriose said, but quickly moved on to attack ordinary citizens: "They shot you just because you were a Tutsi. When they started using machetes, they didn't even bother to ask for ID cards. It was as if they had carried out a census; they knew you were a Tutsi."

Gloriose's home was one of those invaded. "Around 11:00 a.m. on Sunday [April 10] a large group of interahamwe came to our house. They tried to break the gate. They had difficulties with the gate so they cut through the hedge. They came in and started searching the house." After a while, they prepared to leave— but their leader arrived and ordered them "to go back in and kill." Her family was ordered outside. There, her husband, Deo Rutayisire, and her brother, Maurice Niyoyita, were hacked to death with machetes. Gloriose tried to flee with her 2-year-old daughter in her arms, but the child slipped from her grasp, "and I saw them cutting her up. I ran with all the strength I had."

While she desperately sought a place to hide, Gloriose was stunned to hear her neighbors calling out to the militia members: "Here she is, here she is!" "These were neighbors I had already considered friends, people I felt had been kind to me." Finally she found sanctuary in an abandoned house with an old vehicle parked adjacent. "The bonnet was open and it did not have an engine. I jumped right inside the bonnet and stayed there for about a day and a half." Militia scoured the house, coming close to the car where she was hiding. "I could feel them so near to me. I was terrified to death. I stopped myself from breathing."

When the *interahamwe* moved on, Gloriose begged for refuge from a neighbor who had been friendly with her sister. But the neighbor demanded that she leave. She decided to return to her house, only to run into an "ambush [that] had been set up for me." She was detained for a few hours, until the militia decided to execute her. An *interahamwe* "hit me with the machete. Fortunately it was dark and he could not see very well. He kept trying to aim for my neck but I instinctively put my hands over my neck. He kept hitting my hands, thinking it was my neck. After a while, I decided to let him think I was dead." Finally "they left, thinking they had finished their job."

Gloriose ran to hide in a water-filled ditch. But "some other militia saw me and went to tell my killers that they had not completed their job. The next morning, my killers came back, this time with guns and grenades." They shot and tossed grenades into the trench, but Gloriose was able to evade them. "It was a very long trench. This made it difficult for them to know my exact location because of course I kept moving."

Apparently believing she must have been killed by the fusillade, the militia again moved on. "I spent the night in the trench. The wounds in my arms were not only extremely painful but had come to smell. I decided to come out of the trench for fear that I would die there." She fled to the nearby residence of one of the few surviving Tutsi families in the area: "I found out that the husband had been an invalid for a long time; maybe that's why the killers let them live." Together with her rescuers, she joined a stream of Tutsis heading toward the lines of the rebel Rwandan Patriotic Front in Gitarama district.

On the verge of starvation, she and her companions finally stumbled on an RPF patrol. She was taken to a health center in the city of Rutare. There, her wounds were treated, and she was interviewed by researchers from African Rights, a London-based organization that would go on to publish the most detailed and harrowing account of the Rwandan genocide.[47]

In Kibuye prefecture, some 20,000 Tutsis had congregated at Gatwaro stadium. The stadium was surrounded by soldiers and militia, who began firing into the stadium and at anyone who sought to flee. Twelve thousand people died in a single day. Elsewhere in the prefecture, perhaps the most exterminatory killing of the genocide took place. "Entire Tutsi communities were wiped out with no witnesses left to tell what happened. From a population of 252,000 Tutsi in a 1991 census, by the end of June there were an estimated 8,000 left alive."[48]

Many Tutsis fled to high ground, such as Bisesero mountain in southwestern Rwanda (see Figure 9.4). The "mountain of death" was the scene of unforgettable acts of resistance, as Tutsis sought desperately to fend off the attacks. A survivor, Claver Mbugufe, recalled:

There were constant attempts to kill the refugees at Bisesero. But we were always able to defend ourselves. Towards mid-May, when we were still in the grip of the interahamwe militia and their allies, they received enormous reinforcements. . . . Soldiers also came and set up a camp near Bisesero for three days, during which they killed many refugees. We spent the entire day running up and down. We tried to concentrate our defence in one area in order to break their stranglehold. We did everything possible to kill any one of them who stood in our way. Sometimes, we even managed to wrest guns from soldiers and policemen. We killed many of these aggressors.[49]

Despite such heroism, tens of thousands of people died at Bisesero in April and May. A series of other massacres, notably in Cyahindu prefecture, claimed over

10,000 victims at one time. Then there were the "death camps" such as those in the Kabgayi archbishopric, where some thirty thousand Tutsis congregated. Militia roamed freely through Kabgayi—the site depicted on the cover of this book—selecting Tutsi men and boys for execution, and women and girls for rape.[50] (The gendering of the Rwandan catastrophe is discussed further in Chapter 13.) This horror ended only when the Rwandan Patriotic Front captured Kabgayi on June 2.

Throughout, a remarkable feature of the genocide was its routinized character. The killings were "marked not by the fury of combat or paroxysms of mob violence, but by a well-ordered sanity that mirrored the rhythms of ordinary collective life."[51] Killers arrived for their duties at a designated hour, and broke off their murderous activities at five in the afternoon, as though clocking off.

Another signal feature, as noted above, was the involvement of ordinary Hutus in the slaughter. "Had the killing been the work of state functionaries and those bribed by them," wrote Mamdani, "it would have translated into no more than a string of massacres perpetrated by death squads. Without massacres by machete-wielding civilian mobs, in the hundreds and thousands, there would have been no genocide."[52] In a development perhaps unprecedented in the history of genocide, Hutu women flocked or were conscripted by the tens of thousands to participate

Figure 9.4 A ring of spears outside the Bisesero genocide memorial in southwest Rwanda commemorates the heroic resistance of tens of thousands of Tutsis who fled to these hills when the 1994 genocide erupted. Nearly all were massacred during weeks of raids by Hutu killing squads.

Source: Author's photo, August 2012.

in the killing of Tutsis and the stripping of corpses. To the extent that their violence was directed against Tutsi women,

> there appears to have been a kind of gendered jubilation at the "comeuppance" of Tutsi females, who had for so long been depicted in Hutu propaganda as Rwanda's sexual elite. Otherwise, the motivations for women's involvement as genocidal killers frequently paralleled those of Hutu men: bonds of ethnic solidarity . . . suasion and coercion by those in authority (including other women); the lure of material gain; and the intoxicating pleasure of untrammelled sadism.[53]

It is impossible to know how many of the killers, male and female, would have avoided their role if they could. It is clear, however, that hundreds of thousands of Hutus participated eagerly. "It was as if all the men, women and children had come to kill us," recalled one survivor.[54] Many were motivated by greed—the chance to loot Tutsi belongings and seize Tutsi land (see Chapter 10). And for those at the bottom of the social ladder, there was the unprecedented opportunity to exercise life-and-death power over others. Gérard Prunier captures this element vividly, noting that "social envy came together with political hatred to fire the . . . bloodlust":

> In Kigali the [militias] . . . had tended to recruit mostly among the poor. As soon as they went into action, they drew around them a cloud of even poorer people, a lumpenproletariat of street boys, rag-pickers, car-washers and homeless unemployed. For these people the genocide was the best thing that could ever happen to them. They had the blessings of a form of authority to take revenge on socially powerful people as long as these [victims] were on the wrong side of the political fence. They could steal, they could kill with minimum justification, they could rape and they could get drunk for free. This was wonderful. The political aims pursued by the masters of this dark carnival were quite beyond their scope. They just went along, knowing it would not last.[55]

It did not last—in part because the killers were running out of victims, but in larger part because the genocide distracted the Hutu Power regime from confronting RPF forces. Immediately following the outbreak of the genocide on April 6–7, the RPF contingent in Kigali had moved out of its barracks to establish control over several neighborhoods of the capital, thereby protecting thousands of Tutsis who would otherwise have faced certain death. Rwanda thus witnessed the surreal phenomenon of street battles in the heart of the capital, while the government was extending the holocaust to every corner of the countryside under its control. That control rapidly ebbed, however, as the RPF renewed its offensive. By mid-June, they had decisively defeated Rwandan government forces, which were pushed into a limited zone in the southwest of the country. The offensive was accompanied by large-scale revenge killings of Hutus in territory that RPF soldiers had overrun. Estimates of those killed range as high as 50,000, with many summary executions, particularly of "battle-age" Hutu men who were automatically assumed to have participated in the genocide.[56]

At this point, foreign forces finally staged a decisive intervention—but one that primarily benefited the *génocidaires*. On June 17, France proposed to the UN Security Council that French troops be sent to Rwanda under UN auspices. Four days later, thousands of French troops began assembling on the Rwandan border with Congo—an indication of how rapidly a substantial intervention can be mounted when the political will exists.[57] On July 4, the RPF gained full control of the capital, Kigali; the following day, France, with UN approval in hand, established a "safe zone" in the southwest.

The French intervention, known as Opération Turquoise, may have saved many Tutsi lives. But protecting Tutsis was not the main purpose of the intervention. Rather, the operation was a continuation of the long-standing French support for the Hutu Power government. It permitted the orderly evacuation of nearly *two million* Hutus, including tens of thousands of *génocidaires*, to refugee camps in neighboring Congo. As Gérard Prunier wrote, "the refugees moved to the camps in perfect order, with their *bourgmestres* and communal counsellors at their head. Inside the camps they remained grouped according to their *communes* of origin and under the control of the very political structure which had just been responsible for the genocide."[58] The *génocidaires* certainly thought their saviors had arrived. RTLM hate radio urged "you Hutu girls to wash yourselves and put on a good dress to welcome our French allies. The Tutsi girls are all dead, so you have your chance."[59]

This mass flow of refugees was highly visible to international media that gained access to the camps. The humanitarian crisis—especially outbreaks of cholera and other diseases that killed thousands of refugees—was something the international community could address with minimum risk. The Clinton government in the US, which had spent the period of the mass slaughter instructing its representatives to avoid using the word "genocide" and placing obstacle after obstacle in the path of intervention, now leapt into action. US troops arrived within days to begin distribution of water, supplies, and medical aid to the camps.

"Like a monstrous cancer, the camps coalesced, solidified and implanted themselves" in eastern Congo.[60] Hutu extremists slaughtered local Tutsis and staged cross-border raids into Rwanda, prompting the newly installed RPF regime in Rwanda to launch an invasion of Congo to pacify the border regions and establish a fiefdom for exploitation by Rwanda's new Tutsi elites. According to Filip Reyntjens, it was "the unfinished Rwandan civil war, exported in 1996, and again in 1998, to the DRC" that triggered the cataclysm of the First and Second Congo wars, which combined have likely inflicted the most massive death toll of any conflict since the Second World War.[61]

CONGO AND AFRICA'S "FIRST WORLD WAR"

> The world doesn't look into the forest.
>
> Congolese woman interviewed by Bryan Mealer

Congo was the backdrop for one of the greatest but least-known genocides in modern history—the Belgian "rubber terror" in Congo (Chapter 2). After independence from Belgium in 1960, it fell under the sway of an army colonel, Mobutu Sese Seko, who renamed it Zaïre (it became the Democratic Republic of the Congo in 1997; for readers' convenience, I use "Congo" for all stages of the country's colonial and post-independence history).

Mobutu was notoriously corrupt and megalomaniacal, "a ruthless crook who fitted his palace with a nuclear shelter, hired [the] Concorde for shopping trips and so gutted the treasury that inflation between October 1990 and December 1995 totalled 6.3 billion per cent."[62] Industry and infrastructure collapsed as kleptocracy came to pervade Congolese politics, economic life, and social relations.[63]

The catalyst for Mobutu's downfall came from eastern Congo, thousands of kilometers from the capital, Kinshasa. In the final stages of the 1994 genocide in Rwanda, as Tutsi rebel forces closed in from the north and east, Hutu *génocidaires* staged a mass evacuation of populations under their control, across the Congolese border to the city of Goma. Ironically, it was *this* humanitarian crisis that galvanized the world, not the genocide against Tutsis.[64] Ironically, too, the outside aid that flooded in was instrumental in permitting the *génocidaires* to reconstitute themselves, control the refugee population, and launch attacks against Tutsis in both Congo and Rwanda. This set the stage for the dramatic and destructive events of 1996–1997: the Rwandan invasion and push to overthrow the Mobutu regime; the massive forced repatriation to Rwanda of more than a million Hutu refugees; and one of the most comprehensively-"hidden" genocides of the late twentieth century. This time it would be inflicted by Rwandan Tutsis and their Congolese Tutsi (Banyamulenge) allies against Rwandan Hutus, albeit at killing sites far removed from Rwanda itself.

1996–1997: THE "GENOCIDE OF THE CAMPS"

The mass atrocities inflicted mostly by Rwandan RPA soldiers against Rwandan Hutu refugees in 1996–1997 are intensively little-studied, if such a thing is possible. The United Nations *Mapping Report* of 2010—first leaked, then published in slightly bowdlerized form—is the first comprehensive source available in English. This inattention reflects the complicity of leading international actors in the genocide that unfolded during the First Congo War. As Prunier noted in *Africa's World War*, "there seems to have been an unspoken compact among the various Western actors not to prevent the Rwandese from carrying out their revenge [against Hutus] since it was the West's lack of reaction during the genocide [against Tutsis] that had made it possible in the first place.... The RPF calculated that guilt, ineptitude, and the hope that things would work out would cause the West to literally get away with murder. The calculation was correct."[65] This moral inertia, combined with RPF obstruction, long prevented outside observers from gaining an accurate understanding of exactly what occurred during the genocide—though precious few evinced an interest in the subject.

The UN report for the first time detailed the scale, systematic character, and specific atrocities inflicted by the RPA and its allies, with notable Ugandan support. Invading in October 1996, the RPA first cleared the massive refugee camps

along the Rwandan and Ugandan borders, shelling terrified refugees into evacuating them. Most returned under duress to Rwanda, but hundreds of thousands
fled deeper into the Congolese interior. The RPA and AFDL pursued them across
the eastern half of the country (see Map 9.3), incidentally triggering murderous
anti-Tutsi pogroms in Kinshasa, to topple President Mobutu and install their own
proxy, the longtime rebel Laurent Kabila.[66] It was, wrote Prunier, "the first known
instance of postcolonial imperial conquest in Africa by an African country."[67] The
Rwandans assumed that Kabila would allow them to rule *de facto* over North and
South Kivu provinces in Congo's far east, "protecting" the Banyamulenge Tutsis—
though in fact the Rwandan Tutsi presence greatly exacerbated ethnic tensions in
the Kivus—and looting the territory of its rich mineral resources.

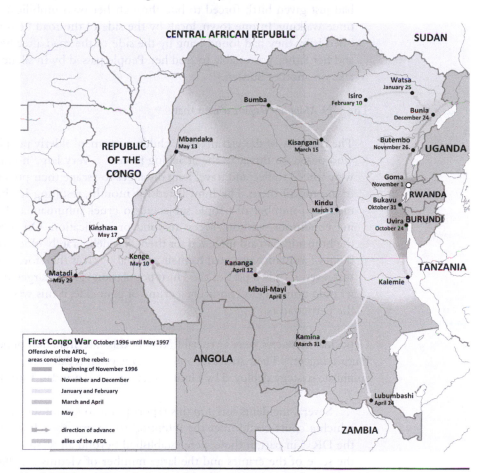

Map 9.3 This map shows the lines of advance by the Rwandan army (RPA) and the Tutsi–Banyamulenge
militia, the AFDL, during the First Congo War of 1996–1997 to topple the Mobutu regime and install
Laurent Kabila as Rwanda's Congolese client. As detailed in the United Nations' 2010 *Mapping Report*,
after "cleansing" the border region, including the massive refugee camps around Goma and Bukavu,
the Tutsi forces pursued Rwandan Hutu refugees deep into the jungles of eastern and finally central
Congo. Hundreds of thousands of refugees succumbed from starvation and disease, or in largescale
genocidal massacres inflicted by the vengeful Rwandans and their Banyamulenge allies.

Source: Don-kun, Uwe Dedering/Wikimedia Commons.

For the Hutu refugees fleeing deep into the interior, exhaustion, starvation, and disease were the greatest threats. They were kept on the move, massacred whenever they sought to settle in large groups. One refugee, Béatrice Umetesi, fled from Goma, later providing a unique account of her experiences in a memoir, *Surviving the Slaughter*.[68] In Jason Stearns's summary:

> Death surrounded them. Chronic diseases, such as diarrhea, malaria, and typhoid, were the biggest killers. Others died of diabetes or asthma, having run out of medicine to treat their chronic illnesses. The smell of rotting bodies filled the air. . . . Beatrice saw flurries of white and blue butterflies alight on fresh corpses, feeding off their salt and moisture. Further on, she saw a woman who had just given birth forced to bite through her own umbilical cord and continue walking. In one town, locals by the side of the road held up a malnourished baby they had found lying by the side of the road after her mother died and her father was unable to feed her. People passed by in silence, unwilling to take on another burden.[69]

The UN *Mapping Report* found that

> The majority of the victims were children, women, elderly people and the sick, who posed no threat to the attacking forces . . . Very large numbers of victims were forced to flee and travel long distances to escape their pursuers, who were trying to kill them. The hunt lasted for months, resulting in the deaths of an unknown number of people subjected to cruel, inhuman, and degrading living conditions, without access to food or medication. On several occasions, the humanitarian aid intended for them was deliberately blocked, . . . depriving them of assistance essential to their survival. . . . It is therefore possible to assert that, even if only a part of the Hutu population . . . was targeted and destroyed, it could nonetheless constitute a crime of genocide, if this was the intention of the perpetrators.

Genocidal massacres were a crucial feature of this extermination of perhaps 233,000 Hutu refugees.[70] Their structure and character often recalled the concentrate-and-annihilate strategy deployed by Hutu Power against Rwandan Tutsis in 1994:

> . . . Several incidents listed in this report point to circumstances and facts from which a court could infer the intention to destroy the Hutu ethnic group in the DRC in part, if these were established beyond all reasonable doubt. Firstly, the scale of the crimes and the large number of victims are illustrated by the numerous incidents described [in the report]. The extensive use of edged weapons (primarily hammers) and the systematic massacre of survivors, including women and children, after the camps had been taken show that the numerous deaths cannot be attributed to the hazards of war or seen as equating to collateral damage. . . . Particularly in North Kivu and South Kivu but also in other provinces, the massacres often began with a trick by elements of the AFDL/APR, who summoned the victims to meetings on the pretext either of discussing their repatriation to Rwanda in the case of the refugees, or of introducing

them to the new authorities in the case of Hutus settled in the region, or of distributing food. Afterwards, those present were systematically killed. . . . Such acts certainly suggest premeditation and a precise methodology. . . . Furthermore, no effort was made to make a distinction between Hutus who were members of the ex-FAR/Interahamwe [Rwandan army/militia] and Hutu civilians, whether or not they were refugees. This tendency to put all Hutus together and "tar them with the same brush" is also illustrated by the declaration made during the "awareness-raising speeches" made by the AFDL/APR in certain places, according to which any Hutu still present in Zaire must necessarily be a perpetrator of genocide, since the "real" refugees had already returned to Rwanda. These "awareness-raising speeches" made in North Kivu also incited the population to look for, kill or help to kill Rwandan Hutu refugees, whom they called "pigs."[71]

In a grim echo of the Jewish Holocaust (Chapter 6), reports indicated that bodies in mass graves were being exhumed and burned to cover the evidence of genocide. ". . . There is much work to do, digging up the bodies and burning them," a soldier told one of Filip Reyntjens's informants. "When the UN eventually comes to investigate, there will be no evidence."[72] Perhaps the most dogged western reporter in Congo, Howard French, found his access blocked "to one of the last refugee-gathering points south of Kisangani, a place of horrific death with no more descriptive name than its distance marker, Kilometer 42. Bulldozers had been sighted heading south down the road from Kisangani, and relief agency officials who had passed nearby on a train said the area reeked of incinerated bodies." In his memoir, *A Continent for the Taking*, French scathingly related:

> Whether it was the United States or the United Nations, no Westerner would ever push hard enough to lift the veil over this crude little Auschwitz. In fact, just a few months later, Washington would be pushing to make sure that no Western investigators ever made it down that road. Tacitly, America had already made common cause with Rwanda's Tutsi-led government, which was counting on the thickness of the bush at the heart of the continent to hush the agonized cries of the massacred, just as it was counting on the unending rains that fed the great [Congo] river to wash away the ashes, along with every last drop of blood.[73]

THE SECOND CONGO WAR

Once installed in power in Kinshasa, Rwanda's client Laurent Kabila fell under the sway of Hutu representatives in Kinshasa, supporting renewed cross-border attacks and killing operations in Rwanda.[74] Rwanda soon began plotting a coup against its former protégé. An attempted drive on Kinshasa by Rwandan forces and anti-Kabila Congolese was halted only by the military intervention of Angola and Zimbabwe. Together with Namibia and Chad, these formed the coalition that maintained Kabila in power until his 2001 assassination. (He was succeeded by his son Joseph, still in power as of early 2016.) Meanwhile, Rwanda, Uganda, and Burundi lined up with the anti-Kabila rebels who dominated the eastern half of the country. Congo had become "Africa's first world war." It was a continental struggle that "reached almost without interruption from the Red Sea to the Atlantic Ocean,"[75] and offered almost unlimited opportunities for looting of precious minerals, especially diamonds and, for a time, coltan (an ore used in cell phones and other devices).

This was also a prototypical "new war" of the type examined in Chapter 12— and a classic "degenerate war," in Martin Shaw's formulation (see p. 118). Clashes between major concentrations of armed forces were rare. Many of the killers were paramilitaries, warlords, and freebooters, cut adrift from more traditional military forces. Of special note was the militia led by the Congolese Tutsi Laurent Nkundabagenzi (also known as Nkunda), operating from a power base among the Tutsi population of North Kivu. Nkunda's "record of violence in eastern Congo includes destroying entire villages, committing mass rapes, and causing hundreds of thousands of Congolese to flee their homes."[76] Other key actors were soldiers of the Congolese army, who felt abandoned by central authorities in Kinshasa: "Paid poorly, if at all, undisciplined and feeling abandoned, these fighters calculate they have more to gain from looting and shooting than maintaining the fiction of an integrated national army."[77] Internecine conflicts between these armed groups provoked refugee flows numbering in the tens of thousands. Warlordism was rife amidst state collapse, with the Congolese government unable to "make [and] enforce laws, maintain order, deliver services, or ensure security."[78] Against this anarchic backdrop, as Prunier noted in his 2009 work *Africa's World War*, "civilians died partly because the soldiers killed them but, more often, because their living conditions (absence of health care, impossibility of steady cultivation, impossibility of trade, lack of shelter during the rainy season, constant displacement) caused their death."[79]

Central to the "self-sustaining" character of the conflict was the rich mineral resources of Congo, which proved an irresistible and enduring lure for foreign powers and their Congolese clients. Competition for the spoils eventually caused a falling out and pitched battles between Rwandan and Ugandan occupiers.[80] Both countries had experienced miraculous leaps in their export of key commodities— diamonds, gold, timber, and coltan—at levels that mysteriously far exceed domestic production.[81]

BOX 9.2 DENYING RWANDA, DENYING CONGO

Since the Rwandan holocaust of 1994, a brazenly denialist discourse has sought to counter the overwhelming evidence of the "Hutu Power" regime's systematic genocide of the Tutsi civilian population. The so-called "double genocide" thesis inflated atrocities by the Rwandan Patriotic Front in 1990–1994 and downplayed the Hutu genocide of Tutsis, to produce a rough and mendacious equivalence between the two. It received a significant airing by French president François Mitterrand,[82] and became a shibboleth for the scattered network of Rwandan Hutu exiles and their admirers, not to mention alleged and convicted *génocidaires* and their lawyers. The Hutu-perpetrated genocide of Tutsis, with its hundreds of thousands of victims, was even "disappeared" completely. In 2010, the longtime leftist critic Edward S. Herman joined with a blogger, David Peterson, to produce a book, *The Politics of Genocide*, for Monthly Review Press. The authors went so far as to contend that the depiction of a Hutu genocide of Tutsis was the *reverse* of what had actually occurred in 1994; that the principal agent of genocidal killing was the RPF; and that Hutus constituted a majority of victims. As I argued upon the book's appearance, this was "the equivalent of asserting that the Nazis never killed Jews in death camps—indeed, that it was really Jews who killed Germans." I accused the authors of "the most naked denial of the extermination of at least half a million Tutsis by agents of 'Hutu Power' that I have ever read in an ostensibly scholarly source." This radically revisionist—one might say fantasist—stance was based "on 'evidence' that, even on cursory examination, proves to be the sheerest gossamer, when it is not simply hearsay and idle speculation."[83]

The denialist project has attracted only marginal attention so far. But it draws some strength and influence from widespread popular ignorance and derision of the Great Lakes region (the "Whoopsie/Tutu" phenomenon); the confusion that prevailed during the 1994 genocide, stoked by the regime's "tribal war" smokescreen, media blackout, and the massive, suddenly visible flow of destitute Hutu refugees to Congo at genocide's end; and the endorsement, explicit or implicit, of generally conscientious individuals like Noam Chomsky and John Pilger, who should know much better.[84]

On the other side of the genocide-denial equation—in a palpable irony—stands the Kagame/RPF regime of Rwanda. It has sought to render itself immune to accusations that it committed genocide and crimes against humanity against Hutus, on a scale of tens of thousands of victims in Rwanda in 1994 and up to three hundred thousand in the 1996–1997 "genocide of the camps." It has aggressively denounced any legal attempt to confront those crimes—not that any significant international or national authority has proposed prosecutions. The shine has worn off the Kagame government in recent years, as international pressure was brought to bear over its depredations in the DRC, and as Kagame pushed through constitutional changes allowing him to remain president until 2036. (This is quite a likely prospect, given the regime's demonstrated capacity to engineer election and plebiscite results approaching 100 percent in its favor.) But it still trades on its status as the force that ended the 1994 genocide, engineered reconciliation and grassroots justice in the aftermath, and advanced a novel and in many ways impressive developmental agenda for twenty-first century Africa (see "Success Stories?," Chapter 16).

The leaking of the UN *Mapping Report* in August 2010, and the furious reaction it evoked from Kagame/the RPF, shed fresh light on "the genocide of the camps," including the unveiling of sickening survivor testimony from dozens of massacre sites. At the 2014 conference of the International Association of Genocide Scholars (IAGS) in Winnipeg, Manitoba, I shared a panel with one of those survivors. During the period set aside for questions and comments, he was subjected to a lengthy and vituperative verbal attack by a Rwandan government representative and her colleague. When he disclaimed a "genocide" framing for the mass crimes committed in Congo by the RPA and its AFDL allies, I interjected to state that I considered the G-word entirely appropriate. The scene was depressing evidence of the Rwandan regime's own denialism, which has landed both Rwandans and foreigners in hot water, sometimes in jail. In the government's eyes, pointing to its actions in Congo promotes a "double-genocide" thesis; it is genocide "revisionism," and subject to criminal sanction. My focus on the Rwandan genocide in this chapter, and my efforts to counter extreme revisionist trends, are sufficient counter to any such accusation. I wonder nonetheless what may happen the next time I apply for a Rwandan visa.

THE BURUNDIAN IMBROGLIO

Burundi and its neighbor Rwanda are "conjoined twins," or so the cliché has it. We have seen that in demographic composition, colonial administration, ethnocratic "capture" of the postcolonial state, and diverse and intertwining eruptions of genocide and mass violence, the countries' destinies are difficult to understand independently of each other.

Whereas in Rwanda the Hutu majority seized control of the post-independence Rwandan state and used it to persecute and marginalize Tutsis, in Burundi the situation was reversed. A Tutsi minority, controlling both the state administration and (crucially) the military, imposed an ethnocratic order under which it eventually "became almost impossible for a Hutu to win—either in secondary school or in the nation's only university, where admission and instruction were totally controlled by the government." Tutsis comprised fully 99 percent of army officers. "Similarly, in every other area controlled by [the] government, Tutsi dominance was near universal: 95 percent of the judiciary, 88 percent of the faculty at the University of Bujumbura, and all thirty-three members of the Comité Militaire de Salut National (or, Military Committee for National Security, which had final authority over national decision making) were Tutsi."[85]

The first massive genocide to afflict Burundi—one that reverberated all around the Great Lakes region—was the "eliticide" launched by the Tutsi-dominated military regime against educated Hutus in 1972. It followed an abortive Hutu-sponsored coup and the selective killing of thousands of Tutsis. In a savage response aimed at subordinating the Hutu masses to Tutsi rule for generations, the army massacred up to 200,000 Hutus. According to Peter Uvin, "these events constitute the defining moments in independent Burundi's history. They crystallized Hutu and Tutsi identities and created a climate of permanent mutual fear."[86]

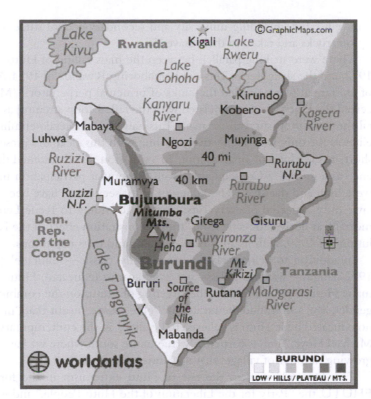

Map 9.4 Burundi.

Source: Map provided by WorldAtlas.com.

Time magazine depicted the genocidal campaign while it was underway, in June 1972:

> The primary targets of the government's continuing "pacification drive" are the Hutu "elite"—meaning not merely the five Hutu cabinet ministers who were summarily executed at the beginning of the rebellion but practically anybody who can write his own name or afford a hut with a corrugated-iron roof instead of a thatched one. At one school, 140 Hutu boys and girls were shot or hacked to death by soldiers. Though the rate of killings had diminished by last week, troops were still descending on isolated villages at night and murdering the local leaders. . . . With their devastating pogrom, the Tutsi overlords have unquestionably bought themselves a few more years in power.[87]

According to Jeremy Greenland, "army units commandeered merchants' trucks and mission vehicles, and drove up to schools removing whole batches of children at a time. Tutsi pupils prepared lists of their Hutu classmates to make identification by officials more straightforward." "In Bujumbura, Gitega, and Nigozi," wrote René Lemarchand, "all administrative personnel of Hutu origins—not only local civil servants but chauffeurs, clerks, and semi-skilled workers—were rounded up, taken to the nearest jail, and either shot or beaten to death with rifle butts and clubs. In Bujumbura alone, an estimated 4,000 Hutu identified as educated or semi-educated, including university and secondary-school students, were loaded up on trucks and taken to their graves."[88]

There were striking parallels between the mass killing of Hutus in Burundi in 1972 and the slaughter of Tutsis in neighboring Rwanda in 1994. An atmosphere of existential fear pervaded the ranks of principal perpetrators: "Many Tutsi perceived the Hutu attacks [associated with the failed coup attempt] as posing a mortal threat to their survival . . . many Tutsi saw the wholesale elimination of Hutu elites as the only way of effectively dealing with this clear and present danger—in short, it was a kind of 'final solution' to a situation that threatened their very existence as a group."[89] Consequently, levels of popular participation in the genocide were high and decisive: "The killing of Hutu seemed to have become part of the civic duty expected of every Tutsi citizen," according to René Lemarchand. This mortal fear derived directly from "the demonstration effect of the Rwanda Revolution" of 1959, with its anti-Tutsi pogroms and mass expulsions.

In addition to being a classic—perhaps *the* classic—"eliticide" (see p. 34), the 1972 slaughter was also a classic *gendercide* against (educated) Hutu males. Though many Hutu females also died, the targeting of Hutus on the combined grounds of gender, age, and imputed educated or "elite" status meant that "in area after area no educated male Hutu is believed to be alive," in the contemporary assessment of Michael Hoyt. "This is particularly true in the south where we have word from [a] growing number of villages that no Hutu males remain at all."[90]

The genocide sparked the rise of Hutu extremism in the form of PALIP-EHUTU, the "Party for the Liberation of the Hutu People," and its armed wing, the FNL. Founded in 1980, the FNL remains the leading armed opposition force in Burundi (see "Great Lakes Aftermaths," below). The attacks it launched against Tutsi civilians in 1988 provoked another brutal state response, with up to 20,000 Burundians killed in the atrocities.

As in Rwanda, the end of the Cold War disrupted longstanding clientelist arrangements with the great powers, and led to ever-greater pressure for democratization in keeping with the "new world order." Burundi, with its Tutsi ethnocracy ruling apartheid-style over a Hutu subject population, and with its heavy dependence on foreign aid, was pushed toward interethnic accommodation. The crowning moment of the process was the installation of the country's first Hutu president, Melchior Ndadaye, in 1993. But within weeks, Ndadaye was murdered by Tutsi soldiers in a coup against the democratically-elected government. The assassination triggered despair among the Hutu masses, spawning "countless atrocities and random killings of Tutsi civilians" across the country.[91] As always, the army's response was merciless. Between 30,000 and 100,000 people were murdered—mostly Hutus, reflecting the disparities between the armed formations. Some 350,000 Burundian Hutus fled to the sanctuary offered by the Habyarimana regime in Rwanda, providing "a powerful stimulus to the crystallization of Hutu Power" and contributing "significantly to the radicalization of Hutu politics on the eve of the carnage."[92] They also leant credence to Hutu Power's propaganda assault on Rwandan Tutsis, which depicted the minority as a "fifth column" poised to join with the RPF invaders to slaughter and re-enslave Hutus. Studies of ordinary genocidal perpetrators and accomplices since the 1994 genocide, above all

Scott Straus's, have reported that these messages were widely believed and generated a sense of mortal fear among Rwandan Hutus.[93]

The 1993 bloodbath inaugurated a decade of civil war amounting to a "creeping genocide."[94] Hutu rebel groups used Congolese territory as a base for attacks against the hard-pressed Burundian army; after July 1994, their ranks were swelled by Hutu *génocidaires* and others fleeing Rwanda. Tutsis fled the countryside for camps run by humanitarian organizations, or for the relative safety of Bujumbura. The capital became "completely mono-ethnic," wrote Christian Jennings:

> The only Hutus who now entered it did so during the day, leaving at night to return to the hills. The agricultural framework and structure of the country had collapsed; many Hutus hid from the army during the day in wooded and swampy areas, only emerging at night to cultivate their crops. The Tutsi were unable to herd or breed their cattle, and food was a major problem. The towns were essentially controlled by the army, Tutsi militias and Tutsi displaced people, while the hills were the land of the Hutu.[95]

As in Congo—and in small part reflecting the presence of Burundian rebels there—Burundi became a "degenerate war" in which Hutu rebel "liberators" seemed as likely to slaughter innocent Hutu as Tutsi civilians, and in which the state sought to compensate for its minimal legitimacy with sheer untrammeled violence. Jennings described a 1996 attack by rebels, described as "a mixture of local men, young stragglers speaking Kinyarwanda in old military uniforms who were ex-FAR [Hutu soldiers] from Rwanda, and Hutu civilians they did not know":

> The army surrounded a number of hills with armoured cars, and took up positions on the tracks running through the forests. . . . Then on the night of 21 and 22 March, they attacked . . . The killing went on all night. . . . In the large, airy bungalows at Bururi hospital, the beds and corridors were all full of the survivors. Pierre Nahibandi had survived the attack. A Hutu, he had lain on the ground in the road and pretended to be dead as the killers went from hut to hut, stabbing the children and mutilating many of them with machetes. Hands and legs were cut off and placed in piles. The young girls and the women were held down. They were raped first by the Hutu attackers, and then with sharpened branches and bayonets. Then they were hacked to death. All of them. The army could hear everything going on [from its base at Bururi] but did not intervene. The people on the hill were half Hutu. Some were pushed into one of two communal latrines to drown. The Hutu attackers then started a huge fire in the centre of the village out of straw and thatch, and threw the remaining wounded onto it along with the corpses. The military arrived at nine the following morning. The death-toll from that night on the three hills of Musenyi alone was 643 people.[96]

Only in 2003, with the political interventions of South Africa's Nelson Mandela and others, did the pervasive climate of violence begin to ease. Yet on a small scale, clashes continued between the army and shadowy rebel elements, with civilians generally the victims.

GREAT LAKES AFTERMATHS

When Hutu Power was crushed in **Rwanda** in July 1994, the country faced a staggering task of material reconstruction, human recovery, restitution, and political reconciliation. Fleeing Hutus had stripped the country almost bare, down to the zinc roofing on houses. Nonetheless, the Tutsi-dominated regime scored notable successes. Economic production was restored to pre-1994 levels. Approximately 1.3 million Hutu refugees were repatriated from Congo.

The basic orientation of the post-genocide government was clear: it was guided by "the conviction that power is the condition of Tutsi survival."[97] Its "Never Again" rallying cry could be interpreted as a pledge that never again would Hutus achieve dominance in Rwandan politics. "The reality," wrote Gérard Prunier as early as 1997, "is that the government is perceived by the average Hutu peasant as a foreign government."[98] Mounting criticism of the RPF-dominated regime's authoritarianism has tarnished Rwanda's "success story" image (see Chapter 16).

In November 1994, the United Nations established the International Criminal Tribunal for Rwanda in Arusha, Tanzania. However, despite an impressive budget of US$1.8 billion, the tribunal launched proceedings only against alleged

Figure 9.5 Lime-shrouded corpses at the Murambi genocide memorial in Rwanda—now the only site in the country where exhumed bodies of victims are on open display. See also the photo essay, photo 6.

Source: Author's photo, August 2012.

perpetrators of genocide against Tutsis and moderate Hutus (that is, no prosecutions were launched of post-1994 Rwandan government leaders for alleged involvement in RPF-inflicted atrocities against Hutus). It also proceeded excruciatingly slowly. The ICTR did not hear its first case until 1997, and as its mandate ended in 2015, Prunier's interim assessment still captured the criticisms of its detractors:

> It was an embodiment of the worst aspects of UN bureaucratic inefficiency; a muted, closed arena for jousting over all the unacknowledged political contradictions of the genocide; and a swamp of nepotistic and corrupt practices. . . . Whereas it had taken the Nuremberg Tribunal one year (from November 1945 to November 1946) to judge twenty-four Nazis and hang ten, the ICTR had managed to carry out only twenty procedures in ten years at a cost of around $700 million.[99]

A central purpose of the court, however, was to refine the law of genocide and crimes against humanity, and contribute to the growing body of case law that was rendering these concepts workable (or manifestly unworkable) for the first time.[100] One of the ICTR's convictions—that of Jean-Paul Akayesu in 1998—was especially significant, with its "historic determination that systematic rape was a crime against humanity and that sexual violence constituted genocide in the same way as any other act." Legal scholar Rebecca L. Haffajee called it "perhaps the most groundbreaking decision advancing gender jurisprudence worldwide."[101] In another case, two former media officials of Rwandan "hate radio" were convicted of using media as genocidal instruments (see Chapter 15).[102] The court wrapped up its operations on December 31, 2015.

In Rwanda itself, some 120,000 accused *génocidaires* languished for years in grim and sometimes murderous conditions in jail, while the country's shattered legal system sought to bring at least some to trial. Finally, in 2003, it was recognized that formal proceedings could never cope with the massive number of accused. Over 20,000 prisoners were released, and others were promised a reduction of sentences in return for confessions. The most interesting form of attempted justice was *gacaca*, or "on the grass," a traditional form of tribunal that sacrificed formal legal procedures and protections for speedy results and a focus on restorative rather than punitive justice (see Chapter 15).

In *Congo*, the genocidal civil war of the late 1990s gradually devolved, like Burundi's mass violence, into the kind of background crisis that kept it out of the global headlines. Probably the most significant development was the sustained pressure by the international community, notably Rwanda's principal patrons in the US and UK, to lever the Kagame regime out of its fiefdom in the Kivus. As early as 2002, according to Jason Stearns, the two countries "went on the offensive with Rwanda and Uganda. Washington abstained from a vote to Renéw the International Monetary Fund's loans to Rwanda, while London privately made clear to Kampala that it would not extend further loans if it did not withdraw its troops." Given Rwanda's fundamental dependence on foreign aid, "in June 2002, President Kagame committed to withdrawing all Rwandan troops within three months.

Figure 9.6 Displaced Congolese flee fighting near the Kibati camp in North Kivu province, eastern DR Congo, November 2008. According to photographer and aid worker Julien Harneis, "I was on the outskirts of [the] camp to oversee our emergency measles vaccination. It was in the same location as an ICRC WFP food distribution. We heard shooting the other side of the camp less than a kilometer away, single shots and automatic for about 15 minutes. People fled the distribution, ran to the camp, picked up their belongings and hurried down the hill to Goma. A crowd gathered around an abandoned food truck and started to loot it until government military police came in to restore order. As we drove back more than 200 very tense government troops trudged up the hill, announcing worse to come."

Source: Julien Harneis/Creative Commons/Flickr.

[Ugandan president Yoweri] Museveni followed suit in November. Journalists lined up at border posts to see a total of 30,000 foreign troops march across, as crowds of Congolese celebrated."[103]

This still left Rwanda's Tutsi client, Bosco Ntaganda, at liberty in North Kivu. Gradually, the pressure on Rwanda, the heavy commitment of UN peacekeepers, and the growing assertiveness of the International Criminal Court, brought about a schism between patron and client. When the Kagame regime withdrew its support, in 2013, Ntaganda—rather than face a more summary form of reprisal—surrendered at the US embassy in Kigali, and was transferred to The Hague to face charges of war crimes and crimes against humanity. His trial began in September 2015.

There was no such reckoning for Ntaganda's patrons in Kigali, or for the genocidal havoc wreaked by the Rwandan Patriotic Army and its AFDL allies in Congo in 1996–1997. The quid pro quo for Rwanda loosening its neocolonial grip on eastern Congo was a willingness to conduct business as usual with the increasingly despotic but development-oriented government in Kigali (see pp. 775–777). Meanwhile, in Kinshasa, Joseph Kabila seemed to be succumbing

Figure 9.7 A policeman patrols by a burning barricade during protests against Burundian president Pierre Nkurunziza in May 2015.

Source: Photo by Goran Tomasevic/Reuters.

to the widespread temptation to institutionalize his personal rule. In January 2015, dozens died in urban protests against the kind of electoral-law manipulations that Rwanda's Kagame was pursuing, to circumvent limits on presidential terms. He had at least refrained from gratuitously stirring up ethnic rivalries in the tumultuous east.

Burundi, which usually received even less international attention than Congo, suddenly leapt into global headlines in 2015. Again the crux of the crisis lay in an attempt to transform a proto-democracy into a personal dictatorship. In the wake of transitional elections to end the civil war and "creeping genocide" in the countryside, the Hutu president, Pierre Nkurunziza, took power in 2005, heading an ostensibly mixed regime: Hutus occupied 60 percent of government posts and Tutsis 40 percent. This arrangement functioned to the extent that a sense of trans-ethnic Burundian nationalism seemed to be taking hold. But when Nkurunziza pushed parliament to scrap presidential term limits, allowing him to contest the 2015 elections, widespread violence erupted (see Figure 9.7). The recalcitrant Hutu FNL militia, which had signed a ceasefire in 2006, again mobilized in opposition to Nkurunziza's power-grab. Attempts by the African Union to defuse the crisis and introduce peacekeeping forces were met with bellicose rhetoric by the Nkurunziza regime. This left the situation on a knife's edge at the time of writing, with Burundi setting alarm-bells ringing in the media, UN circles, and every corner of the genocide-prevention community.[104]

FURTHER STUDY

Rwanda

African Rights, *Rwanda: Death, Despair and Defiance* (rev. edn). London: African Rights, 1995. Immense and harrowing depiction of the Rwandan holocaust; like nothing else in the literature.

Roméo Dallaire (with Brent Beardsley), *Shake Hands with the Devil: The Failure of Humanity in Rwanda*. New York: Carroll & Graf, 2004. Literate and passionate memoir by the Canadian leader of the UN assistance mission in Rwanda (1993–1994).

Alison Des Forges, *Leave None to Tell the Story: Genocide in Rwanda*. New York: Human Rights Watch, 1999. Another indispensable human-rights report on the genocide.

Lee Ann Fujii, *Killing Neighbors: Webs of Violence in Rwanda*. Ithaca, NY: Cornell University Press, 2009. Insightful account of the local dynamics of the killing, and how community and personal bonds sometimes muted it.

Jean Hatzfeld, *Machete Season: The Killers in Rwanda Speak*, trans. Linda Coverdale. New York: Farrar, Straus & Giroux, 2005. Chilling testimony from imprisoned *génocidaires*. See also *Life Laid Bare: The Survivors in Rwanda Speak*; *The Antelope's Strategy: Living in Rwanda After the Genocide*.

René Lemarchand, *The Dynamics of Violence in Central Africa*. Philadelphia, PA: University of Pennsylvania Press, 2009. Places the Rwandan genocide in regional context, with superbly enlightening commentary on Burundi and Congo as well.

Mahmood Mamdani, *When Victims Become Killers: Colonialism, Nativism, and the Genocide in Rwanda*. Princeton, NJ: Princeton University Press, 2001. How political identity was constructed for Hutus and Tutsis.

Linda Melvern, *Conspiracy to Murder: The Rwanda Genocide and the International Community*. London: Verso, 2004. Follow-up to the author's hard-hitting critique, *A People Betrayed: The Role of the West in Rwanda's Genocide* (2nd edn).

Gérard Prunier, *The Rwanda Crisis: History of a Genocide*. New York: Columbia University Press, 1997. The most widely-cited scholarly study of the Rwandan genocide.

Carol Rittner, John K. Roth, and Wendy Whitworth, eds., *Genocide in Rwanda: Complicity of the Churches?* St. Paul, MN: Paragon House, 2004. Insights into the churches' role.

Scott Straus, *The Order of Genocide: Race, Power, and War in Rwanda*. Ithaca, NY: Cornell University Press, 2006. Based on interviews with over two hundred jailed perpetrators; one of the most discussed recent works of genocide studies.

Scott Straus and Lars Waldorf, eds., *Remaking Rwanda: State Building and Human Rights after Mass Violence*. Madison, WI: University of Wisconsin Press, 2010. Critical essays on post-genocide Rwanda under RPF rule.

Congo

Bryan Mealer, *All Things Must Fight to Live: Stories of War and Deliverance in Congo*. New York: Bloomsbury USA, 2008. Extraordinary, frequently gut-churning reportage from the Congo wars.

Gérard Prunier, *Africa's World War: Congo, the Rwandan Genocide, and the Making of a Continental Catastrophe*. Oxford: Oxford University Press, 2009. Magisterial survey of the intricacies and atrocities of war and genocide in Congo.

Filip Reyntjens, *The Great African War: Congo and Regional Geopolitics, 1996–2006*. Cambridge: Cambridge University Press, 2009. A pithy, clear-eyed survey, with a focus (as the title suggests) on the geopolitical dimension.

Thomas Turner, *The Congo Wars: Conflict, Myth and Reality*. London: Zed Books, 2007. Perhaps the best short introduction to the byzantine Congolese conflict.

Marie Béatrice Umutesi, *Surviving the Slaughter: The Ordeal of a Rwandan Refugee in Zaire*. Madison, WI: University of Wisconsin Press, 2004. The only detailed account in English by a Hutu survivor of the "genocide of the camps" (1996–1997).

Michela Wrong, *In the Footsteps of Mr. Kurtz: Living on the Brink of Disaster in Mobutu's Congo*. New York: Perennial, 2002. Journalistic account of life in Congo (then Zaïre) under the Mobutu dictatorship.

Burundi

Patricia O. Daley, *Gender & Genocide in Burundi: The Search for Spaces of Peace in the Great Lakes Region*. Oxford: James Currey, 2008. Masculinities, femininities, and militarism in Burundian politics and genocide. In its way, as viable an overview of this little-studied case as Lemarchand's (see below), and more up-to-date.

Christian Jennings, *Across the Red River: Rwanda, Burundi and the Heart of Darkness*. London: Phoenix, 2001. Vivid reporting from the Great Lakes region in the late 1990s. Most chilling are the chapters detailing Burundi's descent into renewed mass violence.

Ambassador Robert Krueger and Kathleen Tobin Krueger, *From Bloodshed to Hope in Burundi: Our Embassy Years during Genocide*. Austin, TX: University of Texas Press, 2008. A fast-paced and empathetic account by a diplomatic pair who were conscientious about investigating genocidal atrocities during the Burundian civil war of the 1990s and early 2000s.

René Lemarchand, *Burundi: Ethnic Conflict and Genocide*. Cambridge, MA: The Woodrow Wilson Center Press, 1995. Long the standard monograph in English on the causes and course of mass violence in Burundi.

NOTES

1 See Adam Jones, "The Great Lakes Genocides: Hidden Histories, Hidden Precedents," in Alexander Laban Hinton, Thomas La Pointe, and Douglas Irvin-Erickson, eds., *Hidden Genocides: Power, Knowledge, Memory* (New Brunswick, NJ: Rutgers University

Press, 2014), pp. 129–148. The present chapter reworks and reproduces a number of passages from this essay, especially on Burundi. See also my pairing of the Rwandan and DR Congo cases in "Masculinities and Vulnerabilities in the Rwandan and Congolese Genocides," in Amy E. Randall, ed., *Genocide and Gender in the Twentieth Century: A Comparative Survey* (London: Bloomsbury Academic, 2015), pp. 62–79 (e-book).

2 An influential study of Burundian Hutu refugees in Tanzania, escaping the 1972 genocide/eliticide, is Liisa H. Malkki, *Purity and Exile: Violence, Memory, and National Cosmology among Hutu Refugees in Tanzania* (Chicago, IL: The University of Chicago Press, 1995). The Tanzanian city of Arusha was the site of negotiations between the Rwandan Patriotic Front and the Habyarimana regime, leading to the eponymous Accords of 1993. After the genocide of the following year, it was chosen as the base of operations for the International Criminal Tribunal for Rwanda (ICTR).

3 "In addition to inequalities in access to land, the minority Hema, just like the Tutsi, were given a privileged position in education, the administration, politics and the economy during the colonial period." Filip Reyntjens, *The Great African War: Congo and Regional Geopolitics, 1996–2006* (Cambridge: Cambridge University Press, 2009), pp. 215–216; Reyntjens also stresses the need "to take into account . . . the constant renegotiation by elites of the local political, social and economic space, and . . . the impact of these processes on local power structures."

4 John Quigley, *The Genocide Convention: An International Law Analysis* (London: Ashgate, 2006), p. 33.

5 Gérard Prunier, *The Rwanda Crisis: History of a Genocide* (New York: Columbia University Press, 1997), p. 261. A good short overview of the Rwandan genocide is Gerald Caplan, "The 1994 Genocide of the Tutsi of Rwanda," in Samuel Totten and William S. Parsons, eds., *Centuries of Genocide: Essays and Eyewitness Accounts*, 4th edn (London: Routledge, 2012), pp. 447–476.

6 Christian P. Scherrer, *Genocide and Crisis: Conflict Roots, Mass Violence, and Regional War* (Westport, CT: Praeger, 2002), p. 109.

7 Colonel Luc Marchal, UNAMIR commander in Kigali; quoted in *Chronicle of a Genocide Foretold: Part 2, "We Were Cowards"* (Ottawa: National Film Board of Canada [hereafter, NFB], 1997).

8 International Panel of Eminent Personalities (IPEP) report, quoted in Kenneth J. Campbell, *Genocide and the Global Village* (New York: Palgrave, 2001), p. 78. The scenes at the psychiatric hospital, and the Belgian soldier's comment, are available in the NFB documentary *Chronicle of a Genocide Foretold: Part 2*.

9 Quoted in NFB, *Chronicle of a Genocide Foretold*. Samantha Power wrote: "It is shocking to note that during the entire three months of the genocide, [President] Clinton never assembled his top policy advisers to discuss the killings. . . . Rwanda was never thought to warrant its own top-level meeting." Power, *"A Problem from Hell": America and the Age of Genocide* (New York: Basic Books, 2002), p. 366.

10 Quoted in Power, *"A Problem from Hell,"* p. 382.

11 Annan speaking at Memorial Conference on Rwanda Genocide, New York; United Nations Press Release, SG/SM/9223, AFR/870, HQ/631, March 26, 2004, www.un.org/News/Press/docs/2004/sgsm9223.doc.htm.

12 Mahmood Mamdani, *When Victims Become Killers: Colonialism, Nativism, and the Genocide in Rwanda* (Princeton, NJ: Princeton University Press, 2001), pp. 51, 70.

13 Prunier, *The Rwanda Crisis*, p. 39.

14 Ibid., p. 3.

15 Mamdani, *When Victims Become Killers*, p. 66.

16 Prunier notes that "by the end of the Belgian presence in Rwanda in 1959, forty-three [prefectural] chiefs out of forty-five were Tutsi as well as 549 sub-chiefs out of 559." *The Rwanda Crisis*, p. 27.

17 The myth still occasionally surfaces, as when Andrew Bell-Fialkoff refers to "the Hamitic Tutsi." Bell-Fialkoff, *Ethnic Cleansing* (New York: St. Martin's Griffin, 1999), p. 182.

18 René Lemarchand puts this very well: "The Hamitic idea, which presumed the innate cultural superiority of the Tutsi and claimed that Ethiopia was their original homeland, was pressed into service to legitimize Tutsi overrule under the Belgian colonizers. The inversion of this mythical discourse, emphasizing the foreignness, cunning, and perversity of Tutsi 'feudal exploiters,' played an equally decisive role in legitimizing Hutu ascendancy in the last years of colonial rule. It also lent ideological justification to the génocidaires." Lemarchand, *The Dynamics of Violence in Central Africa* (Philadelphia, PA: University of Pennsylvania Press, 2009), p. 92.

19 Christopher Taylor, *Sacrifice as Terror: The Rwandan Genocide of 1994* (Oxford: Berg, 1999), pp. 128–130.

20 See Mamdani, *When Victims Become Killers*, p. 88.

21 Melvern, *A People Betrayed*, p. 42.

22 Scherrer, *Genocide and Crisis*, p. 105.

23 Many commentators have accused the RPF, under then-General, now-President Paul Kagame, of "recklessness" for launching this invasion. Bill Berkeley, for example, contends that "No rational person could have looked at the history of repeated mass slaughters in Rwanda and Burundi since 1959 and doubted for a moment that at least one likely outcome of such an invasion would be massive violence against defenseless Tutsi civilians." Berkeley, "Road to a Genocide," in Nicolaus Mills and Kira Brunner, eds., *The New Killing Fields: Massacre and the Politics of Intervention* (New York: Basic Books, 2002), p. 114. See also Alan J. Kuperman, "Provoking Genocide: A Revised History of the Rwandan Patriotic Front," *Journal of Genocide Research*, 6: 1 (March 2004), pp. 61–84.

24 Alison Des Forges, *Leave None to Tell the Story: Genocide in Rwanda* (New York, Human Rights Watch, 1999), p. 122. According to Danielle de Lame, a Belgian anthropologist, "Already in 1989 [Rwandan] farmers described their situation as apocalyptic." Quoted in Jacques Sémelin, *Purify and Destroy: The Political Uses of Massacre and Genocide* (New York: Columbia University Press, 2007), p. 15.

25 Catharine Newbury, "Ethnicity and the Politics of History in Rwanda," in David E. Lorey and William H. Beezley, eds., *Genocide, Collective Violence, and Popular Memory: The Politics of Remembrance in the Twentieth Century* (Wilmington, DL: Scholarly Resources, Inc., 2002), p. 76.

26 Melvern, *Conspiracy to Murder*, pp. 62–64.

27 Scherrer, *Genocide and Crisis*, p. 122.

28 Quoted in Melvern, *A People Betrayed*, p. 155.

29 This phrase is drawn from the title of ch. 8 of African Rights, *Rwanda: Death, Despair and Defiance* (rev. edn) (London: African Rights, 1995).

30 For more than a decade-and-a-half, controversy has swirled around the critical event of the downing of Habyarimana's presidential jet. It continues at a high pitch. A great deal hinges on whether Hutu or Tutsi forces committed the act: if Hutus, for example, the evidence is stronger for a well-established extermination plan (as in Linda Melvern, *Conspiracy to Murder*); if Tutsis, there is greater support for a reactive and retributive framing, emphasizing Hutu fear and panic after the assassination of "their" president (e.g., Scott Straus, *The Order of Genocide*). At first, something of a consensus reigned that the plane was probably downed by the Hutu Power government, perhaps with the assistance of foreign agents or mercenaries, as part of a *coup d'état* against moderates and the opening salvo of a "final solution" to the Tutsi "problem." This theory then gave way gradually to arguments that the Tutsi-dominated RPF was in fact the party responsible. "Strong circumstantial evidence" for the involvement of the current Rwandan president, Paul Kagame, was outlined by a renegade from Kagame's regime, Lt. Abdul Joshua Ruzibiza, and by a French magistrate, Jean-Louis Bruguière, who investigated the plane crash and issued his findings in 2006. See Ruzibiza, *Rwanda: L'histoire secrète* (Paris: Éditions du Panama, 2005); an English translation of the Bruguière report, posted October 1, 2007, is available at http://cirqueminime.blogspot.

com/2007/10/completed-bruguire-report-translated.html. It recommends that the International Criminal Tribunal for Rwanda (ICTR) charge Paul Kagame "for his presumed participation in the attack of 6 April 1994." René Lemarchand expresses general support for the findings in *The Dynamics of Violence in Central Africa* (pp. xii, 102). On the basis of these allegations, French officials in late 2008 extradited Rose Kabuye, President Kagame's chief of protocol, and charged her with "complicity in murder in relation to terrorism" for her alleged involvement in the downing of Habyarimana's plane. (See "Rwandan Official Charged in France,"*AlJazeera.net*, November 20, 2008.) Kabuye's trial process was ongoing at the time of writing. A new stage, and something of a return to the original consensus, may be indicated by a weighty investigation, the Mutsinzi report, unveiled in January 2010. It was sponsored by the Rwandan government, true, but was based on "more than five hundred interviews with former officers of the Hutu Power regime and other eyewitnesses," and cited the findings of foreign forensic experts that the Falcon jet was downed by missiles fired from a base under Rwandan government (hence Hutu) control. According to Philip Gourevitch, though the report is not conclusive, it "lays out [the] story in remarkably convincing detail," with witness accounts that "describe the events before, during, and after the assassination with convincing consistency." Gourevitch, "The Mutsinzi Report on the Rwandan Genocide," *The New Yorker*, January 8, 2010. See also Robert Marquand, "Rwanda Genocide: Will New Report Close the Book on Who Started It?," *The Christian Science Monitor*, January 12, 2010. Marquand notes that "with French Foreign Minister Bernard Kouchner in Rwanda . . . and with French president Nicolas Sarkozy traveling there this month—French leaders appear to be tacitly accepting the new findings" on the downing of the jet—and, it might be added, accepting the displacement of French influence symbolized by Rwanda's accession to membership in the anglophone Commonwealth of Nations. For an excellent summary of the findings and significance of this latest report, see Gerald Caplan, "Who Killed the President of Rwanda?," Pambazuka News, January 21, 2010, www.pambazuka.org/en/category/features/61625.

31 Richard Dowden, *Africa: Altered States, Ordinary Miracles* (New York: PublicAffairs, 2009), p. 237.

32 Dallaire, *Shake Hands with the Devil*, p. 328. He accords special praise to the stalwart contingent of Tunisian peacekeepers: "I can't say enough about the bravery of the Tunisians. They never shirked their duty and always displayed the highest standards of courage and discipline in the face of difficult and dangerous tasks" (p. 302). The same can be said of the heroic Red Cross staff throughout the genocide.

33 The deaths of the US troops in Somalia were recounted in the book and film *Black Hawk Down*.

34 Prunier, *The Rwanda Crisis*, p. 107. According to Chris McGreal, the pattern continued after April 6, 1994: "When the genocide started, Paris made no secret of where its loyalties lay. The French military flew in ammunition for government forces and, in the following weeks, a stream of Hutu officials travelled to Paris, including Jean-Bosco Barayagwiza, later convicted of genocide by the international tribunal, for meetings with President Francois Mitterrand and the French prime minister. Even as the mass graves filled across Rwanda, Paris engineered the delivery of millions of dollars' worth of weapons to the Hutu regime from Egypt and South Africa." McGreal, "France's Shame?," *The Guardian*, January 11, 2007, www.guardian.co.uk/world/2007/jan/11/rwanda.insideafrica. A book-length examination is Daniela Kroslak, *The French Betrayal of Rwanda* (Bloomington, IN: Indiana University Press, 2008).

35 Scherrer, *Genocide and Crisis*, p. 364.

36 Melvern, *Conspiracy to Murder*, p. 182.

37 Ibid., p. 168.

38 "The officers of UNAMIR believe to this day that had the European troops that came to rescue the expats stayed on in Rwanda, the killing could have been stopped

there and then. . . . Together with the moderates in the Rwandan army and with the peacekeepers there would have been ample troops to restore calm. There were already 2,500 peacekeepers with UNAMIR, there were 500 Belgian para-commandos, part of the evacuation force, together with 450 French and 80 Italian soldiers from parachute regiments. In neighbouring Kenya there were 500 Belgian para-commandos, also a part of the evacuation operation. In Burundi there were 250 US Rangers, elite troops, who had come to evacuate the US nationals. There were 800 more French troops on standby." Ibid., p. 188.

39 Cited by Adam LeBor, who adds: "There are few, if any, more succinct summaries of the Clinton administration's responses to the genocidal crises of the early and mid-1990s." LeBor, "*Complicity with Evil*": *The United Nations in the Age of Modern Genocide* (New Haven, CT: Yale University Press, 2006), p. 178.

40 US Department of State, Daily Press Briefing, Friday, June 10, 1994. Full official transcript at http://dosfan.lib.uic.edu/ERC/briefing/daily_briefings/1994/9406/940610db. html. These are the comments referenced on p. 76, note 91, in partial justification of a slight shift in my preferred definition of genocide. As James Woods, the US Deputy Assistant Secretary of Defense at the time of the genocide, later stated: "I think it was a sort of a formal spectacle of the US and disarray and retreat, leading the international community away from doing the right thing and I think that everybody was perfectly happy to follow our lead—in retreat." Quoted in Timothy Murithi, "The Role of Regional Organizations," in Adam Lupel and Ernesto Verdeja, eds., *Responding to Genocide: The Politics of International Action* (Boulder, CO: Lynne Rienner Publishers, 2013), p. 164.

41 Dallaire, *Shake Hands with the Devil*, p. 325.

42 According to Christian Scherrer, "the map showing the places where the largest massacres occurred was almost identical with that of the religious centers in the various dioceses and parishes of Rwanda." Scherrer, *Genocide and Crisis*, p. 113.

43 African Rights, *Rwanda: Not So Innocent: When Women Become Killers* (London: African Rights, 1995), p. 26, emphasis added.

44 The death tolls usually cited for these cases are 36,000 (Odessa) and 33,000 (Kiev); according to Eugen Kogon, the highest number of killings in a single day at Auschwitz-Birkenau was 34,000, and other estimates are lower. Kogon, *The Theory and Practice of Hell* (New York: The Berkley Publishing Company, 1980), p. 241.

45 African Rights, *Death, Despair and Defiance*, p. 922. As one *génocidaire* recalled: "The white priests took off at the first skirmishes. The black priests joined the killers or the killed. God kept silent, and the churches stank from abandoned bodies." Quoted in Jean Hatzfeld (trans. Linda Coverdale), *Machete Season: The Killers in Rwanda Speak* (New York: Farrar, Straus & Giroux, 2005), p. 142. On the churches' role more generally, see Chris McGreal, *Chaplains of the Militia: The Tangled Story of the Catholic Church during Rwanda's Genocide* (London: Guardian Shorts, 2014); Timothy Longman, *Christianity and Genocide in Rwanda* (Cambridge: Cambridge University Press, 2010); Carol Rittner, John K. Roth, and Wendy Whitworth, eds., *Genocide in Rwanda: Complicity of the Churches?* (St. Paul, MN: Paragon House, 2005).

46 Dona Tella Lorch, "Children's Drawings Tell Horror of Rwanda in Colors of Crayons," *The New York Times*, September 16, 1994.

47 African Rights, *Rwanda: Death, Despair and Defiance*, pp. 590–595.

48 Melvern, *Conspiracy to Murder*, p. 224.

49 African Rights, *Rwanda: Death, Despair and Defiance*, p. 665.

50 For an account of the genocidal killing at Kabgayi, see African Rights, *Death, Despair and Defiance*, pp. 708–718. The primary and secondary schools in the Kabgayi complex became the sites of two of the four main camps for displaced and terrified Tutsis. The killers reportedly rampaged most freely through the primary school, raping women and girls, and selecting boys and men for execution. As RPF forces approached Kabgayi, the killing of Tutsis grew more frenzied and generalized (see testimony, p. 711).

51 Darryl Li, "Echoes of Violence," in Mills and Brunner, eds., *The New Killing Fields*, p. 125.

52 Mamdani, *When Victims Become Killers*, p. 225.

53 Adam Jones, "Gender and Genocide in Rwanda," in Jones, ed., *Gendercide and Genocide* (Nashville, TN: Vanderbilt University Press, 2004), p. 123.

54 African Rights, *Rwanda: Not So Innocent*, p. 88.

55 Prunier, *The Rwanda Crisis*, pp. 231–232.

56 See Des Forges, *Leave None to Tell the Story*, p. 734.

57 Linda Melvern wrote that "the French operation included everything UNAMIR needed. There were more than 2,500 elite soldiers from the French Foreign Legion, paratroopers, marines and special forces, all equipped with state-of-the-art weaponry, communications, one hundred armoured vehicles, heavy mortars, helicopters, and even jet aircraft. There was an armada of cargo aircraft." Melvern, *Conspiracy to Murder*, p. 243.

58 Prunier, *The Rwanda Crisis*, p. 267.

59 RTLM broadcast quoted in Martin Meredith, *The Fate of Africa: A History of Fifty Years of Independence* (New York: PublicAffairs, 2005), p. 520.

60 Michela Wrong, *In the Footsteps of Mr. Kurtz: Living on the Brink of Disaster in Mobutu's Congo* (New York: HarperCollins, 2001), p. 245.

61 Reyntjens, *The Great African War*, p. 7.

62 "Africa's Unmended Heart," *The Economist*, June 11, 2005. For an accessible overview, see Georges Nzongola-Ntalaja, *The Congo from Leopold to Kabila: A People's History* (London: Zed Books, 2003).

63 Bryan Mealer, *All Things Must Fight to Live: Stories of War and Deliverance in Congo* (London: Bloomsbury, 2008), gives a sense of Congo's infrastructural breakdown following the Belgian departure, particularly in the book's final section, a journey through barely-tracked forest (see the epigraph to this section). A haunting and elegiac portrait of contemporary eastern and central Congo is achieved by Anthony Bourdain in a peerless short travel documentary, a highlight of his *Parts Unknown* series on CNN (season 1, episode 8). See www.cnn.com/video/shows/anthony-bourdain-parts-unknown/episode8/ for a description; trailers are available online, but not the full program. It can be viewed on the Netflix subscription service at the time of writing.

64 "The abject suffering [of Hutus in the Congolese camps] inverted the moral standing of the refugees and even soldiers—they became victims, not killers." Moreover, "aid workers and local groups, who spent months living with and talking to the refugees became influenced by the revisionist concept of a double genocide—that the Habyarimana government and the RPF had both killed in equal proportions. . . . Paralyzed during the political crisis [of the genocide], military forces were suddenly mobilized for the 'humanitarian' disaster, transforming the genocide into a 'complex emergency' in which there was no good and bad side, only victims." Jason K. Stearns, *Dancing in the Glory of Monsters: The Collapse of the Congo and the Great War of Africa* (New York: PublicAffairs, 2011), p. 38, 40–41. For more on denial of the genocide of Rwandan Tutsis, see Box 9.2.

65 Filip Reyntjens especially takes to task the United States and its ambassador in Rwanda, Robert Gribbin: "Through its diplomatic and military support, the United States gave the signal or at least the impression, to the Rwandan government and the AFDL[,] that anything was permitted, and that they were ensured impunity. By action and omission, they therefore bear part of the responsibility for the crimes committed by their allies. In that sense, their position toward the new Rwandan regime was comparable to that of France towards the old one." Reyntjens, *The Great African War*, pp. 78–79.

66 Kabila's rambling history of rebellion extended all the way back to the early 1960s. The Argentine revolutionary Ernesto Guevara knew him in the days when "Che" was quixotically seeking to spread the Cuban revolution to central Africa. Che considered him a buffoon and wastrel. What Kabila thought of Che is unknown. See Juan O. Tamayo, "Kabila Didn't Impress Che Guevara," *The Seattle Times*, May 11, 1997, http://community.seattletimes.nwsource.com/archive/?date=19970511&slug=2538521.

67 Gérard Prunier, *Africa's World War: Congo, the Rwandan Genocide, and the Making of a Continental Catastrophe* (New York: Oxford University Press, 2009), p. 333.

68 See Marie Béatrice Umutesi, *Surviving the Slaughter: The Ordeal of a Rwandan Refugee in Zaire* (Further Study).

69 Stearns, *Dancing in the Glory of Monsters*, p. 130.

70 Estimate cited in Reyntjens, *The Great African War*, p. 93.

71 "Key Excerpts from UN Report on Rwandan Army Genocide in DR Congo," BBC Online, August 27, 2010, available at www.congoplanet.com/article.jsp?id=45261725. The full title of the report is *Democratic Republic of the Congo, 1993–2003: Report of the Mapping Exercise Documenting the Most Serious Violations of Human Rights and International Humanitarian Law Committed within the Territory of the Democratic Republic of the Congo between March 1993 and June 2003* (Geneva: Office of the High Commissioner of Human Rights [UNHCHR], 2010). The full text as published in October 2010, with minor wording changes in some sensitive passages, is available online at www.ohchr. org/Documents/Countries/CD/DRC_MAPPING_REPORT_FINAL_EN.pdf. The quoted passages are from sections 512–517. I have delved more deeply into the report's findings in my essay, "Masculinities and Vulnerabilities in the Rwandan and Congolese Genocides." It was the UN's deployment of the G-word that most infuriated Rwandan officials. Their protests, and perhaps an autonomous reconsideration by the UNHCHR, led to the language being slightly watered down in the final report. For example, a reference to "a number of damning elements that . . . could be classified as crimes of genocide" was altered to "a number of *inculpatory* elements." Left intact, however, was the reference to "crimes of genocide" that had so riled the Rwandans. It was notable that none of the threatened retaliated by Rwanda (e.g., withdrawal of its UN peacekeepers) in fact resulted.

72 Quoted in Reyntjens, *The Great African War*, p. 95.

73 Howard W. French, *A Continent for the Taking: The Tragedy and Hope of Africa* (New York: Alfred A. Knopf, 2004), p. 219.

74 Scherrer, *Genocide and Crisis*, p. 267.

75 International Crisis Group (hereafter ICG), "How Kabila Lost His Way: The Performance of Laurent Desire Kabila's Government," background paper, May 21, 1999. See also Jeremy M. Weinstein, "Africa's 'Scramble for Africa': Lessons of a Continental War," *World Policy Journal*, 17: 2 (Summer 2000), pp. 11–20; Thomas M. Callaghy, "Life and Death in the Congo: Understanding a Nation's Collapse," *Foreign Affairs*, 80: 5 (2001), pp. 143–149.

76 Howard W. French, "Kagame's Hidden War in the Congo," *The New York Review of Books*, September 24, 2009, www.nybooks.com/articles/23054. In January 2009, Rwanda suddenly turned on Nkunda and had him arrested. According to French, "the arrest took place just after the release of a UN report documenting Rwanda's close ties to the warlord, and concluding that he was being used to advance Rwanda's economic interests in Congo's eastern hinterlands. The report stated that Rwandan authorities had 'been complicit in the recruitment of soldiers, including children, have facilitated the supply of military equipment, and have sent officers and units from the Rwandan Defense Forces,' while giving Nkunda access to Rwandan bank accounts and allowing him to launch attacks on the Congolese army from Rwandan soil."

77 Rory Carroll, "Violence Threatens to Engulf Congo," *The Guardian*, November 26, 2004, www.guardian.co.uk/world/2004/nov/26/congo.rorycarroll.

78 Weinstein, "Africa's 'Scramble for Africa.'"

79 Prunier, *Africa's World War*, p. 338.

80 See Lara Santoro, "False Dawn," *The New Republic*, July 3, 2000; French, "Kagame's Hidden War."

81 Bryan Mealer notes that the uranium in the atomic bombs that exploded over Hiroshima and Nagasaki in August 1945 (see Chapter 1) came from Congolese mines. Mealer, *All Things Must Fight to Live*, p. 232. On the economic/extractive dimension

of the Congolese conflict, see Peter Eichstaedt, *Consuming the Congo: War and Conflict Minerals in the World's Deadliest Place* (Chicago, IL: Lawrence Hill Books, 2011); for historical context, see "The Political Economy of Pillage," in Thomas Turner, *The Congo Wars: Conflict, Myth and Reality* (London: Zed Books, 2007), pp. 24–48. According to Jason Stearns, "some researchers estimate that net profits made by Rwandan companies could have been as high as $150 million [from June 2000 to July 2001], while other researchers calculate total profits made off the minerals trade at $250 million per annum throughout their occupation. For Rwanda, whose entire annual budget was $380 million at the time, this income made its expensive involvement in the Congo possible. President Kagame himself described their involvement in the Congo as 'self-sustaining.'" Stearns, *Dancing in the Glory of Monsters*, p. 300.

82 See pp. 492–494 for discussion of Mitterrand's and others' denialist "double genocide" framing of Rwanda.

83 See the material compiled as "Denying Rwanda," in Adam Jones, *The Scourge of Genocide: Essays and Reflections* (London: Routledge, 2013), pp. 346–359. My detailed "Response to Herman & Peterson" is available online at http://jonestream.blogspot.ca/2010/11/denying-rwanda-response-to-herman.html.

84 Pilger supplied an endorsement and Chomsky an introduction for the Herman/Peterson book. Pilger called it a "brilliant exposé of great power's lethal industry of lies" and a defense of the collective right "to a truthful historical memory"—a description so blithely ignorant and mendacious that it leaves one slack-jawed. See Jones, "Denying Rwanda," and my "Open Letter to John Pilger," www.genocidetext.net/pilger.htm.

85 Ambassador Robert Krueger and Kathleen Tobin Krueger, *From Bloodshed to Hope in Burundi: Our Embassy Years during Genocide* (Austin, TX: University of Texas Press, 2008), p. 57 (e-book).

86 Peter Uvin, "Ethnicity and Power in Burundi and Rwanda: Different Paths to Mass Violence," *Comparative Politics*, 31: 3 (1999), p. 258.

87 "Burundi: Double Genocide," *Time*, June 26, 1972. See also Romain Forscher, "The Burundi Massacres: Tribalism in Black Africa," *International Journal of Politics*, 4: 4 (1972–1973), pp. 77–87; and Warren Weinstein, "Ethnicity and Conflict Regulation: The 1972 Burundi Revolt," *Africa Spectrum*, 9: 1 (1974), pp. 42–49.

88 René Lemarchand (and Greenland quoted in Lemarchand), "Burundi 1972: Genocide Denied, Revised, and Remembered," in Lemarchand, ed., *Forgotten Genocides: Oblivion, Denial, and Memory* (Philadelphia, PA: University of Pennsylvania Press, 2011), p. 41.

89 René Lemarchand, *Burundi: Ethnic Conflict and Genocide* (Cambridge: Cambridge University Press, 1994), p. 101.

90 Hoyt quoted in Lemarchand, *Burundi*, p. 103.

91 René Lemarchand, *The Dynamics of Violence in Central Africa* (Philadelphia, PA: University of Pennsylvania Press, 2009), p. 146.

92 Lemarchand, *Dynamics*, p. 58.

93 Straus found "that most [Hutu] perpetrators participated in violence because they feared the consequences of not doing so ...What comes through [in interviews with perpetrators] ... is a sense of acute insecurity, even panic." Scott Straus, *The Order of Genocide: Race, Power, and War in Rwanda* (Ithaca, NY: Cornell University Press, 2006), p. 157.

94 Krueger and Krueger, *From Bloodshed to Hope*, p. 17 (e-book).

95 Christian Jennings, *Across the Red River: Rwanda, Burundi and the Heart of Darkness* (London: Phoenix, 2001), p. 144.

96 Ibid., pp. 214–215. Ambassador Robert Krueger wrote of this period: "I had not respected the Hutu rebels before. Now I detested them ... Small in number and inefficient, they made futile raids against the Burundi Army and then fled. In their wake, the Tutsi military swept the hillsides surrounding the area of the attack, killing innocent Hutu men, women, and children who had had no part in the rebel incursions. These

bandes armées brought more pain and heartache to their ethnic kinsmen than they ever prevented." Krueger and Krueger, *From Bloodshed to Hope*, p. 204 (e-book).

97 Mamdani, *When Victims Become Killers*, p. 261.
98 Prunier, *The Rwanda Crisis*, p. 370.
99 Gérard Prunier, *Africa's World War: Congo, the Rwandan Genocide, and the Making of a Continental Catastrophe* (New York: Oxford University Press, 2009), p. 349.
100 For a first-rate overview, see L.J. van den Herik, *The Contribution of the Rwanda Tribunal to the Development of International Law* (Leiden: Martinus Nijhoff Publishers, 2005).
101 Haffajee quoted in David M. Crowe, *War Crimes, Genocide, and Justice: A Global History* (London: Palgrave Macmillan, 2014), p. 356.
102 On the so-called "media trials," see Dina Temple-Raston, *Justice on the Grass: Three Rwandan Journalists, Their Trial for War Crimes and a Nation's Quest for Redemption* (New York: The Free Press, 2005).
103 Stearns, *Dancing in the Glory of Monsters*, p. 317.
104 See, e.g., Barbara F. Walter, "Burundi Is on the Verge of a Mass Atrocity. Will We Ignore It Again?," *Political Violence @ a Glance*, November 11, 2015, http://politicalvio lenceataglance.org/2015/11/11/burundi-is-on-the-verge-of-a-mass-atrocity-will-we-ignore-it-again/; Tom Miles, "U.N. Says Ill-Prepared for Rwanda-Style Descent in Burundi," Reuters dispatch, November 10, 2015, http://in.reuters.com/article/burundi-politics-un-idINKCN0SZ2FI20151110; "Burundi 'Genocide' Will Not Be Allowed to Happen: African Union," Agence France-Presse dispatch in *Yahoo! News*, December 17, 2015, http://news.yahoo.com/burundi-genocide-not-allowed-happen-african-union-111911096.html.

BOX 9A DARFUR, SOUTH SUDAN, SOUTH KORDOFAN

For half a century, Sudan was racked by a civil war that many observers have characterized as genocidal—between the Muslim Arab-dominated north (home to the capital, Khartoum) and the predominantly Christian and animist south. In recent decades, northern imposition of Arabic and *sharia*, or Islamic law, has fueled southern rebellion. The conflict exacted "a huge and terrible human toll," with possibly two million killed. Francis Deng, soon to be appointed the first UN Special Adviser on the Prevention of Genocide, characterized Sudan in 2001 as "the worst humanitarian disaster in the world today."[1]

Perhaps unexpectedly, it was a smaller-scale tragedy elsewhere in Sudan—in the remote region of Darfur, bordering Chad—that captured world attention in 2004. Darfur also provoked the most voluble debate over application of the "genocide" label since Rwanda in 1994.

For decades, sporadic conflict had flickered in Darfur between Arab pastoralists and African agriculturalists. The onset of recurring drought exacerbated tensions, pushing Arab northerners deeper into the African heartland. Feelings of marginalization, invasion, and exploitation provided a constituency for the rebellion that first erupted in June 2003, led by two rebel groups, the Sudan Liberation Army (SLA) and the Justice and Equality Movement (JEM).

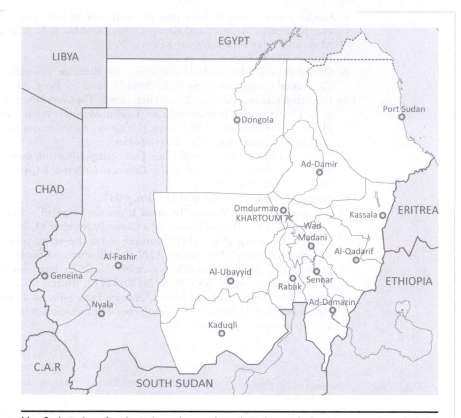

Map 9a.1 Sudan after the independence of South Sudan, with the western region of Darfur shaded.

Source: Wikimedia Commons.

Rebel attacks on Sudanese government offices, police, and military bases provoked an indiscriminately violent response from the military government in Khartoum, led by General Omar al-Bashir. Employing time-honored counterinsurgency strategies (precisely those that Khartoum had used for decades in the conflict with South Sudan), the government equipped an Arab militia, the *Janjaweed*, to mount attacks on African villages. (The name *Janjaweed* "translates roughly as 'evil men on horseback,' [and] was chosen to inspire fear.")[2] The assaults were carried out with the participation of Sudanese military forces, equipped with bombers and helicopters. The most violent of the militia leaders, Musa Hilal, wrote in August 2004 to a regional commander, "citing orders from President Bashir himself": "You are informed that directives have been issued . . . to change the demography of Darfur and empty it of African tribes."[3]

The *Janjaweed* behaved much as Serb paramilitary units did in invading Bosnian Muslim or Albanian Kosovar villages (see Chapter 8). Adult male noncombatants were rounded up and murdered in gendercidal massacres.[4]

African women were raped on a large scale, by assailants who called them "black slaves" and "rap[ed] them so that they [would] bear Arab children."[5] Civilian populations were dispossessed, starved, and put to flight:

> Government and Janjawiid forces destroyed everything that made life possible. Food that could be carried away was; the rest was burned. Animals that could be taken away were; the rest were killed. The simple straw buildings that served as clinics and schools were destroyed . . . and everything in them was stolen or torched. Pumps were smashed and wells polluted—often with corpses. Mosques were burned and Qurans desecrated.[6]

A US State Department report of September 2004 found that 61 percent of refugees interviewed had witnessed a member of their family killed (overwhelmingly a husband, son, or brother); 67 percent had seen others outside their family killed.[7] Up to 2,000 villages had been destroyed, damaged, and abandoned, leaving two million people uprooted and too terrified to return. With the collapse of agriculture, millions were dependent on outside food aid. As food supplies ran desperately short, "genocide by attrition" began to replace direct killing.

In the face of the systematic atrocities, a consensus emerged among many nongovernmental organizations, and some governments, that the campaign was genocidal.[8] According to the Aegis Trust in Britain, this conclusion was unavoidable. "Was the killing intentional? Yes. Was it systematically organised by the al-Bashir regime using government-armed Janjaweed militias, bombers and helicopter gunships? Yes. Were the victims chosen because of their ethnic and racial identity? Yes. This, in short, is genocide. The genocide continues."[9] Notably, in September 2004, US Secretary of State Colin Powell agreed. "We concluded that genocide has been committed in Darfur, and that the government of Sudan and the Janjaweed bear responsibility and that genocide may still be occurring."[10] However, as *The New York Times* pointed out, Powell's statement came "with the quick assurance that this didn't mean the United States was prepared to take any further action."[11]

"By the beginning of 2005, almost 2 million people had been driven to camps and towns inside Darfur and another 200,000 had sought refuge in Chad."[12] This, however, appears to have marked the peak of the devastation, as is considered further below. The death toll remains a subject of fierce dispute. Flint and de Waal estimated a total of 200,000 killed from all causes, the great majority in 2003–2004. This was in keeping with UN estimates, at least through to April 2008, when John Holmes, the UN Under-Secretary General for Humanitarian Affairs, sparked controversy by claiming that up to 300,000 had died. The assertion was rejected by the Khartoum authorities, but it also "reportedly surprised UN agencies and NGOs operating in Darfur."[13]

After the widespread accusations of genocide, an African Union peace-keeping force was deployed to Darfur. But it was just 6,700-strong in a territory as large as France, lacked a clear mandate to intervene to protect civilian lives, and was generally reduced to "watching the tragedy unfold."[14] Peace negotiations produced a tentative accord, the optimistically-dubbed Comprehensive Peace Agreement, in 2005 between the government and the SLA. It was rapidly flouted by both sides.[15] In August 2006, the UN Security Council declared its support for a peacekeeping force, but the Sudanese government bridled, and what emerged was instead a UN–AU hybrid, UNAMID (the UN-African Union Mission in Darfur). The force eventually reached 27,000 personnel, though it was indifferently armed and equipped, and with only a limited ability to protect civilians scattered across the huge territory. It also encountered concerted resistance by the Sudanese authorities, who used every opportunity to impede and reduce its operations.[16] Nonetheless, a somewhat downscaled UNAMID, 20,000 strong, remained in place at the time of writing, its mandate renewed through June 2016.[17]

According to the careful analysis by Julie Flint and Alex de Waal, violent deaths in Darfur peaked in 2003–2004. By 2006, thanks in large part to the heroic efforts of relief workers, "UN officials on the ground, in Darfur, estimated the correct figure at closer to two hundred deaths a month from violence, while mortality from hunger and disease remained comparable to pre-war levels and well below emergency thresholds."[18] By then, though, the "Save Darfur" movement was beginning to crest, with comparisons being drawn to the Jewish Holocaust[19] and the genocide in Rwanda. For all its good intentions, Flint and de Waal accuse the movement of creating "a simplistic moral fable that portrayed the crisis as a battle between good and evil"—skating over, in large part, the role of rebel groups in fueling the violence.[20] The International Criminal Court has included Darfuri rebel leaders in its Sudan-related indictments, though none had been brought to trial as of February 2016.[21] Likewise, Omar al-Bashir, indicted by the ICC on charges of genocide and crimes against humanity, retained his post as Sudanese president following disputed elections in April 2015. "Furthermore," as Samuel Totten noted, "al Bashir has brazenly traveled to numerous countries, many of which have ratified the United Nations Convention on the Prevention and Punishment of the Crime of Genocide (UNCG) and the Rome Statute [of the ICC], but none of the countries have arrested him, and thus impunity continues to reign . . ."[22]

Meanwhile, the humanitarian crisis in Darfur continued unabated. According to Eric Reeves, "some 3 million people have been internally displaced or turned into refugees," with hundreds of thousands displaced in 2014 and 2015 alone.[23]

Figure 9a.1 Sudanese president Omar al-Bashir, reelected in April 2015, continues to travel internationally despite his indictment by the International Criminal Court (ICC) on charges of committing genocide and crimes against humanity in Darfur. What was seen as a step forward—the first indictment of a sitting head of state for genocide—has become the world's leading example of impunity for mass atrocity. He is shown at an African Union summit in January 2009, several months after his original indictment by the ICC (the genocide charge was added in 2010).

Source: Photo by Jesse B. Awalt/US Navy/Wikimedia Commons.

The world's newest state, South Sudan, plummeted into chaos after independence, traumatizing anew millions of the world's poorest people, and driving to distraction those in the international community who had engineered its independence. That sovereign status arose from:

(1) the grinding stalemate of the Sudanese civil war;
(2) the Khartoum regime's apparent conviction that it could keep an independent South Sudan in a weak and destabilized condition, and maintain its hold over the strategic Abyei and South Kordofan regions along the countries' new border;
(3) the designs of the great powers (especially the US and UK) for a new and dependent petro-state in Africa; and
(4) the kind of obscure, unpredictable political machinations that led the Indonesian government to grant a referendum on the status of the East Timor—another recent entrant to the global order of sovereign states (see Box 7a).

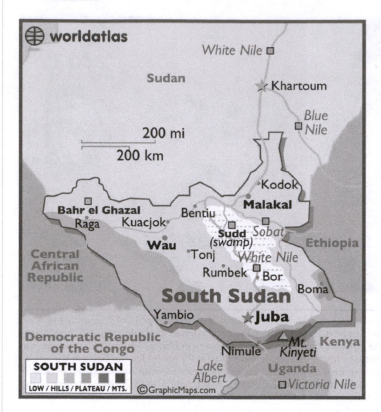

Map 9a.2 South Sudan, the world's newest state (2011).

Source: Map provided by WorldAtlas.com

Shortly after independence, however, conflict erupted anew—this time between South Sudanese political-ethnic factions. In 2013, President Salva Kiir sacked vice-president Riek Machar, accusing him of plotting a coup. That Kiir was from the Dinka tribe, and Machar a Nuer, sparked armed resistance among Machar's supporters, who accused Kiir of seeking to implant a Dinka ethnocracy. A BBC timeline gives a sense of the downward spiral:

2011 January—The people of South Sudan vote in favour of full independence from Sudan.

2011 9 July—Independence day.

2011 August—UN says at least 600 people are killed in ethnic clashes in the state of Jonglei.

2012 January—South Sudan declares a disaster in Jonglei State after some 100,000 flee clashes between rival ethnic groups.

2012 February—Sudan and South Sudan sign non-aggression pact at talks on outstanding secession issues, but Sudan . . . shuts down the South's oil export pipelines in a dispute over fees. South Sudan halves public spending on all but salaries in consequence.

2012 July—Country marks first anniversary amid worsening economic crisis and no let-up in tension with Sudan.

2013 December—Civil war erupts as President Salva Kiir accuses his ex-Vice-President, Riek Machar, of plotting to overthrow him. Rebel factions seize control of several regional towns, thousands are killed and many more flee. Uganda[n] troops intervene on the government's side. Foreigners are evacuated.

2014 May—UN envoy Toby Lanzer says conflict has resulted in slaughter of thousands, displacement of more than a million and five million in need of humanitarian aid.

2014 July—UN Security Council describes the food crisis in South Sudan as the worst in the world.

2015 February—General elections due in June are called off because of the ongoing conflict. China announces the deployment of an infantry battalion on a UN peacekeeping mission . . .[24]

"You have a failed state, and you split it into two," observed Omer Ismail of the anti-genocide Enough project (www.enoughproject.org). "What do you get? You get two failed states."[25]

The "main theatre" of the violence was the inaptly-named Unity state, where "protracted conflict [erupted] over major towns and oil installations," featuring "mass atrocities" and "multiple armed groups operating with their own agendas," in the International Crisis Group's depiction. While Dinka–Nuer divisions were evident in the state, so too was "bitter competition [among] Nuer politicians" themselves.[26]

The principal agent of atrocity, by most accounts, was the Salva Kiir regime, particularly as rebel resistance weakened. In March 2016, Amnesty International documented one of the war's worst crimes: the gendercidal massacre of sixty men and boys, suffocated in a shipping container in the central village of Leer. Amnesty's researchers

> found the remains of many broken skeletons still strewn across the ground. . . . According to witnesses, between 20 and 23 October 2015, government soldiers arbitrarily arrested dozens of men and boys in Luale village and Leer town. They then forced them, with their hands tied behind their backs, into one or more shipping containers located at the Comboni Catholic Church. Witnesses described hearing the detainees crying and screaming in distress and banging on the walls of the shipping container, which they said had no windows or other form of ventilation. They said that civilian and military officials had direct knowledge that the detainees were in distress and dying but did nothing to help them. For example, one witness said that she saw the then area commander order soldiers to open the container and remove

the bodies of four dead men and then close the container again on the remaining detainees who were still alive inside. By the following morning, all but one of the remaining detainees had died. . . . Following their death, government soldiers loaded dozens of bodies into a truck and dumped them in two open pits in Kulier, Juong payam, approximately 1km northeast of Leer town. Family members who visited the area in the following days said the bodies, left in the open, had been eaten by animals and had started to decompose.[27]

Out-group women and girls who were spared extermination were subjected to systematic sexual violence and enslavement, according to an equally disturbing report of the United Nation's Office of the High Commissioner for Human Rights in March 2016. The office described Unity State in South Sudan as "one of the most horrendous human rights situations in the world, with massive use of rape as an instrument of terror and weapon of war. . . . The sexual assaults were characterised by their extreme brutality, with women who tried to resist, or even looked their rapist directly in the eye, being killed in some cases." One witness stated: "If you looked young or good looking, about ten men would rape the woman; the older women were raped by about seven to nine men."[28] In numerous cases, "fighters [were] allowed to rape women in lieu of wages";[29] crimes of kidnapping and forced marriage were also rife.

Limited movement occurred on the political front as this book was going to press. In February 2016, Kiir abided by one of the central provisions of a peace agreement struck the previous August, and appointed Machar—still self-exiled—as his vice-president. It was unclear whether the power-sharing agreement would be implemented, and to what extent it could end the fighting in a classic "degenerate war" (Chapter 12), "between militia forces driven by local agendas or revenge who pay little heed to paper peace deals." Tens of thousands of South Sudanese had been killed, and fully 2.8 million were in dire need of humanitarian aid.[30]

There were direct links among independence for South Sudan, the continuing conflict in Darfur, and the renewed campaign of mass violence against the population of the Nuba mountains in South Kordofan, bordering South Sudan. This had been one of the most afflicted regions during the long Sudanese civil war, with the central authorities imposing a "policy of famine" and of "genocide by attrition," at the same time as they sought to strip the Nuba tribes of their most fertile lands and turn them over to Arab colonists.[31] In 1992, "backed by indiscriminate aerial bombing and shelling, the army destroyed villages, looted, abducted women and children, killed tens of thousands of men and women and displaced hundreds of thousands of Nuba . . . as a prelude to [their] resettlement in so-called 'peace camps' in North Kordofan," which were effectively concentration camps where hunger and destitution were rife.[32] Alex de Waal describes this as manifesting "the most clear-cut . . . genocidal intent in modern Sudan":

> A titanic plan for resettlement of the Nuba out of their homeland distinguished the campaign from the routine cruelties of Sudanese counterinsurgency. The government announced plans to resettle 500,000 people, the entire population of the insurgent area, and by late 1992 had relocated one-third of that number. An adjunct to this was a policy of starving the rebel-held areas into submission. The army and security [forces] disrupted trade and closed markets, destroyed farms and looted animals. Raiding, abduction, and rape prevented any movement between villages and to markets. Thousands died of hunger and disease, while the flow of basic goods (including soap, salt, and clothing) to the rebel areas almost completely dried up. The Nuba Mountains went back in time: people wore home-spun cotton or went naked, could no longer use currency and so instead reverted to barter, and relied upon traditional medical remedies.

"The policy was genocidal in both intent and its possible outcome," writes de Waal.[33] But it failed. Nuba resistance was not crushed, and added its weight to the rebel onslaught against the Khartoum regime, culminating in the Comprehensive Peace Agreement of January 2005. The agreement, however, was far from comprehensive. It froze out the Nuba tribes, who, fearing a reassertion of Khartoum's authority and an imposition of *sharia* law in the territory, rose up in renewed insurrection. Together with Darfuri militia elements—incorporated into an umbrella formation, the Sudan Revolutionary Front (SRF)—they launched raids that "shocked Khartoum" and pushed into North Kordofan.[34] The Sudanese regime responded by recruiting thousands of former *Janjaweed* militia from Darfur and attacking the Nuba by land and air,

> killing people indiscriminately and destroying farms and *tukuls*. Almost immediately many fled into the mountains seeking sanctuary, just as they did in the 1990s. Having left behind their only means of livelihood and source of food, their farms, the Nuba Mountains people faced a repeat of the 1990s in which they had to resort to scouring the rocky mountainsides for leaves, roots, and grasses for something to eat.[35]

The conflict and humanitarian crisis continued at the time of writing. Among genocide scholars, Samuel Totten has advocated indefatigably on the Nuba's behalf, including personally coordinating and supervising deliveries of humanitarian aid. His efforts have been vital to raising awareness (including my own) of the ongoing catastrophe in South Kordofan.

FURTHER STUDY

Darfur

M.W. Daly, *Darfur's Sorrow: A History of Destruction and Genocide*. Cambridge: Cambridge University Press, 2007. Learned history, ranging from the mid-19th century to (quite late in the volume) the genocidal conflict of recent years.

Julie Flint and Alex de Waal, *Darfur: A New History of a Long War*. London: Zed Books, 2008. Introduction to the Darfur conflict, by authors with extensive experience in the region.

Rebecca Hamilton, *Fighting for Darfur: Public Action and the Struggle to Stop Genocide*. New York: Palgrave Macmillan, 2011. A clear-eyed and constructive appraisal of the "Save Darfur" movement.

Mahmood Mamdani, *Saviors and Survivors: Darfur, Politics, and the War on Terror*. New York: Pantheon Books, 2009. Critical study of the Darfur conflict, especially regarding outside intervention strategies.

Gérard Prunier, *Darfur: A 21st Century Genocide*. Ithaca, NY: Cornell University Press, 2008. Third edition of Prunier's insightful short treatment (formerly *The Ambiguous Genocide*).

South Kordofan/Nuba Mountains

Samuel Totten, *Genocide by Attrition: The Nuba Mountains of Sudan*, 2nd edn. New Brunswick, NJ: Transaction Publishers, 2015. Testimony and analysis of the Nuba genocide.

South Sudan

James Copnall, *A Poisonous Thorn in Our Hearts: Sudan and South Sudan's Bitter and Incomplete Divorce*. London: Hurst Publishers, 2014. A readable and highly-informed primer.

NOTES

1 Francis M. Deng, "Sudan—Civil War and Genocide," in William L. Hewitt, *Defining the Horrific: Readings on Genocide and Holocaust in the Twentieth Century* (Upper Saddle River, NJ: Pearson, 2004), pp. 223–224.

2 Scott Straus, "Darfur and the Genocide Debate," *Foreign Affairs*, 84: 1 (2004), p. 126. According to Gérard Prunier, "Sociologically the *Janjaweed* seem to have been of six main origins: former bandits and highwaymen who had been 'in the trade' since the 1980s; demobilized soldiers from the regular army; young

members of Arab tribes having a running land conflict with a neighbouring 'African' group . . . common criminals who were pardoned and released from gaol if they joined the militia; fanatical members of the Tajammu al-Arabi [Arab Union], a militantly racist and pan-Arabist organization which stressed the "Arab" character of the province']; and young unemployed 'Arab' men, quite similar to those who joined the rebels on the 'African' side." Gérard Prunier, *Darfur: The Ambiguous Genocide* (Ithaca, NY: Cornell University Press, 2005), pp. 45, 97–98.

3 Hilal quoted in Flint and de Waal, *Darfur*, p. 128.

4 For a compendium of reportage on gender-selective massacres and other atrocities, see Adam Jones/Gendercide Watch, "Gendercide in Darfur," www.gendercide.org/darfur01.htm.

5 Public International Law and Policy Group (PILPG), "Genocide in Darfur: A Legal Analysis," September 2004, www.africafiles.org/article.asp?ID=6727.

6 Ibid.

7 State Department statistics cited in PILPG, "Genocide in Darfur."

8 "Organizations arguing that the massacres in Darfur fulfil the international legal definition of genocide include Physicians for Human Rights and the UK-based campaigning group Justice Africa. Human Rights Watch and the International Crisis Group have not employed the term 'genocide,' but both say Sudanese government forces and Janjawid militias are responsible for crimes against humanity, war crimes, and 'ethnic cleansing.' Amnesty International has called for the setting up of an international inquiry to examine charges of war crimes and 'allegations of genocide.'" John Ryle, "Disaster in Darfur," *The New York Review of Books*, 51:13 (August 12, 2004), www.nybooks.com/articles/2004/08/12/disaster-in-darfur/. The UN International Commission of Inquiry on Darfur, reporting in 2005, argued that "the crucial element of genocidal intent appears to be missing, at least as far as the central government authorities are concerned," but stressed that "the crimes against humanity and war crimes that have been committed in Darfur may be *no less serious and heinous than genocide*" (quoted in Flint and de Waal, *Darfur*, p. 183, emphasis added)—a phrasing worth keeping in mind for the discussion of genocide versus crimes against humanity in Chapter 15 (pp. 709–712).

9 Aegis Trust report quoted in Anne Penketh, "Darfur: Never Again?," *The Independent*, January 26, 2005.

10 Terence Neilan, "Powell Says Sudan Abuses Qualify as Genocide," *The New York Times*, September 9, 2004.

11 Scott Anderson, "How Did Darfur Happen?," *The New York Times*, October 17, 2004.

12 Ibid.

13 Simon Tisdall, "Suffering Lost in a Numbers Game," *The Guardian*, April 29, 2008.

14 Prunier, *Darfur: The Ambiguous Genocide*, p. 145. See also Steve Bloomfield, "Darfur Peacekeepers Understaffed, Underequipped and Now Under Fire," *The Independent*, April 25, 2007, http://platform.blogs.com/passionofthepresent/2007/04/darfur_peacekee_1.html.

15 See Jonathan Steele, "It Was Meant to Bring Peace. Instead, British-brokered Deal Has Rekindled War," *The Guardian*, September 30, 2006, www.guardian.co.uk/world/2006/sep/30/sudan.jonathansteele.

16 An unnamed diplomat quoted by Al Jazeera called UNAMID "the most dysfunctional peacekeeping mission in the world." "UN Warns of Worsening Situation in Sudan's Darfur," *AlJazeera.com*, June 11, 2015, www.aljazeera.com/news/2015/06/sudan-darfur-security-council-150610235631458.html.

17 See United Nations, "UNAMID Facts and Figures," www.un.org/en/peace keeping/missions/unamid/facts.shtml.

18 Flint and de Waal, *Darfur*, p. 190.

19 See, e.g., Nat Hentoff, "The Black Holocaust," *The Village Voice*, January 2, 2007, www.villagevoice.com/2007-01-02/news/the-black-holocaust/; Hentoff, "Holocaust in Plain Sight," *The Village Voice*, March 28, 2006, www.villagevoice.com/2006-03-28/news/holocaust-in-plain-sight/; "[George] Clooney Warns of 'Holocaust' in Sudan," ITV News, September 15, 2006. On Clooney's activism around Darfur and neighboring conflicts, see Figure 12.4, p. 615. See also Rebecca Hamilton, *Fighting for Darfur: Public Action and the Struggle to Stop Genocide* (Further Study, this chapter).

20 Flint and de Waal, *Darfur*, p. 184. "Whereas the great majority of violent deaths in 2003–04 were due to attacks on civilians by the army and Janjawiid, from 2005 onwards most were caused by fighting among rebel groups and competition for pasture land among Arab militias—both of whom often fought with weapons supplied by the government, whose attacks continued" (p. 187). See also Edmund Sanders, "Death Rate Declines in Darfur," *The Los Angeles Times*, August 26, 2007.

21 *International Criminal Court*, "Situations and Cases," March 2016.

22 Totten, *Genocide by Attrition*, pp. 24–25.

23 Eric Reeves, "The World's Abandonment of Darfur," *The Washington Post*, May 15, 2015.

24 "South Sudan Profile—Timeline" (excerpted), *BBC Online*, August 27, 2015, www.bbc.com/news/world-africa/14019202.

25 Ismail quoted in Elizabeth Dias, "Sudan: The Forgotten War," *Time*, February 23–March 2, 2015, p. 41.

26 International Crisis Group, "Sudan and South Sudan's Merging Conflicts," *Africa Report no. 223*, January 29, 2015, p. ii.

27 Amnesty International, "South Sudan: Government Forces Deliberately Suffocated Dozens and Dumped Bodies in Open Pits," news release, March 11, 2016, www.amnesty.org/en/latest/news/2016/03/south-sudan-government-forces-deliberately-suffocated-dozens-and-dumped-bodies-in-open-pits/. According to the report, South Sudanese forces "appeared to be targeting all of the male cattle keepers who remained in the village," and "were not detaining the men and boys based on individualized suspicion of criminal activity." Amnesty International, "'Their Voices Stopped': Mass Killing in a Shipping Container in Leer, South Sudan" (London: Amnesty International, 2016), p. 10. Available online at www.amnesty.org/download/Documents/AFR6535982016ENGLISH.pdf.

28 United Nations Human Rights, Office of the High Commissioner, "South Sudan: UN Report Contains 'Searing' Account of Killings, Rapes and Destruction," news release, March 11, 2016.

29 John Aglionby, "UN Decries Child Killings and Mass Rape in South Sudan," *Financial Times*, March 11, 2016, www.ft.com/intl/cms/s/0/a8a67432-e777-11e5-ac45-5c039e797d1c.html. See also Nicholas Kristof, "South Sudan: Where the Soldiers Are Scarier Than the Crocodiles," *The New York Times*, March 12, 2016, www.nytimes.com/2016/03/13/opinion/sunday/where-the-soldiers-are-scarier-than-the-crocodiles.html.

30 "Hopes Rise for South Sudan Peace Deal," Agence France-Presse dispatch in *The Guardian*, February 12, 2016, www.theguardian.com/world/2016/feb/12/hopes-rise-for-south-sudan-peace-deal. The article notes that "the peace agreement is increasingly fragile, with Kiir undermining a fundamental pillar of its

power-sharing clauses by nearly tripling the number of regional states. [In February 2016] Kiir also signed into law . . . a controversial non-governmental organisations (NGO) bill, restrict the numbers of foreign aid workers, which has raised fears it will hinder efforts to help millions in need and goes against the peace agreement."

31 A survivor interviewed by Samuel Totten related: "In 1988, Arabs came from the North and settled here in the Nuba Mountains. . . . They were sent here to control the Nuba. I was not happy to see the Arabs, because [later] in 1989 they took the land I farmed. I was forced to move from land that was good to land that was rocky and very difficult to cultivate. The Arabs also took all of my cows and goats, and so I was left with nothing. No land that I used to own, no animals. Nothing! And I had to move up the mountain. Many Nuba experienced this injustice. . . . There was no one to report the thefts to because the Arabs were *the* authorities in the area and they were also *the* ones stealing." Quoted in Totten, *Genocide by Attrition*, 2nd edn (New Brunswick, NJ: Transaction Publishers, 2015), p. 115.

32 Totten, *Genocide by Attrition*, p. 10. Totten's work includes vivid testimony about the most murderous period of war and genocide in the early 1990s. See also the "eyewitness accounts" gathered in Alex de Waal, "The Nuba Mountains, Sudan," in Samuel Totten and William S. Parsons, eds., *Centuries of Genocide: Essays and Eyewitness Accounts*, 4th edn (London: Routledge, 2012), pp. 421–446.

33 De Waal, "The Nuba Mountains," p. 428.

34 International Crisis Group, "Sudan and South Sudan's Merging Conflicts," p. 8.

35 Totten, *Genocide by Attrition*, p. 125.

Photo Essay

How to represent genocide in photographs, beyond clichéd and depersonalized images of corpses and piled-up skulls? The question has intrigued and vexed me as photography has grown more central to my own output and intellectual interests.

"During the past few years, I have roamed the world photographing sites of genocide and mass atrocity and the memorials to which they gave rise . . . . . . It has become a profound calling, and one I hope to pursue for the remainder of my creative life." (Jones, "Seized of Sorrow")

Relics and artifacts (1)

Photo 1 A bomb casing once housing chemical munitions, used in the Halabja massacre, Iraq, now a flowerpot at the entrance to Halabja's memorial museum.

"On March 16, 1988, Saddam Hussein's forces attacked the predominantly Kurdish city of Halabja by the Iranian border with airborne chemical agents, accusing Halabjis of assisting Iran in its war with Iraq. Some 5,000 civilians were killed. The Iranian government arranged for journalists to visit Halabja after the assault, and the photographs they flashed around the world are among the most iconic of those taken in the mass conflicts of the 1980s. . . . Spent munitions from the chemical attack are deployed throughout the dioramas of the Halabja Museum . . . they lend an element of chilling contemporaneity and authenticity amidst the post hoc fabrications. In an apparently more mischievous spirit, or perhaps for simple novelty, the lone bomb casing in this photo is placed inside the main entrance to the museum. It is offset from the main portal to the exhibition area (visible at the rear), suggestive of marginalia and afterthought. It speaks nonetheless to

a common totemistic tendency in societies that have passed through great militarized tragedies and upheavals.

"In a classic feminist essay on war and gender, Carol Cohn described her response to visiting a US nuclear missile base . . . A significant moment came when Cohn and other visitors to the nuclear base were invited to 'pat the missile.' There is something of this fetishism in the Halabja flowerpot. The missile's blatant phallicism, though, has been sundered, rendered concave, receptive, im/emplanted. The genocidal weapon has been transformed not just into a quaint furnishing, but also into perhaps the most symbolically 'feminine' accoutrement of the bourgeois household, in Iraq no less than in Europe. The ghastliness of the crime of which this adornment is an actual relic is—neutralized? femin- ized? sanctified? subverted? satirized? Any and possibly all of these, depending on the disposition of the viewer, and the unknown motives of the curators." (Jones, "Imagi(ni) ng Gender and Conflict")

The photographer here does not "pat the missile," but in order to level with it—necessary to achieve the looming, foregrounded composition—he must kneel/ genuflect before the relic and its deactivated but still latent destructive power.

We should think, also, of the textbook author's *physical* and *temporal* investment in an image. There is the online and/or archival search for the highest-resolution version. There is the correspondence often involved in clearing, licensing, con- firming, or conveying thanks for a Creative Commons usage. There is the con- verting to greyscale and cropping and sharpening as necessary. There is evaluating, and possibly adjusting, its physical presentation at the proofs stage, and otherwise shepherding the shot to publication. Then and forever after, one invests in it as a reader and (in public settings) audience member. It lies, at least, in a realm beyond the ordinary viewing experience.

Source: Author's photo, April 2011.

Relics and artifacts (2)

Photo 2 Exhumed shoes of a child victim of the Anfal genocide. Display at the Third International Conference on Mass Graves in Iraq, Erbil, Iraqi Kurdistan.

"In recent years, social scientists have noted, and probed, the prevalence of children in contemporary humanitarian imagery. Political scientist Kate Manzo has explored how development NGOs mobilize an 'iconography' that draws on the cultural meanings of modern Western childhood to project institutional values and to cultivate a humanitarian identity via strategies of 'innocence-based solidarity.'" (Heidi Fehrenbach, "Children and Other Civilians," in Fehrenbach and Rodogno, eds., *Humanitarian Photography*)

The tug at the heartstrings extends beyond the West, as this image from a genocide exhibit in Iraqi Kurdistan shows. In addition to the iconography of childhood, it has a touch of kitsch, the plastic flower set alongside the cheap child's sandals. Fehrenbach also explores the prominence of woman/girlchild motifs in her essay, noting that "humanitarian photography and its visual and narrative expressions reflect a marked perception of, and sensitivity to, the peculiar experiences of women and children in war." She ascribes this in large part to the prevalence of women in the humanitarian-photography community. But as photo 15 shows, male photographers also seek to activate these tropes—as, indeed, I did here. Perhaps the only non-exploitative image in this selection was taken by the photographer in the Tuol Sleng prison, cataloguing the Khmer Rouge's victims on pain of death himself (Photo 16).

Source: Author's photo, April 2011.

Faces of trauma (1)

Photo 3 "An exhausted American Marine, Pvt. Theodore J. Miller, exhibits the thousand-yard stare after two days of constant fighting on Eniwetok. He was KIA [killed in action] at [age] 19, March 24, 1944 at Ebon Atoll. He is buried at The Punch Bowl, [Hawaii]."

As World War Two Pacific battles went, Eniwetok Atoll in the Marshall Islands was one of the minor and briefer ones, fought "before the Japanese had time to build a formidable defense," according to Donald Miller. It is not even mentioned in Eric Bergerud's 500-page *Touched with Fire: The Land War in the South Pacific* (Penguin, 1996). It nonetheless took the same savage toll as fighting all over the Marshalls and the other Pacific islands and atolls. "In no theater of war during the twentieth century did infantry experience as much combat at point-blank range as they found in the South Pacific," wrote Bergerud.* Miller conveyed something of the challenges:

> "The pitiless heat and suffocating humidity broke the spirits and stamina of strong men; fetid swamps, thick with crocodiles, were breeding basins for mosquito-borne diseases, and the high, interwoven canopy of forest growth—great trees that seemed to reach to the sky—shut out the light, casting men into a perpetual darkness that drove some of them crazy. Soldiers and Marines went

---

* Donald L. Miller (and Bergerud quoted in Miller), *D-Days in the Pacific* (New York: Simon & Schuster, 2005), pp. 127–128.

for weeks without seeing either the sun or the stars; and everywhere there was the smell of death and decay from rotting bodies and vegetation. 'In the jungle, we were enveloped by a matted tangled tree canopy, 200 feet or so up,' an Australian soldier described . . . 'It drove some of our less strong soldiers to total nervous breakdown and weeping frustration.'" (Miller, *D-Days in the Pacific*)

"Canopy," "shut out the light," "enveloped," "perpetual darkness" . . . it is hardly conducive to photographic or cinematic representation, and it reminds one how the USMC battle photos of the Pacific war are generally of subjects snapped on beaches or exposed hillsides, in a harsh daylight glare; or, as here, in stunned post-combat repose. We have been granted almost no visual sense of the jungle war, with the honorable exception of filmmaker Terrence Malick's recreation in *The Thin Red Line* (1998, DP John Toll). Malick's film aestheticizes the natural swamp and jungle settings as it does the rippling grassy hillsides in the central battle scene, but does so unusually and beautifully throughout.*

Source: United States Marine Corps (USMC)/Wikimedia Commons.

---

* There is nothing comparable in US Vietnam war movies, including *The Deer Hunter*, *Platoon*, and so on. Recall that the pivotal battle scene in Coppola's *Apocalypse Now* is a beach attack. Gunshots and arrows are fired *from* the jungle into the river—the narrow band of communication, the symbol of conquest and civilization. On the one occasion that the film tiptoes into the forest, it meets with a ferocious tiger, and skedaddles.

Faces of trauma (2)

Photo 4 Young people at a commemoration ceremony for a new memorial to the Babi Yar massacre outside Kiev, Ukraine, 2009.

The Nazis methodically tabulated and systematically exterminated 33,771 Jewish civilians at Babi Yar (the "Grandmother's Ravine") on September 29–30, 1941. It was the most gargantuan of the *Einsatzgruppen* massacres in the early months of the invasion of the USSR (see "The Turn to Mass Murder," Chapter 6). Almost certainly, it exceeded the death toll of any single-day killing spree in the gas chambers of Auschwitz or in any other Nazi death factory. We have images of the prelude, and somehow even more disturbing *color* images of the aftermath, with the piles of stripped clothing and the filled-in grave. The victims are of course absent in the latter, and they are massified in the former. Clustered in groups, their naked vulnerability is plain and horrifying, but there is a sense in which, in their visual function, they have been reduced to the status determined by the *génocidaires*: chattel for the slaughterhouse. We cannot see their faces closely, as we can see the expressions of these young people. The youths here are a distant mirror, a contemporary reflection. Their imagination—and our imagining of their imagination—is an act of resurrection.

> *"I can look at this picture for minutes on end, exploring the depth of expression and emotion in each of the faces, and pondering what I know of the events that so traumatized them."* (Jones, "Encompassing Genocide")

"Cultures of memory are organized by round numbers, intervals of ten; but somehow the remembrance of the dead is easier when the numbers are not round, when the final digit is not a zero. So . . . it might be easier to imagine the one person at the end of the 33,761 Jews shot at Babi Yar: Dina Pronicheva's mother, let us say, although in fact every single Jew killed there could be that one, must be that one, is that one." (Timothy Snyder, *Bloodlands*)*

Source: AP Photo/Efrem Lukatsky.

---

* Ironically in this context, the number of murdered Jews is a misprint—33,771, not 33,761, was the total reported by the killers. See the image of the *Einsatzgruppen* report on p. 701.

Bodies, corpses, persons (1)

Photo 5 The face of gendercide against "battle-age" men: a victim of Serb killing squads at Srebrenica, Bosnia and Herzegovina, exhumed from a mass grave by forensic investigators.

"The shock lies in the personality of the corpse: its recognizable, agonized/agonizing humanity underneath the dirt and decay. . . . The result, I believe, is a poignant image of horror, as well as (inevitably and appropriately) a repellant one." (Jones, "Encompassing Genocide")

"Photographs show how easily we are reduced to the merely physical, which is to say how easily the body can be maimed, starved, splintered, beaten, burnt, torn, and crushed. Photographs present us, in short, with physical cruelty and our vulnerability to it." (Susie Linfield, *The Cruel Radiance*)

"Let us think of the human as a value and a morphology that may be allocated and retracted, aggrandized, personified, degraded and disavowed, elevated and affirmed. The norm continues to produce the nearly impossible paradox of a human who is no human, or of the human who effaces the human as it is otherwise known. . . . If, as the philosopher Emmanuel Levinas claims, it is the face of the other that demands from us an ethical response, then it would seem that the norms that would allocate who is and is not human arrive in visual form. These norms work to *give face* and to *efface*. . . . There are ways of framing that will bring the human into view in its frailty and precariousness, that will allow us to stand for the value and dignity of human life, to react with outrage when lives are degraded or eviscerated without regard for their value as lives." (Judith Butler, "Torture and the Ethics of Photography")

Source: Photo by Tim Loveless/Courtesy of the International Criminal Tribunal for the Former Yugoslavia (ICTY)/Victoria Enaut.

Bodies, corpses, persons (2)

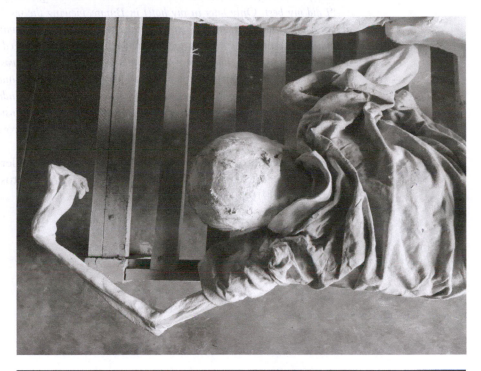

Photo 6 Exhumed, lime–dusted corpse at the Murambi genocide site in Rwanda (see also Figure 9.5, p. 498).

"The photographer is recording a visual image of the scene, approaching it through a frame before which those involved in the torture and its triumphal aftermath also stood and posed. The relation between the photographer and the photographed takes place by virtue of the frame. The frame permits, orchestrates, and mediates that relation." (Judith Butler, "Torture and the Ethics of Photography")

"I often wonder what is involved in representing mass crimes aesthetically. Never was this challenge brought home to me more clearly than in Rwanda, which I finally visited in 2011 after years of study, and again in 2012. On that first occasion, I fought hard to secure the necessary permission of The National Commission for the Fight against Genocide (CNLG), Rwanda's 'genocide ministry,' which now must approve all attempts to photograph the numerous genocide sites scattered around the country. Permit in hand, I approached the site of Murambi, not far from the intellectual capital of Butare, itself home to a powerful genocide memorial.

"Murambi seems to me the worst place in the world. Displayed there in former schoolrooms are the desiccated and lime-shrouded corpses of hundreds of victims of the 1994 genocide. Normally one tours the site in the company of a guide (generally a survivor of the genocide). But because I had the CNLG's imprimatur, I was allowed to roam freely.

You need to understand that this involves negotiating your way around corpses piled so close to your passage that you have to take care not to knock off a stray arm or foot.

"I did my best. Only later in my hotel in Butare, viewing the results, did I begin to absorb what I had seen. And when I returned to the site the following year, this time without the desire or permission to re-photograph the site, I realized how much of a defense the photography had been against the raw horror of what I was witnessing. This visit was shorter, more superficial, guided, but I felt helpless—utterly unable to process the visuals in a way that might inspire or educate others. It makes me wonder to what extent our anti-genocide efforts, distanced as they necessarily are, serve to insulate us from the human catastrophes they seek to confront." (Jones, "Seized of Sorrow")

Source: Author's photo, August 2012. For the complete gallery "Rwanda—Genocide Sites & Memorials," see www.flickr.com/photos/adam_jones/albums/72157630919887160.

Can landscapes speak? (1)

Photo 7 The destroyed Old City of Van, the leading Armenian center of southeast Turkey, which rose in resistance to the Ottoman Turkish genocide, and was reduced to rubble by Ottoman Turkish authorities after it was recaptured from Russian/Armenian defenders.

"Genocides and related crimes against humanity occur in particular places and are targeted at collectivities or identity groups that inhabit those spaces. The creation of an imagined 'other' that is dangerous, dirty, degenerate, or in some other way undesirable is a fundamental element of every genocidal event, and the objective of the perpetrating power is to suppress, remove, or ultimately destroy this dangerous, collective other. Thus, space is transformed in the mind of the perpetrator even before any acts of destruction are carried out—indeed, the creation of an imagined space that no longer suffers the influence, presence, or physical being of the other is a key step along the way to actual genocide, which may be viewed as the spatial imaginary made real. From the victims' viewpoint, on the other hand, these spaces to be cleansed represent geographies of exclusion and fear. . . . Genocide events not only devastate peoples, they also destroy spaces and places: As a culture is eliminated, its impact on the landscape recedes or disappears altogether, and the place as it once was ceases to exist, except perhaps in occasional relict features on the landscape." (Stephen L. Egbert and Shannon O'Lear, "Genocide, Geographies Of," entry in Barney Warf, ed., *Encyclopedia of Geography* [London: Sage Publications, 2010], pp. 1201–1202.)

Source: Author's photo, June 2011.

Can landscapes speak? (2)

Photo 8 The irrigation ditch, preserved at the memorial to the My Lai massacre in Vietnam, where US troops shot villagers *Einsatzgruppen*-style on March 16, 1968.

See Box 10.1, pp. 553–556, on the actions of Hugh Thompson, Jr., the helicopter pilot who witnessed the massacre in the ditch, and who intervened with his fellow crew-members, Lawrence Colburn and Glenn Andreotta, to save a dozen Vietnamese civilians from the massacre.

"Out in the paddy field beside a dike 200 meters south of the village they watched [from their helicopter] a small group of soldiers approach an injured woman, aged about 20. Thompson had marked her with smoke. . . . Thompson and his crew watched as an infantry officer, wearing a captain's bars on his helmet, came up to the woman, prodded her with his foot, and then killed her. Those in the helicopter could hardly believe what they were seeing. Minutes later over on the eastern side of the village they saw dozens of bodies in the irrigation ditch. Movements from the ditch convinced them people were still alive. Not far away a group of infantrymen taking a cigarette break sat around on the ground and relaxed . . .

"Thompson landed the helicopter . . . [he] wanted to know if there was any way they could help the people in the ditch. The sergeant replied the only way to help them was to put them out of their misery. . . . Frustrated, Thompson lifted off again and circled the area for a few minutes. Almost as soon as he took off his worst fears were confirmed. Andreotta reported the sergeant was now shooting people in the ditch. Thompson began thinking about what the Nazis had done in the last war—marching people to a ditch and blowing them away. Furious with himself and everybody else, finally he snapped. . . .

"[After evacuating the rescued civilians,] Thompson made one last pass of the ditch. As he did so Andreotta shouted he could see something moving. They landed and Thompson covered Colburn and Andreotta with a machine gun as they approached to the edge of the ditch. It was a horrendous sight; a hundred dead men, women, and children filled the channel four or five deep [n.b. A plaque at the memorial, visible in the photo, asserts that 170 villagers were massacred in the ditch]. Bodies were scattered along the edges of the ditch. There was blood, filth, and stench everywhere. The corpses looked completely mangled and torn apart. . . . Eventually [Colburn] found what he was looking for: a child, aged about 3, covered in blood and slime but not seriously injured. He had to move a couple of bodies out of the way to get the child completely free. He then handed the little body up to Colburn by the back of its shirt. It was limp and felt just like a rag doll." (Michael Bilton and Kevin Sim, *Four Hours in My Lai* [London: Penguin, 1992], pp. 137–140.)

Source: Author's photo, July 2009.

Can buildings speak? (1)

Photo 9 Adjoining façades, Mostar, Bosnia and Herzegovina.

The battle for the city of Mostar was the crux of a Balkans sideshow. It pitted Bosniaks (Bosnian Muslims) against their erstwhile allies, the Croats, who were now "cleansing" each other's populations in the Croat-majority region of southwestern Bosnia. The Neretva river became an ethnic boundary, as it remains today. The military frontline ran along the main avenue, where these structures stand. To drive home the contention that coexistence was now impossible as well as undesirable, Croat forces shelled the Stari Most, the famous medieval bridge spanning the river, until it collapsed. After the war, the elegant arch was rebuilt with foreign funding, locally-quarried stone, and period construction techniques. Today, in the souvenir shops near the bridge, you can buy decorative items made of artillery shells (shades of Photo 1) and pens made from the cartridges of 7.62mm semi-automatic rifle bullets.

On two visits to Mostar, I have photographed ruins and shellpocked façades surreally juxtaposed with adjoining renovated and repainted properties. (One of these has landed on the cover of James Waller's 2016 book with Oxford University Press, *Confronting Evil: Engaging Our Responsibility to Prevent Genocide*.) For me, they signify renewal, remembrance, and warning all at once.

Source: Author's photo, June 2011.

Can buildings speak? (2)

Photo 10 Hallway with cells at the Tuol Sleng torture and interrogation center, Phnom Penh, Cambodia. The image was used on the cover of the second edition of *Genocide: A Comprehensive Introduction*.

". . . I settled on one of my own photos, taken in mid-2009 at the Tuol Sleng/S-21 prison complex, founded by Cambodia's Khmer Rouge on the site of a former school. Tuol Sleng and nearby Cheung Ek are mandatory stops on the Cambodian 'genocide tour,' but no less moving for that. I remember having the hallway to myself, capturing it in natural light, the tableau punctuated by cell doors swinging open and askew. In imagining it for the cover, I visualized drawing the reader through a doorway (or any kind of entrance/opening—this is a common motif in my photojournalism), and guiding them along a dark passageway. If you wanted to stretch the metaphor, you could see each cell as a chapter or key theme of the book; the doorway itself, with its jagged and irregular contours, seems to me like a wound." (Jones, "Encompassing Genocide")

Source: Author's photo, May 2009.

The death factory

Photo 11 Members of a *Sonderkommando* haul the bodies of Jews murdered by the Nazis to be burned in pits at the Auschwitz–Birkenau death camp.

The *Sonderkommando* workers were nearly all Jewish (men), selected for the infernal task of burning the corpses of their fellow Jews (see Greif, Further Study, Chapter 6). The photo is one of four taken, at enormous risk, during the final mass slaughter of Hungarian Jews in the summer of 1944. A Greek Jew, Alex, is said to have been the photographer.*

"These four pictures . . . represent a moment when the most defiled of men stepped back into humanity: into a decision, into visibility, into a demand that

* For the images and commentary, see https://en.wikipedia.org/wiki/Sonderkommando_photographs.

the civilized world *see* the genocide and account for it. The photographs, as [Georges] Didi-Huberman writes, were 'snatched . . . from a world bent on their impossibility.' They are *in themselves* an act of revolt and an assertion of the human; they are a refusal of absolute helplessness in the midst of an apparently unstoppable death-machine." (Linfield, *The Cruel Radiance*)

Source: United States Holocaust Memorial Museum (USHMM).

Sifting the ashes

Photo 12 Jan Gross used this image as the basis for his book with Irene Grudzińska Gross, *Golden Harvest: Events at the Periphery of the Holocaust* (Oxford: Oxford University Press, 2012).

In Gross's summary, the photo shows local Polish peasants, "gleaners, or, as they were called at the time, 'diggers' (*kopacze*) . . . digging through mass graves at the site of the Treblinka extermination camp" after the end of the Second World War, "looking for pieces of jewelry and dental gold overlooked by the Nazis" in their genocide of the Jews (p. xiii). According to the former director of Treblinka's museum, who supplied the image to Gross, the peasants were photographed after their arrest by police. "I was stunned by the power of the scene caught in the photograph," wrote Jan Gross (p. xiv), "and equally stunned that no one had noticed the picture upon its publication" in the Polish newspaper *Gazeta Wyborcza* in 2008.* The evidence of grassroots-Polish exploitation of Jewish suffering brought some soul-searching domestically, but also media attacks against Gross, including an allegation that he had misrepresented the scene depicted in the photo—that the peasants were merely being good citizens and tidying the landscape!

Source: Wikimedia Commons.

---

* See the English translation of the January 7, 2008 *Gazeta Wyborcza* article by Piotr Gluchowski and Marcin Kowalski, "Gold Rush in Treblinka," at http://holocaustcontroversies.yuku.com/reply/25792/Gold-Rush-in-Treblinka#reply-25792.

The politics of witnessing (1)

Photo 13 Mourners at the Srebrenica reinterment ceremony and commemoration, Potocari, Bosnia and Herzegovina.

I recall walking through the memorial and cemetery for victims of the 1995 Srebrenica massacre, outside the former UN base at Potocari, during the annual commemoration and reburial ceremony in 2007. The exhumed and catalogued remains of recently discovered victims were carried in a procession of mini-coffins to the cemetery, where mourners, mostly women, awaited at graveside. Wielding my camera in their presence felt awkward and invasive at first. Then I realized that my presence, as a foreigner and a photographer, was a meaningful element of the scene. The mourners' mourning was partly *performative*. They wanted to be observed and recorded—to keep alive the memory of their murdered menfolk, to confront the denialists and forgetters with the evidence of freshly-turned earth and raw pain.

"It is not only or exclusively at an affective register that the photograph operates, but through instituting a certain mode of acknowledgment. It 'argues' for the grievability of a life: its pathos is at once affective and interpretive. If we can be haunted, then we can acknowledge that there has been a loss and hence that there has been a life: this is an initial moment of cognition, an apprehension, but also a potential judgment, and it requires that we conceive of grievability as the precondition of life, one that is discovered retrospectively through the temporality instituted by the photograph itself." (Butler, "Torture and the Ethics of Photography")

Source: Author's photo, July 2007.

The politics of witnessing (2)

Photo 14 A Congolese rape and burn survivor tells her story at a gathering in Goma, DRC. "Survivors of rape, supported by UNICEF and VDay, held a day of speeches telling their stories and calling for an end to violence against women. The courage of the women to tell their stories in front of three hundred people was palpable." (Julien Harneis)

"I was glad to discover on Flickr the work of Julien Harneis, who has worked for many years with Médecins Sans Frontières. Julien's page, like my own, supplies a wealth of Creative Commons imagery, and his magnificent image of a rape (and burn) survivor 'telling her story' . . . allowed me to resolve a conundrum I faced in illustrating the discussion of genocidal rape [in the second edition of this book]. How could I do so, while also preserving the anonymity of survivors, as I felt obliged to? Julien, with his unerring eye and discreet composition, lent the testimony—mute on the page—an eloquence that readers and viewers supplemented with their own imaginations." (Jones, "Encompassing Genocide")

When I show the color version in class and in public talks, the survivor's dress leaps to radiant life, becoming the focal point of the composition and the emblem of her enduring vivacity. The dress pattern ironically mimics the scars on her open, expressive, injured, embracing arms. I am also drawn to the audience member at bottom left of the photo. She is peripheral and indistinct in the composition. But her emotionally charged body language—leaning forward, slightly bowed/rocked, hand over her mouth—mutely conveys what we do *not* see, and cannot hear. (See "Faces of Trauma," above.)

Source: Photo by Julien Harneis/Flickr/Creative Commons. The hi-res color version is posted at www.flickr.com/photos/julien_harneis/2858287885/.

The politics of witnessing (3)

Photo 15 "A Starving Child near Ayod, Southern Sudan"

The South African photographer Kevin Carter took this photograph in March 1993, during a devastating famine. It won him the Pulitzer Prize. Shortly after receiving the award, in July 1994, Carter committed suicide by inhaling carbon monoxide in his pickup truck. His suicide note mentioned money troubles, but he also wrote: "I am haunted by the vivid memories of killings and corpses and anger and pain . . . of starving or wounded children, of trigger-happy madmen, often police, of killer executioners . . ."

"Kevin Carter later told the story. Working around a feeding station near the village of Ayod, he had been alerted by the sound of soft, high-pitched whimpering nearby. He ventured out with his camera to find this painfully thin child, swollen with the pregnancy of hunger, collapsed into a tiny heap. Behind her, menacing her utter human frailty, a vulture landed. The photographer watched for a while and took several photographs of her attempts to stand and move on before collapsing again in exhaustion. Smoking a cigarette, he waited twenty minutes, wondering if the vulture would spread its wings. It did not. He took this picture and then wept and thought of his own daughter, whom he longed to hold in his arms. He then shooed away the bird and carried the child to safety and food. . . .

"When published simultaneously in the *New York Times* and the Johannesburg *Mail & Guardian* on March 26, 1993, the photograph released an avalanche of responses. Readers wanted to know immediately why the photographer took the photograph instead of helping the child to the feeding station towards which its desolated being was so abjectly struggling under the grisly eyes of a vile predator. The readers of the *New York Times* also wanted to know what happened to her. Editors reported days later that she had indeed made it to the feeding station; Carter himself delivered her. But what chance an orphan girl under five had to survive beyond that moment remained deeply unclear. We need to ask ourselves what it was about an image, so striking that it led to Pulitzer Prize recognition by fellow photographers for its striking photographic quality, that, nonetheless, suspended mediatized consumption of the master subject of our times—suffering—and released the demand for a narrative beyond its iconicity; that released the child from being but the affecting and tolerable icon of an endemic African condition of famine, over there, the continent's 'tragic destiny,' so that the single life of this one unknown toddler mattered to readers of the *New York Times*, saturated as they are with images of violence. And did their outrage poison or shatter the photographer beyond endurance of what he, in their service, had had to witness for himself?" (Griselda Pollock, "Photographing Atrocity: Becoming Iconic?," in Batchen *et al.*, eds., *Picturing Atrocity*, pp. 74–75.)*

Source: © Kevin Carter/Sygma/Corbis.

---

* Quoted in "The Exchange: Susie Linfield on Photography and Violence," *The New Yorker*, November 22, 2010, www.newyorker.com/books/page-turner/the-exchange-susie-linfield-on-photography-and-violence.

Youth and lunacy

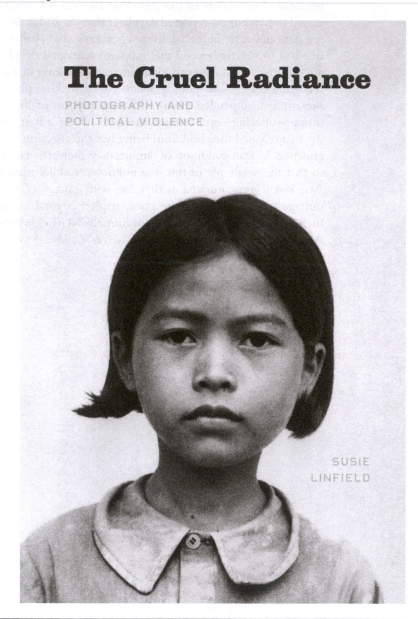

Photo 16 Cover of Susie Linfield, *The Cruel Radiance* (2010).

Linfield: "The cover of my book is a photograph of a young Cambodian girl before she was executed, and probably [first] tortured, by the Khmer Rouge as a so-called enemy of the state. Looking at that photograph could not tell me all or most of what I needed to know about the rise of the Khmer Rouge and their genocidal politics. But it offered me a way into the lunacy of that political regime. We can know the numbers—that an estimated two million Cambodians were killed—but to begin to really think about what it means for a government to torture and execute its own children is, I think, something else."*

"Nhem Ein was the photographer at Tuol Sleng. He took 10,000 pictures and survived because he never spoiled a picture. . . . 'Those that arrived at the facility had no chance of living,' he told AP. . . . Seth Mydans wrote in the *New York Times*: 'He had a job to do, and he did it supremely well, under threat of death, within earshot of screams of torture: methodically photographing Khmer Rouge prisoners and producing a haunting collection of mug shots that has become the visual symbol of Cambodia's mass killings.'" *Nhem Ein:* "They would say, 'Why was I brought here? What am I accused of? What did I do wrong?' . . . 'Look straight ahead. Don't lean your head to the left or the right.' That's all I said . . . I had to say that so the picture would turn out well. Then they were taken to the interrogation center. The duty of the photographer was just to take the picture."†

Source: Courtesy of The University of Chicago Press.

Further Study

The subject of photography and atrocity is polarizing, if you'll excuse the pun. The divide is well exemplified by Susan Sontag's classic *On Photography* (London: Penguin Classics, 2008), and Susie Linfield, *The Cruel Radiance: Photography and Political Violence* (Chicago, IL: University of Chicago Press, 2010). Sontag's crystalline insights are essential, and her skepticism about the capacity of images to represent suffering also shaped her final book, *Regarding the Pain of Others* (New York: Picador, 2003). There, Sontag argued that photographs can "haunt us . . . but they are not much help if the task is to understand." Only supplementary "narratives" could perform this task (p. 89). Linfield accepts many of Sontag's insights as "sharp and true. But it is Sontag, more than anyone else, who was responsible for establishing a tone of suspicion and distrust in photography criticism, and for teaching us that to be smart about photographs means to disparage them." By contrast, Linfield believes "it is photographs . . . that bring us close to those experiences of suffering in ways that no other form of art or journalism can" (p. xv).

---

* See Kimberly Juanita Brown, "Regarding the Pain of the Other: Photography, Famine, and the Transference of Affect," in Elspeth H. Brown and Thy Phu, eds., *Feeling Photography* (Durham, NC: Duke University Press, 2014), pp. 181–203.
† See "Facts and Details: Tuol Sleng Prison," http://factsanddetails.com/southeast-asia/Cambodia/sub5_2b/entry-2859.html; Seth Mydans, "Out from behind the Camera at the Khmer Rouge Torture House," *The New York Times*, October 26, 2007, http://www.nytimes.com/2007/10/26/world/asia/27cambo.html.

Other notable works include:

Geoffrey Batchen, *Picturing Atrocity: Photography in Crisis*. London: Reaktion Books, 2012. A superb and visually-impactful collection, with royalties donated to Amnesty International.

Judith Butler, *Frames of War: When is Life Grievable?* London: Seagull Books, 2009. Includes Butler's important essay "Torture and the Ethics of Photography: Thinking with Sontag," sampled here.

Heide Fehrenbach and Davide Rodogno, eds., *Humanitarian Photography: A History*. Cambridge: Cambridge University Press, 2015. Diverse and readable essays examining photography's use by the Congo Reform Association, US relief agencies, the Red Cross, and others. Especially valuable is Peter Balakian's chapter, "Photography, Visual Culture, and the Armenian Genocide."

David Friend, *Watching the World Change: The Stories Behind the Images of 9/11*. New York: Farrar, Straus and Giroux, 2006. An intimate exploration of key images and their impact.

Adam Jones, ed., *Evoking Genocide: Scholars and Activists Describe the Works That Shaped Their Lives*. Toronto, ON: The Key Publishing House Inc., 2009. Richly illustrated, and including many short tributes to photographs and other works of art, documentation, and memorialization.

David King, *Ordinary Citizens: The Victims of Stalin*. London: Francis Boutle Publishers, 2003. Haunting secret-police mugshots of individuals destined (with rare exceptions) for the execution chamber.

Sharon Sliwinski, "The Childhood of Human Rights: The Kodak on the Congo," *Journal of Visual Culture*, 5: 3 (2006), pp. 333–363. A fine introduction to the dawn of humanitarian photography during the era of the Congo Reform Association (see Chapter 2). The subject is also explored in the Batchen and Fehrenbach/Rodogno volumes (see above).

Eric Stover and Gilles Peress, *The Graves: Srebrenica and Vukovar*. Zurich: Scalo Publishers, 1998. Images and text portraying forensic excavations in Bosnia and Croatia.

Barbie Zelizer, *About to Die: How News Images Move the Public*. Oxford: Oxford University Press, 2010. Asks: "Under what conditions does an image work most powerfully?" and "How does this impact public response to the news?"

Author's note

For my Global Photo Archive, including color hi-res versions of all my photographs in this volume and many thousands of others, see www.flickr.com/adam_jones/sets/. With rare exceptions, my photos are posted under a Creative Commons license, meaning you may freely use them in your own teaching, projects, and publications, with appropriate credit. I have also worked with the International Association of Genocide Scholars to prepare an archive of hi-resolution images pertaining to genocide and crimes against humanity, all under a Creative Commons license, including many of the historical photos, documents, and artworks in this book. See the IAGS Creative Commons Image Bank at www.genocide scholars.org/iags-creative-commons-image-bank/.

My evolving encounter with photographic representations of genocide (as creator, consumer, author, and pedagogue) is explored in three essays. "Encompassing Genocide" and "Imag(in)ing Gender and Conflict" both appear in Adam Jones, *The Scourge of Genocide: Essays and Reflections* (London: Routledge, 2013), pp. 26–55 and 140–148. The latter was first published in *Feminist Review*, 101 (July 2012), pp. 132–141, at the generous invitation of Laura Shepherd. My autobiographical essay, "Seized of Sorrow," in Samuel Totten, ed., *Advancing Genocide Studies: Personal Accounts and Insights from Scholars in the Field* (New Brunswick, NJ: Transaction Publishers, 2015), includes some meditations on my photography from genocide sites and memorials worldwide. The italicized passages in this photo essay are quoted from these sources, as indicated.

Warm thanks to the following for their support and encouragement on the photographic front, and for many nourishing conversations over the years: Kelly Webeck, Mary Lee Webeck, Adam Muller, Rafiki Ubaldo, Matthew Remington, Griselda Ramírez, Julien Harneis, Wayne Emde, and Ami Fagin.

PART 3 SOCIAL SCIENCE PERSPECTIVES

CHAPTER 10

Psychological Perspectives

Any broad historical examination of the phenomenon of genocide cannot fruitfully proceed without engagement with issues of collective human psychopathology.

Mark Levene

Understanding genocide requires probing the minds of those who commit it, and those who seek to prevent or limit it. This is the province of psychology. Not surprisingly, many prominent scholars and analysts of genocide are psychologists and psychiatrists, including Israel Charny, Ervin Staub, Roy Baumeister, Robert Jay Lifton, and James Waller.

In approaching psychological contributions in this chapter, I will set aside one line of inquiry, focusing on the "authoritarian personality" and the mass psychology of fascism. Associated with central twentieth-century figures such as Theodor Adorno, Wilhelm Reich, and Erich Fromm, these investigations located fascism's psychological roots in childhood experiences of parental authoritarianism and repression. They also emphasized mechanisms of psychological projection, displacing onto others the violence derived from a lack of personal self-esteem (or, alternatively, hysterical narcissism), as well as various sexual neuroses. Projection strategies are considered further below, while some of the earlier Reichian attention to familial and social-psychological dynamics is paralleled in the closing discussion of genocidal perpetrators and rescuers.

█ NARCISSISM, GREED, FEAR, HUMILIATION

What motivates *génocidaires?* I see four psychological elements as essential: narcissism, greed, fear, and humiliation.

Narcissism

All or almost all of us prefer comfort to truth.

Tzvetan Todorov

The Greek god Narcissus became so enraptured with his own reflection in a pool that he "fell in love with himself, and not being able to find consolation, he died of sorrow by the same pool."[1] The myth speaks to our propensity for hubristic self-love, a phenomenon first studied in a psychological and psychiatric context by Sigmund Freud (1856–1939). Freud described narcissism as a formative and necessary stage of ego development, but also sketched notes on a *narcissism of minor differences.* This refers, in Anton Blok's summary, to "the fact that the fiercest struggles often take place between individuals, groups and communities that differ very little—or between which the differences have greatly diminished."[2] Scholars of genocide are often struck by how groups that seem close linguistically,

Figures 10.1 and 10.2 Malignant or pathological narcissism, generating a "cult of personality" buttressed by the intensive use of propaganda, is a regular feature of dictatorial and genocidal regimes. *Left:* Hubert Lanzinger's 1930s-era portrait of Adolf Hitler, *Der Bannerträeger* (The Standard Bearer), shows the Fuhrer as a heroic armored knight of old, reclaiming Germany's rightful place in the order of nations. *Source:* US Army Center of Military History, Washington, DC/US Holocaust Memorial Museum. *Right:* Kim Il Sung, absolute ruler of North Korea from 1948 to his death in 1994, is still depicted as a deity-like figure, as in this 2008 photo of a wall painting in the city of Wonsan. The photographer noted: "Paintings like this . . . are found in every city, town and village in the country. Major monuments aside, they are the only things that are illuminated at night[;] there are street lamps, but they are never switched on." Kim Il Sung's grandson, Kim Jong Un, ruled North Korea at the time of writing (March 2016; see Box 5.4 for more on the North Korean regime).

Source: Yeowatzup/Wikimedia Commons.

geographically, and/or religiously can succumb to bitter intercommunal conflict: Hutus and Tutsis, English and Irish,[3] Serbs and Croats, Catholics and Protestants. At a deeper level, Freud observed that "the communal feeling of groups requires, in order to complete it, hostility towards some extraneous minority."[4] The psychological dynamic by which the "Self" and the "We" are defined against the "Other" is fundamental to genocide.[5]

Of equal significance is *malignant* or *pathological* narcissism, in which others exist only to fortify, magnify, and idolize the self.[6] Profound insecurity, anxiety, and unease often accompany this form of narcissism—a fear that without validation by others, the self will be undermined or annihilated.[7] But this seems to vanish at the extremes of malignant narcissism, where true *psychopathy* lies. This is a murderous egotism, incapable of empathy with others, that considers human destruction inconsequential if it increases personal power and glory.

Malignant narcissism and psychopathy are common among *génocidaires* in modern history. Consider Adolf Hitler, whose injured ego found transcendence in Holocaust. (How Hitler, the failed artist and rootless ex-soldier, must have reveled in the version of the Lord's Prayer devised by the League of German Girls: "Adolf Hitler, you are our great Leader. Thy name makes the enemy tremble. Thy Third Reich comes, thy will alone is law upon earth . . ."!)[8] Consider as well Joseph Stalin and Mao Zedong, "fanatics, poets, paranoiacs, peasants risen to rule empires whose history obsessed them, careless killers of millions"[9]—or Serbian ex-president Slobodan Milosevic, responsible for so much human devastation during the Balkan wars:

> US psychiatrists who have studied Milosevic closely describe him as having a "malignant narcissistic" personality. They see Milosevic as "strongly self-centered, vain, and full of self-love." He is also completely indifferent to almost anyone or anything else around him. A malignant narcissist such as Milosevic creates a core personality for himself and then shapes his own perception of the world to fit that personality. . . . Milosevic understands what is really going on, he knows that his own depictions of events that diverge from reality are lies, but at the same time he believes so strongly in his own lies that he sometimes gives the appearance of crossing the line into unreality.[10]

Collective pathological narcissism is also a factor in genocide. Shifting the analysis and diagnosis from the individual to the collective is a controversial move. But it seems appropriate when a majority or dominant minority of a nation's citizens hold that their country is innately superior, chosen by God or destiny, unique bearers of truth, or limitlessly capable. The philosopher Sam Vaknin has summarized the criteria for collective pathological narcissism:

> The group as a whole, *or members of the group* . . . feel grandiose and self-important. . . . [They are] obsessed with group fantasies of unlimited success, fame, fearsome power or omnipotence, unequalled brilliance, bodily beauty or performance, or ideal, everlasting, all-conquering ideals or political theories. . . . [They] are firmly convinced that the group is unique. . . . [They] require excessive admiration, adulation, attention and affirmation—or, failing that, wish

to be feared and to be notorious. . . . [They] feel entitled. They expect unreasonable or special and favorable priority treatment. They demand automatic and full compliance with expectations. . . . They rarely accept responsibility for their actions . . . [They] are devoid of empathy. They are unable or unwilling to identify with or acknowledge the feelings and needs of other groups. [They] are arrogant and sport haughty behaviors or attitudes coupled with rage when frustrated, contradicted, punished, limited, or confronted. . . . [All of] this often leads to anti-social behavior, cover-ups, and criminal activities on a mass scale.[11]

During the nineteenth and early twentieth centuries, one of the countries of which I am a citizen, Great Britain, was probably the world leader in collective pathological narcissism. Generations of schoolchildren grew up imbibing their elders' conviction that Britain was God's gift to humankind, particularly to the darker races it was destined to rule. British culture and civilization were supreme, and British men and women were uniquely noble, brave, virtuous, and incorruptible. Traces of this mentality persist even in the post-colonial era, and can resurge with virulent passion in times of crisis, as I observed firsthand during a visit to Britain during the Falklands/Malvinas War of 1982.[12]

Figure 10.3 A popular Canadian slogan adorns a wall in a Vancouver bookstore. Collective narcissism is the foundation of *nationalism*, which is widely recognized as a central ideological underpinning for modern genocide (see Chapter 16). It also fuels *patriotism*, generally—and dubiously—viewed as a benign and positive emotion. Nearly all states and societies indulge in such narcissistic self-congratulation (see note 11, p. 562). At what point does it become dangerously pathological?

Source: Author's photo, March 2015.

In the past century, the societies that have most dramatically evinced a tendency toward collective pathological narcissism are three totalitarian states—Nazi Germany (1933–1945), Stalinist Russia (1928–1953), and Maoist China (1949–1976)—and, since 1945, a democratic one, the United States.[13] The presence of the US in this list, like its British predecessor, suggests that collective pathological narcissism is not tied to a particular political system or ideology. Psychologist Robert Jay Lifton has analyzed the contemporary US variant in his book *Superpower Syndrome*, pointing to

> a bizarre American collective mind-set that extends our very real military power into a fantasy of cosmic control, a mind-set all too readily tempted by an apocalyptic mission. The symptoms are of a piece, each consistent with the larger syndrome: unilateralism in all-important decisions, including war-making ones; the use of high technology to secure the ownership of death and history; a sense of entitlement concerning the right to identify and destroy all those considered to be terrorists or friends of terrorists, while spreading "freedom" and virtues seen as preeminently ours throughout the world; the right to decide who may possess weapons of mass destruction and who may not, and to take military action using nuclear weapons if necessary against any nation that has them or is thought to be manufacturing them; and underneath all of these symptoms, a righteous vision of ridding the world of evil and purifying it spiritually and politically.[14]

This mindset was fortified by the attacks of September 11, 2001, but it was not a product of them. Rather, distinctively American ideologies of unlimited space and power, combined with the country's unchallenged superpower status since the Second World War, generated a consensus (though very far from a universal view) that the US is destined to dominate the world and prevent any challenge to its hegemony. In past epochs, the mentality has spawned genocidal or proto-genocidal atrocities against Native Americans, Filipinos, Indochinese, and others. In more recent times, it has produced regular bouts of bellicosity and bullying internationally, with consequences that challenge conventional depictions of democratic state behavior, and are examined further in that context in Chapter 12.

Greed

"These people are like vultures swarming down, their eyes bleary, their tongues hanging out with greed, to feed upon the Jewish carcass." So wrote an appalled German businessman, observing the Nazi "Aryanization" of Jewish properties.[15] Yet few Germans shared his scruples. Most viewed the dispossession of the Jews of Germany as a once-in-a-lifetime opportunity, and made the most of it: "Looted Jewish property was a magnet which attracted millions brought up to believe in the myth of the Jewish wealth."[16] In the Nazi death camps, Jews were robbed not only of their few remaining possessions, but of their hair, which was sold for mattress stuffing—and (after death) of the gold fillings in their teeth, melted down for bullion.

Figure 10.4 In a classic activation of personal greed and self-interest, the Nazis used the seizing and plundering of Jewish livelihoods as a means of distributing property and other material items and resources, from luxury goods and clothing to civil-service jobs, to those they favored or whose support they sought. This was true not only for Germans, but to varying degrees across Nazi-occupied Europe. Even despised Slavs were allowed and encouraged to ransack Jewish property and possessions after a mass killing or expulsion of a town's or city's Jewish population. In this more bureaucratized instance from Marseille, France, a few months after the Nazi conquest (July 1940), a Jewish-owned pen-repair shop has been seized and transferred by Nazi directive, almost certainly to a new French owner. The right-hand notice reads "Jewish Enterprise/ Business" in German and French, and was probably applied before or simultaneously with the adjacent one, which reads in French: "Change of Management: From 1 November 1940 [i.e., several months after the fall of France and the Nazi occupation of much of the country], the management of this enterprise is Catholic and French, as are the personnel." (Author's translation; note the sinister implication that being both French and Jewish is no longer possible.)

Source: United States Holocaust Memorial Museum (USHMM).

In his 2005 work *Hitler's Beneficiaries*, German historian Götz Aly showed how critical was this massive apportioning of Jewish property (and goods and belongings seized from other subject populations) to the Nazis' hold on power and popular support. "The Holocaust," declared Aly, "will never be properly understood until it is seen as the most single-mindedly pursued campaign of murderous larceny in modern history." He pointed to "vast numbers of Germans [who] fell prey to the euphoria of a gold rush . . . as the state was transformed into a gigantic apparatus for plundering others" and distributing the bounty.[17] ". . . In Hamburg alone," wrote Frank Bajohr, "more than 100,000 individuals acquired objects formerly in Jewish possession, hundreds of firms changed hands and thousands of pieces of real estate came under new ownership, along with the furnishings of 30,000 Jewish households. A large proportion of these items of furniture and household goods were pilfered from their owners throughout the whole of occupied Europe."[18] The expropriation and extermination of the Jews offered plenty of opportunities for subject populations in the Nazi-occupied territories to grab some precious crumbs, too. An "insatiable greed for money or other spoils" is an important factor, along with "traditional hatred," in explaining the frequently enthusiastic support that Ukrainians and Poles displayed for the Nazi roundups and deportations of Jews.[19] The ancient Jewish community of Salonica, for example, was deported *en masse* for extermination in several waves beginning in March 1943. "...As soon as [the Jews] were marched away, people rushed into their houses, tore up floorboards and battered down walls and ceilings, hoping to find hidden valuables. There was a 'complete breakdown of order' wrote an official at the time, and the second-hand shops of the city began to fill up with stolen goods."[20] In Poland, "After the war, when somebody came to the church in a fur-lined coat, it was usually known that it was 'post-Jewish.'"[21]

But the only unusual feature of this Nazi system was its extent. Greed is "an overriding theme in human affairs,"[22] and a principal motive of genocidal perpetrators and bystanders alike. The opportunity to strip victims of their wealth and property—either by looting it outright, or purchasing it at desperation prices—and to occupy their emptied dwellings appears again and again in accounts of genocide. The Vendée genocide of the 1790s, inflicted by French revolutionaries on the people of a rebellious region (Chapter 1), "was also intended as an asset-stripping enterprise, the final recorded tally of confiscated goods [being] 46,000 farm animals, 153,000 hundredweight of grain, 111,000 pounds of various metals, [and] a vast catalogue of other items, including fifty children's shirts."[23] As Armenians in 1915 were rounded up and massacred or driven away on death marches (Chapter 4), the US consul in Trebizond, Oscar Heizer, reported: "A crowd of Turkish women and children follow the police about like a lot of vultures and seize anything they can lay their hands on and when the more valuable things are carried out of the house by the police they rush in and take the balance. I see this performance every day with my own eyes."[24] At the height of Stalin's purges in the Soviet Union (Chapter 5), there was "frequent house-moving because every execution created a vacant apartment and dacha which were eagerly occupied by survivors and their aspirational Party housewives, ambitious for grander accommodation."[25] In Rwanda in 1994 (Chapter 9), would-be killers of Tutsis sometimes "didn't finish the job," a survivor recalled, "because they were in too much of a hurry to start looting. We could hear them getting into the cars, the vans, loading cases of Primus [beer], fighting over the furniture and everything else, rummaging under the beds for money."[26] "[We] had tasted comfort and overflowing plenty," one Hutu killer recalled. "Greed had corrupted us."[27]

Greed has been defined by Mark Levene as "the drive not only to take more than one needs, but to ingest much more than one could easily or safely manage."[28] It is intimately connected to the existential hunger for power, domination, and prestige. "Man does not strive for power only in order to enrich himself economically," noted the sociologist Max Weber. "Power, including economic power, may be valued 'for its own sake.' Very frequently the striving for power is also conditioned by the social 'honor' it entails."[29] "Functionalist" analysts of the Jewish Holocaust emphasize the eagerness with which underlings sought to implement Hitler's grand plans, generating a dynamic that was to a considerable degree independent of direct orders.[30] Simon Sebag Montefiore noted that in Stalin's USSR, a "Terror entrepreneurialism" reigned, with a "succession of ambitious torturers who were only too willing to please and encourage Stalin by finding Enemies and killing them for him."[31] Often these individuals were designated next for execution; but there were always upwardly mobile men and women waiting to take their place.[32] The direct material rewards were considerable: "When an apartment was vacated by the arrest of its inhabitants, it was often taken over by the NKVD [secret police] officers, or divided up and occupied by other servitors of the Stalinist regime, such as office workers and chauffeurs, some of whom had no doubt been rewarded for giving information on the previous occupants."[33]

Even a brief moment in the sun may be enough to motivate *genocidaires*, as with the "street boys, rag-pickers, [and] car-washers" whom Gerard Prunier described as vengefully targeting Tutsis in Rwanda's genocide (see p. 486).[34] Greed reflects objective material circumstances, but also, like narcissism, the core strivings of ego. Greed is never satiated; but when it is fed, one feels validated, successful—even omnipotent. Perhaps the only force that can truly match it as a motivator for genocide is *fear*.

Fear

"Men cannot look directly at either the sun or death," wrote French *philosophe* François La Rochefoucauld.[35] For women as well, "no power so effectively robs the mind of all its powers of acting and reasoning as fear," in the words of British statesman Edmund Burke.[36]

To grasp the central role of fear and psychological anxiety in genocide, it is worth distinguishing between *mortal terror* and *existential dread*. Mortal terror is largely an "animal" response to a perceived threat to physical survival and integrity. Existential dread revolves around a sense of personal identity, destiny, and social place. It evokes, or threatens to evoke, feelings of shame, dishonor, and humiliation—of ego extinction. On both planes, the threat *mortifies* us (from the Latin *mortificare*, "to put to death").[37]

Mortal terror is "animal fear," perhaps in a double sense. In a form that is often hard to distinguish from simple reflex, it is common across species. We may have derived our first sense of it as humans from animals themselves—predatory ones. In her book *Blood Rites*, Barbara Ehrenreich linked phenomena as disparate as separation anxiety in infants, religious rituals including human sacrifice, and intercommunal warfare to the terrifying encounter of prehumans and primitive humans with predatory beasts. "Nothing gets our attention like the prospect of being ripped apart, sucked dry, and transformed into another creature's meal," she wrote.[38] The predator may have been the original "Other," transformed—as humans gained the upper hand over the animal kingdom—into the predatory out-group. The human "Other" in turn bounded and delineated the in-group (clan, tribe, ethnic group) where one found sustenance and support, including in collective self-defense.[39] Evolutionary psychologists—those who apply evolutionary biology to psychology—deploy such connections to argue that "human behavior is driven by a set of *universal reasoning circuits* that were *designed by natural selection* to solve *adaptive problems* faced by our *hunter-gatherer ancestors*."[40] But social psychologists—studying people in situations of group interaction—have also found that subjects "who believe others will attack them respond with more aggression than they direct against targets who do not elicit such a belief."[41]

Mortal terror attains a particular pitch of intensity in the human animal, owing to our apparently unique capacity to foresee our own extinction, beyond a context of proximate physical threat.[42] In the eyes of some scholars and philosophers, the resulting "death anxiety" is the worm in humanity's psychic apple. It is a key factor, obviously, in religious belief, which offers an escape from death to a paradisiacal afterlife. It is also (frequently via the religious route) central to acts of genocide. In those acts resides an element of psychological projection—a displacement of the perpetrator's own death anxiety onto a scapegoat[43] over whom one wields a "death-defying," and death-inflicting, power. "Driven by nameless, overwhelming fears," wrote Israel Charny, "men turn to the primitive tools of self-protection, including the belief that they may spare themselves the terrible fate of death by sacrificing another instead of themselves."[44] As Ernest Becker likewise argued in what is still the most profound exploration of humans' death anxiety, *The Denial of Death*, "only scapegoats can relieve one of his own stark death fear: 'I am threatened with death—let us kill plentifully.'" Becker pointed to the "transference" of the fear of death onto quasi-immortal leader/*Führer* figures: "the more they have, the more rubs off on us. We participate in their immortality, and so we create immortals," and buttress their pathologies and atrocities with our collective support. We are also led blindly to support "rational," technological solutions, and to fetishize scientific progress, even when it has destructive, indeed (in the nuclear age) species-threatening consequences.[45]

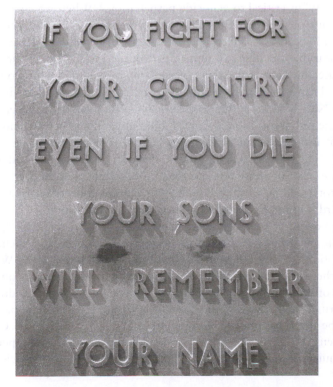

Figure 10.5 A plaque on the Askari war memorial in Dar es Salaam, Tanzania, promises transcendence to African soldiers who served in British forces during World War One. ". . . Binding oneself to the tribe," writes Donald G. Dutton, "serve[s] as a symbolic panacea for avoiding the terror of death," investing it instead with an aura of martyrdom and sacrifice.[46] The militants of Islamic State and Al-Qa'eda supply extreme examples (see chs. 1, 4).

Source: Author's photo, May 2013.

How has mortal terror influenced the course of genocides, both ancient and modern? Two of the central explanations offered for genocidal behavior—*peer pressure* and *fear of contamination/pollution*—merit attention. With regard to the former, both direct coercion and a more diffuse threat of alienation may obtain. In numerous genocides, perpetrators who refuse to kill—or witnesses who protest the killing—are at mortal risk of sharing the fate of victims. In sentencing the Bosnian Serb soldier Drazen Erdemovic in 1998 for his participation in the mass slaughter of Bosnian Muslim men and boys at Srebrenica (Chapter 8), for example, the Trial Chamber of the International Criminal Court for the Former Yugoslavia found in partial mitigation of Erdemovic's crime that "the accused committed the offence in question under threat of death." "Your Honour, I had to do this," Erdemovic had told the tribunal. ". . . When I [at first] refused, they [commanding officers] told me: 'If you are sorry for them, stand up, line up with them and we will kill you too.'"[47] Erdemovic received just five years' imprisonment for his participation. Likewise, in Rwanda in 1994, many Hutus who "were outraged to see such vicious killing and burning" nonetheless refrained from interfering, according to Christine Nyiransabimana, a Tutsi survivor. "But it was quite dangerous to do more than murmur in protest, because the *interahamwe* [genocidal militia] killed—without fooling around—any Hutus having friendly dealings with their Tutsi neighbors."[48] Great Lakes specialist René Lemarchand agreed that "many Hutu were driven to kill their Tutsi neighbors because they knew they had no other option; refusal to comply meant that they themselves would be killed the next day."[49]

With regard to more diffuse forms of peer pressure, Jacques Sémelin has noted "the fear of being rejected by the group and, in a broader sense, of being ostracised by society" as critical to genocide perpetration.[50] When we consider the German "ordinary men" studied by Christopher Browning, leading perpetrators of the Nazi "Holocaust by Bullets" on the eastern front in 1941–1942 (see Chapter 6), it is clear that the desire to remain part of the group (here, Police Battalion 101) was based on more than a sense of solidarity or belonging. In a context of extreme physical danger—in this case, the "barbarized" warfare evident from the first days of the Nazi-Soviet war (see pp. 125–126)—group belonging offered the best, perhaps the only protection available. Shunning and anathematization by the group, even if it did not lead to direct execution or incarceration for refusing to participate in genocidal killing (and it did not), had tangible and possibly mortal implications. Submersion in the group, meanwhile, allowed perpetrators to diffuse the moral burden of their atrocities in actions undertaken by the collective—a standard feature of genocidal praxis, as Sémelin has also noted.[51]

The question of contamination/pollution and the quest for "purity," particularly in an age of science and pseudo-science, are similarly anchored in human perceptions of physical vulnerability and inevitable mortality. We are separated from the world and its multifaceted, often microbial threats by only a thin membrane of skin. The advent of modern biological science has produced a discourse of "viruses" and "cancers" and "bacilli" in the genocides of the past century or so. But the quest for purity through extermination of an impure Other, one who threatens the physical existence and solidaristic bonds of the perpetrator's own community, is lodged deep in the human psyche and human societies.

Mark Levene has argued that genocidal propaganda "fails to mask the underlying, essentially psychopathological nature of the anxiety" over purity and contamination. It produces one of the most prevalent features of genocidal discourse: "a theme of creeping contagion, corruption and contamination of both the individual and the social organism."[52] As usual, the Nazis' anti-semitic propaganda provides no shortage of examples, such as the propaganda poster described by Dawid Rubinowicz, a Polish Jewish diarist, in 1942: "A Jew is shown mincing meat and putting a rat into the mincer. Another is pouring water from a bucket into milk. In the third picture a Jew is shown stamping dough with his feet and worms are crawling over him and the dough."[53]

Daniel Chirot and Clark McCauley ascribed a central significance to this factor in their 2006 volume *Why Not Kill Them All?* "Fear of pollution," they wrote, "is at once the most intense, but also the psychologically most difficult cause to understand for those who do not share the sentiment that a particular group is so polluting that its very presence creates a mortal danger. . . . We cannot understand the horror of Europe's wars of religion, or of Stalin's destruction of millions, without understanding the fear of pollution." Passionate attachment to the in-group "means necessarily hate for the threatening out-group," with an abiding "fear of pollution . . . lead[ing] us to what would otherwise seem to be incomprehensible mass murder."[54]

The quest for purity also takes the form of the "cults of antiquity and agriculture" explored by historian Ben Kiernan in his 2007 study, *Blood and Soil.* "Even as they require technological dominance," Kiernan wrote, "genocide and extermination betray a preoccupation with restoring purity and order. In racial or geographical terms, this often demands eradication of foreign contamination and return to an imagined pure origin."[55] Two vivid examples are the Balkan wars and Rwandan genocide of the 1990s (see Chapters 8 and 9). Prominent among Serbs' historical memories were the genocidal atrocities inflicted upon them by the fascist Ustashe regime in Croatia during the Second World War. The revival of Ustashe-style symbolism and rhetoric by Franjo Tudjman's Croatian nationalist regime both evoked and marshaled deep anxieties, heightened when discrimination began against Serb professionals and officials within Croatia. In these varied ways "the Croats signaled the reasonableness of Serb fears," which was then "manipulated by Slobodan Milosevic, who needed the Croat issue to secure his power."[56]

The Rwandan holocaust of 1994 occurred in the aftermath of a massive (1993) blood-letting in neighboring Burundi, where between 50,000 and 100,000 civilians, overwhelmingly Hutus, were massacred by the Tutsi-dominated military following a failed coup. Some 350,000 Hutus fled to Rwanda, bringing firsthand accounts of atrocities; among these refugees were some of the most unrestrained genocidal killers of Tutsis in 1994.[57] The slaughter revived memories of an even greater killing of Hutus in 1972, when an "eliticidal" attempt was made to exterminate virtually all Hutus who had education or professional status (mainly adult males). Combined with the Tutsi-led rebel invasion of Rwanda in 1990, an "image of the Tutsi as the embodiment of a mortal danger . . . [was] hauntingly evident," according to René Lemarchand.[58] Scott Straus's study of perpetrators found "that most perpetrators participated in violence because they feared the consequences of not doing so. . . . What comes through [in interviews] . . . is a sense of acute insecurity, even panic, in the face of the president's death and the advancing Tutsi rebels."[59]

Even in the prototypical case of genocide against a completely defenseless and objectively non-threatening population—the Jewish Holocaust—mortal terror may have figured, though in heavily hystericized form. As Raul Hilberg notes, "the Germans drew a picture of an international Jewry ruling the world and plotting the destruction of Germany and German life."[60] "If we didn't defend ourselves, the Jews would exterminate us," Nazi propaganda chief Joseph Goebbels declared in March 1942. "It is a life-or-death struggle between the Aryan race and the Jewish microbe."[61] Linking Jews with bolshevism/communism created a fear-evoking dimension that was *not* purely hysterical, in the sense that Soviet Russia and Slavic civilization did pose logical threats to the German heartland.[62] (Ironically, the Jews were also depicted as *capitalist* plutocrats, plotting the subjugation, exploitation, and destruction of non-Jews everywhere. The only consistency in the portrait was thus the psychopathological hatred pervading it.)

Mortal terror contains a strong element of psychological *projection*. One justifies genocidal designs by imputing such designs to perceived opponents. The Tutsis/Croatians/Jews/Bolsheviks must be killed because they harbor intentions to kill us, and will do so if they are not stopped/prevented/annihilated. Before they are killed, they are brutalized, debased, and dehumanized—turning them into something approaching "subhumans" or "animals" and, by a circular logic, justifying their extermination. A central aspect of this psychological dynamic is inflicting acts of mutilation, including on corpses. Sémelin has described this very well:

> Cruelty is truly a mental operation on the body of the other, intended to destroy his humanity. . . . And why stop once one has started? Why not continue dismembering the body, cutting off a woman's breasts, a man's penis, breaking their limbs? The vertigo of impunity hurls the executioner into a bottomless pit of cruelty. This spiral of bodily destruction can even continue after death. Although bereft of life, bodies can still resemble the living. And so they must be scalped, torn into pieces, crushed into unrecognisable objects; or, even worse, arranged in a variety of unimaginably grotesque positions, or carved up into pieces to turn them into waste material or even rubbish. In all these various acts of cutting and disemboweling it is the executioner who is protecting himself. Seen in this way, the perpetration of atrocities is the means by which perpetrators establish their own radical psychological distance from the victims, and convince themselves that these are in no way, and no longer, human beings.[63]

Projection also assists in displacing guilt and blame from genocidal perpetrators to their victims.[64] Wolfgang Sofsky noted that the Nazis designated Jews as the principal guards and hands-on oppressors of fellow Jews in the concentration camps, as well as those (the *Sonderkommandos*) who carried out much of the industrial processing of corpses in the death camps. It is "as though [the Nazi regime] wished to prove that the members of the subrace accepted any degradation and even killed one another: as though it wished to shift the burden of guilt onto the victims themselves."[65] In southwestern Rwanda, where thousands of Tutsis were reduced to hiding lice-ridden in swamps scoured by their would-be killers, a Tutsi survivor,

Innocent Rwililiza, recalled: "I believe that seeing us like that, living like worthless wild things, made the Hutus' work easier for them. Especially for those who were not consumed with a killing hatred." When caught, they were regularly exposed to torture, humiliation, and mutilative atrocity before being killed. "I feel . . . that they cut and mutilated to take humanity away from the Tutsis and kill them more easily that way," Rwililiza said.[66]

The possibility of physical/psychological displacement and dispossession is foundational to existential dread. "Desperation is a theme that runs through a great deal of ethnic violence," wrote Donald Horowitz. "A good many groups are convinced that they are or soon will be swamped, dominated, and dispossessed by their neighbors, perhaps even rendered extinct."[67] Since the physical annihilation of the individual is not impending, existential dread may appear subordinate to mortal terror. To view it as such would be a serious error. Group identity is so supreme a value that many individuals will sacrifice their lives to defend it. Likewise, people will often choose physical death over existential shame, dishonor, or loss of status and "respect" before one's peers.[68] Time-honored codes of warriorhood, masculine honor, and female virginity/sexual fidelity provide examples.

Finally, one should recognize that fear is pivotal to feelings of *humiliation*. As Chirot and McCauley wrote, this linkage is "why 'prestige' is so often important. Those who feel that their prestige has been diminished [i.e., that they have been humiliated] then feel they are vulnerable because they are seen as weak. This might embolden their enemies."[69] We turn to this phenomenon next.

Humiliation

> If I've learned one thing covering world affairs, it's this: The single most underappreciated force in international relations is humiliation.
>
> Thomas Friedman, *New York Times* columnist

What Friedman perceived in global affairs, psychologists and others have explored at the level of the individual. Humiliation is defined by Evelin Lindner as "the enforced lowering of a person or group, a process of subjugation that damages or strips away their pride, honor or dignity."[70] It is increasingly recognized as a primary motivating force in human behavior, particularly violent behavior. Lindner cited Suzanne Retzinger and Thomas Scheff's finding that "humiliated fury" plays a major role "in escalating conflict between individuals and nations."[71] Robert Jay Lifton wrote that "Humiliation involves feelings of shame and disgrace, as well as helplessness in the face of abuse at the hands of a stronger party. These are among the most painful and indelible of human emotions. He who has known extreme shame and humiliation may forever struggle to recover a sense of agency and self-respect."[72] Psychologist James Gilligan, who conducted research among hardened convicts in US prisons, went so far as to argue that "the basic psychological motive, or cause, of violent behavior is the wish to ward off or eliminate the feeling of shame and humiliation—a feeling that is painful and can even be intolerable and overwhelming—and replace it with its opposite, the feeling of pride."[73]

Humiliation thus features prominently in the most extreme manifestations of human aggression: murder, war, genocide. Indeed, it is difficult to find a historical or contemporary case of genocide in which humiliation is not a key motivating force.[74] It suffices to consider the three best-known genocides of the twentieth century:

- In the case of the Ottoman destruction of minority Christians (Chapter 4), the Young Turk authorities in Constantinople were humiliated by military defeats in the Balkans and northern Africa (1909–1913), and by the secession of imperial territories including Serbia, Bulgaria, and Albania. "Turks have awoken a national spirit, a national grudge," wrote the Turkish historian M. Cemil Bilsel. "They have infected people with a spirit that longs one day to settle accounts for the humiliation and oppression suffered by Turkdom."[75] In so doing, they were also humiliated by the presence of religious and ethnic minorities in their midst (overwhelmingly Christian) that played a prominent "middleman" role in the economy, and were supposedly assisting foreign plots against Turkey at a time of great vulnerability (the First World War). Moreover, it appears that Turkish authorities and commentators today would experience a sense of humiliation if they acknowledged and apologized for the Armenian and other genocides. Humiliation is thus a key underpinning of the government's campaign of genocide denial.[76]
- The Nazis rose to national prominence by exploiting national humiliation, which they translated into vengefulness and hatred against Germany's supposed tormentors. After four years of fighting in the First World War, the Germans were stunned by their army's collapse on the Western Front late in 1918. The defeated forces flooding back across the Rhine formed the core of the extreme right-wing groups that proliferated in the early 1920s—including one around Adolf Hitler, whose writings and statements blaze with anger at Germany's humiliation.[77] Outrage and humiliation greeted the imposition of the punitive Versailles Treaty in 1919, further fueling extremist and revanchist movements. Humiliation sought an outlet in scapegoating; the Nazis argued that it was the Jews who had delivered Germany a treacherous "stab in the back" to prostrate the country before the Western Allies, Bolshevism, and capitalism. As Germany moved from hyperinflation in the 1920s to the Great Depression at decade's end, economic pressures and privation added to feelings of humiliation, especially among men whose self-image was intimately bound up with their "provider" status.[78]
- In Rwanda under Belgian colonialism, Tutsis were taught that they were descended from the "civilized" peoples of the Nile region, while Hutus were depicted as unrefined bumpkins. Tutsis were viewed (and came to view themselves) as tall, powerful, educated, attractive; Hutus as the humiliating antithesis. The 1959 revolution establishing Hutu political dominance was represented as a vanquishing of humiliation for the Hutu masses. Now Tutsis would be put "in their place." But when a Tutsi exile movement invaded from Rwanda in 1990, Hutu hegemony was threatened. The descent into economic crisis around the same time meant humiliating unemployment for hundreds of thousands of Hutus—again especially poignantly for adult men, who would be conscripted in huge numbers as agents of the genocide.

Humiliation also figures strongly in subaltern genocide, the "genocides by the oppressed" discussed in Chapter 1. There are, of course, both fantasies and realities of oppression. Nearly every *génocidaire* considers himself or herself oppressed by the target group: Turks by Christians, Germans by Jews, Hutus by Tutsis, Serbs by Kosovars, and so on. In many cases, these framings are the product of mythmaking and paranoia. In other instances, there may be a more objective character to the convictions. Hutus in Rwanda *had* experienced social subordination and humiliation at Tutsi hands. The Kosovar KLA extremists who waged a low-level campaign of persecution and—arguably—genocide against Serbs in Kosovo were motivated by years of Serb brutalization and oppression (Chapter 8). Islamist terrorism (see pp. 60–61) also carries a tinge of subaltern genocide: its exponents keenly feel the humiliation of centuries of conquest and domination by Western "Crusaders." "What America is tasting now is only a copy of what we have tasted," declaimed Osama bin Laden. "Our Islamic nation has been tasting the same for more than 80 years, of humiliation and disgrace."[79] Commentators have often wondered how relatively privileged Arabs—even those directly exposed to and benefiting from the prosperity and cosmopolitanism of the West—can come to plan and perpetrate terrorist attacks that may include genocidal massacres. Humiliation is key to understanding this phenomenon; the educated and privileged may feel it even more powerfully than the masses.[80]

Finally, humiliation mingled with fear is central to an understanding of a commonly noted phenomenon in genocide: the use of dispossessed minorities and rootless refugees as perpetrators of mass atrocities. In considering imperialism and colonialism in Chapter 2, we cited Mark Levene's insight that the Scottish and Irish populations exposed to genocidal or proto-genocidal atrocities at English hands often supplied the vanguard of genocides against indigenous peoples in the Americas and Australia. "Brutalised by their previous experience, still looked down upon by their Anglo 'betters' as little more than savages themselves—the 'Scum of the Earth' and 'Refuse of Mankind,' not to say 'like the Goths and Vandals of old'—it was perhaps not that surprising that some of their number became serious native exterminators in their own right."[81] Other examples include the uprooted Balkan Muslims of the Ottoman Empire, who were readily turned against Christian populations during World War One; and the Burundian Hutus who fled Tutsi-sponsored terror in their homeland, took refuge in neighboring Rwanda, and are considered by some to have been especially eager tormentors of Tutsis during the 1994 genocide (see note 57).[82]

THE PSYCHOLOGY OF PERPETRATORS

> The father of two little kids like [you], how do you shoot babies?
> I don't know. It's just one of them things.
>> Exchange between CBS reporter Mike Wallace and Paul Meadlo,
>> a leading perpetrator of the My Lai massacre in Vietnam,
>> 1968 (see pp. 553–556)

In 1992, Christopher Browning published his groundbreaking book *Ordinary Men*, about a battalion of German police reservists and conscripts—mostly middle-aged men too old for active military service—who functioned as a killing squad on the eastern front in 1941–1942. "The men of Reserve Police Battalion 101 were the unlikeliest of mass murderers. They did not represent special selection or even random selection. . . . They were simply ordinary people who went about completing the murderous tasks assigned them with considerable indifference."[83] As Daniel Goldhagen demonstrated in *Hitler's Willing Executioners*, these tasks included corralling and executing Jews and "saboteurs," including children and women, with rifle shots to the back of the head. Often the men emerged spattered with blood and brain matter. The sheer gruesomeness of their task led some to accept their commanding officer's offer to absent themselves from the slaughter without penalty. But surprisingly few bowed out: Browning estimates that 80 to 90 percent of the battalion eventually participated in close-up mass killings of Jews. Others felt queasy at the outset, but accustomed themselves to the killing, even coming to enjoy it. Some initially excused themselves, then returned. Most numbed themselves with intoxicants—a typical tactic of *génocidaires*, since alcohol and drugs "have the advantage of suppressing the individual's inhibitions and immersing him in an artificial state of well-being or even euphoria that helps him function in the blood and death-stained environment in which he is operating."[84]

How to explain this routinized participation in acts of unimaginable horror? Although criticized by Goldhagen for downplaying the role of Jew-hatred in the murders, Browning *did* acknowledge that the "deluge of racist and anti-Semitic propaganda" played a key role.[85] But he placed additional emphasis on "the mutually intensifying effects of war and racism"; obedience to authority; peer pressure and the "threat of isolation" from the group (with possibly mortal consequences in wartime); machismo; and feelings of obligation, duty, and honor. Browning's student, Waitman Wade Beorn, in a 2014 study of *Wehrmacht* (German regular army) formations during the early stages of the "Holocaust by Bullets" in Belarus, likewise recognized the "ideological penetration of Nazi values as an explanation." He noted importantly that *Wehrmacht* complicity in Jew-killings and "Jew hunts" was evident from the first stages of the war, when the "brutalization" highlighted by Omer Bartov had yet to really take hold (see pp. 125–126). This reflected not only a widespread anti-semitic disposition, but also a culture of atrocity in the German armed forces, evident during the First World War and the genocidal slaughter of the Hereros and Namas (see Chapter 3). In addition, Beorn pointed to the influence of leadership factors, unit culture and peer pressure, gender conditioning, and the typical greed of the *conquistador* for material benefits and coerced sex.[86]

The Milgram experiments

I was speechless. And then I finally said I didn't really feel I was suited for this assignment. He [the superior officer] was, you know, very friendly, very sympathetic . . . He said he understood well that that would be my first reaction but that I had to remember that my being asked to take this job showed proof of their exceptional trust in me. It was a most difficult task—they fully recognized it—but . . . I myself would have nothing whatever to do with the actual [killing] operation; this was carried out entirely by doctors and nurses. I was merely to be responsible for law and order.

> Franz Stangl, commander of the Treblinka death camp, describing his introduction to mass murder as a functionary of the Nazis' T-4 "euthanasia" program of the mentally and physically handicapped (see pp. 372–374). Many of those who worked in the T4 program, like Stangl, went on to higher-profile roles in the Jewish Holocaust.

Among the research highlighted by Christopher Browning in his book *Ordinary Men* was the twentieth century's most famous series of psychological studies. Conducted by Stanley Milgram at Yale University beginning in the early 1960s, it has been known since as "the Milgram experiments."[87] The basic design was elegantly simple, yet open to complex variations. A mild-mannered and agreeable middle-aged man, an accountant by profession, was trained to serve as the "learner" of the experiments (Figure 10.6). He was placed on one side of a wall, and a designated subject (the "teacher") was seated on the other, in front of a generator supposedly capable of administering shocks of increasing voltage to the learner. "The generator had thirty different switches running in fifteen-volt increments from 15 to 450 volts," wrote James Waller. "The higher levels of shock were labeled in big letters as 'Intense Shock,' 'Extreme Intensity Shock,' 'Danger: Severe Shock,' and, ominously, 'XXX.'" To give the subject a taste of the treatment supposedly to be meted out to the learner, he or she was administered a shock of 45 volts—"a level strong enough to be distinctly unpleasant." As the subject asked questions of the learner, incorrect answers were met with commands from a white-coated authority figure (the "experimenter") for the subject to administer "shocks" of ever-greater intensity to the learner. "At 300 volts, the learner vigorously pounded on the laboratory walls in protest. . . . The learner's pounding was repeated after 315 volts. Afterward, he was not heard from again," but the subject was instructed to disregard this, and to continue to turn the dial.[88]

The greatest shock of all was the experiment's results, which have echoed through the disciplines of psychology and sociology ever since. An absolute majority of subjects—twenty-six out of forty—"*obeyed the orders of the experimenter to the end*, proceeding to punish the victim until they reached the most potent shock available on the generator."[89] Sometimes they did so stoically and dispassionately: the face of one subject is described as "hard, impassive . . . showing total indifference as he subdues the screaming learner and gives him shocks. He seems to derive no pleasure from the act itself, only quiet satisfaction at doing his job properly."[90] Most subjects, however, displayed tension, stress, concern, confusion, shame. When the experimental design was altered to make the learner dimly visible, some subjects sought to avoid the consequences of their actions by "avert[ing] their eyes from the person they were shocking, often turning their heads in an awkward and conspicuous manner."[91] But the experimenter assured them that he took full responsibility for the subject's actions. Moreover, the subject was told that he or she had "no other choice"; his or her continued participation was "essential." Despite clear misgivings, as noted above, the majority of subjects not only administered the "shocks" but stayed the course to the end.[92] A fair number projected their

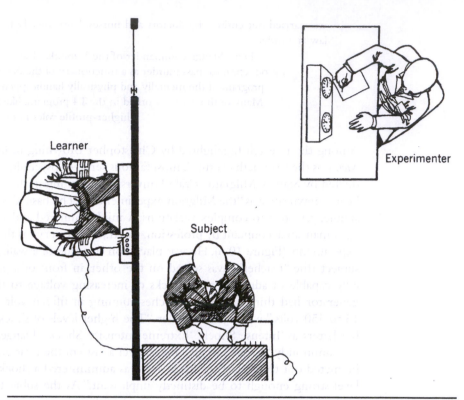

Figure 10.6 The core of the Milgram experiments: an authority figure (the Experimenter, top right) commands a Subject to administer supposed shocks when the Learner answers a question incorrectly. The Subject is instructed to increase the voltage as the Learner (an actor) conveys first pain, then ominous silence. How far will an ordinary Subject turn the dial?

Source: Stanley Milgram, *Obedience to Authority* (New York: Random House, 1995). Used by permission.

own stress and shame on to the learner, blaming him "for having volunteered for the experiment, and more viciously, for his stupidity and obstinacy." Interestingly, the obedience displayed by women "was virtually identical to the performance of men," though "the level of conflict experienced by the women was on the whole higher than that felt by our male [subjects]."[93] Variations on the core experiment helped Milgram to zero in on some of the factors affecting obedience. Subjects placed in greater physical proximity to the learner, even touching him, were less likely to proceed than those more remotely positioned: "the changing set of spatial relations leads to a potentially shifting set of alliances over the several experimental conditions." Christopher Browning noted that "when not under the direct surveillance of the scientist, many of the subjects 'cheated' by giving lower shocks than prescribed."[94] When an ordinary-seeming person was substituted for the white-coated experimenter, "only a third as many [subjects] followed the common man as followed the experimenter." Furthermore, when other "subjects" were added and secretly instructed to rebel against the authority figure, "the effects of [such] peer rebellion [were] very impressive in undercutting the experimenter's authority." This led Milgram to conclude that "the mutual support provided by men for each other is the strongest bulwark we have against the excesses of authority." In a point relevant to our discussion of gender and genocide (Chapter 13), Milgram noted that selecting an adult male for the "learner" role probably affected the outcome. "As victims, [women] would most likely generate more disobedience, for cultural norms militate against hurting women even more strongly than hurting men. . . . Similarly, if a child were placed in the victim's role, disobedience would be much greater."[95]

Milgram summarized his results, which have been confirmed by dozens of subsequent studies:[96]

> What is surprising is how far ordinary individuals will go in complying with the experimenter's instructions. . . . It is the extreme willingness of adults to go to almost any lengths on the command of an authority that constitutes the chief finding of the study and the fact most urgently demanding explanation. . . . Ordinary people, simply doing their jobs, and without any particular hostility on their part, can become agents in a terrible destructive process. Moreover, even when the destructive effects of their work become patently clear, and they are asked to carry out actions incompatible with fundamental standards of morality, relatively few people have the resources needed to resist authority.[97]

Milgram emphasized that "every sign of tension" among the subjects was "evidence of the failure of authority to transform the [subject] to an unalloyed state of agency."[98] There was at least a latent capacity and desire to resist. In this context, it is worth examining the comportment of the minority of subjects who refused to "shock" the learner. One was a professor of Old Testament studies, who may have drawn on his religious convictions:

> EXPERIMENTER: It's absolutely essential to the experiment that we continue.
> SUBJECT: I understand that statement, but I don't understand why the experiment is placed above this person's life.
> EXPERIMENTER: There is no permanent tissue damage.
> SUBJECT: Well, that's your opinion. If he [the learner] doesn't want to continue, I'm taking orders from him.
> EXPERIMENTER: You have no other choice, sir, you must go on.
> SUBJECT: If this were Russia maybe, but not in America.[99]

Another subject, an industrial engineer, grew "incredulous and indignant" when ordered to continue administering the shocks:

> EXPERIMENTER: You have no other choice.
> MR. RENSALEER: I *do* have a choice. . . . Why don't I have a choice? I came here on my own free will. I thought I could help in a research project. But if I have to hurt somebody to do that, or if I was in his place, too, I wouldn't stay there. I can't continue. I'm very sorry. I think I've gone too far already, probably.[100]

To anticipate our discussion of the psychology of "rescuers," below, the resisters demonstrated a high degree of empathy for the learner—and of ego independence, symbolized by their refusal to submit blindly to an authority figure.[101] But they were, to repeat, a minority. Milgram voiced his expectation that outside of the laboratory environment—and especially in conditions of dictatorship or totalitarianism—they would be fewer still.

In his account of the experiments, Milgram moved beyond psychology to the sociology of modernity and bureaucratic complexity, which granted individuals a large measure of physical and psychological distance from the consequences of their actions. It is not surprising, therefore, to find the sociologist Zygmunt Bauman drawing on Milgram's work to support his contention that "the process of rationalization facilitates behaviour that is inhuman and cruel."[102] This theme is explored further in the discussion in Chapter 11 of sociological perspectives on genocide.

The Stanford prison experiments

Other insights into the psychology of genocide and group violence may be drawn from a second classic set of experiments, conducted by a Stanford University team under the social psychologist Philip Zimbardo in 1971. These were described in detail in Zimbardo's 2008 book, *The Lucifer Effect*.

"The rationale is this," Zimbardo told his team of researchers:

> ... Our research will attempt to differentiate between what people bring into a prison situation from what the situation brings out in the people who are there. By preselection, our subjects are generally representative of middle-class, educated youth. They are a homogeneous group of students who are quite similar to each other in many ways. By randomly assigning them to the two different roles, we begin with "guards" and "prisoners" who are comparable—indeed, are interchangeable. The prisoners are not more violent, hostile, or rebellious than the guards, and the guards aren't more power-seeking authoritarians. At this moment "prisoner" and "guard" are one and alike. . . . In two weeks, will these youngsters still be so indistinguishable? Will their roles change their personalities? Will we see any transformations of their character?[103]

Zygmunt Bauman summarized the course and consequences of the experiment as follows:

> In Zimbardo's experiment (planned for a fortnight, but stopped after one week for fear of irreparable damage to the body and mind of the subjects) volunteers had been divided at random into prisoners and prison guards. Both sides were given the symbolic trappings of their position. Prisoners, for example, wore tight caps which simulated shaven heads, and gowns which made them appear ridiculous. Their guards were put in uniforms and given dark glasses which hid their eyes from being looked into by the prisoners. No side was allowed

Figure 10.7 Dr. Philip Zimbardo, creator of the Stanford University prison experiments in 1971, went on to serve as an expert witness in the trials of US soldiers accused of abuses at the Abu Ghraib prison west of Baghdad, Iraq. In both instances, Zimbardo argued, the authoritarian environment of the prison (whether real or experimental) produced aberrant and abusive behavior by otherwise ordinary individuals. He is shown here on the Stanford campus in March 2007.

Source: Photo by Shams Shaikh.

to address the other by name; strict impersonality was the rule. There was [a] long list of petty regulations invariably humiliating for the prisoners and stripping them of human dignity. This was the starting point. What followed surpassed and left far behind the designers' ingenuity. The initiative of the guards (randomly selected males of college age, carefully screened against any sign of abnormality) knew no bounds. . . . The construed superiority of the guards rebounded in the submissiveness of the prisoners, which in its turn tempted the guards into further displays of their powers, which were then duly reflected in more self-humiliation on the part of the prisoners. . . . The guards forced the prisoners to chant filthy songs, to defecate in buckets which they did not allow them to empty, to clean toilets with bare hands; the more they did it, the more they acted as if they were convinced of the non-human nature of the prisoners, and the less they felt constrained in inventing and administering measures of an ever-more appalling degree of inhumanity.[104]

Bauman slightly overstates the case. In fact, the guards divided into three factions, with about one-third assuming "cruel, callous, sadistic, dominating, authoritarian, tyrannical, coercive, and aggressive roles." James Waller described a middle group as "tough but fair," while a final segment "emerged as 'good guards' and tried to help the prisoners when they could."[105] Christopher Browning pointed out that the behavior of Zimbardo's guards was strikingly similar to that of the "ordinary men" he studied for his eponymous book—from the "nucleus of increasingly enthusiastic killers who volunteered," through those who "performed . . . when assigned but who did not seek opportunities to kill," through "a small group (less than 20 percent) of refusers and evaders."[106] However, it must be remembered that Zimbardo's experiment was terminated after only a few days; it is impossible to say how many of the "tough but fair" group and the hold-outs would eventually have behaved sadistically, had it continued.

To the public, Zimbardo's results were as shocking as Milgram's. They depicted "the sudden transmogrification of likeable and decent American boys into near monsters of the kind allegedly to be found only in places like Auschwitz or Treblinka."[107] Contemporary readers are likely to think of the American men and women who abused inmates at Abu Ghraib prison near Baghdad, along with many other sites in occupied Iraq and at the US-run prison at Guantánamo Bay, Cuba. Indeed, in the wake of the Abu Ghraib revelations, many commentators cited the Zimbardo experiments as evidence that (in the words of criminologist David Wilson) "if you give a person power over someone who is powerless, someone who has been demonised or made to seem less human, then that absolute power corrupts absolutely."[108] Zimbardo himself offered expert counsel to the defense in one of the trials of Abu Ghraib perpetrators.

Viewing the lessons of the Stanford experiment from a quarter-century's perspective, Zimbardo wrote that it showed how

> within certain powerful social settings, human nature can be transformed in ways as dramatic as the chemical transformation in Robert Louis Stevenson's captivating fable of Dr. Jekyll and Mr. Hyde.... Good people can be induced, seduced, and initiated into behaving in evil ways. They can also be led to act in irrational, stupid, self-destructive, antisocial, and mindless ways when they are immersed in "total situations" that impact human nature in ways that challenge our sense of the stability and consistency of individual personality, of character, and of morality.... The [experiment] is a clarion call to abandon simplistic notions of the Good Self dominating Bad Situations. We are best able to avoid, prevent, challenge, and change such negative situational forces only by recognizing their potential power to "infect us," as it has others who were similarly situated.[109]

THE PSYCHOLOGY OF RESCUERS

> I simply had to do it, there was nothing else for it, there was no other way. I did not even think long about it, not at all . . . I just couldn't act in any other way.
>
> Otto Jodmin, Holocaust rescuer

> I have to be at peace with myself, what others think about me is not important. It is my own conscience that I must please and not the opinion of others.
>
> Janka Polanska, Holocaust rescuer

Even in the darkest hour, a "Good Self" does seem able to trump Zimbardo's "Bad Situations"—or at least appear regularly enough to be notable. The historical record is replete with accounts of brutal perpetrators, and bystanders whose "neutrality . . . helps the stronger party in an unequal struggle."[110] But it is also filled with testimonials to the brave individuals who interceded to save total strangers (as well as friends and acquaintances) from genocide.

The most famous of these figures are associated with the Jewish Holocaust, in part because that campaign of mass murder is better known and documented than all the others put together. Many readers will be familiar with the extraordinary collective opposition mounted by the people of Nazi-occupied Denmark, which, it should be conceded, had been "awarded a degree of autonomy that was unusual for a region under German occupation." In 1943, Nazi officials encountered "a local population unanimous in its resolve" to preserve Danish Jews from round-up and extermination. Virtually the entire Jewish population, several thousand strong, was successfully transferred by the operators of small boats to safety in neutral Sweden. According to Raul Hilberg, "help came from every quarter. The Danish police shielded the operators by warning them of danger, individuals helped to sell Jewish belongings, taxi drivers transported the Jews to the ports, house and apartment owners offered the victims shelter, Pastor Krohn [an advocate for the Jews] handed out blank baptismal certificates, druggists supplied free stimulants to keep people awake, and so on." It was, wrote Hilberg, "one of the most remarkable rescue operations in history."[111]

Less well known, but comparable in scale, was the preservation of Bulgaria's historic Jewish population. Bulgarian claims to a rescuer role must be qualified. Jews in Macedonia, western Thrace,[112] as well as the Dobrudja region, occupied by Bulgaria under the terms of its alliance with the Nazi-dominated Axis, were surrendered to be deported and murdered. But as the Holocaust raged, the Jewish population of this Axis ally—at least within its prewar boundaries—was totally preserved. "Through a mixture of state stonewalling and widespread elite but also demotic [popular] resistance," noted Mark Levene, the Bulgarian state "not only halted Jewish deportations from Bulgaria *intégrale* but prevented the Germans from attempting to restart them. Indeed, the manner in which Orthodox Church, parliament—the Sobranje—and the wider public mobilized to non-violently thwart the programme, including a plan by leading clergy to lie down on the tracks in front of the deportation trains, is quite exemplary."[113]

Among individual rescuers of Jews, at least before the release of Steven Spielberg's film *Schindler's List*—about the exploits of a German industrialist who saved hundreds of Jews from the gas chambers of Auschwitz-Birkenau (see Figure 10.9)—the most renowned was probably a Swedish representative in Budapest, Raoul Wallenberg:

> In 1944 the United States belatedly established the War Refugee Board (WRB) to aid and rescue the victims of Nazism. Fearing the imminent deportation of Hungarian Jewry, the WRB solicited the help of a number of neutral countries to protect this endangered community. Sweden embraced the American proposal and appointed Wallenberg as a special envoy to Hungary whose sole mission was to avert the deportation of Jews. Taking advantage of his diplomatic immunity and money contributed by private organizations like the American Jewish Joint Distribution Committee, Wallenberg issued bogus Swedish "protective passports," rented apartment buildings to serve as Jewish sanctuaries under Swedish protection, and personally whisked hundreds of Hungarian Jews off German transports on the pretext that they were wards of Sweden. Wallenberg's example inspired other neutral embassies and the International Red Cross office in Budapest to protect Jews too. According to some estimates, the rescue campaign launched by Wallenberg may have saved as many as 100,000 Jews.[114]

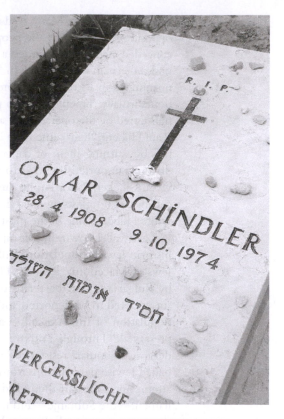

Figure 10.8 Pastor André and Magda Trocmé led the village of Le Chambon-sur-Lignon in its resistance to Nazi and French-collaborationist roundups of Jews in "Vichy" France. The collective efforts of thousands of villagers saved thousands of Jews.[115]

Source: Chambon Foundation.

Figure 10.9 Tombstone of Oskar Schindler in a cemetery in Jerusalem, Israel. Schindler's famous "list" protected hundreds of Jews from the gas chambers, though in postwar life his business ventures failed, and he had to be kept materially afloat by grateful survivors.

Source: Author's photo, May 2011.

In the grimmest of ironies, Wallenberg the rescuer survived the Nazis, only to disappear into the custody of Soviet forces occupying Hungary. For reasons unknown, he appears to have spent years in detention before finally dying in the camps sometime in the 1950s.[116]

Equally striking is the story of Chiune Sugihara (Figure 10.10), the Japanese consul in Lithuania, who received a flood of Jews fleeing the Nazi-Soviet invasion of Poland in 1939. Sugihara

> willingly issued them transit visas by considerably stretching his own government's official rules, allowing the Polish Jews to cross Soviet territory en route to Japan and, from there, to anywhere they wished. Before the Japanese government reassigned him, Sugihara issued some 4,500 visas, many of them handwritten, and he did not stop issuing visas until literally the moment before his train carried him out. . . . His visas were also easy to counterfeit.

Figure 10.10 Chiune Sugihara, the Japanese consul in Kaunas, Lithuania, who defied higher-ups to issue Japanese visas to thousands of Jews in 1941, enabling them to flee the advancing Nazis.

Source: Wikimedia Commons.

Combined with those forgeries, Sugihara's efforts may well have saved some 10,000 Jews.[117]

"I cannot allow these people to die, people who had come to me for help with death staring them in the eyes"—so Sugihara recollected his feelings later. "Whatever punishment may be imposed upon me, I know I should follow my conscience. . . . I acted according to my sense of human justice, out of love for mankind."[118]

Famous rescuers such as these took advantage of (and often risked) their professional positions to undertake their missions; but, of course, millions of people in the twentieth century alone utilized their occupational and bureaucratic positions to kill rather than save. What distinguishes individuals who choose to shelter and assist those at mortal risk of genocide, often at mortal risk to themselves?

In many cases, religious motivations played an important role. At its best and most humane, religion embodies universal values of compassion and mercy (see Chapter 16). Thus we find the Catholic cleric, Dompropst Bernard Lichtenberg of Berlin, rejecting the passivity and anti-semitism of the church hierarchy, and daring "to pray publicly for all Jews, baptized [as Christians] or not." When his efforts failed to save Jews from transportation to the death camps, he "*demanded that he be allowed to join [them] on their journey to the East*." He was imprisoned, and picked up by the Gestapo upon his release; he died *en route* to Dachau.[119] Less demonstrative but no less religiously imbued were the actions of the "kind and gentle" Muslim notably recalled by a survivor of the Armenian genocide, who found refuge in his home:

> The bey followed Islamic law to the letter and was a devout believer. He prayed five times a day and fasted one month out of the year. I used to join him in these [observances]. He had also made a pilgrimage to Mecca and was thus

called "Haji." He was a principled and just man. He felt genuine sorrow for the Armenian massacre and considered it a sin to bring any confiscated Armenian possessions into his home. He used to condemn the Turkish government, saying, "The Armenians are a hardy, intelligent, and industrious people. If there are any guilty among them, the government can arrest and punish them instead of slaughtering a helpless and innocent people."[120]

However, it is also the case that "more intense religiosity is frequently associated with greater prejudice" (Chapter 16);[121] and in any case, religious belief is by no means necessary to rescuers. Often it matters only that someone be "so overcome by the human tragedy of the genocide" that she or he feels impelled to intercede. During the Rwanda catastrophe of 1994, Paul Rusesabagina, Hutu proprietor of the Hotel Mille Collines in Kigali, saved nearly 1,300 refugees—mostly Tutsi, as was his wife—from slaughter by Hutu militias, preserving them for the full two-and-a-half months of the genocide. Rusesabagina "rationed water from the swimming pool, had checkpoints removed, bribed killers with money and Scotch whisky and kept a secret telephone line open to the outside world." "I wanted to keep my people, the refugees, safe," he told a suddenly interested world. "That was my main objective and I tried to keep that up to the end . . . I rather take myself as someone who did his duties and responsibilities, someone who remained until the end when others changed completely their professions, and most of them became killers and others were killed."[122] The 2004 film of Rusesabagina's exploits, *Hotel Rwanda*, brought international attention to this rescuer.

Figure 10.11 Paul Rusesabagina, *Hotel Rwanda* rescuer, at a conference on the Rwandan genocide in Ann Arbor, Michigan, March 2014.

Source: Gerald R. Ford School of Public Policy, University of Michigan/Creative Commons/Flickr.

BOX 10.1 "KEEP YOUR PEOPLE IN PLACE. MY GUNS ARE ON YOU": HUGH THOMPSON, JR. AND THE MY LAI MASSACRE

Figure 10.12 Lt.-Col. Hugh Thompson, Jr., in his official army portrait prior to the My Lai massacre.

Source: US Army/Wikimedia Commons.

The *Einsatzgruppen-style* massacre of hundreds of defenseless civilians at My Lai (see the photo essay, photo 8) produced no shortage of villains. But it also gave rise to a truly heroic act of genocide rescue.

Hugh Thompson, Jr., was a 25-year-old helicopter pilot flying an observation craft on the morning of the slaughter. With him on the morning of March 16, 1968, were crew chief Glenn Andreotta and door gunner Lawrence Colburn, who was just 18 at the time.

Flying over My Lai hamlet, Thompson noted a number of corpses on the ground, including of some people he had previously seen lying injured. At a dike outside My Lai village, Thompson found a wounded young woman, and marked the spot with smoke, indicating that medical attention was urgently required. He took off again and hovered close to the ground, watching as a US infantry captain approached the wounded woman, "prodded her with his foot, and then killed her. Those in the helicopter could hardly believe what they were seeing."[123]

Hovering above the irrigation ditch depicted in the photo essay (photo 8), Thompson and his crew saw that it was filled with dead and wounded civilians. He landed again, exited the helicopter, and confronted a US sergeant. How could they help the civilians? he asked the sergeant. By putting them out of their misery, the sergeant responded. Another officer approached—Lt. William Calley, who would be the only killer convicted (and later pardoned) for the My Lai massacre. Calley told Thompson to mind his own business.

Lifting off again, crew member Andreotta watched soldiers firing methodically at surviving Vietnamese. "My God! They're firing into the ditch!" he yelled. "You've got to be kidding," Thompson responded, then looked himself to see "bodies flinching and blood spurting from the impact of the M-16 bullets." That was the point at which he "snapped," he recalled later. Seeing a group of around ten Vietnamese fleeing toward a shelter, pursued by US soldiers, Thompson announced: "We're going in." "We're with you, boss," Colburn assured him. "Let's do it."[124]

Thompson landed his helicopter, interposing the Huey between the troops and the panicked civilians. Turning to Colburn, he instructed him to train his machine gun on the US forces. "Y'all cover me! If these bastards open up on me or these people, you open up on them. Promise me." "Consider it done," Colburn told him.[125]

"They were the enemy then, I guess," Thompson would recall years afterward.[126] "I could not live with myself unless I took some action to save the innocent."[127]

Exiting the helicopter, Thompson, armed only with a holstered handgun, demanded that the soldiers help him evacuate the civilians from their shelter. ". . . A lieutenant countered that they would be taken out with grenades. Refusing to back down, Thompson replied, 'I can do better than that. Keep your people in place. My guns are on you.' He then ordered two other helicopters to fly in for medical evacuation of the eleven wounded Vietnamese."[128]

Returning to the irrigation ditch, he found "a horrendous sight . . . Bodies were scattered along the edges of the ditch. There was blood, filth, and stench everywhere." "What do you call it when you march 100 or 200 people down in a ditch and line up on the side with machines [machine-guns] and start firing into it?" Thompson demanded later. "Reminds me of another story that happened in World War Two, like the Nazis."[129] He pulled a small child, alive and miraculously unscratched, from the ditch. Weeping, he flew his craft back to Quang Ngai, the nearest city, and deposited the child at a hospital. Then, furious, he reported the massacre to his immediate superiors. This was the point at which instructions went out to the soldiers of Charlie Company to "stop the killing." The massacre ceased, saving untold further lives in nearby villages marked for annihilation. But the massacre cover-up began. It would last for more than a year-and-a-half, until details of the slaughter broke in the US press, sparking a national scandal.

After the veil of silence was lifted, Thompson was awarded the Distinguished Flying Cross for supposedly having "greatly enhanced Vietnamese-American relations in the operational area." "Thompson later threw the decoration away."[130] His reporting of the massacre, and later his testimony before an investigative commission, drew the wrath of many in the United States who viewed him as a traitor to the military. Fellow service-members often shunned him as a snitch. At home, "I'd received death threats over the phone. . . . It was scary. Dead animals on your porch, mutilated animals on your porch some mornings when you get up." He was flooded with hate mail:

> You should be stripped of your stripes, you chicken-livered traitor, for the trouble you have caused our country and our military. . . . Your kind is our worst enemy, the rat commie within our country. . . . *Our country right or wrong*. If you don't believe that way, you are no American; you are no better than the fanatic communist animals . . . You have disgraced us all.[131]

As the thirtieth anniversary of the massacre approached, however, media interest picked up, as did lobbying efforts to have Thompson's heroism recognized. Finally, in 1998, at a moving ceremony with Colburn at the Vietnam War Memorial in Washington, DC, he accepted the Soldier's Medal, crediting him with "heroism above and beyond the call of duty . . . while saving the lives of at least 10 Vietnamese civilians during the unlawful massacre of noncombatants by American forces at My Lai" (see Figure 10.13). Of greater significance were the laudatory letters that now replaced the hate mail and death threats. "I do not want all this talk of 'hero' to frighten you away, Mr. Thompson," wrote one admirer. "It is just a code word for what you did, which was essentially loving your neighbor in a profound way under difficult circumstances." Another stated: "My husband and I recently had our first child, a son, and I have clipped your story from our local newspaper to save, and at the right time, to show our son, so he will understand moral courage and know that once this country was privileged to have a hero in its midst."[132]

Thompson felt he could not have behaved otherwise. "I saved the people because I wasn't taught to murder and kill. I can't answer for the people who took part in it," Thompson said. "I apologize for the ones that did. I just wished we could have helped more people that day."[133]

In 1998, on the massacre's thirtieth anniversary and shortly after receiving the Soldier's Medal, Thompson and Colburn revisited the scene of the massacre. In intensely moving encounters captured by a *60 Minutes* camera crew, they were reunited with two of the villagers they had rescued from the carnage.

Hugh Thompson, Jr. died of cancer in January 2006, aged 62. But the narrative of his and his crewmen's actions at My Lai continue to be used in US manuals of military ethics, and in European countries as well. A Norwegian lawyer and Red Cross advisor, Terje Lund, told Thompson's biographer, Trent Angers, that

> for him, as a teacher, the story of the My Lai rescue has provided a living example, a clear demonstration of legally and ethically correct behavior for other soldiers to see. This example has helped to take the meaning of the Geneva Conventions

and international humanitarian law from the abstract and theoretical into the realm of the real and the concrete, thus enhancing the understanding of these rules by legions of military personnel who have been involved in armed conflicts around the world since the Vietnam War. And, he added without equivocation, as a direct result of the soldiers' better understanding of the laws, countless lives of civilians and prisoners of war, perhaps thousands, have been saved.[134]

SOLDIER'S MEDAL
HUGH C. THOMPSON, JR.
(THEN WARRANT OFFICER ONE, UNITED STATES ARMY)

For heroism above and beyond the call of duty on 16 March 1968, while saving the lives of at least 10 Vietnamese civilians during the unlawful massacre of noncombatants by American forces at My Lai, Quang Ngai Province, South Vietnam. Warrant Officer Thompson landed his helicopter in the line of fire between fleeing Vietnamese civilians and pursuing American ground troops to prevent their murder. He then personally confronted the leader of the American ground troops and was prepared to open fire on those American troops should they fire upon the civilians. Warrant Officer Thompson, at the risk of his own personal safety, went forward of the American lines and coaxed the Vietnamese civilians out of the bunker to enable their evacuation. Leaving the area after requesting and overseeing the civilians' air evacuation, his crew spotted movement in a ditch filled with bodies south of My Lai Four. Warrant Officer Thompson again landed his helicopter and covered his crew as they retrieved a wounded child from the pile of bodies. He then flew the child to the safety of a hospital at Quang Ngai. Warrant Officer Thompson's relayed radio reports of the massacre and subsequent report to his section leader and commander resulted in an order for the cease fire at My Lai and an end to the killing of innocent civilians. Warrant Officer Thompson's heroism exemplifies the highest standards of personal courage and ethical conduct, reflecting distinct credit on him, and the United States Army.

Figure 10.13 The US Army Soldier's Medal citation for Hugh Thompson, Jr. After years of lobbying by Thompson's supporters, the honor was awarded to him, Lawrence Colburn, and Glenn Andreotta, who was killed in action a few weeks after the My Lai massacre. At Thompson's insistence, the ceremony took place (in 1998) at the Vietnam Veterans Memorial in Washington, DC, shortly before Thompson and Colburn flew to Vietnam with a *60 Minutes* crew to be reunited with Vietnamese they had saved thirty years earlier.

Source: Courtesy of The Hugh Thompson Foundation.

With the guidance of some trailblazers in the study of "the rescuer personality," let us dig a little deeper into these rare but precious social–psychological formations. Samuel and Pearl Oliner's *The Altruistic Personality*, Eva Fogelman's *Conscience & Courage*, and Nechama Tec's *When the Light Pierced the Darkness* cumulatively sample hundreds of Holocaust rescuers, mostly Polish.[135] In most cases, the subjects had never told their tales before the researchers inquired about it—indeed, amidst the pervasive "anti-semitism without Jews" in contemporary Poland, it could be dangerous or socially uncomfortable to proclaim one's rescuer role. What did these researchers discover about the motivations of those who aided, sheltered, and protected defenseless Jews, when most around them were turning their backs or actively assisting with the slaughter? Consider some of the testimonies of these otherwise ordinary individuals:

I had contact all the time with people who were against Hitler. They told me the most horrible things—transports, gas chambers, drownings, gassing in trains—I knew that a huge injustice was taking place. I felt tense, I couldn't sleep.

I could smell the smoke from Majdanek [death camp] . . .

. . . When [the Germans] started taking the Jewish people, that really lit my fire. They took them like sheep, throwing them into trains. I couldn't stand it anymore. . . . They took innocent people and I wanted to help.

Somebody had to do it.

If you can save somebody's life, that's your duty.

The hand of compassion was faster than the calculus of reason.

. . . Unless we helped, they would be killed. I could not stand that thought. I never would have forgiven myself.

Can you see it? Two young girls come, one sixteen or seventeen, and they tell you a story that their parents were killed and they were pulled in and raped. What are you supposed to tell them—"Sorry, we are full already?"

. . . I was so ashamed of what other so-called Christians did that I felt I wanted to do the contrary.

The times forced us to give in and be a quisling [collaborator] or to fight back, and we would rather have died than cooperate with the Nazis.

He was my friend. I did not refer to him as a Jew. I did not see a Jew in him.

It wasn't that we were especially fond of Jewish people. We felt we wanted to help everybody who was in trouble.[136]

The personal values and psychological orientations cited again and again revolve around themes identified by the Oliners: *altruism* (from the Latin: literally, "other-ism"), *universalism, care* ("the obligation to help the needy"), *compassion* (literally,

Figure 10.14 Sophie Scholl (center), with her brother Hans (left) and friend Christoph Probst. These German students were at the heart of the "White Rose" conspiracy at the University of Munich during World War Two. The organization distributed leaflets denouncing Nazi rule and atrocities against civilians, including the mass murder of Jews on the eastern front. All three were arrested in February 1943 and guillotined a few days later, after a show trial in the "People's Court" presided over by the fanatical Nazi judge, Roland Freisler.[137]

Source: Wikimedia Commons.

"together feeling"), *empathy, equity/egalitarianism, justice* (defined as "the right of innocent people to be free from persecution"), *respect, fairness, personal honor,* and *patriotism* (understood as "encompass[ing] national acceptance of pluralistic and diverse groups in relationships of equality rather than mere tolerance").[138] It is clear that these orientations have an abiding basis in rescuers' family upbringings. Rescuers were significantly more likely than non-rescuers to describe their parents as *benevolent, loving, kind, tolerant, compassionate, non-abusive,* prone to *explain* rather than punish, *extensive* rather than restrictive in their orientation toward others.[139] They were more likely to possess an "ego orientation" that emphasized these traits, along with *strength, autonomy,* and *independence*—"a certain non-conformity, a moral stubbornness, in refusing to adhere to the norms imposed upon them," as Donald Bloxham put it.[140] Jan Gonski protected Jews in Poland, and told Nechama Tec:

> . . . I have the courage of my own convictions. I have to be able to face myself. Had I not helped, I would have found it unpleasant to be alive. I had to comply with my own rules, to my own expectations, and they ordered me to act. As for other people, I do not bother with what they think about me. . . . Every person depends on the opinion of others, but compared to other people I depend less than they. Of course I like when people approve of me but, when they do, I am only pleasantly surprised.[141]

Many rescuers also had personal experiences of marginalization, suffering, and loss, including "a recent loss of someone close to them or an incapacitating childhood illness which caused them to identify with the Jewish victims."[142] In varied ways, then, when the moment of choice arrived, rescuers were "already attuned to conferring meaning on events through their particular moral sensibilities," which influenced the outcome if they did not precisely determine it. As the Oliners phrased it:

> Already attuned to conferring meaning on events through their particular moral sensibilities, [rescuers] depended on familiar patterns to discern the significance of the unprecedented events at hand. To a large extent, then, helping Jews was less a decision made at a critical juncture than a choice prefigured by an established character and way of life. As Iris Murdoch observes, the moral life is not something that is switched on at a particular crisis but is rather something that goes on continually in the small piecemeal habits of living. Hence, "at crucial moments of choice most of the business of choosing is already over." Many rescuers themselves reflected this view, saying that they "had no choice" and that their behavior deserved no special attention, for it was simply an "ordinary" thing to do.[143]

Even with these strong familial buttresses, the psychology of the rescuer did not necessarily arise "out of the blue" or manifest itself in a purely disinterested way. Geographical proximity, particularly in urban settings, facilitated matters. Nationalist sentiment was not absent: French rescuers were more likely to help Jews who were French citizens than stateless refugees. Frequently, rescuers had had previous positive relationships with Jews: as childhood friends, co-workers, neighbors. Sometimes Christian rescuers perceived Jews as a "chosen people," intimately related through the shared religious tradition. "Several rescuers acknowledged that they became dependent on the Jews they helped," for household chores, assistance with repairs and maintenance, and so on.[144] In some cases, rescuers had little idea what they were getting themselves into; small and low-risk acts of kindness would lead inexorably to acts of long-term and high-risk helping. Sometimes the rescued promised the rescuer a material reward after the war was over. More attractive and traditionally "innocent" Jews (particularly children) were especially likely to receive aid. Sometimes sexually intimate relationships developed, as they frequently do in situations of stress and shared danger.

Something unexpected in the rescuer testimony is the sense of *fun* that accompanied the risk. "It was a continuous game," Hiltgunt Zassenhaus told Eva Fogelman. "I was like an actor playing a part." "The development of a rescuer self helped these rescuers keep their fear under control," Fogelman wrote. "The ego gratification and self-satisfaction gained from successfully outwitting the authorities and protecting others encouraged rescuers to keep up and, in some instances, to expand their activities."[145] This was reflected in the trajectory of Cornelia Knottnerus, a Dutch rescuer who was an adolescent at the time of the Nazi occupation:

> When you are young, you love a challenge. I thought of myself as a little hero against the big Nazis. The best antidote to fear is action, and we did not become brave all at once. Little things added up. We brought this paper there for the

underground . . . we took in these [Jewish] children . . . we made out false passports . . . our involvement got deeper and deeper . . . but we were not brave all at once.[146]

Often, rescuers felt disappointed or disillusioned by the response of the rescued when the danger was over. "While some Jewish survivors kept in touch with their rescuers," Fogelman found, "many others, desperate to reestablish their own family bonds and forget the horror-filled past, did not maintain relations with their saviors. The abrupt rupture of what often had been intense and caring relationships left rescuers feeling bereft and lost."[147] But rescuer–rescued relationships could also endure for life—sometimes through marriage.[148]

This serves as a reminder that rescuer psychology is not to be romanticized. I do believe, however, that it is to be *idealized*, in the profoundest sense of the word. These people, who usually considered themselves utterly ordinary, point us to the human motivations that may one day bring an end to genocide in our world. Let us hope they are indeed ordinary—or at least more common than is generally realized. Because "if humankind is dependent on only a few autonomously principled people, then the future is bleak indeed."[149]

FURTHER STUDY

Roy F. Baumeister, *Evil: Inside Human Violence and Cruelty*. New York: W.H. Freeman, 1999. An engaging and wide-ranging inquiry.

Svetlana Broz, *Good People in an Evil Time: Portraits of Complicity and Resistance in the Bosnian War*. New York: Other Press, 2004. Portraits of Balkan rescuers.

Peter Grose, *A Good Place to Hide: How One French Community Saved Thousands of Lives in World War II*. New York: Pegasus Books, 2015. Portrait of the remarkable collective rescue of Jews in Le Chambon-sur-Lignon and nearby Huguenot/Protestant villages.

Thomas Kenneally, *Schindler's List*. New York: Touchstone, 1993. Fact-based novel about the German rescuer of Jews; basis for the classic film. See also *Searching for Schindler*.

Ernst Klee, Willi Dressen, and Volker Riess, eds., *"The Good Old Days": The Holocaust as Seen by Its Perpetrators and Bystanders*. New York: Konecky & Konecky, 1988. The "banality of evil" seems an appropriate term for these cheerful reminiscences of parties and sunny holidays, while millions were murdered.

Robert J. Lifton, *The Nazi Doctors: Medical Killing and the Psychology of Genocide*. New York: Basic Books, 1986. Analyzes the complex psychology of medical workers/murderers at Auschwitz.

Stanley Milgram, *Obedience to Authority: An Experimental View*. New York: HarperPerennial, 1995. "The Milgram Experiments": a classic of social-scientific investigation.

Sönke Neitzel and Harald Welzer, *Soldiers: German POWs on Fighting, Killing, and Dying*. Toronto: Signal, 2013. Fascinating insights into the minds of German soldiers held as prisoners-of-war, whose conversations were secretly recorded and transcribed by British intelligence.

Leonard S. Newman and Ralph Erber, eds., *Understanding Genocide: The Social Psychology of the Holocaust*. Oxford: Oxford University Press, 2002. Essays on perpetrators and bystanders in the Jewish and other genocides.

Samuel P. Oliner and Pearl M. Oliner, *The Altruistic Personality: Rescuers of Jews in Nazi Europe*. New York: The Free Press, 1988. Intensely moving large-sample study. See also Samuel P. Oliner, *Do Unto Others: Extraordinary Acts of Ordinary People*.

Eyal Press, *Beautiful Souls: Saying No, Breaking Ranks, and Heeding the Voice of Conscience in Dark Times*. New York: Farrar, Straus & Giroux, 2012. Short, sharp meditation on the conscientious minority of resisters during the Holocaust and in contemporary Israel and Croatia; especially interesting is the closing chapter on corporate whistleblowers.

John Rabe, *The Good Man of Nanking: The Diaries of John Rabe*, trans. John E. Woods. New York: Alfred A. Knopf, 1998. Searing diary of the "Rape of Nanjing" by Japanese forces in 1937–1938, and the "International Safety Zone" established by Rabe and others to save Chinese civilian lives.

Paul Rusesabagina, *An Ordinary Man: An Autobiography*. London: Penguin, 2006. Memoir of the rescuer who inspired the film *Hotel Rwanda*.

Jacques Sémelin, Claire Andrieu, and Sarah Gensburger, eds., *Resisting Genocide: The Multiple Forms of Rescue*. Oxford: Oxford University Press, 2013. Encyclopedic collection examining rescuer behavior in the Armenian, Jewish, and Tutsi genocides.

Ervin Staub, *The Roots of Evil: The Origins of Genocide and Other Group Violence*. Cambridge: Cambridge University Press, 1989. Early study of the psychology of genocide. Staub's magnum opus, *Overcoming Evil: Genocide, Violent Conflict, and Terrorism*, is still on my reading list.

Nechama Tec, *When Light Pierced the Darkness: Christian Rescue of Jews in Occupied Europe*. Oxford: Oxford University Press, 1984. Rescuer behavior in Poland. See also *Resistance: Jews and Christians Who Defied the Nazi Terror*.

Samuel Vaknin, *Malignant Self-love: Narcissism Revisited* (5th rev. edn). Skopje: Narcissus Publications, 2003. Lengthy work by a leading authority on narcissism.

James Waller, *Becoming Evil: How Ordinary People Commit Genocide and Mass Killing*, 2nd edn. Oxford: Oxford University Press, 2007. The best social-psychological study of genocide, literate and engaging throughout.

Emmy E. Werner, *A Conspiracy of Decency: The Rescue of the Danish Jews*. Boulder, CO: Westview Press, 2002. The story of another extraordinary rescue from under Nazi noses.

Philip Zimbardo, *The Lucifer Effect: Understanding How Good People Turn Evil*. New York: Random House, 2007. Career-summarizing work by the designer of the Stanford prison experiments.

▌ NOTES

1　Greek Mythology Link, "Narcissus," http://andrejkoymasky.com/liv/fam/bion1/narcis01.html.

2　Anton Blok, "The Narcissism of Minor Differences," in Blok, *Honour and Violence* (Cambridge: Polity Press, 2001), p. 115. Michael Ignatieff's exploration was influential in bringing Freud's concept to bear on ethnic conflict and genocide: "The Narcissism of Minor Difference," in Ignatieff, *The Warrior's Honour: Ethnic War and the Modern Conscience* (London: Penguin, 1998), pp. 27–65.

3 As Mark Levene noted, "it is striking . . . the degree to which the slanderous invocations made against American and later, antipodean 'first peoples' simply replicated Anglo venom directed at what were nearly always referred to as the 'wild' Irish." Levene, *Genocide in the Age of the Nation State, Vol. 2: The Rise of the West and the Coming of Genocide* (London: I.B. Tauris, 2005), p. 48. The real-world consequences were also comparable, in that "considered overall, an Irish population collapse from 1.5 or possibly over 2 million inhabitants at the onset of the Irish wars in 1641, to no more than 850,000 eleven years later represents an absolutely devastating demographic catastrophe" (p. 54).

4 Freud quoted in Blok, *Honour and Violence*, p. 117.

5 Raphael Lemkin himself noted in his unfinished history of genocide: "On the group level such hostility exists most often between groups who have much in common and thus have ample opportunity to offend one another. There is much latent hostility between French and German, Hindu and Moslem in India, Chinese and Japanese which has often flared up into actual aggression. Examples such as these could be greatly multiplied. . . . At times of intense hostility differences between the groups are exaggerated and similarities are minimized; imaginary offenses and insults are often added to real ones." Lemkin, *Lemkin on Genocide*, ed. Steven Leonard Jacobs (Lanham, MD: Lexington Books, 2012), p. 29.

6 See Samuel Vaknin, *Malignant Self-love: Narcissism Revisited* (Skopje: Narcissus Publications, 2003).

7 "A narcissist openly reveals his megalomania, but craves admiration, praise, and flattery. He has little sense of humor, he cannot form significant relationships, and blows to his self-esteem can elicit violent anger. He has a paranoid distrust of others. He can appear self-confident and secure, but deep down feels shame, insecurity, and inferiority. . . . He may, at one moment, appear a charming, benign benefactor, and the next moment turn into a raging, aggressive attacker. . . . He has a distorted conscience. Depression is common." Neil J. Kressel, *Mass Hate: The Global Rise of Genocide and Terror* (New York: Plenum Press, 1996), p. 133.

8 Quoted in Barbara Ehrenreich, *Blood Rites: Origins and History of the Passions of War* (New York: Metropolitan Books, 1997), p. 210.

9 Simon Sebag Montefiore, *Stalin: The Court of the Red Tsar* (London: Phoenix, 2004), p. 617. In Maoist China, the cult of personality was all-pervasive, surpassing even the Stalinist exemplar. Gao Xingjian, later a Nobel laureate, described the ritual: "At six o'clock in the morning, the bugle call got people up, and they had twenty minutes to brush their teeth and have a wash. They then stood before the portrait of the Great Leader on the wall to seek 'morning instructions,' sang songs from Mao's *Sayings* and, holding high the little red book [of Mao's collected aphorisms], shouted out 'long live' three times before going to the dining room to drink gruel. Assembly followed, and Mao's *Selected Works* were recited for half an hour before people shouldered their hoes and pickaxes to work on the land." Quoted in Roderick MacFarquhar and Michael Schoenhals, *Mao's Last Revolution* (Cambridge, MA: The Belknap Press of Harvard University Press, 2006), p. 263. All of this must have been wonderful for Mao's ego; so too the endless stream of young female consorts handpicked for him (and by him) from the military and theater troupes. Chang and Halliday are merciless on this point (in *Mao: The Unknown Story*; see Chapter 5, Further Study)—justifiably, given that the debauchery occurred in what was otherwise one of the most austere and sexually puritan regimes in the world.

10 Louis Sell, *Slobodan Milosevic and the Destruction of Yugoslavia* (Durham, NC: Duke University Press, 2002), p. 173.

11 Vaknin, "Collective Narcissism," http://samvak.tripod.com/14.html; emphasis added, to stress that the "collective" character of such narcissism need not require unanimity or even a majority among the afflicted group. Precisely when ordinary grandiosity

becomes pathological narcissism is difficult to discern. To some degree inherent in modern nationalism, as Mark Levene has noted, is *sacro egoismo:* "'the egotistic pursuit of the interest of one's own group, even if it involves the disregard and abuse of another,' the former, moreover, always being deemed 'sacred' and hence morally self-sufficient." Levene, *Genocide in the Age of the Nation State, Vol. 2*, p. 185, quoting George Mosse. An American correspondent, Kathleen Morrow, wrote: "An assumption of superiority is part of *every* national character. . . . If you listen long enough to any citizen of any nation, you will detect a trace of narcissistic unreality . . . part of the cultural mythology that holds the group together. (The French think they invented 'culture,' the Italians are sure they are the only people who really know how to 'enjoy life,' etc.) I tend to assume this almost universal tendency to national grandiosity is innocent enough—as long as the nation or group does not accumulate enough power to begin to try to impose its internal mythology on the rest of the world. . . . I suppose I'm arguing that US collective pathological narcissism is not a cultural or psychological problem as much as a systemic one. By systemic, I mean the global system, which at this point exhibits a number of power vacuums into which a too-powerful US can narcissistically rush." Morrow, personal communication, May 5, 2005.

12 For a pointed analysis of the collective narcissism of my other country of citizenship, see Clifford Krauss, "Was Canada Just Too Good to be True?," *The New York Times*, May 25, 2005.

13 Cambodia under the Khmer Rouge (see Chapter 7) is another candidate, but I consider Khmer Rouge fanaticism to have been too shallowly rooted in society as a whole to merit inclusion.

14 Robert Jay Lifton, *Superpower Syndrome: America's Apocalyptic Confrontation with the World* (New York: Thunder's Mouth Press/Nation Books, 2003), p. 190.

15 Quoted in Saul Friedlander, *Nazi Germany and the Jews, Volume 1: The Years of Persecution, 1933–1939* (New York: HarperCollins, 1997), p. 259.

16 Alexander Donat, *The Holocaust Kingdom* (Washington, DC: Holocaust Library, 1999), p. 197.

17 Götz Aly, *Hitler's Beneficiaries: Plunder, Racial War, and the Nazi Welfare State* (New York: Holt Paperbacks, 2005), pp. 285, 324. See also Martin Dean, *Robbing the Jews: The Confiscation of Jewish Property in the Holocaust, 1933–1945* (Cambridge: Cambridge University Press, 2008).

18 Frank Bajohr, "Expropriation and Expulsion," in Dan Stone, ed., *The Historiography of the Holocaust* (London: Palgrave Macmillan, 2004), p. 54.

19 Saul Friedländer, *The Years of Extermination: Nazi Germany and the Jews, 1939–1945* (New York: HarperCollins, 2007), p. 535.

20 Mark Mazower, quoted in Jan Tomasz Gross, *Golden Harvest: Events at the Periphery of the Holocaust* (Oxford: Oxford University Press, 2012), pp. 43–44. Gross's book, a study of the grassroots Polish pillaging of Jewish livelihoods and property during and after the Holocaust, is an important recent source on greed in genocide (see also the photo essay, photo 4).

21 Anna Bikont, quoted in Gross, *Golden Harvest*, p. 112.

22 Patricia Marchak, *Reigns of Terror* (Montreal, PQ: McGill-Queen's University Press, 2003), p. 21.

23 Levene, *Genocide in the Age of the Nation State, Vol. 2*, p. 105.

24 Heizer quoted in Levon Marashlian, "Finishing the Genocide: Cleansing Turkey of Armenian Survivors, 1920–1923," in Richard G. Hovannisian, ed., *Remembrance and Denial: The Case of the Armenian Genocide* (Detroit, MI: Wayne State University Press, 1999), p. 115. (Heizer's statement dates from July 1915.) The US consul in Mamouret-ul-Aziz, Leslie A. Davis, similarly reported that "The scenes of that week [of deportation] were heartrending. The [Armenian] people were preparing to leave their homes and to abandon their houses, their lands, their property of all kinds. They were selling their possessions for whatever they could get. The streets were full of Turkish women, as well as men, who were seeking bargains on this occasion, buying organs, sewing

machines, furniture, rugs, and other articles of value for almost nothing. . . . The scene reminded me of vultures swooping down on their prey. It was a veritable Turkish holiday and all the Turks went out in their gala attire to feast and to make merry over the misfortunes of others." Davis quoted in Marchak, *Reigns of Terror*, p. 166.

25 Montefiore, *Stalin: The Court of the Red Tsar*, p. 265.

26 Marie-Louise Kagoyire, quoted in Jean Hatzfeld, *Life Laid Bare: The Survivors in Rwanda Speak* (New York: Other Press, 2006), p. 126.

27 Quoted in Jean Hatzfeld, *Machete Season: The Killers in Rwanda Speak*, trans. Linda Coverdale (New York: Farrar, Straus & Giroux, 2005), p. 87.

28 Levene, *Genocide in the Age of the Nation State, Vol. 2*, p. 241.

29 H.H. Gerth and C. Wright Mills, eds., *From Max Weber: Essays in Sociology* (New York: Oxford University Press, 1954), p. 180.

30 Michael Burleigh, *Ethics and Extermination: Reflections on Nazi Genocide* (Cambridge: Cambridge University Press, 1997), p. 164.

31 Montefiore, *Stalin*, p. 626.

32 "Everybody could hope for speedy advancement because every day somebody was plucked from their midst and had to be replaced. Of course, everybody was also a candidate for prison and death, but during the day they did not think about it, giving full rein to their fears only at night." Nadezhda Mandelstam, *Hope Against Hope* (New York: Modern Library, 1999), p. 282.

33 Orlando Figes, *The Whisperers: Private Life in Stalin's Russia* (New York: Metropolitan Books, 2007), p. 265. Brian Moynahan likewise notes that under Stalinism, "Denouncing a neighbor meant the chance of more living space. A student at the Leningrad Technical School told how his mother had welcomed the expulsions. 'Mama says, "Damn them. Let them all be exiled. Maybe then we'll be given an apartment sooner."' Apartment hunters attended factory meetings eager to denounce those with a choice room or space." Moynahan, *Leningrad: Siege and Symphony* (London: Quercus, 2014), p. 28.

34 Gérard Prunier, *The Rwanda Crisis: History of a Genocide* (New York: Columbia University Press, 1997), pp. 231–232.

35 La Rochefoucauld quoted in Eva Fogelman, *Conscience & Courage: Rescuers of Jews during the Holocaust* (New York: Anchor Books, 1994), p. 50.

36 Burke quoted in Linda Green, "Fear as a Way of Life," in Alexander Laban Hinton, ed., *Genocide: An Anthropological Reader* (Malden, MA: Blackwell), p. 307.

37 Dictionary.reference.com definition, http://dictionary.reference.com/browse/mortified.

38 Ehrenreich, *Blood Rites*, p. 76.

39 On the psychology of "in-group-out-group differentiation," see Ervin Staub, *The Roots of Evil: The Origins of Genocide and Other Group Violence* (Cambridge: Cambridge University Press, 1989), pp. 58–62.

40 James Waller, *Becoming Evil: How Ordinary People Commit Genocide and Mass Killing*, 2nd edn (Oxford: Oxford University Press, 2007), p. 149. Emphasis in original.

41 Donald L. Horowitz, *The Deadly Ethnic Riot* (Berkeley, CA: University of California Press, 2001), p. 151.

42 See J.S. Piven, *Death and Delusion: A Freudian Analysis of Mortal Terror* (Greenwich, CT: IAP Publishers, 2004).

43 In the Hebrew religious tradition, the scapegoat was "a live goat over whose head Aaron confessed all the sins of the children of Israel on the Day of Atonement. The goat, symbolically bearing their sins, was then sent into the wilderness." (*Answers.com*)

44 Charny quoted in Leo Kuper, *The Prevention of Genocide* (New Haven, CT: Yale University Press, 1985), p. 196. See also the discussion of psychological research on "mortality salience" and "terror management" in Kate Douglas, "Death Defying," *New Scientist*, August 28, 2004.

45 Ernest Becker, *The Denial of Death* (New York: The Free Press, 1973), pp. 148–149, 284. Jacques Sémelin argues along similar lines in *Purify and Destroy*: "Beyond fear and hatred, [there] thus appears a fantasy of all-powerfulness in which this 'us' is victorious: it is

regenerated by destroying 'them.' The death of an evil 'them' makes possible the omnipotence of 'us.' Such a psychological posture may seem 'primitive' or archaic—which, in fact, it is. We are still here in the realm of the *imaginaire*, but unlike that of death, it is one of omnipotence and glory. The two are inextricably linked. The two of them can be terribly effective because they affect the very foundations of the human psyche as explained, for example, by psychoanalysis." Sémelin, *Purify and Destroy: The Political Uses of Massacre and Genocide* (New York: Columbia University Press, 2007), p. 17.

46 Donald G. Dutton, *The Psychology of Genocide, Massacres, and Extreme Violence: Why "Normal" People Come to Commit Atrocities* (Westport, CT: Praeger Security International, 2007), p. 24.

47 "Prosecutor v. Drazen Erdemovic, Sentencing Judgement," March 5, 1998. From the Documentation Site of the Netherlands Institute of Human Rights, http://sim.law.uu.nl.

48 Nyiransabimana, quoted in Hatzfeld, *Life Laid Bare*, p. 140.

49 René Lemarchand, "Disconnecting the Threads: Rwanda and the Holocaust Reconsidered," *Journal of Genocide Research*, 4: 4 (2002), p. 513. A similar dynamic was evident in the Nazi SS, where (by contrast with the Order Police) not only was disobedience generally punished by execution, but a loss of employment in the camps could mean transfer to the mortal danger of the eastern front. Hence, according to Christopher Fettweis, "cowardice played an important role" in motivating SS members. "These men and women were well aware that to request a transfer might mean a trip to the Russian front, from which few people returned. The Jew-killing duties, while perhaps unpleasant, were relatively safe and provided a solid chance to survive the war. The Russian front must have provided quite an effective incentive to perform for those assigned to guard the trains, or to man the towers, or to work in the rear in the *Einsatzgruppen*." Fettweis, "War as Catalyst: Moving World War II to the Center of Holocaust Scholarship," *Journal of Genocide Research*, 5: 2 (2003), p. 229.

50 Sémelin, *Purify and Destroy*, p. 262.

51 "One thing is immediately obvious [in genocidal situations]: the killers are in a *group*. . . . Killings are thus carried out by battalions, gangs, crowds. Each group has a different story, and operates under different circumstances. But one thing is certain: It is the group that acts as the collective operator of mass murder. It is the group that gives rise to individuals transformed into killers." Ibid., pp. 240–241. Sémelin also points out (p. 273) that the forcible submersion of *victims* is frequently adopted as a strategy "to de-individualize them. Quantity depersonalizes and consequently desensitizes."

52 Mark Levene, *Genocide in the Age of the Nation State, Vol. 2*, p. 140.

53 Rubinowicz quoted in Friedländer, *The Years of Extermination*, p. 385.

54 Daniel Chirot and Clark McCauley, *Why Not Kill Them All? The Logic and Prevention of Mass Political Murder* (Princeton, NJ: Princeton University Press, 2006), pp. 36, 86.

55 Ben Kiernan, *Blood and Soil: A World History of Genocide and Extermination from Sparta to Darfur* (New Haven, CT: Yale University Press, 2007), p. 27.

56 Horowitz, *The Deadly Ethnic Riot*, p. 548.

57 The fact that these highly frustrated and alienated individuals were also outsiders made them additionally useful in jump-starting genocidal killing at the local level. An unidentified survivor of the Rwandan genocide, interviewed by Lee Ann Fujii, described killing sprees in Ngali, south of Kigali, in which "the Burundians would set an example for the Rwandan Interahamwe [genocidal militia] to kill and show them how to kill someone because the people from here in Ngali were scared and ashamed of killing their neighbors, their friends." Fujii, *Killing Neighbors: Webs of Violence in Rwanda* (Ithaca, NY: Cornell University Press, 2009), p. 86. This is just one example of "the transformation of refugee-generating conflict into conflict-generating refugees," in René Lemarchand's mordant phrasing (Lemarchand, *The Dynamics of Violence in Central Africa* [Philadelphia, PA: University of Pennsylvania Press, 2009], p. 20.) Lemarchand also notes that following the Burundian genocide of 1972, "It is not a matter of coincidence that the few Hutu elites who survived the Burundi carnage were the first to articulate a stridently anti-Tutsi ideology . . ." (p. 58).

58 Lemarchand, "Disconnecting the Threads," p. 507.

59 Scott Straus, *The Order of Genocide: Race, Power, and War in Rwanda* (Ithaca, NY: Cornell University Press, 2006), pp. 139, 157.

60 Raul Hilberg, *The Destruction of the European Jews* (3rd edn), *Vol. 3* (New Haven, CT: Yale University Press, 2003), p. 1093. Mark Levene also points disparagingly to the fantastic "notion that worldwide Jewry, despite its dispersal, minority status and history of persecution, was actually spearheading an international, even cosmic conspiracy to emasculate and ultimately wipe out not only the German people but all western civilization." Levene, "Why Is the Twentieth Century the Century of Genocide?," *Journal of World History*, 11: 2 (2000), p. 323.

61 Goebbels, quoted in Friedländer, *The Years of Extermination*, p. 335.

62 Such propaganda had a duly fear-evoking effect on German fighting forces, who came to view their mission of occupation and genocide as a fundamentally defensive one, especially with regard to the Slavic enemy. One soldier wrote in August 1941: "Precisely now one recognizes perfectly what would have happened to our wives and children had these Russian hordes ... succeeded in penetrating into our Fatherland. I have had the opportunity here to ... observe these uncultivated, multi-raced men. Thank God they have been thwarted from plundering and pillaging our homeland." Cited in Omer Bartov, *Hitler's Army: Soldiers, Nazis, and War in the Third Reich* (New York: Oxford University Press, 1992), p. 156.

63 Sémelin, *Purify and Destroy*, p. 297.

64 A Hutu killer in the Rwandan genocide also recalled: "The perpetrators felt more comfortable insulting and hitting crawlers in rags rather than properly upright people. Because they seemed less like us in that position." Quoted in Hatzfeld, *Machete Season*, p. 132.

65 Wolfgang Sofsky, *The Order of Terror: The Concentration Camp* (Princeton, NJ: Princeton University Press, 1999), p. 267.

66 Rwililiza quoted in Hatzfeld, *Life Laid Bare*, pp. 102, 113.

67 Horowitz, *The Deadly Ethnic Riot*, p. 393.

68 According to Terrence Des Pres, immersion in filth and excreta has much the same character, violating psychological taboos so deeply held that they are almost instinctive. "The shock of physical defilement causes spiritual concussion, and, simply to judge from the reports of those who have suffered it, subjection to filth seems often to cause greater anguish than hunger or fear of death. 'This aspect of our camp life,' says one survivor [of the Nazi camps, Reska Weiss], 'was the most dreadful and the most horrible ordeal to which we were subjected.' Another survivor [Leon Szalet] describes the plight of men forced to lie in their own excreta: they 'moaned and wept with discomfort and disgust. Their moral wretchedness was crushing.'" Des Pres, *The Survivor: An Anatomy of Life in the Death Camps* (Oxford: Oxford University Press, 1976), p. 66.

69 Chirot and McCauley, *Why Not Kill Them All?*, p. 28.

70 Evelin Lindner, "Gendercide and Humiliation in Honour and Human-rights Societies," in Adam Jones, ed., *Gendercide and Genocide* (Nashville, TN: Vanderbilt University Press, 2004), p. 40. Daniel Chirot and Clark McCauley define humiliation as "the emotion experienced when a public loss of status is imposed by another. This imposition is usually perceived as unfair and undeserved." Chirot and McCauley, *Why Not Kill Them All?*, p. 79; see their broader discussion of "Shame and Humiliation," pp. 77–80.

71 Retzinger and Scheff cited in Lindner, "Gendercide and Humiliation," p. 45.

72 Lifton, *Superpower Syndrome*, p. 103.

73 James Gilligan, "Shame, Guilt, and Violence," *Social Research*, 70: 4 (Winter 2003), p. 1154.

74 Donald Horowitz likewise wrote of "deadly ethnic riots" that "the reversal of invidious comparisons, the retrieval of imperiled respect, and the redistribution of honor are among the central purposive ideas embedded in the dramaturgy." Horowitz, *The Deadly Ethnic Riot*, p. 431.

75 Belsil quoted in Taner Akçam, *A Shameful Act: The Armenian Genocide and the Question of Turkish Responsibility* (New York: Metropolitan Books, 2006), p. 116.

76 Akçam is definite on this: "Turkish nationalism arose as a reaction to the experience of constant humiliations. Turkish national sentiment constantly suffered from the effects of an inferiority complex. . . . Critical . . . was the fact that the Turks not only were continuously humiliated and loathed, but they were conscious of this humiliation. . . . A nation that was humiliated in this way in the past and is also conscious of that experience, will try to prove its own greatness and importance." Taner Akçam, "The Genocide of the Armenians and the Silence of the Turks," in Levon Chorbajian and George Shirinian, eds., *Studies in Comparative Genocide* (London: Macmillan, 1999), p. 129. See also Akçam, *From Empire to Republic: Turkish Nationalism and the Armenian Genocide* (London: Zed Books, 2004), chs. 2 and 3.

77 "Nazi doctors told me of indelible scenes, which they either witnessed as young children or were told about by their fathers, of German soldiers returning home defeated after World War I. These beaten men, many of them wounded, engendered feelings of pathos, loss, and embarrassment, all amidst national misery and threatened revolution. Such scenes, associated with strong feelings of humiliation, were seized upon by the Nazis to the point where one could say that Hitler rose to power on the promise of avenging them." Lifton, *Superpower Syndrome*, p. 111.

78 I explored the link between "Humiliation and Masculine Crisis in Iraq," focusing on the invasion of 2003 and subsequent occupation and uprising, in an article by this title in *Al-Raida* (Beirut: Institute for Women's Studies in the Arab World), Vol. 21, July 2004, available at www.iiav.nl/ezines/email/AlRaida/2004/No104–105.pdf.

79 Quoted in Gilligan, "Shame, Guilt and Violence," p. 1162. Jessica Stern's interviews with Palestinian suicide bombers provide further evidence of humiliation as a motivating force. See Stern, *Terror in the Name of God: Why Religious Militants Kill* (New York: Ecco Press, 2003).

80 This is also evident, with generally more positive outcomes, in the history of movements for national autonomy or independence. Clearly, the educated and otherwise privileged are disproportionately represented among the leaderships of such movements.

81 Levene, *Genocide in the Age of the Nation State, Vol. 2*, p. 60.

82 Scott Straus, however, rejected "the claim that Burundian refugees instigated the killing in Rwanda," contending that the population of Butare in southern Rwanda, where Burundian refugees were concentrated, arrived late and mostly unwillingly to the genocide. Straus, *The Order of Genocide*, p. 61.

83 Waller, *Becoming Evil*, pp. 72–73.

84 Sémelin, *Purify and Destroy*, p. 267.

85 Christopher Browning, *Ordinary Men: Reserve Police Battalion 101 and the Final Solution in Poland* (New York: Perennial, 1993), p. 184.

86 Waitman Wade Beorn, *Marching Into Darkness: The Wehrmacht and the Holocaust in Belarus* (Cambridge, MA: Harvard University Press, 2014), pp. 234–245.

87 See Thomas Blass, *The Man Who Shocked the World: The Life and Legacy of Stanley Milgram* (New York: Basic Books, 2004).

88 Waller, *Becoming Evil*, p. 108.

89 Stanley Milgram, *Obedience to Authority: An Experimental View* (New York: HarperPerennial, 1995), p. 33; emphasis added.

90 Ibid., p. 40.

91 Ibid., p. 34. "Subjects seemed able to resist the experimenter far better when they did not have to confront [the 'victim'] face to face" (p. 62).

92 One might expect a degree of trauma to have resulted to the subjects from learning their capacity to do harm, but according to Milgram, this was not the case. Nearly all subjects expressed gratitude for the insights that the experiments had provided them. The comment of one subject in a follow-up interview was: "I think people should think more deeply about themselves and their relation to their world and to other people." Ibid., p. 196.

93 Ibid., pp. 63, 161.

94 Browning, *Ordinary Men*, p. 172.

95 Milgram, *Obedience to Authority*, pp. 40, 62–63, 97, 118, 121.

96 See Waller, *Becoming Evil*, pp. 109–111. For recent evaluations of Milgram's work, see Thomas Blass, "Perpetrator Behavior as Destructive Obedience: An Evaluation of Stanley Milgram's Perspective, the Most Influential Social-Psychological Approach to the Holocaust," in Leonard S. Newman and Ralph Erber, eds., *Understanding Genocide: The Social Psychology of the Holocaust* (Oxford: Oxford University Press, 2002), pp. 91–109; and Philip Zimbardo, *The Lucifer Effect: Understanding How Good People Turn Evil* (New York: Random House, 2007), p. 275, citing "a recent comparative analysis . . . of the rates of obedience in eight studies conducted in the United States and nine replications in European, African, and Asian countries." This found "comparably high levels of compliance by research volunteers in these different studies and nations"; but see also the critique by Augustine Brannigan in *Beyond the Banality of Evil: Criminology and Genocide* (Oxford: Oxford University Press, 2013), pp. 5–21.

97 Milgram, *Obedience to Authority*, pp. 5–6. In a personal letter to Henry Riecken of the National Science Foundation, Milgram was more cynical: "In a naïve moment some time ago, I once wondered whether in all of the United States a vicious government could find enough moral imbeciles to meet the personnel requirements of a national system of death camps, of the sort that were maintained in Germany. I am now beginning to think that the full complement could be recruited in New Haven." Quoted in Thomas Blass, *The Man Who Shocked the World: The Life and Legacy of Stanley Milgram* (New York: Basic Books, 2004), p. 100.

98 Ibid., p. 155.

99 Ibid., p. 48.

100 Ibid., p. 51.

101 However, as Roy Baumeister notes, while "empathy may prevent cruelty in some cases . . . it can also serve it. The true sadist is not lacking in empathy—on the contrary, empathy helps the sadist to derive maximum pleasure and inflict the greatest pain." Roy F. Baumeister, *Evil: Inside Human Violence and Cruelty* (New York: W.H. Freeman, 1999), p. 247.

102 Zygmunt Bauman, *Modernity and the Holocaust* (Ithaca, NY: Cornell University Press, 2000, p. 155. For more on the psychology of torture and sadism, see Elaine Scarry, *The Body in Pain: The Making and Unmaking of the World* (New York: Oxford University Press, 1985), especially ch. 1; and John Conroy, *Unspeakable Acts, Ordinary People: The Dynamics of Torture* (New York: Alfred A. Knopf, 2000).

103 Zimbardo, *The Lucifer Effect*, p. 33.

104 Bauman, *Modernity and the Holocaust*, pp. 166–167.

105 Waller, *Becoming Evil*, p. 238.

106 Browning, *Ordinary Men*, p. 168.

107 Bauman, *Modernity and the Holocaust*, p. 167.

108 Ryan Dilley, "Is It in Anyone to Abuse a Captive?," *BBC News Online*, May 5, 2004, http://news.bbc.co.uk/1/hi/magazine/3683115.stm.

109 Zimbardo, *The Lucifer Effect*, pp. 210–11.

110 Hilberg, *The Destruction of the European Jews*, Vol. 1, p. 318.

111 Hilberg, *The Destruction of the European Jews*, Vol. 2, pp. 589, 597–598.

112 See "NGO: Bulgaria Must Take Responsibility for Thracian, Macedonian Jews' Deportation," *Novinite.com*, February 14, 2013, www.novinite.com/articles/147841/NGO%3A+Bulgaria+Must+Take+Responsibility+for+Thracian,+Macedonian+Jews'+Deportation.

113 Mark Levene, *The Crisis of Genocide, Vol. 2: Annihilation: The European Rimlands 1938–1953* (Oxford: Oxford University Press, 2013), p. 174. For a detailed account of this remarkable case, see Michael Bar-Zohar, *Beyond Hitler's Grasp: The Heroic Rescue of Bulgaria's Jews* (Holbrook, MA: Adams Media Corporation, 1998). For less dramatic but equally effective acts of resistance, at least until the Nazis occupied Italy directly,

see Susan Zuccotti, *The Italians and the Holocaust: Persecution, Rescue, and Survival* (New York: Bison Books/University of Nebraska Press, 1996).

114 Samuel P. Oliner and Pearl M. Oliner, *The Altruistic Personality: Rescuers of Jews in Nazi Europe* (New York: The Free Press, 1988), p. 20. Wallenberg's story has overshadowed those who facilitated his acts of rescue, such as the Swedish diplomat Per Anger. According to historian Henry Huttenbach, it was Anger who first "hit on the idea of issuing Jews temporary Swedish passports and identity cards. . . . Anger's undivided cooperation allowed Wallenberg to succeed. . . . It is safe to say that Wallenberg's mission to save Hungarian Jews from deportation would not have got off the ground had Wallenberg not had the total support from the Swedish Embassy, that is, from Per Anger." Henry R. Huttenbach, "In Memoriam: Per Anger, 1914–2002," *Journal of Genocide Research*, 5: 2 (2003), p. 191. Saul Friedländer notes also the role of "the Swiss diplomats, Carl Lutz, and the delegate of the ICRC, Friedrich Born; the Italian Giorgio Perlasca, impersonated a 'Spanish chargé d'affaires'; [and] the Portuguese, Carlos Branquinho. . . ." Friedländer, *The Years of Extermination*, p. 642.

115 See Peter Grose, *A Good Place to Hide: How One French Community Saved Thousands of Lives in World War II* (New York: Pegasus Books, 2015), and Philip Hallie's earlier, rather preachy treatment, *Lest Innocent Blood Be Shed: The Story of the Village of Le Chambon and How Goodness Happened There* (New York: HarperPerennial, 1994). Caroline Moorhead's book, *Village of Secrets: Defying the Nazis in Vichy France* (New York: Harper, 2014) explores the responses of villagers in the wider region around Le Chambon-sur-Lignon. It has sparked considerable controversy with its claim to dispel "myths" surrounding the rescues, and its harsh treatment of André Trocmé. One can gain a sense of the strong reactions from the comments on the book's Amazon .com page, www.amazon.com/Village-Secrets-Defying-Resistance-Trilogy/dp/ 0062202472.

116 A concise and readable account of Wallenberg's efforts to save Hungarian Jews and his subsequent fate is John Bierman, *Righteous Gentile: The Story of Raoul Wallenberg, Missing Hero of the Holocaust* (rev. edn) (London: Penguin, 1995).

117 John G. Heidenrich, *How to Prevent Genocide: A Guide for Policymakers, Scholars, and the Concerned Citizen* (Westport, CT: Praeger, 2001), p. 122.

118 Sugihara, quoted in Samuel P. Oliner, *Do Unto Others: Extraordinary Acts of Ordinary People* (Boulder, CO: Westview Press, 2003), p. 50; also in Hillel Levine, *In Search of Sugihara: The Elusive Japanese Diplomat Who Risked His Life to Rescue 10,000 Jews from the Holocaust* (New York: The Free Press, 1996), p. 12. "Sugihara's ordinariness is perhaps what is so extraordinary about this story," writes Levine. "In illustrating for us how a common person can perpetrate a most uncommon act, he empowers us all as he challenges us to greater responsiveness and responsibility" (p. 284).

119 Hannah Arendt, *Eichmann in Jerusalem: A Report on the Banality of Evil* (New York: The Viking Press, 1965), p. 130; emphasis added.

120 Survivor testimony quoted in Donald E. Miller and Lorna Touryan Miller, *Survivors: An Oral History of the Armenian Genocide* (Berkeley, CA: University of California Press, 1999), p. 13.

121 Oliner and Oliner, *The Altruistic Personality*, p. 155. The Oliners consider religious belief "at best . . . only weakly related to rescue" of Jews during the Second World War (p. 156).

122 Mike Collett-White, "'Rwanda's Schindler' Saved 1,268 Lives," *The Scotsman*, December 30, 2004. Rusesabagina's alienation from the post-genocide regime in Rwanda is revealing: see Arthur Asiimwe, "'Hotel Rwanda' Hero in Bitter Controversy," Reuters dispatch, April 18, 2007.

123 Michael Bilton and Kevin Sim, *Four Hours in My Lai* (New York: Penguin, 1992), pp. 138–139, 204.

124 Trent Angers, *The Forgotten Hero of My Lai: The Hugh Thompson Story* (Lafayette, LA: Acadian House Publishing, 1999), pp. 120–121, 123. A revised (2014) edition is available, but my second-hand copy is signed by Thompson personally!

125 Thompson quoted in ibid., p. 124.

126 Thompson quoted in Oliner, *Do Unto Others*, p. 118.

127 Zimbardo, *The Lucifer Effect*, pp. 474–475.

128 Rebecca Leung, "An American Hero: Vietnam Veteran Speaks Out About My Lai," *CBSNews.com*, May 9, 2004. www.cbsnews.com/stories/2004/05/06/60minutes/main615997.shtml.

129 Bilton and Sim, *Four Hours in My Lai*, p. 205. For excerpts from a televised interview with Thompson on *BBC Hardtalk*, see www.youtube.com/watch?v=hkFa2lSNAGc.

130 Leung, "An American Hero."

131 Quoted in Angers, *The Forgotten Hero of My Lai*, p. 178.

132 Correspondence quoted in ibid., pp. 202, 229.

133 Leung, "An American Hero."

134 Angers, *The Forgotten Hero of My Lai*, p. 221.

135 Nechama Tec, *When Light Pierced the Darkness: Christian Rescue of Jews in Nazi-Occupied Poland* (New York: Oxford University Press, 1986); Samuel P. Oliner and Pearl M. Oliner, *The Altruistic Personality: Rescuers of Jews in Nazi Europe* (New York: The Free Press, 1988); Eva Fogelman, *Conscience & Courage: Rescuers of Jews during the Holocaust* (New York: Anchor Books, 1994).

136 The quoted testimony is drawn from Oliner and Oliner, *The Altruistic Personality*, pp. 119, 134, 138, 143, 159, 168–169, 197, 209, 216–218, and Fogelman, *Conscience & Courage*, p. 144. I am struck as well by this almost surreal vignette from the Warsaw Ghetto, recorded by the diarist Emmanuel Ringelblum: "There is a policeman who is renowned as a model German. Nicknamed 'the gentleman,' he is the soul of honesty. He permits wagons through the gates of the Wall, refusing to take a bribe. He also permits Jewish children to pass to the Other Side by the dozen to buy food … Examples of his wondrous decency and honesty are recounted daily. He plays all sorts of games with the smuggler children. He lines them up, commands them to sing, and marches them through the gates." Ringelblum, *Notes from the Warsaw Ghetto: The Journal of Emmanuel Ringelblum*, ed. and trans. Jacob Sloan (New York: Schocken, 1974), p. 265.

137 See Frank McDonough, *Sophie Scholl: The Real Story of the Woman Who Defied Hitler* (Stroud: The History Press, 2010); Annette Dumbach and Jud Newborn, *Sophie Scholl and the White Rose* (Oxford: Oneworld, 2009). Marc Rothemund's Oscar-nominated 2005 film, *Sophie Scholl: The Final Days*, is edge-of-your-seat stuff, with a galvanizing performance by Julia Jentsch as Sophie (see www.imdb.com/title/tt0426578/). It has consistently been a student favorite in iterations of my International Politics on Film course at the University of British Columbia. An astonishing literary treatment of anti-Nazi resisters, based on the true story of Otto and Elise Hampel, is the 1947 novel by Hans Fallada, *Every Man Dies Alone*, trans. Michael Hofmann (New York: Melville House, 2010), also available in English under the title *Alone in Berlin* (London: Penguin Modern Classics, 2010). This is also an intimate, documentary-style portrait of the Nazi police state in malignant operation.

138 See also Barbara Coloroso's exploration of genocide's links to bullying—the "conscious, willful, deliberate activity intended to harm, to induce fear through the threat of further aggression, and to create terror in the target." Coloroso, *Extraordinary Evil: A Brief History of Genocide* (New York: Viking, 2007), pp. 51–80 (quoted passage from p. 55).

139 Donald Bloxham, *Genocide, The World Wars, and the Unweaving of Europe* (London: Vallentine Mitchell, 2008), p. 238.

140 Oliner and Oliner, *The Altruistic Personality*, p. 222. Such values and character traits may also be manifested collectively, as with the "conspiracy of decency" among Danes to preserve the country's Jewish population.

141 Gonski quoted in Tec, *When Light Pierced the Darkness*, p. 163.

142 Oliner and Oliner, *The Altruistic Personality*, p. 136.

143 Ibid., p. 86.

144 Ibid., p. 257.
145 Ibid., pp. 78–79.
146 Knottnerus quoted in ibid., p. 144.
147 Ibid., p. 282.
148 See the intensely moving portrait of Marianna and Stanislaw Ramotowski—Jewish rescued and Polish rescuer, then husband and wife—related in Anna Bikont's *The Crime and the Silence*. "I didn't marry for love, that came later. I just liked her. I wanted to save a life," Stanislaw Ramotowski told Bikont. The marriage allowed Marianna to be baptized and "Polonized," rescuing her from the Holocaust. "When the war was over, I said to my wife: 'Now, my sweetheart, you're free; go where you will.' She said she wasn't going anywhere. 'Well,' I said, 'if that's the way it is, we'll be together ever after.' And that's how it has been." Bikont adds, "For the next sixty years they didn't part . . . When I saw them the first time, they looked as if they were posing for a portrait. He was sitting near her, holding her hand. Later I saw that this was how they spent most of the day." Bikont, *The Crime and the Silence: Confronting the Massacre of Jews in Wartime Jedwabne*, trans. Alissa Valles (New York: Farrar, Straus and Giroux, 2015), pp. 81, 93 (e-book).
149 Oliner and Oliner, *The Altruistic Personality*, p. 257.

CHAPTER 11

The Sociology and Anthropology of Genocide

The 'genos' is . . . a primary and universal institution of mankind, whatever its actual evolution may be, and it is clear that mankind spent most of its history within the framework of this social unit. It was here that the original esprit de corps, the way of life, the traditions, the forces of cohesion and solidarity were born. It was also here that the spirit of exclusiveness, suspicion, and hatred of other groups was bred. . . . Thus the genos is both the unit against which the crime is directed and the unit from which it originates. . . . Here we are dealing not with casual events but with deeply entrenched anthropological and sociological patterns.

Raphael Lemkin

INTRODUCTION

The disciplines of sociology and anthropology are distinguished by the types of societies studied. Anthropologists have carried out work on the non-industrialized "Third World" or Global South, while sociologists have focused on social patterns and processes within the industrialized "First World" or Global North.[1] Anthropology also possesses a distinctive methodology: fieldwork. Nonetheless, the disciplines are linked by a common concern with societal and cultural processes, and it is appropriate to consider them together.

Sociologists and anthropologists also shared a reluctance, until fairly recently, to engage with the themes of genocide and state terror. "Many sociologists," stated Irving Louis Horowitz in the late 1980s, "exhibit a studied embarrassment about these issues, a feeling that intellectual issues posed in such a manner are melo-dramatic and unfit for scientific discourse."[2] Nancy Scheper-Hughes similarly described "the traditional role of the anthropologist as neutral, dispassionate, cool and rational, [an] objective observer of the human condition"; anthropologists tra-ditionally maintained a "proud, even haughty distance from political engagement."[3]

Fortunately, Horowitz's evaluation is now obsolete, thanks to a host of soci-ologists who have contributed seminally to genocide studies. They include Kurt Jonassohn, Helen Fein, Zygmunt Bauman, Michael Mann, and Daniel Feierstein. Anthropological studies came later, but recent years have been the first antholo-gies on anthropology and genocide, as well as groundbreaking works by Alexander Laban Hinton, Victoria Sanford, and Christopher Taylor, among others.[4]

In examining sociological perspectives, this chapter focuses on three key themes:

1. the sociology of modernity, which has attracted considerable interest from genocide scholars in the wake of Zygmunt Bauman's *Modernity and the Holocaust*;
2. the sociology of "ethnicity" and ethnic conflict; and
3. the role of "middleman" or "market-dominant" minorities.

It then addresses anthropological framings of genocide, focusing also on the work of forensic anthropologists.

SOCIOLOGICAL PERSPECTIVES

The sociology of modernity

Is genocide a modern phenomenon?[5] At first glance, the question seems banal. We saw in Chapter 1 that the destruction of peoples on the basis of group identity extends back to early history, and probably to prehistory. Yet we also know that in recent centuries, and especially during the past hundred years, the prevalence of genocide has taken a quantitative leap. The central issue is: Has that leap also been *qualitative*? Is there something about modernity that has become *definitional* to genocide?

In one of the most discussed works on the Jewish Holocaust, *Modernity and the Holocaust*, sociologist Zygmunt Bauman delivered a resounding "yes" to this question. "Modern civilization was not the Holocaust's *sufficient* condition; it was, however, most certainly its *necessary* condition. Without it, the Holocaust would be unthinkable."[6] Bauman's argument revolved around four core features of modernity: nationalism; "scientific" racism; technological complexity; and bureaucratic ration-alization. Modern nationalism divided the world "fully and exhaustively . . . into national domains," leaving "no space . . . for internationalism" and designating "each scrap of the no-man's-land . . . [as] a standing invitation to aggression." In such a world, European Jews—with their international and cosmopolitan identity—could be construed as alien. They "defied the very truth on which all nations, old and new alike, rested their claims; the ascribed character of nationhood, heredity and natu-ralness of national entities. . . . *The world tightly packed with nations and nation-states abhorred the non-national void. Jews were in such a void: they were such a void.*"[7] This existential unease toward the Jew was combined with scientific racism, which Bauman depicted as a modern phenomenon,[8] overlaying traditional intercommunal antipathies with a veneer of scientific and medical rationality. This brought with it an impetus to total extermination of the racial Other: "The only adequate solution to problems posited by the racist world-view is a total and uncompromising isolation of the pathogenic and infectious race—the source of disease and contamination—through its complete spatial separation or physical destruction."[9]

How could such a totalizing project be implemented? For Bauman, the advent of modern technology and bureaucratic rationality was essential. The mass death that the Nazis developed and inflicted relied on products of the Industrial Revolution. Railway transport, gas chambers, Zyklon B cyanide crystals administered by men in gas masks—all were essentially modern inventions and had to be managed by a bureaucracy of death. The great German theorist of modern bureaucracy, Max Weber, emphasized "its peculiar, 'impersonal' character," which "mean[s] that the mechanism "is easily made to work for anybody who knows how to gain control over it." Weber also argued that "the bureaucratization of all [social] domination very strongly furthers the development of 'rational matter-of-factness' and the personality type of the professional expert," distinguished by his or her cool

Figure 11.1 Sociologist Zygmunt Bauman's *Modernity and the Holocaust* argued for an intrinsic grounding of the Nazis' destruction of the Jews in modern ideologies of racism and nationalism, and the distancing/fragmenting character of highly bureaucratized genocide. He is pictured in September 2013.

Source: Wikimedia Commons.

amorality and devotion to efficiency. Moreover, bureaucracy cultivates secrecy: "the concept of the 'official secret' is the specific invention of the bureaucracy."[10]

The processing of millions of "subhumans" for anonymous death was unthinkable in the absence of such a culture, according to Bauman:

> By its nature, this is a daunting task, unthinkable unless in conjunction with the availability of huge resources, means of their mobilization and planned distribution, skills of splitting the overall task into a great number of partial and specialized functions and skills to co-ordinate their performance. In short, the task is inconceivable without modern bureaucracy.[11]

Moreover, this "splitting [of] the overall task" into isolated and fragmented units of time, space, and work created a vital psychological distance between the victims and those participating in their annihilation. No individual—except, by reputation, the distant and semi-mythical *Führer* figure—exercised overall authority or bore overall responsibility. One did not commit mass murder *per se*. Rather, one operated a railroad switch, or dropped a few cyanide crystals into a shaft: "a cool, objective operation . . . mechanically mediated . . . a deed performed at a distance, one whose effects the perpetrator did not see," in Wolfgang Sofsky's words.[12] Much the same set of values, procedures, and behaviors characterized the nuclear mentality, with its potential for rationally administered omnicide (Chapter 2).[13]

More recently, historian Mark Levene, in his magisterial work *Genocide in the Age of the Nation State*, has argued that "the problem of genocide lies in the very nature of modernity."[14] This, together with the subtitle of his second volume (*The Rise of the West and the Coming of Genocide*), suggests that genocide is *essentially* modern and inextricably linked to the West's imperial expansion from the fifteenth century on (see Chapters 2 and 3): "the crystallization of the phenomenon we call 'genocide'—as opposed to other categories of mass murder—could only be really achieved in the context of an emerging, global, interlocking system of nation-states which finally came to its *fullest* fruition in the twentieth century."[15] While this was "accompanied by no overarching political agenda for the annihilation of foreign peoples," for Levene, it established "a broader cultural discourse in which such annihilation was considered perfectly acceptable." The bureaucratic features which Bauman emphasized resurfaced in Levene's contention that "we normatively name people as members of given tribes, nations, races, religions" because of "modernity's facility for reducing and simplifying complex phenomena—humans included—'into a more manageable and schematized form,'" while failing or refusing "to imagine human beings as potentially possessing multi-layered identities and loyalties."[16]

Two main criticisms of this modernity-of-genocide thesis may be advanced. First, the supposed dividing line between historical and modern genocide seems more stylistic than substantive. It is simply not the case that "the Holocaust left behind and put to shame all its alleged pre-modern equivalents, exposing them as primitive, wasteful and ineffective by comparison," as Bauman contended.[17] Rather, the clear conviction of the founder of genocide studies, Raphael Lemkin, was that "genocide is not an exceptional phenomenon, but . . . occurs in

Figure 11.2 Are the technologies, ideologies, and state capabilities of modernity inextricably linked to genocide? Some argue that the connection is so intimate that we should find another word for the mass killings of pre-modern ages. Even those who take a longer view, like this author, acknowledge distinctive features of genocide in the modern age. Pictured: a canister of Zyklon B, the insecticide that the Nazis adapted to murder Jews and others in gas chambers.

Source: Author's photo of museum display, Yad Vashem, Jerusalem, May 2011.

intergroup relations with a certain regularity like homicide takes place between individuals."[18] Lemkin's own historical analysis of genocide encompassed millennia: he opens his unfinished history of genocide by declaring his intent "to prove that genocide has always existed in history."[19] The UN Genocide Convention that resulted from Lemkin's lobbying efforts likewise recognized in its preamble "that *at all periods of history* genocide has inflicted great losses on humanity" (emphasis added). Levene, for his part, is far too good a historian to ignore the continuities, so he hedges his bets at points—referring to "our phenomenon, *at least in its modern and contemporary manifestations*"; "genocide—*or at least a modern variant of it*"; "any *broad historical examination* of the phenomenon . . ."[20]

To explore the distinctively "modern" features of modern and contemporary genocides is a worthwhile inquiry, and both Bauman and Levene have made foundational contributions to the field. But precisely the same line of inquiry could be launched into the human institution most intimately allied with genocide—war. While we could note all manner of modern expansions and deadly innovations, we would not, I think, suggest that war thereby is *essentially* a modern creation.[21] So, too, with genocide. As Alex Alvarez argued, "What modernity has done is reshape genocide into a more efficient and rational endeavor capable of killing on an industrial scale. The modern age has not created genocide; rather it has altered its nature, application, and efficiency."[22]

Another criticism of the modernity-of-genocide thesis may be summarized in one word: Rwanda (see Chapter 9). There, around one million people were hunted, corralled, and exterminated in *twelve weeks*—a rate of killing exceeding by a wide margin that of the "modern" Nazi holocaust. Yet the genocide was not only more modern in chronological terms; it was carried out by men and women armed with little more than guns and traditional agricultural implements.[23] It involved no appreciable role for scientific or technical experts. And *the killing was conducted up close, often face-to-face, publicly*, with no resort to the physical and psychological distancing strategies and official secrecy supposedly necessary for "modern" mass slaughter.[24] One can argue that the Rwandan holocaust depended on a complex administrative apparatus; a racist ideology tinged with pseudo-science; and the industrial mass production of machetes, hoes, firearms, and grenades. But are these inherently "modern"? Bureaucracy is ancient, as various Chinese dynasties remind us.[25] One suspects that the ideology of hate developed by Hutu Power would have been just as functional without its vaguely modernist overtones.[26] With regard to Rwanda's technology of death, the basic implements of guns, machetes, and explosives all pre-date the Industrial Revolution. Even in the Jewish Holocaust, "the million or so Jews asphyxiated at Auschwitz were killed by hydrogen cyanide, a compound isolated in the eighteenth century. The 1.6 million or so Jews killed at Treblinka, Chelmno, Belzec, and Sobibor [death camps] were asphyxiated by carbon monoxide, which even the ancient Greeks knew was lethal."[27]

ETHNICITY AND ETHNIC CONFLICT

Loe, this is the payment you shall get, if you be one of them they terme, without.

Thomas Merton, 1637

Few concepts are as amorphous and yet important as ethnicity. On one hand, ethnic identifications seem so fluid and mutable as to lack almost any "objective" character. On the other hand, ethnicity is arguably the dominant ideological impetus to conflict and genocide worldwide.

Three historical phenomena account for the prominence of ethnicity in today's "global society." The first is nationalism, touched on in Chapter 2. As medieval Europe moved away from a quilt of overlapping sovereignties and toward the formation of modern states, it first fell under the sway of strong, centralizing monarchs. With the onset of the democratic age via the American and French Revolutions, sovereignty was held increasingly to reside in "the people." But *which* people? How defined? The popular thrust gave rise in the nineteenth century to modern ethnic nationalism, as Western rulers and their populations sought an ideology to unify the new realms. The result was what Benedict Anderson called "imagined communities": geographically disparate but mutually identified agglomerations defining themselves as "French," "German," "British," "Italian," and so on.[28] The core idea was that the "imagined community" required a particular political form, the "nation-state," to achieve true realization.[29]

On what basis were these communities imagined? It is worth pausing briefly to consider the bases or foundations of ethnicity, as they have been listed by a prominent scholar of the subject. Anthony Smith cited six foundations of ethnic identity: "1. a collective proper name, 2. a myth of common ancestry, 3. shared historical memories, 4. one or more differentiating elements of common culture, 5. an association with a specific 'homeland,' 6. a sense of solidarity for significant sectors of the population."[30]

While a refined concept of ethnicity is often considered to be a Western invention, this is open to challenge. Han Chinese, for example, had a well-developed ethnic sensibility well before the West's rise to dominance.[31] So too, clearly, did the peoples of the ancient Middle East, whose ethnic rivalries and extermination strategies were quite well-advanced, if the relevant religious texts are granted credence. (Even if the genocides mentioned in Chapter 1 were fantasies, the fact that people felt drawn to fantasize them speaks to ethnoreligious distinctions and divisions as sharp as any in modern times.) Indeed, it could be argued that ethnicity is at least latent in all societies, independent of Western penetration and influence. Other social units—notably extended family, clan, and tribe—evince many of the same solidaristic bonds as ethnicity; they may be considered proto-ethnic groupings. Like ethnic groups, moreover, these identifications are meaningless without an Other to define against oneself. There are no in-groups without out-groups, with what anthropologist Fredrik Barth has called "boundary maintenance mechanisms" serving to demarcate the two.[32]

When a dominant ethnic collectivity is established as the basis of a "nation-state," a quandary arises in dealing with the out-groups—"ethnic minorities"—that also find themselves within the boundaries of that state. Such minorities exist everywhere; even supposedly unified or organic nation-states (Japan is the most commonly cited example) have them. This often carries explosive consequences for intercommunal violence, including genocide, as we have had numerous opportunities to witness in these pages.

The second historical factor is the spread of Western imperialism and colonialism around the world (Chapter 2), which shaped the present-day configuration of nationalisms in important ways. Most obviously, it spurred the idea of ethnic nationalism (though some nationalisms, and a wide range of ethnic *identifications*, clearly existed independently of it). Despite the best efforts of colonizers to preserve those they subjugated from such dangerous influences, ethnic-nationalist ideologies were gradually absorbed and integrated into the anti-colonial movements that arose from the mid-nineteenth through mid-twentieth centuries. In addition, following the time-honored strategy of divide and rule, aimed at *preventing* nationalism, the colonialists typically gathered a host of clans, tribes, and long-established "national" entities into a single territorial and administrative unit. A glance at the ethnic composition of countries such as Nigeria, Congo, and Indonesia suffices to remind one of the enormous diversity of peoples that comprised the deliberately unimaginable "communities" of colonialism.

The nationalist leaders who sprang to prominence in the colonized world in the 1920s and 1930s were thus confronted with the crushing challenge of either forging a genuine sense of national community among diverse peoples, or negotiating a peaceful and viable fragmentation of the colonial unit. For the most part, they chose to maintain the colonial boundaries. In some cases, this produced viable multiethnic states (see Chapter 16), but in many instances it did not. Sometimes the managed breakup of multiethnic entities led to massive violence (India, Palestine); in states where the leadership chose to preserve an artificial unity, time-bombs were set for the future (Nigeria, Indonesia, Yugoslavia). The ethnic violence associated with the collapse of the Soviet empire in 1991 is a recent example of this trend.

A final historical conjuncture, often overlooked, is *globalization*. Although globalizing trends can be traced back many centuries, they have reached a new stage of complex interconnectedness at the turn of the millennium. One advantage of ethnic identifications is that they offer a strong sense of psychological rootedness amidst change and upheaval. Given the rapid transformations associated with globalization, where is a stable sense of "we," and therefore of "me," to be found? The anthropologist Clifford Geertz has argued that "during the disorienting process of modernization . . . unintegrated citizens, looking for an anchor in a sea of changes, will grab hold of an increasingly anachronistic ethnic identity, which bursts onto the scene and then recedes as the process of structural differentiation moves toward a reintegrated society.[33]

One can question, though, whether such ethnic resurgence is a transitory phenomenon. As globalization is accompanied by intense nationalist sentiment in many parts of the world, the "transition" seems to be taking rather longer than expected. Part of the misunderstanding may lie in a tendency to believe that ethnic identifications are not primordial but fictional—created and manipulated by self-interested elites to mobilize their followers. (This line of argument has been bolstered by recent "postmodern" orientations in the humanities and social sciences.)

There *is* an important sense in which ethnic identifications are "imagined" or "mythical."[34] As I will show below, they are also subject to endless manipulations by elite figures and violence specialists. Ethnic identifications are protean in the sense that all of the six "bases" that Anthony Smith identifies for ethnicity can be altered, though not always at will or completely. One can change one's territorial base and recast one's primary ethnic identification, as generations of immigrants to the ethnic "melting-pot" of the United States have done (while often maintaining a secondary attachment to the previous identification). Ancestral myths can be revised, reinterpreted, or abandoned. Historical memory, language, culinary taste, forms of artistic expression—all are highly mutable.

Over time, however, ethnic identifications often achieve intergenerational stability. They assume a practical force in individual and group psychology, societal structure, and political behavior that is impossible to ignore, least of all by those seeking to understand and confront genocide and other mass violence.[35] In *Becoming Evil*, James Waller presented evidence from psychology, sociology, and anthropology to show that these identifications originate deep in human social behavior: "Knowing who is kin, knowing who is in our social group, has a deep importance to species like ours." Moreover, "We have an evolved capacity to see our group as superior to all others and even to be reluctant to recognize members of other groups as deserving of equal respect." Members of a cannibal tribe in Irian Jaya, Indonesia, convey this pointedly: they define themselves as "the human beings," and all others as "the edible ones."[36]

Ethnic conflict and violence "specialists"

Some defining work on the dynamics of mass violence has pointed to the role of organizational actors and their representatives in provoking and channeling violent outbreaks. The founder of genocide studies, Raphael Lemkin, wrote in his unfinished history of genocide that "vested interest groups often foster or actually supervise the carrying out of genocide for reasons of expediency. They may want to distract the people on whom their power depends from certain grievances or gain other advantages from the destruction of the victim group."[37] The contemporary sociologist Donald L. Horowitz emphasizes the role of

> organizations, often tied to ethnically based political parties, [that] reflect and reinforce interethnic hostility through propaganda, ritual, and force. They run the gamut from civilian to proto-military organizations, operating under varying degrees of secrecy and with varying degrees of coherence and military training. Their raison d'être is the alleged danger from the ethnic enemy.[38]

Within such organizations and associations, Paul R. Brass stressed the role of violence "specialists" operating within "institutionalized . . . systems" of violence:

> The kinds of violence that are committed in ethnic, communal, and racial "riots" are, I believe, undertaken mostly by "specialists," who are ready to be called out on such occasions, who profit from it, and whose activities profit others who may or may not be actually paying for the violence carried out. In fact, in many countries at different times in their histories, there have been regions or cities and towns which have developed what I call "institutionalized riot systems," in which known actors specialize in the conversion of incidents between members of different communities into ethnic riots. The activities of these specialists are usually required for a riot to spread from the initial incident of provocation.[39]

The significance of this category of actors to the fomenting and implementing of genocide should be recognized.[40] Note some of the "specialists" that Brass identifies: "criminal elements and members of youth gangs," "local militant group leaders," "politicians, businessmen, religious leaders," "college and university professors," "pamphleteers and journalists . . . deliberately spreading rumors and scurrilous propaganda," "hooligans" (ranging from Nazi thugs to modern soccer hoodlums), "communal political elites."[41] Add to this list the violence specialists cited by Charles Tilly in his study of *The Politics of Collective Violence:* "Pirates, privateers, paramilitaries, bandits, mercenaries, mafiosi, militias, posses, guerrilla forces, vigilante groups, company police, and bodyguards."[42] Beyond the essential (and universally acknowledged) role of state officials and security force commanders, what we have here is a veritable who's-who of the leading *agents provocateurs* of genocide, its foot-soldiers, and its ideological defenders.

BOX 11.1 GENOCIDE AND CRIMINOLOGY

Figure 11.3 Cover of Augustine Brannigan, *Beyond the Banality of Evil* (2013).

Source: Courtesy of Oxford University Press.

In the sociological field of criminology, wrote Augustine Brannigan, "mass murder, atrocities, and genocide appear to attract little attention. Instead, there is a preoccupation with individual-level predatory behaviour." This "has led to a mindset in which we have become almost incapable of grasping the phenomenon of state-initiated crimes, such as those associated with inter-ethnic conflict."[43] His 2013 book *Beyond the Banality of Evil* is one of a number of recent contributions that aim to address this gulf in the field.[44]

Defining "crime" as "the use of force or fraud in the pursuit of self-interest," Brannigan notes that it has tended to be depicted as "deviant" behavior, transgressing societal norms. But what if an entire society, or at least its dominant elites, *sanction* mass killings, rendering them perfectly legal under the laws and norms inculcated by the state? Brannigan deployed Jack Katz's concept of "righteous slaughter" to denote killings that "are undertaken in a sense of righteousness, and reflect the defence of a communal good, or a value that the victim is seen to transgress." Such "righteous" killing is powerfully connected to a sense of *humiliation* (see Chapter 10), as when a man finds his lover in bed with another: "The perpetrators face a challenge that threatens to degrade or humiliate them. . . . They transcend the humiliation, and seek satisfaction in violence by making a last stand in defence of The Good."

In such instances, perpetrators "rarely exhibit signs of guilt or remorse," and "the legal system typically minimizes their culpability"—as killing an "unfaithful" woman has generally been accepted as a mitigating circumstance in prosecuting and sentencing the murderer. In the same way, Brannigan contended, "throughout history, genocide and war crimes have been conventionalized, and . . . their perpetrators have largely escaped the illegalities of murder." Thus, the crimes for which senior Nazis were sentenced and often hanged after the Second World War were paradoxical in that they "were not viewed as crimes when they were planned and executed. They were state orders . . . adopted as government policy."

Criminologists likewise have tended to adhere to "the control perspective pioneered by Norbert Elias," in which inadequate socialization of youth by familial and educational institutions leads to diminished self-control and delinquent actions. But in the Nazi case, Brannigan argued, "mass murder results not from a lack of self-control, *but from quite the opposite: over-control*." In a society driven toward genocidal outcomes, citizens are inculcated to express "what might be called genocidal altruism." A ubiquitous emphasis upon the threat that the homeland or in-group faces, and the veneration that elites claim to merit, drives ordinary people toward "a politics that reflect[s] the highest human aspirations, the highest honour that individuals could bestow on their country and their legacy," and transforms the "crime of crimes" into a noble and self-sacrificial endeavor.

Critical here, for Brannigan, are political formations "that put individual choices at the disposal of the sovereign, the leader, or the larger social collective." However, such elite strategies involve high levels of organization, command, and coordination of the general population—offering numerous opportunities for disruption, both by domestic dissidents making individual stands, and key international actors who can coordinate outside interventions.

The more fundamental counter to "righteous slaughters," explored further in Chapter 16, is a range of preventive strategies aimed at "the cultivation of social structures in which the sovereign's aspiration for political transcendence is restrained." This requires "populations of engaged citizens who will not permit their states to silence their voices, reduce their heterogeneity, and further their interests in disregard for the plurality of interests in society." The rise of a cosmopolitan worldview, also discussed in this book's conclusion, may offer a "way forward . . . to renegotiate the supremacy of the sovereign state and to lay the foundations for future cosmopolitan governance, nationally and transnationally, that makes politically motivated mass murder ideologically indefensible and strategically impossible. This will take decades, but globalization makes this course of action not only feasible, but also unavoidable."

"Middleman minorities"

> The Greeks and Armenian merchants have been the leeches in this part of the world sucking the life blood out of the country for centuries.
>
> Admiral Mark L. Bristol, US High Commissioner to Turkey, 1922

Perhaps no collectivities are as vulnerable to hatred and large-scale killing as those "characterized as possessing an excess of enterprise, ambition, energy, arrogance, and achievement by those who believe themselves lacking such traits."[45] Such minorities are not necessarily immigrants or descendants of immigrants, but often they are, and this foreignness is a key factor in their targeting. Worldwide, reflecting both centuries-old patterns and more recent globalizing trends, populations have arrived or been introduced from outside the established society. Lacking access to land, as well as the network of social relations that dominant groups can utilize, such groups normally settle in the cities or towns—often in neighborhoods or zones that quickly acquire a minority tinge. Even when they are brought in by a colonial power as indentured laborers (as with the Indians whom the British imported to Uganda, South Africa, Fiji, and elsewhere), there is a strong tendency for such groups to establish themselves in commercial trades.

Occupying an inherently vulnerable minority position, these sectors historically have been attractive to colonial powers as local allies and intermediaries. Such alliances allowed colonizers to "divide and rule," with the aid of a minority that was (1) less anchored to the territory and dominant culture in question, and therefore less prone to push for autonomy or national independence; and (2) heavily dependent on colonial favor, and therefore more likely to be loyal to the colonizers. Colonial favor often translated into greater educational opportunities and positions in lower and middle sectors of the bureaucracy. However, even in the absence of such colonial backing, and in the face of strong opposition from the dominant society, such groups almost universally emphasize education as a means of moving beyond their marginal position and attaining prosperity. They typically display strong bonds of ethnic, cultural, and material solidarity among their members, and they may have the advantage of access to capital and trading relationships through remaining ties with their (or their ancestors') countries of origin.

A frequent result is that these minorities establish a high degree of prominence, sometimes even outright dominance, in key sectors of the national economy. Well-known examples include Jews, whom Amy Chua refers to as "the quintessential market-dominant minority,"[46] and the Chinese of Southeast Asia. East Indians achieved a similar position in many East African economies, while Lebanese traders came to dominate the vital diamond trade in West Africa. The Dutch, British, and Portuguese-descended Whites of southern Africa may also be cited, along with the White "pigmentocrats" who enjoy elite status in heavily indigenous countries of Latin America. The potential for conflict, including for the violent or genocidal targeting of middleman minorities,[47] is apparent, though far from inevitable.[48] Through their common and preferential ties to colonial authorities, these minorities were easily depicted as agents of the alien dominator, opponents of national liberation and self-determination, and cancers in the body politic. Even today, their frequently-extensive international ties and "cosmopolitan" outlook may grate on the majority's nationalist sentiments. Moreover, their previous relationship with a colonial power has often translated into a quest for alliances with authoritarian regimes in the post-colonial era. Elite Chinese businessmen in the Philippines and Indonesia, for example, were among the most enthusiastic and visible backers of the Marcos and Suharto dictatorships. When authoritarian rule collapsed, the mass hostility, resentment, and humiliation could be vented under democratic guise—a pattern that Chua has described well:

> In countries with a market-dominant minority and a poor "indigenous" majority, the forces of democratization and marketization directly collide. As markets enrich the market-dominant minority, democratization increases the political voice and power of the frustrated majority. The competition for votes fosters the emergence of demagogues who scapegoat the resented minority, demanding an end to humiliation, and insisting that the nation's wealth be reclaimed by its "true owners." Thus as America toasted the spread of global elections through the 1990s, vengeful ethnic slogans proliferated: "Zimbabwe for Zimbabweans," "Indonesia for Indonesians," "Uzbekistan for Uzbeks," "Kenya for Kenyans," "Ethiopia for Ethiopians," "Yids [Jews] out of Russia," "Hutu Power," "Serbia for Serbs," and so on. . . . As popular hatred of the rich "outsiders" mounts, the result is an ethnically charged political pressure cooker in which some form of backlash is almost unavoidable.

Among the strategies of backlash, the "most ferocious kind . . . is ethnic cleansing and other forms of majority-supported ethnic violence," up to and including genocide.[49] Rwanda in 1994 is the best example of democratization helping to spawn genocide against a relatively prosperous minority. However, if we remove the democratic element from the equation, we can also add to the list the two other "canonical" genocides of the twentieth century. The relative wealth, industriousness, and educational attainment of the Armenian minority, even under conditions of discrimination and repression in the Ottoman lands, made them an easy target for the fanatical nationalism of the Young Turks (Chapter 4). Similar hatred or at least distaste toward Jews in Germany and other European countries contributed to popular support for the Holocaust against them (Chapter 6). Note that all three of these genocides featured massive looting and plundering along with mass

Figure 11.4 "Many homes and businesses owned by ethnic Chinese in Jakarta were looted and burned in the riots" of 1998 that overthrew the Suharto dictatorship in Indonesia. In times of political turbulence, ethnic "middleman" minorities and their property are especially vulnerable to mob violence and destruction. For more on this period of Indonesian history, see Box 7a.

Source: Office of the Vice President, Republic of Indonesia/Wikimedia Commons.

murder (see the discussion of genocide and greed in Chapter 10). Genocide offers an unprecedented opportunity to "redress" an economic imbalance by seizing the wealth and property of the victims, and to inflict on them the kind of humiliation that the majority population may have experienced.

ANTHROPOLOGICAL PERSPECTIVES

A confession: I have long been envious of anthropologists. Political scientists like myself are commanded to maintain a detached, "objective" view of their subject. Our research stratagems are usually confined to the library and the office, with only occasional forays into the outside world. Anthropologists, by contrast, are allowed and encouraged to get their hands dirty. The defining method of anthropology—fieldwork—commands them to wade into the thick of their subject matter, and get to know the people they study. They may "emerge from the field exhausted," but they carry with them "a material of extraordinary richness and depth."[50] Reading anthropological case studies, one sees and hears the subjects, smells the air, tastes the food.

Anthropology "calls for an understanding of different societies as they appear *from the inside*,"[51] where anthropologists are seen as inevitable and integral participants in the cross-cultural encounter. They are expected to describe the impact of the experience on their own subjectivity. Assisting with the forensic excavation of mass graves in Guatemala, Victoria Sanford reported: "I'm not vomiting, I haven't fainted, what a beautiful valley, everything is greener than green, those are real bones, my god 200 people were massacred here, their relatives are watching."[52] It would be hard to describe such an experience as enjoyable. But it is certainly *revelatory*, both to author and reader, in a way that more detached analyses rarely are.

Consider the approach adopted in another recent and impressive work on the anthropology of genocidal conflict: Ivana Macek's *Sarajevo Under Siege: Anthropology in Wartime* (2009). In April 1992, Bosnian Serb forces closed a ring around the cosmopolitan city of Sarajevo, beginning a siege that lasted for nearly four years (see pp. 434–436). Macek—a Croat scholar from Zagreb whose anthropological research had previously focused on Africa—found herself drawn not to "aggressive Croatian nationalism," but to the besieged multiethnic population of Sarajevo, which was "being hit hardest by a nationalistic war." She decided "to let individuals' lived experiences of violence stand at the center of research and from that point to trace the effects of war on society and culture." In so doing, she consciously took "a poet's approach to fieldwork, as well as to writing." In contrast to the emotional disengagement and bloodless prose of most social-science writing, Macek proclaimed the anthropologist's right to adopt "a disciplined subjectivity [which] becomes not a flaw or obstacle but a crucial element for creating meaningful knowledge."

For six months over the period of the siege, during several visits, Macek shared the struggle and toil of Sarajevans, "employ[ing] all of my faculties . . . in order to manage from day to day, as well as record what they and I were undergoing." She emerged with a unique perspective: both insider/participant and rigorous scholarly observer. She documented the "deep sense of shame and humiliation" that always lurked, as people desperately clawed the means of subsistence from their austere and dangerous environment. But she also documented the strategies of coping and resistance: from the "fantastically inventive solutions to wartime shortages"; to the "magical thinking and small private magic routines" which people adopted as a "'childish' solution to an objectively unbearable situation"; to the gallows humor that citizens indulged in ("What is the difference between Sarajevo and Auschwitz? There is no gas in Sarajevo"). Perhaps surprisingly, and inspiringly, an outpouring of creative talent occurred as a reaction to the siege, resulting in "an amazingly active artistic life": as one Sarajevan told her, "arts became the fount of the lifeforce. It gave back life to people, gave birth anew to optimism and strength, and gave meaning in a time when it looked as if life had lost all meaning." But Macek also witnessed expressions of "the emotional numbness and irrationality that followed an excess of pain": "People I saw who simply stood in open places during the shelling as if nothing was going on . . ."

Perhaps most poignantly, Macek captured the slow erosion of the cosmopolitan and interethnic identity that the overarching designation of "Sarajevan" had long sponsored and permitted. Increasingly, Sarajevans grew

> divided along ethnonational lines into Muslims, Serbs, and Croats. Eth-
> noreligious identities became politicized and grew more salient in everyday
> life. . . . Family members, friends, colleagues, and neighbors were judged by new,
> wartime standards, as people almost invariably tried to understand whether

or not others' actions were influenced by their national identity. . . . Sarajevans started to "remember" the ethnoreligious traditions that most of them had lost during the secularization of society following the Second World War.[53]

The result of Macek's investigations was a portrait of a community under siege, with acts of genocide and urbicide underway (and resisted), with identities and memories summoned and reshaped. It provided further evidence that, in historian Anton Weiss-Wendt's assessment, it is anthropologists who "have made probably the most valuable contribution to genocide studies in . . . recent years."[54] However, this emergence of an anthropological critique in genocide studies required, and derived from, a broader shift in the discipline's focus: "a theoretical and ethnographic move away from studying small, relatively stable communities toward looking at those under siege, in flux, and victimized by state violence or insurgency movements."[55] The declaration issued in *Anthropology Today* in 1993, "Anthropologists Against Ethnic Violence," stated that "we must not shirk the responsibility of disputing the claims of demagogues and warning of the dangers of ethnic violence."[56]

The declaration, and the broader paradigm shift it represented, also reflected a conviction that anthropology had been deeply compromised, in the past, by its alliances with European imperialism and Nazism.[57] Most nineteenth-century anthropologists took for granted European dominance over subject peoples. Their schema of classification tended to revolve around hierarchies of humanity: they sifted and categorized the peoples of the world in a way that bolstered the European claim to supremacy. Modern "scientific" racism was one result. Even the most liberal anthropologists of the pre-First World War period, such as Franz Boas, viewed the disappearance of many primitive civilizations as preordained; "salvage ethnography" was developed in an attempt to describe as much of these civilizations as possible before nature took its supposedly inevitable course.[58]

Perhaps neither before nor since have anthropologists played such a prominent role in state policy as during the Nazi era (Chapter 6). Gretchen Schafft noted that "German and, to a lesser extent, Austrian anthropologists were involved in the Holocaust as perpetrators, from its beginning to its conclusion . . . Never had their discipline been so well respected and received. Never had practitioners been so busy . . . while the price for not cooperating was 'internal exile,' joblessness, or incarceration."[59] Prominent anthropologists such as Eugen Fischer, Adolf Würth, and Sophie Ehrhardt flocked to lend a scientific gloss to the Nazis' preposterous racial theories about Jews, Roma, and Slavs; many of these "scholars" continued their work into the postwar period.[60]

However, contradictorily and simultaneously, anthropology was emerging as the most pluralistic and *least* ethnocentric of the social sciences. Under the influence of the discipline's leading figures—Franz Boas, the revolutionary ethnographer Bronislaw Malinowski, the Englishman A.R. Radcliffe-Brown, and the American Margaret Mead—a methodology was developed that encouraged nonjudgmental involvement in the lives and cultures of one's subjects. Hierarchies of "development" were undermined by anthropologists' nuanced study of "primitive" societies that proved to be extraordinarily complex and sophisticated. And the supposedly scientific basis for racial hierarchy was powerfully challenged by work such as that of Boas, who "researched the change in head shape across only one American generation," thereby "demonstrating to the world how race, language, and culture are causally unlinked."[61] Anthropologists played a notable and little-known role in drafting the Universal Declaration of Human Rights, cautioning the UN Commission devoted to the task against "ethnocentrism, the assumption of the superiority of one's own cultural values."[62] With the great wave of decolonization after the Second World War, it was anthropologists above all who went "into the field" to grapple with, and in a sense validate, diverse "Third World" societies.

Anthropology's guiding ideal of cultural relativism requires that the practitioner "suspend one's judgement and preconceptions as much as possible, in order to better understand another's worldview." In studying genocidal processes, the relativist approach emphasizes "local understandings and cultural dynamics that both structure and motivate genocide," and examines them in their broader cultural context. Rather than "simply dismissing *génocidaires* as 'irrational' and 'savage,'" the approach "demands that we understand them and their perspective regardless of what we think of perpetrators."[63]

Arguably, though, cultural relativism has its limits. At some point, if one is to confront atrocities, one must adopt a universalist stand (i.e., that atrocities are always criminal, and cannot be excused by culture). Nancy Scheper-Hughes, among others, has criticized cultural relativism as "moral relativism" that is "no longer appropriate to the world in which we live." If anthropology "is to be worth anything at all, it must be ethically grounded." [64] Alexander Hinton likewise suggests that relativism "played a key role in inhibiting anthropologists from studying genocide," together with other forms of "political violence in complex state societies."[65]

Partly because of relativist influences, and partly because of its preference for "studying small, relatively stable communities,"[66] anthropology's engagement with genocide came relatively late. Only recently has a "school" begun to coalesce, developing a rich body of literature, particularly on terror and genocide in Latin America, Africa, and Southeast Asia. Deploying fieldwork-based ethnography (literally, "writing about ethnic groups"), these researchers have amassed and analyzed a wealth of individual testimonies about the atrocities. In Victoria Sanford's estimation, this "is among the greatest contributions anthropology can make to understanding social problems—the presentation of testimonies, life histories, and ethnographies of violence."[67] Together with the reports of human rights organizations and truth commissions (see Chapter 15), these provide important evidence, for present and future generations, of the nature and scale of atrocity.

Anthropologists go further still, to analyze how atrocity is ritualized within cultures, and how when collectively "performed," it serves to bolster communal identity and solidarity. A wide range of commentators have noted, for example, the atmosphere of festive cruelty that regularly pervades genocidal frenzies. Where the killing and celebrations of it are not tightly circumscribed, limited to a core genocidal cadre, they often assume a carnival-like flavor. In a North American context, one can recall the party atmosphere that prevailed among all-white spectators at the lynching of African American men and women, or the Colorado militia perpetrators of the Sand Creek Massacre of Cheyenne (see p. 157), who "put their accomplishments on public display, a deliriously received victory parade through Denver providing the opportunity for them to bedeck their horses, uniforms and other accoutrements with the various bodily parts—mostly female genitalia—that they had garnered as trophies."[68] In both cases, the performance and ritual celebration of genocidal acts helped to fortify white tribal solidarities, constructed against a threatening tide of "savage" Indians or "depraved" black males. Where these subaltern identifications are not fantastical but actual, one sees not only a similar ritual quality to acts of vengeance against (real) oppressors, whether localized or generalized, but the incorporation of *fantasies* of vengeance into cultural rituals and performances located along a continuum of subaltern genocide. My own exploration of this theme in *Genocides by the Oppressed* was strongly influenced by anthropological inquiries into ritual performances of retributive victory and atrocity.[69]

Questions of genocide and memory, explored further in Chapter 14, are also informed and interpreted by anthropological researchers: how coping strategies are adopted in the aftermath of mass atrocity;[70] how atrocities may become literally "part of the landscape" for communities, attached to familiar objects, irrupting to the forefront of consciousness at unexpected moments:

> [The] living memory of terror can reinvoke the physical and psychological pain of past acts of violence in unexpected moments. A tree, for example, is not just a tree. A river, not just a river. At a given moment, a tree is a reminder of the baby whose head was smashed against a tree by a soldier. The tree, and the memory of the baby it invokes, in turn reinvoke a chain of memories of terror, including witnessing the murder of a husband or brother who was tied to another tree and beaten to death—perhaps on the same day or perhaps years later.[71]

Culturally specific practices of terror are especially well suited to anthropological investigation. In his study of the Rwandan genocide, *Sacrifice as Terror*, Christopher Taylor showed how cultural dynamics, rituals, and symbolism may help to explain the particular course that the holocaust took. His analysis demonstrated—in Alexander Hinton's summary—that anthropological methods "explain why the violence was perpetrated in certain ways—for example, the severing of Achilles tendons, genital mutilation, breast oblation, the construction of roadblocks that served as execution sites, bodies being stuffed into latrines." The violence "was deeply symbolic," representing cultural beliefs about expulsion and excretion, obstruction and flow.[72] For example, Taylor pointed out the symbolism of the Nyabarongo River as a route by which murdered Tutsis were to be "removed from Rwanda and retransported to their presumed land of origin," thereby purifying the nation of its internal "'foreign' minority." Figure 9.2 on p. 481 shows the grim results. In Taylor's interpretation,

> Rwanda's rivers became part of the genocide by acting as the body politic's organs of elimination, in a sense "excreting" its hated internal other. It is not much of a leap to infer that Tutsi were thought of as excrement by their persecutors. Other evidence of this is apparent in the fact that many Tutsi were stuffed into latrines after their deaths.[73]

An intimate familiarity with day-to-day cultural praxis allows anthropologists to draw connections between "exceptional" outbursts of atrocity, such as genocide, and more quotidian forms and structures of violence. The leading theorist in this regard is Nancy Scheper-Hughes, whose classic study of a Brazilian village, *Death without Weeping*, explored the desensitization of women-as-mothers to the deaths of their infant children amidst pervasive scarcity.[74] This extended even to complicity in their offspring's deaths through the deliberate withholding of food and care, with the resulting mortality viewed as divinely ordained. Subsequently, Scheper-Hughes outlined a *genocidal continuum*, composed

> of a multitude of "small wars and invisible genocides" conducted in the normative social spaces of public schools, clinics, emergency rooms, hospital wards, nursing homes, court rooms, prisons, detention centers, and public morgues. The continuum refers to the human capacity to reduce others to nonpersons, to monsters, or to things that give structure, meaning, and rationale to everyday practices of violence. It is essential that we recognize in our species (and in ourselves) *a genocidal capacity* and that we exercise a defensive hypervigilance, a hypersensitivity to the less dramatic, *permitted*, everyday acts of violence that make participation (under other conditions) in genocidal acts possible, perhaps more easy than we would like to know. I would include all expressions of social exclusion, dehumanization, depersonalization, pseudo-speciation, and reification that normalize atrocious behavior and violence toward others.[75]

Scheper-Hughes explored how such everyday forms of violence, social marginalization, and repression can "prime" societies for more visible outbreaks of mass atrocity. She noted, for instance, that Brazilian "street children" experience attacks by police "that are genocidal in their social and political sentiments." The children "are often described as 'dirty vermin' so that unofficial policies of 'street cleaning,' 'trash removal,' 'fly swatting,' and 'pest removal' are invoked in garnering broad-based public support for their extermination." Through such practices and rhetoric, genocide becomes "socially incremental," something that is "experienced by perpetrators, collaborators, bystanders—and even by victims themselves—as expected, routine, even justified."[76] There seems a clear connection between such everyday rhetoric and the propaganda discourse of full-scale genocide, in which Native American children were referred to as "nits [who] make lice," Jews as "vermin," and Rwandan Tutsis as "cockroaches."

In closing this brief account of anthropological framings and insights, it is worth considering the role of *forensic anthropologists*. Bridging the natural and social sciences, they "have worked with health professionals, lawyers, photographers, and nongovernmental organizations to analyze physical remains and gather evidence with which to prosecute perpetrators."[77] Their core activities consist of the "search for, recovery, and preservation of physical evidence at the outdoor scene" of crimes and mass atrocities. They document how evidence relates to its "depositional environment," and use the data collected to reconstruct the events surrounding the deaths of the exhumed victims.[78]

Photo 11.5 (above) The "preserved ruin" of the Eastern State Penitentiary in Philadelphia, USA, a nineteenth-century prison in which inmates were held incommunicado for twenty-three hours daily; some went insane. The penitentiary was closed in 1971.

Source: Author's photo, March 2011.

Photo 11.6 Anthropologist Nancy Scheper-Hughes, who coined the term "the genocidal continuum," did the bulk of her fieldwork in Latin America, where homeless people—like these youths sleeping rough in Buenos Aires, Argentina—are highly vulnerable to harassment and even murder by state "security" forces and off-duty "death squads."

Source: Photo by Hernán Piñera/Creative Commons/Flickr.

BOX 11.2 "THE BONE WOMAN": CLEA KOFF

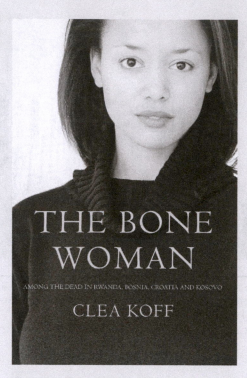

Figure 11.7 Cover of Clea Koff, *The Bone Woman*.

Source: Courtesy of Atlantic Books.

Clea Koff was an anthropology student, spending her summer digging for ancient skeletons in Greece, when she realized she "didn't want to exhume . . . people [who] had been buried 'properly.' " Instead, "I wanted to investigate clandestine graves and the surface remains of crime victims, or of people whose deaths were accidental. My real interest was people who'd been recently killed and whose identities were unknown."

Her passion led Koff to combine her Master's studies with four years (1996–2000) working in the field with the United Nations' newly-created forensics team, first in post-genocide Rwanda, then in the Balkans: Bosnia, Croatia, and Kosovo. Her memoir, *The Bone Woman*, describes her first encounters with the human detritus of genocidal killing.[79] She grew used to autopsy reports containing phrases like "putrefied, smelly mass of residual unidentifiable viscera." She learned that "bodies in the state of decomposition known technically as saponified have a tender skin. If you punctured it, something not dissimilar to cottage cheese came foaming out, and then you had to clean that away as well."

The sheer horror of genocide's indiscriminate slaughter often afflicted Koff, in her waking thoughts and her dreams alike. In Kibuye, Rwanda, she excavated tiny corpses from a mass grave that her team called "the nursery" because of the number of children and infants unearthed there. Later, near Vlasenica in Bosnia, "I 'saw' this young guy, there at Cerska, on the hillside where we had just been digging, and I 'felt' the pain of the bullet entering his thigh just above the knee; I could sense his youth and the tragedy of it all and I thought of his family and what they were missing . . . . I lost an element of self-control." She berated herself for letting her emotions impede "whatever it is that allows me to work with dead bodies without feeling tragedy as I work."

Koff grew familiar with the daily "aches and pains" of forensic work: "I had Trowel Thumb, Gravedigger's Back, Left Knuckle Callus, Inner Thigh Pick Bruise, and Right Index Finger Trowel Callus." There were deeper discomforts as well, like the threat posed by the minefields that littered the Bosnian countryside. "We were told that if we stepped on a mine with a lift-off trigger (as opposed to a pressure trigger), the best thing to do is stand absolutely still. Even if you have to stand still for two days, you are better off waiting for help than trying to disengage from the mine."

She nevertheless found it "inordinately satisfying to lift bodies I've excavated out of their grave. These are people whom someone attempted to expunge from the record, the very bodies perpetrators sought to hide. I particularly cherish helping to carry my bodies on their stretchers away from the grave. It is as though I've seen the bodies through, from initial uncovering to liberation." She took comfort, as well, in the solidarity of her fellow forensic investigators. "When I'm sitting in a vehicle at the end of a long, hot day and I reek of decomposing tissue and my back is aching from lifting bodies and I'm trying not to think about everything I just saw wrenched from the ground that day, I feel better looking around me and seeing my teammates, just as grimy and absorbed in their thoughts, people who have just gone through everything I've just gone through. Even if we never talk about it, we understand one another's experiences that day as no one else could."

Most of all, there was the satisfaction of contributing, as Koff saw it, to processes of truth, justice, and post-conflict reconciliation. Of the victims of the 1995 Srebrenica massacre exhumed at Cerska, Koff wrote: "these bodies, by their very presence, were dismantling years of the perpetrators' propaganda that the grave didn't exist, that the missing men were probably larking about in Italy, that a crime against humanity hadn't taken place . . ." It fortified her conviction that "the global role of forensic science is not only to deter killing but also to contribute, in a postconflict setting, to improved and real communication between 'opposing' parties. This is done by helping to establish the truth about the past— what happened and to whom—which in turn strengthens ties between people in their own communities."

In recent years, forensic anthropologists have become the most visible face of anthropology in genocide investigation and adjudication. Among the pioneers of the field was Clyde Snow, a US specialist who in the 1990s oversaw the exhumations at the Balkan massacre sites of Vukovar and Srebrenica. As Snow described his task:

> When [societies] choose to pursue justice, we forensic anthropologists can put the tools of a rapidly developing science at the disposal of the survivors. We can determine a murder victim's age, sex and race from the size and shape of certain bones. We can extract DNA from some skeletons and match it with samples from the victims' relatives. Marks on the bones can reveal signs of old diseases and injuries reflected in the victims' medical histories, as well as more sinister evidence: bullet holes, cut marks from knives, or fracture patterns produced by blunt instruments. Taken together, such clues can tell us who victims were and how they died—clues crucial to bringing the killers to justice.[80]

Snow's earliest digs were conducted in Argentina during the 1980s, where he helped to train the Argentine Forensic Anthropology Team (Equipo Argentino de Antropología Forense, EAAF) that exhumed victims of the "Dirty War." "Ample forensic evidence" underpinned the report of the Argentine truth commission, *Nunca Más* (Never Again), and the prosecutions of former *junta* leaders.[81] The team went on to conduct exhumations in El Salvador, at the site of the military massacre of some seven hundred civilians at El Mozote.[82] With assistance from the American Association for the Advancement of Science (AAAS), Snow subsequently trained members of the Guatemalan Forensic Anthropology Team.[83] The team's investigations were equally vital to the truth commission report that labeled the military regime's campaign against Mayan Indians in the Guatemalan highlands as genocidal (see Box 3a), and assigned responsibility for more than 90 percent of the atrocities of the "civil war" to the government and the paramilitary forces it mobilized.[84] Its activities have now encompassed some thirty countries worldwide, from Ethiopia and Iraq to the Philippines and French Polynesia.[85]

"Bones are often our last best witnesses," Clyde Snow said; "they never lie and they never forget."[86] His comment on the nature of his investigations summarized the work of the conscientious anthropologists—and many others—who have informed our understanding of individual genocides: "You do the work in the daytime and cry at night"[87] (see also Box 11.2). The pathbreaking forensic anthropologist died in May 2014, aged 86.[88]

FURTHER STUDY

Zygmunt Bauman, *Modernity and the Holocaust*. Ithaca, NY: Cornell University Press, 2000. Influential sociological interpretation of the Jewish Holocaust.

Pierre L. van den Berghe, ed., *State Violence and Ethnicity*. Niwot, CO: University Press of Colorado, 1990. Today obscure, but one of the best sociological works on genocide and state terror.

Paul R. Brass, ed., *Riots and Pogroms.* New York: New York University Press, 1996. Vigorous edited volume on the dynamics of ethnic violence.

Amy Chua, *World on Fire: How Exporting Free Market Democracy Breeds Ethnic Hatred and Global Instability.* New York: Anchor, 2004. Provocative overview of "market-dominant minorities."

Daniel Feierstein, *Genocide as Social Practice: Reorganizing Society under the Nazis and Argentina's Military Juntas.* New Brunswick, NJ: Rutgers University Press, 2014. Now in English, a sophisticated sociological essay by the leading light of the "Argentine school" in genocide studies.

Helen Fein, *Genocide: A Sociological Perspective.* London: Sage, 1993. Short, influential treatise.

H.H. Gerth and C. Wright Mills, eds., *From Max Weber: Essays in Sociology.* New York: Oxford University Press, 1954. Writings of the great German theorist of authority, modernity, and bureaucracy.

Alexander Laban Hinton, ed., *Annihilating Difference: The Anthropology of Genocide.* Berkeley, CA: University of California Press, 2002. A groundbreaking anthology; see also *Genocide: An Anthropological Reader, Genocide: Truth, Memory, and Representation* (ed. with Kevin Lewis O'Neill).

Donald L. Horowitz, *The Deadly Ethnic Riot.* Berkeley, CA: University of California Press, 2001. Massive, eye-opening treatise on ethnic violence.

Irving Louis Horowitz, *Taking Lives: Genocide and State Power* (4th edn). New Brunswick, NJ: Transaction Publishers, 1997. Rambling sociological pontifications.

Clea Koff, *The Bone Woman: A Forensic Anthropologist's Search for Truth in the Mass Graves of Rwanda, Bosnia, Croatia, and Kosovo.* New York: Random House, 2004. Vivid self-portrait of one of the world's leading forensic investigators.

Michael Mann, *The Dark Side of Democracy: Explaining Ethnic Cleansing.* Cambridge: Cambridge University Press, 2005. Sprawling study of modernity and "murderous ethnic cleansing."

Victoria Sanford, *Buried Secrets: Truth and Human Rights in Guatemala.* New York: Palgrave Macmillan, 2003. Sanford worked alongside the Guatemalan forensic anthropology team.

Gretchen E. Schafft, *From Racism to Genocide: Anthropology in the Third Reich.* Urbana, IL: University of Illinois Press, 2004. Explores anthropologists' complicity in Nazi social engineering.

James C. Scott, *Seeing Like A State: How Certain Schemes to Improve the Human Condition Have Failed.* New Haven, CT: Yale University Press, 1998. Fascinating political-sociological study of "high-modernist" social planning, relevant to studies of state terror and totalitarian systems.

Jeffrey A. Sluka, ed., *Death Squad: The Anthropology of State Terror.* Philadelphia, PA: University of Pennsylvania Press, 2000. Another important anthology.

Anthony D. Smith, *National Identity.* London: Penguin, 1991. Fine primer on the ethnic and cultural roots of nationalism.

Wolfgang Sofsky, *The Order of Terror: The Concentration Camp*, trans. William Templer. Princeton, NJ: Princeton University Press, 1999. Essential work on the dynamics of death and life in the Nazi camps.

Christopher C. Taylor, *Sacrifice as Terror: The Rwandan Genocide of 1994*. Oxford: Berg, 1999. Anthropological insights into the Rwandan holocaust.

Sarah E. Wagner, *To Know Where He Lies: DNA Technology and the Search for Srebrenica's Missing*. Berkeley, CA: University of California Press, 2008. Moving anthropological study of the exhumation of victims of the 1995 Srebrenica massacre, and continuing attempts to identify the dead.

█ NOTES

1 See Thomas Hylland Eriksen, *Small Places, Large Issues: An Introduction to Social and Cultural Anthropology* (London: Pluto Press, 2001), p. 29.

2 Horowitz quoted in Helen Fein, *Genocide: A Sociological Perspective* (London: Sage, 1993), p. 6.

3 Nancy Scheper-Hughes, "The Primacy of the Ethical: Propositions for a Militant Anthropology," *Current Anthropology*, 36: 3 (1995), pp. 410, 414.

4 See Alexander Laban Hinton, ed., *Annihilating Difference: The Anthropology of Genocide* (Berkeley, CA: University of California Press, 2002); Alexander Laban Hinton, ed., *Genocide: An Anthropological Reader* (London: Blackwell, 2002); Nancy Scheper-Hughes and Philippe Bourgois, eds., *Violence in War and Peace: An Anthology* (London: Blackwell, 2004); Jeffrey A. Sluka, ed., *Death Squad: The Anthropology of State Terror* (Philadelphia, PA: University of Pennsylvania Press, 1999).

5 "Modernity," as Hinton notes, "is notoriously difficult to define," but "can perhaps best be described as a set of interrelated processes, some of which began to develop as early as the fifteenth century, characterizing the emergence of 'modern society.' Politically, modernity involves the rise of secular forms of government, symbolized by the French Revolution and culminating in the modern nation-state. Economically, modernity refers to capitalist expansion and its derivatives—monetarized exchange, the accumulation of capital, extensive private property, the search for new markets, commodification, and industrialization. Socially, modernity entails the replacement of 'traditional' loyalties (to lord, master, priest, king, patriarch, kin, and local community) with 'modern' ones (to secular authority, leader, 'humanity,' class, gender, race, and ethnicity). Culturally, modernity encompasses the movement from a predominantly religious to an emphatically secular and materialist worldview characterized by new ways of thinking about and understanding human behavior." Hinton, "The Dark Side of Modernity: Toward an Anthropology of Genocide," in Hinton, ed., *Annihilating Difference*, pp. 7–8. For an ambitious anthology, see Stuart Hall *et al.*, eds., *Modernity: An Introduction to Modern Societies* (Malden, MA: Blackwell, 1996).

6 Zygmunt Bauman, *Modernity and the Holocaust* (Ithaca, NY: Cornell University Press, 2000), p. 13.

7 Ibid., pp. 53, 55; emphasis in original.

8 "As a conception of the world, and even more importantly as an effective instrument of political practice, racism is unthinkable without the advancement of modern science, modern technology and modern forms of state power. As such, racism is strictly a modern product. Modernity made racism possible." Ibid., p. 61.

9 Ibid., p. 76.

10 Max Weber, "Bureaucracy," in H.H. Gerth and C. Wright Mills, eds., *From Max Weber: Essays in Sociology* (New York: Oxford University Press, 1954), pp. 229, 233, 240. Lester R. Kurtz notes that bureaucracy evinces a tendency "to promote formal rather than substantive rationality, that is, the kind of thinking that emphasizes efficiency rather than moral or contextual considerations." Quoted in Robert Jay Lifton and Eric Markusen, *The Genocidal Mentality: Nazi Holocaust and Nuclear Threat* (New York: Basic Books, 1990), p. 180.

11 Bauman, *Modernity and the Holocaust*, p. 76.

12 Wolfgang Sofsky, *The Order of Terror: The Concentration Camp* (Princeton, NJ: Princeton University Press, 1999), p. 264. "Modern terror has no need of big criminals. For its purposes, the small-time tormentor suffices: the conscientious bookkeeper, the mediocre official, the zealous doctor, the young, slightly anxious female factory worker" (p. 278).

13 The classic study is Markusen and Kopf, *The Genocidal Mentality*.

14 Mark Levene, *Genocide in the Age of the Nation State, Vol. 1: The Meaning of Genocide* (London: I.B. Tauris, 2005), p. 10.

15 Ibid., p. 144. See also the emphatic formulation that "the specificity of genocide cannot be divorced from the very modern *framework* within which it occurs" (p. 155).

16 Levene, *Genocide in the Age of the Nation State, Vol. 1*, pp. 12–13, quoting Alexander Hinton.

17 Bauman, *Modernity and the Holocaust*, p. 89.

18 Lemkin, letter of July 22, 1948, quoted in John Docker, "Are Settler-Colonies Inherently Genocidal?," in A. Dirk Moses, ed., *Empire, Colony, Genocide: Conquest, Occupation, and Subaltern Resistance in World History* (New York: Berghahn Books, 2008), p. 87.

19 Raphael Lemkin, *Lemkin on Genocide*, ed. Steven Leonard Jacobs (Lanham, MD: Lexington Books, 2012), p. 3.

20 Levene, *Genocide in the Age of the Nation State, Vol. 1*, pp. 20, 130, 145. Emphases added.

21 Likewise with racism: though Levene correctly points to a modern scientific or pseudo-scientific discourse, he also acknowledges that "differentiating people on the basis of gradations of skin colour, and other physical attributes, as a tool whereby a dominant group legitimizes its social control over other groups is very old in history. It is certainly not exclusive to Europeans. One only has to look at the caste system in India to note its longevity and invidiousness." Levene, *Genocide in the Age of the Nation State, Vol. 2: The Rise of the West and the Coming of Genocide* (London: I.B. Tauris, 2005), p. 189.

22 Alex Alvarez, *Governments, Citizens, and Genocide: A Comparative and Interdisciplinary Approach* (Bloomington, IN: Indiana University Press, 2001), p. 2.

23 Michael Mann similarly notes that in the Nazi genocide against the Jews, "foreign collaborators, Romanian and Croatian fascists, used primitive techniques to almost as devastating effect" as high-tech gas chambers. Mann, *The Dark Side of Democracy: Explaining Ethnic Cleansing* (Cambridge: Cambridge University Press, 2005), p. 241.

24 "As for the supposedly desensitizing effects of bureaucratic distancing, the brutal face-to-face murder of the Tutsis by tens of thousands of ordinary Hutus, many of them poor farmers, utterly disproves that thesis." Marie Fleming, "Genocide and the Body Politic in the Time of Modernity," in Robert Gellately and Ben Kiernan, eds., *The Specter of Genocide: Mass Murder in Historical Perspective* (Cambridge: Cambridge University Press, 2003), p. 103.

25 Levene likewise acknowledges "the military-bureaucratic power and organizing outreach of *pre-modern* states" (his emphasis). Levene, *Genocide in the Age of the Nation State, Vol. 1*, p. 148.

26 For a contrary view, defining the core features of the Rwandan holocaust as "manifestations of the modern world," see Robert Melson, "Modern Genocide in Rwanda: Ideology, Revolution, War, and Mass Murder in an African State," in Gellately and Kiernan, eds., *The Specter of Genocide*, pp. 325–38.

27 Timothy Snyder, *Bloodlands: Europe between Hitler and Stalin* (New York: Basic Books, 2010), pp. xiv—xv.

28 Benedict Anderson, *Imagined Communities: Reflections on the Origins and Spread of Nationalism* (London: Verso, 1991).

29 Dan Stone wrote that "the history of nation-building is inseparable from the 'memories' that nations create, in the shape of the narratives or monuments they construct. Indeed, collective memory does not emerge after the process has come to an end but is an essential part of the process whereby a group constitutes itself as a group." Stone, "Genocide and Memory," in Donald Bloxham and A. Dirk Moses, eds., *The Oxford Handbook of Genocide Studies* (Oxford: Oxford University Press, 2013), p. 117.

30 Anthony D. Smith, *National Identity* (London: Penguin, 1991), p. 21.

31 I am grateful to Benjamin Madley for this insight.

32 Barth cited in Andrew Bell-Fialkoff, *Ethnic Cleansing* (New York: St. Martin's Griffin, 1999), p. 73. As Alexander Hinton notes, "It is one of the most vexing problems of our time that imagined sociopolitical identities are so often forged out of hatred toward contrasting others." Hinton, *Why Did They Kill? Cambodia in the Shadow of Genocide* (Berkeley, CA: University of California Press, 2005), p. 220. For a famous reading of the phenomenon, examining the constitutive impact of the "Orient" upon the "West," see Edward Said, *Orientalism* (New York: Vintage Books, 1979).

33 Geertz quoted in Ray Taras and Rajat Ganguly, *Understanding Ethnic Conflict: The International Dimension* (New York: Longman, 1998), p. 14.

34 See John R. Bowen, "The Myth of Global Ethnic Conflict," in Hinton, ed., *Genocide: An Anthropological Reader*, pp. 334–343.

35 Nancy Scheper-Hughes wrote sardonically: "'Race,' 'ethnicity,' 'tribe,' 'culture,' and 'identity' were dutifully deconstructed and de-essentialized in Anthropology 101, where they were taught as historically invented and fictive concepts. Meanwhile . . . South African Xhosas and Zulus (manipulated by a government-orchestrated 'third force') daily slaughtered each other in and around worker hostels in the name of 'tribe,' 'ethnicity,' and 'culture.'" Scheper-Hughes, "The Primacy of the Ethical," p. 415.

36 James Waller, *Becoming Evil: How Ordinary People Commit Genocide and Mass Killing* (Oxford: Oxford University Press, 2002), pp. 153–154. He also points out (pp. 241–242) that in social-psychological experiments, "complete strangers arbitrarily assigned to groups, having no interaction or conflict with one another, and not competing against another group behaved as if those who shared their meaningless label were their dearest friends or closest relatives," and would rapidly come into conflict with those defined differently, but equally meaninglessly.

37 Lemkin, *Lemkin on Genocide*, p. 26.

38 Donald L. Horowitz, *The Deadly Ethnic Riot* (Berkeley, CA: University of California Press, 2001), p. 243.

39 Paul R. Brass, "Introduction," in Brass, ed., *Riots and Pogroms* (Washington Square, NY: New York University Press, 1996), p. 12.

40 Horowitz makes explicit the link between ethnic rioting and genocide: "The deadly ethnic riot embodies physical destruction combined with degradation and the implicit threat of genocide. . . . The random, brutal killing of targets based merely on their ascriptive identity has . . . a proto-genocidal quality about it; it is an augury of extermination." Horowitz, *The Deadly Ethnic Riot*, pp. 432, 459.

41 Brass, "Introduction," pp. 12–13.

42 According to Charles Tilly, these actors "operate in a middle ground between (on one side) the full authorization of a national army and (on the other) the private employment of violence by parents, lovers, or feuding clans." Tilly, *The Politics of Collective Violence* (Cambridge: Cambridge University Press, 2003), p. 19.

43 Augustine Brannigan, *Beyond the Banality of Evil: Criminology and Genocide* (Oxford: Oxford University Press, 2013). The quotes in this box text are drawn from pp. 2, 23, 27, 31, 41, 79 (emphasis added), 82, 84, 85, 221.

44 See, e.g., Andrew Woolford, "Making Genocide Unthinkable: Three Guidelines for a Critical Criminology of Genocide," *Critical Criminology*, 14: 1 (2006), pp. 87–106; Claire Moon, "The Crime of Crimes and the Crime of Criminology: Genocide, Criminology and Darfur," *The British Journal of Sociology*, 62: 1 (2011), pp. 49–55. A survey published as this edition went into production is Nicole Rafter, *The Crime of All Crimes: Toward a Criminology of Genocide* (New York: New York University Press, 2016).

45 Horowitz, *The Deadly Ethnic Riot*, p. 187. See also Walter P. Zenner, "Middleman Minorities and Genocide," in Isidor Wallimann and Michael N. Dobkowski, eds., *Genocide and the Modern Age: Etiology and Case Studies of Mass Death* (Westport, CT: Syracuse University Press, 2000), pp. 253–281. Pioneering genocide scholar Leo Kuper refers to these as "hostage groups"; that is, "hostages to the fortunes of the dominant group."

Kuper, "The Genocidal State: An Overview," in Pierre L. van den Berghe, ed., *State Violence and Ethnicity* (Niwot, CO: University Press of Colorado, 1990), p. 44. See also the discussion in Kuper's *The Prevention of Genocide* (New Haven, CT: Yale University Press, 1985), p. 201.

46 Amy Chua, *World on Fire: How Exporting Free Market Democracy Breeds Ethnic Hatred and Global Instability* (New York: Anchor, 2004), p. 79.

47 Genocidal massacres may also be cited, such as the centuries of pogroms against European Jews, Indian uprisings against Whites in Upper Peru and Yucatan (Chapter 1), and the Hindu slaughter of Sikhs in India in 1984. Short of genocide or genocidal massacre, the strategy most commonly adopted against market-dominant minorities is mass expulsion. Idi Amin's banishing of Indians from Uganda in 1972 (Chapter 1) is an example; another is the "Boat People" expelled from Vietnam following the nationalist victory of 1975, aimed at "the elimination of ethnic Chinese and bourgeois Vietnamese from Vietnamese society." Richard L. Rubinstein, *The Age of Triage: Fear and Hope in an Overcrowded World* (Boston, MA: Beacon Press, 1983), p. 176. This was also, of course, the dominant Nazi policy toward German Jews between 1933 and 1938 (Chapter 6).

48 Horowitz, for example, argues that "in comparative perspective," the targeting of "unusually prosperous or advantaged ethnic groups . . . is only a minor factor in target selection [for deadly ethnic rioting], operative under certain, specific conditions of riot leadership. Quite often, prosperous minorities are not targeted even during the most brutal riots." Horowitz, *The Deadly Ethnic Riot*, p. 5.

49 Chua, *World on Fire*, pp. 124–125. Martin Shaw makes a similar point: "Elections are . . . often flashpoints both for elite rivalries and for conflicts between population groups supporting rival parties. Since most societies are plural in terms of ethnicity, nationality, religion, etc., and most parties mobilize along these lines . . . electoral processes open up possibilities of violent conflict, often turned against ethnopolitically or religiopolitically defined sections of the population. Where elections are not accompanied by entrenched citizen rights and institutional accountability, they can be as dangerous as no elections." Shaw, *Genocide and International Relations: Changing Patterns in the Transitions of the Late Modern World* (Cambridge; Cambridge University Press, 2013), p. 158.

50 Eriksen, *Small Places, Large Issues*, p. 27.

51 Ibid., p. 7.

52 Victoria Sanford, *Buried Secrets: Truth and Human Rights in Guatemala* (New York: Palgrave Macmillan, 2003), p. 31.

53 Ivana Macek, *Sarajevo Under Siege: Anthropology in Wartime* (Philadelphia, PA: University of Pennsylvania Press, 2009). The quotes in these passages are drawn from pp. x, 4, 8, 11, 12, 31, 48–49, 53, 54–55, 62, 123, 161.

54 Anton Weiss-Wendt, "Problems in Comparative Genocide Scholarship," in Dan Stone, ed., *The Historiography of Genocide* (London: Palgrave Macmillan, 2008), pp. 42–70.

55 Alexander Laban Hinton, "The Dark Side of Modernity: Toward an Anthropology of Genocide," in Hinton, ed., *Annihilating Difference*, p. 2.

56 Declaration quoted in Macek, *Life Under Siege*, p. 28.

57 "The work of anthropology, in its earliest instances of practice, composed a necessary first step that gave substance and justification to theories of 'natural' hierarchy that would eventually be employed to rationalize racism, colonialism, slavery, ethnic purifications and, ultimately, genocide projects." Wendy C. Hamblet, "The Crisis of Meanings: Could the Cure be the Cause of Genocide?," *Journal of Genocide Research*, 5: 2 (2003), p. 243.

58 See also the discussion of Patrick Brantlinger's *Dark Vanishings* in Chapter 3.

59 Gretchen E. Schafft, "Scientific Racism in Service of the Reich: German Anthropologists in the Nazi Era," in Hinton, ed., *Annihilating Difference*, pp. 117, 131. See also Schafft's full-length book, *From Racism to Genocide: Anthropology in the Third Reich* (Urbana, IL: University of Illinois Press, 2004).

60 See Sybil Milton, "Holocaust: The Gypsies," in Samuel Totten *et al.*, eds., *Century of Genocide: Eyewitness Accounts and Critical Views* (New York: Garland Publishing, 1997).

61 Paul A. Erickson and Liam D. Murphy, *A History of Anthropological Theory* (Toronto, ON: Broadview Press, 2003), p. 76.

62 Geoffrey Robertson, *Crimes Against Humanity: The Struggle for Global Justice* (New York: The New Press, 2000), pp. 31–32. An anthropologist, W.G. Sumner, first used the term "ethnocentrism" in 1906, defining it as "the technical name for [a] view of things in which one's own group is the center of everything, and all others are scaled and rated with reference to it. ... . Each group nourishes its own pride and vanity, boasts itself superior, exalts its own divinities, and looks with contempt on outsiders." Quoted in Waller, *Becoming Evil*, p. 154.

63 Alexander Hinton, personal communication, July 24, 2005.

64 Scheper-Hughes, "The Primacy of the Ethical," p. 410.

65 Hinton, "The Dark Side of Modernity," in Hinton, ed., *Annihilating Difference*, p. 2.

66 Ibid.

67 Sanford, *Buried Secrets*, p. 210. In anthropological parlance, individual testimonies constitute the "emic" level of analysis, academic interpretations the "etic" level. See Eriksen, *Small Places, Large Issues*, p. 36.

68 Mark Levene, *Genocide in the Age of the Nation State, Vol. 2: The Rise of the West and the Coming of Genocide* (London: I.B. Tauris, 2005), p. 94.

69 Adam Jones, "'When the Rabbit's Got the Gun': Subaltern Genocide and the Genocidal Continuum," in Nicholas A. Robins and Adam Jones, eds., *Genocides by the Oppressed: Subaltern Genocide in Theory and Practice* (Bloomington, IN: Indiana University Press, 2009), pp. 185–207; see especially pp. 187–188.

70 See, e.g., Antonius Robben, "How Traumatized Societies Remember: The Aftermath of Argentina's Dirty War," *Cultural Critique*, 59 (Winter 2005), pp. 120–164.

71 Sanford, *Buried Secrets*, p. 143.

72 Hinton, "The Dark Side of Modernity," p. 19. Hinton argues that symbolism "mediate[s] all our understandings of the world, including a world of genocide" (personal communication, July 24, 2005). Jacques Sémelin also points to "the ways in which bodies are taken over, twisted, cut into pieces" as constituting "wholly cultural acts, through which the perpetrator expresses something of his own identity." Sémelin, *Purify and Destroy: The Political Uses of Massacre and Genocide* (New York: Columbia University Press, 2007), p. 301.

73 Christopher C. Taylor, *Sacrifice as Terror: The Rwandan Genocide of 1994* (Oxford: Berg, 1998), p. 130. The phenomenon has its counterpart in other genocides; as early as 1940, the English novelist and essayist H.G. Wells pointed to "the victims smothered in latrines" in Nazi concentration camps, exemplifying "the cloacal side of Hitlerism." Quoted in Robertson, *Crimes Against Humanity*, p. 23. For another fascinating study of violent ritual and symbolism, see Antonius Robben, "State Terror in the Netherworld: Disappearance and Reburial in Argentina," in Robben, ed., *Death, Mourning, and Burial: A Cross-Cultural Reader* (London: Blackwell, 2005), which explored the symbolic violation of "disappearance" in a culture that ascribes great significance to the physical corpse and rituals of burial.

74 Nancy Scheper-Hughes, *Death without Weeping: The Violence of Everyday Life in Brazil* (Berkeley, CA: University of California Press, 1993).

75 Nancy Scheper-Hughes, "Coming to Our Senses: Anthropology and Genocide," in Hinton, ed., *Annihilating Difference*, p. 369. See also Scheper-Hughes, "The Genocidal Continuum: Peace-time Crimes," in Jeannette Marie Mageo, ed., *Power and the Self* (Cambridge: Cambridge University Press, 2002), pp. 29–47.

76 Scheper-Hughes, "Coming to Our Senses," pp. 372–373.

77 Hinton, "The Dark Side of Modernity," p. 33.

78 D.C. Dirkmaat and J.M. Adovasio, "The Role of Archaeology in the Recovery and Interpretation of Human Remains from an Outdoor Forensic Setting," in William D. Haglund and Marcella H. Sorg, eds., *Forensic Taphonomy: The Postmortem Fate of Human Remains* (New York: CRC Press, 1997), p. 58.

79 Clea Koff, *The Bone Woman: A Forensic Anthropologist's Search for Truth in the Mass Graves of Rwanda, Bosnia, Croatia, and Kosovo* (New York: Random House, 2004). The quotes in this box text are drawn from pp. 8, 16, 51, 55, 76, 104, 124, 153–154, 181, and 192.

80 Clyde Snow, "Murder Most Foul," *The Sciences* (May/June 1995), p. 16.

81 Ibid., p. 20.

82 See Leigh Binford, *The El Mozote Massacre: Anthropology and Human Rights* (Tucson, AZ: University of Arizona Press, 1996); Mark Danner, *The Massacre at El Mozote: A Parable of the Cold War* (New York: Vintage, 1994).

83 "Originally a five-member group, the Guatemalan Forensic Anthropology Foundation now employs more than 60 people and has carried out more than 200 exhumations." Victoria Sanford, personal communication, June 15, 2005.

84 The activities of the Guatemalan forensic team are movingly described by Victoria Sanford in her book *Buried Secrets*, centering on exhumations in the Mayan village of Acul.

85 For an overview of the EAAF's global work, see Mercedes Doretti and Clyde Snow, "Forensic Anthropology and Human Rights: The Argentine Experience," in Dawnie Wolfe Steadman, ed., *Hard Evidence: Case Studies in Forensic Anthropology*, 2nd ed. (London: Routledge, 2015), pp. 303–18. See also the EAAF's website at http://eaaf.typepad.com/eaaf__sp/.

86 Snow quoted in Elizabeth Neuffer, *The Key to My Neighbor's House: Seeking Justice in Bosnia and Rwanda* (New York: Picador, 2001), p. 76.

87 Snow quoted in Michelle Green, "Dr. Clyde Snow Helps Victims of Argentina's 'Dirty War' Bear Witness from Beyond the Grave," *People* magazine, December 8, 1986, www.people.com/people/archive/article/0,,20095200,00.html.

88 See "Stories in Bones," *The Economist* (obituary), May 24, 2014, www.economist.com/news/obituary/21602660-clyde-snow-forensic-anthropologist-died-may-16th-aged-86-stories-bones.

CHAPTER 12

Political Science and International Relations

> Genocide is . . . the ultimate failure in politics. Genocide reflects a decision to reject accommodation, to inflict maximum violence, and to extinguish future social interaction in a shared territory. Rather than manage a social contract, negotiate difference, devolve power, distribute goods, and compromise through accommodation or negotiation—the promise of politics, however flawed in all its myriad applications and however constrained by limited means—genocide is about destroying human populations so that they can and will not make demands or pose threats.
>
> Scott Straus

The core concern of political science is power: how it is distributed and used within states and societies. International relations (IR) examines its use and distribution among the state units that compose the international system. Historically, IR's overriding concern is with peace and war, though in recent decades the discipline has grappled increasingly with the growth of international "regimes": norms, rules, and patterns of conduct that influence state behavior in given issue areas.

The relevance to genocide studies of all these lines of inquiry is considerable. We have already drawn upon the contributions of political scientists and IR theorists, notably in Chapter 2 on "State and Empire; War and Revolution." The present chapter explores four further contributions of PoliSci and IR frameworks: empirical studies of genocide; the changing nature of war; the putative link between democracy and peace; and the role of ethical norms and moral entrepreneurs in constructing "prohibition regimes" worldwide, including the regime against genocide.

EMPIRICAL INVESTIGATIONS

The most influential empirical investigators of state-directed mass killing are the US political scientists R.J. Rummel, Barbara Harff, and Ted Gurr, the latter two often working in tandem. Their studies have clarified the scope and character of genocidal, "politicidal," and "democidal" murder in modern times. As with nearly all genocide scholars, their work is preventionist in orientation (see Chapter 6). They seek to determine the explanatory variables that can assist in identifying the genocide-prone societies of the present, and in isolating positive and constructive features that may inoculate societies against genocide and other crimes against humanity.

Rummel's book *Death by Government* (1997) coined the term "democide" to describe "government mass murder"—including but not limited to genocide as defined in the UN Convention. Examining the death toll from twentieth-century democide, Rummel was the first to place it almost beyond the bounds of imaginability. According to his study, somewhere in the range of *170 million* "men, women, and children have been shot, beaten, tortured, knifed, burned, starved, frozen, crushed, or worked to death; buried alive, drowned, hung, bombed, or killed in any other of the myriad ways governments have inflicted death on unarmed, helpless citizens and foreigners."[1] If combat casualties in war are added to the picture, "Power has killed over 203 million people in [the twentieth] century."[2]

Rummel identified the "most lethal regimes," in terms of numbers of people exterminated, as the Soviet Union under Lenin and Stalin (Chapter 5), communist China (Chapter 5), Germany under the Nazis (Chapter 6 and Box 6a), and Nationalist China (touched on briefly in Chapter 2). If the "megamurder" index is recalculated based upon a regime's time in power (i.e., as deaths per year), then Cambodia under the Khmer Rouge (Chapter 7), Turkey under Kemal Ataturk, and the Nazi puppet state in Croatia (1941–1945) top the list.

Rummel discerned an underlying "Power Principle" in this human catastrophe, namely that "Power kills; absolute Power kills absolutely":

> The more power a government has, the more it can act arbitrarily according to the whims and desires of the elite, and the more it will make war on others and murder its foreign and domestic subjects. The more constrained the power of governments, the more power is diffused, checked, and balanced, the less it will aggress on others and commit democide.[3]

Accordingly, for Rummel, liberal democracies are the good guys. Only in situations of all-out international war, or when their democratic procedures are subverted by conniving elites, do they engage in democide on a significant scale. This argument ties in with the "democratic peace" thesis, and I will return to Rummel's work in addressing that thesis below. His significance, for the present, lies in his systematic attempt to tabulate the gory toll of twentieth-century mass killing, and to tie this to the exercise of political power (or "Power") worldwide.

Barbara Harff, working alone and with Ted Gurr, has approached genocide and "politicide"—mass killing on the basis of imputed political affiliation[4]—through the study of ethnopolitics and ethnic conflict. In 1988, the authors first published data for genocides and politicides, and sought to isolate where, and under what conditions, outbreaks were likely to occur. Harff summarized the findings as follows:

> Revolutionary one-party states are the likeliest offenders. Genocides occur with alarming frequency during or shortly after the revolutionary takeovers. Especially dangerous are situations in which long-standing ethnic rivalries erupt and radicalized groups armed with a revolutionary ideology gain the upper hand. Communist ideologues tend to be most aggressive in their dealings with potential or past opposition groups. Interestingly enough, the length of democratic experience is inversely related to the occurrence of geno/politicides.[5]

In recent years, Harff has conducted research at both the US Naval Academy and the University of Maryland's Center for International Development and Conflict Management, utilizing statistical data of the US government-sponsored Political Instability Task Force, with which she worked in the 1990s and early 2000s.[6] Her important article for the *American Political Science Review* maintained a distinction between genocides and politicides that some find problematic;[7] but her findings have both buttressed and extended her earlier work. "Empirically, all but one of the 37 genocides and politicides that began between 1955 and 1998 occurred during or immediately after political upheavals . . . 24 coincided with ethnic wars, 14 coincided with revolutionary wars, and 14 followed the occurrence of adverse regime changes."[8] She concluded that "the greater the magnitude of previous internal wars and regime crises, summed over the preceding 15 years, the more likely that a new state failure will lead to geno-/politicide." Among the key explanatory variables located by her study are:

- *Presence or absence of genocidal precedents:* "The risks of new [genocidal/politicidal] episodes were more than three times greater when state failures occurred in countries that had prior geno-/politicides."
- *Presence or absence of an exclusionary ideology:* "Countries in which the ruling elite adhered to an exclusionary ideology were two and a half times as likely to have state failures leading to geno-/politicide as those with no such ideology."
- *Extent of ethnic "capture" of the state:* "The risks of geno-/politicide were two and a half times more likely in countries where the political elite was based mainly or entirely on an ethnic minority."
- *Extent and depth of democratic institutions:* "Once in place, democratic institutions—even partial ones—reduce the likelihood of armed conflict and all but eliminate the risk that it will lead to geno-/politicide."
- *Degree of international "openness":* "The greater their interdependence with the global economy, the less likely that [national] elites will target minorities and political opponents for destruction."

Harff's research also turned up surprises. Ethnic and religious cleavages, in themselves, were strongly relevant only when combined with an ethnic minority's capture of the state apparatus. Poverty, which many commentators view as a virtual recipe for social conflict including genocide, could indeed "predispose societies to intense conflict," but these conflicts assumed genocidal or politicidal proportions only in tandem with features of the political system (a minority ethnicity in charge, the promulgation of an exclusionary ideology, and the like).

Harff concluded by arguing that "the risk assessments generated . . . signal possible genocides." Updating the risk assessments in 2012, she cited progress in "systematic risk assessment" of genocide, but "not enough to indicate more precisely when genocidal violence is likely to begin. What high risk profiles tell us is that a country is in the latter stages of upheaval that may result in genocide. This alone should be enough to focus on preventing escalation."[9]

According to the "Country Risks of Genocide and Politicide," the dozen states at greatest risk of outbreaks were, in order: Myanmar, Syria, China, Sudan, Pakistan, Ethiopia, Zimbabwe, Rwanda, Iran, the Democratic Republic of the Congo (DRC), Somalia, and Saudi Arabia. Those judged at highest "risk of future instability" in the 2011 dataset were Syria—a prediction tragically borne out almost as the data was appearing—Pakistan, Ethiopia, and the DRC.

In keeping with preventionist discourse (see Chapter 16), Harff urged that "early warning efforts should be revived," accompanied by "preventive tools . . . tailored to the specific needs of particular communities at a particular time. The next big challenge for early warning research is to learn more about what works to prevent genocidal violence in which kind of situations and at which time."[10]

▌ BOX 12.1 THE POLITICAL SCIENCE OF GENOCIDE

Figure 12.1 Ernesto Verdeja, at the Kroc Institute for International Peace Studies, explores the political science of genocide prevention and intervention, transitional justice, and restitution/reparations.

Source: Courtesy of University of Notre Dame/Kroc Institute for International Peace Studies.

"Aside from a few important exceptions," notes University of Notre Dame genocide scholar Ernesto Verdeja, "mainstream political scientists rarely engage with the most recent work on comparative genocide." He ascribes this in part to genocide studies' "roots in the humanities (especially history) and reliance on methodological approaches that have had little resonance in mainstream political science, as well as the field's explicit commitment to humanitarian activism and praxis." In his 2012 article, "The Political Science of Genocide,"[11] Verdeja draws on recent PoliSci investigations of mass violence to suggest how genocide scholars could learn from their insights, in order to better understand "the conditions under which genocide is likely to occur, the multilevel processes of violent escalation and de-escalation, and the ways in which these processes are shaped by, connect to, reinforce, accelerate and impede one another." Political scientists, too, can benefit from the contributions of genocide scholars:

I argue that scholars should, 1) model elite and follower radicalization processes by disaggregating genocidal "intent" over time and space and exploring how it emerges, rather than taking it as pregiven. Doing so will permit researchers to, 2) situate genocide research within a broader context of political violence to understand how they are related temporally (in terms of sequencing) and spatially, as well as decenter analytical domains beyond the standard country-level and single victim group to gain insight in[to] the dynamics of genocide, including how perpetrator policies vary by group; 3) draw on recent advances in microanalyses of civil war to theorise about subnational patterns of violence diffusion; 4) move beyond reductive contrasts between ideology and rationality to analyze how ideologies frame the strategic choices "available" to genocidal elites. . . .

I agree that elite strategic behavior is crucial for understanding genocide, but I argue that it is important to move beyond elite theories to systematically explore variation in genocidal violence within cases . . . Subnational analyses can inform—and revise—elite theories by showing how micro- and meso-processes may be only loosely linked to elite policies. . . .

I contend that subnational analyses can inform—and revise—elite theories by showing how micro- and meso-processes may be only loosely linked to elite policies. . . . I argue for a robustly *comparative* approach to questions of variation. Such an approach can advance research in political science in several ways. First, by treating genocide as a process rather than an outcome, we can better model the contexts and scenarios in which genocide occurs, and thus understand what conditions and interactions may make genocide more likely. Second, placing genocide firmly in the domain of political violence significantly widens the cases available for comparative study and permits researchers to assess which causal processes are unique to genocide and which are not, advancing theoretical knowledge on various trajectories of the onset, diffusion and abeyance of mass violence. Third, this agenda's focus on subnational and microanalytical perspectives furthers our understanding of basic concepts in the study of large-scale political behavior, including "intentionality," "ideology," "rationality," and "identity," which are often reified in country-level research on violence with problematic consequences for causal theorizing. . . .

Genocide research, in short, needs to be brought back into the fold of political conflict analysis and of comparative politics more generally. For while genocide is an extreme form of violence that understandably generates stark moral, political, and legal responses, it is also a complex historical outcome no less amenable to nuanced analysis than other forms of violence or indeed other forms of general political conflict.

THE CHANGING FACE OF WAR

Kalash au bilash; kalash begib al kash.
(You're trash without a Kalashnikov [automatic rifle]; get some cash with a Kalashnikov.)
Popular saying in Darfur, Sudan (see Box 9a)

Methods of warfare have varied greatly over centuries and across human societies. Representatives of all of the disciplines explored in this section have provided a rich body of conflict case studies, and important exercises in comparative theory building.[12]

War in "primitive" societies ranges from the brutal and destructive (as with the Yanomami of Brazil and various New Guinean societies) to the largely demonstrative and symbolic (as among many native nations of North America).[13] The great empire builders of Central Asia laid waste to entire civilizations, but in Europe in the early modern period, war came to be waged by and against professional armies, with exemptions granted to civilians—in theory, and often in practice. Yet the two most destructive wars in history were centered precisely in civilized, modern Europe, where clashes of ideologies and national ambitions targeted principally the civilian population.

With the advent of the nuclear age, the potential destructive power of "total wars" grew limitless. The superpowers stepped back from the brink, confining their clashes to wars at the peripheries of their respective spheres of influence. One IR scholar even wondered whether an "end to major war" was nigh.[14] That speculation may have been valid—and may still be valid—in the case of international wars pitting centralized states against one another. Yet a tectonic shift in the nature of war occurred during this period. Most wars were now *civil* wars, pitting armed groups (usually guerrillas) against other armed groups (usually state agents and paramilitaries) within the borders of a single country. Often, too, these conflicts demonstrated a strong ethnic element, although this tended to be downplayed in commentary and scholarship, which focused on the government–guerrilla dyad. Examples are the wars in Burma, Ethiopia, Kashmir (divided between India and Pakistan), and Guatemala; many others could be cited.

Some scholars of international relations declared that the end of the Cold War marked a break in the trajectory of modern war. In fact, the civil wars and "limited" imperial wars of the Cold War era arguably laid the foundations for war as it is waged around the world today. Conflicts in Central America (Guatemala, Nicaragua, El Salvador) and Africa (Angola and Mozambique) were incredibly destructive—the Southern African conflicts alone killed well over a million people combined, and made refugees of millions more. Restraints on the targeting of civilians were either lax or non-existent. Terror strategies were widely employed, and by diverse actors: armies, paramilitary forces, freebooters, and mercenaries, with wide scope granted to criminal and profiteering elements. In Africa, the weapon of choice was the AK-47 automatic rifle—one of the rare Soviet products preferred over the capitalist competition.

The Cold War's demise magnified these trends, and added new ones. It is a truism that the withdrawal of the superpowers from extensive military engagement in the Third World "lifted the lid" from simmering or dormant ethnic conflicts in many countries. Ethnically-fueled wars have increased worldwide—although it may be debated whether this primarily reflects older tensions and conflicts, or "more immediate and remediable causes: political manipulation, belief traps and Hobbesian fear."

Many states that had been propped up by one of the superpowers (or had played off the US and Soviet Union against each other) collapsed in the face of popular resistance. This produced the great wave of democratization in East Asia, Latin America, and Eastern Europe at the end of the 1980s and into the 1990s, but it also led to "failed states," in which no central authority exerted effective control. Power and the means of violence devolved to decentralized networks of paramilitaries, warlords, freebooting soldiers or former soldiers, and brigands.

In such cases, these groups were often at odds or at war with one another—and usually with the civilian population as well. To shore up their power base, warlords and freebooters sought "rents" from the civilian population—in the form of mafia-style "protection money" or simple robbery—and from the sale of natural resources, so that wars in Congo, Liberia, Sierra Leone, and Colombia, among many others, were sustained by the windfall profits to be made from diamonds,[15] gold,[16] timber, oil, and drugs. These spoils were marketed internationally; the world had truly entered an age of *globalized* warfare, in which consumer decisions in the First World had a direct impact on the course and outcome of Third World conflicts.[17]

Gérard Prunier, who has witnessed the emergence and evolution of many such conflicts over four decades of academic work in Africa, described these "new wars" in 2009:

> Here economic predation, trafficking of all kinds, and looting both at the individual and at the collective level become essential features of the conflict because they are essential means of financing it. This has massive consequences

Figure 12.2 The new face of war: demobilized child soldiers in the Democratic Republic of the Congo, 2002.

Source: Courtesy Dimitri Falk.

Figure 12.3 The Nyakabanda transit camp for Congolese refugees outside Kisoro, southwestern Uganda.

Source: Author's photo, July 2012.

[for] the way the war is fought. Because civilians are the ones from whom the military can take its means of survival, armed violence is more often directed at civilians (including, at times, those of one's own camp) than at the enemy army. Direct armed confrontation is often avoided, and straightforward military victory is only one of the various options in the field. It is actually this nonstate, decentralized form of violence that makes the conflicts so murderous and so hard to stop. Looting and its attendant calamities (arson, rape, torture) become routine operations for the "combatants," who are soon more akin to vampires than to soldiers.[18]

As Prunier's account suggested, the implications of these trends for genocides of the present and future are likewise "massive":

- The fact that most "new wars" are civil wars means that norms of state sovereignty are less powerful inhibitors than with international wars. The latter may be muted or suppressed by collective security strategies deployed in recent decades. In any case, international wars are viewed as "threats to the system," and nearly always provoke an international outcry. No such effective "prohibition regime" exists in the case of civil conflicts (though one might be nascent). Contrast, for example, the response to Saddam Hussein's invasion of Kuwait with his much more severe depredations against Iraqi Kurds (mentioned in Box 4a).
- New wars feature a profusion of actors and agents, often making it difficult to determine who is doing what to whom. The most destructive war of recent times, in Congo (Chapter 9), has killed millions. But with a mosaic of local and outside forces, apportioning responsibility for genocide and other atrocities—and bringing effective pressure to bear on perpetrators—are tasks even more daunting than usual.
- To lend moral and political legitimacy to activities usually fueled by greed and power lust, new-war actors often play up ethnic and particularist identities. Campaigns of persecution against national and ethnic groups, including genocide, become a standard *modus operandi*. The wars of the 1990s in West and Central Africa and former Yugoslavia (Chapter 8) are prominent examples.
- The globalized arms trade and caches left over from Cold War struggles have flooded the territories in which new wars occur with cheap, light weaponry. In many countries, an AK-47 may be purchased for a few dollars. The loss of superpower sponsorship, and political-material competition among the various actors, spawn ever greater demands on the civilian population. Civilians may be mass-murdered if held to be in allegiance with one of the opposing groups, or insufficiently cooperative with extraction and taxation measures, or simply in the way.
- The ambiguous, uncertain, and shifting control over territories and populations that characterizes these wars vastly increases the complexity of conflict suppression and humanitarian intervention. IR scholars speak of "complex

humanitarian emergencies" in which war, genocide, social breakdown, starvation, refugee flows, and internally displaced populations all combine to produce a downward spiral of suffering and destruction. Aid agencies, journalists, and human rights monitors are all at greater risk, and may be correspondingly more reluctant to enter the field or remain there. Without their expert witnessing and evaluations, events on the ground are further obscured, and considerable interventionist potential is squandered.

- If sufficient sources of "rent" can be extracted from the land and its population, these wars can become self-perpetuating and self-sustaining. The longer they drag on, the likelier is massive mortality from hunger and disease—and the likelier that the only viable source of income and self-respect (for young men but also, increasingly, for young women) is to join a warring faction.

It is difficult to say whether the new wars are more likely to produce genocide, but at the very least, they contain a strong genocidal *potential*. And, all too frequently, a genocidal dynamic is central to the unfolding conflict.

DEMOCRACY, WAR, AND GENOCIDE/DEMOCIDE

> Societies are known by their victims.
>
> Richard Drinnon

Are democracies less likely to wage war and genocide against each other than are non-democracies? Are they less likely *in general* to wage war and genocide?

These issues have provoked arguably the most vigorous single debate in the international relations literature over the past three decades—the so-called "democratic peace debate." They have also given rise to one of the few proclaimed "laws," perhaps the *only* one, in this branch of the social sciences. Democracies, it is claimed, do not fight each other, or do so only rarely. Why might this be so? As IR scholar Errol Henderson summarizes:

> Theoretical explanations for the democratic peace emphasize either structural/ institutional factors or cultural/normative factors in preventing war between democracies. The former posits that institutional constraints on the decision-making choices of democratic leaders make it difficult for them to use force in their foreign policies and act as a brake on conflict with other democracies. The latter assumes that democracies are less disposed to fight each other due to the impact of their shared norms that proscribe the use of violence between them.[19]

A "harder" version of the democratic peace hypothesis, advanced by R.J. Rummel, argues that democracies are far less likely than authoritarian states to commit democide, whether against their own populations or against others. Rummel conceded that democracies sometimes perpetrate democide, but "almost all of this . . . is foreign democide during war, and consists mainly of those enemy civilians killed in indiscriminate urban bombing." Acknowledging other examples, he claimed that they are the exceptions that prove the rule: "In each case the killing was carried out in a highly undemocratic fashion: in secret, behind a conscious cover of lies and deceit, and by agencies and power holders that had the wartime authority to operate autonomously. All were shielded by tight censorship of the press and control of journalists." In order for democratic states to become democidal, therefore, what makes them democratic has to be suspended, at least temporarily.[20]

There is much that is intuitively appealing about Rummel's formulations, and those of other proponents of the democratic peace hypothesis. First, it seems evident that genocides inflicted by democracies *against their own populations* are rare. One can think of exceptions—Sri Lanka is sometimes cited—but they do not come readily to mind. By contrast, this book is replete with examples of authoritarian, dictatorial, tyrannical, and totalitarian governments slaughtering their own populations (the USSR under Lenin and Stalin; China before and after the communist revolution; Cambodia under the Khmer Rouge; and so on). At a glance, too, the "law" that democracies do not fight each other seems empirically robust.

Things become more complicated, however, when we consider the history of colonizing liberal democracies; the nature of some of the indigenous societies they attacked; the secretive and anti-democratic character of violence by *both* democratic and authoritarian states; and the latter-day comportment of democracies, including the global superpower and non-Western democracies.

As we saw in Chapter 3, the strategy adopted toward indigenous peoples by Western colonial powers—in most cases, the most democratic states of their age—was frequently genocidal. Other, less democratic states were less likely to aggress internationally than the liberal democracies of the time (which were also the most technologically-advanced countries, hence best equipped to impose violence on others).[21]

The character of the indigenous societies that the colonialists confronted, moreover, was often no less democratic than the colonial states themselves—sometimes more so. As sociologist Michael Mann has noted:

> The "democratic peace" school have excluded groups like the [North American] Indian nations from their calculations on the somewhat dubious grounds that they did not have permanent differentiated states of the "modern" type. Though this is convenient for the self-congratulatory tone of much of their writings . . . it is illegitimate even by their own definitions. For Indian nations did develop permanent constitutional states through the mid-nineteenth century—for example, the Cherokee in 1827, the Choctaw, Chickasaw and Creeks in the period 1856–1867.[22]

Thus, when genocidal campaigns were waged against these nations, "liberal democracies were actually committing genocide against other democracies, repeatedly." In fact, Mann suggested, "If we counted up separately the cases where 'the people' of the United States, Canada and Australia committed mass murder on the individual Indian and aboriginal nations, we could probably tip Rummel's statistical scales over to the conclusion that democratic regimes were more likely to commit genocide than were authoritarian states."[23] In *Genocide in the Age of the Nation State*, historian Mark Levene similarly argued that "in the time of intense nation-state formation, specifically in the late eighteenth and early nineteenth centuries . . . arguably the two most notable repeat-perpetrators of genocide were Britain and the United States."[24] This phenomenon pervades the contemporary age as well. In examining *international* involvement in mass violence and atrocity, there is little doubt that the most consistently and aggressively violent country over the past fifty or sixty years is also the world's leading liberal democracy. Whatever the brutality of the Soviets in Hungary (1956) or in Afghanistan (see Chapter 2), no power approaches the United States when it comes to instigation of, and complicity in, conflicts and atrocities worldwide. The majority of this violence, moreover, was not conducted through formal participation in formally declared wars, but organized "covertly."[25] As we saw, Rummel generalized about this theme, claiming that democratic democide represents a stark departure from democratic norms. But then, wonders Errol Henderson, should these agents of mass violence really be classed as democracies?[26]

Mann, for his part, pointed out that the enabling variables which Rummel cited for "democratic democide"—secrecy, censorship, lying, deceit—are also those which have typically enabled mass killing by non-democratic states. Authoritarian genocides similarly tend to be inflicted in wartime, with attempts at secrecy. "Hitler committed almost all his murders during the war, and he did not dare make them public—indeed, nor did Stalin."[27]

Henderson, revisiting the dataset on democratic peace compiled by John Oneal and Bruce Russett (1997), pointed to sharp differences among Western liberal democracies, on one hand, and those he classified as "Hindu" democracies (India and Sri Lanka) and "Other" democracies (notably Israel), on the other. By retabulating Oneal and Russett's numbers, Henderson found that "Western democracies were significantly less likely to initiate interstate wars," but Hindu and other democracies "were significantly *more* likely to initiate them."[28]

On balance, and crucially including "extrastate" wars (wars against non-state entities, usually in a colonial and imperial context), "democratic states [are] in fact significantly *more likely* to become involved in—and to initiate—interstate wars and militarized international disputes," according to Henderson.[29] With regard to extrastate wars, "Western states—including the Western democracies—are more likely" to initiate and involve themselves in such conflicts. He concluded, provocatively and counterintuitively, that "for all of its positive value as an egalitarian form of government, one of the key threats to peace for individual states is the presence of a democratic regime."[30]

What can we take away from these diverse arguments? First, even the skeptical Henderson acknowledged the "positive value" of democracy "as an egalitarian form of government." As Rummel argued, consolidated democratic regimes are much less likely to wage war and genocide against their own populations than are tyrannical states.

On the other hand, liberal democracy is no guarantee against domestic killing, as millions of indigenous peoples discovered. Nor, in a world where the greatest perpetrator of international violence is the liberal-democratic superpower, can democracy be seen as a cure-all.[31]

NORMS AND PROHIBITION REGIMES

[My story] ... shows how a private individual almost single-handedly can succeed in imposing a moral law on the world and how he can stir world conscience to this end.
Raphael Lemkin

International relations scholars have studied the role of norms and regimes in global affairs, notably (for our purposes) *humanitarian norms* and *prohibition regimes.* Regimes were defined by Stephen Krasner as "principles, norms, rules, and decisionmaking procedures around which actor expectations converge in a given issue-area." Norms are "specific prescriptions or proscriptions for action," while principles are "standards of behavior defined in terms of rights and obligations."[32]

Ethan Nadelmann defined prohibition regimes as sets of "norms ... which prohibit, both in international law and in the domestic criminal law of states, the involvement of state and nonstate actors in particular activities." Such regimes emerge

> like municipal criminal laws ... for a variety of reasons: to protect the interests of the state and other powerful members of society; to deter, suppress, and punish undesirable activities; to provide for order, security, and justice among members of a community; and to give force and symbolic representation to the moral values, beliefs, and prejudices of those who make the law.[33]

The key player in transforming norms into international regimes, especially prohibition regimes, is the *norm (or moral) entrepreneur,* "an individual or organization that sets out to change the behaviour of others,"[34] and the *principled-issue networks* that such entrepreneurs create. The moral entrepreneur may take advantage of his or her celebrity, as US actors ranging from George Clooney and Angelina Jolie to Don Cheadle, Mia Farrow, and Ashley Judd have leant their names, time, and fame to the anti-genocide cause (see Figure 12.4).

The history of the prohibition regime against genocide, weak and underdeveloped as it currently is, provides an excellent example of such entrepreneurship. Raphael Lemkin's decades-long campaign to develop a norm against genocide eventually generated a principled-issue network of scholars, government representatives, legal specialists, and human-rights activists; this network has grown exponentially, and exerted a real though limited influence on global politics.

Lemkin's campaign was described in general terms in Chapter 1. Here, I want to examine the nuts and bolts of Lemkin's anti-genocide strategy, to demonstrate how successful norm entrepreneurship proceeds.

First, Lemkin perceived a void in existing international law. While legislation and even military intervention were countenanced in cases of interstate violence, states had free rein to inflict violence on their own populations. To generate a

Figure 12.4 Contemporary celebrities, as "superempowered individuals" in a wired and interconnected world, often leverage their fame to serve as "moral entrepreneurs," seeking to draw attention to humanitarian causes and crises. The anti-genocide cause is no exception, and the struggle against such grim atrocities mostly benefits from an infusion of celebrity initiative—and glamour. A leading advocate and "entrepreneur" is the actor George Clooney, pictured here discussing genocide in Sudan with President Obama at the White House in October 2010. "Celebrity can help focus news media where they have abdicated their responsibility," Clooney told *Newsweek* in 2011. Of the photographers pursuing his convoy in South Sudan (see Box 9A), he said, "If they're going to follow me anyway, I want them to follow me here." Journalist John Avlon described Clooney as "a man unconstrained by bureaucracy, with access to power and the ability to amplify a village's voice onto the world stage."[35] For more on his satellite remote-sensing project, see www.satsentinel.org. The anti-genocide advocacy efforts of Angelina Jolie, Mia Farrow, Ashley Judd, Don Cheadle, and (for US Indians) the late Marlon Brando[36] also merit mention.

Source: Pete Souza/White House/Wikimedia Commons.

norm and prohibition regime against such actions, a powerful existing norm, and a defining regime of world affairs, had to be eroded. This was the norm of state sovereignty, and the international regime (the Westphalian state system) that it underpinned. As long as states forswore intervention in the "internal" affairs of other states, a principal cause of human suffering could not be confronted.

To define a new norm and sell it to the world, Lemkin invented a word that addressed the "crime without a name," as Winston Churchill had described Nazi atrocities in Eastern Europe. Lemkin struggled to find "a word that could not be used in other contexts (as 'barbarity' and 'vandalism' could) . . . one that would bring

Figure 12.5 Jody Williams was a little-known US activist who spearheaded an International Campaign to Ban Landmines (ICBL), leading to the 1997 Mine Ban Treaty, also known as the Ottawa Convention. She was awarded the Nobel Peace Prize in the same year. Perhaps only Raphael Lemkin's "norm entrepreneurship" around genocide was so singlehanded and rapidly successful in engineering a "prohibition regime" in international affairs.[37] Williams is pictured at a hearing on "Preventing Sexual Violence and Gender-based Crimes" at the United Nations General Assembly, New York, in September 2012.

Source: Photo by Catianne Tijerina, UN Women/Creative Commons/Flickr.

with it 'a color of freshness and novelty' while describing something 'as shortly and as poignantly as possible.'"[38] The term he finally settled on—genocide—proved to be one of the core *catalyzing ideas* of the twentieth century. With unprecedented speed, it led to the drafting of an international Convention against genocide, the foundation of a prohibition regime that today exhibits growing strength and complexity.

With his evocative term in hand, Lemkin physically planted himself at the heart of postwar international legislation and regime formation. In the surprisingly informal surroundings of United Nations headquarters, then housed in an abandoned war plant on Long Island, Lemkin obsessively lobbied delegates to the new organization, spending "endless hours haunting the drafty halls."[39] Few delegates escaped his (usually unwanted) attentions. From his one-room Manhattan apartment, Lemkin fired off literally thousands of letters to government officials and politicians, religious and cultural figures, newspapers and their editors and assistant editors and reporters. In addition, "friends, friends of friends, and acquaintances of acquaintances" were drafted to the cause, providing background information and fresh contacts. Yet despite the reams of contacts, true friends were few. "I was condemned to loneliness. This was an essential condition of my life"— words that will resonate with many norm entrepreneurs, who are not always the most gregarious of people. "... I felt that only lonely persons can reach the borders of the unconscious and achieve the state of intuition which were so necessary for appraising situations at once and acting quickly. This intuition was a most valuable part of my equipment for many years."[40]

Throughout his campaign, Lemkin engaged in *norm grafting*. The task of the norm entrepreneur is eased if s/he can point to previous, congruent norms that have achieved wide acceptance. If A, why not B? (If slavery is wrong, why not forced labor? If voting rights are extended to all adult males, why not to women?) Such grafting presumes a desire for moral and rhetorical consistency on the part of policymakers and publics.[41] Thus, Lemkin pointed to the huge gap in the evolving prohibition regime against war crimes and crimes against humanity. "If piracy was an international crime, he could not understand why genocide was not." In a similar vein, Lemkin wrote in *The New York Times:* "It seems *inconsistent* with our concepts of civilization that selling a drug to an individual is a matter of worldly concern [i.e., the basis for an international prohibition regime], while gassing millions of human beings might be a problem of internal concern."[42]

Norm entrepreneurs frequently exploit historical moments that provide a favorable environment for norm adoption and regime creation. These moments usually follow major upheavals that weaken preconceptions and undermine established frameworks. Lemkin's fortunate conjuncture was the "multilateral moment" (Power's phrase) immediately following the Second World War. In a few years, many of the international organizations, legal instruments, and regimes of today were first developed (often grafted onto previous institutions and regimes, as the UN grew out of the League of Nations). The revelation of the full horror of Nazi rule, especially the reports and images from the death camps, undermined the

Figure 12.6 "Our Countrymen in Chains": illustration for an 1837 poem by the Quaker activist John Greenleaf Whittier. Slavery was once even more deeply embedded in human society than genocide is today—indeed, while few people defend genocide as such, most people saw slavery as the natural order of affairs through to the nineteenth century. What changed minds, and finally pushed slavery to the margins of international society, were the slave uprisings in Haiti and elsewhere (see pp. 64–65) and the abolitionist movement launched in the West in solidarity with the enslaved. If slavery can be abolished, why not genocide? This iconic image of the abolitionist movement displays tropes that have been common in "norm entrepreneurship" through to the present: the appeal to common humanity and empathy; a sentimental and religious dimension; and (unfortunately) the paternalistic portrayal of the victim as supplicant, dependent on the charity and good will of the privileged viewer.

Source: US Library of Congress Prints and Photographs Division/Wikimedia Commons. The image of the kneeling and prayerful slave was first deployed in England in the 1780s as the official seal of the Society for the Abolition of Slavery.

legitimacy of state sovereignty as a shield against intervention and prosecution on humanitarian grounds.

Lemkin's greatest achievement was the UN Genocide Convention. "Just four years after Lemkin had introduced 'genocide' to the world, the General Assembly had unanimously passed a law banning it." Lemkin duly entered hospital and stayed for three weeks, diagnosing his condition as "genociditis: exhaustion from the work on the Genocide Convention."[43] Then he turned his efforts (which by this point were undermining his health) to lobbying for ratification of the treaty, and the transformation of his norm into an effective prohibition regime. Using classic tactics of the norm entrepreneur, Lemkin crafted his messages and appeals carefully, individually, and with an eye for utilitarian impact. "He sent letters out in English, French, Spanish, Hebrew, Italian, and German. Long before computers or photocopiers"—two of the most powerful tools of the contemporary norm entrepreneur—"he handcrafted each letter to suit the appropriate individual, organization, or country. . . . He wrote to the leaders of the most influential political parties, the heads of the private women's or civic groups, and the editors of prominent newspapers." He also "attempted to mobilize American grassroots groups" and "enlisted a panoply of American civic organizations, churches, and synagogues."[44] With few material resources of his own, he "borrowed stationery from supportive community organizations, applied for grants to pay for postage, and sent thousands of letters to absolutely anybody whose moral heartstrings he felt he might tug or on whose connections he might prey to get the ear of a US senator."[45]

According to Power, Lemkin "varied his pitch," tailoring his message carefully and sometimes cynically to the object of his appeal. "If a country had experienced genocide in the past, he reminded its citizens of the human costs of allowing it. But if a country had *committed* genocide in the past, as Turkey had done [against minority Christians], Lemkin was willing to keep the country's atrocities out of the discussion, so as not to scare off a possible signatory" to the convention.[46] For similar reasons, Lemkin avoided pushing for the inclusion of political groups in the UN definition of genocide. This, he feared, would provoke resistance among states fearful of having their political persecutions labeled as genocide. (In any case, Lemkin had never cared much about political groups. He did not consider them to be bearers of human culture in the same—archaic?—way that he viewed ethnonational groups.)

With his reluctance to include political groups, Lemkin contributed to some of the conceptual and legal confusion that has since surrounded the UN Convention.[47] On balance, though, it is hard to disagree with his own self-estimation (in pitching his story to publishers): that his life "shows how a private individual almost single handedly can succeed in imposing a moral law on the world and how he can stir world conscience to this end."[48]

IR theorists of norms and regimes describe a *tipping point* followed by a *norm cascade* in the diffusion of norms, analogous to the paradigm shifts in scientific knowledge studied by Thomas Kuhn.[49] One norm displaces another, decisively and definitively. At this point, norms become strongly entrenched in international regimes, including effective prohibition regimes.

With respect to the norm against genocide and crimes against humanity, we can observe that it has partially, not decisively, displaced the norm of state sovereignty. It appeared possible, in the immediate postwar period, that a tipping from sovereignty to cosmopolitanism and international governance could occur, but this idealistic vision faded rapidly with the onset of the Cold War, and does not seem a great deal closer today. Thus, while the drive to suppress and prevent genocide has indeed spawned a norm and a prohibition regime, it is applied only weakly and inconsistently compared, say, with norms against state-sponsored slavery, nuclear proliferation, assassination of foreign leaders, or piracy and hijacking.[50] The anti-genocide movement is best classed with a range of other norms and regimes that have made significant strides, but have yet to entrench themselves in international affairs: those against capital punishment, trafficking (in human beings, drugs, and ivory), and theft of intellectual property, to name a few.

Nadelmann has developed a five-stage model for the evolution of prohibition regimes. At first, "most societies regard the targeted activity as entirely legitimate"; indeed, "states are often the principal protagonists." Then, the activity is redefined as morally problematic or evil, "generally by international legal scholars, religious groups, and other moral entrepreneurs." Next, "regime proponents begin to agitate actively for the suppression and criminalization of the activity." If this stage is successful, "the activity becomes the subject of criminal laws and police actions throughout much of the world." In the fifth and final stage, "the incidence of the proscribed activity is greatly reduced, persisting only on a small scale and in obscure locations."[51] Using this model, we can position the anti-genocide regime—and the other comparatively weak regimes mentioned above—between Nadelmann's third stage, with "regime proponents . . . agitat[ing] actively for the suppression and criminalization of the activity," and stage four, in which the regime is "the subject of criminal laws and police actions throughout much of the world."

Most weaker prohibition regimes suffer from a number of debilities. They may be relatively recent (many were at Nadelmann's first stage of evolution just a few decades ago). Their core concepts or "catalyzing ideas" may be prone to ambiguities of definition and application. Enforcement mechanisms are underdeveloped, and often corrupt—suggesting a lack of political will, and attesting to the failure of activist mobilization to spur political actors to meaningful effort. All of these factors are evident in the case of the anti-genocide regime.

Prohibition regimes are also hampered where strong counter-incentives exist. It remains in the interest of vast numbers of ordinary people (or smaller numbers of powerful people) to undermine the regime and weaken its application. Just as the lure of illegal drugs for both consumers and vendors outweighs the ability of states to suppress these substances, so genocide holds an enduring appeal as a problem-solving strategy for states and other actors.[52]

According to Nadelmann, however, prohibition regimes are *more* likely to succeed when the targeted activity has a strong transnational dimension; when unilateral and bilateral means of enforcement are inadequate; when a norm "reflects not just self-interest but a broadly acknowledged moral obligation"; and when the activity is vulnerable "to global suppression efforts by states."[53] IR theorists Margaret Keck and Kathryn Sikkink point out additionally that prohibition regimes are boosted when "the causal chain [is] short," when "causes can be assigned to the deliberate 'intentional' actions of identifiable individuals," and when a universalistic "concern with bodily harm" underlies the prohibition effort.[54] In all these respects, the anti-genocide regime holds considerable potential. This may bode well for its future strengthening.

FURTHER STUDY

Susan Burgerman, *Moral Victories: How Activists Provoke Multilateral Action*. Ithaca, NY: Cornell University Press, 2001. Concise study with a Latin American focus.

Errol A. Henderson, *Democracy and War: The End of an Illusion?* Boulder, CO: Lynne Rienner, 2002. Myth-shattering analysis of democracies' involvement in international conflict.

Adam Hochschild, *Bury the Chains: Prophets and Rebels in the Fight to Free an Empire's Slaves*. Boston, MA: Houghton Mifflin, 2005. Study of the abolitionist movement, with many lessons for anti-genocide "norm entrepreneurs" today.

Kalevi J. Holsti, *The State, War, and the State of War*. Cambridge: Cambridge University Press, 1996. Arguably the best introduction to global transformations in warfare.

Adam Jones, ed., *Genocide, War Crimes and the West: History and Complicity*. London: Zed Books, 2004. "The most comprehensive treatment of Western responsibility for mass atrocity yet published" (Richard Falk); naturally I agree.

Mary Kaldor, *New and Old Wars: Organized Violence in a Global Era*. Stanford, CA: Stanford University Press, 2001. Like Holsti (above), a core text of the new security studies.

Stathis Kalyvas, *The Logic of Violence in Civil War*. Cambridge: Cambridge University Press, 2006. Now-classic work exploring the kind of "subnational" and "micro- and meso-" actors and processes referenced by Ernesto Verdeja (Box 12.1).

Margaret E. Keck and Kathryn Sikkink, *Activists Beyond Borders: Advocacy Networks in International Politics*. Ithaca, NY, and London: Cornell University Press, 1998. The role of transnational nongovernmental networks in norm entrepreneurship and regime formation.

Manus I. Midlarsky, *The Killing Trap: Genocide in the Twentieth Century*. Cambridge: Cambridge University Press, 2005. Major study from a political-science perspective, emphasizing the contingency of genocidal processes.

R.J. Rummel, *Death by Government*. New Brunswick, NJ: Transaction Publishers, 1994. Comprehensive survey of government-directed mass killing, marred by some dubious cheerleading for Western democracies.

Martin Shaw, *Genocide and International Relations: Changing Patterns in the Transitions of the Late Modern World*. Cambridge: Cambridge University Press, 2013. Stimulating discussion that "emphasizes the international context of genocide" and "the relationships between genocide and the international system." (From the back-cover blurb.)

Ward Thomas, *The Ethics of Destruction: Norms and Force in International Relations*. Ithaca, NY: Cornell University Press, 2001. Elegantly-written study of normative constraints on war-making.

Benjamin A. Valentino, *Final Solutions: Mass Killing and Genocide in the 20th Century*. Ithaca, NY: Cornell University Press, 2004. Nuanced study of the insurgency–counterinsurgency dynamic in many genocidal campaigns; also strong on revolutionary ideologies and "communist mass killings."

NOTES

1 R.J. Rummel, *Death by Government* (New Brunswick, NJ: Transaction Publishers, 1994). He considers this a fairly conservative estimate: "The dead could conceivably be nearly 360 million people." Rummel maintains an extensive website on democide at www.hawaii.edu/powerkills/.

2 Ibid., p. 13. "If all these dead were laid out head to toe, assuming each to be an average of 5 feet tall, they would reach from Honolulu, Hawaii, across the vast Pacific and then the huge continental United States to Washington DC on the East Coast, *and then back again almost twenty times*" (emphasis in original).

3 Ibid., pp. 1–2.

4 It is interesting to note that in her earlier writing (1987), Harff subsumed politicide under genocide: "My definition of genocide differs from the official definition . . . insofar as it broadens the scope of the victims and perpetrators. Thus, political opponents are included in my definition, though they lack the formal legal protection of the Convention on Genocide." Harff, "The Etiology of Genocide," in Michael N. Dobkowski and Isidor Wallimann, eds., *The Age of Genocide: Etiology and Case Studies of Mass Death* (Westport, CT: Greenwood Press, 1987), p. 44.

5 Harff quoted in Helen Fein, *Genocide: A Sociological Perspective* (London: Sage, 1993), p. 40.

6 Barbara Harff, personal communication, June 12, 2012.

7 Barbara Harff, "No Lessons Learned from the Holocaust? Assessing Risks of Genocide and Political Mass Murder since 1955," *American Political Science Review*, 97: 1 (2003).

8 Ibid.

9 Barbara Harff, "Assessing Risks of Genocide and Politicide: A Global Watch List for 2012," in J. Joseph Hewitt, Jonathan Wilkenfeld, and Ted Robert Gurr, eds., *Peace and Conflict 2012* (Boulder, CO: Paradigm Publishers, 2012), p. 56.

10 Ibid., p. 56 and Table 6.1, p. 55.

11 Ernesto Verdeja, "The Political Science of Genocide: Outlines of an Emerging Research Agenda," *Perspectives on Politics*, 10: 2 (2012), pp. 307–308, 316.

12 For an extensive interdisciplinary sampling, see my "Bibliography of War" at http://adamjones.freeservers.com/bibliography_of_war.htm.

13 According to David Kertzer, "In many parts of the world, warfare itself is highly ritualized, with a special permanent site for the hostilities, special bodily adornment, special songs and verbal insults, and rules about the actual conduct of combat. In many of these cases, as soon as an individual is seriously wounded, hostilities cease and a round of post-battle ritual begins." Kertzer, quoted in Charles Tilly, *The Politics of Collective Violence* (Cambridge: Cambridge University Press, 2003), p. 86.

14 See John E. Mueller, *Retreat from Doomsday: The Obsolescence of Major War* (New York: Basic Books, 1989).

15 See Greg Campbell, *Blood Diamonds: Tracing the Deadly Path of the World's Most Precious Stones* (Boulder, CO: Westview Press, 2002).

16 See, e.g., Human Rights Watch, *The Curse of Gold*, June 2005, www.hrw.org/reports/2005/drc0505/.

17 This too has a precedent in the "limited" wars of the 1980s, when Nicaraguan *contra* rebels and the *mujahadeen* Islamists in Afghanistan trafficked drugs to finance weapons purchases, with the tacit approval and sometimes active complicity of the US government. See Peter Dale Scott and Jonathan Marshall, *Cocaine Politics: Drugs, Armies, and the CIA in Central America* (Berkeley, CA: University of California Press, 1991). For an overview of contemporary trends in historical context, see Peter Dale Scott, *Drugs, Oil, and War: The United States in Afghanistan, Colombia, and Indochina* (Lanham, MD: Rowman & Littlefield, 2003).

18 Gérard Prunier, *Africa's World War: Congo, the Rwandan Genocide, and the Making of a Continental Catastrophe* (New York: Oxford University Press, 2009), p. 337.

19 Errol A. Henderson, *Democracy and War: The End of an Illusion?* (Boulder, CO: Lynne Rienner, 2002), p. 4. See also Tarak Barkawi and Mark Laffey, *Democracy, Liberalism, and War: Rethinking the Democratic Peace Debate* (Boulder, CO: Lynne Rienner, 2001).

20 Rummel, *Death by Government*, pp. 14, 17. Among the other cases of "democratic democide" that Rummel cited in passing (pp. 14–16) were: "the large-scale massacres of Filipinos during the bloody US colonization of the Philippines at the beginning of [the twentieth] century, deaths in British concentration camps in South Africa during the Boar [sic] War, civilian deaths due to starvation during the British blockade of Germany in and after World War I, the rape and murder of helpless Chinese in and around Peking in 1900 [while crushing the Boxer Rebellion], the atrocities committed by Americans in Vietnam, the murder of helpless Algerians during the Algerian War by the French, and the unnatural deaths of German prisoners of war in French and US POW camps after World War II." However, as Mark Levene noted, Rummel displayed "an almost wilful myopia about mass murders committed directly or indirectly by liberal democratic regimes," especially more recent ones committed by his own country, the United States (Levene, *Genocide in the Age of the Nation State, Vol. 1: The Meaning of Genocide* [London: I.B. Tauris, 2005], p. 54). For example, while acknowledging that US forces did commit "democide" in Vietnam (Chapter 2), he suggested with a straight face that "the US democide in Vietnam seems to have killed at least 4,000 Vietnamese civilians, POWs, or enemy seeking to surrender, maybe as many as 10,000 Vietnamese"—this in a war that killed two to three million people, certainly including at least a million civilians, and kills them to this day through unexploded ordnance and environmental poisoning (Rummel, *Death by Government*, p. 277). In 2005, Rummel revised upward *more than fifty-fold* his estimate of all "colonial democide" in "colonized Africa and Asia [from] 1900 to independence," from an initial toll of 870,000 (a small fraction of the casualties in the Belgian Congo alone) to include *an additional 50 million victims.* Rummel, "Reevaluating Colonial Democide," December 11, 2005, www.ciolek.com/spec/rummel-on-democide-2005.html. Rummel died in 2014, without (to my knowledge) having conducted a similar reexamination of his Vietnam findings.

21 I do not mean to suggest that *only* democracies aggressed in this fashion——the counterexamples of tsarist Russia and imperial Japan may be cited——but rather that democracy seems to have provided no check to such aggression.

22 Michael Mann, "The Dark Side of Democracy: The Modern Tradition of Ethnic and Political Cleansing," *New Left Review*, 235 (May–June 1999), pp. 18–46.

23 Mann, "The Dark Side of Democracy," p. 26. On the same page, Mann argues that "deliberate genocidal bursts were more common among British than Spanish or Portuguese settlers. In both cases, we find that the stronger the democracy among the perpetrators, the greater the genocide."

24 Levene, *Genocide in the Age of the Nation State, Vol. 1*, p. 162.

25 I have prepared a table of "Key Instances of US Involvement in Mass Violence against Civilians since 1953" to buttress this claim: see www.genocidetext.net/us_violence.pdf. In the decade since the first edition of this book was published, no one has publicly challenged this claim and its supporting data, to my knowledge. See also the bibliography of much of the "dissident" literature on US state violence supplied in Adam Jones, "Introduction: History and Complicity," in Jones, ed., *Genocide, War Crimes and the West: History and Complicity* (London: Zed Books, 2004), pp. 26–30. This essay also introduces the concept of "democrisy," i.e., "the stain of hypocrisy that attaches to regimes that are avowedly democratic in character, that allow comparative freedom and immunity from naked state violence domestically, but that initiate or participate in atrocious actions beyond their borders" (p. 9).

26 See Henderson, *Democracy and War*, p. 82. One should also note the overwhelming US dominance in foreign sales of the armaments that fuel wars and genocides worldwide. In 2015, the US was still the world's largest seller and supplier of weaponry, by far. Indeed, just as until quite recently the US military budget exceeded that of the rest of the world combined, America today commands over 50 percent of the global arms

market. See Denver Nicks, "The US Is Still No. 1 at Selling Arms to the World," *Time*, December 26, 2015, http://time.com/4161613/us-arms-sales-exports-weapons/; Lauren Carroll, "Obama: US Spends More on Military Than Next 8 Nations Combined," *Politifact.com*, January 13, 2016, www.politifact.com/truth-o-meter/statements/2016/jan/13/barack-obama/obama-us-spends-more-military-next-8-nations-combi/. For arms sales per capita, no country approaches democratic Israel, and "Peace-loving Sweden and Switzerland are [also] among [the] Top Arms Exporters Per Capita in the World" (Allison Jackson, *GlobalPost.com*, May 23, 2014, www.globalpost.com/dispatch/news/regions/europe/140522/peace-loving-sweden-and-switzerland-are-among-the-top-arms-exporters-per-capita).

27 Mann, "The Dark Side of Democracy," p. 20.

28 Henderson, *Democracy and War*, p. 66; emphasis added.

29 Ibid., p. 17.

30 Ibid.

31 It is also worth recalling the destruction inflicted by global capitalism under a liberal-democratic aegis, as noted in Chapter 1's discussion of structural violence.

32 Stephen Krasner, "Structural Causes and Regime Consequences: Regimes as Intervening Variables," *International Organization*, 36:2 (1982), pp. 185–205.

33 Ethan Nadelmann, "Global Prohibition Regimes: The Evolution of Norms in International Society," *International Organization*, 44: 4 (1990), pp. 479–526.

34 Ann Florini, "The Evolution of International Norms," *International Studies Quarterly*, 40 (1996), p. 375.

35 John Avlon, "Clooney's Not Kidding: Actor Adds 'Arrested Activist' to Credit Roll," *Newsweek*, February 20, 2011, www.newsweek.com/clooneys-not-kidding-actor-adds-arrested-activist-credit-roll-68527.

36 On Brando's multifaceted advocacy efforts, see Bill Raden, "Marlon Brando: The Actor as Activist" (interview with Susan Mizruchi), *Capital & Main*, June 26, 2014, http://capitalandmain.com/latest-news/issues/culture-and-media/marlon-brando-the-actor-as-activist/; Mizruchi, *Brando's Smile: His Life, Thought, and Work* (New York: W.W. Norton & Company, 2014).

37 See Richard Price, "Reversing the Gun Sights: Transnational Civil Society Targets Land Mines," *International Organization*, 52: 3 (Summer 1998), pp. 613—644.

38 Samantha Power, *"A Problem from Hell": America and the Age of Genocide* (New York: Basic Books, 2002), p. 42.

39 Ibid., p. 51.

40 Raphael Lemkin, *Totally Unofficial: The Autobiography of Raphael Lemkin* (New Haven, CT: Yale University Press, 2013), p. 163.

41 The concept is similar to Keck and Sikkink's formulation of "moral leverage" as exercised by activist networks: "Material leverage comes from linking the issue of concern to money, trade, or prestige, as more powerful institutions or governments are pushed to apply pressure. Moral leverage pushes actors to change their practices by holding their behavior up to international scrutiny, or by holding governments or institutions accountable to previous commitments and principles they have endorsed." Margaret E. Keck and Kathryn Sikkink, *Activists Beyond Borders: Advocacy Networks in International Politics* (Ithaca, NY: Cornell University Press, 1998), p. 201.

42 Power, and Lemkin quoted in Power, "A *Problem from Hell*," p. 48; emphasis added. In similar fashion, activists seeking to memorialize certain genocides may also draw upon genocidal precedents. Thus, "proliferating Armenian discourses on [the genocide of] 1915 were coloured by connections with the Jewish Holocaust. This was entirely natural, given the proximity of the 'final solution,' the growing public awareness of it in the 1960s in the aftermath of the trial of Adolf Eichmann, and the fact that the Nazi campaigns of genocide had given decisive impetus to the establishment of the genocide convention." Donald Bloxham, *The Great Game of Genocide: Imperialism, Nationalism, and the Destruction of the Ottoman Armenians* (Oxford: Oxford University Press, 2005), p. 217.

43 Lemkin, *Totally Unofficial*, p. 179.

44 Power, *"A Problem from Hell,"* p. 72.

45 Ibid., p. 71.

46 Ibid., pp. 63–64. John Cooper described similar strategies in his study of *Raphael Lemkin and the Genocide Convention* (London: Palgrave Macmillan, 2008): "Lemkin carefully avoided upsetting the Arab supporters of the genocide convention by . . . not singling out the fate of the Jews during the Second World War" (p. 147), and skated over Turkish crimes against the Armenians when wooing the Turkish government. He was also a grand flatterer. To the Mexican Ambassador to the UN, Padilla Nervo, Lemkin wrote: "Certainly, the great humanitarian tradition of your country, and the great prestige of its leaders throughout Latin America, in the United Nations, and in the world at large, qualifies Mexico as a natural champion and leader for the genocide convention" (p. 178). To the Haitian Foreign Minister, Dr. Vilfort Beauvoer, Lemkin eloquently declared: "Your ancestors, Excellency, were brought as slaves to this hemisphere. They were tortured and beaten; now you are a free people. . . . Your government should be in the forefront of this action" (p. 179). Meanwhile, in correspondence with a representative of the same French nation that had once enslaved the Haitians, Lemkin argued that "Quick ratification by France would start a strong ratification movement in the entire world because every country looks to France for guidance in matters of international law and new ideals" (p. 181). "The approach to every nation must be made by stressing values peculiar to it," Lemkin wrote in his autobiography. "The correspondence must be in the language of the nation approached and in appealing to the traditions of her people. A bridge of sympathetic understanding and 'at home' feeling must be established." Lemkin, *Totally Unofficial*, p. 187.

47 Nor did Lemkin draw the line at behavior that many found boorish, if it would advance his cause. Power describes his "mix of flattery and moral prodding . . . [which] sometimes slipped into bluntly bullying his contacts and demanding that they acquire a conscience." *"A Problem from Hell,"* p. 71.

48 Lemkin quoted in ibid., p. 77.

49 The term "norm cascade" was coined by Martha Finnemore and Kathryn Sikkink in "International Norm Dynamics and Political Change," *International Organization*, 52: 4 (Autumn 1998), pp. 901–902. See also Thomas S. Kuhn, *The Structure of Scientific Revolutions* (Chicago, IL: University of Chicago Press, 1996).

50 "Piracy may be regarded as the very first 'crime against humanity,' its peculiarly barbaric quality derived from the taking of lives which were especially vulnerable while outside the protective realm of any nation." Geoffrey A. Robertson, *Crimes against Humanity: The Struggle for Global Justice* (New York: The New Press, 2000), p. 208. Accordingly, the international regime against piracy might be regarded as the first in history, with the possible exception of that prohibiting assassinations of state leaders and diplomatic representatives.

51 Nadelmann, "Global Prohibition Regimes," pp. 484–486.

52 See Catherine Barnes, "The Functional Utility of Genocide: Towards a Framework for Understanding the Connection between Genocide and Regime Consolidation, Expansion and Maintenance," *Journal of Genocide Research*, 7: 3 (September 2005), pp. 309–330.

53 Nadelmann, "Global Prohibition Norms," p. 491.

54 Keck and Sikkink, *Activists Beyond Borders*, pp. 27, 53, 195.

CHAPTER 13

Gendering Genocide

It is recommended that the definition [of genocide] should be extended to include a sexual group such as women, men, or homosexuals.

> Benjamin Whitaker, *Revised and Updated Report on the Question of the Prevention and Punishment of Genocide* (the UN Whitaker Report), 1985

Gender is about gender, it is not about men on their own or women on their own . . . it is about relationships and interactions, and when you work on these issues it should be in an inclusive fashion.

> Chris Dolan

The gender dimension of genocide and other crimes against humanity has only recently attracted sustained attention. Leading the way were feminist scholars, who paid particular attention to rape and sexual assault against women, and pressed for such crimes to be considered genocidal. Other scholars and commentators have concentrated on the gender-selective killing of infant girls through female infanticide, or the denial of adequate nutrition and health care resources to females at all stages of life.

The term "gender" is one of the most contested in the social sciences. Not long ago, it was assumed that gender could be clearly distinguished from biological/ physiological sex. Gender referred to the way that societies and cultures ascribed particular "feminine" and "masculine" roles, expectations, and values to (biological) males versus females. This vocabulary still has its strong proponents.[1] In the past couple of decades, however, the distinction between biological/physiological sex and cultural gender has begun to break down. Increasingly, scholars and activists argue that sex and gender overlap and are mutually constitutive. Such is the view of international relations scholar Joshua Goldstein, who views a strict gender-sex distinction as "construct[ing] a false dichotomy between biology and culture." Goldstein accordingly "use[s] 'gender' to cover masculine and feminine roles and bodies alike, in all their aspects, including the (biological and cultural) structures, dynamics, roles and scripts associated with each gender group."[2] His definition also guides discussion in this chapter. It allows us to explore the gendering of genocide both in its destructive impact on male and female bodies, and with regard to the cultural practices that shape embodied experience.

Gender is not synonymous with women/femininity, despite its close association with feminist-influenced scholarship and policymaking. Some feminists have contended that gender *means* the oppression of women by men,[3] resulting in a certain tone-deafness to the ways in which men and masculinities are often targeted, including in genocide. This chapter adopts a more inclusive view of gender. Indeed, it begins with one of the least-studied aspects of contemporary genocide: the gendercidal (gender-selective) killing of males.

GENDERCIDE VS. ROOT-AND-BRANCH GENOCIDE

> I saw the militias running in all directions, chasing men and boys to kill them.
> Eyewitness in East Timor (Box 7a), September 1999

The gendercidal targeting of a community's adult males, usually accompanied by slavery and/or concubinage for out-group women, has deep roots. In Homer's *Odyssey* (9:39–61), the hero Odysseus describes his raid on Ismaros: "I pillaged the town and killed the men. The women and treasure . . . I divided as fairly as I could among all hands."[4] The Greek historian Thucydides (fifth century BCE) recorded a dialog between Athenian representatives and delegates from Melos, resisting Athenian control. In the military show-down that resulted, wrote Thucydides, "the Melians surrendered unconditionally to the Athenians"; the latter then "put to death all the men of military age whom they took, and sold the women and children as slaves."[5] It is impossible to know how common this pattern of gender-selective slaughter of males was, compared with the root-and-branch extermination of every member of the opposing group—women, children, and the elderly along with adult men. The term "root-and-branch" is also implicitly gendered: the root is the female that gives birth to the branch, the child. Thus, root-and-branch genocides are those that expand *beyond* adult males to remaining sectors of the targeted population.[6] When they do, the "branches"—children—are targeted in part because they may grow (a) to fight and take revenge, or (b) to give birth to new generations of resisters. The "roots"—women in their child-bearing years—may be slaughtered for their potential as bearers of the same new generations. ("Why were women and children considered enemies?" Scott Straus asked a convicted *génocidaire* in Ruhengeri,

Rwanda. "The children and women would reproduce," he was told. "And if they reproduced?" "They would kill us again as they killed before, as is said in history."[7])

In the modern era, gendercides against "battle-age" males have been more frequent than campaigns of root-and-branch annihilation. There is a brutal logic in this. Genocide usually occurs in the context of military conflict, or precipitates it. Males are everywhere those primarily designated to "serve" in the military. A deranged form of military thinking dictates that all men of battle age, whether combatant or non-combatant, are legitimate targets.[8]

In general, then, men are cast as "provocative targets," in Donald Horowitz's phrase:

Experimental data indicate that provocative targets are more likely victims of aggression than are nonprovocative targets and that aggression may be regarded as less legitimate when the victim is weak or fails to retaliate. Men are attacked in riots and singled out for atrocities much more than women are, just as males are attacked more frequently than females are in experiments, and the skewing in both seems positively related to the strength of the target.[9]

Men are also standardly—and indiscriminately—the targets of *hostage-taking* and *reprisal* policies. Nazi policy everywhere in German-occupied territories was to respond to the killings of German soldiers and personnel by exacting vengeance upon randomly chosen males of the community where (or near where) the attack occurred. "I came home from shopping on 9 June 1944 to find my husband and my son hanging from the balcony of our house," a French woman related. "They were just two of a hundred men seized at random and killed in cold blood by the SS [after the killing of forty German soldiers by *Maquis* resistance fighters]. The children and wives were forced to watch while they strung them up to the lamp-posts and balconies outside their own homes. What is there for me to say?"[10]

As this suggests, there is also a logic to the physical preservation of women. They are deemed to pose no military threat, or a lesser one. They may have value as slaves and/or concubines. In addition, male-dominant society is overwhelmingly *patrilineal*, with descent traced through the father. The woman may be viewed as a "blank slate," able to adopt, or at least provide a conduit for, the ethnicity of a male impregnator; women may even be held to contribute nothing to the genetic mix *per se*. (This was a prominent theme as recently as the Rwandan genocide of 1994.)[11]

Reflecting such gendered assumptions and social structures, many cultures—perhaps most pervasively those of the Western world between the medieval era and the twentieth century—evolved norms of war that dictated protection for "civilians." This term also carried gendered connotations, so that even today the phrase "women and children" seems synonymous with "civilians."[12] Of course, once women and children have been removed from the equation, only adult men remain, implicitly consigning this group to non-civilian status and rendering it "fair game"—though degrees of protection may be extended on the basis of (old) age or demonstrable non-combatant status (e.g., handicapped or injured men).

A key question with regard to gender and mass killing is, therefore: Will genocidal forces view the slaughter of "battle-age" males as a sufficient expression of

Figure 13.1 The gendercidal massacre of a community's males, often in acts of gender-selective "reprisal," is a standard feature of genocides throughout history. A frieze at the memorial museum in Lidice, Czech Republic, depicts the 1942 massacre by Nazi soldiers of 190 village males, in revenge for the assassination of Reinhard Heydrich (a key figure in planning the Holocaust of European Jews) in nearby Prague. Such mass execution scenes were repeated during the Armenian genocide (Chapter 4); by the Japanese at Nanjing in 1937–1938 (Chapter 2); in Dhaka, Bangladesh in 1971 (Box 8a); and at Srebrenica in Bosnia-Herzegovina in 1995 (Chapter 8), to cite just a few examples. The children and women of Lidice were transported to concentration camps and death camps, where most were eventually killed. The gendercidal massacre of able-bodied males implies no long-term preservation of women, children, and the disabled. Instead, as in the Nazi case, it often serves as a precursor to "root-and-branch" genocide against entire populations.

Source: Author's photo, November 2009.

Figure 13.2 Gender-selective roundups and detentions of a community's men, often under conditions of torture and abuse including sexual violence, are among the most reliable indicators that a campaign of full-scale genocide may be impending (see further discussion in Chapter 16, p. 757). In the wake of the Nazis' *Kristallnacht* pogrom against Jews on November 9–10, 1938, some thirty thousand Jewish men were arrested and incarcerated, like these prisoners being inducted at the Buchenwald concentration camps. Hundreds died from physical abuse and suicide.

Source: United States Holocaust Memorial Museum.

the genocidal impulse? Or will they also target children, women, and the elderly? The resolution to the question usually unfolds sequentially: *once* the younger adult male population group has been targeted, will remaining population groups *then* be slaughtered? Obviously, removing the group most closely associated with military activity, and hence military resistance, makes targeting other group members easier, logistically speaking. It may be much *harder*, however, to motivate genocidal killers to do their work, given norms against targeting these "helpless" populations.

The twentieth and twenty-first centuries have witnessed both core types of genocide, as we have seen throughout this volume. Typical of gendercidal strategies was the war in Bosnia-Herzegovina, with its crowning mass slaughter at Srebrenica (Chapter 8). To the Bosnian case we can add literally dozens of others in which gender selectivity channeled, and significantly limited, the *strictly murderous* dimension of the genocide (which is the critical one, by my preferred definition). They include Bangladesh in 1971; Cambodia between 1975 and 1979; Kashmir/Punjab and Sri Lanka in the 1980s and 1990s; the genocidal massacres of Sikhs in New Delhi in 1984; Saddam Hussein's Anfal Campaign against Iraqi Kurds in 1988; Kosovo and East Timor in 1999; Chechnya in the 1990s and 2000s; and Iraq after 2003.[13] The death toll in the "degenerate war" in the Democratic Republic of the Congo (see Chapter 9) has been inflicted mostly indirectly, as the consequence of the collapse of agricultural cycles, health services, transportation and evacuation routes, and so on. One would not expect a massively gender-disproportionate death toll under such circumstances. Likewise, there is no shortage of chilling evidence of largescale, gender-indiscriminate massacres of the kind that prevailed in the Rwandan holocaust. But to the extent that *direct, gender-selective* mass killing has occurred—and they have certainly accounted for tens if not hundreds of thousands of Congolese lives—it seems overwhelmingly to have targeted males, in the typical gendercidal pattern. At the outset in 1996, for example, ethnically Tutsi Banyamulenge males in eastern Congo were targeted for "reprisals" by the army of the tottering Mobutu regime (they were assumed to be allies or operatives of Tutsi-ruled Rwanda, which was seeking to install its own client in Mobutu's place). In his book *Dancing in the Glory of Monsters*, Jason Stearns recounted the story of one of them, "Alex":

At dawn, Mobutu's soldiers separated the men from the women and children. . . . The soldiers loaded their guns and shouted that all men over the age of fourteen had to come to one side. As a tall thirteen-year-old, Alex was a borderline case. Picking him out of a lineup, where he was standing next to his brother, a soldier took pity on him and pushed him brusquely toward where his mother and sisters were waiting, knotting their skirts up between their fingers. They watched together as his father and older brother were bound with sisal ropes, their arms tied behind their back and their legs together. The soldiers dumped them "like sacks of cassava" into the boat, which they then paddled out into the lake. It was a big vessel; Alex estimated there to be around thirty or forty captives onboard. At around two hundred meters from shore, still within sight of their frantic families, the men were thrown into the water. Alex could see splashes of water where the men flopped and struggled in vain to keep their heads above water before they drowned. Some managed to keep afloat by wiggling their bodies for several minutes. On the beach, their families screamed out and cried but couldn't do anything. His mother fainted. The soldiers watched, their rifles on their shoulders.[14]

In New Delhi in 1984, where more than 5,000 Sikhs died in days of genocidal massacres, the gendered targeting of males was carried to almost surreal extremes:

> The nature of the attacks confirms that there was a deliberate plan to kill as many Sikh men as possible, hence nothing was left to chance. That also explains why in almost all cases, after hitting or stabbing, the victims were doused with kerosene or petrol and burnt, so as to leave no possibility of their surviving. Between October 31 and November 4, more than 2,500 men were murdered in different parts of Delhi, according to several careful unofficial estimates. There have been very few cases of women being killed except when they got trapped in houses which were set on fire. Almost all of the women interviewed described how men and young boys were special targets. They were dragged out of the houses, attacked with stones and rods, and set on fire. . . . When women tried to protect the men of their families, they were given a few blows and forcibly separated from the men. Even when they clung to the men, trying to save them, they were hardly ever attacked the way men were. I have not yet heard of a case of a woman being assaulted and then burnt to death by the mob.[15]

Delhi and, with it, Bangladesh, appear in Donald Horowitz's compendium of "deadly ethnic riots," which are closely linked to genocide (see also Chapters 11 and 12). Horowitz is emphatic about the gender dimension of such slaughters, and his comments may be used without qualification to describe genocide as well:

> While the violence proceeds, there is a strong, although not exclusive, concentration on male victims of a particular ethnic identity. The elderly are often left aside, and sometimes, though less frequently, so are children. Rapes certainly occur in ethnic riots, sometimes a great many rapes, but the killing and mutilation of men is much more common than is the murder or rape of women. Women are sometimes pushed aside or forced to watch the torture and death of their husbands and brothers. . . . Sometimes women are even treated courteously by their husbands' killers.[16]

It is important to point out that, whatever some denialists might claim, targeting "only" adult men for massacre is sufficient, under international law, to constitute genocide. This was confirmed in April 2004, when appeal judges of the International Criminal Tribunal for the Former Yugoslavia (ICTY) overturned a 2001 verdict against Bosnian Serb General Radislav Krstic, who had been found guilty "not of genocide but of aiding and abetting genocide" during the Srebrenica massacre. The appeals chamber determined that "by seeking to eliminate a part of the Bosnian Muslims"—those living in Srebrenica, and specifically by exterminating "the male Muslim" component of that group—genocide had indeed occurred under Krstic's supervision.[17] The original judgment outlined the legal justification as follows:

> The Bosnian Serb forces could not have failed to know, by the time they decided to kill all the men, that this selective destruction of the group would have a lasting impact upon the entire group. Their death precluded any effective attempt by the Bosnian Muslims to recapture the territory. Furthermore, the Bosnian Serb forces had to be aware of the catastrophic impact that the disappearance of two or three generations of men would have on the survival of a traditionally patriarchal society . . . The Bosnian Serb forces knew, by the time they decided to kill all of the military aged men, that the combination of those killings with the forcible transfer of the women, children and elderly would inevitably result in the physical disappearance of the Bosnian Muslim population at Srebrenica.[18]

In its way, the verdict was as significant as that rendered earlier by the International Criminal Tribunal for Rwanda (ICTR) against Jean-Paul Akayesu. This established that the systematic rape of women could be considered genocidal when part of a broader campaign of group destruction (see the discussion of genocidal rape, below).

A very common result of gendercides against men is a glaring demographic disparity in the proportion of surviving women versus men. This is exemplified by cases such as Iraq, Cambodia, highlands Guatemala, and Rwanda—although one must be careful in evaluating the extent to which data truly reflect disproportionate male mortality, or alternatively an undercounting of males who may be in exile (as refugees or fighters), or in hiding to escape persecution and evade conscription.[19]

In the "root-and-branch" holocausts that the general public tends to view as the paradigm of genocide, a sequential progression is apparent along the lines described earlier. It is striking that all three of the "classic" genocides of the twentieth century—by the Turks against the Armenians; the Nazis against the Jews; and Hutus against Tutsis—followed roughly this pattern. The time separating the different stages was sometimes brief (in the Nazi case, only a few weeks), and the Rwandan case cannot be incorporated without serious qualification. Readers are invited to peruse the chapter-length treatments of these genocides through a "gendered" lens, to see how the progression from gendercidal to root-and-branch strategies occurred.

As noted in the Jewish Holocaust chapter, the shift from targeting "battle-age" non-combatant males, usually viewed as legitimate targets, to targeting children, women, and the elderly, may result in substantial emotional stress to killers. "While unarmed men seem fair game," wrote Leo Kuper, "the killing of women and children arouses general revulsion"[20]—though not in all situations, and not necessarily for long. Hence the escalation of Nazi killing of Jews, moving from adult males to other population groups;[21] hence, too, the development of distancing technologies such as gas vans and gas chambers, to reduce the trauma for murderers of women and children. One can also note the degeneration of more centralized control over genocidal killing in Rwanda. This appears to have been linked, in part, to concerns of ordinary Hutus that the murder spree was moving beyond "acceptable" victims.[22]

WOMEN AS GENOCIDAL TARGETS

The focus so far on the mass-murder component of genocide may have the undesirable effect of implying that women are exempted from the worst genocidal violence. Nothing could be further from the truth. First, root-and-branch genocides throughout history have killed tens or hundreds of millions of females. Many structural cases of genocide—such as mass famine, economic embargo, and so on—have an equal or greater impact on women and girls than on men and boys.

Second, the micro-managed gender strategies employed, for example, at Srebrenica, are fairly rare, especially in the contemporary era of "degenerate war" (see Chapters 2, 12). It is more common, as it was even in the Balkan genocides, for women to be exposed to direct abuses and atrocities. While these may be on average less deadly, they are no less "gendered." They range from verbal assault and humiliation, to physical attack and individual rape, to multiple and gang rape (often under conditions of protracted sexual servitude), to rape-murder on a large scale.

In December 1937, one of the most savage instances of genocidal rape inaugurated the so-called Rape of Nanjing. When Japanese forces seized the Chinese capital, up to a *quarter of a million* Chinese men were corralled and massacred, often after torture. Tens of thousands of women were also killed—usually after extended and excruciating gang rape. Kenzo Okamoto, a Japanese soldier, recalled: "We were hungry for women! Officers issued a rough rule: if you mess with a woman, kill her afterwards."[23] Another soldier stated: "Perhaps when we were raping [a female victim], we looked at her as a woman, but when we killed her, we just thought of her as something like a pig."[24] A Chinese eyewitness, Li Ke-hen, described "so many bodies on the street, victims of group rape and murder. They were all stripped naked, their breasts cut off, leaving a terrible dark brown hole; some of them were bayoneted in the abdomen, with their intestines spilling out alongside them; some had a roll of paper or a piece of wood stuffed in their vaginas." Almost no female was safe. Girls as young as eight, along with elderly women, were raped and killed. Even those not murdered immediately were liable to be "turned loose in such a manhandled condition that they died a day or two later."[25]

The Japanese rape of women in the Asian-occupied territories featured in the indictment at the postwar Tokyo Tribunal—though the systematic conscription and sexual exploitation of Korean, Indonesian, and other women (the so-called "comfort women"—see Chapter 14, p. 670) was not addressed. This may be because the victorious powers had overseen somewhat similar systems of female exploitation in their own spheres. Likewise, when invading Soviet forces raped "as many as 1.4 million women" in the eastern German territories—"some 18 per cent of the female population of those regions"[26]—the mass crimes went unmentioned at the Nuremberg war crimes trials. The Soviets, of course, would never have permitted an investigation of the subject; nor did the other Allied occupiers press for one, guilty as they were of their own largescale sexual attacks on German women.

Feminist author Susan Brownmiller's book *Against Our Will* (1975) marked the first systematic exploration of rape. It publicized the large-scale sexual violence against Bengali women during the Bangladesh genocide of 1971 (Box 8a), and the social rejection that raped women confronted in the aftermath. It was the Balkan wars of the 1990s, though, that exposed the issue of mass rape of women to international visibility (see the account of 16-year-old "E.," cited in Chapter 8). The term "genocidal rape" began to be widely employed to convey the centrality of sexual assault to the wider campaign of group destruction. Although rejected by some who argued that rape and genocide were distinct crimes, the concept gained further credibility with the events in Rwanda in 1994. As the UN Special Rapporteur on Rwanda, René Degni-Segui, pointed out, "rape was the rule and its absence the exception" during this genocide.[27] While estimates of women raped in the Balkan genocides ranged between 20,000 and 50,000, in Rwanda they were *ten times* higher—between 250,000 and 500,000. Moreover, as at Nanjing, rape was standardly accompanied by "extreme brutality" above and beyond the specific sexual assault. "Rape accompanied by mutilation [was] reported to include: the pouring of boiling water onto the genital parts and into the vagina . . . the cutting off of breast(s) and the mutilation of other parts of the female body."[28] And rape was very often followed by death—sometimes (and still) many years later, owing to the high proportion of Hutu rapists infected with the HIV virus. General Roméo Dallaire, recollecting the Rwandan holocaust years after he had failed meaningfully to impede it, found himself haunted above all by "the death masks of raped and sexually mutilated girls and women." But "even in the whitened skeletons" of the memorial sites, "you could see the evidence" of the masculine pathologies inscribed on their defenseless bodies:

> The legs bent and apart. A broken bottle, a rough branch, even a knife between them. Where the bodies were fresh, we saw what must have been semen pooled on and near the dead women and girls. There was always a lot of blood. Some male corpses had their genitals cut off, but many women and young girls had their breasts chopped off and their genitals crudely cut apart. They died in a position of total vulnerability, flat on their backs, with their legs bent and knees wide apart. It was the expressions on their dead faces that assaulted me the most, a frieze of shock, pain and humiliation.[29]

In part as a result of the scale and savagery of the Rwandan rapes, and reflecting years of feminist-inspired mobilization around the issue, in September 1998 the ICTR convicted Jean-Paul Akayesu for acts of genocide including sexual violence. As Human Rights Watch noted, this marked "the first conviction for genocide by an international court; the first time an international court has punished sexual violence in a civil war; and *the first time that rape was found to be an act of genocide [intended] to destroy a group.*"[30] (See also the photo essay, photo 14.)

Astonishingly, the record of mass rape in the Rwandan genocide was matched and even surpassed in the years following the holocaust—in neighboring Congo, where sexual violence has raged through to the present day. "Tens of thousands of women, possibly hundreds of thousands, have been raped in the past few years," wrote Jeffrey Gettleman of *The New York Times* in 2008.[31] Those responsible include virtually all the military and paramilitary forces operating in the east of the country—and even some of the "Blue Helmets" of MONUC, the UN peacekeeping force dispatched to restore order and protect civilians. John Holmes, coordinator of emergency relief for the UN, stated in 2007 that rape in Congo had become "almost a cultural phenomenon . . .The intensity and frequency is worse than anywhere else in the world."[32] "It's like a contagion," reported the advocate and actor Ashley Judd after a visit to eastern Congo. "When one man does it, it activates other men, and then the more brutal it becomes—looking for pregnant women to rape, and children. It's so unbelievably heinous that it's hard for us to wrap our minds around." As in Rwanda, apart from the psychological trauma and humiliation of rape, severe and often life-threatening physical injuries were the norm:

> The vagina will tear when being forced to accommodate either a rapist's anatomy or objects that are introduced: wood, rock, sticks, guns, bayonets. There will be perforation of the vaginal walls, perforation and ripping of the cervix, potentially, based on the extent of the penetration into the uterus. The wall between the rectum and vagina is ripped apart. The urethra, which goes to the bladder, is damaged. There is incontinence. The urine is constantly seeping out, because the muscles and mechanisms that hold the bladder intact are ruined; there is faecal incontinency, which of course can introduce faecal matter into the gut, which results in horrific infections. Does that paint the picture?[33]

In the past decade, attention has begun to be paid to the previously taboo subject of rape and sexual violence against men and boys in war and genocide. A handful of scholars, including myself, noted as early as the mid-1990s that males were also being targeted for systematic sexual violence in the wars in former Yugoslavia.[34] Amalendu Misra notes that "of the 6,000 Serb-held concentration camp interns in the Sarajevo Canton, 5,000 were men and 80 per cent of them had been raped either by their captors or were forced to rape each other."[35] Sexual mutilation of Rwandan Tutsi men was widespread in the holocaust of 1994. Virtually any conflict situation that involves the widespread roundup and gender-selective detention of men and adolescent boys will feature sexual violence on an epidemic scale within the regime's jails. Misra interviewed a Sri Lankan survivor, "Jeychandran," who

> still wakes up several nights a week sweating. His nightmares are always the same: being dragged out of his house by Sri Lankan soldiers and gagged and raped by soldiers in uniform in the barracks; someone binding his hands and legs before fixing two metal clips to his scrotum and penis and then putting the wires in the plug. He twitches as he speaks about his experience . . . He disappears into his thoughts in the middle of the conversation. Small beads of sweat build up on his temple and neck. When he wakes up from this nightmare and returns to the conversation his throat is dry and his voice affected.[36]

Examples of the sexual victimization of males from Africa (especially Uganda and DR Congo)[37] have received study, while Human Rights Watch and others have documented almost ubiquitous rape and sexualized torture against detainees in Bashar al-Assad's despotic Syria.[38] International organizations like the Red Cross, and nongovernmental initiatives such as the Refugee Law Project at Kampala University (where leading advocate Chris Dolan was long based),[39] have begun to reconceptualize rape in war and genocide to incorporate attention to male victims and survivors. This has not occurred without pushback in institutional-feminist ranks, as advocates for female rape victims fear a diminution of resources for their cause. But it contributes, in my view, to a necessary broadening of "gender-based violence" (GBV) to acknowledge that "gender against men"[40] is also a real-world configuration, and to draw the relevant policy conclusions.

GENDERCIDAL INSTITUTIONS

An appreciation of female vulnerability to genocide is greatly increased if we expand our framing beyond politico-military genocides, to the realm of "gendercidal institutions." I refer here to patterned behavior, embedded in human societies, that exacts a death toll sufficiently large in scale and systematic in character to be considered gendercidal.

For females, probably the most destructive such institution throughout history is female infanticide and neonaticide. The selective killing of newborn and infant girls reflects a culturally ingrained preference for male children. A nineteenth-century missionary in China, for example, "interviewed 40 women over age 50 who reported having borne 183 sons and 175 daughters, of whom 126 sons but only 53 daughters survived to age 10; by their account, the women had destroyed 78 of their daughters."[41] The Communist Revolution of 1949 made great strides in reducing discrimination against women and infant girls, but such millennia-old traditions are extremely difficult to root out. Today, numerous reports speak of large demographic disparities between males and females in parts of rural China, leading to widespread trafficking in women and adolescent girls as Chinese men seek to import wives from outside their regions.

The country where female infanticide and neonaticide are most widespread at present is India. For example, a study of Tamil Nadu state by the Community Service Guild of Madras found that "female infanticide is rampant" among Hindu families: "Of the 1,250 families covered by the study, 740 had only one girl child and 249 agreed directly that they had done away with the unwanted girl child. More than 213 of the families had more than one male child whereas half the respondents had only one daughter."[42] Among wealthier families in both India and China, however, infanticide is being replaced by sex-selective abortion, following *in utero* screening procedures that have spread even to isolated rural areas.

Among other gendercidal institutions targeting females are gendered deficiencies in nutrition and health care (reflecting the prioritizing of male family

Figure 13.3 Female infanticide and female foeticide (sex-selective abortion) are among the most destructive of "gendercidal institutions." The practices are especially widespread in India and China, the world's most populous countries. A sign outside the maternity hospital in Pondicherry, India, encourages a progressive approach to gender equality.

Source: Author's photo, June 2008.

members for these resources); "honor" killings of women and girls, particularly in the Middle East, South Asia, and the Caucasus; and dowry killings and *sati* in India, the former referring to murders of young women whose families cannot provide sufficient dowry payments to the family of their designated spouse, while the latter institution consigns women to die on the funeral pyres of their husbands.

Gendercidal institutions have also targeted males throughout history, and exacted a vast death toll. Military conscription is a striking example.[43] Less widely appreciated is *corvée* (forced) labor, which is both intimately related to and analytically distinct from military conscription. *Corvée* has overwhelmingly targeted adult men throughout history, killing in all likelihood hundreds of millions. There are grounds, in fact, for considering *corvée* the most destructive of all human institutions, even outstripping war. Ironically, forced labor remains legal today under the relevant international convention—but only when its targets are able-bodied adult males between the ages of 18 and 45.[44]

BOX 13.1 GENDERCIDE AND VIGILANTISM AGAINST GAY AND TRANS PEOPLE

Figure 13.4 A demonstrator from the Westboro Baptist Church wields anti-gay placards in a protest outside the United Nations, New York City, April 2008. The WBC is a fringe outfit, unaffiliated with the US Baptist community, but such hateful views are shared by uncounted millions of people—and many governments—worldwide. The result is discrimination, persecution, and violence against gay and trans individuals, at times amounting to gendercide, as in Brazil and Iraq/Islamic State.

Source: David Shankbone/ Wikimedia Commons.

The phenomenon of discrimination and violence against homosexuals—especially gay men—and trans women and men is a pervasive occurrence worldwide. It is linked to the collective policing of gender, in which those who opt out of heterosexuality are seen as "asocial" threats. In the Nazi case (Box 6a), gay males were viewed as violating eugenic tenets. While the mentally handicapped were "useless eaters," gays were condemned as superfluous for their "failure" to help replenish the *Volk*.

In this book's first edition, I wrote that "perhaps only in the Nazi case has violence against homosexual men attained a scale and systematic character that might be considered genocidal." That judgment may still hold, but it has been challenged by the murderous campaign against homosexuals launched in post-2003 Iraq. In 2005, the leading Shia cleric, Grand Ayatollah Ali al-Sistani, issued a *fatwa* (religious injunction) calling for gay men and lesbians to be killed "in the worst, most severe way" (he lifted the decree against gay men the following year, but the *fatwa* against lesbians remained in place).[45] What had been one of the Arab world's livelier and more open gay scenes was replaced by a campaign of religious-fundamentalist terror that had killed an estimated four hundred people for alleged homosexual acts by 2007.[46] In that year, the United Nations Assistance Mission in Iraq (UNAMI) reported that "Islamic groups and militias have been known to be particularly hostile towards homosexuals, frequently and openly engaging in violent campaigns against them. There have been a number of assassinations of homosexuals." At "religious courts . . . presided over by young, inexperienced clerics," homosexuals were given summary trials and sentences ranging "from 40 lashes to the death penalty."[47] In 2009, the UK *Observer* profiled a would-be judge and executioner, a young man who passed his days "cruising" Web sites to uncover hidden gays. The Net, he said, "is the easiest way to find those people who are destroying Islam and who want to dirty the reputation we took centuries to build up." "Animals deserve more pity than the dirty people who practise such sexual depraved acts," declared another member of the group. "We make sure they know why they are being held and give them the chance to ask God's forgiveness before they are killed."[48]

Those gays that had not fled the terror lived in fear, as related to *The New York Times* by "Mohammed [and] his friends":

> They described an underground existence, eked out behind drawn curtains in a dingy safe house in southwestern Baghdad. Five people share the apartment—four gay men and one woman, who says she is bisexual. They have moved six times in the last three years, just ahead, they say, of neighborhood raids by Shiite and Sunni death squads. Even seemingly benign neighborhood gossip can scare them enough to move. "We seem suspicious because we look like a cell of terrorists," said Mohammed, nervously fingering the lapel of his shirt. "But we can't tell people what we really are. A cell, yes, but of gays."[49]

In Uganda, repeated attempts have been made to introduce bills that would impose the death penalty or life imprisonment upon those engaging in homosexual relations.[50] The measures are emblematic of a distressing trend in Africa toward anathematizing and criminalizing gays—again spurred by religious fundamentalism, this time predominantly of a Christian stripe.[51] In Latin American countries still reeling from the death-squad violence of the 1970s through the 1990s, gay males—especially male prostitutes and transvestites—remain at extraordinary risk of vigilante-style killings in some Latin American societies. In the past two decades, however, the region has undergone a "gay rights revolution," with most countries decriminalizing homosexuality and some, like Uruguay and Mexico (City), becoming world leaders in promoting LGBT rights.[52]

In post-apartheid South Africa, the country that first enshrined such rights in its constitution, lesbian women—and gay men—have been targeted in an epidemic of "corrective rape," aimed at punishing them for their transgressive sexual identity.[53] Globally, Amnesty International reports sampled by Stefanie Rixecker demonstrate that a wide range of violence is "directed at queer individuals based upon their actual or perceived sexual preference":

> The types of abuses range from complaints of ill treatment while in police custody to rape, sexual abuse, sexual realignment surgery, extrajudicial executions and disappearances, and state-sanctioned execution. The murder of gays and lesbians due to their sexuality, or to associated behaviors and illnesses (e.g. HIV and AIDS), not only means that the individuals are targeted, but also—due to the relatively small numbers of gays and lesbians—becomes tantamount to genocide and now, more specifically, gendercide.

"Although a full complement of the gay community is not murdered in such acts," Rixecker wrote, "the relatively small statistical populations of gays and lesbians overall means that the annual toll of queer identities can be regarded as a genocidal act."[54]

In recent years, as gay rights have become gradually more accepted and respected, the burden of atrocity has increasingly targeted transgender women and male transvestites. The country with by far the highest—unquestionably gendercidal—levels of such violence is Brazil, where "an estimated 326 trans people were reported killed" in 2014, or "one person every 27 hours."[55] A report by Transgender Europe found that "military police continued to hunt down gender variant/trans people, now with the support of so-called death squads and vigilante groups." In 2015, the trans-rights group Transrevolução, based in Rio de Janeiro, estimated that "the life expectancy for trans people in Brazil is about 30 . . . while the average Brazilian lives to age 75." The prominence of trans Brazilians among street populations and in the sex industry—reflecting their social marginalization and lack of employment options—places them at additional risk. "If I didn't have my mother and father to help me, I'd probably turn to prostitution to support myself," said Maria Clara Araújo, "the first black transsexual to go to a federal university in Brazil." "If we had homes, jobs, an education, we would not be so prone to [living on the streets]. If families supported them and society gave these girls a chance, they would die less."[56]

Figure 13.5 August 2008: a display of crosses outside a convention center in the Brazilian capital, Brasilia, part of a demonstration against homophobia and transphobia with the rainbow colors of the LGBT flag. Evidence suggests that more LGBT people, especially gay men and trans women, are murdered in Brazil than in any other country.

Source: Agenciabrasil.gov.br/Wikimedia Commons.

GENOCIDAL MEN, GENOCIDAL WOMEN

A cursory examination of classical and contemporary genocides shows that the overwhelming majority of genocidal planners, killers, and rapists are men, just as men predominate as architects and wagers of war. There is also the lesser, but still striking, disproportion of men among murderers worldwide (especially mass and serial murderers). One wonders, in fact, whether for many people, a *sufficient* explanation of genocide (and war, and murder) would not be simply: "Boys will be boys." Likewise, when we focus on disproportionate male *victimization*, at least for genocide's most lethal strategies, patterns of intramale competition and conquest seem significant. They are evident not only in most human societies, as anthropologists have shown, but among the higher primates that are humanity's closest relatives.

Explanations for these tendencies and uniformities have spawned enduring, interdisciplinary, and so far inconclusive debates. Some of the most intriguing, but also ambiguous, data come from sociobiological investigations. In their book *Demonic Males*, Richard Wrangham and Dale Peterson drew direct comparisons between chimpanzee societies—in which prevail patterns of male bonding and hegemony-seeking, raiding, sexual assault, infanticide, and violent bloodlust—and human beings, a species that shares some 99 percent of its genome with chimpanzees. Some of the questions they asked about male chimps translate directly to human genocide, especially those pertaining to apparently "irrational" forms of violence: "Why kill the enemy, rather than simply drive him away? Why rape? Why torture and mutilate?"[57]

In *The Dark Side of Man* (which includes a chapter on "Genocide"), another researcher, Michael P. Ghiglieri, described a frankly stomach-churning act of massed killing of an isolated male chimp, comparable in central respects to a scene from the Rwandan genocide or a frenzied ethnic pogrom. He likened the results to the aftermath of a Nazi death-squad operation:

> In Gombe and Mahale [districts of Tanzania], after all the adult males in each vanquished community had been killed and all the adolescent males had sickened and died, seemingly from depression, the young females shifted their allegiance and home ranges and mated with the victorious males. The victors instantly expanded their territories to include part (Gombe) or most (Mahale) of the territories of the dead males. Both defeated communities ceased to exist, having been wiped out by genocidal warfare. Tanzanian chimps, like Hitler's storm troopers, had fought for lebensraum [living space].[58]

There are at least powerful common patterns, then, between these two closely-related species. Behavior such as bonding among in-group males to destroy out-group males; kidnapping and rape of females; frenzied/"sadistic" violence; and infanticide, all seem to some degree genetically coded, evolving over time amidst resource scarcity (which provokes "colonial"-style foraging along frontiers), and intramale competition for female mates, especially multiple mates.

How does this shape an understanding of nature versus nurture, physiology versus environment, in understanding gendered roles, identities, and performances? Ghiglieri made a case for hardwired male behavior, sardonically noting that "none of these apes learned these violent behaviors by watching TV or by being victims of socioeconomic handicaps—poor schools, broken homes, bad fathers, illegal drugs, easy weapons, or any other sociological condition." Only strict and lifelong discipline, he contended, would ever rein in males' basically "ethnocentric and xenophobic" disposition, their innate urge "to fight and kill other men genetically more distant from them in genocidal wars aimed at seizing or usurping what those other men possess, including the reproductive potential of their women."[59]

However, Wrangham and Peterson—along with Joshua Goldstein in his essential contribution *War and Gender*—considered the nature-versus-nurture argument a dead end. In their view, *both* physiology and environment are influential. In the ape world, another species also shares 99 percent of its genetic code with humans: the bonobo. But the bonobo is "the gentle ape"; there are "no reports of males forcing copulations, battering adult females, or killing infants," and they seem overall an amazingly benevolent bunch. Part of the explanation may lie in their more varied and plentiful food supply, contrasted with that of the foraging chimpanzee populations. This limits male intergroup and intragroup violence, as does the fact that bonobo females do not have manifestly fertile "periods," encouraging less territorial expansion for reproductive purposes, less competition (and rape) to access females during fertile periods, and a more relaxed and playful attitude toward sexuality (including homosexuality).

In addition, and in part for these reasons, female bonobos appear to act as a potent restraining force against male aggression and violence. If males "throw their weight around and become overly aggressive, they are liable to be suppressed by females . . . [who] form alliances that effectively protect them against male aggression."[60] This led the authors to stress (as did Ghiglieri) that females play a vital role in *validating* male violence by mating with the violent male—even in the context of a coercive "patriarchal bargain." "Women's evolved strategic responses to male demonism have included countermeasures and defiance, but they have also included collaboration. That is to say, while men have evolved to be demonic males, it seems likely that women have evolved to prefer demonic males . . . as mates."[61] The ubiquitous phenomenon of females "cheerleading" for male violence, addressed below, thus has its counterpart in the primate world. For Wrangham and Peterson, therefore, the resolution to the dilemma lay in humans' intelligence and capacity for empathy, which together could allow the human race to transcend its inbred and acculturated—and everywhere male-dominated—tendency to violence. This was not so far from elements of Ghiglieri's own "antidote to men's violence in America."[62]

In human societies, male hegemony is enshrined as the institution of *patriarchy*—"rule by the fathers," that is, rule by men as heads of family units and by older and more powerful men within communities, rather than rule by men as an undifferentiated gender class. However, in contrast with the chimpanzee "alpha male" who must constantly defend his status against challengers—or lose it—we see in human societies a displacement of the hegemonic struggle onto subordinate males. It is the patriarchs who choose to wage war and genocide against out-groups; but to this end, they must mobilize younger, subordinate males to inflict the actual violence. They are assisted by women as mothers and nurturers, who help to educate, train, and prepare younger generations of males for service as soldiers, cannon-fodder, and *génocidaires*. If they survive and succeed, they too are eligible to join patriarchal ranks, with all its consequences—including the privilege of mating with the most desirable females.

It is notable that while in some cultures, men flock to perform their assigned role as subordinate agents of violence, in most others they must be dragged unwillingly into these duties. The long, little-studied history of masculine resistance to military conscription, and the brutality of the "basic training" to which conscripts are exposed, suggest that male violence is not automatically activated—even, in many cases, that a more peaceable disposition must be broken down and reconstructed for warlike or genocidal purposes.

It is likewise the case among humans that, while those who commit murder, rape, and other violent crimes are overwhelmingly male, the majority of men in most cultures do *not* engage in such heinous acts. Nonetheless, the majority of men do partake, consciously or unconsciously, in the benefits of patriarchy, notably the subordinate and submissive role to which it consigns most females. And we must not pass over the human male's near-monopoly of the most violent crimes—like murder, rape, and genocide—quite so lightly. Psychologically-complex humans have developed the psychologically-complex ideology of *misogyny*—fear and hatred of females—as a key buttress of patriarchy. When combined with the active desire *for* females, as mates and cheerleaders, the mix is toxic indeed. No male is more dangerous than the frustrated and alienated male; and though he may ordinarily seek validation and a sense of superiority through the targeting of out-group males, he is also prone to seek it through existential violence against females. Allan D. Cooper has argued that "when men suffer from [an] acute masculine identity crisis, that is when they experience relative deprivation of masculinity, they often seek to end the crisis by destroying the desired object beyond their reach: a woman."[63] Thus the serial murderer or rapist of women is generally a dysfunctional and humiliated male. Thus too, perhaps, some of the wanton and mutilative savagery that attends male violence—both against females, as we have just seen, and against other males—occurs in societies at "peace," and in times of war and genocide as well.

In the specific context of genocide, Cooper has contended that most outbreaks of mass killing can be linked to an "emasculating moment," in which males, especially leaders, feel humiliated by a challenge to their masculinity, and react viciously—both to buttress the gendered status quo, and to reclaim an existential sense of masculine prowess.[64] Elisa von Joeden-Forgey has carried this analysis a step further, with her study of ideologies of "genocidal masculinity." She sees such ideologies as aimed *not* at preserving patriarchy, but at destroying it. Genocide relies upon subordinate and marginalized males who rebel against a patriarchal order which has frozen them out, denying them (among other things) access to females as the site of biological reproduction. In reacting to this sense of marginalization and humiliation, genocidal masculinity "rejects the old patriarchy and embraces an expression of power based on killing rather than life-giving." The result is a "ritualized cruelty" which often takes the form of what von Joeden-Forgey calls "life force atrocities": "violence that targets the life force of a group by destroying both the physical symbols of the life force as well as the group's most basic institutions of reproduction, especially the family unit." She depicts these atrocities as falling into two broad categories:

> The first are inversion rituals that seek to reverse proper hierarchies and relationships within families, and thereby to destroy the sacred bonds that give our

lives purpose and meaning. Such acts include forcing family members to watch the rape, torture and murder of their loved ones, and forcing them to participate in the perpetration of such crimes. Common versions of such atrocities includes fathers being forced to rape their children, mothers being forced to kill their children, children being forced to kill their parents, children being pulled screaming from their parents' arms to be killed, and parents being forced to watch as their children are slowly tortured and murdered. The second category of genocidal atrocity is the ritual mutilation and desecration of symbols of group reproduction, including male and female reproductive organs, women's breasts as the sites of lactation, pregnant women as the loci of generative powers, and infants and small children as the sacred symbols of the group's future. The evisceration of pregnant women and the use of infants for target practice are common examples. What ties these two categories of life force atrocity together is that in each, perpetrators betray a pronounced obsession with the destruction of the life force of a group—not just the group's biological ability to bring children into the world, but also the structures of tenderness, love, protectiveness and loyalty that sustain family, and community, life.[65]

Figure 13.6 "Russian atrocities in Livonia in XVI century (using women for archery target practice)." Anonymous woodcut published by Dariusz Kupisz, Psków, in 1581–1582. Scholars including Elisa von Joeden-Forgey and Christopher Taylor have explored how sexualized and mutilative atrocities in genocide are used to "inscribe" patriarchal power and misogynist ideologies upon women's bodies, generally as a preface or postscript to their murder.

Source: Wikimedia Commons.

Is, then, women's significance to genocide and gender primarily that of victims, as "objects" on which males write their genocidal "scripts"? Far from it: a perpetrator/bystander dimension is also prominent. In fact, as Daniel Jonah Goldhagen has argued, "when we look to the populations in whose name eliminationist politics are perpetrated, women are no less supportive than men, and are no less desirous of the broader political and social transformations undergirding such politics than the men are."[66] Under patriarchy, women are generally reduced to supporting roles; but they perform them with enthusiasm. As "cheerleaders" for genocide, they offer moral and material support to male perpetrators; assist in ostracizing males who seek to evade involvement in the slaughter;[67] and provide political support, sometimes exceeding that of men, for genocidal leaders.[68]

Whatever the genetic and sociobiological inheritance, when women, along with men, are *mobilized, forced, encouraged, allowed* to participate in genocide and other atrocious violence, they generally display no more reluctance than (often reluctant) males. Readers' minds might leap to the revelations from Abu Ghraib prison near Baghdad, where female guards were prominent as agents of abuse. The scholar of genocide, moreover, encounters the direct involvement of women at many points in history: torturing and executing prisoners-of-war (as was standard in Native American civilizations); joining men in attacking and pillaging refugee convoys (as Kurdish women did in the Armenian genocide); and actively involving themselves in "euthanasia" killings and concentration-camp atrocities under the Nazis (female camp guards "murdered as easily [as men]; their sadism was no less," notes James Waller).[69]

Most dramatically, and at levels perhaps unprecedented in history, women actively participated in perpetrating the Rwandan holocaust of 1994. "I had seen war before, but I had never seen a woman carrying a baby on her back kill another woman with a baby on her back," said a stunned officer with the United Nations Assistance Mission for Rwanda (UNAMIR).[70] Hutu women ululated their men into genocidal action, and were prominent after massacres in "finishing off" those still clinging to life: "Some were dead, some alive," one Hutu girl remembered. "We beat the ones who were not dead. The other women killed one each."[71] They gleefully looted the corpses afterward, "fighting over the fabric and the trousers," in the recollection of one Hutu perpetrator.[72] Nor were women limited to these subordinate roles: they assumed leadership positions at national, regional, and local levels. The most notorious (and high-level) case is Pauline Nyiramasuhuko, indicted by the International Criminal Tribunal for Rwanda (ICTR) for "personally direct[ing] squads of Hutu men to torture and butcher Tutsi men, and to rape and mutilate Tutsi women."[73] ("Before you kill the women, you need to rape them," Nyiramasuhuko reportedly urged the *interahamwe* militiamen whom she supervised.)[74]

Rwanda, indeed, can serve as something of a test for the proposition that human females are more reluctant participants in violence and genocide than are males. Laura Sjoberg and Caron Gentry contend that "women, like men, are capable of violence. As women's freedoms increase, so will their violence."[75] James Waller likewise argues that "the challenge . . . is to transcend our gender expectations that women are basically innocent by nature, so that their acts of cruelty are viewed as deviant and abnormal, and instead approach their perpetration of extraordinary

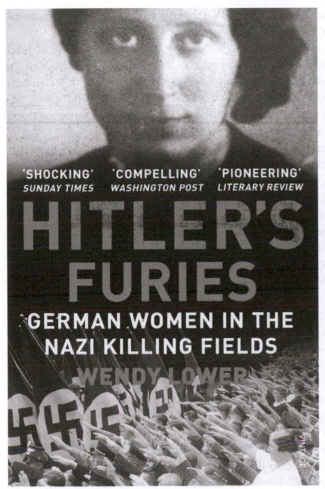

Figures 13.7 and 13.8 Wendy Lower's groundbreaking study, *Hitler's Furies: German Women in the Nazi Killing Fields*, examined women's complicity in the Nazi enterprise, as "zealous administrators, robbers, tormentors, and murderers in the bloodlands" (see Box 2.3 for more on the "Bloodlands" under Nazi occupation).[76] Lower noted that "emerging feminist views stressed the victimization of [German] women," for example as the victims of rape at Red Army hands, "not their criminal agency." But fully "a third of the female population [of Nazi Germany], thirteen million women, were actively engaged in a Nazi Party organization, and female membership in the Nazi Party increased steadily until the end of the war. Just as the agency of women in history more generally is underappreciated," Lower cautions, "here too—and perhaps even more problematically, given the moral and legal implications—the agency of women in the crimes of the Third Reich has not been fully elaborated and explained." Female concentration camp guards—and "about one-tenth of camp personnel was female"—were often eager volunteers for the "gruesome work," seeing "these mass-murder sites as places of employment and opportunity. The uniform was impressive, the pay was good, and the prospect of wielding power was appealing." (Andrew Charlesworth noted that at Auschwitz-Birkenau, "there was a lawn where the women workers could sunbathe as the captives filed past on their way to the gas chambers.")[77] "Multitasking secretaries were both desk murderers and sadists: some not only typed up liquidation orders but also participated in ghetto massacres and attended mass shootings," wrote Lower. Nurses, meanwhile, "counseled ordinary women about 'racial hygiene' and hereditary diseases. In Germany, they participated in selections of the mentally and physically disabled in asylums and escorted these victims to their deaths in gas chambers or administered lethal injections." And then there were the women who "were among [the] prime agents and beneficiaries" of "the biggest campaign of organized robbery and economic exploitation in history"—the dispossession of Jews in Germany and the Nazi-occupied territories. "The greed of German men and women who gained access to the plunder was seemingly insatiable. The wife of a policeman in Warsaw, for instance, stockpiled so much that she lacked the space to hide it; she simply piled up the booty outside, around her house."

Sources: Courtesy of Vintage Books/Random House UK (cover); Bjørn Marquart (author photo).

evil the same way we have that of men—as ordinary people influenced by cultural, psychological, and social constructions."[78]

In examining these constructions, can we discern specifically "feminine" roles, psyches, and personae among female perpetrators of genocide, and cheerleaders for it? The attempt is somewhat speculative, for the simple reason that the male perpetrator has overwhelmingly been the focus of inquiries into gender and violence, while female perpetrators have tended to be exoticized and sensationalized. However, several observations can be ventured.

First, we saw at the outset of this section that in male-dominant society, there may be a biological and cultural logic to female support for male violence, including its genocidal manifestations. Moreover, women under patriarchy are designated as the guardians of "home and hearth," especially children—meaning that they may feel especially keenly any threat to that domestic order, of the kind that designated "enemies" allegedly pose. A personal sense of vulnerability to violence—to sexual assault in particular—seems to have underpinned female support for genocidal actors and institutions, as with the US white women who willingly participated (as denouncers, spectators, and symbolic icons of female purity) in the lynchings of African-American men.

In asserting themselves as agents *beyond* the roles reserved for them under patriarchy, women may lay claim to a specific "female masculinity," according to Judith Halberstam[79]—appropriating and performing the kind of identities (as strong, potent, cruel) that are normally mapped onto males. Though no "matriarchal" society probably ever existed, some cultures have permitted women substantial public roles as social and economic actors, and these may facilitate greater and more direct female involvement in violence as well. Such cultures sometimes supply iconic images of the violent female, arguably validating and encouraging female expressions of violence—as the place of the bloodthirsty goddess Kali in Hindu culture has been linked to the prominent role women have played in the Hindu extremist movement.[80] Finally, to the extent that women are targeted in genocide, intrafemale rivalries may produce a kind of "gendered jubilation" at the destruction and humiliation of female rivals. This was powerfully evident in Rwanda, for example, where Hutu women had long been depicted as less attractive and desirable than their Tutsi counterparts. Many Hutu women accordingly took pleasure in Tutsi women's "comeuppance," and proved more than willing to assist in inflicting it.[81]

A NOTE ON GENDERED PROPAGANDA

A useful application of a gender perspective in genocide studies is to genocidal propaganda, so central in mobilizing populations to support and commit atrocities. This issue may be approached from various angles.

If men, overwhelmingly, must be mobilized to do the "dirty work" of genocidal killing, how are their gender sensibilities exploited? Perhaps the most common strategy is to accuse males who evince qualms about participation of being cowards—failed bearers of masculinity. A Rwandan official visiting a commune that was deemed "negligent" in its genocidal duties demanded to know "if there were no more men there, meaning men who could deal with 'security' problems."[82] Men who "shirked" their duties were denounced in terms little less venomous than those employed against Tutsis: "What are those sons of dogs fleeing from?"[83]

Men's designated role as "protectors" of women and children fuels potent propaganda strategies. Nazi troops dispatched to the firestorm of the eastern front were exposed to speeches from their commanders, demanding to know "what would have happened had these Asiatic Mongol hordes succeeded to pour into . . . Germany, laying the country waste, plundering, murdering, raping?"[84] By implication, the German troops were justified in laying waste, plundering, murdering, and raping, as they did to an extent unseen since the days of the "Mongol hordes."

Women, as noted, are generally cast in supporting roles in genocidal campaigns. Propaganda directed at them emphasizes their role as guardians of home and children. This has the added advantage of bolstering the self-image of males as protectors of (passive, defenseless) "women and children."

A further important aspect of genocidal propaganda is the demonization of outgroup men as a prelude to gender-selective round-ups and mass killing. The classic case is the construction of the "Eternal Jew" in Nazi propaganda, which paved the way for the Holocaust of 1941–1945. This propaganda entrenched an image of the "wretched, disgusting, horrifying, flat-footed, hook-nosed dirty Jew"[85]—virtually always a *male* Jew. As Joan Ringelheim notes: "Legitimation for targeting Jewish men was plentiful in Nazi anti-Semitic and racist propaganda and, more to the point, in Nazi policy. The decision to kill every Jew did not seem to demand special justification to kill Jewish men. They were already identified as dangerous," thanks to years of grotesque imagery such as that depicted in Figure 13.9. "This was not so for Jewish women and children."[86] Jewish men were also depicted as sexually rapacious and invasive. Peter Fritzsche notes that "it was usually Jewish men who were imagined to prey on German women: the gender of the Jewish peril was male, while Aryan vulnerability was female."[87] It comes as little surprise, then, that adult male Jews were the first to be rounded up and executed *en masse* on the eastern front, thereby acclimatizing the killers to subsequent root-and-branch genocide.[88]

In a similar vein, consider the language typically directed at population groups to mark them out for persecution or genocide: terms such as "monster," "beast/bestial," "devil/demon," "bandit," "criminal," "rapist," "terrorist," "swindler," "vagabond," "subhuman," "vermin," "exploiter". . . . Now, though the task may be unpleasant, assign a human face to these caricatures. Is it a male or a female face that automatically leaps to mind?[89]

When women are targeted in genocidal and proto-genocidal propaganda, this tends to occur (1) on a smaller scale, (2) with a lesser variety of imagery, and (3) with a heavy concentration on the female's imputed sexual power (including her reproductive capacity) (see Figure 13.10). Hence the regular use of terms such as "seducer," "prostitute," "whore," "baby factory." This emphasis on sexual power and capacity no doubt fuels the rampant sexual violence against women and girls, including extreme humiliation and "life force atrocities," that is a regular feature

Figure 13.9 Poster for the Nazi propaganda exhibition *Der Ewige Jude* (The Eternal Jew), 1937. The sinister-looking male Jew is shown as addicted to lucre (the coins in his outstretched hand), oppressive (the whip in the other), and allied with international communism (Germany with the hammer-and-sickle crooked under his arm). Depictions of the Jewish male as dangerous and malevolent were central to their selective targeting at early stages of Nazi campaigns of persecution and, ultimately, genocide. More generally, such demonized depictions of out-group males are central to both genocidal propaganda and gendercidal massacre.

Source: Hoover Institution Archives Poster Collection.

Figure 13.10 "General Dallaire and his army have fallen into the trap of fatal women." Tutsi women, with badges/tattoos of support for the FPR (Rwandan rebel forces), are depicted seducing UN force commander Gen. Roméo Dallaire in this cartoon from the Hutu Power propaganda paper *Kangura* (February 1994). Genocidal propaganda against women often emphasizes their imputed sexual powers; in the Rwandan case, this paved the way for massive sexual violence against Tutsi women during the 1994 genocide.

Source: From Christopher Taylor, *Sacrifice as Terror: The Rwandan Genocide of 1994* (Oxford: Berg, 1999).

of genocidal campaigns. Women, and men, may also be targeted for their supposed links to the supernatural ("witch" and, relatedly, "baby-killer").

The implicit gendering of much genocidal propaganda seems fundamental to marshaling support for gendercide and all-out genocide. As such, it would seem to have implications for strategies of genocide prevention. I return to this subject in the concluding chapter.

FURTHER STUDY

African Rights, *Rwanda: Not So Innocent: When Women Become Killers*. London: African Rights, 1995. Taboo-shattering account of women's participation in the 1994 genocide.

Anonymous, *A Woman in Berlin: Eight Weeks in the Conquered City: A Diary*. New York: Picador, 2006. An account by a 34-year-old journalist of her experience of Soviet conquest and occupation, including the mass rapes of German women. Antony Beevor calls it "a victim's eye view . . . one of the most important personal accounts ever written about the effects of war and defeat."

Maria Eriksson Baaz and Maria Stern, *Sexual Violence as a Weapon of War? Perceptions, Prescriptions, Problems in the Congo and Beyond*. London: Zed Books, 2013. Short, much-discussed volume challenging core assumptions about conflict-related sexual violence and its perpetrators.

R. Charli Carpenter, *"Innocent Women and Children": Gender, Norms, and the Protection of Civilians*. London: Ashgate, 2006. Innovative study of gender and humanitarian intervention, focusing on the vulnerabilities of civilian males.

Michael P. Ghiglieri, *The Dark Side of Man: Tracing the Origins of Male Violence*. Cambridge, MA: Perseus Books, 2000. Argues that men are biologically programmed to wage war and commit genocide.

Joshua S. Goldstein, *War and Gender: How Gender Shapes the War System and Vice Versa*. Cambridge: Cambridge University Press, 2001. A captivating interdisciplinary overview.

Sonja M. Hedgepeth and Rochelle G. Saidel, eds., *Sexual Violence against Jewish Women during the Holocaust*. Waltham, MA: Brandeis University Press, 2010. Disturbingly but necessarily dispels notions that the Nazis' pathological racism precluded acts of specifically sexual violence against Jewish women. The chapters on concentration camps and brothels are especially revelatory.

Human Rights Watch, *Shattered Lives: Sexual Violence During the Rwanda Genocide and Its Aftermath*. New York: Human Rights Watch, 1996. Examines the targeting of women for rape in the Rwandan holocaust; available on the Web at http://hrw.org/reports/1996/Rwanda.htm.

Adam Jones, ed., *Gendercide and Genocide*. Nashville, TN: Vanderbilt University Press, 2004. The most wide-ranging book on gender-selective killing. See also *Gender Inclusive: Essays on Violence, Men, and Feminist International Relations*.

Claudia Koonz, *Mothers in the Fatherland: Women, the Family and Nazi Politics*. New York: Basic Books, 1987. Influential inquiry into the diverse roles of German women under Nazism.

Rohit Lentin, ed., *Gender and Catastrophe*. London: Zed Books, 1997. Essays on the gendering of genocide, slavery, poverty, and famine, with an emphasis on women.

Lois Ann Lorentzen and Jennifer Turpin, eds., *The Women and War Reader*. New York: New York University Press, 1998. Anthology of writings on women's victimization and agency in wartime.

Wendy Lower, *Hitler's Furies: German Women in the Nazi Killing Fields*. Boston, MA: Houghton Mifflin, 2013. Groundbreaking study of female complicity in the Holocaust and Nazi colonizing schemes; see Figures 13.7 and 13.8.

Amalendu Misra, *The Landscape of Silence: Sexual Violence Against Men in War*. London: Hurst & Company, 2015. The first book-length analysis of the subject, exploring its human, legal, and "biopower" aspects.

Amy E. Randall, ed., *Genocide and Gender in the Twentieth Century: A Comparative Survey*. London: Bloomsbury, 2015. A stimulating and inclusive collection; features my essay "Masculinities and Vulnerabilities in the Rwandan and Congolese Genocides" (ch. 2).

Carol Rittner and John K. Roth, eds., *Rape: Weapon of War and Genocide*. St. Paul, MN: Paragon House, 2012. "One of the most nuanced, illuminating, and grimly engaging volumes on rape and mass violence yet published"—from my back-cover endorsement.

Alexandra Stiglmayer, ed., *Mass Rape: The War against Women in Bosnia-Herzegovina*. Lincoln, NE: University of Nebraska Press, 1995. A standard source on sexual violence against women in the Balkan wars.

Laura Sjoberg and Caron E. Gentry, *Mothers, Monsters, Whores: Women's Violence in Global Politics*. London: Zed Books, 2007. Critiques patriarchal and feminist-essentialist framings of female violence.

Nechama Tec, *Resilience and Courage: Women, Men, and the Holocaust*. New Haven, CT: Yale University Press, 2003. A sensitive, gender-inclusive examination by a Holocaust survivor and researcher of rescuers.

Klaus Theweleit, *Male Fantasies, Volume 1: Women, Floods, Bodies, History*, trans. Stephen Conway. Minneapolis, MN: University of Minnesota Press, 1987. Profound psychoanalytical study of fascist and paramilitary masculinities.

Samuel Totten, ed., *Plight and Fate of Women During and Following Genocide*. New Brunswick, NJ: Transaction Publishers, 2009. Very useful contribution to a series of "critical bibliographic reviews" of genocide.

Mary Anne Warren, *Gendercide: The Implications of Sex Selection*. Totowa, NJ: Rowman & Allanheld, 1985. Coined the term "gendercide," with a focus on reproductive technologies, especially female feticide (sex-selective abortion).

NOTES

1 See, e.g., R. Charli Carpenter, "Beyond 'Gendercide': Operationalizing Gender in Comparative Genocide Studies," in Adam Jones, ed., *Gendercide and Genocide* (Nashville, TN: Vanderbilt University Press, 2004), pp. 230–256, esp. pp. 232–238. The classic argument for gender as wholly constructed (all nurture, no nature) is Judith Butler, *Gender Trouble* (London: Routledge, 1990).

2 Joshua Goldstein, *War and Gender* (Cambridge: Cambridge University Press, 2001), p. 2. Elizabeth Grosz argues along similar lines: "I will deny that there is the 'real,' material body on the one hand and its various cultural and historical representations on the other . . . These representations and cultural inscriptions quite literally constitute bodies and help produce them as such. . . . The body must be regarded as the site of social, political, cultural and geographic inscriptions, production, or constitution. The body is not opposed to culture . . . it is itself cultural, *the* cultural, product." Quoted in Jan Jindy Pettman, "Body Politics: International Sex Tourism," *Third World Quarterly*, 18: 1 (1997), pp. 99–100.

3 For instance, Mary E. Hawkesworth wrote: "In principle, a gendered practice could privilege men or women. But the history of male dominance has resulted in systematic male power advantages across diverse social domains. Feminist usage of the adjective 'gendered' reflects this male power advantage. *Hence a gendered practice is synonymous with androcentric* [male-centered] *practice* in common feminist terminology." Hawkesworth, "Democratization: Reflections on Gendered Dislocations in the Public Sphere," in R.M. Kelly *et al.*, eds., *Gender, Globalization, and Democratization* (Lanham, MD: Rowman & Littlefield, 2001), p. 235, n. 2; emphasis added. For a more recent articulation of this gender framing—equally constraining and self-serving, in my view—see the 2014 comments by the UN Special Rapporteur on Violence against Women, Rashida Manjoo: "Violence against women is a systemic, widespread and pervasive human rights violation, experienced largely by women because they are women. The concept of gender neutrality is framed in a way that understands violence as a universal threat to which all are potentially vulnerable, and from which all deserve protection. This suggests that male victims of violence require, and deserve, comparable resources to those afforded to female victims, thereby ignoring the reality that violence against men does not occur as a result of pervasive inequality and discrimination, and also that it is neither systemic nor pandemic in the way that violence against women undisputably [*sic*] is. The shift to neutrality favours a more pragmatic and politically palatable understanding of gender, that is, as simply a euphemism for 'men and women', rather than as a system of domination of men over women. Violence against women cannot be analysed on a case-by-case basis in isolation of the individual, institutional and structural factors that govern and shape the lives of women. Such factors demand gender-specific approaches to ensure an equality of outcomes for women. Attempts to combine or synthesize all forms of violence into a 'gender neutral' framework, tend to result in a depoliticized or diluted discourse, which abandons the transformative agenda. A different set of normative and practical measures is required to respond to and prevent violence against women and, equally importantly, to achieve the international law obligation of substantive equality, as opposed to formal equality." Manjoo, "Report of the Special Rapporteur on Violence against Women, Its Causes and Consequences" (advance edited version), United Nations Human Rights Council, May 28, 2014. I am grateful to Heleen Touquet for bringing this source to my attention. For a recent and forceful critique of such mindsets, though the author acknowledges feeling "frankly somewhat terrified of rejection by the very people whose cause I aim to support with my work," see Elissa Helms, "The Challenge of Gendering Genocide: Reflections on a Feminist Politics of Complexity," *European Journal of Women's Studies*, 22: 4 (2015), pp. 463–469 (quote p. 467).

4 Excerpts in Kurt A. Raaflaub, handout for Brown University Classics course (CL56), "War and Society in the Ancient World."

5 Thucydides, *The Peloponnesian War*, quoted in Frank Chalk and Kurt Jonassohn, *The History and Sociology of Genocide: Analyses and Case Studies* (New Haven, CT: Yale University Press, 1990), p. 73.

6 See Adam Jones, "Why Gendercide? Why Root-and-Branch? A Comparison of the Vendée Uprising of 1793–94 and the Bosnian War of the 1990s," *Journal of Genocide Research*, 8: 1 (2006), pp. 9–25.

7 Scott Straus, *The Order of Genocide: Race, Power, and War in Rwanda* (Ithaca, NY: Cornell University Press, 2006), p. 164.

8 A disturbing strand of just-war theory even justifies gender-selective extermination of males. Michael Walzer wrote: "a soldier who, once he is engaged, simply fires at every male villager between the age of 15 and 50 . . . is probably justified in doing so." Quoted in Carpenter, "Beyond 'Gendercide,'" p. 252, n. 13.

9 Donald L. Horowitz, *The Deadly Ethnic Riot* (Berkeley, CA: University of California Press, 2001), p. 148. Horowitz added that "In experiments, males are also more selective in their choice of targets; females distribute shocks more equally among targets. Perhaps selective targeting itself is a sex-skewed phenomenon"; that is, males are more likely to aggress against males selectively and disproportionately than are women (p. 148).

10 Quoted in Andrew Roberts, *The Storm of War: A New History of the Second World War* (London: Penguin, 2009), p. 479. See also the "reprisal" massacres detailed, gut-wrenchingly, in Mark Mazower, *Inside Hitler's Greece: The Experience of Occupation, 1941–44* (New Haven, CT: Yale University Press, 2001), e.g., at pp. 173–181; and in Ben Shepherd, *Terror in the Balkans: German Armies and Partisan Warfare* (Cambridge, MA: Harvard University Press, 2012), especially ch. 6, "Settling Accounts in Blood."

11 See Adam Jones, "Gender and Genocide in Rwanda," in Jones, ed., *Gendercide and Genocide*, p. 111. Jennie E. Burnet notes a related pattern in the Rwandan genocide, and probably others: "Women's land rights were sometimes part of the 'reward' for militiamen. One survivor recounted how the head of the local militia gave her and her sisters to militiamen as 'wives,' and their father's land was split among the 'husbands.' Women's and girls' greater survival rates can in part be explained through this use of women and girls as economic pawns to acquire land and property through so-called 'marriage.'" Burnet, "Rape as a Weapon of Genocide: Gender, Patriarchy, and Sexual Violence in Rwanda," in Amy E. Randall, *Genocide and Gender in the Twentieth Century: A Comparative Survey* (London: Bloomsbury, 2015), p. 132 (e-book).

12 See R. Charli Carpenter, "'Women, Children and Other Vulnerable Groups': Gender, Strategic Frames and the Protection of Civilians as a Transnational Issue," *International Studies Quarterly*, 49 (2005), pp. 295–334.

13 Most of these cases receive extended treatment on the Gendercide Watch site, www. gendercide.org. A question commonly asked is whether in such cases, men are being targeted "as a group" or "as such," rather than (for example) as combatants or potential combatants. The question is a valid one, in part because as noted in the discussion of "Multiple and Overlapping Identities" in Chapter 1 (pp. 45–48), *gender always combines with other variables* to produce genocidal outcomes. The most obvious are *ethnicity/nationality/ race/religion/perceived political affiliation* (that is, there is no targeting of males as a global gender group, but rather of males belonging to one of these designated groups); *age* (with "battle-age" males more liable to be targeted than very young or very old ones); *community prominence* (the disproportionate representation of men among elites means that when "eliticides" occur, as in Burundi in 1972, the victims are overwhelmingly male); and *perceived military capacity* (given the prevailing cultural and practical identification of males with combatants). Often implicit in the question, however, is the notion that women and girls *are* victimized "as such"—primarily because they are female. In my view, this is untenable. When women are the victims of politico-military genocide, it is similarly on the basis of their ethnicity, perceived political affiliation, and so on (or because of their family relationship with men of these designated groups). The Nazis who killed Jewish women *en masse* did not kill German women—in fact, their slaughter of the Jews was often justified by the supposed need to protect German women. Even in the cases where a misogynistic worldview seems predominant, other variables are crucial. Female infanticide does not target females as a group, but rather those of a particular age, and usually of a particular (poorer) social class. The European witch hunts of the medieval and early modern era, which resulted in a death toll of about 75 percent female, likewise did not designate all women as targets, but women perceived as a threat for their supposed liaisons with dark powers. *Age* and *marital status* were other important variables, with the majority of women designated as "witches" being older and more likely to be widows. Clearly, however, the

gender variable is decisive in all these cases—as it is in the case of gendercidal killings of men. Finally, does the gendered hatred of women—misogyny—that factors in all these cases have a counterpart for male victims (misandry)? I contend that it does, and that it is evident, for example, in gendered propaganda. For further discussion, see Adam Jones, "Problems of Gendercide," in Jones, ed., *Gendercide and Genocide*, pp. 257–271.

14 Jason K. Stearns, *Dancing in the Glory of Monsters: The Collapse of the Congo and the Great War of Africa* (New York: PublicAffairs, 2011), pp. 101–102. Elsewhere (p. 137) Stearns describes Rwandan-backed "AFDL soldiers separating about five hundred men from women and children and murdering them" in the Chimanga camp west of Bukavu: "In the Hutu villages I visited north of Goma a decade later, villagers consistently spoke of [Rwandan] RPF commanders calling meetings and then tying up and executing dozens of men. They showed me cisterns and latrines with skeletal remains still showing." For more on these gendercidal atrocities, see Adam Jones, "Masculinities and Vulnerabilities in the Rwandan and Congolese Genocides," in Amy E. Randall, ed., *Genocide and Gender in the Twentieth Century: A Comparative Survey* (London: Bloomsbury, 2015), pp. 62–79 (e-book).

15 Madhu Kishwar, "Delhi: Gangster Rule," in Patwant Singh and Harji Malik, eds., *Punjab: The Fatal Miscalculation* (New Delhi: Patwant Singh, 1985), pp. 171–178.

16 Horowitz, *The Deadly Ethnic Riot*, pp. 73, 123, n. 261.

17 Ian Traynor, "Hague Rules Srebrenica was Genocide," *Guardian*, April 20, 2004, www.guardian.co.uk/world/2004/apr/20/warcrimes. See also the comments by Daniel Goldhagen concerning the Nazis' early gendercidal massacres of Jewish males on the Eastern front: "Even if . . . the initial order was to kill 'only' teenage and adult Jewish males—the order was still genocidal and clearly was understood by the perpetrators as such. . . . The killing of the adult males of a community is nothing less than the destruction of that community." Daniel J. Goldhagen, *Hitler's Willing Executioners: Ordinary Germans and the Holocaust* (New York: Vintage, 1997), p. 153.

18 Judgment of August 2, 2001, cited in John Quigley, *The Genocide Convention: An International Law Analysis* (London: Ashgate, 2006), p. 197.

19 See, e.g., the discussion of the Rwandan case in Jones, "Gender and Genocide in Rwanda," pp. 123–125; and of the Cambodian case in May Ebihara and Judy Ledgerwood, "Aftermaths of Genocide: Cambodian Villagers," in Alexander Laban Hinton, ed., *Annihilating Difference: The Anthropology of Genocide* (Berkeley, CA: University of California Press, 2002), pp. 275–280.

20 Leo Kuper, *Genocide: Its Political Use in the Twentieth Century* (London: Penguin, 1981), p. 46. Richard Rhodes also noted that "Men prepared to kill victims who are manifestly unthreatening—the elderly, unarmed women, small children, infants—behave differently from men prepared to kill victims such as men of military age who can be construed to be at least potentially dangerous." Rhodes, *Masters of Death: The SS-Einsatzgruppen and the Invention of the Holocaust* (New York: Alfred A. Knopf, 2002), p. 69. According to Rhodes (p. 167), the Nazis even "established mental hospitals and rest areas" to care for SS men "'who [had] broken down while executing women and children.'" "I must admit openly that the gassings had a calming effect on me," confessed Rudolf Höss, the former commander of the Auschwitz death camp. ". . . I was always horrified of death by firing squads, especially when I thought of the huge numbers of women and children who would have to be killed. . . . Now I was at ease. We were all saved from these bloodbaths." Quoted in Mark Levene, *Genocide in the Age of the Nation State, Vol. 1: The Meaning of Genocide* (London: I.B. Tauris, 2005), p. 102.

21 See the analysis of this escalation in Goldhagen, *Hitler's Willing Executioners*, pp. 149–151.

22 On this phenomenon, see Jones, ed., *Gendercide and Genocide*, pp. 24–25, 117–118.

23 James Yin and Shi Young, *The Rape of Nanking: An Undeniable History in Photographs* (Chicago, IL: Triumph, 1996), p. 188.

24 Iris Chang, *The Rape of Nanking: The Forgotten Holocaust of World War Two* (London: Penguin, 1998), pp. 49–50.

25 Historian David Bergamini, quoted in Yin and Young, *The Rape of Nanking*, p. 195.

26 Ian Kershaw, *Hitler, 1936–1945: Nemesis* (New York: W.W. Norton & Company, 2000), p. 763.

27 Quoted in Elenor Richter-Lyonette, "Women after the Genocide in Rwanda," in Richter-Lyonette, ed., *In the Aftermath of Rape: Women's Rights, War Crimes, and Genocide* (Givrins: Coordination of Women's Advocacy, 1997), p. 107. See also Patricia O. Daley, "Constructing a Paradigm of Violence: A Feminist Perspective on Genocidal Politics," in Daley, *Gender & Genocide in Burundi: The Search for Spaces of Peace in the Great Lakes Region* (Oxford: James Currey, 2008), pp. 21–39.

28 Ibid., p. 107.

29 Roméo Dallaire, *Shake Hands with the Devil: The Failure of Humanity in Rwanda* (New York: Caroll & Graf Publishers, 2003), p. 430.

30 "Human Rights Watch Applauds Rwanda Rape Verdict," Human Rights Watch press release, September 2, 1998, www.hrw.org/en/news/1998/09/02/human-rights-watch-applauds-rwanda-rape-verdict; emphasis added. See also Teaching Human Rights Online, "Rape and Genocide in Rwanda: The ICTR's Akayesu Verdict," http://home pages.uc.edu/thro/rwanda/RwandaRapeCase2.htm.

31 Jeffrey Gettleman, "Rape Victims' Words Help Jolt Congo into Change," *The New York Times*, October 17, 2008, www.nytimes.com/2008/10/18/world/africa/18congo.html.

32 Stephanie McCrummen, "Prevalence of Rape in E. Congo Described as Worst in World," *The Washington Post*, September 9, 2007. See also "Rape a Weapon of War in Congo, Activists Say," *CNN.com*, October 17, 2009, www.cnn.com/2009/WORLD/africa/10/16/amanpour.congo.rape.documentary/index.html.

33 Judd quoted in Christopher Dickey, "Ashley Judd's Heart of Darkness," *Newsweek*, October 30, 2008, www.newsweek.com/id/166488. See also Anna Husarska, "The Hidden Wounds of Congo's Wars," *Slate.com*, January 4, 2008, www.slate.com/id/2181274. On efforts to help survivors, see Stephanie Hanes, "Life after Rape in Congo," *The Christian Science Monitor*, April 25, 2007, www.csmonitor.com/2007/0425/p13s02-woaf.html.

34 The principal legal scholar on sexual violence against men and boys is Sandesh Sivakumaran: see, e.g., his article "Sexual Violence Against Men in Armed Conflict," *The European Journal of International Law*, 18: 2 (2007), pp. 253–276, available online at http://ejil.org/pdfs/18/2/224.pdf. See also Ellen Anna Philo Gorris, "Invisible Victims? Where Are Male Victims of Conflict-Related Sexual Violence in International Law and Policy?," *European Journal of Women's Studies*, 22: 4 (2015), pp. 412–427; and Lara Stemple, "Male Rape and Human Rights," *Hastings Law Journal*, 60: 605 (February 2009), pp. 605–647 (a PDF version can be searched online). Amalendu Misra, *The Landscape of Silence: Sexual Violence Against Men in Armed Conflict* (London: Hurst & Company, 2015), is the first monograph in English, to my knowledge. For intervention strategies, see Callum Watson, *Preventing and Responding to Sexual and Domestic Violence against Men: A Guidance Note for Security Sector Institutions* (Geneva: DCAF, 2014), www.dcaf.ch/content/download/174011/2714016/file/SDVAM_FINAL%20online.pdf. My own edited volume, *Sexual Violence against Men in War and Genocide*, is in preparation.

35 Misra, *The Landscape of Silence*, p. 14.

36 Ibid., pp. 172–173.

37 See Will Storr's exemplary and much-cited report, "The Rape of Men: The Darkest Secret of War," in *The Guardian/The Observer*, July 17, 2011, www.theguardian.com/society/2011/jul/17/the-rape-of-men.

38 See, e.g., "Syria: Sexual Assault in Detention," *Human Rights Watch* press release, June 15, 2012, www.hrw.org/news/2012/06/15/syria-sexual-assault-detention.

39 "Dolan has been working on the issue [of male survivors of conflict-related sexual violence] since 2008, when he collaborated with a young filmmaker on a first ever documentary on the issue, released in 2009 and titled *Gender Against Men* [see www.youtube.com/watch?v=mJSl99HQYXc]. The same year RLP [the Refugee Law Project in

Kampala, Uganda] also organized an open call for a first ever men–only workshop on Sexual and Gender-Based Violence, which was attended by 150 survivors from five different language backgrounds. Since then more patients and clients came to the[m], and in 2011 a small group of men started a support group, today known as Men of Hope with over 80 members. RLP's work has been featured in a number of media outlets, and Dolan was also commissioned by the UNHCR to draft humanitarian guidelines on working male victims, published in 2012 [see www.refugeelawproject.org/files/working_papers/Working_with_Men_and_Boy_Survivors_of_Sexual_and_Gender-Based_Violence_in_Forced_Displacement.pdf], and was asked to write the final report on the UN Forum. For more information, see www.refugeelawproject.org/."

40 "Gender against men": see previous note.

41 Ansley J. Coale and Judith Banister, "Five Decades of Missing Females in China," *Demography*, 31: 3 (August 1994), p. 472.

42 Malavika Karlekar, "The Girl Child in India: Does She Have Any Rights?," *Canadian Woman Studies*, March 1995.

43 For one of hundreds of possible examples, see Matthew White's description of Peter the Great's military conscription policies in Russia: "Peter's relentless maintenance of a huge standing army was just as deadly as his wars. Disease, malnutrition, neglect, and brutal discipline cut through his troops; so did the frigid cold of an empire that stretched all the way across the north of Asia. The draft was so dreaded that peasants mangled themselves to be ineligible. They knocked out their own teeth so they couldn't bite open cartridges to load their muskets. They severed their own toes so they couldn't march and fingers so they couldn't shoot." White, *Atrocitology: Humanity's 100 Deadliest Achievements* (Edinburgh: Canongate, 2011), p. 244. The British institution of "the press gang" effectively kidnapped young men, especially in port cities, for indefinite servitude in the Royal Navy—often they would never see their families and communities again. This proved fertile ground for the seeds of the early anti-slavery movement of the late eighteenth and early nineteenth centuries. These working–class coastal populations, who might be expected to view emancipated slaves as economic competitors and threats, instead strongly backed the abolitionist cause. Their own communities' vulnerability to kidnappings and involuntary servitude seems to have been a central factor. See Adam Hochschild, *Bury the Chains: Prophets and Rebels in the Fight to Free an Empire's Slaves* (Boston, MA: Houghton Mifflin Company, 2005), pp. 222–225. For detailed analyses of the press gang/impressment, see Denver Brunsman, *The Evil Necessity: British Naval Impressment in the Eighteenth-Century Atlantic World* (Charlottesville, VA: University of Virginia Press, 2013), and Nicholas Rogers, *The Press Gang: Naval Impressment and Its Opponents in Georgian Britain* (London: Continuum, 2007).

44 For detailed case studies of gendercidal institutions against females and males, see the Gendercide Watch website.

45 Cara Buckley, "Gays Living in Shadows of New Iraq," *The New York Times*, December 18, 2007, www.nytimes.com/2007/12/18/world/middleeast/18baghdad.html.

46 Ibid.

47 Doug Ireland, "UN Human Rights Report Confirms Iraqi Gay Killings," ZNet.org, January 27, 2007. See also Rasha Moumneh, "Iraq's New Surge: Gay Killings," *Foreign Policy*, September 9, 2009, www.foreignpolicy.com/articles/2009/09/09/iraqs_new_surge_gay_killings.

48 Afif Sarhan and Jason Burke, "How Islamist Gangs Use Internet to Track, Torture and Kill Iraqi Gays," *The Observer*, September 13, 2009, www.guardian.co.uk/world/2009/sep/13/iraq-gays-murdered-militias.

49 Buckley, "Gays Living in Shadows."

50 See Jeffrey Gettleman, "After Americans Visit, Uganda Weighs Death for Gays," *The New York Times*, January 3, 2010, www.nytimes.com/2010/01/04/world/africa/04uganda.html (the accompanying photo by Marc Hofer of anti-gay demonstrators in Kampala is also striking).

51 Fran Blandy, "Homosexual Africans Face Prison, Intolerance and the Death Penalty," *The Telegraph*, January 11, 2010, noting that "38 out of 53 [African] countries have criminalised consensual gay sex." See also the June 2013 Amnesty International report, *Making Love a Crime: Criminalization of Same-Sex Conduct in Sub-Saharan Africa*, www. amnestyusa.org/sites/default/files/making_love_a_crime_-_africa_lgbti_report_emb_6.24.13_0.pdf. Thanks to Jill Mitchell Nielsen for bringing this source to my attention.

52 Omar G. Encarnación, "Latin America's Gay Rights Revolution," *Journal of Democracy*, 22: 2 (2011), pp. 104–118.

53 LaToya Peterson, "Corrective Rape: The Epidemic of Violence Against South Africa's LGBT Community," *TheRoot.com*, May 23, 2015, www.theroot.com/articles/culture/2015/05/corrective_rape_the_epidemic_of_violence_against_south_africa_s_lgbt_community.html.

54 Rixecker, "Genetic Engineering and Queer Biotechnology," p. 188.

55 "At Least 48 Transgender Women Killed in Brazil in January [2016]," *Feministing.com*, February 3, 2016, http://feministing.com/2016/02/03/at-least-48-transgender-women-killed-in-brazil-in-january/.

56 Donna Bowater and Priscilla Moraes, "Brazil: Targeting Trans People with Impunity," *AlJazeera.com*, April 22, 2015, www.aljazeera.com/indepth/features/2015/04/brazil-targeting-trans-people-impunity-150413210248222.html.

57 Richard Wrangham and Dale Peterson, *Demonic Males: Apes and the Origins of Human Violence* (New York: Mariner, 1996), p. 23.

58 Michael P. Ghiglieri, *The Dark Side of Man: Tracing the Origins of Male Violence* (Cambridge, MA: Perseus Books, 2000), p. 173.

59 Wrangham and Peterson, *Demonic Males*, p. 214.

60 Ibid., pp. 208, 227.

61 Ibid., p. 239.

62 Ghiglieri called "for the vast majority of US citizens to make the individual decision to cooperate as a group . . . to teach children, all children, from day one, self-control, self-discipline, and self-responsibility in a world where we ourselves show that offensive violence is wrong. . . . Boys becoming young men must already have been socialized with these deep human values (in a palatable form, more or less as Boy Scouts of America wishes to do) *by their parents*. Second, we must decide to cooperate to make felonious violence—rape, murder, offensive war, genocide, and terrorism—not only 'not pay' for the perpetrator but also reap pain. In short, to stop violence, we must decide that our justice is *lex talionis* justice"—at which point Ghiglieri's prescriptions cease to persuade me (*The Dark Side of Man*, p. 256). See also the discussion in John Docker, "Genocide as Ancient Practice: Chimpanzees, Humans, Agricultural Society," in Docker, *The Origins of Violence: Religion, History and Genocide* (London: Pluto Press, 2008), pp. 13–38. After surveying some of the same terrain explored by Wrangham/Peterson, Ghiglieri, and Joshua Goldstein, Docker expressed support for a "sophisticated anti-determinism . . . which allows a powerful space for plasticity of brain and mind, the capacity not to be predetermined, the talent to be transformative, to be able to change and reverse and invert, to be unpredictable. In these terms, while there may be shared characteristics between chimpanzees and early humans, these may act in human history as potentialities, as possibilities, rather than as inevitable or binding; and they may not be carried through at all" (p. 28).

63 Allan D. Cooper, *The Geography of Genocide* (Lanham, MD: University Press of America, 2009), p. 42.

64 Ibid.; see ch. 6, "The End of Masculinity," and the lengthy appendix (Appendix 2) exploring "The Emasculating Moment of Historic Genocides."

65 Elisa von Joeden-Forgey, "Genocidal Masculinity," in Adam Jones, ed., *New Directions in Genocide Research* (London: Routledge, 2012), p. 89.

66 Daniel Jonah Goldhagen, *Worse Than War: Genocide, Eliminationism, and the Ongoing Assault on Humanity* (New York: Basic Books, 2009), p. 215. See also Alan Hall, "Behind

Every Nazi Mass Murderer Was a Woman: New Book Claims Women under Hitler Were Just as Ruthless as Men," *The Daily Mail*, February 3, 2009, profiling the research of German historian Kathrin Kompisch (*Täterinnen: Frauen im Nationalsozialismus*, 2008), not yet published in English.

67 "In Britain and America during [World War One], women organized a large-scale campaign to hand out white feathers to able-bodied men found on the streets, to shame the men for failing to serve in combat. . . . The white feather campaign was briefly resurrected in World War II, and the British government had to issue badges for men exempt on medical grounds." Goldstein, *War and Gender*, p. 272. See also Nicoletta F. Gullace, "White Feathers and Wounded Men: Female Patriotism and the Memory of the Great War," *The Journal of British Studies*, 36: 2 (1997), pp. 178–206. Barbara Ehrenreich notes: "Many feminists, such as England's Isabella Pankhurst, set the struggle for suffrage aside for an equally militant jingoism, and contented themselves with organizing women to support the war effort. 'The war is so horribly exciting but I cannot live on it,' one British suffragette wrote. 'It is like being drunk all day.'" Ehrenreich, *Blood Rites: Origins and History of the Passions of War* (New York: Metropolitan Books, 1997), p. 13.

68 It seems that at least as many women as men, perhaps more, supported Hitler and the Nazi regime; Tim Mason wrote that "a variety of different sources convey the impression that in the later 1930s the Third Reich enjoyed a large measure of active and passive support among women, *a larger measure than it gained from among men*" (quoted in Robert Gellately, *Backing Hitler: Consent and Coercion in Nazi Germany* [Oxford: Oxford University Press, 2001], p. 16, emphasis added). Gellately explained this as follows: "Conservative, Catholic, and even liberal women by and large shared the point of view advocated by the Nazis, as to a 'naturally' determined sexual division of labour, and that it was important to reconstruct a 'community of the people' in which they would be involved primarily as wives and mothers, and 'not be forced to compete with men for scarce jobs and political influence'" (p. 10, citing Ute Frevert, *Women in German History*). Owing to gender-separated voting booths, we also know that more women than men voted in favor of perpetuating Augusto Pinochet's dictatorial rule in Chile in a 1989 plebiscite; "51% of women and 58% of men voted 'no'" to the dictator. (See the fine documentary, *In Women's Hands*, PBS/Annenberg Project, *Americas* series, 1993.) In both cases, one wonders whether the fact that it was predominantly men who were targeted for harassment, detention, incarceration, torture, and murder by the regimes in question (the Jewish Holocaust apart) may have prompted a greater proportion of men to express opposition to those regimes when it was safe to do so. Finally, the recent prominence of women in the proto-genocidal Hindu-extremist movement in India has received increasing scholarly attention (see note 80).

69 James Waller, *Becoming Evil: How Ordinary People Commit Genocide and Mass Killing*, 2nd edn (Oxford: Oxford University Press, 2007), p. 267.

70 Quoted in Alison Des Forges, *Leave None to Tell the Story: Genocide in Rwanda* (New York: Human Rights Watch, 1999), p. 261. For numerous examples, see the groundbreaking African Rights report, *Rwanda: Not So Innocent: When Women Become Killers* (London: African Rights, 1995). For more on Nyiramasuhuko, see Carrie Sperling, "Mother of Atrocities: Pauline Nyiramasuhuko's Role in the Rwandan Genocide," *Fordham Urban Law Journal*, January 1, 2006. Nyiramasuhuko was sentenced to life imprisonment in June 2011; according to Wikipedia, she "is the first woman to be convicted of genocide by the ICTR, and the first woman to be convicted of genocidal rape" (see https://en.wikipedia.org/wiki/Pauline_Nyiramasuhuko).

71 Quoted in *Crimes against Humanity*, film produced by the Imperial War Museum, London, December 2002 (from the official transcript).

72 Leopord Twagirayezu, quoted in Goldhagen, *Worse Than War*, p. 102. A Hutu woman, Consolée Murekatete, who challenged her husband's participation in the genocide, told Jean Hatzfeld: ". . . Myself, I don't see any great disagreement between the Hutu men and women during those tumultuous days. The men cut [people] zealously in the marshes; the women burned with the same zeal in pillaging the fields and

houses. . . . Frankly, one never heard a pitying word for the Tutsi women who had been our neighbors. No complaint from wives about the Tutsi women our husbands might be raping—as long as our men performed their dirty deeds in the papyrus of the marshes, sheltered from prying eyes and gossiping tongues." Quoted in Hatzfeld, *The Antelope's Strategy: Living in Rwanda After the Genocide*, trans. Linda Coverdale (New York: Farrar, Straus and Giroux, 2009), pp. 138, 140.

73 Kimberlee Acquaro and Peter Landesman, "Out of Madness, A Matriarchy," *Mother Jones*, January/February 2003. Available at http://motherjones.com/politics/2003/01/out-madness-matriarchy. The article is a good overview of women's position in Rwanda after the genocide, including the "unplanned—if not inadvertent—movement of female empowerment driven by national necessity."

74 For a lengthy profile of Nyiramasuhuko, see Peter Landesman, "A Woman's Work," *The New York Times Magazine*, September 15, 2002, www.nytimes.com/2002/09/15/magazine/a-woman-s-work.html.

75 Laura Sjoberg and Caron E. Gentry, *Mothers, Monsters, Whores: Women's Violence in Global Politics* (London: Zed Books, 2007), p. 4.

76 Wendy Lower, *Hitler's Furies: German Women in the Nazi Killing Fields* (Boston, MA: Houghton Mifflin, 2013; the cover pictured is the UK paperback edition). The quoted passages in this caption are drawn from pp. 6, 7, 10, 11, 21, 43, 101–102.

77 Andrew Charlesworth, "The Topography of Genocide," in Dan Stone, ed., *The Historiography of the Holocaust* (London: Palgrave Macmillan, 2004), p. 223.

78 Waller, *Becoming Evil*, pp. 268–269.

79 Judith Halberstam, *Female Masculinity* (Durham, NC: Duke University Press, 1998); cited in von Joeden-Forgey, "Genocidal Masculinity."

80 On Hindu women's militancy, see Parita Mukta, "Gender, Community, Nation: The Myth of Innocence," in Susie Jacobs *et al.*, eds., *States of Conflict: Gender, Violence and Resistance* (London: Zed Books, 2000), pp. 163–178; Atreyee Sen, "Reflecting on Resistance: Hindu Women 'Soldiers' and the Birth of Female Militancy," *Indian Journal of Gender Studies*, 13: 1 (2006), pp. 1–35.

81 See Adam Jones, "Gender and Genocide in Rwanda," in Jones, *Gender Inclusive: Essays on Violence, Men, and Feminist International Relations* (London: Routledge, 2009), p. 123.

82 Quoted in Des Forges, *Leave None to Tell the Story*, p. 459.

83 Quoted in African Rights, *Rwanda: Death, Despair and Defiance* (rev. edn) (London: African Rights, 1995), p. 82.

84 Commander of the *Wehrmacht's* II Corps to his troops, late December 1941; quoted in Omer Bartov, *Hitler's Army: Soldiers, Nazis, and War in the Third Reich* (New York: Oxford University Press, 1992), p. 132.

85 Saul Friedländer, *Nazi Germany and the Jews, Volume 1: The Years of Persecution, 1933–1939* (New York: HarperCollins, 1997), p. 124.

86 Joan Ringelheim, "Genocide and Gender: A Split Memory," in Ronit Lentin, ed., *Gender and Catastrophe* (London: Zed Books, 1997), p. 19. See also the heavily-gendered depiction of the Jew in Adolf Hitler's *Mein Kampf* (Boston, MA: Houghton Mifflin, 1943), pp. 300–327.

87 Peter Fritzsche, *Life and Death in the Third Reich* (Cambridge, MA: The Belknap Press of Harvard University Press, 2008), p. 129. Jeffrey Herf's portrait of the "Jewish enemy" was gendered throughout, both in presenting exclusively male Jews in the propaganda images reproduced as color plates, and in numerous passing references throughout the text (Herf, *The Jewish Enemy: Nazi Propaganda during World War II and the Holocaust* [Cambridge, MA: The Belknap Press of Harvard University Press, 2006]; see, e.g., pp. 32, 33, 128, 143, 222). However, Herf did not explore gender as an overarching theme or variable.

88 Peter Longerich's classic study *Holocaust* is the only work I know that specifically devotes a chapter to "The Mass Murder of Jewish Men" (ch. 11 in Longerich, *Holocaust: The Nazi Persecution and Murder of the Jews* [Oxford: Oxford University Press, 2010],

pp. 192–205). Longerich emphasizes the "reprisal" trope which was used as a cover for the gender-selective slaughter of Jewish men—a quite typical pattern in war and genocide (see also note 10). He cites an incident report from *Einsatzgruppe* C on August 20, 1941, stating: "In Januszpol, a city with more than 25 per cent Jewish inhabits, Jewish women have in recent days displayed impertinent and insolent behavior with respect to the restrictions currently imposed on them. They tore their own and their children's clothes from their bodies. As an interim reprisal measure, the commando that arrived, once order had been re-established, shot 15 male Jews. Further reprisals will follow" (pp. 200–201). The conflation of Jewish men with "partisan" forces—an identification subsequently extended to Jewish women, though less persuasively to the perpetrators—is explored in *Marching into Darkness*, Waitman Wade Beorn's excellent study of *Wehrmacht* complicity in the "Holocaust by Bullets" in Belarus (Cambridge, MA: Harvard University Press, 2014). Beorn shows how minimal was the actual partisan threat to German forces in these early stages of the "Holocaust by Bullets," by contrast with the much more organized resistance of 1943–1944 (and with Nazi-occupied Yugoslavia, where the partisan war was waged with particular ferocity, and used as a cover for the extermination of Jewish men—see Longerich, pp. 300–301). According to Longerich, the decisive shift from a gendercidal to "root-and-branch" genocidal strategy (see discussion on pp. 626–632) occurred "at the end of August or the beginning of September [1941]," when a policy was revealed to *Einsatzgruppen* commandos "that there is now an order from the Führer according to which all Jews are to be killed indiscriminately" (p. 227). By the closing months of 1941, the policy had shifted in a newly-gendered direction: "During the summer, the victims of mass shootings had principally been Jewish men of military age; but, from the autumn onwards, the selection principle was reversed and Jews capable of work [disproportionately male] were exempted from the annihilation measures" (p. 209).

89 See Adam Jones, "Genocide and Humanitarian Intervention: Incorporating the Gender Variable," *Journal of Humanitarian Assistance*, February 2002, www.jha.ac/articles/a080.htm.

PART 4 THE FUTURE OF GENOCIDE

CHAPTER 14

Memory, Forgetting, and Denial

...What to forget and what to remember is a political choice, more often than not dictated by the need to erase the past to legitimize the present.

René Lemarchand

"You speak about history," Soviet dictator Joseph Stalin told a gathering of his subordinates. "But one must sometimes correct history."[1] Never was that task pursued more surreally than under Stalin. Old photographs were doctored to eliminate Stalin's former Bolshevik colleagues, now labeled "saboteurs" and "enemies of the people" (see Chapter 5). The history of the Communist Party was rewritten to accord Stalin a central and heroic role. Inconvenient evidence was expunged, such as Lenin's warning shortly before his death that Stalin should be distrusted and marginalized. When the Nazi-Soviet pact was signed in August 1939, the erstwhile epitome of evil—the fascist German regime—became a friend and business part-ner. Less than two years later, Germany had launched the most destructive invasion of all time against the Soviet Union. Overnight, Soviet public opinion and official history had to shift again to accommodate total war against the former friend (and, prior to that, mortal enemy).

As satirized by George Orwell in *Nineteen Eighty-Four*, Stalinism and other totalitarianisms have become classic cases of the manipulation of history and memory. Usually, however, things are not as clear-cut as dictatorial imposition. Rather, memory and history reflect an ongoing contestation and evolution, within both societies and individual hearts and minds. Elizabeth Jelin has written of "'legitimacy' struggles over memory—who has what rights to determine what should be remembered and how":

> Such moments of contestation over commemorations and memorials are markers which provide clues to the processes of remembrance at the subjective and the symbolic levels, where the memories of different social actors are enacted and become "the present," making it easier to analyze the construction of collective, social and public memories.

At these points, Jelin adds, "memories are multiple and at times in conflict."[2] In large part, this reflects one's positioning in the historical drama. Is one an older person, with direct memories of the events? Is one younger, seeking to uncover the secrets of one's elders, or alternatively to "let the past take care of the past" and move on? Is one a former collaborator with the repressive regime, anxious to justify the collaboration or mitigate one's guilt through confession and public repentance? Is one a victim of the regime who feels that personal suffering constitutes "the basic determinant of legitimacy and the claim to truth"?[3] Or does such suffering mean that one is unable to adopt an "objective" approach to the events?

The answers to these questions tell us something about how individual identities are constructed through selective memory (as all memory is). Cumulatively, they also say a great deal about how a society remembers, and *why* it remembers: that is, with what collective or public purpose.[4] To understand this more deeply, let us consider three cases in which genocide and crimes against humanity, or forceful allegations thereof, have spawned far-reaching debate, self-analysis, and denial.

CONTESTED MEMORIES: THREE CASES

I. Germany

Germany's reckoning with its Nazi past may be divided into three principal phases. The first, extending from the war's end to about the mid-1960s, was one of willful amnesia, as Germans sought to put the war behind them. It has been argued that this act of forgetting (see further below) was significant in allowing West Germans to build a prosperous and democratic state, while in Soviet-controlled East Germany, Nazi sins could be displaced onto "fascism" and the communist entity depicted in a heroic light. In West Germany, to the extent that victims were memorialized and commemorated, they were overwhelmingly *German* victims—such as the hundreds of thousands of German POWs who remained in Soviet camps, in many cases into the 1950s. The West German government under Konrad Adenauer did initiate substantial reparations payments to Jews in the form of tens of billions of deutschmarks in financial transfers to Israel. This evoked some public opposition, but most Germans appear to have welcomed it as a means of bolstering their alliance with the West—rather than as an *entrée* to memorialization of Jewish suffering and German guilt.

Figure 14.1 A visitor at the open-air Memorial to the Murdered Jews of Europe in central Berlin, designed by Peter Eisenman. Is the German capital the most memory-saturated space in the world?

Source: Author's photo, June 2013.

The upheavals of the 1960s radically destabilized this historical narrative. Survivors and scholars of the genocide against the Jews explored the Holocaust systematically for the first time. German scholars asserted historical continuities between the Nazi and post-Nazi periods, including the role of large capitalist enterprises that had managed the transition smoothly from fascism to democracy. Many younger Germans made pilgrimages to Israel to atone for the sins of their forebears. The *Schuldfrage* (guilt issue) took center stage, symbolized by Chancellor Willi Brandt's famous kneeling apology for Nazi crimes (the so-called *Kniefall*) on a July 1970 visit to Poland.[5] In academia, the ferment spilled over into the *Historikerstreit* (historians' debate) of the 1970s and 1980s, "a scholarly controversy over the place and significance of National Socialism and the Holocaust in the narrative of modern German history."[6] An older generation concerned with maintaining, for example, a distinction between Nazi and German Army practices was confronted by mostly younger scholars who challenged the assumptions and evasions of their seniors (see also Chapter 6).

This second phase saw the German and Nazi past rendered more complex and problematic to ordinary Germans. Society was prone to "irruptions of memory" of the kind described by Alexander Wilde: "public events that break in upon [the] national consciousness, unbidden and often suddenly, to evoke associations with symbols, figures, causes, ways of life which to an unusual degree are associated with a political past that is still present in the lived experience of a major part of the population."[7]

BOX 14.1 *STOLPERSTEINE*: THE "STUMBLING STONES"

Figure 14.2 "Here lived Fritz Hauser, born 1892. Arrested 1940. Sentenced in Freiburg. Flossen-bürg concentration camp. Dachau [concentration camp]. Murdered 14 April 1944 at Majdanek [death camp]." This "stumbling stone" at Zunfstrasse 5 in Freiburg, Germany, commemorates a victim of the Nazis' persecution and incarceration of homosexual men (see Box 6a, "The Nazis' Other Victims").

Source: Photo by James Steakley/Wikimedia Commons.

Europe's most ubiquitous memorialization project began as the brainchild of Gunter Demnig, a German artist with a longstanding interest in "laying Spuren—'traces' or 'tracks' or 'evidence'—of the past as art." Demnig conceived of the *Stolpersteine*—"stumbling stones"—as "a decentralized monument" or "social sculpture." The first was laid, illegally, in Berlin in 1996. Dozens more followed on a single street. When the authorities learned of them, they appreciated their cultural potential—and perhaps feared the outcry that would accompany an attempt to remove them. Demnig's actions were thus legalized retroactively, and the "stumbling stones" proliferated.[8]

As described by Andreas Kluth, the *Stolpersteine* "are brass plates sitting on concrete cubes of ten centimetres on each side. Printed into each plate are the details of one victim of National Socialism—Jewish, gypsy, homosexual or other—who had his or her last address at this spot. The information is deliberately kept terse." The "stones" are sponsored by private citizens. "Germans who are curious about what transpired in their building, schoolchildren doing a project, surviving relatives of a victim, anybody who is interested—conduct their own research about a victim at a specific address." Demnig then crafts each of the *Stolpersteine* by hand, "because, he says, any form of mass-manufacturing would remind him of the mechanized and bureaucratic murder at Auschwitz." As for the "stumbling," as a teenage boy insightfully told Demnig, "You're not stumbling physically, you're stumbling with your head and heart."

Demnig anticipated that the brass "stones" would be polished by constant footfalls, "refreshing the memory each time," in his words. But according to Kluth, pedestrians instead "usually step around the plates, perhaps associating them with gravestones, which they are not. This means that the metal oxidises and turns brown or even black, which in turn, ironically, makes it look as though the Stolpersteine were left untended. Often, residents then polish them the old-fashioned way." A woman in Kluth's apartment building, for example, "regularly lights candles and strews white roses around the Stolpersteine in our street." When Kluth and his children first arrived to view the apartment—in the ritzy Charlottenburg district, prewar home to many upper-class German Jews—they noticed five "stones" in the street. "We bowed down and I read the inscriptions out loud. My seven-year-old daughter wondered what this might be about. Since she asked, I began to tell them, for the first time, about the Holocaust. As I did so, some of our neighbours-to-be paused and joined us and an ad hoc conversation arose—all before we had even moved in."

As of early 2016, there were an astounding 56,000 *Stolpersteine* distributed around Europe, "most in Germany, thousands in Berlin alone." They have evoked both huge interest and some criticism, including from far-right figures who denounce the project as "harken[ing] back to a time that is now passed" and "a moneymaking scheme for their creator"[9]—and, less expectedly, some German Jews, who consider the *Stolpersteine* "undignified because pedestrians are in effect trampling on a victim's name." Demnig, by contrast, argues that "the more people walk over a Stolperstein, the greater the honour to the person who lies there." Moreover, "when you want to read [the 'stone'], you have to bow, before the victim"—for him, "one of the most beautiful" aspects of this unique grassroots initiative.

One such irruption belonged to the realm of popular culture: the January 1979 broadcast of the US television miniseries *Holocaust*, starring Meryl Streep and James Woods, which despite its soap-opera stylings offered Germans perhaps their first sustained depiction of Jewish persecution under Nazism. Quite unexpectedly, it was *Holocaust* that first rent the public fabric in a decisive way, as Heinz Höhne noted in *Der Spiegel*:

An American television series, made in a trivial style, produced more for commercial than for moral reasons, more for entertainment than for enlightenment, accomplished what hundreds of books, plays, films, and television programs, thousands of documents, and all the concentration camp trials have failed to do in the more than three decades since the end of the war: to inform Germans about crimes against Jews committed in their name, so that millions were emotionally touched and moved.[10]

Another irruption was prompted by the visit of US President Ronald Reagan to the Bitburg military cemetery, where German soldiers, including SS officers, were interred. The German soldiers were "victims of Nazism also," Reagan proclaimed. "They were victims, just as surely as the victims in the concentration camps."[11] His comments sparked a furor among US military veterans, as well as among Jewish intellectuals and activists. In Germany, they provoked intense public discussion over whether Jewish and German victimization should be mentioned in the same breath.

A third, somewhat amorphous phase began in the 1990s, in the wake of the *Historikerstreit*, and carried over into the new millennium.[12] It centered on the public debate over three controversial books. Daniel Jonah Goldhagen's *Hitler's Willing Executioners* accused "ordinary Germans" of perpetrating many of the genocidal atrocities of the Second World War. The book attracted a huge audience in Germany, especially among the younger generation. Günter Grass's *Im Krebsgang (Crabwalk)*, meanwhile, described events at the end of the war, when the *Wilhelm Gustloff* cruise liner was torpedoed by a Soviet submarine, killing thousands of German civilian refugees.[13] Jörg Friedrich's *Brandstätten (Fire Sites)* provided grisly photographic evidence of the effects of Allied fire-bombing of German cities. (See Box 6a for more on Grass's and Friedrich's books.) Friedrich ably described the public's response to his book in terms that captured the emotional stress of suppressing memories, and the catharsis of expressing them:

> The bombing left an entire generation traumatised. But it was never discussed. There are Germans whose first recollections are of being hidden by their mothers. They remember cellars and burning human remains. It is only now that they are coming to terms with what happened . . . [But] Germans in their seventies and eighties have not forgotten. Their memories are still vivid. People stand up in my public lectures and describe what befell their families. They have tears in their eyes and they can't breathe.[14]

Also significant was the late 1990s controversy over a traveling exhibition of photographs, organized by the Hamburg Institute for Social Research, that provided vivid and chilling evidence of German Army participation in atrocities against Jews, Soviet prisoners-of-war, and others. The longstanding distinction between Nazi "evil" and army "honor" was decisively and probably permanently undermined.[15] At the same time, a victim-centered memorialization proceeded apace for the millions of ethnic Germans expelled to Germany at the war's end, and in its aftermath (see Figure 14.3).

Can a new, usable collective memory or public history be constructed out of these diverse strands and fragments? Robert Moeller, a leading scholar of the subject, appeared to believe so. He favored narratives that "move beyond a language in

Figure 14.3 A banner with an image of ethnic-German refugees, uprooted from formerly Nazi-occupied territories between 1945 and 1947, adorns a building in central Berlin destined for a refugee documentation center.

Source: Author's photo, June 2013.

which the categories of victim and perpetrator were mutually exclusive," seeking instead "to capture the complexities of individual lives and 'mass fates' by exploring how during the Third Reich it was possible both to suffer and to cause suffering in others."[16] Yet any such project is, it is fair to say, in its early stages.

II. Japan

Japan's struggles over memory mirror in key respects those in Germany, the other major Axis power defeated in the Second World War. Postwar German governments, however, offered both effusive apologies and tens of billions of dollars in restitution payments, while German scholars often took a lead in exposing German crimes. By contrast, Japanese authorities have only grudgingly conceded that their overseas empire was founded on slave labor, and with rare exceptions have resisted formal apologies. Japanese scholars and activists, too, have often sought to paper over the country's criminal record, while glorifying the actions of the Japanese military.

In the 1980s and 1990s, Asians enslaved either in the Japanese homeland or the wartime empire—Koreans and Chinese above all—launched a concerted campaign to win restitution from the Japanese government. They were joined by former Allied prisoners-of-war, some three hundred of whom petitioned in 2008 for recognition of the unpaid labor they had been forced to perform for the Aso Mining Company in 1945. The claim was particularly volatile, given that Aso was the family firm of the then-prime minister, Taro Aso. Aso was additionally notorious for "his combative reputation as a historical revisionist," centered on what *The New York Times* denounced as "nostalgic fantasies about Japan's ugly past." Apart from the relatively small number of POWs, some 10,000 Koreans had also "worked under severe conditions in the company's mines between 1939 and 1945; many died and most were never properly paid." Nonetheless, the Aso Group's official corporate history "omitted all mention" of the forced laborer, and bluntly refused to provide details about both the POWs and Koreans enslaved there.[17]

The cases of slave labor that received the greatest attention were those of the so-called "comfort women": tens of thousands of women tricked and coerced into serving as sex slaves to Japanese soldiers throughout the "Greater Asian Co-Prosperity Sphere." Following the Japanese invasion of Manchuria in 1931, the Japanese army began to construct a network of hundreds of "comfort stations" across the occupied territories, "dup[ing] or forc[ing] Korean, Taiwanese, Chinese, Indonesian, Filipino, Japanese and Dutch women to work in them." Estimates of the number dragooned and exploited in this fashion range between 140,000 and 200,000.[18] Those who survived (about one in six did not) faced continued shame and suffering upon their return home, and like so many atrocity survivors, kept their experiences quiet for decades. Only in the 1980s did they begin to seek compensation for their suffering from the Japanese government.

In 1993, in a rare and groundbreaking move, the Japanese government officially recognized the system of sexual slavery, and established a small private fund for compensation.[19] Disbursements ended in 2007, however, and in that same year, Japanese prime minister Shinzo Abe sparked an international outcry by effectively rescinding Japan's recognition of the sexual slavery. The women, he claimed, had willingly served as prostitutes, in order to earn money for their families. "There is no evidence to prove there was coercion, nothing to support it," Abe declared. "So, in respect to [the 1993] declaration, you have to keep in mind that things have changed greatly."[20] In December 2015, however, South Korea and Japan proclaimed a "final and irreversible resolution" of the issue. Abe (in the words of Japanese foreign minister Fumio Kishida) "expresse[d] anew sincere apologies and remorse from the bottom of his heart to all those who suffered immeasurable pain and incurable physical and psychological wounds as 'comfort women.'" Restitution payments totaling US $8.3 million were also announced. The agreement was roundly denounced by women survivors, NGOs, and opposition figures in South Korea, who argued "that the accord fell far short of the women's long-standing demand that Japan admit legal responsibility and offer formal reparations." The Korean Council for the Women Drafted for Military Sexual Slavery in Japan declared it "nothing but a diplomatic collusion that thoroughly betrayed the wishes of comfort women and the South Korean people."[21]

The "comfort women" controversy attested to a wider memory struggle in Japan, played out in the fields of political and religious ritual, education, and popular culture. For decades, it had been customary for Japanese political leaders to visit the Yasukuni shrine in Tokyo (see Figure 14.4), to pay tribute to the nearly two-and-a-half million soldiers, officers, and government functionaries who are not only memorialized there, but designated as deities in the pantheon of the Shinto religion. Over time, the shrine became a brazen monument to Japanese militarism, with an attached museum full of weaponry and housing a statue honoring Japanese *kamikaze* (suicide pilots)—with no mention of the atrocities inflicted by Japanese forces throughout the "Greater Asian Co-Prosperity Sphere." Right-wing extremists, proclaiming they are defending Japanese "honor," have made the shrine a point of pilgrimage, sparking counter-demonstrations by communists and other anti-imperialists.[22]

The contemporary controversy arose after 1959, when the names of more than a thousand war criminals convicted and executed for atrocities committed during World War Two were added to Yasukuni's rolls. In 1978, fourteen "Class A" war criminals were similarly honored, including wartime prime minister Hideki Tojo, executed by the International Military Tribunal for the Far East in 1948. For a Japanese prime minister to visit Yasukuni and pay homage to those memorialized there "could be likened to [a German] Chancellor . . . paying his respects at monuments to Himmler and Goebbels, or even Hitler himself," wrote Christopher Reed.[23] But it became a tradition to do so, thereby setting an official seal on what, since the war, has been a privately-owned memorial. In 2001, Prime Minister Junichiro Koizumi prayed at the shrine, repeating the ritual five times more before leaving office in 2006.[24] His successor, however—Shinzo Abe, already under fire for his comments about slave laborers—initially avoided those same ceremonies, while expressing remorse for the "tremendous damage and suffering" Japan had inflicted on neighboring nations.[25] Abe, however, turned up at the shrine ceremonies in December 2013; "about 10 percent of the combined membership of the upper and lower houses of Parliament" joined him in the pilgrimage, mostly from Abe's conservative Liberal Democratic Party. At the most recent ceremony in October 2015, he was again absent, sending instead "a ritual offering of evergreen branches to the shrine"—and three cabinet members.[26]

In the course of 2015, both Abe and the figurehead emperor Akihito had publicly expressed their "profound grief" and "sincere condolences" (Abe), and "deep remorse" (Akihito), for the victims of Japanese militarism.[27] The prime minister's ambivalent stance, and the will-he-or-won't-he speculation attached to every Yasukuni commemoration, exemplified the conflicting pressures on Abe. *VOA News* noted that he sought "to balance appeasing regional concerns with maintaining support from fervent nationalist supporters who believe Japan's war crimes have been exaggerated, or that the country has apologized enough." The regional dimension was evident in the "three-way meeting among high-ranking leaders from Japan, China and South Korea" planned for the month following the Yasukuni ceremony; Abe's attendance "would have jeopardized" the summit. His branch-offering itself was enough to draw a rebuke from a Chinese Foreign Ministry spokesperson, who urged Japan "to face up to and deeply reflect on [its] history of militarism." South Korea, for its part, accused Abe of "glorifying Japan's forcible colonization and war of aggression."[28]

Figure 14.4 The Yasukuni shrine in Tokyo—a homage to Japanese war dead that has become a key site in the struggle over memories of Japan's World War Two-era atrocities.

Source: David Monniaux/Wikimedia Commons.

Domestically, arguments raged in the 2000s over what constituted "acceptable" forms of cultural expression and public criticism concerning Japan's imperial past. Perhaps the most notable furor erupted over another documentary film—this one a brazenly revisionist account of the "Rape of Nanjing" (see Chapter 2, p. 100) directed by Satoru Mizushima, a prominent TV mogul. After allegedly conducting "exhaustive research" on the subject, Mizushima emerged with the conclusion that not a single Chinese had been massacred by Japanese troops: "The evidence for a massacre is faked. It is Chinese Communist propaganda . . . If we remain silent, anti-Japanese propaganda will spread across the world. What is important is to correct the historical record and send the right message."[29] *The Truth of Nanjing*, released in 2008, prompted angry protests from the Chinese government, but it catered to a substantial constituency of Japanese convinced that the country's honor was being besmirched by its enemies. That this constituency encompassed senior figures in the Japanese establishment was demonstrated by a "true modern history" essay contest held in 2008. The winning entry was authored by none other than General Toshio Tamogami, air force chief of staff. Tamogami considered it "certainly a false accusation to say that our country was an aggressor nation" in the war. Rather, "many Asian countries take a positive view" of Japan's wartime policies, which, he alleged, had actually promoted positive race relations: "If Japan had not fought the Great East Asia War at that time, it might have taken another 100 or 200 years before we could have experienced the world of racial equality that we have today."[30] This, though, was too much for a government increasingly sensitive to international criticisms of its war record and the failure to acknowledge atrocious conduct. Tamogami was fired from his post within a day of the prize announcement.

III. Argentina

In 1976, against a backdrop of mounting social and economic chaos, a military regime under General Jorge Rafael Videla took power in Argentina. A state of siege was declared. For the next seven years, Videla and his fellow generals presided over the most brutal of South America's modern military dictatorships. Between 10,000 and 30,000 people—suspected of involvement with leftist guerrillas, or vaguer subversions—were "disappeared" by the authorities. Generally, they were tortured to death or executed; in many cases their bodies were dumped out of airplanes and into the Atlantic Ocean (see further below). Pregnant detainees were often allowed to give birth before being killed; the infants were then turned over to be adopted by military families.[31] In 1982, following Argentina's defeat by Great Britain in the war over the Falkland Islands,[32] military rule began to crumble. In 1983, the state of siege was lifted, and free elections held. Raul Alfonsín of the Radical Civic Union (UCR) was sworn in as president in December. That month also saw the creation of the National Commission on Disappeared People (CONADEP), which investigated the fate of those who vanished under the military regime. Its report was released in 1984 under the title *Nunca Más* (Never Again)—echoing the call of those who memorialize the Jewish Holocaust. The report "catalogued 8,960 unresolved 'disappearances,' but warned that the true figure might be higher. It also listed 340 clandestine abduction centers in Argentina, which it said were in use at the height of the repression."[33] In Argentina, the events are regularly referred to as "genocide," although the designation would be disputed by some genocide scholars.[34]

The most notorious of the state detention facilities was the Naval Mechanics School (Escuela Mecánica de la Armada, ESMA) in the Palermo suburb of Buenos Aires. Over time, the movement to memorialize the disappeared and compensate survivors began to push for the creation of a museum on the forty-two-acre property. In 2004, the government of Nestor Kirchner bowed to the pressure. It expropriated the site and declared it would house a "Museum of Memory," to educate current and future generations about the period of state terror.

But which memories, and whose, should be reflected? Was this form of memorialization even appropriate, with the atrocities still fresh in the national consciousness? An account by journalist Larry Rohter in *The New York Times* described "sharp differences" over these issues among human-rights activists.[35] The Mothers of the Plaza de Mayo had gathered throughout the military dictatorship in the central square of Buenos Aires, demanding information and the return of their disappeared loved ones. Some members of the group argued that "museums mark the end of a story, and we haven't reached that point in Argentina yet," in the

Figure 14.5 The façade of the Escuela Mecánica de la Armada (Naval Mechanics School) in Buenos Aires, Argentina. A principal detention and torture center during the years of military dictatorship (1976–1983), its operations gave rise to the largest-ever trial of accused perpetrators of atrocity crimes under the *junta*—sixty-eight former officials in all.

Source: Author's photo, January 2005.

words of one leader, Hebe de Bonafini. "It's much too soon to be setting up a museum, because the historical events in question are too recent." Other organizations, however, strongly supported the project. One, called *Memoria Abierta* (Open Memory), compiled an archive of over 4,000 photographs and a range of oral histories for deposit in the museum. According to Patricia Valdez, director of the project: "We do not want this museum for ourselves, but for Argentine society. It has to be a place that transcends the fluctuations of Argentine politics and lets the facts speak for themselves."

Even among those who generally supported the initiative, the appropriate range and limits of this "memory space" *(espacio para la memoria)* aroused controversy. In announcing the museum's creation on March 24, 2004, the anniversary of the 1976 *golpe (coup)*, President Kirchner "seemed to be suggesting that the focus will be on the military dictatorship that dominated the country from 1976 to 1983." Kirchner was leader of the Peronist Party, whose activists had been targeted during the so-called "Dirty War." But Peronism, too, stood accused of atrocities during the 1970s. They included the formation of paramilitary organizations and death squads blamed for some three hundred

Figure 14.6 An image from a rainy winter's visit to Olimpo, another of the detention and torture centers in Buenos Aires that is now a memorial to the "disappeared" and genocided, like the young man pictured in the window.

Source: Author's photo, July 2011.

murders, as well as bombings and kidnappings. Limiting the museum's coverage to the 1976–1983 period "would only distort historical realities," argued the Peronists' conservative opponents. Mabel Gutierrez of the Group of Relatives of the Disappeared and Detained rejected the criticisms. "We are going to try to be as impartial as possible in telling the story, but if those on the other side don't like it, let them make their own museum. They have the money of the reactionaries of the right."[36]

The struggle took place against a backdrop of on-again, off-again attempts to prosecute Argentina's military leaders and their henchmen for crimes committed under the dictatorship. After a series of "demonstration coups" by disgruntled military officers following the return to democracy, President Alfonsín declared a *punto final* (full stop) to the prosecutions in 1985. Those already jailed were pardoned by his Peronist successor, Carlos Meném, who declared he was acting in the interests of national unity and reconciliation.[37] But as in neighboring Chile, as the country stabilized, as a new generation of once-repressed youths took power,[38] and as electorates responded favorably to justice-seeking measures, initiatives were relaunched. The Argentine Supreme Court in 2005 lifted the immunity granted to officials of the former regime. The military reacted vengefully. Key witnesses to the dictatorships' crimes were "disappeared" or killed.[39] When they finally evacuated the ESMA site in 2007, reported the

UK *Telegraph*, "soldiers nailed a shooting-target to the front door of one of the buildings and then systematically wrecked the place . . . Signs of this destruction are everywhere still: ripped floors, flooded basements and destroyed bathrooms, with only the sound of water dripping from broken pipes coming from inside. This havoc has dashed hopes that the entire ESMA complex, apart from the two buildings that have just opened, will be accessible to the public in the near future."

Disagreements among the groups struggling to define collective memory continued to "mak[e] matters worse," with "little agreement on how to develop the rest of the complex. Some insist that certain buildings should be brought down; others want to preserve the place as it stands." According to Nenina Bouliet of the Memory Institute, "Besides divisions on what to include, we're swamped with proposals from Argentinian artists . . . Unfortunately, we lack museum experts in Argentina with experience on how to transmit the horrors that took place here."[40] Though this author was granted tours of the ESMA complex in 2007 and 2011, along with selected others, the public opening of the "Museum of Memory" had yet to materialize at the time of writing (early 2016).

In the meantime, the controversy over military-era crimes and contemporary trials only increased in intensity. In November 2012, "the biggest trial of human rights abuses in the history of Argentina" opened in Buenos Aires, targeting, in many cases, military figures who were "already serving life sentences in jail." Former navy officers Jorge Eduardo Acosta, Alfredo Astiz ("The Blond Angel of Death"), and Ricardo Miguel Cavallo were the defendants in a proceeding that "recognized 789 victims, and will consider testimony from around 900 witnesses." Two civilians were also tried, a "very important" element, according to human-rights advocate Silvina Stimemann. For the first time, the macabre "death flights," in which drugged prisoners were killed by being pushed out of planes and helicopters, took center stage. Their prominence was bolstered by new evidence released by the Uruguayan government in 2011: "classified photographs from its defence department" showing "corpses . . . their hands and feet bound" that had washed ashore on the Uruguayan coast.[41]

"It's one thing looking at them from the other side of the glass in the viewing gallery," said Graciela Palacio Lois, "whose husband Ricardo never returned from a meeting of the Peronist University Youth movement in 1976." "But it's another thing sitting in the witness area with them in front of you."[42] The trial, originally scheduled to take two years, was still ongoing as this edition went into production. But renewed controversy erupted in late 2015 in the wake of the departure of Peronist president Cristina Kirchner, when the prominent *La Nación* newspaper, "historically close to the military establishment," published an editorial titled "*No más venganza*" (No More Vengeance), calling for a new *punto final* in criminal proceedings against present and future defendants. Outraged *La Nación* staff protested by issuing "a photo showing journalists in the paper's newsroom holding placards reading 'I condemn the editorial'" (see Figure 14.7).[43]

Figure 14.7 Journalists and other staff of the conservative *La Nación* newspaper in Buenos Aires assemble to repudiate an editorial calling for an end to trials of officials accused of crimes against humanity under the 1976–1983 military regime.

Source: *La Nación* staff (public post), November 2015.

FORGETTING

On an individual level, perpetrators seek to consign their atrocities to memory's dustbin. Forgetting may represent a final stage of revision, reinterpretation, and denial, canceling any dissonance with one's preferred self-image. A common strategy is to displace others' victimization onto oneself. Atrocities that one perpetrated, supported, or ignored are crowded out by memories of personal and collective victimization, whether experienced or imagined. However, victims too may seek to forget: whether because it is painful to remember; because remembering prevents them from "getting on with their lives"; or because they are convinced no one will listen to their stories. Such was the case with many survivors of the Armenian and Jewish holocausts, who spent decades after the events seeking to consign them to the past and build new lives. Today, genocide survivors are often encouraged to tell their stories, on the assumption that this will bring them relief. But whatever the benefits of doing so for a public audience, the emotional and psychological implications for the survivors are more uncertain. Relating their experiences may bring to the surface trauma that survivors had long worked to suppress.

Moreover, while many people welcome survivors' accounts for the unique perspective they supply on atrocious events, some—perhaps only a vocal fringe; perhaps the majority—will accuse them of falsification or exaggeration. Such testimonies upset the delicate project of forgetting within perpetrators' societies. And they destabilize a central strategy in such forgetting: *denial*. Assertions of genocide denial have surged in recent years, as ever more historical events have come to be labeled as "genocide." I explore the phenomenon of genocidal denial in the next section, together with the vexing issue of how best to confront and counter it.

BOX 14.2 "HISTORY WARS" AND THE CANADIAN MUSEUM FOR HUMAN RIGHTS

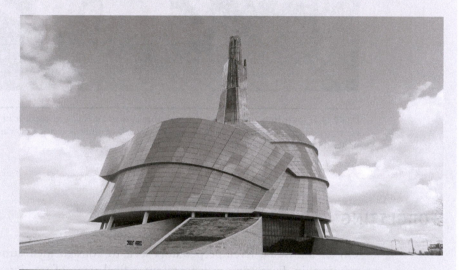

Figure 14.8 The Canadian Museum for Human Rights in Winnipeg, Manitoba, designed by Antoine Predock.

Source: Photo by Robert Linsdell/Creative Commons/Flickr.

The project that became the Canadian Museum for Human Rights, and the "history wars"[44] that have swirled around it, began with efforts to introduce a dedicated Holocaust gallery to the Canadian War Museum in the Canadian capital, Ottawa. This later morphed into an initiative to establish two museums, one for the Jewish Holocaust, one for other genocides and mass atrocities. Jewish-Canadian advocates strongly promoted the *Shoah* as "unique," both as a historical phenomenon and as a foundation for education about genocide and human-rights violations (see Chapter 6, pp. 353–355). Sheldon Howard of B'nai Brith, Canada argued in 2000 that the Holocaust should be "the central reference point" in any remembrance project. It was, said Howard, "the pinnacle" of the "crimes against humanity witnessed in the past 100 years," and "unique" in the "universal lessons" it taught.[45] In the end, it was a Canadian-Jewish media tycoon, Israel Asper, who offered to fund a Canadian Museum for Human Rights in the city, Winnipeg, where his Asper Foundation was based. Its executive director, Moe Levy, pledged that it would be a "museum for human rights, not the Holocaust," and would "be totally apolitical and antiseptic in terms of trying to preach a message of one kind of inhumanity over another." In 2008 the Canadian Museums Act was adjusted to include "the country's fifth national museum and the first outside Ottawa,"[46] and construction on the museum, now with mixed federal and foundation financing, began in downtown Winnipeg, Manitoba in April 2009. After numerous delays, and with the project still hounded by "controversy and protests," the CMHR opened its doors in September 2014.[47]

Throughout, the most voluble opposition to the museum's framing of holocaust and genocide arose from the Ukrainian-Canadians. In Canada and elsewhere, Ukrainian remembrance strategies vis-à-vis the Stalinist "terror-famine" of the 1930s (Chapter 5) are fascinating, though little-studied.

From the start, Ukrainian advocates have confronted a quandary posed by the centrality of the Holocaust to understandings of genocide and the kind of mega-atrocity that warrants recognition, commemoration, and some form of restitution even many decades later. Advocates sought to "graft" the Ukrainian onto the Holocaust in revealing ways. As with all such "memory work," there was also a contemporary political component. Ukrainians' genocidal experience at Soviet/Russian hands was deployed as a nation-building strategy in independent Ukraine (notably in its renewed confrontation with Russia), and as a binding cause of the global diaspora. The parallels with diaspora-Jewish politics and nation-building in Israel are apparent (see Chapter 6, pp. 349–353). It was no coincidence that the evocative name chosen for the famine-crime—the *Holodomor* ("hunger-extermination")—shared its first two syllables with the Holocaust. Equally revealing was the canonizing of a death toll, a strategic debate that nearly all such memory projects engage in, sometimes with a questionable inflationary bent. Poles, for example, settled on an iconic "six million" figure for their genocide at German hands, around the time that this became widely accepted as the human toll of the *Shoah*. This masked the fact that some three million of the victims were Jews—Poland, as we have seen, was at the epicenter of both the European Jewish population and the Nazi Judeocide—and the toll of ethnic Poles was likely significantly lower than three million.[48] Some Ukrainian advocates took this undignified strategy a step further, claiming that at least *seven* million of their people (Figure 14.8), even *ten million or more*,[49] had succumbed in the famine. (It is at least certain that the higher estimates of famine victims in 1932–1933 must include millions of non-Ukrainians—in the lower Volga, northern Caucasus, and especially Kazakhstan.[50] Their populations were decimated at levels comparable to or even exceeding those for Ukrainians: see the discussion in Chapter 5.) At times, such advocacy carried more than a whiff of Ukraine's entrenched anti-semitism, as with assertions that the *Holodomor* was "the real holocaust," or claims that a "Jewish mafia" was responsible (an echo of the "Jewish-Bolshevik" myth propounded by the Nazis; see Figures 1.7 and 13.9). Even mainstream advocates staunchly avoided mention of the extensive atrocities against Jews perpetrated by Ukrainian partisans of the Organization of Ukrainian Nationalists (OUN) and the Ukrainian Insurgent Army (UPA),[51] as well as the involvement of many Ukrainian individuals in the Nazi Holocaust, whether as camp personnel, auxiliaries to genocidal massacres, or denouncers of Jews in hiding.[52] Indeed, early activism by the Ukrainian Canadian Congress (UCC) focused on defending Ukrainian-Canadians who were sought for extradition to the Soviet Union and other countries for their alleged involvement in Holocaust atrocities. A focus on Ukrainian victims stifled mention of Ukrainian *génocidaires*, not only against Jews, but against ethnic Poles during the vicious war triggered by the Soviet occupation of eastern Poland (historically western Ukraine) in 1939–1941.

The mainstream Ukrainian Canadian Congress (UCC) generally adopted a wait-and-see attitude, but a breakaway faction, the UCCLA, took the "consistent view that the Asper plan was a Holocaust museum in disguise."[53] Their fears were confirmed by the exhibit plan put forward by the CMHR in 2008. The Jewish Holocaust was to occupy the museum's central gallery, with the Holodomor and other mass crimes "lumped" in a separate "mass atrocity gallery."[54] So it happened that when the nascent Canadian Museum for Human Rights held its first public meeting in

Figure 14.9 Advocates for recognition and commemoration of the Ukrainian *Holodomor* ("hunger-extermination") in 1932–1933 "grafted" their campaign onto remembrance strategies for the Jewish Holocaust, in part by alleging that the Stalinist famine took an even greater toll of human lives. As in this 2009 poster, the figure of "7,000,000" is regularly circulated, surpassing the iconic six-million figure for the Jewish Holocaust. Even death tolls reaching ten million or more are sometimes proclaimed. Such statistics can only be generated through (a) inflation and (b) incorporating millions of out-group victims. The tactic is distressingly common among groups seeking recognition and memorialization of their historical suffering.

Source: Poster by Leonid Denysenko/Wikimedia Commons.

December 2011, its staff was confronted by challenges and skepticism, most prominently from Ukrainian advocates:

> . . . There were shouts about why the museum's *Examining the Holocaust* gallery will be devoted almost entirely to the genocide of European Jews . . . The Ukrainian Canadian Civil Liberties Association (UCCLA) and Ukrainian Canadian Congress have previously raised concerns about the lack of a full exhibit to mark the Holodomor . . . "How did you concretely address some of these concerns that were raised by the UCC, regarding the . . . possibly too much concentration on the Holocaust, vis-a-vis the other tragedies of the world?," Ostap Hawaleshka, a Ukrainian-Canadian and retired professor asked museum officials . . . Museum CEO Stuart Murray responded by saying they are listening carefully to many groups and have done extensive consultation—and the process is still evolving. . . . Museum spokesperson Angela Cassie added the exhibition plan has changed significantly in response to concerns raised by the Ukrainian community, as well as other genocide-affected national groups, such as Rwandans and Armenians.[55]

Other constituencies vied for attention to their cause. Armenian-Canadians were particularly vocal about the need for an inclusive and comparative approach to modern genocides. Perhaps the most poignant criticisms, however, came from indigenous Canadians, the subjects and agents of Canada's most visible, and arguably influential, rights claims over the past quarter-century. The "history wars" over the museum occurred in tandem with restitution claims for the devastation wreaked by the residential-school system (RSS), and the broader Truth and Reconciliation process culminating in 2015, profiled in the final chapter (pp. 726–730). Indigenous advocates brought their own "uniqueness" claim to the discussion, and a powerful one, as is evident in Tricia E. Logan's critique of the CMHR declaration that it would not house permanent galleries for indigenous people, or others:

> In a theoretically impermanent institution, how do you reconcile the need for a permanent, prominent statement about the respected rights won and violated *on the very piece of land on which the museum stands?* Indeed a permanent statement is being made by the geographical presence of the institution. The Museum physically sits at the forks of the Red and Assiniboine rivers, which remains a deeply sacred space for First Nations and Métis* peoples in Canada. As such, I believe there is museum content that is not at all "changeable" or

---

* The mixed-race Métis are a separately-recognized Aboriginal people, concentrated in the fur-trade regions of initial indigenous–European contact around Hudson Bay, and spreading further west. Their twin uprisings against federal authority in the nineteenth century (the Red River Rebellion in Manitoba, 1869–1870, and the North West Rebellion in Saskatchewan, 1885) are touchstones in Canadian history, for mainstream and revisionist historians alike. See Tricia Logan, "Settler Colonialism in Canada and the Métis," *Journal of Genocide Research*, 17: 4 (2015), pp. 433–452.

fluid, insofar as the Museum is situated in a space that is rooted in Indigenous histories. These stories tell a narrative of rights that does not get changed out with curatorial or interpretive museum practice. . . . A 4,500-square-foot gallery on the Holocaust, placed at the heart of a human rights journey through the Museum, makes a significant statement in this "ongoing dialogue," insofar as it suggests Canada's primary connection to genocide is via the Holocaust.[56]

This was indeed the solution adopted by the Canadian Museum for Human Rights when it opened its doors in late 2014. At the time of writing, I had no personal impressions to offer. But a student and friend from Winnipeg, who requested anonymity, kindly reported to me on her visit to the CMHR in December 2015:

I think "weighting" the Holocaust as the all-encompassing genocide was reflected in the space. The Holocaust space was large, imposing, and stark (black and white). Very intricate, almost modernist architecture for the seating/theatre area. The rest of the genocides were separated by a lighter exhibit on human rights which led into a low-ceilinged genocide room. Different genocides were lined up in cubicles containing very few objects from the [genocidal] incidents. I found the objects weren't as emotive as the ones from the Holocaust exhibit, kind of like the museum took whatever they could get. The placards were a lot less comprehensive, simply because every genocide was contained in a small space that didn't allow for the journey that the Holocaust space had. Overall, it felt like an organized hodge-podge. Still highly emotional, but more passive in terms of what the museum-goer could do. . . . All of the Holocaust victims were covered in depth, with giant portraits of the various groups dominating the large space. All of structural and ideological aspects of the Holocaust were covered, so it seemed more vast and sinister than the genocides in the separate exhibit.

The writer also noted:

I think the exhibit on Canadian Human Rights and the exhibit on Residential Schools ("Indigenous Perspectives") make the CMHR less like a Holocaust museum overall. . . . Aside from the genocide floor, various human rights issues are focused on pretty evenly. A temporary exhibit with a residential school art installation was one of the most striking floors to me. I wish it was permanent.[57]

The debate continues, but the museum itself has been an unexpected "hit." The *Toronto Star* called it "the cultural good news story of the year" in December 2015: "Its target for annual attendance was 250,000, but in its first year it drew 400,000. Meanwhile, it has won international, national and regional awards." The New York-based *Travel and Leisure* magazine anointed it "one of the top five coolest destinations in the world." It was, said the *Toronto Star*, "a fairy-tale ending to a brutal set of obstacles, most conspicuously a vitriolic and long-running chorus of hostility."[58]

GENOCIDE DENIAL: MOTIVES AND STRATEGIES

Denial is the final stage of genocide, and an indispensable one from the viewpoint of the *génocidaires*. "The perpetrators of genocide dig up the mass graves, burn the bodies, try to cover up the evidence and intimidate the witnesses. They deny that they committed any crimes, and often blame what happened on the victims."[59] As Richard Hovannisian has written:

> Following the physical destruction of a people and their material culture, memory is all that is left and is targeted as the last victim. Complete annihilation of people requires the banishment of recollection and the suffocation of remembrance. Falsification, deception, and half-truths reduce what was to what may have been or perhaps what was not at all.[60]

The phenomenon of genocide denial is overwhelmingly associated with the Jewish Holocaust. Since this resurged in the public consciousness in the early 1960s, a diverse and interlinked network of Holocaust deniers has arisen. In Europe, a centuries-old tradition of anti-semitism (see Chapter 6) underlies their activities, which overlap with neo-Nazi violence against Jews and their property. In North America, the neo-Nazi element is also strong. In both "wings" of the denialist movement, however, academic figures—such as Arthur Butz in the US, Robert Faurisson in France, and David Irving in Great Britain (jailed for three years for Holocaust denial in Austria in 2006)[61]—have also sought to lend the enterprise a veneer of respectability.

We will consider specific denial strategies below, but before we do, it is important to stress that the Jewish Holocaust is not officially denied by any state or national elite (though denial is common intellectual currency in the Arab and Muslim worlds).[62] Thus, in the West at least, deniers of the Jewish catastrophe remain relatively marginal figures, with little access to the mainstream.

However, the broader phenomenon of genocide denial is far more deeply entrenched, often representing a societal consensus rather than a fringe position. Individual and collective narcissism (Chapter 10) plays a pivotal role. In many contexts, a denialist stance heads off "cognitive dissonance" between one's preferred view of self and country, and the uglier reality. There is also generally an element of material self-interest. Denial can pay well, since it fortifies the status quo and serves powerful and prosperous constituencies, both political and corporate. Positive rewards are combined with sanctions. Failure to deny (that is, a determination to acknowledge) may result in loss of employment, decreased social standing and career prospects, dismissal as a "kook" or a "radical," and so on.

Among the most common discourses of genocide denial are the following:

"Hardly anybody died." Reports of atrocities and mass killings are depicted as exaggerated and self-serving. (The fact that some reports *are* distorted and self-interested lends credibility to this strategy.) Photographic and video evidence is dismissed as bogus or staged. Gaps in physical evidence are exploited, particularly an absence of corpses. Where are the bodies of the Jews killed by the Nazis?

(Incinerated, conveniently for the deniers.)[63] Where are the bodies of the thousands of Kosovars supposedly killed by Serbs in 1999? (Buried on military and police bases, or dumped in rivers and down mineshafts, as it transpired.) When the genocides lie far in the past, obfuscation is easier. Genocides of indigenous peoples are especially subject to this form of denial. In many cases, the groups in question suffered near-total extermination, leaving few descendants and advocates to press the case for truth.

"*It was self-defense.*" "The onset of [genocidal] killing," wrote Jacques Sémelin, "almost always seems to involve this astounding sleight of hand that assimilates the destruction of civilians with a perfectly legitimate act of war. From that moment on, massacre becomes an act of self-defense."[64] Murdered civilians—especially adult males (Chapter 13)—are depicted as "rebels," "brigands," "partisans," "terrorists." The state and its allies are justified in eliminating them, though unfortunate "excesses" may occur. Deniers of the Armenian genocide, for example, play up the presence of armed elements and resistance among the Armenian population—even clearly defensive resistance. Likewise, deniers of Nazi genocide against Jews turn cartwheels to demonstrate "that *Weltjudentum* (world Jewry) had declared war on Germany in 1933, and the Nazis, as the ruling party of the nation, had simply reacted to the threat."[65] Jews were variously depicted as predatory capitalists, decadent cosmopolitans, and leaders of global communism. The organizers of the third canonical genocide of the twentieth century, in Rwanda, alleged that the assault on Tutsis was a legitimate response to armed invasion by Tutsi rebels based in Uganda, and the supposed machinations of a Tutsi "fifth column" in Rwanda itself.

Genocide may also be depicted as an act of *pre-emptive* self-defense, based on atrocities, actual or alleged, inflicted on the perpetrator group in the past—sometimes the very distant past. Semelin, for example, has explained Serbs' "insensitivit[y] to the suffering they caused" in the Balkan genocide of the 1990s in terms of their inability to perceive any but "their own woes, as a martyred people who had themselves been victims of 'genocide' during the Second World War." Former Serb president Biljana Plavsic, then on trial at the International Criminal Tribunal for the Former Yugoslavia (ICTY; see Chapter 15), acknowledged that the "obsession with no longer being victims transformed us into bullies"—and in some cases *génocidaires*.[66]

A sub-strategy of this discourse is the claim that **"*the violence was mutual.*"** Where genocides occur in a context of civil or international war, they can be depicted as part of generalized warfare, perhaps featuring atrocities on all sides. This strategy is standard among the deniers of genocides by Turks, Japanese, Serbs, Hutus, and West Pakistanis—to name just a few. In Australia, Keith Windschuttle used killings of whites by Aboriginals to denounce "The Myths of Frontier Massacres in Australian History."[67] (See also *"We* are the real victims," below.) Sometimes the deniers seem oblivious to the content of their claims, reflecting deeply-embedded stereotypes and genuine ignorance, rather than malicious intent—as with the CNN reporter who blithely referred to the world standing by and "watch[ing] Hutus and Tutsis kill each other" during the Rwandan genocide of 1994.[68]

"*It wasn't intentional.*" The difficulties of demonstrating and documenting genocidal intent are exploited to deny that genocide occurred. The utility of this strategy is enhanced where a longer causal chain underpins mass mortality. Thus, when diverse factors combine to cause death, or when supposedly "natural" elements such as disease and famine account for many or most deaths, a denialist discourse is especially appealing. It buttresses most denials of indigenous genocides, for example (see Chapter 3). Deniers of the Armenian and Jewish holocausts also contend that most deaths occurred from privations and afflictions that were inevitable, if regrettable, in a wartime context—in any case, not genocidal.

"There was no central direction." Frequently, states and their agents establish deniability by utilizing off-duty death squads, or employing freelance forces such as paramilitaries (as in Bosnia-Herzegovina and Darfur), criminal elements (e.g., the *chetes* in the Armenian genocide), and members of the targeted groups themselves (Jewish *kapos* in the Nazi death camps; Mayan peasants conscripted for genocide against Mayan populations of the Guatemalan highlands). State attempts to eliminate evidence may mean that documentation of central direction, as of genocidal intent, is scarce. Many deniers of the Jewish Holocaust emphasize the lack of a clear order from Hitler or his top associates to exterminate European Jews. Armenian genocide denial similarly centers on the supposed freelance status of those who carried out whatever atrocities are admitted to have occurred.

"There weren't that many people to begin with." Where demographic data provide support for claims of genocide, denialists will gravitate toward the lowest available figures for the targeted population, or invent new ones. The effect is to cast doubt on mortality statistics by downplaying the victims' demographic weight at the outbreak of genocide. This strategy is especially common in denials of genocide against indigenous peoples, as well as the Ottoman genocide of Christian minorities.

"It wasn't/isn't 'genocide,' because . . ." Here, the ambiguities of the UN Genocide Convention are exploited, and combined with the denial strategies already cited. Atrocious events do not qualify as "genocide" . . . because the victims were not members of one of the Convention's specified groups; because their deaths were unintended; because they were legitimate targets; because "only" specific sectors of the target group (e.g., "battle-age" men) were killed; because "war is hell"; and so on.

"We would never do that." Collective pathological narcissism (see Chapter 10) hinders recognition, or even conscious consideration, of genocidal culpability. When the state and its citizens consider themselves pure, peaceful, democratic, and law-abiding, responsibility for atrocity may be literally unthinkable. In Turkey, notes Taner Akçam, anyone "dar[ing] to speak about the Armenian Genocide . . . is aggressively attacked as a traitor, singled out for public condemnation and may even be put in prison."[69] In Australia, "the very mention of an Australian genocide is . . . appalling and galling and must be put aside," according to Colin Tatz. "A curious national belief is that simply being Australian, whether by birth or naturalisation, is sufficient inoculation against deviation from moral and righteous behaviour."[70] Comedian Rob Corddry parodied this mindset in the context of US abuses and atrocities at Abu Ghraib prison near Baghdad. "There's no question what took place in that prison was horrible," Corddry said on *The Daily Show*. "But the Arab world has to realize that the US shouldn't be judged on the actions

of a . . . well, we shouldn't be judged on actions. It's our principles that matter, our inspiring, abstract notions. Remember: just because torturing prisoners is something we did, doesn't mean it's something we *would* do."[71]

"*We are the real victims*." For deniers, the best defense is often a strong offense. With its "Day of Fallen Diplomats,"Turkey uses Armenian terrorist attacks against Turkish diplomatic staff to preempt attention to the Turkish genocide against Armenians. In the case of Germany and the Nazi Holocaust, there is a point at which a victim mentality concentrating on German suffering leads to the horrors that Germans inflicted, on Jews and others, being downgraded or denied. In the Balkans, a discourse of genocide was first deployed by Serb intellectuals promoting a nationalist-xenophobic project; the only "genocide" admitted was that against Serbs, whether by Croatians in the Second World War (which indeed occurred), or in Kosovo at the hands of the Albanian majority (which was a paranoid fantasy). Notably, this stress on victimhood provided powerful fuel for unleashing the genocides in the first place; the discussion of humiliation in Chapter 10 is worth recalling.

DENIAL AND FREE SPEECH

What are the acceptable limits of denialist discourse in a free society? Should *all* denial be suppressed? Should it be permitted in the interest of preserving vigorous debate in a liberal public sphere?

In recent years, many countries in the West have grappled with these questions. Varied approaches have been adopted, ranging from monitoring denialist discourse, to punitive measures including fines, imprisonment, and deportation. At the permissive end of the spectrum lies the United States. There, notorious deniers of the Jewish Holocaust, as well as neo-Nazi and Ku Klux Klan-style organizations, operate mostly unimpeded, albeit sometimes surveilled and infiltrated by government agents. A much harder line has been enforced in France and Canada. In France, Holocaust denier Robert Faurisson was stripped of his university teaching position and hauled before a court for denying that the Nazi gas chambers had existed. Eventually, in July 1981, the Paris Court of Appeals assessed "personal damages" against Faurisson, based on the likelihood "that his words would arouse in his very large audience feelings of contempt, of hatred and of violence towards the Jews in France."[72] In Canada, Alberta teacher Jim Keegstra "for twelve years . . . indoctrinated his students with Jewish conspiracy explanations of history . . . biased statements principally about Jews, but also about Catholics, Blacks, and others."[73] In 1982, Keegstra was dismissed from his job and, in 1984, charged with promoting racial hatred. In 1985, he was convicted, and sentenced to five months in jail and a $5,000 fine. The decision was overturned by the Alberta Court of Appeal, citing Canada's Charter of Rights and Freedoms, but Canada's Supreme Court delivered a seminal 1990 decision in Keegstra's case, ruling that hate speech was *not* constitutionally protected.[74]

Undoubtedly the most famous trial involving a genocide denier is the libel case brought in 2000 by David Irving, an amateur historian of some repute who nonetheless cast doubt and aspersions on the genocide of the Jews. Deborah Lipstadt accused Irving of genocide denial in her book *Denying the Holocaust*, referring to him as a "discredited" scholar and "one of the most dangerous spokespersons for Holocaust denial."[75] She also pointed to his links with neo-fascist figures and movements. Irving exploited Britain's loose libel laws to file a suit for defamation. The resulting trial became a *cause célèbre*, with prominent historians taking the stand to outline Irving's evasions and obfuscations of the historical evidence, as well as the character of his personal associations. The final, 350-page judgment by Judge Charles Gray cited Irving for nineteen specific misrepresentations, and contended that they were deliberate distortions to advance a denialist agenda. Irving's suit was dismissed, leaving him with a £2 million bill for legal costs—though he was subject to no legal sanction *per se*.

The spectrum of policies toward deniers, from permissive to prosecutory, is mirrored by the debate among genocide scholars and anti-genocide advocates. Those who call for punitive measures against deniers stress the link between denial and genocide, including future genocides, as well as the personal suffering that denial inflicts on a genocide's survivors and their descendants. This argument was made eloquently by Roger Smith, Eric Markusen, and Robert Jay Lifton, who held that

> denial of genocide [is] an egregious offense that warrants being regarded as a form of contribution to genocidal violence. Denial contributes to genocide in at least two ways. First of all, genocide does not end with its last human victim; denial continues the process, but if denial points to the past and the present, it also has implications for the future. By absolving the perpetrators of past genocides from responsibility for their actions and by obscuring the reality of genocide as a widely practiced form of state policy in the modern world, denial may increase the risk of future outbreaks of genocidal killing.

They especially condemned the actions of some professional scholars in bolstering various denial projects:

> Where scholars deny genocide, in the face of decisive evidence that it has occurred, they contribute to a false consciousness that can have the most dire reverberations. Their message, in effect, is: murderers did not really murder; victims were not really killed; mass murder requires no confrontation, no reflection, but should be ignored, glossed over. In this way scholars lend their considerable authority to the acceptance of this ultimate human crime. More than that, they encourage—indeed invite—a repetition of that crime from virtually any source in the immediate or distant future. By closing their minds to truth such scholars contribute to the deadly psychohistorical dynamic in which unopposed genocide begets new genocides.[76]

The opposing view does not dispute the corruption of scholarship that genocide denial represents. However, it rejects the authority of the state to punish "speech crimes"; it stresses the arbitrariness that governs *which* genocide denial is prohibited; and it calls for proactive engagement and public denunciation in place of censorship and prosecution. A leading exponent of such views is the linguistics scholar and political commentator Noam Chomsky, whose most bitter controversy revolves around a defense of the right of Robert Faurisson to air his denialist views. In an essay titled "Some Elementary Comments on the Rights of Freedom of Expression," published (without his prior knowledge) as a foreword to Faurisson's *Mémoire en défense*, Chomsky depicted calls to ban Faurisson from teaching, even to physically attack him, as in keeping with authoritarian traditions:

> Such attitudes are not uncommon. They are typical, for example, of American Communists and no doubt their counterparts elsewhere. Among people who have learned something from the 18th century (say, Voltaire) it is a truism, hardly deserving discussion, that the defense of the right of free expression is not restricted to ideas one approves of, and that it is precisely in the case of ideas found most offensive that these rights must be most vigorously defended. Advocacy of the right to express ideas that are generally approved is, quite obviously, a matter of no significance ... Even if Faurisson were to be a rabid anti-Semite and fanatic pro-Nazi ... this would have no bearing whatsoever on the legitimacy of the defense of his civil rights. On the contrary, it would make it all the more imperative to defend them.[77]

Each of these perspectives brings important ideas to the table. To expand on Smith *et al.*'s reasoning: in most societies, some speech is subject to legal sanction—libelous, threatening, and obscene speech, for instance. It can reasonably be asked whether genocide denial does not do greater harm to society, and pose a greater threat, than personal libel or dirty words. Does not genocide denial libel an entire people? And is the threat it poses not extreme, given that denial may sow the seeds of future genocides?

The case is a powerful one, and yet I find myself generally in agreement with Chomsky. Free speech *only* has meaning at the margins. Banning marginal discourses undermines liberal freedoms. Moreover, only a handful of deniers—principally those assailing the Jewish and Armenian genocides—have attracted controversy for their views. One wonders, as well, whether the names and views of people such as Irving, Faurisson, and Keegstra would be remotely as prominent if prosecutions and other measures had not been mounted against them.[78] (Indeed, it makes me queasy to print them here.) Deborah Lipstadt, for one, thinks not. The scholar who defended her work against David Irving's charge of libel told the BBC in 2006: "I am uncomfortable with imprisoning people for speech ... I don't find these laws efficacious. I think they turn Holocaust denial into forbidden fruit, and make it more attractive to people who want to toy with the system or challenge the system."[79] In my view, denialist individuals, and the initiatives they sponsor, are best confronted with a combination of monitoring, marginalization, and effective public refutation. Such refutation can be accomplished by visible and vocal denunciation, informed by conscientious reportage and scholarship, as well as by proactive campaigns in schools and media.

While genocide denial in the public sphere may be destructive, for genocide scholars and students its consequences may actually be productive. Professional deniers have spurred scholarship in areas that otherwise might not have attracted it.[80] Moreover, not all "denial" is malevolent. Whether a genocide framework should be applied in a given case is often a matter of lively *and legitimate* debate. In recent decades, the character and content of mass killing campaigns in Bosnia and Kosovo, Darfur, Biafra (Nigeria), East Timor, Guatemala, and Vietnam have been intensively analyzed and hotly disputed. I believe this is to be encouraged, even if I find some of the viewpoints disturbing and disheartening. Keeping denial of *all* genocides out of the realm of crime and punishment may be the price we pay for this vigorous exchange.[81]

FURTHER STUDY

Ian Buruma, *The Wages of Guilt: Memories of War in Germany and Japan.* London: Atlantic Books, 2009. Originally published in 1994, Buruma's book explores how World War Two's main aggressors came to terms with their past—or failed to.

Stanley Cohen, *States of Denial: Knowing about Atrocities and Suffering.* Cambridge: Polity Press, 2001. Insights into denial, and efforts to counter it, on both personal and societal levels.

Richard J. Evans, *Lying About Hitler: History, Holocaust, and the David Irving Trial.* New York: Basic Books, 2001. Brisk account of Irving's defamation suit, by a historian who served as a defense witness.

John R. Gillis, ed., *Commemorations: The Politics of National Identity.* Princeton, NJ: Princeton University Press, 1994. How collective memory shapes national identity.

Jeffrey Herf, *Divided Memory: The Nazi Past in the Two Germanys.* Cambridge, MA: Harvard University Press, 1997. Intricate rendering of Germany's "search for a usable past."

Herbert Hirsch, ed., *Genocide and the Politics of Memory: Studying Death to Preserve Life.* Chapel Hill, NC: University of North Carolina Press, 1995. Early and wide-ranging collection.

Richard G. Hovannisian, ed., *Remembrance and Denial: The Case of the Armenian Genocide.* Detroit, MI: Wayne State University Press, 1999. Armenian genocide denial and its place in collective memory.

Adam Jones, ed., *Evoking Genocide: Scholars and Activists Describe the Works That Shaped Their Lives.* Toronto, ON: The Key Publishing House Inc., 2009. Explores, in sixty mini-essays, how genocide was memorialized and interpreted in cultural works, and how those works in turn influenced genocide educators and anti-genocide advocates.

Edward T. Linethal and Tom Engelhardt, eds., *History Wars: The Enola Gay and Other Battles for the American Past.* New York: Holt, 1996. Vigorous, fair-minded essays on US historical controversies during the 1980s and early 1990s.

Deborah E. Lipstadt, *Denying the Holocaust: The Growing Assault on Truth and Memory.* New York: Plume, 1994. Survey of denial's exponents that prompted David Irving's failed legal action against Lipstadt.

David E. Lorey and William H. Beezley, eds., *Genocide, Collective Violence, and Popular Memory: The Politics of Remembrance in the Twentieth Century.* Wilmington, DE: Scholarly Resources, 2002. Still the best primer on genocide and memory.

Peter Novick, *The Holocaust in American Life*. Boston, MA: Mariner Books, 2000. Engaging exploration of how the Jewish Holocaust was remembered and deployed by American Jews and others.

George Orwell, *Nineteen Eighty-Four*. London: Penguin, 1983. Classic bleak satire of the manipulation of history and memory under totalitarianism.

Michael Shermer and Alex Grobman, *Denying History: Who Says the Holocaust Never Happened and Why Do They Say It?* (rev. edn). Berkeley, CA: University of California Press, 2000. Carefully-documented rebuttal of Holocaust deniers.

Jay Winter, *Sites of Memory, Sites of Mourning: The Great War in European Cultural History*. Cambridge: Canto, 1998. History, memory, and memorialization in post–First World War Europe.

John C. Zimmerman, *Holocaust Denial: Demographics, Testimonies and Ideologies*. Lanham, MD: University Press of America, 2000. Like Shermer (above), a systematic and effective counter to denialist claims.

NOTES

1 Stalin quoted in Simon Sebag Montefiore, *Stalin: The Court of the Red Tsar* (London: Phoenix, 2004), p. 142.
2 Elizabeth Jelin, "The Minefields of Memory," *NACLA Report on the Americas*, 32: 2 (September/October 1998), p. 25. Martha Minow wrote: "Memorials can name those who were killed; they can depict those who resisted and those who rescued. They can accord honor and confer heroic status; they can express shame, remorse, warning, shock. Devoting public space to memories of atrocities means devoting time and energy to decisions about what kinds of memories, images, and messages to embrace, critique, and resist . . . Vividly capturing and recasting memory, fights over monuments in the streets and in debates usefully disturb congealed memories and mark important junctions between the past and a newly invented present," Minow, *Between Vengeance and Forgiveness: Facing History after Genocide and Mass Violence* (Boston, MA: Beacon Press, 1998), pp. 138, 140.
3 Jelin, "The Minefields of Memory," pp. 26, 28.
4 For some nuanced and cautionary comments on public memory, see Jay Winter, "The Generation of Memory: Reflections on the 'Memory Boom' in Contemporary Historical Studies," *GHI Bulletin*, 27, www.ghi-dc.org/publications/ghipubs/bu/027/b27winterframe.html.
5 For text and a vivid photograph, see https://iconicphotos.wordpress.com/2009/05/25/warschauer-kniefall/.. "The event made Brandt widely unpopular in Germany, especially among conservatives and liberals but also many social democrats, and he was heavily criticized by the press for being unpatriotic . . . Eventually, [however,] even many Germans came to see it as a courageous and honorable decision."
6 Robert G. Moeller, "War Stories: The Search for a Usable Past in the Federal Republic of Germany," in David E. Lorey and William H. Beezley, eds., *Genocide, Collective Violence, and Popular Memory: The Politics of Remembrance in the Twentieth Century* (Wilmington, DE: Scholarly Resources, 2002), pp. 206, 211.
7 Alexander Wilde, "Irruptions of Memory: Expressive Politics in Chile's Transition to Democracy," in Lorey and Beezley, eds., *Genocide, Collective Violence, and Popular Memory*, p. 4.
8 Andreas Kluth, "Stumbling over the Past," *Intelligent Life*, May/June 2013, www.intelligentlifemagazine.com/content/places/andreas-kluth/stumbling-over-past. Quoted passages in the box text are drawn from this source except where indicated.

9 Lisa Lampert-Weissig, "The Vanished Stumbling Stones of Villingen," *Tablet*, June 3, 2015, www.tabletmag.com/jewish-news-and-politics/191167/vanished-stumbling-stones. As of December 2015, municipal authorities in Munich, responding to the accusations of "disrespect" pressed by some members of the city's Jewish community, still forbade the placing of *Stolpersteine*. See Joanna Slater, "Dispute Rises as Munich Continues Ban of Stumbling Stones Honouring Holocaust Victims," *The Globe and Mail*, December 6, 2015, www.theglobeandmail.com/news/world/dispute-rises-as-munich-bans-stumbling-stones-honouring-holocaust-victims/article27627683/.

10 Hoehne quoted in Ian Buruma, *The Wages of Guilt: Memories of War in Germany and Japan* (London: Atlantic Books, 2009), p. 88.

11 Quoted in Moeller, "War Stories," p. 210. On Bitburg, see also Jeffrey Herf, *Divided Memory: The Nazi Past in the Two Germanys* (Cambridge, MA: Harvard University Press, 1997), pp. 350–354.

12 For an incisive overview of the *Historikerstreit* and related debates, see A. Dirk Moses, *German Intellectuals and the Nazi Past* (Cambridge: Cambridge University Press, 2009).

13 The controversy, late in Grass's life, over his admitted membership (as an adolescent) in a Waffen-SS unit toward the end of the war, provided another opportunity for German soul-searching. See Neal Ascherson, "Günter Grass: The Man Who Broke the Silence," *The Guardian*, April 18, 2015, www.theguardian.com/books/2015/apr/18/gunter-grass-tributes-man-broke-silence.

14 Friedrich quoted in J.M. Coetzee, "Victims" (review of Günter Grass, *Crabwalk*), *New York Review of Books*, June 12, 2003.

15 See the companion volume for the exhibition: Hamburg Institute for Social Research, *The German Army and Genocide: Crimes Against War Prisoners, Jews, and Other Civilians in the East, 1939–1944* (New York: New Press, 1999). An excellent documentary on the controversy surrounding the *Wehrmacht* exhibition is *The Unknown Soldier*, dir. Michael Verhoeven (First Run Features, 2008).

16 Moeller, "War Stories," p. 216. See also Nicholas Kulish, "Facing German Suffering, and Not Looking Away," *The New York Times*, February 26, 2009, www.nytimes.com/2009/02/27/world/europe/27poland.html.

17 William Underwood, "WWII Forced Labor Issue Dogs Aso, Japanese Firms," *The Japan Times*, October 28, 2008, http://search.japantimes.co.jp/cgi-bin/fl20081028zg.html. By contrast, as Christopher Reed notes, "Germany has chosen a path of reconciliation by proactively settling wartime forced labor accounts. The 'Remembrance, Responsibility and the Future' Foundation was established in 2000, with funding of some $6 billion provided by the German federal government and more than 6,500 industrial enterprises. As reparations payments drew to a close in late 2005, about 1.6 million forced labor victims or their heirs had received individual apologies and symbolic compensation of up to $10,000. Similarly, the Austrian Reconciliation Fund recently finished paying out nearly $350 million to 132,000 workers forced to toil for the Nazi war machine in that country, or their families" (Reed, "Family Skeletons: Japan's Foreign Minister and Forced Labor by Koreans and Allied POWs," *The Asia-Pacific Journal: Japan Focus, May 6, 2006, http://apjjf.org/-Christopher-Reed/1627/article.html*).

18 The "comfort women" experienced treatment that "was almost universally barbaric. They were forced to have sex with as many as 50 men a day, some were tied to beds with their legs open, and many were beaten by drunken soldiers." Velisarios Kattoulas, "No Comfort for the Women," *Far Eastern Economic Review*, March 15, 2001. According to George Hicks, "The comfort system consisted of the legalised military rape of subject women on a scale—and over a period of time—previously unknown in history." George Hicks, *The Comfort Women: Japan's Brutal Regime of Enforced Prostitution in the Second World War* (New York: W.W. Norton, 1994), pp. 16–17.

19 David McNeill, "Korea's 'Comfort Women': The Slaves' Revolt," *The Independent*, April 24, 2008; Norimitsu Onishi, "Japan's 'Atonement' to Former Sex Slaves Stirs Anger," *The New York Times*, April 25, 2007.

20 Norimitsu Onishi, "Abe Rejects Japan's Files on War Sex," *The New York Times*, March 2, 2007, www.nytimes.com/2007/03/02/world/asia/02japan.html.

21 Choe Sang-Hun, "Japan and South Korea Settle Dispute Over Wartime 'Comfort Women,'" The New York Times, December 28, 2015, www.nytimes.com/2015/12/29/world/asia/comfort-women-south-korea-japan.html.

22 For an overview of the controversy surrounding the Yasukuni shrine, see John Breen, ed., *Yasukuni, the War Dead and the Struggle for Japan's Past* (New York: Columbia University Press, 2008); and Buruma, *The Wages of Guilt*, pp. 219–228.

23 Christopher Reed, "When the Victors Memorialize Their Massacres: Koizumi and the Rape of Nanking," *Counterpunch*, October 19, 2005.

24 Chisaki Watanabe, "Suit Over Japan War Shrine Visits Rejected," Associated Press dispatch in *The Guardian*, September 29, 2005.

25 Miwa Suzuki, "Japan's Leader Shuns Controversial War Shrine," *The Sydney Morning Herald*, August 16, 2007.

26 Jonathan Soble, "Shinzo Abe Stays Away as Japanese Lawmakers Visit Contentious Yasukuni Shrine," *The New York Times*, October 20, 2015, www.nytimes.com/2015/10/21/world/asia/japan-yasukuni-shrine-shinzo-abe.html.

27 Brian Padden, "Abe Expresses 'Deepest Remorse' on WWII Anniversary," *VOA News*, August 14, 2015, www.voanews.com/content/abe-expresses-deepest-remorse-on-wwii-70th-anniversary/2917748.html; Jonathan Soble, "Emperor Akihito Expresses 'Deep Remorse' for Japan's Role in World War II," *The New York Times*, August 15, 2015, www.nytimes.com/2015/08/16/world/asia/emperor-akihito-expresses-deep-remorse-for-japans-role-in-world-war-ii.html.

28 Soble, "Shinzo Abe Stays Away."

29 Mizushima quoted in David McNeill, "Propaganda War is Declared in Cinemas over Nanking Massacre," *The Independent*, December 4, 2007, www.independent.co.uk/news/world/asia/propaganda-war-is-declared-in-cinemas-over-nanking-massacre-762821.html; and Justin McCurry, "China Angered by Nanjing Massacre Film," *The Guardian*, January 25, 2007, www.guardian.co.uk/film/2007/jan/25/china.world.

30 Tamogami quoted in Blaine Harden, "WWII Apologists Persist Despite Japanese Policy," *The Washington Post*, November 3, 2008.

31 An essential source is Antonius C.G.M. Robben's *Political Violence and Trauma in Argentina* (Philadelphia, PA: University of Pennsylvania Press, 2005). Two English-language overviews are Martin Edwin Andersen, *Dossier Secreto: Argentina's Desaparecidos and the Myth of the "Dirty War"* (Boulder, CO: Westview Press, 1993), and Paul H. Lewis, *Guerrillas and Generals: The "Dirty War" in Argentina* (Westport, CT: Praeger Publishers, 2002). A concise early summary from a genocide studies perspective is "The Disappearances: Mass Killing in Argentina," in Ervin Staub, *The Roots of Evil: The Origins of Genocide and Other Group Violence* (Cambridge: Cambridge University Press, 1989), pp. 210–231. The case has become a central one, predictably, for the "Argentine school" of genocide studies, and the contributions of Daniel Feierstein and others (see his index entry). The kidnapping of infants was the subject of an Oscar-winning Argentine film, *The Official Story* (1985).

32 The Falkland Islands are known as Islas Malvinas to Argentines.

33 Amnesty International, "Argentina: The Military Juntas and Human Rights," in William L. Hewitt, ed., *Defining the Horrific: Readings on Genocide and Holocaust in the Twentieth Century* (Upper Saddle River, NJ: Pearson, 2004), p. 247.

34 In November 2003, together with a small group of other foreign scholars, I attended what was probably the first international conference on genocide in South America, held at the University of Buenos Aires. At a guess, 75 or 80 percent of the presentations dealt with the "genocide in Argentina" under military rule. Without exception, all the presenters took it as a given that the events in question had constituted genocide. This

would be much more controversial among genocide scholars in the West, given the limited number of victims, and the fact that the violence was targeted against alleged members of a political group. In conversation with some of the Argentine scholars, though, it became clear to me that not only did they consider the term valid, but they regarded its application as *vital to memorializing the events and validating victims' suffering*.

35 Larry Rohter, "Debate Rises in Argentina on Museum of Abuses," *The New York Times*, April 19, 2004. Unless otherwise specified, all quotes in this discussion of the Museum of Memory are drawn from Rohter's article.

36 Quoted in ibid.

37 However, *junta* leader General Videla was jailed in June 1997 for the kidnapping of children, which was held to lie beyond the boundaries of the *punto final*.

38 As noted in Chapter 15, Chile's outgoing president at the time of writing, Michele Bachelet, was a political prisoner under General Augusto Pinochet's military regime (1973–1990).

39 "Police Probe Death of Witness in Argentina Human Rights Trial," *CNN.com*, October 20, 2009, www.cnn.com/2009/WORLD/americas/10/20/argentina.witness/index.html; Tom Hennigan, "'Dirty War' Torture Witness Goes Missing," *The Times*, September 28, 2006, www.thetimes.co.uk/tto/news/world/americas/article2000588.ece.

40 Alfonso Daniels, "Argentina's Dirty War: The Museum of Horrors," *The Telegraph*, May 17, 2008, www.telegraph.co.uk/culture/3673470/Argentinas-dirty-war-the-museum-of-horrors.html.

41 "Argentina Tackles 'Dirty War' Crimes at Epic Trial," *France24.com*, November 29, 2012, www.france24.com/en/20121128-argentina-dirty-war-trial-death-flights-buenos-aires-justice-military-junta. See also "Largest Trial of 'Dirty War' Crimes Starts in Argentina," *BBC Online*, November 28, 2012, www.bbc.com/news/world-latin-america-20523955.

42 *BBC Online*, "Largest Trial."

43 Alexandre Peyrille, "Argentina Daily Shocks with Call to Scrap 'Dirty War' Trials," Agence France-Presse dispatch on *Yahoo! News*, November 24, 2015, http://news.yahoo.com/argentina-daily-shocks-call-scrap-dirty-war-trials-225650894.html.

44 David MacDonald defines history wars as "debates over collective memory within a national territory, between those separated by generational, ethnic, ideological or other divisions deemed to be of fundamental importance to members of the groups involved." MacDonald, "Canada's History Wars: Indigenous Genocide and Public Memory in the United States, Australia and Canada," *Journal of Genocide Research*, 17: 4 (2015), p. 412.

45 Howard quoted in A. Dirk Moses, "The Canadian Museum for Human Rights: The 'Uniqueness of the Holocaust' and the Question of Genocide," *Journal of Genocide Research*, 14: 2 (2012), p. 222.

46 Moses, "The Canadian Museum for Human Rights," p. 224.

47 Joseph Brean, "Canadian Museum for Human Rights Opens Amidst Controversy and Protests," *National Post*, September 19, 2014, http://news.nationalpost.com/news/canada/canadian-museum-for-human-rights-opens-amidst-controversy-and-protests.

48 Some feminist advocates and others have likewise propounded a figure of *nine million women* killed in the European witch-hunts of the early modern period. In fact, the total death toll of the hunts was more probably 40–50,000, and is extremely unlikely to have exceeded 100,000. About a quarter of the executed "witches" were men. See the excerpts from Wolfgang Behringer, "Neun Millionen Hexen: Entstehung, Tradition und Kritik: Eines Populären Mythos," at https://archive.is/Y9Tp#selection-409.0–417.55; Gendercide Watch/Adam Jones, "Case Study: The European Witch-Hunts, c. 1450–1750," www.gendercide.org/case_witchhunts.html; Adam Jones, "Witch-Hunts and Genocide" (review of Wolfgang Behringer, *Witches and Witch-Hunts: A Global History*), in Jones, *The Scourge of Genocide: Essays and Reflections* (London: Routledge, 2013), pp. 239–243.

49 See, e.g., the poster produced by the League of Ukrainian Canadians, "Holodomor Genocide by Famine," at http://faminegenocide.com/kuryliw/hires/page1.jpg, and the image by the Ukrainian Genocide Famine Foundation—USA, www.ukrainiangenocide.org/sitebuilder/images/holodomor_0–903x1180.jpg.

50 The point is well made in Mark Levene, *The Crisis of Genocide, Vol. 1: Devastation: The European Rimlands 1912–1938* (Oxford: Oxford University Press, 2013), p. 336.

51 See J.P., "Eastern Approaches: The Tragic Massacre in Volyn Remembered," *The Economist*, July 15, 2013, www.economist.com/blogs/easternapproaches/2013/07/polish-ukrainian-relations: ". . . Both communist and nationalist elements among the Ukrainians called for ethnic cleansing of Poles from Volyn, even though the Soviet mass starvation, known as the Holodomor, or death by hunger, had just cost millions of Ukrainian lives across the border. 'It was worse than a crime, it was a stupidity,' [Ukrainian historian Yarislav] Hrytsak says. 'You had a terrain that was ready to explode.' What followed was genocide, he says, but it must be viewed within the context of a pyramid of genocidal acts committed on the territory of Ukraine in the 1930s and 1940s, starting from the Holocaust and ending [with] Akcja Wisla [Operation Vistula], the forced deportation of tens of thousands of Ukrainians" by Poland's postwar, Soviet-installed authorities.

52 For more on "the memory politics which has led Ukrainian-Canadian lobby groups to ignore or whitewash Ukrainian atrocities against the Jews," see Karyn Ball and Per Anders Rudling, "The Underbelly of Canadian Multiculturalism: Holocaust Obfuscation and Envy in the Debate about the Canadian Museum for Human Rights," *Holocaust Studies*, 20: 3 (Winter 2014), pp. 33–80 (quote from p. 35).

53 Moses, "The Canadian Museum for Human Rights," p. 224. As the factional politics played out, the UCC called for "a Holodomor gallery that bore comparison with the Holocaust one, while the UCCLA advocated twelve galleries that are 'thematic, comparative and inclusive,' in which no genocide predominated; where the UCC wanted to elevate the Holodomor to the Holocaust's lofty status, the UCCLA wanted to bring the Holocaust down to the same level" (Moses, p. 229).

54 Ibid., pp. 228–229.

55 CBC News release quoted in ibid., pp. 215–216.

56 Tricia E. Logan, "Memory, Erasure, and National Myth," in Andrew Woolford, Jeff Benvenuto, and Alexander Laban Hinton, eds., *Colonial Genocide in Indigenous North America* (Durham, NC: Duke University Press, 2014), pp. 157–158.

57 Personal communications, January 1, 2016.

58 Martin Knelman, "Canadian Museum for Human Rights is a Hit," *The Star*, December 12, 2015, www.thestar.com/entertainment/2015/12/12/canadian-museum-for-human-rights-is-a-hit.html.

59 Gregory H. Stanton, "Eight Stages of Genocide," www.genocidewatch.org/aboutgenocide/8stagesofgenocide.html.

60 Richard G. Hovannisian, "Denial of the Armenian Genocide in Comparison with Holocaust Denial," in Hovannisian, ed., *Remembrance and Denial: The Case of the Armenian Genocide* (Detroit, MI: Wayne State University Press, 1999), p. 202.

61 See Ian Traynor, "Irving Jailed for Denying Holocaust," *The Guardian*, February 21, 2006, www.guardian.co.uk/world/2006/feb/21/thefarright.highereducation.

62 For a summary, with many examples, see Anti-Defamation League, "Holocaust Denial in the Middle East: The Latest Anti-Israel Propaganda Theme," www.adl.org/holocaust/denial_ME/Holocaust_Denial_Mid_East_prt.pdf. For a consideration of the broad trends in the Arab world, see Meir Litvak and Esther Webman, *From Empathy to Denial: Arab Responses to the Holocaust* (London: Hurst and Company, 2009).

63 Thus, in the context of the "Holocaust by Bullets" just discussed, German Reichsfuhrer Heinrich Himmler issued an order in July 1942 that "all mass graves [on the eastern front, mostly filled with Jewish victims] were to be opened and the corpses burned. In addition the ashes were to be disposed of in such a way that it would be impossible at some future time to calculate the number of corpses burned." A similar

procedure was followed at the Auschwitz-Birkenau death camp in Poland: "Elevators carried the corpses to the ground floor [of the gas chamber/crematorium complex], where several ovens reduced them to ashes. After the grinding of bones in special mills, the ashes were used as fertilizer in the nearby fields, dumped in local forests, or tossed into the river, nearby." Both passages from Saul Friedlander, *The Years of Extermination: Nazi Germany and the Jews* (New York: HarperCollins, 2007), pp. 404, 503.

64 Jacques Sémelin, *Purify and Destroy: The Political Uses of Massacre and Genocide* (New York: Columbia University Press, 2007), p. 248.

65 Michael Shermer and Alex Grobman, *Denying History: Who Says the Holocaust Never Happened and Why Do They Say It?* (Berkeley, CA: University of California Press, 2002), p. 40.

66 Ibid., p. 213. The point of *reductio ad absurdum* was reached with the Kosovo conflict of 1998–1999, during which Serb acts of genocide against Kosovar Albanians were justified by the Albanian "occupation" of historic Serb lands. Serb extremists traced the alleged trend back no fewer than six centuries, to the Battle of Kosovo Polje in 1389, and used it to justify the first public accusations of "genocide" occurring in a contemporary Balkans context—that is, by Kosovar Albanians against Serbs! (See Chapter 8.) For Sémelin, such tropes serve as a reminder that "the word [genocide] is used as much as a symbolic shield to claim victim status for one's people, as a sword raised against one's deadly enemy" (p. 313).

67 For a summary and debunking, see Ben Kiernan, "Cover-up and Denial of Genocide: Australia, the USA, East Timor, and the Aborigines," *Critical Asian Studies*, 34: 2 (2002), pp. 180–182.

68 CNN International broadcast, December 31, 2004.

69 Taner Akçam, *From Empire to Republic: Turkish Nationalism and the Armenian Genocide* (London: Zed Books, 2004), p. 209.

70 Colin Tatz, *With Intent to Destroy: Reflecting on Genocide* (London: Verso, 2003), p. 137.

71 Corddry quoted in Alan Shapiro, "American Treatment of Iraqi and Afghan Prisoners: An Introduction," *TeachableMoment.org*, http://www.teachablemoment.org/high/prisoners.html. From another *Daily Show* alumnus, Stephen Colbert, we get the concept of "truthiness": "an epoch-defining coinage for the belief that if something feels true in your gut, then it is true." James Poniewozik, "Stephen Colbert's Night Vision," *TIME*, September 7–14, 2015, http://time.com/4012855/stephen-colberts-night-vision/.

72 Paris court judgment cited in Shermer and Grobman, *Denying History*, pp. 10–11. In 2007, the European Union adopted hate-crime legislation that "urges EU nations to impose prison sentences of up to three years for individuals convicted of denying genocide, such as the mass killing of Jews during World War II or the massacres in Rwanda in 1994. The rules would require countries to prosecute offenders in connection with killings that have been recognized as genocides by the International Criminal Court in The Hague." Molly Moore, "EU Ministers Agree on Rules against Hate Crimes, Racism," *The Washington Post*, April 20, 2007.

73 David Bercuson and Douglas Wertheimer, quoted in Luke McNamara, "Criminalising Racial Hatred: Learning from the Canadian Experience," *Australian Journal of Human Rights*, 1: 1 (1994). Available online at www.austlii.edu.au/au/journals/AJHR/1994/13.html.

74 See McNamara, "Criminalising Racial Hatred." The case of Ernst Zündel, a German-born denier of the Jewish Holocaust, has also generated controversy. Zündel became "a political hot potato to immigration officials in Canada and the United States." Moving from Canada to the US when the Canadian government denied his application for citizenship, Zündel was then deported back to Canada, and then on to Germany, where in 2007 he was convicted on "14 counts of inciting racial hatred and for denying that the Nazis killed six million Jews during World War II." See "Jail for German Holocaust Denier," *BBC Online*, February 15, 2007, http://news.bbc.co.uk/2/hi/europe/6364951.stm. He was freed in March 2010.

75 Richard J. Evans, *Lying About Hitler: History, Holocaust, and the David Irving Trial* (New York: Basic Books, 2001), p. 6. Evans was one of the historians who testified at the trial; his book provides an excellent overview of the proceedings.

76 Roger W. Smith, Eric Markusen, and Robert Jay Lifton, "Professional Ethics and the Denial of the Armenian Genocide," in Hovannisian, ed., *Remembrance and Denial*, pp. 287, 289.

77 Noam Chomsky, "Some Elementary Comments on the Rights of Freedom of Expression," www.chomsky.info/articles/19801011.htm. Much controversy attached to Chomsky's comment in this essay that "As far as I can determine, he [Faurisson] is a relatively apolitical liberal of some sort."

78 After the David Irving decision, historian Andrew Roberts claimed the judgment against Irving was at best a partial victory, since "the free publicity that this trial has generated for him and his views has been worth far more than could ever have been bought for the amount of the costs." Quoted in Evans, *Lying About Hitler*, p. 235.

79 Lipstadt quoted in "'Irving? Let the Guy Go Home,'" *BBC Online*, January 4, 2006, http://news.bbc.co.uk/1/hi/uk/4578534.stm. See also Michael Shermer, "Free Speech, Even If It Hurts," *The Los Angeles Times*, February 26, 2006; Ben MacIntyre, "We Can't Deny the Deniers," *The Times*, January 20, 2006.

80 According to Colin Tatz, "for all the company they keep, and for all their outpourings, these deniers assist rather than hinder genocide and Holocaust research," in part by "prompt[ing] studies by men and women of eminence . . . who would otherwise not have written on genocide." Tatz, *With Intent to Destroy*, pp. 139–140.

81 For a discussion of responsible versus malicious denial of a genocide framework in the Cambodian case, see Ben Kiernan, "Bringing the Khmer Rouge to Justice," *Human Rights Review*, 1: 3 (2000), pp. 92–108. In fact, Jörg Menzel's article, "Justice Delayed or Too Late for Justice? The Khmer Rouge Tribunal and the Cambodian 'Genocide,' 1975–79," *Journal of Genocide Research*, 9: 2 (2007), pp. 215–233, strongly questions the "genocide" appellation for the Cambodian case, as the quote marks in the title suggest. "It is . . . far from clear if the criteria of genocide, as established under current international criminal law, are met by the crimes of the potential candidates of the ECCC . . . The genocide question may therefore be relevant more on a dogmatic and a psychological level" (ibid., pp. 222–223). I would consider Menzel's critique a "responsible" one in Kiernan's terms; yet it is notable that his skeptical and quite dismissive framing appeared in the leading journal of comparative genocide studies.

CHAPTER 15

Justice, Truth, and Redress

What can justice mean when genocide is the issue?

Terrence Des Pres

The legal strictures against genocide constitute *jus cogens:* they are among the laws "accepted and recognized by the international community of States as a whole from which no derogation is permitted." *Jus cogens* is associated with the principle of *universal jurisdiction (quasi delicta juris gentium),* which "applies to a limited number of crimes for which any State, even absent a personal or territorial link with the offence, is entitled to try the offender."[1]

There is theory, however, and there is practice. After the UN Convention came into force in 1951, genocide was all but ignored in international law. In the international arena, the word was commonly deployed for propaganda purposes. For example, the resurgence of interest in the Jewish Holocaust, and the roughly contemporary rise of Israel to major-power status, made "genocide" an attractive verbal weapon for Palestinians and their Arab allies. National-level trials occasionally utilized the legal concept, as with Israel's prosecution of Adolf Eichmann in 1961 (at least initially), and Ethiopia's proceedings against members of the Dergue regime (see below). Yet overall, a conspiracy of silence prevailed in diplomatic quarters and at the United Nations. Diplomatic norms militated against such grave accusations, while states' bloody hands meant that there was always a danger that allegations could rebound on the accuser, through the defense of *tu quoque*—"a plea that the adversary committed similar atrocities."[2]

Despite this passivity, the twentieth century *did* produce revolutionary new forms of international justice. Formal mechanisms ranged from the humanitarian law of the Hague Conventions (1899, 1907) and Geneva Conventions (culminating in 1949); to war crimes tribunals at Nuremberg and for Yugoslavia, Rwanda, and Sierra Leone; and most recently to an International Criminal Court (ICC) with universal jurisdiction though, alas, not yet universal membership. These were accompanied by less formal institutions, such as the "truth commissions" mounted under both national and international aegis, and investigative bodies that may blow the whistle on genocide, whether past, present, or incipient. Such efforts also feature substantial public involvement, especially by religious and human rights NGOs, academics, and legal professionals—a phenomenon that can be traced back to the international campaigns against slavery and the Congo "rubber terror" in the nineteenth and early twentieth centuries.

This penultimate chapter explores the interrelation of justice, truth-seeking, and redress as they have evolved both nationally and internationally.

LEIPZIG, CONSTANTINOPLE, NUREMBERG, TOKYO

> Persons charged with Genocide or any of the other acts enumerated in Article III shall be tried by a competent tribunal of the State in the territory of which the act was committed, or by such international penal tribunal as may have jurisdiction with respect to those Contracting Parties which shall have accepted its jurisdiction.
>
> UN Genocide Convention, Article V

The move toward tribunals for war crimes and "crimes against humanity" reflected the growing institutionalization and codification of humanitarian instruments during the latter half of the nineteenth century. This was evident in the formative efforts of Henri Dunand and his International Committee of the Red Cross, founded in 1864. The Red Cross was a pioneering institution in addressing suffering that offends the human conscience. Leaders were also becoming aware of "crimes against humanity" (Box 15.1), albeit selectively. Consider British politician William Gladstone's 1870 fulmination against Ottoman atrocities in the Balkans:

> Certain it is that a new law of nations is gradually taking hold of the mind, and coming to sway the practice, of the world; a law which recognises independence, which frowns upon aggression, which favours the pacific, not the bloody settlement of disputes, which aims at permanent and not temporary adjustments; above all, which recognises, as a *tribunal* of paramount authority, the general *judgment of civilised mankind*?[3]

Much the same speech could have been given for the drafting of the Rome Statute of the International Criminal Court (1998), suggesting that Gladstone was overly optimistic in his assessment. But his generation did witness substantial advances in human freedom. The abolition of slavery in the United States (1861) and Brazil (1888) were high-water marks. They were accompanied by campaigns against the Congo "rubber terror," pogroms against Russian Jews, and early Ottoman massacres of Armenians (1894–1896), presaging the genocide of Christian minorities during World War One.

At century's end, Russian Tsar Nicholas convened an international conference on war prevention at The Hague in Holland. This led to two seminal conventions, in 1899 and 1907, that placed limits on "legitimate" methods of warfare, including bans on civilian bombardments and the use of poison gas.[4] All sides abrogated the agreements only a few years later, during the First World War (1914–1918). But the new framings shaped the postwar world—including the 1927 Protocol against chemical and biological warfare, which remains in force.

As part of the punitive peace imposed on Germany at Versailles, a few desultory trials of alleged war criminals took place before German courts at Leipzig. They ended in fiasco, with the Allies divided, and German opposition to the initiative effectively unchallenged. A similar dynamic prevailed in the trials that Allied occupiers imposed on Turkey, described in Chapter 4.[5]

More high-profile and successful were the international tribunals at Nuremberg and Tokyo following the Second World War.[6] Trials were by no means foreordained as a strategy for dealing with German and Japanese war criminals. Intense debates on this topic occurred among members of the Allied coalition during 1943–1945. Both Winston Churchill and Joseph Stalin pushed for summary executions of those in the Nazi leadership strata.[7] Franklin Roosevelt considered the wholesale demilitarization, deindustrialization, and dismemberment of Germany (the so-called "Morgenthau Plan"). This was in keeping with public opinion in the Allied countries: few people viewed tribunals as the optimal way of dealing with enemy war crimes.

However, a legal process was finally settled upon in both the German and Japanese cases. This was, indisputably, a major advance in international jurisprudence. Nuremberg featured "the first official mention of genocide in an international legal setting," as all the German defendants were accused of "conduct[ing] deliberate and systematic genocide, viz., the extermination of racial and national groups, against the civilian populations of certain occupied territories."[8] Raphael Lemkin's tireless lobbying reaped dividends, though, as noted in Chapter 1, "genocide" formed no part of the Nuremberg verdicts. (Nor could it have, since it was not at the time a crime under international law.)[9]

Both tribunals were flawed. Leaders were tried only for crimes committed in wartime. Nazi actions against the Jews prior to September 1, 1939, for example, were absent from the Nuremberg indictments. Nazi crimes against Jews, Roma, and other groups were downplayed, while charges of waging aggressive war were stressed. Japanese atrocities against Chinese and other Asian civilians were similarly underemphasized, by contrast with allegations of the murderous abuse of Allied prisoners-of-war.

BOX 15.1 NUREMBERG: BENJAMIN FERENCZ, THE *EINSATZGRUPPEN*, AND THE STORY OF COURTROOM 600

Figure 15.1 Benjamin Ferencz at a press conference in Courtroom 600 of the Palace of Justice, Nuremberg, Germany.

Source: Author's photo, August 2012.

A muggy summer day in Nuremberg, Germany. I was in a small, still-functioning courtroom—but a veritable arena of history, only recently opened to the public. Courtroom 600 of Nuremberg's Palace of Justice was where the most famous war-crimes trials in history were held—where Nazi leaders including Hermann Göring, Wilhelm Keitel, and Albert Speer were tried in 1946. They were usually convicted, sometimes sentenced to death (Göring, Keitel), sometimes treated quite leniently (Speer, Hitler's personal architect and later Minister of Production for the "total war" period of fanatic Nazi war-making, including the working to death of uncounted slave laborers—sentenced to twenty years and destined for further global celebrity).[10] As I sat there, I noticed a film crew setting up its equipment. Then a small, spry, very elderly man strolled into the room. He chatted briefly with the filmmakers, and wandered out. Who was that, I wondered? The woman at the ticket booth enlightened me. "That's Benjamin Ferencz. He was the chief prosecutor in the *Einsatzgruppen* trial in the forties. They're making a documentary about his life, and they've invited him back to the courtroom where the trial took place."

My jaw dropped. I ran upstairs to the museum exhibition, found the man, and shook his hand. Later I had the chance to sit in on Ferencz's press conference, and watch him hold forth in the very room where he had confronted some of the most evil and efficient mass killers of the twentieth century. The film being shot that day, *A Man Can Make a Difference*, was released in 2015.

The *Einsatzgruppen*, and the police-battalion units seconded to them, have become iconic in Holocaust and genocide studies, through works such as Christopher Browning's *Ordinary Men* and Patrick Desbois's *The Holocaust by Bullets* (see Further Study, ch. 6). They were the principal perpetrators of the first phase of the Jewish Holocaust, in which well over one million Polish and Soviet Jews were murdered by point-blank rifle and pistol fire in 1941 and early 1942, before the first gas vans and chambers became operational at Belzec and Chelmno. Their numbers were small—only about 3,000 men in four widely-dispersed *kommando* units. But they were relentlessly efficient at genocide—and at record-keeping.

```
- 2 -

Einsatzgruppe C.

Standort  K i e w .

    Das Sonderkommando 4a hat in Zusammenarbeit mit
Gruppenstab und zwei Kommandos des Polizei-Regiments
Süd am 29. und 30.9.41 in Kiew  33.771 Juden exekutiert.

Einsatzgruppe D.

Standort  N i k o l a j e w .

    Die Freimachung des Gebietes durch die Kommandos
von Juden und kommunistischen Elementen wurde fort-
gesetzt. Insbesondere wurden in der Berichtszeit die
Städte Nikolajew und Cherson von Juden freigemacht
und noch vorhandene Funktionäre entsprechend behan-
delt. Vom 16.9. bis 30.9. wurden 22.467 Juden und
Kommunisten exekutiert. Gesamtzahl  35.782. Ermitt-
lungen ergaben wiederum, dass sich die hohen kommuni-
stischen Funktionäre fast überall in Sicherheit ge-
bracht hatten. Gefasst wurden in erster Linie führende
Partisanen oder Führer von Sabotagetrupps.

    Ermittlungstätigkeit über Partisanengruppen wurden
fortgesetzt. Fahndungen ergaben, dass Sowjets schon
seit Jahren in Versammlungen nicht nur zum Eintritt
in die Rote Armee, sondern auch zur Bildung von Par-
tisanengruppen aufforderten. Kampf der Partisanen
und ihre Ausbildung waren wichtige Schulungsthemen.
Rekrutierung zunächst freiwillig, nach Ausbruch der
Kampfhandlungen wurden Aushebungen ähnlich wie zu
Baukompanien auch für Partisanengruppen von Männern
im wehrpflichtigen Alter vorgenommen. Aufteilung in
Dreier-, Fünfer- und Zehner-Gruppen sollte rasches
und sicheres Arbeiten ermöglichen. Es besteht der Ein-
druck, dass Ausbreitung des Partisanenkriegs dadurch
vermindert, dass höhere Partisanenführer vielfach ge-
flohen und Initiative der einzelnen Angehörigen durch
jahrzehntelange Erziehung zur Unselbständigkeit und
das Warten auf Anweisung weithin erloschen ist.
```

Figure 15.2 Initial page of the Nazi *Einsatzgruppen* report confirming the genocidal massacre of 33,771 Jews at the Babi Yar ravine outside Kiev, Ukraine, on September 29–30, 1941 (see also photo essay, photo 4). A trove of such reports enabled the Allies to mount a second major set of Nuremberg trials, targeting key *Einsatzgruppen* commanders and killers, prosecuted by Benjamin Ferencz.

Source: Holocaust Research Project.

For the first Nuremberg trials of the senior Nazi criminals, prosecutors undertook a rigorous sifting of the documentary spoor left by the most rigorously bureaucratic *génocidaires* in history. It was during this time that a chilling trove of *Einsatzgruppen* documents was uncovered. They were reports to headquarters from the field, "highly detailed, indicating exactly how many 'Bolsheviks,' 'Jews,' and 'Gypsies' they killed, including the dates of killings and their locations."[11] The person who found the motherlode, Fred Burin, was a researcher for a 26-year-old, Hungarian-born lawyer from New York. Benjamin Ferencz had served with General George Patton's army invading Europe. He returned to the US at the end of 1946, but with his Harvard Law training, German language skills, and all-around tenacity, he was quickly recalled to Berlin to serve on the legal team of Telford Taylor, the US chief prosecutor for the Nuremberg trials.

When Ferencz laid eyes on the *Einsatzgruppen* documents, he could scarcely believe their contents. "The reports went on for almost two years," wrote Michael Bazyler and Frank Tuerkheimer. "When Ferencz started to total up the number of persons murdered reported in these documents he stopped at one million and flew to

Figure 15.3 Benjamin Ferencz in his mid-twenties, during the *Einsatzgruppen* trial in Courtroom 600 in 1947–1948.

Source: United States Holocaust Memorial Museum (www.ushmm.org).

Nuremberg. There he proposed to Taylor that an additional trial be added to those already planned."[12] The result was what media dubbed "the biggest murder trial in history," and the second (after Nuremberg's main proceedings) to deploy the new concept of *genocide* in the indictment, referencing "a systematic program . . . aimed at the destruction of foreign nations and ethnic groups by murderous extermination." As Hilary Earl notes in her absorbing monograph, the *Einsatzgruppen* trial was also "the only Nuremberg war crimes trial that dealt exclusively with the Final Solution to the Jewish Question," that is, the Holocaust (Chapter 6).[13]

The trial began in September 1947. The preeminent defendant was Otto Ohlendorf, commander of *Einsatzgruppe* D. This seemingly suave figure had testified at

Figure 15.4 Defendants during proceedings in the *Einsatzgruppen* trial, January 1, 1948. At left in the first row is Otto Ohlenhdorf, who admitted orchestrating the murder of tens of thousands of Jewish civilians in the Nazi-occupied east, and expressed no regret for his crimes. Ohlendorf and three others were hanged, but many of those convicted had their sentences commuted, and were released after just a few years. As with the Constantinople trials after World War One, considerations of *Realpolitik*—in this case, the claimed need to integrate Germany into NATO and democratic Europe—soon derailed the quest for justice.

Source: Photo by unknown US Signal Corps photographer/Wikimedia Commons.

the initial Nuremberg trials, "calmly describ[ing] his responsibility for the murder of ninety thousand civilians. He had reviewed the field reports and was certain that his numbers were accurate."[14] The discovery of the documents changed that, and led to Ohlendorf being tried alongside twenty-one accused perpetrators, all of them accused of directly participating in acts of murder, as well as broader exterminatory conspiracies. "Astonishingly Ohlendorf thought he was acting humanely in circumscribing the manner in which his victims were killed. He stated that he would not permit his men to bash the heads of infants against hard surfaces, but rather had his men instruct mothers to hold their children close to their chests so that one bullet through the head of the child would kill both the child and mother."[15]

Ferencz secured the conviction of all trial defendants, and the death penalty against fourteen. Four of them, including Ohlendorf, were hanged. But already the political winds were shifting. The Allied occupiers were working to build up West Germany as a buttress against communism. "Denazification" and justice-seeking procedures were seen as unnecessarily provocative, and best left to German national jurisdiction. After the initial executions, none further were carried out. "By mid-1958, the remaining sixteen defendants were either paroled or released to spend the balance of their lives in freedom." When Ferencz read of the release of three of the killers in December 1951, he wrote acerbically to former prosecutor Taylor, noting that one of the "Einsatzgruppen boys, Schubert . . . confessed to personally supervising the execution of about 800 Jews in a humane manner to avoid the moral strain on the execution squad. You may recall that the deadline for cleaning up Simferopol [in Crimea, Ukraine] was Christmas 1941 and that Schubert managed to kill all the Jews by then. So for Christmas ten years later he goes Scot free. Who says there is no Santa Klaus?"[16]

The dissipating of the momentum for justice and punishment of the *Einsatzgruppen* killers hardened in Ferencz a resolve similar to Raphael Lemkin's: to create a fresh legal institution, in this case an International Criminal Court. Ferencz made this, and the jurisprudence surrounding the international crime of aggression, the cornerstone of his life. His 1975 book, *Defining International Aggression: The Search for World Peace*, first made the case for a world court to try genocide and crimes against humanity.[17] (Ferencz had used the word "genocide" at various points in the *Einsatzgruppen* trial, most prominently in the indictment. But since the UN Convention did not become law until 1951, none of the Nuremberg defendants could be formally tried for it. He met Raphael Lemkin at Nuremberg, and remembered him as a somewhat wild-eyed and even "crazy" character. Lemkin had, after all, recently learned of the murder of dozens of his family members in the Holocaust.)[18]

When the International Criminal Court finally tried its first case, against Congolese militia leader Thomas Lubanga, Benjamin Ferencz was invited to deliver the closing statement for the prosecution, in August 2011.[19] The following year, Lubanga was convicted of war crimes and sentenced to fourteen years in the ICC's cells at The Hague. Ferencz continues to thrive, aged 96 at the time of writing.[20]

The long-established principle of *nullum crimen sine lege*—no crime without an accompanying law—was implemented in "an extremely loose and controversial" way at Nuremberg. Leaders were tried for crimes that had not formally existed when they were committed.[21] In addition, prosecutors at both the Nuremberg and Tokyo tribunals avoided charging Germans and Japanese with atrocities that the Allies had also inflicted. Thus, while indiscriminate bombardment of civilians was long established as a core war crime, it could not be prosecuted without providing the accused with a ready-made *tu quoque* defense. Even so, an Indian judge at Tokyo, Rahadbinod Pal, dissented from the majority verdict, labeling the trial a sham for its inattention to the Allies' own crimes.[22] In one case—that of unrestricted submarine warfare—the charges manifestly *did* overlap with Allied practice. Here, German Admiral Karl Dönitz's *tu quoque* defense was successful, leading to his acquittal, though Dönitz was convicted on "counts . . . [of] crimes against peace and war crimes—and sentenced to 10 years in prison."[23]

For the Tokyo trials, the Allies did not prosecute Emperor Hirohito, the man who "had personally approved all his country's barbaric military ventures" before and during the Second World War. They allowed him to remain on the Japanese throne, albeit de-deified.[24] Nor was Hirohito the only accused war criminal allowed to evade justice. The US was particularly interested in military technology, including biological weapons. Thus, Japanese scientists associated with the Unit 731 biological experiments—which led, among other things, to the release of live plague bacilli over Chinese cities—were granted immunity from prosecution, in return for sharing their research and expertise with the Americans. In Europe, police and security forces were deemed vital to both sides in the emerging Cold War struggle, regardless of the role they had played in fascist persecutions. Soviet occupiers, for instance, incorporated Nazi-era personnel wholesale into the new Stasi security force of East Germany.

The trials were victor's justice, but they were also "groundbreaking," "perhaps the most important war crimes tribunal in history," in the estimation of legal scholar David Crowe, who calls Nuremberg a "transformative trial in history."[25] It established "two central precedents: that of individual criminal responsibility, and that of the universal jurisdiction over crimes against humanity."[26] Out of twenty-four indictments, two were dropped and three defendants acquitted; another seven were imprisoned and not executed. (In the Tokyo proceedings, seven defendants were sentenced to death, sixteen to life in prison, and two others to lighter terms.) There is also no discounting the bonanza that the tribunals represented for historical scholarship and the documentation that underpins it. Alan Bullock called Nuremberg, with its bounty of Nazi documents on public display, "an absolutely unqualified wonder . . . the greatest coup in history for historians."[27]

THE INTERNATIONAL CRIMINAL TRIBUNALS: YUGOSLAVIA AND RWANDA

It is one of history's ironies that the International Criminal Tribunal for the Former Yugoslavia (ICTY) was created to deflect accusations of Western complacency in the face of genocide.[28] In spring 1992, with war raging in Bosnia, voices were raised for the establishment of a UN-sponsored tribunal to try the perpetrators of atrocities. In May 1993, the Security Council created the ICTY at The Hague (hence, "the Hague tribunal"). For some time following, this was as far as the West was willing to go. The Balkan wars continued for another three years, with the worst single atrocity occurring near their end (the Srebrenica massacre of July 1995). The tribunal's creation did not prevent a new eruption of conflict in Kosovo in 1998–1999.

Following the Dayton peace agreement of 1996, the ICTY process gradually gathered steam. The unwillingness of occupying forces to seize indicted individuals, for fear of destabilizing the transition process, gave way to a more assertive attitude. The pace of arrests and prosecutions picked up substantially. With growing cooperation from Croatian authorities, more than half of the ICTY's indicted figures were in custody by 2001. In that year, the process climaxed with the extraordinary transfer of former Yugoslav President Slobodan Milosevic to the tribunal. "For the first time in human history, a head of state was brought to international legal accountability for crimes committed as a result of his rule."[29] Though Milosevic died before a conviction could be rendered, by 2009 his partner in crime, Bosnian Serb president Radovan Karadzic, was gazing dolefully from the dock (Figure 8.6, p. 448), en route to being convicted for genocide at Srebrenica and other crimes.

Unlike the ICTR for perpetrators of atrocity crimes in Rwanda, the ICTY won measured praise for its impartiality. The tribunal's first conviction was issued against a Croatian (albeit one who served with Serb forces). Indictments of Croatian General Ante Gotovina and Kosovo prime minister Ranush Haradinaj helped to balance the emphasis on Serb crimes against Bosnian Muslims, Croats, and Kosovar Albanians. As with the Nuremberg trials, it was a victory for "transparency," in Paul Mojzes's estimation:

> The court slowly confronted the populations of the various states with the undeniable truth of what was secretly or under false pretenses done in their name—that, indeed, many of their heroes had innocent blood on their hands. The voluminous documentation that runs into the hundreds of thousands of pages and videos, as well as the televised transmission of the trials, have convinced many that it was not merely "an evil time" but that "evil people" were in charge and that events could have been very different had these individuals made better choices.[30]

However, the ICTY was criticized for ruling out war crimes prosecutions of NATO leaders of the Kosovo war, accused of attacks on civilian targets and other breaches of international law.[31] Serbs and their allies also protested the treatment of Bosniak militia leader Naser Oric, whose forces "destroyed about fifty Serb villages" in the prelude to the 1995 genocide, massacring and expelling Serbs in the process, "all done from the 'safe haven' [of] Srebrenica, that was supposed to have been disarmed." Oric was indicted and arrested by the ICTY, but released on grounds of insufficient proof, despite the fact that "Dutch researchers and filmed evidence attest to his prior systematic killing of all Serbs he could lay hands on."[32]

With the Hague tribunal in place, the UN could hardly avoid establishing a tribunal for the Rwandan genocide of 1994. The International Criminal Tribunal for Rwanda (ICTR) was housed at Arusha, Tanzania, where the abortive 1993 peace agreements had been signed (Chapter 9). The ICTR's gears ground painfully slowly, however. Understaffed and underfunded, it was prone to allegations that it focused exclusively on Hutu killers of Tutsis, with no consideration of Tutsi reprisal killings of Hutus.[33] Its operations also appeared distorted by the more extensive genocide trials in Rwanda. These imposed the death penalty, while ICTR proceedings did not, leading to the paradox that *génocidaires* could escape execution at the ICTR, while their underlings could be (and were) sentenced to death by Rwandan judges.[34] In Gérard Prunier's scathing 2009 assessment, the Rwanda tribunal

> combined three different evils: it was an embodiment of the worst aspects of UN bureaucratic inefficiency; a muted, closed arena for jousting over all the unacknowledged political contradictions of the genocide; and a swamp of nepotistic and corrupt practices. . . . The result was that, whereas it had taken the Nuremberg Tribunal one year (from November 1945 to November 1946) to judge twenty-four Nazis and hang ten, the ICTR had managed to carry out only twenty procedures in ten years at a cost of around $700 million.[35]

On December 31, 2015, "after 21 years, 93 cases and $2 billion" in expenditures,[36] the ICTR wrapped up its operations. News reports spoke of a final squabble over its legacy—specifically, the destiny of the huge archives it had compiled over the two decades of its existence. As with the Nuremberg document haul, it was expected that "the ICTR's archives will prove an indispensable resource to students, scholars, historians, and journalists hoping to establish a detailed and accurate account" of the 1994 holocaust. The Tutsi-dominated RPF government in Rwanda considered itself the natural inheritor of the archives, and of the broader legacy of the tribunal. "After all, this is the history of the people of Rwanda and not that of a now-extinct tribunal. It was Rwandans who lived these crimes and who undoubtedly deserve ownership over the documents which spell out, in harrowing detail, the forensic and factual truths behind" the genocide. Who could object?

But "pertinent fears" existed that another agenda underpinned the Rwandan government's eagerness for control over the archives. Mark Kersten wrote that the ICTR "is in possession of substantial evidence relating to crimes perpetrated by the [Paul] Kagame-led Rwandan Patriotic Front (RPF) during the 1994 Genocide—evidence that it has never used for prosecutions." This "ongoing threat" is one that the Kagame regime cannot counter by "hunting down, intimidating, and assassinating political figures opposed [to] the regime." (See Chapter 16, pp. 775–777, for more on the RPF government in post-genocide Rwanda.) Any archival evidence implicating the RPF in atrocities might be destroyed or otherwise suppressed if it fell into the Rwandan government's hands.

The issue would remain unresolved for the time being. The archives were to be housed at "the tribunal's residual mechanism, the so-called Mechanism for International Criminal Tribunals," also based in Arusha.[37] According to *The New York Times*,

> The Mechanism, as United Nations officials call it, will continue to run an office in Arusha, but it will be about a tenth of the size of the tribunal at its height. The Mechanism has been preparing for this transition for several years.

It will also track residual issues from the United Nations court for the former Yugoslavia when it closes, most likely in late 2017.[38]

Juridical contributions

Archival/historical contributions of the Nuremberg variety would, then, be a significant aspect of the Rwandan and Yugoslav tribunals. But at least as significant are the contributions of these trial proceedings to interpreting and sharpening the international law of genocide and crimes against humanity. Some examples:

- *Jurisdictional issues.* For decades, applications of international humanitarian law were impeded by the difficulty of determining which legal instruments could be imposed on sovereign states, and when—in peacetime, or solely in war? In civil wars, or only international ones? These matters are now largely resolved. In its "exhaustive analysis of customary and conventional international humanitarian law," the Hague tribunal concluded by decisively "severing . . . the category of crimes against humanity [including genocide] from any requirement of a connection to international wars, or indeed to any state of conflict."[39] In the estimation of legal scholar Christopher Rudolph, this ICTY precedent "opened the door to international adjudication of internal conflicts."[40] It was seized upon by the Arusha tribunal in extending relevant international law to a "civil conflict" (the Rwanda genocide). The precedent has become a touchstone for advocates of universal jurisdiction in cases of genocide and other crimes against humanity.
- *The concept of a victim group.* Many have criticized the UN Genocide Convention's exclusion of political and other potential victim groups. Moreover, the four core groups that the Convention *does* recognize—"national, ethnical, racial, and religious"—are notoriously difficult to define and distinguish "as such." Confronted with genocide in Rwanda, where populations sharing most of the usual ethnic markers—language, religion, a common history—descended into savage intercommunal killing, the ICTR chose to define an ethnic group as "one whose members share a common language and culture; or, a group which distinguishes itself as such (self-identification); or, *a group identified as such by others, including perpetrators of the crimes (identification by others).*"[41] Identities may now be *imputed* to a collectivity, as well as avowed by one (see also Chapter 1, note 83).
- *Gender and genocide.* According to Steven Ratner and Jason Abrams, the ICTY's "indictments and jurisprudence have highlighted the role of sexual violence in the Balkan conflict and more clearly defined the status of such offenses in international criminal law."[42] For instance, in the Celibici case, the ICTY ruled that rape could constitute torture. The ICTR went further still. With the Akayesu decision of 1998, the Arusha tribunal, "in one of its significant innovations, defined rape as a form of genocide, in that it constitutes serious bodily or mental harm in accordance with article II(b) of the [UN]

Convention."[43] Rape was also depicted as a form of "preventing births within the group," both physically and through inflicting psychological trauma on women.[44] From both perspectives, female rape victims are now viewed as victims in their own right, rather than as a medium through which dishonor and dislocation are visited upon a family or community. This new sensitivity, "a significant advance in international jurisprudence,"[45] reflects decades of successful feminist mobilization around the issue of rape, including groundbreaking analyses of rape in war and genocide.[46] Neither the ICTY nor the ICTR has accompanied these advances with systematic attention to rape and sexual violence against males, especially in detention centers and prison camps. The ICTY tribunal reacted with unease to forays on the subject, while the ICTR has ignored it altogether.[47] However, the tribunals did make one essential contribution to legal understandings of gendercidal atrocities against men. In 2001, Bosnian Serb General Radislav Krstic became the first person to be convicted by the ICTY of aiding and abetting genocide. Krstic's lawyers had argued that because "only" adult males were killed at Srebrenica, the strategy was not genocidal against the community as a whole. In its 2004 verdict on Krstic's appeal, the court rejected these arguments, contending that selective killing of males constituted destruction of the Bosnian-Muslim population "in part," and this was sufficient to characterize the slaughter as genocide.[48]

BOX 15.2 "GENOCIDE" VS. "CRIMES AGAINST HUMANITY"

Figure 15.5 The International Criminal Court building in The Hague, Netherlands.

Source: Photo by Vincent van Zeijst/Wikimedia Commons.

The concept of "crimes against humanity" predates that of genocide. It was first used in an international context in 1915. As the Ottoman genocide against Christian minorities raged (see Chapter 4), the Allies of the Triple Entente—Russia, France, and Great Britain—gathered to issue a statement of protest and concern. The proposed Russian wording condemned "crimes . . . against Christianity and civilization," but the other Allies felt this could bring yet more persecution upon the ravaged Christian populations of Anatolia. Accordingly, an agreement was struck to change the text to denounce instead crimes "against humanity and civilization."

Thus was born one of the most potent concepts of human rights and, eventually, of international law. The Nuremberg tribunal of 1945–1946 employed the language of crimes against humanity, along with "crimes against peace" and "war crimes," to prosecute Nazi war criminals for acts that included "murder, extermination, enslavement, deportation, and other inhumane acts committed against any civilian population, before or during the war . . ." The Rome Statute of the International Criminal Court, adopted in 1998, added the crimes of torture, "rape, sexual slavery, enforced prostitution, forced pregnancy, enforced sterilization, or any other form of sexual violence of comparable gravity"; "persecution against any identifiable group or collectivity on political, racial, national, ethnic, cultural, religious, gender . . . or other grounds"; "forced disappearance of persons"; and "the crime of apartheid." It also emphasized that the "other inhumane acts" referenced at Nuremberg consisted of those "of a similar character [to those cited] intentionally causing great suffering, or serious injury to body or to mental or physical health."[49]

For genocide scholars and students, the areas of conceptual crossover and divergence with the UN Genocide Convention are worth noting. Crimes against humanity are characterized by two main requisites: they must be "widespread or systematic," and they must be committed in the course of an attack "directed against any civilian population" (Rome Statute). Neither of these requirements is found in the Genocide Convention, though in practical application and prosecution, genocide has generally been viewed as targeting civilians (or at least non-combatants). The "widespread" scale and "systematic" character of atrocities likewise supply important evidence that a campaign of genocide is underway.

Importantly, the "murder" and "extermination" provisions of crimes against humanity legislation do *not* require that the civilian victims be members of a particular national, ethnic, racial, or religious collectivity, as the Genocide Convention does. Moreover, the Rome Statute's prohibition against "persecution" of "identifiable group[s]" references a wider range of collectivities than does the Convention, including "political," "cultural," and "gender" groups.

There is an intriguing overlap between the "extermination" provisions of crimes against humanity legislation and Article 2(c) of the Genocide Convention, which bans "deliberately inflicting on the group conditions of life calculated to bring about its physical destruction in whole or in part." The Rome Statute defines "extermination" in similar, at times identical, language: it is "the intentional inflic-tion of conditions of life, inter alia [among other things] the deprivation of access to food and medicine, calculated to bring about the destruction of part of the popula-tion." Like Article 2(c), therefore, "extermination" emphasizes *indirect* destruction through denial of the means of subsistence, especially "food and medicine." Fami-nogenic crimes (see Figure 2.2, p. 96), as well as certain strategies of blockade and ghettoization, can either be considered genocidal under international law (when directed against members of one of the groups designated in the Convention), or exterminatory under crimes against humanity provisions (so long as they are "wide-spread or systematic" and target a civilian population).

In international-legal practice, crimes against humanity after Nuremberg faded into the background—as indeed did the Genocide Convention after it entered into law in 1951. When mass killing and other crimes erupted in the Balkans, Rwanda, and elsewhere in the 1990s, it was allegations of genocide which cap-tured the imagination of publics, political leaders, and legal specialists—in part because the interethnic dimension of the killing was so pronounced. However, prosecutors at the Yugoslavia and Rwanda tribunals—and at those that have fol-lowed—quickly ran up against limitations and ambiguities in the Genocide Con-vention, most notably its requirement that *intent to destroy a particular group* be demonstrated. Not only does crimes against humanity legislation incorporate a much wider range of crimes (notably including torture, forcible deportation, and sexual assault), but a prosecutor need only demonstrate that acts were intention-ally inflicted against civilians, rather than a designated group.[50] If she or he *can* so demonstrate, then the punishment imposed on the perpetrator—usually life imprisonment or incarceration for decades—will likely be similar to that imposed for genocide.[51]

The result has been a subtle but noticeable shift in international tribunals away from genocide and toward crimes against humanity as the preferred legal framework. This was prominently displayed in the International Criminal Court's indictment of Sudanese president Omar al-Bashir in 2008 (as well as a former Sudanese interior minister and *Janjaweed* militia leader) for crimes allegedly committed in the Darfur region of western Sudan (see Box 9a). Prosecutors requested an indictment for genocide, along with war crimes and crimes against humanity. But the ICC's pre-trial chamber at first demurred: "the material provided by the Prosecution in sup-port of its application for a warrant of arrest failed to provide reasonable grounds to believe that the Government of Sudan acted with specific intent to destroy, in whole or in part, the Fur, Masalit and Zaghawa groups" of Darfur.[52] (On appeal, however, the charge was added to the indictment in 2010.) The former Liberian leader and warlord, Charles Taylor, was similarly tried and convicted by the UN-sponsored Special Court for Sierra Leone in 2010 for war crimes and crimes against humanity—but not for genocide (see further below). Likewise with the ICC's cases against Congolese and Ugandan warlords, and the Kenyan president and deputy president, Uhuru Kenyatta and William Ruto.

The trend might be expected to grow in coming years. In some ways, this strikes me as an important validation of a concept which has generally been sidelined by the recent emphasis on genocide. "Crimes against humanity" is, on its own terms, a revolutionary notion. It suggests that the atrocities in question target not only the proximate victim, but the entire human collective and its core values. It is thus an elegant and rather moving encapsulation of the tendency toward universalism and cosmopolitanism, from which ideas of "human rights" derive.

The growing prominence of crimes against humanity in legal and public discourse also points to something I have long sensed: that the most significant deployment of "genocide" may *not* be as a legal-prosecutorial device, but as an intellectual concept and—recognizing the term's unequaled rhetorical power—an advocacy tool to arouse public concern, shame perpetrators, and press for intervention.[53] This may also free the term from its unnecessarily restrictive framing in the UN Genocide Convention, with its limited target groups and high evidentiary requirement of genocidal intent.

Readers interested in the concept of crimes against humanity are invited to consult my short 2008 book, *Crimes Against Humanity: A Beginner's Guide* (Oneworld Publications).

NATIONAL TRIALS

Prosecution of genocide and other crimes at a national rather than international level carries certain advantages. Mechanisms for indictment, prosecution, and adjudication usually exist, at least in name: this is a definitional feature of the modern state. Moreover, in countries where genocide and crimes against humanity have been committed, the matter is deeply personal:

> Where trials take place in the country where the offenses occurred, the entire process becomes more deeply connected with the society, providing it with the potential to create a strong psychological and deterrent effect on the population. This factor, combined with the greater access to evidence, witnesses, victims, and perpetrators, gives such tribunals a significant potential advantage over international tribunals.[54]

Unfortunately, perpetration of genocide on a national territory often correlates with underdeveloped and compromised legal institutions. Thus, the capacity for administering justice may be sorely lacking. In Ethiopia, for instance, President Meles Zenawi's government charged more than 5,000 representatives of the brutal Dergue dictatorship with offenses that included crimes against humanity and genocide; but these "highly ambitious" prosecutions suffered from a "judicial system [that was] weak and lacking any tradition of independence."[55] Rwanda's formal post-genocide trials, as distinct from the *gacaca* experiment (see below), aroused strong international criticism for their selective and sometimes shambolic character.

National trials can also arouse national sentiment, to the detriment of the proceedings. This derailed the tribunals at Leipzig and Constantinople after the First World War. Even contemporary, advanced legal systems may be unduly swayed by such sentiment. Israel, for example, mishandled the trial of John Demjanjuk, a US citizen extradited on charges of having served as a brutal guard ("Ivan the Terrible") at the Treblinka death camp. According to Geoffrey Robertson, some Israelis "wanted so badly to convict Demjanjuk that three experienced judges ignored exculpatory evidence and presided over an outrageously unfair show trial," sentencing the prisoner to death. Only when incontrovertible proof of mistaken identity was submitted at the appeal stage was Demjanjuk "grudgingly" cleared.[56]

In addition to Ethiopia's proceedings against the Dergue and Israel's against Demjanjuk, some major national trials for war crimes and crimes against humanity include:

- Poland's numerous trials of leading and subordinate Nazis. Result: the conviction and frequently execution of, inter alia, Hans Frank (head of the Nazis' murderous "General Government" in occupied Poland), and Rudolf Höss and Amon Göth (commanders of the Auschwitz-Birkenau death camp and Krakow–Plaszow slave-labor camps).[57]
- Proceedings against thousands of accused war criminals in Germany after World War Two, following on the Nuremberg tribunal but conducted by German courts. Result: minimal "denazification," with most former Nazi functionaries left unprosecuted.
- Israel's abduction and trial of leading Nazi bureaucrat Adolf Eichmann (1960–1961). Result: Eichmann's conviction and execution (1962).[58]
- Argentina's prosecution and incarceration, in the mid-1980s, of leaders of the former military *junta*. Result: five leaders convicted and jailed, but pardoned several years later; renewed prosecutions in the 2000s as immunity is lifted (see Chapter 14).
- Trials of accused *génocidaires* in Rwanda. Result: some trials and executions, general chaos, and the introduction of less formal *gacaca* proceedings (see below).
- The trials in post-2003 Iraq of Saddam Hussein and several of his henchmen for genocide against Shias and Kurds (Box 4a). Result: Saddam and his cousin, Ali Hassan al-Majid ("Chemical Ali"), convicted and hanged; others on death row.

Domestic legislation on genocide is sometimes intriguing for its application of the Genocide Convention. Incorporation of the Convention into national law can be restrictive, based on "reservations" that are often self-serving.[59] But domestic framings can also be expansive and inclusive, perhaps charting a course for

Figure 15.6 "Adolf Eichmann in the yard of his cell at Ayalon Prison in Israel, 1961." Israeli agents abducted Eichmann in Argentina, where he had fled at war's end after supervising the extermination of Hungarian Jews in 1944. He was tried in Jerusalem in 1961 for "crimes against the Jewish people," and hanged at Ramla prison in May 1962.

Source: Israeli Government Press Office (GPO)/Flickr/Wikimedia Commons.

developments at the international level. This is especially notable in the case of designated victim groups for genocide. Bangladesh—with memories of the 1971 genocide still fresh (Box 8a)—added political groups to the Convention definition, as did Costa Rica in 1992 and Panama in 1993. Peru includes social groups, while Finland adds "a comparable group of people" to the Convention's core list of collectivities.[60] Another distinctive example is Cambodia, where, in light of the Khmer Rouge's strategies, genocide was defined in a Decree Law of July 1979 as including "planned massacres of groups of innocent people; expulsion of inhabitants of cities and villages in order to concentrate them and force them to do hard labour in conditions leading to their physical and mental destruction; wiping out religion; [and] destroying political, cultural and social structures and family and social relations."[61]

THE "MIXED TRIBUNALS": CAMBODIA AND SIERRA LEONE

The tribunals established for Cambodia and the West African nation of Sierra Leone provide an innovative "mixed" model that combines national and international representation. The trendsetter is Cambodia, where the model emerged after hard bargaining between the United Nations and the Cambodian government. The UN—supported in this by human rights NGOs in Cambodia and abroad—declared the country's post-genocide legal system incapable of administering justice. Not only was the system ramshackle and underfunded, the argument ran, but it was vulnerable to intervention and control by the authoritarian Hun Sen government. Government representatives, by contrast, stressed the importance of homegrown justice. After tortuous twists and turns a compromise was reached, and a UN–Cambodia Agreement was signed in June 2003. According to Tom Fawthrop and Helen Jarvis, the mixed tribunal was "a carefully crafted structure designed to provide sufficient checks and balances. International jurists, lawyers and judges will occupy key roles as the co-prosecutor, co-investigating judge and two out of five trial court judges, and must be a party to conviction or exoneration of any accused."[62]

For a summary of the proceedings of the Extraordinary Chambers in the Courts of Cambodia through to early 2016, see pp. 413–415. The trial targeted a handful of senior figures only, so as not to risk destabilizing the process of recovery and reconciliation underway in Cambodian society. The Khmer Rouge roots of a number of Cambodian leaders—including the prime minister, Hun Sen—has also reduced enthusiasm for a more far-reaching process. As Jörg Menzel summarized it, "the Cambodian approach to transitional justice is minimalist in nature: a symbolic criminal trial against a few main perpetrators. This is not much, but probably better than nothing."[63]

Although it took the Cambodian framework as its guide, the Special Court for Sierra Leone was the first to initiate proceedings. It, too, includes both national and foreign justices, adjudicating under both domestic and international laws. But in a unique twist, two cities on different continents hosted the proceedings. Trials of the leaders of three different militia formations (the RUF, CDF, and AFRC) took place in Freetown, the Sierra Leonean capital. But a chamber of the International Criminal Court at The Hague was employed as the venue for Charles Taylor's trial—a special case, owing to Taylor's role as former president of Liberia (he was charged with orchestrating atrocities in Sierra Leone), and his status as a highly divisive figure in this traumatized region of West Africa. The possibility that a public trial would destroy nascent processes of reconciliation and reintegration of former combatants prompted the United Nations to approve the move. Taylor's trial process concluded in 2012 with his conviction and sentencing to life imprisonment, a verdict upheld on appeal in 2013.[64] The court's most notable legal contribution, perhaps, were the convictions of AFRC figures for forcibly conscripting children, and of RUF leaders for inflicting forced marriage on women. These were the first times such verdicts had been rendered under international law.[65]

ANOTHER KIND OF JUSTICE: RWANDA'S *GACACA* EXPERIMENT

Following the seizure of power in Rwanda by Paul Kagame's RPF rebels, well over 100,000 detainees were jailed for years without trial, in squalid and overcrowded conditions. Their incarceration was usually based on genuine suspicion of involvement in the genocide; some accusations, though, were surely concocted to settle personal scores or seize property. Clearly, the country's shattered legal system could not hope to clear the backlog of cases.

The solution eventually settled upon was *gacaca* (ga–CHA–cha). The word refers to a patch of grass traditionally used for community gatherings. Here it references the open-air proceedings chaired by "260,000 lay judges—old and young, men and women, Hutu and Tutsi," elected by popular vote in October 2001.[66] *Gacaca* tribunals, which began to function in 2005, were established at four levels, from cell through sector and district to province. The lowest-level tribunal handled Category 4 offenses, those against property only. Sector tribunals assessed crimes involving injury, while district-level trials handled cases of killing, but not—at the outset—the organization and direction of killing (Category 1 crimes). Until 2008, these latter crimes fell outside the *gacaca* framework, but in that year the tribunals' mandate was extended to include local-level planners and organizers of genocidal crimes. Provincial tribunals served as courts of final appeal for all *gacaca* cases.[67]

At the trials, victim and perpetrator were brought face to face, with witnesses speaking for each, and with each allowed an opportunity to address the tribunal. The "array of participants . . . include[d] all those affected by the crimes and also those who will be affected by the suspect's return to the community."[68] Judges, nine in number, were volunteers, usually community notables.

The ensuing procedure "clearly contains elements that are distinctly retributive in nature," such as the emphasis on individual guilt and the imposition of

Figure 15.7 "It's Vestine's turn to talk about what happened to her family before the gacaca, the village court."

Source: Mark Vuori/World's Children's Prize/www.worldschildrensprize.org.

punishments, as legal scholar Nicholas A. Jones acknowledged. However, *gacaca* also featured important elements of *restorative* justice:

> An offender who willingly accepts responsibility, takes ownership of his or her actions, and demonstrates his or her contriteness and willingness to tell the truth about the events that occurred, may receive a reduced sentence and an earlier return to the community through the application of the community service aspect of the plea. The *[gacaca]* legislation provides the accused with an avenue through which they may attempt to make amends for the harm they have caused. Additionally, this may present offenders with an opportunity to increase their likelihood for re-integration into the community, because other members of the community witness those attempts at restitution.[69]

In the evaluation offered by one of Jones's interviewees,

> I think that the Gacaca can bring people together because once you bring people together to dialogue, to discuss the issues that affect them directly, to discuss about whether they took part—one accused of murdering another, the other saying "you did this," "I didn't do this," "I did this, I'm sorry, can you forgive me?" That's a very important dialogue, and finally, starting from the hard facts is difficult, but finally you reach a consensus, whatever the case. Once people come together, you will definitely come up with a changed attitude. Previously people didn't want to even look at one another, but now they can hope to, they can hope to sit down and they can discuss issues.[70]

Critics of *gacaca* pointed to the political selectivity of the process—Tutsi killers of Hutus during and after the genocide against Tutsis were not called to account—as well as to the lack of Western-style judicial safeguards, such as defense lawyers and a presumption of innocence, and the "low standards of evidence" that left "ample room for manipulation and corruption."[71] There was the perpetual problem of post-genocide justice: individuals' exploitation of inadequate legal infrastructure, and the prevailing confusion, fear, and paranoia, to saddle innocent people with genocide-related charges, thereby displacing them as political, professional, or even romantic rivals. And legitimate concerns were raised about whether such a process could ever provide more than a superficial salve for the deep, indeed permanent wounds inflicted by the 1994 holocaust. Many Tutsi survivors perceived *gacaca* (not without reason) as a process engineered by, and for the benefit of, the "Ugandan" Tutsi component that took power at the end of the 1994 genocide (see Box 15.4).

Gacaca proceedings were wound up in June 2012; henceforth, any accused perpetrators or participants in the genocide will be handled by the Rwandan court system. How to evaluate this distinctive strategy of justice-seeking by a poor country confronting widespread complicity in barely-imaginable crimes? In a 2011 assessment, David Simon acknowledged the many flaws of *gacaca*, but cited it as a contribution to the wider task of "mak[ing] politics possible in a world where it has not been since the genocide, and even before it. *Gacaca* did not complete that task, but it began it." For Simon, the process served as an exercise in "civic citizenship." It did so "by creating a shared experience, providing a forum for discourse, creating an opening for social reintegration and generating a record of what happened." He also credited it with contributing to Rwanda's "economic transformation," in that it "has disposed of the backlog of legal cases and helped to reduce the population of previously overcrowded prisons. It thereby freed up labor for production—at a minimum, to help Rwanda feed itself."[72]

THE PINOCHET CASE

General Augusto Pinochet was first among equals in the military *junta* that overthrew the elected regime of Salvador Allende in Chile on September 11, 1973.[73] The coup was followed by a campaign against the Left, in which several thousand Chileans died. Many more were scarred physically and psychologically by torture, and tens of thousands forced into exile. Activists who fled one Southern Cone* country for refuge in another were hunted down and murdered in death-squad operations coordinated jointly by the region's dictators, Pinochet included.

In 1974, Pinochet appointed himself president. Repression, torture, and death-squad activity continued, albeit on a reduced scale. In 1989, confident that his free-market reforms and social conservatism would sway a majority of Chileans, Pinochet submitted to a plebiscite. A majority—though not a large one—rejected him. Pinochet duly left office in 1990, and a centrist government took power.

Pinochet lived on, wealthy and comfortable except for persistent back problems. In search of relief, he consulted physicians in London, where the former Conservative Prime Minister, Margaret Thatcher, was his regular visitor; she had staunchly backed Pinochet during her years in power. For its part, the Blair government dispatched Foreign Office staff to attend to the aging dictator's needs and concerns.

Press reports had alerted Spanish judge Baltasar Garzón to Pinochet's presence in Britain. In October 1998, Garzón procured a warrant for Pinochet's extradition. The former dictator, aware that legal proceedings were afoot, was preparing to flee when police detained him. He would remain under house arrest while the British considered Garzón's extradition request.

On March 24, 1999, the same day that NATO bombs began falling on Kosovo (Chapter 8), a panel of the House of Lords—the supreme British tribunal—voted 6–1 that norms of diplomatic immunity did not extend to Pinochet in his current situation.[74] British domestic opinion was divided over the detention and extradition request, however, with Lady Thatcher leading a chorus of protest. In the end, *Realpolitik* (loosely, "realistic politics") won out. In March 2000, a year-and-a-half after Pinochet's arrest, UK Home Secretary Jack Straw released him by government fiat on "compassionate" grounds.[75]

---

* The "Southern Cone" of South America consists of Argentina, Chile, Paraguay, and Uruguay.

This seemed an abortive conclusion. Nonetheless, the Pinochet case was recognized as a watershed in international humanitarian law.[76] For the first time since the legally-ambiguous Eichmann case,[77] a former leadership figure, accused of committing grave abuses in one state (but not of war crimes *per se*), was detained in another state for possible extradition to a third. Considerations of sovereign immunity were no longer determinant. As one of the British Law Lords wrote: "The trend was clear. War crimes had been replaced by crimes against humanity. The way in which a state treated its own citizens within its own borders had become a matter of legitimate concern to the international community."[78]

In a neat example of a political "feedback loop," international legal proceedings against Pinochet influenced the Chilean domestic agenda.[79] In closing his 2000 account of the Pinochet case, Geoffrey Robertson opined that Pinochet was "as likely to go to trial [in Chile] . . . as he is to heaven."[80] But in 2004, the Chilean Supreme Court suddenly declared Pinochet fit to stand trial, at age 89, for murders committed under his aegis. Shortly after the renewed legal process was announced, Pinochet entered hospital with a supposed "stroke." The Supreme Court was unimpressed. In the first days of January 2005, it reiterated that the process should go ahead, and placed the former dictator under house arrest. In September 2005, Pinochet was formally stripped of his immunity from prosecution. His death in December 2006 brought relief, but not for his surviving colleagues. In November 2015, Reuters journalist Gram Slattery described a "doubl[ing] down on prosecutions for Pinochet-era crimes," with some four hundred cases referred to prosecutors in the previous two years. Under activist Supreme Court president Sergio Muñoz, "Chile's courts [were] racing to address dictatorship-era crimes before the deaths of witnesses, victims, and the accused makes doing so impossible." "Chile has evolved from turning away from these issues to taking them on," Muñoz said. "For the victimizers, this means the state has not forgotten what you've done, and you will be punished. . . . There will be no closed doors behind which you can hide."[81]

Where would it all end? In the wake of Pinochet's detention prosecution, and Yugoslavia's surrender shortly thereafter of Slobodan Milosevic for trial at The Hague, a certain vulnerability attended dictators and their henchmen worldwide.[82] Former Peruvian president Alberto Fujimori was repatriated from Chile, put on trial, and convicted in April 2009 of kidnapping and murder for death-squad massacres and "disappearances" of leftist opponents. He was "sentenced to 25 years in what was described as a landmark ruling for human rights cases in Latin America."[83] Sudanese president Omar al-Bashir's indictments for crimes against humanity and genocide in Darfur seemed to solidify the trend.

Even for those who did not face courts or formal indictments, travel arrangements were disrupted. Cuban President Fidel Castro allegedly "cancelled at least two trips out of Cuba, apparently fearing he could be arrested on US criminal charges." The former chief of Ethiopia's Dergue regime, Mengistu Haile Mariam, "faced an arrest threat in South Africa while receiving medical treatment there, causing him to return to safer exile in Zimbabwe."[84] Alleged architects of Israeli atrocities against Palestinians cancelled trips to the United Kingdom for fear of detention and arrest under universal jurisdiction provisions.[85] Not even the policy elite of the world's leading democracy was safe from such challenges. In March 2009, none other than Baltasar Garzón, "the crusading investigative judge who ordered the arrest of the former Chilean dictator Augusto Pinochet," moved to open an investigation of "six former high-level Bush administration officials" accused of "violat[ing] international law by providing the legal framework to justify the torture of prisoners at Guantanamo Bay, Cuba . . ." Those named included former attorney general Alberto R. Gonzales, and various legal specialists who had bent the law to permit the torture of prisoners in US custody.[86] This, however, was a step too far for Spain's attorney general. He promptly moved to squelch the investigation, cautioning that US courts were the appropriate venue for such charges, and Spain's should not become "a plaything" for political agendas.[87]

The veto was widely seen to mark a cresting of the universal-jurisdiction movement that Spain, and Garzón, had done so much to spearhead. Indeed, momentum appears to have stalled since the last edition of this book appeared. Probably the most prominent development is a negative and now ritualized one: the same Omar al-Bashir whose indictment seemed a promising advance now mocked the universal-jurisdiction regime with every foreign country and Genocide Convention signatory that he visited (see Box 9a and Figure 9a.1).

THE INTERNATIONAL CRIMINAL COURT (ICC)

> Implicit within the logic of the term "crime against humanity" is the need for an international court.
>
> David Hirsh

The concept of a permanent international tribunal for war crimes and crimes against humanity is a venerable one. According to legal scholar William Schabas, Gustav Moynier of the Red Cross outlined an early plan in the 1870s.[88] But for most of the twentieth century, the one court with a claim to global jurisdiction—the International Court of Justice (ICJ) at The Hague, also known as the World Court—was limited mostly to territorial claims and resource disputes. When Nicaragua launched proceedings against the US in the 1980s for acts of material sabotage and support for *contra* rebels, the US at first argued that the ICJ lacked jurisdiction. When the ICJ begged to differ, the US withdrew from the proceedings and refused to abide by any judgment against it. The ICJ ruled in Nicaragua's favor, but was impotent to enforce its decision. "A court with teeth" in the humanitarian and human rights arena existed only in the Western European regional context: the European Court of Justice's decisions are binding on all European Union members. However, the mounting impetus for a global prohibition regime against genocide, war crimes, and crimes against humanity led, in 1994, to the UN drafting a statute for a legal body along the lines of the Yugoslavia tribunal, but with global jurisdiction. A final version was agreed on in Rome, with the "Rome Statute" passed on July 17, 1998. In April 2002, sixty-six countries—six more than required—voted to adopt the Statute, and it entered formally into force. By early 2010, 108 "state parties" had ratified it in their national legislatures.

Eighteen judges, including seven women, were appointed, and Luis Moreno Ocampo was selected as the first chief prosecutor. He was succeeded by Fatou Bensouda (Figure 15.8) in 2011.

The court was envisaged as an adjunct to legal proceedings at the national level. Only when national mechanisms prove incapable of handling a case can the ICC come into play. Individuals from states who are not signatories to the Rome Statute may still be tried, though only if referred to the Court by a signatory state. In general, ICC proceedings are to be activated only by a request from a member state, though some loopholes do exist. The chief prosecutor can initiate investigations on his or her own *(proprio motu)*, while the UN Security Council may command the prosecutor to apply the court's jurisdiction even if s/he is reluctant to do so. A Pre-Trial Chamber will then issue warrants for the arrest of indicted individuals (it is individuals, not states or other entities, that are the focus of the ICC's operations).

The Court's mandate extends to genocide, war crimes, crimes of "aggression," and crimes against humanity. The definition of "genocide" adopted by the ICC is identical to that of the UN Convention. Worth noting also is the emphasis on

Figure 15.8 Fatou Bensouda, chief prosecutor of the International Criminal Court, at the Global Summit to End Sexual Violence in Conflict, London, June 2014. Bensouda, who has worked at the court since 2004, was formerly justice minister of The Gambia.

Source: Foreign and Commonwealth Office, UK/Wikimedia Commons.

"crimes against humanity" in the Rome Statute. As we saw above (Box 15.2), this category of crimes overlaps with the Genocide Convention in some measure, and is likely—for practical and conceptual reasons—to figure more prominently than genocide in future legal prosecutions.

Despite the broad international consensus behind the ICC, many governments, including the US, have shied from it. The Clinton government signed the Rome Statute in the knowledge that it was unlikely to be ratified by Congress.[89] The issue of universal jurisdiction, along with the semi-independent role of the prosecutor, were key sticking points. In May 2002, the Bush administration renounced the treaty, and declared that it would not tolerate the detention or trial of any US national by the ICC. Later the same year, Bush signed into law the "American Service-Members Protection Act," authorizing the US president "to use all means . . . necessary to bring about the release of covered US persons and covered allied persons held captive by or on behalf of the [ICC]."[90] Some wryly referred to this as the "Invade The Hague Act," conjuring images of US troops descending on Dutch detention centers to free Americans accused of abuses and atrocities. The tone was certainly eased by Barack Obama's inauguration in 2009, but the new civility did not extend to the US actually becoming a state party to the court.

The ICC is "the body that may ultimately play the greatest role in interpreting the prohibition against genocide."[91] To this point, though, "its power as part of the atrocities [prohibition] regime remains contested and indefinite."[92] Its broad mandate and intended permanence bode well, as does its popularity in most countries of the world. On the other hand, concessions made to placate US and other concerns (including an opt-out clause lasting seven years) provoked concern that the ICC might become just another toothless legal body.

A striking aspect of the court's operations was its near-exclusive concentration on African crimes and conflicts—indeed, in twenty-three cases launched by early 2016, not a single person had been indicted from outside the continent.[93] Only *two* convictions had been entered in the court's first eleven years, both of Africans (Congolese warlords Thomas Lubanga and Germain Katanga). This led to accusations that the "African Criminal Court" was deliberately limiting itself to the least politically-contentious cases, to avoid ruffling great-power feathers. Even within Africa, the continuing impunity enjoyed by Sudanese president Omar al-Bashir despite his ICC indictments for genocide and crimes against humanity, and fiascos surrounding attempted prosecutions of Kenyan president Uhuru Kenyatta and deputy president William Ruto,[94] prompted charges that the court was vulnerable to pressure by relatively-powerful countries and leaders.

Supporters of the ICC riposted, however, that

although all eight sets of cases in progress are African, five were initiated by African governments themselves, and two (concerning Sudan and Libya) were referred to the court by the UN Security Council. The Kenyan cases were agreed to by Kenya's government of the day, at the urging of the UN's former head, Kofi Anna, a Ghanaian, who had mediated an end to Kenya's post-[2007] election chaos. As for the charge that the court is run by white imperialists, its president is South Korean. The chief prosecutor is Gambian. The main director in her office is from Lesotho. And Sidiki Kaba, . . . [the] president of the assembly of member countries . . ., is Senegal's justice minister.

The Economist added that "several investigations are under way outside Africa, too":

> They include cases in Afghanistan, Colombia, Georgia and Honduras, as well as Iraq, where allegations against British soldiers are being examined with the co-operation of the British government. It seems increasingly likely that Palestine, thanks to its advance towards statehood within the UN, will refer Israel's settlements on the West Bank and military actions in Gaza to the court—which could mean that Hamas, the Palestinian Islamist movement, also comes under scrutiny for firing rockets indiscriminately at Israeli civilians. And Ukraine, though not a signatory [to the Rome Statute], has accepted the court's jurisdiction to investigate crimes alleged to have been committed on its territory.[95]

INTERNATIONAL CITIZENS' TRIBUNALS

Often called "international people's tribunals," these bodies substitute accusations and public shaming for due process and enforcement. The formation of a citizens' tribunal implies that regular means of justice are inadequate—corrupt or compromised. "The people"—certain interested people—seize the initiative and stage a quasi-trial. This may publicize atrocities, raise public consciousness, or shatter taboos, for example about Western state involvement. (It is usually Western democracies that are both hosts and subjects of the proceedings.) Tribunals can place vital evidence on the public record, and point to gaps between legislation and its application, highlighting the immunity often extended to sovereign states and their representatives.

Citizens' tribunals received a rare comparative analysis in a book by political scientists Arthur and Judith Klinghoffer.[96] The authors pointed out that, in many ways, the most remarkable and successful citizens' tribunal was the first. In February 1933, the month after Adolf Hitler came to power, the Reichstag Parliament building in Berlin was burned down. Three foreign and one German communist, along with the Dutchman Marinus van der Lubbe, were charged with the crime. The Nazis seized on the fire to declare a state of emergency, suspend the Weimar Constitution, and begin their mass round-ups of communist suspects (Box 6a). Fearing that the German courts were too cowed to try the matter fairly, various public intellectuals, along with prominent socialists and communists, convened "The Commission of Inquiry into the Origins of the Reichstag Fire" in London in September 1933. Held a week before official proceedings were due to get underway in Germany, the tribunal pulled the rug out from under the Nazis' planned show-trial. Placed in the hot seat by international media attention, a court in Leipzig convicted only van der Lubbe (he was subsequently executed). The four communists were acquitted. "The first international citizens' tribunal had taken on Nazi Germany, and had won," wrote Arthur Klinghoffer. "Intellectuals had confronted a totalitarian state, and had successfully used public opinion as a weapon to further their cause."[97]

Four years later, supporters of exiled Russian communist Leon Trotsky organized a citizens' tribunal at his new (and final) home in Coyoacán, a Mexico City suburb. The intent of the Dewey Commission, chaired by the eponymous philosopher, was to denounce Soviet show-trials and accusations against Trotsky. The tribunal achieved some success in countering Stalinist propaganda, although its geographic remove from centers of Western public opinion limited its impact.

Much more visible was the International War Crimes Tribunal to judge US actions in the Vietnam War in 1967, known as the Russell Tribunal. Delegates voted unanimously that US actions did constitute genocide against the Vietnamese and other Indochinese peoples (for more on the US war in Vietnam, and these findings, see Chapter 2). According to Ann Curthoys and John Docker, "the Tribunal made a significant and eventually influential contribution to debates over the morality and conduct of the war in Vietnam."[98] However, "this decision on genocide had little impact on the American public and was generally viewed by the press as verbal excess."[99]

Since the 1970s, tribunals have publicized the restitution claims of indigenous peoples; the Japanese "comfort women" issue; Western wars and sanctions against Iraq;[100] and alleged "crimes against humanity and nature" by the global multinational corporation Monsanto.[101] As these examples suggest, "In essence, tribunals have become a weapon of the radical left in its battle with 'global capitalism.'"[102] It has been argued that "these tribunals do make some contribution to the pathetically limited possibilities of action for the punishment of genocide."[103] However, many observers consider them to be kangaroo courts: their "investigations sometimes seem perfunctory, and the verdict seems preordained," in Leo Kuper's words.[104] Richard Falk referred to the Russell Tribunal as "a juridical farce."[105] Law Professor Peter Burns likewise argued that "the desired conclusion[s]" of such tribunals are "inextricably woven into the accusations and process itself." He considered them "a form of overt morality play, relying upon polemic and theatre to achieve results that may be desirable ethically, but may or may not be desirable legally."[106]

TRUTH AND RECONCILIATION

Like *gacaca* in Rwanda, truth and reconciliation commissions are driven by a vision of restorative justice that "seeks repair of social connections and peace rather than retribution against the offenders." As such, these commissions have become the preferred option for societies (or at least their decision-makers) who wish to avoid arduous and possibly destabilizing trials. For victims, such commissions provide a forum, perhaps the first they have had, for speaking of the horrors inflicted upon them or upon those whom they loved. Ideally, the result is *catharsis*—in this context, the mastering of one's pain through its articulation. "By confronting the past, the traumatized individuals can learn to distinguish past, present, and future. When the work of knowing and telling the story has come to an end, the trauma then belongs to the past; the survivor can face the work of building a future."[107] Validation may also lie in having one's testimony heard, corroborated, and integrated into a commission's published findings. A degree of moral order is restored to the world when one's suffering is taken seriously, and its perpetrators viewed with obloquy. (Truth-telling may also have a darker side, however, considered below.)

Key questions for truth commissions include the following. *For how long will the commission operate?* The general trend is from a few months to a couple of years. *Who will fund it?* Significant resources may be available domestically, as in South Africa. In other cases foreign funding is crucial, and in a pair of instances the UN has played a formative role (El Salvador) or a prominent one (Guatemala). *Who will staff the commission?* The emphasis has been on prominent public figures from the country in question, widely seen as fair-minded and compassionate. *Will the commission examine alleged abuses by all sides in a given conflict, or by one side only?* The strong tendency has been toward examining all sides' conduct, since this greatly bolsters the credibility of the commission's proceedings and final report. *Will the commission have the power to dispense justice and grant amnesty?* Justice, no; and only South Africa's commission could grant amnesty to those who confessed before it.

In conducting its operations, *how will the commission elicit testimony?* Sessions may be held in public or behind closed doors. Anonymous testimony might be permitted, especially in the case of sexual crimes. *What standard of evidence will be required to draw publishable conclusions?* According to Hayner, the trend is toward "the 'balance of probabilities' standard for basic conclusions of fact. This . . . suggests that there is more evidence to support than to deny a conclusion, or that something is more likely to be true than not based on the evidence before the commission."[108] *Will the commission's report include prescriptions and recommendations?* In general, yes. Special attention is often paid to reforming the state security forces. Commissions may also provide critical documentation for subsequent criminal trials. *Will the commission name names?* More rarely.[109] There is a delicate balance to be struck between holding individuals accountable while risking (1) disrupting a delicate political transition, or (2) provoking threats and acts of violence against witnesses and commission staff. The UN-sponsored commission in El Salvador *did* name names, despite intense opposition from the Salvadoran government and military. The Guatemalan commission, by contrast, chose not to, though it left no doubt that state agents had committed the overwhelming majority of the atrocities (see Box 3a).

Will truth commissions consider the roles of foreign actors? Generally not, though when such investigations *are* conducted, they may be revelatory. The 1992 report of the Chad truth commission, for example, produced a hard-hitting assessment of US aid to the goons of the Habré regime. The US also came under close scrutiny by the Guatemalan Commission for Historical Clarification. The commission obtained extensive documentation of the US role in overthrowing a democratic government in Guatemala (1954), then installing and sustaining the military dictators who eventually turned to full-scale genocide against Mayan Indians and domestic dissenters.

However, "most truth commissions have not investigated this international role at any depth; few have addressed the issue at all in their final report."[110] This reflects material and evidentiary constraints, as well as the complexity of some international involvements. (One balks at assessing the international dimension of the

Congo conflict, for example, if a truth commission is ever struck with this man-date.) Sometimes the reluctance may derive from practical considerations. Many truth commissions, as noted, rely on international financial support—frequently from the United States.

BOX 15.3 CANADA: TOWARD TRUTH AND RECONCILIATION ON "TURTLE ISLAND"[111]

On June 3, 2015, the Truth and Reconciliation Commission of Canada wound up its hearings with a festive public concert featuring Canadian Cree singer and icon Buffy Sainte-Marie (see Figure 3.10, p. 174). The commemorations capped a for-mal process that had begun in 2008 with Prime Minister Stephen Harper's apology for the abuses of the residential school system (RSS, see pp. 160, 162–163). The TRC, like others worldwide, would investigate those abuses, hear testimony from survivors and others—some seven thousand people in all—pass a form of judg-ment, and issue recommendations for reform and national reconciliation.

The commission's summary report, *Honouring the Truth, Reconciling for the Future*, was released on December 15, 2015. The three commissioners—two of them

Figure 15.9 Audience members listen to testimony at a hearing of the Truth and Reconciliation Commission of Canada in Victoria, BC, April 2012.

Source: Photo by Chad Hipolito/Canadian Press.

Aboriginal Canadians (Justice Murray Sinclair, "Manitoba's first Aboriginal Judge," and Chief Wilton Littlechild of the Maskwacis Cree nation), the other (Dr. Marie Wilson) partnered with one—had fulfilled their stated mandate of exploring "the history, purpose, operation and supervision of the residential school system" in Canada, together with "the effect and consequences of the system, and its ongoing legacy . . ."[112]

The commission's investigation of the Indian Residential Schools (IRS) reflected a growing mountain of evidence and testimony concerning indigenous children's experiences at these institutions, touched on in Chapter 3 (see pp. 160, 162–163). In 1990, indigenous leader Phil Fontaine detailed sexual and other abuses inflicted at the Oblates of Mary Immaculate and Assiniboia schools.[113] His brother, Theodore Fontaine, described the emotional and existential impact of his own residential-school incarceration in a 2010 memoir, *Broken Circle*:

> Those of us from residential schools were mentally crippled by the experience and clueless about what we were or were supposed to be. Most survivors left school in their teens or early 20s, and most didn't live long. They were trapped at age seven or slightly older in psychological, emotional and spiritual age. For many, it has proved difficult or impossible to recover. . . . In most cases, we came to see our keepers as saviours and protectors from hunger, isolation and abandonment. We watched parents and family leaving the school on that first day and blamed them for leaving us. We blamed ourselves for being left behind, abandoned because we weren't wanted or had been bad. We blamed ourselves for still being hungry, isolated and alone. . . . They pounded into our little minds that our families couldn't look after us as well as the school could. This was the biggest hoax and tragedy bestowed on Indian people and their children in Canada by residential schools. . . . Most residential school survivors avoid direct eye contact. The blame that's mostly turned inward has caused shame. We don't want anyone to see what's happened.[114]

A landmark set of class actions was settled—for legal purposes, at least—by the Indian Residential Schools Settlement Agreement of 2006, which included a provision to strike a Truth and Reconciliation Commission. After six years of hearings, in which over six thousand witnesses testified, the TRC concluded that the residential schools should be viewed against the backdrop of policies that aimed to destroy Canadian indigenous civilizations, *through a form of genocide*:

> For over a century, the central goals of Canada's Aboriginal policy were to eliminate Aboriginal governments; ignore Aboriginal rights; terminate the Treaties; and, through a process of assimilation, cause Aboriginal peoples to cease to exist as distinct legal, social, cultural, religious, and racial entities in Canada. The establishment and operation of residential schools were a central element of this policy, which can best be described as "cultural genocide." . . . States that engage in cultural genocide set out to destroy the political and social institutions of the targeted

group. Land is seized, and populations are forcibly transferred and their movement is restricted. Languages are banned. Spiritual leaders are persecuted, spiritual practices are forbidden, and objects of spiritual value are confiscated and destroyed. And, most significantly to the issue at hand [the residential school system], families are disrupted to prevent the transmission of cultural values and identity from one generation to the next. In its dealing with Aboriginal people, Canada did all these things. Canada asserted control over Aboriginal land. . . . These measures were part of a coherent policy to eliminate Aboriginal people as distinct peoples and to assimilate them into the Canadian mainstream against their will.[115]

Several months earlier, TRC chairperson Murray Sinclair had telegraphed the Commission's interpretation, stating:

I think as commissioners we have concluded that cultural genocide is probably the best description of what went on here. But more importantly, if anybody tried to do this today, they would easily be subject to prosecution under the genocide convention. . . . The evidence is mounting that the government did try to eliminate the culture and language of indigenous people for well over a hundred years. And they did it by forcibly removing children from their families and placing them within institutions that were cultural indoctrination centres. That appears to us to fall within the definition of genocide under the UN convention.[116]

As whenever "the G-word" is prominently employed, Sinclair's declaration provoked voluble and sometimes bitter debate. Conservative commentators dismissed Sinclair's "cultural genocide" formulation as a "blood libel" (Conrad Black),[117] or took refuge in the others-were-a-lot-worse defense (Jeffrey Simpson).[118] Others disputed the characterization of the genocide as "cultural." "The word," wrote Jesse Staniforth, "seems to suggest that the IRS system was designed to destroy cultures but not people." This was "far from the reality," and attested to a desire to "cling tightly—and childishly—to the idea that Canada has always been on the side of goodness and justice":

Canada did not pack Indigenous people onto train cars and send them to be gassed, or march them into fields and execute them with machine-gun fire. However, our country committed not 'cultural' genocide, but just regular genocide. We forcibly took children from families—sometimes at gunpoint—and flew them to remote locations they could not escape—sometimes in tiny handcuffs—where they were submitted to a program of forced labour and 'education' designed to destroy their cultures and civilizations." . . . Residential Schools were predicated on the notion that Indigenous children were less human than other children, so they were worked like animals in the slave labour many schools mandated. For the same assumption of their lesser humanity, children in the IRS system were often deliberately malnourished and kept in cramped, filthy quarters. When they subsequently fell sick as a result of this racially motivated neglect and mistreatment, they were not provided adequate medical treatment and died by the thousands. The Canadian government was happy to leave these children to die because they were Indigenous. . . . Which part of this sounds civilized enough that it deserves to be mitigated by the adjective "cultural"?[119]

An evaluation of Canada's TRC process should acknowledge that, along with renewed indigenous activism under the "Idle No More" banner,[120] it helped to keep indigenous peoples and issues at the forefront of the national agenda for several years. It provided a public voice and perhaps a measure of catharsis and healing to survivors, and educated generations of non-indigenous Canadians about the devastating assault on Canada's native peoples.[121] With regard to the commission's eliding of a genocide framework, genocide scholar David Bruce MacDonald suggested that the TRC had at least "created a ground floor for proceeding further in discussing and describing now the native Canadian experience is consistent with the definition of the UN Genocide Convention." This, he continued, offered "considerable scope for survivors, community leaders, and educators to articulate how the UNGC reflects Canadian history and the schools." For example, lobbying efforts might now be directed at "provincial legislatures or the federal parliament," to seek recognition of genocide at those levels.[122]

Many survivors and their advocates expressed skepticism, however. Criticism focused on the time-bound, government-sponsored character of the TRC; the constrained forms of apology and restitution that it offered or encouraged; and the abiding emphasis on "closure":

> . . . Survivors appear to be all too aware of the government's desires to make their suffering legible, calculable, and manageable, so that it no longer represents a burden on the government. They also sense that they are meant to find closure through these apologies and payments and to no longer be 'a problem' for the government. . . . In this case, redress transfers the legitimate justice demands of Indigenous peoples into tidy boxes of repair, removing them as a challenge to the legitimacy of the settler colonial nation and potentially hiding the violence of settler colonialism within a language of reconciliation.

Instead of—or in addition to—this limited project, Andrew Woolford argues that Canada's dominant non-indigenous population must confront a deeper, more discomfiting challenge: "[H]ow do we radically alter a way of life that has resulted in such attempts at Indigenous destruction and remains with us today? How do we redress the fact that we live and have benefited from our lives upon Indigenous lands?"[123] Or, as the TRC commissioners eloquently phrased it:

> Getting to the truth was hard, but getting to reconciliation will be harder. It requires that the paternalistic and racist foundations of the residential school

system be rejected as the basis for an ongoing relationship. Reconciliation requires that a new vision, based on a commitment to mutual respect, be developed. . . . Reconciliation, in the context of Indian residential schools, is similar to dealing with a situation of family violence. It's about coming to terms with events of the past in a manner that overcomes conflict and establishes a respectful and healthy relationship among people, going forward. . . . Reconciliation must support Aboriginal peoples as they heal from the destructive legacies of colonization that have wreaked such havoc in their lives. But it must do even more. Reconciliation must inspire Aboriginal and non-Aboriginal peoples to transform Canadian society so that our children and grandchildren can live together in dignity, peace, and prosperity on these lands we now share.[124]

—With research assistance by Jill Mitchell Nielsen.

Truth commissions resemble citizens' tribunals in compensating for a lack of "teeth" in their deliberations by creating ripples in the public sphere. In the commissions' case, this can produce a kind of quasi-legal sanction against offenders. Some of those named by commissions may avoid foreign travel, fearing arrest. At a more informal level, Hayner has vividly described the treatment accorded to leaders and high-profile agents of the former *junta* in Argentina. Many were never formally tried; some were jailed but released under an amnesty. Nevertheless, the revelation of their deeds, primarily through the Argentine truth commission and its *Nunca Más* report, carried lasting consequences for these individuals. "Whenever they venture into the streets or public places, [Generals] Videla, Massera, Campos, and several others have experienced spontaneous though nonviolent acts of repudiation: waiters refuse to serve them, other patrons leave the place or sit far away from them, some actually defy their bodyguards and confront them with the opinion that most Argentines have of them."[125]

A question remains: Is the truth always desirable? In personal terms, truth-telling about atrocity is often deeply traumatizing for the teller. Yael Fischman and Jaime Ross describe the "recurring themes" of torture survivors in therapy:

Fear of destroying others, such as relatives and therapists, by relating the trauma; fear of loss of control over feelings of rage, violence, and anxiety; shame and rage over the vulnerability and helplessness evoked by torture; rage and grief at the sudden and arbitrary disruption of individual, social, and political projects, and at the violation of rights; guilt and shame over surviving and being unable to save others; guilt over bringing distress on self and family and over not protecting them . . . fear and rage at the unpredictability of and lack of control over events; grief over the loss of significant others, through both death and exile; and loss of aspects of the self, such as trust and innocence.[126]

Outside a formal therapeutic environment, though, almost no mechanism to elicit truth-telling—be it a truth commission, a human rights investigator, or a journalist—provides meaningful follow-up to traumatized survivors. Truth-divulging may also be "dangerous and destabilizing" on a national level, according to Hayner, "disrupt[ing] fragile relationships in local communities recently returned to peace."[127] She cited Mozambique, where "people across the political spectrum, including victims, academics, government officials and others . . . said, 'No, we do not want to reenter into this morass of conflict, hatred, and pain. We want to focus on the future. . . . We prefer silence over confrontation, over renewed pain. While we cannot forget, we would like to pretend that we can.'"[128]

These attitudes were not ostrich-like. Rather, they signaled a process of peace and reconciliation that had come about "remarkably quickly" in Mozambique, many observers describing it "with a sense of wonder." From the day a peace agreement was signed ending one of Africa's most brutal twentieth-century wars, "the former warring enemies have lived in peace virtually without incident." Rituals of purification and reconciliation were performed at the village level, beyond the reach of state initiatives.[129] "We were all thinking about how to increase peace and reconciliation," said one Mozambican official, "but when we came to the grassroots, they were reconciling already. Our ideas were only confusing and stirring up trouble."[130] In 2009, Malangatana Ngwenya, a renowned Mozambican poet and artist who lost many members of his family in the war, told the UK *Guardian:* "If we had had a truth commission, it would just have caused tension. I don't want to know who killed my family. It would be stupid to know. And even if by chance I learned who took my brother's life, I wouldn't waste time on starting to hate."[131]

A similar reconciliation process prevailed in East Timor following the final expulsion of Indonesian forces from the territory in 1999 (Box 7a). While the Indonesian architects of genocide in East Timor enjoyed immunity in their homeland, the quarter-century-long occupation also drew many Timorese onto the Indonesian side as collaborators. For those accused of "nonserious crimes," the post-independence Timorese authorities sponsored a community reconciliation program (PRK) described by anthropologist Elizabeth F. Drexler:

> Individuals wishing to be reconciled with particular communities (deponents) submitted statements of nonserious crimes. These statements were reviewed by the deputy general prosecutor for serious crimes to establish that the deponent applying for reconciliation was not sought on other charges of more serious crimes. In the community hearings deponents testified to their actions, often emphasizing their lack of power or control in an overall system of intimidation and forced participation in the campaign of terror orchestrated by infamous militia leaders who remained just over the border in Indonesia. Community members in attendance had the opportunity to question what happened, often producing responses that attributed culpability to other militia members who remain in West Timor. . . . Most communities agreed to accept the deponent and promised to no longer ostracize him or her after the symbolic act of reconciliation was fulfilled (e.g., cleaning the church). Thus in community reconciliation hearings, testimony had immediate effects, and the community was bound to act as if the narrative given were true.

While "some victims . . . criticized the process because they felt pressured to accept statements from the perpetrator that were not as complete or remorseful as they had hoped," the program has nonetheless "been celebrated as a major innovation," according to Drexler.[132]

There is nothing automatic or inevitable about "reconciliation," however. Surface processes can obscure enduring divisions and antipathies, as reflected in the skeptical comments sampled by Jean Hatzfeld in Rwanda (see Box 15.4).

BOX 15.4 "RECONCILIATION" AND "REINTEGRATION" IN RWANDA

Concepts such as "forgiveness" and "reintegration" are fraught with complexity— perhaps nowhere more so than in Rwanda, where both the post-1994 government and the international community have promoted and supervised a process that now sees thousands of killers and survivors living side-by-side. How genuine and far-reaching is the reconciliation thus achieved? Some of the most revealing testimony of Tutsi survivors was compiled by Jean Hatzfeld for his book The Antelope's Strategy: Living in Rwanda After the Genocide.[133] *Hatzfeld returned to Rwanda to*

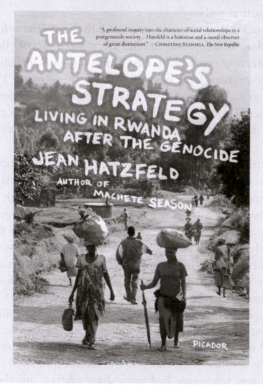

Figure 15.10 Cover of Jean Hatzfeld, *The Antelope's Strategy* (2009).

Source: Courtesy of Picador USA.

interview both the survivors and the killers he had profiled in Machete Season *and* Life Laid Bare *(see Further Study, Chapter 9). Among the responses:*

If you think about it, who is it talking about forgiveness? The Tutsis? The Hutus? The freed prisoners, their families? None of them. It's the humanitarian organizations. They are importing forgiveness to Rwanda, and they wrap it in lots of dollars to win us over. There is a Forgiveness Plan just as there is an AIDS Plan. . . . As for us, we speak of forgiveness to earn their good opinion—and because the subsidies can be lucrative. But when we talk among ourselves, the word *forgiveness* has no place; I mean that it's oppressive. For example: You see Adalbert return. He led the killings on Kibungo Hill [in Nyamata district], he was pardoned, he parades around Kigali, he wields his machete once more in his fields. You, you're from Kibungo, living five hundred meters from his house, and you lost your mama, papa, two sisters, wife, and little boy. You run into Adalbert downtown. He to you, you to him—who's going to say that word *forgiveness*? It's outside of nature. The times we live in just shove everything down our throats. . . . The survivors, they wind up frustrated, under a crippling inhibition, and they murmur . . . Being powerless to voice one's anger, sadness, and longing for what is lost, and unable to tell one's whole story for fear of offending a Hutu or annoying the authorities—this inability to reveal one's heart is sheer torture. (Innocent Rwililiza)

Some Hutus behave nicely because they feel ashamed, but others speak on the sly about starting it up again. Some Tutsis murmur words of vengeance. If lips repeated what the heart is whispering, they would sow panic, revenge, and killings in every direction. It's best to mute your sorrow and hide your resentment, or share them with a companion in misfortune. (Cassius Niyonsaba)

. . . A gentleman came into the bakery holding a little boy by the hand. . . . He was sweating. He had just gotten out of prison and moved like an old man. When we chatted, he said, "I'm sad now because I have a son I haven't watched grow up. . . . I was a respectable person and no one greets me anymore. Evil has ruined my life." I thought, Fine, this man is speaking sincerely. If all the Hutus went wrong, each and every Hutu, what could be the point of learning what this one did in particular? If he shows remorse or offers to be friends with me, I'll say yes from my heart, because life must go on. He kept speaking plaintively about his misfortunes, saying courteous things in a pitiful voice, but he neither asked for nor offered anything. These people cannot take us into consideration, cannot ask for our forgiveness. Why? I don't know. (Sylvie Umubyeyi)

. . . Two people came to me at home to ask forgiveness. They did not come sincerely but to try to avoid prison. It's difficult to tell a father how you cut his daughter, or for the father to ask those people how they cut her. So we said nothing, just exchanged civilities. They offered a little drink; we promised to help one another with our farmwork. Listening to them, not listening to them, it was all the same. I listened so that they would go away sooner and leave me with my grief. As they left, those people topped off the visit by saying they had done me a kindness by failing to catch me [during the genocidal massacres] in the marshes. I pretended to be grateful. (Jean-Baptiste Munyankore)

We, too, tend to want to forget a little. Embroidering memories, rehashing stories, comparing details—that can be bothersome, that can complicate an already burdensome day. But the Hutus—they evade absolutely everything. They only want to speak about the wonderful present. So we prefer to joke around. The more we talk, the more they tell us how nice they are, the more we let ourselves be softened up by niceness. That eases our anger. Not our distrust or suspicions, but the anger, yes. (Francine Niyitegeka)

THE CHALLENGE OF REDRESS

The *Concise Oxford Dictionary* defines redress as to "set right, remedy, make up for, get rid of, rectify . . . [a] distress, wrong, damage, grievance, [or] abuse." Political scientist Colin Tatz, summarizing the arguments of Mari Matsuda, cited "five prerequisites for a meritorious claim for redress: a 'human injustice' must have been committed; it must be well-documented; the victims must be identifiable as a distinct group; the current members of the group must continue to suffer harm; and such harm must be causally connected to the past injustice."[134]

Forms of redress are numerous, and sometimes amorphous. *Reparations*, as defined by Ernesto Verdeja, consist of "policies and initiatives that attempt to restore to victims their sense of dignity and moral worth and eliminate the social disparagement and economic marginalization that accompanied their targeting, with the goal of returning their status as citizens." Founded on notions of distributive justice, they generally contain a "collective material" element, "seek[ing] to provide resources to victimized groups with the aim of creating the material basis and security necessary for them to become full participants in social, political, and economic life," such as housing and job-creation programs. It may also have an "individual material component," featuring such strategies as "familial rehabilitation through access to medical, psychological, and legal services, compensation for financially assessable losses, economic redress for harms that are not easily quantifiable, and restitution of lost, stolen, or destroyed property."[135] Penalties imposed by official tribunals, such as the ICTR and ICTY, certainly qualify, as do the decisions of less formal processes (such as *gacaca* in Rwanda). The healing that ideally accompanies truth commissions and formal acts of reconciliation may also constitute redress. Compensation is a regular feature. It may take the form of:

- *Monetary payments*. The most prominent case is surely the decades-long reparations payments by Germany to the state of Israel, amounting to

US$89 billion by 2012.[136] In that year, the German government announced an additional US$1 billion in payments "for the homecare of Holocaust survivors around the world."[137] Recent settlements with Japanese Americans interned during World War Two, "comfort women" abused and exploited throughout the Japanese wartime empire, and Canadian Native peoples victimized in the residential school system (see Box 15.3) have all featured substantial reparations payments. The debate over reparations for Atlantic slavery have likewise focused on largescale infusions of money and material resources to African-American communities and populations.[138] As debt "restructuring" negotiations between Greece and the German-dominated European Union reached a critical point in spring 2015, the Greek government called on Germany to pay hundreds of billions of dollars in reparations for wartime atrocities and material destruction.[139] The demand, however, has not been seriously pursued since.

- *Territorial agreements*. These are of special significance to indigenous peoples, for whom the recovery of a land base is often essential to the broader viability of these groups and communities. Perhaps the most dramatic such agreement in recent years created a new Canadian territory, Nunavut, in April 1999, as the homeland of the Inuit people of the eastern Arctic. It was only one of dozens of claims adjudicated or still disputed in Canada.[140]

- *Restitution of property or cultural objects*, especially from museum collections. Again such measures are of particular importance to indigenous peoples worldwide. The world-renowned Smithsonian Museum "began to repatriate American Indian bones in the late 1980s, and in 1990 the United States passed legislation to enforce the return of those remains by museums that benefit from federal funds." As well, the museum "independently returned remains to Australia in 2008 and 2010"[141]—part of a global trend. *The Sydney Morning Herald* reported in 2009 that "since 1996, more than 1000 indigenous remains have been brought back to Australia," though "more than 1000 are still held in museums worldwide."[142]

- *Co-management of resources and profit sharing*. The 1995 Waikato-Tainui settlement in New Zealand includes provisions for "joint management" of natural resources.[143] Profits from these sources significantly boosted Maori incomes. In Canada, a "patchwork of revenue-sharing arrangements" established with First Nations communities has prompted calls for "Aboriginal revenue sharing" as a broader, federal policy.[144]

- *Affirmative action measures in politics, education, and the employment/corporate sectors*. The best-known example is the Black Economic Empowerment law passed in post-apartheid South Africa, to redress the massive racial inequalities in the "rainbow nation"; they have had only limited success so far.[145] Debates over race-specific university admissions policies in the US, and over quotas for women's political and corporate representation in Scandinavia and elsewhere, have also centered on affirmative action as a means of redress for past (and enduring) discrimination and injustice.[146]

The Role of Apology

Apologies and forgiveness-seeking are significant elements of reparation and redress—but how significant?[147] Martha Minow emphasizes "the communal nature of the process of apologizing," which "requires communication between a wrongdoer and a victim. . . . The methods for offering and accepting an apology both reflect and help to constitute a moral community."[148] Some memorable apologies for the past several decades include:

- German Chancellor Willi Brandt's *Kniefall* (kneeling apology) at a Polish war memorial in 1970.
- Queen Elizabeth's 1995 *mea culpa* to New Zealand Maoris for British violation of the Waitingi Treaty of 1840: "The Crown expresses its profound regret and apologizes unreservedly for the loss of lives because of hostilities arising from this invasion and at the devastation of property and social life which resulted."[149]
- The annual "Sorry Day," instituted by white Australians after the publication of *Bringing Them Home*, the report of the Aboriginal and Torres Strait Islander Commission (Chapter 3).[150]
- President Bill Clinton's 1998 half-apology at Kigali airport for Western inaction during the genocide in Rwanda.[151]
- The 2004 statement by Heidemarie Wieczorek-Zeul, Germany's development aid minister, to Namibian Hereros for "atrocities . . . [that] would have been termed genocide" (see Chapter 3).
- Australian prime minister Kevin Rudd's February 2008 apology, "without qualification" and as his government's first act of parliament, for the forcible transfer of Australian aboriginals to white-run institutions that sought to extirpate the native culture from their hearts and minds. Rudd apologized "to the mothers, the fathers, the brothers, the sisters, the families and the communities whose lives were ripped apart by the actions of successive governments under successive parliaments" (see Chapter 3).[152]
- The apologies to African Americans by the US House of Representatives and Senate, separately in 2008 and 2009, for slavery and the "Jim Crow" apartheid measures that followed its formal repeal. The Senate wording, which passed unanimously, "acknowledges the fundamental injustice, cruelty, brutality, and inhumanity of slavery and Jim Crow laws" and "apologizes to African-Americans on behalf of the people of the United States." However, the Senate tacked on a disclaimer that "Nothing in this resolution authorizes or supports any claim [for compensation/restitution] against the United States."[153] Remarkably, the separate House and Senate bills "were never reconciled or signed" by President Obama.[154]

Perhaps the most unusual of this century's welter of apologies was Denmark's to Ireland. On an August 2007 visit to Ireland, Danish culture minister Brian Mikkelson expressed remorse for brutal Viking raids in Ireland, "pillaging monasteries and massacring inhabitants"—some 1,200 years ago! ". . . We are not proud of the damages to the people of Ireland that followed in the footsteps of the Vikings," Mikkelson told his hosts. "But the warmth and friendliness with which you greet us today . . . show us that, luckily, it has all been forgiven."[155]

One can question whether genuine issues of reparation and restitution arise in the Viking case. With regard to more recent atrocities, however, there remains a danger that apology may serve as a cheap substitute for meaningful redress. Does it not "merely whitewash the injustice?" wondered Elazar Barkan.[156] In the wake of Kevin Rudd's historic apology to the "Stolen Generations," Tony Barta also inquired whether the terms of the *mea culpa* in fact served to "bur[y] a history of genocide."[157]

However, apologies may also serve as the *entrée* to significant material compensation, memorialization, and institutional transformation. A US congressional apology to Japanese Americans for their internment during the Second World War came as part of a Civil Liberties Act, under which the US government paid out 80,000 claims worth $1.6 billion, in addition to opening a Japanese American National Museum in Los Angeles. Britain's apologies to the Maoris of Aotearoa/ New Zealand led to the co-management arrangements already cited, while Canada's successive apologies to First Nations peoples were followed by substantial restitution payments, both for individual survivors and for "community-based healing initiatives."

By contrast, a failure or refusal to apologize usually signifies intransigence toward material and institutional forms of redress. Notable *non*-apologies of recent times include Turkey's for the genocides of Christian minorities during World War One; Central European countries' for the mass expulsion of ethnic Germans at the end of the Second World War and after; and Israel's for the "ethnic cleansing of Palestine" in 1947–1948 and since.[158] Nonetheless, the apologetic trend prevails, suggesting a strengthening of the humanitarian regime first forged in the mid-nineteenth century.

FURTHER STUDY

Hannah Arendt, *Eichmann in Jerusalem: A Report on the Banality of Evil.* New York: The Viking Press, 1965. Arendt's controversial account of the trial in Israel of Adolf Eichmann, the ultimate bureaucratic killer.

Elazar Barkan, *The Guilt of Nations: Restitution and Negotiating Historical Injustices.* New York: W.W. Norton, 2001. Wide-ranging overview of contemporary forms of redress.

Michael J. Bazyler and Frank M. Tuerkheimer, *Forgotten Trials of the Holocaust.* New York: New York University Press, 2014. Informative, highly-readable account of the little-known successors to Nuremberg's trials of Nazi leaders.

David M. Crowe, *War Crimes, Genocide, and Justice: A Global History.* New York: Palgrave Macmillan, 2014. An excellent, encyclopedic overview, moving briskly despite its considerable length.

Priscilla B. Hayner, *Unspeakable Truths: Transitional Justice and the Challenge of Truth Commissions*, 2nd edn (New York: Routledge, 2011). Energetic insider account and evaluation of truth commissions.

L.J. van den Herik, *The Contribution of the Rwanda Tribunal to the Development of International Law*. Leiden: Martinus Nijhoff, 2005. Overview of the ICTR's shaping of the law of genocide and crimes against humanity.

Alexander Laban Hinton, ed., *Transitional Justice: Global Mechanisms and Local Realities after Genocide and Mass Violence*. New Brunswick, NJ: Rutgers University Press, 2010. Examines cases including Guatemala, Indonesia/East Timor, Rwanda, and British Columbia.

David Hirsh, *Law against Genocide: Cosmopolitan Trials*. London: Glasshouse Press, 2003. Focuses on four recent trials related to genocide and crimes against humanity.

Michael J. Kelly, *Nowhere to Hide: Defeat of the Sovereign Immunity Defense for Crimes of Genocide and the Trials of Slobodan Milosevic and Saddam Hussein*. New York: Peter Lang, 2005. How the immunity previously granted to leaders of sovereign states eroded in the twentieth and twenty-first centuries.

Antjie Krog, *Country of My Skull: Guilt, Sorrow, and the Limits of Forgiveness in the New South Africa*. New York: Three Rivers Press, 2000. Searing study of the truth and reconciliation process after apartheid.

Martha Minow, *Between Vengeance and Forgiveness: Facing History after Genocide and Mass Violence*. Boston, MA: Beacon Press, 1998. A good introduction to issues of truth and redress.

Nunca Más: The Report of the Argentine National Commission on the Disappeared. New York: Farrar Straus Giroux, 1986; Spanish version online at www.nuncamas.org/index.htm; English version at http://web.archive.org/web/20031004074316/nuncamas.org/english/library/nevagain/nevagain_001.htm. The groundbreaking investigation of crimes committed by the Argentine military *junta* (1976–1983).

Steven R. Ratner and Jason S. Abrams, *Accountability for Human Rights Atrocities in International Law: Beyond the Nuremberg Legacy* (2nd edn). Oxford: Oxford University Press, 2001. Best read alongside Schabas (see below), with a useful Cambodia case study.

W. Michael Reisman and Chris T. Antoniou, eds., *The Laws of War: A Comprehensive Collection of Primary Documents on International Laws Governing Armed Conflict*. New York: Vintage, 1994. Core texts with commentary.

Geoffrey Robertson, *Crimes against Humanity: The Struggle for Global Justice* (3rd edn). New York: The New Press, 2007. Thin on genocide, but elegantly written and bracingly opinionated.

Philippe Sands, *East West Street: On the Origins of "Genocide" and "Crimes Against Humanity."* New York: Alfred A. Knopf, 2016. Fascinating and intimate study of the intersecting lives of Raphael Lemkin and Hersch Lauterpacht. The latter pioneered the concept of "crimes against humanity" in international jurisprudence.

William A. Schabas, *Genocide in International Law: The Crime of Crimes* (2nd edn). Cambridge: Cambridge University Press, 2009. Comprehensive and massively detailed; an indispensable reference work.

Sarah B. Sewall and Carl Kaysen, eds., *The United States and the International Criminal Court: National Security and International Law*. Lanham, MD: Rowman & Littlefield, 2000. Essays analyzing the ICC initiative in historical context.

Adam M. Smith, *After Genocide: Bringing the Devil to Justice.* Amherst, NY: Prometheus Books, 2009. Wide-ranging portrait of the accomplishments and travails of the international search for justice.

Eric Stover and Harvey M. Weinstein, eds., *My Neighbor, My Enemy: Justice and Community in the Aftermath of Mass Atrocity.* Cambridge: Cambridge University Press, 2004. Now-classic collection of essays with a grassroots emphasis and expertise, focusing on the Bosnian and Rwandan cases.

NOTES

1   William A. Schabas, *Genocide in International Law: The Crime of Crimes* (Cambridge: Cambridge University Press, 2000), p. 354. Some examples of crimes that command universal jurisdiction are "hijacking and other threats to air travel, piracy, attacks upon diplomats, [threats to] nuclear safety, terrorism, *apartheid* and torture." Elsewhere, Schabas notes that "although no treaty authorizes universal jurisdiction over genocide, and there is as yet no determination of its legitimacy by the International Court of Justice, there now seems little doubt that it is permitted by international law." Schabas, "The Law and Genocide," in Donald Bloxham and A. Dirk Moses, eds., *The Oxford Handbook of Genocide Studies* (Oxford: Oxford University Press, 2013), p. 129.

2   Schabas, *Genocide in International Law*, p. 341.

3   Gladstone quoted in Gary Jonathan Bass, *Stay the Hand of Vengeance: The Politics of War Crimes Tribunals* (Princeton, NJ: Princeton University Press, 2000), p. 33; emphasis added.

4   Mark Levene writes of the Hague process: "It was as if an approximation of the Genocide Convention was being propounded at the end of the First, not the Second, World War." Levene, *The Crisis of Genocide, Vol. 1: Devastation: The European Rimlands, 1912–1938* (Oxford: Oxford University Press, 2013), p. 172.

5   See Vahakn N. Dadrian and Taner Akçam, *Judgment at Istanbul: The Armenian Genocide Trials* (New York: Berghahn Books, 2011).

6   The official names of the tribunals were the International Military Tribunal (Nuremberg, created in August 1945) and the International Military Tribunal for the Far East (Tokyo, created in January 1946). For more on the tribunals, see Joseph E. Persico, *Nuremberg: Infamy on Trial* (London: Penguin, 1995), and Arnold C. Brackman, *The Other Nuremberg: The Untold Story of the Tokyo War Crimes Trials* (New York: William Morrow, 1987).

7   See Richard Overy, "Making Justice at Nuremberg, 1945–1946," www.bbc.co.uk/history/worldwars/wwtwo/war_crimes_trials_01.shtml.

8   Samantha Power, *"A Problem from Hell": America and the Age of Genocide* (New York: Basic Books, 2002), p. 50 (quoting the Nuremberg indictments).

9   "Genocide was mentioned at Nuremberg, but was not included in the charges against the defendants and was not an operative legal concept." Arthur Jay Klinghoffer and Judith Klinghoffer, *International Citizens' Tribunals: Mobilizing Public Opinion to Advance Human Rights* (New York: Palgrave, 2002), p. 195 (n. 5).

10 See Albert Speer's two wily, fascinating volumes of autobiography, drafted secretly in prison: *Inside the Third Reich*, reissue edition (New York: Simon & Schuster, 1997) and *Spandau: The Secret Diaries*, trans. Richard and Clara Winston (New York: MacMillan, 1976); and Gitta Sereny's classic deconstruction of the Speer myth, *Albert Speer: His Battle with Truth* (New York: Vintage, 1996).

11 Michael J. Bazyler and Frank M. Tuerkheimer, *Forgotten Trials of the Holocaust* (New York: New York University Press, 2014), pp. 162–163.

12 Ibid., p. 163.

13 Hilary Earl, *The Nuremberg SS-Einsatzgruppen Trial, 1945–1958: Atrocity, Law, and History* (Cambridge: Cambridge University Press, 2010), pp. 79, 93, 179. Earl notes that while genocide featured in the indictment, "in the end, the issue was largely avoided at trial and the prosecutors thereby missed an early opportunity to develop the legal concept into positive law" (p. 95).

14 Bazyler and Tuerkheimer, *Forgotten Trials*, p. 165.

15 Ibid., p. 168.

16 Ibid., p. 193.

17 The first full-length biography is Tom Hofmann, *Benjamin Ferencz, Nuremberg Prosecutor and Peace Advocate* (Jefferson, NC: McFarland & Company, 2014).

18 Hilary Earl, "Prosecuting Genocide before the Genocide Convention: Raphael Lemkin and the Nuremberg Trials, 1945–1949," *Journal of Genocide Research*, 15: 3 (2013), p. 323.

19 The video of Ferencz's ICC summation can be viewed at www.youtube.com/watch?v=TI3JhJOhBQo.

20 For a recent interview with Ferencz, see "'World Powers Betrayed the Spirit of Nuremberg,'" *France24.com*, December 4, 2015, www.france24.com/en/20151119-nuremburg-anniversary-ben-ferencz-interview-world-powers-holocaust-icc.

21 Steven R. Ratner and Jason S. Abrams, *Accountability for Human Rights Atrocities in International Law: Beyond the Nuremberg Legacy* (2nd edn) (Oxford: Oxford University Press, 2001), p. 22. Martha Minow points out that "no prior law made it clear that individuals could be charged with the crime of waging aggressive war; the same held true for crimes against humanity, including murder, extermination, enslavement, and persecution on the basis of views or identities." Minow, *Between Vengeance and Forgiveness: Facing History after Genocide and Mass Violence* (Boston, MA: Beacon Press, 1998), p. 33.

22 Geoffrey Robertson, *Crimes against Humanity: The Struggle for Global Justice* (New York: The New Press, 2000), p. 224.

23 David Hirsh, *Law against Genocide: Cosmopolitan Trials* (London: Glasshouse Press, 2003), p. 42.

24 Robertson, *Crimes against Humanity*, p. 222.

25 David M. Crowe, *War Crimes, Genocide, and Justice: A Global History* (New York: Palgrave Macmillan, 2014), pp. 160, 193.

26 Hirsh, *Law against Genocide*, p. xvi.

27 Bullock quoted in Richard J. Goldstone and Gary Jonathan Bass, "Lessons from the International Criminal Tribunals," in Sarah B. Sewall and Carl Kaysen, eds., *The United States and the International Criminal Court: National Security and International Law* (Lanham, MD: Rowman & Littlefield, 2000), p. 54.

28 Bass wrote that the ICTY "was an act of tokenism by the world community, which was largely unwilling to intervene in ex-Yugoslavia but did not mind creating an institution that would give the *appearance* of moral concern." Bass, *Stay the Hand of Vengeance*, p. 214.

29 Louis Sell, *Slobodan Milosevic and the Destruction of Yugoslavia* (Durham, NC: Duke University Press, 2002), p. 361.

30 Paul Mojzes, *Balkan Genocides: Holocaust and Ethnic Cleansing in the Twentieth Century* (Lanham, MD: Rowman & Littlefield, 2011), p. 225.

31 For a nuanced examination, see David Bruce MacDonald, "The Fire in 1999? The United States, NATO and the Bombing of Yugoslavia," in Adam Jones, ed., *Genocide, War Crimes and the West: History and Complicity* (London: Zed Books, 2004), pp. 276–298.

32 Mojzes, *Balkan Genocides*, p. 169.

33 Rory Carroll, "Genocide Tribunal 'Ignoring Tutsi Crimes,'" *The Guardian*, January 13, 2005. "A former prosecutor, Carla del Ponte, promised to charge members of the RPF [the Tutsi-led Rwandan Patriotic Front] but before doing so she was removed from her post by a unanimous vote in the UN security council in August 2003. Her successor, Hassan Bubacar Jallow, showed no such zeal."

34 See Minow, *Between Vengeance and Forgiveness*, p. 41.

35 Gérard Prunier, *Africa's World War: Congo, the Rwandan Genocide, and the Making of a Continental Catastrophe* (New York: Oxford University Press, 2009), p. 309.

36 Laura Heaton, "Last Days for UN Court Trying Suspects in Rwanda Genocide," *The New York Times*, December 14, 2015, www.nytimes.com/2015/12/15/world/africa/last-days-for-un-court-trying-suspects-in-rwanda-genocide.html.

37 Mark Kersten, "The Rwanda Tribunal Closes—But Who Owns Its 'Legacy'?," Justice in Conflict, December 18, 2015, http://justiceinconflict.org/2015/12/18/the-rwanda-tribunal-closes-but-who-owns-its-legacy/.

38 Heaton, "Last Days for UN Court."

39 Robertson, *Crimes against Humanity*, p. 296; emphasis added.

40 Christopher Rudolph, "Constructing an Atrocities Regime: The Politics of War Crimes Tribunals," *International Organization*, 55: 3 (2001), p. 667.

41 Yusuf Aksar, "The 'Victimized Group' Concept in the Genocide Convention and the Development of International Humanitarian Law through the Practice of Ad Hoc Tribunals," *Journal of Genocide Research*, 5: 2 (2003), p. 217; emphasis added.

42 Ratner and Abrams, *Accountability for Human Rights Atrocities*, p. 201.

43 Schabas, *Genocide in International Law*, p. 384.

44 Ibid., p. 174.

45 Nicholas A. Jones, *The Courts of Genocide: Politics and the Rule of Law in Rwanda and Arusha* (London: Routledge, 2010), p. 143.

46 See, e.g., Susan Brownmiller, *Against Our Will: Men, Women, and Rape* (New York: Bantam, 1975); Alexandra Stiglmayer, ed., *Mass Rape: The War against Women in Bosnia-Herzegovina* (Lincoln, NB: University of Nebraska Press, 1994).

47 On the rape of males in conflict and genocide, see pp. 634–635.

48 Judge Meron stated: "By seeking to eliminate a part of the Bosnian Muslims, the Bosnian Serb forces committed genocide. They targeted for extinction the 40,000 Bosnian Muslims living in Srebrenica, a group which was emblematic of the Bosnian Muslims in general. They stripped all the male Muslim prisoners, military and civilian, elderly and young, of their personal belongings and identification, and deliberately and methodically killed them solely on the basis of their identity." Ian Traynor, "Hague Rules Srebrenica Was Genocide," *The Guardian*, April 20, 2004, www.theguardian.com/world/2004/apr/20/warcrimes.

49 For the full text of the Rome Statute, see http://legal.un.org/icc/statute/romefra.htm.

50 See Robert Marquand, "Why Genocide is Difficult to Prosecute," *The Christian Science Monitor*, April 30, 2007, www.csmonitor.com/2007/0430/p01s04-wogi.html.

51 L.J. van den Herik has written of the Rwanda tribunal (ICTR) that "an examination of the legal description of crimes against humanity . . . reveals that this crime has been formulated to serve as a kind of safety net in case genocide could not be proved." Van den Herik, *The Contribution of the Rwanda Tribunal to the Development of International Law* (Leiden: Martinus Nijhoff Publishers, 2005), pp. 254–255.

52 Zachary Manfredi, "Implications of the Absence of Genocide Charges for Bashir," *ICC Observers*, March 5, 2009, http://iccobservers.wordpress.com/2009/03/05/icc-observers-commentary-implications-of-the-abscence-of-genocide-charges-for-bashir.

53 As Daniel Jonah Goldhagen argues, "We should use 'genocide' . . . regularly and liberally for mass murders," since "more than any other term, [it] conveys the magnitude of the horror of what perpetrators do to their victims." Goldhagen, *Worse Than War: Genocide, Eliminationism, and the Ongoing Assault on Humanity* (New York: Basic Books, 2009), p. 525.

54 Ratner and Abrams, *Accountability for Human Rights Atrocities*, p. 182.

55 Ibid., p. 175.

56 Robertson, *Crimes against Humanity*, p. 240. Demjanjuk died in 2012.

57 "Surprisingly, perhaps, to western Europeans schooled in thinking that communist orthodoxy inevitably prohibited proper investigation of the racist thrust of Nazi genocide, Poland maintained arguably the most consistent record over the post-war decades of trying war criminals. Poland also tried an unusually large number of Germans, as

opposed to the general European record of trying indigenous collaborators: of the 5,450 war criminals tried up to 1977, 5,358 were German nationals and many of these were perpetrators of the Holocaust, including at least 617 former personnel of Auschwitz-Birkenau." Donald Bloxham, "From Streicher to Sawoniuk: The Holocaust in the Courtroom," in Dan Stone, ed., *The Historiography of the Holocaust* (London: Palgrave Macmillan, 2004), p. 403.

58 David Crowe calls the Eichmann trial "the first legal undertaking since the 1940s that addressed the question of genocide in a formal legal context," but notes that genocide was erroneously introduced to the charge-sheet, then changed to charges under the Israeli Nazi and Nazi Collaborators (Punishment) Law, "since [Eichmann's crimes] took place before the [Genocide] convention went into effect." Crowe, *War Crimes, Genocide, and Justice: A Global History* (New York: Palgrave Macmillan, 2014), p. 285.

59 For a complete list, see Prevent Genocide International, "Declarations and Reservations to the Convention on the Prevention and Punishment of the Crime of Genocide," www.preventgenocide.org/law/convention/reservations/.

60 Schabas, *Genocide in International Law*, p. 351 (n. 28).

61 Cited in Tom Fawthrop and Helen Jarvis, *Getting Away with Genocide? Elusive Justice and the Khmer Rouge Tribunal* (London: Pluto Press, 2004), p. 223.

62 Ibid., p. 240.

63 Jörg Menzel, "Justice Delayed or Too Late for Justice? The Khmer Rouge Tribunal and the Cambodian 'Genocide' 1975–79," *Journal of Genocide Research*, 9: 2 (2007), p. 224.

64 Laura Smith-Spark, "Charles Taylor: War Crimes Conviction, 50-year Sentence Upheld," *CNN.com*, September 26, 2013, www.cnn.com/2013/09/26/world/africa/netherlands-charles-taylor-verdict/.

65 See "'Forced Marriage' Conviction a First," IRIN dispatch, February 26, 2009, www.irinnews.org/Report.aspx?ReportId=83160. See also the Special Court's website at www.rscsl.org/.

66 Lyn S. Graybill, "Ten Years After, Rwanda Tries Reconciliation," *Current History*, May 2004, p. 204.

67 George Packer, "Justice on a Hill," in Nicolaus Mills and Kira Brunner, eds., *The New Killing Fields: Massacre and the Politics of Intervention* (New York: Basic Books, 2002), pp. 133–134.

68 Alana Erin Tiemessen, "After Arusha: Gacaca Justice in Post-Genocide Rwanda," *African Studies Quarterly*, 8: 1 (2004).

69 Jones, *The Courts of Genocide*, p. 69.

70 C. Kayitana quoted in ibid., p. 51.

71 Packer, "Justice on a Hill," p. 135.

72 David J. Simon, "The Challenge of Social Reconciliation in Rwanda: Identity, Justice, and Transformation," in Adam Jones, ed., *New Directions in Genocide Research* (London: Routledge, 2012), pp. 265–266. Anne Aghion's 2009 documentary film, *My Neighbor My Killer* (www.gacacafilms.com), powerfully documents the reintegration process, and provides a useful overview of the *gacaca* process as a whole. See also Jennie E. Burnet, "(In)Justice: Truth, Reconciliation, and Revenge in Rwanda's *Gacaca*," in Alexander Laban Hinton, ed., *Transitional Justice: Global Mechanisms and Local Realities after Genocide and Mass Violence* (New Brunswick, NJ: Rutgers University Press, 2010), pp. 95–118. Burnet found that "how well *Gacaca* has functioned varies a great deal from community to community," with "the most important variable" being "the character of the *inyangamugayo* (people of integrity), who serve[d] as judge and jury in the *Gacaca* system" (p. 96).

73 Allende died in the coup, apparently by his own hand as military forces invaded the Moneda presidential palace.

74 A technical consideration dictated, however, that Pinochet could be extradited only for crimes committed after Britain's incorporation of extraterritorial torture as a crime under domestic law. Thus, only offenses from the final two years of Pinochet's rule—not the most repressive—could be extraditable.

75 A good investigation of the events, with many key documents, is Diana Woodhouse, *The Pinochet Case: A Legal and Constitutional Analysis* (Oxford: Hart Publishing, 2000).

76 For a survey, see Roger Burbach, *The Pinochet Affair: State Terrorism and Global Justice* (London: Zed Books, 2003).

77 "Ambiguous," because Eichmann's arrest by Israeli agents was technically a violation of Argentine sovereignty (and was protested as such); furthermore, Eichmann was dispatched clandestinely to Israel to stand trial, rather than being formally extradited. On the search for Eichmann and his kidnapping (at which time he was given a choice between being summarily executed, or tried in Israel), see Neil Bascomb, *Hunting Eichmann: How a Band of Survivors and a Young Spy Agency Chased Down the World's Most Notorious Nazi* (Boston, MA: Mariner Books, 2010).

78 Lord Millet quoted in Robertson, *Crimes against Humanity*, p. 395.

79 Ernesto Verdeja also refers to the Pinochet detention as "an example of how international events can redefine domestic political contours," and this was well before the Chilean Supreme Court's declaration that Pinochet was fit to stand trial. Verdeja, "Institutional Responses to Genocide and Mass Atrocity," in Jones, ed., *Genocide, War Crimes and the West*, p. 339.

80 Robertson, *Crimes against Humanity*, p. 400.

81 Gram Slattery, "Chile Doubles Down on Prosecutions for Pinochet-era Crimes," Reuters dispatch, November 1, 2015, www.reuters.com/article/us-chile-dictatorship-trials-idUSKCN0SQ2D120151101.

82 See Marc Weller, "On the Hazards of Foreign Travel for Dictators and Other International Criminals," *International Affairs*, 75: 3 (1999), pp. 599–617.

83 Rory Carroll, "Former Peruvian President Alberto Fujimori Sentenced to 25 Years," *The Guardian*, April 7, 2009, www.guardian.co.uk/world/2009/apr/07/alberto-fujimori-peru.

84 John G. Heidenrich, *How to Prevent Genocide: A Guide for Policymakers, Scholars, and the Concerned Citizen* (Westport, CT: Praeger, 2001), p. 67.

85 "In 2005, a retired Israeli general, Doron Almog, returned to Israel after landing in London because he was tipped off that police planned to arrest him. The warrant for Almog—who allegedly oversaw the bombing of a Gaza building in which 14 people were killed—was later cancelled. Other Israeli leaders, including former military chief Moshe Yaalon and ex-Shin Bet security chief Avi Dichter, have cancelled trips to Britain in recent years for the same reason." Ian Black, "Tzipi Livni Arrest Warrant Prompts Israeli Government Travel 'Ban,'" *The Guardian*, December 15, 2009, www.guardian.co.uk/world/2009/dec/15/tzipi-livni-arrest-warrant-israeli.

86 Marlise Simons, "Spanish Court Weighs Inquiry on Torture for 6 Bush-Era Officials," *The New York Times*, March 28, 2009, www.nytimes.com/2009/03/29/world/europe/29spain.html.

87 Valerie Nichols, "Spain Rejects 'Bush Six' Torture Trial," Atlantic Council, April 16, 2009, www.atlanticcouncil.org/blogs/new-atlanticist/spain-rejects-bush-six-torture-trial.

88 Schabas, *Genocide in International Law*, pp. 368–369.

89 For a summary of the US position on the Genocide Convention, see Samantha Power, "The United States and Genocide Law: A History of Ambivalence," in Sewall and Kaysen, eds., *The United States and the International Criminal Court*, pp. 165–175.

90 For the complete text of the bill, see http://2001–2009.state.gov/t/pm/rls/othr/misc/23425.htm.

91 Alexander K.A. Greenawalt, "Rethinking Genocidal Intent: The Case for a Knowledge-based Interpretation," *Columbia Law Review*, 99 (1999), p. 2269.

92 Rudolph, "Constructing an Atrocities Regime," p. 678.

93 See the ICC's summary of cases (accessed March 12, 2016) at www.icc-cpi.int/en_menus/icc/situations%20and%20cases/cases/Pages/cases%20index.aspx.

94 See Catrina Stewart, "The Case against Kenya's Powerful Vice-President, William Ruto, That the ICC Must Win to Vindicate Itself," *The Independent*, February 14, 2015,

www.independent.co.uk/news/world/politics/the-case-against-kenyas-powerful-vice-president-william-ruto-that-the-icc-must-win-to-vindicate-10046724.html; "ICC Case against Kenya's Ruto 'In Tatters': Defence," *News24.com*, January 14, 2016, www.news24.com/Africa/News/icc-case-against-kenyas-ruto-in-tatters-defence-20160114–2.

95 "Nice Idea, Now Make It Work," *The Economist*, December 6, 2014, www.economist.com/news/international/21635470-international-criminal-court-struggling-justify-itself-amid-accusations-bias. For a defense of the court along these lines, see Joshua Lam, "How 10 Years of the ICC Have Advanced the Global Struggle for Justice," *The East African*, August 4, 2012.

96 Klinghoffer and Klinghoffer, *International Citizens' Tribunals*.

97 Arthur Jay Klinghoffer, "International Citizens' Tribunals on Human Rights," in Jones, ed., *Genocide, War Crimes and the West*, pp. 350–351.

98 Ann Curthoys and John Docker, "Defining Genocide," in Dan Stone, ed., *The Historiography of Genocide* (London: Palgrave Macmillan, 2008), p. 24.

99 Klinghoffer and Klinghoffer, *International Citizens' Tribunals*, p. 156.

100 See, e.g., the "Criminal Complaint" filed by former US Attorney General to the International Court [People's Tribunal] on Crimes Against Humanity Committed by UN Security Council on Iraq held in Spain in November 1996: Jones, ed., *Genocide, War Crimes and the West*, pp. 270–273; and, most recently, "Declaration of the Jury of Conscience World Tribunal on Iraq," Istanbul, June 27, 2005, www.terrelibere.org/1367-declaration-of-the-jury-of-conscience-world-tribunal-on-iraq/.

101 See Robin Andrews, "Citizens' Tribunal to Investigate Monsanto for 'Ecocide'," *Iflscience.com*, December 7, 2015, www.iflscience.com/environment/citizens-tribunal-investigate-monsanto-ecocide.

102 Klinghoffer and Klinghoffer, *International Citizens' Tribunals*, p. 10.

103 Leo Kuper, *The Prevention of Genocide* (New Haven, CT: Yale University Press, 1985), p. 193.

104 Ibid.

105 Falk quoted in Klinghoffer and Klinghoffer, *International Citizens' Tribunals*, p. 134.

106 Professor Peter Burns of the University of British Columbia, personal communication, May 12, 2005.

107 Minow, *Between Vengeance and Forgiveness*, pp. 60, 67.

108 Priscilla B. Hayner, *Unspeakable Truths: Confronting State Terror and Atrocity* (New York: Routledge, 2001), p. 232.

109 "While most commissions have had the power to name perpetrators, however, only a few have done so: El Salvador, Chad, the second commission of the African National Congress, and the South African Truth and Reconciliation Commission." Hayner, *Unspeakable Truths*, pp. 107–108.

110 Ibid., p. 75.

111 The vision of present-day Canada as "Turtle Island," grounded in Native beliefs, is explored at http://turtleislandeducate.com/about/turtle_island.

112 Letter of the Truth and Reconciliation commissioners, December 31, 2011, in The Truth and Reconciliation Commission of Canada, *They Came for the Children: Canada, Aboriginal Peoples, and Residential Schools* (Winnipeg, MB: Truth and Reconciliation Commission of Canada, 2012), p. iii. The report is available online at www.myrobust.com/websites/trcinstitution/File/2039_T&R_eng_web%5B1%5D.pdf. See the commissioners' profiles at www.trc.ca/websites/trcinstitution/index.php?p=5.

113 Fontaine's 1990 interview on CBC's *The Journal* can be accessed in the CBC Digital Archives at www.cbc.ca/archives/entry/phil-fontaines-shocking-testimony-of-sexual-abuse. At the time, Fontaine was grand chief of the Assembly of Manitoba Chiefs. He subsequently headed the nationwide Assembly of First Nations.

114   Theodore Fontaine, *Broken Circle: The Dark Legacy of Indian Residential Schools: A Memoir* (Victoria, BC: Heritage House, 2010), pp. 120, 132–133, 171. See also the comments of "John," a "Manitoba-based survivor," quoted by Andrew Woolford: "I learned how to suppress my natural feelings, my feelings of love, compassion, natural sharing and gentleness. I learned to replace my feelings with a heart of stone. I became a non-human, non-person, with no language, no love, no home, no people, and a person without an identity. In this heart of stone grew anger, hate, black rages against the cruel and unfeeling world. I was lost in a veil reaching up to the black robes and priests and nuns trying to make sense of all of this anger and cruelty around me. Why were these people so cold? Did they not have parents somewhere who loved them? Why did they despise us so much?" In Woolford, *This Benevolent Experiment: Indigenous Boarding Schools, Genocide, and Redress in Canada and the United States* (Winnipeg, MB: University of Manitoba Press, 2015), p. 199.

115   *Honouring the Truth, Reconciling for the Future: Summary of the Final Report of the Truth and Reconciliation Commission of Canada* (Ottawa: Truth and Reconciliation Commission of Canada, 2015), pp. 1–3. Available online at www.trc.ca/websites/trcinstitution/File/2015/Honouring_the_Truth_Reconciling_for_the_Future_July_23_2015.pdf.

116   McLachlin and Sinclair quoted in John Paul Tasker, "Residential Schools Findings Point to 'Cultural Genocide,' Commission Chair Says," *CBC.ca*, May 29, 2015, www.cbc.ca/news/politics/residential-schools-findings-point-to-cultural-genocide-commission-chair-says-1.3093580.

117   Conrad Black, "Canada is Afflicted by a Pandemic of Defective Moralizing on Native Issues," *The National Post*, June 13, 2015, http://news.nationalpost.com/full-comment/conrad-black-canada-is-afflicted-by-a-pandemic-of-defective-moralizing-on-native-issues.

118   "If 'cultural genocide' were practiced on Indians in Canada, instead of assimilation as 'settlers' assumed would be the best future for aboriginal people, then it was practiced for a long time throughout much of the world, often more violently than in Canada, to the point where the word has lost much of its meaning, except as a rhetorical debating point." Jeffrey Simpson, "Fixating on the Past Makes Progress Difficult," *The Globe and Mail*, June 2, 2015, www.theglobeandmail.com/opinion/fixating-on-the-past-makes-progress-difficult/article24759214/.

119   Jesse Staniforth, "'Cultural Genocide'? No, Canada Committed Regular Genocide," *The Star*, June 10, 2015, www.thestar.com/opinion/commentary/2015/06/10/cultural-genocide-no-canada-committed-regular-genocide.html.

120   See "Idle No More: Indigenous-Led Protests Sweep Canada for Native Sovereignty and Environmental Justice," *Democracy Now*, December 26, 2012, www.democracy-now.org/2012/12/26/idle_no_more_indigenous_led_protests.

121   "In 2013, at the British Columbia National Event in Vancouver, where over 5,000 elementary and secondary school students attended Education Day, several non-Aboriginal youth talked about what they had learned. Matthew Meneses said, 'I'll never forget this day. This is the first day they ever told us about residential schools. If I were to see someone who's Aboriginal, I'd ask them if they can speak their language because I think speaking their language is a pretty cool thing.' Antonio Jordao said, 'It makes me sad for those kids. They took them away from their homes—it was torture, it's not fair. . . . That's one of the worst things that Canada did.' Cassidy Morris said, 'It's good that we're finally learning about what happened.' Jacqulyn Byers told us, 'I hope . . . that a whole lot of people now recognize that the crime happened and that we need to make amends for it.'" Truth and Reconciliation Commission, *Honouring the Truth*, p. 11.

122   David MacDonald, "Five Reasons the TRC Chose 'Cultural Genocide'," *The Globe and Mail*, July 6, 2015, www.theglobeandmail.com/opinion/five-reasons-the-trc-chose-cultural-genocide/article25311423/.

123 Woolford, *This Benevolent Experiment*, pp. 287, 296.

124 Truth and Reconciliation Commission, *Honouring the Truth*, pp. vi, 6, 8.

125 Hayner, *Unspeakable Truths*, p. 111.

126 Fischman and Ross, article on "Group Treatment of Exiled Survivors of Torture," in the *American Journal of Orthopsychiatry;* quoted in Victoria Sanford, *Buried Secrets: Truth and Human Rights in Guatemala* (New York: Palgrave Macmillan, 2003), p. 241.

127 Hayner, *Unspeakable Truths*, p. 185.

128 Ibid.

129 See also Carolyn Nordstrom, "Terror Warfare and the Medicine of Peace," in Catherine Besteman, ed., *Violence: A Reader* (New York: Palgrave Macmillan, 2002), pp. 273–296.

130 Hayner, *Unspeakable Truths*, pp. 190–191. For a similar report from Uganda, see Marc Lacey, "Atrocity Victims in Uganda Choose to Forgive," *The New York Times*, April 18, 2005. "Remarkably, a number of those who have been hacked by the rebels [of the Lord's Resistance Army], who have seen their children carried off by them or who have endured years of suffering in their midst say traditional justice must be the linchpin in ending the war. Their main rationale: the line between victim and killer is too blurred."

131 Ngwenya quoted in Jonathan Steele, "A Healing in Mozambique," *The Guardian*, November 20, 2009, www.guardian.co.uk/commentisfree/2009/nov/20/mozambique-civil-war-peace.

132 Elizabeth F. Drexler, "Addressing the Legacies of Mass Violence and Genocide in Indonesia and East Timor," in Alexander Laban Hinton and Kevin Lewis O'Neill, eds., *Genocide: Truth, Memory, and Representation* (Durham, NC: Duke University Press, 2009), p. 229.

133 Jean Hatzfeld, *The Antelope's Strategy: Living in Rwanda After the Genocide*, trans. Linda Coverdale (New York: Farrar, Straus and Giroux, 2009). The quotes in the box text are drawn from pp. 17–18, 20–21, 83–84, 85, 90.

134 Colin Tatz, *With Intent to Destroy: Reflecting on Genocide* (London: Verso, 2003), p. 105.

135 Ernesto Verdeja, "Transitional Justice and Genocide," in Joyce Apsel and Ernesto Verdeja, eds., *Genocide Matters: Ongoing Issues and Emerging Perspectives* (London: Routledge, 2013), pp. 183–185.

136 David Rising, "Germany Increases Reparations for Holocaust Survivors," *The Times of Israel*, November 16, 2012, www.timesofisrael.com/germany-increases-reparations-for-holocaust-survivors/.

137 See "Holocaust Reparations: Germany to Pay 772 Million Euros to Survivors," *Der Spiegel*, May 29, 2013, www.spiegel.de/international/germany/germany-to-pay-772-million-euros-in-reparations-to-holocaust-survivors-a-902528.html.

138 See, e.g., Ta-nehisi Coates, "The Case for Reparations," *The Atlantic*, June 2014, www.theatlantic.com/magazine/archive/2014/06/the-case-for-reparations/361631.

139 See Daniel Martin, "Athens Demands £200 BILLION from Germany in Reparation for Nazi Atrocities Committed during World War Two . . . Days before Greece is Due to Pay Back £450m of Debt," *Mail Online*, April 7, 2015; Matthew Dalton, "In Greek Town, Reparations Claim Against Germany Hits Home," *Wall Street Journal*, May 19, 2015, www.wsj.com/articles/in-greek-town-reparations-claim-against-germany-hits-home-1432075909. (Reporting from the town of Kalavryta, where "on Dec. 13, 1943, German soldiers gunned down 496 men and boys, the worst of many massacres during their brutal occupation of Greece.")

140 See Christopher Alcantara, *Negotiating the Deal: Comprehensive Land Claims Agreements in Canada* (Toronto: University of Toronto Press, 2013).

141 Doreen Carvajal, "Museums Confront the Skeletons in Their Closets," *The New York Times*, May 24, 2013, www.nytimes.com/2013/05/25/arts/design/museums-move-to-return-human-remains-to-indigenous-peoples.html.

142 Paul Carter, "Aboriginal Remains Repatriated," *The Sydney Morning Herald*, September 21, 2009.

143 See Linda Te Aho, "Power-Sharing and Natural Resources," *PostTreatySettlements.org .nz*, n.d., http://posttreatysettlements.org.nz/power-sharing-and-natural-resources/. See also Joseph J. Spaeder and Harvey A. Feit, "Co-management and Indigenous Communities: Barriers and Bridges to Decentralized Resource Management," *Anthropologica*, 47: 2 (2005), pp. 147–154.

144 Gary Mason, "Aboriginal Revenue Sharing is an Idea Whose Time Has Come," *The Globe and Mail*, January 23, 2015, www.theglobeandmail.com/opinion/aboriginal-revenue-sharing-is-an-idea-whose-time-has-come/article22589275/.

145 See Emilie Iob, "10 Years In, South African Affirmative Action Faces Criticism,"Voice of America, October 29, 2013, www.voanews.com/content/south-african-affirmative-action-faces-criticism-on-tenth-anniversary/1779584.html.

146 See, e.g., Alice Lee, "Gender Quotas Worked in Norway. Why Not Here?," *New Republic*, September 5, 2014, https://newrepublic.com/article/119343/impact-quotas-corporate-gender-equality.

147 A relevant collection, published as this edition was going into production, is Christopher Daase *et al.,* eds., *Apology and Reconciliation in International Relations: The Importance of Being Sorry* (Abingdon: Routledge, 2016).

148 Minow, *Between Vengeance and Forgiveness*, p. 114.

149 Queen Elizabeth quoted in Elazar Barkan, *The Guilt of Nations: Restitution and Negotiating Historical Injustices* (New York: W.W. Norton, 2001), p. 264.

150 "A 'Sorry Day' in Australia," *BBC Online*, May 26, 1998, http://news.bbc.co.uk/1/hi/world/asia-pacific/100476.stm.

151 Clinton's semi-apology ran as follows: "It may seem strange to you here, especially the many of you who lost members of your family, but all over the world there were people like me sitting in offices, day after day after day, who did not fully appreciate the depth and the speed with which you were being engulfed by this unimaginable terror. The international community, together with nations in Africa, must bear its share of responsibility for this tragedy as well. We did not act quickly enough after the killing began. We should not have allowed the refugee camps to become safe haven for the killers. We did not immediately call these crimes by their rightful name: genocide. We cannot change the past. But we can and must do everything in our power to help you build a future without fear and full of hope." See "Text of Clinton's Rwanda Speech," CBS News, March 25, 1998, www.cbsnews.com/news/text-of-clintons-rwanda-speech/.

152 For text and video of Rudd's apology, see www.australia.gov.au/about-australia/our-country/our-people/apology-to-australias-indigenous-peoples. For those inclined to dismiss such apologies as "only words," Hall Greenland captures something of the impact of Rudd's parliamentary declaration: "There were tears in Kevin Rudd's eyes as the parliament, the crowded gallery and huge crowd outside rose to give him a standing ovation. And there was not a dry eye among the thousands that assembled at the open-air broadcast in Eveleigh Street in the Sydney suburb of Redfern—Australia's little Harlem. All over Sydney the Aboriginal flag flew from town halls, schools and even Sydney University two blocks from Eveleigh Street. . . . For many kids this day will be like the day of the moon landing, or the day Martin Luther King was assassinated, or Che [Guevara] murdered, or JFK shot, was for previous generations; they will remember where they were if only because lots of schools watched the apology. It means these rising generations will inherit an Australia which has, if not a clean sheet, at least an honest one." Greenland, "Australia's Finest Hour," *Counterpunch.org*, February 13, 2008, www.counterpunch.org/2008/02/13/australia-s-finest-hour/.

153 See Krissah Thompson, "Senate Backs Apology for Slavery," *The Washington Post*, June 19, 2009; text of the Senate resolution available at www.congress.gov/bill/111th-congress/senate-concurrent-resolution/26.

154 Theodore R. Johnson, "How to Apologize for Slavery," *The Atlantic*, August 6, 2014, www.theatlantic.com/international/archive/2014/08/how-to-apologize-for-slavery/375650/.

155 Owen Bowcott, "Danes Say Sorry for Viking Raids on Ireland," *The Guardian*, August 15, 2007, www.guardian.co.uk/world/2007/aug/16/ireland.

156 Barkan, *The Guilt of Nations*, p. 323.

157 Tony Barta, "Sorry, and Not Sorry, in Australia: How the Apology to the Stolen Generations Buried a History of Genocide," *Journal of Genocide Research*, 10: 2 (2008), pp. 201–214.

158 On Israel-Palestine, see Ilan Pappé, *The Ethnic Cleansing of Palestine* (Oxford: Oneworld, 2006). With regard to the ethnic German expulsions, a small step was taken by the Czech government in August 2005, apologizing to expellees who were "active opponents of Nazism." See "Czechs Apologize for Mistreating German Anti-Nazis in WWII," Reuters dispatch in *Haaretz.com*, August 30, 2005. However, see also the European Court of Human Rights decision of October 2008 "reject[ing] a land claim by ethnic Germans who lost homes in Poland during World War II," on the grounds that "modern Poland bears no responsibility for the expulsion of ethnic Germans by the Soviets . . . because it had no governmental control of the land," and therefore was not obliged "to enact laws providing for rehabilitation, restitution of confiscated property or compensation for property lost by the individual applicants." "Court Throws out Restitution Claim by Ethnic Germans," *Deutsche Welle* dispatch, October 10, 2008.

CHAPTER 16

Strategies of Intervention and Prevention

The slogan "Never Again," said human rights scholar Thomas Cushman, "embodies in crystalline form the preventative discourse" that pervades comparative genocide studies:

> Through empirical and scientific observation of operationally defined cases of genocide, one can isolate the variables and causal mechanisms at work and predict future genocides. Armed with such predictions, one can take specific practical steps to intervene and stop genocides from occurring. The key to success is the development of political mechanisms or structures, which will heed the scientific understanding and possess the political will, which means basically the ability and the physical force necessary to intervene to stop genocide.[1]

Cushman viewed such optimism skeptically. He rejected the notion that all genocides can be prevented or suppressed. But he recognized that *some* can be, and he argued for strategies sensitive to historical context and the practical limitations on key actors. With such cautions in mind, this chapter tries to avoid easy answers and pat solutions. But it recognizes, and indeed typifies, the concern of the vast majority of genocide scholars and advocates, not only with regard to past genocides, but in confronting present genocidal outbreaks and preventing them in the future.

Figure 16.1 Never again . . . but how? Detail of memorial at the Dachau concentration camp in southern Germany.

Source: Massimiliano Giani/Creative Commons/Flickr.

Why should genocide be prevented? For most people who have read this far, the answer may be self-evident: to preserve people and groups at risk of destruction. But what if moral considerations are excluded, and rational self-interest is emphasized? This would at least have the advantage of appealing to a broader range of potential allies.

In his thoughtful book *How to Prevent Genocide*, John Heidenrich addressed this question head-on. He pointed out that genocides typically generate refugee flows that can overwhelm neighboring countries and destabilize whole regions. Today, up to 27 million people may also be "internally displaced" worldwide as a result of genocide. "Such global multitudes of homeless and often stateless people have repeatedly drained the resources of the world's emergency aid services." He added that "every major genocidal crisis also shakes the international order. No one in 1994 expected that, within two years, mass killings in tiny Rwanda would plunge the enormity of Zaire/Congo into a civil war drawing in countries from almost half of Africa—but that is what happened."[2]

It is thus in the interest of humanity—both morally and practically—to oppose the crime against humanity that is genocide. What are the most reliable warning signs and expediting conditions of this phenomenon? What ideas have been proposed for genocide intervention and prevention? What might we add to the mix? And what is the role of central actors, from the international community and its constituent organizations, to nongovernmental organizations (NGOs), civil society, and concerned—or potentially genocidal—individuals?

WARNING SIGNS

> Genocide . . . rarely comes out of the blue anymore [*sic*] than it picks on a group of
> people for no reason whatsoever.
>
> Mark Levene

What are the most reliable indicators that a genocide is impending? Although there is no "general 'essence' of genocide . . . across time and space," some traits and enabling conditions may serve as red flags.[3] In outlining them, I touch on possible intervention strategies, but postpone a more substantial engagement with this theme for later in the chapter.

- *A history of genocide and intercommunal conflict.* As political scientist Barbara Harff reminded us, "perpetrators of genocide often are repeat offenders, because elites and security forces may become habituated to mass killing as a strategic response to challenges to state security."[4] Genocide is frequently dependent on pre-existing patterns of state behavior and state–society relations. Psychologist Ervin Staub pointed to "ideologies of antagonism" among communal groups, "the outcome of a long history of hostility and mutual violence."[5]

- *Severe economic crisis.* Few factors seem so influential in genocidal violence as economic upheaval and catastrophe. When the material base of people's lives is thrown into question, they are prone to seek scapegoats among minorities (or majorities); to heed an extremist political message; and to be lured by opportunities to loot, pillage, and supervene. Economic crisis may undermine the legitimacy and administrative capacity of state authorities, who may lash out genocidally as a means of maintaining power. Such crises also encourage rebellious, revolutionary, and secessionist movements. These movements may fuel the ruling authorities' paranoia, and sometimes contain a genocidal seed and impetus of their own.

- *Mobilization along lines of communal cleavage.* It is natural for people of a particular religion, language, or history—the usual markers of "ethnic" identity—to associate with others who share those traits. Social and political mobilization along such lines is not inherently bad and violence-provoking. Indeed, if successfully managed, it may *forestall* outbreaks of violence. No one anticipates a genocidal outbreak in Belgium or Switzerland, for example— two countries whose political systems are largely structured along communal or "consociational" lines.[6]

   Nonetheless, a healthy and nongenocidal society will, in place of or in addition to such mobilizations, include a range of "cross-cutting" forums, movements, and socialization mechanisms that encourage people to move beyond limited identifications toward a more cosmopolitan vision. Such relations can help offset us-and-them thinking, as Ervin Staub wrote: "To evolve an appreciation of alike-ness and a feeling of connectedness, members of subgroups of society must live together, work together, play together; their children must go to school together. Members of different nations must also work and play together . . . To reduce prejudice requires positive contact."[7]

BOX 16.1 THE UNITED NATIONS OFFICE OF GENOCIDE PREVENTION (OSAPG) AND THE *FRAMEWORK* OF ATROCITY CRIMES

Figure 16.2 Adama Dieng, as of 2016 the United Nations Special Adviser on the Prevention of Genocide.
Source: Photo by Jean-Marc Ferré/UN Photo.

The mission statement of the UN Office of the Special Adviser on the Prevention of Genocide (OSAPG), based at the organization's New York headquarters, "acts as a catalyst to raise awareness of the causes and dynamics of genocide, to alert relevant actors where there is a risk of genocide, and to advocate and mobilize for appropriate action."[8] Founded in the wake of soul-searching over the UN's manifest and often craven failures in the Bosnian and Rwandan genocides (Chapters 8–9), the Special Adviser on genocide—one of around fifty in the UN system—was mandated by the Secretary-General to

(a) collect existing information, in particular from within the United Nations system, on massive and serious violations of human rights and international humanitarian law of ethnic and racial origin that, if not prevented or halted, might lead to genocide; (b) act as a mechanism of early warning to the Secretary-General, and through him to the Security Council, by bringing to their attention potential situations that could result in genocide; (c) make recommendations to the Security Council, through the Secretary-General, on actions to prevent or halt genocide; (d) liaise with the United Nations system on activities for the prevention of genocide and work to enhance the United Nations capacity to analyse and manage information relating to genocide or related crimes.[9]

Under the initial stewardship of Francis Deng, the office quickly attracted criticism and a measure of derision for its rather low-key efforts to confront ongoing and potentially-impending outbreaks of genocide, crimes against humanity, and war crimes.[10] The current Special Adviser, Adama Dieng, is a Senegalese "legal and human rights expert" and former registrar of the Rwandan genocide tribunal (ICTR; see Figure 16.2). His public and institutional profile may be slightly higher than his predecessor's, but there is little doubt that the OSAPG remains notably peripheral in the UN bureaucratic labyrinth. One can cite moments when it set a seal of official concern and definition upon outbreaks of mass atrocity—Syria, Islamic State. But in no specific case, it seems, has the Special Adviser played a decisive or even influential role.

Perhaps most substantial, instead, are the office's little-noticed *conceptual* and *consociational* contributions. I have had the privilege of serving as an expert consultant in several overseas seminars co-sponsored by the OSAPG—mostly in the former Yugoslavia, but also in Jakarta, Bangkok, and Geneva. Delegates from around the Balkans, Europe, or Southeast Asia—mostly younger civil-society activists but also some political, military, and humanitarian representatives—have gathered under UN auspices to share insights, experiences, and (in the Balkan cases) a truly eye-watering quantity of tobacco. Real communication has been generated, along with a smidgen of intercommunal reconciliation and cooperation.

My own presentations at such gatherings, jointly with Yale political scientist David Simon, seek to bring comparative and conceptual clarity to the discussions. Since 2014, UN teams have used a core OSAPG document: the *Framework of Analysis for Atrocity Crimes*. This "integrated analysis and risk assessment tool" draws on scholarly understandings of genocide-as-process, and the insights into genocidal "stages" and warning signs generated by Gregory Stanton's Genocide Watch (www.genocidewatch.org) and other projects. It outlines eight "common" (structural) and six "specific" (situational/dynamic) risk factors, each with a set of onset "indicators":

Common Factors

1. **Situations of armed conflict or other forms of instability** ("International or non-international armed conflict," security and humanitarian crises, political-economic-social tension and instability);
2. **Record of serious violations of international human rights and humanitarian law** ("Past or present serious restrictions to or violations of international human rights and humanitarian law . . . Past acts of genocide, crimes against humanity, war crimes or their incitement. . . . Policy or practice of impunity for or tolerance of serious violations . . . Justification, biased accounts or denial of serious violations . . .");

3. **Weakness of state structures** ("National legal framework that does not offer ample and effective protection . . . Lack of an independent and impartial judiciary . . . Lack of effective civilian control of security forces . . . High levels of corruption or poor governance . . . Insufficient resources . . .");

4. **Motives or incentives** ("Political motives, particularly those aimed at the attainment or consolidation of power . . . Economic interests . . . Strategic or military interests . . . Ideologies based on the supremacy of a certain identity . . . Politicization of past grievances . . . Social trauma");

5. **Capacity to commit atrocity crimes** ("Availability of personnel and of arms and ammunition . . . Capacity to encourage or recruit large numbers of supporters . . . Strong culture of obedience to authority and group conformity . . . Presence of commercial actors or companies that can serve as enablers . . . Armed, financial, logistic, training or other support of external actors . . .");

6. **Absence of mitigating factors** ("Limited or lack of empowerment . . . [of] elements that could contribute to the ability of protected groups, populations or individuals to protect themselves . . . Lack of a strong, organized and representative national civil society and of a free . . . media . . . Lack of or limited presence of the United Nations, INGOs [international nongovernmental organizations] or other international or regional actors . . . Lack of exposure, openness or establishment of political or economic relations with other States . . . Lack of support by neighbouring States . . .";

7. **Enabling circumstances or preparatory action** ("Imposition of emergency laws or extraordinary security measures . . . Suspension of or interference with vital State institutions . . . Strengthening of the security apparatus . . . Increased violations of the right to life [and] physical integrity . . . Imposition of life-threatening living conditions . . . Marking of people or their property . . . Increased politicization of identity . . . Increased inflammatory rhetoric, propaganda campaigns or hate speech . . .");

8. **Triggering factors** ("Sudden deployment of security forces or commencement of armed hostilities . . . Abrupt or irregular regime changes . . . Religious events or real or perceived acts of religious intolerance or disrespect . . . Sudden [economic] changes . . . Acts related to accountability processes, particularly when perceived as unfair.")

Specific Factors

9. **Intergroup tensions or patterns of discrimination against protected groups** ("Segregational, restrictive or exclusionary practices, policies or legislation . . . Denial of the existence of protected groups . . . History of atrocity crimes committed with impunity . . . Past or present serious tensions or conflicts between protected groups . . . Lack of national mechanisms or initiatives to deal with identity-based tensions or conflict");

10. **Signs of an intent to destroy in whole or in part a protected group** (". . . Documents, political manifests, media records . . . through which a

direct intent, or incitement, to target a protected group is revealed, or can be inferred . . . Targeted physical elimination . . . Widespread or systematic discriminatory or targeted practices or violence . . . Attacks against or destruction of homes, farms, businesses or other livelihoods of a protected group and/or of their cultural or religious symbols and property");

11. **Signs of a widespread or systematic attack against any civilian population** ("Signs of patterns of violence against civilian populations . . . Increase in the level of organization or coordination of violent acts . . . Use of the media or other means to provoke or incite to violent acts . . . Establishment of new political or military structures");

12. **Signs of a plan or policy to attack any civilian population** (". . . A State or organizational plan or policy to target civilian populations or protected groups . . . Discriminatory security procedures . . . Alteration of the ethnic, religious, racial or political composition of the overall population . . . Preparation or mobilization of armed forces . . . Involvement of State institutions or high-level political or military authorities in violent acts");

13. **Serious threats to those protected under international humanitarian law** ("Fragmentation of parties . . . Mistrust . . . Increased radicalization . . . Threat of or incitement to violence against those protected under international humanitarian law . . . Refusal to allow inspections . . . Refusal to acknowledge detentions");

14. **Serious threats to humanitarian or peacekeeping operations** (". . . Rules of engagement or legislation that allow the disproportionate or indiscriminate use of force . . . Increased intensity of the conflict . . . Attacks against locations in close proximity to humanitarian or peacekeeping operations and personnel . . . Disrespect, threats or increase in attacks . . . [against] humanitarian or peacekeeping operations").

The specificity of risk factors and warning signs is not matched by a similar array of intervention options. At this point, the office and the United Nations more generally move into highly-contested territory. The *Framework* considers prevention and intervention to be "primarily the responsibility of individual States." It calls in general terms for "efforts to build the resilience of societies to atrocity crimes . . . by ensuring that the rule of law is respected and that all human rights are protected, without discrimination; by establishing legitimate and accountable national institutions; by eliminating corruption; by managing diversity constructively; and by supporting a strong and diverse civil society and a pluralistic media." [11]

As a survey of genocide early-warning signs, however, the OSAPG *Framework* is both concise and comprehensive. It can usefully be paired with the "Responsibility to Protect" and "Will to Intervene" initiatives (Box 16.3), as indeed the OSAPG is institutionally, to generate strategies of intervention and prevention rooted in both case-sensitive analysis and a commitment to action.

- *Hate propaganda.* A standard feature of genocidal mobilization is hate propaganda, including in mass media, public political speech, websites, graffiti, and more diffuse discourse strategies, such as rumor and gossip. The proliferation of media organs and other institutions devoted to hate speech is usually identifiable, though an increase in frequency and/or intensity of annihilationist rhetoric may be harder to measure. To the extent that it can be gauged, it may identify future *génocidaires*—and their targets. Hate speech underpins "exclusionary ideologies ... that define target groups as expendable."[12] And if there is one message I would seek to impart above all others in the study and prevention of genocide, it is: *Let the perpetrators or would-be perpetrators tell you, by their words and deeds, who their targets are. Then confront them accordingly.*

    How does one confront hate propaganda? Pluralistic societies encounter some of the same vexing questions as in the case of genocide denial (Chapter 14), notably: is it legitimate to suppress dissident speech? Whereas denialism can be confronted with logical and empirical refutation, and includes a grey area of legitimate discussion and debate, hate propaganda directly incites violence. But repressing it may only spur the hatred that underlies it, and give publicity to the propagandists. Constructive countermeasures—support for pluralistic media projects and political initiatives; effective use of education systems— are generally preferable. However, while this argument may be comfortably advanced in democratic living rooms, it has different implications in societies where history and current indicators warn of genocide. Suppressing ethnic hate propaganda in Rwanda, for instance, may run counter to cherished liberal principles, but I, for one, would not object to it.

- *Unjust discriminatory legislation and related measures.* Some discriminatory ("affirmative action") legislation may actually help to suppress a potential genocide (see, e.g., the discussion of the *Bumiputra* policy in Malaysia, p. 772).

    In general, though, discrimination embodied in law (and in deliberately unequal systems of "justice") serves to marginalize and isolate designated groups—perhaps as a prelude to their extermination.

    Another kind of discriminatory legislation deserves attention: that aimed at restricting possession of firearms. My liberal sympathies incline me toward effective gun control as a measure of a civilized society. However, the argument advanced by Jay Simkin *et al.*, members of the odd-sounding group Jews for the Preservation of Firearm Ownership (www.jpfo.org), rings true. They contend that most instances of mass killing have been preceded by systematic campaigns to seize arms from intended targets.[13] A reasonable middle ground might lie in allowing restricted firearm ownership in plural societies, while recognizing that campaigns to suppress private gun ownership in illiberal and repressive societies *may* aim to deny a minority the means to resist genocide.

- *Severe and systematic state repression.* Repression and state terror are especially trenchant indicators that a genocidal campaign may be brewing. Regardless of whether genocide ensues, such abuses must be denounced and suppressed. The imposition of emergency measures; restrictions on civil liberties; the banning or harassing of opposition parties and organizations; arbitrary detentions and large-scale round-ups of civilians; the advent or increased use of torture as state policy; substantial flows of refugees and internally-displaced persons (IDPs)—all these should arouse deep concern, and may well presage a genocidal outbreak.

    These acts are predominantly inflicted in authoritarian and developing societies, but citizens of democratic countries should acknowledge that they are not immune to creeping societal repression. They should be alert to violations of democracy and human rights at home and abroad, exploiting liberal democracy's broad freedoms in doing so.

The groups most likely to be targeted for repression include ethnic, racial, and religious minorities; "middleman" groups, especially those occupying an envied place in the economy (see Chapter 11); political dissidents and accused "enemies of the people," especially those involved in nationalist and secessionist movements or class rebellions; and finally, groups labeled as "outcasts," "asocials," and "rootless and shiftless," or depicted as outside the "universe of obligation," as sociologist Helen Fein theorized it (Chapter 1).

My own contribution to early-warning mechanisms revolves around the vulnerability of adult males, notably men of "battle age" (roughly 15–55). As I argued in Chapter 13, there are grounds for claiming that this group, usually described as the most impervious to violence, is in fact *most* vulnerable to genocide and the repression that routinely precedes it—if by "most vulnerable" we mean most *liable* to be targeted for mass killing and other atrocities.[14] The United Nations and other international organizations, governmental and nongovernmental, require a paradigm shift in their thinking on gender, violence, and humanitarian intervention—one that allows specific, inclusive attention to be paid to adult men and male adolescents. How, for example, might greater sensitivity to the vulnerability of "battle-age" males at Srebrenica have assisted in heading off the gendercidal massacres of July 1995?[15]

BOX 16.2 *PAX ETHNICA*: INOCULATING SOCIETIES AGAINST GENOCIDE

KARL E. MEYER AND

SHAREEN BLAIR BRYSAC

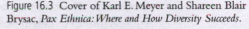

Figure 16.3 Cover of Karl E. Meyer and Shareen Blair Brysac, *Pax Ethnica: Where and How Diversity Succeeds.*

Source: © 2012. Reprinted by permission of PublicAffairs, an imprint of Perseus Books, a division of PBG Publishing, LLC, a subsidiary of Hachette Book Group, Inc.

PAX

ETHNICA

WHERE AND HOW

DIVERSITY SUCCEEDS

What can states and societies do to render themselves less susceptible—perhaps even immune—to genocide? Scholarly interest has recently turned to *negative* cases of genocide: "To know why and when genocide occurs, we need to know why and when genocide does *not* occur, especially when our existing explanations tell us it *should* occur."[16] So argues Scott Straus in his major work, *Making and Unmaking Nations: War, Leadership, and Genocide in Modern Africa* (2015). Another recent Africa-focused volume similarly asked "why some countries avoid mass atrocities despite having much in common with countries that have succumbed to such violence."[17] Stephen McLoughlin's *The Structural Prevention of Mass Atrocities: Understanding Risk and Resilience* (2014) was the first in the series on Genocide and Crimes against Humanity that I will be editing for Routledge Publishers over the life of this textbook.

Building on extensive field research, Straus and McLoughlin explore a wide range of African cases of conflict and successful conflict management. Straus contrasts the genocidal trajectories of Sudan and Rwanda with instances of political restraint/retreat, pluralism, and dialogue in Mali, Côte d'Ivoire, and Senegal. McLoughlin examines Botswana, Zambia, and Tanzania. What do these studies conclude about the strategies that have proved successful in keeping genocide in check?

> *Straus:* I afford a central role to political agency in the process of "making nations." In the African context, most states are ethnically and religiously heterogeneous. The long-term best asset against the risk of genocide and mass categorical [group-targeted] violence is to craft a political vision that incorporates a role for multiple identities as fundamental to the project of the state. . . . Multiethnic nations can be made. In the end, articulating a nationalist narrative of pluralism and inclusion provides the greatest source of restraint. . . .
>
> Another long-term domestic prevention measure is to find ways to avoid or end armed conflict. . . . As a general rule of thumb, finding ways to avoid or mitigate armed conflict remains an imperative—one that has long-term developmental benefits as well.
>
> Diversifying economies, especially those that are reliant on high-value, enclaved mineral exports, is also a long-term [preventive] mechanism . . . The same logic applies to the need for robust and independent civil societies. . . . The more diversified the political and social space, the greater will be the domestic restraint against the escalation of violence. . . . Finally, ensuring accountability for past human rights violations sends a signal that such violence, even if committed in the name of a higher purpose, is not acceptable.[18]
>
> *McLoughlin:* The investigation yielded some key commonalities. First, in the decades preceding independence, the liberation movements in each territory were led by individuals who worked to construct broad and inclusive national

identities. . . . In all three states, the process of decolonization was characterized by amicable relations with the British colonial administrators [thus rendering a violent and destructive "liberation war" unnecessary]. . . . In all three states [Botswana, Zambia, Tanzania], a peaceful transition to independence was followed by the implementation of policies that prioritized the equitable provision of essential services. . . . The three cases . . . highlight how significant were the ideas and actions of the three inaugural leaders [Seretse Khama in Botswana, Kenneth Kaunda in Zambia, and Tanzania's Julius Nyerere] in establishing broad and unifying national identities, and then in initiating a raft of inclusive social policies (albeit with varying degrees of success). . . . The motive of local and national actors in the three cases has never been primarily to prevent mass atrocities, but rather to improve living conditions through better social relations, greater economic opportunities and more representative government.[19]

An eclectic global study of "resilient" societies drew evidence from cases as diverse as Germany and Denmark (they weren't always so friendly), Tatarstan in Russia (see Box 16.4), the polyglot French port of Marseille, and the borough of Queens in New York City. In *Pax Ethnica: Where and How Diversity Succeeds* (2012), Karl E. Meyer and Shareen Blair Brysac cite eleven strategies "for promoting civility in diverse societies":

One. Wherever feasible, choose peace rather than land, since the pains of partition and/or occupation invariably exceed the gains. . . . Two. Take time to make the case—economic, cultural, political—for diversity and do not leave unanswered stereotyped caricatures of currently unpopular minorities. . . . Three. Do not abjure the second passport or demonize hyphenated citizenship. In today's global village, plural citizenship is less a menace than a recognition of a new reality . . . Four. Fear not the persistence of minority tongues. Different languages pose practical problems, especially in schools, but more often than not these are bogus issues puffed up by pseudo-populists. . . . Five. In constructing homes for new immigrants, *horizontal* appears to be more successful than *vertical* [as in Queens, where "most neighborhoods . . . consist of one-family homes amid relatively low-rise brick apartment houses, nurturing street life and identification with neighborhoods"] . . . Six. Do not underestimate the power of professional, parental, and civic associations. Seven. Use public libraries to give immigrant newcomers a welcoming space where not only books but DVDs are available in their mother tongue. . . . Eight. Make empowerment of women a priority, the better to erode barriers between ethnic communities, promote economic growth and smaller families, combat spousal abuse, raise health standards, and provide role models for students. . . . Nine. Celebrate difference of creed and culture with a calendar that records the major religious festivals and national holidays of diverse minorities. . . . Ten. Recognize, celebrate, and elect the political leaders who actively promote diversity . . . Eleven. Do not underestimate the allure of popular culture, rap music, or sports to diminish class differences and foster a [more diverse] society . . . [20]

HUMANITARIAN INTERVENTION

> The reality that interventions may not be able to be mounted in every case where there is justification for doing so is no reason for them not to be mounted in any case.
>
> International Commission on Intervention and State
> Sovereignty (ICISS), 2001

Humanitarian intervention is not a post–Cold War invention. In researching and drafting his history of genocide, Raphael Lemkin drew on the legal scholar Ellery Stowell, who in 1931 defined "humanitarian intervention" as "the justifiable use of force for the purpose of protecting the inhabitants of another state from treatment so arbitrary and persistently abusive as to exceed the limits within which the sovereign is presumed to act with reason and justice."[21] The passage could have been lifted straight from the findings of the International Commission on State Sovereignty's *Responsibility to Protect* report (see p. 764), with perhaps a reduced (but still considerable) emphasis on the use of military force.

The 1990s inaugurated a new age of humanitarian intervention. With the end of the Cold War, the way lay open for hard-nosed *Realpolitik* to be set aside in favor of efforts to help suffering and persecuted peoples. The United Nations would finally come into its own as the arbiter and peace-builder that Franklin Roosevelt originally envisaged. Regional actors would step up to address nearby trouble spots.

At the same time, the collapse of the Soviet empire and of superpower rivalries had allegedly "lifted the lid off" a host of simmering conflicts, mostly ethnonational in nature. One prominent observer warned of a "coming anarchy" of state collapse and untrammeled violence.[22] In many parts of the world—Africa, former Soviet central Asia, the Caucasus, the Balkans—anarchy did indeed arrive.

During this period, "humanitarian intervention" came to be associated with a military response to atrocities, separating warring factions, supervising negotiations, and brokering political settlements. The four key cases of, and debates over, humanitarian intervention in the 1990s—Iraqi Kurdistan (1991); Bosnia-Herzegovina (1992–1995); and Kosovo and East Timor (both 1999)—all featured such interventions. However, might such military interventions instead represent *failures*, in the same way that successful fire-fighting may attest to inadequate fire prevention? In this discussion, I first address non-military intervention strategies. As the former UN Special Adviser on the Responsibility to Protect, Edward Luck, has stressed: "Good policy starts with anticipation and prevention, early engagement, and keeping as many reasonable options open as possible."[23]

Military solutions should be a last resort, although mounted resolutely and with all dispatch when necessary. Strategies of "preventive intervention" include "development assistance and other efforts to help address the root cause of potential conflict; or efforts to provide support for local initiatives to advance good governance, human rights, or the rule of law; or good offices missions, mediation efforts and other efforts to promote dialogue or reconciliation."[24] Lending political support—whether good offices, formal mediation, or simply rhetorical support—to governments that act respectfully toward their citizens is one of the most constructive interventionist measures.

Conversely, *withholding* aid may be a potent intervention strategy. It is essential that military and "security" aid not be provided to forces of repression. However, recent history suggests that such forces are often favored aid recipients. France, for instance, armed and trained the Rwandan *génocidaires* even when their murderous intentions were plain, and continued to support them after they had slaughtered up to a million of their fellow citizens. As noted in Chapter 12, the United States is without equal in the post-World War Two period in supporting forces of atrocity and genocide beyond its borders.

With regard to economic intervention, it is worth abiding by medicine's Hippocratic oath: First, do no harm. Interventionist economic policies such as "austerity" measures and "structural adjustment" programs may increase social stress in a way that contributes directly or indirectly to genocide. Rwanda and, arguably, Yugoslavia in the 1980s and 1990s provide examples. Cosmopolitanism is to be celebrated, but cheerleading for limitless "globalization" should be questioned. As international legal theorist Richard Falk has written, "Economic globalisation . . . weakens the overall capacity and will of governments to address human wrongs either within their own society or elsewhere. . . . It seems appropriate to link economic globalisation with a high threshold of tolerance for human wrongs, at least for now."[25] Moreover, if structural and institutional violence can themselves constitute genocide, then structural adjustment measures and the like may be not only a *cause* of genocide, but a *form* of it.

Sanctions

Economic and political sanctions lie at an intermediate point between "soft" intervention strategies and military intervention. As *The Responsibility to Protect* summarized such measures, they may include "arms embargoes," "ending military cooperation and training programmes," "financial sanctions," "restrictions on income-generating activities such as oil, diamonds . . . logging and drugs," "restrictions on access to petroleum products," "aviation bans," "restrictions on diplomatic representation," "restrictions on travel," and "suspension of membership or expulsion from international or regional bodies."[26] To this list might be added judicial sanctions, such as indictments for war crimes and genocide.

The difficulty with sanctions lies in targeting them to impede a repressive or genocidal leadership, without inflicting general human suffering. In two twentieth-century cases, human destruction caused by malevolent and/or misdirected sanctions could be considered genocidal. The economic blockade imposed on Germany during *and after* the First World War killed up to three-quarters of a million people.[27] The sanctions imposed on the Iraqi population in peacetime provide a second case (see Chapter 1).

Partly as a result of the Iraqi catastrophe, "blanket economic sanctions in particular have been increasingly discredited in recent years," because they impose "greatly disproportionate . . . hardships" on civilians.[28] Appropriately-targeted measures, however, may repress would-be *genocidaires*. These actions can include freezing of bank accounts; travel bans; and (more controversially) sporting, cultural, and academic boycotts.

The United Nations

The UN has a pretty abysmal record in confronting and forestalling genocide. According to Leo Kuper and others, this reflects the organization's founding on Westphalian norms of state sovereignty (Chapter 12), and the desire of most member states to avoid shining a spotlight on their own atrocities, past or present.

There is and always has been another side to the UN, however, typified by its extraordinarily-effective specialized agencies (UNICEF, the World Food Program, the High Commissioner for Refugees [UNHCR], and many others), as well as by the UN's contribution to peacekeeping and peacebuilding around the world. Since the late 1980s, the UN has increasingly stressed *peacebuilding*, described by UN Secretary-General Kofi Annan as

> the creation or strengthening of national institutions, monitoring elections, promoting human rights, providing for reintegration and rehabilitation programmes, as well as creating conditions for resumed development. Peacebuilding does not replace ongoing humanitarian and development activities in countries emerging from crises. Rather, it aims to build on, add to, or reorient such activities in ways that are designed to reduce the risk of a resumption of conflict and contribute to creating conditions most conducive to reconciliation, reconstruction and recovery.[29]

These measures are vital to making "Never Again" a reality. Peacebuilding has been implemented most visibly in three Central American countries (El Salvador, Nicaragua, and Guatemala) after their civil wars. In coordination with nongovernmental organizations, both indigenous and foreign, the UN oversaw the demobilization and reintegration of fighting forces; constructed new societal institutions virtually from scratch; organized and supervised elections; monitored violations of human rights; and assisted in the work of truth-and-reconciliation commissions, among other duties. On balance, this must be counted as a major UN success, providing a wealth of knowledge and practice for future genocide prevention and conflict resolution.

Overall, evidence supports the assertion of *The Responsibility to Protect* that the UN "is unquestionably the principal institution for building, consolidating and using the authority of the international community."[30] As John Heidenrich noted, "by signing the UN Charter, every member has obligated itself to adhere to the most basic norms of civilized conduct, which means that only through outright hypocrisy can a government commit a crime as grievous as genocide." Moreover, "only the United Nations has the Security Council, the only international body with the global legal right to compel countries to adhere to international humanitarian treaties and customs, by force if necessary."[31]

Figure 16.4 A formation of Mongolian UN peacekeepers at a medal ceremony in Bentiu, South Sudan, in November 2013.

Source: Martine Perret/UN Photo/Creative Commons/Flickr.

WHEN IS MILITARY INTERVENTION JUSTIFIED?

What are the core challenges of humanitarian military interventions? Paul Williams summarizes the "prudential considerations" as including:

> What combination of air, sea and/or land forces should be deployed? What is the likelihood that the injection of foreign military forces will make things worse in the short term, and/or harder to resolve in the longer term? Will military action in this particular case jeopardize other important foreign policy goals such as cooperation among the Permanent Five members of the Security Council? How long should the intervention last and what is the exit strategy or political endgame? To what extent should foreign forces engage with and/or transform local political structures?[32]

In the wake of the Kosovo intervention, carried out without UN Security Council authorization, a Swedish-sponsored Independent International Commission was formed under the stewardship of South African Judge Richard Goldstone (who also spent two years as head of the ICTY tribunal at The Hague). A commission member, political scientist Mary Kaldor, summarized the commission's conclusion: "that the Kosovo intervention was illegal, because there was no Security Council resolution, *but legitimate* because it resolved a humanitarian crisis and had widespread support within the international community and civil society." The "illegal but legitimate" verdict was an elegant one, but attested to "very dangerous" gaps and imprecisions in international law and interventionist policies.[33]

BOX 16.3 THE RESPONSIBILITY TO PROTECT (R2P) AND THE WILL TO INTERVENE (W2I)

Mobilizing the Will to Intervene (W2I), a Canadian-sponsored initiative, built upon the influential Responsibility to Protect (R2P) framework developed several years earlier (see p. 761). W2I's framers declared:

First, we must recognize that the United Nations and other international institutions are made up of national governments whose primary concern is the retention of political support from their domestic constituencies. Consequently, the key to mobilizing international support is to first garner domestic support . . . A vocal and broad-based constituency must emerge with the ability to advocate the case for governmental action in a persuasive manner.

"Mobilizing political will" to intervene in mass atrocities relied upon four key elements:

leadership from the executive and legislative branches of government; interdepartmental coordination within the government; well developed civilian and military capacity; and knowledge sharing and pressure by civil society groups and the news media to raise awareness among decision makers and the public.

Communication was essential: not only between public and political spheres, and through the media, but in the need for streamlined communication *within* government bureaucracies. The Will to Intervene initiative, like the Genocide Prevention Task Force, emphasized this latter point. It proposed a Coordinating Office for the Prevention of Mass Atrocities to "create standard operating procedures for disseminating intelligence concerning the risks of mass atrocities throughout the whole of government."

The report urged humanitarian and nongovernmental organizations to "move beyond well-meaning but simplistic calls for the government to 'do something' to prevent mass atrocities, and provide precise proposals for action founded on results-based analysis." These should then be presented to policymakers, through well-maintained channels: "It is imperative that advocates build and sustain long-term relationships with key civil servants, politicians, and members of the executive, so that they may strategically reach all levels of government with their proposals for action."

The Will to Intervene authors lamented that the momentum for humanitarian intervention had notably flagged in the wake of September 11, 2001, and the long, draining invasions and occupations of Iraq and Afghanistan. These, they contended, "have depleted much of Canada and the United States' defense, diplomatic, and development resources, vastly diminishing the political will to engage in humanitarian intervention."[34] The humanitarian justifications offered for the Iraq War, meanwhile, delegitimized appeals for humanitarian intervention, especially as the dimensions of that disaster became clear (Box 4a).

Many commentators, however, have criticized military interventions as currently framed, because they tend to grant *carte blanche* to powerful states (themselves at no risk of military intervention) to dictate to the world's weaker states. In the view of law professor Stephen Holmes, this may extend to mounting invasions on supposedly "humanitarian" grounds. For all the lofty rhetoric that accompanies them, Holmes argued, military interventions are usually selective, self-interested, and counterproductive.[35] A leftwing cottage industry bloomed after the 1999 Kosovo intervention, depicting it as malign US/NATO imperialism rather than an altruistic venture.[36] The broader point—that "humanitarian" intervention often masks imperial motives—is cogent. Calls for intervention may legitimately be analyzed for possible ulterior motives, but the existence of such motives should not necessarily rule out intervention altogether. I personally supported military intervention in Kosovo and East Timor in 1999, and Libya and Syria in the wake of the "Arab Spring" uprisings.[37]

It is worth considering the place of *regional actors* in the intervention equation. Such actors have played *the* key role in virtually all successful interventions against genocide over the past three-and-a-half decades (success being measured by a halt to the killing). In 1971, India, the regional hegemon of south Asia, intervened to stop the genocide against Bengalis in East Pakistan (see Box 8a). In 1979, Tanzania overthrew the Idi Amin government in Uganda, ending his depredations (though installing a new regime under Milton Obote that proved little better). Also in 1979, Vietnam invaded Cambodia and pushed the Khmer Rouge regime to the margins. NATO's 1999 intervention in Kosovo brought an end to Serb genocide in the province, and allowed 800,000 ethnic Albanian refugees to return. Later that year, Australia played the leading role in ending Indonesia's genocidal occupation of East Timor; at the dawn of the new millennium, Nigeria headed the interventions in Sierra Leone and Liberia staged by ECOWAS (the Economic Community of West African States).[38]

Figure 16.5 Skeptical voices are generally raised about military and "humanitarian" interventions, accusing leaders of harboring neocolonial ambitions and *Realpolitik* motivations. Demonstrators march against the bombing of Syria, London (UK), November 2015.

Source: Alisdare Hickston/Creative Commons/Flickr.

In none of these interventions, with the possible exception of Australia in East Timor and the NATO countries in Kosovo, did moral and humanitarian considerations act as primary catalysts—*from the perspective of the intervening state*.[39] Ulterior motives were always present (see Box 16.4). Yet in a world of states that is still run according to classical notions of sovereignty and *realpolitik*, one arguably takes what one can get. Ulterior motives may even be welcome for the added spur they provide to necessary state intervention. And the Timor case (see Box 16.4) shows us, like no other recent instance of successful intervention, how powerfully morally-infused activism can influence the equation.

As Timothy Murithi has argued in a sensitive analysis, such bodies "have the comparative advantage of being in the vicinity of an unfolding crisis and therefore are more likely to act with a degree of urgency than the United Nations." They additionally "have more legitimacy as the collective voice of their member states than individual states when it comes to mitigating against [*sic*] mass atrocities." But Murithi also points out that "regional organizations can suffer from internal political wrangling that can paralyze the ability to act in a timely fashion."[40] And when their mandate is tightly restricted, or their forces inadequate, their presence in a conflict situation may be ineffective or even counterproductive.

Two relatively recent examples—the African Union's peacekeeping force in Darfur, Sudan (Box 9a) and the Arab League's monitors in Syria—caution against viewing regional initiatives as a panacea. The AU forces in Darfur "failed to fulfill their mandate because they had insufficient troops and inadequate equipment and training."[41] In Syria, meanwhile, the 165 monitors were restricted to an observer role, and ended up serving as little more than window-dressing for the Assad regime's depredations, which continued apace. Ali Salem Al-Deqbasi, the head of the advisory Arab Parliament, lamented that "the killing of children and the violation of human rights law is happening in the presence of Arab League monitors." The force was, he claimed, "giving the Syrian regime a cover to commit inhumane acts under the noses of the Arab League observers."[42] Murithi concluded that regional organizations were best suited "to deploy fact-finding and preventive diplomacy missions";[43] until and unless they develop standing forces capable of rapid deployment in emergency situations, he contends, their military role is best utilized in the context of broader UN-authorized forces.

BOX 16.4 "IF YOU LEAVE US HERE, WE WILL DIE": INTERVENTION IN EAST TIMOR, 1999

Figure 16.6 Cover of Geoffrey Robinson, *"If You Leave Us Here, We Will Die": How Genocide Was Stopped in East Timor*. See also Figure 7a.2, p. 427.

Source: Courtesy of Princeton University Press.

"IF YOU LEAVE US HERE, WE WILL DIE"

HOW
GENOCIDE
WAS STOPPED
IN EAST TIMOR

GEOFFREY ROBINSON

In Box 7a, we explored one of the most dramatic of recent humanitarian interventions, in Indonesian-occupied East Timor in September 1999. Violence erupted after referendum results showed a clear majority of Timorese in favor of independence from their powerful neighbor. An unusually rapid, direct, and successful intervention quelled it, however, and set East Timor on course to the independent statehood it had been denied after decolonization from Portugal in 1975. Geoffrey Robinson has supplied a riveting eyewitness account of the 1999 events.[44]

Robinson was a political affairs officer with the unarmed UN team, known as UNAMET, which supervised the referendum and witnessed its aftermath. "In a few short months," he reported, "the vast majority of international UNAMET staff had become so deeply committed to the [referendum] process that they were prepared to work exceptionally long hours and, quite literally, to place their lives on the line to ensure its success." Many were worried, however, by the decision to leave security in the hands of the Indonesian occupiers. Their worst fears were confirmed when it became known that a large majority of Timorese had voted for independence.

The resulting crackdown and killing spree by Indonesian-sponsored militias prompted those at UN headquarters to order a staff pullout from the Dili compound. But some 1,500 terrified refugees had gathered there, and according to instructions issued on September 8, they would be left behind. The announcement provoked "outrage" and "a storm of protest within the compound," wrote Robinson. It "brought to a head fundamental questions about the United Nations' priorities and its responsibilities to the people of East Timor." To many observers, "it seemed that the United Nations was drawing an invidious distinction among its employees, based solely on their race or national origin."

The objections were communicated to New York. In the end, eighty-one UN staffers and others were allowed to remain in the compound, while most foreign and local staff were evacuated on September 10. Remaining staffers and journalists, accompanied by all refugees who wished to leave, departed safely for Darwin on September 14.

Memorable and, one hopes, trendsetting though the rebellion was, it was just one of the factors that encouraged the US superpower and its Australian ally to sponsor an armed intervention in East Timor under UN auspices within days of the outbreak of post-referendum violence (though too late to save hundreds or thousands of Timorese murdered by militias). This overrode the traditional commands of *Realpolitik*, which would have dictated support for Indonesia rather than Timorese independence—as had indeed prevailed in the international community over the preceding quarter-century. According to Robinson, the "unusual conjuncture of events and conditions" encouraging intervention included "dramatic media coverage, the existence of a longstanding network of NGO and church organizations, and the surprisingly effective diplomacy of the UN Security Council and the secretary-general himself. More than anything else, though, it shows that the actions of a relatively small number of people, some but not all of them powerful, profoundly influenced the course of events" not only through the rebellion at the UN compound, but "by keeping the spotlight of media attention on East Timor, and by making a compelling moral case for intervention."

After perhaps wavering before the rebellion of September 8, Annan, recalling the fiascoes in Rwanda and Bosnia (Srebrenica) during his tenure as UN peacekeeping chief, mounted "an extraordinary campaign of personal diplomacy, urging world leaders to contribute to an international force and exert pressure on Indonesia to accept it." He also announced "emphatically" that "the United Nations is [not] abandoning the people of East Timor in their hour of greatest need."

Annan felt obliged to issue the declaration, in part, by the "thousands of messages I have received from all over the world." This attested to the power of the global protests mounted by civil society and nongovernmental organizations, especially in Australia, the UK, North America, and Portugal. A dedicated core of activists had utilized every communications strategy open to the "norm entrepreneur" over the previous quarter-century to publicize Indonesian atrocities and promote Timorese self-determination. Now they activated their networks to bring tens of thousands of demonstrators into the streets of major cities. The flavor of some of these mass protests is captured in a contemporary news account:

In Sydney . . . more than 20,000 protesters took to the streets on Saturday demanding urgent action to end the bloodshed in East Timor, AFP reported. The rally called on a "gutless" Australian government to immediately withdraw recognition of Indonesia's sovereignty over East Timor and to send in an armed peacekeeping force. Wielding banners emblazoned with slogans such as "[Prime Minister] Howard You Coward" and "East Timor—Blood on Howard's Hands," a breakaway group of 30 demonstrators battered their way into the prime minister's Sydney office. To screams of "UN in, Indonesia out" the group rammed the glass sliding doors. . . . During the five-hour rally, dozens of solidarity activists, politicians and union members made emotional pleas to the government to take immediate military action to end the massacres by pro-Indonesia militias. The protest condemned Canberra's refusal to act without Indonesian permission and a UN mandate. Demonstrators, who brought the city to a standstill, vowed to continue to stage mass rallies if an international peacekeeping force was not in the region within a week. They called for a war crimes tribunal and for international financial agencies, such as the World Bank and the International Monetary Fund, to cut funding until peace was restored.[45]

Efforts to marshal a humanitarian response were further assisted by a favorable historical moment. A referendum might never have taken place in East Timor had a new Indonesian president, B.J. Habibie, not replaced the dictator Suharto and shifted policy on the Timor issue. When the consequences of the vote became plain, proponents of intervention could cite the recent confrontation with Serbia over Kosovo, in which NATO intervention was justified by all manner of humanitarian rhetoric which could now be deployed to justify aiding East Timor (Chapter 8). More generally, the 1999 events took place during an unusually propitious post-Cold War phase of international politics, bookended by the US and Allied interventions in Iraq (the first in 1990, establishing a Kurdish protected area on humanitarian grounds; the second in 2003, cloaking adventurism in humanitarian guise, to the detriment of the cause). Such "moments" cannot be predicted in advance, but they can be exploited when they arise, and promoted through patient and dedicated advocacy.

The advantages of intervention by regional actors are several. Geographical contiguity minimizes logistical difficulties, although this may be offset by resource constraints (apart from the Australian case, all the interventions cited above were carried out by poor developing nations). With contiguity often comes a degree of ethnocultural kinship, making it less likely that interventions will be seen as foreign or imperial in nature. Regional powers may also have a vested interest in guarding against the spill-over of genocide, something that more distant actors might not share.

At the same time, however, vested interests operate, and may undermine the intervention. The conflict in Congo—Africa's "first world war" (see Chapter 9)—fed the expansionist and pillaging ambitions of a host of African nations. Logistical difficulties are likely to prevail where regional actors are underdeveloped, with limited resources. In such cases, material assistance from the developed world is critical. Political scientist Alan Kuperman has argued that "only the US military has a large, long-haul cargo air fleet," without which "rapid reaction to most parts of the world is impossible."[46] Journalist Michael Hirsh goes so far as to argue that the "most important future role for the UN" might be that of "a legitimizer for local forces" to intervene, with assistance and logistical backing from the developed countries, primarily the US who supply most of the UN's budget.[47]

A standing "peace army"?

In a contribution to his edited *Encyclopedia of Genocide*, Israel Charny proposed the creation of an International Peace Army as a "standing machinery . . . for responding to eruptions of genocide, at any time or place in the world." Such a force

would move automatically into action any time that authenticated reports are received of the mass killing of any group of unarmed civilians, such as the ethnic cleansing of a village or a region. The basic mandate of the *International Peace Army* would be to take action in the same way that we are accustomed today in democratic countries to call on the police at the first evidence of murder or even possible murderous assault.[48]

The Peace Army would be pluralistic in composition (with "nationals from a very wide range of countries"). Charny divided the Peace Army into three units: one military, another medical and humanitarian, and a third designed "for the Rebuilding of Safe and Tolerant Communities." In a nod to the growing scope and complexity of UN peacekeeping and peacebuilding operations from the late 1980s onward, this last component would bring "skilled administrators and technicians for reestablishing the basic structure of community life." It would also aim to "mobilize indigenous leaders of the peoples involved in the conflict—religious leaders, political leaders, popular folk heroes including media celebrities, sports stars, beloved popular singers, leaders in education, and so on of the indigenous culture—who will agree to speak to the building of a new era of tolerance and reconciliation."[49]

Such a Peace Army might seem utopian, but contemporary developments may make it less so. For one thing, Charny's imagined force would be an "affiliated police arm" of the United Nations.[50] In the new millennium, the UN took steps to establish a standing army that, with the input of humanitarian organizations, could fulfill many of the functions Charny envisaged. The plan called for twelve nations—Canada and Denmark have already signed on—to contribute to a 6,000-strong force on standby for a call from the Secretary-General and the Security Council. A different, possibly complementary, Dutch proposal called for a "fire brigade" of 2,500 to 5,000 soldiers as "a permanent, rapidly deployable brigade" to intervene in genocidal outbreaks. Five thousand troops is roughly the force that Major-General Romeo Dallaire pleaded for in 1994 when the Rwandan genocide was underway. "If I had had such a force available to me while I was the UNAMIR Force Commander sometime in mid-April, we could have saved the lives of hundreds of thousands of people," Dallaire asserted.[51]

The European Union, which after the UN may represent the world's leading force for democracy, peace, and humanitarianism (see below, pp. 780–783), has discussed an "EU Rapid Reaction Force" (ERRF), capable of deploying up to 60,000 soldiers within sixty days and maintaining them in the field for up to one year. The EU also floated the idea of "battle groups" consisting of elite battalions of 1,500 soldiers, able to deploy within fifteen days and stay in the field for a month. Not to be left out, the African Union also sought to develop an African Standby Force consisting of "regionally-based standby brigades, numbering between 3,500 and 5,000 troops," deployable within two weeks.[52] All these initiatives were guided by a perception that the hidebound, bureaucratic process of deploying peacemaking and peacekeeping operations gives *génocidaires* and war criminals too great a head start. For the UN and the Europeans alike, there was the added attraction of developing a military force that does not rely on the US for funding and logistics. Unfortunately, at the time of writing (mid-2016), none of these forces had seen the light of day.

Finally, there is the possibility of an "international legion of volunteers," as Heidenrich discussed. Such corps have played an important role in some conflicts, from the Spanish Civil War to the French Foreign Legion's varied postings. Some proposals even envisage the use of mercenaries in this role, arguing that the unsavory reputation attached to such forces is outdated.[53]

■ BOX 16.5 SUCCESS STORIES?

Any study of genocide must reckon not only with genocidal outbreaks of the kind examined throughout this book, but with cases where genocide has *not* occurred— despite significant ethnoreligious divisions and, often, histories of intercommunal conflict. What can we learn about genocide prevention and intervention from apparent examples of coexistence and successful conflict management? And how must their successes be qualified?

Malaysia

Malaysia (formerly Malaya) achieved independence from Great Britain in 1959, by which point its communal makeup reflected the demographic transformations wrought by colonialism. In addition to a sizable Indian population, originating with the indentured laborers whom the British brought to work the highland tea plantations, roughly a quarter of the population is ethnic Chinese. As elsewhere in Southeast Asia, the Chinese moved into business and industry, particularly after the departure of British capital. Their growing economic power, and allegations of subversive links to communist China, generated the same hostility from native Malays that has occasionally led to rioting in neighboring Indonesia (Box 7a).

Malaysia, too, saw its outbreak of anti-Chinese rioting in 1969, with several hundred killed. The Malay-dominated government, however, responded intelligently, if in a somewhat authoritarian fashion. It launched an affirmative-action campaign—the *bumiputra* ("sons of the soil") policy—to boost the presence of Malays in higher education and the national economy, without alienating ethnic Chinese to the point that they abandoned the country.[54] Just as significantly, they ensured that a rising tide would float all boats—that is, by generating economic prosperity, all communities would benefit. The modernization of the country proceeded apace. "From 1970 to 1995, the per capita Malay income grew by 830 percent while the per capita Chinese income grew by 635 percent," reducing—though not eliminating—the income gap between the two main groups. "Middle-class and entrepreneurial Malays share common interests in Malaysia with middle-class Chinese, and this lessens ethnic conflict," emphasizing the importance of such interests "cut[ting] across ethnic, religious, or regional lines." As a result, wrote Daniel Chirot and Clark McCauley, while "Malaysia has hardly been a model of perfect toleration," it has managed to combine "a relatively accommodating policy toward the more entrepreneurial minority, affirmative action for the poorer major-ity, and acceptance of multiculturalism."[55] Tensions and rivalries remain, with the small Christian minority protesting discriminatory measures that reflect the staunch Islamism of the ruling regime.[56] But although the protests threatened to spill over to rioting and communal violence in 2009, no such full-scale eruption had occurred in the four decades since 1969.

Source: Frederik Holst, *Ethnicization and Identity Construction in Malaysia* (London: Routledge, 2012).

Kazan, Tatarstan Republic (Russia)

In how many other places on earth do Muslims and Christians live peacefully side by side, in similar demographic proportions? In a country like Lebanon, this eventually proved a recipe for communal conflict and civil war. One might expect something similar in Kazan. After all, the fierce rivalry and battles between ethnic Russians and the Bulgar-and Mongol-descended Tatars was a defining feature of Russia's

Figure 16.7 Young women in traditional and Western dress chat outside Kazan's main university. The city, capital of the Tatarstan Republic in Russia, represents a notable example of Muslim–Christian and religious-secular coexistence.

Source: Author's photo, June 2008.

emergence as a modern state. In 1552, Ivan the Terrible besieged and annexed the Tatar Khanate, and a flood of Russian colonists followed, continuing under successive tsarist regimes and during the period of Soviet communism (Chapter 5). Russians now account for fully 40 percent of the population, versus the Muslim Tatars' 50 percent.

Elsewhere in the Russian Federation and beyond, tensions between indigenous Muslim populations and Russians have spawned genocide (in the Caucasus) and secessionist aspirations (not only among Muslims in Chechnya [see Box 5a], but in Crimea and eastern Ukraine, with their large Russian populations). In Kazan, however, an almost surreal coexistence reigns. The minarets of the magnificent Kul-Sharif mosque, opened in 2005, rise adjacent to the steeples of the Russian Orthodox cathedral.

This is the result of enlightened political leadership, interfaith dialogue, and a careful apportioning of material resources among the different ethnoreligious communities. In the post-Soviet period, the Republic of Tatarstan was granted a large measure of political autonomy and control over exploitation of the republic's rich oil and gas resources; Moscow appears to view the republic as a model for its relations with Russian Muslims and the wider Muslim world. The Kul-Sharif mosque, for example, was built on the site of a mosque razed by the sixteenth-century Russian conquerors, as a gesture of reconciliation and restitution. At its dedication, Tatarstan president Mintimer Shaimiev (in some ways a typical post-Soviet strongman, but one of the more collegial) spoke of the mosque's "profound meaning, tied to the aspirations of the multiethnic peoples of the republic, to live in peace and friendship." Nor is this "mere boilerplate," noted Karl Meyer and Shareen Blair Brysac in their engaging global survey, *Pax Ethnica*: "In living memory, there have been no violent eruptions between rival faiths in Tatarstan, an oasis of ecumenical tolerance where remarkably, nearly one in three marriages joins spouses professing different religions and/or ethnicity."[57] The "sovereignty project" that Shaimiev pitched to post-Soviet Russia allowed the republic "symbolic badges of nationhood"[58] and culminated in an agreement that awarded Tatarstan full control over its subsoil (oil and natural gas) resources, including taxation of revenue, and extensive cultural, linguistic, and educational rights. This greatly reduced frictions between region and center.

Internally, Tatarstan's Council for Religious Affairs managed relations among the faiths—ensuring, for instance, that "when the state pays for a mosque to have a new roof structure, it ensures at the same time that a Russian-Orthodox church receives similar funding, for new chairs."[59] One result is that religious fundamentalism, usually fueled by feelings of persecution and humiliation, has found little foothold in Kazan. Among Muslims, women in Western dress mingle easily with more tradition-minded coreligionists (see Figure 16.7). Orthodox Christians and Muslims alike throng the city's beautiful boulevards, and flock to its lively cafes and pizzerias. "When people live directly next to one another they get a feeling for how to respect one another," said Renat Nakifovich Valiullin, head of the Council for Religious Affairs. A skeptic might note that the same was said of Sarajevo in Bosnia—a model of intercommunal harmony until Yugoslavia collapsed into war and genocide in the 1990s (Chapter 8). For now, though, Kazan's example shines brightly.

Source: Karl E. Meyer and Shareen Blair Brysac, *Pax Ethnica: Where and How Diversity Succeeds* (New York: PublicAffairs, 2012), chapter 3: "Tatarstan: The Cave of the Clan Bears."

Rwanda

Most of the "success stories" in this section emphasize pluralism, consociationalism, and democracy as key factors in inoculating societies against outbreaks of genocide and crimes against humanity. The Malaysian example, however, points to a more authoritarian and *dirigiste* framing that can also be judged as "successful," in this respect at least. In both Malaysia and Rwanda, the model has been based on economic development that gives all communities at least some sense, though not necessarily an equal one, of growing prosperity. This can mute the sense of discrimination and marginalization that so often gives rise to social conflict.

In the Rwandan case, however (see Chapter 9), the government is more authoritarian, and a verdict of "success" correspondingly more controversial. Founded on the RPF guerrilla movement which seized power in Kigali in July 1994, it has been classed by many observers as an *ethnocracy*—a political order in which a particular ethnic group is hegemonic. The genocidal "Hutu Power" regime gave way to a Tutsi-dominated one under President Paul Kagame;[60] many would concur with René Lemarchand's evaluation of the government as "a thinly disguised Tutsi dictatorship."[61] But advancing any such argument in Rwanda is bound to land one in trouble—or worse—with the authorities. Officially, after 1994, there are no longer ethnicities in the country. Citizens are neither Hutu nor Tutsi, but Banyarwanda. Acknowledging continuing ethnic tensions and inequalities is viewed as a subversive echo of the genocidal past.

Kagame won 95 percent of the presidential vote in the first post-genocide elections in 2003, and the RPF was returned to power in 2008 in a vote which, again, no opposition party was allowed to contest. According to *The Economist*, Kagame "allows less political space and press freedom at home than Robert Mugabe does in Zimbabwe," while "anyone who poses the slightest political threat to the regime is dealt with ruthlessly."[62] Press freedom is heavily curtailed, with Rwanda ranking 161st out of 180 countries surveyed by Reporters Without Borders in 2016.[63]

Figure 16.8 Rwandan president Paul Kagame, leader of the ruling Rwandan Patriotic Front (RPF), is shown in June 2009 attending the World Economic Forum on Africa in Cape Town, South Africa. Kagame, a Rwandan Tutsi exile from Uganda, has blended harsh authoritarianism with measures to promote economic growth, attract foreign investment and aid, and suppress ethnic mobilizations of the kind that produced the 1994 genocide (see Chapter 9). In December 2015, in stage-managed fashion, the usual overwhelming majority of Rwandans approved constitutional changes that could allow Kagame to stay in power until 2034.[64]

Source: Eric Miller/Wikimedia Commons.

In December 2015, Kagame secured another surreally-favorable result in a national referendum to remove existing limits on presidential terms, paving the way for him to extend his rule until 2034. "What is happening is people's choice," he declared. "Ask people why they want me." He still foreswore any intention of remaining president for life. EU and US representatives wagged a finger; Kenneth Roth, executive director of Human Rights Watch, tweeted that the result was no surprise when "so many dissidents [are] silenced, [and] civil society stifled."[65]

Even with such heavy-handed tactics, however, it is difficult to deny that post-1994 Rwanda has witnessed remarkable transformations. The ban on mobilizing around ethnic constituencies and platforms has helped to suppress civil violence (and ethnically-imbued hate speech), though it has also masked and buttressed what is effectively the hegemony of the Tutsi-exile constituency that seized control in 1994. Internationally, the Kagame regime has positioned Rwanda as a poster child for foreign investment and overseas development assistance.[66] The RPF regime also set a seal on the country's removal from the French zone of influence, securing entry to the British Commonwealth instead, in late 2009. Economic growth has averaged an impressive 6 percent annually—albeit from a very low base, and with a half-acknowledged boost from the looting of eastern Congo's rich resources, following the extension of Rwandan power there in 1996 (see Chapter 9). New industries (such as specialty coffees) have been promoted, and the government has worked hard to attract tourism, depicting the country as an oasis of peace and social order on the troubled African continent.[67] A reservoir of

Western guilt for the genocide was an enormous boon, at least until the Kagame regime's depredations in eastern Congo squandered much goodwill. Meanwhile, the *gacaca* process within (see pp. 715–718) allowed hundreds of thousands of alleged Hutu accomplices to the genocide to be judged by local communities and reintegrate in society, following models of restorative justice rather than, in general, raw retribution.

A striking feature is that Rwanda today has the highest female political representation of any country in the world. The 2003 constitution guaranteed women 30 percent of seats in the national parliament, but in fact they have surged far beyond this point, as *The Washington Post's* Stephanie McCrummen reported:

> Women hold a third of all cabinet positions, including foreign minister, education minister, Supreme Court chief and police commissioner general. And Rwanda's parliament [in September 2008] became the first in the world where women claim the majority—56 percent, including the speaker's chair. One result is that Rwanda has banished archaic patriarchal laws that are still enforced in many African societies, such as those that prevent women from inheriting land. The legislature has passed bills aimed at ending domestic violence and child abuse, while a committee is now combing through the legal code to purge it of discriminatory laws.[68]

For the visitor (I have toured the country twice since the second edition of this book was published), Rwanda poses a nearly surreal dilemma. The regime's accomplishments are everywhere evident: the excellent roads and sanitation; the safety and security of urban and rural areas alike; the boom in construction and investment that is transforming Kigali; the proliferating schools and health centers in the countryside.[69] The political atmosphere is not comparable to that of the stultified, suffocating dictatorships I knew in Cold War East Germany or Guatemala. While domestic media are indeed tightly controlled, Internet and satellite TV access is extensive; the excellent Kenyan-based weekly, *The East African*, which regularly prints harshly-negative stories about Rwandan leaders and policies, is sold at supermarket checkout counters. Yet politics is generally a taboo topic in conversations with Rwandans. And even without leaving the national territory, one can peer across a narrow arm of Lake Kivu at Cyangugu in the far southwest and see, sprouting across hilltops in Bukavu in the neighboring DR Congo, the mansions of Rwanda's military chiefs and their Congolese satraps. These crassly opulent dwellings, looming over tumbledown lakeshore settlements of Congolese, symbolize Rwanda's continued domination and exploitation of eastern Congo.[70] It is tempting to see, in their siting only a few hundred meters from the border, the need for close lines of communication with Rwanda proper, which could offer refuge if the Congolese population rebelled against Rwanda's neocolonial rule.

Source: Stephen Kinzer, *A Thousand Hills: Rwanda's Rebirth and the Man Who Dreamed It* (Wiley, 2008).

India

It may seem strange to cite India as a "success story" of coexistence and conflict management. After all, the country was born of genocide (the Partition violence of 1947–1948, in which half a million to a million Indians perished).[71] Since then, India has experienced a significant—and politically now dominant—strand of Hindu chauvinism and extremism; waves of secessionist and counterinsurgent violence in Punjab and Indian-occupied Kashmir; Maoist guerrilla violence against "class enemies," provoking an indiscriminate state backlash;[72] Muslim-Christian clashes in the desperately-poor states of the northeast; endemic caste violence against marginalized Dalit ("Untouchable") communities; and regular rounds of Hindu-Muslim and Hindu-Sikh violence. The last of these at times has spilled over into genocide—as with the savage Delhi massacre of Sikhs following Prime Minister Indira Gandhi's assassination in 1984,[73] and the mass killings of Muslims in 2002 in Gujarat (see further below).

Running counter to these grim and continuing trends is the tradition of Indian secularism and democratic pluralism inaugurated by the joint leaders of the Congress Party in the pre-independence period: Mohandas (Mahatma) Gandhi and Jawaharlal Nehru. Gandhi, accused of betraying the Hindu nationalist cause, was assassinated by an extremist of the Rashtriya Swayamsevak Sangh (RSS) in 1948. But as India's founding prime minister, Nehru promoted a vision of the vast subcontinent as "an ancient palimpsest on which layer upon layer of thought and reverie had been inscribed, and yet no succeeding layer had completely hidden or erased what had been written previously." Despite the "diversity and infinite variety" of Indians, they were bound by "that tremendous impress of oneness, which had held all of us together for ages."[74]

The other offspring of Partition, Pakistan, quickly fell under military dictatorship, and was sundered (not least thanks to India's efforts) in the genocidal birth of Bangladesh (Box 8a). Other promising young democracies in South and Southeast Asia—including Burma/Myanmar and Sri Lanka—succumbed to militarism, civil war, and genocide against ethnic minorities. But India has soldiered democratically on,[75] with its flamboyant free elections (by far the largest in the world), its vigorous press, its *lingua franca* and connecting railroad network inherited from the British, its centuries-long tradition of village-level coexistence among diverse religions and ethnicities, and its growing and tech-savvy middle class. And then there's cricket . . . [76]!

Communal stability is notably enhanced by the fact that "the Indian Muslim community is perhaps the largest Muslim community in the world that has never produced either a massive fundamentalist movement or a rush to join terrorists."[77] Nearly all the Islamist terrorist attacks launched on the Indian heartland have originated in Pakistan and been carried out by Pakistani agents.

Figure 16.9 Narendra Modi, elected India's prime minister in 2014, is an outspoken advocate of the Hindu–nationalist cause, and stands accused of complicity in the mass murder of Muslims in Gujarat in 2002. His ascent to national power, accompanied by a wide range of anti-secularist measures, raised concerns that he sought to undermine India's longstanding traditions of pluralism and ethnic diversity.

Source: 2008 photo by Norbert Schiller/World Economic Forum/Wikimedia Commons.

The dramatic ascent to national power of the charismatic BJP leader Narendra Modi in May 2014 deeply worried many adherents of a secular and pluralistic India. Modi was an activist in the Hindu-extremist RSS from the age of eight (!). As chief minister of the Indian state of Gujarat in 2002, he played a role—at best culpably negligent, at worst actively complicit—in the genocidal pogrom that murdered approximately 2,000 Muslims. In a fierce October 2015 critique, Sonia Faleiro pointed to the murder of several prominent secular figures—including the 77-year-old academic, M.M. Kalburgi, "an outspoken critic of Hindu idol worship"—as only the tip of the iceberg of an insurgent religious chauvinism:

> . . . The government has purged secular voices from high-profile institutions including the National Book Trust and the independent board of Nalanda University. The government is not replacing mediocre individuals: The chancellor of Nalanda was the Nobel laureate Amartya Sen. It is replacing luminaries with people whose greatest qualification is faith in Hindutva [Hindu-supremacist] ideology. The new appointees are rejecting scientific thought in favor of religious ideas that have no place in secular institutions.

In a particularly symbolic repudiation of Nehru's vision of a pluralistic Indian "palimpsest," the Modi government removed the director of New Delhi's Nehru Museum and Library, "announc[ing] plans to rename the museum and change its focus to highlight the achievements of Mr. Modi. This," Faleiro noted pithily, "is akin to repurposing the Washington Monument as an Obama museum."

Whether India was indeed "undergoing a tectonic shift that will have long-term repercussions," as Faleiro argued, remained uncertain.[78] Relative communal peace reigned at the time of writing, apart from the ongoing Maoist insurgency, unrest among tribal peoples in the northeast, and village-level assaults on vulnerable Dalits. But for a country as immense, fissured, and poverty-stricken as India, any verdict of "success," however merited, must remain provisional.

Sources: Sunil Khilnani, *The Idea of India* (Farrar, Straus & Giroux, 1999); Gautam Adhikari, *The Intolerant Indian: Why We Must Rediscover a Liberal Space* (HarperCollins, 2011).

The European Union (EU)

Figure 16.10 Flags of the European Union (EU) fly outside European Commission headquarters in Brussels, Belgium.

Source: Xavier Hape/Wikimedia Commons.

For hundreds of years, the conflict dyad of Great Britain and France was one of the most war-prone in the world. The entrance of a unified Germany in 1871, and Germany's determination to win "a place in the sun" alongside the other imperial powers, directly contributed to the two world wars of the twentieth century. Yet today, these three countries are at peace, thanks in significant part to a wider union encompassing most of Europe outside Russia. The EU project began in 1951 with the formation of the European Coal and Steel Community, in which erstwhile enemies France and (West) Germany took a leading role. In 1957, these two countries, together with Italy, Belgium, Luxembourg, and the Netherlands, formed the European Economic Community (EEC). It gradually expanded to include, first, Great Britain, and since the fall of communism in 1989, a number of the former Soviet satellite states in central Europe. The European Union (EU) formally came into being in 1993, and comprised twenty-eight members as of 2016.

Today, war between EU members is almost inconceivable. Moreover, member states must agree to respect the rights of ethnic, religious, and sexual minorities enshrined in the Convention for the Protection of Human Rights and Fundamental Freedoms (the European Convention on Human Rights), and to defer to the judgments of the European Court of Human Rights (ECHR)—one of the few international legal institutions with real teeth, and generally considered the strongest rights-protection body in the world.[79] (Whether this has made Europeans in general more tolerant of ethnic and religious minorities is questionable, however, in light of the apparent rise in hate crimes and growing hostility to immigrants—particularly Muslims—reflected in large-sample opinion surveys.)[80]

The benefits of belonging to the EU can also act as a spur to reform and reconciliation in countries aspiring to membership. There is no doubt that Croatia's growing willingness to extradite accused war criminals to the Hague tribunal, and accept the return of Serbs expelled from the Krajina region during "Operation Storm" in 1995 (see Chapter 8), was closely linked to its campaign to join the EU, which was realized with its accession to the Union in 2013. Turkey's on-again, off-again ascent to EU membership is also linked to its repeal, after 2003, of bans on the Kurdish language in education, media, and public discourse.

As this book went to press, to my personal dismay and that of Europeanists everywhere, the union appeared in a state of disarray unprecedented since its founding. Anti-EU parties and movements were ascendant across the continent, exemplified by Great Britain's "Brexit" vote in June 2016. The German-led campaign to force brutal austerity-driven economic policies upon Greece was widely seen as a gratuitous humiliation of a small but cornerstone European democracy. It also brought with it more than a whiff of a previous version of German expansionism, which Greek politicians did not hesitate to leverage by calling for tens of billions of dollars in restitution for atrocities inflicted during the Nazi occupation of Greece.[81] Threatening Europe's boundaries in the east was the civil war in eastern Ukraine, combined with the Putin government's occupation and declared annexation of the Crimean peninsula with its ethnic-Russian majority. Meanwhile, seemingly distant conflicts in Syria, Iraq, and Afghanistan generated an escalating wave of refugees and migrants, risking their lives and losing them by the thousands in overcrowded boats on the Mediterranean. This produced heart-rending scenes in the summer of 2015, and even accusations of genocide for the EU's failure to address the situation.[82] The emergency talks that followed only revealed deep divisions among EU members. More recent entrants (and more corrupt and authoritarian regimes), such as Hungary and Slovakia, bluntly refused to consider absorbing a designated share of refugees and migrants.

There were encouraging moments. As hundreds of thousands of refugees sought access to "the European dream,"[83] German prime minister Angela Merkel rode a wave of pro-refugee sentiment in German society, reflected in huge "Refugees Are Welcome" banners at televised soccer matches, and effusive outpourings of assistance for those arriving on German soil. Germany announced it would accept and process a staggering 800,000 refugees in calendar year 2015, dwarfing the contributions of other western countries (and allowing Merkel to regain the moral high ground after the Greek debacle). In the end, Germany registered over a million.

This open-hearted response was clearly grounded in the collective German soul-searching about the genocidal atrocities of the Nazi era (see Chapter 15) as well as the memory of a time when millions of Germans were themselves desperate refugees (see Chapter 6a). Whether the empathy would endure, even in a more

Figure 16.11 Sign at a pro-refugee demonstration in Vienna, February 2013.
Source: Photo by Haeferl/Wikimedia Commons.

muted form, was highly uncertain at the time of writing. Sweden aside, no other EU member had risen to the challenge. Public sexual assaults by migrant men, in Köln and elsewhere, rocked Germany and fueled nativist strains. Meanwhile, the tide of refugees and would-be migrants continued, fanned by conflicts and impoverishment in the African Sahel and intractable civil wars in Syria, Iraq, and Afghanistan. Paralyzed by its incapacity to manage the human flow, then stunned by the "Brexit" vote in the United Kingdom, the "New Europe" threatened to return to one of borders, walls, and suspicion.

Source: T.R. Reid, *The United States of Europe: The New Superpower and the End of American Supremacy* (London: Penguin 2004), especially ch. 6, "The European Social Model."

The United States and Canada

These two North American countries, which share the longest undefended border in the world, are themselves a model of *international* coexistence. Internally, as we have seen, both countries have wrestled with the consequences of European colonialism: the continuing marginalization of indigenous peoples and, in the US case, the legacy of slavery and discrimination against African Americans. Nonetheless, whether we consider the "melting pot" model in the US or the doctrine of "multiculturalism" which has come to dominate Canadian political discourse, both countries have significantly advanced values of pluralism and cosmopolitanism within their borders. The umbrella appellation "American" has proved a successful device for integrating new waves of immigrants to the US, with a decreasing emphasis on assimilating to the hegemonic (white-Protestant) culture. Even after the horrors of September 11, 2001, there was no significant violent backlash against US Muslims. Nor have present tensions over undocumented migrants, especially from Mexico, led (so far) to widespread vigilantism. The US still naturalizes more immigrants than any other country—over a million annually.

The election of the nation's first African-American president, Barack Obama, was a watershed. In his "Speech on Race," delivered in March 2008, Obama outlined his "own American story" as follows:

I am the son of a black man from Kenya and a white woman from Kansas. . . . I've gone to some of the best schools in America and lived in one of the world's poorest nations. I am married to a black American who carries within her the blood of slaves and slaveowners—an inheritance we pass on to our two precious daughters. I have brothers, sisters, nieces, nephews, uncles and cousins, of every race and every hue, scattered across three continents, and for as long as I live, I will never forget that in no other country on Earth is my story even possible.[84]

Opaque to this outsider is the strange paroxysm the United States was passing through at the time of writing: a bombastic billionaire wrestling with bible-thumpers, and everyone seemingly in agreement that overtures to the outside world were best made through aerial bombing. A spate of low-casualty but high-visibility terrorist attacks by US Islamists, and the reverberations of the November 2015 rampage in Paris, fueled a wave of hate-speech, harassment, and attacks on Muslim people and places of worship. Much as in the European Union, nativist anxieties threatened to overwhelm—or at least undermine—an admirable tolerance.

As for my own country, Canada, it has—despite a major hiccup in 1970[85]—wrestled peacefully with the challenge of nationalism and separatism in the predominantly-French-speaking province of Quebec. In the wake of sweeping policies of accommodation, acceptance of the Parti Québecois's affirmative action measures for francophones following its provincial election victory in 1976, and two referendums on Quebec "sovereignty" which failed (the second only narrowly), the secessionist impetus in Quebec appears to have waned. Meanwhile, Canada's previous emphasis on encouraging immigration from "white" Europe has given way to a much greater openness to the wider world, so that cities like Toronto and Vancouver are today among the most multicultural on the planet. Reconciliation efforts with the country's marginalized aboriginal populations—including recognition of land rights and resource claims—have also proceeded, though natives' standards of living and health remain far below those of non-aboriginals.[86] In 1999, as noted in Chapter 15, the federal territory of Nunavut was carved out of the Northwest Territories, accompanied by a substantial devolution of political authority to the native Inuit population, and an agreement to share the proceeds from the territory's rich mineral resources. Canada also "finali[zed] a C$1.9 billion ($1.7 million) class-action settlement for 80,000 surviving former inmates" of the residential schools,[87] followed by a wrenching truth-and-reconciliation process (see Chapter 15).

Sources: John D. Buenker and Lorman A. Ratner, eds., *Multiculturalism in the United States: A Comparative Guide to Acculturation and Ethnicity*, rev. edn (Greenwood Press, 2005); John Ralston Saul, *A Fair Country: Telling Truths about Canada* (Toronto: Penguin, 2009).

IDEOLOGIES AND INDIVIDUALS

Who am I and of what am I capable?

James Waller

Our analysis now shifts from the national and international-political sphere to the more intimate level of human beings' minds and hearts. What difference can individual witnessing make to genocide? How do ideologies, whether religious or secular, spur us to perpetrate—and prevent—genocide? And how can we confront and mitigate our own potential to inflict or support genocidal acts?

The role of the honest witness

Witnessing and transmitting are central to genocide prevention and intervention. The key is *honest, accurate* witnessing, combined with the capacity to communicate what one has witnessed. The "relentless keepers of the truth," as Russian intellectual Nadezhda Mandelstam called them, are genocide's most powerful opponents, and "the best proof that good, not evil, will prevail in the end."[88] Conversely, those who fail to witness honestly—who turn away, distort, and deny—are reliable allies of the *génocidaires*.

A fascinating contrast in honest versus dishonest witnessing is provided by the terror-famine in Ukraine (1932–1933). At the height of the famine, with millions dying throughout the countryside, British socialists Sidney and Beatrice Webb traveled to the USSR. They kept well away from the starving rural areas, and subsequently wrote "a glowing account" of their visit *(Soviet Communism—A New Civilisation*, published in 1935). *The New York Times*'s Moscow correspondent, Walter Duranty, likewise avoided all mention of the famine and the state's genocidal manipulation of it. Duranty's reports influenced the Roosevelt administration's decision to recognize the Soviet government—in 1933, as famine, collectivization of the countryside, and the crushing of peasant resistance all reached their zenith.[89]

The witnessing of British journalist Malcolm Muggeridge was radically different. Arriving in the Soviet Union in 1933, Muggeridge adopted the simple expedient of buying a train ticket to journey through the heartland of Ukraine and the North Caucasus. *En route*, he witnessed some of the horrific scenes of famine described in Chapter 5. "*Whatever else I may do or think in the future, I must never pretend that I haven't seen this,*" Muggeridge wrote in his diary.[90] He returned to publish, albeit anonymously, an account of "millions of starving peasants, their bodies often swollen from lack of food," struggling with "soldier members of the GPU [secret police] carrying out the instructions of the dictatorship of the proletariat." The Stalinist forces, he wrote, "had gone over the country like a swarm of locusts and taken away everything edible . . . [and] had reduced some of the most fertile land in the world to a melancholy desert."[91] He called it "one of the most monstrous crimes in history, so terrible that people in the future will scarcely be able to believe that it happened."[92] Muggeridge's example was echoed and exceeded by the journalist Gareth Jones (see Figure 16.12), who, as Timothy Snyder noted, appears to be the only figure in the UK press who published exposés of the famine under his own name.

Like Jones and Muggeridge, the diplomats, missionaries, and some German soldiers who witnessed the genocide of the Armenians during the First World War were central to catalyzing international protest, and some small measure of intervention in the Armenian plight. Their writings and photographs are essential to our current understanding of the genocide, and serve as a bulwark against those who deny it (see Chapters 4 and 14). By contrast, the withdrawal of nearly all media and most foreign observers from Rwanda in the early stages of the 1994 genocide meant that only the most fragmentary imagery and testimony of that holocaust reached the outside world. Even in an age of globalized mass communication, the Rwandan *génocidaires* inflicted their horrors with only rare outside witnesses, and no outside intervention.

Figure 16.12 Whether accurate information about genocide is disseminated depends on whether mass media and other actors invest the necessary resources in documenting the events, and whether witnesses report honestly. While many pro-Soviet journalists and intellectuals ignored or covered up the mass famine sweeping the Soviet Union during the 1930s, a small handful of witnesses emerged with their integrity intact. Malcolm Muggeridge of *The Guardian* was one (see main text). Another was Gareth Jones, a British diplomatic attaché who organized his own trip to the Soviet countryside at the height of the famine, and published dispatches like this one, from the London *Evening Standard* (March 31, 1933).

Source: www.garethjones.org.

Often, honest witnessing must be carried out at great risk of capture, torture, and death. At such times it inspires real awe. A dramatic example is Jan Karski, a Polish diplomat in his late twenties, who sought to convey the truth of the Jewish Holocaust to the outside world. Operating throughout Nazi-occupied Poland, Karski "disguised himself as a Jew, donning an armband with the Star of David, and smuggled himself through a tunnel into the Warsaw ghetto. Posing as a Ukrainian militiaman, he also infiltrated Belzec, a Nazi death camp near the border between Poland and Ukraine." One marvels at the danger and deception hinted at in this passage. At the end of 1942, Karski escaped to London. He immediately sought a meeting with representatives of the Jewish community. Passing on Karski's reports to the World Jewish Congress in New York, Ignacy Schwartzbart, a prominent London Jew, urged his audience to *"BELIEVE THE UNBELIEVABLE."*[93] Even leading Jews, however, found the information unfathomable: "I cannot believe you," US Supreme Court justice Felix Frankfurter told Karski in a private meeting. It was not that he was accusing Karski of lying, Frankfurter stressed; it was just that he did not possess the evidence that would allow him to absorb such a mind-boggling account. This serves as a painful reminder that no link need exist between honest witnessing and genocide prevention. A host of unpredictable factors—above all, public attention, political will, and private/elite sponsorship—must come into play if information is to translate into action.[94] In the contemporary age, the witnessing of human rights organizations and activists is indispensable. Global NGOs such as Human Rights Watch, Amnesty International, the Red Cross, and Doctors Without Borders, as well as legions of national and regional projects, provide the most detailed and informed analyses of rights violations and human suffering. One activist describes their core approach as *"promoting change by reporting facts."*[95]

Other activist initiatives preserve past traumas, including genocide, in historical memory—another form of witnessing. One example is the Russian Memorial Society (see Map 5.1). "Memorial was founded by a group of young historians, some of whom had been collecting oral histories of [Gulag] camp survivors for many years," wrote Anne Applebaum. "Later, Memorial would also lead the battle to identify the corpses buried in mass graves outside Moscow and Leningrad, and to build monuments and memorials to the Stalinist era." By the end of the 1990s, Memorial had established itself as "the most important centre for the study of Soviet history, as well as for the defence of human rights, in the Russian federation." Its publications were "known to Soviet scholars around the world for their accuracy, their fidelity to facts, and their careful, judicious archives."[96]

Figure 16.13 Education projects and fieldtrips have become an integral part of genocide-awareness and prevention strategies. A student group meets at the museum of the Dachau concentration camp near Munich, Germany (see Figure 16.1).

Source: Author's photo, October 2012.

Ideologies, religious and secular

> The imagination and the spiritual strength of Shakespeare's evildoers stopped short at a dozen corpses. Because they had no *ideology*.
>
> Alexander Solzhenitsyn, *The Gulag Archipelago*

The role of religious belief in genocide prevention and intervention may be examined from two perspectives. On one hand, religious believers throughout history have derived from their faith an abiding love and respect for humanity. In a practical sense, this has led them to cross lines of religion, ethnicity, and social class to help genocide's victims. In colonial Spanish America, Bartolomé de las Casas denounced atrocities against the Indians with a passion that still cuts through cant nearly five centuries later (though las Casas supported the importation of African slaves to reduce the burden on indigenous peoples). Catholics in Poland during the Second World War regularly sheltered Jews (see Chapter 10). One such rescuer, Irene Gut Opdyke, was a devout believer who wrote in her memoirs: "Courage is a whisper from above: when you listen with your heart, you will know what to do and how and when."[97] Post-genocide Rwanda witnessed a surge of converts to Islam, since the country's Muslim minority, by contrast with its Catholic Church, saved Tutsi coreligionists, rather than assisting in their massacre. Surely, the humane and cosmopolitan vision guiding much religious belief and practice is to be acknowledged and admired.

The case of Rwanda's Catholic Church, however, reminds us that religious believers often act negligently or murderously in genocide.[98] "The very worst things that men have ever done," said British politician William Gladstone, "have been done when they were performing acts of violence in the name of religion."[99] In the opinion of the great sociologist Barrington Moore, Jr.—summarized by his student Charles Tilly—monotheistic religions, in particular, foster "gross intolerance, hence readiness to kill outsiders, because of their sharply drawn distinctions between the worthy and the unworthy, the pure and the impure."[100] But polytheism provides no barrier to fanaticism, as Muslim and Sikh survivors of Hindu nationalist violence can attest.

The distinguishing element here is not religious belief *per se*, but *extremism and exclusivism* passed through a religious filter. There are few more important tasks of genocide prevention than confronting religious extremists and fundamentalists, at home and abroad—not with persecution or bombs, which would only fuel their martyr complexes, but with a pluralistic, humanistic education system, and a cosmopolitan[101] counter-discourse (including by religious moderates).

Secular ideologies are also Janus-faced in relation to genocide. Democratic and pluralistic ideologies are primarily responsible for our concern over genocide and human rights violations. The very idea of "human rights" is a product of the secular Enlightenment in Europe, though it resonates with many religious and philosophical traditions. These ideologies have underpinned enormous positive changes in human civilization. State-sponsored slavery is no more.[102] The most blatant

Figure 16.14 Christian and Muslim schoolmates in Addis Ababa, Ethiopia. Like Kazan in Russia (see "Success Stories?"), Addis is renowned as a cosmopolitan city where ethnoreligious conflict is rare, where diverse populations intermix, and where mosques and churches stand cheek-by-jowl.

Source: Author's photo, May 2013.

forms of colonialism have mostly been expunged from the earth. Major wars and genocides across a range of previously-conflictive "dyads" are now unlikely or unthinkable (France and Germany is the most commonly-cited pairing). Institutions whose gratuitous cruelty has something in common with the sadism of genocide—such as drawing-and-quartering or breaking on a wheel[103]—are also historical relics.

Secular-humanist ideologies have given rise to the idea of global civil society and "world citizenship," vital to transcending the differences of culture, class, and religion that can fuel genocides. A world citizen holds that:

> Everyone is an individual endowed with certain rights and subject to certain obligations; everyone is capable of voluntaristic action seeking rational solutions to social problems; everyone has the right and obligation to participate in the grand human project; everyone is, therefore, a citizen of the world polity. World citizenship is the institutional endowment of authority and agency on individuals. It infuses each individual with the authority to pursue particularistic interests, preferably in organizations, while also authorizing individuals to promote collective goods defined in largely standardized ways.[104]

But secular ideologies have also *underpinned* most genocides of the past two centuries. One thinks of the genocidal expansionists into an economically "unexploited" North America; the Young Turk modernizers of the Ottoman Empire, and their counterparts in Stalinist Russia; the Nazis with their fanatical racism and nationalism; and the Khmer Rouge communists in Cambodia. The genocidal consequences of much secular ideology were eloquently conveyed by a repentant Communist Party activist, speaking about the imposition of famine and collectivization in the Soviet countryside:

> With the rest of my generation I firmly believed that the ends justified the means. Our great goal was the universal triumph of Communism, and for the sake of that goal everything was permissible—to lie, to steal, to destroy hundreds of thousands and even millions of people, all those who were hindering our work or could hinder it, everyone who stood in the way. And to hesitate or doubt about all this was to give in to "intellectual squeamishness" and "stupid liberalism," the attribute of people who "could not see the forest for the trees" . . . I was convinced that I was accomplishing the great and necessary transformation of the countryside; that in the days to come the people who lived there would be better off for it; that their distress and suffering were a result of their own ignorance or the machinations of the class enemy; that those who sent me—and I myself—knew better than the peasants how they should live, what they should sow and when they should plow.[105]

A mirror image of such thinking in the capitalist West depicts those who stand in the way of "modernization" and "development" as backward and disposable, while the millions of casualties inflicted by colonial famines or contemporary "structural adjustment" policies are justified by the noble ends of market liberalism.

It is at this point that secular ideologies blend with religious ones, and begin to realize their true genocidal potential. A replacement is found for the supernatural goals of religion (salvation, paradise, oneness with the creator, and so on). Such bounties are now promised in one's own lifetime, or at least within a few generations. It is in this sense that the English historian A.J.P. Taylor refers to Marx and Engels's *Communist Manifesto* as a "religious book," guided by a figure (Marx) who was "essentially . . . a prophet, not a philosopher"; "if events did not fit in with his system," Taylor wrote, "so much the worse for events."[106]

All of this serves as a reminder that a critical individual dimension—in both senses of the word "critical"—exists in religious and secular ideologies alike. Each person must monitor, as objectively and skeptically as possible, the tendency to hatred and exclusivism that is present in us all. There is always a temptation to believe we are superior and in the right—whether we buttress this with religious belief, a secular stance, or a mixture of the two. Actually, we *might* be "superior" and in the right! I do believe some epistemologies (strategies of knowing), moral frameworks, and social options are superior to others, or I would not be writing this book. But we must guard against hubris. As the US indigenous activist Ruby Plenty Chiefs reminds us: "Great evil has been done on earth by people who think they have all the answers."[107]

BOX 16.6 IS HUMANITY BECOMING MORE PEACEFUL?

Figure 16.15 Steven Pinker, author of *The Better Angels of Our Nature* and numerous other books on human psychology and society.

Source: Cary Lecture Series, Lexington, MA/ Creative Commons.

Steven Pinker shows his colors at the outset of his 2011 volume, *The Better Angels of Our Nature: A History of Violence and Humanity*. The Harvard professor of psychology proclaims that "violence has declined over long stretches of time, and today we may be living in the most peaceable era in our species' existence." Our age, says Pinker, "is blessed by unprecedented levels of peaceful coexistence."[108] His epic-length tome catalyzed further debate over whether humanity was experiencing not just a rare period of relative peace, but the beginning of a new epoch of non-violent relations, at the international, societal, and interpersonal levels. The strength of the evidence for this proposition is clearly of significance to the cause of genocide prevention and intervention.

There is much evidence to submit against Pinker's thesis, as any reader who has reached the final chapter of this book will be aware. Pinker is not unaware of the dangers of hypothesizing on the basis of limited-term evidence: he relates the quip "about the turkey who, on the eve of Thanksgiving, remarked on the extraordinary 364-day era of peace between farmers and turkeys he is lucky enough to be living in." But he marshals a vast range of comparative data to support his contention that a "reduction in violence [is evident] at many scales—in the family, in the neighborhood, between tribes and other armed factions, and among major nations and states." He sees this as the zenith of an essential process of *modernity* (see Chapter 11). One feature was the dissemination of humanist Enlightenment values. It underpinned a globalized "rights revolution," reducing or suppressing such practices as slavery, colonialism, infanticide, vendettas, boxing, and bear-baiting/bullfighting (as part of a rights discourse that now transcended the human species). Like other exponents of the "democratic peace" (see Chapter 12), Pinker argues that liberal-democratic philosophies of rule have "pacifying features" that "penaliz[e] an utter lack of empathy" in leaders or would-be leaders, and impose "checks and balances [that] limit the damage that a grandiose leader can do." The rise of democracy has been accompanied by shifts from "a culture of honor, in which men were respected for lashing out against insults" to "a culture of dignity, in which men were respected for controlling their impulses," including their sexual impulses. New understandings emerged to govern decorum in social and diplomatic relations—limiting the acceptability of everything from assassinating foreign leaders and butchering their emissaries, to belching and farting at the dinner table.

At the macro-level, the focus in genocide studies has typically been on modernity as an enabler of imperialism and the genocidal nation-state, both forces crushing indigenous and minority peoples worldwide (see Chapters 2, 3). Pinker, while hardly oblivious to these processes and crimes, draws on German sociologist Norbert Elias to argue that the modern period is also one of

> the centralization of state control and its monopolization of violence, the growth of craft guilds and bureaucracies, the replacement of barter with money, the development of technology, the enhancement of trade, the growing webs of dependency among far-flung individuals, [which] all fit into an organic control. And to prosper within that whole, one had to cultivate faculties of empathy and self-control until they became . . . second nature.

As for contemporary war-making, Pinker seeks to debunk the frequently-cited claim that we have witnessed a sharp rise in the proportion of civilian casualties in armed conflicts. He supports estimates "that civilians suffer around half of the battle deaths in war, and that the ratio varies from war to war but has not increased over time. Indeed, . . . it has recently decreased by a substantial margin," with cases of indiscriminate "degenerate war" like the Democratic Republic of the Congo (see Chapters 2, 9, 12) serving as statistical outliers.

Among the authors cited in support of Pinker's thesis is noted international relations scholars Joshua Goldstein, whose *War and Gender* was sampled in Chapter 13. The title of Goldstein's subsequent book, *Winning the War on War: The Decline of Armed Conflict Worldwide* makes clear his agreement with Pinker's framing. The work gets off to a retrospectively-unpromising start, when Goldstein cites post-2005–2007 improvements in security and stability in Iraq, many of which have been demolished by Islamic State and other sectarian actors in recent years (see Box 4a). But his broad-sample survey likewise supports a view that

> wars today are measurably fewer and smaller than [even] thirty years ago. By one measure, the number of people killed directly by war violence has decreased by 75 percent in that period. . . . *Interstate* wars have become very infrequent and relatively small. Wars between "great powers" have not occurred for more than fifty years. The number of *civil* wars is also shrinking, though less dramatically, as old ones end faster than new ones begin.

Goldstein does not consider this process "inevitable, irreversible, or part of an immutable trend," but he expresses a conviction that humanity has found violence-control mechanisms that work, at least to the extent that "less of a bad thing is a good thing." "The reduction in war over several decades suggests that the international community is doing something right in trying to tame war," Goldstein writes. He highlights "the efforts of international peacekeepers, diplomats, peace movements, humanitarian aid agencies, and other international organizations in war-torn and postwar countries."[109]

Such broadly optimistic formulations have drawn fire. For some, Pinker's grim depiction of warfare among "primitive" peoples evinces an ethnocentric bias and desire for a new, western-driven "civilizing mission."[110] John Gray, in a long critique of Pinker and Goldstein for *The Guardian*, also challenged Pinker's understanding of "violence [as] a type of backwardness."[111] While acknowledging "that the modern state's monopoly of force has led, in some contexts, to declining rates of violent death," Gray emphasizes the state's role in perpetrating "mass killing" and "state terror" worldwide. He also questioned the authors' reliance on statistical measures of violence, contending that these reflected a scientific fetishism that was incapable of grasping the nature of contemporary "degenerate wars":

> Estimating the numbers of those who die from violence involves complex questions of cause and effect, which cannot always be separated from moral judgments. There are many kinds of lethal force that do not produce immediate death. Are those who die of hunger or disease during war or its aftermath counted among the casualties? Do refugees whose lives are cut short appear in the count? Where torture is used in war, will its victims figure in the calculus if they succumb years later from the physical and mental damage that has been inflicted on them? Do infants who are born to brief and painful lives as a result of exposure to Agent Orange [see Figure 1.4, p. 35] or depleted uranium find a place in the roll call of the dead? If women who have been raped as part of a military strategy of sexual violence die before their time, will their passing feature in the statistical tables?

According to Gray, an overreliance on "murky" data leaves "a vast range of casualties of violence unaccounted for." His examples of mass violence are disproportionately drawn from the period of the "Hemoclysm" identified by Matthew White in *Atrocitology*, closely identified with totalitarian fascist and communist regimes, and the two world wars (see Box 1.2, p. 8). Gray is right to stress the great violence of the western-colonial "unweaving" that followed the Second World War, which continued and arguably still takes the form of "neocolonial" and "proxy" wars. But in my view, Pinker and Goldstein have identified trends, both in the contemporary "globalized" world and over the *longue durée* of modern history, that deserve careful study by genocide scholars and peace advocates.

Personal responsibility

How can you as an individual monitor your beliefs, and reduce (forgive me) your genocidal potential?[112]

- *Educate yourself broadly and deeply.* If your beliefs are congruent with reality and a viable moral framework, they should not collapse in the face of opposed views. Expose yourself to those viewpoints, by consulting a wide range of media—something that is now easier than ever. Learn from contrary-minded others. Surprisingly often, you will find that those who think differently become more familiar, even genuine friends. This may make you less likely to support their persecution and extermination.
- *Travel if you can.* This is also easier than ever, even outside the privileged West. My own most intensive learning has come from traveling as much of the world as time and money have allowed. Talk to people in those distant lands, like-minded and otherwise. The vast majority will be welcoming and receptive, and will open their hearts and lives to you. You are bound to discover strong bonds of community; and again, when you have immersed yourself in a place and interacted with its people, you are probably less likely to want to kill them someday, or support anyone with that agenda. Travel also serves as an antidote to the kind of narcissistic, triumphalist thinking about one's own nation and culture that is such a vital underpinning of genocidal enterprises (see Chapter 10).[113]

  If you *can't* travel, or won't, then at least read voraciously (history, current affairs, travel accounts, even guides); watch the History Channel and Discovery and National Geographic; surf the Net for relevant perspectives and insights. As always, balance your receptivity with critical thinking and a healthy dose of skepticism.
- *"Keep [y]our consciences soft and vulnerable."* "Only then," wrote Donald and Laura Miller, "will we rise up to challenge the suffering that surrounds us. Denial of evil is a defense mechanism that a just world simply cannot afford."[114] Be open to the distress and persecution of others. As the Argentine

revolutionary Ernesto "Che" Guevara wrote in a 1966 letter to his children: "Above all, be capable always of feeling to your very depths any injustice committed against anyone in any part of the world."[115] Similar were the words of Holocaust survivor and Nobel Peace Prize–winner Elie Wiesel, accepting his award in 1986:

> Sometimes we must interfere. When human lives are endangered, when human dignity is in jeopardy, national borders and sensitivities become irrelevant. Whenever men or women are persecuted because of their race, religion, or political views, that place must—at that moment—become the center of the universe.[116]

It is easy to allow crimes like genocide and other mass violence to slide into abstractions. Aid agencies speak of "compassion fatigue." Allen Feldman pointed to a "cultural anesthesia" born of "generalities of bodies—dead, wounded, starving, diseased, and homeless . . . pressed against the television screen as mass articles."[117] Soviet dictator Joseph Stalin famously commented, "One death is a tragedy; a million deaths is a statistic."[118]

The solution lies in empathy and learning.[119] I recall sitting in a restaurant in Colombia in 1994, watching fragmentary images on TV of dozens of bodies floating down a river somewhere very far away. These are today among the indelible images of the Rwandan holocaust (see Figure 9.2). My thought at the time? "Oh jeez, more tribal violence in Africa." Only after plowing through a few thousand pages of testimony and reportage on the genocide, material that stunned and changed me, did I feel I had expiated the shame of that first ignorant reaction.

- **Question authority.** I do not say "Reject authority." Much authority is *authoritative* rather than *authoritarian*. It derives its legitimacy from suasion and moral appeal. On the other hand, the great majority of genocides are carried out under authoritarian rule of one kind or another, and formally-democratic societies are far from immune to these temptations—especially in times of proclaimed emergency. Many if not most readers of this book will be called upon, at some point in their lives, to decide whether to support a call to large-scale collective violence. Is that call warranted, or is it a summons to atrocity? All authority rests on conformity, and conforming *may* be immoral, or inhuman. When this is the case, move beyond questioning to active opposition. ". . . Any form of domination, hierarchy, control has a burden of proof. It's not self-justifying. It has to demonstrate that it's legitimate, just as any use of force or coercion does. Therefore it deserves to be challenged. And if it's challenged, and it cannot justify itself, it should be dismantled."[120]

"Learn to think and to judge for yourself, responsibly," wrote Rudolf Höss. "Don't accept everything without criticism and as absolutely true, everything which is brought to your attention. Learn from life. The biggest mistake of my life was that I believed everything faithfully which came from the top, and I didn't dare to have the least bit of doubt about the truth of that which was presented to me. Walk through life with your eyes open."[121] The advice, sincere or not, was delivered in a final letter to his children before Höss, one of the most heinous *génocidaires* of the twentieth century, was hanged for his crimes on the grounds of the Auschwitz-Birkenau death camp that he had commanded.

- **Support worthy causes.** You know a few already. Some of those devoted specifically to genocide prevention may be found on the webpage for this book (www.genocidetext.net). Consider supporting by *participating*, not just by contributing money. Participation brings you into contact and solidarity with other human beings. This is essential to building a global movement against genocide and other mass crimes.

Proponents of worthy causes may sometimes use violence to achieve their goals—typically, to bring an end to violence (including structural violence) by an oppressor. These actions may not be pretty, but neither, unfortunately, are they obsolete. Violent resistance to the planners and perpetrators of genocide, *while it is underway,* is an incontestable right. Likewise, all people have the right to resist aggressive war waged against them, if their resistance does not descend into atrocity.

Beyond this, I offer only tentative comments about whether to support a given movement that practices violence. In my life, I have strongly backed movements that used violence to defend civilian populations, for positive social revolution, and for national independence (the Sandinistas in Nicaragua; the FMLN guerrillas in El Salvador; South Africa's ANC; Fretilin in East Timor). I have also supported state-led military interventions that suppressed genocide—Vietnam in Cambodia, or NATO in Kosovo (though in the latter case, I criticized the military strategy, based on high-altitude bombing, as cowardly and ineffective).

As Alan Kuperman has pointed out, however, violent resistance and military intervention may provide just the "provocation" that would-be *génocidaires* seek to justify implementation of their "final solution." Thus, violence should be employed, and such movements be supported, only *in extremis:* as a defensive response to manifestly intolerable treatment or (Kuperman) "grossly disproportionate" state attack or counterattack.[122] It is a cliché to say that non-violent means should be tried first, second, and third. It becomes less of a cliché when we appreciate the demonstrable power of non-violent resistance, which has toppled dictatorships around the world.[123]

CONCLUSION

This book has endeavored to provide an introduction to the concept and practice of genocide. We have considered both genocide's roots in antiquity and its manifestations in modern and contemporary periods. The intimate relationships between genocide, war, imperialism, and social revolution have been explored, together with diverse social science perspectives on the phenomenon. We have examined how legal institutions and mechanisms evolved to confront genocide; how genocides worked their way into collective memory; and the role that gender plays.

One might express optimism or pessimism about the chances of establishing an effective anti-genocide regime. While a mood, by itself, changes nothing, there are many relatively-recent historical grounds for some optimism. ". . . Despite various setbacks," writes Micheline Ishay, "the history of human rights shows a clear dimension of progress: slavery has been abolished (even if vestiges, intolerable though they may be, remain), women in most of the world have been granted the right to vote, and workers are endowed with more social and economic protection than ever before."[124] Gary J. Bass argues along similar lines:

All the preconditions for a new era of human rights are there, if we only want it. In the world's liberal democracies, we have a more wide-ranging and well-educated press than ever, if we could stop slashing foreign bureaus; we have a public that is freer to express its political opinions than ever, if it could be bothered to figure them out; and we have military forces that could in many cases protect the victims of genocide, if the order came. The idea of protecting human rights is increasingly commonplace, but today's leading democracies have not yet shouldered the responsibilities that previous great powers did. We are all atrocitarians now—but so far only in words, and not yet in deeds.[125]

My own conviction is that anything in the human order that can be understood can also be confronted, if not entirely vanquished. In the case of a blight as pernicious and enduring as genocide, we are morally compelled to do so. Actions taken today carry special significance, with so many human and planetary issues demanding attention. To stage an effective confrontation, we need to be aware of the linkages between genocide and other pressing challenges. Hence, in part, my preference for a broad and inclusive genocide framework, rather than a conceptually-restrictive or narrowly-legalistic one. Meaningful "peace" cannot exist alongside massive inequalities in wealth, health, and education. And it will do us little good to suppress genocide and establish amity among peoples, if the earth itself finally rebels against the species that has caused it so much ecocidal damage. (This edition is published in the wake of "the hottest year on record by far," a phenomenon that the vast majority of scientists link to climate change caused by human resource consumption and environmental exploitation.)[126]

The odds of overcoming these multifarious challenges are impossible to estimate, but I believe we have an obligation to face them squarely. I hope I have persuaded you, if you needed persuading, that the effort to confront and suppress genocide deserves a prominent place on the human agenda. May I welcome you to the struggle?

FURTHER STUDY

Gary J. Bass, *Freedom's Battle: The Origins of Humanitarian Intervention.* New York: Alfred A. Knopf, 2008. The dawn of "humanitarian" interventions in the nineteenth and early twentieth centuries.

Timothy W. Crawford and Alan J. Kuperman, eds., *Gambling on Humanitarian Intervention: Moral Hazard, Rebellion and Civil War.* Abingdon: Routledge, 2006. Cautionary tales of "moral hazard" in humanitarian interventions.

John G. Heidenrich, *How to Prevent Genocide: A Guide for Policymakers, Scholars, and the Concerned Citizen.* Westport, CT: Praeger, 2001. Emphasizes strategies of military intervention.

Leo Kuper, *The Prevention of Genocide.* New Haven, CT: Yale University Press, 1985. Kuper's second and final book on genocide focuses on UN performance and preventive strategies.

Adam Lebor, *"Complicity with Evil": The United Nations in the Age of Modern Genocide.* New Haven, CT: Yale University Press, 2006. Disturbing overview of the UN's failed interventions in the 1990s and 2000s.

Adam Lupel and Ernesto Verdeja, eds., *Responding to Genocide: The Politics of International Action.* Boulder, CO: Lynne Rienner Publishers, 2013. Stimulating set of essays exploring early-warning systems and the role of the UN and regional organizations, among other themes.

Stephen McLoughlin, *The Structural Prevention of Mass Atrocities: Understanding Risk and Resilience.* New York: Routledge, 2014. An Africa-focused contribution to the literature on political and societal resilience to genocide (see Box 16.2). See also *Mass Atrocities, Risk and Resilience: Rethinking Prevention* (ed.).

Karl E. Meyer and Shareen Blair Brysac, *Pax Ethnica: Where and How Diversity Succeeds.* New York: PublicAffairs, 2012. Engaging and informative profiles of ethnic and religious accommodation, in both the Global South and North (see Box 16.2).

Nicolaus Mills and Kira Brunner, eds., *The New Killing Fields: Massacre and the Politics of Intervention.* New York: Basic Books, 2002. Exceptional essays, with a journalistic tinge.

Mobilizing the Will to Intervene: Leadership and Action to Prevent Mass Atrocities. Report of The Will to Intervene Project (Montreal Institute for Genocide and Human Rights Studies, 2009). Available online at http://migs.concordia.ca/W2I/documents/ENG_MIGS_finalW2IAugust09.pdf. The Canadian counterpart to the US-based Genocide Prevention Task Force, with policy recommendations for both Canadian and US governments, publics, and media.

Prevent Genocide International. Online at www.preventgenocide.org. Indispensable resources and prevention strategies.

Preventing Genocide: A Blueprint for US Policymakers. Report of the Genocide Prevention Task Force, Washington, DC: US Holocaust Memorial Museum *et al.*, 2008. Available online at www.ushmm.org/m/pdfs/20081124-genocide-prevention-report.pdf. Focuses on the US leadership role in prevention and intervention.

Geoffrey Robinson, *"If You Leave Us Here, We Will Die": How Genocide Was Stopped in East Timor.* Princeton, NJ: Princeton University Press, 2009. How an effective intervention was marshaled, by one of the participants and rebels (see Box 16.4).

Henryk J. Sokalski, *An Ounce of Prevention: Macedonia and the UN Experience in Preventive Diplomacy.* Washington, DC: United States Institute of Peace Press,

2003. Detailed inside account of a broadly-successful experiment in preventive deployment, by the leader of the UN force in question.

Peter N. Stearns, *Global Outrage: The Impact of World Opinion on Contemporary History.* Oxford: Oneworld, 2007. Engaging survey of the emergence of global public opinion on humanitarian issues.

Rory Stewart and Gerald Knaus, *Can Intervention Work?* New York: W.W. Norton & Co., 2011. Wrestles with core conundrums of intervention, from both supportive and skeptical viewpoints.

Scott Straus, *Making and Unmaking Nations: War, Leadership, and Genocide in Modern Africa.* Ithaca, NY: Cornell University Press, 2015. Theory and case studies, with genocidal societies set against examples of resilience and pluralism (see Box 16.2).

Nicholas Wheeler, *Saving Strangers: Humanitarian Intervention in International Society.* Oxford: Oxford University Press, 2000. A foundational study.

NOTES

1 Thomas Cushman, "Is Genocide Preventable? Some Theoretical Considerations," *Journal of Genocide Research*, 5: 4 (2003), pp. 528, 531.

2 John G. Heidenrich, *How to Prevent Genocide: A Guide for Policymakers, Scholars, and the Concerned Citizen* (Westport, CT: Praeger, 2001), p. 18.

3 Cushman, "Is Genocide Preventable?," p. 525.

4 Barbara Harff, "No Lessons Learned from the Holocaust? Assessing Risks of Genocide and Political Mass Murder since 1955," *American Political Science Review*, 97: 1 (February 2003), p. 62.

5 Ervin Staub, "The Psychology of Bystanders, Perpetrators, and Heroic Helpers," in Leonard S. Newman and Ralph Erber, eds., *Understanding Genocide: The Social Psychology of the Holocaust* (Oxford: Oxford University Press, 2002), p. 30.

6 For a discussion of consociationalism in the context of a genocide-afflicted region, see René Lemarchand, "Consociationalism and Power Sharing in Africa: Rwanda, Burundi, and the Democratic Republic of the Congo," *African Affairs*, 106 (2007), pp. 1–20.

7 Ervin Staub, *The Roots of Evil: The Origins of Genocide and Other Group Violence* (Cambridge: Cambridge University Press, 1989), p. 274.

8 "Mission Statement," Office of the Special Adviser on the Prevention of Genocide, www.un.org/en/preventgenocide/adviser/.

9 "Annex: Outline of the Mandate for the Special Adviser on the Prevention of Genocide," letter from Kofi A. Annan (S/2004/567), July 13, 2004, www.un.org/en/ga/search/view_doc.asp?symbol=S/2004/567.

10 See Aidan Hehir, "An Analysis of Perspectives on the Office of the Special Adviser on the Prevention of Genocide," *Genocide Studies and Prevention*, 5: 3 (2010), pp. 258–276. Elsewhere, Hehir writes that the creation of the OSAPG was "one of the key, and arguably [the] most prominent, aspects of the 'Action Plan to Prevent Genocide' launched by Kofi Annan in April 2004, and for this reason alone it merits attention. The OSAPG is additionally significant in that the powers vested in, and resources devoted to, this new office are indicative of the extent to which the rhetoric proclaiming the need for UN reform has been implemented in practice." However, these are not sufficient to offset "those aspects of the UN's architecture, which have contributed to inertia." Hence, "it is difficult to identify any tangible reform"—including the OSAPG—"that can enable 'Never Again!' to move from rhetoric to reality." Hehir, "The Special Adviser on the Prevention of Genocide: Adding Value to the UN's Mechanisms for Preventing Intra-State Crises?," *Journal of Genocide Research*, 13: 3 (2011), p. 283.

11 See *Framework of Analysis for Atrocity Crimes: A Tool for Prevention* (New York: United Nations, 2014), available online in PDF format (Google "un atrocity"). The same year that the *Framework* appeared (I believe), the previously-separate Office of the Special Adviser on the Responsibility to Protect was folded into the OSAPG. Adama Dieng thus consults and shares duties with a separately-mandated Special Adviser—originally Edward Luck, currently Jennifer Welsh.

12 Ted Robert Gurr and Barbara Harff, *Ethnic Conflict in World Politics* (Boulder, CO: Westview Press, 1994), p. 80.

13 For an overview of the empirical evidence, see David Kopel, review of Jay Simkin *et al.*, *Lethal Laws* (Milwaukee: Jews for the Preservation of Firearm Ownership, 1994), in *New York Law School Journal of International and Comparative Law*, 15 (1995), pp. 355–398.

14 R. Charli Carpenter has deepened and problematized this framing of "vulnerability" in important respects, emphasizing physical capacity as well as liability to violent victimization. See Carpenter, "Women and Children First: Gender Norms and Humanitarian Evacuation in the Balkans, 1991–1995," *International Organization*, 57: 4 (Fall 2003), pp. 661–694. More generally, Carpenter's 2006 volume, *"Innocent Women and Children": Gender, Norms and the Protection of Civilians* (London: Ashgate, 2006), is an essential and eye-opening contribution.

15 See Adam Jones, "Genocide and Humanitarian Intervention: Incorporating the Gender Variable," in Jones, *Gender Inclusive: Essays on Violence, Men, and Feminist International Relations* (London: Routledge, 2009), pp. 255–282.

16 Scott Straus, *Making and Unmaking Nations: War, Leadership, and Genocide in Modern Africa* (Ithaca, NY: Cornell University Press, 2015), p. 2.

17 Stephen McLoughlin, *The Structural Prevention of Mass Atrocities: Understanding Risk and Resilience* (New York: Routledge, 2014).

18 Straus, *Making and Unmaking Nations*, pp. 323–325.

19 McLoughlin, *Structural Prevention*, pp. 157–159, 163.

20 Karl E. Meyer and Shareen Blair Brysac, *Pax Ethnica: Where and How Diversity Succeeds* (New York: PublicAffairs, 2012), pp. 289–394 (e-book).

21 Stowell quoted in Lemkin, *Lemkin on Genocide*, p. 47.

22 See Robert D. Kaplan, *The Coming Anarchy: Shattering the Dreams of the Post Cold War* (New York: Random House, 2000).

23 Edward Luck quoted in Paul D. Williams, "Humanitarian Military Intervention After the 'Responsibility to Protect': Obstacles and Prospects," in Joyce Apsel and Ernesto Verdeja, eds., *Genocide Matters: Ongoing Issues and Emerging Perspectives* (London: Routledge, 2013), p. 157.

24 International Commission on Intervention and State Sovereignty (hereafter, ICISS), *The Responsibility to Protect* (Ottawa, ON: International Development Research Centre, 2001), p. 19.

25 Richard Falk, "The Challenge of Genocide and Genocidal Politics in an Era of Globalisation," in Tim Dunne and Nicholas J. Wheeler, eds., *Human Rights in Global Politics* (Cambridge: Cambridge University Press, 1999), p. 191.

26 ICISS, *The Responsibility to Protect*, pp. 30–31.

27 "After the Armistice [of November 1918], the blockade was extended to the Baltic ports and continued until the Allies were satisfied with German compliance with their demands. The journalist Walter Duranty visited Lubeck in 1919 and found people living on potatoes and black bread. They had no meat, butter, milk or eggs. A doctor told him that 90 per cent of the children were anaemic or below weight, and that more than half of them had rickets or tuberculosis. . . . The senior German delegate at Versailles, Graf Ulrich von Brockdorff-Rantzau, expressed some of the [German] resentment: 'The hundreds of thousands of noncombatants who have perished since November 11 because of the blockade were destroyed coolly and deliberately, after our opponents had won a certain and assured victory. Think of that, when you speak of guilt and atonement.'" Jonathan Glover, *Humanity: A Moral History of the Twentieth Century* (New Haven, CT: Yale University Press, 1999), pp. 65–66.

28 ICISS, *The Responsibility to Protect*, p. 29.

29 Annan quoted in ibid., p. 40.

30 Ibid., p. 48.

31 Heidenrich, *How to Prevent Genocide*, p. 61.

32 Williams, "Humanitarian Military Intervention," p. 157.

33 Mary Kaldor in "Humanitarian Intervention: A Forum," *The Nation*, July 14, 2003, p. 13. "The commission went on to argue that a gap between legality and legitimacy is very dangerous and needs to be removed by specifying conditions for humanitarian intervention." This was the challenge taken up, not entirely successfully in my view, by the ICISS.

34 *Mobilizing the Will to Intervene: Leadership and Action to Prevent Mass Atrocities*, report of The Will to Intervene Project (Montreal: Montreal Institute for Genocide and Human Rights Studies, 2009). Quoted passages from pp. 2, 32, 37, 52–53, 62; the full text of the report is available online at http://migs.concordia.ca/W2I/documents/ENG_MIGS_finalW2IAugust09.pdf.

35 Stephen Holmes, "Looking Away," *London Review of Books*, November 14, 2002.

36 See Michael Parenti, *To Kill a Nation: The Attack on Yugoslavia* (London: Verso, 2000); Noam Chomsky, *The New Military Humanism: Lessons from Kosovo* (Monroe, ME: Common Courage Press, 1999); Philip Hammond and Edward S. Herman, eds., *Degraded Capability: The Media and the Kosovo Crisis* (London: Pluto Press, 2000); and Diana Johnstone, *Fools' Crusade: Yugoslavia, NATO, and Western Delusions* (New York: Monthly Review Press, 2003).

37 See Adam Jones, "Challenges of Genocide Intervention," *Global Dialogue* (online), 15: 1 (2013), www.worlddialogue.org/content.php?id=546.

38 For a stimulating treatment of "The Sierra Leone Model [of] Multidimensional Peace Operations, 1998–2011," see ch. 6 in Goldstein, *Winning the War on War*, pp. 136–176.

39 India relished the opportunity to deal a blow to its perennial rival, Pakistan, by severing its eastern wing; it also feared that among the flow of millions of mostly Hindu refugees to restive Bengal were many potential supporters of the Maoist "Naxalite" rebellion then raging in the country's northeast. (For a detailed examination of Indian decision-making, see Sonia Cordera, "India's Response to the 1971 East Pakistan Crisis: Hidden and Open Reasons for Intervention," *Journal of Genocide Research*, 17: 1, pp. 45–62.) In *The Blood Telegram*, Gary J. Bass goes further still, accusing "Indira Gandhi and her top advisers [of being] coldly calculating strategists, even if their actions served a humane cause." He assailed the "breathtaking hypocrisy" of India's "demanding freedom for the Bengali people in East Pakistan, while conducting its own repression of restive populations under Indian control in Kashmir, as well as lesser-known groups . . . [including]—with painful irony—leftist Bengalis within India's own volatile state of West Bengal." He does, however, credit "sympathy for Bengalis" with underpinning Indian policy to some degree. Bass, *The Blood Telegram: Nixon, Kissinger, and a Forgotten Genocide* (New York: Alfred A. Knopf, 2013), (e-book, page unknown; see note 14, p. 468). As for Tanzania in 1979, it was also confronted by an unmanageable flood of refugees (and the regime that it installed to replace Idi Amin's in Uganda, that of Milton Obote, was no less murderous than its predecessor). Vietnam, for its part, had deep political rivalries with the Khmer Rouge, close ties to the Vietnamese minority in Cambodia, and desires to establish itself as the regional hegemon. Member countries of NATO were profoundly concerned by the security implications of hundreds of thousands of Kosovar refugees destabilizing neighboring countries in a corner of Europe that had already spawned one world war. Only in the East Timor case, I have argued (Box 7a and Box 16.4), was moral suasion by morally-motivated actors truly decisive in the equation: it persuaded Australia to lead the intervention, when considerations of *Realpolitik* dictated otherwise. However, to the extent that it became politically untenable for the Australian government to act otherwise, we may also argue that practical considerations outweighed humanitarian ones.

40 Timothy Murithi, "The Role of Regional Organizations," in Adam Lupel and Ernesto Verdeja, eds., *Responding to Genocide: The Politics of International Action* (Boulder, CO: Lynne Rienner Publishers, 2013), p. 157.

41 Ibid., p. 169.

42 Ibid., p. 170.

43 Ibid., p. 174.

44 Geoffrey Robinson, *"If You Leave Us Here, We Will Die": How Genocide Was Stopped in East Timor* (Princeton, NJ: Princeton University Press, 2010). The quoted passages are drawn from pp. 155, 175, 179, 186, 191, and 194.

45 "Children of Timor Veterans Protest at Australian and US Embassies," *The Jakarta Post*, September 12, 1999, http://jawawa.id/index.php/newsitem/children-of-timor-veterans-protest-at-australian-and-us-embassies-1447893297.

46 Alan J. Kuperman, "Humanitarian Hazard: Revisiting Doctrines of Intervention," *Harvard International Review*, Spring 2004, p. 67.

47 Michael Hirsh, "Calling All Regio-Cops: Peacekeeping's Hybrid Future," *Foreign Affairs* (November–December 2000), p. 5.

48 Israel W. Charny, "An International Peace Army: A Proposal for the Long-range Future," in Charny, ed., *The Encyclopedia of Genocide* (Santa Barbara, CA: ABC-CLIO, 1999), p. 650.

49 Ibid., pp. 650–652.

50 Ibid., p. 650.

51 Dallaire quoted in Heidenrich, *How to Prevent Genocide*, pp. 200–201. Heidenrich's ch. 12, "The Evolution of an Idea," explores the various proposals for a UN standing force.

52 See Tim Pippard and Veronica Lie, "Enhancing the Rapid Reaction Capability of the United Nations: Exploring the Options," United Nations Association-UK, July 2004.

53 See, e.g., the analysis of a British government Green Paper on the subject in "Peacekeeping 'Role' for Mercenaries," *BBC Online*, February 13, 2002, http://news.bbc.co.uk/1/hi/uk_politics/1817495.stm.

54 On the *bumiputra* policy, and the politics of intercommunal relations more generally, see Michael Schumer, "Malaysia's New Journey," *Time*, September 5, 2010, http://content.time.com/time/magazine/article/0,9171,2013695,00.html.

55 Daniel Chirot and Clark McCauley, *Why Not Kill Them All? The Logic and Prevention of Mass Political Murder* (Princeton, NJ: Princeton University Press, 2006), pp. 166–167.

56 See "Christianity's Modern-Day Martyrs," *Spiegel Online*, February 26, 2010, www.spiegel.de/international/world/0,1518,680349,00.html.

57 Meyer and Brysac, *Pax Ethnica*, p. 98 (e-book).

58 Ibid., p. 117.

59 Verena Hutter, "German–Russian Exchange," Goethe-Institut, July 15, 2009.

60 René Lemarchand, for example, claims that "a fundamental reality of the Kagame regime" is that "one ethnocracy has replaced another." Lemarchand, "A History of Genocide in Rwanda" (review article), *The Journal of African History*, 43: 2 (2002), pp. 307–311.

61 René Lemarchand, *The Dynamics of Violence in Central Africa* (Philadelphia, PA: University of Pennsylvania Press, 2009), p. x.

62 "A Flawed Hero," *The Economist*, August 21, 2008.

63 See the Reporters without Borders Press Index at https://rsf.org/en/ranking.

64 Tracy McVeigh, "Rwanda Votes to Give President Paul Kagame Right to Rule until 2034," *The Guardian*, December 20, 2015, www.theguardian.com/world/2015/dec/20/rwanda-vote-gives-president-paul-kagame-extended-powers.

65 Ibid.

66 For a recent assessment, see Mike Nelson, "Rwanda's dependency on foreign aid," Africa in World Politics (blog), October 21, 2015, http://africanworldpolitics.site.wesleyan.edu/2015/10/21/rwandas-dependency-on-foreign-aid/.

67 For an example of the upbeat media coverage that has resulted, see Shashank Bengali, "Rwanda Economy Thriving as Country Moves Past Genocide," McClatchey Newspapers on *Yahoo! News*, March 1, 2008.

68 Stephanie McCrummen, "Women Run the Show in a Recovering Rwanda," *The Washington Post*, October 26, 2008, www.washingtonpost.com/wp-dyn/content/article/2008/10/26/AR2008102602197.html. As of 2015, women filled "10 of the 26 Senate seats and 51 of the 80 seats in the Chamber of Deputies." *Freedom House*, "Freedom in the World 2015: Rwanda," https://freedomhouse.org/report/freedom-world/2015/rwanda.

69 The gains of the post-genocide Rwandan regime are outlined in boosterish but not inaccurate fashion in Patricia Crisafuli and Andrea Redmond, *Rwanda, Inc.: How a Devastated Nation Became an Economic Model for the Developing World* (New York: St. Martin's Griffin, 2014). Even a uniformly critical survey of post-genocide Rwanda acknowledged at the outset "Rwanda's undeniable accomplishments: visionary leadership, political stability, economic growth, [the] pro-business environment, relative transparency, [the] high proportion of women in parliament, and improved education and health care." It warned nonetheless of "the social and political costs of repression, exclusion, growing inequality, a general climate of fear and intimidation, and impunity for crimes against humanity and war crimes committed in Rwanda and in the DRC." Scott Straus and Lars Waldorf, "Introduction: Seeing Like a Post-Conflict State," in Straus and Waldorf, eds., *Remaking Rwanda: State Building and Human Rights after Mass Violence* (Madison, WI: University of Wisconsin Press, 2011), p. 7.

70 For visuals, see the author's June 2013 photos at www.flickr.com/photos/adam_jones/9009444928/ and www.flickr.com/photos/adam_jones/9008173737/ (panorama).

71 For a survey of recent literature on the Indian Partition and its relevance for genocide studies, see my review article in *Journal of Genocide Research*, 10: 4 (2008), pp. 625–632.

72 See Sudeep Chakravarti, *Red Sun: Travels in Naxalite Country* (New Delhi: Penguin Books India, 2008).

73 See Jarnail Singh, *I Accuse . . . The Anti-Sikh Violence of 1984* (Gurgaon: Penguin Books India, 2009).

74 Nehru quoted in Shashi Tharoor, *Nehru: The Invention of India* (New York: Arcade Publishing, 2004), p. 225.

75 Patrick French noted that "half the people in the world who live in a democracy live in India." French, *India: A Portrait* (New York: Knopf Doubleday Publishing Group, 2011), p. 62.

76 Perhaps you thought I was joking. "In India, cricket is [a] 'religion.' The country comes to a stop when a cricket match is being played—the roads are deserted, parties and weddings are postponed, operations in hospitals are rescheduled, parliament goes in for early closing. North-south, east-west, rich-poor, men-women, rural-urban, Hindu-Muslim—a craze bordering on madness unites the nation when it comes to cricket." Vinod Mehta, "Letter: India's Cricketing 'Religion,'" *BBC Online*, October 14, 2004, http://news.bbc.co.uk/2/hi/programmes/3734038.stm.

77 Martha C. Nussbaum, *The Clash Within: Democracy, Religious Violence, and India's Future* (Cambridge, MA: The Belknap Press of Harvard University Press, 2007), p. 46. Nussbaum's book provides a detailed analysis (chapter 1) of the "Genocide in Gujarat" on Modi's watch, and the Hindu-nationalist ideology that underpins the RSS and the more mainstream BJP.

78 Sonia Faleiro, "India's Attack on Free Speech," *The New York Times*, October 2, 2015, www.nytimes.com/2015/10/04/opinion/sunday/sonia-faleiro-india-free-speech-kalburgi-pansare-dabholkar.html?_r=0.

79 The European Convention is also binding on the forty-seven countries that compose the Council of Europe, including nineteen that are not (yet) members of the EU.

80 See the website of the EU-sponsored Fundamental Rights Agency, http://fra.europa.eu/en.

81 Helena Smith, "Athens Insists 'Open Wound' of German War Reparations Must Be Closed," *The Guardian*, April 8, 2015, www.theguardian.com/world/2015/apr/08/greece-germany-war-reparations-demands.

82 See, e.g., the August 2015 comments of the mayor of Palermo, Leoluca Orlando, quoted in "Palermo Mayor: Refugee Crisis 'A Genocide'," *DW.com*, August 7, 2015, www.dw.com/en/palermo-mayor-refugee-crisis-a-genocide/a-18633896. See also the statement by Maltese prime minister Joseph Muscat in April 2015: "What is happening now is of epic proportions. If Europe, if the global community continues to turn a blind eye . . . we will all be judged in the same way that history has judged Europe when it turned a blind eye to the genocide of this century and last century." Quoted in "Mediterranean Migrants: Hundreds Feared Dead after Boat Capsizes," *BBC News*, April 19, 2015, www.bbc.com/news/world-europe-32371348.

83 See Jeremy Rifkin, *The European Dream: How Europe's Vision of the Future Is Quietly Eclipsing the American Dream* (New York: Tarcher, 2005).

84 "Barack Obama's Speech on Race," *The New York Times*, March 18, 2008.

85 I refer to the "October Crisis" of 1970, when the government of Prime Minister Pierre Trudeau imposed the War Measures Act in response to bombings and kidnappings by the Quebec Liberation Front (FLQ). Some of my first memories of life in Canada are of soldiers and armored vehicles stationed outside the parliament buildings in Ottawa.

86 See, e.g., Bill Curry, "Aboriginals in Canada Face 'Third World'-Level Risk of Tuberculosis," *The Globe and Mail*, March 10, 2010, www.theglobeandmail.com/news/national/aboriginals-in-canada-face-third-world-level-risk-of-tuberculosis/article4352641/.

87 Debora Mackenzie, "Canada Probes TB 'Genocide' in Church-Run Schools," *New Scientist*, May 5, 2007.

88 Nadezhda Mandelstam, *Hope Against Hope* (New York: Modern Library, 1999), p. 383.

89 Ian Hunter, "A Tale of Truth and Two Journalists," in William L. Hewitt, ed., *Defining the Horrific: Readings on Genocide and Holocaust in the Twentieth Century* (Upper Saddle River, NJ: Pearson Education, 2004), p. 134. See also S.J. Taylor's biography, *Stalin's Apologist: Walter Duranty: The New York Times's Man in Moscow* (New York: Oxford University Press, 1990).

90 Muggeridge quoted in Hunter, "A Tale of Truth," p. 135; emphasis added.

91 Muggeridge quoted in Robert Conquest, *The Harvest of Sorrow: Collectivization and the Terror-Famine* (New York: Oxford University Press, 1986), p. 260.

92 Muggeridge quoted in Timothy Snyder, *Bloodlands: Europe between Hitler and Stalin* (New York: Basic Books, 2010), p. 56.

93 Samantha Power, *"A Problem from Hell": America and the Age of Genocide* (New York: Basic Books, 2002), p. 32. See Jan Karski's pulse-pounding 1944 memoir and testament, *Story of a Secret State: My Report to the World* (London: Penguin Classics, 2011).

94 Staub, *The Roots of Evil*, p. 282.

95 Quoted in Margaret E. Keck and Kathryn Sikkink, *Activists Beyond Borders: Advocacy Networks in International Politics* (Ithaca, NY: Cornell University Press, 1998), p. 19; emphasis added. For an overview of the history and activities of Amnesty International, see Jonathan Power, *Like Water on Stone: The Story of Amnesty International* (London: Penguin, 2002).

96 Anne Applebaum, *Gulag: A History* (London: Penguin, 2003), p. 497. The contribution of artists, writers, and other shapers of culture also provides a potent form of witnessing, albeit usually at some remove from events. It would be hard to overstate the importance of films such as *Schindler's List* and *The Killing Fields* to increasing public consciousness of the Jewish and Cambodian genocides, respectively. "Norm entrepreneurs" (Chapter 12) frequently write and use books—both non-fiction and fiction—to confront genocide and other crimes against humanity. Sometimes these can become true "culture carriers." Harriet Beecher Stowe's *Uncle Tom's Cabin* alerted millions of nineteenth-century readers to slavery's depredations; for a fascinating study of its enduring impact, see David S. Reynolds, *Mightier Than the Sword: Uncle Tom's Cabin and the Battle for America* (New York: W.W. Norton & Co., 2012). On a more modest scale, works like Rigoberta Menchú's autobiography (Further Study, Box 3a),

Jonathan Schell's anti-nuclear manifesto *The Fate of the Earth* (Further Study, Chapter 2), Samantha Power's *"A Problem from Hell"* (Further Study, Chapter 1), and Adam Hochschild's book on the Belgian Congo, *King Leopold's Ghost* (see Chapter 2, note 19) have played something of the same "culture carrier" role. In the visual arts, I think of Picasso's *Guernica* (1937), and some of the iconic photographs sampled in this book, notably of Nazi crimes and African famine victims.

97 Irene Gut Opdyke with Jennifer Armstrong, *In My Hands: Memories of a Holocaust Rescuer* (New York: Anchor Books, 2001).

98 The controversy over the Catholic and Protestant churches' actions during the Jewish Holocaust may be revisited in this context (see Chapter 6).

99 Quoted in Peter Balakian, *The Burning Tigris: The Armenian Genocide and America's Response* (New York: HarperCollins, 2003), p. 121.

100 Charles Tilly, *The Politics of Collective Violence* (Cambridge: Cambridge University Press, 2003), p. 8; see also Barrington Moore, *Moral Persecution in History* (Princeton, NJ: Princeton University Press, 2000).

101 The term "cosmopolitan" was first deployed in the modern era by Immanuel Kant in *Perpetual Peace* (1795). Mary Kaldor "use[s] the term . . . to refer both to a positive political vision, embracing tolerance, multiculturalism, civility and democracy, and to a more legalistic respect for certain overriding universal principles which should guide political communities at various levels, including the global level." Kaldor, *New and Old Wars: Organized Violence in a Global Era* (Stanford, CA: Stanford University Press, 2001), p. 116. See also Peter Singer, *The Expanding Circle: Ethics, Evolution, and Moral Progress* (Princeton, NJ: Princeton University Press, 2011); the discussion of "the re-emergence of cosmopolitanism" in David Hirsh, *Law against Genocide: Cosmopolitan Trials* (London: Glasshouse Press, 2003), pp. 13–17; and S. Vertovec and R. Cohen, eds., *Conceiving Cosmopolitanism* (Oxford: Oxford University Press, 2002).

102 Ethan Nadelmann claims that "no other international prohibition regime so powerfully confirms the potential of humanitarian and similar moral concerns to shape global norms as does the regime against slavery and the slave trade." Nadelmann, "Global Prohibition Regimes: The Evolution of Norms in International Society," *International Organization*, 44: 4 (Fall 1990).

103 For a famously-stomach-churning description of the type of public execution common in "civilized" Europe as recently as the eighteenth century, see the opening pages of Michel Foucault's *Discipline and Punish: The Birth of the Prison* (New York: Vintage, 1979)—but not before lunch.

104 John Boli and George M. Thomas, "INGOs and the Organization of World Culture," in Boli and Thomas, eds., *Constructing World Culture: International Nongovernmental Organizations since 1875* (Stanford, CA: Stanford University Press, 1999), pp. 39–40. See also Peter N. Stearns's study of the emergence (and limitations) of "world opinion" in *Global Outrage: The Impact of World Opinion on Contemporary History* (Oxford: Oneworld, 2007); Micheline R. Ishay, *The History of Human Rights: From Ancient Times to the Globalization Era (Berkeley, CA: University of California Press, 2008);* Lynn Hunt, *Inventing Human Rights: A History* (New York: W.W. Norton & Co., 2007).

105 Testimony quoted in Conquest, *The Harvest of Sorrow*, p. 233. Nadezhda Mandelstam wrote of "this craving for an all-embracing idea which would explain everything in the world and bring about universal harmony at one go." Under Stalinism, "Life was deviating from the blueprints, but the blueprints had been declared sacrosanct and it was forbidden to compare them with what was actually coming into being." Mandelstam, *Hope Against Hope*, pp. 115, 163.

106 A.J.P. Taylor, "Introduction," in Karl Marx and Friedrich Engels, *The Communist Manifesto* (Harmondsworth: Penguin, 1970), pp. 27, 46. Hence also state socialism in practice (Stalin, Mao, the Kims of North Korea, and others; see Chapter 5). Christopher Hitchens notes that "Communist absolutists did not so much negate religion, in societies that they well understood were saturated with faith and superstition, as seek to *replace* it. The solemn elevation of infallible leaders who were a source of endless

bounty and blessing; the permanent search for heretics and schismatics; the mummifi-cation of dead leaders as icons and relics; the lurid show trials that elicited incredible confessions by means of torture ... none of this was very difficult to interpret in tra-ditional terms." Hitchens, *God is Not Great: How Religion Poisons Everything* (Toronto, ON: McClelland & Stewart, 2007), p. 246. See also the discussion in Mark Levene, *Genocide in the Age of the Nation State, Vol. 2: The Rise of the West and the Coming of Geno-cide* (London: I.B. Tauris, 2005), pp. 200–206. John Gray has explored the ideological and programmatic connections among utopian projects which claim both religious and secular inspiration in *Black Mass: How Religion Led the World into Crisis* (Toronto, ON: Anchor Canada, 2007). The quasi-religious character of contemporary capitalist thinking about "development," "modernization," "freedom," and other lofty themes has been critiqued by Karl Polanyi, Noam Chomsky, Vandana Shiva, Amartya Sen, Naomi Klein, and many others. How a hubristic faith in such prescriptions produced disaster (and arguably genocide) in Vietnam is captured by David Halberstam in *The Best and the Brightest* (New York: Ballantine, 1993). The title has become a catch-phrase for the technocratic mindset and bright-eyed naïveté that produced hecatombs of dead and debilitated in the "developing" world.

107 Ruby Plenty Chiefs quoted in Martha Minow, *Between Vengeance and Forgiveness: Fac-ing History after Genocide and Mass Violence* (Boston, MA: Beacon Press, 1998), p. 8.

108 Steven Pinker, *The Better Angels of Our Nature: A History of Violence and Humanity* (Lon-don: Penguin, 2011), p. xix. The remaining citations in this box text are to pp. xx–xxi, 93, 221, 231, 382–383, 560, 715, 628.

109 Goldstein, *Winning the War on War*, pp. 3, 5–6, 7.

110 See, e.g., Stephen Curry (of Survival International), "Why Steven Pinker, Like Jared Diamond, Is Wrong," *Truthout.org*, June 11, 2013, www.truth-out.org/opinion/item/16880-the-case-of-the-brutal-savage-poirot-or-clouseau-or-why-steven-pinker-like-jared-diamond-is-wrong.

111 John Gray, "Steven Pinker is Wrong about Violence and War," *The Guardian*, March 13, 2015, www.theguardian.com/books/2015/mar/13/john-gray-steven-pinker-wrong-violence-war-declining.

112 Jacques Sémelin wrote: "The eternal question always crops up: how on earth is it possible? How can human beings suddenly become executioners of their fellow man [and woman]? Yet if our own country sank into an increasingly serious economic crisis, with dismal parades of millions of unemployed, if it was harassed by a rise in ter-rorist attacks, each one bloodier than the last, how long would we remain impervious to this way of thinking? We would have to find enemies, not only beyond our borders but also within them, and—who knows?—maybe even right where we live: in our town, village, street, our own building." Sémelin, *Purify and Destroy: The Political Uses of Massacre and Genocide* (New York: Columbia University Press, 2007), p. 9.

113 "Travel is fatal to prejudice, bigotry, and narrowmindedness, and many of our people need it sorely on these accounts. Broad, wholesome, charitable views of men and things cannot be acquired by vegetating in one little corner of the earth all one's lifetime." Mark Twain, *The Innocents Abroad* (1869). Thanks to Jennie Walker for this source. Unfortunately, Twain's views were not always in keeping with these lofty senti-ments, especially with regard to US indigenous peoples (see p. 149).

114 Donald E. Miller and Lorna Touryan Miller, *Survivors: An Oral History of the Armenian Genocide* (Berkeley, CA: University of California Press, 1999), p. 5.

115 Guevara letter in the Museo Ernesto Che Guevara, Alta Gracia, Argentina; author's transcription and translation. Kurt Gerstein, a Nazi SS officer, witnessed the stripping, brutalization, and murder by gassing of a transport of Jews to the Belzec death camp in 1942. He subsequently made a greater effort than perhaps any other German "Aryan" to alert the world to the Nazi extermination campaign. In a March 1944 letter to his staunchly pro-Nazi father, Gerstein wrote: "However tight the limitations on a man may be and however much, in many things, he may follow the principle that discre-tion is the better part of valor, he must never lose his standards or his ideas. He must

never exonerate himself before his conscience and before the higher order of things to which he is subject by saying: that is not my business, I can do nothing to change things. . . . He keeps silent but he thinks: that is my business. I am involved in this responsibility and guilt, having knowledge of what is happening and a corresponding measure of blame." Quoted in Saul Friedländer, *The Years of Extermination: Nazi Germany and the Jews, 1939–1945* (New York: HarperCollins, 2007), pp. 539–540. However, Gerstein continued to deliver Zyklon B gas pellets to the death camps, thus remaining a "member of the extermination system," albeit "a morally tormented and 'treasonous'" one (Friedländer, p. 540).

116 Wiesel quoted in Samuel P. Oliner, *Do Unto Others: Extraordinary Acts of Ordinary People* (Boulder, CO: Westview Press, 2003), p. 159.

117 Feldman quoted in Liisa H. Malkki, "Speechless Emissaries: Refugees, Humanitarianism, and Dehistoricization," in Alexander Laban Hinton, ed., *Genocide: An Anthropological Reader* (Malden, MA: Blackwell, 2002), p. 353.

118 Stalin quoted in David Remnick, *Resurrection: The Struggle for a New Russia* (New York: Vintage, 1998), p. 288.

119 Timothy Snyder offers a resonant proposal for personifying the dead who are rendered invisible by brute statistics. In his much-discussed book *Bloodlands* (see Box 2.3), he writes: "Cultures of memory are organized by round numbers, intervals of ten; but somehow the remembrance of the dead is easier when the numbers are not round, when the final digit is not a zero. So within the Holocaust, it is perhaps easier to think of 780,863 different people at Treblinka: where the three at the end might be Tamara and Itta Willenberg, whose clothes clung together after they were gassed, and Ruth Dorfmann, who was able to cry with the man who cut her hair before she entered the gas chamber. Or it might be easier to imagine the one person at the end of the 33,761 Jews shot at Babi Yar [in Ukraine in 1941]: Dina Pronicheva's mother, let us say, although in fact every single Jew killed there could be that one, must be that one, is that one." Snyder, *Bloodlands: Europe between Hitler and Stalin* (New York: Basic Books, 2010), p. 408. Ironically, perhaps, Snyder misstates the number of the Nazis' victims at Babi Yar: it was 33,771 (see the report by the murderers, Figure 15.2, p. 701).

120 Noam Chomsky, BBC *Hardtalk*, November 3, 2009. "Authoritative" interpretations of history, enshrined for example in school textbooks, must also be critically examined and regularly challenged, lest they "reinstil the ideological seeds of tomorrow's conflicts," according to Jacques Sémelin. "Therefore the prevention of mass-scale violence must include work on the memories of the past memories that could just as well serve to stir up passions as to contain them in working for reconciliation." Sémelin, *Purify and Destroy*, p. 372. Taner Akçam wrote along similar lines that "all studies of large-scale atrocities teach us one core principle: To prevent the recurrence of such events, people must first consider their own responsibility, discuss it, debate it, and recognize it. In the absence of such honest consideration, there remains the high probability of such acts being repeated, since every group is inherently capable of violence; when the right conditions arise this potential may easily become reality, and on the slightest of pretexts. There are no exceptions. Each and every society needs to take a self-critical approach, one that should be firmly institutionalized as a community's moral tradition regardless of what others might have done to them." Akçam, *A Shameful Act: The Armenian Genocide and the Question of Turkish Responsibility* (New York: Metropolitan Books, 2006), p. 2. For a case study of an attempt to write a collaborative, consultative, pluralistic regional history of the Balkans, and the quite inspiring results, see Nicole Itano, "To Avoid 'Us vs. Them' in Balkans, Rewrite History," *The Christian Science Monitor*, March 14, 2007, www.csmonitor.com/2007/0314/p01s02-woeu.html, describing an initiative in which "more than 60 scholars and teachers from around the Balkans have joined to create a new series of history books that tackle some of the most controversial periods in the region['s history]." In the Balkans, Itano wrote, "history is often served up as a nationalistic tale that highlights the wrongs perpetrated by others." The new history books, "which are being translated into 10 regional languages,

present history from various perspectives and excerpt historical documents to challenge interpretations of key events like the Ottoman conquest of Constantinople." They will provide an alternative to "government-issued texts in which wars—and there have been many in the region over the centuries—are portrayed in 'us versus them' terms with ancient wrongs visited again and again." Such initiatives deserve imaginative extension and enthusiastic support.

121 Rudolph Höss, *Death Dealer: The Memoirs of the SS Kommandant at Auschwitz*, ed. Steven Paskuly (New York: Da Capo Press, 1996), p. 194. For a vivid narrative juxtaposing Höss's life and crimes with the trajectory of the young German Jew, Hanns Alexander, who brought him to justice after the war, see Thomas Harding, *Hanns and Rudolf: The True Story of the German Jew Who Tracked Down and Caught the Kommandant of Auschwitz* (New York: Simon & Schuster, 2013). A film is apparently in the works: see http://thomasharding.com/blog/2014/5/7/hanns-and-rudolf-optioned-by-ink-factory.

122 Alan J. Kuperman, "Wishful Thinking Will Not Stop Genocide: Suggestions for a More Realistic Strategy," *Genocide Studies and Prevention*, 4: 2 (August 2009), pp. 191–199. Kuperman argued (p. 193) that "the international community should refuse to intervene in any way—diplomatic, economic, or military—to help sub-state rebels unless state retaliation is grossly disproportionate. This would discourage militants within vulnerable sub-state groups from launching provocative rebellions that recklessly endanger civilians in hopes of garnering foreign intervention. At the same time, by retaining the intervention option for cases of disproportionate retaliation, this reform also would discourage states from responding to rebellion by intentionally harming civilians. All sides in civil conflicts would thus have incentives for less violent action."

123 The lives and writings of twentieth-century figures such as Mahatma Gandhi, Martin Luther King, the Dalai Lama, and Aung San Suu Kyi provide important insights and inspiration, as does Jonathan Schell's study, *The Unconquerable World: Power, Nonviolence, and the Will of the People* (New York: Metropolitan Books, 2003). See also Adam Hochschild, *To End All Wars: A Story of Loyalty and Rebellion, 1914–1918* (Boston, MA: Houghton Mifflin Harcourt, 2011); Peter Ackerman and Jack DuVall, *A Force More Powerful: A Century of Nonviolent Conflict* (New York: Palgrave, 2000); Joseph Lelyveld, *Great Soul: Mahatma Gandhi and His Struggle with India* (New York: Alfred A. Knopf, 2011).

124 Micheline R. Ishay, *The History of Human Rights: From Ancient Times to the Globalization Era* (Berkeley, CA: University of California Press, 2008), p. 12. Matthew White described the anti-slavery regime as "the strongest taboo in international law." White, *Atrocitology: Humanity's 100 Deadliest Achievements* (Edinburgh: Canongate, 2011), p. 171.

125 Gary J. Bass, *Freedom's Battle: The Origins of Humanitarian Intervention* (New York: Alfred A. Knopf, 2008), p. 382.

126 Justin Gillis, "2015 Was Hottest Year in Historical Record," *The New York Times*, January 20, 2016, www.nytimes.com/2016/01/21/science/earth/2015-hottest-year-global-warming.html. The environmental/ecocidal crisis has received increasing attention in genocide studies. See Mark Levene, "Predicting Genocide in an Age of Anthropogenic Climate Change: An Interim Report," *Crisis Group*, 2009, www.crisisforum.org.uk/publications/Levene_genocide_climate.doc. A shorter version of the argument is found in Mark Levene, "From Past to Future: Prospects for Genocide and Its Avoidance in the Twenty-First Century," in Donald Bloxham and A. Dirk Moses, eds., *The Oxford Handbook of Genocide Studies* (Oxford: Oxford University Press, 2010), pp. 638–659. See also the special issue on "Climate Change, Environmental Violence and Genocide" edited by Jürgen Zimmerer, *The International Journal of Human Rights*, 18: 3 (2014). For a general critique, see Naomi Klein, *This Changes Everything: Capitalism vs. the Climate* (Toronto: Knopf Canada, 2014).

INDEX

Note: Page numbers in italic indicate a figure or table on the corresponding page.